General Insurance

*The Irwin Series in
Insurance and Economic Security*
Davis W. Gregg
Consulting Editor

11th edition

General Insurance

David L. Bickelhaupt
Professor of Insurance and Finance
College of Administrative Science
The Ohio State University

1983

Homewood, Illinois 60430

With love to my wife, Lee,
and to Tina, Janet, Paul, and Carol

© BUSINESS PUBLICATIONS, INC., 1936

© RICHARD D. IRWIN, INC., 1942, 1947, 1953, 1957, 1961, 1964, 1970, 1974, 1979, and 1983

ISBN 0-256-02821-4
Library of Congress Catalog Card No. 82–84265
Printed in the United States of America

890 K 09876

Preface

I love to read, and hope you do, too—but writers and books have tough competition these days. Reading books is harder than watching television or playing video games. Andy Rooney summed up his feelings by saying that whenever he has time enough to sit down and read a book, he gets up and does something else. Perhaps I should also entice my readers with a title such as "A Few Minutes with General Insurance."

Purpose. The fact is, however, that more than a few minutes is needed to understand insurance, which is what I want you to do. I can't promise all the momentary pleasures of TV: the nostalgia of old movies, the excitement of sporting events with replays of the best parts, the allure of the soaps, or the laughs with your favorite entertainers. The surest guarantee I can make is that you will *learn* more, hour-for-hour, from this book than from television. Particularly, you'll know more about how *insurance* can help *you* obtain greater security in a world otherwise filled with uncertainties.

Uses. This book is the 11th edition of *General Insurance,* which to my knowledge is a record for any college insurance text. The previous edition was adopted for courses in more than 300 colleges and universities. Usually, it is used as a comprehensive introduction to all the fields of insurance and risk management. I believe its *breadth* and *depth* of knowledge is its greatest asset, for insurance courses vary from an average of about 45 hours of classroom instruction to as few as 30 hours and as many as 60 hours or more. Good teachers want students to be able to describe *what* is, but also to know *why* things are and *why* they are important. The treatment of subjects here is sufficient to achieve those results for courses of varying lengths. In shorter courses, some chapters can be omitted or used as supplementary assignments or special class reports (see the suggested assignment schedules that follow this preface).

Not all insurance education takes place in college-credit courses. This book has also been used in professional insurance programs of the Insurance Institute of America (IIA), the Casualty Actuarial Society (CAS), the Certified Financial Planner (CFP), various insurance company courses, and in many states for insurance agents' licensing examinations.

Organization and changes.   Risk is the basis for insurance. *Part One* of this text builds a concise foundation for insurance study by relating risk, risk management, and insurance in the first four chapters. This emphasizes the *consumer viewpoint,* which is most important to you. *Part Two* continues this approach by analyzing more specific consumer needs and insurance solutions in six chapters explaining life and health insurance. A separate chapter stresses the *social insurance viewpoint* of government insurance programs, and a review chapter shows how private and social insurance are coordinated in these fields. *Part Three* similarly treats the many different kinds of property and liability insurance, including the significant fire, liability, automobile, and homeowners' exposures and insurance contracts. Recognizing that students and consumers also need to understand the *insurer viewpoint, Part Four* has been changed to follow the fundamental principles, terminology, and contract analysis of all the various lines of insurance. A more meaningful understanding of insurance operations is achieved by this arrangement, with separate chapters on insurance marketing, underwriting, loss payment, and regulation. *Part Five* reviews consumer, business, and social issues, in a chapter that was the first of its kind in basic insurance texts to emphasize a look to the future. In total, a *balanced* approach to insurance and risk management from all major viewpoints is the objective of the five parts of this book.

The new subject matter in this edition is extensive. Every chapter is updated with current topics. Hundreds of footnote references indicate sources of ideas and readings for further information. Frequent use of tables and figures review and summarize significant concepts in the changing world of insurance. Examples of new developments discussed include risk measurement techniques, "captive" insurers, universal life insurance, the effects of new tax laws on life insurance and annuities, social security changes and problems, "cafeteria" employee benefit plans, retroactive insurance, pollution liability, financial services conglomerates and supermarkets, insurer investments, "homeowners plus" contracts, open competition rating, and many others.

Teaching aids.   The "outline of concepts" at the beginning of each chapter is recommended for the close attention of readers, both *before* and *after* reading the chapters. These highlight the major ideas and are helpful in reviewing the relationships among major and subtopics. Selected excerpts from the most important insurance contracts for consumers are included, but many teachers will want to obtain complete sample contracts for their classes from the Insurance Information Institute (110 William St., New York, N.Y. 10038), the American Council of Life Insurance (1850 K St., N.W., Washington, D.C. 20006), or the Alliance of American Insurers (20 N. Wacker Dr., Chicago, Ill. 60606).

Teachers may also obtain from Richard D. Irwin (1818 Ridge Rd., Homewood, Ill. 60430) a 350-page *Solutions and Visual Aids Manual* with full answers to all "For Review and Discussion" questions at the end of each chapter. It contains about 150 enlarged-print tear-out pages and new visual aids prepared by Michael M. Delaney of the University of Nebraska at Omaha. These are designed for use with an opaque projector or for making copies, transparencies, or slides to enhance classroom presentation of major concepts. Teachers should write on their department stationery or ask Irwin sales representatives for their *free* copy.

Acknowledgments.   The past 20 years and five editions of this text have been typed with expert care by Eleanor B. Sapp, who deserves my personal thanks and admiration. I also thank my colleagues and many students and friends for thoughtful suggestions for improvement. Particular thanks are due Dr. Robert J. Myers for very helpful review of Chapter 11. Several other anonymous reviewers also made valuable chapter-by-chapter recommendations. I welcome further reactions—general or specific, long or short, immediate or belated—from any readers of this edition.

David L. Bickelhaupt

Suggested assignment schedule
for different course lengths

* The length and number of class sessions are based on the assumption that the normal course will contain either 30 or 45 individual classes of about 60–90 minutes each, with outside reading assignments in preparation for the classes averaging about two hours each. Some variation of the suggested timing is natural, depending upon the interests of students and teachers, and the desire to use other supplementary materials. Several of the assignments may be easily shortened, if necessary, by omitting a portion of some chapters. In some survey or introductory courses, the teacher may wish to consider omitting Chapters 14, 15, 17, 18, 21, 22, 24 and increasing emphasis on the other chapters.

Contents

PART ONE
RISK, RISK MANAGEMENT, AND INSURANCE

1 Risk and risk management   2

The values with which risk is concerned. Different reactions to risk. What risk is: *Uncertainty and risk. Economic risk.* Risk-related terms: *Perils. Hazards. Losses.* Classifications of risk: *Speculative and pure risks. Personal, property, and liability risks. Insurable risks.* Why treat risk? *Security a natural goal. Losses from pure risk. Other costs of pure risk.* Scope and objectives of risk management: *Scope of risk management. Objectives of risk management.* The place of the risk manager.

2 Risk-management decision making   26

The steps in risk management and risk-treatment alternatives: A summary. Basic methods of treating risk: *Risk control methods. Risk financing methods.* Individual steps in risk management: *Risk identification. Risk measurement. Choice and use of methods of risk treatment. Risk administration.* An example of risk-management decision making. A case study for business risk management.

3 Insurance and its significance   64

How insurance works: *The insurance equation. Probability and uncertainty. The principle of large numbers. Adequate statistical data.* A brief history of insurance: *Ancient insurance ideas. The Middle Ages and the merchant era. The 18th century and insurance in early America. The expanding 1800s. 20th-century growth.* The fields of insurance: *General. Social (government) insurance. Voluntary (private) insurance.* The benefits and costs of insurance: *Benefits of insurance. Costs of insurance. Statistical evidences.*

Social insurance programs in the United States. Old-Age, Survivors, Disability, and Health Insurance: *Eligibility. Benefits. Administration. Financing.* Unemployment Compensation: *Eligibility. Benefits. Administration. Financing.* Workers' Compensation: *Eligibility. Benefits. Administration. Financing.* Temporary-disability (nonoccupational) insurance laws: *Eligibility. Benefits. Administration. Financing.* Summary of four major social insurance programs. Other social insurance programs: *The Railroad Retirement and Unemployment Acts. Government employee retirement systems. Veterans' benefit programs. The future.* Proposed national health insurance plans: *The need. The objectives. The proposals.*

12   Coordinating life and health insurance   352

Human life and health values. Life and health risk management. Personal life and health insurance planning: *Personal life insurance programming. A case study example of family life insurance needs and costs. Personal health insurance programming. A case study example of family health insurance needs and costs. Personal estate planning.* Business life and health insurance planning: *Buy-and-sell agreements. Key person life and health insurance.*

PART THREE
PROPERTY AND LIABILITY INSURANCE

13   Fire insurance   382

The standard fire insurance contract: *The need for standardization. Methods. Development. Benefits.* The declarations. The insuring agreement: *Inception and termination. Property and location. Personal nature. Actual cash value. Perils insured against. Assignment.* The conditions and exclusions: *Concealment or fraud. Excluded property. Excluded perils. Suspension. Added perils and provisions. Cancellation. Loss provisions.* Fire insurance forms: *Purpose. Preparation and use. Types.* Clauses: *Purpose and use. Nuclear clause. Water exclusion clause. Liberalization clause. Standard mortgage clause. Coinsurance clause. Pro rata distribution clause.* Endorsements: *Purpose. General use. The extended coverage endorsement. The broad form endorsement. The special form endorsement.* A review of the fire insurance contract. Special and allied fire lines. Concurrency.

14   Indirect loss insurance   430

General purposes. Classification of types of indirect loss insurance. Time element losses: *Business interruption insurance. Contingent business interruption insurance. Rents and rental value insurance. Extra-expense insurance. Tuition fees insurance.* No time element losses: *Profits insurance.*

27 Insurance loss payment   834

Significance. Purposes. Insurance adjusters: Types and organizations: *Agents as adjusters. Staff adjusters. Independent adjusters. Adjustment bureaus. Public adjusters.* Claims procedures: *Fire insurance losses. Liability insurance losses. Life insurance losses.*

28 Insurance regulation   856

Why insurance regulation is needed. Methods of insurance regulation: *Self-regulation of insurance. Government regulation of insurance.* Kinds of insurance regulation by the states: *Formation and licensing of insurers. Insurer operations. Rehabilitation and liquidation of insurers.* Some current regulatory issues: *Insurer guaranty funds. Federal versus state regulation. Other regulatory issues.*

PART FIVE
THE FUTURE OF INSURANCE

29 Consumer, business, and social issues   884

Three major viewpoints. Consumer issues: *Significance of insurance to consumers. Potential effects on insurance. Current examples of the consumer trend.* Business issues: *Internationalism. Marketing methods in insurance. Arson problems. Insurance exchanges. Insurer investments. New types of insurance.* Social issues: *The ethical pillars of insurance. Government regulation. Other social issues.*

APPENDIXES

List of figures

List of tables

Part One

RISK, RISK MANAGEMENT, AND INSURANCE

Why does this insurance text emphasize the concepts of risk and risk management in Part One? The reasoning is that without risk there would be no insurance. Thus, a good understanding of risk is essential to the study of insurance, before more extensive discussion of insurance contracts and the functions of insurance companies.

The rationale is first to establish a foundation of knowledge about *risk*—a basic characteristic of life resulting from uncertainty or variation in regard to financial losses. Chapter 1 explains what risk is, the major types of risk, why risk should be treated, the scope and objectives of risk management, and the place of the risk manager.

Chapter 2 presents the increasingly popular concept of *risk management* as a decision-making process. It includes the basic methods of treating risk, the steps in the risk-management process, and examples of coordinated risk treatment.

Insurance becomes significant because it is a major alternative helping to solve many of the problems that risk creates. Chapter 3 reviews how insurance works and the importance of insurance in terms of its history, its various fields, its benefits, and its place in our economic society. Chapter 4 introduces the basic product of insurance—*the insurance contract*—including the general and special legal characteristics which determine the rights and responsibilities of insurers and insurance consumers.

With the background of Part One, the relevance and organization of the other major parts of this text are clarified. The text proceeds to emphasize the consumer viewpoint in the more specific analysis by types of insurance (Parts Two and Three), the insurer viewpoint (Part Four), and to look ahead to the future of insurance (Part Five).

Chapter 1

Outline of concepts

Risk is *uncertainty of financial loss,* in brief, but there are many kinds.

Values with which risk is concerned are based on human needs.

Different reactions to risk and insurance (which reduces risk) occur.

What risk is becomes the foundation for insurance: differentiated on the basis of *objective* (measurable) and *subjective qualities,* and *variation* between expected and actual results.

Risk-related terms often confused with risk include: *perils* (causes), *hazards* (acts or conditions which increase loss), and *losses* (decreases in value).

Classifications of risk are needed in order to study risk properly.

Speculative and pure risks are distinguished by *loss or gain* versus *loss or no loss* situations (to which insurance applies).

Personal, property, and liability risks are major types of pure risk.

Insurable risks must, in total, be substantially *important, accidental, calculable,* and *definite,* and *not excessively catastrophic.*

Why treat risk is a basic question, answered by the facts that *security* is a natural goal, that *direct and indirect losses* are high, and that *other costs of potential losses* (fear and worry, less than optimum use of resources) are also great.

Risk management is introduced by explaining:

The scope and objectives of risk management, which briefly are coordinated risk treatment: systematically analyzing and deciding on the best alternatives. Its *purpose* is to reduce the adverse effects of risk by conserving the assets and income of businesses, institutions, and individuals. It uses the two basic risk-treatment methods of *risk control* and *risk financing.* It is *not* all management, nor all risks, but it is much more than mere *insurance* management. Both *general goals* and *specific risk-management goals* are considered in setting objectives.

The place of the risk manager is presented as a growing position of significance within the *organizational framework* of managerial decisions, with broad *responsibilities* and *qualifications* for performing tasks well in a professional manner.

Risk and risk management

Risk is the basis of insurance. Although every person, business, or organization faces risk each day, a sound understanding of the concept of risk is the foundation upon which an insurance book should begin. Generally, risk has to do with the uncertainty of losing, or not gaining, something of value. Risk occurs because of the variation in outcomes or results. Insurance emphasizes the variable results of financial losses. Uncertainty rather than certainty characterizes risk; unpredictability rather than predictability; not knowing rather than knowing.

THE VALUES WITH WHICH RISK IS CONCERNED

What values does risk concern? Many different kinds, including all the goals of life and life itself. These goals begin the complex explanation of human motivation. A well-known psychologist, Abraham Maslow, states a theory of motivation that views behavior as dominated by five levels of needs or wants: (1) survival, (2) safety and security, (3) love and belongingness, (4) esteem, and (5) self-actualization.[1] Once the physiological drives for survival, such as hunger and thirst, are met, decisions are based upon a quest for the other goals. Note that the second level of needs, which is very closely related to the idea of risk, centers on safety and security. A reasonable level of security, including economic, emotional, and other types of stability, is a very common need. Often, attaining this goal in life helps reduce the risk of losing happiness or success.

The third level of needs emphasizes that "no man [or woman] is an island." A successful life, whether measured in dollars or happiness or inner peace, is rarely complete without approval by, or relationship to, other persons or groups. Here love is an excellent example of risk. Like risk, love is all around us, tremendously important, yet difficult to define or predict and hard to get along with—or without. Too much love is

---

[1] Abraham H. Maslow, _Motivation and Personality,_ 2d ed. (New York: Harper & Row, 1970).

3

bad, and too little is worse. Love can miraculously inspire, or hopelessly frustrate. Risk is much the same in its uncertainty.

Esteem, the fourth level of needs, requires an ego built upon respect, from yourself as well as others. It involves prestige and recognition for achievement, which are difficult goals in the face of natural fears and feelings of inferiority. Self-actualization, the final level in this hierarchy of needs explaining motivation, is the most elusive of all. Trying to change and grow as a person toward personal satisfaction, fulfilling one's highest potential, is perhaps life's most uncertain goal.

All of these motivational needs determine the values with which risk is concerned. The many uncertainties surrounding such goals are the essence of numerous risks. Sometimes these many risks seem contradictory in nature.

DIFFERENT REACTIONS TO RISK

Risk is sometimes desirable and, at other times, undesirable. Linus, in the famous *Peanuts* comic strip, doesn't want risk. He drags his "security blanket" around continuously in order to have the comfort of something he knows and avoid the unknown real world. His friend Charlie Brown has a perplexing risk, too, as he never knows whether or not the unpredictable Lucy will pull the ball away from him as he attempts to kick off the new football season. This example illustrates the undesirable features of risk—unpredictability or not knowing, insecurity, and some resulting discontent or loss.

But ask business persons about risk! They want it, and it is important to them. They like risk and live by the creed of "nothing ventured, nothing gained." They invest their time, effort, and money for the uncertain profits which may result from their entrepreneurship. Business persons buy and sell, hire and fire, with the hope of profit and the threat of loss in mind. They are risk seekers rather than risk dodgers, with an attitude oftentimes of "What a dull world this would be if everything were known and there were no risks." The feeling is not limited to the business field. The skydiver, the astronaut, and the dragracer have a similar idea. Sir Walter Scott did, too, when he said: "One hour of life . . . filled with noble risks, is worth whole years of paltry decorum."[2]

Why is risk so important, yet different, to business persons and to Linus or Charlie? The influence of risk is apparent in the many attitudes toward it, varying from negative to positive reactions. It may result in substantial losses, worry, and inefficiency. The difference is briefly stated in differentiating between *speculative* risk (uncertainty about *profit or*

---

[2] Sir Walter Scott, *Count Robert of Paris,* chap. 25.

loss situations) and *pure* risk (uncertainty about *loss or no loss* situations). These are discussed further on later pages in this chapter.

The above examples illustrate the problem of using such a word as *risk* without first finding out what it is. That difficulty describes *insurance,* too, because a tremendous variety of ideas emerges in our everyday use of the term. Basically, it is a system for *reducing risk.* The surprising thing is that insurance is almost hated by some persons, yet highly desired by others. One person thinks of insurance as a tricky legal contract, while to another it is a valuable business, and to still another an important and necessary part of the family budget. The many different connotations suggest that further definitions should be deferred until a basis for understanding has been established.

WHAT RISK IS

A logical basis for such understanding is the concept of *risk,* which is the foundation for insurance. Without risk, there would be no need for insurance. Basically, risk is *uncertainty, or lack of predictability.*[3] It concerns values (usually monetary ones) which may be lost or not gained, and it is the *variation in possible results* which causes risk to occur in so many situations. And what widespread risks do exist! No one ever reaches the state of absolute certainty. From the moment of birth until life has ceased, every individual constantly faces the possibility of unexpected and unwanted happenings.

Examples of risk are everywhere, ranging from the unavoidable to those assumed by choice. Human existence itself creates such risks as not knowing when death, ill health, injury, or unemployment will occur. Examples of risk by choice would be the formation of any business enterprise, drilling a new oil well, or investing money in real estate. Indeed, anyone who owns property automatically assumes the risk of such perils as fire, windstorm, theft, or liability lawsuits. The inability to predict when or if these perils may cause losses is a risk that property owners acquire with their ownership.

Persons in the insurance business often use the word *risk* in a different manner to describe the object of potential loss, or the *object insured.* Thus, a building may be referred to as "the risk" in a fire insurance contract. This is a technical use of the term which should not be confused with the more important general description of what risk is.

---

[3] This aspect of risk, predictability, is emphasized in some definitions. See Davis T. Ratcliffe, "Teaching the Meaning of Risk," *Journal of Risk and Insurance* 38, no. 3 (September 1971), p. 455. For more thorough discussion of the definition of risk, see *Essays in the Theory of Risk and Insurance,* ed. J. D. Hammond (Glenview, Ill.: Scott, Foresman, 1968).

Uncertainty and risk

Risk concerns *variations* in possible outcomes in a situation. *Uncertainty* is often used as a synonym for risk, although when so used, it usually refers to *objective* (measurable or quantified) uncertainty.[4] Economists and statisticians use this concept when they measure variation in occurrences. One such measure of variation called the *standard deviation* helps predict expected variations from a norm. The predictability of an expected probability actually occurring is increased as the number of events is increased, as will be seen later in the discussion of the principle of large numbers.

Insurance is closely related to variations in losses. Note that risk is *not* merely chance of loss, for anything that is absolutely certain not to happen (0 percent chance of loss) or absolutely certain to happen (100 percent chance of loss) does not involve objective risk. Anywhere between the points of certainty, 0 percent and 100 percent probability of loss, involves some uncertainty and thus risk. For example, the chance of loss may be 10 percent, or 1 out of 10, that a person will be in the hospital in a given year. Risk exists in this situation because some variation from the 1-in-10 probability will occur.

The *degree* of risk is measured by variation between the expected (probable) results and the actual results. In the above example, there is a greater degree of risk when the percentage of variation is high. If one employer has 10 employees, he cannot be very certain that only 1 will be in the hospital that year. However, an employer with 100,000 employees can reasonably predict that 10,000, or very close to this number, will be in the hospital. The actual variation from the expected number hospitalized will be slight (a lower percentage than in the case of only 10 employees), and the degree of risk will be low.

Subjective uncertainty, which involves a feeling or state of mind as to expected results, differs from the above concept of objective uncertainty. Lack of knowledge as to the real facts, prejudices, unwarranted high hopes, and other factors can cause different predictions. Therefore different subjective risks occur, and these often deviate from the underlying objective risk. This kind of uncertainty is not readily measurable and is not usually what is meant when the term *risk* is used.

Economic risk

Are all risks economic? One might rush to answer yes, but a second thought would suggest that although most risks have financial conse-

---

[4] The classic treatment of this subject is found in Alan H. Willett, *The Economic Theory of Risk and Insurance* (Philadelphia: University of Pennsylvania Press, 1951), pp. 5–6; and Frank H. Knight, *Risk, Uncertainty, and Profit* (Boston: Houghton Mifflin, 1921), pp. 233–34.

quences, not all necessarily do. Moral, spiritual, and other risks could be identified, as well as the more obvious loss of economic values. <u>Many definitions of risk refer to it as uncertainty *of financial loss*. For insurance, this is the major concern about risk.</u>

RISK-RELATED TERMS

Terminology becomes important in the serious study of any subject. It is the basis for communication and understanding. Terms that are loosely used in a general or colloquial sense can lead only to misunderstanding in a specialized study area such as insurance. See Figure 1–1, showing the relationship among these terms and risk.

Perils

In contrast to risk, which is the uncertainty of loss (or results or happenings), the word *peril* should be used to identify the *cause* of risk. Examples of perils are commonplace and include fires, automobile accidents, thefts, earthquakes, windstorms, forgeries, water, illness, and hundreds of other causes of uncertainty.

Figure 1–1. The terminology of risk

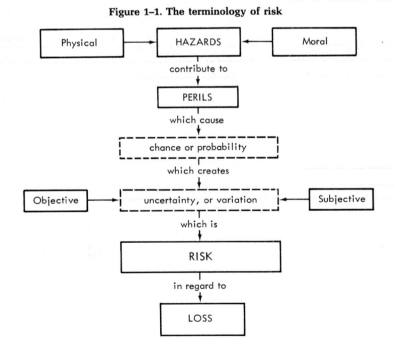

A classic use of the word is that in the *"Perils* of Pauline," the hair-raising silent movie melodramas in which poor Pauline was caused great uncertainty as to her life and limb.

The law has coined the term *acts of God* to describe perils operating without human agency or intervention and not preventable by human foresight or care. Fires caused by lightning are often so considered, as are storms, extraordinary floods, and other forces of nature.

Hazards

The various *acts or conditions which increase the likelihood or severity of a loss* are termed *hazards*. Ordinarily, many separate hazards attach to any particular object or person. The sum total of the hazards constitutes the perils which cause the risk.

A practice of the insurance business divides hazards into two major classifications. The first of these is termed *physical hazards*, and this classification includes everything relating to location, structure, occupancy, exposure, and the like. The term *moral hazards* is applied to those factors that have their inception in mental attitudes. Included in this second group are the hazards created by dishonesty, insanity, carelessness, indifference, and other causes that are psychological in nature.

Physical hazards.   Physical hazards include conditions such as these: wastepaper piled under a staircase, gasoline stored on the premises, weak construction which may fail in a heavy wind, unsafe brakes on a car, holes in a sidewalk, inadequate inventory checks in a store, and improper water drainage systems. Each of these conditions, as well as many others, would increase the chance of a loss occurring in regard to a specific peril such as fire, wind, water, theft, or other accident.

Insurance involves an evaluation of all the hazards and of the loss-prevention facilities for minimizing the loss in the event of the happening of the peril insured against. Measuring the hazard is the task of insurance rating or pricing.

Moral hazards.   The term *moral* is applied to that group of hazards which grows out of the *mental attitudes* of individuals. Carelessness or mental instability most decidedly contribute to a risk. While the term *psychological* might be more apt, a reason for the term *moral* is found in the fact that particular emphasis is given to dishonest acts and to fraud through the deliberate destruction of insured property. The term *moral hazard* is in no way limited, however, to cases involving moral instability but includes in its scope all factors contributing to risk that are mental in their nature.

Appraisal of moral hazard requires the study of the character and reputation of the person under consideration for insurance. Evidence pointing to the fact that an insured ever defrauded any other person, or had a previous bankruptcy record, is an indication of possible moral hazard in regard to insurance. Investigators also concern themselves with insureds' reputation in trade, their rating with the banks, their standing with competitors, and finally the regard in which they are held by those with whom they transact business. Individuals who have a reputation for taking unfair advantage of legal technicalities or who have repudiated contracts in the face of possible financial loss are regarded as likely to resort to other unethical methods. Finally, in the moral hazard category are to be found those abnormal mental cases known as "pyromaniacs," individuals who act under an irresistible impulse to set fires.

A distinction is sometimes made between *moral* and *morale* hazards, including as examples of increasing chance of loss such morale conditions as carelessness and indifference. Laziness, disorderliness, and lack of concern for others are termed morale problems rather than moral problems (problems involving dishonesty). Leaving car doors unlocked increases automobile thefts; bad smoking habits increase fire losses; and hurried, unthinking action can cause many personal injuries.

Losses

An economic *loss* is the undesirable end result of risk. It is the *decrease or disappearance of value,* usually in an unexpected or at least relatively unpredictable manner. In general terms, not all losses are related to risk; some losses are the result of intentional actions, as for example the gift of property to someone. Other losses may be expected because they are known always to occur, such as depreciation of physical properties which can be expected as well as predicted fairly accurately. Many losses, however, cannot be predicted and become the result of risks. Illustrations include loss of property due to fire or theft or other perils, loss of income due to property destruction or personal perils of death or disability, increased expenses such as medical costs, and loss of assets due to legal liability for losses affecting other persons.

It is important to note that there are two types of losses: (1) losses that *actually* occur and (2) losses that *might* occur.[5] Losses that prospectively might occur are often called *loss exposures* and are much more numerous than actual losses that result from the different possibilities of loss. Both types of loss must be considered, for the cost of risk includes not only the real losses but also the cost of the uncertainty involved in exposure to loss. (See section "Why treat risk?")

---

[5] C. Arthur Williams, Jr., George L. Head, Ronald C. Horn, and G. William Glendenning, *Principles of Risk Management and Insurance,* vol. I, 2d ed. (Malvern, Pa.: American Institute for Property and Liability Underwriters, 1981), p. 10.

An example of the relationship among the terms discussed in this section is as follows: Mr. Rich owns a Chris-Craft cabin cruiser. He knows that some (1) *hazards* (contributing factors) such as the captain's negligence or structural faults of the ship contribute to (2) *perils* (causes of risk) such as fire, collision, or sinking, which cause (3) *risk* (uncertainty of financial loss), which results in, or might result in (4) *loss* (decrease in value). The hazard of the captain's inattention to rocks and shallow water may contribute to the peril of collision and the risk or uncertainty of having a financial loss or repair bill of $5,000 to the ship.

CLASSIFICATIONS OF RISK

Speculative and pure risks

Two basic kinds of economic risks are *(a)* speculative risks and *(b)* pure risks.[6] See Figure 1–2 for a diagram of the classifications of risk in this section. *Speculative* risks involve the chance of *loss or gain,* whereas in *pure* risks there is only the chance of *loss or no loss.*

Pure risks are "pure" in the sense that they do not mix both profits and losses. The business of insurance is concerned with the economic problems created by pure risk. The introduction to this chapter contrasted the businessperson's attitude toward risk with that of Linus and Charlie Brown in the comic strip *Peanuts*. The risk seeking by businesspersons is for speculative risk, with the purpose being the prospect of gain if the business venture is successful. The risk aversion by the comic strip characters is for pure risk, with the prospect of loss being the unhappy result of the giving up of Linus' "security blanket" or Charlie's football-kicking episodes. A more common example of pure risk is that found in ownership of property. In regard to such a peril as windstorm, the owner may either suffer a loss or not have a loss. There cannot be a gain from having the loss (if insurance is involved, it is assumed that payment is *not* for more than actual loss).

Because *speculative risk* involves an element of both profit and loss, it may sometimes be nullified by a process known as *hedging*. Hedging is a procedure by which two compensating or offsetting transactions are used to assure a position of "breaking even." For example, a manufacturer who buys raw material may suffer a loss if the price of the raw material rises before the finished product is offered on the market. If the price of the raw material falls, a speculative profit will result, but a manufacturer is in business to make a profit on production and not

---

[6] Basic types of risk are also differentiated as "fundamental" (those universal and impersonal) and "particular" (those individual and personal). Another distinction is sometimes made between "dynamic" and "static" risks, but an understanding of "speculative" and "pure" risks is more meaningful in most discussions about risk.

Figure 1–2. The classifications of risk

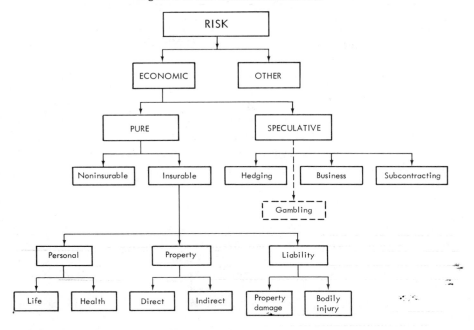

on cost changes. The speculative risk may be avoided by "selling short" a commodity contract for delivery of an equal amount of raw material at a stated price at about market time for the finished product. The manufacturer will lose on the short sale if prices of raw materials advance, but gain if prices of raw materials decline. The net result of the hedging contract of short sale is to eliminate speculative risk on the cost of raw material when the goods are sold.

The hedging process is not always available, for it depends on the existence of an active commodity futures market. The futures market is well developed for some goods within certain time limits, but unavailable for many other goods. The result of hedging is similar to a "hedged" bet, where after a bet is made, the bettor doesn't want to keep the risk and makes an opposite bet for exactly the same amount and odds.

Subcontracting is another example of avoiding speculative risk, in which a general contractor obtains contracts at fixed prices for parts of the total job to be completed in the future.

The presence of a risk as an *existing* condition is the factor that removes insurance from the category of a *gambling* risk, a special type of speculation. Insurance does not create risk, but transfers and reduces risk already in existence. Contrasted to this is a bet; no risk exists before, but one is *created* at the time of the gambling transaction, putting values at risk that were not in jeopardy before the bet.

Gambling operations may involve many of the attributes of insurance, such as large numbers, spread and homogeneity of risk, and predictability. Probably this is the reason so many uninformed persons think of insurance as gambling and sometimes even feel that they have "lost the bet" if they fail to have a loss equal to the cost of insurance. The distinction is not in the method of operation, which may appear similar, but in the fact that insurance concerns itself with an existing risk. Speculation and insurance are both based upon socially and economically useful risks, too, while gambling is generally regarded as a less desirable method of speculation.

Personal, property, and liability risks

The risks confronting human beings are ordinarily divided into three classifications: *(a)* risks involving the person, *(b)* risks involving loss or damage to property (including indirect loss of income), and *(c)* risks involving liability for the injury to the person or property of others. Figure 1–2 shows this relationship.

The first of these classifications of risk is ordinarily termed *personal* and is chiefly concerned with the time of death or disability. Of death there is no uncertainty; but the time of its occurrence is uncertain. And aside from death, there is the risk of incapacity through accidental injury, illness, or old age. Personal risks are often divided into *life* and *health* risks. Sometimes they are called "personnel" exposures.

The second classification of risk is that which arises from the destruction of *property.* The possible loss of a cargo or ship at sea is considered a risk to those engaged in maritime operations. *Direct* losses by fire, lightning, windstorm, flood, and other forces of nature offer a constant threat of loss to real estate, as well as all kinds of personal property and property involved in any form of transportation. *Indirect* losses also may occur, including the loss of profits, rents, or favorable leases.

The third classification of risk is occasioned by the operation of the law of *liability.* An individual may be legally liable for an injury to another, as, for instance, through an accident when the driver of an automobile is negligent and injures a pedestrian, or when a person is injured on someone's property. Such a risk is termed a "third-party" risk because when insurance is used to shift the burden of responsibility, the insurer and the insured person have agreed that a "third party" (the injured person) will be paid for injuries for which the insured is legally liable. The liability risk includes both *bodily injury* and *property damage* risks.

SOME BENEFITS OF PROPERTY CONTRACTS INCLUDE PERSONAL LOSS RECOVERY ARISING FROM LIABILITY; I.E. MEDICAL IN HO & AUTO

Insurable risks

Not all risks are *insurable*. In order to be considered insurable, a risk must substantially meet the five requirements outlined below: (1) importance, (2) accidental in nature, (3) calculability, (4) definiteness of loss, and (5) no excessively catastrophic loss.[7] Many insured risks do not meet each of the requirements perfectly, but when considered as a whole they may meet the requisites adequately.

Importance. Because of the element of expense in carrying on the business of insurance, premiums include a charge to provide for this cost. In the case of small risks that involve a threat of no great consequence, the cost of handling the business would make the rate prohibitive. For example, a pen may be lost or eyeglasses broken. To make a risk insurable, the amount of loss must be of such *importance* as to make the cost element a minor factor in the premium charged.

Accidental nature. Insurable risks must also normally be *accidental* in nature. Insurance is intended to cover fortuitous or unexpected losses. The loss need only be accidental *from the standpoint of the insured.* (It could, for example, be intentionally caused by someone else, such as a thief or a vandal.) Intentional losses caused by the insured are usually uninsurable because they cannot be reasonably predicted, and payment for them would violate public policy by encouraging such actions as fraud or arson. Other losses are so common as to be expected rather than unexpected. Wear and tear and depreciation are examples.

Calculability. A third requisite of an insurable risk is that it be *calculable*. It must permit a reasonable statistical estimate of the chance of loss and possible variations from the estimate. Losses may sometimes be unpredictable to an individual but be predictable in the aggregate and thus become insurable for a group. As a corollary to this requirement, the risk must be one of which there are a *large number* in existence, though insurers occasionally cover isolated risks concerning which there is no previous experience. For example, aviation insurers are faced with the necessity of providing insurance that will keep pace with the rapid advances in the field. The advent of jet- and rocket-propelled aircraft created a need for insurance in a field where statistical data were entirely lacking. The same is now true for the supersonic (SST) aircraft, where $50 million or more may be the cost of each plane. Most insurance is written, however, to cover risks where losses may reasonably be expected and where mathematical treatment or judgment based upon experience permits an estimate of losses sufficiently exact to make possible a workable estimate of their probable cost. When experience extends over a

---

[7] The objective measurement of the dimensions of insurability are discussed in Baruch Berliner, *Limits of Insurability of Risks* (Englewood Cliffs, N.J.: Prentice-Hall, 1982).

GO TO PAGE 42

number of years and the number of risks is great enough, a premium can be computed that will assure a sum sufficient to pay losses, compensate the insurer, and provide stability and permanence in the business. When new insurance forms are instituted, it becomes necessary to make rates that are dependent upon what is sometimes called "underwriting judgment," and in some instances this is nothing more than an approximation or guess to be adjusted with the accumulation of experience.

Other requirements for an insurable risk also relate to the prime requisite that the risk must be reasonably calculable. The need for large numbers applies not only for total risks accepted by an insurer but must also be met within each class of risks. Thus a large number of *homogeneous,* or similar, exposures to loss must be present to make a risk insurable. The exposures must also be *independent* of one another, so that reasonable estimates of loss can be made.

Definiteness of loss.   The losses should be *definite,* otherwise estimates of possible loss are difficult. Many insurance contract provisions have the objective of making the insured losses as clear and definite as possible. The perils as well as the losses must be clarified in the contract. Whether or not the loss actually occurred, and if so how many dollars of loss were involved, must be discernible.

No excessively catastrophic loss.   Ordinarily, no excessive *catastrophe* (very large) possibility of loss should be associated with an insurable risk. Accepting a few such risks together with smaller risks would make accurate predictions of loss impossible and could destroy the financial stability of an insurer. Today many losses are called catastrophic if they exceed $5 million,[8] but for most insurers losses are not excessively catastrophic unless many millions of dollars are involved. Nuclear and war risks are examples. What size loss is deemed catastrophic depends upon the financial resources available.

In total.   The student should note that these requirements for an insurable risk are not absolute. Insurability is best described as a relative matter in which the insurable quality of the risk is determined by appraisal of all the requirements together. The size and ability of the insurer are also important. Many common kinds of insurance do not meet each of the requirements perfectly. Consider, for example, the following: Is theft insurance "definite" (that is, was the item really stolen, or just lost)? Are all drivers "similar" in regard to risk of automobile accidents? (Obviously not, though they may be relatively similar within age, type of car, and other classifications.) Is a fire caused by carelessness always "accidental"? Aren't windstorms such as hurricanes and tornadoes "catastrophic" in nature?

Careful analysis in applying each of the requirements for an insurable

---

[8] *Insurance Facts* (New York: Insurance Information Institute, 1981–82), p. 49.

risk to a particular peril shows that few, if any, are "perfect" insurable risks. Most are only relatively good ones, and some are fine examples of bad ones. Many contract and insurer underwriting restrictions deal with this problem, trying to improve the insurability of a peril by such methods as limitations on the amount of coverage and locations, prohibited types, specific contract definitions, deductibles, and reinsurance. What is "insurable" may change over time and with the use of such limitations. Flood damage, for example, was considered uninsurable for many years, but it may now be insured in many areas through a federal government insurance program.

WHY TREAT RISK?

Studying risk and insurance is suggested in Part One to answer the following questions: *What* is risk, *why* treat risk, and *what* is risk management? (Chapter 1). *How* are risk-management decisions made? (Chapter 2). *How* significant is insurance in this process? (Chapter 3), and *what* are the fundamentals of *insurance contracts* (Chapter 4)?

In classifying the types of risk, some possible answers to these questions have already been suggested. Speculative and pure risk were distinguished, so that the emphasis was placed upon pure risks, involving chance of loss or no loss, but not those risks having profit as a predominant feature. Hedging was explained as one example of a method for dealing with speculative risk. Gambling risks were excluded from consideration because they involve the creation of risk rather than the treatment of existing economic risk. The concept of insurable risks was emphasized. One might think that an insurance text could stop right there and conclude that insurance is *the* answer to the problem of handling risk. No such easy, pat answer is intended, for no risk in theory or in practice should be handled with insurance as a perfunctory solution. After an understanding of why treating risk is so often necessary, a proper solution should include full consideration of *all* the available alternatives for dealing with risk.

Security a natural goal

The quest for security, or reasonable certainty, is a basic human drive. The concern is natural—a desire for knowing that the future will provide the necessities of life (and perhaps some luxuries, too).

Risk, or uncertainty of financial loss, is a threat to those future needs and wants. The values with which risk is concerned were discussed at the beginning of this chapter. Perils can destroy or damage assets and interrupt or terminate income. Such losses can decrease the future enjoyment of life, and this is why most persons prefer to do something about risk rather than merely accept it as is.

Losses from pure risk

This reaction to risk is particularly appropriate in regard to pure risk. The future result is either loss or no loss. The *actual losses* may be serious, crippling a business or causing an individual or family great financial hardship. One type of loss is *direct* physical loss, such as fire damage, which results in more than $5 billion of *property* loss each year in the United States. *Indirect* loss is also considerable, such as lost profits following a direct loss. Billions of dollars are lost, too, because of the loss of human *life* values due to such perils as death and disability.

Other costs of pure risk

In addition to actual losses, other undesirable results stem from risk. Uncertainties in regard to the possibilities of loss, or *loss exposures,* are costly. *Even if no losses ever occur* as anticipated, at least two factors add to the cost of risk: (1) *fear and worry* and (2) *less than optimum use of resources.*[9]

Fear and worry are very costly. The time spent in thinking about real or imagined chances of loss is expensive. The "opportunity cost" of worry time and effort is probably staggering when one considers the many other things that could be done if there were no fear of loss. "If we only could work as hard as we worry" is an expression that indicates the cost of lost peace of mind.

In addition, exposures to loss create adverse effects on the behavior of individuals, organizations, and societies. Uncertainty involves many situations where estimates of the probability of loss are necessary. Most persons will not predict the chance of loss correctly: some will be pessimistic and overestimate; others will be optimistic and underestimate. The result is either wasteful preparations for losses that are not as likely as expected or lack of preparation for unexpected losses that may have serious financial consequences.

Investments are frequently influenced by the exposures to loss with which they are associated. Sometimes activities or investments are completely avoided because the exposure to loss is high, in spite of excellent earnings potential. That amount of money "put away for a rainy day" may have to be put in very safe investments in order to be readily available if and when it does rain (or some other peril causes loss). Without such uncertainty, perhaps the money could be invested in a much more

---

[9] Williams et al., *Principles of Risk Management,* p. 11.

productive capacity with consequent greater return. Investments may also be diverted to more liquid, or safer, types of assets than are really necessary. Thus, returns in relation to true loss exposures are less than optimum, and these reduced earnings are an additional cost of risk.

There also is a tendency because of loss exposures to concentrate planning on the near future, rather than on the significant benefits of long-range planning. The cost of risk is increased by the extent to which exposures to loss cause this misemphasis in planning.

SCOPE AND OBJECTIVES OF RISK MANAGEMENT

Understanding risk and why risk should be treated are fundamental to full appreciation of the significant trend toward adoption of the *risk-management concept*. The idea is that risk must be properly managed in order to achieve various individual and organizational goals. Perhaps no other trend related to insurance has caused more concern and changes during the past two decades than this logical movement toward a systematic analysis of risk and the alternative methods of treating risk.

This part of Chapter 1 concentrates on introducing the *scope and objectives of risk management*—what it is and what it tries to do. The next section explains the *place of the risk manager*—who performs the functions of risk management. These sections lead to discussion in Chapter 2 of the *risk-management decision-making* process—how risk management is achieved.

Scope of risk management

The two basic methods of treating risk—risk control and risk financing—are integrated in a process known as *risk management*.[10] *Risk control* minimizes losses and loss exposures, while *risk financing* pays for losses that do occur. Risk management is also the use of the steps in risk management (see Chapter 2) and particularly concerns the use of the various methods of risk treatment. In effect, it is *coordinated risk treatment*.

Risk management is basically a problem of decision making for either a *personal* or an *organizational* situation. Each situation is unique in the sense that none is exactly the same, even though some common characteristics may be identified. Both personal and organizational risks can be taken care of, or "managed," but most efforts and principles of risk management have centered on the risks of organizations, including

---

[10] Robert I. Mehr and Bob A. Hedges, *Risk Management in the Business Enterprise* (Homewood, Ill.: Richard D. Irwin, 1963), p. vii. This is the first use of the term in the title of a textbook. The 1974 edition is titled *Risk Management: Concepts and Applications*.

those of business firms, nonprofit organizations, or government institutions. With increasing consumer education in family finance, it is expected that the personal consumer will increasingly use the risk-management technique.

The term *risk management* is a relatively new and popular one, though its exact meaning and scope are neither fully understood nor fully accepted.[11] It is not all management of a business. In fact, it does not concern all risk, and the term as it has evolved thus far is really "(pure) risk management," it being understood that the process does not deal with speculative risks. Management reluctance to accept the term *risk management* sometimes stems from executives not understanding that the field is limited to pure risks and primarily to protecting the organization's assets and income from accidental losses.

Management is the whole process of planning, organizing, and controlling people and things. Risk management is only a part of this process but an extremely important one. It has been correlated with the "security" function, one of the six principal functions of businesses: (1) technical, (2) commercial, (3) financial, (4) security (protection of property and persons), (5) accounting, and (6) managerial.[12] Even in this limited concept, risk management is estimated to be 10 percent or more of all business activity of managers.

Risk management is clearly more than just *insurance management,* a concept which would be primarily limited to decisions of when, how much, how, and where to insure the uncertainties previously described as insurable-type risks. Certainly, insurance as *one* of the techniques of handling risk is needed. In fact, it may remain as the principal method of treating the many risks of business. But without careful study of *all* the alternatives in risk management in a coordinated decision-making process, insurance may oftentimes be used where it shouldn't be used, or not used where it should be used. Although some risks usually must be insured, to deserve the title of *risk manager* a person must do much more than merely be an "insurance buyer."

Objectives of risk management

If risk managers are asked, "What is the goal of risk management in your organization?", the answers are likely to vary greatly. However,

---

[11] The origin of the term is not precise. One of the earliest uses appeared in chap. 35 of the fourth edition of Albert H. Mowbray and Ralph H. Blanchard, *Insurance* (New York: McGraw-Hill, 1955). Newer editions give a fuller explanation of the functions and principles of risk management.

[12] Credit for this concept belongs to Henri Fayol, *General and Industrial Management* (New York: Pitman Publishing, 1949); and to C. Arthur Williams, Jr. and Richard H. Heins, *Risk Management and Insurance* (New York: McGraw-Hill, 1964), table 2–1, pp. 13 and 77, who first used it in an insurance text. A fourth edition discusses this idea on p. 24.

many risk managers might summarize by saying that the objective is "to preserve the assets and income of my organization by providing protection against the risks of accidental loss."

Implicit is the idea that preservation includes *all* assets—those of physical property and of employees. Also, it is probable that the idea of protection encompasses *many different methods of treating risk,* including risk control by loss prevention and risk financing through retention and transfers, especially insurance. Finally, it is understood that the risk manager is concerned not with speculative risks of loss or gain but only with *pure* risks related to loss or no loss due to an unexpected accident.

Putting all the possible objectives of risk management in a few words or one sentence is very difficult. Individuals and families have different goals as compared with organizations. Each may have specific goals that are paramount, while others may not feel that some of these goals are important at all.

Risk managers, in further describing the objectives of their organization, should first consider its *general goals.* Is it *profit,* as a profit-seeking enterprise? Is it a good *reputation,* as a solid corporate citizen of the community and society? Or is it other *personal satisfactions* which the owners and managers have, such as being the biggest, best, or most worthwhile organization of its kind? Organizations usually have all or several of these goals but vary as to which is of highest priority. Because one goal often conflicts with another, each organization is characterized by what it considers the best combination of objectives. Risk managers, as part of the management team, must coordinate their own goals in risk management with the overall goals of their particular organization.

More specific risk-management goals have been identified for an organization as: (1) survival, (2) peace of mind, (3) lower costs (or higher profits), (4) stable earnings, (5) minimal interruption of operations, (6) continued growth, and (7) satisfaction of social responsibility with a good public image.[13] Some of these are pre-loss objectives, meaningful before a loss has occurred; some are post-loss objectives for after a loss; and several are significant both before and after a loss.

THE PLACE OF THE RISK MANAGER

The changing function of *risk managers* toward the broader risk-management concept began to occur during the early 1960s.[14] Acceptance of this wider perspective was gradual, but the "risk-management trend" has escalated rapidly in the past decade. The only trade journal of the

---

[13] Robert I. Mehr and Bob A. Hedges, *Risk Management: Concepts and Applications* (Homewood, Ill.: Richard D. Irwin, 1974), Chaps. 1–2.

[14] One of the earliest books that compiled articles describing the increasing duties of risk managers was *The Growing Job of Risk Management* (New York: American Management Association, 1962).

professional society of risk managers, now representing almost 3,500 of the larger U.S. businesses, institutions, and governmental bodies, was called *The National Insurance Buyer* until the early 1970s. Now it is titled *Risk Management,* and it is published monthly by the Risk and Insurance Management Society (RIMS).

RIMS has provided a strong impetus toward making risk managers key executives on the management team. An educational emphasis is providing opportunities for fundamental and advanced preparation for the expanding job of risk manager. The Insurance Institute of America has designed a series of courses in cooperation with RIMS, leading to the professional designations of Associate in Risk Management (ARM), and Loss Control Management (LCM). In addition, regular national and regional conferences, and publications and research grants sponsored by the RIMS Risk Studies Foundation have aided the growth possibilities in this field considerably.

American businesses and institutions are rapidly recognizing the need for professional risk managers. Increasing insurance costs, the broadening scope of liability exposures, governmental legislation tightening safety standards, and other factors are creating a fuller appreciation for the value of risk-management activities. Major business publications have featured risk management as a need for small and medium-sized companies as well as the larger corporations.[15] Risk-management decision making may include much more than traditional tasks related to property and liability insurance. It now often comprises the whole spectrum of protection, including safety and employee benefit administration problems.[16]

To carry out risk-management decision making, many business firms and institutions have created the position of risk manager as a specialist performing this function for management. Only a few of these specialists have this exact title, and the majority are still known instead as "insurance manager," "corporate insurance director," or by other titles. Increasingly, the position is a full-time one, particularly in organizations with more than 1,000 employees. In many other firms (about one fourth of the RIMS members), the risk manager (by whatever the title held) is performing risk-management functions as a part-time job in connection with other duties within the organization.

In a fairly large firm, the risk manager's *position within the organization* usually involves reporting to a top-level financial executive. In

---

[15] See "The Risk Management Revolution," *Fortune,* July 1976, p. 36; "Big Push in Risk Management," *Dun's Review,* June 1977, p. 62; and "Risk Management," *Dun's Review,* July 1981, p. 65.

[16] Thomas B. Morehart and John J. O'Connell, "The Risk Manager's Role in Employee Benefits Administration," *Risk Management,* October 1977, p. 42, and H. Wayne Snider, *Employee Benefits Management* (New York: Risk and Insurance Management Society, 1980).

Figure 1-3. Organization chart showing the place of the risk manager

smaller firms, the risk manager probably operates more in a staff function, reporting directly to the president. Studies show that about one third of the risk managers consider themselves to be members of top management, while more of the others are part of middle management.[17] Almost 80 percent report to top managers—the president, vice president, controller, or secretary—of their organization. More than half of RIMS members were risk managers for organizations with more than 2,000 employees and $100 million annual gross sales. Figure 1-3 shows the place of the risk manager for a typical RIMS member. New corporate risk-management organization systems are also appearing, tying insurance and safety functions more closely together.[18]

The *responsibilities* and authority of the risk manager are quite broad. They cut across many phases of the activities of an organization, and often the risk manager shares the responsibility for certain functions with other executives. The risk manager of larger firms has, in a majority of the cases, *full* responsibility for property and liability: (1) risk identification and evaluation, (2) selection of insurer, (3) approval of insurance

---

[17] A 1978 study prepared for RIMS, *The Risk and Insurance Manager: A Study of Responsibilities and Compensation* (Princeton, N.J.: Sission), compares changes and shows the risk manager's increasing importance.

[18] A series of three articles by Russell A. Drake, Jr., Richard S. Johnson, and James A. McCullough illustrates new organizational and administrative structures for risk management in the October 1977 issue of *Risk Management*.

renewals and amounts, (4) negotiation of insurance rates, (5) seeking competitive insurance bids, (6) insurance record keeping, (7) choosing deductibles, and (8) insurance claims handling. The risk manager usually *shares* authority for: (1) deciding whether or not to insure or retain (including self-insurance) risks, (2) selection of insurance broker, (3) instituting safety expenditures, and (4) reviewing contracts other than insurance.

Increasingly, the risk manager is also becoming involved in self-insurance administration; safety administration and compliance; working with the personnel manager on workers' compensation and in designing and arranging for employee benefit plans of group insurance and pensions; and coordination of the total risk-identification, analysis, and control functions of the organization. There are few areas in which the risk manager has not been acquiring a greater degree of control over the decision-making process. Size of the organization is not the only factor determining the extent of risk management activities. Often times, greater degree of risk because of the work environment and activities creates more need for increased risk-management responsibility and authority of the risk manager.[19]

One other important role of the risk manager is to encourage and help management to formulate a *policy statement* on the objectives and responsibilities of risk management. Having such a written policy statement approved by the president and the board of directors can aid the risk manager greatly in defining the scope and limitations of the job. The objectives, responsibilities, authority, and general policies of his or her department should be clearly stated. Setting broad guidelines in this way improves the risk manager's relationships with other executives and departments. It also helps obtain the cooperation of many persons within the organization who are crucial to a risk manager for information. For the supervision of risk management in the firm, a policy statement is essential as a basis for performance measurement and review.

The *qualifications* for good risk managers are determined by the extent of their important and usually broad responsibilities. They usually have a college education, as well as insurance and other business experience of many years, and often technical background in accounting, engineering, or law. Personal characteristics which enhance their effectiveness are leadership abilities, initiative, tact in working with others, and sound decision-making judgment.

Risk managers should understand the particular insurance needs of

---

[19] John J. O'Connell, "Changing Responsibilities and Activities of Risk Managers—1969 vs. 1975," *Risk Management,* January 1976, pp. 19–22. The data are from his 1975 Ohio State University dissertation, "Variables Related to Differences in the Risk Management Function in Large Organizations."

their organizations, because of their day-to-day contact and experience in their own firms. They should be familiar with and well trained in analyzing insurance coverage, rates, and markets. They are *not,* however, substitutes for good insurance agents or brokers. Agents should be able to supplement the work of risk managers and to provide many essential services in aiding them to locate insurance markets and loss-prevention services and to obtain fair loss settlements. Other advisers may often be used by or in conjunction with the insurance agent. Examples include safety engineers, accountants, attorneys, and trust experts.

Sometimes *the insurance agent,* particularly for small and medium-sized firms, serves in effect as the risk manager for an organization which has no one person assigned to these responsibilities. Larger agencies, especially, offer to serve in this capacity. Care must be taken to see (1) that the services are much broader than mere insurance coverages and include a real risk-management scope of loss prevention and other risk-treatment alternatives, and (2) that the insurance agency knows the special individual needs of the organization. The agent or broker cannot be expected to have a sufficiently accurate knowledge of all the ramifications of the insurance and risk needs of a huge business organization on a continual basis. With a large organization, a very small rate differential may mean a difference of thousands of dollars in premium. The expense of surveys to determine necessary improvements to secure even a minor adjustment in rate will pay where the premium volume is large. With reference to coverages, the large concern may quite safely eliminate certain risk from the insurance program and carry other risks on a deductible or catastrophe basis. While the professional agent and broker can cooperate with the insurance buyer in solving such problems—in fact they are quite essential—it is nevertheless true that the final responsibility for the risk-management program rests with the concern itself. It is because of this that the trained risk manager is coming to occupy an important position in the field of administration.

For international organizations the growing task of *international risk management* is another area of great challenge for risk managers. Foreign operations bring many new problems, including conflicts in corporate goals, different legal and cultural environments, and communication difficulties. A landmark study shows how risk-management practices vary for multinational companies.[20] Protecting worldwide investments is a growing task for risk managers of multinational organizations.[21]

---

[20] Norman A. Baglini, *Risk Management in International Corporations* (New York: Risk Studies Foundation, RIMS, 1976).

[21] Los Angeles Chapter, CPCU, "How to Protect Your Overseas Investment," *CPCU Journal* 35, no. 2 (June 1982), p. 112.

Note to students: It is hoped that you will follow the advice given in the Preface, which recommended as a regular procedure in reading this text: (1) First read the "outline of concepts" on the left-hand page at the beginning of the chapter; (2) Read the chapter; and then (3) *Go back to reread the outline* in order to review how the basic parts and subparts fit together.

FOR REVIEW AND DISCUSSION

1. Why is an understanding of risk important to the study of insurance?

2. Risk often has a different meaning to different persons or to the same person in different situations. Illustrate this statement with the three examples and explain why this paradox is so common.

3. Explain why you agree or disagree that "chance of loss is an inadequate description of risk."

4. Paul states: "Speculative risk is what I want." Carol says: "Not me, I'd rather have pure risk because . . ." How do you think Carol would finish her sentence, and what might be Paul's reasoning?

5. Distinguish between the use of the terms *risk, uncertainty, peril, hazard,* and *loss.* Why should they be differentiated?

6. An author has said: "The *risks* which families and businesses face are all pervasive. For the study of insurance it is meaningful to *classify risks* in several *different* ways. By doing so, one can learn for *which* risks the insurance techniques are best adapted to provide a *solution* to the important *problems* of risk." How would you explain the reasons why each of these statements is true, with particular reference to each of the italicized terms?

7. Why is it necessary to distinguish between:
    a. "Pure" and "speculative" risks?
    b. "Preventable" and "insurable" risks?
    c. "Gambling" and other risks?
    d. "Personal," "property," and "liability" risks?

8. Are all risks insurable? Why or why not?

9. Mr. I. M. Secure is purchasing a home and knows he will acquire several new risks. Classify and describe these risks.

10. Both physical and moral hazards may be involved in many risks. What are the purposes and problems of identifying these types of hazards?

11. Are each of the requisites for an insurable risk met by risks that are insured? Why or why not? Explain each of the requirements briefly and give an example of a risk which is sometimes insured that does *not* satisfy each requirement very well.

12. Do you think a risk such as traveling to and from the moon will ever be insurable? Upon what rationale do you base your answer?

13. *Insurance Facts* says that last year (a) "aggregate property loss in the United States from fire was more than $5 billion" and (b) "total dollar cost of traffic accidents was $60 billion." Explain whether or not you feel that these figures are the complete cost of fire and automobile accidents.

14. What is risk management, and how does it relate to insurance?

15. How have risk management and the risk manager's job changed in the past decade?

16. Suppose you are a merchant just beginning a new drive-in restaurant. You own the building and several vehicles and have 30 employees. What property and liability risks would you think it most important to insure? (Rank in order of importance along with brief reasons.)

17. In learning about risk and insurance, principles or basic ideas should be stressed. Explain two significant ideas which you believe will be of lasting value to you as a consumer in each of the following areas:
    a. The scope of risk management.
    b. The objectives of risk management.
    c. The place of the risk manager.

18. Indicate some of the responsibilities and services which professional risk managers are able to render to their employers. How do risk managers usually fit into the organization of their firm?

Chapter 2

Outline of concepts

Risk-management decision making is explained in terms of:

The steps in risk-management and risk-treatment alternatives: a summary, which establishes a framework for the whole sequence of decisions.

Basic methods of treating risk are two: (1) *risk control* (minimizing losses) and (2) *risk financing* (paying for losses that do occur).

Risk control methods are four:

Risk avoidance is helpful but limited in application.

Combination, segregation, and diversification, often used together.

Loss prevention and reduction, often the first consideration.

Noninsurance transfers, such as subcontracting and licensing.

Risk financing methods include two types: (1) *risk retention* and (2) *risk transfer.*

Risk-retention methods are five:

Absorption in current operating expense, which is common.

Funding and reserves, which help meet some perils.

Deductibles and excess plans, a form of partial retention.

Self-insurance, sometimes used, but often a misnomer.

Captive insurers, which may have some tax or other benefits.

Risk transfer methods include three:

Credit arrangements, difficult for unpredictable losses.

Noninsurance transfers, such as hold-harmless agreements.

Insurance, the predominant method of treating pure risk, is described by *economic* definition as a method of reducing risk by transfer and combination, but also as a *legal* contract, a *business* institution, a *social* device, and a *mathematical* technique.

The individual steps in risk management are the decisions made in regard to:

Risk identification, through the use of *risk and insurance surveys* using *loss-exposure charts, financial statements, flow charts, systems analysis,* and *personal inspections.*

Risk measurement, calculating loss *frequency, severity,* and *variation;* maximum probable loss; and using mathematical tools and computers.

Choice and use of methods, reviewing the basic alternatives of risk treatment, and using *traditional insurance priority listings, loss-matrix tables,* and *risk-management information systems.*

Risk administration, *coordinating the steps and objectives of risk management,* and monitoring *choices and coverages* in order to meet continually changing needs.

An example of risk-management decision making illustrates the four steps in risk management for a plastics manufacturer.

A case study for business risk management of a modern shopping center includes questions reviewing the total process of risk-management decision making.

Risk-management decision making

The challenging world of risk management is approached by answering two basic questions: (1) *Why* is risk management important? and (2) *Who* makes risk-management decisions? These questions were answered by explaining the scope and objectives of risk management, and the place of the risk manager within various organizations. Although individuals and families also must make risk-management decisions, systematic risk management most directly concerns professional risk managers.

The understanding of risk and risk management as presented in Chapter 1 leads to the major decision-making process of the persons or organizations facing the problems of risk. *How* risk management is performed is the focus of this chapter.

There is a dilemma in deciding on the sequence of presenting ideas in regard to risk management: (1) Should the alternatives of risk treatment be discussed first, and then the steps in the risk-management process? or (2) Should the steps in risk management be presented to the student first, and then the risk-treatment alternatives?

Because no perfect solution exists, this chapter adopts a combined approach. First, a brief *summary* of the steps in risk management *and* risk-treatment alternatives establish a framework for the whole sequence of decisions which must be made by the risk manager. Next, the basic *methods of treating risk* are presented, because the major objective of risk management is the coordination of these various alternatives. The *individual steps of risk management* are then discussed in more detail. Finally, an *example* of risk-management decision making and a *case study* for business risk management serve to review the entire risk-management process.

THE STEPS IN RISK MANAGEMENT AND RISK-TREATMENT ALTERNATIVES: A SUMMARY

The risk-management function is perhaps best described and understood in terms of the decisions which are a part of it. The process begins with a recognition of the existence of various risks. Basically this is the *identification or classification* of risks. Then the risks of loss must be *measured, analyzed, and evaluated* in terms of frequency, severity, and variability. Next a decision must be made as to the *choice and use of the methods* for meeting each specific risk identified. Some risks may be avoided, some retained under planned programs, and some transferred by such a method as insurance. Once the methods of treatment are chosen, plans for *administration* of the program must be instituted. This last step includes both the implementation of the methods used, as well as monitoring the choices to see that they are effective.

The above decisions are summarized as the key steps in the total process of treating risk:

1. Identification.
2. Measurement.
3. Choice and use of methods of treatment.
4. Administration.

Figure 2–1 shows these steps and the important relationship to risk-treatment alternatives, or basic methods of treating risk, which are discussed next.

BASIC METHODS OF TREATING RISK

A danger exists in thinking of each of the methods of treating risk as a single and complete solution to the problem of risk. In practice, it is much more common to find all, or at least several, techniques used together to provide the best answers for meeting the financial problems of risk.

Two basic methods of treating risk are: (1) *risk control,* in order to minimize losses, and (2) *risk financing,* in order to reduce the costs of those losses which do occur.[1] In almost all cases it is not merely a choice of using risk control *or* risk financing, but good risk management requires the use of some of *both* methods of treating risk.

Risk *control* involves a number of alternatives, and here again the choice is not limited to just one of them. The goal is the proper *choices,* using all the methods which result in benefits that exceed the costs. Many organizations use all or many of the techniques in order to best handle the diverse types of risk that are discussed in this chapter. The alternatives include: (1) *risk avoidance;* (2) *separation, diversification,*

---

[1] The development of this classification of methods for treating risk is credited to Dr. George L. Head. It has been adopted by the Insurance Institute of America for its RM 54, 55, and 56 courses leading to the Associate in Risk Management national professional designation. For a thorough treatment of these concepts, see Dr. Head's *The Risk Management Process* (New York: Risk and Insurance Management Society, 1978).

Figure 2–1. The steps in risk management and risk-treatment alternatives

or *combination* of loss exposures; (3) *loss prevention and reduction;* and (4) some *noninsurance transfer of loss.*

Risk *financing* also includes many alternatives which can be used separately or in conjunction with one another and with the previously identified risk control measures. Financing methods are subdivided into two categories: *risk retention* and *risk transfer.* Risk retention helps provide different types of funding when paying for losses: absorption in expenses, special reserves, funds, deductibles, "self-insurance," and "captive" insurers. The most common technique of risk transfer is *insurance,* but some *noninsurance transfers* of risk and *credit* mechanisms are also useful.

The following sections discuss each of the methods of risk control and risk financing separately. Chapter 2 emphasizes these methods of treating risk in the context of the process of *risk management,* a decision-making process by which risks are identified and measured, and then the choices among risk control and risk financing methods are made and carried out. This relationship is summarized in Figure 2–1.

Risk control methods

Different ways of subdividing the major methods of risk control are possible. A four-fold subdivision is discussed within this section of the chapter. The emphasis of each method is on achieving the purpose of minimizing losses which might occur to assets and income.

Risk avoidance. One of the most obvious methods of handling risk is to *avoid* as many risks as possible. If one does not want to have economic losses, *some* losses can be avoided by various decisions in which risks are either not assumed, or are abandoned. A family can decide to rent rather than buy a home, thereby avoiding the risk of losing the home value through the peril of fire. A business may lease its automobiles and avoid assuming the risk of losing those values (even though it may be accepting in the lease another risk—that of legal liability for returning the automobiles in good condition). A manufacturer may decide not to produce a chemical which has many potential product liability claims. A person who is worried about poisonous snakebites or heat exhaustion can live in the Arctic, or at least locate in areas with a minimum of risk from such perils. The risk of airplane accidents, drownings, and sports injuries can be avoided largely by keeping away from airplanes, water, and sport events, respectively.

However, avoidance of risk is no practical solution to the many risks that are involved in normal activities. True, some unusual risks with high chance of loss can be avoided, but realistically the avoidance of risk is only an alternative in regard to a restricted number of economic risks. Some risks may be impossible to avoid; others may not be economically desirable, either because the benefits outweigh the costs, or because avoiding one risk may create another. For all such unavoidable risks, other solutions must be considered.

Combination, segregation, and diversification. *Combination,* or pooling, of exposures to loss is a common method of risk control. This method broadens the units of exposure and may aid in predicting future losses. It may "spread the risk" and create more stability in loss experience. Combination is a basic principle of insurance and "self-insurance," and it may also be used in many other business situations. For example, the corporation as a typical form of doing business combines the assets of many stockholders and spreads exposure to loss from a few individuals to thousands of investors. Also, mergers of companies combine many different exposures to loss. Growth within a business firm also combines and extends the scope of loss exposures, when, for example, a business expands its marketing by adding new sales outlets. Employees, too, use combination as a method of reducing risk when they join to practice collective bargaining through unions.

The examples are numerous, but usually the combination process has to be used in conjunction with other methods described here. For example, in order to be most effective, combination of exposures is used *with* segregation and diversification or with other methods of risk financing. The mere combining of exposures is not effective in reducing risk. In fact, it may increase more than it decreases risk if the added exposures are more concentrated or variable than the previous exposures.

Among the simplest but most important methods of risk control are segregation and diversification. *Segregation,* the separation or dispersion of loss exposures, is often an effective way of limiting the severity of loss by reducing the concentration of exposures. It may also increase the number of exposure units. *Diversification* uses different types of loss exposures, as opposed to having only one type, in order to improve on predictability (usually frequency). When assets or activities are duplicated at different locations, the diversification technique is being used.

Common business examples of segregation and diversification (in parentheses) are:

1. Physically separating buildings (and using masonry as well as wood buildings).
2. Using fireproof interior building construction, such fire walls and incombustible and smokeproof stairwells and elevators.
3. Storing inventory in several locations (and types of buildings).
4. Maintaining duplicate records to reduce accounts receivable losses (and using paper as well as microfilm records).
5. Transporting goods in separate vehicles instead of concentrating high values in single shipments (and shipping by truck, railroad, and air).
6. Limiting money exposures at any one location.

7. Prohibiting key employees from traveling together (and using different transportation conveyances).
8. Limiting legal liability by forming several separate corporations.

Classic examples of the *failure* to use segregation and diversification are found in catastrophic fires, such as those that took place at a Linden, New Jersey, oil refinery (1970—$50 million), a New York telephone central office (1975—$70 million), and an English spare parts depot (1981—$150 million). The Tokyo airplane crash which killed over 70 key employees and agents of one sales firm a number of years ago and explosions in large grain elevators are also examples of catastrophic losses due to the lack of segregation and diversification.

Loss prevention and reduction. Two methods of risk control, loss prevention and loss reduction, could be discussed separately, but they are combined in this section because they are so closely related to each other. Techniques which help prevent or reduce loss are often logical and important, for losses are seldom completely taken care of by any one method of treating risk. The total effects of loss are usually much greater than the indemnification available through insurance or any other alternative; thus, preventing or reducing the loss is just good common sense if it can be done with reasonable cost in relation to its potential benefits. In some cases, such as saving lives or preventing human injury and suffering, cost may be a secondary factor.

Loss prevention may involve the elimination of the chance of loss and thus *risk;* more often, a reduction in the *probability* of loss is accomplished. *Loss reduction* has the goal of reducing the severity of loss, and it includes steps taken to accomplish this either before or after loss.

Loss prevention and loss reduction are not the same thing as *risk* reduction. The uncertainty (risk) of variable losses may still be the same, even though the chance of decreasing value (loss) is reduced or there is a reduction of the conditions increasing the ratio of the likelihood of loss (hazards) to the cause of loss (peril). For example, reducing the probability of loss from 10 percent to 5 percent does not necessarily reduce either risk or the variation in expected as compared with actual results at these two loss probabilities.

The topic of loss prevention and reduction is so large that only a brief mention can be made here of the many techniques available to agents, brokers, consultants, insurers, and insureds. Fire-resistive structures are built. Protective devices are installed in boilers. Lightning rods are installed. Safety devices guard much industrial machinery. Such firms as Underwriters' Laboratories inspect most electrical appliances. Construction is aimed at the reduction or elimination of tornado, earthquake, and hurricane losses. Most of these activities take place *before* losses occur. Loss-reduction methods that are used after losses happen include the prompt investigation, reporting, and settlement of claims. Another method is the use of salvage companies to sell damaged goods.

Steps to prevent and reduce losses are the result of both private and community undertakings. Some of the larger projects, such as those involving flood control, are carried on by the federal government. Public measures for loss prevention and reduction also include police and fire protection and municipal building codes. An important question in regard to these activities is to determine who should be *responsible* for them. In total, it becomes in most cases a joint responsibility of (1) government, (2) insurers, (3) private organizations, and (4) the insureds themselves.

The sources of information on loss prevention and reduction are myriad: hundreds of booklets on specific problems in loss prevention are available through the National Fire Protection Association, the Insurance Institute for Highway Safety, engineering journals, and many other sources. A new government source is the National Highway Traffic Safety Administration. Another is the Occupational Safety and Health Administration, which has made thousands of inspections of workplaces in order to reduce employee accidents and sicknesses. Given sufficient funds and ingenuity, the extent of loss prevention and reduction can be almost limitless. Insurers, agents, and specialized loss prevention businesses can aid their clients considerably in this process.

Noninsurance transfers.   The final method of risk control involves *noninsurance transfers.* Such transfers are effected by means of a contract, other than insurance, in which one party transfers to another *legal responsibility* for property or employee losses. A later section will discuss other noninsurance transfers which are methods of risk financing rather than risk control. These transfer the *financial burden* of the transferor.

Subcontracting is one important example. As an illustration, a contractor may wish to transfer the possibility of injury to the contractor's employees in a particularly dangerous part of a construction project. This may be done by hiring subcontractors to do that work, under contracts in which the subcontractors hire their own employees. The responsibility for these employees is, by contract, transferred to the subcontractors, who would be obligated to pay workers' compensation losses. The exposure to these losses is eliminated for the original contractor.

A manufacturer could use another method of noninsurance transfer, that of *licensing.* If the manufacturer does not want to produce or sell certain goods, and wishes to transfer some of the responsibilities of these tasks to someone else, this may be done in licensing contracts. Under these arrangements, the manufacturer would receive only a royalty or fee for licensing others to do the work. The licensees would have the responsibility for injuries to their own employees. In addition, some protection might be achieved in reducing the exposure to liability losses from the public, either in the manufacturing or the distribution of the product.

Risk financing methods

In most cases, losses are only lessened by the methods of risk control just discussed. The one exception is risk avoidance, in which the probability of loss, and thus risk, is eliminated. Under all the other techniques, losses still occur—and some additional choices are necessary in deciding how to pay for them. These alternatives are the methods of *risk financing,* explained in the following sections.

Most losses of any importance require a combination of these alternative financing methods, often in conjunction with risk control measures as well. Risk financing may be divided into two major types: (1) risk retention and (2) risk transfer. In each of these major areas, several significant methods of risk financing are recognized.

Risk retention.   If risk has not been avoided, you may decide to keep it. Sometimes this is called "risk assumption," but *risk retention* seems the better term because you retain rather than newly assume the many risks which you already have. The residual risks must in some way be paid for, or financed. Five basic methods are discussed in this section: (1) absorption in operating expenses, (2) funding and reserves, (3) deductibles and excess plans, (4) "self-insurance," and (5) "captive" insurers.

Probably more pure risks are retained due to *lack* of planning than due to any rational process of planning. Some risks are retained because the existence or significance of the risks is not known. Lack of knowledge or inability to reach the right decision (even with adequate knowledge) may result in retention of risks. Information may be available and not used, or perhaps the necessary information is unavailable. An illustration is retaining the risk of loss to property by falling meteors (or perhaps flying saucers?) because of (1) not knowing anything about meteors, or that a possibility of loss from this source exists, or (2) not knowing that insurance could be obtained for such a peril. *Unplanned* retention of risk might also result from unintentional or irrational action or from passive behavior due to lack of thought, laziness, or lack of interest in discovering uncertainties of loss.

Some *unimportant* risks may be intentionally ignored. This is not considered a method of treating risk but instead a method of *not* treating it. For example, the loss of a glove or pen may cause no financial hardship to an individual, so the risk of loss is ignored and no plan for occurrence of the loss is made. Similarly, a business may decide that smaller buildings or properties are of relative unimportance and knowingly ignore any payment plans for such insignificant risks.

Important risks regarding those losses that could cause financial hardship for a family or business must be paid for in some appropriate manner. *Planned* risk retention is one method, occurring when it is the result of purposeful, conscious, intentional, and active behavior.

The *why* of risk retention is based upon this fundamental question: "What reasons are there for using retention?" These include (1) necessity, where other alternatives are not possible; (2) control or convenience; and (3) cost. The first reason is that risk retention must be used; the second and third should result from a conscious effort to analyze the benefits of retention in terms of control, convenience, or cost, and the ability of individuals or business firms to handle their own risks effectively.

Some pure risks can only be financed by retention. They are knowingly retained by *necessity,* or default, as it is impossible to transfer them. Typical examples of such risks are responsibility for criminal acts and unusual obsolescence of property. Occasionally, a peril that is normally insured against may be uninsurable because of high probability of loss or bad loss experience. This category of retained risks is relatively small, for the transfer of most risks (at some price, even if very high) is usually possible. Sometimes markets for insurance are temporarily unavailable, and retention is necessary until the competitive world markets make adjustments permitting risk transfer. Examples are offshore oil drilling equipment in recent years and extremely poor substandard housing in blighted urban areas.

Retention of risk may be practiced by some individuals or organizations because they wish to have the *control or convenience* of paying their own losses. Regardless of cost comparison, some firms may wish to have the benefits of direct and complete control. Hospital expenses of employees, for example, may be paid directly by the employer in order to obtain the most rapid payment possible and employee goodwill. Or, a manufacturer in a competitive technical field might decide to retain both property and products liability exposures in connection with highly secret inventions of a research laboratory.

The economics of alternative risk treatment are a major consideration in most decisions to retain risk. A comparison of the *cost* involved in each alternative method of financing losses is necessary. If insurance against earthquake damage is available, how much will it cost? If earthquake damage could be prevented by extra-strong building construction, how much would this cost? Would a "self-insurance" program with a reserve fund be feasible, and what would its cost be? In each of these comparisons the need for complete evaluation is obvious. Not only loss frequency and severity but *all* costs of the various alternatives, including indirect as well as direct costs, are needed for fair comparisons.[2] A new cost factor of increased importance is the high cost of money, which

---

[2] The principle of "indirect" costs often exceeding the "direct" loss by as much as four or five times was pioneered by H. W. Heinrich in his book *Industrial Accident Prevention* (New York: McGraw-Hill, 1931).

makes risk-retention plans more desirable because assets are held until losses actually occur.

The time, effort, and cost required to make a reasonable cost comparison among alternatives is an important factor. Unfortunately, many organizations do not try to make such a comparison. The process is not necessarily a complex one; with experience, the *idea* can be put into effect with relatively little trouble or expense. A later section includes a comparison table to illustrate how this can be done as part of risk-management decision making. Exact comparison for larger exposures and numerous perils may be more complicated in practice.

Almost everyone may use each of these methods of financing losses to some extent. For a business firm, many factors are often important, such as the firm's size; its overall objectives; its philosophy; its capacity to absorb losses from assets, operating funds, or credit expansion; and its ability to predict losses.

Does a small firm face the same problems of risk that a larger firm does? Basically, yes, for the small firm probably has the same major perils which may cause loss, such as fire, windstorm, negligence, liability, crime, and so on. (A few exceptions exist, such as on-location steam boiler exposure and radioactive isotopes.) A larger firm, however, may be able to use risk-retention plans to a greater degree because it *may* be able to (1) better predict its larger number of diversified losses, and (2) if it does err in prediction, it *may* have larger reserves or surplus to absorb unexpected losses. A basic question is: "How much change in earnings, before and after taxes, can the organization reasonably accommodate?" Some firms use 5 percent as a benchmark, while others may use as low as 1 percent or more than 10 percent.

Absorption in current operating expense. Looking more closely at each of the methods of risk financing used by business firms, one finds that the most common method is to absorb losses as a part of regular operating expense. In a highly recommended research study, *Corporate Self-Insurance and Risk Retention Plans,* Goshay found that of 156 risk-retention plans by large corporations (most with assets of between $25 million and $300 million) for fire, liability, and workers' compensation perils, almost half maintained no reserves, all losses being paid as a current expense when the occasion demanded.[3] Recent studies have determined that more than two thirds of large U.S. companies retain some property risks.[4]

In smaller firms, it is less likely that current operating expenses can

---

[3] Robert C. Goshay, *Corporate Self-Insurance and Risk Retention Plans* (Homewood, Ill.: Richard D. Irwin, 1964), p. 112.

[4] Mitchell York, "RIMS/TIME Magazine Survey—Where Are We Headed?" *Risk Management,* June 1981, p. 13.

withstand the potential losses. Some other perils which might be considered for absorption in current operating expenses are glass breakage, transportation shipment damage, and automobile physical damage. Many other exposures might be added to this list in particular situations. It is essential that the potential loss severity be low in relation to the assets, surplus, or working capital of the business firm, and that loss frequency be high in order to achieve some measure of predictability of future losses. These same attributes should be carefully considered in any of the risks retained, even where reserves are maintained, as discussed in the next section.

Funding and reserves. Irregular drains of substantial amounts of assets, surplus, or working capital are not desirable or practical for business. A fund (of actual segregated assets) or a reserve (usually a bookkeeping entry of earmarked surplus) may be used to offset some irregular losses which are too large to be absorbed in current operating expenses but small enough that the business firm can reasonably retain them.

There are many difficulties in connection with funds or reserves maintained for risk-retention plans. Funds in particular usually represent an ideal rather than actual practice. Most businesses use a bookkeeping reserve rather than an actual cash fund. The major disadvantage of reserves is that they do *not* guarantee that cash will be available to meet losses. Other problems include: (1) How large should the fund be? (2) How can it be accumulated without intervening losses that might be disastrous? and (3) How can the fund be maintained, without the temptation to use it for other emergencies or in regular operations of the business? If liability or earmarked surplus reserves are used, the general tendency is to find the assets representing the reserves tied up in nonliquid assets, and inadequate for the irregular, larger losses for which the reserves are intended.

The income tax laws are another disadvantage, for a current business deduction is not allowed (except in some workers' compensation "self-insured" plans and bad debt reserves) for the formation of a reserve to meet most losses. Losses are only deductible as they are actually paid, which means deductions may vary considerably. Several federal bills have recently proposed that reserves for some liability lines should be deductible.

In all, funding and reserves, although better than not having them at all, have limited application to most of the perils faced by individuals, families, and small businesses. It is only for *some* type of losses of *some* situations, *with* careful and continuing efforts to maintain the objectives of the plan, that full risk retention with reserves is a satisfactory solution. However, high interest rates and "cash flow" analysis have increased interest in recent years in this method of risk retention.

Deductibles and excess plans. It is in the area of *deductibles,* a form of *partial* risk retention, that many of the most exciting current applications of risk retention are being considered and practiced. The principle of having the policyholder receive payment only for losses over a stated amount (or percentage figure) has been accepted for many years in certain types of insurance, such as marine, credit, collision, and windstorm coverages. It has been widely adopted for many personal lines, such as automobile collision, homeowners, and disability income.

The large commercial buyers of insurance, too, have had access to large deductibles for some years. The growth of interest in, and availability of, deductibles in the $1,000 to $10,000 or more per loss range had been one of the most significant changes in the insurance market during the past decade.[5] One special type, called an *excess plan,* usually has a deductible of more than $100,000. The deductible amount is chosen to approximate the maximum probable loss, and insureds usually provide their own loss-prevention services. The Fire Insurance Research and Actuarial Association publishes tables of recommended fire and windstorm insurance rate credits for $10,000, $25,000, $50,000, and $100,000. The Industrial Risk Insurers and the Factory Mutuals use deductibles of some kind in almost all of their plans.

The size of the deductible to be chosen varies according to a number of factors: the nature of the perils, including the frequency and severity of loss patterns; the financial ability of the insured to withstand losses; the existence of reserves or funds to help finance the deductible portion of losses; the desire for claims handling by the insured or the insurer; the need for loss-prevention services; the insured's degree of risk aversion; and many other criteria.[6] The total circumstances and objectives must be appraised: a deductible of $500 may be too large for some situations, while one of $50,000 may be too small for others. Oil companies and other large companies with diversified exposures often use deductibles of $1 million or more.

A review of the reasons for using deductibles given by insureds might include:

1. *Cost* economies.
   a. Precluding small claims and maintenance expenses.
   b. Omitting regular, expected normal losses that can be handled effectively by other means.
   c. Avoiding state premium taxes.
   d. Avoiding regulated rates or excessive class rates.

---

[5] The insurer problem of determining rates to charge for various deductible plans is discussed in Michael L. Smith and George L. Head, "Guidelines for Insurers in Pricing Deductibles," *Journal of Risk and Insurance* 45, no. 2 (June 1978), p. 217.

[6] Harris Schlesinger, "The Optimal Level of Deductibility in Insurance Contracts," *Journal of Risk and Insurance* 48, no. 3 (September 1981), p. 465.

  e. Not "trading dollars" with the insurer.[7]

2. *Control* purposes.

  a. Of claims payment, for speed and convenience.

  b. Of loss-prevention activities.

  c. To encourage safety consciousness of employees.

  d. To help employee relations.

3. *Coverage.*

  a. To obtain coverage by meeting underwriting requirements.

  b. To separate primary and excess insurance.

  c. To improve loss experience and relations with the insurer.

  d. To meet legislative requirements.

  e. To help management realize its stake in loss prevention and the value of insurance for catastrophic losses.

  f. To supplement self-insurance plans.

"Self-insurance." Only the most complete and formal plans for financing risk are properly described as *self-insurance* plans, as used by some organizations. In most cases, these plans are only partial methods of keeping risk within the firm. Briefly, to deserve the designation of self-insurance, a plan must include certain requisites which apply similarly for sound insurance company operation.

Some of these requirements have already been discussed under the heading of *insurable* risks. To be self-insurable, the same characteristics are necessary. These include the need for large numbers of important, homogeneous, accidental risks, which have the quality of being definite and calculable and do not involve the chance of too large a catastrophic loss. *High frequency* and *low severity of losses* in order to have reasonable *predictability* are essential. For the most part, large organizations are the only ones that can meet these requirements properly. Self-insurance is not realistic for individual or family risk problems.

It is essential to distinguish between self-insurance and no insurance. There can be self-insurance only if the risks are sufficiently spread such that a severe loss will not adversely affect the company or the funds set up for the losses. Most of these funds come from current earnings and current cash flows, which become important considerations.[8] Going without insurance (even with an adequate fund available to pay all losses) is simply placing the fund at risk. An uninsured building valued at $1 million and $1 million on deposit to meet any fire loss means inviting the loss of $1 million in cash instead of the loss of the building. Such

---

[7] This refers to the fact that insurers necessarily have operating expenses, often 30–40 percent of each dollar paid in by policyholders for property-liability insurance.

[8] Ralph E. Gentry, "Assessing a Company's Ability to Self-Assume Risk," *Risk Management,* February 1977, p. 38.

a situation cannot be said to be self-insurance. The insurance premium may be saved, but a serious loss might spell financial disaster.

An example of the failure of what was purported to be a self-insurance fund is the state office building that was presumably covered under the Michigan state fire fund. It was destroyed with an estimated loss of $4.5 million. It is interesting to note that the state library located in the destroyed building was insured in private companies for a total of $2 million for a premium slightly in excess of $3,000. Other examples of the failure of pseudo "self-insurance" plans by business or government units have been observed. Although 22 states now have self-insurance funds for insuring fire and extended coverage perils, six states which once had them have abandoned them.[9]

Self-insurance also requires attention to other points. The plan must have *management's full support* and understanding; it should provide essential *loss-prevention activities* whenever economically feasible; it should normally involve a *savings fund* (not just a "reserve" on the balance sheet) to meet unanticipated losses; and it should provide important recordkeeping and *loss-analysis data*. The size of the funds necessary depends on many factors, including the financial stability of the firm, the maximum probable losses expected, the possible repetition of losses within a certain period, and tax considerations.

The main consideration is care in setting up and administering the self-insurance plan, not beguiling oneself into a feeling of security when the plan is not adequate. This solution can be used successfully by larger firms when judicious steps are taken to assure that the plan is really one of self-insurance. The most common example of self-insurance is in the field of workers' compensation (for industrial injuries and diseases), while some of the largest businesses also use this method for meeting part of their automobile, fire, or health insurance risks.[10]

"Captive" insurers. One risk financing method, closely related to self-insurance, has gained in popularity in recent years as a method of obtaining some tax advantages and closer control of contract design and loss payment. This is the *captive insurer,* a separate subsidiary insurance company that is organized by a firm or organization to write its own insurance. Special tax savings can be achieved by licensing the insurer in Bermuda or other foreign countries, and several hundred captive insurers were formed by the mid-1970s.[11]

---

[9] Mark R. Greene and Michael L. Murray, "Self-Insurance of State Property," *Journal of Risk and Insurance,* March 1978, p. 109.

[10] A monograph analyzing many of the self-insurance techniques is *Self-Insurance: A Risk Management Alternative* (Malvern, Pa.: Society of CPCU, March 1978).

[11] A concise summary of the definition, types, advantages, feasibility, expenses, and locations of captive insurers is found in *The John Liner Letter* (Wellesley Hills, Mass.: Shelby Publishing), 14, nos. 10 and 11 (September and October 1977). Also recommended is George L. Head, "Captives: A Make or Buy Choice," *National Underwriter,* March 5, 1982, p. 27.

Today more than 1,000 captive insurers are operating, and many write insurance for unrelated outside firms as well as for their own parent company or group. This expansion has been encouraged by IRS rulings which usually deny deductibility of insurance premiums if a wholly owned captive insurer accepts only, or primarily, its own parent company's risks. Diversification of loss exposures has also been recently achieved by the formation of several hundred *association captives* which combine insurance for company members of an association. Growth through *pools* of captive companies that reinsure each other's risks, such as within the oil industry, has also occurred.

Thus, although captive insurers began with larger companies that had widespread risks and could afford the cost of the extra arrangements necessary, many smaller companies now can participate in the captive insurer trend. Even someone else's captive insurer can be used to obtain a tax shelter and to reduce costs in a *rent-a-captive* arrangement.

The potential *advantages* of captive insurers, which overcome some of the drawbacks of self-insurance, derive from (1) tax factors, (2) savings on reinsurance, (3) better cash flow and (4) potential profits.[12] Instead contributing to its own reserve, the parent company can insure its risks with a captive insurer, and premiums paid may be deductible if it meets IRS revenue rulings. State premium taxes of about 3 or 4 percent can be avoided by "offshore" captives or lowered by U.S. captives domiciled in several states. The improved access to the reinsurance market through captive insurers may permit cheaper coverage for large or difficult risks to insure. The parent company control over premium dollars, loss payments, reserves, and earnings on investments can improve its cash flow, an important consideration in today's high interest rate economy.

The *disadvantages* of captives should not be overlooked. Prospective savings are not always achieved, for losses may be greater or more eratic than predicted, capital start-up and servicing costs of the captive must be considered, and complex tax uncertainties may actually add to the risk. The *Carnation* case, upheld in 1981 on appeal, disallowed a tax deduction for premiums paid by that company and its affiliates to its wholly owned captive insurer.[13] The decision was based on the totality of the relative distribution of risks (percentage of insureds and premiums unrelated to Carnation) and the degree of control over the captive, which leaves some IRS rulings requiring 50 percent unrelated business as an uncertain standard.

Bermuda has emerged as a major insurance and reinsurance center for more than 700 captive insurers and some $4 billion of premiums, but other foreign locations such as the Cayman Islands, Cyprus, and

---

[12] Chris Welles, "The Captives: Turmoil in Insuranceland," *Institutional Investor,* April 1979, p. 99.

[13] *Carnation Co.* v. *Commissioner,* 71 T.C. 400 (1978), affd. 640F. 2d 1010 (9th Cir., 1981).

Gibraltar are competing for this business.[14] At least three states—Colorado, Tennessee, and Vermont—have passed laws encouraging captive insurers to be domiciled in the U.S.[15] Capital requirements are also a considerable factor for many organizations considering the formation of a captive insurer. Bermuda and the Cayman Islands set a minimum of $120,000–$370,000 of capital and surplus, depending on the duration of contracts written; Vermont defines five types of captives and requires $250,000–$750,000.[16]

Risk transfer. Some of the most important risks and losses which must be financed by individuals and organizations cannot be retained. The sole method left for consideration is the transfer of as much as possible of the unpredictability, or the losses, to someone else. Three methods are possible: (1) credit arrangements, (2) some noninsurance transfers, and (3) insurance.

Credit arrangements. The use of credit contracts to pay for losses may be considered as one method of risk transfer. However, borrowing money usually has other primary purposes, such as financing homes or business expansion. Since credit is always limited, depending upon the financial situation and capabilities of the borrower ("When you need it most is when it's hardest to get"), it seems generally unwise to use credit for relatively unpredictable needs. Pure risks, especially for larger and infrequent types of losses, are difficult to handle by borrowing *after* the need arises. Unless prior arrangements are made (such as letters of credit from banks), you may be adding the additional risk of not being able to obtain credit instead of actually transferring these losses to others.

Other noninsurance transfers. Risks may be shifted to others by several other types of noninsurance transfers. In a risk financing method, it is the *financial burden* of property, employee, or liability losses that are transferred, not the ultimate legal responsibility (which is transferred in the noninsurance methods of risk control discussed previously).

A *hedging contract* has been shown to be a method of transferring some speculative (loss *or* gain) risks. Sometimes this balancing of possible profit and loss through two offsetting contracts is called "neutralization." The method cannot be used for pure risk, which involves no possibility of gain.

Most noninsurance transfers for risk financing deal with *liability* risks, and the best example is the *hold-harmless agreement.* In this contract

---

[14] J. Richard Barnes, "The Colorado-Captive—An Answer to IRS Objectives?" *Risk Management,* April 1977, p. 40; and James F. Johnson, John J. Sarchio, and Richard E. Beane, "Captive Insurance Companies: The Vermont Alternative," *Risk Management,* June 1981, p. 20.

[15] Welles, "The Captives."

[16] P. Bruce Wright, "Domestic vs. Offshore Captive Insurer Domiciles," *Risk Management,* June 1982, p. 24.

clause, the transferee agrees to hold the transferor harmless in the case of legal liability to others. The transferee agrees to pay claimants (or the defense costs of claims or lawsuits), or to repay such losses if they fall on the transferor. If the transferee is unable to pay the losses, the ultimate responsibility remains with the transferor.

Several types of legal contracts commonly use hold-harmless agreements. In *lease contracts* a wide variety of legal responsibilities are transferred from one party to another in this manner. For example, proper maintenance is often stated in a lease to be under the care of the transferee (lessee) who rents property from an owner. Homes, apartments, automobiles, and many other types of leased property are common today.

Construction contracts also often use hold-harmless agreements to transfer the financial burden of some (but seldom all) of the legal liability losses from the owner to the contractor. *Supply* contracts are a further example, with the supplier usually agreeing to hold the manufacturer or distributor harmless in claims resulting from the supplier's negligence. The extent of the transfer of risk may occasionally extend further to include all of the manufacturer's negligence as well.

Bailees, or persons holding property of others temporarily, often accept by *bailment contract* or common law some risks from the property owners. Liability for damage to goods is shifted from owner to bailee in hundreds of everyday business situations, such as railroad or airline tickets, truck shipments, laundries, warehouses, parking lots, and repair shops.

Most risk transfer methods are far from complete. The uncertainty in regard to *some* perils in *some* circumstances for a *limited* length of *time* for a *limited amount* may be transferred to others. Still, the major risks of families and businesses remain with them unless the final method of risk transfer, *insurance,* is used.

Insurance.   Among the methods of risk transfer, by far the most common is *insurance*. This requires an understanding of (1) what it is, (2) how it works, and (3) its significance. The first concept is developed here, while the second and third concepts are covered in Chapter 3.

A definition of *insurance* may be developed from several viewpoints: economic, legal, business, social, or mathematical. Regardless of which viewpoint is taken, a full interpretation should include both a statement of its objective as well as the technique by which the purpose is achieved.

There is no one brief definition that does justice to the many important viewpoints of insurance. It may be an economic system for reducing risk through transfer and pooling of losses; a legal method of transferring risk in a contract of indemnity; a business institution providing many jobs in a free enterprise economy; a social device in which the losses of few are paid by many; or an actuarial system of applied mathematics. It is all of these and more, depending upon how one views the major

Table 2–1. Definitions of insurance

Viewpoint	Objective	Technique
Economic	Reduction of uncertainty	By transfer and combination
Legal	Transfer of risk	Through payment of a premium by insured to insurer in a contract of indemnity
Business	Sharing of risk	By transfer from individuals and businesses to a financial institution specializing in risk
Social	Collective bearing of losses	By all members of a group contributing to pay losses suffered by unfortunate ones
Mathematical	Predicting and distributing losses	By actuarial estimates based upon principles of probability

purposes, methods, and results of insurance. Table 2–1 summarizes the five viewpoints from which insurance can be defined.

Probably the most widely used definition of insurance is an *economic* one. In this sense, insurance is a method which *reduces risk* by a *transfer* and *combination* (or "pooling") of uncertainty in regard to financial loss. Depending on whether the viewpoint is that of the insured or the insurer, it may be that only transfer is needed in order to have an insurance plan (transfer of risk reduces the *insured's* risk), or only combination (as in the "self-insurance" plans discussed previously). Usually, however, the economic concept of insurance involves both transfer and combination of risk.

From a *legal* standpoint, an insurance *contract* or *policy* is used to transfer risk for a *premium* (price) from one party known as the *insured* or *policyholder* to another party known as the *insurer*. By virtue of a legally binding contract, the insured exchanges the possibility of an unknown large loss for a comparatively small certain payment. It is not really a guarantee against losses occurring, but a method of assuring that repayment, or *indemnity,* will be received for losses that do occur as the result of risk.

Why is it important whether or not a plan is determined legally to be insurance? It is significant because many types of regulation and taxation apply specifically to insurance. Warranty service contracts, for example, are commonplace today for automobiles, tires, and appliances. If such warranties are not legally defined as insurance because of the all-loss (not merely risk of accidental losses) nature of their promises, the companies offering the warranties need not organize an insurance company, hold reserves, or pay state insurance premium taxes. Variable annuity contracts, if not defined by the courts as exclusively insurance contracts, become subject both to state insurance laws and to the federal securities legislation of the Securities Exchange Commission. These legal

Go To page 65

decisions, and others in regard to such contracts as employee benefit plans and hospital and medical benefit plans, have become very important in insurance.

As a *business* institution, insurance has been defined as a plan by which large numbers of people associate themselves and transfer risks that attach to individuals to the shoulders of all. Insurance may also be looked upon as an important part of the financial world, where insurance serves as a basis for credit and a mechanism for savings and investments. Insurance as a business is a common way of thinking about what insurance is, for many persons have contact with the thousands of insurance organizations and their almost 2 million employees. It has become a major part of the free enterprise economy.

An adequate *social* definition giving recognition both to the end of insurance and to the means for effecting it has been admirably stated thus: "We should define insurance, then, as that social device for making accumulations to meet uncertain losses of capital which is carried out through the transfer of the risks of many individuals to one person or to a group of persons. Wherever there is accumulation for uncertain losses or wherever there is a transfer of risk, there is one element of insurance; only where these are joined with the combination of risks in a group is the insurance complete."[17]

To effect insurance, persons who are exposed to loss agree to contribute to indemnify or repay whichever member of the group shall suffer loss. All members contribute to a common fund, and payments are made out of this fund to those who have suffered loss. Thus, for the payment of a definite sum (the insurance premium) the financial consequences of a $100,000 total fire loss to a homeowner are eliminated by exchanging an uncertain large loss for a certain small cost. The sum total of such individual transactions makes insurance a social method by which unfortunates (those having losses) are compensated by the whole group.

In the strictest interpretation of the term, contributions to a fund are not essential. It is conceivable for private groups to rely entirely upon assessments after losses to indemnify the sufferers, and in such instances no funds may be accumulated in advance. In the case of the government functioning as the insurer, a fund may be accumulated, or the beneficiaries may depend for their insurance payments upon the taxing power.

In a *mathematical* sense, insurance is the application of certain *actuarial* (insurance mathematics) principles. Laws of probability and statisti-

---

[17] A. H. Willett, *The Economic Theory of Risk and Insurance,* Columbia University Studies in History, Economics, and Public Law, vol. 14 (New York: Columbia University Press, 1901), p. 388. See also reprinted edition published under the auspices of the S. S. Huebner Foundation for Insurance Education (Philadelphia: University of Pennsylvania Press, 1951), p. 72.

cal techniques are used to achieve predictable results. The details of how this is done are covered in Chapter 3.

INDIVIDUAL STEPS IN RISK MANAGEMENT

With the background of the basic methods in treating risk, the individual steps in risk management are presented in this section. These are: (1) *risk identification,* (2) *risk measurement,* (3) *choice and use of alternative methods of treatment,* and (4) *risk administration.* Figure 2–1 shows the relationship among these steps and how the various risk-treatment alternatives of risk control and risk financing just discussed become the central focus of decision making in step 3.

Risk identification

The process of risk management begins with the first step of risk identification, which involves the careful and systematic discovery of all of the risks of loss and potential loss (loss exposure) which confront an organization. Oftentimes, the identification is combined with a specific notation as to which of the methods of risk treatment is available or is being used for each of the losses or loss exposures. Because insurance is usually the primary method used, the document generally is known as a *risk and insurance survey.*

Risk and insurance surveys. Chapter 1 has already presented the fundamental ideas of what risk is and the classifications of risk, which are the basis for risk identification. Closely akin to the life-health insurance programming process discussed in Chapter 12 is the *risk and insurance survey* made in regard to the property-liability risks for a given establishment. Although most often used in business situations, the term is also appropriate in the individual or personal area. The survey is not limited to property-liability risks, but can and often does include life-health risks as well, even though many of the forms and methods used emphasize the property-liability aspects of risks.

Risk and insurance surveys are known under a variety of names. They are called *plans, abstracts, analyses, audits, fact-finders,* and other such names.[18] In practice all are essentially designed to identify the risks and perils and then plan for providing methods (including insurance) for meeting them. They may also uncover points of weakness in existing insurance programs, suggesting rearrangements of amounts and coverages. The plans should indicate risks that the insured may carry, losses

---

[18] For example, see the various "Risk Analysis" forms published by the Insurance Division of the American Management Association and by the Risk and Insurance Management Society. For specific industrial groups, see Bernard Daenzer, "Risk Discovery Guide" (New York: AMA, 1978).

that may be prevented, and where insurance is, therefore, not needed.

The *need* for risk and insurance surveys is found in many organizations. Although they are basically designed for businesses, nonprofit institutions, including government divisions, also need and can use the same principles to advantage. State and city officials, corporation directors, guardians, executors, and trustees subject themselves to grave criticism or direct personal liability if without verification they are satisfied that the risk and insurance programs are sufficient. Frequently such persons have but the vaguest idea of the risks that threaten the institutions under their care. Verbal recommendations or suggestions may be misunderstood or misinterpreted. The carefully prepared risk and insurance program, coordinated by professional life and property insurance counselors, presents a logical solution of the problem.

The risk and insurance plan, while of special interest and value to large businesses and institutions, is by no means limited in value to large enterprises. Many small and medium-sized businesses need a good risk and insurance survey as much as do the larger firms. It is the smaller businesses, in fact, that are particularly vulnerable to financial ruin as the result of a mistake or an omission in good insurance protection. In a small business it might be possible to follow the rule "When in doubt, insure." This practice *might* prove to be less expensive and provide as much protection as would result from an expensive program of insurance and risk administration within the firm. However, small businesses must also plan to take advantage of all insurance cost reductions that are economically advisable. Otherwise, small profit margins can turn into business losses. The lack of full-time, or even part-time, "risk managers" (such as might be found in the larger business firms) also emphasizes the need for organized and systematic action by small businesses.

The risk and insurance survey involves risk detection, identification, and classification. Sometimes it also includes estimates of the risk or loss values, which are part of risk measurement. The insurance agent or broker may help in the planning and may to a large degree be able to prepare the survey. The work, however, will often require the close cooperation of representatives of the business firm or institution.

The *method* of risk identification varies according to the particular information available, type of organization, and desires of the risk manager. The form may be simple or complex, depending upon the size of the organization and the sophistication of the persons implementing this step. Five different but effective methods of risk identification are used, such as (1) *loss-exposure charts,* (2) *financial statement analysis,* (3) *flowcharts* analyzing the firm's functions and operations, (4) *systems analysis,* and (5) *personal inspections.*

Loss-exposure charts. One of the most common methods used is a detailed list of loss exposures. Sometimes the list of possible sources of loss contains many pages, organized in separate major sections so that exposures will not be overlooked. A chart may be drawn, sometimes known as a *loss-exposure chart*. A brief example is shown in Figure 2–2. Property losses (both direct and indirect), liability losses, and personnel losses are included.

Elaborate survey charts have been prepared to meet the needs of different types of business establishments. Special survey forms have been prepared by insurers, insurance consultants, and insurance agencies. These published "checklists" serve as a starting point for analysis. Applying the general lists to the risk manager's own organization is always required as a second step to make the checklist worthwhile.

An organized risk and insurance survey is considerably more than the completion of a published checklist or the arbitrary insertion of recommendations in a set of blank forms. It includes (1) perils or loss identification and (2) diagnosing the particular firm's exposures. An impressive-

Figure 2–2. Loss-exposure chart accompanying risk and insurance survey

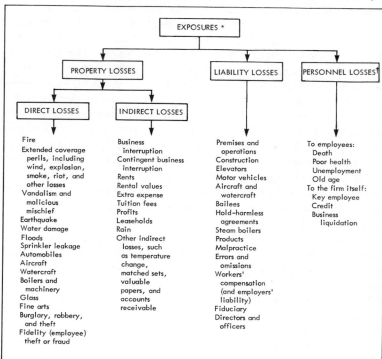

* Note that this is a *partial* listing of only some of the possible loss exposures.

† The "personnel" classification was first developed in C. Arthur Williams, Jr., and Richard M. Heins, *Risk Management and Insurance* (New York: McGraw-Hill). The latest edition appeared in 1981.

looking survey delivered by an incompetent person may give a false sense of security if it has not been tailored to the special needs of the individual organization.

Financial statement analysis. In the method of *financial statement analysis,* each account title in the balance sheet, the profit and loss statement, and other financial statements are listed separately and analyzed to determine the potential perils that might cause losses. Real estate, cash, inventories, personal property, accounts receivable, income accounts, and so on have special characteristics that effect loss.

For example, the *cash* item for the property assets shown on the balance sheet might be one of the listings. Opposite this item the many perils which could cause loss of cash are enumerated: fire, windstorm, explosion, vandalism, water damage, burglary, robbery, theft (including embezzlement by employees), and mysterious disappearance. Cash at different locations, such as in the office, retail stores, or in safes, are separately analyzed to identify special perils to which cash is exposed in different circumstances.

The items on the *income statements and budgets* will also pinpoint the sources of past and future profits subject to indirect loss when direct property losses occur. A comprehensive analysis of financial statements thus becomes a very useful method for identifying both direct and indirect losses.

Flowcharts. Using *flowcharts* is another systematic method for identifying risks and losses for an organization. Charts showing the entire operations in detail are prepared, and each step in the production and distribution of goods and services is analyzed to consider the potential losses that might occur at each point or location in the process.

For a manufacturer, a flowchart shows in diagram form how and where the raw materials are received and stored, the location of the separate steps in the production process, the inventory of finished goods, and the packaging and distribution loss exposures. Each of the steps is analyzed in order to identify the particular possibilities of loss to the various assets during each stage of the operations.

Systems analysis. The new concept of *systems analysis* can also be applied in identifying risks, as the firm's total systems of responsibility and authority are evaluated.[19]

In this method of risk identification, the work system is perceived as a collection of work activities within the overall objective of an organization. The components of each of the work subsystems are analyzed. For each subsystem the separate loss sources are isolated and systematically identified.

---

[19] The concept summarized here is from Christopher M. Dawson, "The Subsystem Approach to Identifying Loss Services," *Risk Management,* May 1982, pp. 12–15.

Four approaches to defining the subsystems are used, either individually or together: (1) processes or departments, (2) physical areas, (3) groups of employees, and (4) classes of machinery or equipment. Next, the relationships among the components of personnel, materials, machinery, and environment are shown in tables which compare the subsystems as to loss sources, current controls, associated loss experience, and control deficiencies. The information thus gathered is used to establish priorities for critical and other classifications of losses pertaining to the various work tasks.

Personal inspections. All of these methods of risk identification are of value as checks against possible exposures, but none of them will replace the technical knowledge that is applied by consultants or insurance agents, and by the specialized information that can be derived from risk managers. *Personal inspections* of premises and operations remain a significant source of knowledge to the risk manager of an organization.

Risk managers must be aware of the total operations of their organizations. They may rely heavily on second-hand reports from all departments, but these must be supplemented by actual visits to many areas to observe the particular conditions which result in exposures of assets and income to loss. In no other way can some of the risks be discovered and identified in the five methods just described.

Risk measurement

Risk measurement is the second step in risk management. Several aspects of risk measurement have already been presented, and others will be discussed in the next chapter. In Chapter 1 risk was examined as to basic speculative (loss or gain) and pure (loss or no loss) types. Degree of risk was shown to be measured by variation between expected and actual losses. In describing how insurance works, in Chapter 3, the concepts of probability of loss and variation are explained in further detail.

Loss frequency, severity, and variation. Briefly, probability of loss can first be measured in three basic ways: (1) *frequency,* (2) *severity,* and (3) *variation.* It is important for risk managers, on the basis of the past loss experience of their firms or that of similar classes of risk exposures, to estimate losses that may be expected. They must also try to predict variation (risk) in future losses, as to both frequency and severity. The primary purpose is to help them decide what to do about various loss exposures.

Properly carried out by the risk manager, risk measurement can aid greatly in suggesting the risks and losses that are most important to treat. For example, if an organization owns 100 automobiles that have averaged 25 losses a year, a loss "frequency" of 25/100 (or ¼) can be calculated. If it is also known that an average loss "severity" of $1,000 in each loss has occurred, then an "annual dollar loss" of $25,000 has resulted. With additional information about losses over a period of years, the trends and "variation" in losses expected in the future may be estimated. Predictions of loss frequency, severity, and "expected annual loss" are fundamental dimensions of significant value to the risk manager.

Some losses may be found to be so infrequent that it would be uneconomic to try to deal with them. Damage to property by "flying saucers" or "unidentified flying objects" (UFOs) may be an example of this type of loss probability. At the other extreme, some other losses may be so frequent as to be regularly anticipated. If small in amount, relative to a firm's assets or income, then the situation may suggest that the risk manager take steps to retain them by absorption in normal expenses or by setting up a reserve to handle them as they occur. Not only must the frequency of loss be high and the severity low, but the variation of losses must be regular and predictable within ranges that the firm can handle.

Maximum possible and probable loss.   If complete data are lacking, or the cost of making more precise estimates is too high, then other methods of measuring risk may be advisable. For example, risk managers often divide potential losses into various categories of importance to their firm. Classifications may be established, such as those losses which are of high, moderate, or slight importance. Estimates of *maximum possible loss,* the worst that *could* happen, and *maximum probable loss,* the worst that is *likely* to happen, are valuable measures. In this way the solutions for the most significant kinds of loss can be tackled first and others of minor importance can be disregarded in the process of risk management.

Most useful to the risk manager is the concept of *maximum probable loss.* By using some actual or hypothetical loss data, the probability that severe losses might occur can be observed. Some extreme probabilities that are possible but not likely are disregarded in the estimate of maximum probable loss. For example, the risk manager might determine that "there is only a 2 percent probability that loss will exceed $100,000." If it is reasonable to exclude such a remote probability, then the maximum probable loss of those that *are likely to occur* becomes $100,000. The risk manager then concentrates on providing for the 98 percent probability that loss could reach that amount.

Several dimensions of maximum probable loss are pertinent. In order to determine the effect of losses on an organization, it is worthwhile to estimate not only the maximum probable loss for a *single* loss exposure such as one building but also for *multiple* losses that could occur together, such as a fire conflagration or windstorm over a large area. In addition, the maximum probable loss *per year* is of special interest to the risk manager because of its financial effect on resources, budget planning, and taxes of the organization.

Mathematical and computer tools. This section has presented only a few of the mathematical tools of risk measurement. Measuring losses by using these and other quantitative tools to analyze loss statistics is becoming much more common today.[20] Sophisticated mathematical studies and models are not always necessary or appropriate, but the risk manager can develop the techniques relatively easily for measuring probability and risk, forecasting losses, and for using present value and linear regression concepts and break-even models.[21]

Computers are becoming an important tool of risk managers.[22] They make quantitative methods of risk and loss measurement both feasible and practical from a cost standpoint. Loss data can be collected, stored, and analyzed better than ever before both for risk-management and general-management decisions.

On the other hand, from a security and safety standpoint computers bring a whole new set of problems to an organization. The computer room is a concentrated area with extremely valuable equipment and with records that are vital to many organizations. New "Halon" and CO_2 fire extinguishing systems are needed, sabotage and vandalism must be prevented, tape erasure problems avoided, employee fraud and espionage by competitors checked, and loss of electric power to the computers anticipated with backup alternative power sources. A challenging specialized area of loss prevention for risk managers has emerged in the past decade.

Choice and use of methods of risk treatment

The third step in risk management is taken after risks have been identified and measured. It is one of the most crucial and difficult phases, because it involves careful evaluation of both the suitability and the cost of various alternatives.

The most significant characteristic of the risk-management concept is that it is a *synthesis* of all methods of dealing with risk. Even the

---

[20] One of the earliest articles advocating such applications was Jack E. Brucker and John J. O'Connell, "Quantitative Techniques and Risk Management," *Risk Management,* May 1975, p. 16. A more complete review is found in J. David Cummins and Leonard R. Freifelder in a series of articles, "Statistical Analysis in Risk Management," in *Risk Management,* beginning in September 1978 and concluding in April 1979.

[21] Mark R. Greene, *Decision Analysis for Risk Management* (New York: Risk and Insurance Management Society, 1977).

[22] See "Risk Management and the Computer," *Risk Management,* August 1976, p. 7; and Michael D. Gantt and James Gatza, *Computers in Insurance* (Malvern, Pa.: American Institute for Property and Liability Underwriters, 1980).

consideration of one peril, such as fire, usually requires that a risk manager integrate the two basic methods of *risk control* and *risk financing*. The many alternative types of these methods of treating risk were discussed individually in the first part of this chapter and were summarized in Figure 2–1, together with the steps in the process of risk management.

How these methods of treating risk are chosen is the pertinent question here. The choice among alternatives is based on understanding each of the various types, including the conditions under which each should be considered, their advantages, and limitations. Can the risk be avoided, or can it be controlled by other means such as loss prevention or reduction? If not, can it be financed by risk retention or risk transfer? More important, if several methods are feasible, which one is best, or as is often the case, what combination of methods provides the most desirable result?

The objective is to reduce the adverse effects of risk, which implicitly are concerned with costs, both before and after losses have occurred. Cost comparisons are the key, and at least three techniques are identifiable: (1) traditional insurance priority listings, (2) loss-matrix tables, and (3) risk-management information systems.

Traditional insurance priority listings.   Probably easiest because of familiarity with the insurance coverages already in use, the *traditional insurance priority listing* starts with the losses identified in step 1 of risk management. For example, the loss-exposure chart of Figure 2–2 might be chosen as a basis and each potential loss related to insurance contracts. Then these coverages are separated into several categories: (1) *essential* (for compulsory, or very large exposures), (2) *desirable* (for large exposures with some serious financial effects), and (3) *available* (for smaller exposures where insurance is convenient).

The advantage of the resulting categories is that they suggest preliminary priorities of those loss exposures for which insurance contracts are useful. However, the decisions as to which insurance coverages are merited are largely subjective, even when related to various contract coverages, amounts, and costs. At best, and including some consideration of possible deductibles with the contracts, the emphasis is too much on insurance, which is only one of the alternative risk-treatment methods.

Loss-matrix tables.   A more comprehensive technique for choosing the best method of risk treatment is the use of *loss-matrix tables*. Rather than priority groups of insurance coverages only, matrix tables force a comparison among several (or all) alternative treatment decisions. Each decision as to risk treatment is compared with each possible outcome of that decision. Summary tables of the *decisions and outcomes* stress a *quantitative* approach which requires cost estimates for the various results in a much more objective and systematic manner.

A simple example of how a matrix table can be used in risk-management decision making is shown in Table 2–2. Only two of the most common methods of risk financing—retention and insurance—are summarized in this example. Assuming that there is a building exposed to loss by fire, and that only two possible outcomes are possible (fire, or no fire), the table shows the estimated dollar value of the resulting costs. For example, under the *retention* decision, the costs are $56,000 in case of a fire: (1) $50,000 insurable loss, (2) $5,000 uninsured losses, and (3) $1,000 worry. In the case of no fire, the only cost is that of worry, or $1,000. Under the *insurance* decision, the costs of a fire are $7,100: (1) $2,000 cost of insurance, (2) $5,000 uninsured losses, and (3) $100 worry for *uninsured* losses. In the no-fire outcome, the costs are $2,100: (1) $2,000 cost of insurance, and (2) $100 worry for uninsured losses.

The comparison in Table 2–2 does not indicate a definite decision between the two alternatives compared. If the risk is retained, the costs could be as much as $56,000 if fire occurs, or as little as $1,000 if fire does not occur. If the building is insured, the costs could vary from $7,100 if fire occurs to $2,100 if there is no fire. What other factors might help in the decision? Most important is the consideration of the probability of fire. If loss statistics for similar buildings show the probability of a total loss is 10 percent, and the probability of no fire is 90 percent, then the "expected loss" could be included in the table: under retention, $5,600

Table 2–2. Comparison of the alternative cost of retention and insurance

Decision	Outcome*	
	Fire	No fire
1. Retention	Potentially insurable losses $50,000 Uninsured† losses 5,000 Worry 1,000 Total $56,000	Worry $1,000 Total $1,000
2. Insurance	Cost of insurance $ 2,000 Uninsured losses 5,000 Worry (uninsured losses) 100 Total $ 7,100	Cost of insurance $2,000 Worry (uninsured losses) 100 $2,100

* To simplify the illustration, only two outcomes are assumed: total loss by fire or no fire.
† Uninsured losses are those losses that cannot be insured, such as inconvenience, loss of customers, and perhaps depreciation and credit costs for rebuilding.
Source: The first textbook to use such a comparison, from which this is adapted, is C. Arthur Williams, Jr., and Richard M. Heins, *Risk Management and Insurance* (New York: McGraw-Hill, 1964), pp. 62–63. In their 1971 edition (p. 228), these authors add the probabilities of losses, and the use of deductibles with various amounts of insurance. In their 1981 edition (pp. 249–54) they evaluate tax factors for both insured and uninsured losses, and retention with and without the use of loss-control measures such as sprinkler systems.

(or 10 percent of $56,000) for a fire, and $900 (or 90 percent of $1,000) for no fire; under insurance, $710 (or 10 percent of $7,100) for a fire, and $1,890 (or 90 percent of $2,100) for no fire. A decision in favor of insurance would emerge, because the total costs of both outcomes under retention would be $6,500 versus $2,600 under the insurance decision.

In the table, some arbitrary judgment figures must be used, such as the cost of worry. However, if some attempt is made to predict reasonable amounts, the decision to retain or insure becomes more rational than when little or no attempt to compare costs is made. The table is simplistic in its assumptions, but it does show the method of using a loss-matrix table to aid in making decisions. As additional factors are included such as estimating aftertax losses and comparing other methods of risk treatment, the tables necessarily become more complex. The resulting decision, on the other hand, may be easier to see and justify as the cost comparisons are broadened and improved.

Risk-management information systems.   The increased use of computers as a tool for aiding quantitative methods of measuring losses and risk was noted earlier. In addition, computer capabilities have made practical a whole new field of *risk-management information systems* to risk managers. These systems coordinate the compilation of loss and other data with rapid availability of the information for analysis and ultimate use for decision making.

Four phases in the evolution of these systems are described: (1) transaction processing, (2) standard reporting, (3) random data access, and (4) decision-making support.[23] One of the greatest potential values appears to be in the last phase. The choice and use of methods of risk treatment should be improved greatly with a complete risk-management information system in operation.

Objective analysis based on wider-based and more accurate data will enhance the future ability of risk managers to make cost projections and comparisons for alternative risk-treatment methods. Additional financial techniques are beginning to attract the attention of risk managers, too. One example is "capital budgeting."[24] This procedure, useful for long-term investments such as installation of sprinkler systems, determines cash flows and profitability measures in order to compare alternative rates of return on investment.

---

[23] James D. Blinn, Mitchell J. Cole, and Douglas G. Hoffman, "Risk-Management Information Systems: Catalysts for Progress," *Risk Management*, April 1982, p. 12; "Building a Risk-Management Information System," May 1982, p. 12; and "Justifying a Risk-Management Information System's Cost," July 1982, p. 28.

[24] C. Arthur Williams and Richard M. Heins, *Risk Management and Insurance* (New York: McGraw-Hill, 1981).

Risk administration

Once the choice of risk-treatment alternatives has been made, the risk manager must devise a system for implementing and periodically monitoring the details of risk management.[25]

Coordination of the steps and objectives of risk management. Actually, the risk-management process must be carried out in conjunction with each of the first three steps of risk management. The total process should be coordinated to agree with whatever written *policy statement* has been adopted and with the *objectives* of risk management. Both of these ideas were discussed earlier in Chapter 1. These serve as guidelines and standards for the risk manager's job, against which compliance is checked, and performance is compared and measured. If inadequate, corrections should made.

Internal communication procedures for obtaining continuous information from all executives and departments of the firm must be well established. Only by adapting the formal and informal communication channels for overseeing risk identification, measurement, and choice of treatment alternatives can the risk manager achieve success in his or her challenging task.

Monitoring choices and coverages. New risks must be continually identified, and all risks must be frequently remeasured. Treatment alternatives, too, must be reconsidered and reviewed for their effectiveness and their actual and potential costs.

One important part of risk administration in regard to the choice of insurance is to arrange for the actual issue of the *contracts* of protection. Sometimes this requires the use of *binders* for temporary coverage, particularly of property-liability insurance. This makes insurance effective immediately, even though the complete written contract may be obtained weeks later. This procedure must be carried out carefully by arriving at a clear understanding of when the protection is effective and what the scope of the coverage will be when the completed contract is written. Some binders may be given orally, but it is the best practice to have such agreements put into written binders as soon as possible.

Sometimes the process of initiating and reviewing insurance coverages involves the use of *competitive bidding.* Specifications for the desired contracts are drawn up, and bids are solicited from various insurers. Agents, brokers, or consultants are often helpful in contacting the available markets. Lowest costs are not the only factor to consider, as financial strength, reputation, claims services, loss prevention, and other work

---

[25] Dr. George L. Head divides the administration step into two parts—the implementing of the techniques and the monitoring of the results. See *The Risk-Management Process* (New York: Risk and Insurance Management Society, 1978); and C. Arthur Williams, George L. Head, Ronald C. Horn, and G. William Glendenning, *Principles of Risk Management and Insurance,* vol. I (Malvern, Pa.: American Institute, 1981).

of the insurer are important. Normally, competitive bidding is useful to compare markets periodically, but not every year because of the value of continued services and consideration of the costs involved.

The administration of existing insurance coverages is another task of the risk manager. Precise *renewal and expiration records* are essential in order to prevent any lapse in needed coverage. Amounts of coverage are kept up to date by frequent appraisals. Rate classifications and costs are checked.

If choices of risk treatment other than insurance have been made, risk administration includes additional procedures and review. For example, if *loss prevention* is significant, the risk manager must be certain that their own loss-control programs, as well as those provided by insurers, agents, or other loss and safety specialists are performing well. Loss data and trends are analyzed regularly to determine if desired results are being achieved.

The technique of risk-management administration involves the coordination of many persons and much information. It is the continual problem, and opportunity, of good risk management to put the whole process together in the most effective manner possible.[26]

An introductory text in the field of risk and insurance should not lose sight of its major premise, namely, that for most personal situations and for many business situations, insurance is one of the most effective methods of meeting important risks. If this were not true, then the subject for study in this whole text might be called risk management. The predominant method of treating pure risk *is* insurance, however, and it is here that this book places its emphasis. Given a familiarity with the process of risk management, from which decisions to insure stem, the student needs most to discover and evaluate the wide scope, techniques, and benefits of insurance. It is on the insurance method that many of the following chapters concentrate, though the insurance choices made should be considered within the context of the risk-management process. Insurance should usually be the final consideration, after proper appraisal of the possible benefits of other risk-treatment alternatives through the risk-management process outlined in the preceding section.

AN EXAMPLE OF RISK-MANAGEMENT DECISION MAKING

In reviewing the above steps, an example may be helpful. Consider the problem of a small manufacturer of plastic toys. The risk manager for such a firm might put together a package of risk management that would include:

---

[26] A helpful source of current information is a looseleaf service compiling risk-management subjects in Matthew Lenz, Jr., ed., *Risk Management Manual* (Santa Monica: Merritt).

I.   *Step 1—Risk identification*
     Fire and explosion are relatively obvious as two major risks of loss, and
     the answers below emphasize these. Other risks are classified by using a
     checklist of perils, and comparing these with financial statement accounts.

II. *Step 2—Risk measurement*
     By using past company records, the risk manager finds out that there
     has been extreme variation in both the number and amount of losses during
     the past 20 years. The degree of risk and maximum probable loss is therefore
     high. Industry loss probability is also found to be higher than that for
     most manufacturers. Values of buildings, machinery, inventory, and other
     property are appraised.

III. *Step 3—Choice and use of method of treatment.*
     A. *Risk control methods* are used:
         1. *Avoiding some risks:* in order to conserve working capital and avoid
             risk, three trucks are *leased* by the firm, with the rental company
             taking care of the fire, theft, and collision coverage. The same tech-
             nique is chosen in leasing a new computer to replace an outdated
             one.
         2. *Segregating* the storage of finished goods in a separate building,
             located away from the more hazardous production facilities, is de-
             cided upon.
         3. *Diversifying* the product line, so that destruction of one type of
             specialized machine would not shut down the production process,
             is adopted by management at the risk manager's recommendation.
         4. An intensive *loss-prevention and loss-reduction* program against
             the perils of fire and explosion is adopted. A sprinkler system, a
             fire patrol, night security guards, the training of employees in fire
             prevention habits and the use of fire-fighting equipment, regular
             inspections and proper building construction are each used to ad-
             vantage.
         5. A *noninsurance control* of risk is accomplished by subcontracting
             with another firm to produce one of the more toxic plastics neces-
             sary in the company's research department.
     B. *Risk financing methods* are used:
         1. *Retaining* some risks by the following actions:
             a. A *reserve* is set up in the corporate accounts to take care of
                 smaller losses up to $5,000. (Such losses might have been just
                 absorbed in the operating expense account.)
             b. A *deductible* of $5,000 is purchased in connection with the fire
                 insurance contract. Letting the supervisors know that this has
                 been done may encourage the prevention of losses.
             c. *Self-insurance* is considered but decided against as a method
                 of treatment because values are concentrated at one location.
         2. *Transferring* some risks is chosen for the following:
             a. The building and its contents are *insured,* including fire and
                 explosion coverage, for $1,000,000, with a $5,000 deductible.
                 Consultation with several different insurers and agents helps
                 determine the proper perils and the amounts of coverage.

        b. A *noninsurance transfer* of risk is made by means of a hold-harmless agreement with the firm's major sales distributor, in which the distributor agrees to pay for any product liability losses caused by negligence in the distribution process.

IV.

    Step 4—Risk administration

    A. The above choices of risk-treatment alternatives are carefully checked for conformity with objectives stated in the written policy statement of the firm.

    B. The choices are implemented by communication and discussion with other departments of the firm: rental of the trucks through the purchasing department; segregating finished goods by consultation with the inventory control section; diversification of product line with the production department; reserve accounts with the accounting department and the treasurer's office; deductibles explained to the supervisors of various departments; loss-prevention program coordinated with the safety and security department; sale of the unneeded computer with the accounting and property departments. Fire insurance is also purchased through a carefully selected agent who will provide appraisal services for property values at stated time intervals.

    C. An annual, or more frequent, review of the risk-management decisions in regard to choices of methods and values is scheduled for the future. A consultant is to be hired at five-year intervals to evaluate the decisions and to arrange for competitive bids on the insurance.

A CASE STUDY FOR BUSINESS RISK MANAGEMENT

The following final example may be useful to the student in reviewing the technique of business risk management.[27] From the facts given, a risk and insurance survey for the shopping center owner can be developed to aid in determining the answers to the kinds of questions which are raised at the end of the case study information.

The Riskee Shopping Center

The Facts:

    Mr. I. M. Sure is the developer and chief financier of a new shopping center to be located on the outskirts of a fast-growing residential suburb near a major metropolitan city. He has organized the enterprise under the legal title of Success, Inc., and though construction has not yet begun, he is asking your advice in regard to the risks and insurance he should

---

[27] Other case study examples are available in William M. Howard, *Cases on Risk Management* (New York: McGraw-Hill, 1970); Jerry S. Rosenbloom, *A Case Study in Risk Management* (New York: Appleton-Century-Crofts, 1972), which provides an in-depth treatment of a large chemical company's risk-management programs; and Mark R. Greene and Oscar N. Serbein, *Risk Management: Text and Cases* (Reston, Va.: Reston Publishing, 1978).

consider necessary during the developmental and operating stages of his business venture.

The center will provide 88,000 square feet of store space, and the purchase of the land has just been completed. An architect has been retained and has begun plans for a slanted L-shaped line of stores set at an angle to an important traffic route.

Preliminary arrangements have been made for leasing space to a large supermarket chain, a branch department store, a well-known national restaurant, a theater, a variety store, and several auxiliary service-type operations, including a barbershop, a dry cleaner, a branch bank, and an insurance agency.

Twenty-four tenants in all will occupy the premises under 15-year leases which stipulate a minimum rental plus a sliding percentage of sales agreement. The lease relieves the tenant of liability for rent if the premises are substantially damaged by fire.

The flat-roof building will be a "fire-resistive" construction. The largest section of the building will be the 18,000 square feet of open space for the supermarket. The heating equipment is designed to be placed at the rear of the building and will provide steam heat for all the stores in the center.

Eighty thousand square feet of macadam parking space are to be provided, with painted 45-degree parking stalls for about 400 cars. Floodlights on aluminum pylons and attendants for the parking lot were considered but decided against.

Storage space is to be kept at a minimum in order to provide maximum selling space. Each tenant is to be responsible under its lease for its own (1) snow removal; (2) trash removal; (3) repair of fire damage to the building; (4) air conditioners, if the tenant desires them; and (5) fire extinguishers.

A small rental and maintenance office is to be maintained in the shopping center, and 10 office and service employees will be employed.

Some questions for case study:

1. What risks does Mr. I. M. Sure have at present, while he owns the vacant land that is to be used as the shopping center site? Are these "speculative" or "pure" risks? Should he have some form of insurance to meet these risks?

2. After construction is under way, what risks does Mr. Sure face? What insurance should he consider?

3. Assuming the shopping center to be complete, make a hypothetical risk analysis for Mr. Sure. What risks does the locational factor alone suggest? Are there any life and health risks?

4. Complete the risk and insurance survey that might be performed by a risk manager for Mr. Sure by outlining with brief explanations a business insurance survey for the Riskee Shopping Center. Include the following:

   a. Possible risks which Mr. Sure might *avoid.* Give specific examples.

   b. Possible losses which Mr. Sure might try to *prevent or reduce.* Give examples.

    c. Possible risks which Mr. Sure might *self-insure.*

    d. Possible risks which Mr. Sure might *transfer* by some method *other than* insurance.

    e. An insurance proposal as to the coverages you would recommend to Mr. Sure. Separate the essential, desirable, and available coverages.

5. Now, assuming that the shopping center is complete and that the tenants have moved in, discuss the exposures and special insurance problems which each of the following tenants might have:

    a. The department store.

    b. The supermarket.

    c. The restaurant.

    d. The branch bank.

    e. The dry cleaner.

    f. The insurance agency.

The coordination of insurance and risk programs for the Riskee Shopping Center is a modern example of the great need for extensive planning in the process of risk management. Only after alternatives to insurance have been carefully analyzed and integrated into the total system for meeting risk can the result deserve to be called risk management. The intelligent business (and personal) consumer of insurance will aim at achieving the many benefits of the risk-management process, through insurance purchased and coordinated with other alternatives included in the risk-management concept.

FOR REVIEW AND DISCUSSION

1. Explain the two basic alternatives for treating risks.
2. What factors *should* determine the method of risk treatment that is chosen in order to take care of a particular peril?
3. Can an *insurer* use both of the basic methods of risk treatment? Illustrate each basic method.
4. *a.* Why is *planned* risk retention a common practice?
    b. Under what circumstances can it be used?
5. Whose responsibility is loss prevention and loss reduction, and why?
6. An adequate description of "insurance" requires an explanation of *what it is, its purpose,* and *how it accomplishes its goal.* Explain.
7. *Why* is the legal definition of insurance important in our society?
8. Explain how risks are transferred by means other than insurance.
9. Under what circumstances, and from whom, is "self-insurance" advantageous?
10. Several different definitions of insurance are not only possible but also necessary to really understand insurance. Explain this statement.

11. There are several ways in which each of the different risks may be handled. One method is not adopted to the exclusion of others, but each method may be most useful for particular risks. Explain, differentiating between the methods of *risk control* and *risk financing*.

12. Describe, with at least two examples for each, how the risk-management concept might be applied by *(a)* a personal insurance consumer and *(b)* a business insurance consumer.

13. Refer to the "Case Study for Business Risk Management" near the end of this chapter, and have different groups of students consider Questions 1 through 5. Have the class as a whole discuss the proposed answers from each group.

14. How might the insurance and risk problems of a municipality differ from those of an individual? Of a business? Of a nonprofit organization?

15. If an insurance agent makes a survey for a client and the client adopts the program in its entirety, as recommended, what is the position of the agent if a loss develops that proves not to be fully covered by insurance?

16. How are risks identified in the first step in risk management?

17. How are risks and losses measured in the second step in risk management?

18. Explain the traditional way of making choices among insurance coverages and contrast it with one other way of choosing among risk-treatment alternatives.

19. Coordination is one of the desirable attributes of a good personal or business insurance and risk program. What have you learned about the *kinds* of coordination that are needed and *how* they can be achieved?

20. In what ways are risk managers important to the insurance business, and how would you predict their future?

21. Have separate groups of students discuss and report to the class how risk managers are becoming more involved in broadening responsibility for loss prevention, safety administration, and employee benefit plans.

22. Appoint different class members to answer questions about risk management by playing the roles of *(a)* President, *(b)* VP—Finance, *(c)* VP—Production, *(d)* VP—Personnel, *(e)* VP—Marketing, *(f)* VP—Legal, *(g)* VP—Accounting, *(h)* Risk Manager, *(i)* Employee Benefits Manager, *(j)* Safety Manager, *(k)* Insurance Agent, and *(l)* Risk Management Consultant. The role-playing can be aided by preparing identification signs that show the whole class which students have each of the above titles.

Chapter 3

Outline of concepts

The significance of insurance is seen in understanding *how it works*, its *history*, its many *fields*, its numerous *benefits*, and its *statistical evidences*.

    How it works is explained by (1) the *insurance equation*, (2) *probability and uncertainty*, (3) the *principle of large numbers*, and (4) *adequate statistical data*.

    A brief history of insurance summarizes how growing needs have been met:

        Ancient insurance ideas of loan-risk contracts and risk sharing.

        The Middle Ages and the merchant era of fire-marine risks.

        The 18th century and early America, when U.S. insurers began.

        The expanding 1800s, which saw catastrophic fires in many cities.

        Twentieth-century growth, paralleling industrial expansion in the automobile, aircraft, and space ages.

    The fields of insurance are classified for better understanding:

        Social (government) insurance is *compulsory*, is either *federal* (such as OAS-DHI) or *state*, encompasses *large groups*, and aims at providing *minimum benefits* for economic security from *some universal perils* such as old age, injury, sickness, death, and unemployment.

        Voluntary (private) insurance includes:

            Commercial insurance, the "insurance business," which is:

            Personal insurance, for loss of *earning power* and added *expenses* of death or disability, in *life* and *health* insurance,

            Property insurance, for loss of ownership use or value of assets, insured in *fire, marine, casualty,* and *surety* insurance.

            Multiple-line and all-lines insurance, *important trends.*

        Cooperative insurance, such as *nonprofit* Blue Cross–Blue Shield.

        Voluntary government insurance, which is government administered but *not* compulsory.

    The benefits and costs of insurance are reviewed with the inquiry as to what our society would be like *without* insurance.

        Benefits of insurance are *peace of mind, paying losses* that prevent financial strain, *increasing marginal utility* of assets, providing a *basis for credit, stimulating saving,* providing *investment capital,* the *advantages of specialization, loss prevention,* and many others.

        Costs of insurance include *operating expenses, profits, opportunity costs,* and some *increased losses.*

Statistical evidences of employment, assets, sales, and other figures show the powerful force of insurance in our free enterprise economy.

Insurance and its significance

Risk and risk management have purposely been the primary subjects of the first two chapters of this book. In the broad picture *insurance* is only one method of solving some of the problems of risk, but its place is a *substantial* one. By all measures—assets, income, investments, insurers, employees, insureds, direct and indirect benefits—insurance looms as a giant in our society today.

For example, did you know that insurance costs the average U.S. worker a *month's pay every year,* or 12 percent of disposable income? That estimate comes from the National Insurance Consumer Organization and does not include Social Security taxes and much of the insurance costs of businesses.

A brief look at *how insurance works* is presented first in this chapter. Next, to see how insurance has grown, its *history* is reviewed. Then an overview of the *fields* of insurance is given, indicating the immense scope of the entire subject. In the final section of the chapter, the general and specific *benefits* of insurance are summarized.

HOW INSURANCE WORKS

How can any organization assume a large risk for a comparatively small premium and then soon thereafter make a large loss payment? For example, life insurance pays some death claims on policies issued and in force for less than a year. Fire insurance on buildings may result in the payment of thousands of dollars in return for the payment of a few dollars in premiums.

Four concepts help explain how insurance works: (1) the insurance equation, (2) probability and uncertainty, (3) the principle of large numbers, and (4) adequate statistical data.

The insurance equation

The equality between the receipts taken in and what is paid out constitutes what may be termed the "insurance equation." The receipts include

(1) _premiums_ (or insurance payments from policy holders), (2) _interest earnings,_ and (3) _other income._ The cost factors that enter into what is paid out may be listed as follows: (1) the cost of _losses;_ (2) the cost of doing business or _expenses;_ and (3) the cost of capital, or _profits._

Losses.   Insurers deal primarily with groups. In the case of the life insurer, it is not concerned with when one person will die but with how many will die each year out of a large group. Knowing this within reasonable limits, the life insurer sets its rates so that it will take in enough money to be able to pay all _losses._ In the case of other forms of insurance, the procedure is the same. The fire insurer is interested not in whether specific buildings will burn but in what the ratio of losses to premiums will be when a large group of buildings is insured.

These costs vary with the different kinds of insurance contracts written. The loss cost may be as much as or more than 90 percent of total premiums (as it is for hospitalization insurance), or about 65 percent (as for automobile insurance). It may be as little as 5 percent in such kinds of insurance as title, steam boiler explosion, or fidelity bonds, in which loss-prevention services are more feasible and important than payment of losses.

Insurers set up specific loss reserves required by state laws and also reserves for catastrophes. Losses are based upon average expected losses, but from time to time abnormal losses occur. For example, various fires have from time to time destroyed large areas in our important cities, windstorms have damaged wide areas, and accidents have caused the death of a large number of people at one time. Catastrophes of this sort must be taken into consideration by insurers in computing the premium.

Expenses.   In addition to securing sufficient funds to meet all losses, insurers must collect enough money to pay _expenses_ such as salaries, rentals, supplies, taxes, and agents' commissions—all of which form a part of the cost of doing business. Certain insurers also provide special services in engineering, rate making, and loss prevention that are designed to save property and lives. The cost of doing business is affected greatly by the marketing system used and the services rendered to the policyholder by the agents of insurers.

Profits.   There must also be some source to pay the cost of capital, or _profits._ Profits are the amounts left after all losses and expenses have been paid out. Some profits are usually retained by insurers to increase surplus; some are currently distributed to owners. Stockholders who invest funds in insurance do so for a profit, and, accordingly, in the computation of the premium some provision must be made to compensate the owner of the capital invested in the enterprise. Surplus and stockholders' capital also help to assure financial solvency, and, occassionally, an assessment is made on policyholders (used by some smaller mutual insurers). Capital and assessment costs are variable according to the legal type of insurer and the state laws.

Stated in more complete terms than just that premiums and costs must be equal, the insurance equation as illustrated in Figure 3–1 is a revision of a basic accounting concept that total outgo and income must be equal. For an insurance business, total income (that is, premiums, interest earnings, and miscellaneous income) must in the long run equal total payments (that is, losses, expenses, and profits). Reserves and surplus are items that temporarily restrict outgo.

Probability and uncertainty

Another explanation of how insurance works centers on the application of the essential concepts of probability and uncertainty. The function of insurance is to assume the burden of the risks which individuals are unwilling to carry. The insurer is able to reduce the sum total of all the uncertainties (risk) to a reasonable degree of certainty. Within calculable limits the insurer is able to foresee the normal losses and estimate the catastrophe losses so that the premium charge to pay all losses as well as to cover expenses and profits can be computed.

The ability to do this places the insurer on a footing quite different from the insured. Were it not for this ability, insurance would be nothing more than the accumulation of many small chances into one enormous chance. While in each individual case the element of uncertainty is extreme, in total a reasonably definite loss may be predicted. The uncertainty element is not entirely eliminated. Some insurers are more successful than others. Although every insurer endeavors to achieve reasonable

Figure 3–1. The insurance equation

predictability, some companies will err and suffer losses and expenses beyond what they take in.

Probability measures the chance of occurrence of a particular event. In the field of insurance, the theory has proved to be of great importance in measuring (predicting) losses. The probability of loss *(p)* is expressed algebraically by means of a fraction whose numerator is the number of unfavorable possibilities and whose denominator is the total number of all possible events.

If we let
  $n =$ Total number of units, or separate events (favorable and unfavorable)
  $a =$ Number of ways considered unfavorable (loss)
  $b =$ Number of ways considered favorable (no loss)
  $p =$ Probability of an unfavorable outcome (loss)
  $p_1 =$ Probability of a favorable outcome (no loss)

Then

  $p = a/n$

and

  $p_1 = b/n$

A simple illustration of another probability formula is found in the experiment of tossing a coin. There are but two ways in which a coin may fall: either heads up or tails up. The probability that it will fall heads up is found by using the number of possible successful chances as the numerator of the fraction and the total number of chances as the denominator. Thus, given a large enough number of tosses, we have the probability of tossing a head as ½.

With relation to any given event, the two extremes are certainty and impossibility. Between the two there are varying degrees of probability. It will be recognized, however, that the degree of uncertainty (risk) and the degree of probability do not represent similar concepts. If a thing is certain to happen, then its probability is represented by unity, or 1. If it is impossible that it should happen, there is no probability, or probability is represented by 0. Impossibility, then, is negative certainty. The event is certain not to happen.

Uncertainty of loss (risk) is a more difficult concept. Basically, however, the idea is that of *variability* of the chance (probability) of loss. A number of statistical methods are helpful in measuring the variability of expected losses, which is what insurers must do when they issue insurance contracts promising to pay for future losses. Most students who have had a basic course in statistics should recall concepts such as normal distribution and standard deviation, which are used to measure objective risk.

The principle of large numbers

In addition, one principle in particular is of great importance to insurance. This is the *principle of large numbers,* or "law of averages," which briefly states that, relatively, *actual results tend to equal expected (probable) results* as the number of independent events increases. In other words, as a larger number of such events are included, the difference between actual and expected results becomes a smaller percentage (though not in absolute numbers) of the expected results.

Insurance is concerned with the number of times an event, or loss, may be expected to happen over a series of occasions. Certain happenings occur with surprising regularity when a large number of instances are observed. The regularity of the happenings increases as the observed instances become more numerous. The concept is that of "credibility," which indicates the degree of reliability that one can place upon the use of past experience to predict what will happen in the future.

Applying these conclusions to insurance in a hypothetical case, assume that we are considering the predictability of automobile accidents in a given city for a group of Toyota car owners. From data gathered on all cars in a city over the past several years, we can construct a "probability distribution" such as Case 1 in Figure 3–2. This shows the relative likelihood (percentage probability) of each possible outcome in terms of the accidents occurring, expressed as a percentage of all the cars in the city which are involved in an accident during a year. Case 1 distribution

Figure 3–2. Probability of losses (hypothetical)

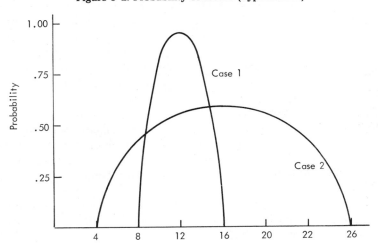

Percent of cases involved in automobile accidents per year

Case 1: 10,000 cars (entire group of car owners in the city).
Case 2: 100 cars (Toyota car owners only).

shows that experience to have varied from 8 to 16 percent of all the cars. From other data, suppose we learn that the Case 2 distribution depicts the experience of Toyota car owners, with accidents ranging from 4 to 26 percent in different years. From Figure 3–2 we can observe that the smaller group of Toyota owners exhibits wide variation in results. If we were using these data to predict future accidents for this group, we could only predict within a wide range of percentages, with relatively low probability of actual experience being equal to expected experience. Case 1 shows that the variation of results is much less for the entire group of car owners in the city, and our predictions for the future could be made with greater likelihood of the accidents occurring within a smaller range of percentages. With the use of the principle of large numbers, Figure 3–2 shows that the reliability of our predictions increases for the larger group.

This is the "magic" of insurance, increasing predictability and reducing risk through the use of the principle of large numbers.[1] Insurers have learned the wisdom of insuring the largest number of similar risks possible. A great number ensures more regular and more accurately predictable losses.

Adequate statistical data

In using the mathematical laws of probability, uncertainty, and large numbers, it is apparent that there is a need for adequate statistical data. Unless accurate statistical information is available, predictions in the form of probabilities will be defective. Therefore, in each of the fields of insurance, carefully compiled statistics are assembled to accumulate experience as a basis for rate making. For example, the statistical data used in estimating the number of deaths for life insurance purposes are arranged in a "mortality" table showing how many persons at a given age will probably die during each year. In fire insurance, statistics are developed on details of construction, occupancy, protection, and exposure pertaining to different types of buildings. For automobile insurance, data for many classifications of type and use of car, territory, age of driver, and other factors are collected. The proper classifications and use of trend factors to anticipate changing loss factors help to achieve equity or fairness in the rates charged to many insureds with different loss probabilities.

It is the constant aim to reduce judgment factors to a minimum and to set rates as far as it is possible upon a scientific basis which rests on the use of statistical data in applying known laws of probability,

---

[1] Called the "miracle of averages" by Winston Churchill, as quoted in H. A. L. Cockerell, *What Goes On In Insurance?* (Cambridge, England: Woodhead-Faulkner, 1982), p. 10.

uncertainty, and large numbers. This, then, is how insurance works. It applies mathematical tools in using statistical data on groups, in order to achieve better predictions than can be made by individuals. The success of insurers in doing this explains why insurance, among the several alternatives discussed in Chapter 2, has become the predominant method of treating risks.

The student should note that the explanation of how insurance works could apply either to private insurance or to social insurance. Consideration of the differences between these two major fields of insurance is presented later in this chapter. Social, or government, insurance could have been discussed as a separate alternative method for treating risk, but the broader concept of insurance is explained here as a single risk-treatment method.

A BRIEF HISTORY OF INSURANCE

In the light of the common lack of understanding about insurance, an appropriate title for this section might be "the mystery with a history." Will and Ariel Durant in their provocative book, *The Lessons of History*,[2] have observed, with words that are surprisingly appropriate to the field of risk and insurance, that

> most history is guessing; the rest is prejudice. . . . we must operate with partial knowledge, and be content with *probabilities.* . . . perhaps, within these *limits*, we may ask what history has to say. . . . It is a *precarious* enterprise, and only a fool would try to compress a hundred centuries into a few pages of *hazardous* conclusions. We proceed.

We proceed to *insurance*, where history is important in obtaining proper perspective because the roots of the insurance idea go far back in the pages of history. This section merely serves as an introduction to the wealth of knowledge which history contains about insurance. By learning more about the past, one can better understand the present and appraise the future of insurance.

Ancient insurance ideas

Insurance has a rich and colorful history. It is a part of many ancient civilizations, and almost any economic history contains references to practices which can be identified as the forerunners of modern insurance techniques.

The evolution of insurance is not so precise that one can point with confidence at a single civilization, or year, or transaction, and say: "That

---

[2] New York: Simon & Schuster, 1968, pp. 12–13. Emphasis by italics added here.

was the beginning of insurance." Certainly, however, the origins were present in biblical times. Some authors even describe insurance arrangements thousands of years before the Christian calendar began (perhaps not as it is known today, but, nevertheless, with similarities of purpose and method).

The Babylonians and Hindus used contracts known as "bottomry" loans to shift the burden of risk from owners of ships and cargoes to moneylenders who agreed to cancel the loan if the ship or cargo were lost during a voyage. If the venture was successful, the charge for the bottomry loan was a high one which combined both interest and the cost of risk. Insurance has been called "the handmaiden of commerce," for it was with early commercial activities and the great dangers of travel and trade that such contracts appeared. The Phoenicians, Greeks, and Romans developed agreements that correspond in most essentials to written contracts used 2,000 years later in marine ventures to the New World. Moneylenders and traders used these loan-insurance agreements in their vast negotiations throughout the ports of the Old World.

Not only were risks shifted from one party to another in ancient times, but the idea of sharing and pooling risks was also used. Chinese merchants divided their cargoes among several ships for perilous voyages on the rivers of ancient China, for the purpose of not having any one merchant suffer a total loss of cargo because of one disaster. The famed storage of grain during the "Seven Fat Years" in preparation for the "Seven Lean Years" is adequately explained in the Bible to denote a clear recognition of the principle of community and group sharing of risk.

Life insurance, too, can be traced to ancient civilizations such as Rome. Burial funds were common in those days. In Greece religious organizations collected and dispersed funds for burial costs of members. The Egyptians left many evidences in the tombs of the pyramids that burial societies were then in existence. Feudal guilds included burial costs in their system of dues, although documentation is difficult in the tracing of their use through the Dark Ages.

The Middle Ages and the merchant era

Perhaps the real origins of insurance stem from the advances made in commerce during the Middle Ages. Venetian decrees in the 15th century regulated marine insurance contracts, and the Hanseatic League used indemnity contracts for trade with all of Europe. The Mediterranean trade with Europe and the Near East rapidly expanded the need for specialized services in the guaranteeing of financial solvency in the face of navigation disasters.

New financial specialists, known as "underwriters," appeared. They wrote their names under contracts of insurance as they accepted maritime risks. In the coffeehouses of England, particularly, the individual insurer grew in significance as England and France forged to the peak of their naval supremacy. Lloyd's of London became the best-known center of marine insurance and remains today as an important source of worldwide insurance on ships and cargoes.

Fire insurance appeared in the 17th century, prompted by a disastrous fire which destroyed 85 percent of London in 1666. The failure of several insurance schemes in this period led to increased desire by the public for stronger insurance plans. One famous plan by Nicholas Barbon, a dentist turned builder who guaranteed to repair houses he built if they were later damaged by fire, was doomed to early failure because of lack of recognition of the substantial risks assumed in the agreement.

The 18th century and insurance in early America

The beginnings of corporate insurance, as opposed to individual insurers whose guarantees were limited to their personal fortunes, appeared in 1720. The "Bubble Period," during which speculators and insurers alike failed in a financial panic of widespread repercussions, brought forth restricted charters from Parliament for two insurance companies, the London Assurance Corporation and the Royal Exchange Assurance Corporation. These companies had a monopoly on corporate insurance, and perhaps the wisdom of the royal charters is evidenced by the fact that these two insurers are still strong companies today.

Colonial America naturally took ideas from England for the first companies in the United States. Much of the early insurance was written by branch offices of English insurers. But new American companies sprang up to meet the needs of a growing America. Benjamin Franklin organized the first incorporated fire insurance company, the Philadelphia Contributionship, in 1752. The Mutual Assurance Company (1784) was known as the "Green Tree" because of the emblem on its "fire mark," a plaque fastened to the outside of insured houses to identify them for the fire-fighting companies maintained by the insurance company. The oldest joint stock company was formed in 1794 to do a fire and marine business (and for a few years, life insurance, too) under the name of the Insurance Company of North America. In life insurance, other companies were started but remained small until after 1800: the Presbyterian Ministers' Fund in 1759 and the Episcopal Corporation in 1769.

THE CORPORATION FOR RELIEF OF POOR AND DISTRESSED PRESBYTERIAN MINISTERS AND OF THE POOR AND DISTRESSED WIDOWS AND CHILDREN OF PRESBYTERIAN MINISTERS,

The expanding 1800s

Economic expansion in the 1800s found more life insurance companies ready for business: the Pennsylvania Company for the Insurance on Lives

(1809), the New York Life Insurance and Trust Company (1830), the New England Mutual Life Insurance Company (1836), and the Mutual Life Insurance Company of New York (1843). The beginnings of scientific actuarial mortality tables appeared, and life insurance quadrupled in the decade following the Civil War.

The fire insurance business prospered also, while growing pains developed in the form of concentrated city construction and expanding market problems as the first agency systems were developed. Disastrous city fires tested the strength of the fire insurance companies and pointed toward crucial needs for improved building codes and fire-fighting equipment. The Chicago Fire in 1871 is famous as it resulted in a property loss of over $150 million, which was an especially huge loss for that time. Almost $100 million of the losses was insured. Numerous other fire disasters were almost as important, however, as each tried the resources and services of the insurance companies: fires in New York in 1835; New Orleans in 1854; New York in 1862; Portland, Maine, in 1866; and Boston in 1872 ($75 million property loss, just one year after the Chicago fire!).

State regulation of insurance began about 1850 as several states established boards or commissions for the supervision of the business. Solvency and tax revenues were the prime objectives of the new laws, through deposit, investment, reserve, and premium tax requirements. The first separate insurance departments were established in 1855 (Massachusetts) and 1859 (New York). Men such as Elizur Wright became the stalwart proponents of better insurance regulation as abuses were corrected and mathematical standards improved in many phases of the insurance business.

20th-century growth

The development of insurance in the 1900s has paralleled the major economic changes of the times. The expansion of the railroads, the advent of the automobile age, the mass production techniques of modern industry, the wars, the introduction of the airplane, and the changing social consciousness of an affluent society—all of these factors and many more closely affected the rise of insurance as a major business of the 20th century.[3]

---

[3] Some excellent insurance company biographies clearly show how insurance reacted to the major events of the 19th and 20th centuries. The author has seen nearly a hundred such insurance history books. Representative are: Nicholas B. Wainwright, *A Philadelphia Story* (New York: Frederick Fell, 1952); Thomas C. Chubb, *And There Were No Losses* (New York: John B. Watkins, 1957); Hawthorne Daniel, *The Hartford of Hartford* (New York: Random House, 1960); R. Carlyle Buley, *A Study of the History of Life Insurance: The Equitable Life Assurance Society of the United States*, vols. 1 and 2 (New York: Appleton-Century-Crofts, 1953 and 1967); William Cahn, *A Matter of Life and Death* (New York:

Some of the landmarks in fire and windstorm insurance were the San Francisco earthquake and fire of 1906 (property loss of $350 million), the New England hurricane of 1938, the Texas City ship explosion of 1947 (3,500 killed or injured), and the East Coast windstorm of 1950 (over 1.5 million separate insurance claims). In more recent years there have been a number of windstorm catastrophes, such as Hurricanes Betsy ($715 million insured loss in 1965), Agnes ($100 million, 1972), and Frederic ($750 million, 1980), and tornadoes through 17 Southern and Central states ($430 million, 1974).

Transportation risks changed as the railroads encountered competition from the motortruck and airline industries. New chemicals, radioactive materials, and industrial processes have caused continual risk analysis innovations for property insurance. Riot insurance coverage assumed major importance as part of the fire insurance contract with the multimillion-dollar losses at hundreds of cities in the late 1960s and again at Miami in 1981.

Major developments in casualty insurance have been the rise of workers' compensation insurance since the early 1900s and the growth of automobile insurance to insure more than 150 million drivers today at a cost of $41 billion per year. Negligence laws have increased the need for many other forms of liability insurance, especially medical malpractice and products liability. Modification in liability laws, such as no-fault automobile insurance, appeared in the 1970s. Concentrated valuable properties have expanded crime insurance needs. High medical costs and loss of income have skyrocketed health insurance to a multibillion-dollar part of the insurance field. Multiple-line insurance, combining property and casualty coverages in homeowners' and business contracts, was a major change for the current generation of policyholders.

Life insurance, too, has undergone significant change since 1900. Many new companies have competed for the growing needs of a prosperous economy until today 2,000 life insurers are in business. Group insurance through employers for their employees has shown rapid growth, and today group pension, life, and health insurance play an important part in labor negotiations. New mortality tables have been adopted and merchandising methods changed to encompass "variable" life contracts to meet inflation needs and "universal" life contracts to increase returns on investment. The life insurers had a most remarkable record for a financial institution during the Great Depression of the 1930s, with less than one tenth of 1 percent of policyholder funds lost during that period. Life insurance amounts in force have grown nearly 10-fold in the past

Random House, 1970); Humbert O. Nelli, *A Bibliography of Insurance History* (Atlanta: Georgia State University, 1971); Donald J. Cannon, ed., *Heritage of Flames* (Garden City, N.Y.: Doubleday, 1977); and David Tregoning and Hugh Cockerell, *Friends for Life* (London: Henry Melland, 1982).

25 years, to over $4 *trillion* today in 400 million contracts with 150 million insureds. Many insurers by the 1980s had expanded their corporate structures to include broadened financial services in providing mutual funds, variable annuities, IRAs, and even stock purchases.

THE FIELDS OF INSURANCE

General

The *total* field of insurance is described briefly in this section. The basic classification emphasizes the difference between *social* and *voluntary* insurance. In essence, this is the distinction between compulsory *government* insurance and voluntary *private* insurance. Voluntary insurance includes the major category of commercial insurance, which is what persons usually have in mind when they refer to *the insurance business*.

Commercial insurance is divided into personal (life and health) and property types of protection, and traditionally in property insurance the major groupings of fire-marine and casualty-surety insurance have been important. With recent trends toward broader insurance operations and contracts, the terms *multiple-line insurance* and *all-lines insurance* have become significant.

Another useful method of studying the fields of insurance is to analyze the legal types of insurers and their organization. Chapter 25 will use this approach in studying the marketing of commercial insurance.

Figure 3–3 shows the relationship among the fields of insurance discussed in this section. In terms of taxes or premiums, the total sales volume is about $485 *billion* a year.[4] The relative sizes of the parts of this gigantic total field should be noted. A current perspective is needed, as well as the historical one presented in the preceding section of this chapter.

Social (government) insurance

Social insurance is compulsory and is designed to provide a minimum of economic security for large groups of persons. It concerns itself primarily with providing basic needs in the event of the unfavorable losses (income and costs) resulting from the universal perils of accidental injury, sickness, old age, unemployment, and the premature death of the family wage earners. In total, social insurance is about 49 percent of all insur-

---

[4] We see figures in billions so often today that comprehension of just how large an amount a "thousand million" is becomes difficult. An example may help: if you spent $1 million at the rate of $1,000 a day, it would take nearly three years to spend it all. How long would it take to spend $1 *billion* at the same rate? (Answer: More than 2,700 years!)

Figure 3–3. The fields of insurance and premium (or tax) volume

* All figures are in *billions* of dollars for the year 1981. Some estimates are included.

† Social insurance figures are "taxes"; voluntary insurance figures are "premiums."

‡ Life insurance includes *insured* annuities with about $29 billion of premiums, but intentionally excludes uninsured private pension contributions.

§ Casualty premiums excludes about $4 billion of health insurance premiums written by property insurers. This amount is included in health total. Workers' compensation (about $15 billion written by casualty insurers) is included in casualty total but could be classified as health insurance. Note also that BC–BS premiums are separately noted above as part of cooperatives.

‖ Homeowners' and commercial multiple-peril premiums apportioned one half to fire, one half to casualty.

¶ Another method of dividing the property field (including liability) is on the basis of who pays the premium dollar. *Business* consumers purchased approximately one half and *individual or family* consumers purchased one half of the total.

Sources: The 1982 publications of *Insurance Facts, Best's Aggregates and Averages, Life Insurance Fact Book, Source Book of Health Insurance Data,* and *Budget of the U.S. Government.*

ance in the United States, as measured by combining social insurance contributions (taxes) and voluntary insurance premiums.

The term *social insurance* could conceivably include all insurance, since all insurance possesses widespread social implications and involves large groups. However, the concept is limited here to those insurance plans which are required by government, are usually administered by federal or state governments, and have as their object the provision of a minimum standard of living. The element of compulsion is based upon the experience that some persons cannot or will not voluntarily purchase insurance, and thus could become dependent on society. The obligation of the government derives from its duty to protect the general welfare of its citizens.

Social security legislation provides for programs of social insurance and public assistance. There are at present 10 programs embraced by the general term *social security*. They comprise five forms of social insurance and five of public assistance.

The *social insurance* plans include (1) federal Old-Age, Survivors, Disability, and Health Insurance (OASDHI); (2) state workers' compensation systems (and several federal); (3) federal-state systems of unemployment compensation; (4) state-sponsored (in five states) temporary disability income insurance; and (5) health insurance, added to the OASDHI in 1966 with the Medicare program for the elderly. A rationale for including automobile liability insurance as a sixth category can be developed, especially in several states where it is compulsory before obtaining a license plate. It is excluded here, however, because the compulsion is not universal in the United States and because private insurers are the primary source of the liability protection.

In contrast to social insurance, *public assistance* includes no contributions or payments directly from the individuals or employers. It is financed by general tax revenues, and recipients of social assistance programs must meet certain standards of "need" to become eligible for benefits. Examples include the federal-state programs for (1) old-age assistance, (2) aid to the blind, (3) aid to dependent children, (4) Medicaid for medical care to the needy, and (5) institutional care for the aged, destitute, and other groups.

Contributions for social insurance benefits are compulsory for covered groups. Social insurance thus limits the freedom of the individual. In a strict sense, it is not an undemocratic process; rather, it changes the method of reaching a desirable objective. It requires every individual not only to provide for himself and his family but also to contribute, if able, to the needy in the community.

Social insurance is treated separately in Chapters 11 (Government Life and Health Insurance) and 24 (Government Property and Liability Insurance). The remainder of this section stresses the kinds of voluntary insurance and especially commercial insurance, which is the basis of the private sector of insurance.

Because social insurance usually provides compulsory basic benefits rather than total protection needs, it is important for insureds to understand its costs and its limitations. Private insurers, too, should know how its cost influences their business, and how social insurance provides a foundation upon which total insurance needs are met.

Voluntary (private) insurance

Voluntary insurance is not based primarily upon governmental compulsion and is sought by the insured to meet a recognized need for protection. Voluntary insurance divides itself into three groups: (1) *commercial* insurance, (2) *cooperative* insurance, and (3) *voluntary government* insurance. Total premiums are nearly $250 billion annually.

Voluntary insurance includes a wide range of insurance protection. Commercial insurance represents that division of the field usually thought of as the "insurance business," including those privately formed insurers which are organized with profit as a normal business objective. In addition to the commercial insurers there are certain nonprofit associations that form a class known as *cooperative* insurance. Blue Cross–Blue Shield hospital and medical insurance associations are the largest examples of this type. Other examples include some fraternal lodges and unions. Finally, the government appears in the voluntary field by making insurance available where the hazards are so great that private insurers cannot well assume the risk. Examples include the federal insurance program for crops (against droughts, floods, and other perils), riot, crime, and flood insurance by the Federal Insurance Administration, and the mortgage guarantee insurance of such organizations as the FHA. These types of insurance have important social implications but are all classed as *voluntary government* insurance because the protection is not compulsory.

Commercial insurance.   The most important of the kinds of voluntary insurance and the most highly developed of all the forms of available insurance protection is called *commercial* insurance. A vast number of insurance forms have been developed to meet the needs of individuals, families, businesses, and other organizations. When the term *insurance* is used, it is usually commercial insurance to which reference is made.

In contrast to the cooperative plans, commercial insurance receives its motivating force from the profit idea. Agents located throughout the country present their insurance plans to prospects and receive as their compensation a commission on the business they produce.

Two major classifications are parts of commercial insurance: (1) *personal* insurance and (2) *property* insurance. This division is based on the nature of the *perils;* that is, whether they are more directly concerned with losses due to loss of (1) earning power of a person or (2) values of a physical property. Another classification of all kinds of insurance might contrast "individual or family" versus "business" insurance, depending on the nature of the *purchaser.*

Partly as the outgrowth of historical development and partly as the result of legal restrictions, commercial insurers have specialized in particular kinds (lines) of insurance. Traditionally, many insurers wrote business only in such categories as life and health, fire and marine, or casualty and surety insurance. Today many insurers include several or all of the categories. These insurers have become known as multiple-line or all-lines insurers.

Personal insurance. The loss of earning power by persons results from their death, injury, illness, old age, or loss of employment. The branches of insurance covering some of these contingencies have not, it seems, acquired names in keeping with their purposes, so that death is a contingency covered by life insurance, injury and sickness are contingencies covered by health insurance, old age is insured by annuities or pensions, and unemployment insurance indemnifies for the loss of part of income and is a type of social insurance. Life insurance, including annuities, and health insurance are important parts of the personal category of commercial insurance.

Life insurance in its simplest form protects the insured's family, creditors, or others against the loss of earning power caused by death of the insured. The permanent loss of current earning capacity amounts to an "economic death." From an economic standpoint, death may be (1) actual, (2) living, or (3) retirement. The first classification represents the so-called casket death. Permanent disability is "living death," while living beyond the period of earning capacity represents "retirement death."[5]

Health insurance provides benefits for medical expenses or for time lost because of injury or illness. Although health insurance is written by life insurers, injury and illness are also viewed as casualties, and casualty and multiple-line insurers write some of this type of business. Some insurers limit their business only to forms of health coverages, including accident insurance.

Property insurance. Property, used here as a synonym for *ownership,* is the right to use and dispose of an animal or thing for a legitimate end without the interference of any other person.[6] *Property* insurance

---

[5] These concepts of economic death were developed by one of the early academic pioneers of life insurance, Dr. Solomon S. Huebner.

[6] Although a sound argument can be made for including a person's earning power as one of his valuable "properties," the distinction here between personal and property insurance seems justified on the basis of more generally accepted use of the term *property.*

against loss arising from the ownership or use of property includes two
general classifications. The first indemnifies the insured in the event
of loss growing out of damages to, or destruction of, his or her *own*
property. The second form pays damages for which the insured is legally
liable, the consequence of negligent acts that result in injuries to *other*
persons or damage to their property. This is known as "liability insurance."

Recently many writers and data have been using the separate categories of property and liability insurance, but the practice is not universal.
In the general sense used here, property insurance protects both physical
and financial assets. Traditionally, the more usual division of property
insurance has been the major groupings of fire and marine, casualty
and surety insurance. Most states have permitted insurers to write *multiple-line* insurance since the early 1950s, and now many insurers write
all of these major kinds of property insurance.

Fire insurance in its simplest form provides indemnity for loss or damage caused by fire. It may be written to cover not only direct loss but
consequential (indirect) loss as well, such as loss of profits resulting from
a fire which closes a business for several months. The fire field has also
been extended to include a number of perils closely allied to fire, such
as windstorm, explosion, smoke, earthquake, and riot. Damage to property from these perils frequently results in further damage caused by
fire following the initial cause of loss. It is not always easy to establish
a line of demarcation between one cause and the other, and it was a
natural consequence that fire insurance should be extended to cover
both classes of peril. Thus fire insurance policies also cover the so-called
allied lines.

Marine insurance covers goods primarily while they are in the process
of transportation. It includes protection against the perils of fire and
allied lines and also many other perils of navigation and transportation,
such as theft, sinking, and collision. Although often written by fire insurers, marine insurance and its contracts are quite unique in their flexible
and broad protection. They may insure one's own property while in transit or one's legal liability for others' property (such as a railroad, airline,
or trucking firm has for goods in its care).

Casualty insurance is not as easy to define. Such insurance started
with accidental injury insurance (1850) and steam boiler explosions
(1867). Accepting "casualty" to mean "accident"—that is, a violent
mishap proceeding from an unknown or unexpected cause—casualty insurance might be presumed to include any loss or damage when an accident is the cause of the loss.

However, this could apply to almost any kind of insurance. The better
explanation is to recognize the meaning of the term *casualty* (1) by a
process of elimination (all insurance not classified as fire, marine, or

life) or (2) by reference to statutes, in which the states define the kinds of insurance which a casualty insurer can write.

The major kinds of casualty insurance today are shown in Table 3–1. Automobile insurance is by far the most important category, including more than one half of the total premium volume. A wide variety of other kinds of insurance are also a part of casualty insurance.

Surety insurance, or surety bonds, are often included with casualty insurance. Many casualty insurers are licensed to write "fidelity" (employee dishonesty) bonds and many types of "surety" bonds. These contracts are basically guarantees of performance of an expressed obligation and cover not only dishonest acts but also negligence or lack of ability. Examples include contract, executor, and many kinds of judicial bonds.

Multiple-line and all-lines insurance.   For many years, the business of property insurance was carried on chiefly by insurers that devoted their efforts to a single "line," or major kind, of insurance. A fire insurer wrote only fire insurance, and a casualty insurer only the various kinds of casualty insurance mentioned above. Mono-line insurance companies were the normal method of operation in American insurance. The "American" system of separating insurance into fire and casualty lines was strengthened by state laws which licensed insurers for one or the other of these major fields of property insurance, but not both.

The combination of traditional fire and casualty insurance lines occurred in what has been called the *multiple-line insurance trend.* The convenience of, and the need for, broader automobile, aircraft, and other contracts were two of the factors causing the breakdown of the legislative barriers. (See Chapter 23 for a more complete discussion of this change.) Many insurer *groups* have written some multiple-line insurance since

Table 3–1. Kinds of casualty insurance

Kind of insurance	1981 premiums (in $ billions)
Automobile	$41.1
Workers' compensation	14.6
Multiple-peril*	9.1
Miscellaneous liability	7.4
Accident and health	3.6
Fidelity and surety	1.3
Crop-hail	0.5
Boiler and machinery	0.3
Burglary and theft	0.1
Credit, glass, aircraft	0.3
Total	$78.3

* Not included in this figure are $9.1 billion of premiums apportioned as the property insurance part of multi-peril contracts.

Source: *Insurance Facts* (New York: Insurance Information Institute, 1982–83), p. 13.

the 1920s. *Individual* insurers have often been licensed for the broad fire-casualty market since legislation permitted them to do so (1950 in most states).[7] The real multiple-line insurance change has centered in the last three decades on combinations of coverages in a single multiple-line package *contract*. The homeowner's policy is the best example, combining fire, theft, and liability protection in one insurance contract for the family. Many new business multiple-line contracts for stores, industries, and service businesses have also evolved.

The second major trend in broader insurance organizations and contracts is the *all-lines* trend, which combines *personal* and *property* insurance. Thus it integrates most of the basic types of insurance, including some of each of the traditional fire, casualty, life, and health lines. The all-lines trend so far has been evident mostly in the formation of many large all-lines insurer *groups*. Most major property insurers have formed or bought life insurance subsidiaries. Many of the larger life insurers in the 1970s became all-lines groups by adding property-liability affiliated companies. All-lines insurance *contracts* are not yet permitted in most states, though life and disability insurance for a homeowner's mortgage has been combined with the homeowner's and automobile policies in a few new contracts. Many states, however, still prohibit personal life insurance from being combined in the same contract with property insurance. The differences in purpose, duration, and form of the contracts are given as reasons. It appears, however, that the benefits of cost reduction, greater convenience, and better coverage will eventually be recognized in more flexible laws to permit more all-lines insurance contracts.

Cooperative insurance. The term *cooperative* is usually applied to associations operating under hospital, medical, fraternal, employee, or trade-union auspices. The associations are organized without regard to the profit motive and represent, in fact, an effort to accomplish the ends of social insurance by private enterprise.

By far the most important example of cooperative insurance, comprising 90 percent of the total business of cooperatives, are the Blue Cross, Blue Shield, and other medical insurance plans (see Figure 3–3). These cooperatives are an interesting combination of social and private insurance. They emphasize the *nonprofit,* cooperative objective and are administered in most states under special state statutes which essentially remove them from the commercial category of voluntary insurance. The associations are not incorporated or licensed as insurance companies, and some of the usual state taxes and regulations do not apply to them. Such plans include representative membership in their boards of directors from medical groups and the public. They write more than half of

---

[7] In all states by 1955, usually by specific statute but in a few states by insurance department rulings. See David L. Bickelhaupt, *Transition to Multiple-Line Insurance Companies* (Homewood, Ill.: Richard D. Irwin, 1961), p. 37.

all hospital insurance and a significant portion of other medical cost insurance in the United States.

Fraternal societies sometimes provide life or health insurance benefits for their members. The associations are ordinarily small, to a large extent local in their operation and management, and they bring together persons having a common ethnic origin or religious belief. Employee associations and unions sometimes also provide cash payments to members when sick and at the time of death.

Voluntary government insurance. Insurance that falls into this category of voluntary insurance is principally distinguished from social insurance in that there is no complete element of compulsion. The various plans offered are designed to benefit the entire community but are used only by those persons who wish to use the available benefits.

In this category are to be found such plans as the insurance of mortgage loans by the Federal Housing Administration, the insurance of growing crops by the Federal Crop Insurance Corporation, and government life insurance, administered by the Veterans Administration for members of the armed forces. Also, one state (Wisconsin) offers life insurance, and one state (Maryland) writes automobile insurance, through a state fund.

Because the plans are required for most chartered banks, the Federal Deposit Insurance Corporation (FDIC) and a similar plan for savings and loan associations (FSLIC) are not included here as voluntary government insurance systems.

Voluntary government insurance usually provides protection in fields that private insurance cannot safely enter. This is because of lack of experience in the field or because of the catastrophic perils connected with the insurance. Coverage of such perils on a safe basis is beyond the capacity of private enterprise.

In some instances there is an overlapping of government voluntary insurance and insurance offered by commercial insurers. One example is crop insurance, which today is available through either the FCIC or commercial insurers. The crops and areas covered, however, may not be the same.

More recent examples have appeared with federal insurance programs for riot, flood, and crime insurance through the Department of Housing and Urban Development. The insured does not usually have to purchase the coverage and the federal insurance administrator oversees these plans. (See also Chapter 24.)

THE BENEFITS AND COSTS OF INSURANCE

What would our society be like without insurance? If one ponders the answers to that provocative question, many of the benefits of insurance are highlighted.

Would banks loan money on homes or businesses if they were uncertain as to whether or not the collateral value could be lost due to fire, wind, or other perils? Would finance companies approve installment loans for automobiles or other household goods? Or would anyone *want* to own an automobile if liability for losses caused to others could not be insured? Or to own a home that could be destroyed in a few hours without any recovery for the loss? Would workers choose hazardous but important occupations if it were uncertain whether the employer could pay for a work injury? How could a young family man or woman provide an income for dependent children without life insurance? Or for payment of large medical bills?

The examples are many, and they range throughout the basic parts of our society, from agriculture to commerce, banking, manufacturing, transportation, and communication. The business of insurance provides the factor of protection now regarded as essential throughout our economic and business environment.

While there is scarcely anyone who does not at some point or other make contact with the business of insurance, there are few indeed who without some reflection and investigation have an adequate idea of the great size and importance of the total field. There is no business or individual that does not owe it substantial credit for daily comforts and conveniences.

Benefits of insurance

Some examples of the wide scope and benefits of insurance have already been presented in the first chapter. A summary of the most important benefits of insurance would include all of the concepts discussed in the following sections.

Peace of mind. Almost everyone has a basic desire for some security or peace of mind. To the extent that insurance provides certainty or predictability, it improves the efficiency of individual or business decisions by reducing anxieties. This is a psychological factor that is difficult to measure in terms of specific benefits. It is nonetheless important in our everyday life, irregardless of whether or not losses actually occur.

Pays losses. The existence of insurance often supplies the financial aid which permits a family or organization to continue despite serious losses that have occurred. The death or disability of a "breadwinner" can bring financial disaster to a family. With family income stopped, the spouse or children may have to give up their home and accept undesirable alternatives such as foster homes, living with relatives, or accepting relief payments. A fire or a liability suit can cause the failure of an organization. Such perils can be met through insurance, which provides *indemnification* or repayment at the time of need in order to keep the family or business intact. Insurers pay benefits in excess of $150 billion every year.

Increases marginal utility of assets.   From an economic standpoint, insurance serves as an intermediary between those who have small need for a minor amount of capital or income (i.e., the cost of insurance) and those who have great needs for the immediate use of large sums to meet losses they have suffered. Marginal utility refers to the use value of the last (marginal) unit. Basically, insurance takes the least useful "last" dollar of low marginal utility from all policyholders and repays the important "first" dollars of high marginal utility to those unfortunate persons who have suffered severe losses.[8]

Provides a basis for credit.   One finds it impossible to visualize the credit economy of today without insurance. Several kinds of insurance are invaluable as the foundation for credit transactions. Personal and business bank loans of many kinds use life insurance (either face values or cash values) as a guarantee that the loan will be repaid in spite of uncertain contingencies such as the death or disability of the borrower. Fire insurance is invariably required by mortgagees who loan money with real or personal property as collateral. Creditors must know that their collateral will not disappear in a fire, windstorm, or other loss, and this security is accomplished by having debtors purchase proper amounts of insurance for their homes or automobiles.

Stimulates saving.   Many kinds of insurance are important because they encourage thrift. An insurance premium, though small in relation to the possible loss it protects against, is basically a prepayment in advance of potential loss. All the payments are gathered together to form a fund from which those few who do suffer losses are paid. In essence, the plan of insurance encourages all to save so that unfortunates can be repaid for their losses. In addition, life insurance has special advantages in stimulating savings. The long-term contracts, often over a whole lifetime, build substantial cash, emergency, or retirement values. Policyholders treat their regular premium payments as an obligation to their families or beneficiaries, and greater savings result than in other good-intentioned but irregular savings programs.

Provides investment capital.   The savings held as assets by insurance companies are not stagnant. They provide a gigantic source of important capital for our economy. The American Council of Life Insurance reviews the creative force of $526 billion of life insurer assets in 1982 by showing how these funds are used: *government securities,* $39 billion, or 8 percent; *mortgages,* $138 billion, or 26 percent; *corporate bonds,* $194 billion, or 37 percent; *stocks,* $48 billion, or 9 percent; *loans to*

---

[8] An exception to this statement is the use of deductibles, which may not pay the policyholder until after the loss has exceeded a specified minimum.

policyholders, $49 billion, or 9 percent; *real estate,* $18 billion, or 3 percent; and *cash and miscellaneous,* $40 billion, or 8 percent.

Another measure of life insurers' investments is provided by recent data which separate investments made for "socially desirable purposes." These include investments for environmental improvements, hospitals, family housing, and education. The life and health insurance business now publishes an annual breakdown of statistics on the more than $1 billion a year spent on such projects.[9]

In addition to the large sums invested by life insurers, property insurers had about $228 billion in investments. These insurers have heavy investments in bonds and much greater investments in stocks than the life insurers. Not including the assets of social insurance programs, in 1982 the investments of private insurers in the United States totaled over $750 billion. Such assets and their investment have a tremendous impact on families and businesses through the money and capital markets of the United States. (See Chapter 29 for further investment details.)

Advantages of specialization.   It is common sense that an insurer that specializes in risk bearing can usually perform its services more efficiently than someone else. When a business or organization transfers its risk to an insurer it says in effect: "Here, you take care of those bothersome, unpredictable risks of loss, and we'll pay attention to the main purposes of our organization." The productive aspect of insurance thus emerges as an incentive to organizations or individuals, relieving them of accidental losses so that more effort, personnel, and capital can be directed toward the work for which they are best suited. For example, a department store is normally better off to shift its pure risks to an insurer and then to concentrate its efforts on greater sales or other merchandising services. Insurance also aids competition, because it permits smaller organizations to transfer risks that they cannot safely retain themselves. The alternative of "self-insurance" or do-it-yourself insurance is better only when a very large store with diversified risks can do a better job than the insurer. Even in such a case, the store must further consider the loss of profits it has in effect given up (the "opportunity costs" in an economic sense) because it is using time and personnel to provide its own insurance program.

Loss prevention.   Insurance benefits society by fostering considerable effort to prevent losses (see Chapter 2). This result is a subsidiary goal for most kinds of insurance, but undoubtedly more loss-prevention work occurs because of insurance than would occur without it. The net effect is advantageous, as lives are saved or property values preserved.

---

[9] See the annual *Social Report of the Life and Health Insurance Business* (Clearinghouse on Corporate Social Responsibility), and the bi-monthly *Response* (Center for Corporate Public Involvement) published by the American Council of Life Insurance, Washington, D.C.

Examples are fire prevention campaigns, motor vehicle safety research, health education by life insurers, elevator and boiler inspections, and many others. Also important in this work are associations sponsored by insurers, such as the National Automobile Theft Bureau, Underwriters' Laboratories, and many others.

 Special benefits of individual kinds of insurance. In addition to the above eight general benefits of many kinds of insurance, each particular kind has some special benefits which make it significant to our economy. For example, consider some of the special purposes and achievements of life insurance: it establishes an immediate and liquid estate, encourages gifts to charity, aids in planning for education costs, reduces mortgage worries, offers safe and tax-deferred investments, and provides retirement income. For each particular kind of insurance a supplementary list of special benefits might be developed. The student should think about such fields as transportation insurance, theft insurance, nuclear insurance, and health insurance to provide additional examples of such benefits.

New types of insurance are also constantly being developed for specialized insurance needs. For example, the space age created the need for insurance of communications satellites that are valued at $30 to $100 million each. If insurance was unavailable, it is unlikely that such space shots would be commercially feasible. With insurance available, more than 60 satellites have been insured—and several have failed, including one loss of $77 million.[10]

Have you heard about other large potential losses that have been insured, such as the health of TV's Lassie ($1 million), the life of Pope John Paul II during his trip to Brazil ($2 million), or the disability of Bill Walton of the San Diego Clippers basketball team (on whom more than a million-dollar loss was paid)? Or do you like fish stories, such as the $1 million insurance policy written with a premium of $30,000 for a Puget Sound auto supply store that promised such a prize to the lucky fisherman who could catch a tagged coho salmon on one specific day?[11] Special insurance contracts have been written for all these, and many more, unusual risks.

Costs of insurance

It would be unfair to consider only the benefits of insurance without mentioning possible negative considerations. The institution of insurance is not maintained without costs to the policyholders. The costs of insur-

---

[10] Harmut Hesse, "Insurance Demand Lifts Off Canaveral Pad, Too," *National Underwriter,* April 17, 1981, p. 92.

[11] "One That Got Away," *Sports Illustrated,* September 1981, p. 13.

ance include its (1) *operating costs*, (2) *profits*, (3) *opportunity costs* and
(4) *possible increased losses*.

Operating costs.   In the beginning of this chapter, one of the methods
used to explain how insurance works was the "insurance equation." This
comparison shows that insurers cannot pay out more dollars than they
take in. Of the dollars paid out, not all are paid to the policyholders
or beneficiaries of the insurance contracts. In fact, *operating expenses*
which enable insurers to do business are approximately one fourth of
each dollar that insurers take in. The proportion varies by type of insurance: on average it is less than 20 percent for life-health insurance (and
less than 10 percent for insurance written in group insurance contracts);
and more than 30 percent for property-liability insurers.

Operating expenses include many different types of costs, including
agents' commissions, home office and field administrative expenses, loss-
adjustment expenses, and taxes. These costs of operating insurers, their
agency systems, and other services must be balanced against the benefits
of insurance enumerated in the preceding section.

Profits.   Also mentioned in the insurance equation were *profits*. These
amounts are small, perhaps less than 5 percent on average, in relation
to the total premium dollar. However, they are necessary because otherwise no capital would be attracted to insurers in order for them to do
business.

Profits are paid to owners. In some insurers, such as mutual companies,
the profits (or part of them) are paid back to the policyholders as dividends. These payments reduce net costs, although the policyholders have
temporarily given up the time value of the money. In stock companies,
profits are paid to the stockholders as a return on the capital they have
invested in the insurer.

Opportunity costs.   From an economic viewpoint, the capital, personnel, and materials required by insurers could be used elsewhere if they
were not devoted to the insurance business. Other productive contributions to our economy and society could be made by these alternative
uses. Therefore, the use by insurers represents costs, or other opportunities that are given up, in order to have insurance institutions. These
opportunity costs foregone must be considered one of the potential costs
of insurance.

Increased losses.   Insurance, like other worthy institutions, occasionally has some direct adverse effects. *Increased losses* may sometimes
result because insurance can increase moral hazard, as explained in
Chapter 1. The encouragement of fraud to collect losses caused intentionally by insureds or to exaggerate claims beyond actual losses are two
examples. The increases in carelessness that occur when people feel completely insured is another cost of insurance. It is hoped that such effects
are relatively minor; but some, such as fires caused by arson, are a major

and increasing problem. Although the costs are difficult to measure precisely, constant effort to control these possible added costs of the insurance system is necessary.

Statistical evidences

The major contributions of insurance can be summarized concisely in sales, employment, asset, and other figures which show its size and diversification throughout our economy. The *sales* volume of the total fields of insurance, in terms of premiums and taxes, has already been noted as more than $400 billion.

Two million persons are employed in the voluntary sector of insurance in the United States by 5,900 insurers and many more thousands of agencies and related businesses. This means that about one out of every 50 *employed persons* directly receives a livelihood from insurance. Not all of these persons are in insurance sales work, either, for almost two thirds of insurance employment is nonsales work.[12] Many men and women are needed by insurance for such jobs as underwriters, claimspersons, computer programmers, accountants, secretaries, clerks, statisticians and actuaries, advertising experts, research specialists, investment counselors, and management positions from top executives to personnel managers to field managers of many types. Few people realize that insurance employment exceeds that found in many other major parts of our economy, such as banking or mining or chemical products.

Another measure of significance has already been introduced in referring to the *assets* controlled by insurance organizations and the *investments* which stem from the use of these assets. (See tables in Chapter 29 for life and property insurer investments) Few other institutions, even financial ones, can compare with the several hundred billion dollars of funds put to use by insurers. Virtually every area of our economy receives some capital from investments made by the insurance business. In the race into space in which the United States placed men on the moon, life insurance funds provided capital for the development and manufacture of jet spacecraft. Another major use of the assets held by insurers is the payment of *losses*. Each year life insurers alone pay more than $30 billion to policyholders and beneficiaries, including more than one half in "living benefits" such as annuities and policy dividends.

The conclusion is clear. By any measure of employment, assets (and their use), or premium volume, the institution of insurance is of major significance in the economic activity of the United States. The private sector alone employs 2 million persons, holds some $750 billion of assets,

---

[12] *Life Insurance Fact Book* (New York: American Council of Life Insurance, 1982), p. 91.

and has an annual income of more than $200 billion. The interests of everyone are closely affected by the giant size and scope of insurance. Insurance is the cornerstone of the private property system and an essential element of our free enterprise economy.

A warning is also pertinent. The insurance business can operate efficiently only in an environment in which it can effectively accumulate data on the whole range of risk problems, from risk probabilities and loss control to a system of total risk management which assures the solvency of insurers as well as the clients that insurance serves. This interdependency of risk, risk management, and insurance is emphasized in the first three chapters of this text.

FOR REVIEW AND DISCUSSION

1. Paul is explaining what insurance is to his friend Terri. Briefly describe several methods he might use to explain how insurance works and why you think one method might be better than another to do this.

2. A newspaper article recently concluded that if an insurer received $1,000 in premiums and paid out $600 in losses, it made a profit of $400. Does this seem reasonable? Is the conclusion correct?

3. Explain how predictability is achieved through the use of insurance.

4. How can the history of the "insurance idea" help you understand its current use? Cite several examples of early insurance ideas.

5. Divide the class into about seven groups. Let each group discuss for five minutes any examples which illustrate the significance of insurance. Then have each group, through one person chosen as the reporter, present to the class what it considers to be the two *best* examples.

6. Why is it of some importance *to the insured* whether a type of insurance is part of the *social* or the *private* field of insurance?

7. In terms of size, what is the approximate *relationship* of—
   a. Voluntary and social insurance?
   b. Federal insurance as a part of social insurance?
   c. Commercial insurance as a part of voluntary insurance?
   d. Personal and property insurance as a part of commercial insurance?
   e. Life insurance as a part of personal insurance?
   f. Automobile insurance as a part of casualty insurance?

8. "The development of social insurance is in fact a threat to the insurance business." Explain why you agree or disagree with this statement.

9. How do social and voluntary forms of insurance differ? Identify the basic kinds of each as to their purposes and methods of operation.

10. What kinds of perils (causes of loss) are included in fire insurance? Marine insurance? Casualty insurance? Personal insurance? Multiple-line insurance? All-lines insurance? Why are the last two types important?

11. How do cooperative types of insurance vary from commercial and voluntary government types? Give examples of each.

12. Why is the term *casualty insurance* misleading? How did casualty insurance evolve?

13. How does insurance differ from assistance? Why is this important?

14. How has the scope of social insurance changed over the years? Give examples of some of the changes of greatest significance.

15. What are some of the benefits of insurance—
    a. To the individual?
    b. To the business economy?
    c. To society?

16. "Over-insurance leads to fraud, full insurance to carelessness, and even partial insurance to some diminution of watchfulness." This statement is made by Willett in *The Economic Theory of Risk and Insurance.* Justify insurance in light of the statement, explaining how the benefits of insurance usually exceed its costs.

17. "Insurance is one of the most fundamental parts of our entire economy," said a well-known businessman recently. If he were speaking to a group of college seniors, how would you *outline* his talk on this subject?

18. Insurance is available throughout the world today. Why do you think insurance has become of tremendous significance in the United States, whereas in other countries its position varies greatly?

Chapter 4

Outline of concepts

Insurance contract fundamentals are the basis for the rights and obligations of the insurer and the insured and are sometimes the source of perplexities and misunderstandings.

The relationship of insurer functions explains *consumer* and *insurer* (or *functional*) viewpoints on insurance in this text.

The insurance contract or policy is the tangible means by which private insurance is created.

The basic characteristics of being a *future, contingent, service, risk* contract describe the unique combination which is insurance.

General legal requirements must be met to establish valid and enforceable insurance contracts.

Special legal characteristics of the insurance contract are very important in understanding its purposes and the laws and legal interpretations which help achieve these goals:

Its personal nature, which affects its assignability.

Its conditional nature, the promises for one party's obligation being based upon the other party's actions.

Its strict compliance nature, resulting from the fact that the insurer usually prepares the contract. Even though the "benefit of the doubt" goes to insureds in case of the lack of clarity, insureds who do not read their policies are foolish, for oral evidence usually cannot contradict the written contract.

Its indemnity nature, for the purpose of repaying insureds as nearly as possible for the *actual losses* they have sustained—not more, not less. The contrast with *valued policies* is noted.

Insurable interest supports the concept of indemnity, although its requirements vary among the types of insurance.

Subrogation rights also maintain indemnity and hold wrongdoers responsible for the results of their actions.

Concealment, representations, warranties, and **fraud** differ in their effect on the insurance contract. There should be *utmost good faith* between the insurer and the insured, especially for *material* or important facts. **Fraud** involves the *intent* to deceive, such as claims "padding."

Agency-law principles assume importance to the insured in insurance contracts, which are largely marketed through agency systems.

Insurance contract fundamentals

Insurance contracts sometimes become "bestsellers," but even the new shortened and improved insurance policies are unlikely to become "best-read," in spite of the thousands of dollars they may mean to consumers of insurance.

In your insurance contracts, should you read *(a)* every word, *(b)* only the important words, or *(c)* none of the words? A practical person, and those who know multiple-choice tests, would sensibly choose the middle-of-the-road answer *(b)*. But what are the important words?

That's the goal of this chapter—to learn about the basic product of insurance, the insurance contract, and about some of the important legal words and fundamentals upon which it is based. Hopefully, you will then feel that you can and should read more of an insurance contract, without a dictionary and an insurance agent at your elbow.

THE RELATIONSHIP OF INSURER FUNCTIONS

The *consumer viewpoint* of insurance is often emphasized in this text. In fact, the risk-management concept as discussed in the first two chapters is essentially looking at what options the consumer has in taking care of risks. The significance of the insurance option presented in Chapter 3 leads to studying next the fundamentals of insurance contracts, the basic product seen by insurance consumers.

As a consumer of insurance, however, you should recognize that a broader perspective is also important—that of the *insurer viewpoint*. It is the insurer that develops the insurance contract and brings it to the purchaser. In doing so the insurer must perform several basic functions: (1) product design, (2) marketing, (3) underwriting, and (4) loss payment. This *functional* viewpoint of the insurer is summarized in Figure 4–1 which also relates these functions to the control of insurance activities through regulation as the insurance contract is brought to the consumer.

Only the first function is discussed in this chapter, providing the necessary background for more specific discussion of the common types of life-health insurance in Part Two and property-liability insurance in

1) ALEATORY - MORE MAY BE GAINED THAN GIVEN
2) UNILATERAL - PROMISE MADE BY ONLY ONE PARTY
3) INFORMAL - NOT LIMITED TO A PARTICULAR FORMAT
4) CONTRACT OF ADHESION - ONE PARTY CONSTRUCTS THE TERMS

96   Chapter 4

Figure 4–1. The functional viewpoint of insurance

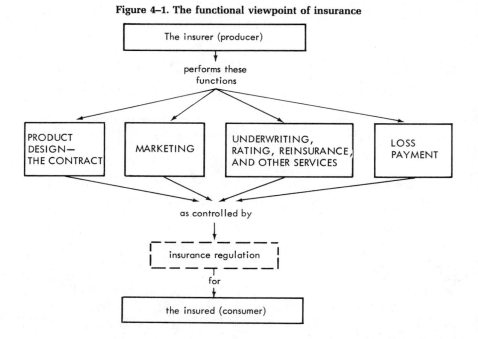

Part Three. Then the other functions are presented in Part Four, after the student has become familiar with the many types of insurance and the relevant terms included in insurance contracts.

THE INSURANCE CONTRACT OR POLICY

Contract law is of extreme importance to the field of insurance. Private insurance is usually created by a written contract or *policy*. Sometimes insurance begins with an oral agreement between the insurer (or its agent) and the insured and later is completed by a written contract. The most tangible product resulting from the insurance system is the written contract which transfers the risk of financial loss from the insured to the insurer. Thus, <u>insurance is fundamentally dependent upon the legal principles of contracts.</u>

Many persons think of the physical piece of paper upon which the insurance contract is written as the whole of insurance. Since this document is what the insurance purchaser sees, he or she may unconsciously assume that this is all there is to it. One tends to forget that there are many other parts of insurance. The risk transfer, the application of the law of large numbers, the freedom from worry, the inspections and the loss-prevention services, the advisory functions—all of these services tend to be forgotten when only the contract of insurance is considered. Even the payment of losses in dollars of currency is neglected in such thoughts by insurance purchasers, that is, unless they happen to suffer losses for which reimbursement is paid! The contract is significant in insurance, but the "service beyond the contract" is also of tremendous importance to the consumer.

Before studying more specifically the principles of insurance law in this chapter, other basic attributes of insurance are reviewed.

INSURANCE: A FUTURE, CONTINGENT, SERVICE, RISK CONTRACT

Is insurance an "intangible" product? Many writers characterize it as such, in contrast to such goods as clothing or automobiles, which can be seen, felt, and frequently used in everyday life. The description is not a sufficient answer as to why insurance is different from other economic products. Insurance *is* tangible in many ways, such as in the form of a contract or a loss-payment check. It is more than a mere piece of paper, for it is also a promise to pay money. The real differences that characterize the insurance product and its marketing can be summarized by saying that the insurance contract is unique in that it is a *future, contingent, service, risk* contract.

Unlike most of the physical goods that one purchases for immediate enjoyment, insurance is usually thought of as providing *future* benefits when loss payments are made. The policyholder does not, however, realize that he or she is using the insurance by obtaining a significant benefit immediately and continually throughout the contract period of protection. The relief from anxieties and freedom from worry as to financial losses are real insurance benefits. The policyholder often forgets this, however, and contemplates only that the insurance is purchased to obtain a loss payment sometime well into the future. A fire, an automobile collision, a death, or a retirement are all future considerations to the insurance purchaser.

More than that, policyholders buy insurance against many perils with the conviction that such perils will not really cause losses to them. They buy it "just in case" but at the same time thinking that "it will never happen to me." This quality of insurance emphasizes its *contingent* nature. The feeling of contingency is supported by fact, too. Only the unfortunate minority who actually suffer loss see that benefit of insurance. Families may continue insurance for many years without an automobile loss, or for a lifetime without a fire or theft loss to their home. A business may continue through millions of worker-hours without a disabling injury to any of its employees. The very nature of many kinds of insurance is based on contingencies that may or may not occur and that normally occur only infrequently.

The preceding comments have suggested the need for considering insurance as a *service* contract rather than a single physical product. It is, in fact, a bundle of services. Insurance becomes a unique product because the policyholder needs help in understanding its varied benefits. That is why in the marketing of insurance the personal service of an agent is so often necessary. Even though it is the ultimate responsibility of the insured to understand the contract, agents can be most helpful. Through them prospective insurance buyers learn about needs in regard to risks and how insurance prevents losses, transfers risks, and pays benefits in the case of losses. They learn how liability insurance pays the legal cost of defense in lawsuits. They find out how life insurance serves as a basis for credit, creates a liquid estate, and offers alternatives for using capital in the form of life income guarantees. In return for the cost of the contract, the policyholder receives many advisory services, some at the inception of the policy, others during the term of the contract or at the time of loss, and some at the end of the contract period. Many of the services of insurance are provided before the real needs for it are realized—at the time of loss.

The *risk* of financial loss is a final characteristic that differentiates insurance from other goods and services. The basis of the insurance contract is uncertainty about many perils which may cause accidental loss. Insurance transfers the risk of such losses to the insurer, a professional risk bearer. Other service contracts may be future and contingent, but they do not involve payment for unexpected perils such as fire, collision, and death. The characteristic that the insurance contract is based upon chance or fortuitous events is also closely related to it being called an "aleatory" contract, in which the values exchanged (i.e. a small premium for a large loss payment) are not equal.

GENERAL LEGAL REQUIREMENTS

The rights and obligations of the parties to an insurance agreement are determined largely by reference to the general laws which govern contracts. The agreement by which insurance is effected is a contract in which the insurer in consideration of the payment of a specified sum by the insured[1] agrees to make good the losses suffered through the

---

[1] Historically the term *insured* was distinguished from *assured* and *insurance* from *assurance*. Assurance concerned the duration of life where death either occurred or did not. Insurance related to uncertainties that could result in either whole, partial, or no losses at all, such as fires, collisions, and similar events. The distinction is no longer common, although the word *assurance* is used by a few companies in the United States and quite a number in Europe.

happening of a designated unfavorable contingency. The insurance contract need not be in writing, but as a matter of business practice such agreements are ordinarily written. Even social insurances, such as workers' compensation, are written, though the terms appear in a state law rather than in a private agreement.

A contract has been defined as "an agreement enforceable by law." A more complete definition would include certain essentials which the law requires: (1) the *offer* and its *acceptance;* (2) the *object* of the agreement must be *legal;* (3) the *parties* must be *competent;* and (4) generally a *consideration,* or payment, is essential. A lack of any of the essential elements prevents the enforcement of the agreement. To be valid and enforceable, insurance contracts must meet these four general legal requirements.

Offer and acceptance

A legally binding agreement, or contract, requires both an offer by one party and an acceptance by another party. In insurance the *offer* is usually made in a request for coverage by the prospect, or applicant. The simplest method, used for many types of property and liability insurance, is an oral request to an agent, either in person or by telephone. In life and many forms of health insurance the offer must be made in a written application.

Before a contract is effective, *acceptance* of the offer is necessary. In property-liability insurance, the agent usually has authority to "bind" or accept the offer, even without receiving any payment from the applicant. The protection may commence immediately, if desired, based entirely on the oral request of the applicant and the oral acceptance by the agent. A written "binder," or temporary contract, may be issued by the agent, pending later writing of the actual contract (usually within 15–30 days), but this is not essential in order for the agreement to be effective.

In life insurance the method and timing of legal acceptance are different. The written application and the first premium payment are usually submitted by the applicant as the offer to the agent, who issues a "conditional receipt." Acceptance is held by most courts in such cases to be as of the time when the applicant meets the underwriting standards of the insurer, including a medical examination if required. Then the coverage requested is made effective as of the time of the application and premium payment. If the premium is not paid with the application, the offer to insure is made by the insurer. The insurance is not accepted and does not become effective until the contract is delivered to the applicant while in good health and the premium is paid. If the applicant does not meet the underwriting standards of the insurer, the insurer

may make a counteroffer with a different contract, which the prospect
may accept or reject upon delivery by the agent.

Legal purpose

The second requirement of a legally binding contract is that it must
have a *legal purpose* or object. The courts will not enforce an insurance
contract, for example, if it has an illegal purpose or is contrary to public
policy. Examples include a thief attempting to insure stolen property;
life insurance taken out by the applicant with the proven intention of
murdering the insured in order to collect payment; or fire insurance
taken out by you on your neighbor's house in the hope that it will burn
(this would lack an "insurance interest," as discussed later in this chapter, and it would be against public policy because it would be a gambling
contract).

Competent parties

Valid contracts also require that the parties making the offer and
those accepting the contract be legally *competent* to make the agreement.
In insurance, the most common problem arises in connection with applicants who are minors (under age 18, or 21 in some states). Such applicants
may have the option of repudiating contracts, up to the time they reach
legal adulthood, unless the contracts are for necessities, such as food,
shelter, or clothing. Some insurance contracts are thus voidable by applicants who are minors, and these applicants would receive a full return
of the premiums paid. Some states have made exceptions for life and
health insurance contracts by establishing special age limits of 14–16,
beyond which age minors are considered to have the legal capacity to
insure themselves and the contract is binding.

A similar problem may occur in insurance contracts written for insane
or intoxicated persons, who cannot make legal contracts because they
fail to understand the agreement.

Insurers, too, must be competent to enter into a legal contract by
meeting charter and license requirements of the states. In cases where
such legal capacity is lacking, many courts have nevertheless held the
contracts binding on the insurer, or on its corporate officers personally.

Consideration

The final requirement for a valid contract is some *consideration* exchanged by both parties to the agreement—a right or something of value
given up, or an obligation assumed. In insurance, the applicant typically
makes a premium payment, or the contract may become effective on

the basis of the applicant's promise to pay and to meet other conditions of the contract. The insurer's consideration is its promise to pay for specified losses or to provide other services to the insured.

SPECIAL LEGAL CHARACTERISTICS

The remainder of this chapter concerns special legal characteristics of the insurance contract. These are not necessarily unique to insurance contracts, but in total they help describe the fundamental ideas upon which insurance contracts are based. A good understanding of the characteristics should aid the insurance consumer in reading insurance contracts and in comprehending the underlying legal concepts which are essential to most insurance contracts. Figure 4–2 summarizes the characteristics.

Personal nature

The insurance contract is *personal* and follows the person rather than the property concerned. We speak of "insuring property." Yet this is not technically the situation. Insurance actually provides repayment of a loss arising out of some undesired happening. It is impossible to guarantee to a person that possessions will not be lost, or even to guarantee to replace them with like and kind. It is possible, however, to provide for indemnification to the person who has incurred the loss. Hence, if

Figure 4–2. Special legal characteristics of insurance contracts

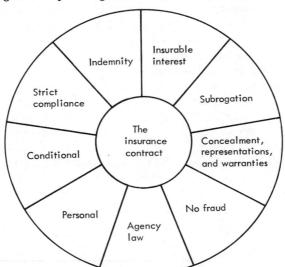

an individual should pay for a fire insurance contract and subsequently sell the property without arranging with the insurer to transfer the insurance to the new owner, there would be no payment by the insurer in case of fire because there would be no loss on the part of the original insured. The measure of insurance payment is loss to the insured, not loss of specified property.

One result of the personal nature of insurance is that many insurance contracts are not freely assignable by the policyholder to other parties. Most insurance contracts (life insurance being an exception) represent a personal agreement between insurer and insured. To permit a fire or automobile insurance contract to be assignable without the insurer's approval would be unfair to the insurer. Only by knowing and investigating each policyholder it insures can the insurance company correctly appraise the risk it is accepting. A parallel illustration of a personal contract in the entertainment field may help the student realize the value of this aspect of insurance. Bob Hope's manager could not fulfill a personal appearance contract by Bob Hope by sending someone else to appear for him.

Conditional nature

The obligation to perform on the part of one of the parties to an agreement may be conditioned upon the action of the second party. A clause in an insurance contract requiring such performance is usually referred to as a *condition*. Failure of one party to perform relieves the other party of obligation.

Where an insurance contract is subject to a condition, the condition is usually regarded as either precedent (before) or subsequent to (after) the time at which a promise becomes binding on the promisor. An illustration of a common *condition precedent,* which must take place before a promise becomes binding, is the requirement in many insurance contracts that an insured who suffers a loss must give proper notice and proof to the insurer before the claim is payable. Note that the insured does not have to file a claim but that the insurer is not obligated to pay unless the insured does so in the proper manner. An example of a *condition subsequent* is an insured's failure to cooperate with the insurer in defending a liability claim. Here the promise of the insured is not fulfilled, and that failure subsequently relieves the insurer of its earlier promise to pay.

Strict compliance nature

Contracts of adhesion. The insurance contract is said to be a "contract of *adhesion"* in that it is ordinarily prepared in all its details by the insurer and the insured has no part in drawing up its clauses or determining its wording. In applying for insurance, the applicant either accepts the policy as prepared by the insurer, does not purchase the insurance, or contacts another insurer that may use some different contract wording. Contracts are sometimes modified to meet individual needs, but even when so modified, the contract with its amendments is prepared by the insurance company. A contract of adhesion is contrasted to a "bargaining contract" in which both parties contribute to the terms and conditions.

The insurer does not always draw up the contract. Sometimes legislation requires that specific wording be used. Other times the insured may be a large corporation that is in a position to ask for and obtain special contract provisions. In such cases, the intent of the entire contract and of both the insurer and the insured would probably be considered in interpretations of the contract by the courts.

Benefit of doubt to insured. Since the insurer has the advantage in drawing up the agreement and is expected to represent clearly the intent of all the parties, it is generally enforced that where the terms of the policy are ambiguous, obscure, or susceptible of more than one interpretation, the construction most favorable to the insured must prevail.[2] The rule is based on the assumption that the insurer is under a duty to make its meaning clear. When the insurer has failed to be clear, the "benefit of the doubt" goes to the policyholder. This applies, however, *only* when the *court* decides the contract is unclear, not every time the insured misinterprets or does not understand a provision. Sometimes, however, this principle may help insureds, offsetting their lack of participation in drawing up the contract.

Insureds should read contract. Where there is no ambiguity, the contract is to be enforced in accordance with its terms. If the contract is clear and understandable, its meaning may not be distorted by interpretations. Consideration must be given to the generally understood meaning of the terms used and to the entire context to determine the nature and extent of coverage.

A corollary to the strict compliance rule is that the law holds persons to be bound by the terms of a written contract which they sign or accept, regardless of whether or not they have taken the trouble to acquaint themselves with all its terms and conditions.[3] Too many insurance contracts are complicated and difficult to understand. It is probably safe to state that regardless of the clarity or obscurity of the terminology, most people do not read their policies. Insureds assume that a policy

---

[2] *Knouse* v. *Equitable Life Insurance Company of Ohio,* 181 Pac. (2d) 310.

[3] This is the general rule. See *Grace* v. *Adams,* 100 Mass. 505. However, some recent cases seem to say that the insured does *not* have to read his or her policy. Special situations sometimes occur, such as those in which the insured has reasonably relied upon advice of a professional agent, but it is unwise for policyholders to assume that courts will be lenient in excusing them from a contract's written terms.

meets their needs and let it go at that. It is no defense, however, when the loss occurs, to claim ignorance of the terms of the policy because of failure to read the agreement. The insured's failure to read the contract does not change or extend the rights of the insured as stated in the written policy. The advice to insurance buyers should be: "To avoid problems (and uncertainties!), *know* what is in your insurance policy by reading it, or having it explained, or both."

Oral evidence. In connection with the insurance contract, the rule of law applying to *parole* or oral evidence has been expressed in a leading case: "It is a fundamental rule, in courts both of law and equity, that parole contemporaneous evidence is inadmissible to contradict or vary the terms of a valid written instrument."[4] Thus, an insured cannot usually contradict the written contract by saying that the agent *said* the policy covered a specific type of loss.

Although the contract in the ordinary course is not subject to modification by parole evidence, the language of the policy is nevertheless not binding in clear cases of mutual mistake of fact or where there is a mistake on one side and fraud inducing it on the other. In such cases, the injured party has an equity right to ask that the contract be reformed to the true agreement. An example might be a contract which is written, with incorrect oral information from a prospective insured, for insurance on a wrong building.

Parole evidence also can be helpful to the insured: usually, when information is given to the insurance agent at the time of an application or loss, this knowledge is also assumed to be knowledge of the insurer.

Indemnity nature

Many property, liability, and health insurance contracts are essentially contracts of *indemnity* or repayment. For example, property contracts promise to pay losses on the basis of "actual cash value." By this it is meant that insurance provides reimbursement for actual damage sustained by the insured but no more. This being the case, the total policy amount (face value) is not the amount payable in the event of a loss but rather represents a maximum limit to the liability of the insurer. Under the indemnity rule, if a property is valued at $50,000 and insured for $100,000, the insurance company would pay $50,000 to the policyholder who suffers a total loss. If the insured receives reimbursement for part or all of the loss from any other source, the liability of the insurer is often reduced in the same amount.[5] An exception to the use

---

[4] *Northern Assurance Co.* v. *Grand View Building Assn.*, 182 U.S. 308 (1902).

[5] The U.S. Supreme Court has set forth the basic rule by stating that where there is a contract of indemnity, such as fire insurance, and a loss happens, anything that reduces or diminishes that loss reduces the amount which the indemnifier is bound to pay (*Chicago,*

of indemnity in property insurance is the "valued policy," where the full policy amount is paid for a total loss under certain circumstances described in a later section of this chapter.

Property insurance. The destruction or damage of the *property* described in the contract of insurance is not the contingency upon which the insurer promises to indemnify the insured; it is only when the insured has suffered a loss that the insurer may be called upon to make a payment under the contract.[6] In most cases of property insurance the approximate value of the property can be estimated before a loss, or determined after a loss, within reasonably narrow limits. Some cases present special problems, however, such as older buildings that are now used for different purposes than when they were built. For example, a large stable or coach house now used as a garage at the rear of a residence would probably never be replaced as it was if it were destroyed by fire. Here the functional value of the building is more important than the replacement value. The insurer would usually limit the insurance amount written to its functional value.

Liability insurance. *Liability* policies paying for damage to other persons or their property are a special example of indemnity. They were formerly written as contracts of indemnity. If insureds were declared bankrupt and therefore did not pay the injured parties to whom they were legally liable, then insurers were not obligated to pay. In such situations the insureds suffered no loss; therefore indemnification by the insurers could not be made.

The liability policies as now issued are regarded not as contracts of indemnity against loss but as contracts of indemnity against liability. The insurer pays if the insured is liable for damages within the scope of the contract, even if the insured is declared bankrupt and technically could not pay the injured party.

In setting the limits of insurance for liability policies, care must be taken to write the policy amount high enough to take into consideration the unknown nature of jury verdicts. In buying liability protection, the policyholder should often purchase higher limits than the minimum or standard limits available.

One of the most difficult applications of the idea of indemnity in liability situations is the determination of reasonable payment for such items in the claim as "pain and suffering," "mental anguish," and so on. Actual medical costs and loss of income are much easier to justify on the principle of indemnity.

Life and health insurance. *Life* insurance and many *health* insur-

---

St. Louis & New Orleans R.R. Co. v. *Pullman Southern Car Co.,* 139 U.S. 79). Exceptions to this rule may be found, particularly in some indirect loss insurance and in many types of individual health insurance.

[6] *Draper* v. *Delaware State Grange Mutual Fire Ins. Co.,* 91 Atl. 206.

ance contracts are not based upon the indemnity principle.[7] Here it is the difficulty of determining precise values that prevents the contract from being, strictly speaking, based upon indemnity. One cannot say that the life of a person is worth (or not worth) precisely $10,000 or $50,000 or $300,000. Thus the life insurance contract is a *valued policy,* and agrees to pay a certain stated amount rather than an amount determined after the loss to be a repayment for the loss. There can be no question raised by the insurer paying the loss as to whether or not the loss of life actually resulted in an equivalent economic loss to the insured or the beneficiaries of the life insurance contract.

Valued policies. A special case of the indemnity doctrine concerns the *valued policy* in property insurance. There are properties that are extremely difficult to appraise accurately. Thus, the valued policy is used, just as in life insurance. In this category fall works of art, antiques, rare collections, and family heirlooms. Because of the difficulty of arriving at any satisfactory agreement as to value following a loss, it is deemed advisable in this class of business that the insurer and the insured agree upon a value at the time the policy is issued.

The valuation agreed upon must be fair to both insurer and insured. It should not be so high as to create a desire by the insured to have a loss payment rather than the object insured, yet it should be high enough to compensate the insured reasonably if loss should occur.

Thus the Picasso monument in Chicago's Civic Center Plaza has reportedly been insured for $300,000. If total loss results, the policy amount will determine the amount of the insurance claim payment. Even if the 160-ton, 50-foot-high sculpture actually turns out to be worth only $200,000, at the time of loss the full amount of $300,000 would be paid. Another example is Leonardo da Vinci's famous painting, *Mona Lisa,* which was recently insured for $40 million.

In writing a contract of this type, there is no violation of the indemnity idea. Rather, an agreement is made in advance as to the amount necessary to indemnify the insured in the event of loss or damage to the property. The use of the valued policy in such situations is regarded as sound practice because such articles of unique value may be subject to honest differences of opinion at any particular time. Many valuable items should be insured in this manner.

Valued policy laws. From time to time there develops a demand by the public for *valued policy laws* in connection with the insurance of other types of property, such as homes. The opportunity to use such policies to overinsure has caused insurance authorities to frown upon

---

[7] Recommended for more information on legal aspects pertaining to life insurance is Janice E. Greider and William T. Beadles, *Law and the Life Insurance Contract* (Homewood, Ill.: Richard D. Irwin, 1979).

the general use of this contract. Nevertheless, several states have enacted statutes that make valued policies mandatory for insurance on homes or other *real estate* property. Some of these laws apply only when an insured property is *totally* destroyed, and only for certain perils, such as *fire or windstorm*. The amount of insurance in force is then taken as conclusive evidence of the true value of the property and the loss, regardless of the actual value. Property owners reason that it is unjust for them to pay for insurance over a number of years and then to get less than the face of the policy if their property is destroyed. The reasoning has its appeal. However, experience in the insurance business indicates that there is less injustice if the responsibility for fixing a reasonable amount of insurance is placed upon insureds than if insureds are permitted to make a profit through the destruction of their property. Valued policy laws are believed to invite carelessness and fraud, stimulate overinsurance, and violate the indemnity rule.

Insurable interest

Closely related to the concept of indemnity is the requirement that all insurance contracts contain an element of *insurable interest*. An insurable interest is a right or relationship in regard to the subject matter of the insurance contract such that the insured can suffer *financial* loss from damage, loss, or destruction to it. The subject matter might be a property, a life, or another interest.

The purposes of requiring an insurable interest in insurance contracts are to prevent gambling, to decrease moral hazard, and to help measure the actual loss. Without an insurable interest, a contract is a wager or gambling contract. It also could be an undesirable incentive for some persons to cause losses or injuries on purpose. When an insurable interest exists, no profit results, for insureds merely receive repayment for the loss they have suffered.

A clear example of insurable interest is ownership of *property*, with a fire, windstorm, or other peril causing a financial loss. However, many other types of insurable interest are common. Mortgagees, bailees, and creditors may have insurable interests, and oftentimes there are several persons who have insurable interest in the same property. A homeowner may insure his or her interest in property, for example, while at the same time the policy insures the mortgagee's interest up to the value of the mortgage.

Liability creates many insurable interests. Either an automobile owner or driver may be held responsible for losses caused by the car; thus each has an insurable interest. Employers may also be liable for employees' automobiles. Tenants oftentimes are liable for injuries caused to the public on the premises. Property owners may be held responsible for the actions of contractors and contractors for the actions of subcontractors. All such losses may be the basis of an insurable interest.

The continuance of *life and* good *health* serves as the basis for many other examples of insurable interest. Death, injury, or sickness may result in financial losses to the persons insured, or to their families, creditors, business partners, or employers. The right of persons to insure their own lives, as well as the right of close family members to insure blood relatives, is based on a presumed insurable interest. Other insurable interests for life or health insurance are based upon actual losses (either increased expenses or reduced income potential) resulting from the relationship to the insured. For example, a creditor can insure the life of a debtor, normally up to the amount of the loan, or a businessperson may insure a partner's life for the potential loss this would cause the partnership.

The question of *when* an insurable interest is required is also important. Generally, property insurance has the legal requirement that an insurable interest exist at the time of loss, whereas life insurance requires an insurable interest only at the time the contract is purchased.

↑ *BEADLES — PAGE 130*

Subrogation rights

The doctrine of *subrogation* gives the insurer whatever rights the insured possessed against responsible third parties. It is basically a process of substitution, the insurer taking over the rights of the insured that existed at the time of the loss.[8] From the time of the loss the insured may not release any rights that might prove beneficial to the insurer.

In common law it is held that a person who causes a loss or who is primarily liable ought ultimately to be made responsible for the damages sustained. In connection with the law of insurance, it is a matter of equity that upon paying the insured the amount of the loss, the insurer has a right of action against any other person who may have caused the loss. In some cases, the insurer has subrogation rights because of a specific subrogation clause in the contract, rather than from equitable or common-law rules.

The right of the insurer against other negligent persons usually does not rest upon any contractual relationship but arises out of the nature of the contract of insurance as one of indemnity. If the insured is indemnified, it would be inequitable for him or her also to try to collect from the parties responsible for the loss. If the insured were permitted to do this, a double collection of the loss, from both the insurer and the

---

[8] For an extensive treatment of the idea and use of the principle of subrogation, see Ronald C. Horn, *Subrogation in Insurance Theory and Practice* (Homewood, Ill.: Richard D. Irwin, 1964).

responsible party, might result in a profit to the insured. Subrogation is also a fair principle in that it holds wrongdoers responsible for the results of their wrongful actions instead of permitting them not to pay only because an insurance contract was in force. The overall cost of insurance to policyholders is also reduced in this manner.

The right of subrogation by the insurer is limited in amount to the loss payment which has been made to the insured. The insurer cannot make a profit by subrogating against the person who caused the loss. In fact, oftentimes subrogation rights are of little value to the insurance company. There may be no doubt that someone else was responsible for the loss, but in order to recoup its loss payment the insurer must (1) prove the liability of the wrongdoer and (2) the negligent party must have the financial ability to pay for the loss he or she caused. In many cases the expense or difficulty of legal proof may prevent the insurer from using its subrogation rights. If it might cost $1,000 to collect a $600 claim, the subrogation right may be worthless.

The importance of subrogation varies greatly for the various types of insurance. In life insurance it is not used. Limited use is found in fire insurance, where proof of the case of fire is often difficult. However, tenants can be held liable, for example, when their carelessness causes a fire loss to rented property. A more common illustration of subrogation is in automobile insurance, where the insurer first pays under collision coverage for damage to the insured's car. Then the insurer takes over the rights of the policyholder by subrogation and brings suit against the other driver involved in the accident to receive reimbursement. If the insured did not receive full payment from the insurer because of a deductible in the policy, the insured would retain the right to sue the responsible party for the deductible amount. Sometimes a joint suit for the full amount is filed, but the insurer is not obligated to do this.

Effect of concealment, representations, warranties, and fraud

BEADLES - PAGE 272

Concealment. Since the contract of insurance concerns itself with risk and uncertainty, it has been established as a fundamental doctrine of insurance law that neither party practice *concealment*. The contract is said to be one of "utmost good faith." Both parties to the agreement must stand on an equal footing. This doctrine makes mandatory the affirmative disclosure to the insurer of all *material* or important facts that are the exclusive knowledge of the insured. For example, if there is knowledge on the part of the owner that the property insured was in grave danger of destruction at the inception of the agreement and if this information is not disclosed to the insurer, an unbalanced agreement will result.

The concealment of a material fact need not be intentional or fraudulent in order to make a policy voidable, and it is no defense to plead mistake or forgetfulness. If the insurer would have declined the risk or accepted the policy upon different terms if it had possessed all the facts, the policy is voidable.

The terms *void* and *voidable* are sometimes used interchangeably, but such use is not correct. A *void* agreement is one that is entirely without legal effect, and neither party can enforce it. For example, the law makes certain requirements essential for the validity of a contract, and in the absence of these essentials the contract is void. Thus, a contract having an illegal object cannot be enforced at law by either party.

A *voidable* contract is one that may be affirmed or rejected at the option of one of the parties but is binding on the other. If the insured has failed to comply with a condition of the contract, the insurer may elect to fulfill its part of the agreement or may choose to treat the contract as voidable. There are frequent instances in which the insurer has a technical right to claim a forfeiture but in the interests of equity and good public relations decides not to exercise that right. Only seldom does the insured have the right to treat a contract as voidable—perhaps in a case where the insurer has grossly misrepresented the contract benefits.

The concealment doctrine had an early start in ocean marine insurance, and due to the nature of the business a strict interpretation applies even today. A ship or cargo may be insured in London, yet the property may be located in some far corner of the globe. Since the property is beyond the possibility of inspection by the insurer, full reliance and dependence must be placed upon the insured for all pertinent facts.

In the case of other types of insurance, the property or persons insured are ordinarily convenient for inspection, and consequently the material facts essential for an appraisal of the risk are within the range of the insurer's observation. When it is not made the subject of express inquiry, the concealment must be intentional to make the policy voidable. The insured needs only to answer fully and in good faith all inquiries made by the insurers. One exception to the rule provides that when important facts bearing on the risk are so unusual that they would not ordinarily be inquired about or readily discovered by the insurer, the obligation of affirmative disclosure is present, whether or not express inquiry has been made.

Representations. A *representation* is a statement made by the insured to the insurer at the time of or prior to the formation of a contract. Since it is the right of the insurer to have full knowledge of the subject of insurance, it frequently becomes necessary to depend upon statements of the insured, from whom it is most convenient to ascertain the pertinent facts. A *misrepresentation* (false statement) on the part of the insured of any *material* (important) fact has the same effect as a concealment and affords a basis for making the contract voidable by the insurer.

The difference between concealment and misrepresentation is that the insured conceals if a silence is maintained when there is an obligation to speak and misrepresents if a statement is made which is not true. The determination of what is material is based on the same ideas as apply in the cases of concealment illustrated earlier. Each set of facts must be evaluated in the given situation, by the courts if necessary. For example, a response of "No" by a businessperson applying for theft insurance to the question "Have you had any theft losses?" might be considered a material misrepresentation if, in fact, the applicant carelessly forgot a large loss that occurred two years earlier—but perhaps it would not be considered such if the only previous loss was a very small one which happened five years earlier.

Warranties. When the application for the insurance contract is made a part of the policy, the answers to specific questions on the application are deemed *warranties*. If false, they make the policy voidable by the insurer. Some warranties may also be specifically added in the policy, such as the promise of the insured in a burglary policy that an alarm system or security guards will be maintained.

The difference between a warranty and a representation is that a warranty is a part of the contract itself and must therefore be strictly complied with, whereas a representation is usually an incidental statement preceding the contract and not actually a part of it, though it may be an inducement to it. The difference, in effect, is that in order to make the contract voidable a warranty need only be false, whereas a representation must be both false and material.

In order to constitute a warranty, a statement must not only be intended as such but must be definitely indicated as a warranty either through its incorporation into the policy or through being specifically referred to as such. Where there is any doubt as to whether a warranty was intended, the statement is to be regarded as a representation and must be shown to be material in order to defeat the policy.

Many states have modified by legislative act the strict application of the doctrine of warranties for most kinds of insurance except marine. Where the doctrine has been thus modified, the insurance is sometimes voidable only if a loss occurs during a breach of warranty, or is caused thereby, or if the breach materially increases the risk. This, in effect, causes *most warranties* in insurance contracts *today* to be *considered as representations*. It is wise, however, not to tamper with warranties incorporated into insurance policies, but to comply with them to the letter, for it is still the tendency of some courts to enforce the original strict rule, declaring the policy voidable when a warranty is breached, regardless of how trivial or immaterial to the loss it may be.

Effect of fraud. A false representation or the concealment of a material fact *with the intent and result* that it be acted upon by another party may constitute *fraud*. A concealment amounts to a false representation if active steps are taken to prevent discovery of the truth. This is the case if a representation is made that is in part true, but certain facts are suppressed.

To constitute fraud the representation must be of past or existing acts. It follows, therefore, that expressions of opinion, belief, expectation, or intention do not constitute fraudulent statements. The representation must be of material fact that would lead to reliance upon it by the party to whom it is made. Commendatory expressions of value or false representations made where the parties deal on an equal footing and have equal means of knowledge are not held to be fraudulent. For example, if an applicant for automobile insurance said, "I am a very good driver," there could be no fraud, as this was merely an expression of opinion. However, if an applicant said, "I have never had an accident," where in fact the applicant had several recent accidents and was making the statement with the idea of getting a lower insurance cost, fraud might be provable.

An active intent to deceive or the intentional misleading by one person of another is usually present. The person making the statement must know that it is false or make the statement in reckless disregard of whether it is true or false. Finally, in order to constitute fraud the misrepresentation must be relied upon by and injure the other party. In such cases a contract becomes voidable at the option of the injured party.

The requirements for proving fraud are difficult to meet. An insurer must prove intent to defraud on the part of the insured. Intent involves premeditation, and it is hard to show what a person thought before an action, unless intent is very clearly indicated by present or repeated past actions or statements. If proved, however, fraud is a serious matter. It may permit the insurer to rescind the contract. For example, if in order to obtain a lower rate the insured purposely misstates in an automobile insurance application that no young family members use the car, the coverage may be lost because of the fraudulent action of the insured. A more common but perhaps equally serious example is the intentional exaggeration of any insurance claim for the purpose of receiving overpayment for a loss.

Summary. In order to review the concepts of concealment, representations, warranties, and fraud, the requirements for making an insurance contract voidable by the insurer are shown in Table 4–1.

Agency-law principles   *Beadles · page 65*

Much of the business of insurance is conducted by corporations that rely upon representatives, known as *agents,* to sell insurance contracts to applicants and insureds. The predominance of agency systems is seen

Table 4–1. The effects of concealment, representations, warranties, and fraud

Concept	Requirements for voidability	Example
Concealment	Must be silence which is material (or important).	Applicant for windstorm insurance fails to tell agent that a tornado is known to be approaching the property.
Representations	Must be statement (oral or written) which is false *and* material	Applicant for theft insurance falsely states that no recent losses have been suffered, when in fact a loss occurred a few months previously.
Warranties	Must be false and incorporated and identified in the contract or application as a warranty.	Applicant for marine insurance answers question in the application falsely, by stating that the ship is used on inland rather than ocean waters.
Fraud	Must be false, with an intent to deceive, and be relied upon by and cause injury to the other party.	Insured purposely overstates a claim in order to obtain a larger loss payment than is justified.

in the later chapter on insurance marketing. Specific business firms, known as insurance agencies, are retailers through whom insurance contracts are sold. However, in the present chapter the term *agency* refers to the *legal relationships* among insurers, their agents, and insurance consumers, as based upon principles of agency law.

How an insurance contract comes into effect is thus frequently determined by agency law. Two types of agency relationships are important: (1) *agency by agreement,* and (2) *agency by other means.* The rights and responsibilities of all the parties are dependent upon these methods, and applicants or insureds need to understand how their insurance contracts are affected by these agency relationships.

Agency by agreement.   Agency involves a *principal* who authorizes a second party, an *agent,* to create, modify, or terminate a contract with a third party. The agent acts on behalf of the principal. In insurance, the insurer is the principal who hires an insurance agent to deal with the applicant or insured.

An agency relationship could be created by an oral agreement, but most agency agreements are reduced to writing. In the business of insurance, a written document, the *agency contract,* or "commission of authority," usually designates the parties and outlines the specific authority of the agent to act for the principal, or insurer, in dealing with the insurance buyer. Most agency relationships are created in this manner.

Agency by other means.   By operation of law or court interpretation, other agency relationships may be created. If the principal permits someone to act in such a way that third parties may reasonably believe that an agency relationship exists, reliance on the agency thus created is said to be an *agency by estoppel*. This means that the principal is pre-cluded, or stopped, from using the right to deny that an agency relation-ship exists.

The application of this principle to insurance prevents an insurer from denying a fact which has been admitted by the insurer's previous action. For example, suppose an employee (who is not an agent) of an insurer was carelessly given some numbered and signed policies. Even though the insurer did not intend the employee to be an agent, if the contracts were filled in by the employee, the insurer might be estopped or prevented from later denying coverage.

Estoppel is closely connected with the principle of *waiver*, the inten-tional relinquishing or abandonment of a known right. Thus an insurer or an agent may accept a premium payment from the insured, knowing of a violation of a policy condition, such as the storage of large amounts of gasoline on the premises. The condition may be waived by the act of accepting the premium. A waiver may also occur after a loss. The insurer may waive such rights as the requirement for written proof of loss by the insured. Suppose the insurer denies liability for the loss. Then the insurer's right to receive proof within a specified number of days after the loss may be held to have been relinquished, or waived.

Sometimes a person may claim to have authority to act for a given principal without actually having such authority. If, however, the princi-pal later ratifies the act of the unauthorized agent, the agreement be-comes effective and binding upon the principal from the inception of the original agreement. This situation creates an *agency by ratification.* Ratification may be either expressed or implied from any act, expression, or conduct which would definitely indicate the intent of the principal to adopt the transaction. Assume that an insurer tells an agent not to write a liability insurance contract for more than $100,000 but that later the agent does and the insurer accepts the payment of the premium. That acceptance would ratify the agency relationship for the transaction.

The scope of *apparent authority* assumes an extremely important place because the responsibility of the principal for acts of the agent often exceed the powers expressly conferred in definite instructions to the agent. Incidental powers for which the agency was created are often implied, and the general uses and customs of the community tend to expand or limit the agent's authority. An agent's actions bind the princi-pal if they fall within this apparent authority.

For example, insurers issue to their agents lists of "prohibited risks" that the company will not write, such as amusement parks, nightclubs, sawmills, and bowling alleys. In addition to listing prohibited risks, some insurers list properties which may be insured only after specific referral to the company and special inspection. If the applicant is unaware of such limiting instructions given to the agent, and an agent writes a policy anyway, the insurer would have to pay the applicant for a loss unless it had canceled the policy. However, the insurer would have a right of action against the agent for violating his or her agency contract.

FOR REVIEW AND DISCUSSION

1. Lee, in frustration, states: "I'll never read all those legal words in my insurance contracts, but I always have the feeling I should do so." Is there a solution to this dilemma? Explain.

2. One person says that insurance is "intangible," while another states that it is "a future, contingent, service, risk contract." Which description do you prefer, and why?

3. Identify three special legal characteristics of insurance and explain the reason for the importance of each to the policyholder.

4. From the insurer's standpoint, why are the following important in the insurance transaction:
   a. Its strict compliance nature?
   b. Its indemnity nature?
   c. Insurable interest?
   d. Subrogation?
   e. Agency law?

5. Must insurance contracts be in writing? Why or why not?

6. Why do you think the application of the concept of subrogation varies among the different types of insurance? Give examples from the property and life insurance fields.

7. The strict compliance rule is justified by the fact that the insurer has an advantage in drawing up the insurance agreement. In your opinion, are insurance contracts sufficiently complex to concede a real advantage on the part of the insurance company?

8. Distinguish between a "warranty," a "representation," a "concealment," and "fraud" and explain the importance of each to the insurer and the insured.

9. Mr. B. Scottfree is an agent.
   a. He is suspended by the Careful Insurance Company. The company takes its supplies from the agent's office. The agent reissues an expired policy, collecting and retaining the premium. Is there any liability on the part of the insurer, or must the policyholder suffer the loss?
   b. Suppose that after suspension but before the supplies are taken, Mr. Scottfree issues a policy. The company accepts the premium. Upon what theory is the agent's act validated?
   c. Suppose the agent is not suspended but has instructions not to insure certain prohibited properties. Carelessly, he issues a policy on a prohibited risk. Before notice reaches the home office of the company, the property burns. Discuss the questions of liability involved.

10. What examples can you give of possible violations of the concept of indem-

nity in insurance? Indicate *how and why* they deviate from the indemnity approach.

11. Match the following description in column 2 with the most appropriate term from column 1, by pairing the letters with the correct numbers:

Column 1	*Column 2*
a. Insurable interest	1. Important in insurance marketing
b. Concealment	2. Thus, not all insurance is assignable
c. Subrogation	3. If material, may make contract voidable
d. Valued policy laws	4. Must include intent to deceive
e. Agency law	5. Insurance amount paid for total loss
f. Personal nature	6. Without it, insurance would be a profit
g. Fraud	7. Insurer takes over insured's rights
h. Ambiguity	8. Insured should read contract
i. Contract of adhesion	9. Insurer prepares the contract
j. Strict compliance rule	10. Benefit of doubt may go to insured

12. What two types of agency relationships are important in insurance, and why are these important to insurance agents and to insurance consumers?

Part Two

LIFE AND HEALTH INSURANCE

Part Two is "a matter of *life and death*" . . . and *health and disability* as well. The insurance systems that are used to protect families and businesses against *loss of income* or *increased expenses,* due to death or disability, are the subject of Chapters 5–12 on *life and health insurance.* Part One introduced the risk-management viewpoint. Part Two is the first part of this book to emphasize the "by line" approach of studying the major types of insurance separately.

Chapters 5–8 discuss the field of *life* insurance (and annuities), beginning with *general principles* underlying the protection and investment aspects of this important part of the insurance business. What a student and rational consumer should know is stressed in regard to actuarial base, legal doctrines, and cost. Basic *types of contracts* are analyzed to learn that all life insurance policies are fundamentally of these types: term, whole life, and endowment. *Contract features* provide considerable flexibility to meet changing consumer needs, and *annuities* and pensions protect the consumer against "living too long" instead of "dying too soon."

Health insurance in a wide variety of *individual* contracts is the subject of Chapter 9. The *group* insurance technique is discovered in Chapter 10 to be one of the fastest-growing parts of both life and health insurance.

Government insurance systems for life and health insurance (Chapter 11), including the extensive social security and workers' and unemployment compensation plans, are seen as a social insurance base in the U.S. insurance picture. The *coordination* of all government, group, and individual life-health insurance is the challenging task of Chapter 12.

Chapter 5

Outline of concepts

Life insurance principles are basic ideas to understanding:

Its nature is *protection* against the financial *loss of income* earning ability caused by death, or *investment* for similar loss in old age.

Compared with other insurance contracts, it is *not indemnity;* it is *unique* in combining long-term protection and investment; and it has *insurable interests* based on family relationships or financial losses.

Fundamental financial and actuarial concepts include:

The life insurance equation (Premium cost = Mortality + Expenses − Interest earnings).

Comparison of basic *term, whole life, endowment* and *annuity* contracts.

Development from assessment plans, often unsuccessful ventures.

Level premium plan, which creates reserves and cash values.

Investment functions, which offer immediate creation of estates; stable yield with high safety; managerial, tax, and other advantages.

The mortality table, including discussion of:

What it is—a compilation of probable mortality at each age.

Where it comes from and its purposes, as aided by *actuaries.*

Its basic construction in which death rates are calculated.

Different mortality tables for many different groups of insureds.

Development of the 1958 CSO table, the most widely used today.

Life insurance premium calculations:

Advancing premiums as age increases, a basic characteristic.

The interest factor, compounding of premium payments.

The gross premium, net premiums plus loading expenses.

Life insurance reserves:

Origin, the level premium plan of overpayment in the early years.

Definition, present value of future benefits less future premiums.

The reserve account, mostly "legal reserves."

Underwriting of life insurance, which includes:

Medical examinations for many applicants.

Other factors and sources of information, such as inspection reports.

Substandard or extra risks, with occupational or physical ratings.

Nonmedical life insurance, increasingly used today.

War clauses, restricting payment for war deaths of military personnel.

Legal doctrines of *divorce, common disaster, presumption of death, presumption against suicide, rights of creditors, murder, fraud,* and *legal execution.*

Life insurance principles

How important is *life insurance?* Ask any widow or widower left with a family to raise, or any businessowner who needs a loan, or any retired person living on a relatively low income! Life insurance helps in these crucial situations, and many more, every day.

As an alternative, consider the gigantic size of the life insurance business. To the insurance consumer, it annually means more than $100 *billion* in insurance premiums paid and about $50 billion in current benefits received. In addition, future benefits are guaranteed by assets of $700 billion held by life insurers, and these funds are a substantial part of investments in the U.S. economy. In terms of the values insured by life insurance, it can even be called a $4 *trillion* business, which is the amount of "life insurance in force" held by more than 150 million policyholders.

The reasons why life insurance has grown to such prominence in the United States today are explored in the next four chapters—its actuarial and legal principles, its types of contracts and their uses, and the specific contract features which insurance purchasers should understand. Chapter 5 establishes the principles upon which life insurance depends: its nature, financial and actuarial concepts, mortality tables, premium calculations, reserves, underwriting techniques, and legal doctrines.

THE NATURE OF LIFE INSURANCE

The basis for life insurance is *income earning ability*, the economic part of total "human life value." The potential earning power of the individual is one of the greatest assets that any family or business owns. A person 25 years old, with an average annual income of $25,000 during the 40 years until age 65, will earn $1 million. Earning power is worth many times more than the buildings, automobiles, or other assets that we think of as most valuable. Life insurance protects the insured's family, creditors, or others against financial loss growing out of the death of the insured. The largest loss is that of future earnings, but other losses

119

may be incurred because of medical, funeral, legal, or tax costs following death.

Definition

Legal status was given long ago to the definition which indicates the life insurance agreement to be:

> A contract by which the insurer, for a certain sum of money or premium proportioned to the age, health, . . . and other circumstances of the person whose life is insured, . . . if such person shall die within the period limited in the policy, will pay the sum specified . . . to the person in whose favor such policy is granted.[1]

Policies provide methods for payment of the proceeds in installments or in some manner other than a lump sum; the choice is made by the insured or by the beneficiary if the insured has not made a choice. The choices are termed "optional modes of settlement" or "settlement options."

In addition to the life policy, which has as its purpose creating capital (payment in the event of a death), the life insurance business has developed another type of contract termed "the annuity." The annuity furnishes systematic liquidation of capital and is especially useful protection in the event of old age, when a guaranteed lifetime income is needed after earning capacity has decreased or stopped.

Compared with other insurance contracts

The essential difference between life insurance and other forms of insurance designed solely to protect against an uncertain peril is that life insurance has the added function of accumulation. (The type of life insurance known as "term insurance" is usually an exception to this.) A considerable part of the premiums paid for permanent life insurance represents a payment on the part of the insureds to a fund to be administered by the insurer. The dual role of creation of an estate *and* its management and investment in the interest of the insured are features peculiar to the business of life insurance.

Not a contract of indemnity. Strictly speaking, one cannot say that the life insurance contract is one of indemnity. In buying life insurance, an insured undertakes to compensate his or her estate, dependents, or others for the loss occasioned by untimely death. However, when settlement is made, the beneficiaries under the policy are under no obligation to demonstrate, as a condition precedent to collecting the insurance, a

---

[1] *Ritter* v. *Mutual Life Insurance Company,* 169 U.S. 139 [1898].

direct financial loss as a result of the death of the insured. The insured's value as a producer may have long since ceased, yet the beneficiaries have the right to participate fully in the policy in accordance with its terms.[2] Life insurance pays a specific amount of money, without regard to actual monetary loss.

Although the basic use of life insurance is the protection of life values, life insurance contracts have found additional uses. They are used for holding and accumulating assets, as a means for transferring business ownership, and in connection with the establishment of a trust. All these uses lend value to the services of the life insurance business. In many instances the secondary uses supplement and merge with the primary use.

A unique risk. In all forms of insurance except life insurance, the happening of the unfavorable contingency which gives rise to the loss is uncertain. In life insurance the contingency is death, which is universal and certain. Because the happening of the contingency insured against is certain, life policies provide for certain payment, unless written only for a term. The uncertain element is the time when such payment must be made.

Insurable interest required. Although the life insurance contract is not one of indemnity, this fact does not preclude the requirement basic to all insurance of an *insurable interest,* as explained in Chapter 4. In life insurance, insurable interest is only required at the time when the contract is purchased, not at the time of death.

The doctrine of insurable interest is considerably broader in the field of life insurance than in other fields of insurance. Some state statutes apply, and court cases vary considerably. Generally, however, so far as a person's *own life* is concerned, there is no precise monetary limit. The courts have held that any person has an insurable interest in his or her own life for any amount. Persons may, therefore, buy as much insurance as an insurer is willing to write and as they are willing and able to pay premiums on.

To establish insurable interest in close family relationships, there must be pecuniary (or financial) interest in the continuance of the life of the insured. In the case of *husband and wife,* pecuniary interest is presumed. Actual pecuniary loss growing out of the death of an insured, as well

---

[2] Life insurance in the early days was widely used as a vehicle for gambling, with policies taken out on the lives of important men in public life. Early opposition to life insurance included many who felt that insurance on the life of a person was a thing to be abhorred, and in some instances it was absolutely prohibited by law. A turning point was reached in 1774, with the enactment of the famous statute 14 Geo. III, c. 48, *An Act for Regulating Insurance upon Lives, and for Prohibiting all such Ins. except in cases where the Persons Insuring shall have an Interest in the Life or Death of the Person Insured.*

as an expectation or presumption of pecuniary advantage in the case of certain near relationships, will support an insurable interest. This is particularly the case where the policy has been obtained in good faith and not for the purpose of speculation, and where natural affection would normally operate to protect the life of the insured.

A *creditor* may have an insurable interest in the life of a debtor to the extent of the debt. Typical examples of such insured debts in today's "credit economy" are automobile loans; installment loans for television sets, furniture, and household appliances; and small personal loans. Credit life insurance is one of the fastest-growing areas of life insurance and is discussed further in a later chapter. If the policy is one taken out by a debtor and is used as collateral for a loan, the debtor may take out the policy for any amount and deliver it to the creditor. The right of the creditor to the benefits under the policy is limited to the amount of the indebtedness. If, however, the creditor takes the policy out, the amount of insurance must not be largely in excess of the amount of the debt. In any case, the debtor must consent to the issuance of the policy.

There are other relationships from which a pecuniary interest arises sufficient to establish an insurable interest under a life contract. A substantial amount of life insurance is written insuring the life of a *partner* in a business venture for the benefit of the surviving partner or partners. Sometimes the proceeds of such a policy are payable to the firm, and in other instances the proceeds provide a fund with which the surviving partners buy the deceased partner's interest. A firm may also insure the life of a *key person,* such as an important officer upon whose life a substantial portion of the earnings of the firm depend. In the case of employees, insurable interest is dependent upon the value of the employee to the business. An employee who could be easily replaced would hardly be one in whom the employer could reasonably claim an insurable interest. However, a business usually has an interest in any employees occupying key positions, such as the president, executive officers, and department heads. In the event of doubt, however, valid insurance may be written if the employee (instead of the employer) applies for the policy and designates the employer as beneficiary. In the case of a small corporation where the stock is closely held, the lives of *primary stockholders* may be insured, the proceeds to be used to buy the stock of a deceased stockholder.

In summary, in the field of life insurance, in addition to the insurable interest every person has in his or her own life, there are both *monetary* and *nonmonetary* losses that will meet the requirement for an insurable interest. Some may be partially related to replacing financial losses, while others cover situations involving a presumed natural affection or a reasonable expectation of benefit.

FUNDAMENTAL FINANCIAL AND ACTUARIAL CONCEPTS

The life insurance equation

In Chapter 3 the concept of how insurance works was explained in terms of an equation in which the incoming premiums and investment earnings of an insurer equal the outgoing payment of losses, expenses, and profits. For individuals, death is certain, but the time of death is uncertain. For large groups of persons, however, the insurer can predict accurately the number of deaths to be expected. The life insurer cannot predict *who* will die, but it can predict *how many* persons will die within a given time. The key to the insurer's ability to reduce uncertainty is that it uses the principle of large numbers to deal with many persons.

In its simplest form, here is the method of computing a life insurance premium, assuming that 10,000 individuals aged 58 wish to insure their lives for a period of one year for $1,000. Reference to a standard mortality table indicates that the death rate per 1,000 is 17. The life insurer, therefore, will count on 170 deaths during the year, or payments equal to $170,000. Since there are 10,000 in the group to pay the losses at the beginning, if a premium of $17 is collected from each of these and the death experience is exactly that of the expectation, the insurer will have $170,000 with which to pay claims. In the interest of simplicity, the costs of doing business are not considered at this point.[3]

Since there is no assurance that the death rate will exactly follow the expectation in the given year, insurers collect somewhat more than they need to pay the expected claims. In addition to this, they must add a "loading" to the mortality cost in order to have enough to pay the operating expenses of the company. Finally, funds held for reserves or surplus are invested, and the investment income is used to reduce the cost of insurance. If the insurer is able to operate at an expense less than it calculated, or if the death claims do not equal the expectations, the savings are accumulated, and, at the end of the business year, they may be apportioned to policyholders as a dividend or to stockholders as profits. Thus, in the long run, the equation balances. Premiums collected and interest earned equal the total of death claims, expenses, and dividends or profits paid.

To summarize, the insurance premium is predicated upon the following assumptions: *(a) mortality, (b) loading* for expenses and contingencies, and *(c) interest* to be earned on reserves. In terms of the *life insurance equation* these factors are stated as: *premiums + interest earnings = mortality + expenses*. The insurer expects the mortality experience to

---

[3] The mortality table used for this calculation is the Commissioners' 1958 Standard Ordinary Mortality Table, generally referred to as the "1958 CSO Table." This table appears in Table 5–1 in a later section of this chapter.

be less than the assumed tabular experience; an effort is made to keep expenses under the amount assumed in the rate calculations; and the interest rate is conservative. All of these margins provide safety factors.

Comparison of basic contracts

The standard forms of (1) term, (2) whole life, (3) endowment, and (4) annuities are the bases of all calculations. The mathematical work is done by persons who are called *actuaries*. For each of these basic contracts, actuaries calculate the different premium charges. The premium for the term policy is the lowest, and there are increasingly higher rates for other forms up to the highest cost short-term endowment. In every case the premium is computed upon the basis of the coverage afforded in the contract.

The *term policy* promises to pay the face of the policy if the insured dies during the stated policy period, such as 5, 10, or 20 years, or perhaps before a certain age, such as 65 or 70. Term life insurance provides *temporary* protection only for the number of years designated in the contract, or to a specified age. If the policyholder outlives the term indicated in the policy, the coverage is terminated and no payment is made.

When the insurance is for the whole life of the insured, the insurer pays a definite sum whenever death may occur. Because of this, such a contract is known as a *whole life policy*. The protection is *permanent*, as long as the premiums due are paid. Which insureds will die within a comparatively short time and which will live to very old age, no one knows. The actuary does, however, have a very close approximation of how many will die and how many will be paying premiums each year. By computing the annual premium payments and decreasing them by the amount of interest expected to be earned, the actuary is able to determine how much must be received in premiums to have on hand funds to pay the death benefits. The "limited-payment policy" is a whole life form, but it is distinguished from the "ordinary life" policy, which provides for premium payments for as long as the insured shall live, in that its premium payments are made only for a definite number of years or until a certain age. The usual premium payment periods are 10, 20, or 30 years, or to age 65. The policy does not mature (pay the face value) until death occurs.

The usual *endowment policy* differs from the whole life policy in that the face of the policy is paid if the insured is living at the end of the term indicated in the contract. If the insured dies during this term, the face of the policy is paid to the designated beneficiary. Thus, with a 20-year endowment contract for $10,000, if the insured lives to the end of the term, he will receive $10,000, but if the insured dies before the end of the term, $10,000 will be paid to whoever is designated as beneficiary.

The *annuity* provides for a periodic payment for a number of years or for life. The annuity idea is the opposite of life insurance in that the annuity is concerned not with accumulation but with the liquidation of funds. Chapter 8 discusses annuities separately from other life insurance contracts.

The actuary is able to combine term insurance with whole life, whole life with an annuity, and so on, in order to work out in a single contract any needed combination of savings and protection. The special contracts are the actuarial sum of the combined basic contracts. It is evidence of the competitive nature of the insurance business that many combinations or special policies (discussed further in Chapter 6) are made available to the insured.

Development from assessment plans

Life insurance in its simplest form provides for insurance written on a year-to-year basis. Based upon the mortality experience, a group of insureds of a given age may each be charged a premium sufficient to provide a sum that is adequate to meet death claims for a year. Each succeeding year the premium will be higher since the survivors will be older and will have a higher death rate.

In early life insurance associations, the *assessment plan* of life insurance paid all benefits out of current premiums. Proponents of this plan failed to recognize that as the years went by, there would be a natural increase in claims unless sufficient new younger members could be obtained to maintain the mortality rate of the group on an even basis. Because the death rate increases more rapidly for older persons, the average age of the group was very difficult to maintain. Another problem was that assessment companies usually collected equal annual assessments from each member, regardless of age. The lowest cost occurred when the majority of members were young, but young people began to drop out when the assessments became higher. The greater the average age of the group, the more difficult it became to secure new members. The inevitable result was an even higher rate of assessment and not infrequently a collapse of the organization. The loss to those old members who all their lives had contributed to the benefits of others was disheartening and often tragic.

The assessment method of writing life insurance has proved unworkable. The requirement of low premiums in the younger productive years and high premiums in the older years of lessening productive capacity tends *(a)* to defeat the purpose of life insurance and *(b)* to affect mortality experience adversely. As premium charges increase, if the insurance is dropped at a time when the insured has real need of it, the plan has defeated its purpose. The second disadvantage is that policyholders drop their insurance because rates are high—only when they feel themselves to be in reasonably good health. Insureds suffering from poor health that may shorten their lives usually struggle to keep their insurance in force, regardless of increased cost. As the well members drop out and the ill remain, the mortality figures will soar, and the premiums predicted on normal experience will not produce funds adequate to meet the claims. For both these reasons, assessment insurance no longer occupies an important place in the field of life insurance.

The level premium plan for permanent protection

One-year renewable term insurance policies are available with premiums calculated on the basis of the amount necessary to insure a person for one year. At younger ages, the premiums appear particularly attractive, but as permanent insurance the contracts manifest the same defects of increasing costs and adverse selection as assessment plans. To correct these defects, a plan that would not increase the premium with the age of the insured was devised and has become familiar to life insurance policyholders. The number of deaths still rises with increasing age, but the premium paid by the insured is constant throughout the premium-paying life of the contract. This disposes of the disadvantage of an increasing premium each year. The plan is one of averaging or leveling; hence the term *level premium*. Premiums substantially in excess of the cost of protection are collected in the earlier years of the policy. The excess is invested, and the accumulated sum reduces the amount of risk each year. (See Figure 5–2 in a later section of this chapter.)

Reserves. The state law establishes a minimum amount that the insurer must have available to guarantee future obligations with respect to all policies. This amount is known as the *reserve,* and it is quite often called the "legal reserve." These accounts are *liabilities* on the balance sheet of insurers. As the insured grows older, the reserve reduces the risk for the insurer so that a constantly increasing premium is not required to meet the increased mortality rate (see Figure 5–1). Under the level premium plan, the *net amount at risk* to the insurer is the face of the policy less the policyholder's reserve increased by interest earned from investments.

Permanent life insurance combines a saving or accumulation feature with the element of pure insurance. Basically the contract is composed of two elements: *(a)* the reserve and *(b)* pure life insurance. The reserve represents invested savings. The amount of the savings or investment account increases each year as premium payments are made. Since pure

Figure 5–1. Diagram showing decreasing amount at risk, first 20 years of whole life policy issued at age 35

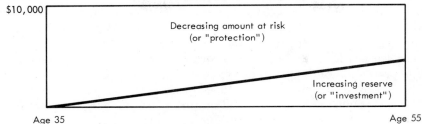

$10,000

Decreasing amount at risk
(or "protection")

Increasing reserve
(or "investment")

Age 35   Age 55

life insurance, that is the net amount at risk, is on a decreasing basis, if the insured lives long enough, the investment element would ultimately equal the face of the policy.

Cash and loan values. Although the reserve is a group matter, parallel with it is a *cash value* allocated to each individual policy. The cash value, which also builds up from year to year, may be withdrawn by the policyholder or borrowed against. The amount of the *loan value* is based on the cash value.   *WOODSON ARTICLE*

Borrowing is quite different from withdrawal, and it sometimes occasions misunderstanding. A loan requires interest, and the question is frequently put: "Why should a policyholder pay interest on his or her own money?" The question points up a difference between the reserve and the cash value. The reserve is a group asset and must continually be increased at the rate of interest contemplated in rate calculations if the insurer is to meet future policy obligations. A policyholder loan is just another investment (at a fixed and guaranteed rate) to the insurer. Interest is required because of the interest-earning assumptions underlying the contract. If the cash value is withdrawn and the insurance terminated, that part of the reserve designed to meet the maturity of the policy is freed. Withdrawing the cash value, then, means the termination of insurance. Borrowing the cash value with a loan at interest keeps the insurance in force.

The investment functions of life insurance

Interest is one of the assumptions upon which the calculations of life insurance premiums are based. Hence, the investment of the reserve takes on importance. The continued accumulation of life insurance funds is inherent in the level premium system. The investment of these funds in a manner that will earn the necessary interest and assure the contract payments is one of the major functions of level premium insurance.

Protection and/or investment. Life insurance replaces income lost in the death of policyholders, to dependents or others, or replaces income to policyholders in old age. To the extent that life insurance is purchased for *protection,* it is a contract of insurance. To the extent that life insurance is purchased as a source of income, it becomes an *investment.* Annuities, discussed in Chapter 8, are also fundamentally investments.

The protection and investment elements of life insurance vary greatly by the type of contract purchased. Term insurance contracts are primarily for protection; endowments and annuities emphasize the investment purpose. Whole life contracts combine both protection *and* investment while the policy is in effect, as explained in discussing the reserve. From the insured's viewpoint, however, the whole life policy may be said to be protection *or* investment. The loss of potential income is protected against death by the payment of the face value to beneficiaries. Or, while the insured is living, a decision may be made to receive the investment value in the form of cash value or retirement income, and protection ceases. By withdrawing the cash value, the insured gives up the protection. If the cash value is borrowed as a loan, however, some of the protection may continue.

Forms of life insurance having an element of investment give policyholders the benefit of investment skill and management. The insured has an ownership in a diversified cross section of the accumulated reserve of the life insurance company writing the contract. The unique feature is that the investment function is combined with protection.

Investment yield or rate of return. The investment yield is comparable to that offered by savings accounts in banks and savings and loan associations or by some tax-free government securities. The yield is sometimes less than that offered by many other taxable investments such as corporate stocks and bonds, real estate, or U.S. Treasury notes. Valid comparisons among investments are difficult, for often there are substantial differences in the size of the investment needed and in the duration and guarantees of the yield promised. In addition, the safety of the principal often varies. The requirements and goals of investors must also be carefully considered in order to choose proper investments. In total, the yield of life insurance is relatively low as compared with many other investments today. However, the gross yield comparisons are often misleading, and the policyholder should compare *net* yields for comparable *long-term, safe* investments with built-in minimum *guarantees* and *tax* advantages.

In evaluating the yield or return on life insurance as an investment, the net *aftertax* and *after-investment-expense* returns are important. Improper comparisons are often made which try to equate life insurance yield with returns on other investments. Oftentimes, the effect of income taxes and the expenses of making alternative kinds of investment are neglected in the comparisons. For middle- and higher-income investors, the tax factor can mean 5 (or more) percent less on a net basis, with perhaps an additional 1 percent reduction from the gross return because of the expense element. Thus a gross return of 14 percent becomes 8 percent (or less) on a net basis. <u>The substantial advantage of life insurance is that current income taxes are not payable on the interest buildup of the cash values, the so-called inside interest.</u>

An interest rate of about 3.5 percent is guaranteed on the life insurance policy, but this is not the real rate of return on the savings portion of the contract. The policyholder usually receives a greater return through dividends. The guaranteed amounts are only minimums used to calculate the basic reserves and cash values. In cash-value life insurance, the contract is a package of protection *and* savings. The *cost of protection* must be subtracted from the package, taking into consideration each year's cost of protection on the basis of the yearly renewable term insurance premium. This cost is relatively small at the younger ages, and for this reason a short-term (5–20 years, perhaps) comparison makes investments other than life insurance appear favorable. For longer investment periods of 20 years or more, the life insurance contracts show a better relative rate of return because the rapidly rising yearly cost of guaranteed protection at the older ages is built into the package contracts at a guaranteed price. _BELTH PAGE 52/53_

One authority flatly states that "there is no such thing as *the* rate of return on the savings element of a cash-life life insurance policy."[4] There are many ways of calculating the return, and many of the methods used by life insurance agents may be incorrect. An assumption of high cost for the protection element in the contract can make the savings return look very high, and an assumption of low cost can make it appear very low. Belth suggests that the rate of return be viewed as equal to the rate of return on comparable savings methods, such as the 5 or 6 percent paid by large mutual savings banks. A correct comparison of investment yield in life insurance contracts is a very technical and complicated matter. Improvements in the calculations used in past years are available from several sources now, including Belth's own suggested method.[5] For a discussion of term as opposed to permanent types of life insurance, which implicitly involves the investment alternatives to life insurance, see Chapter 6.

Another way of looking at life insurance earnings is to consider the net rate of return earned by life insurers on their total invested assets.

---

[4] Joseph M. Belth, *Life Insurance: A Consumer's Handbook* (Bloomington: Indiana University Press, 1973).

[5] See *Life Rates and Data* (Cincinnati: National Underwriter, 1981, p. xii); and "Contract Cost and Benefit Comparisons," in *Life and Health Insurance Handbook*, ed. Davis W. Gregg and Vane B. Lucas, (Homewood, Ill.: Richard D. Irwin, 1973), chap. 16.

In 1982 this was nearly 9 percent. Note that this is a return based upon investments which are required to be placed largely in bonds and mortgages (approximately three fourths of the total assets in recent years) with high safety. The earnings rate has increased steadily each year for almost 40 years. For individual life insurers, of course, it varies. The earnings rate above the lower guaranteed rates upon which cash values are based has been a primary source of substantial returns to policyholders of "participating" contracts, upon which dividends are paid.

Summary of advantages. The usefulness of life insurance as an investment is dependent entirely upon the financial position, resources, and investment needs of the investor. However, for most investors the advantages of life insurance are:

1. *Safety* of principal and income.
2. Steady reasonable aftertax *yield* (low relative to some other investments, but with at least minimum guarantees).
3. Ready marketability or *liquidity* (the cash values).
4. *Protection of assets from creditors.*
5. *Liquidation* options, especially lifetime annuity income.
6. Use of *loan values or* use as *collateral* for loans.
7. *Convenience* of purchase amounts, premiums, and investment management.
8. *Semicompulsory* nature, assuring *completion* of investment plans and an "instant estate."

Life insurance is always available as high-grade collateral for a loan. It may be purchased in face amounts that are convenient, and when used as an investment, it frees the owner from the responsibility for the selection of individual investments. Installment purchases are available to fit the convenience of the buyer. The investment is protected by the state regulation to which the life insurance business is subject. No other institution can equal the service of life insurance in providing protection against losses growing out of life risks. It creates many estates which, with or without the good intentions of the person insured, would otherwise never be accomplished. As soon as the life insurance contract is in force, an "instant estate" is created. The premium-payment plan encourages continuance of the contract which, in effect, becomes a "self-completing" program over a long period of time. If investment is the primary need, life insurance may provide not only that the income will be regular and sure but that the period of income cannot be outlived by the recipient. For the inexperienced investor, life insurance eliminates reinvestment problems, expenses, and risks. Investments in life insurance may be arranged so that there will be freedom from seizure from the insured's creditors (see last section of this chapter). It is the only form of investment that may be liquidated on installment plans that involve life contingencies, and the investment objective is protected against the failure of completions because of death.

Coordination with other investments. Life insurance does not meet all investment needs. Increasingly it is being used by many persons in coordination with other investments in order to achieve the best investment results. For small investors the combined goals of protection *and/or* investment are reasonably achieved through the use of life insurance as the primary purchase. Many average or larger investors should consider a combination of investment media, using life insurance as a partial base for the total program. Including some high-yield and capital growth potential investments may help meet the need for accumulating large amounts of capital for retirement or other purposes. Stocks or real estate may help serve as a hedge against the erosion of dollar values through inflation. Reasonable diversification among various types of investments is a logical general objective for investors with sizable capital in order to balance maximum yield and safety of principal.

THE MORTALITY TABLE

Life insurers must estimate the price of their insurance contracts in a safe and equitable manner. The goal requires analysis of *mortality* costs, *interest* earnings, and other *expense* factors. Because of a wealth of statistical information and of favorable mortality trends during the 20th century, the pricing of life insurance contracts is sometimes considered one of the easiest of all insurance rating tasks. However, accomplishing the safety of principal and fairness among all policyholders is not always simple. The long-range nature of the necessary predictions for many whole life insurance contracts spans 50 years or more. Very few businesses attempt to guarantee a fixed price for their product for such a long time into the future as life insurance does. Even most other insurance policies are based upon predictions of costs for only a limited period of one or a few years.

What it is

The basic obligation of life insurers is to pay death benefits, so they must know the expected life span of an insured group. The *mortality table* summarizes conveniently the probability of living or dying. It shows the probable death rate at each age, and by starting with a given number at a given age it shows how many persons will probably die during each succeeding year.

Where it comes from and its purposes

Life insurance *actuaries*[6] construct tables showing the mortality experience of large groups of people. Applying the principles of probability and large numbers, they can predict rather closely the number of deaths and the time of their occurrence in any large group. The greater the number of cases under observation, the greater is the accuracy of predictions. Large numbers permit variations from the average to cancel one another, the actual results tending to equal the expected results.

Statutory enactments prescribe the table to be used for certain *purposes*. The actuary needs mortality tables to calculate *(a)* premium rates, *(b)* nonforfeiture benefits on lapse or surrender, *(c)* reserve liabilities, *(d)* gains and losses from insurance operations, *(e)* dividends on participating contracts, and *(f)* annuity income options and contracts.

A department known as the actuarial department is headed by the company actuary, who is frequently a company officer. The actuarial staff varies with the size of the organization, its needs, and the nature of the business. There may be an associate actuary or a number of assistant actuaries and mathematicians. The work of the actuarial department is closely allied with that of the medical department.

Basic construction

A completed mortality table seems to suggest that in its construction the actuary started with a number of lives and then followed the history of that group from year to year until there were no survivors. Actually, the actuary determines the actual mortality rates for all the ages to be included in the table, and from these a table is built based upon such radix as is selected. The mortality table is an assemblage of data that show the probabilities of death and survival. The number of living at the youngest age is called the "radix" of the table. The radix is an arbitrary figure. (See Table 5–1, number living at age 0.) The completed table shows how many persons die at each age and how many survive out of a given number of persons under observation.

By knowing the number of persons in a group of a given age and the number of persons dying during the year, the probability that a person of a given age will live one year can be calculated. Applying the probability that a person of that age will live one year to the number living at any given age, the number who are expected to be alive at the beginning of the next succeeding year is determined. The process is repeated for each age.

---

[6] The title "actuary" within a company is one which may or may not indicate that the person has achieved the professional designation as a Fellow of the Society of Actuaries (FSA). Although many persons may perform actuarial functions, only those who have completed the rigorous examinations of the society are entitled to use the designation FSA following their names.

Table 5–1. 1958 CSO (Commissioners Standard Ordinary) Mortality Table

Age	Number Living	Number Dying	Death Rate Per 1,000	Expectancy, Years	Age	Number Living	Number Dying	Death Rate Per 1,000	Expectancy, Years
0	10,000,000	70,800	7.08	68.30	50	8,762,306	72,902	8.32	23.63
1	9,929,200	17,475	1.76	67.78	51	8,689,404	79,160	9.11	22.82
2	9,911,725	15,066	1.52	66.90	52	8,610,244	85,758	9.96	22.03
3	9,896,659	14,449	1.46	66.00	53	8,524,486	92,832	10.89	21.25
4	9,882,210	13,835	1.40	65.10	54	8,431,654	100,337	11.90	20.47
5	9,868,375	13,322	1.35	64.19	55	8,331,317	108,307	13.00	19.71
6	9,855,053	12,812	1.30	63.27	56	8,223,010	116,849	14.21	18.97
7	9,842,241	12,401	1.26	62.35	57	8,106,161	125,970	15.54	18.23
8	9,829,840	12,091	1.23	61.43	58	7,980,191	135,663	17.00	17.51
9	9,817,749	11,879	1.21	60.51	59	7,844,528	145,830	18.59	16.81
10	9,805,870	11,865	1.21	59.58	60	7,698,698	156,592	20.34	16.12
11	9,794,005	12,047	1.23	58.65	61	7,542,106	167,736	22.24	15.44
12	9,781,958	12,325	1.26	57.72	62	7,374,370	179,271	24.31	14.78
13	9,769,633	12,896	1.32	56.80	63	7,195,099	191,174	26.57	14.14
14	9,756,737	13,562	1.39	55.87	64	7,003,925	203,394	29.04	13.51
15	9,743,175	14,225	1.46	54.95	65	6,800,531	215,917	31.75	12.90
16	9,728,950	14,983	1.54	54.03	66	6,584,614	228,749	34.74	12.31
17	9,713,967	15,737	1.62	53.11	67	6,355,865	241,777	38.04	11.73
18	9,698,230	16,390	1.69	52.19	68	6,114,088	254,835	41.68	11.17
19	9,681,840	16,846	1.74	51.28	69	5,859,253	267,241	45.61	10.64
20	9,664,994	17,300	1.79	50.37	70	5,592,012	278,426	49.79	10.12
21	9,647,694	17,655	1.83	49.46	71	5,313,586	287,731	54.15	9.63
22	9,630,039	17,912	1.86	48.55	72	5,025,855	294,766	58.65	9.15
23	9,612,127	18,167	1.89	47.64	73	4,731,089	299,289	63.26	8.69
24	9,593,960	18,324	1.91	46.73	74	4,431,800	301,894	68.12	8.24
25	9,575,636	18,481	1.93	45.82	75	4,129,906	303,011	73.73	7.81
26	9,557,155	18,732	1.96	44.90	76	3,826,895	303,014	79.18	7.39
27	9,538,423	18,981	1.99	43.99	77	3,523,881	301,997	85.70	6.98
28	9,519,442	19,324	2.03	43.08	78	3,221,884	299,829	93.06	6.59
29	9,500,118	19,760	2.08	42.16	79	2,922,055	295,683	101.19	6.21
30	9,480,358	20,193	2.13	41.25	80	2,626,372	288,848	109.98	5.85
31	9,460,165	20,718	2.19	40.34	81	2,337,524	278,983	119.35	5.51
32	9,439,447	21,239	2.25	39.43	82	2,058,541	265,902	129.17	5.19
33	9,418,208	21,850	2.32	38.51	83	1,792,639	249,858	139.38	4.89
34	9,396,358	22,551	2.40	37.60	84	1,542,781	231,433	150.01	4.60
35	9,373,807	23,528	2.51	36.69	85	1,311,348	211,311	161.14	4.32
36	9,350,279	24,685	2.64	35.78	86	1,100,037	190,108	172.82	4.06
37	9,325,594	26,112	2.80	34.88	87	909,929	168,455	185.13	3.80
38	9,299,482	27,991	3.01	33.97	88	741,474	146,997	198.25	3.55
39	9,271,491	30,132	3.25	33.07	89	594,477	126,303	212.46	3.31
40	9,241,359	32,622	3.53	32.18	90	468,174	106,809	228.14	3.06
41	9,208,737	35,362	3.84	31.29	91	361,365	88,813	245.77	2.82
42	9,173,375	38,253	4.17	30.41	92	272,552	72,480	265.93	2.58
43	9,135,122	41,382	4.53	29.54	93	200,072	57,881	289.30	2.33
44	9,093,740	44,741	4.92	28.67	94	142,191	45,026	316.66	2.07
45	9,048,999	48,412	5.35	27.81	95	97,165	34,128	351.24	1.80
46	9,000,587	52,473	5.83	26.95	96	63,037	25,250	400.56	1.51
47	8,948,114	56,910	6.36	26.11	97	37,787	18,456	488.42	1.18
48	8,891,204	61,794	6.95	25.27	98	19,331	12,916	688.15	.83
49	8,829,410	67,104	7.60	24.45	99	6,415	6,415	1,000.00	.50

Since the radix of the table is arbitrary, the numbers in the columns headed "Number Living" and "Number Dying" are significant only as they serve as a basis for determining the proportion between the number living and the number dying. The column headed "Death Rate per 1,000" is the mortality rate, the basic feature of the table, and from it the other columns are derived. These columns are usually arranged under headings such as those appearing in the 1958 Commissioners Standard Ordinary Mortality Table, which appears in Table 5–1. The final column, "Expectancy, Years," is often included to show the expected number of years of life at each age.[7]

CSO

Different mortality tables for different needs

A difference in mortality tables does not mean that one is accurate and the other incorrect. Different tables are computed for different needs. The rate that is important for life insurance premium calculations is the mortality rate of *insured* lives rather than the mortality rate of a mixture of insured and uninsured lives. It is also important that the group of insured lives be representative of the group to be insured. At first thought, it might seem reasonable to use the mortality rates based upon insured lives to construct tables for both life insurance and *annuities*. Since, however, annuities provide for periodic payments from a given date throughout the lifetime of the annuitant, the longer the annuitant lives, the greater will be the cost of the insurer. In the case of life insurance on the other hand, the longer the insured lives, the greater will be the income in the form of premium payments for the life insurer. Hence, although a decreasing trend in mortality rates is a factor of safety for life insurance computations, it makes the table unsafe for annuity computations.

Annuity computations are essential in determining the value of optional settlements. The mortality data of insured lives prove inadequate for two reasons: *(a)* adverse selection of lives and *(b)* financial adverse selection. First, if the beneficiary in poor health has a choice, some form of settlement other than a life income will be selected. When impaired risks through self-selection are eliminated from the averages, the life expectancy of the remainder will be considerably longer than the average of the entire group. As to financial adverse selection, when investment yields are high, beneficiaries tend to elect lump-sum or short-term op-

---

[7] Don't be too discouraged by the life expectancy for your own age, for the trend is toward increasing longevity. To better the averages, consider the findings of one recent study: mortality rates seem to decrease if you are married, have many close friends and relatives, are a church member, and belong to many groups. "Longevity Linked to Social Contacts," *Columbus* (Ohio) *Dispatch*, February 2, 1978.

tions. An upward trend in investment returns prompts the withdrawal of policy cash values. The tendency to leave funds with the insurer in a period of low yield causes an investment burden when it may be difficult to secure the required yield. The withdrawal of funds as interest rates increase may necessitate the sale of securities and thus disrupt a long-term investment program.

Annuity tables have been constructed based upon the experience of annuitants. A table called the Annuity Table for 1949 was published by the Society of Actuaries. Another annuity table, the 1955 American Annuity Table, is used by many companies. For group employee annuitants, the Group Annuity Table for 1971 is often used. For reserve calculations, 1971 Individual and Group Annuity Tables are available. Projection scales to account for the declining mortality trends are used in order to update many of these tables.

In the _group_ insurance field, for life insurance contracts such as are written on employees through employers, the insurers use the Commissioners 1960 Standard Group Mortality Table. In the _industrial_ life insurance field, for smaller policies, the Commissioners 1961 Standard Industrial Table is used.

As indicated, there are more than a half-dozen mortality tables in current use for the differing needs of life insurers writing the various basic forms of life insurance (ordinary, group, industrial) and annuities (individual, group).

Development of the 1958 CSO Table

The life insurance business is highly competitive, and from year to year mortality improvement has been reflected in lower premium costs to the individual buyer. Since the turn of the century, life expectancy at birth has risen by more than 25 years. Most of the improvement occurred in the early 1900s with control of communicable diseases. Lower costs come about among mutual insurers through increased dividends and among stock insurers as a result of competitive rates. Both classes of insurers predicate their _rates_ on _current actual_ mortality experience. In calculating _reserves and cash surrender values,_ however, one of the _mortality tables_ mentioned below (or in the previous section) is used, as made mandatory by legislation of the states.

The American Experience Table in 1867 was adopted as an early standard. A mortality table presented to the National Association of Insurance Commissioners became known as the Commissioners 1941 Standard Ordinary Mortality Table (1941 CSO Table). The Commissioners 1958 Standard Ordinary Table (1958 CSO Table), based upon the mortality experience of 15 large companies for the years 1950–54, has been adopted for use by all states for policies issued after 1965. A new 1980 CSO

Table is available but has not yet been adopted for general use by the states. Therefore, the 1958 Table is appropriate for the text examples.

LIFE INSURANCE PREMIUM CALCULATIONS

The pricing of life insurance is an example of applied mathematics. The mortality tables, interest tables, and basic formulas are used to calculate the charge to be made for the life insurance contract.

Advancing premiums as age increases

The problem of computing the cost of insuring a group at any age for a period of a year is a matter of simple arithmetic. For example, reference to the 1958 mortality table shows that of 9,373,807 individuals living at the age of 35, 23,528 will die within a year. To insure all the members of the group at age 35 for $1,000 for one year will require a fund sufficient to pay $1,000 for each member dying during the year—$23,528,000 ($1,000 × 23,528). The premium each insured must pay to contribute his or her part to all the claims is $2.51 ($23,528,000 ÷ 9,373,807). To insure the survivors for another year, the charge must be higher since there are fewer members of the group (9,350,279) to pay the premiums and the number of deaths (24,685) will have increased the mortality rate. The 1958 CSO Table reflects a decreasing mortality rate for age zero through nine years and an increasing rate after age ten.

see page 138

Thus insurance premiums, following the mortality rate for each year, advance each year. As the advanced ages are reached, the cost becomes prohibitive. For example, at the age of 85, of 1,311,348 survivors there will be 211,311 deaths. Hence, to pay the claims will require $211,311,000 ($1,000 × 211,311). Thus to insure a person at the age of 85 will cost $161.14 ($211,311,000 ÷ 1,311,348). While the pure premium charge for mortality is comparatively small when the insured is young, this charge increases sharply during the latter part of the life of the surviving members of a group.

The interest factor

All life insurance policies provide for the payment of the first premium before the insurance becomes effective. Since premium payments begin at the inception of the contract and benefits are payable at some future date, the element of interest must be introduced into the calculations to establish an equality between sums now due and sums to be due in the future.

Life insurance calculations are performed upon the basis of compound interest, that is, interest upon interest. The annual rate is expressed in simple interest. At the end of the first interest term, the amount of interest is added to the principal, and the interest rate is applied to the sum to find the interest due at the end of the succeeding term. Interest may be compounded annually or oftener.

For example, if $1,000 is invested at 2.5 percent for one year, $1,025 will be due at the end of the year.[8] At compound interest, the amount due at the end of the first year is treated as a new principal, and the interest for the second year is $25.62, which added to $1,025, equals $1,050.62, the amount due at the end of the second year. *Interest earned* is the difference between an accumulated amount at interest and the principal invested. Continuing the process for a third year, the amount due is $1,076.89. The *principal,* or amount invested, is $1,000. The interest earned at the end of the three years is $76.89. Appendix A contains a compound interest table and is used to indicate the sum that a principal amount at compound interest will produce in a given number of years at 2.5 percent and other selected interest rates. For better understanding, the student should take a different interest factor (3.5 percent or 5 percent), for a longer period of years, and see how large a sum results.

The process of finding the *present value* of an amount due in the future is called *discounting.* The system is the opposite of that used in compound interest calculations. Any debt due in the future is worth less now than the promised debt amount, because of the element of interest. We have just seen that $1,000 at 2.5 percent compound interest has a value of $1,076.89 at the end of three years. Applying the principle of compound discount, $1,076.89 at the end of three years has a present value of $1,000. As with compound interest, mathematicians have calculated compound discount tables which show the present value of $1 at the end of any number of years. Appendix A shows the present value of a sum payable years hence, at 2.5 percent and other selected interest rates.

The net premium   MORTALITY ONLY

Since life insurance benefits are sums payable at a future time, the premiums are due and payable at an earlier date than the due date of the benefits. In establishing the equivalence of benefits and premiums, the discount calculations are basic. The premium is adjusted to the benefit and not the reverse. One buys, as a rule, a policy for a given number of dollars, say $10,000, rather than as much insurance as a given premium

---

[8] Although this interest rate is low in comparison with many assumptions made for *investment* decisions today, the 2.5 percent rate is used here because it is a *minimum standard* for life insurance premium calculations based upon *reserves* required by state laws. The actual interest rates used for *pricing* contracts are higher but vary considerably.

will buy. It becomes necessary, then, to know the present value of the benefits to establish the equivalence of premiums.

In computing the net premiums up to this point, only the actual mortality cost has been considered. By reducing the amount of the death claims to their value at the beginning of the policy year, the factor of interest is introduced and an accurate figure secured. Hence, at the age of 35 the actual cost of insuring all the members of the group for one year will be $2.44 ($23,528,000 × 0.975610 ÷ 9,373,807). This is the *net premium* for a $1,000 policy written for a term of one year at the age of 35.

To recapitulate:

One-year term, age 35 net premium

Number living	No interest		With interest
	Number dying	Amount of policy	
9,373,807	23,528	$1,000	$23,528,000 × 0.97560976 = $22,954,146.43
	$\dfrac{\$23,528,000}{9,373,807} = \$2.51$		$\dfrac{\$22,954,146.43}{9,373,807} = \$2.44$

The process of life insurance premium calculation is illustrated in its basic form in this example for a one-year term policy. In order to determine the price for other insurance contracts, a *net single premium* (NSP) that would pay for the duration of the entire policy, with interest earnings, is calculated. The technique of doing this for a five-year term policy and a whole life policy is shown in Appendix B. Also explained there is the process of converting the NSP to a net level premium (NLP), an annual premium cost figure which is needed because most policies are purchased on an annual (or more frequent) payment basis. An annuity calculation is used to convert the NSP to a NLP. Appendix B illustrates this process for a five-year term policy and a whole life policy.

The gross premium   MORTALITY + EXPENSE + CONTINGENCY

The discussion of premium computation has for simplicity omitted operating costs. The expense of carrying on the business is estimated on the basis of past experience; this amount is added to the net premium and is known as the *loading*. The *net premium plus* the *loading* is the *gross premium*.

Nature and purposes.   The loading added to the net premium for known expenses and unknown contingencies is not uniform among companies. Among mutual insurers the loading is frequently heavier than among stock insurers. The additional premium strengthens the financial position of mutual insurers, and inequity is avoided through a return of any excess beyond needs for growth in the form of dividends to the policyholders.

The element of loading provides, first, for operating expenses and, second, for contingencies unforeseen in the calculations. The expense element includes such items as the cost of getting business and the cost of collecting premiums. Principal among these items are commissions on new business, subsequent commission payments for a term, and the state tax levied on premiums. Other expense items include the cost of settling claims and such general business expenses as salaries and the cost of keeping records.

Calculations. The loading is an amount per $1,000 of insurance, and it varies with the kind of policy and age at issue. To arrive at an equitable distribution of the loading requires complex actuarial calculations. These calculations involve the classification of expenses and a determination of the proportion of particular expense items to be charged to each class of policyholder.

Experience shows that expenses may be grouped into one of three broad categories: (a) those that vary with the size of the premium, (b) those that vary with the amount of the policy, and (c) those independent of both. Commissions that represent a proportion of the premium or premium taxes levied on the amount of the premium will vary as the amount of the premium varies. For example, the amount of tax and the amount of commission on an endowment policy for $1,000 will be higher than on a whole life policy issued at the same age. Home office expenses, including salaries, research, accounting, and the like, represent fixed costs that have no direct relationship to either the premium or the policy amount but are to be distributed among all the policyholders. An equitable loading system considers all the variable and fixed factors.

LIFE INSURANCE RESERVES

Insurance cost is computed to meet the death claims from year to year, plus the cost of carrying on the business. The natural premium increases from year to year. Up to this point in the computation of premiums, one side of the equation has consisted of benefits to be received and the other side of premiums to be paid. The aggregate of all premiums, increased by the assumed rate of interest, must produce a fund sufficient to pay all the benefits as policies mature.

Origin

The *level premium plan* introduced the element of *overpayment*. During the early policy years, a net premium considerably larger than is necessary to meet the mortality costs for these years is collected. The excess premium over calculated costs for each year is reserved for use in the later policy years when the net level premium payments are insufficient for meeting mortality costs. The reserve, then, does not represent a profit but is an insurer *liability* held to meet the claims of policyholders.

A comparison of the natural with the level premium illustrates graphically the need for a reserve under the level premium plan. Figure 5–2 illustrates the trend of a *natural* premium. The vertical lines represent the premium charge of each succeeding year. *Level* premium payments for the same age are also shown.

Superimposing one curve upon the other, one sees at once the extent to which excess payments are made during the earlier years (Figure 5–2). The area *ABC* represents the excess premiums paid during the earlier years. The larger area *CDE* represents the deficiency during the later years of the amount actually collected from the current level premium. This, plus the interest derived from the investment of premiums, represents the reserve accumulated to carry the policy until paid. In computing the adequacy of a reserve, the insurer considers all the policyholders of a group. If an individual carries a policy a few years and dies, the insured pays more than the natural premiums (mortality costs). The excess is not a profit to the insurer since the reserve is necessary for the solvency of the group.

Figure 5–2. Natural premium trend and level premium trend

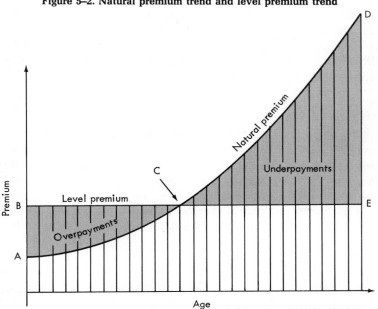

Definition

PERSISTENCY ↗

Very simply, the *reserve* is an amount which, augmented by premium payments required under outstanding contracts and interest earnings, will enable the life insurer to meet its policy obligations. More specifically, it is that portion of premiums paid on level premium life insurance policies which is held to pay future death benefits, policy loans, surrender values, and the like. It is represented by assets which the insurer invests, but it is, in fact, an *insurer liability* to be disbursed to meet the obligations of the policy contract.

For the purpose of computing the reserve, present value calculations as explained previously are necessary. The basic equation used for the computation of premiums during the policy term is as follows: The present value of future premiums plus the reserve equals the present value of future benefits, or $PVFP + R = PVFB$.[9] Transposing the equation, the reserve equals the present value of future benefits minus the present value of future premiums, or $R = PVFB - PVFP$. The reserve is the difference between what will be paid out, and what will be taken in, by the insurer.

With reference to each policy, the reserve grows as the years pass. The difference between the reserve and the face of the policy at any given time represents an amount termed the "net amount at risk." As time runs, therefore, the net amount at risk decreases until it ultimately vanishes, unless death intervenes to mature a claim (see Figure 5–1).

The reserve account   "*ADMISSABLE*" *ASSETS*

The fundamental purpose of the reserve is to have assets available to meet the obligations of the insurer in years to come. The premium calculations contemplate that the reserve will earn interest for the benefit of policyholders and beneficiaries, and it is accordingly invested in government securities, bonds, mortgages, stocks, and real estate. The financial statement of an insurer will show an amount under the heading "Admitted Assets." This represents investments and other credits approved by the state insurance department. The *legal reserve,* plus other liabilities and required capital or surplus, must not exceed the admitted assets if the insurer is to be permitted to continue business.

The ability of the insurer to meet all claims as they mature depends upon the adequacy of the reserve account. The legal reserve should never be regarded as an extra amount to meet contingencies or as a profit

---

[9] For technicalities of the various methods used to determine the legal reserves required by the states and further explanation of the arithmetic of life insurance, its contracts, and its legal aspects, see S. S. Huebner and Kenneth Black, Jr., *Life Insurance*, 10th ed. (Englewood Cliffs, N.J.: Prentice-Hall, 1982).

above mortality experience, for on the basis of the calculated experience the mortality costs will ultimately absorb the entire reserve. Only to the extent that actual experience is more favorable than the calculations will there be any excess over claims from the reserve account.

The mortality tables used as a basis for policy valuation in determining minimum legal reserves make no provision for contingencies other than reasonable margins against adverse mortality fluctuations. They do not provide for investment losses, changing expense ratios, or unfavorable mortality experience due to wars or epidemics. A satisfactory method for providing for such contingencies is the accumulation of special *contingency reserves*. The account so accumulated is over and above policy legal reserve and is actually part of the "surplus."

UNDERWRITING OF LIFE INSURANCE

Medical examinations

In computing premiums, life insurers use only tables based upon insured lives. Since life insurance premiums are computed on the basis of the expected mortality of such a group, the solvency of the insurer requires that the group of insureds be so selected that the actual mortality experience will be no greater than was anticipated when the rates were set.

The *medical examination* is one method that is used to avoid insuring applicants whose health is worse than a normal standard. The purpose of the medical examination is not to find a perfect group for insurance. The examination undertakes, however, to eliminate from the group those who are suffering from ailments that tend to increase the mortality beyond that which the mortality table anticipates. It also helps classify the impaired risks into groups to which premiums adequate to the risk may be assigned, and it detects fraud such as that of an applicant who is aware of a serious health problem.

Exceptions to the practice of requiring a medical examination are common. They are usually made for group policies (see Chapter 10), for annuities (Chapter 8), and for industrial policies (Chapter 7), which are ordinarily sold for small amounts. Also, today many individual policies are written that make use of a "nonmedical" plan which places an increased burden on sources other than the medical examiner for required underwriting information. For much of the insurance that is written, however, the medical examination supplies information for determining whether or not, or on what basis, the applicant is acceptable for insurance.

The medical examiner appointed by the insurer usually takes less than an hour for the life insurance examination and filling out Part II of the application form. The physician reports the applicant's physical characteristics; general condition; any abnormalities of primary systems such as the heart, the lungs, and the digestive and reproductive organs; and the result of blood pressure and urinalysis tests. X rays or electrocardiograms are sometimes required for larger policy applications, or where the applicant's medical history indicates possible abnormal conditions.

If everyone in a community or country were insured, a medical examination would be unnecessary. Since, however, life insurance is usually a matter of volition on the part of the individual, without medical examination there would be a tendency for the unhealthy to seek insurance and for others to neglect or postpone it. Where such a situation exists, there is said to be a condition of "adverse selection," or selection against the insurer.

Other factors and sources of information

Numerous other factors are considered by the insurer in the total underwriting process. *Personal health history* and *habits* are inquired about in the application; *family history* is also important; *occupation, morals, type of insurance, build* (relation of height and weight), and *residence* (U.S. or foreign) are among other information evaluated. *Aviation* interests as a private pilot may result in increases of $3 to $5 per $1,000 of insurance, but no increases are usually charged for any flying as a passenger (even crew members of scheduled commercial airliners receive standard rates). *Sex* is a major factor in the underwriting of life insurance contracts, as many insurers use special lower rates for females. The use of lower rates for *nonsmokers,* which a number of insurers have offered with good sales success during the past decade, may reduce premiums by 2 percent or more.

The sources of information include several in addition to the *insured,* the *application,* the *agent,* and the *medical examination:* the *inspection report,* by an independent company (such as Equifax, Inc., or the American Service Bureau) check on the financial status, reputation, and habits of the applicant; and the *Medical Information Bureau* (MIB), a central clearinghouse of all major health impairments noted for past applicants for life insurance.[10]

Substandard or extra-risk life insurance

An impaired or *substandard risk* is a person in whom the hazard may be presumed to be increased because of the existence of unfavorable physical condition, family history, habits, or occupation. Through the

[10] For the interesting story of this important underwriting interchange among life insurers, see William B. Swarts, "A Decade of Change at MIB," *CLU Journal* 31, no. 2 (April 1977), p. 48.

development of the "extra-risk" type of policy, the benefits of life insurance have been extended to many persons who were formerly ineligible
because of their classification as impaired risks. By means of actuarial
studies, insurers were able to determine what extra premium should
be charged to compensate for the extra risk. The result has been the
reduction of declined applications for life insurance, to a point today
where they account for only 2 percent of total applications, and extra-
risk policies are 4 percent of ordinary contracts issued.[11] Liberalization
of underwriting rules over the years means that today even cancer victims who have fully recovered may receive standard rates.

Impaired risks fall into two groups. In the first group, an extra premium
is charged to compensate for the hazards of *occupation*. The mortality
range for occupational hazards varies from an additional charge of one
third to three times normal mortality. Both accident and disease factors
affecting potential mortality are considered. A window cleaner at the
United Nations building has an obvious increased mortality risk. So do
miners (lung disease and accidents), construction workers, and many
other occupational groups. Even hobbies, such as skydiving or motorcycle
racing, affect the decisions made by insurers, but not all sports affect
the rate. Skin diving, for example, usually does not.

The second group of substandard risks includes those with *physical
impairments*. Those of most frequent occurrence are cardiovascular-renal
disease (31 percent of all extra-risk policies), weight problems (18 percent),
and other physical impairments (29 percent). Occupation and other reasons make up the remaining 22 percent.[12]

A *numerical rating system* is used by most insurers to evaluate the
total effects of physical condition, build, family history, occupation, habits, and other factors. Rating scales based upon debits and credits for
these items are developed. A standard class may fall between 75 and
125, while numerous substandard classes (some as high as 500 to 1,000
percent of normal mortality) are identified. An example might be:

Average person's mortality	100%
Favorable family history	(−10)
Unfavorable occupation	+20
Unfavorable build and overweight	+15
Blood pressure	+35
Total	160%

Several methods of increasing premiums for substandard or impaired
risks are used by life insurers. Most common are (1) adding an extra
flat charge, such as $2 per $1,000 of insurance, and (2) increasing the

---

[11] *Life Insurance Fact Book* (Washington, D.C.: American Council of Life Insurance,
1982), p. 98.

[12] *Life Insurance Fact Book,* p. 99.

insured's age, or "rating up" the policy by using the premiums charged to a person one or more years older than the insured.

Nonmedical life insurance

The plan of issuing a policy without requiring a medical examination by a physician, or *nonmedical life insurance*, reduces acquisition expense, eliminates delay, and overcomes any objection some prospects may have to a physical examination. In Canada, where nonmedical life insurance made its first appearance, many life insurance applications were received in rural districts where the services of a physician were not always readily obtainable. The unavailability of doctors for medical examinations was also an important contributing factor to the further extension of nonmedical life insurance business during and after World War II.

For the nonmedical application, agents must secure much of the information otherwise obtained by the medical examiner. They secure direct from the applicants specific replies to carefully drafted questions concerning the personal and family history and physical condition. The agent also determines as far as possible that the applicant is in sound health and able to work regularly. This information is carefully verified through an independent inspection report, which checks particularly such matters as intemperance and immoral habits. Infrequently the information obtained by the nonmedical application or by this inspection may indicate the possibility of an impairment; in such circumstances a medical examination is required.

The objective of nonmedical life insurance is the same as that of contracts written following a medical examination, that is, to secure an average mortality for the group instead of an abnormally high mortality rate caused by adverse selection. The elimination of the medical examination cost permits a slightly higher mortality experience for the nonmedical life insurance contracts.   *SHOW EXAMPLES FROM RATE CARDS*

In nonmedical coverages, the insurer limits the amount of insurance and the age range. Many insurers make no differentiation between men and women. The trend is definitely toward liberalization of limits. Most life insurers today write $50,000 or more on a nonmedical basis at the younger ages. Some insurers have extended the nonmedical procedure to all applications through age 40 for amounts of $25,000 or less. For ages up to 50, the limit may be reduced to a maximum of $5,000 or $10,000. More and more insurers are writing individual plans, including term insurance and many special contracts on a nonmedical basis. The practices vary greatly by company, but increasing use of nonmedical life insurance is readily apparent.

Some companies issue a special type of nonmedical life insurance called "guaranteed acceptance." Usually written by mail for older insureds (such as ages 40–80), these contracts require no physical examination and eliminate most or all health questions in the brief application form. The amount of protection is limited to perhaps $1,000–$25,000 and automatically decreases with age if the premium cost remains level. For natural deaths during the first several years, only a return of premiums plus interest may be payable. Higher than normal mortality experience increases the typical cost of these policies.

War clauses

Life insurance mortality tables do not reflect death rates to be expected from major military operations. Life insurers have usually attached the so-called war clause to policies issued at the younger ages during wartime. The most common type of war clause excludes death resulting from war.

War clauses cannot be attached to policies already in existence. Insurers follow different rules with respect to new business. It is generally the practice, however, to use the war clause for members of the armed forces. Sometimes insurers attach the clause to all policies issued to younger applicants who might enter military service. The protection provided by the group life insurance of $20,000 automatically provided to military personnel now relieves life insurers of some of the need to provide for the war risk.

LEGAL DOCTRINES

Several legal doctrines applied in the field of life insurance are fundamental to an understanding of how life insurance works and how it is used by policyholders to accomplish certain goals.[13]

Effects of divorce

Where there is no statute covering the situation, the general rule is that a *divorce* does not deprive the irrevocable beneficiary of rights under a life insurance policy. In a few jurisdictions, however, the statutes make provision for terminating the interest of an irrevocable spouse-beneficiary following a divorce from the person whose life is insured, and a new beneficiary may be named. With a revocable beneficiary, which is very common, the spouse may, of course, change the beneficiary as he or she sees fit.

With the divorce rate doubling during the last decade, the importance of life insurance in divorce situations has increased dramatically. Di-

---

[13] Recommended for further information is Janice E. Greider and William T. Beadles, *Law and the Life Insurance Contract* (Homewood, Ill.: Richard D. Irwin, 1979).

vorced mothers, for example, have a greater need for life insurance because there is only one spouse who may provide earned income for the family. The legal and tax treatment of life insurance in divorce settlements also creates a need for careful financial planning and use of life insurance contracts. Existing policies are sometimes used, but more favorable results may be obtained if new life insurance is obtained on the husband by divorced mothers before the divorce settlement.[14]

Common disaster

In the event of a disaster in which both the insured and the beneficiary lose their lives, there is no common-law presumption as to the survivor. So far as the rights of the estate of each are concerned, much may depend upon establishing which of the two outlived the other. The courts have held that the burden of proof rests upon the representatives of the beneficiary. For example, if a husband insures his life naming his wife as beneficiary and both are killed in a disaster under doubtful circumstances as to which died first, the benefits of the insurance will not go to the wife's estate unless it can be shown that she actually survived her husband. Because many insurance policies today, if they do not have a contingent beneficiary, provide for the reversion of the beneficiary's interest to the insured when the beneficiary dies first, proof of survivorship by the beneficiary is required. However, the need is taken care of in many policies by including a *common disaster clause*. This states that in case of death in a common accident (or within a specified number of days, such as 60) the insured shall be presumed to have survived the beneficiary. This prevents the payment of the insurance to the beneficiary's estate and permits the proceeds to be distributed through the insured's estate or as otherwise provided in the common disaster clause. This usually reduces estate taxes, because the amounts are not taxed in both estates.

In almost all states, legislation called the *Uniform Simultaneous Death Act* has been passed in order to reduce the problem of proving who died first.[15] This provides that when the insured and the beneficiary

---

[14] Mary Ann Noecker Guadagno, David L. Bickelhaupt, and Francis C. Noecker, "Life Insurance in Divorce: Financial Considerations for the Divorced Mother," *CLU Journal* 37, no. 3 (July 1982), p. 32.

[15] This act has been enacted in 47 states and the District of Columbia. It has not been adopted in Georgia, Louisiana, or Ohio. However, Georgia and Louisiana have insurance law provisions which stipulate that in the case of simultaneous death the proceeds will be distributed as if the insured survived the beneficiary—unless the policy provides otherwise. Thus, although in form three states have not adopted the Uniform Law, as a practical matter the principle contained in this law has been enacted in all jurisdictions except Ohio. Ohio uses a set of presumptions as to who died first, such as older before younger persons, female before males, and other rules.

have died and there is not sufficient evidence that they have died at
different times, the proceeds of the policy shall be distributed as if the
insured had survived the beneficiary.

Presumption of death

The question arises as to the rights of a beneficiary under a life insurance policy *if the insured disappears* and is assumed to be dead but
actual proof of death cannot be presented. Unexplained absence for *seven
years,* with no communication with those who might be expected to hear
from a person if the person were alive, raises the presumption of the
death of the absent party. "The presumption of the duration of life with
respect to persons of whom no account can be given ends at the expiration
of seven years from the time when they were last known to be living."[16]

The presumption of death is prima facie; that is, it is rebuttable. Evidence may always be introduced to show that the person presumed to
be dead was seen alive or that a reasonable explanation can be advanced
for the absence. In most cases involving life insurance, therefore, the
beneficiary must prove by a preponderance of evidence the time that
such death took place. Insurers sometimes make voluntary payments
before the seven-year period has passed, as for example they did to the
beneficiaries of the Navy men who lost their lives in the disappearance
of the submarine *Thresher* a number of years ago. Deaths in airline
crashes and multiple drownings have been treated similarly.

Presumption against suicide

Life insurance policies do not pay their full face value if the insured
meets death as the result of *suicide* within a limited period, usually
one or two years from the date of issue of the policy. Instead, in order
not to encourage suicide (which is against public policy), only a return
of premiums is paid if suicide occurs within the one- or two-year period.
If the insurer writing a life insurance policy denies liability on this
ground, the burden of proof rests upon the insurer to show that there
was, in fact, a suicide. "The love of life is ordinarily sufficient inducement
for its preservation, and, in the absence of proof that death resulted
from other than natural causes, suicide will not be presumed."[17] When
the evidence permits reasonable doubt between the conclusion that death
was caused by suicide and the conclusion that it was the result of an
accidental or natural cause, the presumption operates against a finding
of suicide.[18] Suicide is established when the evidence indicates that death

---

[16] *George* v. *Jesson,* 6 East. 80, 85; and *McCartee* v. *Camel,* 1 Barb., chap. 455.

[17] *Union Casualty and Surety Co.* v. *Goddard,* 75 S.W. 832.

[18] *White* v. *Prudential Insurance Company,* 120 App. Div. 260.

was self-inflicted and permits no other reasonable inference. Drug over-doses and automobile carbon monoxide deaths are examples of situations in which difficulties arise in differentiating between accidental and intentional deaths.

Rights of creditors to life insurance values

Since life insurance represents the accumulation of a fund for investment, the rights of *creditors* in the case of the insolvency of the insured are frequently perplexing. There is no fraud of creditors by the insured when reasonable insurance premiums are paid upon policies and the beneficiaries designated are such dependents as wife or children.[19] State statutes exempt the life insurance proceeds from the claims of creditors, and the tendency has been to liberalize exemptions.[20]

State exemption statutes vary greatly but fall into one of several broad classifications: *(a)* statutes exempting close relatives, *(b)* statutes exempting all insurance from creditor claims if effected in favor of a person other than the insured, *(c)* statutes exempting a limited amount of protection, *(d)* unlimited exemption, and *(e)* special statutes. The most widely used exemption statute is *(b)*, which provides that the *beneficiary, other than the insured or the person effecting the insurance,* shall be entitled to the "proceeds and avails" of the policy without any limitation (based on the amount of premium or the face amount of the policy) against the creditors and representatives of the insured.[21] The law provides no protection against creditors of a beneficiary. *Special statutes* may apply for: *(a)* group insurance, *(b)* fraternal insurance, *(c)* recipients of relief, *(d)* annuitants, and *(e)* recipients of disability income. Protection against creditors of beneficiaries is a characteristic of these statutes.

Fraud, murder by beneficiary, and death by execution

In case of *fraud by the insured misappropriating funds to pay premiums,* the defrauded person may usually obtain reimbursement from the proceeds of the policy. In the event of *murder of the insured by the beneficiary,*

---

[19] Under the terms of the Bankruptcy Act, the bankrupt is permitted to retain his or her insurance and keep it in force but is required to turn over an amount equal to the cash value to the trustee in bankruptcy. The United States Supreme Court has ruled that if the state statutes exempt a policy, it is exempt in bankruptcy proceedings.

[20] For complete analysis of the types, extent, and reasons for the protection of life insurance against creditors, as discussed in this section, see Stuart Schwarzschild, *Rights of Creditors in Life Insurance Policies* (Homewood, Ill.: Richard D. Irwin, published for the S. S. Huebner Foundation for Insurance Education, 1963).

[21] The exemption is justified upon the theory that an obligation to beneficiaries may rightfully precede that of personal creditors. Laws of this type make an exception in protecting the proceeds of insurance against claims of creditors by providing that the amount of any premium paid to *defraud* creditors shall go to the benefit of the defrauded creditors from the proceeds of the policy. "Avails" includes cash value, dividends, and other values.

the courts have ruled that the beneficiary cannot collect the life insurance policy proceeds. The murderer should not profit from the criminal act, so the policy is paid instead to the estate of the insured. The insurer is exempted from payment only when there is no beneficiary who is free of the taint of crime or when the policy is obtained by the beneficiary with the intent of defrauding the insurer. In the past, life insurance policies often excluded payment for *death of the insured by execution.* Now practically all policies pay for death by legal execution just as they would for any other kind of death.[22]

FOR REVIEW AND DISCUSSION

1. The greatest asset that an individual or a family owns is not a house or a car. What is it, and how does it become the basis for life insurance?

2. In what ways does life insurance differ from other types of insurance? Why are these differences important to the insurer and to the insured?

3. Legally and technically, life insurance is not a contract of indemnity. Why not? Is there a relationship between life insurance and the *idea* of indemnity? Explain your answer.

4. Many situations give rise to an insurable interest in life insurance. Give an example of at least four different insurable interests.

5. The cost of life insurance is based upon three fundamental estimates that must be made by an insurer. What are they, and how accurately can they be predicted? Indicate any special problems, including trends which have been helpful or harmful.

6. How is the actuarial basis for the basic life insurance contracts *(a)* similar and *(b)* different?

7. What are the fallacies in the assessment plan when it is applied to life insurance? Can they be solved by a different premium-paying plan? (This concept can also be explored by having students assume that the class is forming an assessment company. Then have them discuss the likely problems as they become older.)

8. How would you explain the advantages and disadvantages of life insurance *as protection* and/or *investment* to a newly married couple? What factors would be important in determining your recommendations?

9. Explain how a mortality table is constructed. Why are different mortality tables used rather than just one?

10. The Commissioners Standard Ordinary (CSO) 1958 Mortality Table has higher mortality or death rates than are actually being experienced among insured lives today. What is this table used for, and why does this mean that policyholders are not overcharged for their insurance contracts?

11. Why is it not possible to use the same mortality table to compute a life

---

[22] *Weeks* v. *New York Life Insurance Company,* 122 S.E. 586–35 A.L.R. 1482.

insurance premium and the purchase price of an annuity? How are annuity tables used in connection with the life contract?

12. Where does the life insurance reserve come from? How would you describe the purpose of the reserve? To what is it equal?

13. What are the sources of surplus to a life insurer from which it may return a dividend to its policyholders? Should the entire surplus be returned?

14. Name two classes of extra-risk hazards that may result in the classification of an applicant for insurance as substandard. Give examples.

15. Are medical examinations always required before life insurance is issued? If your answer is *yes*, explain why they are necessary. If your answer is *no*, explain why they are not needed.

16. Tom and Joe are not related. Tom wishes to insure his life, naming Joe's children as beneficiaries, but is told he cannot do this. Do you agree or disagree? Why?

17. Mike carries $50,000 life insurance with his wife Mary as beneficiary. Both perish in an aviation disaster. To whom will the insurance be paid? Could the problem be avoided by any special provisions in the insurance policy?

18. Mr. MacDonald disappears without any explanation. When will his wife receive payment as beneficiary under his life insurance policy?

19. What significant advantage do life insurance contract values have to the insured and his or her beneficiaries, if the insured has debts owed to a creditor?

Chapter 6

Outline of concepts

Individual life insurance contracts are analyzed by these characteristics:

Major classes: (1) *individual,* including industrial, and (2) *group,* including creditor life.

Basic traditional types of life insurance contracts:

Whole life insurance policies: permanent contracts are paid by (1) *single premiums,* (2) *limited-payment* premiums, (3) level premiums throughout life (the popular *straight life* or *ordinary life* contract), and (4) smaller initial, then larger, premiums (*modified life* contract).

Term insurance policies have increased in popularity.

Nature: temporary protection for a stated term or duration.

Uses: mortgages, business obligations, families, and students.

Misuses may rely on low short-run costs and "buying term and investing the difference" *without careful long-run analysis.*

Conversion privileges to permanent contracts are important.

Endowment insurance policies emphasize the savings element.

Usual types combines term insurance (pays if you die) with a *pure endowment* (pays if you live).

Uses and misuses depend upon one's goals and protection needs.

Cost comparisons: net cost, interest-adjusted, and other methods help the buyer compare contract costs.

Special riders and policy combinations are plentiful, such as:

Guaranteed purchase option, permitting young policyholders to purchase additional standard insurance at stated ages;

Other combinations, such as double protection and joint life contracts.

Special life insurance markets aim at limited but important markets:

Family insurance plans include three types: (1) *Family income,* combining decreasing term and whole life, (2) *Family maintenance,* with level term; and the (3) *Family policy,* insuring the entire family.

Juvenile insurance plans, including the "jumping juvenile" policy.

Larger plans: minimum amounts, preferred risks, graded sizes.

Employer-employee plans offer low after tax costs in *split-dollar* and *split-life* insurance.

Variable life insurance, an equity-based product in which the face value is not fixed but changes with investment returns.

Adjustable life insurance, permitting both premium and insurance amount changes to meet "life cycle" needs.

Universal life insurance, a recent innovation with strong market potential if tax rulings are clarified favorably, in which relatively large-amount contracts combine term insurance and flexible-premium annuities, permitting changes in face value and anticipated increases in cash value at current higher interest rates.

Individual life insurance contracts

One of the key decisions of life insurance consumers centers on selecting among the many types of *individual life insurance contracts*. Based on the life insurance principles just discussed, the purpose of this chapter is to explain the characteristics of the major contracts available. Thus the uses for which the contracts are designed can be related properly to the needs of life insurance buyers.

The *types* of contracts are but one of the decisions to be made. Later chapters seek answers to important related questions: "What *contract features* are significant? What *other life insurance products,* such as *annuities, health, group,* and *government* insurance are offered by life insurers—and how can all these coverage be *coordinated* to determine *how much* each should contribute to total financial security?

Many life insurers, as part of an escalating *diversification* of product lines, are also typically selling much more than only life insurance contracts. In fact, the most discussed topic of the 1980s may well be the trend toward very *broad financial services,* including all types of insurance and investments, as well as banking, credit, and trust services of many kinds (see Chapter 23). The basic question is how far life insurers can extend in an *efficient* manner their range of consumer products and services.

Will life insurers all become "financial supermarkets" that offer their clients comprehensive financial advice and services without the need to go to other institutions? Although some larger insurers are already reorganizing to do so, it is doubtful that most of the 2,000 life insurers in the United States can or will make such a fundamental change in the 1980s. There also are more than 150 million life insurance policy holders, many of whom need only the specialized services of life insurance rather than broader financial services.

Although this trend is accelerating, it is necessary to study life insurance as a separate subject. The life insurance contract as a distinct, unique, and one of the most widely used of all legal documents deserves such separate treatment. More than two out of three persons in the United States have life insurance—more than an astounding 150 million of the total population. Men buy nearly twice as many policies and more than three times as much life insurance as women, although women are purchasing more than ever before. Both groups should become better buyers. The significance of life insurance as a basic part of financial protection and savings remains high.

THE MAJOR CLASSES OF LIFE INSURANCE

The life insurance business has developed two basic methods of dis- tributing life insurance contracts: (1) *individual* insurance and (2) *group* insurance. The purpose of utilizing more than one system of marketing life insurance is to reach the largest possible number of insureds. No one technique has proved best in selling the idea of life insurance to all markets. The two basic methods are called the major classes of life insurance.

Four categories have been identified for many years: *(a) ordinary* life insurance, *(b) industrial* life insurance, *(c) group* life insurance, and *(d) credit* life insurance. The first two categories involve a separate policy contract for each purchaser and are therefore discussed in this chapter on *individual* life insurance contracts. The third category, *group* life insurance, concentrates its sales efforts by combining many individuals, usually in one group contract for employers. The group technique for providing life and health insurance protection is studied in Chapter 10, and group annuities are studied in Chapter 8. The fourth category, *credit life* insurance, is included in the group insurance totals because almost 85 percent of these contracts, sold through banks and finance companies (often in connection with installment loans), are sold on a group basis.

Table 6–1 shows the growth of the two major classes of life insurance. Today the individual class includes $1,796 *billion,* or 51 percent of the

Table 6–1. Growth of the major classes of life insurance in the United States (by life insurance in force; in billions of dollars and percentages)

End of year	Individual*		Group†		Total	
	Amount	Percent	Amount	Percent	Amount	Percent
1920	38.9	96.0	1.6	4.0	40.5	100.0
1940	100.2	86.8	15.3	13.2	115.5	100.0
1960	379.8	64.8	206.6	35.2	586.4	100.0
1980‡	1,796.4	50.7	1,744.6	49.3	3,541.0	100.0

* Individual insurance includes industrial life insurance, which was only 1 percent of individual insurance in recent years.

† Group insurance includes credit life insurance, of which almost 85 percent was group.

‡ Credit life figures added to group include only loans on life insurance of 10 years' duration or less.

Source: *Life Insurance Fact Book* (Washington, D.C.: American Council of Life Insurance, 1982), p. 15.

total, and the group class accounts for $1,745 *billion,* or 49 percent of the total life insurance in force in the United States. Group insurance increased its percentage of the total from 4 percent in 1920, to 13 percent in 1940, to 35 percent in 1960, and to 49 percent at the beginning of 1981. In total, life insurance in force has grown from $41 billion in 1920, to $116 billion in 1940, to $586 billion in 1960, and to $3,541 billion at the beginning of 1981. (1982 total is just over $4,000 billion.)

Only the two types of individual life insurance—ordinary and industrial—are discussed in this section. Group and credit life insurance are treated in later chapters.

The life insurance business has to a large degree emphasized the sale of *ordinary life* insurance. The protection is issued on the basis of individual applications through life insurance agents and may be adapted to almost every insurance need. Today it accounts for about 50 percent of all life insurance in force. It is usually written in units of $1,000, and the average new policy is for over $30,000, having more than doubled in the past 10 years. Premiums are computed on an annual basis but may be paid monthly, quarterly, semiannually, or annually. Premiums are due and collectible at the home office or the branch office of the insurer. The emphasis of this chapter is placed on this type.

In contrast to ordinary life insurance, *industrial life* insurance is written in small face amounts, usually less than $1,000. Premiums are normally payable weekly or monthly and are collected by company representatives at the home of the policyholder. Historically of substantial importance, industrial life contracts introduced the uses of life insurance and the habit of thrift to many millions of policyholders. To meet the requirements of the industrial classes, insurers provide insurance with premium payments adjusted to the needs of workers, such as a small weekly payment of $0.10, $0.25, or more.

Although industrial life insurance in force has leveled off in recent years at about $35 billion and now represents less than 1 percent of life insurance outstanding as opposed to 18 percent 40 years ago, it remains the sole vital source of protection for many families. Some 58 million policies are still in force, averaging about $630 per policy.[1] Industrial life insurance (or "debit" insurance as it is sometimes called because of the method of accounting for the weekly collections) has declined in relative importance because of: the increased affluence of most families, which now can purchase much larger amounts of insurance than $1,000; the family policy (see later section); the availability of group insurance to most employees; and the death benefits paid under the federal social security plan.

---

[1] *Life Insurance Fact Book* (Washington, D.C.: American Council of Life Insurance, 1982), p. 30.

Many of the larger insurers that once sold primarily industrial life insurance have changed to issuing regular policies on a "monthly debit ordinary" basis. This popular form is called *home service life* insurance, and some $115 billion is included in the current ordinary life figures.

Most industrial insurance is issued without a medical examination, the insurer relying upon statements in the application by the applicant and the agent. Many policies are written on entire families, including each of the children. The method of collecting the premium and the expense of handling small sums cause the rate for industrial life insurance to be several times more than the rate for ordinary life insurance. However, for many insureds the collection service is just as real a benefit as the insurance itself, enabling many persons who otherwise could or would carry no insurance to have some protection. There are now few differences between the provisions in an industrial life insurance policy and those in most ordinary policies. Industrial life policies, of which 90 percent are permanent rather than term coverage, usually have cash values. They also frequently include double indemnity provisions without extra premium. Industrial life insurance is in the strict sense not a different form of insurance protection but rather a plan adapted to a particular market.[2] Industrial life insurance provides for the immediate needs (last expenses and burial) of low-income families.

BASIC TRADITIONAL TYPES OF LIFE INSURANCE CONTRACTS

A great many different life insurance policies are offered to meet the varying needs of individuals. All are either whole life, term, or endowment policies or a combination of one or more of these. Such combinations may include the annuity principle, since annuities are a part of the life insurance business. This being the case, there are four traditional contracts basic to the life insurance business: (1) *whole life* insurance, (2) *term* insurance, (3) *endowment* insurance, and (4) *annuities*.

Whole life insurance includes those forms in which the face amount is paid on the death of the insured whenever death occurs. This is a permanent form of insurance and covers the insured for life. ("Ordinary life" is one type of whole life insurance where premiums are paid throughout life.) *Term* insurance pays on the death of the insured only if the insured dies during the term covered. If the insured outlives the period, there is no obligation on the part of the insurer with respect to benefits of any kind. *Endowments* provide insurance coverage during a stated period and emphasize the savings element. The face of the policy is paya-

---

[2] Robert A. Marshall and Eli Zubay, *The Debit System of Marketing Life and Health Insurance* (Englewood Cliffs, N.J.: Prentice-Hall, 1975).

ble at the end of the endowment period to the insured if living *or* to the beneficiary if the insured dies during the period. <u>Annuity contracts provide for periodic income payments to be made for a fixed period or as long as the annuitant or annuitants</u> live. Annuities are separately treated in Chapter 8.

These four basic traditional contracts form the foundation of the many life insurance coverages offered in the market. No matter how complex a coverage may seem or how many benefits or options are available, the policy effects its objectives by incorporating in a single contract the features of one or more of the basic contracts. Different and newer combinations of life insurance continually are developed, often for special markets. These contracts and the recent emerging "universal life" policy are discussed at the end of this chapter.

Summary comparison

A summary comparison of the basic and common life insurance contracts, not including annuities, is given in Table 6–2. Note that the cost comparisons emphasize the extreme differences in cost which may be chosen by an insured, from $25 to $426 or more for a $10,000 contract at age 20. The differences are the result of the period for which protection is provided, when the benefits are payable, and the length of the premium-paying period. The uses depend upon the goals of the insured in regard to savings, protection, or a combination of savings and protection.

Also note that "cost" is used here to mean the same thing as "premiums" paid for the various contracts. "Net cost" is a more technical concept. Net cost is calculated by subtracting cash surrender values (and dividends paid on participating policies) from the premiums paid over a period of time. This concept is discussed after the basic contracts are explained.

In forms of insurance other than life, the contingency insured against may or may not happen. The policies are issued for a term and may run to expiration with no claim made. Some life policies are similarly written for a term, providing only temporary protection for a designated time period. Many life insurance contracts are written on a permanent or whole life basis; if such contracts are kept in force, the benefits provided must ultimately be paid. Life insurance policies thus are classified as *(a)* permanent and *(b)* temporary.

Whole life insurance policies

<u>Three types of permanent or whole life insurance are differentiated according to *how long the premiums are payable*.</u>

<u>Whole life insurance may be written *(a)* on a straight life basis, *(b)*</u>

Table 6–2. Comparison of basic and common life insurance contracts

Basic type	Protection period	When benefits are payable	Approximate costs for $10,000 at age 20*	How long premiums are paid	Uses
1. Whole life	Permanent	At death, any time	—	—	Combination of moderate savings and protection
a. Straight or ordinary life	"	"	$115	Throughout life	"
b. 20-payment life	"	"	$198	For 20 years	Paying up premiums during working life
c. Life paid up at 65	"	"	$127	To age 65	"
2. Term	Temporary	At death, only during term			Protection only
a. Yearly renewable term	"	"	$25 increasing each year	Varies—can be to age 60–70	Maximum protection
b. Five-year level term (renewable and convertible)	"	"	$53	5 years	Very high protection for limited period
3. Endowment	Temporary or long term	At death, or if living, at end of endowment period			Combination of higher savings and protection
a. 20-year endowment	"	"	$426	20 years	"
b. Retirement income at 65	"	"	$177	To age 65	"

* Costs are necessarily approximate for such general comparisons. Participating policies would be slightly higher, with net costs reduced by annual dividends. Nonparticipating policies would be somewhat lower. Smaller policies under $10,000 will be slightly higher; those over this amount may have a lower rate per $1,000. Those insuring women will also be somewhat lower in cost. Extra policy features such as waiver of premium, accidental death benefits, and so on, would increase these estimates. See "Life and Health Insurance: A Guide for Young Adults" (Washington, D.C.: American Council of Life Insurance, 1980), p. 11.

on a limited-payment basis, or *(c)* on a single-premium basis. The whole
life contract with premiums payable throughout life is known as the
straight life policy and is also called the *ordinary life policy*.[3] This has
been termed the "bread-and-butter" policy of the industry. Benefits are
payable at the death of the insured, though a policyholder may stop
paying premiums and take the accumulated equity in the form of cash
or a reduced paid-up policy. Gain of cash value received over aggregate
premiums paid in is taxable as ordinary income when amounts are received for reasons other than death.

A whole life form known as the *limited-payment policy* provides for
premium payments for a designated term or until the prior death of
the insured. At the end of the premium-payment term, the insurance
is *paid up* for the life of the insured, and no further premiums are
required. Under the *single-premium life policy,* the premium is paid at
the outset of the policy term in a lump sum, but almost all contracts
are paid by periodic installments. Thus, in actual practice, whole life
forms may be reduced to two classes: (1) straight life and (2) limited-
payment life. These forms pay the beneficiary only on the death of the
person whose life is the subject of the insurance. Termination of the
policy prior to death through nonforfeiture or surrender values precludes,
of course, a death settlement. In contrast, term insurance pays on the
death of the insured *if* the insured dies during the term covered.

The ordinary life insurance policy.   The *ordinary, or straight,* life
contract is the most widely sold whole life insurance policy. Not including
group or industrial life insurance, the popularity of the various types
of contracts, as measured by life insurance amounts in force, is shown
in Table 6–3. About 58 percent of ordinary individual contracts, as measured by amounts in force, are whole life contracts. Three fourths of
these are straight life. Term insurance accounts for 38 percent of all
ordinary insurance in force, and endowment types account for about 4
percent.

The *changes* in the use of the various types of contracts are most
important. These proportional changes are shown in Table 6–4. During
the decade of 1971–81, within the ordinary class, the *purchases* of individual whole life and endowment policies have decreased dramatically from
45 to 34 percent of the total amount of coverage, while term life insurance
has increased from 22 to 50 percent. Combination policies such as family
policies, whole life with term, and other combinations also have decreased
in popularity. Estimating the term life insurance components of these
combination policies, the proportionate amount of term life purchased

---

[3] Efforts have been made to limit the use of the term *ordinary life policy* to the straight
life policy and to use the term *ordinary insurance* to apply to all of the contracts in the
ordinary group. As a matter of actual practice, this line of demarcation is not well maintained.

Table 6–3. Life insurance in force by individual basic types of contracts

		Amount*	Percent
1.	Whole life		
	a. Straight life	934	47
	b. Limited-payment life and paid-up life	214	11
2.	Term life	760	38
3.	Endowment and retirement income	70	4
	Total	1,978	100

* Figures for amounts are in billions of dollars.

Source: *Life Insurance Fact Book* (Washington, D.C.: American Council of Life Insurance, 1982), p. 19, based on 1981 figures.

increased from 41 percent in 1970 to 59 percent in 1981. Measured by number of policies purchased, however, permanent insurance of some type was included in more than three out of four policies.

The ordinary life policy is used not only for protection but as a means for savings. The policy values are available to the policyholder when the need for insurance protection has been outlived. Even on contracts calling for continuous premium payments to death, the insured may stop payments at any time. On retirement the policyholder may elect to discontinue premium payments on permanent insurance and take cash or keep a substantial amount of insurance in force; or, if preferred, the cash value may be used to augment retirement income by electing an annuity settlement instead of cash.

The flexibility of the whole life form accounts for its appeal. Basic in

Table 6–4. Life insurance purchases by individual basic types
of contracts, 1971 and 1981

		Percent of policies		Percent of amount	
		1971	1981	1971	1981
1.	Whole life				
	a. Straight life	32	39	27	24
	b. Limited-permanent life	19	13	9	4
	c. Modified life	4	5	4	5
	Total whole life	55	57	40	33
2.	Term life	11	23	22	50
3.	Endowment and retirement income	9	2	5	1
4.	Combinations*	25	18	33	16
	Total	100	100	100	100

* Direct comparison of this table with the earlier figures of Table 6–3 are not possible because family, whole life with term, and other combination policies are not shown there.

Source: *Life Insurance Fact Book* (Washington, D.C.: American Council of Life Insurance, 1982), p. 11, based on a sample survey by the Life Insurance Marketing and Research Association.

the whole consideration, the contract is permanent unless the premium is not paid. Although the net protection element decreases (face value less cash value) as the older ages are reached, the insured has very long-term protection for such purposes as last expenses, income to beneficiaries, or estate liquidity. Future uninsurability, the attainment of advanced age, or other contingencies cannot terminate the protection. There is no necessity for conversion or for redrawing the plan to keep the insurance in force for life.

The ordinary life policy affords the lowest cost permanent protection plan available. The policy is issued on a level-payment premium basis, and the premiums continue throughout the lifetime of the insured. Many object to the requirement of the ordinary life policy that premiums be paid until death. In the declining years of a life, productive capacity diminishes, so it is sometimes considered desirable that premiums cease as in the limited-payment life policy.

Limited-payment policies. The *limited-payment* whole life contract differs from the ordinary life policy in that premium payments are charged for a limited number of years only. After the stipulated number of annual premiums have been paid, the more usual number being for 10, 20, or 30, the policy then becomes a fully paid-up policy. Some are paid up at a specified age, such as age 65 or later.

Frequently, policyholders confuse the limited-payment life policy with an endowment form, and after making the stipulated payments, they expect to receive the face of the policy from the insurer. The face of the policy is not paid until the death of the insured, although the cash, loan, and reserve values are higher than under an ordinary life form, the difference depending upon the number of payments called for in the contract. The fewer the payments, the faster these values will accumulate during the premium-payment period under a limited-payment life form. A policyholder who dies during the early policy years will have paid more than for an ordinary life policy. On the other hand, the policyholder may find sufficient compensation for the extra outlay in the knowledge that at a later age, when income will be curtailed, the burden of paying life insurance premiums will also be eliminated.

In arranging the life insurance program, the question of the relative merits of the ordinary life policies and the limited-payment life policies is inevitable. As a general rule, when funds available for insurance premiums are scarce, the ordinary life form will prove preferable, since more insurance may be obtained for the amount available for premiums. Moreover, if the economic status of the insured improves, the insurance may be rearranged to a limited-payment plan. In the case of participating policies, an insured may elect to utilize dividends by applying them to premium payments to convert the policy into a paid-up form.

If cost is not a determining factor in the arrangement of the life insurance program, the insured may wish to eliminate further life insurance premium payments upon retirement through the limited-payment life policy. If some change of situation causes the insured to use the nonforfeiture (cancellation) provisions of the limited-payment policy, the nonforfeiture values are greater. The increased cash values will carry the policy fully paid for a longer period than would have been the case otherwise.

The single-premium policy is the extreme of the limited-payment contract. The premium under this contract is paid in a single sum. Because such premiums represent substantial amounts of money, most insureds are unwilling to take the risk of the large single payment. The policies do meet a need, however, in that they provide wealthy persons with an opportunity to provide for some future purpose in a manner that requires no further annual premium payments. Gifts or charitable bequests of life insurance are examples.

Modified life policies. To offset the advantages of the ordinary life policy (moderate cost, level premium, and the savings element), there are certain shortcomings. There is a tendency for those influenced primarily by cost and for those with large protection needs, such as young families, to be attracted from the ordinary life policy to the term policy. This may unduly delay the inauguration of a permanent program. To supply an immediate permanent policy with an initial premium that is lower than the ordinary life premium, a *modified life policy* is offered by many companies. For a three- or five-year period the cost is lower than that of the ordinary life policy; thereafter it is slightly higher. Such policies are particularly attractive to young professional persons as they start their careers or while they are in school prior to beginning fairly high-income jobs. Modified life policies have become quite popular and account for about 5 percent of the amount of new contracts purchased today.

Term insurance policies

The earliest form of life insurance contract on record provided insurance only for a stated period, or term.[4] Today term insurance is one of the popular forms. Its proportion of the amounts of individual life insurance purchased annually, either in separate or combination contracts, increased from 40 percent to approximately 60 percent during the past decade.

Nature. Term insurance is precisely what the name would imply, insurance for a term, or *temporary* period. This may be contrasted to

---

[4] One of the earliest policy forms was written by the London Assurance in 1720. This policy provided insurance for one Thomas Baldwin on the life of Nicholas Browne for a term of 12 months.

whole life insurance, which is permanent insurance and covers as long as the insured lives. If term insurance is written for a year, it provides protection equal to the face of the policy for one year, no longer. If it is written for five years, the insurance covers for five years. At the end of the term, whether for one year, five years, or any other period, coverage terminates, and the policy has no value whatever. If the contingency insured against happens, the policy pays in accordance with its terms. If the contingency fails to happen, the premium paid is fully earned, and, at the end of the term, the insurer is under no obligation to the insured. One way of summarizing term insurance is to say that it is "renting" rather than "owning" the insurance.

Uses. Term insurance is popular and sensible whenever it is used for temporary purposes. When protection for a limited period is the element sought in the purchase of a policy, then the term insurance contract has the lowest possible immediate cash outlay. Because the proportion of loading expense to premium is highest, this form of insurance is not the least expensive. The low premium for term insurance reflects the limited time covered by the policy, particulary because the higher percentage of deaths occurring in the higher age brackets are not covered.

In light of the low cash outlay required for immediate protection, particularly in the younger age groups, term insurance is recommended for two major uses: *(a)* to provide temporary insurance where there is the need for large amounts of protection and *(b)* to obtain an option on a permanent program. Sometimes term insurance is the only contract alternative that will provide sufficient amounts of life insurance to meet the consumer's large needs.

One use of term insurance is to provide protection during a period of unusual financial strain. An individual may assume heavy obligations as part of a *business* venture. An untimely death and forced liquidation might seriously cripple the business. The prudent businessperson will frequently buy a term policy to cover the amount of the unusual liabilities for the length of time that is required for their liquidation.

Term insurance is also used to provide a fund for the liquidation of some particular *debt*. Frequently a term policy is carried in connection with a *mortgage loan* upon the home, with the insurance amount decreasing as the loan decreases. In order to see that dependents have a home without encumbrances in the event of the untimely death of the wage earner, a term policy is carried to provide the necessary funds for liquidation. With the growing number of two-income families, new policies are now available so that both wage earners can be included in joint mortgage redemption life insurance contracts. Many new term policies are also available that are designed to conform with shorter-term, growing-equity, and other new trends in home mortgages.

Term insurance finds an important use in supplying adequate insurance at a low cost during a period when a large amount of insurance is most needed but when funds for meeting its cost are limited. A young man with *family dependents* who was recently graduated from college wishes the maximum insurance that money will buy, with the privilege of converting it to another form at a later date. In this instance, the term policy is, in effect, an option upon a later permanent insurance program. In the meantime, dependents are provided with a maximum of protection.

The *student* with small current income but large potential future needs for life insurance is another of these situations. Beware of the life agent who advocates *only* permanent insurance or advises taking out loans or notes to pay the early premiums on such contracts. High cost for unneeded coverage, with harsh penalties for discontinuing the contract (the full loan becoming payable immediately), may be the result of some typical campus life insurance sales.[5] For the typical student, term insurance is the primary need, for it protects insurability in case of health deterioration and guarantees the option of converting later to permanent coverage at standard rates.

Misuses.   Much has been said about term insurance and its relative merits as compared with a whole life plan written on a level-premium basis. Advocates of term insurance may suggest several different forms of term insurance, from the smallest premium form of one-year term insurance to a much larger premium form of long-term insurance, such as term to age 65 or 70. In comparison with that of a level-premium plan, the cost of one-year term insurance (often with a renewable feature to certain ages) is low in the younger age brackets. As the years go on, it becomes increasingly higher, until in the later years of life it is for all practical purposes prohibitive.

Level-term plans illustrate the importance of the *duration of the term* protection to its cost. At ages 20–30, for example, a "term to 65" policy will cost approximately double that of a "five-year term." Term protection beyond age 70 is seldom available because of the sharply increasing cost at the advanced ages. Cost comparisons must also be careful to denote whether a policy is *level* (same face value throughout the contract) or *decreasing* (lower face value each month as the contract continues). For example, a 30-year decreasing term policy for $10,000 would pay only approximately $5,300 if death occurred during the 15th year. Other features that must be compared are the *convertibility* and *renewability* of

---

[5] See Robert A. Hershbarger, "Life Insurance Sales Policies in American Colleges and Universities," *Journal of Risk and Insurance,* March 1977, p. 463; "Campus Life Insurance," *Consumer Reports,* March 1977, p. 168; and Tilton L. Willcox and Phillip A. Harris, "The Effect of Intense Selling of Premium-Loan Insurance on the Attitudes of College Students Toward the Insurance Industry," *The Journal of Insurance Issues and Practices,* Winter 1980, p. 39.

the contract. Most term contracts are convertible to permanent contracts, without a medical examination, for all or most of their term. Renewability of the contract, which is at a higher premium, is often a needed feature to guarantee continued insurability, especially for the shorter term contracts of 1 to 15 years. It does add to the cost of the contract, however.

Because of the apparently low premium in the earlier years, the attraction of term insurance decreases in the later years of life. In the earlier years the insured is in a better income position to pay the premiums, but the premiums are low because the probability of death during these years is slight. As the insured reaches the age when earnings have a downward trend, the premium charges for term insurance are rising . very rapidly. No matter how painstaking the explanation, policyholders tend to discount the high premiums of later years as too remote to be of importance when, in their younger years, they are attracted to term insurance by the comparatively low premium charges. There is a tendency toward abandonment of the term insurance plan when premiums reach a level that the insured cannot or will not pay. *APPROX 2% BECOME CLAIMS*

We sometimes hear it stated that term insurance is an inferior type of coverage, and that a "cheap" coverage cannot be the better product that a higher premium will buy. The reasoning is not sound. The term contract is as safe, as adequate, and in every sense as satisfactory *for the purposes for which it is devised* as any one of the many types of contracts offered by life insurance companies. For many insureds, term insurance should be a major part of their life insurance purchases.

It is also wrong to say that everyone should automatically *"buy term only and invest the difference."* For policyholders such a system rests on several fallacies, primarily: (1) term insurance cannot always be purchased, for poor health or older age make it either difficult or impossible to buy; and (2) the "difference" (between permanent and temporary protection cost, which may range from $5 to $10 per $1000) cannot always bring greater returns at comparable safety, for this depends on size, diversification, costs, mandatory nature, taxes, timing, types, and many other features of the alternative investment program.

The above disadvantages of buying term insurance and having a growing investment portfolio have been reduced in the recent years of higher interest rates and investment returns. A long-term policy, to age 65 or 70, may accomplish the protection needs and objectives of a person up to retirement age. Some of the protection may be converted before the end of the term. The disadvantage of not continuing to "invest the difference" may be overcome by resolute and knowledgeable investors with long-run perseverance and ability to resist the temptation to spend the difference currently. The two objectives for a good investment program, however, must also be balanced—the delicate objective of achieving high safety of principal and the objective of greater returns (after expenses and taxes) over a long period. (See section in Chapter 5 on the investment functions of life insurance.)

No life insurance company or agent should have the slightest objection to the use of the term policy in those situations where its use is indicated. It is not the term policy to which opposition is expressed, but its misuse. The most important point to consider is that term insurance was not designed to be permanent insurance. For temporary protection to cover temporary needs, the policy is admirable. For careful use in connection with moderate-length investment programs, it may be beneficial. To augment a permanent life insurance plan during a period when the need for coverage is greatest, term insurance is indicated. A number of combination policies (see later section of this chapter for special riders and policy combinations) have been worked out by life insurers making judicious and generous use of term coverage.

Conversion privileges.   Life insurance companies have extended certain privileges in connection with the writing of term insurance with a view to encouraging insureds under this form to convert their coverage to a more permanent form. The one-year term policy may ordinarily be renewed without medical examination or may be converted into a permanent-type policy within a given number of years. A potential disadvantage of term insurance, however, is allowing the policy to run to a point where another medical examination is required, and of being rejected or rated as a substandard risk upon application for further insurance.

When issued for a term of five years, the policy may often include the privilege (at any time during the term) of converting the insurance without medical examination to a permanent form. Renewal rates increase at each five-year renewal: when taken out at age 25, the costs are about $5 per $1,000; when renewed at age 30, $6; at 40, $8; at 50, $15; at 60, $33; and at 65, $48. Longer term policies of 10 or 20 years may permit the policy to be converted at any time except during the last several years of the term. Under the longer term policies, unlike the yearly renewal form, a level premium is charged instead of a premium that increases annually. Convertible term insurance finds particular favor with those who intend to make the coverage a part of a permanent program but require low-cost protection for their immediate needs.

Term insurance finds a primary use in providing a means whereby applicants may secure an option on the amount of permanent insurance necessary, before they are in a position to pay for it. For example, most young persons can afford to purchase *decreasing* or *level* term insurance to age 65 in adequate amounts (perhaps $100,000 for about $600 or $900, respectively, per year). There are, however, a number of other situations for which term insurance is admirably adapted, and numerous special policies have been devised to fit these needs.

When a term policy is converted, there are two options. The new permanent policy may carry the date of the conversion, in which case the premium is charged on the basis of the then *attained age* of the insured. Alternatively, the policy may be dated back to the original date of the term policy on the basis of the *original age,* which permits a lower premium. The insured, however, then must pay the difference between the term premium and the premium charge for the new policy, plus interest, from the date of issue of the term policy until the date of conversion. Because this extra, lump-sum payment is often substantial, most term policies that are converted to permanent policies choose the option using the premium for the attained age.

Endowment insurance policies

The ordinary life policy provides for the payment of the amount of the insurance to a designated beneficiary upon the death of the insured. The *pure* endowment reverses the process and pays the amount of the insurance only if the insured is *living* at the end of a specified period. The insurer pays nothing if the insured dies before the end of the period. There are few uses for pure endowments. Sometimes they are written for a child's education or for other specific purposes.

Usual types.   Most endowment policies offered by insurers incorporate the features of a term life insurance policy. The usual endowment policy is thus a combination of pure endowment and term insurance. Most endowment contracts are temporary in terms of the length of the policy, but some are for long periods of 20 years or more. If the insured lives to the end of the term, the face of the policy is paid under the pure endowment feature. On the other hand, if the insured dies during the endowment term, the term feature of the contract pays the face of the policy. The two features are combined in a single plan.

Endowment insurance is written under a number of different forms, each designed to meet particular needs. The terms for which they are written may vary from 5 to 30 years or more, or they may be written to mature at a designated age, such as 60 or 65 years. There are also limited-payment endowments. For example, an endowment payable at death or at age 65 may be written so that premium payments stop at the end of 20 years.

Uses.   The use of endowment insurance has decreased rapidly in today's high interest rate economy. From more than 5 percent of the annual amount of life insurance purchased a decade ago, it is now only 1 percent. Endowment contracts are only 4 percent of all life insurance in force.

The investment feature of endowment insurance makes the premium charge substantially higher than for ordinary life insurance. Obviously, the shorter the term, the higher the premium. Table 6–2 earlier shows that at age 20 the premium for a retirement income endowment at age 65 is more than 50 percent higher, and a 20–year endowment premium is nearly four times higher than that for an ordinary life policy. For the same premiums that insureds pay for endowment policies, they could secure much greater protection under ordinary life or term contracts. Because of this, it is important to recognize the uses of endowment insurance and to buy it only when *saving* for a particular purpose is to be coupled with insurance.

Higher yields of alternative savings or investments often make endowment insurance unattractive. However, some persons find saving money irksome and difficult but regard an insurance premium as an obligation and pay it regularly at fixed periods. Thus, these insureds may accumulate a fund that they might not be able to accumulate in any other way.

One use of an endowment policy is to provide for the *old age* of an insured. Some endowment contracts pay a lump sum at a selected age, such as 65. As an option, a monthly income for the insured's lifetime or for a specified time can be paid starting at age 65, the amount being dependent on the lump sum accumulated. If the insured dies before 65, the face value of the contract is paid to the beneficiary. Another special form of endowment for old age is known as the *retirement income* policy. This contract has the unique advantage of paying a monthly life income, the exact amount of which is known by the insured before retirement, such as $10 per month for each $1,000 of insurance. If the insured dies before retirement income begins, the face amount (or the cash value, if larger) is paid.

Endowment insurance is also used to accumulate funds for other specific purposes. Notable in this class are policies designed to provide funds for the education of *children,* or to enable an insured to make a substantial *gift* to a college, church, or some charity. Through an endowment policy the fund may be accumulated gradually over a period of years and, at the same time, be guaranteed in the event of an untimely death.

A controversial use of the endowment feature, usually offered by smaller life insurers, is *deposit term* insurance. Many variations are available, but one typical policy combines a modest endowment payment with 10–year term insurance. The first-year premium is several times higher than for subsequent years, and this "deposit" is returned with interest at the end of the 10 years. Then the policy can be continued by renewing it for another period or converted to term, whole life, or endowment contracts. Cost comparisons with traditional separate policies are very difficult and often inconclusive, and regulation by the states has varied greatly.[6]

---

[6] Harold Skipper, Jr., "Perspectives on Partial Endowment Type ("Deposit Term") Life Insurance: Implications for Regulators," *CLU Journal,* July 1979, p. 10.

Misuses. Of all the policies offered by the life insurers, perhaps none has been misused and caused greater misunderstanding than the endowment contract. Much of the criticism that is leveled at endowment insurance is based upon the high premium charge. If the endowment policy is purchased only for protection, the insured is paying more for the protection than is necessary. The situation is particularly serious if the resources that the insured can apply to insurance premiums are limited and the need for protection is great. If the endowment policy is purchased only for savings, the insured probably could obtain higher yield elsewhere.

The endowment policy is misused except in the particular kinds of situations noted above. Then the combination of protection and substantial savings may have offsetting advantages of encouraging savings or of providing a guaranteed lifetime income at retirement.

COST COMPARISONS: NET COST, INTEREST-ADJUSTED, AND OTHER METHODS

One of the most perplexing problems for life insurance consumers is that choosing the type of contract, as has been discussed in the preceding section of this chapter, is only part of the necessary comparison. When purchasing life insurance, the buyer should also want to know how much the same contract will cost from one insurer as compared with others. Contrary to normal public opinion, life insurance prices do vary considerably, so consumer efforts in cost comparison are worthwhile.[7]

For nonparticipating term insurance, which does not pay annual dividends, the problem is relatively simple. The premium cost paid each year by the policyholder can be directly compared, being sure to compare exactly the same type of term contract, that is, one-year contracts with one-year contracts, five-year with five-year, term to 65 with term to 65, and so on. Care must be taken to see that the contracts compared contain similar convertibility and renewability features.

For participating term insurance, the comparison must include consideration of the dividends paid annually to the policyholder. This can be done only on the basis of past dividends actually declared and paid, but usually the buyer is attempting to calculate what the future cost will be. This requires *estimates* of prospective dividends which are likely to be paid, but are not guaranteed, over a future period of time. Premiums paid less dividends equal "net payment."

For whole life and endowment insurance, there is the further complication of cash surrender values to consider. (Term policies usually do not have these guaranteed amounts payable to the policyholder if the contract is not continued.) These amounts must also be subtracted from

---

[7] Differences of 10–20 percent are not uncommon, and the ranges may be much greater.

the premiums paid, along with dividends if it is a participating contract, in order to know the "net cost" of the contract. Therefore, the *traditional method* of comparing the costs to policyholders of permanent contracts has been (for a 20-year comparison, $1,000 participation contract):[8]

1.	Premiums paid for 20 years, at $24 per year		$480
2.	Less dividends* estimated for 20 years	$130	
3.	Less cash surrender value in 20th year	342	472
4.	Net cost (total for 20 years)		$ 8
5.	Annual net cost ($8 divided by 20)		$ 0.40

   * Omit this figure if contract is nonparticipating.

   Basically, this calculation shows the average amount of each premium not returned if the policy is surrendered for its cash value. (Many contracts will show a net gain rather than a net cost, particularly if the time is longer than 20 years.)
   But is this the real cost of life insurance for the policyholder? No, for the time value of the money paid to the insurer, the time that elapses before the insurer pays back the dividends, and the cash surrender value (assuming that the contract is canceled after 20 years) are not considered in this method. Thus the comparison can be misleading.
   How can the comparison be improved? A better method, called the *interest-adjusted method,* is generally recognized as a fairer cost comparison because it does take into account the time value of the money received and paid out by the insurer. Many life insurance agents now use this method to show prospective buyers how their contract costs compare with those of other companies. In a few states such a comparison is mandatory in life insurance sales, but in most states it is authorized but only furnished to the consumer on request. An example of the interest-adjusted method, for a situation similar to the one shown above, is:[9]

1.	Premiums paid for 20 years, at $24 per year, accumulated at 4 percent		$743.30
2.	Less dividends* estimated for 20 years, accumulated at 4 percent	$180.70	
3.	Less cash surrender in the 20th year	342.00	522.70
4.	Interest-adjusted cost (total for 20 years)		$220.60
5.	Annual interest-adjusted cost index ($220.60 divided by 30.969, which is the result of the accumulation of $1 per year at 4 percent for 20 years)		$ 7.12

   * Omit this figure if contract is nonparticipating.

   [8] *The Interest-Adjusted Method* (New York: Institute of Life Insurance, 1976), p. 4. *See also Life Rates and Data* (Cincinatti: National Underwriter, 1982).
   [9] *The Interest-Adjusted Method,* p. 5. (Note the interest assumption of 4 percent, which for average persons is a relatively low assumption of aftertax secure savings return. Five percent or more is sometimes used in other comparisons today.)

Several comments about the resulting interest-adjusted figure are pertinent. First, it is not what the consumer actually pays for the contract, which would be merely the premiums paid in each year less the annual dividends (if taken in cash). Second, it is an *index* and therefore useful only in comparing similar contracts at a fixed time under specified assumptions. Third, if you wanted to calculate your actual total outlay for the contract, this would depend upon whether you keep the policy as long as you live (or when it is surrendered for cash value), when the policy ends (by death or surrender), and what the actual dividends are. Finally, this method of cost comparison has the disadvantage of increased complexity for the average consumer.

The interest-adjusted cost index of $7.12 per $1,000 in the preceding example is a truer cost figure than the traditional net cost of $0.40. It does consider the time value of money. However, it is not a perfect comparison, and several other measures have been recommended. Belth suggests a "level price method," and a "retention method," to make still more accurate comparisons.[10] These refinements consider additional factors such as the decreasing amount of protection (as cash values increase), the probabilities of survival and lapse during the period of time studied, and the insurer's retention out of the expected value of premiums to be paid.

A consensus as to the one best cost comparison measure is lacking. The National Association of Insurance Commissioners (NAIC) has recommended a model bill for adoption by the states. This changes the term *interest-adjusted cost* to the "surrender cost index" and the term *net cost* to "net payment index," uses a 5 percent interest assumption, and would require agents to provide 10- and 20-year cost comparisons. (The possibility of insurer manipulations of dividends and cash values to make specific periods of comparison more favorable to their contracts would still exist.) Several federal price disclosure bills have been proposed for enforcement by the Federal Trade Commission.[11]

The consumer's dilemma is still real, even for the relatively few consumers who can, and would, use all the available data. The best general advice seems to be that the policyholder should use the interest-adjusted cost index to at least determine whether a specific insurer has a reasonable price which is among the lower cost index categories.[12] The time-consuming quest for the absolute lowest cost may be fruitless. It is perhaps much more important for consumers to be sure that they have

---

[10] Joseph Belth, *Life Insurance: A Consumer's Handbook* (Bloomington: Indiana University Press, 1973). A recent formula method emphasizing cash-value changes is suggested by this author in his monthly publication, *The Insurance Forum*, June 1982.

[11] Particularly by the late Senator Hart. These have been labeled "truth-in-life insurance" bills.

[12] This follows the NAIC model legislation and is available annually for each insurer in *Interest-Adjusted Index* (Cincinnati: National Underwriter).

selected the best type of contract to meet their own needs. Also, consumers might well concentrate on selecting insurers of proven financial strength, with an established reputation and well-trained agents. After all, the ultimate goal should be to obtain the best combination of reasonable cost *and* security and services provided by life insurance.

SPECIAL RIDERS AND POLICY COMBINATIONS

Guaranteed purchase option   *NOT TRUE !*

The *guaranteed purchase option* can be attached to ordinary life and endowment (but not term) contracts. Under this "rider," which is an endorsement or added part to the basic contract, the policyholder is guaranteed the right, *without medical examination,* to increase the amount of his or her life insurance of standard rates at specified times or ages.

Some people find optioning permanent insurance in this way more satisfactory than convertible term insurance. The cost is low, and the additional amounts of permanent insurance are added gradually over a number of years. For example, an insured taking a $10,000 ordinary life policy at age 25 may be given five separate options (an added total of $50,000) to purchase an additional $10,000 contract at ages 28, 31, 34, 37, and 40. Some insurers permit six options or have four-year option intervals. Others permit the options to be exercised upon the marriage of the insured and at the birth of each child. One disadvantage of the purchase option is its relative inflexibility as compared with comparable term insurance amounts. The options can only be exercised at the stated ages or events, in the specified amount, and in the form of a whole life contract.

The time ultimately comes when many persons become partially or totally uninsurable because of a deterioration of physical condition or other changes. The applicant may obtain some insurance as an impaired risk for a cost higher than the standard rates, but total uninsurability prevents the further purchase of any life insurance. The guaranteed purchase option provides protection against the possibility of being forced to pay more than the standard rates and guarantees the availability of insurance regardless of impairment. The popularity of this feature has increased rapidly during the past generation. It is often a desirable option for younger persons to add to their life insurance. The cost is relatively low—about $2 per $1,000 of the basic contract amount.

Other combinations   *TERM RIDERS*

Another form of permanent insurance that incorporates the term idea is known as the *double protection policy.* This policy provides for the

DOESN'T HAVE TO BE "DOUBLE."

payment at death of the sum insured and for doubling the amount of insurance payable if death occurs within a period specified when the policy is taken out. The usual periods are 10, 15, and 20 years. The policy combines a level amount of term insurance with the basic permanent insurance coverage. The double protection is to supply extra insurance when the need to provide for dependents is the heaviest. At the end of the period of double protection, the basic amount remains in full force to the end of life for the person covered. Premiums may be leveled throughout the lifetime of the insured or, when the double protection feature expires, they may be reduced substantially.

There are numerous other life insurance contracts. Many of them are infrequently used but available from insurers if the insured has a special need or desire for them.[13] Two such policies aim at overcoming a common policyholder objection that death causes the policyholder to forfeit the cash values or the premiums that have been paid on the policy up to that time. Such a comment indicates a misunderstanding of the level-premium plan, which does take the cash values accumulated and the premiums paid into consideration. However, if the insured wants more than the face value paid at death, a combination of ordinary life plus increasing term insurance for the cash values or paid premiums may be written in what is called a *return of premium policy* and a *face amount plus cash value policy*. "RETURN OF VALUE."

Life income policies are sometimes issued to provide the beneficiary with a stated income amount, beginning at the insured's death. A guaranteed number of payments may be included, such as 20 years. The beneficiary named may not be changed, except for the guaranteed portion, which is based on an amount of whole life insurance. The rest of the contract, the life annuity to the beneficiary, is a deferred life annuity, such as is discussed in Chapter 8.

A contract called the *principal and income policy* pays at the death of the insured an income for the life of one beneficiary and then a principal amount to a second beneficiary. A man with children, for example, may provide for a life income to his wife and then distribution of the principal to his children.

Joint life policies are sometimes written for whole life or endowment forms of life insurance. The face value is payable upon the death of any one of the lives insured. Such a policy may be used by husband and wife or by partners in a business. Less flexibility for the individuals involved (for conversions, cash values, and so on) is a potential disadvantage. Joint life contracts have recently also become popular for paying off mortgages upon the death of a spouse. These are a form of decreasing term insurance. Sometimes these are called "contingent life" contracts,

---

[13] See chap. 9 of S. S. Huebner and Kenneth Black, Jr., *Life Insurance* (Englewood Cliffs, N.J.: Prentice-Hall, 1982).

and they may be adapted to either family or business situations covering two or more lives. The concept is based upon coverage for "next death," or paying for each death as it occurs, with automatic continuance of life insurance on each survivor. Premium savings of one fourth to one half can be obtained by this form, although the contract has the disadvantage of somewhat increased complexity to the buyers.[14]

SPECIAL LIFE INSURANCE MARKETS

Many life insurance contracts are designed mostly in order to appeal to certain markets. They are combinations of the traditional whole life, term, and endowment contracts, and they often offer special features which make them more attractive to specific kinds of policyholders. Examples of the contracts aimed at special markets are the family plans, juvenile plans, larger policy plans, split-dollar employer-ee plans, split-life insurance, variable life, and adjustable life insurance. Universal life insurance is one of the newest and most controversial contracts and thus far has been aimed at the higher-income market of life insurance consumers.

Family insurance plans

There are three family plans: *(a)* the *family income policy, (b)* the *family maintenance policy,* and *(c)* the *family policy.* These plans are a different combinations of ordinary life and term insurance. Although quite popular during the last two decades as separate policies, as discussed here, the first two types of family contracts are now more often sold as riders or additions to basic life policies.

Family income policy. This contract, written on the breadwinner of a family, provides that if the insured dies within an agreed period from the date of the policy, an income (usually $10 per month for each $1,000 of face value) will be paid the beneficiary for the balance of the term and that the face amount of the policy will then be paid. It is thus a combination of *decreasing* term insurance (for the income benefit) and ordinary life insurance (for the face value). A policy, for example, may be written to provide the income feature if the insured dies within 10, 15, or 20 years from the date of the policy. If the insured died 5 years after the contract was taken out, a $20,000 20-year family income policy would pay the family $200 per month for 15 years and then pay $20,000 in a lump sum. If the insured outlived the period indicated, the premium would be reduced, and the beneficiary would receive only the face amount of the insurance immediately upon the insured's death.

---

[14] "An Alternative to Multi-Life Selling," *Insurance Marketing,* September 1977, p. 58.

Thus, a young man can provide his wife with an income rather than a lump sum that could be used up before the children are independent. A similar use could be made of this contract if the wife instead of the husband is the wage earner of the family.

Family maintenance policy. This policy is less common but much like the family income policy. It differs in that the term during which income payments are to be made is a fixed period which commences with the death of the insured. Policies may provide the income feature for a selected period, usually 10, 15, or 20 years from the death of the insured. Regardless of the date of death, if the insured dies within the selected period, income will be paid for the number of years specified. Unless otherwise provided, the face amount of the contract is then payable at the end of the period selected for income payments. The family maintenance policy is a combination of ordinary life insurance and *level* term insurance. Term insurance is provided for an amount based on the specified number of monthly payments. ⟋ CAN BE TERM

Family policy. This is a package form providing life insurance coverage for the *entire family*. It covers the father, the mother, and all the children. Coverage on the father is usually ordinary life insurance. Protection on the mother and the children is for a lesser amount than for the coverage on the father and is usually term life insurance. Such a package might provide $5,000 ordinary life on the father with term coverage of $1,000 on the mother and each of the children. Coverage on the father may be increased in units of $2,500, with insurance on other members of the family increasing proportionally.

Newborn children are insured (at no additional cost) when they become 15 days old, and this includes stepchildren and adopted children. If the father dies, the family receives the insurance on his life, and the premiums on their insurance cease. When the children reach a designated age, usually 21, their insurance terminates, but they have the privilege of buying up to five times that amount of permanent insurance at their attained ages without medical examination. The wife's insurance is often term insurance to the husband's age 65, but some forms insure the wife with permanent ordinary life insurance. Premiums are usually waived if the husband dies or is totally disabled. Accidental death benefits are sometimes included automatically, but this is often optional coverage.

Some authorities would point out that sometimes the premium cost which goes toward purchasing the insurance on the lives of the wife and children would be better used in purchasing larger protection on the "breadwinners" (the husband or the wife, if working) of the family if they are inadequately insured. However, the small difference in cost (about $10 a year for the basic $5,000 amount), as compared with the cost of insurance on the breadwinner alone, makes the family policy convenient and salable.

Juvenile insurance plans

Insuring juveniles (usually identified as under age 15) offers families an opportunity to start an insurance program for their children at an early age.

Juvenile insurance is not in the strict sense a separate type of policy. It is rather a form modified to meet the needs of young children. The usual forms are: (a) 20-year endowment, (b) educational endowment at age 18, and (c) ordinary life policies.

Juvenile policies may now be written, subject to some differing laws of the states, to pay the full face amount of the policy on the death of the insured child. The former practice and laws scaled cash benefits to the child's age, and this still may be required. Insurers may require that the child be at least one month old. No medical examination is usually required for normal amounts of insurance. Ownership of the contract usually remains with the applicant (the parents, in the typical case) until the insured child reaches age 18 or 21. Some insurers and state statutes permit life insurance to be purchased by the children themselves if they are over age 15.

A feature peculiar to juvenile insurance may provide for the continuance of the insurance in the event of the death of the adult who applies for the policy and who assumes the responsibility for the payment of the premiums. The clause covering this provision, sometimes referred to as the "payor clause," provides for a *waiver of premiums* in the event of the death or the total and permanent disability of the adult applicant. If a payor benefit is desired, the applicant is sometimes required to have a medical examination.

A popular form of juvenile insurance has come to be known as *jumping juvenile* and derives its name from the fact that the face amount of the policy jumps to five times its original value at no added premium or medical examination when the insured child becomes 21 years of age. The initial policy is usually made available in units of $1,000 of permanent life insurance, up to $10,000 or $15,000. The advantage of this insurance is that it guarantees standard life insurance of a child at the age of 21. Poor health before age 21 cannot prevent that child from purchasing any insurance at all or increase the cost because of substandard classification. The premium paid per $1,000 at the age of issue remains constant throughout the life of the policy and does not increase when the child attains the age of 21. Finally, the policy builds up reserves rapidly, providing attractive cash or loan values. Instead of buying an educational policy, some parents purchase this form of coverage with the thought that the loan values will be available for education if needed; otherwise the coverage will serve as a start to a permanent life insurance estate for the young person.

As a comparison, the cost of "jumping juvenile" insurance at age 1 is about $40 for $1,000 (for life paid up at age 65), while a comparable policy without the jumping feature at age 21 would be about one fourth as much. After age 21, however, the cost remains at $40 per $1,000, while a comparable policy at that age will cost approximately twice as much.

Larger policy plans

A comparatively recent development, the outgrowth of competition, is the group of policies known as "specials." A distinguishing feature of the specials is that they are for larger than normal amounts and are issued at lower premium rates than the similar basic type of contract. In effect, these contracts use the idea of a quantity discount.

The specials generally follow one of three patterns and are known as (a) minimum amount policies, (b) preferred risk policies, and (c) graded policies, with premiums based on size. At the outset, special policies were limited to whole life policies. However, many insurers now have special policies available in almost every basic insurance plan.

Minimum amount policies. As the name indicates, this form requires a policy written in an amount equal to or in excess of a minimum established by the company. This could be $25,000 or more. A part of the premium reduction may flow from a lower commission rate paid the agent; the balance is derived from a distribution of certain of the expense items that are fixed on a policy basis. Costs that are often the same regardless of policy size include the cost of medical examination, bookkeeping, research data, and general administration. The cost of such fixed expenses is lower for each $1,000 of insurance as the size of the policy increases.

Preferred risk policies. Policies in this category justify a lower premium charge on the basis of rigid selection. Certain classes may be selected, such as businesspersons and professionals, whose mortality experience is expected to be better than average. Usually, the contracts are also larger in size than the normal contract and require a medical examination. A policy designed as an "executive policy," for example, would often be for $100,000 or more. While there may be some justification for a differentiation based upon flat expense items for the larger policies, cutting the preferred risks out of an ordinarily standard group must ultimately result in higher costs for those who are left.

Graded policies, with premiums based on size. This plan of pricing is a logical consequence of the minimum amount policy plan. The same argument is advanced that certain fixed costs do not vary with policy size. This plan usually provides for size groups, or "bands," and as the amount of insurance moves from one group to another, the larger

BANDED RATES

the amount of insurance reflected in the particular group, the less is the cost of each $1,000 of insurance. The price variation differs among insurers; but, for example, for one well-known insurer the rate reduction for an over-$50,000 policy as compared with an under-$5,000 policy is approximately 10 percent. A further premium reduction is allowed on many policies issued on the lives of females.[15]

Employer-employee plans

Two employer-employee plans using individual life insurance contracts have the purpose of providing lower aftertax costs: *split-dollar* and *split-life* insurance.

Split-dollar insurance. The *split-dollar insurance* policy involves an agreement between an employer and an employee under which the employer purchases a single life insurance contract on the life of the employee.[16] Any form of permanent life insurance contract may be utilized. The plan is made effective by attaching the split-dollar endorsement to the life insurance contract of which it becomes a part.

By use of the plan employers can provide junior executives with a substantial amount of financial security at reasonable prices. The person whose life is insured pays the entire first-year premium, and then each subsequent year, the premium is reduced by any dividends declared and by the amount the cash value of the policy is increased. The employer pays each year an amount equivalent to the increase in cash value. The payment made by employers, however, is more of an investment than an expense since the cash value of the policy is always returned to them when benefits are paid or the policy is surrendered for any reason. The plan provides low, net cost life insurance to an employee, whose designated beneficiary receives the face value less the cash value. The employer provides an incentive benefit that will tend to encourage the continued employment of a valued employee.

Split-life insurance. Not to be confused with the split-dollar plans just discussed for employer-ee situations, which use a single contract to divide cash values and term protection, is a life insurance product

---

[15] Some participating companies attain the object of coordinating net cost with size of policy by dividend adjustment rather than by a decrease in gross premiums. Graded dividends are distributed on the basis of size groups. To reflect the better mortality experience of female lives in the case of policies over a given minimum, an additional dividend is sometimes provided over and above that paid on male lives.

[16] The same type of plan is available and is sometimes useful in family situations. A father, grandfather, or other relative may purchase insurance on and for a young man, for example, helping him to buy whole life insurance on a split-dollar basis. The insured young man pays the net cost of protection, while the older person pays the increase in cash value (which is an investment, returned to him when the policy matures or is discontinued).

called *split-life insurance*.[17] The concept has been approved by most states. Basically, the idea is to obtain tax benefits through the use of *two separate contracts* of life insurance. One is an annual *deferred annuity* (see Chapter 8) to be held by an organization, such as a business corporation, an HR–10 (Keogh) Plan for self-employeds, or a nonprofit charitable institution, permitting premium payments to be made with tax-free dollars. The second contract is a *yearly renewable level term* insurance policy which can be purchased in the amount of $1,000 of insurance for each $10 of annuity payment by the purchaser. The low term cost (about $3 per 1,000 at age 45) is only available in connection with the annuity purchase.[18]

Split-life contracts make it possible to use the cash value from the annuity, after it has been in force for 10 years and the insured is at least 60 years old. Contrary to a whole life contract, where taking the cash value would discontinue the life insurance protection, the term life protection of the split-life contracts can be maintained by continuing payment of the yearly renewable term premium or by conversion to a whole life policy. The annuity and term life can be written on the same lives or on different insureds. The market possibilities for split-life include helping fund children's education, providing estate liquidity, purchasing key-person life insurance on important employees of business firms, and making gifts to charity.

Variable life insurance

Another innovation in life insurance is the *variable life insurance* contract. Early progress was blocked by legal complications, but in late 1976 the Securities and Exchange Commission ruled that individual life insurance contracts with an *equity base* would be subject to the Securities Acts of 1933–34 and the Investment Company Act of 1940. This ruling complicates the marketing of such contracts, for agents must also be licensed as security salespersons, and a prospectus with much detailed information must be given to the prospective buyer. This has slowed the impetus for the development of such contracts.

The fundamental idea is to change traditional (fixed-dollar-value) whole life insurance, in which the insurer pays a stated face value. The problem is that this specified face value does not attempt to guarantee any particular purchasing power for the consumer. In an era of continuing inflation, this is a real disadvantage to the life insurance beneficiary.

---

[17] The originator, about 15 years ago, was Con G. Demmas. See The *Split Life Story* (St. Louis: Commerce Publishing, 1975).

[18] Joseph M. Belth, "A Note on the Price of Split-Life Insurance," *Journal of Risk and Insurance* 39, no. 3 (September 1972), p. 501. The author concludes that there are some cost benefits, particularly in the net cost *after* taxes.

To offset this disadvantage, the variable life contract has a *variable policy amount* dependent upon earnings from investments such as common stocks. The theory is that as inflation raises common stock values and dividends in a "separate account" maintained for the variable life policies, the dollar values paid under the contract will also increase. Hopefully, the increases will counterbalance decreases in the purchasing power of the dollar. The death payments are guaranteed not to fall below a *minimum* face value but could increase if the equity values increased. Cash values are *not* guaranteed, however, and loan values are usually only 75 percent of the cash values instead of the full amount. The premiums are fixed and *level* for the whole of life.

Early groundwork in such countries as the Netherlands, Canada, and Great Britain indicate that the concept is workable. In the United States, for example, if you had bought a $10,000 contract in 1950, the benefits might have increased to about $18,000 in 1967, dropped to $14,000 in 1970, and then risen to $20,000 by the end of the decade. The individual experience of insurers will probably vary greatly, and this is why each contract will require careful study by the insured of the prospectus required by law. The Equitable Life Assurance Society was the first major American insurer to offer individual variable life insurance contracts, in 1976. Other insurers had sold a similar product earlier but only on a group basis.

The potential disadvantages of variable life insurance should not be minimized. The premiums are higher than those for whole life insurance. The fixed guarantees of traditional life insurance have been of significant value to the reputation of the business for security. Consumer misunderstanding as to how much the variable life values might decrease (or not be as large as expected), if equity returns are not favorable, could endanger this reputation.[19] Expected policy loan values may not be available to policyholders. The contracts increase consumer perplexity about life insurance. Start-up costs for these new contracts in terms of insurer research and agent retraining will be high. Variable life insurance has been approved for sale in all but a few states. However, the number of insurers writing variable life insurance is small, and only about $4 billion was in force by the end of 1981.[20] Many of the arguments pro and con are similar to those discussed further in Chapter 8 in connection with variable annuities.[21]

---

[19] For an analysis that concludes they have been disappointing to date, see Jane Bryant Quinn, "Variable Life, Examined," *Newsweek*, November 16, 1981, p. 113.

[20] *Life Insurance Fact Book*, p. 26.

[21] For a review of both products, see Bernard G. Werbel ed., *Variable Annuities and Variable Life Insurance Primer* (Smithtown, N.Y.: Werbel Publishing, 1977).

Adjustable life insurance

One of the major breakthroughs in the need of the consumer for modifying life insurance amounts to accommodate "life cycle" changes occurred in the late 1970s. This was the introduction by several insurers (Bankers Life and Minnesota Life are early examples) of the *adjustable life insurance* contract. The idea is somewhat like variable life insurance, in that a policy is sold that you can change as your needs change. However, instead of having the life insurance amount vary with the prospective increased earnings of an equity-based account, the *policyholder makes the choices* on changing the policy amount, upward or downward.

The usual whole life and term types of life insurance are combined, with a wide flexibility as to when and how changes can be made. Most important, the *premiums* can be changed as well as the insured values. This is accomplished by increasing or decreasing the length of the term coverage, or by reducing or lengthening the premium-paying period of the whole life coverage.

In addition, the policy amounts can be increased by several methods. Two of them are traditional methods already used in many other life insurance contracts ("guaranteed purchase options," as explained earlier in this chapter, and "dividend options," as discussed in Chapter 7). The new feature is "cost-of-living" increases, by which the insured up to age 55 is permitted to buy additional life insurance every three years, without a medical examination. The increases are limited to about 30 percent of the face value and a maximum of $30,000 and are reduced by life insurance amounts purchased through other contracts during the given three-year period.[22]

The adjustable life contract can help solve the problems of meeting the changing needs of consumers and the effect of inflation on fixed-dollar life insurance values. It may have some of its own problems, too, as the premium is up to 10 percent higher than that of traditional life insurance. On the other hand, it may enable the consumer to save some of the time and costs of buying new policies or dropping old, separate policies.

The most difficult problem is probably the increased difficulty of selling a more complicated product. However, adjustable life insurance avoids the dual-regulation (SEC *and* state insurance departments) problem of variable life insurance. Because of this, the application of the concept may be one of the most significant changes for life insurance in the 1980s. "Its imaginative design and advanced technology will not in themselves make adjustable life an instant success, unless life agents and

---

[22] "Adjustable Life Insurance," *Changing Times,* October 1977, pp. 17–19; and Mary Greenebaum, "Personal Investing," *Fortune,* June 16, 1980, p. 205.

the insuring public like what they see. As with other products, the ultimate test will take place within the marketplace."[23]

As evidence of the rapid changes occurring, more than 50 life insurers are now writing a variation of adjustable and variable life insurance, in which only the *premiums* (but not the policy amounts) change with their financial experience. This is called *variable premium life insurance*.[24] The initial premium is *lower* than for traditional whole life insurance and is guaranteed for the first two or three years. Then the premium may decrease or increase up to a maximum specified amount.

Other *cost-of-living insurance* is offered by some insurers. These policies or riders permit the insured to increase their coverage at the same rate that the consumer price index rises, up to specified maximums, such as 20 percent or $50,000 per year. Unlike adjustable life, the premiums can increase at a faster rate than the benefits because the buyer is older.

The most controversial life insurance product in decades emerged in the late 1970s with the introduction of the "universal life insurance" policy discussed next.

Universal life insurance   AND INTEREST SENSITIVE WHOLE LIFE

Evolutionary nature. After less than five years of very modest growth by variable and adjustable life insurance, a new product called *universal life insurance* burst upon the decade of the 1980s with a wave of publicity and controversy. Sometimes mistaken as a revolutionary change, "universal life insurance policies are evolutionary life insurance products which have been enhanced to provide a lower cost and greater degree of flexibility to the policyholder."[25] Universal life adapts the traditional life insurance and annuity contracts. Lower costs may result primarily because cash values are credited with current interest rates which are variable but anticipated to be higher than traditional, long-term guaranteed rates. Flexibility is achieved by permitting changes in both premium payments and death benefits, as opposed to fixed amounts. In insurance terms, universal life insurance aims at providing both protection and savings through the combination of yearly renewable term insurance and a flexible-premium annuity.

The roots of the universal life insurance *concept* extend much further back than the much publicized appearance in 1979 of a universal life

---

[23] Charles L. Trowbridge, "Adjustable Life—A New Solution to an Old Problem," *CLU Journal* 31, no. 4 (October 1977), p. 20.

[24] "Variable Premium Insurance Plans," *Changing Times,* October 1981, p. 46.

[25] J. Timothy Lynch, "Universal Life Insurance: A Primer," *CLU Journal,* July 1982, p. 44.

insurance *policy* marketed by E. F. Hutton Life Insurance Company. Actuaries, some 20 years ago, discussed the general ideas, and G. R. Dinney is credited with developing the earliest product proposals in the 1960s.[26] One design was a group pension combining term insurance, a cash fund, and a deferred annuity. The most important was a fundamental "Universal Life Insurance Plan" from which different individual contracts with flexible interest rates applying to the savings component could be adapted. It was universal in the sense that many variations could be developed. James Anderson[27] popularized one specific "universal life insurance policy" proposal in 1975, and by the early 1980s the rush to the marketplace by numerous life insurers was on. Among the companies offering the new policies were Transamerica, Life of Virginia, Hartford, Travelers, and others.

Comparison with traditional insurance. The life-plus-annuity approach of universal life insurance is not, however, as simple as merely combining existing traditional contracts. The most important difference is the addition of *cash values* which build up in the life insurance policy at *variable* current interest rates, rather than in predetermined and guaranteed long-term cash values such as in whole life insurance. Close to a 4 percent minimum interest rate is usually guaranteed, with excess interest determined by money market rates or sometimes by external indexes. Each year the insured pays a *flexible premium* which is sometimes called a "contribution" because the amount is voluntary above certain minimums. Each month the insurer, after deducting for expenses and a risk charge for the term insurance protection, credits the remainder to the cash value.

The potential use of the cash value is also different than in traditional contracts which only permit full cash-value withdrawal when the policy is surrendered or loans up to the cash-value amount. The universal life insurance policy adds the option of *partial withdrawals,* sometimes with extra fees charged. These withdrawals are not loans, but they do reduce the policy's face and cash values. The general purpose of the buildup of the cash values is not intended for sporadic emergency withdrawals at the younger age, however. These values are needed for paying the increasing cost of term protection as the insured grows older. Prospectively, they also are expected to permit some optional withdrawals at middle ages (for such expenses as the children's education) and to provide annuity income at the advanced ages.

[margin annotation: "TARGET" "PREMIUM"]

---

[26] G. R. Dinney, "Who Invented Universal Life? I Did," *Canadian Journal of Life Insurance,* March 1982, p. 9. His claim has been supported by others in the newsletter of the Society of Actuaries. A 272-page, 1982 loose-leaf notebook, titled *Scenario 2001,* explains in detail the rationale for development of his Universal Life Insurance Plan.

[27] In a paper, titled "The Universal Life Insurance Policy," presented at the 7th Pacific Insurance Conference.

Another difference is that universal life insurance policies have *adjustable death benefits*. Initially, policyholders select one of two basic forms: (1) a fixed face value, such as $100,000, which when paid at death includes the cash value, or (2) a face value which will pay the face value purchased *plus* the accumulated cash value. Policyholders can at any time thereafter *decrease* the face value (to specified minimum amounts), or they can *increase* it, with evidence of insurability, without rewriting the contract.

Thus, the comparisons as summarized in Table 6–5 are generally advantageous to policyholders: (1) *flexibility* in premiums, benefits, and withdrawals, and (2) *cash-value increases* that reflect current interest earnings and mortality. However, the advantages do not occur without potential problems.

Table 6–5. Comparison of term, whole life, and universal life insurance features

Feature	Term insurance	Whole life insurance	Universal life insurance
Cash and loan value	Usually none	Increases with guaranteed, known amounts	Variable amount
Premium	Initially low, rising with increasing age	Level throughout lifetime	Flexible amount
Withdrawals	Usually none	Full withdrawal only, with policy surrender	Full or partial withdrawals
Death benefits	Fixed amount	Fixed amount	Adjustable amount

Problems. *Flexibility* may be a two-edged sword. Thoughtful policyholders will only make changes when they are warranted by real needs or economic adversity. Universal life insurance, however, permits good changes as well as bad ones. Will the premiums paid in be maintained rather than reduced unnecessarily? Will face values be reduced or withdrawals taken only when they should be? Will long-term savings be accomplished in spite of normal temptations to spend or other difficulties to save? Too much flexibility may be a disadvantage for average universal life insurance policyholders who attempt to achieve the proper balance between protection and saving throughout a lifetime. It will require good education, sufficient income, and unusual discipline to make the right choices.

How about those projected *cash-value increases*? As one of the most enticing sales appeals, companies advertise yields of 10–13 percent or higher but guarantee only about 4 percent. Most important is how long economic conditions will sustain such rates. Policyholders must also be aware that the calculated yield does *not* apply to the entire premiums paid—only to what is left *after* expenses and term insurance coverage is subtracted. Expenses include high first-year fees (often $300–$500 but sometimes $1,000 or more on a $100,000 policy) and a recurring fee of 5–10 percent on all subsequent premiums paid. Term insurance costs also rise rapidly with the older ages. The quoted yields provide another problem: most insurers pay the higher yields only on cash values of more than $1,000, with much smaller minimums paid on lesser amounts. Finally, the calculation of yields in universal life policies is based on cash values after deducting expenses. These yields "are *gross* rates of return, not net rates"[28] which could be compared with yields on the savings element in other insurance contracts or with alternative investments.

Another disadvantage of universal life insurance is *uncertain tax issues.*[29] Although private letter IRS rulings (which apply only to specific cases) have been issued on several points, it may be several years before general rulings, legislation, and court cases provide definite answers. For *policyholders,* will the benefits paid be tax-free, escaping income tax at death? Will the excess interest (earned above the guaranteed interest rates) on the cash values be tax-deferred and thus taxed as income only when received rather than as credited? Also, will withdrawals be taxed only to the extent that they are greater than premiums paid in? These benefits apply now to traditional life insurance policyholders. *Probably* they will apply to universal life insurance policyholders, based on private letter rulings through 1982. However, for *insurers* considerable uncertainty remains in regard to whether or not the excess interest payments will be deductible in computing the company's income tax. (*Note:* As of late 1982, the Tax Equity and Fiscal Responsibility Act of 1982 (TEFRA) favorably settled most of the above tax questions. Universal life contracts issued before 1984 will be taxed under traditional rules if they are "substantially similar" products to the whole life policy.)

Marketing prospects. Most of the larger life insurance insurers have been slow in developing universal life insurance contracts, although there are now various such policies offered by some 50 or more companies. Existing contracts are not yet aimed at the average consumer, for many of them require minimum face values of $100,000 or more. Lower minimum-size policies are anticipated. The wait-and-see attitude of many insurers is based on a reluctance to change from traditional term and whole life insurance contracts, as well as concern for some of the unsettled tax effects of the new policies on both insurers and on policyholders.

Universal life insurance may provide insurers with a product more

---

[28] "Universal Life Insurance," *Consumer Reports,* January 1982, p. 43.

[29] Tax implications are discussed further in Lynch, "Universal Life Insurance: A Primer," pp. 48–50.

competitive with recent high investment returns of other popular alternatives such as money market, bonds, stocks, and real estate. It also may offer another option for higher-income policyholders who contemplate pros and cons of buying life insurance on the basis of "buy term and invest the difference" (see earlier section of this chapter). The competitive aspects go further, however. Universal life insurance is inherently a product which competes directly with both existing and newly issued whole life insurance. As such, for established life insurers who consider whole life as their fundamental product, it should be no surprise that many insurers are being cautious in introducing universal life insurance.

Tremendous changes in marketing life insurance may occur if universal life insurance is expanded to the general market. Agents will have a big stake in the increased opportunities it offers for them to compete and in the increased competition it causes for them. Either way, traditional commission systems are likely to be challenged. Reevaluation of compensation to agents should parallel charges in the services they provide. There will be need for explanation of the new contracts; analysis of the annual computer printout of benefits, costs, and cash values; and advice on how to use the flexible options to best advantage.

The policyholder is and should be a dominant factor in the changing marketplace for life insurance. If inflation and high interest rates continue, life insurance consumers are likely to increase their search for higher returns and flexibility to meet changing needs. As tax uncertainties are clarified, universal life insurance may be the answer in that search for some policyholders, particularly those with higher incomes and need for larger insurance amounts. Most observers do not expect it to replace completely the traditional forms of life insurance, because consumers have many different needs to fulfill. Protection will remain paramount among those needs. Only a relatively small proportion of the public are good long-term savers, particularly when the savings plan is optional. The growth of universal life insurance will be dependent upon how well it meets the combined protection and savings needs of the future consumer.

FOR REVIEW AND DISCUSSION

1. How has the trend toward product diversification and broader financial services by life insurers occurred, and what advantages do you see for the insurer and for the consumer?

2. Indicate which of the following statements are false. *Explain* your reasoning.
   a. Individual life insurance is larger than group life insurance in terms of life insurance amounts in force.

      b. Life insurance premiums can be reduced by buying "modified life" or "limited-payment life" instead of "ordinary life" insurance contracts.

      c. The usual kind of "20-year endowment" pays the face value only if the insured lives for 20 years.

      d. Joint life insurance contracts pay the beneficiary if both of the insureds die in the same accident.

3. The whole life policy is said to be the most important of all life insurance contracts. Explain *why* this statement may be considered accurate. What qualifications might you attach to this statement?

4. Term, whole life, and endowment life insurance are sometimes misused. Give an example of *(a)* a proper use and *(b)* an improper use of each of the basic types of life insurance contracts.

5. Evaluate the concept of "buy term and invest the difference," indicating what "difference" is referred to and what the primary strengths and fallacies of the technique are for the average life insurance policyholder.

6. If Betty purchased a 20-year endowment, a 20-payment life, a whole life, or a term policy, she would pay a different premium for each contract. If she dies while any of the contracts are in force, each contract pays the same amount of insurance. Thus it has been said, that life insurers charge different prices for the same thing. Show why this is not true.

7. Today's society might be characterized as one of *(a)* affluence, *(b)* inflation, and *(c)* consumer orientation. What effect on the types of individual life insurance contracts sold by insurers would you expect each of these factors to have in the next 10 years?

8. Some life insurance agents sell very little term life insurance, while others sell this type of contract almost exclusively (and become known as "termites!"). Can you justify this wide difference?

9. Joe was recently graduated from law college. He has a wife and child and is at present earning approximately $25,000 annually. He is able to save, above his living expenses, $3,000 annually. He contemplates buying a home but has been advised that he should spend the major part of his savings on life insurance. What would you recommend?

10. Don is a young man, aged 24, earning an exceptionally good salary. He is unmarried and has no dependents. Don contends that he has no need for life insurance. Why would you agree or disagree?

11. Pat Nelson has purchased a house valued at $90,000. The monthly payment covers principal, interest, taxes, and property insurance. Assume Pat to be 25 years of age and married, and her loan to be for $60,000. What kind of life insurance might Pat consider to strengthen her position?

12. Differentiate between *split-dollar* and *split-life* contracts.

13. What are the purposes of the guaranteed purchase option? What alternatives are there in achieving these purposes?

14. Differentiate among the three primary life insurance contracts designed for families. Explain at least one advantage and one disadvantage of each.

15. Life insurance agents usually find less sales resistance to juvenile life insur-

ance than to any other contract form. Is there a danger in this natural tendency to care more about one's children than about oneself?

16. How are large-amount life insurance policies issued, and what are the advantages to the policyholder?

17. Divide the class into two groups: one to justify the traditional fixed benefit life insurance contract, and the other to explain the potential merits of *variable* and *adjustable* life insurance policies.

18. Why is the "interest-adjusted" index method of comparing life insurance costs better than the traditional "net cost" method? What disadvantages may it still have?

19. "The new *universal life* insurance policies *may* have considerable sales appeal and advantages for policyholders." Explain this statement and discuss three potential problems for insureds or insurers which may influence the future market for this product.

Chapter 7

Outline of concepts

Life insurance contract features include many provisions for *flexibility*.

General form of the policy is adaptable to many needs.

Insuring agreement and face of policy contain basic agreements.

Application usually includes *medical examination* report in the contract.

Standard provisions provide some uniformity of major clauses:

Payment of premiums sets *inception* of coverage and *grace period*.

The beneficiary, *primary* and *contingent,* should be carefully designated; usually they are *revocable* for flexibility.

Ownership of policy and changes differ in contracts.

Assignment is permitted, effective when in *writing* at home office.

Dividends and dividend options are important in many contracts:

Participating policies pay dividends; **nonparticipating** do not.

Dividend options: *cash, premium reduction, paid-up additions, interest deposits, one-year additional term insurance.*

Policy form changes to other contracts are permitted.

Lapse and reinstatement (within five years) requires *insurability*.

Misstatement of age requires *adjusted face value* amount.

Suicide within two years results in *return of premiums* only.

Indebtedness reduces *settlement* amounts.

Incontestability for *fraud* or other reasons is usually after two years.

Cash, loan, and nonforfeiture benefits include:

Cash values, which are *basic amount* available, or

Policy loans at stated *8 (sometimes 5, 6, or variable) percent* interest.

Automatic premium loan option to prevent mistaken lapse.

Extended term insurance for *full face value.*

Reduced paid-up insurance of *permanent* insurance.

Optional methods of settlement in *supplementary contracts:*

Types permit a choice, in place of a lump sum, of:

Specified amount installments.

Specified period of installments.

Life income payments (unique to life insurance).

Interest payments.

Uses are many, with proper planning and recognition of benefits.

Disability and accidental death benefit extensions:

Waiver-of-premium benefit for total and permanent disability.

Accidental death benefits.

Total disability income benefits.

Life insurance contract features

Nine out of ten U.S. families, or two out of three Americans, have some life insurance today—but how many do a good job in purchasing a life insurance contract by knowing what features it includes?

A family spending $200 per month on staple groceries at a favorite market devotes countless hours every year to the process of shopping. Much time is used in reading labels and asking questions in order to determine the quality, cost, and potential uses of the products purchased. Yet what happens when the same family purchases a life insurance contract? Probably a part of only one or two evenings is set aside to permit a life insurance agent to visit their home. The agent tries desperately in a limited time to understand their needs and explain how life insurance can provide a solution to the basic family problems of savings and protection. Frequently, the meeting with the agent is the first time the husband and wife have taken time together to consider seriously their financial goals and needs. Few families talk with more than one agent.

A logical purchasing system for a major item in the family budget? Hardly, but then the typical method could be rationalized in terms of the many other hasty and uninformed decisions that consumers make. But wait, shouldn't at least the most important uses of family income be approached with at least some knowledge of the fundamental parts of what is being purchased? Not many persons buy an automobile without knowing at least its size, style, kind of engine, and color. Yet people often spend (or worse yet, don't!) an equal amount of income on life insurance without really knowing what the basic features of the contract are.[1]

This chapter introduces the more important provisions of a life insurance contract.[2] Every potential and actual policyholder should know about the features discussed here, for these rights and benefits are what the contract provides in return for its cost.

---

[1] In approximate figures, an $8,000 automobile purchased once every five years costs an average, after salvage, $1200 a year, or $100 a month. At about age 23, ordinary life insurance of $80,000 or more could be purchased for the same monthly cost.

[2] For further information, the student is referred to Janice E. Greider and William T. Beadles, *Law and the Life Insurance Contract* (Homewood, Ill.: Richard D. Irwin, 1979).

The analysis centers on the provisions found in the usual, individual whole life, or permanent life, insurance contract. Some of the features treated may not be found in policies issued as industrial or group life insurance; for example, under such policies, limited or no cash and loan values may be present, or the settlement options may be limited to fewer choices.

GENERAL FORM OF THE POLICY

Basically, the life insurance policy is a promise by the insurer to pay a stated amount of money to the policyholder (or the beneficiary). The conditions under which the benefits are paid are significant. These conditions may include death, some types of disability, and in the case of endowments, a certain maturity date set in the contract.

In connection with the fundamental benefits, many important options and privileges are granted to the policyholder. These features combine to make the life insurance contract one of the most flexible agreements ever designed. The owner of the contract, or sometimes the beneficiary, has the right to: (1) stop or change premium payments, (2) change the recipient of the benefits, (3) assign the contract rights, (4) change the use of the dividends, (5) change to a different policy, (6) reinstate coverage, (7) take cash or loan values, (8) cancel the policy and receive accumulated benefits in a variety of ways, and (9) use the policy proceeds by receiving lump-sum or installment payments.

The parts of the life insurance contract discussed in this chapter include its: (1) *declarations* (found on the "policy face" and in the "application") and *insuring agreement;* (2) mandatory *standard provisions;* (3) mandatory *cash, loan, and nonforfeiture benefits;* (4) *optional methods of settlement; and* (5) optional *disability and accidental death benefit extensions of coverage.*

INSURING AGREEMENT AND FACE OF POLICY

On the first page of the policy appear the name of life insurer, the name of the insured, the amount of the policy (termed the "face amount"), and the names of the beneficiary or beneficiaries. In the insuring agreement the insurer agrees to insure the life of the person named as the insured and to pay to the beneficiary the face amount of the policy upon the notice and proof of death of the insured while the policy is in force.

The type of policy purchased, the policy number, the age of the insured at the time the policy is issued, and the date of issue appear on its face. The face of an endowment policy will indicate that the policy proceeds are payable to the insured if he or she is living a given number of years from the date the policy is issued. The requirements for premium payments are stated, primarily the date when premiums are due and whether they are payable annually, semiannually, quarterly, or monthly. Any special features of the contract are mentioned, and a statement is made that provisions on subsequent pages form part of the contract. The New York insurance law requires a summary description of the contract at the bottom of the face and on the outside of the folded policy. The signatures of the officers authorized to issue the policy appear at the bottom of the first page.

APPLICATION   *B EABLES   202*

As a basis for accepting or rejecting an applicant for insurance, life insurers require certain information. This is contained in an *application*, which becomes a part of the contract. Insurers wish to know, for example, the name, residence, age, and occupation of the applicant as well as the plan of insurance applied for, when premiums are to be paid, the beneficiary and the contingent beneficiary, and other insurance in force. In addition, they wish to know the family record as to longevity and to have evidence of the physical fitness of the applicant. All of this appears in the application. Legally the application constitutes an offer for the purchase of insurance which the insurer may accept or reject.

If a medical examination is required, there are two parts to the application. The first is a questionnaire completed and signed by the applicant. The second consists of a report of the physical examination of the applicant made by the examining physician.

The representations by applicants in the part of the application which they sign and to the examining physician should be accurate and carefully considered. Except for fraud, the information supplied need only be substantially true and not literally so.[3] Persons who have no records and cannot recall all pertinent facts—for example, concerning past physical conditions—meet the requirements if their answers are conscientious and reveal all the information at their command.

Statutes controlling life insurance usually require that the insured be furnished with the contract. Policies make the application a part of the contract, and a photostatic copy is attached. Together they are stated to constitute the entire contract between insurer and insured. The policy ordinarily provides that no statement shall void the policy or be used in defense of a claim under it unless it is contained in the written application endorsed, or attached, to the policy when issued. The insurance

---

[3] The law in most jurisdictions now requires, in the absence of fraud, that statements in the application be considered representations which must be "material" (or important) and not warranties. If not technically correct, representations made in good faith and without intent to defraud do not afford the insurer grounds for canceling the policy or refusing to pay a claim.

buyer should beware of the practice of having the agent ask questions and fill out the application for the buyer—or at least should carefully check the application before signing.[4]

STANDARD PROVISIONS

There is no standard policy form required by statute for life insurance contracts, but instead all newly issued life insurance policies must include the *standard provisions* (sometimes called "general provisions" in the policy) prescribed by the state statutes. New forms of policies are issued only when these have been approved by the state insurance department. It was early felt that a standard form of policy resulted in too much uniformity of available coverages. To provide more leeway with respect to coverages and at the same time adequately safeguard the interests of the policyholders, laws were enacted making certain standard provisions mandatory.[5]

Indicative of the nature of the standard provisions now universally required is the following summary of the ordinary life provisions of the New York law: (1) that there shall be a grace period of either 30 days or one month; (2) that the policy shall be incontestable after it has been in force during the lifetime of the insured for two years from the date of issue; (3) that the policy shall constitute the entire contract between the parties; (4) that if the age of the insured has been misstated, the amount payable under the policy shall be such as the premium would have purchased at the correct age; (5) that participation must be on an annual dividend basis; (6) that options shall be specified to which the insured is entitled in the event of default of premium after the payment of three annual premiums; (7) that loan values shall be stated; and that, for participating policies, the insurer shall annually apportion any accrued divisible surplus.

Since the standard provisions establish minimum requirements only and an insurer may file policies with more liberal provisions, the legislation permits more flexibility in life insurance contracts than would be permitted under a standard policy requirement. At the same time, a considerable degree of uniformity has developed in the contracts offered by most insurers.

---

[4] But for an exception to the rule, when the applicant gives correct answers to the agent, who fills in the application with false statements, and then the insurer collects premiums on such a contract, the insurer cannot use the incorrect answers as a defense. *National Aid Life Association* v. *Clinton*, 176 Okl. 372, 55 P [2d] 781. See also *Atlas Life Insurance Company* v. *Chastin*, 12 CCH Life Cases 5.

[5] Through the activities of committees of the National Association of Insurance Commissioners, as well as the work of such groups as the Committee on Insurance Law of the American Bar Association, most of the important laws governing the business of life insurance are to be found in the statutes of all jurisdictions.

The contract and payment of premiums

Taken together, (1) the face of the policy with the insuring clause, (2) the application, and (3) the subsequent pages containing options, privileges, extensions, or limitations constitute the complete contract of life insurance.

Since premium payments are of vital importance to the validity of life insurance, the policy carefully states how and when premiums are payable. Policies require the payment of the first premium in advance, while the applicant is in good health. Premiums after the first are also payable in advance. Ordinary insurance premiums are computed on an annual basis, though they may be paid semiannually, quarterly, or monthly. Many policies will for comparative purposes include in the contract the premium amount if it is paid on these various bases.

The first premium paid satisfies the requirement for a consideration essential to the validity of the contract and makes the insurance effective. There is no obligation by the insured to pay subsequent premiums, but the payment of such premiums is a condition before the insurer must fulfill its part of the contract.

Premiums are required to be paid either at the home office of the insurer or to an agent authorized to receive payment. The scope of an ordinary agent's authority will extend to the collection of the first premium, but the authority of the delivering agent to collect extends no further. (Industrial insurance is an obvious exception.)

Life insurers allow a *grace period* following the due date of a premium during which the insurance remains in force. The grace period is now usually expressed in days, and 31 days are most often allowed. If the insurance policy becomes payable by the death of the insured during the period of grace, any overdue premiums are deducted from the amount payable. If the premium is not paid before the end of the grace period, the policy becomes void, unless the automatic premium loan provision (see later section) applies.

The beneficiary

The *beneficiary* is the person or interest designated in the contract to receive the proceeds. Oftentimes this is simply done by naming the beneficiary on the face of the policy. If the designation is a complicated one, or if a change is made after the policy is first written, a beneficiary clause may be used, attached in the form of a rider or endorsement to the contract. There are many variations in the beneficiary clause. The final form depends upon the objective of the insured. While the life insurance agent will cooperate and advise, in the end the arrangement of beneficiary designations is the responsibility of the applicant. A beneficiary may be *(a)* primary or *(b)* contingent. The *primary* beneficiary is the beneficiary that is first entitled to the benefits of the policy following the death of the insured. A *contingent* beneficiary is entitled to the benefits only after the death of the primary beneficiary and is often included in contracts.

Designation of beneficiary. The beneficiary designation is, in effect, a will making disposition of life values. An advantage of life insurance is that the funds are paid quickly, without having to go through the legal probate of a will. The owner should give it as careful consideration as is given to the disposition of physical property by will. The designation is crucial in determining who will collect the money promised in the life insurance contract.

The beneficiary may be designated as *(a)* the *insured or his or her estate, (b)* a *specifically named person* or persons, *(c)* a *class* or classes of persons, *(d)* a *business or other organization,* and *(e)* a *trustee.* Because each has its advantages, the form used is important. A careless or thoughtless selection may defeat the whole objective of the insurance.

If a policy is made payable to the *insured or* his or her *estate,* the proceeds of the policy are subject to the claims of creditors upon the death of the insured. If no beneficiary is sufficiently designated, the policy becomes payable to the estate of the insured. If the estate is designated as beneficiary, the distribution of the insurance may be made by the insured's will or if there is no will, in accordance with the inheritance laws of the state.

Most beneficiary designations indicate *specifically named person or persons.* Usually these persons are wives, husbands, children, or other relatives of the insured. Wives are named in about 50 percent of the number of ordinary life policies, children in 20 percent, husbands in 10 percent, other relatives in 10 percent, and estates, trusts, and others in 10 percent.[6] When a wife is designated a beneficiary without indicating her name, in the case of the death of the first wife, a second wife succeeds as beneficiary. In order to avoid any possible question, it is customary not only to designate the relationship as wife but also to state her name. The insurer in making payment is under no obligation to investigate the validity of the marriage.

When "children" are designated as *class beneficiaries* and when it is apparently the intent of the insured, the term *children* will extend to include an adopted child. An insurance policy made payable to children includes all children, whether by the wife designated as beneficiary or by a former wife. If it is intended that only the children by the wife designated as beneficiary shall participate, the words "our children" or "children born of this marriage" should be used. Most companies limit

OR ADOPTED

---

[6] *Life Insurance Fact Book* (Washington, D.C.: American Council of Life Insurance, 1982), p. 42.

the use of class designations and permit only a few types. Carelessly worded clauses create a strong possibility that certain individuals may unintentionally be excluded or included.

A *business organization* such as a partnership or a corporation may be named as a beneficiary. The settlement options may be limited in such cases, for obviously a life income provision is impossible for a corporate beneficiary. A *trustee* may be designated as a beneficiary, when discretionary power is desired in the distribution of the insurance proceeds.

Change of beneficiary. With reference to the beneficiary, life insurance policies are written under two forms. Under the first, the beneficiary is named without right of change on the part of the insured, and the insurance designation in such cases is said to be *irrevocable*. A second method of designating the beneficiary (used by all but a few percent of the contracts) retains the right of change for the insured. Here the beneficiary is said to be *revocable.*

If the right to change the designation of beneficiary is reserved, the interest of the beneficiary is limited to an expectancy during the lifetime of the insured. The revocable beneficiary has no right to the proceeds until the death of the insured. The irrevocable beneficiary has a fixed or vested right in the contract.[7]

If the insured wishes to have flexible use of the policy and wishes to be under no obligation to secure the consent of a beneficiary, the revocable form is the proper form to use. The policy amount is then included in the insured's estate for federal estate tax purposes but is not subject to income tax. This is the usual situation.

Policies as written now usually provide that if the beneficiary dies before the insured, even if the beneficiary is originally designed as irrevocable, the insured may proceed to name a new beneficiary.

Most policies provide a simple procedure for effecting a change. The beneficiary may be changed as often as desired by *filing a written request* for endorsement accompanied by the policy at the home office of the insurer. Upon endorsement on the policy the change becomes effective as of the date of the request.

Ownership of policy and changes

Some policies indicate a life owner. A policy naming a life owner offers the applicant the option of retaining control of the policy or of placing

---

[7] This represents the general rule, but it is an oversimplification of the situation. A revocable beneficiary may have a vested interest if the beneficiary acquires an equitable interest. Such an interest may follow from (a) a contract or (b) a gift. Equitable interest, for example, may arise between partners who agree to maintain policies each for the benefit of the other (*Smith* v. *Schoelkopf*, 68 S.W. [2d] 346). Completed gifts of policies have been upheld in the courts against beneficiaries named after the time of the gift (*McEwen* v. *New York Life Insurance Company*, 183 Pac. 373; 42 Cal. App. 133).

this control with another. A clause is used providing that during the lifetime of the insured the right to receive all cash values, loans, and other benefits accruing under the policy and the rights to exercise all options, changes, or amendments to the policy shall vest in the life owner alone. Ownership may usually be changed by following a procedure stated in the policy. Such a change is the best way to make a gift of a policy, divesting the owner of all "incidents of ownership" in order to exclude the policy values from the estate of the owner.

Assignment

A life policy may be freely assigned, and the consent of the insurer is not required. Thus the contract rights may be transferred to others in a sale, gift, or loan. It is usually provided under the terms of the policy, however, that no assignment shall be effective until the insurer has been notified in writing. The assignment relieves the company of any responsibility arising out of the assignment before the receipt of written notice.

It is not required that the assignee have an insurable interest in the life of the insured, though it is essential that the policy be so written at its inception that it is not invalidated for want of an insurable interest. A valid life insurance policy is assignable like any personal property. The U.S. Supreme Court has specifically stated that to deny the right to assign a life insurance policy or to restrict it to a person having an insurable interest, is to diminish the value of the contract appreciably. However, transferring a policy to an assignee without an insurable interest, with the intent of providing a wager contract, has been held to be objectionable by the courts.

An assignment is to be distinguished from a change in the designated beneficiary. The power to change the beneficiary is a contractual power to appoint.[8] The right of assignment grows out of the nature of life insurance as property.[9] Depending on the purpose for which it is made, an assignment may take one of two forms: *(a)* conditional or *(b)* absolute.

The *conditional* assignment, sometimes known as a "collateral assignment," is used in connection with loans or other forms of indebtedness when a policy is used to provide security. Such assignments may be fixed at an amount sufficient to liquidate the indebtedness. They may also cover the extent of the creditor's interest and follow the amount of the debt as it increases or decreases. As a result of cooperation between the American Bankers Association and life insurance interests, a standard form has been devised. The form, known as the "ABA Form," is

---

[8] *Mutual Benefit Life Insurance Company* v. *Swett,* 222 Fed. 200.

[9] *City National Bank* v. *Lewis,* 74 Okla. 1; 76 Pac. 237.

widely used and has introduced equity and uniformity in setting forth the rights reserved and transferred by the assignment.

An *absolute* assignment conveys to the assignee all right, title, and interest that the insured or policyholder may hold. The assignee is placed in the position of the original assignor and has the right to exercise all the powers and privileges of the contract.

After the death of the insured, the interests of the beneficiary can be assigned without the consent of the insurer and without regard to the conditions in the assignment clause of the policy.

Dividends and dividend options

The importance of the dividends available to many life insurance policyholders is obvious from the fact that about two thirds of life insurance is written on a *participating* basis. Dividends often reduce the original purchase price of a life insurance contract by as much as 20 percent or more over the life of the policy. The original cost is usually higher, but the use of dividends provides the *chance* of lowering "net cost" if the insurer does well.

Participating and nonparticipating policies.   Not only mutual insurers issue policyholder dividends, but many stock companies also give their insureds a choice between purchasing participating and nonparticipating contracts. The policies are alike in their essentials. The difference lies in the fact that the excess earnings of a participating contract are returned to the insured, whereas the earnings of a nonparticipating contract are retained by the insurer as profit for distribution to the stockholders.

Participating policies make provision for the distribution of dividends. The dividends represent a return of a part of the premium collected after *mortality* losses, *interest* earnings, and *expenses* have been determined. Dividends are distributed annually and are payable after the policy has been in force for a given period, usually one or two years.

Dividend options.   Policies provide several options with reference to the use of dividends. The options are not the same in all policies, but they follow a general pattern. They may provide for (1) cash; (2) reduction of the current premium; (3) paid-up additional whole life insurance, increasing the face of the policy; (4) accumulated deposits with the insurer, at a current rate of interest of 5 percent or more; and in many policies, or (5) additional one-year term insurance amounts (the so-called fifth-dividend option).   *PEP Policy with expanded protection*

The amount of additional insurance that dividends will buy (in options 3 and 5) depends upon the attained age of the insured and upon the size of the dividends. Possible advantages of the paid-up option are that purchases do not require that commissions be paid, and that the increased coverage may automatically increase coverage to meet inflation needs. Some policies also provide for conversion of the basic policy to a paid-up basis, or for maturing the policy as an endowment, at the request of the policyholder, if the accumulated dividends and the policy reserve are sufficient to do so. The accumulation of the normal dividends currently issued by most insurers will permit many policies to become paid up after about 25 years.

Policyholders may withdraw dividend accumulations at any time to take the cash value of any paid-up dividend additions that their policies have purchased. The initial choice on the way in which dividends are to be used is made on the policy application form. Many insurers permit a change from one option to another, although a change to the additional insurance options may require a medical examination to determine insurability.

There is no one "best" answer on how to use your dividends. Much depends on the various needs of policyholders for cash (or reduced premiums) as opposed to their health condition, tax bracket, and their need for additional insurance protection. However, a careful comparison of the aftertax benefits of using the different options is recommended before choices are made.[10]

In recent years life insurance policyholders have used dividend options involving approximately $8 billion annually, as shown in Table 7–1.

Table 7–1. Use of various methods of dividend options

Type of option	Percent of total dividend dollars
1. Cash	18
2. Reduction of premiums	18
3. Purchase of additional life insurance protection (whole life or term)	38
4. Left as deposit at interest	26
Total	100

Source: *Life Insurance Fact Book* (Washington, D.C.: American Council of Life Insurance, 1982), p. 43.

Policy form changes

Prior to an indicated age, usually 55 years, the insured may exchange his or her policy without medical examination for any *higher* premium-paying permanent policy issued by the insurer. This may be advantageous if there has been a change in the policyholder's needs or ability to pay premiums.

---

[10] Donald R. Dann and Herbert J. Davis, "Dividend Selection—Art or Science?" *CLU Journal,* April 1981, p. 22.

To make an exchange to a higher premium plan, the insured is required to surrender the policy for rewriting and to pay the difference between the premiums on the new policy and premiums on the policy being surrendered, together with accumulated interest. Premiums would be as required for the original age of the insured. A change of this character betters the position of the insurer in that the reserve on the policy is increased and the amount at risk accordingly lessened. Thus, no medical examination or other evidence of insurability is required.

Other policy changes may be made by mutual consent of the insurer and the policyholder. If a change is made from a higher to a *lower* premium form, not only are future premium payments lessened, but frequently the insurer is required to make a cash payment representing the reduction in the cash value and thereby increasing the actual amount at risk. The policyholder has no contractual right to insist on such a change. Before approving the change, the insurer will require the insured to furnish satisfactory evidence of insurability. The evidence required may be a full or short-form medical examination, or the change may be granted on the basis of a current statement by the insured.

Lapse and reinstatement

Insurance companies are ordinarily willing to revive most policies lapsed for nonpayment of premium. The *reinstatement clause* usually stipulates in the contract that unless the policy has been surrendered for cash, it may be reinstated at any time within *five years* after default. Some policies specify three years.

Payment of premium and of all overdue premiums, with interest, is required. Evidence of insurability satisfactory to the insurer must be submitted at the time the request for reinstatement is made. The older clauses required evidence of "good health," and the change of terminology to "insurability" indicates a requirement somewhat broader than evidence of good health. For example, a criminal condemned to death might be in perfectly good health yet be determined to be uninsurable.[11]

Misstatement of age

Since the annual premium on a policy written with a level premium is based upon the attained age at the inception of the policy, applicants have sometimes deliberately misstated their age. In other instances, the misstatement has been the outgrowth of a mistake.

Life policies contain a special *misstatement-of-age* clause that is equita-

---

[11] *Kallman* v. *Equitable Life Assurance Society,* 248 App. Div. 146; 288 N.Y.S. 1032; 272 N.Y. 648; 5 N.E. [2d] 375.

ble to both the insured and the insurer. The clause provides that, if the age of the insured has been misstated, the amount payable under the policy shall be such as the premium paid would have purchased at the correct age. This is determined by the application of simple proportion. If an applicant states his or her age to be such that the premium for $1,000 insurance at that age is $20 and at the time of the insured's death it turns out that the correct premium should have been $25, the amount of proceeds payable (x) is determined as follows:

$$\$25 : \$20 = \$1,000 : x$$
$$\text{Hence, } \$25x = \$20,000$$
$$x = \$800$$

Since age misrepresentation is covered by a special clause, it cannot fall within the scope of the incontestable clause. Age discrepancies are most frequently discovered when proofs of death are being filed. Regardless of the time of discovery, the amount due under the policy is adjusted to coincide with the amount that the premium would have purchased had the age been correctly stated. If the applicant's age is uncertain or if verification may be difficult, arrangements may be made with the insurer when the policy is issued to accept the age given in the application. The insurer is said to "admit" the age and by so doing agrees not to raise the question at the time of settlement.[12] If any difficulties in proving age are anticipated, it is logical for the insured to do this, for after his or her death the beneficiary may have considerable difficulty in locating the necessary proof.

Suicide

In some of the older policies, suicide claims were paid only when the suicide was the result of insanity, but the dividing line between a sane and an insane suicide was extremely difficult to establish. Also, from a social point of view, the dependents of a suicide, sane or insane, are in as great need of the proceeds of life insurance as they would be if the insured had died as the result of an accident or illness.

Suicide today does not have any effect upon the life insurance proceeds except that the policy provides that it shall be in effect for a designated period of time before the full policy benefits become payable. The purpose is thus twofold: (1) to provide payment, regardless of suicide, after the

---

[12] An insured may take steps to do this at any time. Sometimes buildings containing public records are destroyed by fire or the records are otherwise lost. The following sources are listed in the order of preference: (a) a certificate of birth, (b) a certificate of baptism, (c) a legally certified copy of the entire page of the family Bible, (d) a school record, (e) a confirmation record, (f) a certificate of marriage, (g) a naturalization record, (h) a passport, and (i) an Army or Navy discharge paper. If none of the foregoing is available, other available evidence should be submitted.

stated period; and (2) to limit the payments for suicide within the stated period. The second purpose discourages premeditated suicide by an insured in order to have life insurance benefits paid. A typical *suicide clause* is: "In the event of suicide of the insured, while sane or insane, within two years from the Date of Issue of this policy, the insurance under this policy will be a sum equal to the premiums paid to the Company."

Sometimes the stated period is one year, but the effect is the same—return of premiums is made rather than payment of the full face value.

Indebtedness and settlement

These provisions simply state that any indebtedness and *policy loans* outstanding to the insurer will be deducted from the face value or other benefits when the insurer makes a settlement with the insured. *Settlement* includes payments (1) when a policy has become payable due to the death of the insured, (2) when an endowment has reached its maturity date, or (3) when a policy has been surrendered for cash value. The policy is given to the insurer in exchange for the settlement. Policyholders should always remember when taking a policy loan that they are reducing the amount which will be paid to beneficiaries (unless the loan is repaid prior to death).

Incontestability   *Beadles   190   Start 10-5-87*

After the death of the insured, which may occur many years after the policy was issued, it may not be easy for a beneficiary to justify statements made by the insured when the policy was issued. For this reason, a denial of liability by the insurer on the grounds of fraud could complicate and delay settlements and possibly deprive a beneficiary of payment.

To put an end to the possibility of involving the beneficiary in expensive litigation in life insurance settlements, life insurance contracts provide that the policy shall be *incontestable* after a certain designated period. The incontestable clause is a statutory requirement. *Two years* is the period more frequently used, though some policies are incontestable after one year.

Courts have usually held that *if* a stated period has been reserved in the policy within which the contract may be contested, fraud must be discovered within that time. A policy procured through fraud is not void but is voidable at the option of the insurer. Under the incontestable clause, the insurer is held to have abandoned voluntarily after one or two years its option to contest the contract.

To become incontestable, the period must elapse during the lifetime of the insured. If the insured dies during this period, the policy is always contestable. The clause protects both insureds and beneficiaries because after the period has expired technical defenses may not be advanced as a ground for denying payment. If the insurer has a defense, it must present that defense within a reasonable time, presumably when the insured is still alive and can answer it.[13]

Some policies exclude accidental death benefits (see later section of this chapter) from the incontestable clause. Thus the insurer may still contest the extra benefits for accidental death, even after the stated one- or two-year period. Life insurance policies that have been reinstated (see earlier section) may be contested during a new one- or two-year period, usually only on the basis of false statements made in the reinstatement application.[14]

CASH, LOAN, AND NONFORFEITURE BENEFITS

Among the most important provisions in a life insurance contract are those which state the rights that the policyholder has in case the premiums are not paid. The insured does not lose the values accrued in the contract. The statutory standard provisions require that *nonforfeiture benefits* be provided for in the policy. Thus the policyholder whose premiums are not paid does not forfeit all of his or her benefits but may exercise certain options at the time the contract is surrendered to the insurer: (1) *cash values*, (2) *extended term insurance*, and (3) *paid-up insurance*. Also, *loan values* are available, even without surrendering the policy.

Cash values

The amount of cash available to a policyholder on the surrender of the policy is called its *cash value*. Insureds who surrender their policies cannot receive back the full amount of the premiums they have paid in. During the years that their insurance has been in force, there has been deducted from their premium payments the cost of paying the claims of insureds whose policies matured. They have also contributed their share to the cost of the insurer's operations.

Some cash values are usually available after the first year of a permanent-type life insurance contract. In the early years of the policy the cash values are small, but as the policy becomes older, they increase more rapidly. A table of the cash values at the end of various years is

---

[13] Some companies have modified the clause: "This policy shall be incontestable after one year from its date of issue unless the insured dies in such year, in which event it shall be incontestable after two years from its date of issue."

[14] Greider and Beadles, *Law and the Life Insurance Contract,* p. 478.

included in the contract so that the insured will know the values at
any point if the policy is discontinued. The cash value forms the basis
for the determination of all the nonforfeiture values. Each is the mathematical equivalent of the other. Table 7–3 in the summary at the end
of this section provides a comparison of the cash, loan, and other nonforfeiture benefits available in a typical contract.

Policy loans

Under insurance contracts with cash values, the insured may borrow
from the insurer at a specified rate of interest. The table of cash values
also shows the *loan value.* From it the insured may learn the amount
which may be borrowed from year to year. (See examples in Table 7–
3.)

Policies do not have a loan value until a sufficient period of time has
elapsed to permit the building up of an appreciable policy value. Most
contracts have a loan value after premiums for two full years have been
paid, although many policies have some cash and loan values after one
year.

The interest rate is provided in the policy. A rate of 8 percent is usual
today, although 5 percent will be found in some older policies and 6
percent in some other policies. Some states now permit a flexible loan
rate, varying with current market interest rates, to be used in new contracts. The interest charge is added to the premium payments after the
loan has been made or is sometimes paid in advance when the loan is
made.

The loan does not have to be repaid by the insured but will be deducted
from the policy proceeds when they are paid to the beneficiary. In this
respect, the policy loan is unlike most other loans which require periodic
repayment or renewal. Failure to repay the loan or to pay interest does
not void the policy unless the total indebtedness, including accrued interests, equals or exceeds the cash value of the policy.

The policy-loan feature of permanent life insurance contracts has become a very valuable right in the current state of our high interest
economy. The specified interest rate in the contract cannot be changed
by the insurer. Many insureds fail to recognize that they have built up
these loan values gradually and now are entitled to loans of perhaps
several thousand dollars at the very favorable annual interest rates of
5 to 8 percent. With mortgage and automobile loans at 15 percent or
more, and personal loans at 20 percent or more, the right is indeed
one which should be considered when necessary. That some persons are
using this benefit is apparent from the growth of policy loans during
the 15-year period shown in Table 7–2.

The growth of policy loans is of some concern to insurers. To accommo-

Table 7–2. Growth of policy loans, 1965–1982

	At beginning of			
	1965	1970	1975	1982
Dollars (in billions) of policy loans held as assets by U.S. life insurers	$5.2	$16.1	$24.5	$48.7
Policy loans as a percentage of all assets of U.S. life insurers	4.4	7.8	8.5	9.3

Source: *Life Insurance Fact Book* (Washington, D.C.: American Council of Life Insurance, 1982), p. 68.

date immediate loans, usually only a few days, insurers must maintain more liquid investments and also forgo other investments with greater returns. Tight money markets, with general interest rates on other loans at a high level, will encourage more policy loans. During the 17 years prior to 1982, loans by life insurers to policyholders increased from $5 to almost $50 billion, and loans as a percentage of assets more than doubled. The figures for some specific individual insurers are alarmingly higher. One partial solution to the policy-loan problem is to use variable interest rates based on current bond index yields. Another possible solution suggested is to link dividends paid on policies, paying smaller dividends on contracts with loans outstanding.[15]

Automatic premium loan option

With the *automatic premium loan* provision, overdue premiums (beyond the grace period) are treated as a loan. The policy remains in force for its full amount until the total loans, plus interest against the policy, equal the cash surrender value. Not all policies contain this feature, but it is generally available on request without any additional charge in the premium until the option is used.

This feature is generally a desirable one for the insured to choose when application for the insurance is made. Usually all that is needed is for the applicant to check a box in the application which indicates that this feature is to be included. It prevents unintentional or unavoidable lapsing of the contract should the premiums not be paid during the stated grace period.

Extended term insurance

The *extended term* insurance option provides continued life insurance protection, after premium payments have been stopped, for the *full face*

---

[15] Michael L. Smith, "Linking Dividends to Policy-Loan Usage: A Solution to the Policy-Loan Problem?" *Best's Review*, December 1981, p. 18.

amount of the policy less any existing indebtedness. It will provide, for such a time as the net cash value of the policy will purchase (with a single-premium payment), term insurance at the attained age of the insured. See Table 7–3 for examples of the number of years for which protection is provided under this option.

Usually, extended term insurance goes into effect upon lapse *automatically if no other option is selected*. The special mortality table to be used because mortality is higher than usual and the rate of interest for the computations is stated in the policy for this option and the one following. This option provides the maximum amount of continued protection for the insured.

Reduced paid-up insurance

If insureds elect to have their insurance continue in force for life or to the end of an endowment period, they may use their cash value for that purpose. In a whole life, a *reduced amount* of insurance is continued and paid to the designated beneficiary upon the death of the insured. In an endowment form, protection in the reduced amount is continued to the maturity date of the original policy, and then the insured receives the reduced amount in cash.

The distinction between the extended term insurance option and the reduced paid-up insurance option should be clear. In extended term insurance, the face value of the contract is continued in force but the protection is temporary. In reduced paid-up insurance, the protection is permanent but the amount is for a reduced face value policy. See Table 7–3 for examples of the reduced paid-up insurance amounts provided by this option.

The delay clause

Life insurance policies written today usually provide that the insurer may defer the payment of surrender or loan values for a definite period,

Table 7–3. Cash, loan, and other nonforfeiture values
(for each $1,000 of face value in the contract)

Years the policy has been in effect	Cash, or loan, value	Extended term insurance (years)*	Reduced paid-up insurance
5	$ 68	13	$164
10	172	19	369
15	269	20	514
20	372	19	639
30 (age 65)	550	16	786

* Rounded to full years.
Source: Sample life insurance policy, American Council of Life Insurance, 1980.

usually six months. The clause affords the insurer protection against a "run" and is virtually identical with the protection afforded mutual savings banks by state legislation. Neither type of institution, except in the face of a drastic run, would ever need the delay privilege. It has rarely been used by insurers.

Summary of cash, loan, and nonforfeiture benefits

The major choices that an insured has if the life insurance contract is lapsed (not continued) are three: (1) the *cash value,* (2) the *extended term insurance option,* or (3) the *reduced paid-up insurance option.* All of these options are based upon the cash values indicated in the contract by a table similar to Table 7–3. The *loan* option is also directly related to the cash values, but when the policyholder chooses to borrow against the cash values, the life insurance contract is *not* surrendered to the to the insurer but continues in force. (Technically, this is not one of the nonforfeiture values but is closely related to them.) Interest is paid on the loan, and if the loan is not repaid before the policy matures, it is subtracted from the policy payment. The best choice for the policyholder depends upon a careful appraisal of his or her age, health status, and need for the continued protection of the contract. If cash is needed, a policy loan would probably be the first choice, or perhaps canceling the contract and taking the cash value. If insurance is still needed, the choices are to take a loan and leave the policy in effect, or to cancel the policy and take the extended term insurance (for the full face value) or the reduced paid-up amount for a specified time period. Table 7–3 is a typical table of *guaranteed* nonforfeiture values for a whole life policy *issued at age 35.*

OPTIONAL METHODS OF SETTLEMENT

The values that accumulate or mature in life insurance contracts are called *proceeds* when they are paid out. Of all life insurance proceeds (death, matured endowments, and surrender value payments), about 5 percent are used each year to purchase *supplementary contracts* from insurers.[16] The proceeds are exchanged for a new contract with the insurer which provides regular income or interest payments to the owner. The available alternatives to taking the proceeds as a lump sum are also called *optional methods of settlement* or *settlement options or modes.* Approximately $10 billion of accumulated policy proceeds have been left with life insurers and are now set aside under these supplementary contracts.

---

[16] *Life Insurance Fact Book,* p. 46.

If a policy has proceeds available in the amount of $1,000 or more, insurance contracts usually have options giving the insured the right to have the insurance made payable in installments.[17] During his or her lifetime, the insured may elect to have the proceeds of the insurance paid under one of the optional plans instead of as a lump sum. However, usually the beneficiary makes this choice among the settlement options after the insured has died.

Types OF OPTIONAL METHODS OF SETTLEMENT

Four basic plans have developed from which are derived the clauses of the life insurance policy providing optional modes of settlement.[18] The specific wording in the contracts and the company practices do vary, however. The basic plans are: (1) specified amount installments, (2) specified period installments, (3) life income payments, and (4) interest payments. Examples of the use of these benefits are included in Chapter 12, where life insurance programming and estate planning are discussed.

Specified amount installments. Under this plan, periodic installments are paid to the beneficiary in *amounts specified* in the election, as long as the proceeds last. The policy benefits are distributed periodically to the beneficiary in a fixed amount until the principal and interest are exhausted. The guaranteed minimum interest rate is usually 3.5 percent or more, and additional amounts may be paid by many insurers if interest earnings justify a higher rate.

Specific period of installments. Under this option specified installments are paid to the beneficiary for a *specified number of years.* Payment is made in periodic installments for the number of years elected. Installments are increased by participation in excess interest earned by the insurer over the guaranteed rate. The payments are in such an amount that the proceeds of the insurance, together with interest, are entirely distributed over a stated period. This becomes a useful option in planning life insurance programs when the time for which an income is needed is definitely established. For example, $10,000 of proceeds will provide about $100 a month for 10 years, or $60 a month for 20 years.

Life income payments. Instead of receiving a fixed amount (or being paid for a fixed period) so long as the money lasts, the beneficiary may receive installments under a *life income option.* The objective is the distribution of income for the entire lifetime of the beneficiary. This gives beneficiaries protection against outliving their financial resources.

---

[17] Because of the expense factor, many policies restrict the right of the insured to ask for installments of less than $10 a payment.

[18] Newer policies sometimes make available as many as seven options—dividing the life income option into several types. The insurers offering these options on their newer policies ordinarily permit the same choices under all older policies.

The option is made available in the following forms: (1) the life annuity, (2) the refund annuity, (3) life income with period certain, and (4) joint and survival life income.

The *life annuity* pays installments only while the beneficiary lives, and no return of principal is guaranteed. The *refund annuity* provides for the payment of installments so long as the beneficiary lives. If the beneficiary dies before the sum of the installments received equals the principal sum of the insurance, the difference will be paid in a lump sum or installments to another beneficiary. The *life income with a period certain* pays annuity installments so long as the beneficiary lives. If the beneficiary dies before all of the certain payments have been received, the installments are continued to another beneficiary for the balance of the certain period (or the remaining payments are paid in a lump sum). In the *joint and survivorship life income* option, installments are not only payable over the life of one person but may be continued over the remaining lifetime of a second person. This option appeals to married couples with the idea that payments will continue during the lifetimes of both.

Annuity payments may be made annually, semiannually, quarterly, or monthly. If an annuity option is selected, it is not required that the entire proceeds of the insurance be used for that purpose, nor the beneficiary limited to the use of a single option. Annuity plans may be combined with other optional methods of settlement to the end of working out a tailor-made settlement plan that fits the requirements of any beneficiary.

Interest payments. Under this plan, the proceeds of the insurance are left with the insurer. A guaranteed rate of *interest* (3 percent or more) is paid to the beneficiaries, plus any excess interest earned under participating contracts. The interest is payable periodically during the lifetime of the payee, usually from the date of the insured to death. This option is like leaving the funds in a savings bank account, and the interest received is taxable in both cases.

The person entitled to the proceeds of the insurance may, therefore, leave the money on deposit with the life insurer, at interest, until it is needed. If that person dies, then the face value or other proceeds of the policy (accumulated dividends, for example, less any loans outstanding) become payable to the designated beneficiary of the payee. Oftentimes this option is named as automatic as of the date of the insured's death, pending later choice of another settlement option. This assures immediate interest earnings on the principal. The primary beneficiary is often given flexibility to meet emergencies or changing needs by being granted limited or full *rights of withdrawal* of part or all of the proceeds. For example, a limited withdrawal right might be specified as "up to $5,000 per year."

Uses

The optional methods of settlement are available whether the proceeds are payable as a death claim, or upon maturity as an endowment, or upon surrender on the policy for its cash value.[19] Settlement options assume an important place in determining the type and amount of insurance to be purchased when the insurance program is being set up and correlated with social security benefits.

If substantial amounts of life insurance proceeds are payable beyond the immediate need for lump-sum amounts, settlement options can serve a real purpose in providing for *systematic liquidation* of capital. The breadwinner of a family, for example, may urge (or partially require) that the beneficiary choose some form of installment or life income payments in order to assure continued income to the family. Not all of the proceeds have to be committed to settlement options, but in some cases it is logical to use part of the total available as a basis for future income. If this procedure is followed, then the beneficiary can, for example, supplement the guaranteed income from the settlement options with higher yielding investments of other types.

The *life income option* is one of the most important benefits of a life insurance contract, for no other investment can assure an income for a period which will exactly equal an uncertain lifetime. Any other investment asset must either use its income only or use up some principal as well; and then one cannot know whether the principal will be used up before life ends. A life income option chosen by a female at age 65, with 10 years certain, will pay the beneficiary about $6 per month for each $1,000 of life insurance.

Valuable rights to life income may exist in many older life insurance contracts, for these benefits may have been calculated on the older mortality tables, which assume higher death rates than actually exist today. The life income options available under such older contracts may be favorable choices for the insured or the beneficiary.

DISABILITY AND ACCIDENTAL DEATH BENEFIT EXTENSIONS OF COVERAGE

Three major types of health insurance benefits are included in many life insurance contracts. The most common are (1) the *waiver-of-premium* benefit for total and permanent disability and (2) the *accidental death* benefit. The third type, *disability income,* is less frequently included.

---

[19] Death claims do require proof of death from a physician. Don't try to collect, as one woman recently did, by merely having her name printed in the obituary column of a newspaper! *Equifax Journal,* January 1982, p. 15.

It is, however, a very important and much-needed coverage, and recent years have brought added attention to this optional feature of many life insurance policies.

The waiver-of-premium benefit

Under the terms of the waiver-of-premium benefit, if the insured becomes totally and permanently disabled by bodily injuries or disease (not self-inflicted or occurring before the insurance took effect), the payment of subsequent premiums is waived by the insurer. Virtually all insurers today write the waiver-of-premium coverage with many policies.

For the insured to qualify for the waiver-of-premium benefit, the usual policy requires that the disability: (1) be permanent, (2) be total, and (3) commence before a stated age.

Permanent disability is presumed after the insured has been totally disabled *continuously* for a period of at least *six months*. Later recovery may be evidence that the disability did not continue as a permanent handicap. Premium payments due during the period of disability for the rest of the insured's life are waived.

Total disability is usually defined during the first two years of disability, as "the occupation of the insured at the time such disability began." Thereafter, it is inability to perform activities "in any occupation for which the insured is reasonably fitted by education, training, or experience." The courts have given reasonable and not strict interpretation to these phrases. The irrecoverable loss of the entire sight of both eyes or the total and permanent loss of use of both hands, of both feet, or of one hand and one foot are automatically considered to be total disability. Many other disabilities may be shown to be total in their effect.

Total and permanent disability must commence before the anniversary date of the policy nearest the *60th* birthday. This requirement is necessary because nearly everyone would become disabled and eligible for these benefits at some point in old age were an age limit not specified. Some contracts provide limited waiver benefits (to age 65, or for two years) if a disability occurs between age 60 and age 65.

The benefits and values—such as the sum insured, the loan and cash surrender values, and in the case of participating policies, the dividends—all remain the same as if the premiums had actually been paid in cash. Under the waiver-of-premium provision, the insurer in effect pays premiums due from the insured during the period of total disability. Indirectly the benefit represents a payment to the disabled insured.

It is an important benefit to add to most life insurance contracts, for it enables the protection to be maintained at a time when it is perhaps most needed. It is, in essence, "insurance for continued insurance." A lengthy disability often reduces one's income substantially, to a point where life insurance premiums could not be paid otherwise. The cost is relatively small, usually under $0.50 per $1,000 when added to the policy before age 35.

Accidental death benefits

A popular feature of life insurance is the provision for the payment of additional benefits in the event of *accidental death.* Not all accidental deaths are covered by this clause, which supplies a seemingly endless variety of plots for television dramas. The extra amount payable is usually double the face value of the policy (thus the common term *double indemnity*), but it may be triple or more.

Specifically, the accidental death benefit is payable in the usual policy if death occurs *"before* the anniversary date of the policy following the insured's *70th* birthday; *directly and independently* of all other causes, as a result of *accidental bodily injuries,* and occurs within 90 days from the date of such accident."[20] *Excluded risks* usually listed are death from *suicide* while sane or insane; or resulting from *war;* or resulting directly or indirectly from *disease* in any form; or occurring while *outside the Earth's atmosphere,* or in any kind of *aircraft or spacecraft except as a passenger* (thus most aviation deaths are covered).

On the basis of the needs of the beneficiary, it is hard to justify a greater payment if insureds die as the result of an accident than if they die of disease or other natural death. In fact, the cost of a sudden death may actually be less than that of a lingering one with extensive medical costs.

The accidental death benefit appeals particularly to individuals who feel their insurance program to be inadequate, or to those who feel a need for high-limit accident protection. There may be some justification for some extra coverage on the basis that accidental deaths occur suddenly, when insureds are less likely to have provided adequately for their families. The premium is comparatively small, often under $1 per $1,000, on whole life policies begun before age 45. Thus, the insured may, for a relatively small additional premium, get extra protection in the event of accidental death. Life agents often point out that under the age of 40 accidents are the cause of death in more than 50 percent of the cases. Because people are becoming more and more accident-conscious, the accidental death feature of life insurance has a wide appeal.

This coverage affords an extra insurance protection *only* on a limited basis. When considering the benefits for accidental death as a part of a life insurance program, one should remember (1) that cause of death

---

[20] Many variations in the wording, exceptions, and age limits (65 was common for many years) of the accidental death benefit clause are used by different companies.

usually has nothing to do with the needs of dependents, and (2) that the accidental death provision oftentimes gives a false sense of security. Persons may feel that they have, for example, $100,000 face value of life insurance in force whereas (except in the case of death caused by accident) they have only $50,000. There is no objection to including the coverage so long as its extent and nature are understood. Of the total death benefits of about $14 billion paid by U.S. life insurers last year, it is estimated that less than 2.2 percent were extra payments for accidental death.[21]

The accidental death benefit is not included in the paid-up or extended term insurance provision of the life insurance policy in the event of premium default. The coverage may be discontinued upon the written request of the insured, and the extra premium charge discontinued.

Double indemnity for accidental death, like waiver-of-premium coverage, is widely written. Health and occupational hazards are determining factors in both disability and double indemnity coverages. For example, persons in certain occupations are in every sense acceptable for life insurance at standard rates, but the accidental death rate is considerably higher than normal. In this group are to be found farmers, carpenters, machinists, and many others. Then there are persons suffering from a medical impairment who may be accepted for life insurance, but whose defect may make an accident more likely. If there is a loss of vision in one eye or an amputation that does not seriously handicap the applicant, then accidental death benefits may be written at an advance in premium. Insurers tend to reject risks when the hazard is unusual, as in violent sports. Foreign travel is not now regarded as an increased hazard but may make investigation of the claim difficult or expensive.

Total disability income benefits

Some policies provide for monthly *disability income* payable in case of *total and permanent disability*. The types of disability coverage vary widely. There has been a tendency at times to restrict the scope of disability coverage under life insurance policies, and some insurers do not write this form of coverage.[22]

---

[21] *Life Insurance Fact Book*, p. 40. On page 95 the deaths by natural causes are shown as 92.3 percent of all insured deaths. Deaths by external causes, many of which may *not* meet the specific criteria of the accidental death clause, included motor vehicle accidents (3.0 percent), other accidents (2.3 percent), and suicide and homicide (2.4 percent).

[22] Life insurance income benefits for disability were introduced in the early 1900s, providing an annual income of $100 for each $1,000 of insurance, but the benefit was soon changed to $10 monthly. The disability business expanded rapidly but the depression brought with it economic pressure, and dishonest claimants used the disability clause as a source of income. Benefits were then sharply curtailed and premiums were advanced.

Under the more recent policies, insurers providing a monthly income benefit pay to the insured an amount equal to $10 for each $1,000 of life insurance upon receipt of proof that the insured is *totally* and *permanently* disabled *before the age of 55 or 60*. Evidence is required that the insured has become totally disabled, usually as defined earlier in the discussion of the waiver-of-premium benefits. Many variations in wording are used in some policies, however. Disability is presumed to be permanent only after six months or more of continuous disability; then the income is paid during disability up to age 70. The policy does not cover if the disability arises from bodily injury or disease occurring before the insurance took effect, if known to the policyholder and not disclosed in the application.

Generally, "disability" is much more difficult to define than "death." However, interesting legal problems are beginning to arise with many state laws where "brain death" is accepted as a definition of death. In other states both the heart *and* the brain must cease to function. A recent American Bar Association recommended definition of death is: "For all legal purposes, a human body with irreversible cessation of total brain function, according to usual and customary standards of medical practice, should be considered dead."   NOT TRUE

Income benefits are not written in connection with term insurance policies. When the insured has reached the age of 55 or 60 and the income disability provision of the policy no longer applies, future premiums on the policy are reduced by the amount of the premium charge for the disability benefits.

Disability income is not written by all insurers, and the insurers which write the coverage have established underwriting rules that tend to restrict its availability to carefully selected applicants who are employed. Some insurers may also insure housewives for smaller disability income coverage. Policies now written with the $10-per-month clause may provide for the termination of the disability payments at the age of 65.

Life insurance disability income protection may be used to augment other forms of health coverage. It is expensive in relation to the other health benefits in life contracts. As an example, disability income (including the waiver-of-premium benefit) may cost about $5 per $1,000 at age 30, but the cost increases as age advances to over $15 per $1,000 at age 50. Life insurance underwriters carefully watch disability income limits in relation to income earned by the applicant. Aside from this, life insurers usually establish an arbitrary upper limit of disability income for anyone insured. For example, the limit might be set at $3,000 per month, not exceeding 75 percent of earned income. More discussion on the importance of disability income protection is included in Chapters 9–12.

FOR REVIEW AND DISCUSSION

1. Indicate the *number* of the phrase in column B which is most closely related to the term in column A:

Column A	*Column B*
a. Beneficiaries	1. Face value of policy corrected
b. Dividend option	2. Life income
c. Nonforfeiture option	3. Up to cash value, at about 6 to 8 percent
d. Unique settlement	interest
option	4. Accidental death before age 70
e. Misstatement of age	5. Paid-up additions
f. Policy loans	6. Becomes part of the contract
g. Waiver-of-premium	7. May be primary or contingent
benefit	8. Conditional or absolute
h. Double indemnity	9. Only for permanent, total disability
i. Assignment	10. Extended term insurance
j. Application	

2. Indicate whether the following statements are true or false (with reasons, if false):

    a. Life insurance contracts are not very flexible, because they must be in writing and because they are important legal documents.

    b. Suicide results in full payment of the face value of a life insurance contract during the first (or sometimes the first two) years of the policy.

    c. Beneficiaries are usually revocable, rather than irrevocable, in life insurance contracts.

    d. Policyholders who cancel their life insurance contracts can obtain reduced paid-up insurance, or even insurance for the full face value, under the extended term insurance option.

    e. Disability income benefits are more common in life insurance contracts than are disability waiver-of-premium benefits.

3. What reasons can you give for the lack of a standard life insurance policy? In what sense is there such a contract today?

4. Identify the following found in most life insurance contracts: *(a) dividend* options, *(b) nonforfeiture* options, and *(c) settlement* options.

5. Describe a specific instance in which each of the usual settlement options would be appropriate. Do the same for the normal nonforfeiture options.

6. To what extent are the rights of a beneficiary of a life insurance contract affected by an assignment of the contract to a bank?

7. Explain why each of the three types of disability or accident insurance coverages added to many life insurance contracts is valuable to the life insurance buyer. Do these coverages provide permanent protection? Which type is most common? Most important? Most neglected?

8. A friend of Mrs. Harnack tells her: "The *settlement options* and *policy-loan option* of life insurance contracts are almost worthless in today's economy of high investment returns." How would you *disagree*? Why may these options provide increasing problems for *insurers*?

9. Y insures his life for the benefit of his wife and children. Upon his death, will only the children living at the time of policy issue participate? Or children born after the policy was written? Or children by a former marriage of Y?

10. X insures his life for the benefit of B and later takes a policy loan. X dies, and B contends that he is entitled to the full face of the policy and that the insurer should collect the loan from the estate of X. Is B correct?

11. What is the *suicide clause?* In your opinion, should the usual period of two years be lengthened or shortened?

12. Mrs. King is the beneficiary of Mr. King's policy, written for a face of $50,000 with an *accidental death* benefit. He dies due to an accidental gunshot wound. How much will be paid and why?

13. Few contracts (if any) are more flexible than the typical life insurance contract. Explain at least seven features of the life insurance contract which make it adaptable to changes in the needs or abilities of the policyholder.

14. Mr. and Mrs. Erwin have decided to cancel some life insurance, but they are afraid that they will forfeit all of their contract benefits if they do. How would you advise them?

15. "The problems of defining 'disability' are greater than those of defining 'death.'" Why would you agree, or disagree?

16. What kinds of flexibility in the life insurance contract, *in addition to* the features of typical ordinary life policies discussed in this chapter, might the policyholder desire to have?

Chapter 8

Outline of concepts

Private insurance annuities are a part of the life insurance business.

    Compared with other life insurance contracts, however, they emphasize *liquidation* rather than creation of assets.

    Importance and growth are shown by the number of persons covered by and assets of *individual* and *group* annuities or insured pensions.

    Definition is that of a promise of a *periodic payment* to an *annuitant.*

    Purposes and uses include *settlement options* and *pension* plans.

    Cost factors include age, sex, special mortality tables, and interest.

Types of individual annuities are classified:

    By plan of distribution—*straight (pure),* or *guaranteed refund life.*

    By parties in the contract—*single,* or *joint and survivorship* life.

    By time when benefits begin—*immediate,* or *deferred.*

    By method of purchase—*single,* or *installment* payment.

    By amount of payment—*fixed,* or *variable* annuities.

Contract conditions of individual annuities include:

    General provisions, much like other life insurance contracts.

    No medical examination, as poor health favors the insurer.

    Participation in dividends in many annuity contracts.

Group annuities (under pension plans) are very important:

    Types and growth include *social* and *private, insured* and *noninsured* plans involving a significant $700 billion of assets.

    Nature and purposes center on the guarantee of benefits to employees.

    Eligibility usually requires a waiting period.

    Retirement may be on either *normal* or *optional retirement date.*

    Benefits are determined by: *basic plans* (fixed benefit or money purchase), *past service credits, variable annuity plans* (based on stock equity earnings, or cost-of-living indexes), *death benefits, vesting clause* (right to employer's contributions), *change,* or *discontinuance.*

    Financing sources: *contributory* and *noncontributory* plans determine *who* pays.

    Financing methods determine *how* benefits are financed:

        Noninsured pension plans: *pay-as-you-go,* and *trust fund* (or "trusteed").

        Insured pension plans: *individual policy, group permanent life, deferred group annuity, deposit administration.*

    Combination of methods, also used frequently.

    The Pension Reform Act (1974), or ERISA, is bringing tremendous changes and opportunities to the pension field.

    IRAs, Keogh Plans, and TSAs have tax-deferred annuities as one of the choices for individual pension plans.

Annuities and pensions

"Retire—who, *me?*" expresses the feelings of many persons about retirement. As "the Great American Dream," it's one of those good thoughts—for *tomorrow!* It is easy to lack interest in annuities and pensions—after all, most of us are not ready to retire. But that's the reason everyone should be interested, because even when we are *old* enough to be ready to retire, few of us are *financially* prepared to do so. In reply to a question asking how he liked old age, the French actor Maurice Chevalier once said: "It's pretty good, considering the alternative!" Retired persons everywhere would probably agree, but they might add that it could be a lot better with a little more money.

Living too long (that is, beyond the income-producing years,) may be as great an economic problem as not living long enough (premature death while still working). It also involves more persons, for at the age of 25 more than two out of three persons can expect to live to age 65 or beyond. The significance of this chapter on annuities is apparent.

The attitudes of individuals toward retirement vary greatly. Some persons insist that they never want to retire from their careers. Others can't wait to retire and even hope to retire before normal retirement at age 65. Most workers anticipate retiring at 65, but they have done very little preretirement planning and only minimal savings to provide funds for their retirement years.

Annuities and pensions are periodic income payments that can help make retirement financially possible. This chapter emphasizes *private insurance* annuities, those insured by life insurance companies, of two basic types: (1) *individual* annuities, based on separate individually owned annuity contracts, and (2) *group annuities,* an important part of the pension field. Not all group pensions (usually purchased through employers) are insured, but all pensions use the annuity concept. Many private pension plans use insured group annuities to guarantee the payment of pensions. Other private plans are not insured. Also a part of the total pension field are government or social insurance pensions, which are discussed in Chapter 11.

PRIVATE INSURANCE ANNUITY CONCEPTS

Definition

An *annuity* may be defined as a periodic payment.[1] It may commence at a stated or contingent date, and it may be continued to a designated person for a fixed period or for the life or lives of the person or persons entitled to receive payment.[2] The person entitled to receive payment of an annuity from an insurer is the *annuitant*.

In this brief description, several preliminary observations are implicit. An annuity may be paid as an annual payment, but it most often involves a monthly payment. It may start at a fixed future date, or it may start on an unknown future date depending upon a death. Once payments have begun, they may be continued for a limited number of years. However, in one of its most useful forms, the *life annuity*, the duration of the payments is conditional upon the continued life of the annuitant.

Annuities compared with other life insurance contracts

Private annuities are *like* life insurance contracts in many ways. Actually, they are part of the life insurance business because many life insurers write annuities. Annuity contracts are based upon similar concepts already discussed in Chapters 5–7, such as mortality tables, present value discounting, reserves, and beneficiary designations. Both life insurance and annuities help meet the peril of old age and are important in estate planning. They can be participating policies (paying dividends) or nonparticipating policies. Private annuities, like life insurance, are sold through individual or group contracts, and the policy provisions are quite similar.

On the other hand, private annuities are *unlike* life insurance contracts in very important characteristics. They are different in that they: (1) emphasize *liquidation*, rather than creation, of assets; (2) often *stop*, rather than begin, payments at death; (3) frequently use lump-sum or *single-premium purchase*, rather than installment purchase; (4) usually require *no medical examination* before issuance; (5) use *different mortality tables*, which result in *much higher rates for females* than for males; (6) issue contracts much more often on *joint lives*, instead of individual lives; and (7) use the *group* method for issuing contracts rather than individual sales (for two thirds of annuity premiums, as opposed to one fourth of life insurance premiums).

---

[1] Sometimes it is also defined to be a *regular* or *fixed* amount of payment.

[2] Annuities antedate by many centuries the contract of life insurance. In ancient Rome in the year 40 B.C., Roman jurists developed the first-known life annuity values graduated with reference to age. Loans in the Middle Ages were repaid in the form of annuities.

Importance and growth

Life insurers write private insurance annuities either as separate contracts or as "supplementary" contracts (which use the proceeds of life insurance policies to purchase annuities). The separate contracts are issued on an individual or group contract basis. Thus, three types of these annuities are identified as (1) *individual,* (2) *group,* and (3) *supplementary* contracts.

The relative *importance* of the number of annuities and persons covered by these three private insurance annuities is seen in Table 8–1. There were more than 5 million individual, 21 million group, and less than 1 million supplementary contract annuities in force with U.S. life insurers at the beginning of 1981. These figures, however, are relatively small compared with Table 8–2, which shows more than 150 million persons covered by the OASDHI (Social Security) program, 20 million persons in other government pension programs (railroad, U.S. civil service, state, and local plans), and more than 30 million in noninsured pension plans. Thus, almost all persons have some kind of private annuity or government pension annuity, and many may have rights to retirement income from several different plans.

All private types of insurance annuities have had impressive *growth* during the past three decades, with group annuities (see later section of chapter) growing fastest and now covering 10 times as many persons today as were covered 30 years ago. Individual annuities have been encouraged by tax-sheltered Keogh, IRA (Individual Retirement Accounts), and other plans. Government pension programs have grown even more rapidly than private insurance plans. The growth of other private methods of saving for retirement has also been significant. Examples include the growth of stock market investments, savings and loan associations, and mutual funds during the 1960s and 1970s. More recently, the 1980s have seen tremendous growth in money market certificates and funds.

Table 8–1. Number* of private insurance annuities† in force,
U.S. life insurance, 1950–1980 (in thousands)

	Individual annuities	Group annuities	Supplementary contracts
1950	1,235	2,210	217
1960	1,159	4,533	428
1970	1,708	7,260	607
1980	5,402	21,610	642

* Numbers of persons covered (for group annuities), at year-end. Duplication prevents meaningful combination of the totals of these three types of annuities.

† Does not include variable annuities, covering more than 2 million persons, whose returns are not guaranteed amounts.

Source: *Life Insurance Fact Book* (Washington, D.C.: American Council of Life Insurance, 1981), pp. 37 and 54.

In all, the number of choices among alternatives for meeting retirement needs are almost bewildering in their rapid growth. Consumers have a vital need for integrating their rights to Social Security benefits (explained in Chapter 11), and perhaps to other public pension programs, with careful choices of private individual and group annuities. Together with proper coordination of life and health insurance, as outlined in Chapter 12, the goal of satisfactory retirement is within the reach of everyone.

The place of private annuities in today's financial picture reflects a combination of factors, of which some have caused growth in annuities and others have limited the use of annuities. Several basic growth factors are: the increased emphasis on individual retirement needs; the growth of group pension plans through employer and union help and interest; the fundamental growth of life insurance contracts; general economic trends, such as higher incomes, inflation, and affluence; favorable tax treatment of annuities permitting employers a business deduction for their costs; and taxsheltered plans, since the mid-1970s, by which individual employees postpone income tax on their annuity income.

Some of the limiting factors include: increasing social insurance coverage for retirement, a prime purpose of annuities; effective competition from private noninsured pension plans; continued inflation, which favors the variable-type annuity that insurers are just beginning to market; the psychological emphasis of our younger generations on *now* as opposed to the *future;* and the Pension Reform Act of 1974, which increased the federal regulation of group pensions considerably.

Purpose and uses

In their basic use of liquidating assets, annuities occupy an important place in estate planning and insurance programming. The settlement options of life contracts (see Chapter 7) are examples of one of the important uses of annuities. For those whose emphasis is on retirement needs, the various forms of annuities written by life insurers are one of the most certain, convenient, and complete protections against old age that can be arranged through voluntary action. It substitutes for speculative income a sound and secure return for one's own old age or that of another. The security of a sound life insurer, fortified by legally prescribed supervision, relieves the annuitant of the uncertainties of management and investment.

A second important function of the annuity is to use the capital of annuitants so that it will last them throughout their lives. Given a substantial fortune coupled with investment skill, some persons prefer to handle their own investments and are able to obtain an adequate income for living without drawing upon principal. However, many persons find it necessary to use at least a part of their capital upon retirement. The annuity provides a means by which this capital distribution can be spread over a lifetime.

The matter of capital distribution assumes grave importance for individuals who have accumulated some, but relatively modest, capital. Persons 65 years old with $100,000 have somewhat of a problem in securing the maximum benefits of the fund for themselves during their lifetimes. Invested at a net of 8 percent, their interest income will amount to only $8,000 a year, or $666 per month.[3] If they apportion a certain amount of their principal to be spent each year, they may reach a point at which income and principal are depleted and they find themselves dependent and in need. Even if this point is never reached, it is psychologically distressing to know that one's resources are constantly decreasing.

Where the bare income from capital is insufficient to meet its owner's needs, the investment of the capital in a life annuity will yield, particularly at advanced ages, a sum substantially in excess of the interest yield, and in addition the income is paid for life, regardless of how long the annuitant lives. The purchase price of a single-premium life annuity for a male, age 65, is about $1,100 for $10 monthly. On this basis an annuitant may obtain an income of about $910 per month for life for the payment of $100,000. (The comparable cost would be $1,200 for females, and the monthly income about $830.) Thus, the annuitant has the confidence of an assured income for life, leading to a serene mental attitude. It is contended that freedom from financial worry tends to prolong the life of the annuitant, and this has given rise to the insurance adage "Annuitants never die." A paraphrase of the same idea states: "Annuitants live longer than people!"

Cost factors

Interest earnings are not the only cost factor that determines the amount charged for annuity benefits. The cost is not ordinarily called the "premium," but rather the "purchase price." Of a given group of annuitants, some of the contract holders will die in a short time and others will live for a long time, but the number dying each year will follow closely the predictions of the mortality table. The cost of an annuity is based upon the mortality rates of annuitants, just as life insurance is based upon the mortality rates of insureds.

To determine the cost of an annuity by a mortality table based upon _insured_ lives would dangerously underestimate the risk. Individuals who know they have serious health impairments rarely, if ever, purchase

---

[3] The _net_ interest rate chosen here for illustrative purpose is based on the assumption of a 12 percent gross interest return, reduced an estimated one third for taxes and expenses.

annuities. In life insurance groups there will be many impaired lives at retirement age. At that point in life, only persons who feel in good health would willingly make a substantial payment of principal in return for a life annuity. Thus, a smaller number of deaths than is expected under other life insurance contracts would be experienced. Annuity payments would continue longer than anticipated, and the annuity insurer would soon be in financial trouble. Annuitants, therefore, represent a selected group, and *special mortality tables* must be used in predicting their deaths. Earlier annuity tables may be used by some insurers and consultants, but most use 1971 tables developed separately for individual and for group annuities. These tables are modified in several different versions in order to reflect the improving longevity trend that has already occurred and the anticipated continuance of decreasing mortality.

It has been noted that in computing the life insurance premium, the younger the *age* of the insured when the policy is written, the lower the annual premium. In the case of an annuity, the reverse is true. The younger the annuitant, the greater must be the purchase price for the annuity to pay a designated sum for life. Obviously $10,000 will purchase a greater income for life for a person of 70 than it will for a person of 50. Annuities have a particular appeal to elderly people without dependents who are concerned with providing a guaranteed income for life on the basis of available resources.[4]

The *sex* of the annuitant is also important. Females have greater longevity than males and thus receive annuity payments of about the same amounts as males who are five to seven years younger.

In the remaining parts of this chapter, annuities are divided into two basic types for discussion: *individual* and *group*. Major sections treat the types of individual annuities, their conditions, and the annuity as used today in many large group pension plans.

TYPES OF INDIVIDUAL ANNUITIES

There are several approaches to the classification of annuities. The method used will depend upon the purpose of the classification. Basically, all annuities may be classified *(a)* as to the *plan of distribution* of proceeds, *(b)* as to the *parties in the contract, (c)* as to the *time distribution commences, (d)* as to the *method of purchase,* and *(e)* as to the *amount of the annuity payment.* Under each of these categories, the annuity is divisible into two or more subclasses as shown in Figure 8–1, which summarizes the classification of the types of individual annuities discussed in the following sections of this chapter.

---

[4] Various *refund* or *guaranteed* benefits are included in many annuities so that dependents or other beneficiaries can have some of the benefits of an annuity.

Figure 8–1. Classification of types of individual annuities

By plan of distribution

The *straight or pure life* annuity provides an income to the annuitant for life, without any guarantee of a minimum amount or number of income payments to the annuitant or a beneficiary. In contrast to the straight life annuity, most annuity plans provide payments either for a guaranteed amount, period, or cash refund.

Straight or pure life annuity. This agreement provides payments to the annuitant which continue throughout the life of the annuitant but terminate with his or her death, regardless of how soon that death occurs. Payments are made to the annuitant annually, semiannualy, quarterly, or monthly. Under this type of contract there is no guarantee of a definite number of payments, no cash value, and no provision for refund of any sort upon the death of the annuitant. The form is not popular, but under it annuitants are able to receive the largest possible payments and continue to receive those payments for life. The straight life annuity appeals particularly to persons of advancing age without dependents and of limited means who wish to secure the maximum benefit from their accumulations for their remaining days.

Guaranteed refund life annuities. Most annuities are issued with some guaranteed features which assure the annuitant (or the beneficiaries) a part or all of the cost of the annuity.

In the *installment refund life annuity,* if the annuitant dies before the aggregate of payments equals the purchase price, payments will continue to a designated beneficiary until an amount equal to the full sum of the single payment has been returned. The annuitant, or the designated beneficiary, is certain to receive an amount equal to the purchase price without interest. The annuitant, on the other hand, may live long enough to receive payments that will aggregate a sum substantially in excess of the purchase price. The annual payments under this form are somewhat less than the annual payments under the straight life annuity.

Another form, the life annuity with *number of payments guaranteed,* is similar to the installment refund life annuity. The payments continue during the life of the annuitant, with a guaranteed minimum number of years of payment. The form is thus called an *annuity certain.* For example, if payment is guaranteed for 20 years and the annuitant dies at the end of 5 years, payment will be made for a period of 15 years more to a designated beneficiary. If the annuitant, however, outlives the number of years guaranteed, payments are made until the death of the annuitant occurs, but nothing is paid to the beneficiary.

It sometimes happens that the purchaser of an annuity wishes to make provision for final expenses, such as funeral costs. Special contracts provide an annuity for life, with the additional provision of a lump-sum *cash refund* guaranteed to a designated beneficiary.

The reluctance to risk securing a return in annuity payments that is less than the cost of the annuity may operate to the disadvantage of annuitants. Knowing that the straight life annuity provides the maximum lifetime income for each dollar paid for an annuity, annuitants must decide *(a)* whether they need to leave funds for dependents or *(b)* whether their lifetime needs require their entire capital. Annuitants who have no need to provide for dependents can augment their income by electing an annuity without a refund.

By parties in the contract

Annuities are usually written on the *single* life of one person. They can, however, be written on several, or *joint,* lives. Both kinds of contracts are considered individual annuities because there is just one contract even when more than one life is included as the contingency for payments. Group annuities, written for many employees of a common employer, could be identified as another major division of annuities, as regards the number of parties in the contract. However, these annuities are given separate treatment in the final major section of this chapter.

Single life annuity. The basic annuity is based only on the *single* life of one person. The payments under the annuity are contingent on the continued life of the individual identified as the annuitant.

Joint life and survivorship annuity. In many cases the income need involves more than one person, such as when spouses wish to make provision for the old age of both. The *joint life* contract provides an annuity for the joint duration of more than one life. In a contract that is not often used, payments stop at the death of the first person. A contract widely used guarantees an income for two persons during the lifetime of both, and upon the death of one of them, it continues without reduction until the death of the *survivor*. After the first death, some policies reduce the survivor's annuity payments to two thirds or one half. The contract may also be written to involve more than two persons; and when so written, the income is payable without reduction until the death of the last survivor of the group.

By time when benefits begin

Annuities classified as to when the first payment is made to the annuitant are either *immediate* or *deferred.*

Immediate annuity. Although the title is confusing, an *immediate* annuity provides its first payment at the *end* of the initial payment period after purchase. If the payments are annual, the first annuity payment would be due the annuitant one year after the contract began. If the payments are monthly, the first payment would fall one month after purchase.

Deferred annuities. Under most annuity contracts, probably four out of five, income to the annuitant does not commence until after a certain number of years or until the happening of some event. A *deferred* annuity may be written to provide an income at a certain age, or it may be written to provide an income to a beneficiary upon the death of the insured. A deferred *pure life* annuity can be written, but it is rare because no payment at all is made if the annuitant dies before the first payment comes due.

The *deferred refund* annuity, which is the usual type, includes the stipulation that the aggregate of the amount payable by the company to the annuitant shall equal the aggregate of the payments made for the annuity. Payments may be made in periodic installments, or a single cash payment may be made.

The *retirement* annuity is a deferred annuity which enables an individual to provide an income for retirement by making convenient payments during the productive period of life. The annuitant selects a date for the commencement of payments. The amount of the income is based on the purchase price and the date selected. Retirement income contracts are written with the following provisions for optional settlements: life annuity, a cash refund annuity, or a life income with payments guaranteed for a number of years certain. This contract usually provides for a cash surrender value if the contract is surrendered before the payments to the annuitant commence. Some contracts provide for loans during this same period. An automatic paid-up annuity in a reduced amount becomes effective upon default in the payment of premiums.

The *endowment* annuity, also known as the "retirement endowment," provides for a payment to the named beneficiary if the insured dies prior to the maturity date. If the insured lives to the maturity date, the insured may elect either a monthly income for life or a lump-sum settlement. The contract is, in fact, a retirement annuity coupled with decreasing term insurance running to maturity. The amount of the term insurance each year is the difference between the face amount of the policy and the cash value.

By method of purchase

Single payment annuity. The annuitant can pay a lump sum in return for a regular income for life or for a term. The contract is known as a *single payment* annuity. No further payments by the purchaser are necessary.

Installment payment annuity. However, the single payment is not always convenient, nor will the single payment annuity always meet the needs of the applicant. Life insurers, therefore, often sell the *installment payment* annuity. Arrangements may be made to make the payment annually, semiannually, quarterly, or monthly.

Immediate annuities must be single payment annuities, and they require the deposit of a substantial sum at once. A deferred annuity may be a single payment annuity or an installment payment annuity.

By amount of payment—fixed and variable annuities

An annuity was defined as a periodic payment for a fixed period or for life. Although annuities sold by life insurers are usually for a *fixed* number of dollars, actually nothing in the term *annuity* requires that each of the payments be equal.[5]

---

[5] Nothing in theory, at least. In practice, however, the term is thought by some persons to convey the impression of a *fixed* payment. This idea bothers some life insurers who feel a *variable* payment promise causes a perplexing situation when one calls a payment (understood to be fixed in amount) a "variable annuity."

One of the principal criticisms of annuities has been that fixed amount payments do not adjust themselves to inflation. To meet this situation, in part at least, a strong movement has been started in the life insurance business to write what has been termed *variable annuities.*

The variable annuity contemplates that part or all of the funds of the life insurer set aside to meet annuity payments shall be invested in *equities* instead of bonds and mortgages. The payments will be dependent upon the income that the equity investments produce. The variable income of the annuity would be similar to that of a diversified mutual investment fund.

Variable annuities are often written as deferred annuities. This means that payments for the annuity take place over an extended period. Investment in common stocks over such a period would tend to minimize losses that might otherwise occur if all the equities were purchased at any one time.

The idea of the variable annuity is to make it possible for the purchaser of the annuity to obtain the benefit of a diversified equity investment as a basis for higher retirement income without losing the benefit of the annuity principle that guarantees income for life. The purpose is to try to offset the decrease in purchasing power of the dollar, which has dwindled from $1 in 1940 to $0.58 in 1950, to $0.47 in 1960, to $0.36 in 1970, and to less than $0.20 today.

Variable annuities are written both as *individual* and *group* annuities (see later section of this chapter). Most plans so far have been group plans, but the individual variable contract is now becoming more widely available. Most of the principles apply to either type.

One of the pioneers in the field of variable annuities is the College Retirement Equities Fund, a subsidiary of the Teachers Insurance and Annuity Association of America.[6] An individual participant may elect 0, 25, 50, 75, or 100 percent of premiums to be applied to the purchase of a variable annuity in CREF. The remainder is used to purchase an annuity in TIAA. About half of the participants choose to have 50 percent of their premiums go to CREF. The fixed-annuity part provides a guaranteed monthly income, while the CREF portion is not guaranteed, varying with the investment experience. TIAA–CREF has had success in marketing variable annuities on a group basis to members of educational and research institutions. A recent annual report shows a growth of assets and reserves to approximately $11 billion from more than 3,500 institutions that have benefit plans. The annuity unit value more than tripled during the period, 1957–72, from $17 to $53, fell to $28 in 1974, and rose to about $48 by the beginning of 1982. Long-range participation

---

[6] See William C. Greenough and Francis P. King, *Retirement and Insurance Plans in American Colleges* (New York: Columbia University Press, 1959); and *TIAA–CREF Annual Report,* 1981.

over many years is emphasized as a necessity for success in the use of variable annuities.[7]

Other consumers have access in most states to many group and some individual variable annuities. The legal and other adjustments required by insurers slowed the trend in the 60s. However, by 1982 the number of persons covered by group variable annuities was about 1.6 million, and the number covered by individual variable annuities was 0.8 million. Reserves for the variable funds totaled $4.1 billion for group contracts and $3.5 billion for individual contracts. Most of the plans were based on the performance of equity funds, but a few plans based the variable results on other indexes, such as the consumer price index.[8]

Early companies entering the variable annuity market were the General American Life Group with the Variable Annuity Life Insurance Company (VALIC), and the Aetna Life and Casualty Group with the Participating Annuity Life Insurance Company. The Prudential Life Insurance Company, too, led the battle for court and SEC approval. Several hundred other life insurers now offer these contracts to consumers. Tax-deferred variable annuities are also being offered through many nonprofit organizations under Section 403 *(b)* of the Internal Revenue Code, and to self-employeds in HR-10 plans under the Keogh Act. Individual Retirement Accounts (IRAs) now available to all employees have broadened the market considerably in the 1980s.

Some life insurers do not wish to offer such contracts in connection with life insurance. They say, in effect, that any future *reduced* annuity payment will be difficult if not impossible for the insured to understand. They offer the solution of *additional* life insurance purchases as the method by which to hedge against the decreased purchasing power of the dollar.

A special problem faces those life insurers that write individual variable annuities. The decision has been rendered that the life insurer must meet state laws as well as the organization and prospectus requirements of the Securities and Exchange Commission.[9] An exception has been made in the case of *group* variable annuities sold under the provisions of the Investment Company Act of 1940. Such plans are exempt from the SEC jurisdiction, and regulation is provided by the life insurance laws of the states.

Undoubtedly, the movement toward variable annuities will continue to be one of the most closely watched developments in the field of life

---

[7] Roger R. Conant, "Inflation and the Variable Annuity—Revisited," *CLU Journal* 30, no. 4 (October 1976), p. 12.

[8] *Life Insurance Fact Book* (Washington, D.C.: American Council of Life Insurance, 1982), p. 36.

[9] *Prudential Insurance Company* v. *S.E.C.*, 377 U.S. 953 (1964).

insurance. If current high fixed-interest rates fall and equity returns rise in the U.S. economy, the growth of variable annuity plans is likely.

The consumer has a widening choice of purchase decisions to make. Mutual funds, whose assets grew more than tenfold during the last 20 years, now have strong competition from money market and other funds. Variable annuities will have to be evaluated carefully by life insurance consumers in relation to fixed-dollar annuities, as well as to all other alternative investments. Many factors will need to be considered for the proper choice and coordination of these plans.

CONTRACT CONDITIONS OF INDIVIDUAL ANNUITIES

The conditions of annuity agreements vary with companies and with types of annuity. There are certain clauses, however, that either are legally required standard provisions or have been adopted by most companies. The insuring clause sets forth the promises of the insurer and outlines the types and conditions of payment.

General provisions

Most of the usual provisions are quite similar to those found in life insurance contracts. All companies reserve the right to require evidence that the annuitant is living before any annuity payment is made. They make every effort to save the annuitant from annoyance and usually accept the personal endorsement of the annuitant on the company's check or draft as satisfactory evidence. If because of misstatement of age an excess amount has been paid the annuitant, it is charged against current or subsequent payments. It is customary to issue annuity contracts providing for incontestability after one year from issue. The policy and application constitute the entire contract. The reserve basis is stipulated by indicating the annuity table used together with the interest assumption. The contract may be assigned, but the insurer assumes no obligations unless the assignment is filed at the home office. Nonforfeiture values are usually limited to a paid-up annuity for such an amount as the accumulated payments will buy as set forth in the contract.

No medical examination

No medical examination is required for the purchase of the usual annuity. In the case of life insurance, the medical examination serves to forestall unfavorable selection through the insurance of an undue proportion of impaired risks. Since in the case of an annuity, impairment can in no way adversely affect the interests of the insurer, a medical examination can serve no purpose. The risk lies in the annuitant's living an unusually long life. Consequently, contrary to the situation in the life insurance contract, insurance companies do not need to require a medical examination to determine any physical impairment that may tend to shorten life.

Participation

Both participating and nonparticipating annuities are written by life insurers. The lengthening of the average life of annuitants has made necessary an upward revision of annuity rates. Partly because it offsets this change, the principle of the participating annuity has become more popular. The idea is to guarantee payments based upon conservative interest and mortality rates, with a view to returning to annuitants any extra savings over the calculations in the form of a dividend. Retirement income plans written by participating companies usually provide for the payment of dividends during the purchase price payment period. These plans also provide that the holder of the annuity contract may elect to receive the dividends in cash, apply them to payments due, or deposit them with the insurer at interest, to be withdrawn on demand.

GROUP ANNUITIES (UNDER PENSION PLANS)

Types and growth

The concept of annuities has been explained in terms of individual annuity contracts. The major application of the annuity principle, however, has been in the area of *group annuities* issued under *pension* plans for employees.

Table 8–1 showed the relative importance of annuities written by *private* insurers in the form of individual, group, and supplementary life insurance contracts. More than three fourths of the number of annuity contracts is provided by group annuities.

Both *social* insurance and *private* plans use annuities to provide retirement benefits. The private annuity plans may be *insured* or *noninsured*. The larger employee groups tend to operate their own pension funds, while the smaller ones often use insurers to guarantee their benefit payments and provide investment, payment, and advisory services.

The comparison in Table 8–2 shows the relative position and growth of these parts of the total pension field between 1960 and 1980 in terms of the number of persons covered. It shows more than a doubling in the number of persons covered by the various pension plans, including private, public, and OASDHI systems. The more than $700 billion in assets represented in these plans in the early 1980s is a potent force

Table 8–2. Major pension and retirement plans in the United States
(by number of persons covered, in millions)

	Private			Public*	OASDHI†	Grand totals
	Insured	Noninsured	Total			
1960	5.5	17.5	23.0	9.5	73.8	106.3
1965	7.0	21.1	28.1	11.6	87.3	127.0
1970	10.6	25.5	36.1	13.9	98.9	148.9
1975	15.2	30.3	45.5	16.9	110.1	172.5
1980	26.1	N.A.	N.A.	19.9	153.6	229.9‡

N.A. Not available yet due to changes in reposting requirements.
* Includes railroad, federal civilian, and state and local employees.
† Includes persons employed with coverage in effect at year end (including self-employeds), workers retired for age or disability, and their dependents receiving periodic benefits.
‡ Noninsured figures for 1975 added in this total because later data is not available yet.
Source: *Life Insurance Fact Book* (Washington, D.C.: American Council of Life Insurance, 1981), p. 50.

in the investment and capital markets of the United States.[10] Rapid as the growth in the public and OASDHI plans has been, the private pension area has exceeded the percentage growth of the government plans in terms of people covered. Assets, too, have soared for the private pension plans, quadrupling from 1970 to 1980. Nearly one half of all private employees and close to three fourths of government civilian workers have some retirement plan benefits other than OASDHI.[11] In total, pension funds are one of the largest and fastest-growing sources of wealth in the U.S.

The original purposes of pension plans were to improve morale and decrease labor turnover by offering faithful employees the prospect of security in old age. Other factors, such as tax inducements, pressure from organized labor, and increasing social and political pressures, became influential forces in the rapid growth of pensions plans.[12]

Nature and purposes

Group annuities are an important type of insurance contract used in order to guarantee the retirement benefits of employer-employee private pension plans. Private pension plans are not all insured; in fact, only

[10] A potential danger of such growth is pointed out in Peter F. Drucker, *The Unseen Revolution: How Pension Fund Socialism Came to America* (New York: Harper & Row, 1976).

[11] The relationship between the private and social insurance parts of the total pension field is thoroughly explored in Dan M. McGill, *Social Security and Private Pension Plans: Competitive or Complementary?* (Homewood, Ill.: Richard D. Irwin, 1977).

[12] For a concise explanation of the underlying forces and factors, see Dan M. McGill, *Fundamentals of Private Pensions* (Homewood, Ill.: Richard D. Irwin, for the Pension Research Council, 1979), chap. 1.

about 40 percent of the total private pension plan assets of more than
$423 billion in 1980 were protected by insurance. As a matter of theory,
there is no reason why any business institution might not set up its
own pension plan and administer the fund itself. As a matter of actual
practice, many difficulties have been encountered. Privately administered
pension plans have in many instances been wrecked by unsound management. Considerable dissatisfaction has resulted because of the uncertainty of employees concerning the solvency of the plans and the rights
they have in their pensions. The Pension Reform Act of 1974 was passed
in order to correct these deficiencies. (See section at end of this chapter.)

It is natural for many organizations to turn the entire problem over
to life insurers. Life insurers are equipped to make investments and
have the statistical information that is needed to determine payments
adequate to meet future problems. When employers lack adequate actuarial or investment facilities, it is regarded as good business to turn the
administration of a pension fund over to an insurer. Uninsured pension
plans, however, have become so large and so important as to be able
to command actuarial and management facilities that are in all respects
adequate.

The real purpose of a group annuity as used in a private pension
plan is the third-party guarantee it provides for both employer and employee that the benefits will be paid. The administrative and investment
services are important auxiliary purposes. The appeal of the insured
pension plan is particularly strong for small and medium-sized companies, and for many business institutions it affords the only sound basis
for the establishment of a pension plan.

When a retirement income plan is put into effect, a master contract
is issued to the employer by the insurer. As with other group contracts,
it is usual to give insured employees a membership *certificate* that outlines the benefits in detail. Circulars and booklets describing the benefits
of the plan are usually distributed to employees. These are for convenience only and always refer employees to the master group annuity
contract for full details.

Eligibility

Employers are primarily interested in providing for employees who
reach retirement age while in their employ. They are, therefore, not
particularly interested in including temporary labor. This being the case,
many private pension plans provide a *waiting period,* such as one year,
for eligibility. Other plans require not only a waiting period but a minimum salary or an attained age, such as 25. The waiting period must
be adjusted to fit the individual business. Some employers have little
difficulty with labor turnover, and their retirement plan can be made

effective immediately, with all employees eligible. For other employers the elimination of high turnover groups from the coverage simplifies administration and reduces costs.

Retirement dates

Two basic types of retirement dates are included in most group annuities, the normal retirement date and the optional retirement date.

Normal retirement date. "Normal retirement date" means the first day of the month nearest to the attainment of the established retirement age, which is usually 65. Employees are ordinarily expected to retire and begin receiving annuity payments at the normal retirement age. Factors that affect the selection of the normal retirement age are: *(a)* the age at which social security benefits are available, *(b)* the age at which superannuation (old age) occurs in relation to the employee's occupation, and *(c)* the relative cost of providing retirement at different ages. A majority of plans follow the social security program and provide normal retirement for males at 65 and females at 62, even though reduced OAS-DHI benefits are now available at 62 for males and at 60 for females. Pension plans must recognize other situations, but to provide a maximum annuity from the available funds, the normal retirement age should remain as near 65 as possible.

Optional retirement date. Pension plans ordinarily also provide for *(a)* an *early* annuity date or *(b)* a *postponed* annuity date. Some pension trends are encouraging early retirement, while others, including inflation, are causing more retirements after age 65.

It may sometimes be advisable, or desirable, for an employee to retire before the normal annuity date. Some plans allow the employee to retire within the 10-year period preceding the normal annuity date, or at stated ages such as 60 or earlier. Virtually all plans make some provision for early retirement. An employee who retires early receives a reduced income, often about one half at age 60 or less for earlier retirement. This is so because the period for the accrual of benefits is shortened and the period of annuity income payments is lengthened. Some plans require the employer's approval for early retirement, but others do not.

Arrangements may also be made to have annuity payments commence at a date later than the normal annuity date, known as a "postponed annuity date." Some plans provide the same rate of annuity payments as would have been payable on the normal annuity date, in order to encourage retirement at the normal annuity date. In all cases, a postponed annuity date requires the consent of both the employee and the employer. Late retirement provisions have become more important following 1978 amendments to the Age Discrimination in Employment Act, which prohibits mandatory retirement before age 70 for most employees.

Types of annuities used

When a plan is established, an employer has to choose a particular form of annuity. The normal form may be *(a)* a *refund* annuity or *(b)* a *pure life* annuity. (See earlier discussion on types of individual annuities.) Most insurers writing group annuity contracts also provide optional retirement benefits, such as the joint and last-survivor type.

Benefits

The benefits under group annuities are determined by (1) the basic kind of plan, (2) the treatment of past service credits, and by such other important conditions as (3) the inclusion of variable annuity provisions, (4) death benefits, (5) vesting clauses, and (6) change or discontinuance provisions.   *oʀ DEFINED*

Basic plans. There are two basic benefit plans: *(a)* the *fixed benefit plan* and *(b)* the *money purchase plan*. Under the fixed benefit plan, the benefit is determined in advance, and variables such as age and sex determine the cost. The situation is reversed under the money purchase plan; here the cost is fixed, and the variables determine the benefit.

The fixed benefit (also called "defined benefit") plan receives the widest acceptance and is regarded as equitable in its application. Under the plan, benefits are based upon a formula. The benefit formula must give consideration to the tax status of the plan. Certain forms of apparent discrimination are permitted, such as limitation to salaried employees. A benefit formula is not considered discriminatory if benefits are integrated with social security benefits. Higher paid employees should not receive benefits proportionately greater than those of the lower paid employees. Such rules determine whether the plan is "qualified," so that the employer can deduct pension costs as a normal business expense.

An example of a defined benefit formula might provide a monthly retirement income of 1.5 percent of the monthly average income times the number of years of service. Thus a 30-year employee earning $2,000 a month would receive a $900 monthly annuity. The basis for calculating average income may vary: some plans use career average, but many use the most recent, or highest, average income for a 3–10-year period.

Under the money purchase (also called "defined contribution") plan, both the employee and the employer contribute a fixed percentage of the employee's earnings. Frequently their contributions are equal. The joint contributions are applied to purchase whatever annuity credits they will buy for the individual employee at the time of purchase and at the rates then in effect.

Under a fixed benefit plan based on earnings, retirement income is more readily estimated than under a money purchase plan. The fixed benefit plan appeals to employees because under it they can more readily determine in advance the amount of their retirement income.

Past service credits. Many employees with long service will receive little in the way of a retirement annuity if their only benefits are those that accrue for services from the beginning of a plan. Therefore, most retirement plans provide annuity credit not only for future service rendered following the inauguration of the plan but also for past service. *Past service credits* will depend largely upon the relative ages of the group. In some instances, a maximum period of past service is set as well as a maximum salary for the computation of past service annuities. For example, a plan may provide that the maximum period of past service to be recognized will be the most recently completed 25 years and that the maximum salary to be considered will be $20,000.

One of the most perplexing problems in instituting a retirement plan involves the handling of the *accrued liability* of the employer for past service. Employees nearing the retirement age will remain with the employer only a short period before reaching retirement status; and during this time the employer must build up, from some source, capital sums sufficient to meet the accrued liability. The accrued liability is usually so large that, for most organizations, a single payment to the trustee or the insurer is out of the question. Quite as important today is the fact that ordinarily only 10 percent of the accrued liability for past services is deductible by the employer for income tax purposes in a single year. For these reasons, installment funding is the common method. The plan to be adopted depends upon the immediate needs of the older employees and the financial position of the employer.

Variable annuity plans. In the field of pension planning, where both employer and employee are conscious of changing living costs, it is to be expected that the variable annuity will be given full attention. Employers from time to time have voluntarily adjusted their pension plans so as to raise benefits, but the variable annuity undertakes to accomplish revisions *automatically* by means of the investment portfolio.

In the group field there are two approaches: *(a)* variables reflecting *stock market trends* and *(b)* variables reflecting changes in the *cost-of-living index*. The first of these follows the pattern already noticed in the discussion of individual variable annuities; the second is not dependent upon market movements in determining pension amounts.

Variables that reflect stock market trends are sometimes known as "equity unit plans." A part of the money available for employees' pensions is invested in equities. As the market value of the equity portfolio rises or falls, the income of the retired employee follows. Underlying this type of investment is the conviction that with the continued growth of the country, share values will continue to increase in value and thereby offset simultaneous increases in living costs.

The weakness in the plan is to be found in the fact that there is often no correlation between stock values and the cost of living. For example, the cost of living continued to rise during the 1974–75 recession, when the stock market plunged by 30 percent or more. Again, this has occurred in the early 1980s. To eliminate a downward revision of pensions in times of a declining stock market without an accompanying lowering of living costs, the variable annuity geared to the cost of living was devised. A part of the employer's allocation to purchase retirement income is used to provide benefit adjustments linked to the cost-of-living index.

Pensioners receiving retirement income based upon a variable annuity are freed to at least some degree from cost-of-living worries that may haunt others retired upon a conventional plan. It is interesting to note the increasing popularity of cost-of-living adjustments in pension plans.[13] In 1963 a major impetus was given to the idea by legislation which provided cost-of-living changes in the pensions paid to federal employees and to retired members of the armed forces. Many public employee retirement systems, including the New York State system and the Canada Pension Plan, use the cost-of-living approach. Even some life insurers, such as Aetna Life, have adopted such plans for their own employees. A cost-of-living plan was adopted in 1972, effective in 1975, for the OAS-DHI benefits. The possible inflationary effect of such changes is one disadvantage of the broader use of this idea. Another problem is increased cost. Even a COL benefit limited to a maximum of 3 percent per year can increase overall pension costs by 50 percent or more.

Death benefits. If employees die before retirement and they have contributed to a pension plan, a sum equal to their contributions is paid to their beneficiaries, oftentimes with interest. The accumulations under any annuity plan are substantial, and the death benefit may be a sizable amount. If the death of the annuitant occurs shortly after retirement, the heirs may react unfavorably if they learn that there are no annuity benefits payable to survivors. For this reason, insurers recommend a refund annuity as the normal form. If death occurs before the retired employee has received payments totaling his or her contributions, the balance is paid to a named beneficiary.

Vesting clause. If the pension plan contains a *vesting* clause, employees withdrawing from the plan prior to retirement are entitled to the benefits of the *employer's contributions* during the period of actual service. If the plan contains no vesting clause, the employee is entitled only to a cash refund of his or her own contributions with or without interest.

---

[13] See Robert J. Myers, *Indexation of Pensions and Other Benefits* (Homewood, Ill.: Richard D. Irwin, 1979).

Most pension plans today contain a vesting clause. Through it, the employee has greater job mobility by securing full title to whatever annuity has been accumulated by both the employee's and the employer's contributions. The clause has proved valuable to employers because it encourages employees to carry a greater part of the cost than they might under a plan without such a clause. On the other hand, employers no longer consider payments made for withdrawing employees as losses but as additional salary paid during years of actual service. The Pension Reform Act of 1974 (see later section), requires minimum vesting under several alternatives, such as partial vesting for 5 to 10 years and full vesting after 15 years.

Change or discontinuance. Few employers would be willing to enter upon a pension plan that would bind them irrevocably to its continuation. Yet, pension plans are designed to be permanent. Employers usually point out their intention to continue the retirement plan indefinitely but reserve the right to change or discontinue it at any time. It is usual to protect the employee by providing that discontinuance will not adversely affect the total retirement income credits earned, including the part contributed by the employer. These rights are insured today in many plans under the Pension Benefit Guaranty Corporation. Contracts ordinarily prohibit any cash return to the employer after a plan has terminated. Since the insurer, however, obligates itself only for the amount of annuity for which payment is received, if the past service benefit has not been fully purchased when the plan terminates, the paid-up annuity will not reflect these benefits.

Financing sources

In retirement annuities, *who* pays the costs is important. The employer may pay the entire cost in a *noncontributory* plan, or employees may pay part of the cost in a *contributory* plan. In recent years more than 80 percent of the total cost of all private pension plans has been paid by employers.

The premise that human effort is a production cost has led to the inference that the employer should bear the entire responsibility for providing pensions. Some feel, however, that the cost of pensions should derive in part from the employee. Those who favor a *contributory* form contend that wages are sufficiently high to warrant *employee* contributions. Such contributions, added to employer contributions, substantially increase the amount of the annuity. The contributory plan follows the pattern set by social security legislation. It invites employee interest, removes pensions from the category of paternalism, and gives the employee a sense of independence. Finally, employee participation creates a price consciousness. The employee who asks for increased benefits will be more conscious of their cost if part of that cost shows up as a wage deduction. The controlling argument for a contributory plan is that it usually provides more liberal retirement.

The advocates of a *noncontributory* plan contend that the *employer* should pay all costs because a pension represents a reward for service and is a form of deferred compensation. Employee contributions are made from income after taxes, and net income is thereby reduced by the amount of the contributions. Employer contributions are usually deductible, and the actual reduction of net profits is less than the actual amount of the contribution. The noncontributory plan provides coverage for younger employees who might not participate in a contributory plan. In addition, it gives the employer more freedom in determining the nature of the plan, its benefits, and the method of operation. The early trend toward contributory plans was reversed in favor of the noncontributory plan by the impact of the federal income tax law, which provides that in a qualified plan the contributions of the employer are currently deductible without imposing a current tax burden on the employee. Unions have generally preferred noninsured plans because such plans afford them greater administration and control and because noninsured plans are usually on a noncontributory basis.

Financing methods

A final major characteristic of pension plans is the method by which benefits are financed.[14] Methods of paying for retirement plans include: *(a)* a pay-as-you-go plan, *(b)* a trust fund plan, *(c)* an individual policy plan, *(d)* a group permanent plan, and *(e)* a group annuity plan. The first two methods are *noninsured;* the others are *insured* plans. The pay-as-you-go plan is *unfunded;* all others are *funded* plans. The group annuity plan may be under (1) a deferred annuity contract or (2) a deposit administration contract.

Noninsured pension plans. A *pay-as-you-go* plan has no pension fund established and makes payments to employees out of current income. The plan may be formal or informal. An informal pay-as-you-go plan could be quite unsatisfactory. Since there is no predetermined plan, there is always the pressure to reduce retirement payments if the employer is in an adverse financial position, and some employees may be unfairly treated. A formal pay-as-you-go plan is only slightly better. Although there may be no discrimination as to payments, there is, however, no assurance that the plan will be in effect at retirement or throughout

---

[14] A thorough analysis of the contract provisions and cost factors is available in Everett T. Allen, Jr., Joseph J. Melone, and Jerry S. Rosenbloom, *Pension Planning* (Homewood, Ill.: Richard D. Irwin, 1981).

the lifetime of the employee. Continuation of the plan is at the employer's discretion, and retirement costs may become a burden impossible to carry. The trend is definitely away from pay-as-you-go plans and toward retirement income security through insurance or other means.

A *trust fund plan* may be established for the advance funding of a pension plan. Definite rules govern the fund. Funds are paid to the trustee, such as a bank or a trust company, that invests and administers them. For the fund to be sound, payments must be based on mortality, severance, disability expenses, and investment earnings. Actuarial advice is essential, and a consulting actuary is usually retained to make the original estimates and periodic examinations of the fund.

Two major categories of trust fund plans are used: (1) a *pattern* plan, providing a flat dollar benefit at retirement which often varies with length of service, and (2) a *conventional* plan, providing benefits which vary according to both length of service and rate of compensation. The trust fund method of financing has become the most common type for retirement plans. Approximately 60 percent of private pension assets and covered employees are in noninsured, or trust fund, plans.[15] More than 32 million participants are covered.

Trust fund plans are usually called "self-administered plans" because the employer retains responsibility, directly or indirectly, for their operation. The investment of the fund is governed by the trust agreement. Investment decisions are usually made by a committee composed of company executives or representatives of both employees and management. As an alternative, investment decisions may be left to a trustee alone or to a pension committee and a trustee.

The trust agreement outlines the administration of the plan. Payments may be made directly to retired employees from the trust fund, or the trustee may be authorized to purchase annuities for them. The appeal of the plan lies in the hope that the investment experience of the particular employer will be more favorable than the average investment earnings of insurers. If investments are limited to U.S. government bonds and securities legal for trust funds or life insurers, the margin in favor of the trust tends to disappear. The agreement, however, may include preferred and common stocks. A trust plan is flexible, and the benefits may be revised from time to time as the needs of employees change or, more significantly, as changing conditions dictate.

Generally, the trusteed plans have been successful in their objective of securing somewhat higher investment returns. Their flexibility and their leeway to invest in stocks may be advantageous, for overall pension costs are reduced if investments bring greater returns. The life insurers have improved the competitive position of insured pension plans against

---

[15] Allen, et al., *Pension Planning,* p. 241.

the trusteed plans in recent years. Legislation in many states since the early 1960s has permitted life insurers to keep *separate accounts* for some part of the total assets of the insured pension plans. Common stock investments are made, often averaging about 50 percent of the account.

Insured pension plans. In contrast to the noninsured pension plans (pay-as-you-go and trusteed) are the *insured* pension plans. The major types include (1) the *individual policy* plan, (2) the *group permanent* life plan, and two types of group annuities, (3) the *deferred annuity* plan and (4) the *deposit administration* plan. The relative position of these insured plans is summarized in Table 8–3.

The importance of the group annuity plans (including the deposit administration type) is apparent: these plans comprise about 70 percent of the persons covered, account for over two thirds of the payments into plans, hold three fourths of the reserves, and make about 85 percent of the pension payments currently paid to annuitants.

Under the *individual policy plan,* a trustee arranges for an individual policy for each eligible employee but retains control of it by means of an assignment. Note that this is not the same purpose for which a trustee is used in the "trusteed" plans discussed above, where the trustee exercises broad administrative and investment powers. A retirement annuity contract may be utilized; but if the employer wishes to provide a more sizable death benefit, whole life or other policies may be purchased. The individual policy pension trust plan is most useful in providing pensions for groups too small to be eligible under a group plan. Table 8–3 shows that individual policy pension trusts account for a large proportion of all insured plans but for only about 9 percent of the persons covered.

Table 8–3. Insured pension plans (beginning of 1981)

	Number of plans (in thousands)	Persons covered (in millions)	*In billions of dollars* *		
			Payments into plans	Reserves, end of year	Pension payments
Individual policy pension trust†	210.1	2.4	$ 1.9	$ 11.9	$0.5
Group annuities‡	91.4	19.2	14.8	127.2	4.2
HR-10 (Keogh) plans	n.a.	0.5	0.4	2.5	—
Tax-sheltered plans	n.a.	1.8	2.0	10.3	0.1
Individual retirement accounts	n.a.	1.1	0.7	3.0	—
Other plans	n.a.	1.1	1.8	11.0	0.1
Totals		26.1	$21.6	$165.9	$4.9

* Dash indicates less than $50 million.
† Includes group permanent plans, which are about 6 percent of total plans.
‡ Includes immediate participation guarantee and deposit administration plans.
Source: *Life Insurance Fact Book* (Washington, D.C.: American Council of Life Insurance, 1981), p. 54.

The annuities are based upon the earnings of the employee. Each year the trustee purchases additional contracts. The normal form of the individual annuities purchased under this plan provides payments for 10 years certain and life thereafter. Many insurers which write individual policy plans offer a "guaranteed issue" plan, which generally means that each covered employee is issued life insurance in connection with the pension plan up to a specified amount, such as $10,000.

Aside from providing permanent life insurance protection, *group permanent life insurance plans* have come to be used in connection with retirement plans. When so used, they may provide retirement income insurance or life insurance that can be converted to retirement income. The life insurance protection is available, up to certain limits, without a physical examination. Insurers writing group permanent life insurance require a minimum number of lives to be covered with a minimum amount of insurance on each life.

The most important type of insured pension plan is the *group annuity plan*. By contractual agreement with a life insurer, the benefits of the pension plan are guaranteed to the employee. Two types are used.

The *deferred group annuity* involves the purchase for each employee, *each year*, of a paid-up deferred annuity. At retirement the employee receives the income from the sum of all these annuities. The yearly contribution of the employer consists of both future service contributions and past service contributions. Under this plan, the employer can take no credit for anticipated termination due to employee turnover. The life insurer calculates the contributions of the employer, considering the expected mortality. The employer future service contributions each year, with employee contributions, if any, must be sufficient to purchase all future service benefits that accrue in the year. If the plan is terminated, the insurer administers all benefits previously purchased. Future service benefits are fully guaranteed as they accrue. Past service benefits are guaranteed as purchased and are based on past service contributions. These guarantees appeal to employees.

The *deposit administration group annuity* plan uses an unallocated fund of contributions from the employer to purchase each retiring employee an annuity *as the employee retires*. Certain types of businesses have a very large labor turnover, and most of the workers withdraw before retirement age. The deposit administration group annuity plan was devised to provide a method that would not call for the payment into the fund of sums to provide annuities for employees who would inevitably withdraw. Under this plan, the employer makes monthly deposits into a life insurance fund which accumulates at a guaranteed interest rate in an undivided employer fund. Employee contributions, if any, accumulate in individual employee accounts. As an employee is retired, the accumulation in the individual account is used to purchase a part of the employee's retirement income, and the balance of the employee's retirement income is purchased by a transfer from the employer fund. At retirement a single-premium retirement annuity is provided for the retiring employee.

The insurer makes no guarantee to the employee that the full amount of the annuity outlined in the original plan will be forthcoming. The employer may fail to provide sufficient funds. The insurer can pay only such annuity as the funds it has actually received will permit. On the other hand, the plan saves the employer the necessity of advancing payments for members of the group who almost surely will leave before retirement. The employer may build up the fund during periods of favorable business and may make smaller contributions during periods of business recession. The deposit administration plans are especially popular with larger firms (several hundred employees or more) that desire a flexible plan, with insurance guarantees as of retirement age for their employees.

Combination of methods. It is entirely feasible to use more than one method of providing annuity coverages. A usual combination is a group annuity contract and individual annuity contracts. A group annuity contract may be used to provide benefits based on salary up to a given amount, such as $10,000 or $15,000, for all employees. Benefits for employees earning more than the established limit could be provided through individual annuity contracts.

The distinction between insured and noninsured plans is not always definite. The deposit administration plans use noninsured accumulations prior to retirement and insured annuities thereafter. A trust is often used for noninsured plans (most of which are called "trusteed" plans) as well as insured plans. Some trusteed plans insure part of their total pension obligations.

Another trend of importance to the topic of combining pension methods is the growth of *multiemployer* pension plans.[16] Most prominent are the negotiated plans involving the larger national unions of construction workers, teamsters, longshoremen, miners, clothing workers, and others. The potential benefits of pooling experience and costs and the problems of coordinating numerous plans are illustrative of the gigantic decisions that must be made today in connection with pension plans such as these.

The Pension Reform Act (1974)

One of the most important federal decisions related to insurance in the past decade occurred in 1974, with the passage of the *Employee Retire-*

---

[16] See Joseph J. Melone, *Collectively Bargained Multi-Employer Pension Plans* (Homewood, Ill.: Richard D. Irwin, published for Pension Research Council, University of Pennsylvania, 1963). Any researcher in the pension field should find good use for the nearly 20 books published by the council.

ment Income Security Act (ERISA). This has become commonly known as the *Pension Reform Act,* because it was aimed at correcting well-publicized failures of some pension plans to pay expected benefits to retired employees. A broad and complex set of regulations for private pension plans has emerged.[17]

The general purposes of the act are to strengthen the guarantees and the contractual nature of pension agreements with employers and to raise the fiduciary responsibilities and conduct of pension plan managers. Minimum standards of vesting (nonforfeitable rights to the employer's contributions), prohibition of investment and loan transactions involving potential conflicts of interest by pension fund managers, and a government plan to insure pension plan terminations are among the important provisions of this 208-page act.

Problems. The problems of adjusting to the provisions of the law have been troublesome and costly. Regulations to implement the law have been issued gradually during the past several years, and they have sometimes been in conflict with one another. The Department of Labor and the Treasury Department (IRS) have both been involved in setting these detailed rules. The *dual administration* of the law has created duplication and excessive paperwork for many employers, but gradually the rules for fuller disclosure and reporting requirements are being clarified and simplified. Temporary rules set in 1976 were eased somewhat, especially for smaller pension funds, by rules in final form that were issued in 1978.

In brief, ERISA applies to both insured and noninsured pension plans. It does not require employers to set up pension plans. It has undoubtedly been of value in strengthening existing pension plans for employees. However, its added rules and costs appear to have slowed the adoption of new pension plans considerably. Average pension plan costs are estimated to have increased 15 percent as a result of ERISA, but for some plans the increase may be much greater. Pension plan starts in 1976 were less than 6,000, less than one fifth of the number begun just two years earlier. In addition, pension plan terminations have been occurring at a rate of about one third more than was expected.

Major provisions. The *major provisions* of ERISA cover a number of important areas.[18] *Participation* rules broaden coverage by prohibiting plans from excluding certain employees (age 25 or over, or after one–

---

[17] ERISA basically exempts government (public) pension plans. However, a House Pension Task Force Report in 1978 called for sweeping reforms in the standards of public pensions for federal, state, and local employees. In 1982 the Public Employee Pension Plan Reporting and Accountability Act (PEPRA) was passed, requiring public plans to disclose assets and liabilities (including unfunded ones) to all participants and other interested parties.

[18] See *Pension Facts* (Washington, D.C.: American Council of Life Insurance, published annually).

three years of employment). *Vesting* requirements must be included in the pension plans, meeting one of three alternative guarantees: (1) 100 percent vesting after 10 years of employment; (2) 25 percent after 5 years of employment, increasing by 5 percent each year for 5 years and 10 percent for the next 5 years, so that there is 100 percent vested by 15 years; or (3) 50 percent vesting when age and length of service total 45 years (with a minimum of 5 years of service), plus 10 percent a year thereafter. Many pension plans have adopted the first 10-year vesting alternative minimum standard because it is the easiest to administer and explain to employees. Spouses must be given an option of choosing a continuing pension of at least half the employee's pension, if the retired employee dies before his or her spouse.

The *funding standards* of ERISA require certain minimums, such as being sufficient to meet current costs and amortize past service liabilities over 30–40 years. The *portability* of pension benefits is encouraged, if workers change jobs, by the tax deferment of vested accumulations put in individual annuities or the new employer's plan. *Plan termination insurance* is provided for in a federal Pension Benefit Guaranty Corporation. Defined benefit plans (but not other types) are guaranteed by an assessment plan paid annually by employers, plus a potential liability of up to 30 percent of the net assets of the employer terminating a plan. Some 33 million workers are now covered by PBGC, which has deficits of more than $200 million resulting from terminations of plans by such large firms as White Motors, International Harvester, and Braniff during the early 1980s.

Fiduciary standards are enforced by the DOL and the IRS by making pension trustees, investment advisors, and anyone else with discretionary authority over a pension plan or its assets, personally responsible for carrying out their duties according to the "prudent man" rule. Conflicts of interest with the plan participants and certain types of transactions and conduct are prohibited, unless specifically exempted. The pension funds must be held in trust, or fully insured, to provide the plan's benefits and costs. Extensive *reporting and disclosure requirements* must be followed, both in reports to the IRS and the PBGC and in booklets of explanation given regularly to the employees. *Maximum pensions* for qualified plans are currently set by the law at 100 percent of final average compensation or, if less, at $75,000.[19]

The future. The massive amending process which private pensions are undergoing in order to meet ERISA requirements is still continuing. Many of the regulations required by ERISA have not been issued in final form. The detailed regulations have been slow in forthcoming, but

---

[19] This maximum was increased by cost-of-living indexes to $124,500 in 1981, but current changes are expected to reduce this amount sharply for 1983.

each causes many thousands of changes. Definitions of "prohibited trans-actions" and of the "parties-at-interest" in pension funds are examples of the difficulties. A whole new field of pension experts is emerging, suggesting that the tongue-in-check description of ERISA as "The Accountants, Actuaries, and Attorneys Relief Act of 1974" is not too much of an exaggeration. In addition, employee benefit and risk managers for many firms are evaluating the need for pension fund liability insur-ance. In many ways ERISA should be an impetus to *insured* pension plans by the life insurance business, particularly among smaller compa-nies that must now meet higher fiduciary standards for their pension plans.

The Pension Benefit Guaranty Corporation has had a busy start, with requests for plan determinations (to see whether assets are inadequate and whether it is necessary to appoint a trustee) running into the thou-sands each year. The employer's assessed cost of $1 per worker per year originally set has increased to $2.60 and is expected to go to $6.00 or more. Failures by multiemployer plans, usually through unions, are likely to be high if some of the delayed requirements for them are not implemented soon.

In all, many parts of ERISA may become crucial to the continuation of pension plans in the 1980s. At the same time, the life insurance busi-ness should benefit from the stimulus provided by a law which mandates the prudent and careful actuarial funding of pension plans.[20]

IRAs, Keogh Plans, and TSAs

One provision of the Pension Reform Act has tremendously expanded the incentive for individuals to use individual annuities in their own pension plans. *Individual Retirement Accounts (IRAs)* were permitted by ERISA, starting in 1975, for workers who are not covered by a private pension plan where they are employed. IRAs are now available to all employees, even if they have other pension plans. Under the 1981 Tax Act, the individual may make annual contributions of 15 percent of salary or wages up to a maximum of $2,000 (with nonemployed spouse, $2,250). The contributions paid in are currently tax deductible, and accrued earn-ings and capital gains on the funds held also escape taxes, until with-drawn at age 59½ or after. Life insurance companies are competing with other financial institutions to enroll participants in IRAs. Annuities, mutual funds, stocks, special IRA government bonds, and even savings accounts can be purchased for investment in IRA accounts. In effect, the IRA is a do-it-yourself pension plan, but the rules for purchasing,

---

[20] Charles C. Hinckley, "ERISA and the Life Insurance Industry," *CLU Journal* 30, no. 1 (January 1976), p. 44; and John G. Mulock, "The Positive Side of ERISA," *CLU Journal* 32, no. 3 (July 1978), p. 29.

AVOIDS ERISA

SIMPLIFIED EMPLOYEE PENSION

ALO SEPS

reporting, and withdrawing must be carefully followed to avoid tax penalties.

For self-employed persons, *Keogh (also called HR-10) plans* have been available since 1963. The maximum amounts deductible were sharply increased by ERISA in the 1970s to $7,500 a year or 15 percent of earned income, if less. The maximum dollar limit was raised to $15,000 in 1982 and will be $30,000 in 1984. Tax benefits and investment choices similar to those of the IRAs are available. Mutual funds and life insurance annuities (fixed or variable) have been the popular investment choices. The Tax Reform Act of 1976 introduced changes that also permit estate tax savings if the proceeds of Keogh plans are distributed to a beneficiary over more than one year. Table 8–3 shows that nearly 2 million persons have Keogh or IRA pension plans today, with 5 billion dollars invested. However, the potential market for these two types of individual pensions is estimated at 40 to 50 million persons, so considerable growth is predicted for the 1980s.

A third form of tax-deferred annuities, limited to academic employees and employees of nonprofit organizations, is available under Internal Revenue Code Section 401(c)3. These are called *tax-sheltered annuities, or TSAs.*[21] A payroll deduction method of collecting the contributions through the employer must be used. Maximum limits for the annual tax-deductible contributions are determined by special formulas. Many life insurance companies are now selling both fixed and variable annuity contracts to this market.

The appeal of IRAs, Keogh plans, and TSAs lies in the *tax incentives* for individuals to build their own pension plans for retirement. Conversely, it has been said that the Pension Reform Act of 1974 "denoted a shift in public policy regarding private pensions from a tax-based orientation to one fundamentally related to *employee security.*"[22] Annuities as discussed in this chapter can be used to achieve the benefits of both these objectives. However, consumers must combine knowledge and preretirement planning well before retirement age in order to reach their goals.

FOR REVIEW AND DISCUSSION

1. How important are annuities, and in what parts of the life insurance business are they used?

2. How are annuities *(a)* like and *(b)* unlike other life insurance contracts?

---

[21] Also called tax-deferred annuities, or TDAs. See Saul W. Adelman and Mark S. Dorfman, "A Comparison of TDA and Non-TDA Investment Returns," *Journal of Risk and Insurance* 44, no. 1 (March 1982), p. 73.

[22] William C. Greenough and Francis P. King, *Pension Plans and Public Policy* (New York: Columbia University Press, 1976), p. 67.

3. Are annuities an important savings medium today? Illustrate your answer with comparisons with other savings media and with reference to any general trends that are observable.

4. What classifications of annuities are important to an understanding of the various uses to which annuities may be put?

5. A fairly common type of individual annuity is a *deferred, installment payment, refund, single life* annuity. Explain the italicized terms, and note why the use of these features might be expected in an annuity.

6. Annuities and life insurance both involve life contingencies. Why is the usual medical examination dispensed with in writing annuities?

7. The 1958 CSO Table of Mortality is conservative for use in computing life insurance premiums. The use of this table for the purpose of computing the cost of an annuity would, therefore, be disastrous. Why?

8. Mr. Julian claims that a sound bond is a better type of investment than an annuity since it provides income and the principal remains intact. Is this statement correct? Explain why or why not.

9. Frank says: "I'm not worried about income for my old age because other things will take care of that. I won't need a private pension." Explain what "other things" Frank may be thinking about, and state why you agree or disagree with his conclusion about a private pension.

10. If you were an employee, what factors would you stress in explaining to a co-worker why you were in favor of (a) an insured pension plan or (b) a noninsured pension plan?

11. An insurance executive states: "Our advocacy of variable annuities stems from the dilemma of many persons now retired on pension plans and annuity incomes that often fail to meet the buyer's needs, primarily because of the impact of inflation on the purchasing power of the dollar." How does the variable annuity remedy this situation? How successfully?

12. From the standpoint of the business of insurance, indicate why the variable annuity should or should not be written by a life insurer.

13. Explain briefly the basic methods by which benefits are (a) determined and (b) funded under pension plans.

14. Why are various retirement dates used in pension plans?

15. What advantages and disadvantages do group annuities have for pension plans as opposed to such alternatives as (a) trusteed plans and (b) individual policy plans?

16. "The Pension Reform Act of 1974 (ERISA) has brought many problems to pension plans, but it has also provided new opportunities for the life insurance business." Explain.

17. Many new incentives for consumers to save are available today. Explain how the Individual Retirement Accounts (IRAs) and other tax-sheltered annuities (TSAs) may help in reaching the goal of retirement security in spite of continued inflation.

Chapter 9

Outline of concepts

Individual health insurance is rapidly growing, perplexing in variety.

  Significance is its needed coverage for many insureds, by many insurers.

  Classification and purpose are important to its understanding.

    Definitions must distinguish accident, sickness, and disability.

    Purpose is benefit payments for *medical expenses* and *loss of income*.

    Classes of health insurance include:

      Method of underwriting, *individual* and *group* health insurance.

      Health perils, accident insurance for *injuries,* and sickness insurance for *illness;* also divided into occupational and nonoccupational types.

      Health insuring organizations include choice among many private insurers, Blue Cross–Blue Shield associations, and other plans.

      Health policies: commercial, industrial, mail-order, special-purpose.

      Health losses and protection are included in *three basic contracts:*

        Hospital, surgical, and regular medical expenses;

        Major medical expenses; and

        Loss-of-income protection, very important and much underinsured.

    Relationship to life insurance is close, for life insurers write more health insurance than casualty or specialized health insurers.

  Provisions in a typical health policy are the:

    Application and policy face, including the "accident insuring" clause.

    Cancelability and renewability, a basic policy feature:

      Cancelable contracts.

      Contracts continued at option of insurer.

      Contracts continued at option of insured.

    Benefit provisions are the heart of the contract and may include benefits for *death, dismemberment or loss of sight, total disability, partial disability, elective indemnity, double indemnity, medical expense,* and *waiver of premium.*

    Exclusions and limitations on benefits are often necessary through:

      Exceptions, for particular perils or losses;

      Reductions, limiting benefits for some injuries or diseases; and

      Riders for substandard health risks, excluding preexisting conditions.

    The standard provisions help provide at least minimum uniformity.

  Underwriting problems and special contracts:

    Overinsurance requires the evaluation of potential moral hazard.

    Factors affecting premiums are *benefits, occupation, sex,* and *age.*

    Special health contracts: *professional, homeowner's disability.*

Individual health insurance

What do you want most in life? Well and poor persons tend to say *wealth*, but sick and rich persons invariably say *health*. Many of us in between probably choose "happiness" as a general goal, hoping that it means some of both.[1] This chapter concerns both goals, too, for the effect of ill health is increased expenses and loss of income, which result in less wealth—*unless* you have proper *health insurance*. If you don't, then some of that happiness may be lost, especially in today's era of high medical care costs.

SIGNIFICANCE OF PRIVATE HEALTH INSURANCE

If one were asked to name the major type of voluntary insurance which is a faster-growing type of protection, covering more persons, through more insurers, in more contract forms than *life* insurance, the only answer would be *health* insurance. The vast scope of this field of insurance is evident in its nearly 2,000 insuring organizations that cover almost 190 million (more than 8 out of 10) Americans in thousands of different policy contracts.[2] Premiums for health insurance have quadrupled in the past 10 years to more than $80 billion a year.

The above comments relate to the *private* health insurance business. The Social Security Amendments of 1965, which included the Medicare program of health insurance for the elderly, were a significant landmark in the expansion by government into insuring against health losses. Some observers predicted that this legislation would mean the continual erosion of the health insurance market. However, today more than two thirds of persons age 65 or older have private insurance policies to supplement Medicare benefits. This chapter and the next relate only to the private health insurance field. Chapter 11 discusses the developments in social health insurance.

---

[1] The statesman Disraeli appropriately said 100 years ago that "the *health* of a people is really the foundation upon which all their *happiness* and all their powers. . . . depend." (In 1877 speech, italics added.)

[2] *Source Book of Health Insurance Data* (Washington, D.C.: Health Insurance Association of America, 1981–82), pp. 6–7.

CLASSIFICATION AND PURPOSE

Definitions

The term *health insurance* applies to those forms of insurance that provide protection against the financial impact of illness or injury. Originally a casualty insurance line, the earliest health protection offered was known as "accident insurance." Later, when sickness coverages were added, it was natural to extend the name of the coverage to "accident and sickness insurance" or "accident and health insurance." The term *disability insurance* has also been used. The older names have by no means been entirely replaced as a part of insurance terminology. However, taken as part of a personal insurance program with life insurance covering life contingencies, *health* insurance is the logical term to apply to health contingencies.

[margin note: NOT TO BE CONFUSED WITH DISABILITY INCOME]

Purpose

Health insurance has as its purpose the payment of benefits for loss of *income* and *expenses* arising from illness and injury. Not only is the loss of time from productive enterprise the source of loss to the insured, but the cost of the care and necessary medical attention adds to the amount of the loss. Health insurance provides protection against *(a)* the loss of time or earning power and *(b)* the added expense of medical care.

Since most persons are dependent on the current income derived from their own efforts, time is their most valuable asset. Health insurance protects this asset as it is reflected in earning power and in so doing protects the independence and welfare of the persons depending upon it. The function of health insurance for the family has been compared to that of business interruption insurance in business operations. It provides income when potential earnings are lost through disability.

Incapacity from illness or injury may also draw heavily upon savings to meet the costs of medical, nursing, or surgical care. Health insurance serves to preserve savings, paying for current expenses and making unnecessary the liquidation or mortgaging of the car or the home in order to pay heavy medical or surgical expenses. In this respect health insurance provides property protection.

Classes

Health insurance includes such a wide variety of insurers, contracts, underwriting methods, perils, and losses that the student should pay particular attention to the classes into which the total field is divided. As a summary, Figure 9–1 shows the organization of all health insurance

Figure 9–1. The types of health insurance

into separate categories according to the different criteria used in the following sections of this chapter. Frequent reference to this breakdown of the field should be helpful in reading the chapter and in understanding the relationships within the whole field of health insurance.

Method of underwriting.   Health insurance is written in one of two ways: *(a)* policies covering the *individual* insured and in certain instances his or her family and *(b)* policies covering *groups* of persons. *Group* forms of health insurance are discussed in Chapter 10. Although many of the basic principles of health insurance are introduced in this chapter on individual contracts, because more than four out of five persons are covered by group contracts the student should also carefully consider the further explanation of coverage in Chapter 10.

Health perils.   In regard to the causes of losses or perils, health insurance may be divided into *(a) accident* insurance, for sudden and unexpected injuries and *(b) sickness* insurance, for illness or diseases. This division was the basis for the traditional description of the fields. The terms have been supplanted to a large extent by the newer term *health* insurance, describing in one word both of the major perils.

Another way of dividing the perils of good health is to describe the source of the injury or illness as being *(a) occupational* or *(b) nonoccupational.* The distinction is useful in several forms of insurance, especially in social insurance plans established by government. Here the classification centers on describing the danger of poor health as one resulting from the work situation (covered under workers' compensation insurance in many cases) and all other situations. The outside-of-work causes would usually be provided for by the individual's own voluntary insurance, but in five states they might be compensated under "nonoccupational" or "temporary" disability laws (see Chapter 11).

Health insuring organizations.   The policyholder has a wide choice among types of voluntary insuring organizations. Totaling approximately 2,000, there are 1,000 insurance companies, 110 Blue Cross or Blue Shield plans, and more than 800 independent plans available. The independent plans include those sponsored by communities, unions, employers, colleges, private health clinics, and the health maintenance organizations (HMOs), which are primarily group plans and are discussed in the next chapter.

It is not to minimize the importance of the many other types of insuring organizations that this chapter analyzes only the policy forms of the insurance companies. The sheer scope of the complete discussion that would be required in order to discuss all the Blue Cross, Blue Shield, and independent plans necessitates confining the emphasis in this chapter to insurance contracts issued by licensed health insurance companies.[3]

The major differences between Blue Cross–Blue Shield and insurance companies are:

1.   *Formation and sponsorship.*   Blue Cross plans are community-sponsored, *nonprofit* associations organized under special state *enabling legislative acts* that exempt them from many of the insurance laws. AND TAXES The impetus for Blue Cross plans has usually come from the *hospitals.* Blue Shield plans are basically sponsored by *physicians* through the medical societies and formed in a similar manner.

2.   *Operation.*   The Blue Cross–Blue Shield plans usually make direct

---

[3] Those students desiring further information about health insurance are referred to: O. D. Dickerson, *Health Insurance* (Homewood, Ill.: Richard D. Irwin, 1968); and Davis W. Gregg and Vane B. Lucas, eds., *Life and Health Insurance Handbook,* 3d ed. (Homewood, Ill.: Richard D. Irwin, 1973).

payments to *the participating hospitals or doctors* for the *services* rendered, in contrast to the insurance companies which pay specified dollar amounts *(indemnity)* to the insureds for their medical expenses. Sometimes Blue Cross–Blue Shield rating procedures vary from those of the insurers, which emphasize "class" rating as opposed to "community" rating plans.

Blue Cross–Blue Shield plans, and other hospital-medical plans, are a significant part of the health insurance field. In 1980 more than $34 billion in "subscriptions" (or premiums) was received by these plans, or about 45 percent of the total health insurance premiums of more than $77 billion in that year. In the hospital-surgical-medical expense area alone, Blue Cross and Blue Shield are even more important that the indicated proportion. For major medical expenses they are less important, and they do not write health insurance for loss of income.[4]

The "Blues" have come into their share of criticism in recent years during the rapid escalation of health care costs, which have risen from $68 a year for each American in 1950 to an estimated $1,225 for 1981, or a total public and private cost of $287 billion.[5] The Federal Trade Commission has resisted attempts by Blue Cross and Blue Shield to merge, citing possible monopoly consequences. Blue Cross and Blue Shield have also been criticized, along with other insurers, for a failure to help control and contain health cost increases. Their boards of directors are under increasing pressure to broaden their representation of the public, as most associations are now heavily controlled by doctors and hospital representatives, who thus can assert too much control over the prices charged for the services they provide. The Blues are also prime contractors for much of the Medicare program, and the need for tighter cost controls is also evident there.

Health insurance policies. Individual or family health insurance policies include: (1) commercial policies, (2) industrial policies, (3) mail-order policies, and (4) special-purpose policies. The *commercial policies* are written on selected risks with large medical expense indemnity limits, and they provide three fourths of the total income protection. The premiums are usually payable annually, semiannually, quarterly, or monthly. Because of their much broader coverage, commercial policies deserve the primary attention in this text. Except for the brief summary of the following three other types, this chapter discusses the usual commercial policies.

Industrial policies are quite similar to commercial policies but more restricted in the amount and variety of their coverage. They are designed for the low-income groups, and premiums are often collected at the home.

---

[4] *Source Book of Health Insurance Data*, p. 28.
[5] "Soaring Costs," *Time*, August 1982, p. 42.

Mail-order policies are quite common, though the tremendous number of these forms and their great variability prevent their detailed discussion here. Since these policies are often very limited in the scope of their protection, consumers should be very careful in purchasing them. Most of them cover only a small part of the health coverage needed. They may cover only accidents, or only income while in the hospital, which provides very short-term protection. They are sold only through the mail or by extensive advertising, without the use of agents.

The *special-purpose policies* should be mentioned more fully here, as examples of the wide variety of coverages. Many special policies are written to cover travel. Some cover only one form of travel, such as travel by airplane, and others cover all travel accidents. Aircraft accident insurance is purchased through vending machines located in airports. Much broader travel accident policies on an annual basis are available through many insurance agents. Many of the major oil companies have made such travel accident insurance available for purchase through their credit cards and monthly billing. American Express and other credit card companies have done likewise.

Another type of special-purpose policy, the so-called dread disease policy, covers medical expenses in connection with one or a number of specific diseases, such as poliomyelitis and cancer, that involve large amounts for medical expenses but occur infrequently.

Dread disease policies and many of these special-purpose contracts are sometimes referred to as "limited policies," which may provide either benefits restricted in amount or duration or broad coverage limited to a specified hazard. Some policies pay so small a proportion of benefits in relation to premium cost that they are banned by state laws.

Special-purpose policies are also written to cover some injuries sustained while participating in sports, on vacation, in summer camps, or on duty as a volunteer fire fighter. Policies are also written providing insurance for students.[6] Limited policies are offered to many newspaper subscribers, with the coverage usually restricted to very small amounts for accident injuries only. Generally, special-purpose policies are *not* recommended because they are so limited in coverage and because they are not needed if the broader commercial forms are used.

Health losses and protection. A final method of classifying the various parts of health insurance is by reference to the kinds of losses caused by the interruption of good health.

Health insurance losses fall into one of two major categories: insurance against (1) the cost of *medical care* and (2) the *loss of income*. Three

---

[6] Many university students have group health policies (see Chapter 10) available to them while in school. Now is a good time to look at your coverage. Some of these group health policies are quite limited, but many provide more coverage at less cost than do individual policies.

important types of insurance protection have emerged. These are *(a)* *hospital, surgical,* and *regular medical* expense protection; *(b)* *major medical* expense protection; and *(c)* *income* protection. The first two of these types help pay the cost of health care. The third type helps replace earnings lost as the result of illness or injury. Income protection policies are written on one person, while policies covering the cost of medical care are written on an individual or a family basis. *→ AS COMPARED TO MAJ MED*

Hospital, surgical, and regular medical expense protection. There are two objectives of *hospital expense* insurance: *(a)* to help pay for the costs of room and board and *(b)* to help pay charges for extra hospital services. The policy limits the amount to be paid each day of hospital confinement, and there is a limit with respect to the number of days that coverage applies. Today policies providing $200 per day for 70–365 days are common and needed. Average room-and-board charges in the United States in 1982 were approximately $170 per day and in some areas were as high as $250 per day, for semiprivate accommodations. Other specified miscellaneous benefits, up to $500–$2,000, are included, such as operating room fees and payment for Xrays, laboratory tests, drugs, anesthetics, and the like. Sometimes the limit of coverage is set as a multiple (10 or 20 times) of the daily hospital room-and-board benefit. Broader contracts include maternity benefits, usually limited to a maximum of $300–$1,200. Many policies include the whole family in one contract. *MOST COMMON NOW IS USUAL + CUST*

The costs of specified operations are covered under the *surgical expense* form. The protection includes surgery in a hospital, and it may include surgical procedures performed in the office or home. Policies generally list the operations for which benefits are provided together with a maximum amount payable for each, from $50–$2,000, perhaps. The schedule of operations generally includes all but the most unusual, and many insurers provide an equitable payment toward the cost of surgical procedures not specifically listed in the contracts. Not all policies covering hospitalization expenses include surgical benefits, but most do.

The *regular medical expense* form is designed to help pay for doctors' fees for nonsurgical care in a hospital, at home, or at the physician's office. It is usually written as an optional coverage in conjunction with the basic hospital and surgical benefits. Some policies may provide preventive services, home nursing, Xray treatment, laboratory and other diagnostic tests, and ambulance service, among other benefits.

Major medical expense protection. Catastrophe coverage against medical care costs is the purpose of *major medical expense* insurance. Instead of providing so-called first-dollar coverage, major medical insurance aims at paying only quite large medical losses. The usual hospital and surgical contracts provide for normal medical expenses. There are, however, illnesses and injuries that are a catastrophe. The serious operation, such illnesses as cancer, multiple sclerosis, and the like, and injuries resulting in total and permanent disability may involve a person or a family in expenses running to thousands of dollars.

Because it is designed to meet health losses of this type, the major medical form has grown rapidly in popularity. Even as compared with other fast-growing health insurance fields, major medical policy growth has been phenomenal during the past 20 years:[7] (1) major medical plans, from 33 million to 155 million persons protected; (2) hospital expense plans, from 123 million to 186 million; (3) surgical expense plans, from 112 million to 175 million; and (4) regular medical expense plans, from 83 million to 167 million persons.

One example illustrates the need for major medical insurance, as the various types of costs for one illness are totalled:

Insured—husband, age 42, lung cancer	
Expenses:	
Hospital room and board 30 days @ $170 =	$ 5,100
Hospital miscellaneous expenses, 30 days =	3,000
Hospital—special nursing, 10 days @ $150 =	1,500
Surgery, removal of one lung =	3,500
Home nursing care, 40 days @ $60 =	2,400
Miscellaneous—doctor, medicines at home =	2,500
Total	$18,000

Because more than 90 percent of major medical policies are written today in group (see Chapter 10) rather than individual contracts, only a brief description is presented here. There are four identifying characteristics of major medical insurance: *(a)* the *deductible, (b) participation* or *coinsurance,* and *(c) high maximum limits,* for *(d) blanket medical expenses.* EXCLUSIONS ARE IN CONTRACT.

The *deductible* feature obligates the insured person to pay the initial part of the expenses, which is called the deductible amount. Under individual and family major medical policies, the common range of the deductible is between $100 and $1,000, and sometimes it goes as high as $2,000. The purpose is to avoid frequent small loss payments (usually covered by hospital insurance) and thus to keep the cost of the insurance low. Most deductibles apply to a calendar year; they may apply to each individual or to the entire family. ⤷ ALSO PER DISABILITY DEDUCTIBLE

25,000

When expenses exceed the deductible amount, the policy benefits begin. Under a *coinsurance* feature (or "participation agreement"), the insurer then pays its share. For example, if the insurer is obligated to pay 80 percent of all hospital, doctor, and other medical bills in excess of the deductible sum, the remaining percentage, or 20 percent, is paid by the

---

[7] *Source Book of Health Insurance Data,* p. 12.

policyholder. The purpose of the coinsurance feature is to prevent overuse
or excessive costs of medical facilities and treatment.

Policy benefits are payable up to a *high maximum* specified amount.
$50,000 or more limits are common today; $250,000 or unlimited amounts
have also been written. The maximum benefit may be written to apply
to each illness or injury, and a lifetime maximum is frequently also
used. Today's rapidly rising medical costs suggest frequent reevaluation
of the limit carried.

All types of medical expenses are covered, on a *blanket* basis, including
hospital, surgical, doctor, nursing, and miscellaneous medical costs. There
are no individual limits that apply for the various types of expense.

The deductible and the coinsurance features operate together as follows: With a policy carrying a $500 deductible, in the event of a medical
expense of $5,500 the insured pays the first $500 of expenses. With an
80 percent coinsurance feature, the insurer pays 80 percent of the balance
($5,000), or $4,000, and the insured pays $1,000. The total cost to the
patient would be $1,500, and much of this may be covered by other
basic hospital-surgical policies which most insureds have.

Loss-of-income protection.   Income loss is often the most important
result of injury or illness, in many cases exceeding the cost of medical
care. *Loss-of-income* protection becomes an essential part of any good
health insurance program. This form, sometimes known as "disability
income" protection, is designed to help replace loss of income or earning
power because of illness or injury.

It is a major peril. For a person aged 22 the probability of a serious
disability (90 days or more) is more than *seven* times as great as the
probability of death; at age 42 it is more than four times as great; and
at age 62 it is more than twice as great. Disability income loss payments
by insurers are more than $6 billion a year.

Income benefits are usually expressed as a weekly or monthly sum,
such as $200 per week, or $800 per month. Sometimes the maximum
amount payable is also limited, for example, to 80 percent of regular
gross income. The definition of "disability" used in the contract is extremely important, as this determines the extent of benefits payable
under the contract. The differences between "total" and "partial" disability, and other features, are discussed later in this chapter.

Contracts offered by the various insurers vary greatly. Because there
are many different forms of coverage and many differences among insurers, there tends to be much competition with respect to selling. Sometimes, emphasis is placed upon the protection afforded rather than upon
the premium charged. If emphasis is placed upon a particularly low
premium, the coverage under the contract may be expected to be limited.
In this field, as in others, it is unreasonable to expect to get more than
what is paid for. The policyholder should give careful attention to the

IT IS BETTER TO PAY MORE THAN YOU PLANNED
THEN TO PAY LESS THAN YOU SHOULD

details of the contract because failure to understand the limitations of the policy may lead to disappointment.   Z

Almost every individual or family should have *three basic health insurance contracts:* (1) *hospital-surgical-medical,* (2) *major medical,* and (3) *disability income.* The first two are often available through group plans (discussed in Chapter 10), but individual purchase of proper disability income contracts is usually necessary.

Relationship to life insurance

More life insurance insurers write health insurance than casualty insurers or insurers that specialize in health insurance only. Also, even though health insurance is a major kind of insurance written by casualty insurers (over $3.5 billion in premiums a year), life insurance insurers write more than four fifths of the total health insurance in the United States, excluding Blue Cross–Blue Shield coverage.

For a considerable time there was some reluctance on the part of life insurers to write health insurance coverages. Limited protection in the form of total and permanent disability income and a waiver-of-premium benefit during total disability represented the first attempts on the part of life insurers to recognize health impairments as a part of the life insurance business. However, in the course of analyzing the personal insurance needs of families, it became readily apparent that loss of time and income attributable to injury or illness could disrupt family finances, as could expensive medical care. Health insurance appeared to be the answer.

Thus most life insurers today offer health insurance as an endorsement or "rider" to the life insurance contract, as in total disability waiver-of-premium and disability income benefits, and in extra payments for accidental death. (See Chapter 7.) Also, many life insurers write, under regular forms of individual or group health insurance, benefits for *(a)* hospital, surgical, and medical expense; *(b)* major medical expense; and *(c)* loss of income due to disability.

The close relationship of life insurance, health insurance, and social security benefits suggests that many of the features of these plans should be analyzed together. A complete estate planning program for the family necessitates a coordination of these voluntary and governmental insurance fields to provide the policyholder with an integrated arrangement for meeting personal insurance risks. Chapter 12 discusses this need further.

PROVISIONS IN A TYPICAL HEALTH POLICY

Although a "typical" health contract is as hard to find as the hypothetical "average" person of the U.S. Census Bureau statistics, this section endeavors to describe some of the more important provisions of such a policy. No one specific contract is used as a model; health contracts vary too much among companies and kinds of policies. The best advice that can be given to health insurance policyholders is to read *their* contract, for only then can they tell exactly what their rights and obligations are—and they will probably need the help and advice of good insurance agents to do that.

Many of the provisions discussed in this section are those of the usual commercial health insurance contract for medical expenses and loss of income (which the student should now recognize as having many variations in the health insurance field). For most individuals or families it is a contract purchased in addition to (1) a hospital-surgical policy and (2) a major medical expense policy. The *loss-of-income benefit* becomes the *predominant feature* of the contract. Oftentimes, the contract may still be titled as an "accident and health" or "accident and sickness" policy. Normally, the provisions discussed here are those found in the conditionally renewable type of contract, that is, the kind which may be renewed at the option of the insurer. The provisions, except for the renewability feature, may be quite similar in most of their details to the noncancelable and guaranteed renewable contracts discussed later.

The general form and content of the health insurance policy may be divided into four principal divisions: *(a)* the *application and policy face, (b) cancelability and renewability, (c)* the *benefit provisions,* and *(d)* the *standard provisions.*

Application and policy face

Briefly, the policy face contains the essential elements of an insuring agreement between the insurer and the insured. A summary of the coverage and benefits, a statement of the renewability features, and a reference to the application are usually found here.

The application.   The *application* is required as a basis for the contract, and the insurer relies upon the statements made therein for much of its underwriting information. All states require that the application be attached to the policy form; and both together constitute the contract. There is no standard form of application for a health insurance contract, although the applications of most companies follow a general pattern. They supply the underwriter information that will *(a)* identify the applicant, *(b)* give adequate information to determine the occupational exposure, *(c)* list health insurance benefits from all other sources and indicate whether insurance will exceed earnings, and *(d)* show the applicant's past and present physical condition. The insured acknowledges that false answers in the application may be used to bar recovery in the event that the answers are material to the acceptance of the risk assumed by the insurer.

The policy face. The printed *policy face* contains the name of the insurer, and it should state the times when the insurance takes effect and terminates. The entire consideration for which the policy is issued should appear in the contract. A summary of the benefit provisions (discussed in next section) usually appears on this first page. As an example of one clause which is normally found on the policy face, because of its extreme importance, the accident-insuring clause deserves special attention.

Differences in wording in the *accident-insuring clause* that may seem inconsequential to the layperson may have the effect of limiting the scope of the coverage. The clause may provide benefits for "bodily injury sustained through accidental means," or the clause may read "accidental bodily injuries," thus covering all unintended injuries that are accidental. The importance of the difference is that nearly half of all injuries are the consequence of an intended act and therefore not caused by accidental means. The "accidental bodily injuries" coverage is the broader and preferable form.

The popular notion of an "accident" as anything unexpected is not enough to qualify for loss payment in some contracts. This difference is illustrated by the following example. A man piling wood strains his back and as a result is unable to work. In piling the wood, he did exactly what he intended to do, though the injury to his back was a consequence. There was no accident; therefore, the injury would not fall within the insuring clause covering losses attributable to accidental means. If while piling the wood, the man had slipped and injured himself or had dropped a piece of wood with a resulting injury, there would have been an injury effected through accidental means.

The policy does cover losses attributable to disease or losses to which disease contributed. The phrase "independently of all other causes" that appears in the insuring clauses of many accident policies is very broad, and if interpreted literally it might nullify the intent of the contract. For this reason court interpretations have tended to favor the insured. If an infection is a natural or inevitable consequence of an accident, the accident is regarded as the cause of the infection or death. The courts have held that an injury that might naturally produce death in a person in a poor state of health is the cause of death even if the person would not have died had his or her previous health been different.[8]

Finally, there is the situation in which there is little evidence of the cause of a death except that it involved violence. For example, when an insured dies from injuries received at the hands of another, the legal

---

[8] Justice Cardozo, in the now-often-quoted case of *Silverstein* v. *Metropolitan Life Insurance Company* (254 N.Y. 81; 171 N.E. 914), stated: "A policy of insurance is not accepted with the thought that its coverage is to be restricted to an Apollo or a Hercules."

doctrine of presumptions operates to hold that the injuries were accidental rather than intentionally inflicted.[9]

CONDITIONALLY RENEWABLE
"NON-CAN"

Cancelability and renewability

One of the most important features of health insurance policies is
the right of insureds to keep the contract in force. Most individual health
policies are sold on an annual renewal basis. However, in some contracts
the insurer or insured can cancel the policy at any time during the
year with short notice. In most health contracts, the *insurer* has the
option of not continuing the protection at renewal date. Less common,
but more certain for the insured, are those contracts in which coverage
is continued at the option of the *insured.* Unfortunately, these types
of health insurance are also the most expensive. Thus, the coverage of
most health insurance is usually limited in duration, in contrast to life
insurance which is often permanent.

Health insurance policies written today may be divided into three
groups:[10] (1) those which are *cancelable,* (2) those which are continued
at the option of the *insurer,* and (3) those which are continued at the
option of the *insured.*

Cancelable contracts. Policies that are *cancelable* afford the insurer
the right to cancel the policy *at any time* on five or more days' written
notice to the insured. The insured may also cancel the coverage with
similar notice to the insurer. Such contracts are not common. Thus,
for most policies the feature that is most likely to be of importance is
whether it is the insurer or the insured who has the option to continue
the coverage from year to year.

Contracts which are continued at the option of the insurer. Usually, these contracts *do not have to be renewed by the insurer,* although
they may not be canceled during the policy term. Two types of policies
are used, those which are "optionally" renewable and those which are
"conditionally" renewable.

In the *optionally renewable type,* the insurer may refuse to renew
the contract, may increase the premiums, or may add restrictions to
the coverage. This is the most common provision in health insurance

---

[9] *Sheppard* v. *Midland Mutual Life Insurance Company,* 13 CCH Life Cases 1001; 152
Ohio 6; 87 N.E. (2d) 156. The court stated: "One of the well-recognized presumptions of
the law is that, where it is shown that death resulted from bodily injury caused by violent
and external means without showing as to how the injury was in fact sustained, there is
a presumption that death did not result from suicide."

[10] Other sources may add additional categories. "Term" contracts, which have no renewal
rights and terminate at the end of the policy period, are mostly used in air travel accident
or group student contracts. "Collectively renewable" contracts are similar to "conditionally
renewable" policies but are only issued on a group basis. See S. S. Huebner and Kenneth
Black, Jr., *Life Insurance* (Englewood Cliffs, N.J.: Prentice-Hall, 1982), pp. 266–67.

policies. Although the contract usually is renewed (even if the insured has changed occupations, has filed a claim, or is in worse health than the previous year), the insured has no right to demand that the coverage continue. However, the initial cost of an optionally renewable contract is the lowest of those continued at the option of the insurer.

Also frequently used, policies that are *conditionally renewable* give the insurer the right to refuse to renew the contract but usually only if *all* contracts of the same class are not renewed. The insurer cannot refuse to renew, however, solely on the basis of declining health by the individual policyholder. Conditionally renewable contracts are not as bad for the insured as it may seem. The premium cost is low, and among most reputable insurers the cases of nonrenewal are infrequent (often a fraction of 1 percent per year). Premium increases are applied only when losses for a whole class justify the change. For the insured who loses his or her coverage during failing health, however, the effect is serious. Consequently, there is an increasing interest in contracts where the insured rather than the insurer have the option to continue health insurance protection.

Contracts which are continued at the option of the insured.   Two types of health insurance contracts provide a guarantee to insureds that they have the option to continue the protection. Typically, the option is available up to a specified age such as 65, when most policyholders will become eligible for the federal Medicare plan.

The first type is a *guaranteed renewable* contract. If the premiums are paid when due, the insured has the option to continue protection. The insurer cannot refuse to renew the policy according to the specified conditions. Some states laws specify that a contract of this type issued before or at age 44 must be renewable, as a minimum, to age 50; after age 44, it must be renewable for at least 5 years and provide maximum benefits for at least 10 years or to age 65. Most important, however, is that the *premiums may be changed by classes*. With the rapidly increasing cost of medical care, this provision is reasonable for medical expense contracts. The insurer may not increase the premium solely for the individual policyholder but can do so for an entire class of policies. No illness or injury of the insured will terminate the coverage. The option of the insured to continue protection is guaranteed as specified, although the premium cost is not.

The second type of option for the insured is found in a *noncancelable* contract, which by statute in many states has been defined as one in which the *insured has the right to continue protection for a given period at guaranteed premium rates*. The insurer cannot cancel the policy except for nonpayment of premium. Usually, up to the insured's age 65, the insurer cannot refuse to renew it and cannot increase the premiums.

Table 9–1. Cancelability and renewability provisions in individual health insurance policies

Provision	Who has the right to cancel or renew, and when?	Can the policy premium or coverage be changed?
Cancelable contracts*	Insurer or insured may cancel, anytime during policy period (with 5 days' or more written notice).	No, but the contract can be canceled. Premium and coverage is fixed for the policy period (usually 1 year).
Contracts continued at the option *of the insurer:*		
Optionally renewable	Insurer's option, at renewal date.	Yes. Insurer may increase the premium or may add other coverage restrictions.
Conditionally renewable	Insurer's option, at renewal date, *but only for all contracts of the same class.*	Yes. Insurer may increase the premium, *but only for all contracts of the same class.*
Contracts continued at the option *of the insured:*		
Guaranteed renewable	Insured's option, at renewal date (if issued at or before age 44, to age 50; otherwise for minimum of 5 years).	Yes. Insurer may increase the premium, *but only for all contracts of the same class.*
Noncancelable†	Insured's option, at renewal date, usually up to age 65.	No. Insurer cannot cancel or refuse to renew (except for nonpayment of premium) and cannot increase the premium.

* Note that cancelable contracts may sometimes also have renewable provisions, but that most renewable policies are not cancelable during the policy period.

† Noncancelable contracts, as the term is usually used, are also guaranteed renewable.

Source: Adapted with major revisions from Robert I. Mehr and Emerson Cammack, *Principles of Insurance* (Homewood, Ill.: Richard D. Irwin, 1981), p. 419.

Noncancelable contracts are used ~~occasionally~~ *often* in writing disability income insurance but seldom are used for medical expense insurance. Noncancelable contracts provide better coverage for the policyholder but are often several times more expensive than contracts in which the premiums can be changed, or in which the insurer can refuse to renew the protection. Because disabilities increase with the age of insureds, reserves similar to those for level premium life insurance are required for noncancelable contracts. Usually, however, there are no cash values as in life insurance, although a few health insurers have offered a contract which pays a refund of excess premiums to policyholders who have had few claims after a specified number of years.

The benefit provisions

The benefit provisions are the heart of the health insurance contract. These provisions indicate the amount and nature of the benefits for which the insurer is liable for stated disabilities. Benefits payable under a health insurance policy are payable directly to the named insured, except that in the case of death benefits payment is made to a beneficiary designated in the contract. It is through the benefits that the policy attains its objective of protecting incomes and reimbursing insureds for medical expenses. Some of the various available benefits will be treated individually. The more important of these are found in disability policies under the classifications: *(a) death* benefits, *(b) dismemberment, (c) total disability, (d) partial disability, (e) elective indemnities, (f) double indemnities, (g) medical expense benefits,* and *(h) waiver-of-premium* benefit. Since the first benefit, for death, is similar to the accidental death benefits already discussed in Chapter 7, no further mention of it will be made here.

Dismemberment or loss of sight benefits. Many health insurance policies contain a provision for the payment of lump sums for loss of sight or limbs instead of the weekly or monthly income benefits, but only if the disability is caused by an accident. It is customary to express the lump sums so provided in a multiple of the weekly or monthly benefit. Column 1 in Table 9–2 gives an example. If no weekly indemnity is provided, it is customary to indicate the indemnity for dismemberment and loss of sight in terms of the principal sum (or death benefit), as shown in column 2 of Table 9–2.

Table 9–2. Dismemberment and loss of sight benefits

For loss of	*(1)* Sum equal to indemnity for:	*(2)* Sum equal to:
Both hands, both feet, or sight of both eyes	200 weeks	Principal sum
Hand and foot	200 weeks	Principal sum
Hand or foot and eye	200 weeks	Principal sum
Hand or foot	100 weeks	½ principal sum
Sight of one eye	65 weeks	⅓ principal sum
Thumb and index finger	50 weeks	¼ principal sum

Blindness and dismemberment benefits are often given prominence in the policy and may be mistakenly regarded as an added and attractive feature. As a matter of fact, if the policy gives the insurer the right to substitute a lump-sum payment for continued income payments, it may not be as broad as a policy providing long-term income payments for sickness as well as accident.

Total disability benefits. There is a wide range in the coverages afforded by the various health policies in the market. The definition of "total disability" under one policy may differ entirely from that under a second. For example, a few contracts may require house confinement for total disability, while most contracts define the condition as "inability on the part of the insured to perform any of the duties of *his or her* occupation." A third policy may define total disability as the "inability to perform the duties of *any* occupation whatsoever."

Over the years judicial decisions have broadened the more limited definitions. The courts have tended to interpret the "any gainful occupation" clause to mean something more than selling lead pencils on the street corner. If insureds were unable to engage in occupations for which they were reasonably fitted by education and experience and which would yield them a reasonable livelihood, then the policy was held to cover.

Largely as a result of these court decisions, the common statement of total disability appearing in modern health policies is: (1) a period of one or two years in which the insured is "unable to perform any and every duty pertaining to his or her own occupation"; (2) after which period it is "complete inability to engage in any and every gainful occupation for which reasonably fitted."

It is customary to further classify health loss-of-income policies as those requiring an elimination, or "waiting," period, and those without an elimination period. The elimination period is that period at the beginning of a disability for which no benefits are paid. A policy may provide that benefits are not payable for the first several days, weeks, or months of disability. The waiting period reduces the cost of insurance considerably and is also justified because coverage for short-term disability often may be taken care of by an employee's sick-leave plan at work or by his or her savings.

Some policies, including mail-order ones, base benefits upon the first visit of a physician; others to the time when insureds are in a hospital. The highly restricted nature of such benefits is obvious when one knows, for example, that the average hospital stay is only about one week.

Partial disability benefits. Certain policies may make payments of income at a reduced rate if disability is determined to be partial. Accident policies often recognize partial disability. A policy that requires disability to be continuous and total from the time of the accident is too limited, since frequently real disabilities evidence themselves sometime after the accident. For partial disability a percentage of the weekly or monthly benefit is provided. Fifty percent of the benefit is usual, though sometimes the percentage is lower. *SAME % AS LOSS OF INCOME SO LONG AS MINIMUM IS MET.*

Insurers cover partial disability attributable to sickness much less frequently. The dividing line between no disability and partial disability is difficult to define. The test of partial disability rests upon the inability of the insured to perform a part of his or her work. The policy usually sets a limit to the period for which the insured is entitled to partial disability, such as a number of weeks, months, or years.

Elective indemnity benefits. In some instances the insured may be offered an elective indemnity in the form of a lump sum instead of income payments during disability. Table 9–3 gives a schedule indicating the nature of the options offered under this clause.

Table 9–3. Accident policy schedule

For complete dislocation of joints:		For complete fracture of bones:	
Hip	$1,000	Skull	$1,200
Knee (patella excepted) or ankle	500	Thigh or arm above elbow	1,000
Wrist or elbow	400	Pelvis	800
Shoulder	350	Shoulder blade, leg, or kneecap	600
One or more fingers or toes	150	Collarbone or forearm	500

Double indemnity benefits. Accident policies frequently provide for double indemnity in the event that injuries or deaths are sustained under specified circumstances, such as (a) while the insured is a passenger in or upon a public conveyance provided by a common carrier for passenger service; (b) while the insured is a passenger in an elevator car provided for passenger service only; (c) while the insured is in a building whose outer walls collapse or in a building that burns; and (d) if injuries are received by the explosion of a steam boiler, by a hurricane or tornado, or by a stroke of lightning.

As with the double indemnity feature in the life insurance contract, this benefit is devoid of logic. Dependents of a deceased insured have the same needs whether the accident that causes death is lightning, providing double indemnity, or a fall down a flight of stairs, where only the principal sum is paid. Or to cite another example, an accidental death in one's own car provides only single indemnity. Some of these benefits take on the characteristic of "window dressing." The chance of securing the additional benefit is often extremely remote, yet it is frequently held out as an attractive feature to encourage purchase of the particular contract.

Medical expense benefits. Medical expense benefits are included in many health policies. Some contracts cover only medical expenses, while others cover loss of income too. Many contracts of insurers cover only certain types of medical expenses, such as hospital-surgical expenses similar to those in Blue Cross–Blue Shield contracts. The contract usually provides hospital coverage as a per diem allowance for daily room and board with extra allowances for miscellaneous purposes for a maximum number of days.

Table 9–4. Schedule of indemnities for operations

Abdomen	$1,200	Chest—cutting into thoracic cavity	$750
Amputation of:		Ear, nose, or throat	300
Thigh	1,000	Eye—removal of	800
Arm, leg, or entire foot	800	Inflammation of joint	500
Forearm or entire hand	600	Paracentesis—tapping of abdomen	400

When surgical benefits are found in the policy, the amounts indicated are payable in addition to other indemnities. Table 9–4 gives a partial list as an example of a schedule of indemnities for operations.

Waiver-of-premium benefits. Policies are written containing a clause which waives the premium payments after total disability has run for a given time during the indemnity paying period, such as 90 days. If premiums are paid up to that time, the policy cannot thereafter lapse during the total disability period. This provision is valuable because during a period of disability the needs of insureds may call for all their resources and they are not required to divert any of them to premium payments.

Exclusions and limitations on benefits

Contracts are often issued on insureds who for one reason or another are expected to have a greater chance or amount of loss than usual. Many contracts contain exceptions, reductions, or riders that limit benefits in either frequency or amount.

Exceptions. An *exception* in a health policy is a provision whereby coverage for a specified hazard is entirely eliminated. It is a statement of a risk not assumed. For example, the policy may not cover hernia. Some policies provide that losses caused by sunstroke, freezing, or injuries where there are no visible wounds are to be considered only under the sickness provisions of the policy. Other policies except coverage while the insured is in, or if the loss results from, military or naval service. Some policies specifically limit coverage to the United States and Canada or Europe. Because of the protection that workers' compensation and occupational disease statutes afford to most people actively employed, some insurers issue policies excluding occupational injuries and disease. These policies are known as "nonoccupational."

It is customary for individual health insurance policies to provide that benefits will be payable for disabilities occurring after the policy becomes effective. The intent is to exclude from coverage *preexisting conditions*—conditions that have their origin prior to the commencement of coverage under the policy. Since it is not always easy to determine the exact time of onset of sickness, the usual policy says that benefits will be paid only for sickness contracted and commencing from 15–30 days or more following the policy date. This time is known as the *probationary period* or the "qualification period." The provision safeguards the insurer against applicants who fail to disclose fully their knowledge of an existing disease or impairment.

Reductions. A *reduction* is a provision which takes away some portion, but not all, of the coverage of the policy under certain specific conditions. For example, the statement that disability income for hernia is limited to one month where the policy provides indemnity for longer than a month for other conditions is a reduction. Policies sometime provide for payment of only a percentage of the full benefits after the insured reaches a designated age. For particular sicknesses or specified conditions, there can be extra waiting periods, such as 9 or 12 months for maternity benefits. Disability income policies often have a deductible or waiting period of several weeks or months after disability begins, before benefits start.

Riders for substandard health risks. Normal health is usually required for a standard risk. However, policies are issued today to persons with impaired health, with the specific condition not covered or otherwise qualified. Some contracts provide for full coverage with an increased premium. Where an unrestricted policy cannot be issued, the *impairment rider* or endorsement attached to the policy provides protection against all disability hazards, excluding only the causes of disability which exist at the time the policy is issued. The rider is an important factor in providing disability insurance. Without its use many more applications would be rejected. When a rider has been attached to a policy (for example, following an operation), the rider may be removed, after a period to be determined by the insurer, if no ill effects of the condition covered by the rider have evidenced themselves. Insurance for impaired risks is now available for many types of cardiac conditions, cancer, diabetes, epilepsy, and the like.

Sometimes, instead of issuing a policy with a rider, the underwriter finds it necessary to ask the applicant for a *postponement* of the application for a period of time following recovery from a disease or an operation. If the applicant shows continued recovery over a period of six months or a year, then he or she may be accepted for insurance with or without a rider.

The standard provisions

There is no standard health policy; competition has brought scores of contracts to the market. The nearest approach to a standard policy is to be found in the requirements for *uniform or standard provisions* adopted by the various states. Although there are some deviations in the laws as enacted, these laws are substantially in accord with the Uniform Individual Accident and Sickness Policy Provisions Law, approved by the National Association of Insurance Commissioners in 1950. Sometimes these clauses are called "general provisions" in the contract. They may include some 11 optional provisions in addition to the 12 mandatory "standard provisions" adopted by almost all states.

The standard provisions do not standardize benefits. They are concerned only with operating conditions of the policy. Policies must be approved by the insurance department of the state of issue, and exceptions in the policy must be given the same prominence as the benefits. Although each policy must contain the required provisions or approved corresponding provisions of different wording, the law is sufficiently flexible to permit the insurer to experiment with more liberal policies and claim procedures. The purpose of the standard provisions is to effect a reasonable degree of uniformity in policies and to phrase important conditions in such a way as to make them understandable. The provisions serve to eliminate confusion and misunderstanding. As has been noted, there is no requirement with respect to a literal wording of the provisions.

The more important standard provisions concern rights of the policyholder to: (1) policy changes, (2) incontestability (after two or three years, usually), (3) a grace period for premium payments, (4) reinstatement, and (5) change of beneficiary. The insurer is given the following rights in the standard provisions: (1) written notice of loss (usually within 20 or 30 days), (2) proofs of loss, and (3) right to examine the insured and to autopsy. An example of an optional provision that is sometimes included is a clause which reduces benefits to conform with the proper rating classification if the insured misstates his or her age or changes to a more hazardous occupation. Other common optional provisions used today are: "other insurance" clauses, which reduce payments if there are other contracts of which the insurer has not been notified; "average earnings" clauses, which reduce or prorate loss-of-income benefits if all such benefits exceed the insured's recent earnings (see section on "overinsurance"); and "coordination of benefits" clauses, which determine the order of payment (up to 100 percent of expenses) among several medical expenses contracts that may apply.

UNDERWRITING PROBLEMS AND SPECIAL CONTRACTS

For the insurer, the disability risk involves considerable difficulty. Malingering and fraudulent claims have tended to swell the cost of benefits far beyond the expectations upon which premiums were predicted. Overinsurance has aroused the temptation to extend periods of disability that would unquestionably be shorter without insurance. In periods of unemployment, unwarranted claims have increased sharply. Careful selection and rating and the strict elimination of overinsurance have been suggested as solutions to underwriting difficulties. These measures, together with a realistic attitude toward claim adjustment, will unquestionably help but have proved difficult in application.

This section discusses the problem of overinsurance, the basic factors affecting the premium cost, and several special health insurance contracts.

Overinsurance

Many insurance contracts limit the payment to an amount that will indemnify the insured for his or her loss. In property insurance, the face amount of the policy is the maximum benefit; but if the actual loss to the insured is less than the face of the policy, the liability of the insurer is limited to the actual loss. In life insurance, a specific valued amount rather than indemnity is paid. As for health insurance, its intent is to make good to the insured (1) the cost of medical care and (2) the loss of earnings directly attributable to the disability.

Overinsurance in paying for *medical care costs* is infrequent because most individual contracts are based on services provided, or on actual reimbursement for expenses paid by the policyholder. However, in some *group* contracts a special provision called the *coordination-of-benefits* (COB) clause is used. This clause avoids double payment in such cases as two-income families where both spouses might be covered as dependents. Then both group insurers coordinate their payments by determining which insurer should pay first, and which should pay only after the other's benefits have been exhausted. In spite of increased administrative costs, some employers using the COB clause find that this is a fair method of reducing loss payments.

Reasonably estimating the amount of *disability income* lost by the insured is the major problem in individual health contracts. Because neither the number of disability income contracts that an insured may obtain nor the total amount payable under several contracts is limited, control of overinsurance is primarily the underwriter's job. In terms of adequate insurance coverage, there is nothing to be said for overinsurance. In the light of its dangers, there is much to be said against it. Since the contract itself is not usually limited to indemnity (that is, the insured does not have to prove the loss of a specified amount of income, and even an unemployed disabled person is entitled to collect under disability income contracts), the proper underwriting limits assume major importance in preventing overinsurance.

Overinsurance creates a continuing moral hazard in the disability income insurance field. There is overinsurance when the aggregate benefits exceed the loss which the insured suffers. The temptation to prolong a disability is strong if it proves profitable to the insured to do this. However, too drastic a reduction in benefits defeats the purpose of insurance. In an attempt to provide adequate insurance and at the same time protect the insurer against overinsurance, several optional provisions of the Uniform Law often help prevent overpayment.

The *other insurance* provision reduces the benefit payments proportionally if other unreported individual health insurance is found to be in force when a claim is presented. A provision particularly important for the long-term noncancelable or guaranteed renewable policies is the *average earnings clause*. The amount of benefit payable at any time is typically reduced if the insurance in force in all insurers exceeds a specified percentage (such as 80 percent) of the gross earned income of the claimant at the time of the commencement of disability, or his or her average monthly earnings for the two-year period preceding disability, whichever is the greater. The reduction is proportionate, and a minimum monthly benefit may be included. The goal of avoiding overinsurance is best achieved if the disability income contract pays no more than the net take-home pay, after taxes and work expenses of the policyholder are considered. For this reason, health insurance underwriters often limit the amount of disability income insurance written to approximately 80 percent of the applicant's gross income and also use the average earnings clause to prevent overinsurance.

Factors affecting premiums

Benefits. The most important factor varying the cost of health insurance is the amount and the nature of benefits. The scope of some policies is limited to certain kinds of injuries, whereas other policies cover both injury and sickness for almost every conceivable disability. Among the factors that have a bearing upon the cost of benefits are: *(a)* frequency of occurrence, *(b)* cost of benefit, and *(c)* duration. In determining the effect of accidental death benefits on costs, only knowledge of the rate of death by accident is required. In the case of surgical benefits, both the claim frequency and the amount of the average claim have a bearing. Disability income benefits involve the frequency of the disability and its average duration. The premium may vary from as little as $1 a year for a limited accident policy, such as those issued to newspaper subscribers or airplane travelers, to many hundred dollars a year for a broad medical expense and loss-of-income contract for almost all injuries and diseases.

In addition to the amount and nature of the benefits, at least three other factors enter into the computation of the premium of a health policy: (1) occupation, (2) sex, and (3) age.

Occupation. Health insurance manuals have an elaborate system of classification of occupations. Basic rates are computed that reflect the average experience of all occupational classes. A reduction from this average is allowed for the less hazardous occupations, and increased premiums are charged where the loss experience is expected to be above the average. Occupations are grouped into four or more classes which are given alphabetical designations. The premium charge for a policy advances sharply from the lower rated classes to the higher, and some persons employed in the more hazardous occupations may obtain coverage only from Lloyd's underwriters or specialty insurers. Some risks are usually classed as prohibited for occupational reasons, while others are written only after extra careful underwriting.[11]

Sex. The cost for health insurance benefits is considerably higher for women than for men. Separate rate tables are provided for men and women, or premiums for women are quoted as a multiple of those quoted for men. The cost of benefits for females may exceed the cost of similar benefits for males by 50 to 200 percent. Much of the increased cost of benefits for women is due to the fact that the claims of women are not only more frequent than those of men but last for a longer period. This results not only in longer disability income payments but in additional costs for hospital, surgical, and medical care. There are in addition costs attributable to maternity benefits. All of these factors tend to increase disability costs, with the exception of accidental death and dismemberment benefits, for women over comparable charges for men.

Age. The factor of age, while important, does not have the impact in health insurance that might be expected. Particularly under cancelable policies or policies renewable at the option of the insurer in the 50-year-and-under class, premiums do not usually vary with each age. However, age very definitely is a factor of increase under noncancelable and guaranteed renewable policies; there premium charges range upward year by year or by age groups. All premiums are raised for the senior years, this being justified by the morbidity (sickness) experience tables. For accident insurance the rates are often the same for a given manual classification between the ages of 18 and 60. Many insurers increase medical expense insurance premiums above age 50.

Special health insurance contracts

Several health insurance contracts have been designed for special situations which fall outside the normal underwriting practices of most insurers. Some insurers issue health insurance coverages under professional overhead, professional accident, and homeowners' disability plans.

---

[11] Typical prohibited groups are workers who use such substances as lead, acids, poisonous gases, or chemicals, and those engaged in dusty trades, such as woodworkers or granite workers. The carefully underwritten category includes actors, artists, musicians, and others who have no regular working hours or schedule.

Professional overhead policies. There is a *professional overhead policy* that covers expenses incurred during disabilities, usually with a waiting period of 30 days or more. This is a form of loss-of-time protection with benefit payments monthly. The insured is indemnified in an amount equal to actual business expenses for rent, taxes, public utility services, wages of employees, and other expenses normally incurred in the operation of the insured's office. The policy is of particular interest to architects, consulting engineers, dentists, doctors, lawyers, and public accountants, to mention but a few. It does not provide complete disability income protection for the insured, for it covers only business operating expenses.

Professional accident policies. Special *professional accident policies* provide sizable benefits for those whose professional activities would be seriously impaired as the result of an accidental injury. Members of the dental and surgical profession, for example, could suffer a much more serious loss than those engaged in other business operations through the loss of the use of fingers or a hand. Following is an example of such a policy: accidental death, total disability, or loss of a single leg, arm, or both eyes, $300,000; loss of use of one hand, foot, or eye, $150,000; loss of use of two or more fingers on one hand, $75,000.

Homeowners' disability policies. Term life insurance is frequently written on a decreasing basis in connection with the mortgage on the dwelling of the insured. If the insured dies before the mortgage is paid off, insurance will be available to liquidate the loan in full. Some *homeowners' disability policies* also cover mortgage payments in case the insured is disabled due to either injury or illness. The policy provides an inexpensive assurance that given a temporary disability involving considerable expense, the mortgage payments will be met. The benefits are payable for a limited period, usually about two years. This innovation is one of the first examples of a true "all-lines" insurance contract (see Chapter 23) combining fire, casualty, life, and health insurance in a single combination policy. The coverages are usually included without a medical examination, based upon statements about prior and present health conditions made by the applicant.

FOR REVIEW AND DISCUSSION

1. For each of the following most misunderstood facts about health insurance, explain *why* you do *not* agree that:
   a. All health contracts are about the same.
   b. You can't get health insurance if you have a history of illness.
   c. Major medical policies pay for all catastrophic medical expenses.
   e. The best way is to buy many health insurance contracts.
2. How would you outline the various classes of health insurance? Compare the different ways in which the whole health insurance field can be classified.

3. Health insurance contracts are noted for the extreme variability in the scope of the benefits they provide the policyholder. Briefly describe several examples illustrating (a) the narrowest and (b) the broadest types of contracts.

4. Describe the characteristic features of major medical insurance and explain how each benefits the insurer and the insured.

5. Health policies for loss of income are written with waiting periods of one (or several) weeks or months. What reasons can there be for buying a policy with a waiting period as long as three or six months, or longer?

6. Explain which is the more important health insurance protection: (a) indemnity for loss of time or (b) medical, hospital, and surgical benefits?

7. Mary Perry says to Jane Plane: "My husband is 25 years old and healthy, I want him to have all the life insurance we can afford, rather than spend money for the unlikely chance of losing income by being disabled." If you were Jane, explain why you would agree or disagree.

8. What types of health insurance are most closely related to life insurance? Why might disability income *health* insurance still be needed?

9. Explain briefly the renewability feature and four other important provisions in a typical health insurance contract.

10. Is "noncancelable" health insurance really permanent? Explain and indicate why this feature is important to the health insurance policyholder.

11. Are health insurance policies standardized? If so, discuss how; if not, discuss why they are not.

12. Explain the significance of the difference between the insuring clause of an accident policy which provides coverage against injury through "accidental means" and one which reads "accidental injuries."

13. Joe's policy provides for disability income if he is prevented from engaging in *any* work or *any* business for compensation. He becomes deaf, and because of the nature of his business he is obliged to close it out. Is the insurer liable?

14. Mr. Skip A. Beatty has a heart impairment and is told that it is useless to apply for a health policy. To what extent, if any, are persons with heart impairments eligible for health insurance?

15. Explain the difference between an "exception," a "reduction," and a "rider." Discuss the impact of each on the cost of a health policy.

16. Is overinsurance in the field of health insurance a serious problem? Explain how it can occur, its relationship to the concept of indemnity, and what the insurer can do to prevent it.

17. Choose several important factors which affect the cost of health insurance contracts and briefly show how the prices charged by insurers may vary according to each factor.

18. What factors would you discuss in analyzing the possible (a) growth and (b) decline of private health insurance in the future? In your estimation, why would your overall prediction be optimistic *or* pessimistic?

Chapter 10

Outline of concepts

Group insurance as part of employee benefit plans insures persons in group instead of individual contracts and costs one fifth of payroll.

Group life insurance is one of the major classes of life insurance.

    Nature and development: *master group policy, individual certificates.*

    Unique features include: *legal limitations* on size and type of group (10 or more), and *group selection* with *no medical examination.*

    The employer group life insurance contract is analyzed primarily as low-cost *yearly renewable term* insurance, with some growing interest in various types providing permanent insurance.

    Employee certificate provisions concern individual *limited amounts* set *automatically*, often based on one or two times annual *earnings*, and *beneficiary* and *conversion* provisions.

    Financing employer group life insurance involves employer *(noncontributory)* or employer-employee *(contributory)* premiums, and *net costs* based on *group experience.*

    Group creditor life insurance has many reasons for its *growing* use.

    Franchise, or wholesale, and **salary savings plans** insure *small* groups.

Group health insurance is one of the most remarkable developments.

    Nature and importance: about *three fourths of all* health insurance.

    Fundamental characteristics include:

        General types, for *medical expense* or *loss-of-income payments,* as separately discussed below.

        Eligibility provisions: *minimum number* of persons.

        Costs, based on *contributory* or *noncontributory* plans.

    Group hospital-surgical-medical expense insurance is usually *first-dollar coverage* for *hospital* charges and *surgeons'* and *physicians'* fees.

    Group major medical expense insurance is *catastrophe coverage.*

    Basic features: *high maximum "blanket" benefits* ($50,000 to $1 million or more), *deductibles* (sizable amounts such as $100 to $1,000), and *coinsurance,* the insured paying 20 percent of losses.

    Primary types of plans are called: *supplemental* and *comprehensive.*

    Group dental and vision care insurance are the newest and fastest-growing health insurance coverages.

    Group disability income insurance is nonoccupational coverage.

    Group accidental death and dismemberment insurance is common.

    Health maintenance organizations (HMOs) are a new alternative.

    New trends deserve close attention: *Administrative Service Only* (ASO) plans, *cafeteria or flexible-benefit* plans, and the impact of *social security changes.*

Group life and health insurance

Few, if any, developments in life and health insurance compare with the profound effect which the system of *group* insurance has had in the past several decades. The system of providing basic coverages through employers (and other groups) has been one of the most revolutionary and successful changes in insurance during the 20th century. This chapter explores the purposes and methods of group insurance, emphasizing *group life* and *group health* insurance systems. Many of the same ideas apply in both these fields, but the differences are sufficient to recommend separate consideration.

Group life and health insurance provides much coverage for many workers and their families. However, the protection provided by group insurance contracts is limited in two significant ways: (1) it is typically only available *during the working years,* and (2) it is often *not enough* to meet the full cost of death and disability.

GROUP INSURANCE AS PART OF EMPLOYEE BENEFIT PLANS

Did you know that the average annual cost of *employee benefit plans* in the United States now exceeds $6,000 per employee, or more than 37 percent of payroll?[1] For typical companies today at least one half of those costs are *insurance* benefits for employees. These insured benefits include mandated government insurance for such programs as workers' compensation and social security, and other agreed-upon payments for private *group* insurance and pensions. Thus, group insurance is often 20 percent or more of payroll. Paid vacations, lunches, parking, and other extra benefits are provided by many employers without using insurance. But group insurance is "a major component of employee benefit plans and . . . an insurance technique of considerable economic, social, and political significance."[2] Its far-reaching effects include not only the

---

[1] "Benefits Top $6,000 Per Worker," *Business Insurance,* December 21, 1981, p. 3.

[2] Davis W. Gregg, "Fundamental Characteristics of the Group Technique," in Davis W. Gregg and Vane B. Lucas, eds., *Life and Health Insurance Handbook,* 3d ed. (Homewood, Ill.: Richard D. Irwin, 1973), p. 351. See also Bruce Spencer, *Group Benefits in a Changing Society* (Chicago: Charles D. Spencer, 1982).

279

basis and competition it provides for individual policy contracts and agents working under that system, but also its function as a deterrent to further encroachment into voluntary life-health insurance by the social insurance plans of the United States.

The general term, *group insurance,* includes several kinds of insurance. The common principle of group selection has been used extensively for group *annuities* and pensions (discussed in Chapter 8). To a minor but growing extent the concept is being tried in the *property-liability* insurance field, providing automobile or homeowners' insurance for employees, for example (see Chapter 25). The present chapter concentrates on group *life* insurance, including credit life insurance, and group *health* insurance.

GROUP INSURANCE WRITTEN BY LIFE INSURERS

Most major life insurance companies write both individual and group insurance contracts. In terms of premiums paid for these contracts, group insurance has become a very significant part of their premium income. A summary of the growth of group insurance in U.S. life insurance companies is presented in Table 10–1. By the early 1980s, the three major types of group insurance written by life insurers—group life, health, and annuities—together accounted for more than $50 *billion,* or 55 percent, of total premiums of $94 billion. The growth has been spectacular, as the combined group insurance premiums grew by more than nine times those of two decades earlier. The percentage increases in this period were well in excess of 400 percent for group life, almost 800 percent for group health, and more than 1,500 percent for group annuities.

As a percentage of *all group* insurance premiums written by life insurance companies, group health insurance was the leader with 45 percent, followed by group annuities with 35 percent, and group life with 20 percent. *Within* each of these three types, the group premiums were approximately three fourths of total health insurance, three fourths of total annuities, and one fourth of total life insurance premiums.

GROUP LIFE INSURANCE

Group life insurance provides coverage on the lives of a group of persons in one contract. As a primary class of life insurance, it is in contrast to the ordinary and industrial life insurance classes, which use individual contracts and individual selection techniques.

Nature and development

More than 49 percent of the total life insurance in force at the beginning of 1981 in the United States, involving $1,744 billion, nearly 200

Table 10–1. The growth of group insurance premiums written by U.S. life insurance companies, 1960–1980

Type of group insurance	Premiums received (in millions of dollars)						Premium increase (in millions of dollars) 1960–80	Percent increase 1960–80	Percent of group insurance premiums* 1980	Percent of total life and health premiums*
	1960	1964	1968	1972	1976	1980				
Group health†	$2,559	$3,777	$ 6,081	$10,591	$16,422	$23,000	$20,441	799	45	25
Group life‡	1,850	2,645	3,929	5,634	7,511	10,043	8,193	443	20	11
Group annuities	1,088	1,467	2,217	4,044	10,249	17,526	16,438	1,511	35	19
Total	$5,497	$7,889	$12,227	$20,269	$34,182	$50,569	$45,072	820	100	55

* Another significant observation is the percentage for each of these three major insurance types which is written by the individual and group methods. In 1980 the group technique accounted for 78 percent of health, 25 percent of life, and 73 percent of annuity insurance premiums of the above insurance companies.
  † Of a total of $94,000 million total life and health insurance premiums in 1980 by U.S. life insurers (Blue Cross–Blue Shield health insurance figures not included in any of these figures).
  ‡ Credit life and health insurance is included in the group figures, because almost all credit insurance is written in group contracts.
  Source: *Life Insurance Fact Book* (Washington, D.C.: American Council of Life Insurance, 1961, 1965, 1969, 1973, 1977, and 1981), pp. 52, 53, 55, 60, 55, and 57, respectively.

million insureds, and more than 580,000 master contracts, was *group life insurance* protection.[3] Approximately each six years for more than 40 years the amount of group life insurance has doubled, and in the past decade alone it has almost tripled.[4] In terms of sales dollars rather than insurance amounts, group life insurance premium receipts were also significant—more than 25 percent of all life insurance premiums, or over $10 billion. Group life insurance has maintained a record of remarkable growth to become one of the giants of the insurance business.

The reasons for its growth are many, but predominant among the factors have been the industrialization of the population, the desire of both employers and organized labor to develop employee benefit programs, and the tax advantages that are included in group life insurance.

As the group life contract was originally written, the members of the group were employees of a single employer.[5] The group concept has been expanded, and policies may now be issued to cover other groups for creditors, unions, associations, and trusts. Underwriting rules differ with the insurers, but the underlying concept is the same for all groups.

In the broad sense, the form is based upon the same fundamentals as any life insurance; but it is unique in the *group selection* of risks and the method of *mass distribution*. It differs from other life insurance in that selection based on the group is substituted for individual selection. Mass distribution and mass administration supersede contact with individual insureds. Hence, group insurance may be termed "low-cost, wholesale protection." By considering groups of individuals, it has been possible to eliminate medical examinations and most other selection factors. Although there may be impaired lives in a group, adverse selection through an undue proportion of impaired lives is reduced to a minimum by the legal and underwriting regulations.

Under the plan, a *master contract* is issued to the employer, creditor, union, or other person representing the group to be covered. Each person covered in the group receives a *certificate* detailing the protection afforded, such as the amount of insurance, the name of the beneficiary, and the privilege of converting to a standard form of whole life insurance (without evidence of insurability) upon termination of employment. Premiums are the responsibility of the employer or other party that is the policyholder. A portion of the cost may be paid by the persons insured, or the cost may be paid entirely by the policyholder.

---

[3] The figures include credit life insurance, which accounts for about 10 percent. Credit life insurance is discussed later in this chapter, following treatment of the group life insurance written for employers. More than four fifths of credit life insurance is written as group coverage.

[4] *Life Insurance Fact Book* (Washington, D.C.: American Council of Life Insurance 1981), p. 18.

[5] The attention of the business world was first attracted to group insurance when the Equitable Life Assurance Society of the United States issued a policy effective July 1, 1912, covering the employees of Montgomery Ward & Company.

Group life insurance is not to be regarded as a substitute for a program of individual life insurance. It does, however, furnish the bare requirements in the simplest and most economical form. The formula under which most plans are written provides insurance equivalent to one or two years' earnings of the employee, and the average amount per certificate is nearly $20,000. Although not in any sense adequate, this does give the family of the deceased a small fund to meet current expenses while an adjustment is in process. For some employees who are otherwise uninsurable under individual contracts, it may provide their only protection and thus achieves an objective that is desirable from a social viewpoint.

Group life insurance has several disadvantages. One is that the individual employees (or members of the group) do not receive advice about their total life insurance needs. Group insurance usually provides only minimal and "average" benefits for the entire group and not individual analysis of needs and their solutions. The contract is usually temporary, too, and primarily designed to provide basic benefits only while the person continues as a member of the group and only while the *group* continues the insurance contract. This may give some insureds a false sense of security unless they recognize that most group life insurance is fundamentally different in cost and duration from other forms of permanent individual contracts. Because most group life insurance is term insurance, no cash or loan values are ordinarily a part of the plan.

Unique features of selection and distribution

The distinguishing features of group life insurance include (1) restrictive legislation which defines and limits its scope and (2) the impact which group selection has on the insurers and insureds that are a part of the plans.

Legal limitations. Over 65 years ago the National Convention of Insurance Commissioners adopted the following definition of group life insurance:

> Group life insurance is the form of life insurance covering not fewer than 50 employees, with or without medical examination, written under a policy issued to the employer, the premium on which is to be paid by the employer or by the employer and employees jointly, and insuring all of any class of employees, determined by conditions pertaining to all employment, for amounts of insurance based upon some plan which will preclude individual selection, for the benefit of persons other than the employer.

The definition was adopted by most states and by many insurers as a basis for writing this class of business. Over the years, the state legislatures have enlarged the meaning of the terms *employer* and *group*.

To encourage uniformity among the states and to control expansion of the group idea, a model group life insurance law was proposed in 1946 for enactment in the states. The *minimum size of the group* was reduced from 50 to 25 members for employer or labor union groups. In 1956 another model bill lowered the minimum group size to *ten.* These model bills often also limited the amount of group life coverage that could be written on an individual life, but today only a few states have any such statutory limits. *INCOME TAX AFTER $50,000 BASED ON PS58 COST*

Classified by the *nature of the group,* the Model Bill provides for: *(a) employer* group life insurance, *(b) creditor* group life insurance, *(c) labor union* group life insurance, and *(d) trustee* group life insurance. In the first category, the contracting parties are an employer and an insurance company. Employees are insured for the benefit of beneficiaries designated by the employee but not for the benefit of the employer. Credit or group life insurance covers the lives of debtors to the extent of their indebtedness to the creditor, and the creditor is the beneficiary. (See later section of this chapter.) Labor union group life insurance follows the pattern of employer group life insurance, except that the members of a union rather than the employees of an individual firm constitute the group. Trustee group life insurance enables two or more employers or two or more labor unions to provide insurance under a single contract through a trustee that acts for the employers or the labor unions.[6] The last two types are not discussed separately here, for their plans are identical in almost all respects with the normal employer group life insurance contract.

In recent years group life insurance has been expanded in many states to other groups than the four types classified above. Some of the great variety of additional groups permitted by statute in a number of states are: members of professional organizations (doctors, lawyers, accountants, and others), depositors of a bank, student association members, agents of a common principal, and dependents of insured employees. Lending agencies also issue group mortgage insurance. In total, these types have grown in popularity but are only about 5 percent of group life insurance.

The insurance laws of each state customarily provide that no group insurance policy shall be issued until a copy of the contract has been filed with and approved by the insurance commissioner. The National Association of Insurance Commissioners has adopted *standard provisions* for group life insurance. Wherever the recommended law is enacted, the provisions are required as minimum protection. More liberal provi-

---

[6] Group insurance, including group life insurance, has been determined to be a proper subject for collective bargaining between employers and labor unions. The landmark case was the Inland Steel Company case in 1949.

sions may be substituted for the standard provisions if the insurance commissioner having jurisdiction approves.

The standard group life provisions provide for such items as: (1) a grace period, (2) incontestability, (3) the application being made part of the policy, (4) the conditions under which evidence of individual insurability may be required, (5) equitable adjustment of premium or benefits in case of misstatement of age, (6) designation of the beneficiary, (7) the issuance of individual certificates, and (8) conversion of insurance on termination of employment or of the group policy.

Selection of insureds.   It was the intent of those who drew the Model Bills to make the minimum number required for a group sufficiently large to assure the functioning of the law of averages. In those states where groups smaller than 25 are permitted or where no minimum number is specified, the underlying theory is not changed, but the responsibility for determining an acceptable group is shifted from the legislature or the state regulatory authority to the company underwriters.

At one extreme, a few states define a group as any number in excess of two. At the other extreme, very large group contracts have been written. The Travelers Insurance Company provides coverage for more than .5 million railroad employees and their families in one group contract. This contract is said to be "the largest single private group policy in America." This group is exceeded by the group insurance plan for federal government employees which covers more than 5 million persons. Servicemen's Group Life Insurance, under which each person in the uniformed services of the United States is insured for $20,000 on an automatic basis with private insurers, covers an equivalent number of persons.

In *group selection* without medical examination, it would be unwise to allow any practice that would permit personal selection against the insurer. To avoid such adverse selection, all members of the group must be included, or at least a sufficient number to constitute a fairly representative risk. The group need not include all classes of employees. A policy may be issued covering only employees with a number of years of service, CAREFU[or it may cover the workers in a given department. Any arbitrary grouping is permissible so long as all within the group are offered the insurance.

When the premium is paid entirely by the employer, the group is said to be *noncontributory,* and the insurance extends automatically to all the members of the group. The group is *contributory* when the premium is to be paid jointly by the employer and the employee, and to warrant the insurance such a group must include a minimum of 75 percent of the employees in the class.

There is *no medical examination, usually,* of the individuals insured. A sometimes overlooked advantage of group life insurance is that some persons can obtain protection under the group plan when they could not obtain life insurance at standard rates or possibly could not obtain life insurance at all. Because of the size of the groups it is assumed that the element of individual selection is removed, or at least reduced. This justifies the elimination of a medical examination. Another fact is that each of the insureds under a group policy is healthy enough to be in regular attendance of his or her work. Also, many of the larger employers now require at least some preliminary physical examination before hiring new employees. If an occasional poor risk is included, the law of averages tends to offset such a risk with the favorable cases.[7]

There are, however, some instances in which evidences of insurability may be required of individuals in group plans. Some examples are: *(a)* an employee who does not take insurance within a definite period (usually 31 days) after becoming eligible; *(b)* a person who rejoins the insured group after having been dropped for nonpayment of contributions; and *(c)* members of the group who have converted insurance to an individual policy.

The employer group life insurance contract

This section and the two immediately following discuss employer group life insurance in regard to (1) the employer's contract, (2) the provisions of the employee's certificate, and (3) financing.

Types of contracts.   Group life insurance provides for protection *(a)* on a *term* basis and *(b)* on *permanent* plans. The first group life insurance contracts were written on the renewable term plan, and this practice has generally been followed through the years. A comparatively recent demand has created a market for group life policies with permanent values, like those offered, for example, by individual level premium policies or combinations of group term and paid-up life insurance.

Many of the group life contracts include some of the group health insurance coverages analyzed later in this chapter, such as group accident and sickness, accidental death or dismemberment, hospital and surgical, or medical expense.

Group term.   It is surprising to some persons to learn that almost all (97 percent or more) of employer group life insurance is written on a *yearly renewable term* insurance basis. Knowing the disadvantage which this type of contract has when it is used as an individual policy (see Chapter 6), the student may wonder how it has served so well for the vast majority of group plans. The answer lies in the contribution of the employer to the cost. Thus the increasing cost problem is not

---

[7] Many individual life insurance policies are also issued without a medical examination. In these instances, however, each person submits an application which includes some statements as to present and past health.

fatal to the plan should the average age of the group increase or the mortality experience of the plan grow worse. Group term also offers many advantages in simplicity, flexibility, administration, and tax benefits to both employers and employees. Monthly premiums are paid by the employer, although employee contributions through payroll deduction are common. Some states limit employee cost to a maximum such as $0.60 per month per $1,000.

Group term insurance is temporary rather than permanent protection for the employee. The policy could end any year at the renewal date if the employer does not continue it. It also stops when the worker leaves employment for any reason, such as retirement, disability, or resignation, unless the policy is converted to a permanent form of coverage (see the later section which explains the provisions for conversion in the employee's certificate).

The advantages of group term life insurance to the *employer* are summarized as follows: (1) the employer gains a low-cost, impartial method for furnishing death benefits to the family survivors of deceased employees; (2) public and employer-ee relations are improved; (3) competitive hiring and retaining good employees are aided; (4) the employer's cost is tax deductible to the corporation; (5) employee morale and productivity are enhanced; and (6) some government intervention into private insurance has perhaps been delayed. To the *employee,* these are some advantages of group term life insurance: (1) a layer of death insurance protection is added to social and other insurance benefits; (2) it may be the only life insurance of some otherwise uninsurable employees; (3) automatic payroll deduction from the employee or full payment by the employer makes lapses unlikely; (4) the lowest possible cost is attainable through expense reductions; (5) death benefits and the employer's contri- *EXCEPT* butions to the cost are not taxable to the employee as ordinary income; and (6) a conversion privilege permits conversion to a permanent individual contract without a medical examination of the terminated employee.[8]

Group permanent. With the growing appeal of group term life insurance, those protected began to inquire into the possibility of securing the benefits of the permanent plans under group policies. In particular, they desired: values available to employees on termination of employment in addition to the right of conversion, and paid-up insurance before retirement and while the employee was engaged in active employment. If an employee stops working at an advanced age, the conversion privilege may be of little value if the employee is unable to keep the insurance in force on the basis of attained age premiums. At retirement most plans

---

[8] William G. Williams, chap. 26 in Davis W. Gregg and Vane B. Lucas, eds., *Life and Health Insurance Handbook,* 3d ed. (Homewood, Ill.: Richard D. Irwin, 1973), pp. 377–78. See also Robert W. Batten, George M. Hider, et al, *Group Life and Health Insurance,* vols. 1 and 2 (Atlanta: Life Office Management Association, 1979).

only continue the term insurance for a reduced amount. Accumulated values under a whole life premium would considerably lighten the burden of conversion.

Two basic types of group insurance are used to provide some permanent life insurance: (1) *group term and paid-up* plans, and (2) *level premium group permanent* plans. As a proportion of total group life insurance protection, these plans are relatively unimportant—probably less than about 3 percent. However, there is continuing need for and interest in such plans, especially as tax rules change. Illustrative of the trend toward innovations to provide employees with insurance after retirement, based on Internal Revenue Code changes, are two other combinations of group term and permanent insurance, called *Section 79* and *retired lives reserve* plans. NEW TAX ACT (1986) DIMINISHED THESE AGAIN.

The *group term and paid-up plan* each year combines units of single-premium (paid-up) whole life insurance with decreasing units of group term life insurance. The employee's contribution (typically $1.30 per month for each $1,000 of insurance) usually purchases the paid-up whole life insurance, at the attained age of the employee. The employer's contribution purchases an amount of term insurance in decreasing amounts so that the sum always equals the total death benefit for which the employee is eligible under the plan. At retirement the term insurance amount is usually discontinued, although it has a convertible feature permitting it to be changed to permanent individual insurance. The paid-up insurance amount continues without paying further premiums, or after retirement it may be surrendered for the accumulated cash value.

The *level premium group permanent plan* is less common and typically is used for funding benefits at retirement in a pension plan. Whole life, retirement income, paid-up at 65, or endowment forms of permanent insurance are purchased with the employer or combined employer-ee contributions. At retirement the employee continues to pay the level premium in order to keep the protection in force or may have some cash or paid-up insurance values available.

Section 79 plans, usually designed for smaller groups of less than 10 insureds, have been available since the mid-1960s. However, conflicting and unclear tax rulings under this section of the Internal Revenue Code hampered early development of these plans.[9] Basically, the idea is to qualify individual level-premium insurance, sometimes called "group ordinary," as group insurance. The purpose is to permit an allocation of a portion of the premium for up to $50,000 term insurance per employee in order that it be both deductible to the employer and not taxed as

---

[9] See Gerald E. Huthoefer, "Section 79 Group Ordinary Problems Still Remains," *CLU Journal* 30, no. 2 (April 1976), p. 10; and James E. Roberts, "Section 79—In Transition," *CLU Journal* 30, no. 2 (April 1977), p. 54.

income to the employee. The remaining portion of the premium becomes deductible to the employer but is taxable income (based on favorable tables estimating costs) to the employee.

Retired lives reserve plans are the newest product in the area; some 40 life insurers started to sell various plans to small groups during the last four years. The plans combine regular group term insurance with a reserve which funds *post-retirement* term life insurance coverage for the employee. The costs, paid by the employer, are fully deductible by the employer. Only the estimated term insurance cost for more than $50,000 coverage, at low rates, is taxed as income to the employee. Interest earnings on the reserve fund are credited at current rates of the insurer, with guaranteed minimums of 4–7 percent. After retirement, the RLR plan continues to pay the premiums for the rest of the retired employee's life. Some plans guarantee the sufficiency of the fund to maintain full benefits or guarantee that the cost at retirement will not exceed a specified amount. Although some tax implications await final IRS rulings, retired lives reserve plans appear to be a group insurance product with a promising future.[10]

Policy and certificate limits of insurance. Most life insurers fix the *minimum* amount for any one life at $1,000. A minimum of $50,000 is usually established for a group. Other than administrative costs, the primary purpose of requiring minimum limits and setting the maximum insurance per person is to attain a reasonably uniform distribution of insurance within the group. A maximum limitation precludes a concentration of risks in a few lives.

The *maximum* amount available to an individual employee generally depends on the total amount of insurance in force for the entire group. The schedule of maximum individual amounts may show, for example, a $30,000 limit in the case of a group with $1 million total insurance and $100,000 under a plan with a total of $50 million on all employees. Company practices vary the maximums by such other factors as (1) the annual earnings of the employee, (2) the number of persons in the plan, (3) special classes for lower income groups, and many others.

With respect to the tax situation, large amounts of group life insurance paid for by an employer payable to the employee's family without income taxes have resulted in a powerful appeal for this type of insurance in substantial individual amounts. Tax legislation changes under the 1964 Revenue Act limited the tax-free amount of group life insurance on each individual to $50,000. Above this amount the employee is required to pay income taxes on the cost contributed to the plan by the employer.

---

[10] Richard G. Shechtman, "Retired Lives Reserve: The Product," *CLU Journal* 34, no. 4 (October 1980), p. 20; and "Retired Lives Reserve: Tax Consequences and Planning Opportunities," *CLU Journal* 35, no. 3 (July 1981), p. 20.

Probationary period. In order not to build up an undue expense for the insurance of temporary employees, the group contract may provide that the insurance is not to become effective for new employees until after they have been in continuous service for a designated period. The probationary period usually varies between 1 month and 12. An eligibility period of 31 days is normal after the probationary period, and during this time the employee may apply for inclusion in the group life plan without undergoing a medical examination.

Inception and termination of coverage. When group insurance is desired, a form is prepared supplying sufficient information to provide a tentative rate. If the result of the preliminary survey is satisfactory to the employer, an application for the insurance is filed. Upon the insurer's approval of the plan of insurance selected by the employer and upon the payment of the first premium (which is usually paid monthly), the insurance becomes effective. If, however, the policy is to be issued on a contributory form, with the employee sharing the cost, the insurance does not become effective until the required minimum number of employees have authorized their payroll deduction.

Since the policy is usually written on a yearly term basis, the master policy expires, unless renewed, at the end of the policy year. A severance of employment terminates the employee's insurance under the group policy, subject to the conversion privilege. In the case of the employee's temporary absence from the service of the employer because of physical disability or leave of absence, if the premium is paid by the employer, the insurance may be kept in force.

Employee certificate provisions

The employer group life master contract is supplemented by a certificate which is given to each insured employee. This briefly summarizes the contract amount, beneficiary provisions, and conversion privileges available to each individual.

Individual certificate amounts. A schedule of insurance amounts is set up in the contract for the different classes of employees. The individual employee has no choice of insurance amount. Automatic determination of individual coverage is effected in one of several ways: *(a)* a *flat amount* for all employees, *(b)* an amount based on *position, (c)* an amount based on *length of service,* and *(d)* an amount based on *earnings.*

The simplest determination is a *flat* amount of insurance for each employee. This plan has several shortcomings, including the failure to recognize the needs, ability to pay, worth to the business, and period of service of the employee. Group insurance allocated on a *position* basis separates personnel into classes, such as officers, supervisors, clerical

SOME ALLOW FOR ADDITIONAL OPTIONAL AMOUNTS AT EMPLOYEES EXPENSE.

employees, salespersons, and the like. The amount of insurance is the same for all employees of one class, but it differs among the classes. This plan recognizes, within limits, both worth and length of service, but it introduces some administrative difficulties in establishing categories. Scheduling the amount of insurance on the basis of length of *service* rewards employees for long service. It fails, however, to consider differing income levels and provides lower coverage in the younger age groups, where the needs are frequently greatest.

The most widely used base for determining the amount of insurance is employee *earnings*. Payroll brackets are established, and all who fall within a given bracket automatically receive a predetermined amount of insurance; or, very commonly, the amount is set at a figure such as *one or two times annual salary*. This plan recognizes not only ability to pay but also the worth of the employee to the business. It fails to recognize fully the employee's need for protection, however, such as the number of dependents.

Basically, all plans should consider as fully as possible the employee's *(a)* need and *(b)* ability to pay. It may be, and frequently is, necessary to use more than one plan to accomplish these objectives.

Beneficiary provisions. A beneficiary (other than the employer) must be designated. Each *employee designates* his or her own beneficiary. Policies may provide for the payment of the benefits to certain persons if the beneficiary dies before the employee or if no beneficiary has been named. For example, the policy may contain a *facility of payment* provision permitting the insurer to pay the insurance to the wife or husband, if living, or to the surviving children, to the father or the mother, or to the insured's executor or administrators. In some states, the right of relatives to receive payment if no beneficiary is named is governed by statute.

The policy indicates the steps required to change the beneficiary. Ordinarily, all that is required is the filing with the employer of a written notice on a form provided by the insurer. The employee may change the beneficiary from time to time.

Conversion privilege. Each employee insured under a group policy is usually given the right to continue the insurance as an individual *without medical examination* in the event that work with the employer is terminated. The employee has the right to convert to any of the permanent (not term) policies issued by the insurer for a face amount equal ~~OR~~ *LESS* to that of the employee's group certificate. In most states this right of conversion extends for *31 days* after the termination of employment.

When the conversion privilege is exercised, the premium charged for the new policy is based upon current rates for the attained age of the employee at the time of conversion. If the master group policy is termi-

CONTRACT MAY HAVE TO BEEN IN EFFECT FOR A CERTAIN
PERIOD OF TIME &/OR INDIVIDUAL HAS TO BE
INSURED FOR A CERTAIN PERIOD OF TIME.

nated for any reason, an employee who has been insured for five years may convert to an individual policy, without medical examination, in an amount of at least $2,000.

Policies provide that the employee shall be automatically covered without application, during 31 days following termination of employment, for the amount of his or her group coverage.

Knowing that the purpose of the conversion privilege is to protect the employee's right to maintain life insurance protection, it is incongruous to find that very little (probably less than 2 percent of the potential) group life insurance is actually converted. The prime reason may be ignorance of the important value of the conversion right to uninsurable or substandard applicants. Many employees do obtain new group life insurance from their new employer. The higher premium cost, in relation to group term coverage, which the insured must pay for a converted whole life individual contract discourages many. Still, for many substandard insureds the conversion privilege is a valuable right which should not be overlooked, as evidenced by the extra assessments levied against the employer for converted policies. Adverse selection is quite high, as the most unhealthy persons are most likely to convert their contracts. The extra cost to employers is sometimes as high as $170 per $1,000 of converted life insurance, so most employers do little more than notify employees of their right to convert the group coverage.

Financing employer group life insurance

Premiums. Premiums on the group life policy, whether under a contributory or a noncontributory form, are forwarded to the insurer by the employer. When the employees are to share in the cost of the insurance in the *contributory* plan, their contribution is collected by payroll deductions. Under the *noncontributory* plan, the employee pays nothing and the entire cost is assumed by the employer. Employers usually make premium payments to the insurer monthly.

The basic rate for group insurance depends upon the industry in which the employees are engaged. The survey made following the filing of an application for insurance gives attention to the occupation of the various employees, sanitary and health conditions, the condition of the property, and many other employment hazards. The premium for a particular group is based upon the amount of insurance carried by, and the age of, each employee.

Experience has shown that because of the retirement of a certain number of older employees each year, with replacement in the younger brackets, the age of the group changes little from year to year, and hence the premium is practically stationary for the normal large employee group.

In the beginning, the *noncontributory* plan was the general practice, as a gift or additional compensation to employees. The noncontributory form is considerably simpler in that all employees of a group are automatically covered. Also, the problem of apportioning costs among the classes of employees is avoided, and goodwill is engendered by an outright gift. Advocates of the *contributory* plan contend that group insurance is appreciated more if the employee contributes. It may be used to provide higher benefits than could be included in a noncontributory plan. Employee contributions in most contributory plans are limited by state laws as well as by practice to 60 cents (or less) per month per $1,000 of insurance. (See also Chapter 8 for more discussion comparing contributory and noncontributory financing.)

Net costs.   The mortality experience under group life insurance plans has generally been favorable due to the fact that numerous employees drop out of the group with advancing years and to the fact that the entire group must be working when the insurance is effected. The physically unfit and the weaker lives are eliminated, and those who remain are physically fit to carry on their work. Furthermore, favorable selection is found in the care exercised by the insurer in studying the nature of the hazards involved in the industry when the risk is rated.

Certain specific savings are available under group life insurance. Usually no medical examination is required. Also, commissions paid on this class of business are substantially lower than those for other classes, thereby reducing the acquisition cost of the business. Finally, the expense in issuing and handling a group life policy is less than that of handling a large number of individual policies. Hence, the premium for group life insurance is substantially lower than that for individual policies for most persons.

Dividends and rate adjustments based on the *actual experience of the group* are an important factor in the net cost of the plan. In an average industry the insurance cost will be less than 1 percent of the total amount of insurance in force. When the employee contributes even a small amount, and after dividends have been credited, the burden of a group plan upon the employer is relatively light. That burden increases as more benefits are provided and as employers pay the entire cost of many of the plans.

Group creditor life insurance

What kind of life insurance *(a)* has more than tripled in volume in the past 15 years? *(b)* has over 70 million insureds in the United States, although it still accounts for only about 4 percent of all life insurance in force? *(c)* is the only type of group life insurance in which the master contract policyholder is permitted to be the beneficiary? *(d)* has the *maximum* price for the coverage rigidly controlled in many states? *(e)* has achieved all its growth despite the fact that most states restrict the insurance amount per insured to under $10,000? The answer is *group creditor life insurance*.

The definition of group life insurance in the statutes provides for issuing a policy to a creditor to insure the lives of debtors. It covers that group of debtors who borrow on an installment basis, and the creditor is named as beneficiary.

Reasons for use. The policy appeals to lending institutions in that they are guaranteed repayment of the loan even though the borrower does not live to complete the transaction. Regardless of the ability of the borrower, there is a real danger of not collecting the loan if he or she dies. In any event, the lending institution is relieved of the difficulty of pressing an unsecured claim against an estate of limited means. From a second point of view, the coverage serves to increase business. Credit life insurance is used to repay the debt in case the borrower dies. No obligation is left behind for someone else to meet. Thus, credit life is attractive to both the borrower and the lender.

Types of loans and insurance provided. Policies are written to cover debtors making *installment loans* of the following types: *(a)* unsecured personal loans and *(b)* indebtedness secured by (1) conditional sales contracts and (2) lease sales contracts. Although used at first to secure only limited types of smaller loans, group credit life insurance soon became very popular for many automobile loans and then for general personal loans and even credit card charges. While the tendency is to use individual term policies to cover mortgage loans on homes, the group plan has sometimes been extended to include this class of debtors. Credit life insurance statistics include group protection written for mortgages of 10 years or less.

The limitation for each loan set forth in the laws of most states for group credit life insurance is about $10,000; but the amount of insurance is limited in each instance to the unpaid balance of the debt, subject to the stated maximum. Ordinarily, as with employer group life insurance, no medical examination is required. Group creditor life insurance is usually written on a *reducing term basis* so that the amount of life insurance is limited to the amount necessary to pay off the debt.

Costs. The creditor is responsible for the payment of premiums, which are usually based upon the aggregate debts outstanding each month. The premium is relatively small since the amount of insurance in force with respect to any one debt decreases as repayments are made. Lending institutions charge the customer, usually by increasing the service charges, or they may absorb the cost as an operating expense. Due to the expense of maintaining age records, the premium charge is based upon the volume of loans rather than the ages of debtors. The age factor is reflected in the experience rate developed by the losses of the group.

Provisions.   Individual certificates are not issued unless this is required by law. Individual insurance on the life of any particular debtor terminates if the group policy terminates or if the loan is discharged. The insurance also terminates when the loan has become overdue a specified period of time, usually from one to six months. If during any policy year the number of insured debtors falls below the group underwriting requirements of the insurer (100 is usual), it may decline to insure new debtors. The policy covering debtor groups has no conversion provision.

Growth and problems.   Credit life insurance is a phenomenon of the credit economy in which we now live. It has eased the task of borrowing by reducing the risk of loss to lending institutions that would suffer by the death of debtors. There is more than $165 billion of credit life insurance in force, and it has been growing faster than any other type. Most of it is issued through group policies, although some 17 percent results from individual credit policies. The average loan covered is approximately $2,000.[11]

As might be expected, its rapid growth has been accompanied by some problems. One of the most difficult has been a tendency toward great competition in rates, while rates that were too high (with dividends going to the lending institution) were not recognized by the insureds. States such as New York and New Jersey have set recommended scales for the rates charged under group credit life insurance, with the lowest prices permitted for the largest groups. Other states have not legislated the rates to be charged. They have set maximum rates, however, and have exercised close scrutiny over the business. The insurance commissioner watches the relationship of premiums to losses, but in many states the losses paid are not much more than 50 percent, which may indicate excessive profits to insurers and lenders.

A model bill of the NAIC has helped curb the possible rate and contract abuses in about half the states. With such progress, the future of credit life insurance should remain bright in the credit economy of the United States.

Franchise, or wholesale, and salary savings insurance

Although not technically group insurance, since individual contracts are used, several types of distribution through groups have been developed in life insurance. These methods include franchise (or wholesale)

---

[11] *Life Insurance Fact Book,* p. 24. For cost evaluation, see Joseph M. Belth, "Credit Life Insurance Prices," *Journal of Risk and Insurance* 40, no. 1 (March 1973), p. 115.

insurance and salary deduction plans, for groups of fewer than 25 persons which are not sufficiently large to meet the requirement for the normal group policy. The size of the groups eligible for the coverage is usually 5 or more employees of one employer, or 10 or more members of a trade, labor, or professional association.

Franchise insurance is a plan for the mass selling of *individual policies*. The contracting parties are the employee and the insurer, and a policy is issued to each individual included in the plan. The premium may be paid in full by the employee or by the employer and the employee on a cooperative basis. There is usually no medical examination, but evidence of the physical condition of the applicant is obtained from the questions answered in the application. The insurer has the right to deny an application for any reason, so in small groups adverse selection is avoided.

Salary deduction life insurance, also referred to as "payroll deduction" and "salary savings" insurance, is a plan for the sale of the regular forms of life insurance by personal solicitation of individual employees. The employer deducts the amounts agreed upon from the salary of the employees and makes monthly premium payments. Each participant selects the type and the amount of the policy. The premiums are usually paid entirely by the employee. Rather than being a different life insurance product, salary deduction life insurance is primarily a convenient method by which the employer encourages the employees to purchase regular individual contracts of protection.

GROUP HEALTH INSURANCE

Is U.S. Steel, Goodyear Tire and Rubber, or Pittsburgh Plate Glass the largest supplier of General Motors Corporation? Surprisingly, none of these is, for the largest GM supplier sells group health insurance to GM for its employees—more than $840 million worth each year![12] Other employers may also find themselves in a similar situation, a situation which puts group insurance at or near the top of the cost list for all the products and services that business firms purchase.

The group technique of insuring includes not only group life and group annuities (as discussed in Chapter 8) but also group *health* insurance. The amazing growth of group health insurance in the United States is unique in the sense that no other country in the world has developed such a broad private system of protecting its population against the increased medical expense and the loss of income resulting from poor health.

---

[12] William F. Hamilton and Samuel P. Martin, "Benefits Fever," *Wharton Magazine,* Winter 1977, p. 19. Blue Cross–Blue Shield was the largest supplier, Metropolitan Life second, and U.S. Steel third.

Nature and importance

As with the other group plans, master contracts are issued to employers, unions, associations, or trustees for the benefit of individuals and their families. The basic characteristics are summarized as: (1) *three parties*, that is, the insurer, the employer (or other "policyholder"), and the individual members of the group; (2) insurance based on *group underwriting* rather than individual selection; (3) adverse selection reduced by *minimum size* group requirements and by restrictions on the freedom to choose the insurance, amounts, types, and benefits; and (4) simplicity and *economy* of administration achieved by employer cooperation and employer contributions to the cost of plans.

By 1980 the health insurance receipts of all private insuring organizations were estimated at $78 *billion,* which represented more than 4 percent of disposable personal income.[13] The premiums received by insurance companies made up about 56 percent of the total, and the premiums received by Blue Cross–Blue Shield plans made up the remainder. *Group* health insurance accounted for more than 75 percent of the total. Group health insurance approximately quadrupled in the past decade.

Table 10–1 at the beginning of this chapter summarizes the relative growth of the group insurance technique in the fields of health, life, and annuities. Group health premiums written by U.S. life insurance companies (not including Blue Cross–Blue Shield or casualty insurers) are 45 percent of the total group insurance business. The group technique represents more than a $50 billion business today, or 55 percent of all life and health insurance premiums. The growth of group health was almost 800 percent between 1960 and 1980, exceeding the percentage increase of group life but not that of group annuities.

Factors in the rapid growth have included collective bargaining and union requests for more fringe benefits, favorable tax treatment (the premiums are usually deductible to the employer and not taxed as income to the employee), and the skyrocketing costs of medical care.

Health insurance for groups follows the pattern generally established for life insurance. There are three contract forms: *(a)* group, *(b)* franchise, and *(c)* salary deduction plans. Most persons are covered on a group basis. The other two types were discussed at the end of the group life section in this chapter. This section will concentrate on the group health contract forms.

Group health insurance may and often does cover dependents. In many instances an individual is covered by both a group policy and an individual policy. If the group policy does not provide all the coverage required,

---

[13] *Source Book of Health Insurance Data* (New York: Health Insurance Association of America, 1981–82), p. 27.

it may be supplemented by an individual policy. For many, however, the group policy may provide the only form of health protection.

Because of the greater opportunities for industrial employment, urban residents are more frequently covered under group health insurance policies than are rural residents. By 1980 about 180 million persons had group hospital-surgical insurance coverage, 154 million had group major medical, 86 million had group disability income insurance, and 80 million had group dental insurance.[14]

Fundamental characteristics of group health insurance

Following generally the pattern of individual health insurance plans (Chapter 9), the principal kinds of group health insurance may be noted as: (1) *medical expense reimbursement* insurance and (2) *income reimbursement* insurance. The first type provides benefits for all forms of medical care costs; the second pays for temporary or longer term loss of income due to disability and accidental death and dismemberment benefits.

General types of group health insurance contracts. For discussion in this chapter, the above coverages are divided into six classifications of contracts: (1) *group hospital-surgical-medical* insurance, (2) *group major medical expense* insurance, (3) *group dental and vision care insurance*, (4) *group disability income* insurance, (5) *group accidental death or dismemberment* insurance, and (6) the new *health maintenance organizations* (HMOs), which are beginning to provide a broad type of health care expense insurance.

Eligibility provisions. The first Model Group Accident and Health Insurance Bill suggested that the group include at least 25 certificate holders. Subsequent revisions of the model bill since 1940 reduced the number to 10, and the latest bill mentions no minimum size. The setting of minimums for the size of the group is then left up to the underwriting practices of the insurers. Some states do have group health laws or rulings which define group health insurance; some states prescribe minimum percentage participation requirements (usually 75 percent); and many states set the minimum group size from 2 to 10 members. These minimums do not apply to HMO plans, which from a practical standpoint usually start with at least several thousand subscribers.

All employees may constitute a group, or the employer may select a particular "eligibility group" based on: *(a)* the length of time the employee has been with the company, *(b)* a certain salary range, *(c)* occupation, or *(d)* a combination of these bases. In addition to policies purchased by employers to provide insurance for employees, policies are issued to

---

[14] Ibid., p. 12.

such groups as members of labor unions or professional associations. A number of policies issued to associations or trusteeships have been the outgrowth of collective bargaining with a union in an industry or an area.

Group health coverages for medical expenses may in many instances be extended to cover the dependents of the insured employee. Dependents' coverage, usually including children up to age 19 (or 23 if in school), may include hospital, surgical, some forms of medical, and major medical expense. Stepchildren, adopted children, and foster children are included in the dependent category if they are actually dependent upon the employee for support and maintenance.

Costs. Many group health insurance plans, probably about 60 percent, are written on a *contributory* basis, with the individuals paying a share of the cost. In an employer group this means that both the employees and the employer (policyholder) pay part of the cost of the plan. Other plans may be *noncontributory,* with the employer paying the entire cost. The individual plan participants pay the whole cost of their protection in a few cases.

The premium charges for group health plans are based on rates developed for the standard group for the type, size, and duration of benefits; sex; age; geographic variations; and other factors. The charges for the initial year are normally adjusted thereafter on the basis of the *actual experience* of the group, except for very small groups. Dividends may be used in participating contracts in order to vary the charges made each year according to the actual loss experience of the group.

Generally, group health insurance costs are lower than the costs of comparable coverage purchased under individual contracts. The difference may come from several sources: (1) the employer paying part of the premium, which reduces employee cost; (2) the favorable loss experience of a working group of employees; and (3) administrative savings and payroll deductions, as compared with issuing individual contracts and collecting many separate premiums.

Group hospital-surgical-medical expense insurance

The group health plans which provide protection for medical care expenses do so on the basis of two different philosophies. Some plans cover essentially all the specified kinds of expenses "from the first dollar on" and are called *"first-dollar"* coverages. Certain maximums are usually set in terms of days of medical care or of maximum dollar limits. These limits may be set high enough to cover the costs of most normal losses but often do not aim at providing protection for the very large losses. These are the types of contracts discussed in this section as subdivided into group (1) *hospital,* (2) *surgical,* and (3) *regular medical expenses* policies.

An annual survey of group health insurance plans shows: (1) more than 94 percent of the persons covered in group hospital plans are also insured for surgical benefits, and (2) almost 90 percent have some regular medical coverage.[15]

The second philosophy in covering medical expenses under group plans assumes that it is not of prime importance to the insured what kinds of medical care costs are involved. Instead, the plans aim at providing very high ($50,000 to unlimited, for example) maximum limits for *all* medical care expenses. These contracts are called *major medical* (or *catastrophe medical*) policies. Oftentimes a deductible of several hundred dollars applies, and expenses above the deductible are paid to the insureds on a "coinsurance" or participation basis with the insurer. These contracts are treated in the next major section of this chapter.

Group hospital expense insurance. This coverage is designed to provide benefits to an employee (or other members of the group plan) who is confined to a hospital because of injury or sickness. The coverage is ordinarily written on a *reimbursement* basis; that is, benefits are payable to the employee for charges actually made.[16] This is usually written as a nonoccupational coverage to avoid duplication of workers' compensation benefits.

The benefits are classified as *(a)* room-and-board benefits and *(b)* other miscellaneous benefits. Hospital expense benefits are often extended to cover dependents of the certificate holders under the group plan.

For *room-and-board* benefits the policy provides a daily limit. This limit is usually the charge made for semiprivate accommodations in the area in which the insured employee resides. Most new policies have a limit of $50–$150 per day or higher. The employee is reimbursed for the amount of the charges actually made by the hospital. Room-and-board benefits are payable until the limits for any one period of confinement have been reached. The maximum limits may vary from 70 days to unlimited, although two thirds of the new plans specify 120 days or more.[17] Most contracts include treatment for alcoholism, drug addition, and mental disorders, although special maximum limits may apply.

---

[15] Ibid., p. 12.

[16] By insurance companies, that is. The Blue Cross plans differ in that they promise to provide certain *services,* such as semiprivate room accommodations, rather than reimbursement for the hospital charges for such services. The group hospital plans began with service benefits provided to teachers of Baylor University, Texas, in 1929.

[17] "Hospital Cost Shifting; Group Health Insurance," *Society Page,* American Society of CLU, May–June 1982, p. 4.

Other benefits provide for the payment of *miscellaneous hospital charges* (other than those for room and board). The patient is reimbursed on the basis of charges actually made by the hospital for medical care and treatment. Professional services other than the services of an anesthetist and professional ambulance service are not covered. The limit placed in the policy for these hospital charges is sometimes a multiple of the daily limit for other hospital charges, such as 10, 15, or 20 times. For some plans the limit is $500 but it may be $1,000 or more for these costs. Recently the limit for many plans has been set at whatever the "reasonable and customary" charges are for that area.

Pregnancy benefits are now nearly always treated in the same manner as other medical benefits because of amendments to the Civil Rights Act. Newborn children are included in the coverage during the first week or two. Employees and their dependents are eligible. The normal practice is to make employees insured on the policy date or within 31 days thereafter immediately eligible for benefits. Although one may question the "insurability" of such losses as maternity expenses, with the cost of maternity expenses (hospital and physician) now often exceeding $2,000, the need for including maternity coverage is also clear.

Group surgical expense insurance.   Almost all group hospital insurance plans include *surgical* benefits. Like group hospital expense insurance, group surgical expense insurance is a nonoccupational form of protection. Benefits are payable whether or not the surgical operation is performed in a hospital, and the payments are made for "reasonable and customary" fees. The insurer is liable only for the fees actually charged by the surgeon. This liability is sometimes limited by a schedule of maximum surgical benefits that appears in the policy. For serious operations the maximum often goes to $1,000 or more. (See Table 9–4.) Obstetric benefits are almost always provided to both employees and dependents.

Group regular medical expense insurance.   Group hospital insurance plans usually include at least some coverage for *regular medical expenses,* especially physicians' fees for nonsurgical care. Some of the plans provide such insurance only for in-hospital visits by doctors. The payment is limited to "reasonable and customary" fees, or to $10 or more per visit for 31 days or more. Home and office visits to the doctor are sometimes included, with limits on the number of calls paid for by the coverage.

Diagnostic Xray and laboratory expenses may be included in these group contracts. Today such coverage often applies whether the expenses are incurred in connection with a hospital confinement or at separate offices, laboratories, or diagnostic centers. Actual charges up to a maximum annual limit of $100 to $500 are common.

Group major medical expense insurance

Development. The fast growth of group *major medical expense* insurance is seen in its coverage of 33 million persons in 1960 and nearly 150 million today.[18] That growth is derived from (1) the rapid expansion in the use of the group insuring technique, and (2) the increased recognition of the essential need for protection against the burden of large medical expenses as a result of serious injury or illness. Since both group insurance and major medical expense insurance are primarily innovations of the past several decades, group major medical insurance is truly a modern type of health insurance.

The salient features of major medical insurance have already been noted in Chapter 9. In the field of group insurance the appeal for this coverage has been tremendous. Employers and employees alike have come to realize that the financial protection afforded by the usual hospital and surgical coverages is far from adequate if the illness is serious and prolonged. More than 90 percent of the persons who have major medical insurance are insured under group forms and less than 10 percent under individual forms.

Basic features. The methods by which group major medical plans express their basic features may be used to differentiate some of the plans. Special attention is given to provisions that were not discussed in Chapter 9 in regard to the individual major medical policies.

High maximum benefits. The most significant purpose of group major medical insurance is to include payments for *catastrophe-type* injuries or for illnesses. Contrary to group hospital-surgical-medical plans, which are limited as to type and amount of medical expense, the goal is to provide protection for *all* types of medical expenses for the *larger* losses. This is usually accomplished by using deductibles of $50 or $100 dollars while setting the maximum limits payable at high amounts, such as $100,000 or more. More than 90 percent of newly covered employees in 1981 had limits of $100,000 or more. About one half of those persons had maximums of $1 million and over, and one third had unlimited benefits.[19]

Maximum limits are usually set for each individual as a *lifetime* maximum, but some also apply maximums per year or per disability. When the maximum amount has been paid on behalf of any one person, coverage with respect to that person automatically terminates. Since payments on behalf of an individual tend to reduce the amount of effective insurance, many policies gradually reinstate the full maximum amount.

---

[18] *Source Book of Health Insurance Data,* p. 16. About 7 million persons have major medical coverage in individual contracts.

[19] Ibid., p. 9.

Blanket expenses. Benefits are paid for "a bodily disorder, mental infirmity, or bodily injury." It is normal to include coverage for preexisting conditions which cause disabilities during the term of the policy. *All types of medical expenses* are included in the comprehensive "blanket" coverage, with a few exceptions. The more important types for which protection is provided are: (1) hospital room and board; (2) doctors' care and surgery; (3) professional nursing services; (4) prescription drugs and medicines; (5) anesthesia, oxygen, and Xray examination and treatment; (6) blood, plasma, and surgical dressings; (7) rental of wheelchair, hospital bed, crutches, or other therapeutic equipment; and (8) artificial limbs or eyes. The eligible charges are usually limited only by the maximum amount and by a general provision which requires that the services, treatments, and supplies be reasonably necessary for the care of the insured. A few plans set limits of $100–$150 or more on the daily hospital room-and-board charges.

Included in most current contracts are medical expenses for *mental and nervous disorders* (90 percent include this) and *nursing home expenses* (more than half). Special limits often apply.

A few charges are excluded in order to prevent duplicate or unnecessary coverage: (1) charges which are paid for under workers' compensation or state nonoccupational disability laws; (2) confinement in a government-owned hospital (where the insured would not be obligated to pay in the absence of insurance); (3) war injuries; (4) eye, ear, and general health examinations; (5) dental treatment or cosmetic surgery, unless necessitated by an accidental bodily injury; and (6) self-inflicted injuries.

Deductibles. Different companies approach the deductible in different ways. There are *(a)* the *each illness* plan, *(b)* the *each individual* plan, and *(c)* the *family budget* plan. Group plans also use "corridor" and "integrated" forms of deductibles (see next section on "primary types").

Under the *each illness* plan, the deductible applies to each separate disability. Under the *each individual* plan, all expenditures incurred within a definite period of time, usually a year, are subject to but one deductible, regardless of how many different disabilities are involved. The *family budget* deductible applies one deductible for all covered members of a particular family with respect to all eligible expenses incurred within a given year. This last plan may be the best protection, but in order to keep the costs within reasonable bounds a higher deductible is necessary.

The deductible varies among the different group major medical contracts. Most plans use a deductible of $50 or $100. The deductible is designed to eliminate small claims from coverage. Payment of these small medical expenses should impose no serious burden upon the average family. Many plans today recognize this purpose by eliminating the deductible, paying losses in full above a "stop-loss" amount such as $1,000.

Coinsurance. After the deductible amount has been reached, a "coin-surance" or participation factor is applied to all eligible charges. Under this provision the insured pays a stipulated percentage of all charges over the deductible amount, such as 20 percent. The insurer pays the remaining percentage, such as 80 percent. The 80–20 plan is most common, although the 75–25 plan and some other variations are in use. The purpose is quite obvious: to prevent overuse of the medical services provided for in the contract. Requiring the insured to participate in a portion of the cost curbs excessive use.

Primary types. Group major medical insurance plans are also divided into one of two primary types: *(a) supplemental* major medical plans, and *(b) comprehensive* major medical plans.

Supplemental plans. *Supplemental* major medical plans, sometimes termed "integrated or superimposed plans," are written where there is already some group protection for hospital, surgical, or medical benefits. These plans are designed to coordinate major medical insurance with such other group health coverages as are written concurrently. The intent is to eliminate double coverage. About two thirds of persons having group major medical have this type. The deductible feature is retained. A plan in wide use is known as the *corridor deductible*. The plan excludes from eligible expenses covered by the major medical expense insurance all payments under the hospital-surgical-medical plan. Then a deductible known as the "corridor" of uncovered expenses is established. A usual figure is $50 or $100. In the case of an illness calling for an outlay of $3,600, for example, with the hospital-surgical-medical plan covering up to $1,000 and a $100 "corridor" deductible with a 20 percent coinsurance feature, the insurer would pay $2,000. The total out-of-pocket expense to the individual employee is $600, representing $500 coinsurance and the $100 corridor deductible.

Comprehensive plans. *Comprehensive* major medical plans combine basic and catastrophe medical coverage for groups which have no hospital, surgical, or medical benefits in force. They also may be written to replace all other group health coverages (for medical expenses) already in force. These plans are comprehensive (i.e. inclusive of all medical expenses) because there is no underlying group hospital-surgical-medical coverage. Although the amounts and benefits vary, a typical plan provides an initial deductible of $100 for all claims on a calendar year basis. As a concession to expedite admission to hospitals, full coverage for hospital charges is sometimes allowed. All other covered expenses are reimbursed on an 80–20 percent coinsurance basis. There is a lifetime maximum for all claims, with about three fourths of the plans having limits of $250,000 or more.[20]

---

[20] In plans covering salaried employees of U.S. employers, according to a study of larger group insurance plans by the Wyatt Company of Chicago, *Group Benefit Survey,* 1980, p. 29.

Group dental and vision care insurance

The special problems of extending medical care insurance to provide benefits for dental care and vision care expenses are other areas in which group health insurance plans are meeting significant challenges.

Dental insurance. One of the most popular new fields of rapid expansion in group health insurance is *dental insurance*. Although less than 2 million persons had such insurance coverage in 1965, group dental coverage is now available to more than 80 million persons. Coverage is provided through 35 dental service plans (nonprofit associations sponsored by dental societies) and some 100 or more insurers. Many of the dental service plans are affiliated nationally in the Delta Dental Plans which write about 30 percent of the coverage. Insurers have about 60 percent of the persons covered, and Blue Cross–Blue Shield associations have 10 percent.[21]

Unions are stimulating wide interest in the field. Dental insurance *OFTEN EXCLUDED ALSO* coverage is broadening, too, to include most dental services. Diagnostic, preventive, restorative, and even orthodontic care are often all included. Limits do apply, however, such as per person annual, or lifetime maximums; coinsurance participation by the insured of 20–50 percent; and $25–$50 deductibles. Most plans are based upon paying the "usual, customary, and reasonable fees" for regular cleaning, oral exams, and fluoride treatments. Usually, 80 percent or more of expenses for Xrays, fillings, extractions, and surgery is paid, and 50 percent or more for bridges, crowns, and orthodontic work. The annual limit per year is often set at $750–$1,500. An interesting feature is the emphasis on preventive care (often paid in full) as well as payment for other dental expenses. Many plans cover dependents but also require employees to help pay the premiums. The cost is usually a sizable addition to group health insurance expenses, often adding more than $100 per person or $400 per family to annual health insurance costs. The developments will be worth watching, for it has been estimated that more than 110 million persons will be covered by the mid-1980s.[22]

Vision care insurance. The latest development is group *vision care insurance*. Larger employers and unions have been actively promoting the inclusion of such expenses in group health contracts. Many variations exist in this new field, but the preventive and corrective aspects are similar to those of dental insurance plans. Service contracts with optometrists, opticians, and physicians are sometimes used to help control costs. The typical plan includes examinations, fitting, frames, and lenses, but maximum payments for each category of expenses are common. For example, a maximum of $75–$100 for glasses every two years may be included. Such plans offer another interesting example of the trend toward

[21] *Source Book of Health Insurance Data*, p. 21.
[22] *Journal of Commerce*, April 19, 1982, p. 6c.

including "prepayment" of fairly regular medical expenses with group insurance coverage for the larger medical costs.

Group disability income insurance

In addition to covering medical expenses, group health plans often provide *disability loss of income*. These forms are sometimes known as "accident and sickness" insurance, although care should be taken to recognize them as income plans rather than medical expense reimbursement plans. (See also Chapter 9.)

Of a total of more than 84 million persons having disability income protection by 1980, group insurance policies covered about one half, individual policies about one fourth, and one fourth had other noninsured plans such as formal paid sick-leave plans.[23]

Definition of disability. Disability income plans are designed primarily as supplemental coverage to workers' compensation insurance. The insurer agrees to pay the designated benefits "if the employee shall become wholly and continuously disabled as a result of nonoccupational accidental bodily injuries or nonoccupational sickness, and thereby be prevented from performing any and every duty pertaining to his or her employment."

Group disability income insurance is thus usually a *nonoccupational* coverage similar to plans required by five states under "temporary disability laws" (see Chapter 11). There are no conversion rights to continue disability income coverage on an individual policy basis after leaving employment.

It is usual in the case of disability due to injury to have benefits begin with the first day of disability. In the case of sickness, in order to reduce administrative expense attributable to claims originating from minor illnesses, a waiting period is the standard practice. A period of seven days is the most common waiting period for sickness. Substantial reduction in the premium results from the use of such a waiting period because sicknesses are much more frequently the cause of disability than are accidents.[24] Disability income benefits are usually payable only when the employee is under the care of a physician, and there is no provision for partial disability.

Benefit levels and duration. Efforts are made to establish benefits at an *amount* sufficiently high to relieve financial distress. Benefit levels, however, are generally set at some amount less than the full amount

---

[23] *Source Book of Health Insurance Data,* p. 20.

[24] The frequency of disabilities for sicknesses at all ages is 222 per 1,000 persons each year, as compared with 31 for injuries. *Statistical Bulletin,* Metropolitan Life Foundation, January–March 1982, p. 4.

of take-home pay to discourage malingering. Under the *flat* plan, the weekly benefit is the same for all employees. Under the more common *earnings* plan, benefits are based on earnings and are designed to replace a substantial part of the employee's earnings, such as two thirds or three fourths. The *position* plan calls for the allocation of a flat amount of benefit to a person occupying a particular position such as company officer, supervisor, or salesperson.

The policy then establishes a maximum *duration* for the payment of benefits in any one period of disability. Two types of disability income benefits are written: *short-term* (payable for *up to two years*), and *long-term* (payable usually for *at least five years*, but often to age 65 or for life). Some long-term policies, especially individual rather than group contracts, may cover occupational injuries and sicknesses. About two thirds of disability income policies cover only short-term disabilities. A long-term contract may often provide lifetime benefits for accidental injuries but limit benefits for sicknesses to 1, 2, or 5 years. Thus many disabilities of longer duration are uninsured, creating a serious gap in the income protection of individuals and families.

Group accidental death and dismemberment insurance

Another form of group health insurance aimed at replacing lost income is group *accidental death and dismemberment* insurance. This form provides for payment in the event of loss of life, sight, or limb through external, violent, and accidental means. The coverage may be written on either a 24-hour basis or a nonoccupational basis. The insurance is usually written in conjunction with one of the other forms of group insurance.

As an underwriting practice, insurers establish maximum and minimum amounts of insurance. A minimum of $1,000 and a maximum of $10,000 to $100,000 are common. Many plans provide the same amount of insurance for group accidental death and dismemberment insurance as for group life insurance. Typically, one half of the principal sum (payable for death) is paid for the loss of one hand or foot, or the sight of one eye. The insurer is liable for payment under this form only when loss covered by the policy occurs within 90 days after the injuries are sustained. There is no liability for suicide or war.

Health Maintenance Organizations (HMOs)

With personal health care expenditures rising tenfold during the past 10 years, and now nearly $300 billion a year, it is no wonder that tremendous pressure for new cost control measures has been put on the health care delivery system in the United States. One of the important developments has been the emergence of *health maintenance organizations* (HMOs), encouraged by the HMO Act of 1973 and its amendments.

Development.   Basically HMOs are designed as a new group financing alternative to traditional fee-for-service group health insurance. Historically they derive from prepaid group medical practice plans that have had success in limited areas during the past several decades, such as the Kaiser Permanente, the Health Insurance Plan (New York), the Group Health Cooperative (Seattle), and several dozen others. HMOs involve both a different type of contract as well as a new marketing method, but because they are unique to health insurance they are treated in this chapter rather than the later chapter on insurance marketing.

An impetus to the growth of HMOs were federal laws which provided up to $325 million to aid in the planning and formation of such plans and required employers of more than 25 employees to offer a federally certified HMO (if available in the area) as an option to any employee health fringe benefit. Today there are nearly 300 HMOs with combined enrollments of 11 million persons, although most of these are not yet approved as "qualified" under standards set by the Department of Health, Education, and Welfare.[25]

Characteristics.   Many variations of health maintenance organizations exist, but all may be defined as a *comprehensive set of health services* guaranteed to an enrolled population for a *fixed, prepaid fee.* The HMO sells an agreement to its subscribers to provide, not just pay for, a stated range of health services, at fees ranging from perhaps $50 to $150 or more a month per family.

The subscriber buys, in advance, access to a *team of doctors who are employees* of the plan. The services both of general practitioners and specialists are provided in one-stop comprehensive medical care at a single location, sometimes even including dental care. Diagnostic, laboratory, outpatient, and hospital services are all included. Special emphasis is placed upon *preventive care* through regular examinations.

The HMO is usually organized as a nonprofit association rather than as a corporation. In most states it is not regulated as an insurer, but special enabling legislation applies. The owners may be insurers, Blue Cross–Blue Shield associations, hospitals, medical practicioners, or others. Regulation is strict in some states, while it is minimal in others.

Advantages.   Increased competition by insurers, hospitals, and physicians in providing medical care has been an important benefit of HMOs for the consumer. In some states an example of direct response has been the formation of a special type of HMO known as Independent Practice Associations (IPAs) in which a group of physicians contract on a part-

---

[25] *"Health Care: Getting the Best Value," Money,* September 1982, p. 58.

time basis with hospitals to provide employees with medical services at a specific daily rate.

One goal of the HMOs is to reduce hospitalization costs, and hospital days per year for members have been lowered substantially.[26] Some HMOs have also dramatically reduced the number of surgical operations, for example, by as much as one half.[27] Many of these lower costs may result from the incentive for physicians on a fixed salary to encourage care outside the hospital and to discourage other unnecessary medical care and expenses. However, the overall costs of HMOs tend to run higher than traditional health insurance premiums because of the broad services HMOs provide. Early studies indicate that this results in better health for enrollees of HMO plans.

Problems.   Not all HMOs have been successful, as some have undergone considerable financial and other problems in starting up. Success requires good medical management as well as good business management. Some HMOs have had to increase fees significantly, and several have failed. In general, the development of HMOs has not been as rapid as many observers predicted. The relatively small size of new HMOs (often less than 10,000 subscribers) appears to be a handicap for efficient comprehensive service. The medical profession is still widely divided on the issue of whether medical services by salaried physicians can provide quality care, if built-in financial incentives divide profits among the employees of the HMO when costs are held down. Members sometimes dislike being restricted to physicians participating in the HMO and the difficulty of obtaining out-of-the-area services, or complain about impersonal institutionalized care. Many persons are reluctant to change their established family physician.

Prospects.   Insurance companies were active participants in establishing some of the earlier HMOs, and Blue Cross plans have also been involved in HMOs. Some of the cost control methods emphasized by HMOs, such as encouraging doctors to regularly review one another's work through professional service review organizations (PSROs) and paying for "second opinions" before surgery is done, are being adopted by many group health insurers.

Federal government pressure for the continued growth of HMOs has slowed with budget cuts. However, it is still a reasonable prediction that the HMO movement will continue to expand. The relatively rapid growth of health maintenance organizations, with emphasis on preventive care as a good approach to reducing high health care costs, suggests that

---

[26] "The HMO Approach to Health Care," *Consumer Reports,* May 1982, p. 250, cites a 1980 government study showing 418 hospital days a year per 1,000 HMO members in contrast to a Blue Cross–Blue Shield rate of 725 days and a national average of 1,631 days.

[27] "Too Much Surgery," *Newsweek,* April 10, 1978, p. 65.

the HMOs may prove to be a significant alternative in health care delivery through the group insurance technique.

New trends

Several new trends closely related to group health insurance should be mentioned as significant today. These developments include *Administrative Service Only* (ASO) plans, *cafeteria* or *flexible-benefit* plans, and the impact of *social security changes* on group health insurance described in the preceding sections.

Administrative Service Only (ASO) plans. Rapidly increasing medical care costs during the past decade have exerted tremendous pressure on employers to find ways that may reduce costs for health insurance benefits for which they are paying much of the expense. One method which has become quite popular with risk managers responsible for employee benefit plans is *self-funding,* with the purchase of *administrative service only* (ASO) on a fee basis from insurers or other organizations. Under such arrangements the cost of health benefits is paid through these organizations to employees only as claims actually occur. The risk of higher costs than expected remains with the employer, but there is the advantage of retaining the cash flow until losses are paid. In addition to their own losses, employers pay outside organizations only a service fee for administering the claims payments. Some 25 percent of insurance company group coverage is estimated as paid under ASO plans. In order to protect themselves against the unpredictability of large or increasing claims, many employers also purchase *Minimum Premium Plans (MPPs)* in which insurers pay for loss experience exceeding specified minimum levels. More than 20 percent of insurance company group health coverage is so insured today.[28]

Cafeteria or flexible-benefit plans. An interesting trend, only offered to date by about two dozen employers, is experimentation with *cafeteria or flexible-benefit plans.* Basically these "do-it-yourself" plans attack the increasing complexity and rigidity of employee benefit programs by permitting the *employee to choose* among various group insurance options. Usually a common core of minimum benefits is required in the life, health, and pension areas. Beyond these amounts, the employee selects how he or she wants to spend an annual allocation of credits for total employee fringe benefits. This flexibility allows employees to adapt their total program to their own needs and to their particular tax situations. For example, married persons may desire more life insurance; the older generation, higher retirement income; or two-income families, less health insurance to avoid duplication of coverages. Flexible-

---

[28] *Source Book of Health Insurance Data,* p. 8.

benefit plans have a great appeal to some employees and will grow during the 1980s. However, most insurers and employers are cautious because of some of the potential problems. Will employers be criticized for an employee who makes bad choices? Will loss costs of insurers increase with adverse selection by employees choosing only coverages for which they are poorer risks? Overall, will the plans be an administrative night-mare to design and operate?[29] Perhaps the computer era of tomorrow will help provide answers during the coming decade.

Social security changes. The impact of government expenditures on health care in the United States is readily apparent. The public share of total annual health expenses of nearly $300 billion has risen from 30 percent 15 years ago to more than 40 percent today. In particular, the federal government involvement through various social security pro-grams is immense. *Medical care* costs provided since 1966 by Medicare (primarily for persons 65 and older), Medicaid (for low-income categories), and other programs (military and civilian employees, veterans) have swollen to more than one eighth of the federal budget.[30] In addition, *disability income* for long-term disabilities is paid to 4 million persons.

With the budget restrictions of the economy during the early 1980s, changes in these social programs will likely have major effects on the private health insurance field. Increasing Medicare deductibles, for exam-ple, creates greater demand for supplementary medical insurance through private insurance policies. Cutting ineligible disability income recipients or size of benefits causes greater need for private insurance disability income contracts. The challenge of reducing overall health care costs while providing greater protection appears to be shifting back to private insurers and the other new health care organizations. Group health insurance techniques, especially, should be at the forefront of these changes for future generations.

FOR REVIEW AND DISCUSSION

1. "The group insurance method is very important today as a means by which employers provide fringe benefits in employee benefit plans." Explain. How is it also important to life insurance companies?

2. What features help prevent adverse selection against the insurer in the group life and health insurance contract? Explain each briefly.

3. What characteristics make group insurance different from other insurance plans? Explain the importance of at least three such characteristics.

4. Several different types of minimums and maximums are used in connection with group life insurance. Evaluate the need for such limits.

---

[29] "Fringe Benefits A La Carte," *Changing Times*, May 1982, p. 51, suggests that this may be a key factor.

[30] *Source Book of Health Insurance Data*, pp. 31–35.

5. Group life insurance is necessarily designed to meet basic and average needs of the whole group. Explain how three features of the usual group life contract help in achieving these needs.

6. How can *yearly renewable term* insurance be the normal type used in group life policies when the increasing cost during the older ages makes this insurance unsuitable for many individual life insurance policyholders? Why is this type usually used? Discuss one type of group *permanent* life insurance.

7. To what extent do group life insurance plans *(a)* have standard provisions, *(b)* finance costs through employee contributions, and *(c)* have conversion rights (to permanent life insurance) that are actually used?

8. In terms of its advantages to employers and employees, why has group life insurance grown so rapidly in the last 20 years? What disadvantages and what possible limitations do you foresee in the continued growth of this insurance during the next 20 years?

9. What factors have encouraged, and slowed, the tremendous growth of group health insurance coverages by insurance companies?

10. As an employee of I. B. Human Company, what group health insurance "fringe benefits" would you want the personnel manager to explain to you and your family? Briefly list six pertinent questions that you might ask.

11. What makes group health insurance cost the employee less than comparable individual insurance?

12. What. major types of health insurance *losses* may be covered in typical group health insurance contracts? What basic *perils* besides injuries and sickness may be provided for by group insurance?

13. Two opposing philosophies in group health insurance are *(a)* covering all losses on a "first-dollar" basis, and *(b)* covering only the larger losses on a "catastrophe" or "major medical" basis. With which philosophy do you agree most? Can the two ideas be used rationally together?

14. Why can't a policyholder usually be paid for all of his or her medical expenses and loss of income due to health losses? Does this question have particular relevance to group health insurance? Explain why or why not.

15. Group health policies for loss of income frequently provide no waiting period for disability due to accident but provide one for disability due to sickness. Explain the logic of this situation.

16. Today many hospitals participate in group insurance *service* benefits. How does the loss payment differ from that of the plans offered by insurance companies?

17. What is meant by "blanket" protection in major medical expense insurance? How does it compare with other types of group insurance for medical expense?

18. Group major medical has been a fast-growing part of health insurance. Identify three of its primary features and explain its rapid growth.

19. What has been the effect of rising medical costs on Medicare-Medicaid and on private health insurance plans?

20. Why is group disability income insurance usually a nonoccupational cover?

21. Some predictions say that dental insurance coverage will grow from the present 80 million persons to more than 110 million by the mid-1980s. Divide the class into two groups (all those without any cavities in one group!) and discuss whether or not such a prediction is realistic.

22. How do health maintenance organizations (HMOs) differ from other group health insurance plans? What advantages and disadvantages do they have?

23. Choose *one* new trend related to group health insurance and explain its potential relationship to the cost of private health insurance.

Chapter 11

Outline of concepts

Government provides or requires some insurance for large segments of society in many *social insurance programs,* and among these the largest are *government life and health insurance.*

Economic security to assure individuals of minimum necessities is seen in:

The expanding role of government, which clearly shows the growth of social insurance in the United States as well as throughout the world;

The reasons for accelerated change, which are found in changing social, educational, political, and economic factors; and

"Social security," public assistance, and social insurance, which must be differentiated in terms of both *goals* and *methods.*

The social insurance programs in the United States are extensive and often criticized, but four major ones treat the *old-age, death, disability,* and *unemployment perils.*

Old-age, survivors, disability, and health insurance (OASDHI) is by far the *largest* of all the government insurance programs in the United States.

Eligibility is determined by *covered employment* (more than 9 out of 10 workers) and *insured status* ("fully," "currently," or "disability").

Benefits are analyzed by *type* (including Medicare), *size* (related to *average indexed monthly earnings*), and *special earnings* and *disability requirements.*

Administration is by the *federal* government, with *IRS tax collection, individual employee accounts* recorded, and *application* for benefits required.

Financing involves:

Tax on employer and employee, of 6.7 percent *each* in 1983.

Need for understanding and fewer misconceptions.

Pay-as-you-go assessment plan with contingency trust funds.

Income shift among generations, from young to old.

A current recipient bargain, with only partial "earned" right.

Future self-supporting cost estimates, and **needed reform.**

Unemployment compensation is analyzed in terms of:

Eligibility, in covered employment, willing and able to work.

Benefits, aimed at one half normal wages for about 39 weeks.

Administration, basically by the *states,* with some federal standards.

Financing, a wage tax on *employers* (varies by experience).

Workers' compensation for *occupational* injuries and diseases is reviewed.

Temporary-disability (nonoccupational) insurance, in six jurisdictions.

Summary of four major social insurance programs compares major features.

Other social insurance programs briefly described are: the *Railroad Acts, government employee* systems, and *veterans' benefit* programs.

Proposed National Health Insurance plans are discussed as to need and objectives, and current proposals are noted.

Government life and health insurance

The "quest for security"[1] is a life-long pursuit for most individuals, families, and organizations. In a world of uncertainty, only a few reach their ultimate objectives, and many fail miserably in attaining even a reasonable degree of financial independence. For this reason, society often steps in to help or to require systems aimed at assuring that at least minimal basic human needs and wants are met.

Some societies provide for almost all of the fundamental needs of individuals living within their jurisdiction. Other societies provide very little economic security for their members through government plans and programs. Most nations of the world fall between these two extremes. Government, particularily through social insurance programs, meets some but not all of the fundamental needs. Private insurance is also purchased through individual effort in order to achieve the various total goals which often are threatened by economic uncertainties.

How *social insurance* systems provide basic security against some of the universal perils is the subject of this chapter. Three of the perils causing economic insecurity—*death, old age,* and *poor health*—have been introduced in the previous six chapters on private life and health insurance. (*Unemployment* is another peril, one not treated by private insurance.) Understanding why and how these four major perils are partially met by *government life and health insurance* becomes the focus of Chapter 11.

ECONOMIC SECURITY

The concept of individuals banding together as a society in order to achieve security is as old as humanity. The opening scenes of *Space Odyssey–2001* show apelike creatures collectively obtaining food and protecting themselves against earthly predators. The theme of groups organizing to face uncertainties has expanded to the future and to extra-terres-

---

[1] Robert J. Myers, *Social Security,* 2d ed. (Homewood, Ill.: Richard D. Irwin, 1981), p. 3. Special thanks are due Dr. Myers for detailed recommendations on this Chapter 11.

tial scope in more recent popular movies such as *E.T.* and *Star Wars (I* and *II).*

In modern times, the role of society has increased in terms of intent and methods. Its place is to help the individual achieve a minimum *money* income in spite of some perils of loss, thus securing the ability to purchase food, shelter, clothing, good health, education, and other necessities of life. Economic security has increasingly become a governmental rather than an individual function, and government or social insurance is one method by which this change has occurred.

> *OLD AGE, SURVIVORS, DISABILITY & HEALTH INSURANCE*

The expanding role of government

In the United States, government's role in this process has expanded from a relatively modest few billion dollars a year to expenditures of about one half *trillion* dollars for health, education, welfare, housing, and social insurance by the federal government alone.[2] With state and local government expenditures included, the figures practically double.

The government old age and health insurance systems in some European nations preceded those in the United States by several decades. Social insurance in the United States is largely a product of the 20th century, and particularly of the last 45 years. Workers' compensation insurance appeared in the second decade of the century, but the real impetus toward extensive social insurance systems came in the 1930s with the passage of the federal Social Security Act of 1935. The act was the direct means by which the Old Age Insurance system (now OASDHI, including survivors, disability, and health benefits) and the state unemployment compensation plans began. Temporary-disability (nonoccupational) laws created another major division of social insurance in some states during the 1940s.

The student should be aware that the concept of what is or is not social insurance may undergo change over time. Workers' compensation, for example, is a required type of social insurance, even though private insurers are still important in the insuring of workers' compensation perils. Similarly, compulsory automobile plans discussed in Chapter 19 are changing the basically private nature of automobile liability insurance systems. Chapter 24 treats the newer role of government in property and liability insurance.

The reasons for accelerated change

Acknowledging the inevitability of change and the increase in government's role with regard to economic security is merely a first step. One

---

[2] See *Budget of the U.S. Government* (Washington, D.C.: U.S. Government Printing Office). Social insurance expenditures are approximately one half of this total.

must also comprehend the *accelerating rate* of change, and the reasons *why* economic security has become more and more the province of government rather than private enterprise. Some of the answers may be found in studying the background in which changes have taken place. History may help, but as Will and Ariel Durant have said: "Most history is guessing; the rest is prejudice. . . . We must operate with partial knowledge, and be content with probabilities."[3] Thus, insurance people should appreciate this approach.

A better understanding of the role of government in economic security will also be achieved by noting the social, educational, political, and economic changes which have occurred (with possible effects on the government's role in parentheses):

1. Social.
    a. The decline in the agrarian society and the trend toward urbanization (increases dependence on regular money income).
    b. The improvements in communication (aiding information dissemination.
    c. The changing roles of the family, the church, and other institutions.
    d. Changes in individual initiative and reliance on the group.
2. Educational.
    a. The rise in literacy and educational levels (understanding needs).
    b. Increased concern for the future (changing savings attitudes).
    c. Understanding the values of education in implementing other goals.
3. Political.
    a. The growth of a more legalistic society (changing liability).
    b. The increase in federal power as opposed to state-local power.
    c. Changing goals of society: full employment, internationalism, economic stability, and so on.
4. Economic.
    a. The trend toward industrialization (changing work hazards).
    b. Affluence and the rise of the middle-income group (changing needs).
    c. The continuance of long-term inflation (upsetting planning).
    d. The effect of increasing longevity (influencing retirement needs).
    e. Decreased savings because of taxation and other factors.
    f. The two-income family, with more women in the workforce.

Better understanding of environmental changes will result in a more meaningful appreciation of the present and probable future role of government in economic security.

---

[3] Introduction to Will and Ariel Durant, *The Lessons of History* (New York: Simon & Schuster, 1968).

"Social security," public assistance, and social insurance

In general, the idea of society providing or requiring systems for obtaining economic security is popularly expressed as "social security." To many persons "social security" means a particular program, most frequently that of Old-Age, Survivors, Disability, and Health Insurance (OASDHI). Other persons often use the term in a broader sense which could include almost all government activities, from federal employment offices and minimum wage laws to efforts to bring new industry to a certain area. "Social security" is thus not used with precision in our everyday language. However, it ordinarily refers to those *assistance* and *insurance* programs which are required, subsidized, or actually provided by government.

Goals. The primary *goal* of "social security" is simply stated as continued financial income, in spite of some perils, for the members of a society. It is *basic* economic certainty which is the goal.

Although there are few persons who would quarrel with this statement of the overall goal, many observers will differ in defining the more specific objectives and the methods by which the goals should be accomplished. For example, should the objective be certainty in regard to *all* possible causes of financial adversity? Probably not, but society can pick out the major kinds of unpredictable losses which affect a major part of the population. What is a *major* kind of loss and part of the population? Does it include *all* of the old-age population, the disabled, migrant workers, and so on? How can such widespread social risks be differentiated from causes of the same losses which may be essentially individual in their origin?[4]

The difficulty in defining the goals of "social security" is also highlighted by the question of just what constitutes a *minimum level* of well-being. In our industrialized and urbanized society, the minimum "floor of protection" must be translated into a specific income (or certain services) to enable each person to obtain the necessities of life. Obviously the needs include food, shelter, and clothing, but it is no easy task to reach agreement on the quality and quantity of these basic needs. Should the food minimum include steak at least once in a while instead of hamburger? Is housing only a roof and four walls, or should the neighborhood and other factors be considered? Does it today, for example, include education, a television set, an automobile, and travel?

Methods. What about the methods of providing a social solution to problems in which society as a whole will have to bear the costs if nothing else is done? As described in Chapter 3, the two methods used are "public assistance" and "social insurance."

---

[4] Such as, for example, injuries that are nonoccupational or unemployment that results from quitting work for personal reasons.

Public assistance programs are based on the concept of proven "need." Benefits are available to its recipients only after they have shown (by lacking sufficient assets or income, or both) that society should help them in meeting basic minimum standards. Examples include programs for the blind, the disabled, and dependent children.

Social insurance programs are those systems in which (1) the elements of the insurance technique are present, and (2) the plans are required, and often also conceived, financed, and administered, by government with the objective of meeting certain economic security standards for a society. Many social insurance definitions suggest that the insurance technique requires only a combination or pooling of independent, fortuitous risks in sufficient number to provide reasonable predictability. Other definitions add more specific conditions: eligibility derived from contributions to the plan (without proving need) by recipients; benefits determined by law, and not directly related to contributions made; a definite long-range plan for assuring the financial adequacy of the plan; and others.[5]

The major differences between public assistance and social insurance programs are summarized in Table 11–1.

Table 11–1. Summary of differences between public assistance and social insurance programs

Characteristics	Public assistance programs	Social insurance programs
Basic nature	Welfare or charity	Insurance
Eligibility	Discretionary; "recipients" must demonstrate "need"	Not discretionary; "Insureds" must usually be "contributors"
Benefits	Based on "need" only	Based on covered earnings, wages, or actual costs
Financing	General revenue only	Specific separate taxes (or insurance premiums, in several plans)
Administration	By states, or federal government	By federal government, or by state, in various plans

SOCIAL INSURANCE PROGRAMS IN THE UNITED STATES

The U.S. insurance-welfare system designed for meeting economic security goals has attracted *increasing criticism* in recent years. The general public, the press, politicians, liberals and conservatives, recipients and taxpayers, young and old, men and women, and blacks and whites—all appear to be dissatisfied with the present state of welfare programs. The increasing attitude of questioning has also affected the U.S. social insurance system. The reasons are plentiful: (1) a larger young popula-

[5] Yung-Ping Chen, *Social Security in a Changing Society* (Bryn Mawr, Pa.: McCahan Foundation, 1981), p. 90.

tion, (2) sharply rising taxes, (3) discrimination and inequities, (4) fiscal effects, (5) frauds, (6) worry about the system's financial soundness, (7) competition with private insurance systems, and others. This situation emphasizes the problems of coordination among social insurance and welfare systems, and of coordinating these systems with the private insurance business.

In a textbook of this scope, only a limited summary of the major provisions of the basic social insurance programs can be offered. The student desiring additional detail and further information about each of the social insurance systems is referred to more comprehensive publications.[6]

The remainder of this chapter concentrates on the four most important types of social insurance today: (1) Old-Age, Survivors, Disability, and Health Insurance; (2) unemployment compensation; (3) workers' compensation; and (4) temporary disability (nonoccupational) insurance. The section on workers' compensation will be abbreviated since Chapter 18 on employers' liability and workers' compensation will discuss many of its aspects. Several other social insurance programs of lesser importance are included in the final sections of this chapter: railroad and government employee systems, veterans' benefit systems, and proposed national health insurance systems.

The general significance of the four primary social insurance programs is seen in the size of the yearly taxes (or, in the smaller part of the programs, insurance premiums) which now support them. As noted in Figure 3–3 of Chapter 3, the total taxes and premiums are about $236 *billion* a year, or about one half of the combined private and social insurance fields. About three fourths of the annual cost of social insurance today goes for the OASDHI program, for which taxes of about $163 billion were paid in 1981.[7]

Each of the social insurance plans has basic features with which the student of insurance should be familiar. The programs are analyzed in the following sections of the chapter on the basis of (1) eligibility, (2) benefits, (3) administration, and (4) financing.

OLD-AGE, SURVIVORS, DISABILITY, AND HEALTH INSURANCE

The largest and best-known social insurance system in the United States, OASDHI, is often mistakenly believed to be the only part of the 1935 Social Security Act, which actually also provided for nine other

---

[6] John G. Turnbull, C. Arthur Williams, Jr., and Earl F. Cheit, *Economic and Social Security* (New York: Ronald Press, 1973); Robert J. Myers, *Social Security* and *Medicare* (Homewood, Ill.: Richard D. Irwin, 1981 and 1970, respectively); George E. Rejda, *Social Insurance and Economic Security* (Englewood Cliffs, N.J.: Prentice-Hall, 1976, and scheduled for a 1983 edition).

[7] These figures include approximately $10 billion of general revenue contributions to Part B of the Medicare program.

separate programs.[8] Title II of the act created the trust funds and requirements for the OASDHI program. Today about 36 million persons are
receiving social security benefits, including 24 million retired workers
and dependents, 8 million survivors of workers, and 4 million disabled
workers and their dependents. The system covers almost everyone, and
its costs are paid by employer and employee taxes.

The Social Security Act was by far the most outstanding landmark
in the development of social insurance. The depression of the 1930s was
undoubtedly a factor in this legislation, but the reasons for the recognition of the needs and the choice of a gigantic social insurance program
for the solution were more deep rooted. The United States had changed
rapidly from an agricultural and family-oriented society to an urban
and industrial one. The result was to create an increasing interdependence among all wage earners. Instead of depending upon individual
and family initiative, ingenuity, and thrift to provide support in hard
times, individuals turned to the government and to society as a whole
to help them through economic hardships.

The Great Depression focused attention on the plight of the aged and
the unemployed, and from this grew the Social Security Act. The growth
of social insurance from this beginning has been made possible by an
unparalleled economic upswing in recent decades, enabling a high standard of living in the United States to support the continuing interest
in alleviating social problems. The concern is still evident today, with
the federal administration also pledged to major efforts in reducing unemployment and the undesirable economic effects of inflation.

The amendments to the OASDHI program have been steady during
the past 45 years. Survivorship benefits were added for widows and children up to age 18 in 1939, even before the first retirement benefits for
old age began. Liberalization has proceeded in many sessions of Congress,
including 1946, 1950, 1952, 1954, 1956 (when disability benefits were
introduced), 1958, 1960, 1961, 1965 (Medicare), and almost every year
since then until 1974. However, in 1979, 1980, and 1981 the legislative
enactments generally tended to cut back on the benefits.

Eligibility

Covered employment.   About 9 out of 10 employed persons are now
covered by the plan. The only major types of workers not covered by
OASDHI are (1) some civilian government employees, (2) some agricul-

---

[8] These include one other type of social insurance, unemployment compensation insur-
ance, five public assistance programs, and three child welfare services. Portions of the
following sections have been adapted from the *Social Security Handbook* (Washington,
D.C.: Social Security Administration, U.S. Department of Health, Education, and Welfare).
This is reprinted about every three years. Current laws and regulations of the Social
Security Act should be checked in the two-volume series entitled *Compilation of the Social
Security Laws* (Washington, D.C.: U.S. Government Printing Office).

tural and domestic workers, and (3) some employees of nonprofit organizations (those whose employers elected not to become part of the system). Railroad workers have their own system, but it is closely coordinated with OASDHI. Many federal government employees are covered under other retirement systems, and many state and local government workers are included in OASDHI as a result of federal-state agreements with these employers. Thus, very few working persons are not now a part of the program. Both wage earners and self-employed persons are included.

Insured status. To be entitled to benefits it is necessary that a person be engaged in employment covered by the Social Security Act for at least a prescribed minimum number of quarters. Before 1978, one quarter of coverage is generally earned for each quarter in which at least $50 in covered nonfarm wages is paid in a year, or four quarters of coverage are earned for at least $400 of creditable self-employment earnings in a year. For farm wages, each full $100 unit of annual wages gives a quarter of coverage, up to four maximum. For 1978, one quarter of coverage for each full $250 of annual earnings will apply, with a maximum of four quarters of coverage in a year. After 1978, the $250 amount is adjusted on the basis of changes in average annual national wages; for 1982 the amount required is $340.

Workers become eligible for benefits by achieving (1) "fully," (2) "currently," and (3) "disability" insured status. *Fully insured status* gives eligibility for all benefits except disability benefits. It is usually attained by having 40 quarters, or 10 years, of coverage. However, the requirements may also be met by having worked a shorter period, having at least one quarter of coverage for each calendar year after 1950 (or after the year in which age 21 is attained, if later) prior to death or disability, or age 62. A minimum of six quarters is required. *Currently insured status* alone gains eligibility only for the child's, mother's, and lump-sum survivorship benefits, and the worker must have quarters of coverage during at least 6 of the last 13 quarters. *Disability insured status,* which is required for disability benefits, takes fully insured status *and* 20 quarters of coverage in the 40-quarter period ending with the quarter in which disability began. (Special, more liberal rules apply for persons disabled before age 31.)

Benefits

Types of benefits. There are four basic types of benefits available to those persons who achieve eligibility under the OASDHI program. These are: (1) payments for *death,* including a small lump-sum payment and important survivors' income payments to widows with dependent children; (2) income payments for *disability* if it is total and is expected to last at least 12 months; (3) income payments after *retirement* age to either or both husband and wife (or to a child under 18, or 18 if in high school, or any age if disabled); and (4) *hospital and medical* payments under the Medicare program for *(a)* fully insured persons aged 65 *or over*, or 65 before 1968, *(b) disabled beneficiaries* (workers under 65, widows and widowers aged 50–64, and children aged 18 and over disabled before age 22) who have been on the benefit rolls for at least two years, and *(c)* persons, regardless of age, with *chronic kidney disease* requiring dialysis or renal transplant who are fully or currently insured, or are the spouse or dependent children of such a worker, or are a monthly beneficiary. Thus, in essence, OASDHI pays in cases of dying too soon (before the economic lifetime is completed), being disabled to a point which prevents earning an income, living too long (beyond the normal working lifetime), and incurring hospital-medical expenses at age 65 or older.

In reference to the insured status of the worker, the following *types* of benefits are paid:

1. If the worker is *currently* insured:
   a. Lump-sum death payment:
      (1) To widow, widower, or child eligible for monthly benefits.
   b. Survivorship income payments:
      (1) To a widow or widower[9] with one or more dependent children under age 16 (or disabled before 22).
      (2) To an unmarried child prior to age 18 (or 18 if in high school), or if the child is disabled before age 22.
2. If the worker is *fully* insured:
   a. Lump-sum death payment as in 1*(a)*.
   b. Survivorship income payments as in 1*(b)*, and also:
      (1) To widow or widower at age 65 (or reduced amounts at age 60, or at age 50 if disabled).
      (2) To dependent parents at age 62.
   c. Retirement income payments:
      (1) To retired worker at age 65[10] (or reduced amounts at 62).
      (2) To wife or husband of retired worker at age 65 or more, or reduced amounts at 62–64.[11]
      (3) To child of retired worker, prior to age 18, or if the child is disabled before age 22, or at 18 in high school.

---

[9] Income benefits to a widow or widower will stop if she or he remarries; payments to a wife or a husband will stop if a divorce is granted.

[10] Special transitional benefits are payable to certain persons who attained age 72 before 1972 (1970 for women).

[11] Or full amount at any age if eligible child is present (under 16, or disabled before 22).

  d. Disability income payments:
  (1) To disabled worker under age 65.
  (2) To wife or husband of disabled worker at age 62, or when child under 16 or disabled before 22 is present (also to disabled widow at age 50).
  (3) To child of disabled worker prior to age 18, or if the child is disabled before 22, or if 18 and in high school.

Generally, the worker's major benefit in being "currently" insured is that this enables the dependent children and the surviving parent to receive substantial *survivorship* income. If the worker is "fully" insured, these benefits and important other benefits are available: *retirement* income, and *disability* income (if special 20 out of quarters requirement is met, too). The lump-sum death payment ($255) is payable in the case of either a fully *or* currently insured worker if there is a surviving spouse or eligible children. Medicare hospital benefits are available to nearly all persons over age 65 and to certain disabled persons.

One of the most significant programs was added to the provisions of the Social Security Act in 1965. Popularly known as *Medicare,* the program is in two separate parts: (1) compulsory basic hospital insurance (HI), and (2) voluntary supplementary medical insurance (SMI). Benefits began in 1966, and coverage applies to practically everyone 65 or older.[12] Eligibility has been expanded to include persons under age 65, including (1) totally disabled insured workers for at least 24 months, (2) disabled widows (over age 50) and children on the disability benefit rolls for 24 months, and (3) certain chronic kidney cases. Persons over 65 who are not on social security can purchase HI coverage for $113 a month (for July 1982–June 1983). SMI coverage requires a premium payment by all persons covered. The sizable nature of the program is seen in the estimated benefits for 1982 of approximately $50 billion. *Medicaid,* a separate program of federal grants to the states for paying medical bills of "needy" persons, is not an insurance plan. Although begun at the same time as Medicare, under Title XIX of the Social Security Act, the plan is a federal-state *welfare* program. It grew rapidly to a current cost of approximately $23 billion a year.

The basic HI benefits payable are (1) in-hospital services of up to 90 days in each spell of illness with, in 1982, a $260 basic deductible and coinsurance of $65 a day after 60 days paid by the patient;[13] (2) posthospital care in a qualified extended care facility for 100 days, with $32.50

---

[12] Minor exceptions apply to some aliens and government employees otherwise covered.

[13] These deductibles and coinsurance amounts are to be adjusted automatically each year to reflect changes in hospital costs. A lifetime reserve of 60 days with daily coinsurance of $130 is available, in addition to the basic 90-day coverage. Psychiatric hospital care has a 190-day lifetime maximum.

a day after 20 days paid by the patient; and (3) posthospital part-time home nursing or therapy care for 100 visits. Retirement is not necessary in order to have these benefits.

The supplementary medical benefits are optional but have been purchased by almost all persons 65 or over. The charge of $12.20 a month (for July 1982–June 1983) is supplemented by about three times as much from general revenues (federal). Benefits include (1) physicians' services anywhere, (2) home health services, (3) outpatient hospital and physical therapy services anywhere, (4) limited ambulance services, and (5) miscellaneous dressings and medical equipment. An annual deductible of $75 applies, after which 80 percent of charges "allowed" by the Medicare program are paid. Special limitations apply for costs of mental care.

Size of benefits. As to the *size* of the benefits payable under the OASDHI program, two calculations are important. One is the *primary insurance amount* (PIA), which is the amount of monthly income payable to the insured worker at retirement at age 65, or for disability.[14] The benefit rates for all other types of benefits are calculated as percentages of the PIA. Reduced benefits based on the PIA are available, if chosen, to retirees at age 62, spouses at age 62, and widows at age 60.

The benefits are related to the *average indexed monthly earnings* (AIME), with indicated maximum amounts payable.[15] A person's AIME is figured (under the 1951 new-start method) over a number of years equal to the years after 1950, or age 21 if later, then subtracting the five years of lowest earnings and any years of total disability.[16] The earnings record for past years is indexed, so as to bring it up to date with recent earnings levels.[17] The earnings are subject to a specified maximum taxable earnings base in each year, which changed from $3,600 in 1951, to $4,200 in 1955, to $4,800 in 1959, to $6,600 in 1966, and to $7,800 in 1968. Increases each year since 1971 to the present $32,400 (1982) have been rapid, as shown in Table 11–3 later. The scheduled maximum is now subject to automatic changes according to the annual level of earnings in covered employment. Earnings for active duty in the uniformed services of the United States since 1956 are included, and prior military service may earn wage credits of $160 per month.

---

[14] The mathematical complexities of the necessary calculations are compounded by new formulas with each of the OASDHI amendments, but since 1979 the amounts are automatically developed each year according to provisions of the law.

[15] A new system of calculating "average *indexed* monthly earnings" (AIME) began in 1979. Using national average wages to modify actual earnings, it changes the PIA benefit formula.

[16] For persons disabled before age 47, the number of "dropout years" is less than 5.

[17] After indexing, the AIME is computed by selecting the years of highest earnings (omitting 5 lowest) since 1950 and dividing the total of such earnings by 12 times the number of selected years.

The benefit formula is heavily weighted in favor of the low-income worker. For example, the primary insurance amount for persons attaining age 62 in 1982 (or dying or becoming disabled before age 62 in 1982) is 90 percent of the first $230 of AIME, plus 32 percent of the next $1,158 of AIME, plus 15 percent of the AIME in excess of $1,388. The formula will be changed for those attaining age 62 in subsequent years by increasing the dollar "bend points" as wages rise. Under this formula an AIME of $300 gives a PIA of $229,[18] or 76 percent replacement of earnings, while an AIME of $1,000 gives a PIA of $453, or only 45 percent replacement. Special maximum family benefits apply. The average PIA in early 1982 was about $385 for all retired workers. OASDHI benefits are not subject to income taxes although proposals to make some or all taxable have been proposed.

Once every June the initial benefit amount is increased by a cost-of-living "escalator" as measured by the consumer price index (CPI), if the increase has been at least 3 percent. Benefits were raised approximately 10 percent in 1979, 14 percent in 1980, 11 percent in 1981, and 7 percent in 1982.

Caution is advised in using Table 11–2 to estimate your future benefits. The table shows the monthly benefits for the average person now receiving *retirement* benefits; the figures in the AIME column for $500 will be typical, with a PIA benefit of $314 monthly. (Actual average in early 1982 was about $385 for *all* retired workers.) For *new* retirees in 1982, the AIME column figures for $1,000 are more typical. Not until the early 1990s will the AIME column figures for $2,000 indicate average retirement benefits. For younger persons starting to receive disability or survivorship benefits today, the AIME column figures for the higher amounts are more representative because their average indexed monthly earnings are much greater.

Percentages of the PIA are applied in the following manner for the various types of OASDHI payments:

1. Lump-sum death payments—$255.
2. Survivorship income payments—100 percent of the PIA to widow or widower at age 65 (reduced if age 60–64) or 75 percent to a dependent child and to the child's surviving parent.
3. Retirement and disability income payments—100 percent of the PIA to the retired at age 65 (reduced if ages 62–64) or to the disabled worker; 50 percent of the PIA to the elderly spouse at age 65 (reduced if age 62–64) or child of the retired or disabled worker.

Table 11–2 shows the amount of monthly benefits payable under

---

[18] A higher special minimum PIA of $321 for employment of 30 years, with proportionally less for shorter coverage, is provided.

Table 11–2. Examples of OASDHI monthly benefits* at selected average monthly earnings

	Average indexed monthly earnings†			
Types of benefits	$500	$1,000	$1,500	$2,000
Retirement and disability benefits:				
Retired worker—at 65 ⎱ Disabled worker—under 65 ⎰	$314	$492	$ 627	$ 710
Wife at 65‡	157	246	313	355
Combined retired worker at 65, and wife at 65	471	738	940	1,065
Survivorship payments:				
Widow or widower at 60§	224	351	448	508
Widow or widower, and one child‖	460	720	918	1,041
Maximum family payment°	488	891	1,098	1,244

* Automatic cost-of-living adjustment increases benefit amounts shown, which are for early 1982.
† Benefit amounts shown may change slightly with new rounding rules.
‡ As an option, the retired worker and/or wife can obtain proportionally reduced benefits at age 62.
§ As an option, the widow can obtain proportionally reduced benefits at age 60–64. For initial claim at 65, benefits are the same as those of the retired worker at 65.
‖ Unmarried child under 18 or 18 if in high school.
° Maximum family payments for disability cases are somewhat lower.
Source: *Social Security Benefits* (Chicago, Ill.: Commerce Clearing House, 1981).

OASDHI provisions, at selected average monthly indexed earnings, for the more common types of benefits. About 24 million retired beneficiaries (or their dependents) are now receiving OASDHI benefits, as well as more than 8 million survivors and 4 million disabled persons. The annual rate of benefit outgo was about $145 billion at the beginning of 1982.

Special earnings and disability requirements. Some special provisions apply for determining retirement status and amounts payable. Under an annual earnings test, retired persons may have deductions made from OASDHI benefits.[19] Persons aged 65–71 are not considered fully "retired" if they earn wages or self-employment earnings of over certain amounts. If annual earnings exceed $6,000 (in the 1982 tax year), monthly benefits are reduced on the basis of the excess earnings: $1 for each $2 of annual earnings over $6,000. In applying the earnings test, income is counted only if it results from continuing work, that is, it does not include income from investments, other pensions, or other sources not requiring active employment. After a person reaches age 72 (70, beginning in 1983), the earnings test does not apply, and the person may earn unlimited income without reducing OASDHI benefits.

---

[19] The test also applies to all other OASDHI recipients under age 72 (age 70, after 1982) including widows, except disabled persons. The allowable earnings for beneficiaries other than those aged 65 or over are $4,440 a year. Automatic adjustments in these limits will apply in the future.

The requirements for disability income payments also deserve special note. These are cash benefits, not medical care services, for severe, long-lasting disability which prevents a person from earning a living. The benefits are for total disability (inability to engage in any substantial gainful work) which can be expected to result in death or which has lasted or can be expected to last for a continuous period of not less than 12 months. A "waiting period" of five months applies. The disability may be a physical or a mental impairment based upon medical evidence. Examples include the loss of two or more limbs, vision, hearing, or speech, and disease such as multiple sclerosis and severe cancer. A separate wage tax and trust fund provides the disability benefits under OASDHI. The monthly disability benefits for an insured worker are the same as at retirement age 65—the primary insurance amount. Payments stop if the insured person dies, becomes no longer disabled according to the definitions in the law, or reaches age 65.

Administration

The Old-Age, Survivors, Disability, and Health Insurance system is administered by the federal government. More than 150 million individual account records are maintained by the Social Security Administration in Baltimore, Maryland. The Commissioner of Social Security supervises divisions of management, actuarial services, claims, planning, research, hearings and appeals, accounting, and other functions. Regional and field services are performed through district offices located in more than 600 cities.[20] These offices inform the public about its rights and obligations in connection with OASDHI.

Medicare administration involves several other intermediaries because the Health Care Financing Administration in the Department of Health and Human Services, which has responsibility for this program, has entered into contracts with Blue Cross–Blue Shield and some insurance companies for processing claims payments.

Tax collection.   The taxes for the program are collected by the Internal Revenue Service. Employers deduct the required amounts from the wages of their employees and forward these amounts, plus the employer tax, to the district director of internal revenue. Self-employed persons pay their OASDHI taxes directly to the IRS with their income tax statements. All the taxes are credited to four trust funds; the Federal Old-Age and Survivors Insurance Trust Fund, the Federal Disability Insurance Trust Fund, the Federal Hospital Insurance Trust Fund, and the Supplementary Medical Fund (which also receives general revenue sup-

---

[20] The position of the Social Security Administration in the federal government is explained in the annual report of the Department of Health and Human Services.

port). These funds are used only for the administration and benefit payments of the OASDHI program. They are held until needed by investment in securities of the U.S. government.

Individual accounts.   As soon as workers first perform work covered by the Social Security Act, they must apply for a card which identifies each individual by name and number. The assigned account number is used for the worker's entire lifetime of credited earnings. Reports from workers and their employers each year are the source of the earnings credits.

Workers may check at any time on the status and record of their earnings under OASDHI. In fact, they should check regularly to see that their earnings have been reported and recorded properly by writing to the Social Security Administration, Box 57, Baltimore, Maryland, 21203. Forms for this purpose are available through local district offices and many banks and insurance companies. No fee is charged. Unless this is done at least once every three years, it may be impossible under the law to make corrections if mistakes have occurred. Valuable rights to earnings credits may be lost if the individual does not do this.

Application for benefits.   It is also important for each worker and beneficiary to understand that OASDHI benefits must be applied for, as they are not paid automatically. When application is made for benefits, at death, disability, or retirement, certain proofs must be presented to the district offices. Marriage and birth certificates, proof of support for dependents, and medical proof of disability are required before the various benefit payments can be made. Since certain time limits apply, it is important that these proofs be rendered promptly. Usually the applications must be completed within two years after eligibility, but back payments may be limited to one year. Thus delay can be costly to the OASDHI recipients who neglect or postpone proper application and proofs for benefits.

A system for hearings is maintained for reconsideration of any decision in regard to eligibility or amount of OASDHI benefit claims.

Financing

Tax on employer and employee.   The OASDHI program is paid for by taxes levied under the Social Security Act on the earnings of workers. In the case of wage earners in covered employment, both the *employer and employee* each pay an equal tax on the earnings; self-employed persons pay a tax which is slightly less than 1.5 times the tax which a wage earner pays.

Originally the tax began in 1937 at 1 percent on both employer and employee. The schedule of taxes was set up to be increased periodically as the program got under way and the number of OASDHI beneficiaries increased. Revisions in the schedule have occurred many times, and the tax rates were 2 percent by 1956, 3 percent by 1960, about 6 percent by 1978, and 6.7 percent by 1983. Future scheduled increases are for about 7 percent in 1985, and 7.65 percent (or combined employer-employee rate of 15.3 percent) in 1990. These rates include the HI tax. Table 11–3 summarizes these changes since 1970 and projected increases.

The tax rate is applied only up to a maximum annual taxable earnings base, as shown in Table 11–3. Thus the maximum current tax in 1983 is 6.7 percent of $35,700, or $2392 from the employee, and a similar amount from the employer. By the late 1980s the employee tax will be about $4,000 a year. Self-employed persons pay a higher tax, currently 9.35 percent, or an annual amount of about $3,350, which will rise to more than $6,000 by the late 1980s. The combined effect of the increasing tax rate and taxable earnings base has caused sharp escalation of OASDHI costs: about 100 percent between 1970–74, and 165 percent from 1975 to 1982.

Need for understanding. Many of the misconceptions about the OASDHI program are related to its financing. Even though the Social Security Act is so complex as to discourage effort by most people to understand it, it seems imperative that more persons *should* try to learn how the program works. The person who misunderstands the program (or does not attempt to understand it) is certainly not fulfilling an important obligation. Many booklets are available without cost by calling or writing your local Social Security office. Examples include: *Social Security*

Table 11–3. OASDHI (including Medicare) tax rates, maximum taxable annual earnings, and maximum employee annual taxes, since 1970 and projected

	Tax rates				Maximum taxable annual earnings*	Maximum employee annual taxes†
Year	Em- ployee	Em- ployer	Combined employer-ee	Self-em- ployed		
1970	4.8 %	4.8 %	9.6 %	6.9 %	$7,800	$ 374
1971–72	5.2	5.2	10.4	7.5	7,800–9,000	406–468
1973–77	5.85	5.85	11.7	7.9–8.0	10,800–16,500	632–965
1978	6.05	6.05	12.1	8.1	17,700	1,071
1979–80	6.13	6.13	12.26	8.1	22,900–25,900	1,404–1,588
1981	6.65	6.65	13.3	9.3	29,700	1,975
1982–84	6.7	6.7	13.4	9.35	32,400–39,600‡	2,191–2,653
1985	7.05	7.05	14.1	9.9	43,500	3,067
1986–89	7.15	7.15	14.3	10.0	47,700–61,500	3,411–4,397
1990 and after	7.65	7.65	15.3	10.75	‡	‡

* The years in which the maximum taxable annual earnings change was sometimes different than the years in which the tax rate changes, so a range of earnings is shown.
† Rounded to nearest dollar amount.
‡ After 1981, the earnings base is subject to automatic adjustment each year, related to average annual wages in the United States. Figures for 1983–89 are estimated.
Source: Robert J. Myers, *Social Security* (Homewood, Ill.: Richard D. Irwin, 1981), pp. 100–101.

Information for Young Families, A Woman's Guide to Social Security, and many others.

Pay-as-you-go assessment plan with contingency trust funds. One popular misconception concerns the basic purpose and method of the financing system. OASDHI is not based on an actuarially funded plan, as are individual life insurance contracts and annuities issued by the private insurance business. The solvency of the plan rests on the right of the federal government to levy taxes and to change benefits or taxes in the future, if necessary. The financing of OASDHI is nearly a *pay-as-you-go*[21] plan, as is seen in the fact that during recent years current annual contributions (taxes) just about equal current beneficiary payments. The trust funds of about $47 billion in late 1981 began to shrink rapidly, however, and the OASI Trust Fund started borrowing from the disability or health insurance funds in 1982. A fully funded plan is impractical because the estimated fund needed could be more than a trillion dollars. Such a large fund would have undesirable economic and political effects.

The nature of the financing method is thus comparable to an *assessment* system in which the assessments levied on the future working populations will sharply increase as payments from the system expand. The trust funds are similar to a *contingency fund* rather than a full reserve from which to pay future benefits.

Income shift among generations. A most important effect of OASDHI is the shifting of income from one generation of workers to another. Today's taxes on workers are not, as is popularly believed, being set aside in order to prepay the current contributors their future benefits at death, retirement, or disability. Current taxes are used to pay current recipients, which means generally that the working generation today is paying now for the retired (or disabled or dying) generation. The retirement benefits of persons aged 30 today will be paid not from their own taxes for the next 35 years but from the taxes levied on their working children in the year 2017 and thereafter.

A current recipient "bargain." If a recipient of OASDHI retirement payments believes that he or she has fully "earned" the right to benefits (by the taxes paid up to age 62 or 65), the extent of actual contributions should be considered. On the average, the current beneficiary of retirement income has paid for not much more than 10 percent of the value of his or her benefits. Even at maximum tax rates since 1937, total taxes for the last 45 years would be only about $30,000 combined for employer

---

[21] This is a very general description for current years only. Myers points out the technical differences with "current-cost financing" and how outgo may exceed income (with interfund borrowing now permitted) in the next few years, and then how increased tax rates for 1985–90 and beyond should result in greater income to build up the contingency fund thereafter. Myers, *Social Security,* pp. 283–89.

and employee. A retired worker at age 65 under current schedules of social security benefits would receive in this case about $680 a month ($8160 a year), receiving back more than has been paid in at maximum rates in less than four years. (In addition, if the retired worker is married, the spouse over 65 would receive 50 percent more in benefits.) Sound like a bargain? It is—for those currently retiring, and that comparison does not include any of the other survivorship, disability, or Medicare benefits to which retired workers may be entitled.[22]

For the many persons paying less than maximum rates or paying OASDHI taxes for fewer than 45 years, the comparison of cost/benefits would be even more favorable. If accumulated interest on the amounts paid in is considered, many authorities would argue that only the employee's share, or $15,000, should be used in such a calculation. (The employer's portion might not be paid as additional wages, and if it was it would be currently taxed as income to the employee.)

The "bargain" that recipients of social security payments are now receiving is being paid for by the current working generation. Young entrants to the system today will pay for 1½ times the benefits that they will receive on the average at current benefits schedules. The low-cost bargain look of OASDHI benefits will disappear as the scheduled tax increases take effect and as the average insured workers have paid into the program for a longer period before they or their survivors begin to collect benefits. For new entrants today at age 21 who earn the maximum taxable earnings until age 65, the employee taxes paid will total about $100,000.

The sizable benefits in relation to normal contributions are today a function of the fact that the program has not yet reached the mature stage when the number of new beneficiaries each year will be relatively stable. Now, many recipients qualify for benefits with perhaps only a few years of taxes paid. The expansion of the number of OASDHI recipients will continue during the next several decades.

Future self-supporting cost estimates. The financing of the OASDHI program is designed to be self-supporting, although the benefits paid out in a given year may exceed the taxes paid in during the same year. As long as the system continues indefinitely, future estimates of expenditures and receipts (and changes in the law, if necessary) can be made to assure the solvency of the plan. The long-range estimates are difficult to evaluate. The combination of assumptions which must be made in such estimates are fantastically complex. Estimates are based upon at least 27 principal elements and factors, with 75-year projections indicating an actuarial deficit of about 1.5 percent of payroll, or 11 percent

---

[22] An extreme but interesting case is that of Ida Fuller, who in 1940 was the recipient of the first social security check. She died in 1975 at the age of 100 after receiving benefits of about $20,000, in return for taxes paid in of $22.54! *Moneysworth,* March 1975, p. 2.

of average costs.[23] The Advisory Council on Social Security Financing and actuaries of the Social Security Administration review and revise these estimates periodically.

High-cost estimates and low-cost estimates for the future vary by billions of dollars. The differences in the estimates stem from the complexity and the relative unpredictability of the assumptions that must be made. Future mortality, birth,[24] marriage, divorce, remarriage, immigration, and disability rates all have to be included in the estimates, as well as basic employment data, interest earnings, inflation and many other factors. Rapidly rising hospital and medical costs make the Medicare cost estimates so difficult that the HI costs are not even included in the above description of financing.

Needed reform. In late 1981, after the president's proposals for changes in the social security system were largely rejected by Congress, the National Commission on Social Security Reform was created. A 15-member study group, headed by Alan Greenspan as chairman and directed by Robert J. Myers, was charged with making recommendations in order to adjust benefits and financing to assure continued solvency of the system for the future.[25] For the first time, members of Congress were included in such a commission, which in early 1983 recommended proposals to reduce the deficit in the system by about $170 billion over the next 7 years. The major changes included: (1) accelerating tax increases, to begin in 1984 (2) delaying cost-of-living benefits by 6 months, (3) taxing one half of social security benefits for recipients with other income above $20,000 (or families above $25,000), (4) including all new federal civilian employees and employees of nonprofit organizations, and (5) increasing taxes on self-employed persons.

UNEMPLOYMENT COMPENSATION

The impetus for the states to establish unemployment compensation systems was established in the Social Security Act of 1935. A tax-offset device was used in which most employers were required to pay a 3 percent federal payroll tax *unless* the state created a state unemployment plan that met certain standards. As a result, all states within a few years passed unemployment statutes, permitting employers a 90 percent credit

---

[23] Recommended for detailed explanation of the financing basis of the OASDHI system are Chaps. 4 and 10 of Myers, *Social Security*.

[24] Just this one factor alone will have a tremendous effect on the cost burden to a shrinking base of active workers and may require future funding from general tax revenues. See George E. Rejda and Richard J. Shepler, "The Impact of Zero Population Growth on the OASDHI Program," *Journal of Risk and Insurance* 40, no. 3 (September 1973), p. 313.

[25] Illustrative of the seriousness of the needed changes is A. Haeworth Robertson, *The Coming Revolution in Social Security* (Reston, Va.: Reston Publishing, 1981).

on the federal tax. This left 10 percent to provide general administration for the state systems.

The primary *objectives* of unemployment compensation insurance are to help unemployed workers by: providing them with cash payments during involuntary unemployment, maintaining their standard of living, providing them with time to locate or regain employment, and helping them find jobs. Secondary objectives aim at promoting economic efficiency and stability, by achieving desirable countercyclical effects, improved social allocation of costs, and improved utilization of the labor force, and by encouraging employers to stabilize employment.[26]

Eligibility

In order to be eligible for unemployment compensation, an employee must have been working under covered employment and must also meet certain individual requirements.

Covered employment. Not all workers are covered by the unemployment compensation laws of the states. About two thirds of workers are covered, however. The main exceptions are (1) self-employed persons, (2) agricultural workers and domestic servants, (3) employees of some smaller nonprofit organizations and some state and local governments, and (4) maritime and railroad workers. Separate federal legislation covers the last category, and many states have unemployment compensation laws that require (or permit, on an elective basis by the employer) coverage for some domestic servants, employees of nonprofit organizations, and state and local government workers.

Individual requirements. In order to collect unemployment compensation benefits, workers in covered employment must meet several important requirements. They must be *unemployed through no fault of their own,* which ordinarily disqualifies for benefits any worker who has voluntarily quit, has been discharged for misconduct, is involved in a labor dispute, or refuses suitable employment. The states vary considerably in these definitions for disqualification, and some permit unemployment benefits to workers unemployed because of an employer lockout or even a strike by the employees.

Unemployed workers must be *willing and able to work.* As proof of this, they must register for work at a public employment office, file a claim for benefits, not be sick or disabled, and be actively seeking work and available to take a suitable job if it is offered to them.

A third major requirement for benefits is that workers must have a *prescribed minimum amount of recent work* before the unemployment occurred. State laws vary considerably here, also, ranging from those which prescribe minimum earnings standards in a base period to those

---

[26] Rejda, *Social Insurance and Economic Security,* pp. 373–76.

which require a minimum number of weeks of previous employment.[27] The purpose is to show some substantial recent attachment to the active labor force and contributions by the employer to the unemployment system.

Benefits

The laws of each state must be consulted in order to determine the amount and duration of unemployment benefits. Normally, the purpose is to provide a *temporary* replacement of a *part* of the worker's full-time weekly earnings.

Amount. Within stated minimum and maximum limits, the size of the weekly benefits is usually aimed at about one half of normal wages. Because of rising wages in recent years, the maximum limits are most important, and over half of the new claimants have been eligible for maximum payments in many states. The maximums vary from approximately $80 to $230 weekly, with the average payment falling in between these two figures. About a dozen states provide additional dependents' benefits, which increase the range of the above maximums. Increasingly, "flexible" maximums related to 50 percent of the statewide average weekly wage are being used.

Duration. The state unemployment compensation systems do not aim at a solution to long-term or permanent technological unemployment problems. Typically, most states provide benefits for only *26 weeks*. *Extended benefits,* which extend benefits during periods of high unemployment by 50 percent (or 13 weeks), are also required. These are "triggered" by federally determined thresholds of unemployment, and costs are shared equally by the states and the federal government.

Special provisions in most of the states provide (1) some proportional payments for partially unemployed persons who may replace some of their wages with odd jobs, (2) a waiting period of one week before unemployment payments can begin, and (3) payments to claimants attending approved training courses.

Administration

The direct administration of unemployment compensation systems is performed by the *state* governments, with the federal government participating indirectly through the standards it sets for meeting the requirements of the tax-offset law.

---

[27] *Social Security Programs in the United States* (Washington, D.C.: U.S. Government Printing Office, annual). About a dozen states require flat amounts of $300–$1,200, and about the same number specify a multiple, such as 30 times the weekly benefit, or require a multiple, such as 1.5 times the claimant's high-quarter average.

Federal standards. Since all or a portion of the state unemployment administrative expenses (as well as the approximate 90 percent tax offset) depends on the state's conforming to the federal standards, the requirements are usually met. These include provisions that (1) all state unemployment taxes be deposited in an account with the U.S. Treasury from which only benefits can be paid, (2) benefits be paid only through public or federally approved employment agencies, (3) full payments be made promptly when due, (4) workers have the right to appeal decisions of the state agencies, (5) permit workers to refuse unsuitable jobs under prescribed standards, and (6) administrative personnel be employed on a merit basis.

The Manpower Administration's Unemployment Insurance Service in the U.S. Department of Labor has the responsibility of determining whether the states have complied with the federal requirements.

State administration. The area of state administration is still quite broad, for each state must actually carry out the federal requirements as well as make many of its own decisions in regard to the unemployment compensation program. For example, the state decides the major questions of (1) eligibility (what workers are covered and how they qualify for benefits), (2) benefits (how much and for how long), and (3) financing (how much employers will be charged as a tax on payrolls).

The actual administrative work implementing the unemployment compensation law in each state is performed by the *state employment security agency*. Most of the states use independent departments of the state government or independent boards or commissions. In some states these agencies are under the state department of labor. Benefit claims are handled in about 2,100 local offices of the employment agencies of the states.

Financing

The basic source of funds for the state unemployment systems is a *payroll tax* levied on *employers*.[28] The standard tax rate on employers is 3.4 percent of the wages up to $6,000 for each worker, of which 0.7 percent goes to the federal government and the remainder (up to 2.7 percent) goes to the state government under the tax-offset plan mentioned earlier. Administrative expenses are apportioned from the federal share by Congress. The actual average tax rates vary by state and employer from 0.3 to more than 3.0 percent of the taxable payroll, which may be as high as $11,000 (Alaska).

The most significant variation in the employer's cost in the various

---

[28] Ibid. Three states, Alabama, Alaska, and New Jersey, also require a small contribution (less than 0.9 percent) from employees.

states is found in the *experience rating* systems used in most states. Under these plans the tax rate on employers is changed according to the individual experience of each employer. Alternative higher taxes may apply in many states if the reserve funds fall below specified points. The various experience rating plans differ substantially, but most result in the individual employer paying (according to the employer's past unemployment record) rates which vary between perhaps 1 percent and the maximum standard percentage required. Experience rates aim at stabilizing employment, at better cost allocation, and at greater employer interest.

The pronounced social, political, and economic effects of unemployment have necessitated that it be cared for under a social insurance system rather than a private insurance system. In addition to the complexity of defining who really is an "unemployed" person, the sizable funds necessary and the cyclical changes in unemployment are problems of a substantial nature. The many economic effects of the state unemployment compensation systems include countercyclical contributions, benefits adequacy or inadequacy, the impact of unemployment taxes, and interstate competition in unemployment compensation.

For perspective on the importance of unemployment insurance, the economic effects of the taxes collected and the benefits paid out in a given year should be noted. In the 1970s several recession years resulted in several billion dollars more in payments than in taxes collected. Most state plans became insolvent in the past decade, but a federal loan program has permitted continued payment of benefits. The total accumulated debt of the states now is about $8 billion, and five states have serious deficits ranging from $0.5 billion to $1.7 billion each.[29] A payback plan with interest charges by the federal government was instituted in 1981.

WORKERS' COMPENSATION

In an unusual combination of social and private insurance, workers' compensation laws in all the states require employers to provide certain benefits for *occupational* injuries and diseases.[30] Coverage has gradually been broadened to include all occupational diseases. Workers' compensation was the first kind of social insurance to develop widely in the United States, many of the laws being enacted before 1920. Today there are

---

[29] *Economic Commentary,* Federal Reserve Bank of Cleveland, April 19, 1982.

[30] Note that only New Jersey, South Carolina, and Texas have an "elective" rather than "compulsory" law. If the employer chooses to reject the act, the loss of common-law liability defenses to the employer usually provides strong encouragement to choose workers' compensation. If the employee chooses to reject the act (before a loss occurs), the employer retains the strong common-law defenses explained in Chapter 18.

54 different programs in operation in the states and Puerto Rico, as well as three federal employee plans.

The statutory requirement in most states can be fulfilled by the employer purchasing workers' compensation insurance from a private insurer or by qualifying as a "self-insurer." Eighteen jurisdictions have also established workers' compensation state funds for insuring employers, and six of these require that the benefits of the law be insured (unless a qualified "self-insurance" plan for larger employers is maintained) only with such state insurance funds. Self-insurance is permitted in all but six plans, if certain size and bond requirements are met.

Further details of workers' compensation insurance and the derivation of state workers' compensation laws from the former system of employers' liability are presented in Chapter 18. The discussion here will be limited to a brief description of the major features of the programs. Several issues concerning broader eligibility, higher and more uniform benefits, and the proposed federalization of workers' compensation laws are discussed in a later chapter.

Eligibility

Benefits under workers' compensation laws are payable to many but not all workers. From a very restricted list of hazardous occupations 50 years ago, the laws have been extended to apply to most employers. Although not all jobs are covered, about four fifths of the employees do have coverage under workers' compensation, with the following typical exceptions: (1) employees of firms with less than a minimum number of workers (only about a dozen states have these limits now, usually excluding firms with less than 3 or 5 workers); (2) farm workers; (3) domestic servants; (4) casual labor; and (5) employees of nonprofit charitable organizations or religious organizations.

In order to qualify a death, injury, or disease as covered by workers' compensation, the employee or beneficiary must show that it *arose out of and in the course of employment*. In other words, it must be a work-connected loss. Many states exclude losses that are the result of an employee's intoxication, gross negligence, or willful misconduct.

Benefits

Workers' compensation laws provide definite *schedules* of benefits for deaths and disabling injuries or illnesses. The variations among the states are wide, but most statutes require four basic types of benefits: (1) *medical care* costs, (2) *income* payments for disability or death to the worker or the worker's family, (3) *death* benefits, and (4) *rehabilitation* services, providing retraining, education, job guidance and placement, vocational rehabilitation facilities, or other services.

Medical care benefits are provided for all medically required care, with no arbitrary limits on the duration or the amount payable.[31]

Income benefits under workers' compensation laws are usually based upon the worker's wages at the time of death, injury, or sickness. Weekly payments are typically about 70 percent of spendable earnings (after federal taxes) and are paid to either workers or their survivors. Some states limit death payments to the widow or children to specific maximums ranging from about $40,000 to $120,000. Disabilities may be either partial or total and either permanent or temporary. Lifetime payments are available in most states, but some states set a specific maximum duration of payments, such as 4 to 10 years. Both minimum and maximum weekly benefit amounts are also usually set in the laws. Some laws provide lump-sum benefits in place of income payments for certain disabilities. A waiting period of from two days to one week sometimes applies before weekly benefits begin.

Administration

State governments are the administrators of the workers' compensation laws. In most states, this function is carried out through special *state commissions* appointed for this purpose. These commissions work closely with the employers and their insurers in performing the necessary administrative duties. Oftentimes, the work of the commissions takes on an advisory and quasi-judicial nature. The rules and procedures for filing, reviewing, and investigating claims for benefits are set forth in the laws. Decisions are reached, subject to the approval of the commissions, through various methods of direct settlement, formal agreements, or hearings.

Financing

The direct responsibility for financing workers' compensation benefits is placed upon the *employer*. Through the purchase of a private insurance contract, through self-insurance, or through insurance in a state fund, the employer must pay for the benefits as provided in the state laws.

The cost of workers' compensation insurance varies widely from state to state, among the various occupations, and for each individual

---

[31] This is for accidental injuries; only a few states have some limits on coverage for specified occupational diseases. See *Analysis of Workers' Compensation Laws* (Washington, D.C.: Chamber of Commerce of the United States, published annually), Comparison Chart III.

employer.[32] The liability or restrictiveness of the benefits in the state law is an obvious cost factor. More hazardous occupations may have workers' compensation costs which exceed 20 percent of payroll, whereas clerical occupations with minimum industrial injury and disease perils may have costs of well under 1 percent of payroll. From year to year, the average premium cost approximates 1.5 percent of payroll for all occupations combined. Individual employers are given incentive to reduce losses through the many loss-prevention techniques of various experience rating plans, which adjust the insurance costs according to the losses and expenses of each business firm.

One of the issues of concern about workers' compensation is whether the expansion of the disability provisions of the Social Security Act (see earlier section of this chapter) causes unnecessary duplication of some of the income payments for longer term disabilities. Some disabled workers qualify for workers' compensation death benefits, although amendments to the Social Security Act now provide for an offset where total income benefits would exceed 80 percent of a worker's former earnings.

TEMPORARY-DISABILITY (NONOCCUPATIONAL) INSURANCE LAWS

In addition to disability income for occupational injuries or sickness, five states and Puerto Rico have compulsory temporary-disability laws which provide income payments for nonwork-connected disabilities. These states are New York, New Jersey, California, Rhode Island, and Hawaii.

The need for these laws stems from the fact that most state unemployment compensation systems require that the recipient of unemployment benefits be willing *and able* to work. Only a few states permit payments to disabled unemployed workers.

The fact that most states have not adopted such "cash sickness benefit" plans since the first four states named above began to do so in 1942–49 is largely explained by the rapid growth of other methods of paying such benefits. Employers have formalized many paid sick-leave plans, and private insurers have written an increased volume of group disability insurance for nonoccupational short-term disability. In total, about two thirds of wage and salary workers in private employment have some such protection, either through government or private plans. About one fourth of the private labor force is covered by the six temporary-disability laws.

---

[32] There are about 600 industry and occupational classifications. See "Rating Job Hazards," *Journal of American Insurance,* Fall 1980, p. 23.

Eligibility

The coverage of most workers is similar to that found under the usual unemployment compensation system, and a few categories of employment are excluded. The individual worker is required to show that the regular duties of his or her job cannot be performed due to illness or injury. Certain disabilities, such as pregnancy or intentional self-inflicted injuries, may be excluded. In order to qualify for temporary-disability benefits, the worker must also have had specified minimum earnings for a required time before becoming disabled.

Benefits

The weekly benefit rates in the various plans have the purpose of replacing between 50 percent and two thirds of the average weekly wages lost due to short-term disability. The minimum benefits vary from $7 to $50 weekly, and the maximum benefits vary from about $95 to $175.[33] The duration of benefits is limited to a maximum of 26 weeks except in California, where it is 39 weeks. A waiting period of one week (seven consecutive days) generally applies.

Administration

Four of the six programs administer the temporary-disability laws under the supervision of the state unemployment compensation board, commission, or department. New York uses the workers' compensation board to administer the disability payments, and Hawaii uses its Department of Labor and Industrial Relations.

Rhode Island is the only state which requires that the employer must provide the benefits through an exclusive, or monopolistic, state fund. The other programs permit the employer to choose among private insurers providing a group accident and health insurance contract, a state fund, and a self-insurance plan. The alternatives to a state fund must meet the requirements of the law as to the eligibility of workers for benefits and the amounts and duration of the payments.

Overall the proportion of covered workers insured with private insurers is approximately 50 percent, but the proportion varies from more than 90 percent in New York to less than 10 percent in California, where legislation designed to help prevent insolvency of the state fund has restricted the use of private insurers.

---

[33] "Benefit Hotline," New York: Johnson and Higgins, 1982.

Financing

The *employee* is required to pay all or a portion of the costs of the temporary-disability benefits in each of the six plans. The tax is based on payroll, and it varies from 0.3 percent in Puerto Rico to 1.2 percent in Rhode Island. Only the first $8,200–$17,000 of annual wages is usually taxed.[34]

In four jurisdictions, *employers* also bear part of the costs. In New Jersey and Puerto Rico the employer pays 0.5 percent of covered wages (modified by the experience rating), and in New York and Hawaii the employer pays all additional costs of the program beyond the stated employee contribution.

Although many other states have considered temporary-disability bills, only Puerto Rico (1968) and Hawaii (1969) have passed such laws in the past 25 years. It appears that the private insurance business has expanded its efforts for coverage of the nonoccupational disability income peril and has successfully provided the needed coverage in this area of insurance in many states. Temporary disability is thus covered by both social insurance systems in six jurisdictions and as private insurance in the remaining jurisdictions.

SUMMARY OF FOUR MAJOR SOCIAL INSURANCE PROGRAMS

The fundamental characteristics of the four most significant types of social insurance in the United States are summarized in Table 11–4 as to eligibility provisions, benefits, financing, and administration.

OTHER SOCIAL INSURANCE PROGRAMS

Although the four social insurance programs that have been discussed in this chapter are the most important and widespread, other social insurance systems have developed some significance. Among these are the railroad retirement and unemployment plans, the government employee retirement plans, and veterans' administration benefit programs.[35]

The Railroad Retirement and Unemployment Acts

For several reasons, including strong early unionization of employees, the railroads established a pension system before the Social Security

[34] Ibid. New York taxes only the first $60 of weekly wages, and Hawaii's tax is applied to the lesser of the statewide average weekly wage or one half of the cost up to $1.53 weekly.

[35] For more information concerning these insurance systems, chaps. 12, 13, and 16 of Myers' *Social Security* are recommended.

Act of 1935. Therefore, the railroad industry was excluded from the 1935 act, although later provisions have correlated the two systems by permitting combined credits for all monthly benefits under either OASDHI or the Railroad Retirement Act and by providing Medicare benefits.

Railroad workers have one of the most extensive social insurance benefit programs in the United States. Retirement benefits are paid at age 65 (or reduced benefits at age 60 if they have 30 years of service. The amounts are always higher than OASDHI payments and are calculated on a formula which takes into account both monthly earnings and years of service. Survivors' benefits to widow and children are payable in lump-sum and monthly payments. Permanent disability payments are payable under liberal definitions after 10–20 years of service. Unemployment and sickness benefits are payable under the separate Railroad Unemployment Insurance Act.

Table 11–4. Summary of features of four major social insurance programs

Type of program	Eligibility provisions	Types of benefits	Who administers it?	Who and what finances it?
OASDHI	Covered employ-ment* with certain time and earnings to become in-sured	Income for re-tirement, for long-term to-tal disability, and to survi-vors; and med-ical care for aged and long-time dis-abled	Federal govern-ment	Earnings tax on employer and employee, and on self-em-ployed persons
Unemployment compensation	Covered employ-ment with specified indi-vidual qualifi-cation re-quirements	Temporary in-come for 26–39 weeks to willing and able unem-ployed work-ers	State govern-ment	Payroll tax (mostly state) on employer
Workers' compensation	Covered employ-ment and in-jury or disease arising out of and in the course of em-ployment	Medical care costs, death, disability in-come, and re-habilitation; for *work* ill-ness or injury	State govern-ment	Insurance pur-chased by em-ployer, or self-insurance plans
Temporary dis-ability benefit laws	Covered employ-ment with specified time and earnings requirements	Temporary in-come for 26–39 weeks; for *nonwork* ill-ness or injury	State govern-ment (in five states and Puerto Rico only)	Payroll tax on employee or on employee-employer

* Covered employment is work to which the laws apply, which varies among these programs.

The federal government administers the railroad social insurance program through a separate Railroad Retirement Board. The systems are financed by current taxes (which are higher than OASDHI) on employer and employee (for the Retirement Act benefits) and by taxes on the employer only (for unemployment benefits).

Government employee retirement systems

Federal employees, state employees, and some local government employees have separate social insurance programs which provide retirement, disability, and survivorship benefits.

About 3 million federal government employees, excluding members of the armed services, are most often covered under the provisions of the Civil Service Retirement Act. Special programs are used for some groups, such as foreign service officers and members of Congress. Such federal employees not included in these plans are generally included under the OASDHI program.

The Civil Service Commission administers benefits for federal civil service employees who are eligible for (1) retirement and disability annuities (generally much higher than OASDHI benefits in most cases and based on earnings and length of service) and (2) survivorship benefits to widows and children of employees. In contrast to OASDHI, employees who leave government service before retirement, after five years of service, are entitled to withdraw their contributions or to leave them with the program until an annuity is payable at retirement. The system is financed by a combined contribution rate of 14 percent on the employees' base pay and on the employing federal agency plus substantial payments from the General Fund of the Treasury.

The Federal Employees' Group Life Insurance Act in 1954 and the Servicemen's Group Life Insurance Act of 1965 inaugurated group life insurance coverage for federal employees who are covered unless they choose not to be included. In addition, earlier veterans' life insurance programs, including National Service Life Insurance, have about $64 billion of life insurance in force for persons who served in the armed forces. Private insurers underwrite the current coverage in FEGLI and SGLI in very sizable group life insurance contracts. Health insurance benefits are also available to federal employees, with an optional choice among Blue Cross–Blue Shield, a group private insurer plan, and other alternatives. The benefits differ widely. The federal government pays a portion of the costs.

Approximately 14 million state and local government employees are covered by retirement systems with assets of $200 billion, which provide old-age and disability payments.[36] The plans vary widely, but in general they have increased benefits considerably in recent years. Public school and university teachers frequently have retirement systems separately from other state employees.[37] The employee contributions, which most systems require, may be taken by the employee after a minimum number of years of service if the employee retires early or leaves government service. Some of the plans do not include survivors' benefits beyond a return of the worker's contributions, although increasing evidence of the extension of benefits in this area is found in such plans as those for police officers, fire fighters, and others. About two thirds of the states and many local government employees are entitled to OASDHI benefits if the political subdivision has entered into a voluntary agreement with the federal government to have them included.

Veterans' benefit programs

More than 40 different benefits and services are available to veterans of service in the U.S. armed forces.[38] The Veterans Administration administers many of the benefits. These are primarily available to the veteran, but many of them are also paid or available to survivors or members of the veteran's family. A partial list includes: (1) compensation for service-connected deaths or disabilities, (2) pensions for non-service-connected deaths or disabilities, (3) benefits payable under Servicemen's Group Life Insurance, or earlier plans such as National Service Life Insurance, (4) veterans' burial expense payments, and (5) medical services of many kinds through Veterans Administration hospitals. Supplemental and special payments to those payable under the Social Security Act are made to widows of veterans who died of service-connected causes.

Some examples of veterans' benefits administered by other agencies are: (1) retirement pay from the individual branches of the armed services, (2) social security (OASDHI) wage credits for earnings while in the service, (3) burial space in national cemeteries, (4) farm and home loan benefits, (5) special unemployment benefits, (6) educational readjustment assistance, and (7) reemployment rights under the U.S. Department

---

[36] *Pension Facts* (Washington, D.C.: American Council of Life Insurance, 1981), pp. 6 and 9. For more information, see Howard F. Winklevoss and Dan M. McGill, *Public Pension Plans* (Homewood, Ill.: Dow Jones-Irwin, 1979); and Thomas J. Cook, *Public Retirement Systems* (New York: Teachers Insurance and Annuity Association and College Retirement Equities Fund, 1981).

[37] David L. Bickelhaupt, "Current Pension Dimensions and New Developments for Teachers at State Universities," *Journal of Insurance Issues and Practices* 3, no. 1 (Fall 1979), p. 1.

[38] A summary of these benefits and services is available from the Superintendent of Documents (Washington, D.C.: U.S. Government Printing Office) in a booklet titled *Veterans' Administration Fact Sheet, IS–1.*

of Labor, the Civil Service Commission, and state employment offices. In all, the veterans' benefit programs entail a broad and important range of benefits and services for a large segment of the population.

The future

The future of these social insurance programs is apparently well established. It would be hard to conceive of abandonment of any of the major social insurance programs that have been discussed. The typical trend seems to be in the direction of expanding existing programs. Each has developed by increasing its coverage and the application of its requirements to new and wider groups of persons. Benefits have rarely been reduced but often extended as to kind, amount, and duration. The ultimate development in this area, as in all social insurance programs, will be determined by legislation governed by economic, social, and political considerations.

PROPOSED NATIONAL HEALTH INSURANCE PLANS

One of the most controversial topics in social insurance for many decades in the United States has been the topic of *national health insurance*. Based on the general philosophy that everyone should have access to high-quality medical care, most advanced nations except for the United States have adopted some form of universal compulsory health insurance. However, most United States citizens remain skeptical about such programs, including the National Health Service, which has been in effect for Great Britain since 1946, and the Canadian provincial plans of the 1960s, which became a complete national program in 1971.[39]

The proposals advanced in the United States have been frequent and varied, although during the Reagan Administration, few proposals have been given serious consideration. However, an evaluation of the need for a national health insurance plan and of the objectives of such a plan is in order.

The need

The usual rationale for a system of national health insurance for the entire United States population begins with analysis of the need. Most of the public opinion in this regard centers on the concern of most consumers with the high costs of medical care. This concern is to be expected

---

[39] Selected foreign plans are reviewed in U.S. House Committee on Ways and Means, *National Health Insurance Resources Book* (Washington, D.C.: U.S. Government Printing Office, August 1976).

in an era which has seen these costs increase more rapidly than most other products and services.

One difference between medical care costs and such other costs is that medical care costs are not as evenly distributed among individuals and families on a year-to-year basis as are expenses which affect everyone. Although the average costs of medical care per person may not upset personal budgets, the burden falls much more heavily on those who need medical care in any given year as opposed to the many who do not. The health care expenditures in the United States exceed those of any other nation in the world, quadrupling during the past dozen years.

Private health insurance has helped spread the losses among many—and approximately 85 percent of Americans have some health insurance, and about three fourths have some protection against catastrophic health losses. Critics emphasize the negative aspects of these figures, pointing out that 15 percent have no health insurance and that one fourth lack major medical coverage. Some people, of course, have physical deficiencies or lack the financial ability or the desire to purchase needed health insurance. Yet the proportion of persons protected by the private health insurance system in the United States is higher than the proportion protected by voluntary insurance anywhere else.

Nevertheless, a gap exists between the generally accepted idea that everyone should have access to quality medical care regardless of personal circumstances, and the present extensive (but not complete) coverage of voluntary health insurance to help meet this need.

The objectives

In addition to the general need for and "right" to medical care, the rationale for national health insurance seems to rest either on the appraisal of the present voluntary insurance system as inadequate or on the expectation that a compulsory system would be better.[40] The inadequacies stressed are the previously mentioned incomplete coverage and such others as inefficiencies of marketing and lack of cost control. Many of the criticisms emphasize the quest for improvement in our current economy of high health care costs.

The use of national health insurance to improve the delivery of medical care services is the underlying objective. If this is to be used as the means for accomplishing certain goals, the first step is agreement upon the suggested criteria under which such a system should be evaluated.[41]

---

[40] Rejda stresses (1) the basic right, (2) the reform of present systems, (3) the inferior medical care for the poor, and (4) the need for greater redistribution of income. See chap. 11 in *Social Insurance and Economic Security*.

[41] Robert D. Eilers and Sue S. Moyerman, *National Health Insurance: Conference Proceedings* (Homewood, Ill.: Richard D. Irwin, 1971), chap. 1. Similar criteria are discussed in Rejda, *Social Insurance and Economic Security*, p. 255–61.

These include: (1) consumer participation and control; (2) universal eligibility for all (without age, residence, race, income, physical, or other limitations); (3) comprehensive and continuous medical services, both preventive and curative; (4) accessible and available services to all; (5) no cost barriers to needed services; (6) quality controls to assure the best possible care, without waste of funds; and (7) research, for new methods and review of the system. Ideal goals such as these are not easy to put into practice, for many of the subcriteria needed to implement specific parts of a broad plan meeting these objectives are subject to much debate.

The proposals

The United States already has a partial system of national health insurance in operation—the Medicare-Medicaid plans which cover a substantial portion of the medical expenses of the elderly and some disabled persons. In effect, many of the proposals for NHI would replace or extend these plans on at least a partially mandatory basis to all citizens of the United States.

The differences among the proposed plans of the past decade, however, are significant. Some provide for a very broad system of comprehensive "cradle-to-grave" medical services, whereas others would institute only an insurance plan for meeting catastrophic health losses. Some plans would give a predominant place to existing private insurance, whereas others would substitute a completely mandatory program administered entirely by the federal government. The costs in some plans would be borne entirely by taxpayers, whereas other plans would distribute the costs among employers, employees, and taxpayers.

About a dozen NHI proposals during the 1970s received some legislative support.[42] However, detailed analysis is unwarranted now because none are considered likely to be reintroduced and passed during the current Congress. Any future NHI bills given serious consideration will probably involve substantial compromises among many of the major alternatives.

One of the basic reasons why there is little support for national health insurance is the economic effect of increasing government costs during a period when inflation could be escalated or a recession triggered by the considerable expenses of most NHI plans. The political ramifications are readily apparent, too, and will undoubtedly play a large part in whether, when, or in what form national health insurance is legislated.

An interesting development on the state level since the mid-1970s is the passage of several catastrophic health insurance plans. The first, in Rhode Island, covers out-of-pocket family medical costs exceeding

---

[42] Myers, *Social Security,* pp. 507–26.

$5,000 (or $500–$1,250 if qualified insurance policies of various types are carried), or specified percentages of income from 10 to 50 percent. General revenue state taxes finance the benefits, which are administered through private insurers. Georgia, Maine, Minnesota, and Connecticut now have similar plans, and it is possible that these state programs may become models for some future NHI proposals.[43]

FOR REVIEW AND DISCUSSION

1. Social and private (voluntary) insurance in the United States have both grown rapidly in the past 45 years. How has the *purpose* of each of these major areas of insurance affected its growth pattern? How are social and private insurance alike? How are they different?

2. The government plays several roles in regard to insurance. Identify and illustrate each of these roles. *Why* have the government roles in regard to insurance increased, and which branches of government have taken the leadership in this expansion?

3. Paul Samuelson has said that "social security is, by all odds, the most successful program of the modern welfare state." Why do you think he said that? Do you agree or disagree, and why?

4. What specific criticisms are aimed at social insurance, and how do you evaluate the justification for each? (Discuss at least three.)

5. How do the objective and method of "social insurance" differ from those of "public assistance"? Give several examples. How does the Social Security Act of 1935 relate to these two terms?

6. Rapidly rising OASDHI taxes during the past five years are an issue of great economic and political concern. Discuss the needs and effects of these increases.

7. If more than 9 out of 10 workers are now covered by the OASDHI program, why shouldn't or can't everyone be included in this compulsory law?

8. What is the distinction between "fully," "currently," and "disability" insured status under the OASDHI program? What difference does it make?

9. What is the basis for determining the size of the OASDHI benefits payable? What other factors are considered, and how do these help carry out the social objectives of the program?

10. What disability benefits are included in OASDHI? What new benefits did Medicare add?

11. *Explain* the following comments about the OASDHI program:
    a. It is a pay-as-you-go plan, with a contingency trust fund.
    b. It is, basically, a social and economic program which results in a significant shift in income among different generations.
    c. It is a current recipient "bargain."

---

[43] Ibid., pp. 526–27. Hawaii also has a plan which mandates that all employers provide hospital-medical benefits for employees through private insurers, with joint employer-ee contributions.

    d. It now includes four basic perils, but originally only covered one.

    e. Relatively, low-income groups receive higher benefit amounts; but they also pay more, relatively, in taxes.

12. The economist Milton Friedman has said that "OASDHI is a very good buy for people in the older age group, and a very lousy buy for people in lower age groups." Why do you agree or disagree?

13. Briefly explain two common misconceptions about the OASDHI program, pointing out why they exist and why they are fallacious.

14. Compare and contrast unemployment compensation and workers' compensation as to *(a)* eligibility, *(b)* benefits, and *(c)* administration.

15. A state enacts an unemployment insurance law that is best suited to its individual needs. What is the necessity for minimum federal standards? Is there a current crisis in the solvency of unemployment insurance plans in the states?

16. Who pays for *(a)* OASDHI, *(b)* unemployment compensation, *(c)* workers' compensation, and *(d)* temporary-disability (nonoccupational) benefits?

17. Medicare has been a popular addition to the social security program. In what ways is it *(a)* consistent and *(b)* inconsistent with the purposes and methods of the other parts of the OASDHI program? How does Medicare differ from Medicare?

18. What is the relationship among the goals of the OASDHI system, *group* life and health insurance provided by employers, and *individual* life and health insurance contracts? Diagram this relationship.

19. Divide the class into three "buzz groups." After 20 minutes, have a spokesperson for the first group evaluate the *need* for a national health insurance plan, a spokesperson for the second present the *objectives* of NHI, and a spokesperson for the third describe the *proposal* that the group would recommend for adoption by Congress, considering the rapid increases in medical care costs.

Chapter 12

Outline of concepts

Coordinating life and health insurance is the essential element in planning for buying these types of insurance.

Human life and health values are the basis for estimating what financial values are lost due to death or disability; alternatively, the needs caused by these perils can be calculated.

Life and health risk management involves avoidance, loss-prevention, insurance, and programming techniques of *money* management.

Personal life and health insurance planning is a significant part of individual or family financial planning and budgeting.

Personal life insurance programming involves analysis of:

The needs for lump-sum and income requirements and wants.

The method of fact-finding about all assets and income sources.

Integration with social security benefits in a diagram of goals and income needs met by *group* and *individual* life insurance.

A case study example of family life insurance needs and cost shows the process of estimating needs and providing means for achieving family goals for capital and income.

Personal health insurance programming uses a similar technique to plan for future medical expense and disability income losses.

A case study example of family health insurance needs and costs illustrates the significance of group insurance and OASDHI benefits.

Personal estate planning combines the *creation* and *liquidation* of assets.

Estate impairment results from substantial (30 percent or more) estate shrinkage from estate transfer costs, taxes, and other factors.

The estate planning process involves detailed fact-finding and legal procedures to obtain maximum benefits at minimum costs.

The will is an essential key to achieving desired estate objectives.

The marital deduction, permitting the estate to go to the spouse and reducing the taxable estate, is important.

The estate is often larger than expected.

The unified gift and estate tax, under the Federal Tax Reform Act of 1976 and the Economic Recovery Tax Act of 1981 are explained.

Trusts are one method for coordinating estates and minimizing taxes.

The estate planning team uses four types of professional persons.

Business life and health insurance planning requires facts, analysis, and the choice of useful tools, such as:

Buy-and-sell agreements, funded by insurance; and

Key person life and health insurance, for important employees.

Coordinating life and health insurance

Everyone likes easy answers to difficult questions. How about an answer to the persistent query: "What is the secret of long life and good health?" A simple but unrealistic reply might be: "Don't die, don't be sick, and don't be injured!" Unfortunately, the uncertainties of life and health are not that controllable, so better answers must be found. This chapter suggests two practical, but more complex, answers—life and health *risk management,* and life and health *insurance planning.* As a summary of the previous chapters in Part Two, the two techniques are combined in the chapter title as the objective of *coordinating life and health insurance.* This process implies both the coordination of various types of insurance, which is emphasized, as well as the proper combination of other methods of treating perils which endanger life and health.

What are these perils? *Death, old age,* and *poor health* are primary causes of concern because they cause the need for or loss of *money.* [1] That's where insurance comes in, for insurance *is* money. To be useful, the money must be provided in the right amounts at the right times. Budgeting and saving can help, but for large or unexpected losses due to these perils the logic of life and health insurance is clear. Individuals, families, and businesses (or other organizations) must meet these losses by good planning techniques.

Risk management as discussed in Chapters 1 and 2 emphasizes systematic planning. In addition, in life and health insurance, two techniques help persons plan and implement their decisions—*programming* and *personal estate planning.*

HUMAN LIFE AND HEALTH VALUES

Two basic methods of determining the amount of life and health insurance required in order to protect an individual or family against the economic losses of death or disability are: (1) the *human life value ap-*

---

[1] Note that solving the secret of long life may cause another problem—that of living too long instead of not long enough. With old age comes increasing medical care costs and decreased income.

proach, and (2) the *needs approach.* Because it is more precise and easier to understand, the second approach is used in explaining personal life insurance programming in the next section. It answers the question, "What financial *needs* do my family or I have if death (or disability) occurs?"

However, the question can be rephrased: "What financial *values* will be lost?" This is the concept of *human life values,* popularized by Dr. S. S. Huebner in some of the earliest college courses on life insurance in the 1920s. Although the dollar value estimated by this method is crude, it is meaningful in sharing the tremendous losses which occur when earning power is lost, particularly at the younger ages. The potential asset value of future earnings lost through death or disability is larger by far than any other property values (home, autos, etc.) typically owned by individuals or families.

For example, consider the death of a family breadwinner at the age of 25. If average lifetime annual earnings are estimated at $25,000 per year, and taxes and self-maintenance costs are about 20 percent or $5,000, then the family loses a net income of $20,000 annually for the 40 years until normal retirement at age 65. The total income lost is 40 times $20,000, or $800,000. The present value of that lost income stream to the family (calculated as shown in Chapter 5 of this text), at a conservative 4 percent discount, is the equivalent of nearly $400,000 today.[2] Using the human life value approach, this is the amount lost by the family at the breadwinner's death. If OASDHI and group life insurance provide about one half of these lost income values, then an amount of $200,000 individual life insurance is indicated. This assumes that the goal is to protect the family against the full earning power value lost, which is often an ideal rather than a realistic objective. At average- or lower-income assumptions, the indicated needs for life insurance may be close to the amounts shown by the human life value approach. At higher incomes, the values lost may be much greater than the reasonable needs of the family. Thus, the needs approach may provide more practical answers in life insurance programming.

LIFE AND HEALTH RISK MANAGEMENT

It is far easier to talk about one need or a single type of contract than it is to discuss a whole plan. *Risk management* does involve, necessarily, a good plan. In the early chapters, the technique is emphasized as one of *coordinated* risk analysis and treatment. The objective is to take care of risk in the best possible way, and much of that objective,

---

[2] S. S. Huebner and Kenneth Black, Jr., *Life Insurance* (Englewood Cliffs, N.J.: Prentice-Hall, 1981), p. 22.

except for some psychological and sociological effects, may be reduced to taking care of economic or *financial* needs. Money becomes the means to this end.

Insurance is an important part of most life and health risk-management plans. These plans should also be coordinated, both with each other and with the other methods for treating risk. For example, social security benefits should be considered in connection with group and individual life and health insurance programs. Also, the use of insurance should often be seen as an action to supplement *loss prevention* or purposeful *risk retention*. Annual medical checkups and good health habits are a fundamental step in maintaining a family's health condition. Losses that are frequent, small, and regular in their occurrence should be intentionally retained as part of health risk management. Proper family financial planning should coordinate retention, avoidance, savings, and insurance to meet the goals of treating life and health risks.

Persons or businesses as consumers have choices in selecting the various insurance markets and alternatives for treating life and health risks. The buying phase is often preceded by or combined with the planning of insurance purchases. Good planning is an essential step in good insurance buying and, in the broader sense, risk management, for both personal and business situations. In life and health insurance, the technique of good planning is called *programming;* in all other lines of insurance, the process is usually referred to as a *risk and insurance survey,* as treated in Chapter 2.

PERSONAL LIFE AND HEALTH INSURANCE PLANNING

Life and health insurance planning may serve *(a)* the individual and the family or *(b)* a business or other organization. The first category is "personal insurance," and the second is "business insurance," which protects organizations or associates against losses occasioned by the death or disability of members of the firm or key employees. This is a term applied to a specialized use for regular life and health insurance facilities—it is not a special form of policy developed for business purposes. Business life and health insurance will be discussed in a later section of this chapter.

Personal life insurance programming

Life insurance programming for the individual or the family consists of a study of the need for capital resources and income. The study includes: *(a)* present and future needs and obligations, and *(b)* present and future resources, including life insurance, arranged to meet the needs and obligations at the least possible cost.

Life insurance programming may also include the broader aspects of "estate programming," which includes consideration of all assets available to the estate. Cash, investments, and other valuable rights are coordinated with life insurance proceeds. Also to be considered are estate taxes and legal advice for wills and trusts to carry out estate objectives, as explained later in this chapter.

When life insurance programming made its appearance, many felt that it was primarily for persons of substantial means. For those who inherit or acquire great wealth, the problems of taxation, as well as the liquidation of assets for distribution, indicate life insurance as a means for conserving values. However, experience has shown that the individual of modest means, and more particularly the wage earner with dependents, also needs to make plans for the future and to integrate those plans with life insurance protection. One could argue, in fact, that proper planning is even *more* essential for modest estates, because these can least afford to be wasteful in the use of their limited assets. The principal item in many estates is life insurance. Many would die without resources, or even go bankrupt, but for the life estate created immediately with the purchase of life insurance.

The needs. Through a conference or a series of conferences, the life insurance agent develops an outline of all the needs of the individual or family. The initial step in programming is to establish a priority of needs that must be met to satisfy minimum requirements. The necessities for living, food, shelter, and clothing, of course, come first; the amenities or luxuries next.

For necessities, the logical priority is: *(a)* last expenses; *(b)* emergency funds; *(c)* dependency income during the family-raising period; *(d)* life income for surviving spouse; and *(e)* mortgage payment. Next in the order of priority come: *(f)* educational funds; and *(g)* retirement income if the husband or wife live to retirement age. If the estate is large and resources are available, consideration may next be given to such items as life insurance for children, postgraduate work in college, and other special bequests or gifts.

The method. Two steps must be taken before recommending any program: (1) gathering all necessary factual data, and (2) analyzing the data as they apply to the applicant's estate objectives. Information required will include: *(a)* the names and the relationship of all who are to benefit from the estate, *(b)* all the assets and inheritances of beneficiaries from other sources, *(c)* property held jointly, *(d)* life insurance protection, *(e)* all pertinent information touching upon business interests and plans, and *(f)* the amount and nature of all debts or other obligations. In short, the intelligent program requires a complete picture of all the personal and business resources of the person whose estate is being planned.

The trained insurance agent will require complete information on: the sex and age of the individual; his or her health; the age, sex, and number of dependents; personal and present wealth; loan or tax obligations; the applicant's and spouse's income; present insurance owned; and assets other than life insurance. Requiring special consideration will be such items as social security benefits, group insurance with employer, veteran's benefits, and retirement pensions. With insurance programming the problem is largely one of dovetailing any present insurance into the needs of the insured and supplementing where additional protection is needed.

After the data have been assembled and carefully analyzed, the prospect is then invited to estimate the minimum family *needs* if death should occur immediately. When the needs have been established, it is essential to determine the amount of *capital and income* required to accomplish the objective and the *methods* for providing the amount at the time it is needed. The problem then resolves itself into: *(a)* whether the needs indicated are feasible; *(b)* to what extent existing resources will supply the necessary capital to satisfy the requirements; *(c)* additional insurance required, if any; and *(d)* the most effective manner of distributing existing and new insurance between cash payments and income.

Many insurers today are using computers to simplify this process for many standard situations. "Electronic life insurance programming" can oftentimes be accomplished in less than an hour by the agent in the first interview. Immediate estimates of the life insurance amounts needed to meet selected family goals are obtainable on brief one-page forms, which the agent completes by telephoning a centralized computer hookup to get the information required.[3] The computer answers, of course, are only valuable if the assumptions on which the calculations are based have been carefully made.

Assets other than life insurance are studied to determine: *(a)* their money value and *(b)* the monthly income that these assets will produce. Mutual or money market funds, stocks, savings, and assets of every sort are integrated into the program. An individual without capital has no assurance that he or she will live to accumulate investments to provide an income for minimum requirements. This being the case, life insurance, particularly where means are limited, forms the basis of the estate program. Investments and other resources may be utilized to build from the foundation established by the life insurance program.

Insurance policies are studied with a view to determining the maximum policy-paying power. The summation value of settlement option payments represents a substantial increase over the total face value of

---

[3] An example of such computer service used by many insurers is Keypact, by Computone of Atlanta, Georgia.

the insurance. Since *income* is one of the major requirements of any program, it is important to determine the paying power of the available insurance rather than simply list the face amount of the various policies. After the social security, pension, and veterans' incomes have been utilized to their maximum effectiveness, it becomes necessary to determine the amount of new insurance essential to meet the objectives established in the statement of minimum needs. The living values of life insurance contracts, that is, the retirement benefits, may be taken partly in cash, partly in paid-up insurance, and partly in income if desired.

Integration with social security benefits. The original Social Security Act provided only old-age insurance, but later amendments included survivorship benefits, disability income benefits for total and permanent disability, and Medicare-Medicaid benefits. Thus, social security benefits are of four types: *(a)* retirement benefits to elderly covered workers and their families, *(b)* death benefits to survivors of deceased covered workers, *(c)* disability income benefits, and *(d)* medical expense benefits.

It is essential that the full impact of these benefits receive consideration in the life and health insurance program as part of the planned estate. The process of integrating life insurance with other assets and sources of income is apparent, too, but the universality and size of OASDHI benefits is such that special attention is justified here. More than 9 out of 10 persons in the working population are now included. The substantial size of the benefits, often equivalent to more than $200,000 of life insurance and over $100,000 of retirement benefits for some families, is indicated in further detail in Chapter 11 on government life and health insurance and in Figure 12–1.

Figure 12–1 shows the substantial contribution of OASDHI benefits to the needs of a family. The diagram illustrates the income which the family (based on assumptions of age, income, and property owned, as shown) would receive from OASDHI if the husband died at the widow's age 25. Benefits would be $1,000 a month for the widow until her son reached age 18.[4] No further OASDHI benefits would be received until her age 60, when $500 per month becomes payable.[5]

A similar procedure is just as useful for single persons, or for career women instead of families. Lump-sum and income goals, and OASDHI benefits, of course, will be much different and generally less complicated. Income for dependent parents may be considered, as for dependent children in the family example. Given the high likelihood of future marriage and children, understanding the goals and methods of planning for the family life insurance needs and costs is important for all young persons. The techniques of fact-finding, setting capital and income goals, and deter-

---

[4] Based on an assumed average indexed monthly earnings under social security of $2,000.

[5] Age 60 is the earliest age at which benefits can be received for widow's (unless disabled) retirement. Maximum amounts are 100 percent of the husband's PIA; reduced benefits at age 60 are 71.5 percent of this amount.

mining how net needs (after estimating OASDHI and group insurance benefits) can be met by various life insurance policies are necessary in all situations.

A case study example of family life insurance needs and costs

As an illustration of how life insurance is used to help meet the needs of a typical, young family, Table 12–1 and Figure 12–1 show the procedure which might be followed in estimating gross needs, subtracting OASDHI and other benefits, and arriving at net capital and income needs. Six individual life insurance policies are used to provide for the net needs calculated in this example.

The total insurance recommended is $267,000, of which $10,000 for last expenses and $40,000 for retirement are ordinary life insurance to meet permanent needs, and the balance is various types of term insurance to meet temporary needs. The total cost of the suggested program is $1,495 a year, or about 6 percent of the husband's assumed annual income of $24,000. Note that this program includes more ordinary life insurance than would be necessary to accomplish the same benefits with term insurance if the husband dies at an early age. The cash values of the ordinary life contracts would be available at retirement age even if early death did not occur, so this program will help accomplish substantial retirement objectives as well as survivorship protection objectives.

In the earlier years, such a program could be assured for the family (regardless of the husband's health) by purchasing part of the ordinary life insurance amount as term insurance, and planning to convert portions of the coverage during the first 15 years. Term insurance for this period would cost only about one third of the indicated costs for permanent insurance ($4 versus $13 per $1,000), but the contracts, if converted to ordinary life insurance, would be at the attained age of the husband. At age 35 they would cost about $18 per $1,000, or at age 40 about $20 per $1,000. A "guaranteed purchase option" could also be used to assure the purchase of ordinary life insurance equal in amount to the base policy (at standard rates without a medical examination) at five or six stated ages between 25 and 40. The cost of this feature is very low, about $2 per $1,000, so most persons can guarantee at an early age the eventual purchase of adequate amounts of life insurance for their families. Flexibility in meeting the changing needs of young families is aided by these options.

The life insurance program must be fitted to the particular family goals chosen. Considerably more insurance would be needed if the income *goals* after age 40 were raised. In the example, 100 percent of normal income is assumed as the goal during the family dependency period, when help for the widow would be most necessary. About 75 percent of the normal family income is assumed as the goal for the widow period

Table 12–1. Family life insurance program*

		Lump-sum needs		
		Last expenses: Permanent	Mortgage repayment (declining balance): Ages 25–44	Education: At age 40
I.	Estimated gross needs (based on immediate death of husband)	$10,000 (funeral, taxes, pay off loans, etc.)	$50,000 (could be repaid but would not have to be)	$40,000
II.	OASDHI, group life, part-time work, and wife's private pension	—	—	—
III.	Net needs (I less II)	$10,000	$50,000	$40,000
IV.	How individual life insurance might meet these needs	$10,000 Ordinary Life Insurance Contract	$50,000 Decreasing Term Contract	$36,000 Group Life Insurance Contract, at 1½ times annual salary, would be enough for this purpose
	Earnings (interest) from policies, if death occurs before age 60	—	—	—
V.	Approximate annual costs of contracts‡	$130 ($13 per $1,000)	$200 ($4 per $1,000)	Assume employer pays this cost
VI.	Life insurance contracts	Policy A	Policy B	Policy C (certificate)

* The following assumptions are the basis for this table.

Family ages: Husband (28); wife (25); one child (3).

Income: $24,000/year or $2,000/month.

Property: $70,000 home, with $50,000 20-year mortgage; $1,000 cash savings, $4,000 stocks and mutual funds (hold this $5,000 for emergency needs); two cars valued at $12,000, with $6,000 bank loan outstanding.

Employment: Husband, business management junior executive.

Wife was secretary, could go back to work part-time after children are 18.

OASDHI benefits: For AIME of $2,000 a month, the estimates here are based on the benefits shown in Chapter 11, Table 11–2.

after the child or children are age 18 and one half of normal income for the retirement period. Not all families would make these choices, and the results of the indicated needs could increase considerably if higher goals were selected. Each $100 per month of income desired at age 40 for life, for example, requires over $25,000 more of life insurance

24,000 × 15 = ₽360,000   18,000 × 20 = *360,000

Table 12–1 *(concluded)*

Income needs			
Family dependency period (for 15 years): Ages 25–39	Widow support period (for 20 years): Ages 40–59	Widow retirement period (for life): AGE 80 Age 60 on	Total
$360,000 (full salary, or $24,000 a year, or $2,000 a month)	$360,000 (75 percent of salary, or $18,000 a year, or $1,500 a month)	$240,000 (one-half of salary, or $12,000 a year, or $1,000 a month)	$1,060,000 (total gross needs)
$180,000 (OASDHI—$12,000 a year, or $1,000 a month)	$240,000 (no OASDHI during this "blackout" period; this $1,000 a month income is from wife's part-time work) EARNED	$192,000 (OASDHI—$6,000 a year, or $500 a month; wife's pension—$3,600 a year, or $300 a month)	$612,000 (OASDHI, plus wife's part-time work)
$180,000 ($1,000 a month)	$120,000 ($500 a month)	$48,000 ($200 a month)	$448,000 (total net needs)
$76,000 Decreasing 15-year Term Contract D	$55,000† Decreasing Term to Age 60 Contract E	$40,000† Ordinary Life Insurance Contract F	$267,000 (total Life Insurance Contracts)
From Policy F and Pol. E ($95,000 × .06 = $5,700 a year or $475 a month)	From Policy F ($40,000 × .06 = $2,400 a year, or $200 a month)		
$300 ($4 per $1,000)	$385 ($7 per $1,000)	$480 ($12 per $1,000)	$1,495
Policy D	Policy E	Policy F	

† Policy F—at $5 per month *for life* at age 60, per $1,000, $40,000 will provide needed $200 a month income.

Policy E—at $5.50 per month *for 20 years* at age 40, per $1,000, $55,000 will provide needed $300 a month income (other $200 a month comes from Policy E face value held at interest of 6 percent until age 60, if death occurs at ages 40–59).

Policy D—at $6.90 per month *for 15 years* at age 25, per $1,000, $76,000 will provide needed $525 a month income (other $475 a month comes from Policy F and E held at interest of 6 percent until age 60, if death occurs at ages 25–39).

‡ The costs for all of these contracts may vary considerably according to the particular insurers and the contract features chosen. Participating contracts would be about 15 percent higher than the costs shown, and some nonparticipating quotations could be lower.

in order to provide a settlement option with 20 years of guaranteed payments.

Note that the possibility of the widow *remarrying* is not assumed in the example. This is a personal choice. At a young age, particularly without several children, the widow's remarriage is a realistic assump-

Figure 12–1. Family life insurance program

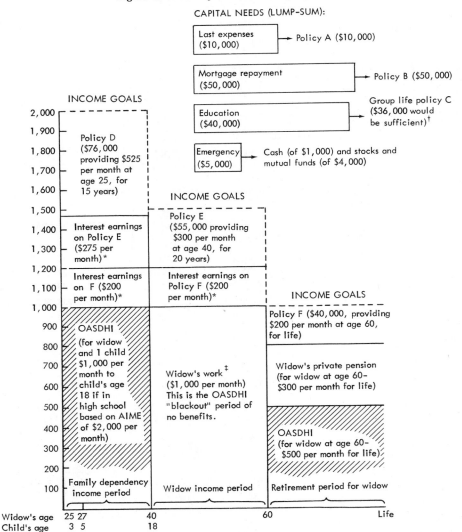

Dotted line shows income goals or objectives; shaded section shows social security (OASDHI) benefits, rounded to nearest $100.

* Interest earnings of about 6 percent, or $5.00 per month, for each $1,000 of proceeds would be available under a participating interest option, for the face values payable at the death of the husband by held until later years in the program.

† With interest earnings on $36,000, for death of the husband during wife's age 25–40.

‡ Under present "earnings test," could disqualify wife for OASDHI benefits if more than about $4,440 a year was earned before *age 40*, which is one of the reasons that work prior to that time is not assumed in this example.

tion. After age 30 or 35, given the financial burdens of raising children, her remarriage is unlikely. Regardless, it is desirable not to leave the widow in the position of feeling an *obligation* to remarry in order to help the financial position of the family. Also, consideration must be given to the *loss* of all or part of the OASDHI mother's benefit if she remarries.

Work by the widow is also subject to much variation in the usual family situation. Many husbands would prefer not to force the widow to seek employment during the family dependency period or at least until the children are well along in school. She would also lose the OAS-DHI mother's benefit if she earned more than about $4,440 a year during this period. The outright assumption that the widow will take on full-time work during that period is oftentimes unrealistic. Her employability later depends on several factors: her work career experience, her educational background, job availability, the retraining or reeducation necessary (probably essential if she seeks work at age 40, after no work experience or after not working for 10–15 years), and her health (what if she is disabled?). The example takes a compromise position, assuming only part-time work with income of $1,000 a month during the ages 40–60.

Group life insurance, usually available in amounts of about 1.5 to 2 times annual salary, or $36,000 in the illustration, is suggested for use in meeting educational needs of the child or children, *if* the father dies prior to the wife's age 40. The father's death would be a serious financial blow to the continuation of education for the children. If the father is still living at age 40, other alternatives may help take care of college education costs: normal salary increases by middle age; the use of cash or loan values of the permanent life insurance contracts; other savings or investments; part-time work by the children or wife; or educational loans secured through grants or through using the life insurance as collateral for other personal loans. Although most employed persons will have some group life insurance in effect, particularly at the younger, more employable ages, consideration should be given to the fact that this protection is not the same as having individual life insurance contracts. The employer may stop the plan, or the employee may be fired or change jobs and lose the benefits of group life insurance, which is usually yearly renewable term protection only.

Particularly important in the illustration is the use of *interest earnings* on contract amounts payable because of the early death of the husband before retirement. The earnings shown are minimums partially guaranteed under the settlement option leaving the proceeds at interest. Additional interest is often paid if the settlement option is participating. Thus the relatively conservative total assumption of 6 percent is used in the example. Higher returns could probably be secured by taking the lump-sum face value and reinvesting it in money market, bonds, stocks, or other media. However, note that the interest earnings estimated in the explanation at the bottom of Figure 12–1 are still several hundred dollars per month for Policies E and F. If the death of the husband does not occur before retirement, these amounts would not be available, nor would they be needed to meet the goals outlined.

The *retirement* assumptions of the illustration consider only the *widow's* situation. Further assumptions could be incorporated into the example to consider the position of the husband and wife, if both are living after age 65. Social security benefits would be about $700 a month (with an assumed AIME of $2,000) for the husband, and about $350 a month for the wife, or a total of $1,050 a month. In addition, the husband may have a retirement income of several hundred dollars a month available from his own private pension. The cash values of the suggested $40,000 of permanent whole life insurance could also be used, if necessary, to supplement retirement income. At age 65, cash values of about $800 per $1,000 of life insurance would be available, or a total of over $32,000. Under a joint and survivor benefit settlement option, about $5.00 per $1,000, or approximately $160 per month, would be payable.

A warning is appropriate in regard to the *changing* needs of the typical family in regard to its life insurance program. Additional children, divorce, changing income, death or disability, job stability, increasing social security benefits, inflation trends, and many other factors should each be reconsidered in a regular and *frequent review* (perhaps even annually on a specific date) of the life insurance program. The goal, too, should encompass a full evaluation of life insurance in coordination with other financial resources, such as investments. Otherwise, the anticipated benefits are unlikely to meet actual needs. The life insurance estate, which often is the majority of the family's assets at the death of the breadwinner(s), is an essential part of any sound financial planning.

The place of the total insurance costs in the *family budget* should be considered. The above example might include the following approximate breakdown of family financial goals:

		Percent of total income of $24,000
1.	Housing	30
2.	Food	20
3.	Clothing, entertainment, and miscellaneous	10
4.	Insurance (life and health)	10
5.	Automobile and transportation	15
6.	Taxes (including OASDHI)	10
7.	Savings	5
		100

Personal health insurance programming

The same technique of planning as used in life estate programming is useful for choosing health insurance coverages. In fact, it is becoming more and more recognized by life and health agents and brokers that both life and health insurance plans must be integrated for successful long-range protection for the policyholder or the family. Social insurance, particularly Medicare and disability income under OASDHI, serve as a foundation but are only part of the total needs of a good health insurance program.

Unless proper health insurance is purchased, the life insurance program is threatened by inability to carry out estate objectives. Without adequate health insurance, a serious injury or illness may cause: (1) extra expenses (or a drain on assets) for medical treatment or (2) loss of income which may prevent the policyholder from keeping life insurance in force.

Medical care coverages should have the following priority: (1) hospital bills, (2) surgical fees, and (3) other medical expenses. Where the amount available for premiums is limited, as it almost always is, some such ranking of importance to the buyer of various health insurance coverages is essential. For middle- or upper-income families, the major or catastrophe medical expenses may assume a priority position, with smaller normal losses of up to a few thousand dollars being taken care of out of savings or other assets.

The most important income losses to be provided for are those of total and permanent disability of the family's breadwinners. Partial income losses, and temporary loss of income up to about a year, are considered of lesser importance.

Equally significant for most policyholders is *major* medical coverage on a "blanket" medical care basis. Many insureds, if they have other assets with which to take care of relatively normal medical costs (up to several hundred dollars, perhaps), may need a major medical contract more than they do a hospital-surgical policy for the more frequent kinds of losses. Medical expenses of several thousand dollars can be a crippling blow to most family budgets, and these catastropic types of health losses should be insured.

One example of the need for coordinating life and health insurance programs is seen in the provision in estate plans for "last expenses." Sometimes these expenses include, in addition to taxes and funeral and cemetery costs, the costs of prolonged and expensive medical care preceding death. If these costs are covered by a permanent life insurance contract, it is unnecessary to duplicate the coverage in health insurance planning, and vice versa.

The loss of income due to injury or illness is a major area of need for coordination between life and health insurance. Part of the loss-of-income problem can be alleviated by waiver-of-premium or disability income "riders" (see Chapter 7) to life insurance contracts. However, it must be remembered that these features are optional and not included in all such contracts. Also very important is the fact that they provide benefits only for *total and permanent* (normally, over six months) disability and not for partial or temporary inability to earn an income due to injury or sickness. There remains a pronounced but oftentimes neglected need for more complete protection against loss of income by having an "accident and health" policy (see Chapter 9) for permanent-partial or temporary-total disabilities. These income benefits should be related to the normal earnings of the insured (perhaps between 50 and 75 percent) rather than to the amount of life insurance in force, as the disability income in life insurance riders must be.

The income benefits of individual and group insurance and the rights under the federal OASDHI program should be coordinated in a diagram similar to Figure 12–1. With objectives set in terms of the monthly or yearly income necessary to support the family when the breadwinner is disabled, the social security benefits (for total and long-term disability only) provide a minimum base. Then the group and individual health policies for loss of income should supplement the program to reach toward the established goals throughout the years following a disability. For the sake of clarity, health insurance needs and possible solutions are summarized in the next section.

A case study example of family health insurance needs and costs

The health insurance program shown in Table 12–2 and Figure 12–2 assumes about the same income goals as are assumed in the life insurance program illustration. The needed hospital-surgical expenses, as well as part of the major medical expense needs (up to $100,000 per illness or injury), are taken care of by a *group* policy available through the husband's place of employment, with the employer typically paying a substantial part of the cost of these plans.[6] Income goals of $2,000 a month before age 40, and $1,500 between ages 40 and 65, are achieved by supplementing assumed OASDHI family benefits between ages 25 and 39, and part-time work by the widow between ages 40 and 65. Policy A, an accident and health contract, provides $500 a month for total and permanent disability on a guaranteed renewable (with rate increases by class permit-

---

[6] A reasonable assumption, since about two thirds of the U.S. population have *group* hospital-surgical coverage, and one half have major medical coverage for limits of $100,000 or more. More than half of these plans are paid in full by the employer, with about 80 percent of total costs being paid by the employer. *See Source Book of Health Insurance Data* (New York: Health Insurance Association of America, 1981–82), pp. 8–9.

Table 12–2. Family health insurance program*

I. Estimate of needs	*Needs (medical expenses and loss of income for disability)*		
	Family dependency period: Ages 25–39	*Wife support period: Ages 40–65*	*Retirement period: Age 65 and over*
A. Medical expenses			
1. Hospital-surgical expenses	Up to $200 per day, for 365 days, with up to $2,000 for miscellaneous charges and $15 per doctor visit up to 30	Same as ages 25–39	Assumes that Medicare benefits will be nearly sufficient, for most of hospital-surgical expenses (HI—Part A) and 80 percent of all other expenses above deductibles (SMI—Part B)
2. Surgical	Scheduled benefits to $2,000 maximum	Same as ages 25–39	
3. Major, or catastrophe, expenses	Up to $100,000 of "blanket"‡ expenses‡ per illness or injury	Same as ages 25–39	
B. Loss of income			
1. Total and permanent	$2,000 per month	$1,500 per month	$1,000 per month
2. Partial and temporary	$1,000 per month, up to 39 weeks	Same as ages 25–39	
II. OASDHI benefits† or part-time work, and wife's pension	IB(1): $1,000 per month to child's age 18 if in high school	None from OASDHI: $1,000 per month from part-time work	Medicare expense benefits plus $500 per month from OASDHI and $300 per month from wife's pension
III. Group health insurance	IA(1), IA(2), and IA(3): full benefits as above; IB(2): full benefits as above	Same as ages 25–39	
IV. Net needs	IB(1): $1,000 per month	$500 per month	$200 per month
V. How individual health insurance might meet these needs	IB(1): Loss of income§ for sickness to age 65, lifetime for accident, or $1,000 per month (Policy A)	Same as ages 25–39	Cash values of permanent life insurance contracts could be used, if needed, to fill in $200 a month gap here
VI. Approximate annual costs of contracts	Policy A: $500 a year; Total $500 a year	Same as ages 25–39	

* Assumptions are same as for Table 12–1.
† These are approximate amounts. Reduced benefits could be obtained at age 60, or after age 50 if the wife is disabled.
‡ Assumes $200 deductible, and 20 percent coinsurance paid by insured, renewable, to age 65, with premium increases by class.
§ Assumes this is for total and permanent disability only; guaranteed renewable, with premium changes, by class, to age 65 and waiting period of one month. Full salary replacement is assumed, although tax benefits and underwriting restrictions probably would make 80 percent of salary, technically, a more precise goal.

Figure 12–2. Family health insurance program

* Approximate rounded maximum benefits. Reduced widow benefits possible at age 60, or age 62, or at age 50 for disabled widow, not shown. Total and permanent disability of husband.

† For total and permanent disability of husband, to age 65 for sickness. If because of accident, benefits would be payable for life. Minor deficiency of $200 a month income during retirement periods are disregarded in this program.

ted) basis. This more than fills in the "blackout period" with no dependent children, during which no OASDHI disability benefits are available to the wife for her husband's disability. Disability income benefits in life insurance contracts could also help meet this need, but here it is assumed that a separate health insurance contract is purchased.

After age 65, Medicare benefits will take care of most hospital and much of the other medical expenses, although some advisers would suggest an individual contract at special rates for the over-65 age group, to supplement these coverages. Income from OASDHI of $500 monthly for the husband's disability and an assumed private pension based on the widow's work ($300 a month) nearly meet the goal of $1,000 lifetime income per month at the older ages in the illustration. Life insurance cash values could be used to provide the $200 per month deficiency.

Total costs for individual Policy A would be about $500 a year, or a little over 2 percent of the annual salary of $24,000. Together with suggested life individual insurance of $1,495 a year, or 6 percent of income, insurance in the family budget shown earlier totals about 8 percent.

This does not include OASDHI taxes, which will be about $1,700 a year, or 7 percent at current rates; nor does it include some employee's participation in group insurance costs.

Naturally, these estimates would be subject to many individual differences. The greatest variation in the insurance costs as a percent of total income would be in the life insurance section. Here the total might be substantially less, depending on how much is budgeted for other savings media.

The personal insurance review examples are an illustration of *insurance programming* on a family basis. The next section of this chapter analyzes total estate planning. While the risks with which the individual is personally concerned are limited, they vary with occupation or profession, income, ownership of other assets, and family needs and personal goals. Again, while cost is of importance in every insurance program, its distribution may be of special interest to the individual. It sometimes happens that heavy premium payments fall due about the same time that taxes, notes, or other extraordinary expenses are payable. If the insured is operating on a budget system, the readjustment of premium payments to fit the financial plan may be necessary. If budgeting is not followed, insurance may be rearranged so that the heaviest premium payments fall due at a time when some particular income is received or in any other manner that will prove most convenient to the insured.

Personal estate planning

The preceding illustrations of life and health insurance programming are but part of the typical family's long-range financial planning. Total *estate planning* is a much broader process which concerns all aspects of the *creation* and *liquidation* of a family's assets. Life insurance is one of the most common methods of creating assets, and it creates an immediate or "instant" estate as soon as it is purchased. It guarantees the goals you want to achieve. The estate includes all assets owned or controlled by a person who dies.

The typical sad situation following a death is increased by the survivors' lack of knowledge about the assets of the estate—what they are, where the ownership documents are kept, and what can and should be done with them. Information on the debts and obligations, too, is usually lacking, as well as information on what procedures must be followed in order to "probate," or have the court approve, any estate settlement. Much is to be recommended in the advice that you should "teach your wife to be a widow (or husband a widower)." It does little good to create a sizable estate without properly planning for its liquidation or use.

The connotations of the term *estate planning* are often misleading. It is more than mere tax planning, and it is more than the mere liquidation or disposition of assets after death because it should include the "wisest and most prudent use of . . . assets during . . . lifetime as well as after death."[7] It is also wrong to assume that only the larger estates require estate planning. The smaller estates are those that can least afford to miss the potential benefits of proper estate planning techniques.

Estate impairment. It is often said that "it is not what you have but what you have left that counts." A recent example of estate shrinkage is that of actress Jayne Mansfield's estate of one-half million dollars, in which several final beneficiaries received less than $2,000 each. This rather extreme example emphasizes that not all the assets of an estate pass to the beneficiaries when a person dies. Another much-publicized example is the estate of Howard Hughes, which was originally estimated at several billion dollars. With lengthy court battles continuing in regard to validity of his will, corrections in property appraisals, and tax complications, the estate value had dwindled to less than one tenth of the original amounts within 2 years after his death.

Primary among the reasons for estate planning is the need for liquidity, providing cash for estate costs within the first year after death. In contrast to other assets, which often shrink with an untimely sale, life insurance provides dollars without forced sale and with no capital gains or income taxes payable at death.

Estate settlement costs often reduce the values going to beneficiaries by 30 percent or more. The substantial cost of estate transfer is one of these factors, but many others exist in the normal situation: inflation erosion of the purchasing power of the dollar, unstable and fluctuating asset values, lack of liquidity to pay immediate estate needs within a few months or estate taxes within nine months of death, and improper use of settlement options under life insurance contracts. Lack of provision for long-term and costly disability losses due to poor health, too, can cause expected estate values to shrink drastically.

The estate planning process. In achieving the objective of transmitting property values with minimum tax burden and maximum effectiveness, a basic understanding of the following concepts are important: the will, the marital deduction, the estate, the gift and estate taxes, trusts, and the estate planning team.

Before these techniques are used, the first step in estate planning involves obtaining facts about the client in regard to domicile (the effect of state laws on the estate vary greatly here), family and dependents, property owned and income rights, wills, and the objectives of the total estate plan.[8] Detailed questionnaires are the method by which these facts are obtained, ranging from checklists of a few items to many pages.

---

[7] Lawrence J. Ackerman, "Estate Planning Principles," in Davis W. Gregg and Vane B. Lucas, eds., *Life and Health Insurance Handbook,* 3d ed. (Homewood, Ill.: Richard D. Irwin, 1973), p. 844.

[8] Ibid., pp. 846–49.

Analysis of the prospective factors tending to impair the estate values and the design of a coordinated estate plan are the next steps in estate planning.

A survey book for the beginning student cannot hope to include all the legal and tax complications of estate planning. However, a few of the more important aspects will be sufficient to explain the major factors to emphasize the critical nature of estate planning. A major message is that good estate plans result only from necessary careful *planning*. This applies both to the *creation* of assets, in which life insurance is almost essential for most families, and to the *disposition* of assets, in which life insurance can be very effective as a secure foundation for the estate plan.

The will. A key role is played in the process by having a legally qualified *will* for both the husband and the wife. Amazingly, thousands of persons die every year without valid wills. The result in these cases is that the state law decides for the family how and when the estate values are to be distributed. The court must appoint an *administrator*, who may not be the *executor* you would have chosen to care for your estate. Many state inheritance laws do not provide for the needs of beneficiaries as one might expect. The typical state inheritance law, for example, allots one third of the estate to the wife, and two thirds to the children (assuming two or more children). This requires a guardianship to be established under the law if the children are under age 18 or 21, and distribution of the *income only* until they reach the age of majority. Other use of the principal is severely restricted and subject to court approval if proven necessary for their essential support and education. The basic question is summarized as: "Would you want the law to specify such uses, or would you rather have your will indicate how much and when your executor (or a trustee) should provide for the children?" It is possible to use estate values according to the deceased's instructions, but only if a valid will is executed in order to carry out these instructions. The will, which may cost only $25–$100, is truly one of the best legal bargains in estate planning.

The marital deduction. From a tax standpoint, the key purpose of a will is to qualify the wife's estate for maximum use of the *marital deduction*. The Economic Recovery Tax Act (ERTA) of 1981 provides that property values, no matter how large, can be given to the spouse outright and be deducted from the taxable estate. As seen above, the intestate (no will) laws will not take advantage of the maximum deduction. It is important to consider both the potential estate tax applying to the spouse's estate, as well as the successive future estate taxes which may apply to the estates of the surviving spouse and the children.

Most tax goals of estate planning, and the examples in this text, concern the *federal estate* tax. The additional *inheritance taxes of the states*, which are much smaller, may also be involved in estate planning, with similar benefits. Income taxes are of lesser importance, although separating principal amounts to have the income separately taxed to children or trusts can also be a wise objective in some of the larger estates.

The estate. Although estates valued at several hundred thousand dollars or more seem large to many persons, the total values accumulated by middle- and upper-class families are often substantial. Invariably they are larger than expected, because all of the items that will be included have never been added up. A recommended procedure is to estimate the total estate values at periodic intervals during one's lifetime, in a "mock" or assumed estate situation, in order to see what approximate tax consequences would be likely. *All* assets owned at the time of death are included, and many other assets over which the deceased has control (such as powers of appointment and revocable gifts) may be considered part of the estate by the tax authorities. Real estate, automobiles, personal property, savings accounts, pension plans, group and individual life insurance (unless there are no "incidents of ownership," such as rights to change the beneficiary, use cash values, and so on), stocks, bonds, mutual and money market funds, business interests, and many other items must all be included. Joint ownership of the home or savings and investment accounts are usually included at the *full* values. Fair market value is the normal amount for federal tax purposes, and many family-type businesses may represent much larger values than anticipated. Inflation has pushed many values higher than is realized.

The unified gift and estate tax. The Federal Tax Reform Act of 1976 changed estate planning considerably. Formerly, there was separate taxation of gift and estate values. Now a *unified tax and tax credit* applies to both cumulative lifetime gifts and deathtime transfers of assets. The combined tax now ranges from about 30 to 70 percent of the *taxable estate* value.[9] The taxable estate excludes assets qualifying for the marital deduction, which is why this is so important. A unified tax credit (for both gifts and estate values) of $79,300 applies in 1983 and is subtracted from the calculated tax.[10] In determining the total taxable estate, the gross estate value is also reduced by the administration expenses, debts, and funeral expenses.

Living gifts can be planned to help reduce the taxes payable. Individual gifts of up to $10,000 annually per donee, or $20,000 if the spouse joins in the gift, can be made without having any gift or estate tax apply to the transfer. Thus a considerable amount can be transferred gradually to the family or others during a lifetime. Other, larger living gifts of

---

[9] New tax provisions are scheduled to reduce the maximum tax rates on estates over $2.5 million to 50 percent by 1985.

[10] The unified tax credit will increase each year until 1987, when it levels off at $192,800.

most kinds of property can also aid in reducing the unified tax at the time of death, for these gifts are not included in the unified taxable estate. *CONTEMPLATION OF DEATH*

Life insurance can be effectively used as gifts in order to reduce estate taxes. Donors can make unlimited gifts of life insurance to the spouse, and such transfers will incur no gift or estate taxes. However, if such gifts are made less than three years before the donor's death, the proceeds of the policies will be included in the donor's estate. If the donor continues to pay the premiums after making the gift, the premiums would be a taxable gift but would usually qualify for the annual $10–$20,000 gift tax exclusion. The donor should not retain any incidents of ownership, such as the right to change the beneficiary, use cash values, and so on.

While it is true that estates with adjusted taxable values of up to $600,000 will pay no tax with the unified tax credit, the importance of using the marital deduction to maximum advantage is emphasized. Leaving the surviving spouse property outright by will reduces the taxable estate and the resulting tax considerably.[11] Also, these examples concern only the federal gift and estate tax, and *state inheritance* taxes would apply in addition.

Estate planning is not a job for a do-it-yourselfer. The advice of attorneys specializing in estate planning is strongly recommended, particularly for larger estates. New rules apply under the 1976 Reform Act— a new "carry-over basis" for valuing estate property on the recipient's tax basis (or on fair market value as of December 31, 1976, which becomes very important), new rules applying taxes to "generation-skipping transfers" in trusts and life estates, and many others.[12] Additional changes by the 1981 ERTA law makes careful estate tax planning and review of estate plans even more essential today.[13]

Trusts. The substantial advantages of *trusts,* to which all or most of the assets are transferred at death, should be of primary concern in many estates. In addition to possible tax savings (often many thousands of dollars), the spouse and children can receive the benefit of professional investment advice and service. A bank trust department is generally used. The advantage of having trustees make or aid in making decisions

---

[11] Careful use is also recommended if the spouse already has substantial assets, in which case it may *not* be advisable from a tax standpoint to utilize the deduction because the tax on the death of the *surviving spouse* may be increased. See Nahum L. Gordon, "The Impact of the Tax Reform Act of 1976 on Estate Planning," *CLU Journal* 31, no. 2 (April 1977), p. 11; and Douglas K. Freeman, "Federal Estate Planning Developments: 1981," *CLU Journal* 36, no. 3 (July 1982), p. 12.

[12] See Roger J. Stalowicz, "The Tax Reform Act of 1976—A Primer," and Alban Salaman, "The Tax Reform Act of 1976: Estate and Gift Tax Provisions," *CLU Journal* 31, no. 1 (January 1977), pp. 13 and 24, respectively.

[13] Herbert Chasman, "Estate Planning After the Economic Recovery Tax Act of 1981," *CLU Journal* 36, no. 1 (January 1982), p. 10.

in regard to use of principal and income is also of real benefit to many spouses unfamiliar with investments and asset conservation.

The goal is easily reached by drawing up a *trust agreement,* for which attorney's fees would usually be only a few hundred dollars. For example, in one common use of trusts, all of the wife's trust income is usually paid to the wife during her lifetime, and she may be given full powers to use the principal as well. Oftentimes, partial powers to invade the principal of the trust are given, restricting her use to a specified dollar amount or percentage of the trust each year. The income of another trust for the children may also be payable to the wife for her life. She may give this to the children (or leave it in the trust at the lower income tax rates applicable there), but according to specifications in the trust she may use the principal only for the direct and essential support and the medical or educational needs of the children.

Many options are available in setting up trusts, and these require professional legal advice. *Revocable* trusts, in which the creator reserves the right to reacquire the property in the trust, are most common. These create transfer taxes at the time of death and do not reduce estate taxes then, but they may be set up to reduce administrative costs and taxes in the estate of the beneficiary and to obtain income tax benefits for the trust income. *Irrevocable* trusts reduce estate taxes by removing the trust property from the taxable estate, but gift taxes are applicable when such trusts are set up, unless the tax is less than the unified gift and estate tax credit.

Life insurance may be a majority of the estate values, and it may be used beneficially to provide liquid assets (without losses if it is sold in a temporarily depressed market). Settlement options such as the life income option can be used to provide a foundation of secure income for the wife as long as she lives and may also save on probate and administration costs. A "pour-over" testamentary (at death) trust can be used to consolidate life insurance and other assets in an *inter vivos* (living) trust, with several legal and administrative benefits.

Executor and legal fees total substantial amounts in estate settlements, often each amounting to 3 to 5 percent of the estate values. Total estate expenses (other than federal estate taxes) and debts are often 10–20 percent or higher. In trust arrangements, the transfer is accomplished largely through the trusts, which may reduce both estate taxes and expenses.

The trust agreement specifies how the trust assets are to be used and invested. If the trustee is a bank trust officer, the assets may be invested in a common portfolio of the bank's trust assets, which are conservatively invested in a wide range of stocks and bonds. *Trust services* are not free; banks will charge about 5 percent (often graduated downward for assets over some figure such as $25,000) of the trust income plus about 0.2 percent of the principal, annually.

The pros and cons of trusts versus other estate settlement methods must be analyzed carefully by comparing costs, the safety of and return on investments, and the restrictions and flexibility of the total plan to meet estate objectives. A balance must usually be struck among estate costs; estate, gift, and income tax savings; freedom from financial management worries; and flexibility.   *NOTE: INVESTMENT ADVISOR IS OMITTED*

The estate planning team. One of the most valuable concepts of estate planning is that with proper forethought the family can have the coordinated services of a whole group of professional experts to help with the complexities of estate creation and liquidation. The *attorney* is, in effect, the captain of the team, which has the goal of building up and using estate values in the best possible manner. The importance of legal documents and procedures makes the attorney's services essential. The accounting and tax aspects may also require the services of an *accountant.* If trusts are used in the estate plan, a bank *trust officer* provides valuable conservation and investment of the estate values. The fourth member of the team, the *life insurance agent,* may be considered one of the most critical choices. Most likely, the agent is the only person who will motivate the family to take the necessary steps to purchase the life insurance that will create much of the estate values and to seek the services of the other estate team members to put the estate plan into effect. As such, the professional agent is indispensable in the usual estate planning process. The agent should not, and cannot, give legal advice or prepare legal documents. However, the life insurance agent should, and can, encourage families to seek the legal help needed to accomplish a sound personal estate plan, using life insurance in many of the ways which have been discussed.

BUSINESS LIFE AND HEALTH INSURANCE PLANNING

Good insurance planning is useful not only in personal estate programming but in many business situations as well. The objective of business life and health insurance is either to maintain a business as a going concern or to retain the values of the business interest for the benefit of an estate following the death or disability of the owner. Insurance is also used to protect the surviving members of a business where the loss or disability of a partner, stockholder, or key employee could: (1) adversely affect control, (2) dissolve the business, or (3) adversely affect its value.

In a closely held business enterprise, numerous relationships must be considered in the event of death and disability. The death or disability of the owner in an individual proprietorship, of one of the owners in a partnership or a small corporation, or of a key employee calls for major financial adjustments. Without adequate funds the disabled person or the deceased owner's estate or the position of survivors, or both, may be adversely affected. Careful planning, combined with the skillful use of life and health insurance, may preserve for all members of a concern substantial values that might be lost otherwise. Two uses of life and health insurance are illustrated by buy-and-sell agreements and key person insurance contracts.

Buy-and-sell agreements

Business life and health insurance, to protect the interest of a deceased or disabled member and at the same time to protect the interest of surviving members, may be arranged in connection with a *buy-and-sell agreement*. This contract provides a sure market for the interest of the deceased or disabled person and a guarantee to survivors of its purchase at a reasonable price with the funds available for payment. It is a form of "business continuation" contract.

The details of the *buy-and-sell agreement*, also known as a purchase-and-sale agreement, must fit the needs of the parties, and will vary with the type of business organization. The names of the parties appear in the agreement, and the purpose is detailed. The agreement will also include either the purchase price or a formula by which it may be determined. All parties commit themselves to the plan for the purchase of the interest of the deceased or disabled associate. The method of financing by the use of life or disability income insurance is set forth; and provision is made for changing the amounts of insurance, if necessary, from time to time. Beneficiary arrangements determine whether the proceeds are to be payable to a trustee who will carry out the transfer or payable directly to the person who, under the agreement, must acquire the business interest of the deceased. There are numerous other details, such as the debts and the rights of termination, withdrawal, or amendment. The agreement, properly drawn, has important benefits for estate tax purposes, for the established values will usually be effective in setting the taxable values at the business interest for the estate. Life and health insurance policies are filed with the agreement. Details are given as to the disposition of the insurance on the life of the surviving associates, as are the rights and privileges under the policies during the lifetime of the insured. The ownership of the contracts may be by the business firm, by the individual partners, or by a trust, depending on the particular business situation.

The carefully drawn buy-and-sell agreement, implemented with life insurance, precludes misunderstanding and provides that the interest of a deceased or disabled associate will be purchased at a fair price. Life and health insurance can be used to make this financially possible at the time of need.

Key person life and health insurance

The principles underlying *key person life and health insurance* for one or more individuals of particular value to a business or organization are essentially the same, regardless of its legal form. The objective of key person insurance is to insure the loss of services caused by the death or disability of a vital employee and to provide resources with which to secure a successor in a competitive market. The insurable value may be determined by estimating the portion of the profits for which the key person is responsible, the cost of replacing and retraining the key person, or the investment that might be lost by the firm. The life and health insurance purchased to cover these costs may be payable to, and be paid by, the organization itself. The premiums are not deductible, but at death of the key person the proceeds paid to the organization are not taxed as income.

Who can be insured as key persons? There can be little doubt of the right of a business or organization to insure its president or manager. Other key employees can likewise be covered: an experienced sales manager; a leading salesperson with many personal clients; a specialist such as an engineer, a chemist, or a researcher; or a person whose management inspires the confidence of financial sources in the business. The list could be expanded to include many other such persons.

In addition to using key person insurance to reimburse the organization for the loss of the services of a particular individual, insurance of this kind has been used as a means for attracting and holding such personnel. Because of the income tax, an increase in salary may be much less attractive than a plan to provide a continuation of salary for a number of years following an employee's death or disability. Frequently, a combination of coverages is provided: indemnity to the organization for the loss of the employee and salary continuation for the employee's dependents. Key person insurance is a valuable and frequently overlooked use of life insurance.

Key person *health* insurance is often neglected. Not only death, but disability as well, can disrupt the operations of a business. Key person disability income insurance can replace the economic loss of an employee's valuable services.

Other life and health insurance which might be considered part of the business field are all the *employee benefit plans* that use insurance as a financing mechanism. These include the *group* coverages for life, health, and annuity insurance, as discussed in Chapters 8 and 10.

FOR REVIEW AND DISCUSSION

1. Insurance programming, as applied to life and health insurance, is part of risk management. Explain this relationship.

2. "Coordination with social security benefits is one of the most important tasks to be accomplished by good life and health insurance programming." Why do you agree with this statement?

3. In planning a life insurance program, explain the extent to which you think the husband should rely upon: (a) investments other than life insurance, (b) work by his wife, (c) his wife's remarriage possibilities in case of his death, and (d) group life insurance coverages?

4. "Health insurance programming is just like life insurance programming." Why would you agree *and* disagree with this comment?

5. Life and health insurance costs for a typical family may average between 5 and 20 percent of annual earnings. Why is there such a substantial difference in the average estimates of cost?

6. "Estate planning is more than merely buying insurance," says a leading estate planning expert. How is this so?

7. Explain how a *will*, the *marital deduction, trusts*, and *gifts* may be used to obtain substantial tax benefits in a family's estate planning.

8. Who are the important members of the "estate planning team," and what part does each play in the estate planning process?

9. A friend of yours comes to you for advice, knowing that you have just completed a course in risk and insurance. He is very confused by the many life and health insurance contracts that are available. Making whatever assumptions are necessary, what recommendations would you give him in regard to:
   a. How should he estimate his life insurance needs and how much life insurance he needs? Show your method of explanation to him as well as the approximate amounts calculated.
   b. What *riders* to the contracts would you suggest or not suggest? *Justify* your recommendations for (or against) at least three riders which are commonly available with life insurance.
   c. Explain the basic health insurance needs he must consider for his family and how you recommend that they be met by insurance.
   d. How might group insurance provide part of the solution to his requirements for life and health protection?

10. Suppose your parents have asked you for advice about social security. What would you tell them about their OASDHI benefits and costs?

11. Mr. Hoenie is 28 years old and has been working for six years since graduating from college. He has a wife and two small children and is employed at an annual salary of $24,000. He has just purchased a home and a new car. The only life insurance he owns is $36,000 of group life through his employer and a $25,000 20-payment life policy that he took out 10 years ago. Making whatever assumptions you consider realistic, discuss the following with reasons for your opinions:

    a. His needs and the types of contracts he should consider so that his family will have proper life and health insurance (outline form).

    b. The relationship of "social security" to his insurance program.

12. You have just had an estate program completed by a qualified chartered life underwriter (CLU).

    a. How could he suggest coordinating your life and health insurance with your savings and investment objectives?

    b. Diagram the relationship of social security (OASDHI) benefits to you and your family as he probably would do in explaining a typical family life and health insurance estate program.

13. What programming benefits can you summarize to a new father, Mr. Z, about his basic *health* insurance needs? What insurance contracts would you recommend? Do you think the "risk manager" at the plant where Mr. Z works could suggest any part of the solutions to his health protection needs?

14. Explain briefly how *business* life and health insurance can be a valuable part of planning by business firms.

15. The Federal Tax Reform Act of 1976 and the Economic Recovery Tax Act of 1981 are said to "have created the need for many changes in estate plans." Cite several examples of why this is true.

Part Three

PROPERTY AND LIABILITY INSURANCE

For the fortunate, their "home is their castle." For many more, their automobile(s) or other personal property are their escape across the moat to independence and mobility. Most persons insure their homes, automobiles, and other property, even before insuring their life and health. Many also make sure that they protect themselves through insurance against the liability they may incur for injuries to other persons or damage to the property of others. Part Three presents the many and varied kinds of *property-liability* insurance which individuals, families, businesses, and other organizations purchase for protection against these risks.

First, the standard *fire* insurance contract and its related forms of *allied lines* are discussed. Next, the forms of *indirect-loss* insurance, which are oftentimes neglected, are presented. *Transportation* (marine) insurance exhibits wide variety. The significant and changing area of *liability* insurance follows. The growing concept of automobile *no-fault* insurance and the *automobile* insurance contract, which everyone needs in our present-day automobile economy, merit treatment in separate chapters. *Crime* insurance and *suretyship,* and *miscellaneous* property and liability insurance, are then discussed, before the popular forms of *multiple-line* personal (homeowner's) and business coverages are treated.

This major section of the text ends with a presentation of the plans of shared private-government protection available through *government*-encouraged insurance for riot, flood, and other perils. In all, a broad package of needed security of the modern consumer of insurance is included for the student to digest and understand.

Chapter 13

Outline of concepts

The standard fire insurance contract is a useful example of one of the most common and relatively uniform insurance coverages. State laws are the most important *method* of achieving the *benefits* of *standardization.*

The basic parts of the New York standard fire policy are presented:

The declarations—statements as to the parties, period, property, perils, and premium of the contract.

The insuring agreement—the heart of the contract as to its: *inception and termination, property and location, personal nature, actual cash value, perils insured against* (*proximate* losses caused by *hostile fires* and *lightning*), and *assignment.*

The conditions and exclusions explain the contract terms as to: *concealment or fraud, excluded property and perils, suspension, added provisions, cancellation,* and *loss provisions* (including *mortgagee* interests, the *pro rata liability* clause, *notice* and *proof* of loss, *appraisal, repair,* and *subrogation* rights).

Fire insurance forms complete the basic fire insurance contract by attachments to the standard policy. These many different forms are illustrated as to their *purpose* (to complete the contract), *preparation and use,* and *types* (specific, blanket, floating, automatic, or schedule).

Clauses, sections of the forms or endorsements, are discussed: *purpose* (to extend, limit, or change the contract); *nuclear, water exclusion, liberalization,* and the *standard mortgage clause;* and the important *coinsurance clause,* discussed as to: *purpose* (to encourage a reasonable relationship of "insurance to value" in order to provide equity among policyholders), *formula and examples* (showing the potential severe penalties), *justification* in the rates, and *valuation problems;* and the *pro rata distribution clause* apportioning coverage among locations.

Endorsements add to the basic contract, for the purpose of modifying it by clarifications, extensions, or limitations, such as *extended coverage* (in most fire insurance contracts, adding such perils as windstorm, riot, explosion, and smoke), *broad form* (broadening and adding new perils), and *special form* endorsements (changing to an "all-risks" basis).

A review of the fire insurance contract shows how, in chart form, the basic parts may be summarized and analyzed.

Special and allied fire lines are: sprinkler leakage, crop, and builder's risk.

Concurrency, the desirable coordination of several insurance contracts through the use of similar wording, is explained in the final section.

Fire insurance

One wonders whether modern society has shown sufficient progress in controlling one of humanity's greatest discoveries—the ability to use fire. Unfortunately, fire is also a formidable enemy. In the United States, more than 5 million fires each year destroy or damage property valued at nearly $7 *billion*. Such losses attest to the cost of carelessness or incomplete control of fire. Examples of current increases in the fire-loss potential permeate our everyday life: high-rise buildings, electricity for modern appliances, billions of cigarettes, arson, and inflammable products of the "plastic age."

Fire insurance is one of the most familiar kinds of insurance. Few persons owning property want to be without its protection. Fire insurance is generally known to its many policyholders, and it is one of the most standardized of all insurance contracts. For many insureds today it is the basis for their homeowner's contract, which is discussed in Chapter 23. Fundamental parts of the basic fire insurance contract, its forms and endorsements, and some "allied lines" are analyzed in this chapter.

THE STANDARD FIRE INSURANCE CONTRACT

The purpose of fire insurance is to indemnify a named insured in the event that certain described properties are destroyed or damaged by the peril of fire. Without insurance, many fire losses could have disastrous financial results for families or businesses. In a contract easily understood by the insurer and the insured, it would appear simple to repay a person for a loss by fire. However, it has taken many years to accomplish today's advantageous uniformity.

The need for standardization

For many years, no standard contract was used by the fire insurers in issuing their contracts, and each home office and sometimes agents were entrusted with this responsibility. Extreme variability appeared, and the contracts became long and complicated. A shorter document, explicit in its provisions and fair to both the insured and the insurer, was vitally necessary to the continued success of the business. Out of the recognition of this need developed the contract which is now referred to as the "standard policy."

Methods

In any field of insurance two basic methods of creating standard insurance contracts are available: voluntary or compulsory. The first is to have insurers by *custom or agreement* use uniform language in the contracts. Many insurance contracts today are standardized to some degree by this method. Even if some of the details of the contract are different, the basic provisions may become quite similar in this way.

The second method is standardization by *legislation* requiring certain contracts or part of contracts to be used by all insurers. In life and health insurance some "standard provisions" are required, although this makes only a small part of such contracts uniform. In property and liability insurance one of the most completely standardized contracts is found in fire insurance. The slow and gradual development of this contract is evidence of the difficulties involved in standardizing a product such as insurance.

Development

An early step toward standardization of the fire insurance contract was undertaken by some insurers, but its adoption was not compulsory. It became evident that in order to be effective, any decided reform must come through legislation. Massachusetts was the first state to adopt a standard policy form (1873), followed by New York (1877), and this form remained unchanged until an amended form was adopted in 1918 and again in 1943. When reference is made to the "standard fire policy" in this text, the "1943 New York form" is indicated. Forty-seven states now make the use of this form mandatory. Massachusetts, Minnesota, and Texas use a somewhat different form, although most of its provisions are similar to those discussed in the following pages.

Benefits

The new form is much simpler and considerably shorter than any of the older standard forms. The standard fire contract benefits the policyholder as follows:

1. Because the basic part of the policy is the same for all contracts, it is unnecessary for the insured to compare every sentence of each contract.

2. A uniform continuity of basic coverage is provided over time and among different insurers.
3. Economy in printing contracts results, because uniform printing of forms is possible for many different insurers.
4. With a standardized form, discrepancies among policies are reduced to a minimum, and loss payments can be made more quickly and easily.
5. The meanings of the terms used in the standard contract are clarified and fixed under a uniform policy as court decisions establish a body of insurance law. Better understanding reduces litigation in regard to policy terms.

Standardization does not extend to all parts of what insureds finally see in their total policy contracts. Parts of the final and complete contract may vary among insureds and insurers. For example, the *declarations* (statements by the insured, rates, property description, etc.) part on the first page will vary in its style and wording. Also, the *forms* and *endorsements* attached to the basic parts of the policy contract may be partially uniform by custom but may be quite different in extending or restricting the coverage to certain perils, places, or properties.

Standardization by law pertains to two essential parts of the contract, the *insuring agreement* and the *conditions and exclusions*. Figures 13–1 and 13–2 in this chapter show the verbatim required language of the 1943 New York standard fire contract. The insuring agreement usually appears on the first page of the policy with the declarations. The conditions (often called stipulations) and exclusions are generally found on the back of the first page of the policy. This chapter discusses in detail the basic parts of the 1943 New York fire contract: first, the declarations; next, the insuring agreement; and then, the conditions and exclusions. The forms, clauses, and endorsements used in connection with the standard contract are introduced in a later section of the chapter.

THE DECLARATIONS

About two thirds of the first page in the New York standard fire policy are devoted to information identifying the insurer and the insured, the duration of the contract, the property and the amounts insured, and the cost for the perils included in the coverage. The section is called the *declarations* because most of the data comes from statements or choices of coverage made by the insured.

Some of the usual information in the declarations section is:

1. The insurer, its address, and the policy number.
2. The insured's name and address.
3. The agent's name and address.

4. A warning that all policies covering the same property must be uniform.
5. A list of the insurance amounts and the rates and premium for each peril which is to be included.
6. The description and location of the property covered.
7. The forms and endorsements attached to the contract.
8. The name of the mortgagee, if there is one, to whom loss will be payable.
9. The date and the signature of the agent writing the contract.

The information in the declarations section may briefly be stated as the *parties, period, property, perils, and premium* of the contract. This classification is often meaningful for analyzing any insurance contract. However, the chronological sequence of the basic parts of the contract is followed here in order to avoid confusion. Under "perils," for example, the discussion would necessarily include part of the declarations, the insuring agreement, the conditions and exclusions, and the forms and endorsements. Toward the end of this chapter, the student may profitably review the whole contract in this type of framework, as shown in Figure 13–3.

THE INSURING AGREEMENT

The fundamental part of any insurance contract is its *insuring agreement,* in which the insurer basically states what it will do and what it will not do. This section of the fire insurance contract is not identified as such, but it is readily discerned as the central part of the agreement. In its paragraphs the insurer obligates itself to indemnify the insured for loss or damage to the described property within a stated period by the specific perils of fire and lightning. The brevity of the insuring agreement as shown in Figure 13–1 should not mislead the student into thinking that it is unimportant. It is the core of the legal agreement between the parties, and each part of the insuring agreement is discussed in the following analysis.

Inception and termination

A contract of insurance need not be in writing. Every day literally thousands of property insurance contracts are made without so much as a scratch of a pen. A policy is ordered by the insured, and the insurance agent agrees that it shall become effective immediately or at a designated time. When insurance coverage of this sort is effected, it is ordinarily for a short period, pending the drawing up and delivery of the formal contract or policy. Insurance in such an instance is said to be "bound."

Figure 13–1. Insuring agreement from first page of 1943 New York standard fire policy

IN CONSIDERATION OF THE PROVISIONS AND STIPULATIONS HEREIN OR ADDED HERETO AND OF the premium above specified, this Company, for the term of *years specified* above from *inception date shown above* At Noon (Standard Time)* to *expiration date shown above* At Noon (Standard Time) at location of property involved, to an amount not exceeding the amount(s) above specified, does insure *the insured named above* and legal representatives, to the extent of the actual cash value of the property at the time of loss, but not exceeding the amount which it would cost to repair or replace the property with material of like kind and quality within a reasonable time after such loss, without allowance for any increased cost of repair or reconstruction by reason of any ordinance or law regulating construction or repair, and without compensation for loss resulting from interruption of business or manufacture, nor in any event for more than the interest of the insured, against all **DIRECT LOSS BY FIRE, LIGHTNING AND BY REMOVAL FROM PREMISES ENDANGERED BY THE PERILS INSURED AGAINST IN THIS POLICY, EXCEPT AS HEREINAFTER PROVIDED,** to the property described herein while located or contained as described in this policy, or pro rata for five days at each proper place to which any of the property shall necessarily be removed for preservation from the perils insured against in this policy, but not elsewhere.

Assignment of this policy shall not be valid except with the written consent of this Company.

This policy is made and accepted subject to the foregoing provisions and stipulations and those hereinafter stated, which are hereby made a part of this policy, together with such other provisions, stipulations and agreements as may be added hereto, as provided in this policy.

* See text for explanation of 1977 change to 12:01 A.M. in many states for new contracts.

Upon receiving an order for insurance, the agent will record the name of the insured, the date on which the insurance is to become effective, the property to be covered, all pertinent information and conditions to be incorporated into the policy, and the amount of insurance (perhaps apportioned among several insurers, with the amount for each indicated). The insurer's liability begins then, unless a future time is stated.

Where written evidence of the agreement is desired, a form called a *binder* is used. Pending delivery of the policy, the binder would ordinarily be given to the insured for a large contract or for one which is to be in effect for a number of days. Fifteen days is a normal maximum of coverage under a binder. When a policy is issued following a binder, it is the custom to date the policy back to the inception date indicated in the original binder.

Under the standard policy, the insurance used to become effective at *noon standard time* (at the place of the property insured) on a given day and was written for a term that expired at noon on a specified day. In 1977 the Insurance Services Office announced revision of most new property insurance contracts to change the inception of coverage to *12:01* A.M. This has been done in most states by statute to conform with liability policies, and the statutes apply to both fire and many package contracts. A few states may still have the old requirement in some of their contracts, but this requirement will gradually disappear.

What happens if a fire has already started in property nearby before the contract becomes effective? The loss is covered as long as the fire reaches the insured property sometime during the term of the policy, regardless of when the fire was originally ignited. An exception might apply if an applicant knew a fire was in progress and concealed this knowledge, for in such case the contract would be voidable by the insurer on the basis of concealment or fraud.

At the time indicated for termination of the policy, the coverage automatically ends—with one exception. If a fire causing damage breaks out before the policy expires, the insurer is liable for all the damage (subject to the maximum policy amount) even though part of the damage is caused by the fire continuing after the normal expiration time.

Most fire insurance contracts are written for one or three years. A discount is not allowed for the longer contracts, and a possible disadvantage of these contracts is that they may increase the likelihood of forgetting to increase the policy amounts to insure changing property values over a period of years.

Fire policies are usually endorsed with a full *reinstatement* of loss clause. The clause is not part of the insuring agreement but is found in added pages of the contract. It provides that any reduction in the amount of the policy because of a loss shall be automatically reinstated to the extent of, and concurrently with, the repair or replacement of the property damaged or destroyed.

Another provision of importance to the determination of the time during which the coverage is in effect is the permission for *cancellation* of the contract. The methods by which cancellation can be accomplished are set forth starting on line 56 of the conditions discussed below.

Property and location

The coverage of *property* is also limited to the listed and described property in the contract. This is usually done in the "declarations" section of the contract, explained previously.

Buildings, machinery, merchandise, household contents, and personal property are all examples of property commonly included in the policy. Both real and personal property may be included in the same contract, but no coverage applies unless the property is named and described.

The contract is also basically a *named location* coverage. It applies only at the location described in the policy, and it would not protect (except with written permission from the insurer) against loss elsewhere if the property were moved. It will be noted later that some of the forms attached to the basic policy do make the coverage applicable automatically to locations other than those specifically named.

Personal nature

The standard fire policy aims at indemnifying the owner of an interest for loss actually sustained to the property insured through the perils insured against. There is no agreement to pay a stated sum. The amount which appears on the face of the policy expresses the limit of the insurer's liability; the amount payable in any situation is determined by measuring the actual loss or damage. This amount is payable, however, not to anyone who may own the property damaged or destroyed but only to the party or parties named in the policy as insured. Property is not insured (as is sometimes stated), but the *person named* in the policy is insured if loss results from the perils covered. The insurance policy is of value primarily to the named insured. Other interests in the property have no interest in the policy or rights under it unless their rights are specifically incorporated into the agreement. Legal representatives, such as heirs or executors of the named insured, are included in the wording of the insuring agreement. Other interests, such as mortgagees, are included only if they are referred to by name in the declarations.

Actual cash value

Fire insurance indemnifies the insured "to the extent of the *actual cash value* of the property at the time of loss. . . ." Regardless of the policy amount, the loss payable is limited to repayment for the real loss sustained. The actual cash value has been defined in many court cases as *the replacement cost new less depreciation.* From the cost of replacing the property new is subtracted a reasonable estimate of actual depreciation due to age, use, and other factors which have reduced the value of the property up to the time of loss. The depreciation amount subtracted is often much less than the "book value" or tax depreciation figures.

Exceptions to the goal of paying actual cash value are the "valued policy" and "valued policy laws" in a few states, as discussed in Chapter 4. Another exception is the *replacement value coverage* sometimes written to insure business buildings, and frequently to insure dwellings, for the full replacement cost (without deduction for depreciation) at the time of the loss. Under the policy terms, replacement value coverage is payable only if the property is rebuilt. Many homeowners' contracts today include this feature if the policyholder has at least 80 percent of the property values insured (see Chapter 23). Some contracts now also insure personal property on a full replacement cost basis, usually for a small additional premium.

However, the basic contract does not undertake to supply "new for old." To do so could create a situation in which the insured might desire to have a loss in order to have new property in place of older property. Such a "profit" could increase the moral hazard of fire insurance and the possibility of arson or fraud.

As used in connection with fire insurance, depreciation includes the element of economic obsolescence. Thus, a property whose "market value" is lessened by changing business conditions, neighborhood changes, and the like, is subject to depreciation when its value is computed for the purpose of loss adjustments. Actual cash value, which represents the actual value of the property destroyed expressed in terms of money, cannot be determined without giving consideration to depreciation of the physical property plus obsolescence.[1]

Repair or replacement costs. Time and other factors frequently become an element in valuation. The policy adds the additional restriction: ". . . but *not exceeding* the amount which it would *cost to repair or replace* the property with material of like kind and quality within a reasonable time after such loss, without allowance for any increased cost of repair or reconstruction by reason of any ordinance or law regulating construction or repair."

When the value exceeds the cost of repairing or replacing, the replacement cost becomes a limit on the amount recoverable. For example, a family moving to a rapidly growing community that is suffering from a housing shortage might be willing to pay considerably more than replacement cost for immediate occupancy. However, this additional cost would not represent insurable value.

The clause limiting the loss to the "cost to repair or replace" is not an option to the insured; rather it expresses a privilege granted *to the insurer.* It places as an upper limit upon the cost, less depreciation, of repairing or replacing the materials that were damaged. The insurer only seldom uses its option to repair or replace, because it is much easier to pay a cash amount than it is to replace or repair property.

The liability of the insurer is not increased if a building law or other factor causes the cost of reconstruction to be more than the normal cost to repair or replace. It sometimes happens that insured property within a municipality fails to meet the requirements of the *local building code* adopted after the building in question was constructed. Fire policies do not cover such increased cost of repairs. For example, rebuilding a frame building in a downtown area may be prohibited. The policy would not pay the increased cost required to rebuild the property with fire-

---

[1] *McCarney* v. *Newark Fire Insurance Co.* et al., 159 N.E. 902.

resistive materials such as brick or steel. Frequently, an ordinance also makes mandatory the demolition of a building when a substantial part of it is destroyed by fire. The New York form thus definitely settles these questions and does not pay for demolition costs or other increased costs incurred because of building codes. A special additional endorsement to the contract is necessary to cover such losses.

Indirect losses.   The insuring clause of the standard fire contract states that it covers "direct loss" and "without compensation for loss resulting from interruption of business." Unless the liability for *indirect* or *consequential* loss is specifically assumed under the contract, such a loss is not covered. Included in the category of indirect losses, which are discussed in Chapter 14, are those arising out of business interruption, such as loss of profit on goods destroyed that might otherwise have been profitably sold. Also, a building rendered unfit for use will deprive its owner of income and its occupant of the use value of the property. Sometimes leases are drawn with a fire clause permitting cancellation by one or both parties in the event of a serious fire. Such a cancellation may deprive an owner or tenant of a valuable long-term lease. Indirect losses may form an important part of any fire loss, but they are not covered in the basic contract unless they are added to the coverage by endorsement.

Insurable interest.   It is the element of insurable interest that takes insurance out of the wagering classification and makes it a contract of indemnity. When the nature of an interest or liability in regard to property is such that the insured would lose financially if a loss occurs, an *insurable interest* exists.

The insuring clause limits the amount that may be recovered to the "interest of the insured." Thus, insureds may not collect unless their interests in the property are such that the damage is actual loss to them. It is the intent of the policy to provide indemnity for loss sustained. A loss payment should not be made to persons who cannot show that they had a financial loss. For example, your neighbors cannot take out insurance on your home and collect for your loss.

Many different persons have insurable interests. Owners of property, mortgagees, bailees, leaseholders, and some creditors are among the more common examples of persons having an insurable interest. Illustrations of the types of losses which can be insured, covering various insurable interests, are: *(a)* loss to buildings, whether the insured has a legal title, an equitable title, or beneficial ownership; *(b)* damage to, or loss of use of, personal property; *(c)* loss of income in the forms of rents; *(d)* the interest of a bailee in the use of property or the bailee's liability for its destruction; *(e)* the interest of a person having a specific lien; *(f)* the interest of a partner in partnership property; *(g)* the liability of a transportation carrier to an owner; *(h)* the interest of a leaseholder if the lease is terminated by fire damage; *(i)* improvements on leased property made by tenants; *(j)* the interest of a mortgagee; and *(k)* the interest of a large majority stockholder in corporate property.

A mere expectancy without a definite legal basis is generally not insurable. A general creditor, therefore, has no insurable interest in the debtor's property unless a secured or specific lien such as a judgment lien has been acquired. A person named in a will as a legatee of property or a relative who may be an heir to an estate has no insurable interest prior to the death. To constitute insurable interest the element of financial loss must be present. If the interest in a property is limited to a hope or an expectancy, there is no insurable interest.

There may be several insurable interests in the same property. Sometimes the loss check is payable to several parties, or "as their interests may appear." The sum of the insurable interests may exceed the total value of the property. Many of the interests described above can be concurrent. Also, insurable interests based on indirect loss to property or on liability are not limited to the value of the property. In order to make the extent of coverage clear, the insurable interest should be definitely stated in the policy contract.

Originally the requirement of an insurable interest was satisfied only if the interest in the property existed both at the time the policy was issued and at the time of the loss. Except in a few states the doctrine has now been modified to recognize as valid a policy issued upon property in which an insurable interest did not exist at the time the policy was issued, but was acquired later and was retained at the time the loss occurred. This rule validates a policy upon a stock of goods that is being increased or changed from time to time. Requiring an insurable interest only at the time of loss also permits coverage on goods in transportation where the insurable interest may not be present now but may come into being as title or responsibility for the goods changes.

Executors, trustees, and heirs are frequently concerned with the validity of the insurance covering the property of the deceased. To make the coverage continuous, the standard contract states in the insuring agreement that the coverage remains effective for the insured's legal representatives in the event of the insured's death.

Perils insured against

The standard fire contract is a *named perils* or *specified* perils contract. This means that it covers only the listed perils described in the contract. In the basic part of the contract, these perils are *"fire, lightning,* and by *removal* from premises endangered by the perils insured against in this policy." Other perils are not covered, unless they are added in the forms or endorsements. The "extended coverage" perils of wind, explosion, smoke, riot, and others are a common addition.

Fire defined. The standard fire policy provides insurance primarily "against all direct loss by fire." The word *fire* is not defined in the contract but has been explained in detail as the courts have interpreted its full meaning. A frequently cited court definition serves as a basis for resolving doubtful cases. The case concerned spontaneous combustion in wet wool. Defining "fire," the court said; "Spontaneous combustion is usually a rapid oxidation. Fire is oxidation which is so rapid as to produce either flame or a glow. Fire is always caused by combustion, but combustion does not always cause fire. The word 'spontaneous' refers to the origin of the combustion. It means the internal development of heat without the action of an external agent. Combustion or spontaneous combustion may be so rapid as to produce fire, but until it does so, combustion cannot be said to be fire."[2]

The presence of heat, steam, or even smoke is evidence of fire, but taken by itself it will not prove the existence of fire. Unless accompanied by ignition, heat sufficient to cause charring or scorching does not constitute fire. To constitute fire, combustion must proceed at a rate sufficiently fast to produce a flame, a glow, or incandescence. Regardless of the amount of heat, there can be no fire until ignition takes place. The loss resulting from a sizable hole burned in a couch would probably be covered even though no one was there to see the fire. A small scorch on a table, caused by a cigarette, would not meet the definition of a fire.

Friendly and unfriendly fires. The insurance contract promises indemnity for loss arising from the happening of an unfavorable contingency. The element of accident in the cause is essential. Hence, a fire deliberately kindled and remaining within the limits intended for it is termed a *friendly fire,* and any damage that it may do is not covered by the fire policy. However, when a fire spreads beyond the confines intended for it and beyond the control of its custodian, it becomes an *unfriendly fire,* and the damage it causes is an insured loss.

The flame of a fire in a stove, a fireplace, or a furnace is regarded as a friendly fire. Damage from such fires in the form of smoke, soot, or heat is not covered by the fire policy. Thus, a cooking fire or an oil stove left burning in a room may smoke and send soot throughout the premises, but the loss is not covered by the basic fire policy. On the other hand, if the fire escapes from the confines in which it is intended that it remain, the fire becomes unfriendly (hostile), and the fire policy covers whatever damage is thus done. Consequently, if a breeze blows a curtain against the flame in a fireplace and the curtain burns, the property thus destroyed is covered.

Direct loss. The insuring agreement specifies that to be covered under the policy a loss must be a *direct* loss. This has been construed by the courts to mean that fire must be the immediate or *proximate* cause

---

[2] *Western Woolen Mills Company* v. *Northern Assurance Co.,* 139 Fed. 637.

of the loss as distinguished from the remote cause. Examples of losses included in the term *direct* or *proximate* are: loss or damage caused by smoke or heat from a hostile fire; damage by water or other materials used to extinguish the fire; damage caused by the fire fighters; and unavoidable exposure at or following the fire.

The proximate cause is held to be the efficient cause; that is, the cause which sets intervening agencies in motion. A proximate cause of loss need not be the nearest in time or in the sequence of events if it is the superior or controlling agency. A fire may be the direct cause of a loss or damage even though some intervening agency may form part of the chain of circumstances set in motion by the fire. For example, it was held that a fire in the tower of a building where it was confined with but slight damage was the proximate cause of a large machinery loss in a part of the building remote from the fire. The fire in the tower burned electric wires that caused a short circuit which in turn caused a general breakdown of the machinery. The entire loss was held to be by fire. In another case a ship caught fire and sank following a collision before the goods on board, which had been insured against loss by fire, had burned. Because the fire prevented the use of the available means for saving the boat, fire was held to be the proximate cause of the loss.

There are numerous examples of cases in which fire has been held to be the direct cause of the damage growing out of the collapse of walls which formed a part of ruins. When a building was destroyed by fire and part of the ruined walls fell two days later, damaging a neighboring property, the insurer covering the second property was held liable for a fire loss. If the walls fall two weeks after a fire, however, fire would not typically be considered the proximate cause of loss.

There are limits to the interpretation of the term *proximate*. If a fire truck on the way to a fire accidentally strikes and damages a store, the fire is not held to be the controlling agency, and the fire insurers of the store owner are not responsible for the loss. The cause of the accident and the cause of the fire are held to be independent. Damage to the store by the fire truck is attributable to the accident or its cause (such as speed, slippery streets, or other factors) and not to the fire to which the fire fighters were going.

It has been held that where fire spreads to an insured building and there causes an explosion, the insurer is liable for all the damage. On the other hand, in the case of an explosion caused by a fire, concussion damage to neighboring properties is not covered by their basic fire policies. (Those contracts including explosion in the extended coverage endorsement, discussed later, would cover such a loss.)

Whether or not the policy covers in a given situation resolves itself into a determination of the intent of the contracting parties. In what is now held to be a leading case on proximate cause, Justice Cardozo says: "Our guide is the reasonable expectation and purpose when making an ordinary contract."[3] Fire must reach the thing insured or come within such proximity to it that the damage is within the compass of reasonable probability. Then, fire is the proximate cause because it was within the contemplation of the contract.

These examples pertain only to property insurance. The basic idea of proximate cause is also applied in liability insurance, but its application to specific examples of how far the responsibility for loss by the wrongdoer or the insurer extends may differ.

Lightning. The 1943 New York standard policy includes loss by *lightning* as well as by fire in the insuring clause of the policy. Lightning is frequently the cause of serious loss, either directly or by setting property on fire. In earlier contracts (which did not cover lightning), the difficulty of determining at what point the lightning damage ended and the fire loss began was eliminated by including both perils specifically in the contract.

Lightning is the natural discharge of electricity from the atmosphere. It does not include artificial electrical energy which sometimes causes damage to television sets, appliances, or other property.

Loss by removal. The loss incurred by removing property endangered by the perils insured against has been definitely assumed under the terms of the New York standard policy. The insured is obligated to do everything reasonable to save threatened property. When damage is sustained in the *removal,* the fire would normally be considered the direct and proximate cause, and the insurer, therefore, is liable. To avoid any doubt the contract specifically lists removal as a covered peril.

The removal must be deemed reasonably necessary, and the threatened danger must be of a nature that would prompt careful and prudent uninsured persons to take like actions in their own interests. Losses caused by breakage and exposure to weather during the process of removal are cause for proper claims. Losses by theft are specifically excluded later in the contract (line 24).[4] However, most courts have allowed coverage for theft in circumstances in which the losses were immediate and the insured acted prudently. A common example is theft by bystanders taking property at or near the scene of the fire.

The insurance follows the property to whatever point it is removed and continues in effect in the new location. The values are covered pro rata, or proportionally, on the old location and on each new location for a period of five days after the fire. When the five-day period has elapsed, insureds will be without insurance as to the new locations, unless they obtain new coverage.

---

[3] *Bird* v. *St. Paul Fire & Marine Insurance Company,* 224 N.Y. 47, 120 N.E. 86.

[4] The following references to lines are to the numbered 165 lines of the back page of the 1943 New York standard fire policy reproduced in Figure 13–2.

Assignment

The transfer of the legal right or interest in an insurance contract to another person is called an *assignment*. Under the terms of the fire insurance contract, an assignment is valid only with the written consent of the insurer. An exception is the case of an assignment of rights to a claim after a loss has occurred. In many other contracts, assignment may be done without the consent of the other party, unless a statute or a contract provision restricts it.

It sometimes happens that with the sale of an insured property, it is desired to transfer insurance to the new owner. This can be accomplished by having the policy endorsed with the insurer's consent as well as the insured's assignment of interest. This can be potentially dangerous, as the new owner cannot take over any more rights than the seller had under the policy. (The seller may have violated some conditions of the policy, for example.) Another method is to have the policy delivered to the insurer or its agent with the request that the insured under the policy be changed and the coverage transferred from the insured named in the policy to the newly designated insured. An endorsement is used, stating that the interest of the named insured has on that date terminated and that the insurance shall continue in effect for the benefit of the new insured. The relationship between the two original parties is terminated, and a new contractual relationship is established. Probably the best method of protecting the new owner's interest in the property is to have a new insurance contract effective when the property is sold and to have the former owner's policy canceled.

THE CONDITIONS AND EXCLUSIONS

Concealment or fraud

It is provided on lines 1–6 (see Figure 13–2) that the entire policy shall be void if, whether before or after a loss, the insured willfully conceals or misrepresents any material facts or circumstances concerning the fire insurance, the property insured, or its interests, or in case of any fraud by the insured. The courts have held that the word *void* should be interpreted as *voidable* (at the option of the insurer).

An example of *misrepresentation* is a false statement in the declarations, such as stating that the building is "brick, with noncombustible roof, used as a single-family dwelling." It might be considered a *material* (important) misrepresentation if the building was actually a frame one, or had a combustible roof, or was occupied by several families.

Fraud frequently occurs in connection with the adjustment of claims. Examples include incorrect loss statements, concealment of salvage, falsification of records, false testimony given under oath, and false written proofs of loss. It has sometimes been offered as a defense that the false statements made in connection with the claim were for some purpose other than to defraud the insurers, such as to substantiate statements previously made to a credit company. The courts have held, however, that such a false statement is still fraud. Another example of fraud is *arson*, in which the insured intentionally sets fire, or has another person set fire, to the insured property for the purpose of collecting a loss payment. Unfortunately, such losses have increased greatly in recent years, with between 11 and 40 percent of fires estimated to have seen set deliberately.[5] The insurer is not liable for such losses, if arson is proved. However, arson by a stranger, not acting under the direction of the insured, is covered.

Excluded property

Certain types of property are excepted from the coverage of the policy, while other types are uninsurable in any case. On lines 7–10, the policy reads: "This policy shall not cover accounts, bills, currency, deeds, evidences of debt, money, or securities; nor, unless specifically named hereon in writing, bullion or manuscripts." If bullion or manuscripts are to be included in the coverage, they must be specifically mentioned. With the exception of these articles, personal property in which an insurable interest exists may be covered.

The forms added to the contract must also be read carefully for excepted property such as automobiles, which are often excluded. Some contracts specifically include coverage on money or other of the above items which are excluded in the standard fire policy. For example, the homeowners' contracts often cover up to $100 on money and $500 on securities. Commercial risks can use the broad form money and securities policy, or accounts receivable or valuable papers contracts to insure such items.

Excluded perils

Lines 11–24 name several perils which are excluded from the standard contract, including *war* (in its various forms), some orders for destruction by *civil authorities, neglect* by the insured to prevent further damage, and *theft*.

---

[5] Based on a 1980 study of 13,418 claims settled in 1980, the All-Industry Research and Advisory Council (AIRAC), the percent of suspected arson fires is 11 percent in the residential voluntary insurance market and 27 percent in the commercial voluntary market. For Fair Access to Insurance Requirements (FAIR) plans, the percent increases to 30 and 40 percent respectively, for a total cost for the claims studied of nearly $600 million. See "Arson: What it Costs, Who's to Blame," *Journal of American Insurance*, Summer 1982, p. 13.

Figure 13–2. Conditions and exclusions from back of first page of 1943 New York standard fire policy

1 **Concealment,** This entire policy shall be void if, whether
2 **fraud.** before or after a loss, the insured has wil-
3 fully concealed or misrepresented any ma-
4 terial fact or circumstance concerning this insurance or the
5 subject thereof, or the interest of the insured therein, or in case
6 of any fraud or false swearing by the insured relating thereto.
7 **Uninsurable** This policy shall not cover accounts, bills,
8 **and** currency, deeds, evidences of debt, money or
9 **excepted property.** securities; nor, unless specifically named
10 hereon in writing, bullion or manuscripts.
11 **Perils not** This Company shall not be liable for loss by
12 **included.** fire or other perils insured against in this
13 policy caused, directly or indirectly, by: (a)
14 enemy attack by armed forces, including action taken by mili-
15 tary, naval or air forces in resisting an actual or an immediately
16 impending enemy attack; (b) invasion; (c) insurrection; (d)
17 rebellion; (e) revolution; (f) civil war; (g) usurped power; (h)
18 order of any civil authority except acts of destruction at the time
19 of and for the purpose of preventing the spread of fire, provided
20 that such fire did not originate from any of the perils excluded
21 by this policy; (i) neglect of the insured to use all reasonable
22 means to save and preserve the property at and after a loss, or
23 when the property is endangered by fire in neighboring prem-
24 ises; (j) nor shall this Company be liable for loss by theft.
25 **Other Insurance.** Other insurance may be prohibited or the
26 amount of insurance may be limited by en-
27 dorsement attached hereto.
28 **Conditions suspending or restricting insurance. Unless other-**
29 wise provided in writing added hereto this Company shall not
30 be liable for loss occurring
31 (a) while the hazard is increased by any means within the con-
32 trol or knowledge of the insured; or
33 (b) while a described building, whether intended for occupancy
34 by owner or tenant, is vacant or unoccupied beyond a period of
35 sixty consecutive days; or
36 (c) as a result of explosion or riot, unless fire ensue, and in
37 that event for loss by fire only.
38 **Other perils** Any other peril to be insured against or sub-
39 **or subjects.** ject of insurance to be covered in this policy
40 shall be by endorsement in writing hereon or
41 added hereto. ·
42 **Added provisions.** The extent of the application of insurance
43 under this policy and of the contribution to
44 be made by this Company in case of loss, and any other pro-
45 vision or agreement not inconsistent with the provisions of this
46 policy, may be provided for in writing added hereto, but no pro-
47 vision may be waived except such as by the terms of this policy
48 is subject to change.
49 **Waiver** No permission affecting this insurance shall
50 **provisions.** exist, or waiver of any provision be valid,
51 unless granted herein or expressed in writing
52 added hereto. No provision, stipulation or forfeiture shall be
53 held to be waived by any requirement or proceeding on the part
54 of this Company relating to appraisal or to any examination
55 provided for herein.
56 **Cancellation** This policy shall be cancelled at any time
57 **of policy.** at the request of the insured, in which case
58 this Company shall, upon demand and sur-
59 render of this policy, refund the excess of paid premium above
60 the customary short rates for the expired time. This pol-
61 icy may be cancelled at any time by this Company by giving
62 to the insured a five days' written notice of cancellation with
63 or without tender of the excess of paid premium above the pro
64 rata premium for the expired time, which excess, if not ten-
65 dered, shall be refunded on demand. Notice of cancellation shall
66 state that said excess premium (if not tendered) will be re-
67 funded on demand.
68 **Mortgagee** If loss hereunder is made payable, in whole
69 **interests and** or in part, to a designated mortgagee not
70 **obligations.** named herein as the insured, such interest in
71 this policy may be cancelled by giving to such
72 mortgagee a ten days' written notice of can-
73 cellation.
74 If the insured fails to render proof of loss such mortgagee, upon
75 notice, shall render proof of loss in the form herein specified
76 within sixty (60) days thereafter and shall be subject to the pro-
77 visions hereof relating to appraisal and time of payment and of
78 bringing suit. If this Company shall claim that no liability ex-
79 isted as to the mortgagor or owner, it shall, to the extent of pay-
80 ment of loss to the mortgagee, be subrogated to all the mort-
81 gagee's rights of recovery, but without impairing mortgagee's
82 right to sue; or it may pay off the mortgage debt and require
83 an assignment thereof and of the mortgage. Other provisions

84 relating to the interests and obligations of such mortgagee may
85 be added hereto by agreement in writing.
86 **Pro rata liability.** This Company shall not be liable for a greater
87 proportion of any loss than the amount
88 hereby insured shall bear to the whole insurance covering the
89 property against the peril involved, whether collectible or not.
90 **Requirements in** The insured shall give immediate written
91 **case loss occurs.** notice to this Company of any loss, protect
92 the property from further damage, forthwith
93 separate the damaged and undamaged personal property, put
94 it in the best possible order, furnish a complete inventory of
95 the destroyed, damaged and undamaged property, showing in
96 detail quantities, costs, actual cash value and amount of loss
97 claimed; and within sixty days after the loss, unless such time
98 is extended in writing by this Company, the insured shall render
99 to this Company a proof of loss, signed and sworn to by the
100 insured, stating the knowledge and belief of the insured as to
101 the following: the time and origin of the loss, the interest of the
102 insured and of all others in the property, the actual cash value of
103 each item thereof and the amount of loss thereto, all encum-
104 brances thereon, all other contracts of insurance, whether valid
105 or not, covering any of said property, any changes in the title,
106 use, occupation, location, possession or exposures of said prop-
107 erty since the issuing of this policy, by whom and for what
108 purpose any building herein described and the several parts
109 thereof were occupied at the time of loss and whether or not it
110 then stood on leased ground, and shall furnish a copy of all the
111 descriptions and schedules in all policies and, if required, verified
112 plans and specifications of any building, fixtures or machinery
113 destroyed or damaged. The insured, as often as may be reason-
114 ably required, shall exhibit to any person designated by this
115 Company all that remains of any property herein described, and
116 submit to examinations under oath by any person named by this
117 Company, and subscribe the same; and, as often as may be
118 reasonably required, shall produce for examination all books of
119 account, bills, invoices and other vouchers, or certified copies
120 thereof if originals be lost, at such reasonable time and place as
121 may be designated by this Company or its representative, and
122 shall permit extracts and copies thereof to be made.
123 **Appraisal.** In case the insured and this Company shall
124 fail to agree as to the actual cash value or
125 the amount of loss, then, on the written demand of either, each
126 shall select a competent and disinterested appraiser and notify
127 the other of the appraiser selected within twenty days of such
128 demand. The appraisers shall first select a competent and dis-
129 interested umpire; and failing for fifteen days to agree upon
130 such umpire, then, on request of the insured or this Company,
131 such umpire shall be selected by a judge of a court of record in
132 the state in which the property covered is located. The ap-
133 praisers shall then appraise the loss, stating separately actual
134 cash value and loss to each item, and, failing to agree, shall
135 submit their differences, only, to the umpire. An award in writ-
136 ing, so itemized, of any two when filed with this Company shall
137 determine the amount of actual cash value and loss. Each
138 appraiser shall be paid by the party selecting him and the ex-
139 penses of appraisal and umpire shall be paid by the parties
140 equally.
141 **Company's** It shall be optional with this Company to
142 **options.** take all, or any part, of the property at the
143 agreed or appraised value, and also to re-
144 pair, rebuild or replace the property destroyed or damaged with
145 other of like kind and quality within a reasonable time, on giv-
146 ing notice of its intention so to do within thirty days after the
147 receipt of the proof of loss herein required.
148 **Abandonment.** There can be no abandonment to this Com-
149 pany of any property.
150 **When loss** The amount of loss for which this Company
151 **payable.** may be liable shall be payable sixty days
152 after proof of loss, as herein provided, is
153 received by this Company and ascertainment of the loss is made
154 either by agreement between the insured and this Company ex-
155 pressed in writing or by the filing with this Company of an
156 award as herein provided.
157 **Suit.** No suit or action on this policy for the recov-
158 ery of any claim shall be sustainable in any
159 court of law or equity unless all the requirements of this policy
160 shall have been complied with, and unless commenced within
161 twelve months next after inception of the loss.
162 **Subrogation.** This Company may require from the insured
163 an assignment of all right of recovery against
164 any party for loss to the extent that payment therefor is made
165 by this Company.

In order to eliminate catastrophic war risks, all fire policies also specifically exclude loss caused by: (1) *Hostile or warlike action*[6] in time of peace or war, including action in defending against an actual, impending, or expected attack by an actual or proclaimed government or sovereign power; or by military, naval, or air forces; or by an agent of any such government or forces; or by any use by such a government of a weapon of war employing nuclear fission or fusion. (2) *Insurrection,* rebellion, revolution, civil war, usurped power, or action taken by governmental authority in hindering, combating, or defending against such an occurrence. The difficulties of defining a term such as war are obvious in the lengthy description of the actions associated with the term.

The importance of the exclusion for insurrection increased following the Los Angeles, Detroit, Newark, Chicago, and other riots of the 1960s and 1970s. An "insurrection" has usually been defined by the courts as including the attempt to overthrow the government, while losses from "riots" are often limited to injury to, damage to, or theft of specific persons or property. Public officials have generally avoided calling any disturbance, however widespread or illegal, an insurrection, for fear of permitting insurers to decline coverage.

The danger of assuming unpredictable risks which are not accidental in nature leads to the exclusion of property *destruction by civil authorities.* The exclusion does not apply to orders for destruction made to prevent the spread of a fire, such as the dynamiting of a block of houses to stop a conflagration. These losses would be covered, but others, such as the condemnation of a building by health authorities, are excluded.

The insured must be reasonably prudent in doing all that can be done at and after a loss to prevent as much damage as possible. The insured cannot *neglect to prevent further damage,* although this does not require unwise exposure to personal danger in a loss. Neither does this require the insured to act with perfect wisdom in the face of an emergency situation. Examples of unreasonable actions which might deny coverage are: (1) not attempting to obtain nearby available help in removing endangered property from a building; (2) failing to turn in a fire alarm as soon as possible; or (3) not arranging to have property, such as machinery, dried off after a fire to prevent rust damage. The cost of removal or protection to prevent further damage after a fire would be includable in the insured's claim for loss.

Theft is specifically excluded as a peril covered in the fire insurance

---

[6] This phrase was tested in the courts in connection with the 1970 hijacking of a $25 million 747 airplane which was flown to Cairo and blown up by several Palestinians. The courts decided that this action was not "war" because it was not performed by governmental groups, but by a small political activist group. See "What Is a War?" *Time,* October 1, 1973, p. 112. Similar acts have caused other aircraft losses, including a DC-10 loss in Pakistan in 1981.

contract. Occasionally such losses may be covered as proximately (closely) related to other covered perils such as fire or riot, but the intent is to exclude all other normal theft losses.

Suspension

In order to protect the insurer with respect to changes in the risk, the coverage is suspended in certain situations. These policy conditions, on lines 28–37, are for the most part concerned with an increase in the hazard. They do not have the effect of voiding the policy permanently but rather act to suspend or restrict the insurance coverage temporarily. When the conditions that suspend the coverage no longer prevail, the insurance reverts to full force and effect.

When the risk is written and the rate fixed, it is assumed that the risk will remain constant during the life of the policy. If there is any important change, the insurer should have the opportunity to either cancel the policy or secure a higher premium. In every case what does constitute an *increase in the hazard* is a matter of fact, and hence in litigated cases it is a matter for the jury to decide. A change in occupancy, for example, having a business such as a dry cleaning shop in a dwelling, would probably be considered sufficient to suspend the insurance. Storage of five gallons of gasoline in the garage of a dwelling would not be called an important increase in hazard, but a thousand gallons might be.

The standard policy definitely incorporates a few special situations which increase the risk to a degree that warrants a suspension of the coverage. *Vacancy* for more than 60 days is one such increased hazard. However, many policies include coverage for some usual or incidental vacancy or unoccupancy in the wording of an attached form.

In the event of *riot* and *explosion,* the policy is not technically suspended but loss is restricted to damage by fire only. The basic policy does not cover sabotage, vandalism, and other like damage that might originate from a riot. In the case of both riot and explosion, if a property is partly demolished and a fire follows, the fire policy is not responsible for the wreckage caused before the fire but only for the loss caused by the fire to the property in its wrecked condition. Today, the difficulty of differentiating such losses is avoided in most contracts because they *include* explosion and riot perils specifically in commonly used endorsements to the fire policy. The best known of these is the "extended coverage" endorsement which is a part of about 9 out of 10 fire insurance contracts.

Added perils and provisions

The standard contract is adaptable to include additional perils, properties, and provisions. Emphasis is placed in lines 38–55 on the fact that such additions must be made in writing and attached to the basic policy. Since the basic policy is designed for use in connection with all classes of property and nearly every known insurable interest, it is impossible to have one complete contract that meets all needs. The policy thus permits covering perils other than fire, lightning, and removal and refers in the insuring clause to "the perils insured against in this policy." To allow for the inclusion of further perils, lines 38–41 provide: "Any other peril to be insured against or subject of insurance to be covered in this policy shall be by endorsement in writing hereon or added hereto."

Insurers have found that it is often necessary to clarify further the extent of the coverage. On lines 42–48 they have incorporated a further clause permitting endorsements. The policy is arranged with a blank page for the attachment of these additions. In this space is attached first of all an addition known as a *form*. It often includes several pages containing a detailed description of the types of property to be insured. Frequently included are a number of *clauses* pertinent to the particular contract and the risk to be insured. These clauses modify the coverage in various ways. *Endorsements* may also be added extending the coverage to include such perils as windstorm or explosion, or to include other extensions or restrictions on the policy coverage.

The standard policy, on lines 49–55, requires that *waivers* be in writing to be effective. The courts have held, however, that just as other provisions of the policy may be waived by anyone with authority to do so, so may the one that requires waivers to be in writing. Thus, in spite of the antiwaiver provision, the insured may occasionally prove that an oral waiver contradicts or modifies the written terms of the policy.

Cancellation

The *insured* may at any time have the policy canceled. No advance notice is required but the policy must be surrendered on demand. A penalty is applied, for the premium to be returned by the insurer represents the balance after charging for the expired term on the *short-rate* basis. For example, a one-year contract canceled after 180 days would cost 55 percent rather than one half of the premium. If the policy has been canceled as a convenience to both parties and is being renewed with the same insurer for the same or a greater amount, it is the custom to charge the earned premium on the *pro rata* rather than the short-rate basis. An example of this distinction follows: Suppose a three-year contract for $300 is canceled after six months. Because proportionally one sixth of the coverage duration has been used up, the pro rata return premium would be $300 less $50, or $250. If the insured requests the cancellation, the short-rate return premium would be $300 less $55, or $245. The smaller return to the insured is justified by expense and adverse selection against the insurer, as the insureds more likely to cancel are those that are less apt to have losses.

When cancellation is ordered by the *insurer,* five days' notice must be given every named insured or interest. In the case of a mortgagee, the policy provides on lines 68–73 that the policy may be canceled by giving such mortgagee a 10 days' written notice of cancellation. When the insurer cancels, only a pro rata premium, as illustrated previously, may be charged.

The New York standard form makes cancellation effective without the insurer actually paying the return premium, provided that the insured is told that a return premium is payable upon request. The cancellation does not become effective until five days after its actual receipt by the insured. The day on which the notice is received is excluded. The insured may be given the notice personally, or it may be sent by mail. Registered mail and return receipts are often used. Some forms fold into envelopes, thereby avoiding the possibility of the insured's claiming to have received an empty envelope.

Loss provisions

All of the remaining conditions and exclusions pertain to rights of and conditions on the parties to the contract after a loss has occurred. The importance of these sections of the required 165 lines in the standard policy is indicated by the fact that more than one half of the lines enumerate provisions which apply following a loss.

Mortgagee conditions after a loss are discussed on lines 74–85. The mortgagee should file proof of loss if the owner does not. If the loss is partial, the insurer may pay the whole mortgage to the mortgagee and take over any rights against the mortgagor. The same subrogation right applies if the insurer pays the mortgagee when the mortgagor is not entitled to payment of the loss, such as in the case of a policy violation. Other mortgage provisions are often included in the forms attached to the basic part of the contract. (See a later section of this chapter for discussion of the standard mortgage clause in the dwelling building and contents form.)

An important limitation on the payment made by the insurer for a loss appears on lines 86–89. The *pro rata liability clause* limits the liability of the insurer by stating that "this Company shll not be liable for a greater proportion of any loss than the amount hereby insured shall bear to the whole insurance covering the property against the peril involved, whether collectible or not." Thus, if insurer A had $100,000 fire insurance on a building and insurer B had $50,000 on the same building, each insurer would pay a proportionate share of any loss. If the loss were $90,000, insurer A would pay two thirds, or $60,000, and insurer B would pay one third, or $30,000, of the loss. The purpose of the pro rata liability clause is to prevent double payment of a loss to the insured, which would be a violation of the indemnity principle. Since more than one policy contract is a common occurrence in fire insurance, it is necessary that insurers specify by the wording that they will pay only their proportionate share of a loss.

Lines 90–122 list certain actions which should be taken following a loss. The acts are conditions which should be met as specified, or the insured may not be able to collect any claim against the insurer. The insured should do the following (or see that they are done by someone else):

1. Give immediate written *notice* of the loss. (Oral notification to the agent is usually held sufficient.)
2. *Protect* the property from further damage.
3. *Separate* the damaged and undamaged property.
4. Furnish an *inventory* of the damaged property, its costs, values, and losses sustained.
5. Render a written *proof of loss* within 60 days, including detailed information about the loss (its time, origin, insurable interests, occupancies, insurance contracts in force, and so on).[7]
6. Exhibit to the insurer the property and books of account.

Although seldom used, *appraisal* proceedings are provided for on lines 123–40. Either insurer or insured may ask for an appraisal if they do not agree on the loss amount. Each selects an appraiser, and the two appraisers choose an umpire who settles any differences in the two appraisals of loss. The method sometimes avoids resorting to the courts for determination of a difficult loss settlement.

The following section (lines 141–47) states again the optional right of the insurer to *repair, rebuild, or replace* the property destroyed or damaged with like kind and quality of materials. As noted earlier, this right is rarely exercised. It does act as a ceiling on payment, however, in case an insured refuses to accept a reasonable loss payment. The insured *may not abandon* damaged property to the insurer and claim a total loss (lines 148–49). The *loss* is *payable* by the insurer *within 60 days after proof of loss* is received (lines 150–56), though most losses are paid well in advance of that required time. According to lines 157–61, the insured *may not sue* the insurer until all the policy requirements have been complied with or *after one year* following the loss.

The final section of the New York standard policy incorporates the doctrine of *subrogation* into the policy with this clause: "This Company may require from the insured an assignment of all right of recovery against any party for loss to the extent that payment therefore is made

---

[7] In New York State, by statute the companies must request the proof of loss from the insured.

by this Company." Though the right of subrogation exists without being expressly stated, the insurer is thus protected from having this right destroyed by action of the insured. The insured should be extremely careful that after a loss no rights of recovery against another party are waived, for such action by the insured might void the policy.

Although subrogation cases are much rarer in fire insurance than in automobile or liability insurance, there are some situations in which the insured's right of action against a negligent third party is extremely valuable to the insurer. For example, a careless neighbor may cause fire damage to your garage by burning leaves too close to your property. Your fire insurer would pay your loss but would expect to take over your rights to sue the neighbor. Likewise, a landlord's insurer may pay the loss but sue a tenant who has carelessly caused a fire. Another example frequently arises when repair or renovation work is done. Suppose the electrician is negligent and sets fire to your property. Again, your insurer will pay your loss but will expect to have the opportunity to bring action against the electrician or the contractor for recovery of its loss payment. The result is fair: the wrongdoer is ultimately held responsible for the loss, and fire insurance cost is kept lower by reducing the loss to the insurer.

FIRE INSURANCE FORMS

Fire insurance contracts are not completely standardized, but state laws make the insuring agreement, conditions, and exclusions uniform in the basic part of the policy. In the total contract, substantial differences appear in the forms, clauses, and endorsements which are attached to and become a part of the fire insurance contract. By these additions the contract is completed, clarified, and extended or restricted to meet the needs of the many different policyholders that purchase fire insurance.

Some of these additional parts of the contract are uniform and used with many policies. Rating bureaus and insurer customs help provide considerable standardization of some forms and endorsements. Most states require the insurance commissioner to approve these additions, and uniformity and fair wording are encouraged. Many other forms and endorsements are highly individualistic, varying among different insurers or insureds to meet specific purposes. This section reviews the more common ones.

Purpose

The statutory fire contract has been seen to include the insuring agreement and the conditions and exclusions. The declarations section precedes the statutory wording. A *form* is usually necessary to complete the contract.[8] It contains information essential to clarifying the terms of the policy, including a description of the types of property to be insured and a number of clauses pertinent to the particular contract. The insuring agreement and the stipulations and conditions are general in their application. By means of the form, the contract is tailored to the specific risks and the particular needs of the insured.

Preparation and use

Standard forms are prepared by rating organizations, each form designed for a particular class of risk. Many rating bureaus prepare 50 or more such forms for different groups or classifications of property. There are forms for dwellings, stores, farms, apartments, manufacturing or mercantile properties, and many others.

The wording of the form is not prescribed by statute. Spaces are often left for typing details, such as the name and address of the insured, the amount of insurance, and special definitions of the property insured. Where this satisfies the needs of an individual insured, the form may be mimeographed, typed, or even handwritten, but for the usual type of risk it is the general practice to use the printed standard forms.

Forms take precedence over the basic standard fire policy, but printed endorsements (see later section for examples of these) override forms. Also, any typewritten or handwritten wording, either in a printed document or its margin, would override printed matter. The wording which is most specific, or which most clearly reflects the intent of the contracting parties, is effective.

If there is no standard form available to meet special needs, it is quite customary in the case of sizable business risks to prepare and print such a form. Where this is done, the approval of the rating authority must be obtained before the form can be used. This approval serves two purposes. The form must afford the benefits of various liberalizing clauses and the protection expected by the insured. On the other hand, the form must also be checked to prevent discrimination against other insureds through an extension of the coverage not provided for in the rating structure.

It is easy to confuse the modifications permitted in the form with the terms and conditions of the basic policy itself. Certain coverages and privileges, as well as certain restrictions and conditions, originate

---

[8] Although still generally true, newer dwelling property forms used in many states under the Insurance Services Office (ISO) program since 1977 feature simplified language and incorporate the provisions of the standard fire policy (previously discussed) *into the form itself.* Several types of these forms are used, including "basic," "broad form," and "special form."

in the form attached to the policy. It is therefore essential where coverage includes a number of policies on the same property to have all the policies carefully checked and to see that the forms are identical.

Types

Although dozens of forms are used in connection with the fire contract, the form will fall into one of the following five categories: *specific, blanket, floater, automatic* or *reporting,* and *schedule.* The individual or family purchaser of insurance will usually be concerned only with the first type, the specific form. The other four types are used mostly for insuring business properties.

Specific coverage. The *specific form* is the most common type in use. It covers primarily one kind of property in one definite location. An example of this type of form is the *dwelling building and contents form,* which has several variations. Sample policy kits containing current editions of these forms are available, as noted in the Preface of this book. (Some newer forms are called *dwelling property* forms.)

The dwelling building and contents forms clarify the coverages, and in addition, they provide some important extensions of coverage. The term *dwelling* as used in the declarations is defined to include the building, attached structures, and outdoor equipment. *Contents* includes all household and family personal property, with a few exceptions such as animals, birds, fish, automobiles, and boats other than rowboats or canoes. Without these definitions, there would be many problems in determining what is covered by these items in the standard fire contract.

Under the Form 2 (broad form), the extensions of coverage are four: (1) the insured may apply up to 10 percent (of the amount of insurance on the building) for *other structures* such as a detached garage or a toolshed; (2) the insured may also apply up to 10 percent (of the building insurance amount) for the loss of *rental value* of part of the dwelling rented to others while it is untenantable due to the perils insured against, with a maximum limit of one twelfth of the 10 percent each month, or for additional living expense to maintain the household's normal standard of living; (3) *worldwide coverage* up to 10 percent (of the amount of insurance on the contents) for losses of family personal property while it is away from the premises, including losses that occur in hotels, college dormitories, summer residences, and so on; and (4) for *improvements, alterations, or additions* by an insured tenant, 10 percent (of the contents insurance amount) may be used. The extensions of coverage noted, in items (1), (2), and (4) only, are an additional amount of insurance in the same loss, beyond the amount stated in the declarations of the standard contract. The cost of *debris removal* is separately noted in this section of the form as covered following a loss, as is *reasonable repairs* to protect the property from further damage, and *property removed* from the endangered premises (for 30 days).

Blanket coverage. A *blanket form* covers by a single amount of insurance the same kind of property in different locations or different kinds of property at a single location. Thus, several buildings in different locations may be insured under a blanket policy, as may stocks of goods or merchandise located in different warehouses or stores, or building and machinery at a single location.

Floating coverage. A *floating form,* termed "a floater" in the insurance business, is used to cover goods in different locations when it is difficult or impossible to furnish an accurate description of the location. One form of floater covers certain specific goods wherever they may be, usually within certain prescribed limits as to territory. For example, the equipment of a traveling theatrical company is located in different hotels, theaters, or storage rooms, or in transportation vehicles. A floater would cover this equipment wherever it might be so long as it remained within the limits prescribed. Such limits might be a single state, the continental limits of the United States, or worldwide.

Automatic or reporting coverage. *Automatic forms* are written with *reporting* requirements for changing values. They are used when it is difficult, if not impossible, to provide the insurer with an accurate statement of values because of changes or fluctuations, even though full insurance coverage is desired. The amounts are automatically adjusted without action on the part of the insured as the insurable values increase or decrease. The multiple-location contracts utilized by chain stores fall within this category. So long as the required reports are accurately made, the insurance adjusts itself to inventory changes within the limits of the policy. The automatic builder's risk form has the same effect. A building in the process of construction adds value day by day. Monthly reports are required, but a loss at a point between two reports will be protected by full insurance as the values of that day show. See Appendix C for more details on these forms.

Schedule coverage. *Schedule forms* are used in some contracts to insure policyholders who own numerous separate properties. All the buildings and their contents belonging to an insured may be grouped on a single printed or typed form covering many specific properties and amounts instead of being written as blanket coverage in a single amount as previously discussed. Separate policies with specific coverage on each item are thus unnecessary. While amounts of insurance are listed for each unit of the property, the policy covers each in proportion to the total values in the schedule. For full coverage the insured must have policies aggregating the total set forth in the schedule. An organization with widely scattered property, such as a state, a municipality, a church, or a university, frequently finds this form to be desirable.

CLAUSES

Purpose and use

Following the descriptive matter in the form, there are a number of short *clauses* modifying the policy conditions. Many clauses are only a few sentences or a paragraph in length. Some of these clauses are also found in the "endorsements" discussed in the next section of this chapter. The endorsements also help explain or modify the basic policy to which they are attached. Clauses are presented at this point in the text because they usually are part of the forms just mentioned or a part of the endorsements treated later.

These clauses differ with the character of the risk, being sometimes permissive, sometimes liberal, yet often restrictive in their nature. Clauses have the effect *(a)* of extending or limiting the coverage provided by the statutory wording of the standard policy and *(b)* modifying the statutory provisions to meet the insured's requirements with respect to the perils covered. Clauses are usually printed in standard forms as separate sections. The first few words of each clause are printed in boldface, and these boldface words are usually the name by which the clause is known. Sample policy kits (or IIA Course Guides) may be referred to for the exact wording of most of the following clauses contained in the dwelling building and contents forms and many other forms.

Several of the many important clauses are discussed separately. The *nuclear clause* and the *water exclusion clause* are significant restrictions on the coverage in many forms. The *liberalization clause* may provide an important extension of coverage to the insured if changes occur in the forms during the policy period. The *standard mortgage clause* is essential whenever the insured property is subject to a mortgage loan. The *coinsurance clause* is used in many property insurance contracts, and it is imperative that insureds understand its purposes and its limiting effect on loss payments. The *pro rata distribution clause* divides coverage under some blanket policies for business properties.

Nuclear clause

A mandatory *nuclear clause* which must be attached to all fire policies provides that the word *fire* does not embrace nuclear reaction, radiation, or radioactive contamination. Whether controlled or uncontrolled or however caused, or any consequence of any of these three perils, are not covered. The intent of the clause is not to limit coverage with respect to other perils enumerated in the policy. Direct loss by fire resulting from the nuclear hazards, for example, is covered.

Insurers provide special facilities for both nuclear energy liability and physical damage coverages. These risks are handled by three insurance pools of several hundred insurers that write up to about $500 million limits for property and liability protection per location.[9] The largest group is called the American Nuclear Insurers. The 1957 Price-Anderson Act supplements private insurance by authorizing a U.S. government agency (now the Nuclear Regulatory Commission) to sell coverage to nuclear reactor operators, to the extent not available by private insurance up to the required $560 million coverage per nuclear incident.

Water exclusion clause

Since the fire policy is commonly extended to include perils other than fire and lightning, to clarify the situation with respect to water damages the *water exclusion clause* disclaims liability with respect to water loss resulting from, contributed to, or aggravated by any of the following: (1) flood, surface water, waves, tidal water, overflow of a body of water, or spray from any of the foregoing, all whether driven by wind or not; (2) water which backs up through sewers or drains; and (3) water below the surface of the ground, including that which exerts pressure on or seeps or leaks through sidewalks, driveways, foundations, buildings, swimming pools or other structures. If fire or explosion ensues, the insurer is liable only for the damage caused by the fire or explosion.

In coastal areas, this clause assumes major importance. Hurricanes in Texas, Louisiana, Florida, New Jersey, and other states have brought public criticism for this exclusion. However, the concentrated and catastrophic nature of water damage by flood and hurricane in low-lying areas makes it nearly impossible to include such coverage in the regular fire insurance contract. (See Appendix C.) Loss prevention through construction techniques designed to meet such special perils is also a reasonable answer to these problems.

Flood damage of millions of dollars in many states during the last decade has focused public attention on the need for some form of insurance to alleviate the disastrous effects of floods. The Department of Housing and Urban Development (HUD) and private insurance companies provide a private-government plan in selected areas for flood insurance. The federal government issues the contracts and establishes rates and limits for coverage marketed by the private insurers. Proper land use and flood control are emphasized. Further discussion is found in Chapter 24.

---

[9] The potential inadequacy of available nuclear insurance is stressed by Norman A. Baglini, "The Nuclear Exposure," *Independent Agent*, September 1982, p. 43. Losses until 1979 were relatively small and few in number, but the Pennsylvania Three Mile Island nuclear mishap in that year attracted worldwide attention. The full $300 million policy limit has been paid by ANI.

Liberalization clause

From time to time rating agencies or insurers extend coverage to include features previously not available. To save the cost of endorsing policies every time a change is made that would benefit the insured, a *liberalization clause* is a part of most of the commonly used forms. Its purpose is to give the insured the benefit of any advantageous change that develops. This is an example of such a clause (from the dwelling building and contents broad form):

> If within 60 days prior to or during the policy period this Company adopts any revision which would broaden coverage under this policy without additional premium, such broadened coverage will immediately apply to this policy.

All of these benefits automatically accrue to the insured without specific mention of each in the contract or by subsequent endorsement. This means that in the event of loss, the insured will get the benefit of any privilege or extension of coverage that has been adopted by the insurer.

Standard mortgage clause

This clause is often found as part of standard forms. It is completed by inserting the name of the mortgagee if there are loans on the property and the interest of the mortgagee is to be insured. The *standard mortgage clause* may also be added to the policy at any time in the form of an endorsement. The clause constitutes a separate and distinct contract between the insurer and the mortgagee. It applies only to the building items insured, not the contents. If a mortgagee is named in the declarations, any loss-payment check is made payable to both the mortgagor and the mortgagee.

The basic purpose of the mortgage clause is to protect the interests of the mortgagee or creditor. The clause gives the mortgagee legal rights as a party in the insurance contract taken out and paid for by the mortgagor or owner of the insured property. The clause avoids the necessity for a separate policy by the mortgagee or for an assignment which is far less certain to protect the creditor. In effect, the mortgagee-creditor rather than the mortgagor-debtor receives the primary benefit from the mortgage clause. To protect the interests of the mortgagee, provision is made that if the owner defaults in premium payment, the mortgagee shall pay on demand for future protection if the insurance is desired to remain in effect. The mortgagee is not liable for payment of premium earned previous to such request.

The most important liberalizing feature of the clause is that which provides that the policy shall not be invalidated by any act or neglect of the mortgagor or owner of the property, or by any foreclosure relating to the property, or by change in ownership or increase in hazard. The mortgagee, which is often a bank or other financial institution that could not keep track of possible violations by many mortgagors, obtains certainty of insurance coverage for the property used as collateral for the loan. The duties imposed upon the mortgagee by the clause are concerned only with changes in ownership, occupation, or hazard when such changes are known by the mortgagee. If the hazard is thus increased, the insurer may request an increased premium.

Coinsurance clause

The *coinsurance clause* aims at an equitable control of the amount of insurance that the insured shall carry. Ordinarily it is used in property insurance for most *business* properties and in some states (such as New York) for dwelling properties. The need for coinsurance requirements is less for many dwellings because the premium differences due to rates and values are less than those for business properties, where both rates and the larger values insured vary greatly. It limits the liability of the insurer to that proportion of the loss which the insurance amount bears to a given percentage of the actual cash value of the property at the time of the loss.

A number of clauses with different names are used to accomplish the same purpose. In fire insurance, with a common requirement of insurance equal to 80 percent of the value, the clause is referred to as the "80 percent coinsurance clause." Because the insured receives a lower rate when this clause is a part of the policy, the coinsurance clause is sometimes termed the "reduced-rate contribution clause." The following coinsurance clause is one now used:

> This Company shall not be liable for a greater proportion of any loss to the property covered than the amount of the insurance under this policy for such property bears to the amount produced by multiplying the actual cash value of such property at the time of the loss by the coinsurance percentage applicable (specified on the first page of this policy, or by endorsement).

The above coinsurance clause is found in many of the printed forms attached to the standard fire contract, such as in the general property form. The clause may also be added to some contracts as a specific additional endorsement if such wording is not already included.

Purpose. The purpose of the coinsurance clause is to provide equity among policyholders by encouraging them to carry a reasonable amount of insurance (usually 80 percent or more) in relation to the full value of their property. The policyholder receives the benefit of a reduced rate as compared with the "flat" rate for fire insurance in return for a promise to the insurer that insurance at least up to the stated coinsurance percentage will be carried.[10] Although the coinsurance clause does not make mandatory the carrying of insurance up to a specified percentage of value, losses are adjusted as if insurance in such an amount were carried. Where there is a deficiency, the insured is said to be carrying that amount of risk and is, therefore, a *coinsurer* to the extent of the deficiency. The coinsurance clause is the simplest and fairest method devised to adjust charges and loss payments on the assumption that reasonable insurance amounts in relation to property values are carried. The insured should carry at least the percentage of insurance specified in the contract. Otherwise the insurer pays only part of the loss.

Adequacy of fire insurance rates (see later section on justification of the coinsurance clause) is another method of explaining the purpose of coinsurance.

Formula and examples.   The application of the coinsurance clause may be expressed in the following formula based on the wording of the clause.

Let

I.C. = Insurance carried (the amount of insurance),

I.R. = Insurance required (the coinsurance percentage × the actual cash value of the property at the time of loss),

L = Amount of the loss.

Then

$$\frac{I.C.}{I.R.} \times L = \text{Amount the insurer pays.}$$

Suppose an insured purchased $60,000 of insurance from company X on a building valued at $100,000. If an 80 percent coinsurance clause were made a part of the contract and a loss of $40,000 occurred, the amount company X would be obligated to pay would be:

$$\frac{\$60,000}{\$80,000} \times \$40,000, \text{ or } \times \frac{3}{4} \$40,000 = \$30,000.$$

The insured would be a coinsurer to the extent of $10,000 since the property was not insured to 80 percent of the value as promised. If the

---

[10] A "flat" insurance rate, which is the alternative to the coinsurance rate, is not based on any assumed amount of insurance in relation to the value of the property. Losses are paid in full up to the amount of the insurance, regardless of whether the insurance amount is close to full value or only a small part of it. The rate is often 50 percent or more, higher than the coinsurance rate.

property was insured for \$80,000, the loss would be paid in full by the insurer:

$$\frac{\$80,000}{\$80,000} \times \$40,000, \text{ or } 100\% \times \$40,000 = \$40,000.$$

The second case, where the insured carried the \$80,000 as required by the coinsurance clause, illustrates the important principle that the insured is *not just paid 80 percent of the loss* when coinsurance is involved.[11] The insured is paid the *full* loss amount (up to the amount of the policy) *if* at least the minimum required insurance amount is carried. The penalty applies *only* if the insured does not have at least the required amount. In the operation of the foregoing formula, the insurer is never liable for an amount in excess of the policies[12] and hence if the insurance was for \$80,000 and the loss was \$90,000, the insurer would be liable only for the \$80,000 policy amount.

It is sometimes incorrectly stated that when the loss is total, the coinsurance clause is inoperative. The clause is operative in every loss. However, when the loss is total, the percentage of the loss that limits the amount the insurer pays will exceed the face of the policies. Because the full amount of the policies is payable in the event of a total loss, the impression follows that the clause is inoperative. Suppose, for example, that the loss was total in our previous case (instead of only \$40,000) when the insurance carried was \$60,000. Then the insurer would pay according to the coinsurance clause:

$$\frac{\$60,000}{\$80,000} \times \$100,000, \text{ or } \times \frac{3}{4}\,\$100,000 = \$75,000.$$

But since the indicated loss payment of \$75,000 exceeds the policy amount of \$60,000, the policy amount becomes the maximum payment, and \$60,000 is paid.

A different example might involve several insurers insuring the same property. Assume:

> Company X has \$20,000 of insurance, with an *80%* coinsurance clause.
> Company Y has \$40,000 of insurance, with an *80%* coinsurance clause.
> Company Z has \$60,000 of insurance, with a *90%* coinsurance clause.
> Value of property is \$200,000. Total insurance is \$120,000.
> Loss of \$96,000 occurs.

---

[11] This is a common mistake made by students who assume that this is how the coinsurance clause works.

[12] Nor an amount in excess of the *loss*. If the insurance amount in the example were \$90,000, the insurer would pay 100 percent, not 90/80 times the loss, up to the \$90,000 insurance amount. Insureds often carry more than the 80 percent required, in order to have enough coverage for serious losses (where the building values are destroyable to that extent), and also in order to be sure to meet the 80 percent requirement if property values are increasing.

Only the lesser limit of liability amount indicated by (1) the coinsurance clause and (2) the pro rata liability clause (discussed previously and found on line 86 of the standard fire policy) would apply. In the case of each of the companies in this example, the coinsurance amount would be the lesser amount, because the insurance required is more than the insurance carried:

$$\text{Co. X would pay} \frac{\$\,20,000}{\$160,000}, \text{ or } \tfrac{1}{8} \times \$96,000 = \$12,000.$$

$$\text{Co. Y would pay} \frac{\$\,40,000}{\$160,000}, \text{ or } \tfrac{1}{4} \times \$96,000 = \$24,000.$$

$$\text{Co. Z would pay} \frac{\$\,60,000}{\$180,000}, \text{ or } \tfrac{1}{3} \times \$96,000 = \$32,000.$$

Total payment $68,000

Justification. To understand the reason for coinsurance, one must consider the function of the insurance *rate,* or the cost per $100 of insurance. Insurance shifts the burden of risk from the individual to many persons. Since a fire in a property need not destroy it totally and since fire losses vary in degree—there being a great many small losses as compared with the number of total losses—unless each insured carries an adequate percentage of insurance to value, the burden of risk will not be equitably distributed.

Insurance premiums have been compared to a tax rate. In every community, taxes to defray community expenses are raised by an assessment levied upon property valued by assessors for that purpose. If each individual were permitted to choose a value upon which to be taxed, the burden would be unfairly distributed. So in fire insurance, if one insured insures in the amount of 50 percent of the property value, another 20 percent, and a third 80 percent, and if each receives a loss payment in full up to the policy amount, those carrying the smaller amounts of insurance to value pay less than their share of the average premiums. To create an equitable situation, the amount of insurance to value carried by each insured should be uniform. The coinsurance clause requires that the insured carry insurance to a certain stipulated percentage of value or, failing to do so, bear a percentage of the loss.[13]

Statistics from the Chamber of Commerce of the United States (Bulletin No. 6) show most fire losses to be small in relation to the values of the properties:

---

[13] There are some situations where insureds may carry less than the required amount on purpose, due to pricing differentials or the deductibles selected. See Michael L. Smith, "A Reexamination of Coinsurance Clauses," *Journal of Risk and Insurance* 47, no. 3 (September 1980), p. 506.

Ratio of loss to value	Percent of building fires
Between 0 and 20 percent of value	86
Between 20 and 40 percent of value	8
Over 40 percent of value	6
Total	100

These data show that if the coinsurance clause were not required, an insured could carry a small amount of insurance and yet be paid for almost all losses. The conclusion is that the insured should be encouraged to carry high amounts of insurance in relation to value (1) in fairness to other policyholders who would otherwise be paying more than their fair share of total premiums and (2) in order to have insurance in adequate amounts for one of its most important purposes, paying for large losses.

Coinsurance valuation problems and solutions.   Since the amount for which the insurer is liable is dependent upon a percentage of the actual cash value of the insured property at the time of the loss or damage, the question of *valuation* is of the utmost importance. Moreover, so far as values are concerned, the entire burden is placed squarely upon the insured. The ways by which values are estimated differ, depending on the type of property.

With *stocks* of merchandise, the value of an inventory can be ascertained within reasonable limits through the record of purchases and sales. Large shifting values of some commodities require close watch, for the coinsurance requirement must be met on the basis of value at the time of loss. Seasonal inventory increases, such as in retail stores before the Christmas holiday season, necessitate insurance increases. In the case of *machinery and fixtures,* values are reduced each year through charge-offs made for depreciation and obsolescence. Tax rules encourage a rapid depreciation program, with the result that fixtures and machinery are carried on the books below their actual cash value. Insurance should be based on actual cash value, not book value.

Real estate affords the most difficult problem in valuation. Because of changing wage scales, material prices, and other market factors, building values are constantly fluctuating. A 10-year-old building that cost $100,000 may have a depreciated new replacement value far in excess of the original cost. Appreciation of value due to increased construction costs often more than offsets the actual depreciation of well-maintained property. Thus, an insurance program based upon the original cost, less depreciation, might be nothing less than disastrous. Another difficult problem is presented when market value and replacement value differ widely. Economic changes in communities sometimes result in properties being offered for sale at a market value very much below the replacement value. If a building would cost $200,000 to rebuild, yet sold for $50,000, how much insurance should be carried to avoid becoming a coinsurer? The answer is that because of economic obsolescence, depreciation, and changing neighborhood conditions, the building has lost 75 percent of its real value.[14] If the sales price is realistic, the building's insurable value is probably $50,000. It is, therefore, wise to eliminate the question of values for coinsurance purposes and to write such a risk flat. Because of the difficulty of agreeing on value and depreciation amounts, insurers are often reluctant to insure buildings on a coinsurance basis where depreciation exceeds 50 percent.

The difficulty of valuation is somewhat eased by a *property exclusions clause* which excludes certain types or parts of property from the valuation for coinsurance purposes. By the use of this clause in many forms, or by endorsements, such items as concrete foundations and the cost of excavations or grading and underground piping are excluded from the total valuation. This reduces the amount of insurance required by the coinsurance clause.

Properties equipped with approved automatic sprinklers and complying with inspection requirements may use a special form containing provision for a *guaranteed amount of insurance clause* as an alternative to the 90 percent coinsurance clause normally available to sprinklered risks. It is usual to require that the guaranteed amount be the full value of the property and that a new statement of values be filed every year. The operation of this clause is identical with that of the coinsurance clause, with the one exception that the amount of insurance to be carried is agreed upon in advance.

The so-called *5 percent waiver clause* usually follows immediately after the coinsurance clause quoted earlier:

> In the event that the aggregate claim for any loss is both less than $10,000 and less than 5 percent of the total amount of insurance applicable to the property involved at the time such loss occurs, no special inventory or appraisement of the undamaged property shall be required.

The purpose of the waiver clause is to relieve the insured of the necessity of taking an actual physical inventory of the undamaged property in the event of small losses. The clause in no way suspends the operation of the coinsurance feature of the contract.

The greatest *disadvantage* of the coinsurance clause is the possibility of *misunderstanding* by the insured.[15] Insurance agents who recognize

---

[14] Suggested annual rates of depreciation depend upon the care of the particular building and the causes of depreciation. A type of building whose life is estimated at 50 years might be considered at the end of 20 years to be 40 percent depreciated. When repairs are neglected, or when some economic change in demand occurs, the building may be almost useless. On the other hand, the element of economic obsolescence and the element of depreciation may be very small.

[15] Dissatisfaction by insureds with the coinsurance clause, particularly where it is used in personal lines, has caused some insurers to abandon its use in favor of requiring under-

the value of coinsurance are sometimes reluctant to advise an insured to adopt it. Insureds who believe they understand the operation of the coinsurance clause frequently forget to keep insurance amounts up to date. If the clause is to be used because of substantial rate savings to the insured, proper education and explanation to the insured are essential. The insured should understand his or her responsibility and possible penalty.

While an insured may secure a reduced *rate* by incorporating the coinsurance clause in the form, it does not always follow that a change from a flat-rate coverage to a coinsurance coverage will result in a lower *total cost*. The requirements of the clause as to the amount of insurance necessary may result in a lower rate per thousand, but because of the necessity of adding additional insurance the total premium charge may be higher. A careful comparison is recommended.

Pro rata distribution clause

Another clause used for some business situations but much less common than the coinsurance clause is the *pro rata distribution clause*. It divides the total coverage under a blanket policy (see previous section on types of forms) to apply specifically upon each separate location in the proportion that the value at each location bears to the sum of the values at all the locations. In connection with this clause, insurers usually require the use of a 90 percent coinsurance clause. The result is a distribution of the coverage that is fair to both the insurer and the insured. The clause is a great convenience in insuring *contents*. Frequently inventories are constantly shifting from one location to another but total value is more or less steady. When the contents may often be shifted from building to building, or when shipments in and out are involved, it is difficult to change specific insurance coverages to follow values. A blanket policy with the pro rata distribution clause automatically shifts the coverage as the relative values shift.

ENDORSEMENTS

Purpose

An *endorsement* is a provision added to the insurance contract by which the scope of its coverage is clarified, restricted, or enlarged. Certain endorsements, such as those that extend the perils covered, may be as long as the form and may be attached when the policy is issued. Other

---

writing appraisals of values, or other alternatives. The insured may also use planned underinsurance as a retention strategy. See Michael L. Smith and David L. Bickelhaupt, "Is Coinsurance Becoming Obsolete?" *Journal of Risk and Insurance* 48, no. 1 (March 1981), p. 95.

endorsements may be brief additions that are added to the contract after the contract goes into effect. A written contract may be completed without an endorsement, but many contracts are not complete without a form being attached. Clauses are sections of either forms or endorsements; they are not required but are very commonly included.

General use

Many endorsements are merely typewritten additions to the contract, changing its amount, rate, or term. Errors may be corrected in the same manner. If a property is sold, the insurance may be continued for the benefit of the new owner by means of an endorsement. Some endorsements are in the nature of permits. For example, a permit may be added to the policy authorizing removal of the insured property and providing for coverage in another location. The policy provides for permission to add endorsements in those parts of the conditions found on lines 38–48.

One of the most common and important uses of endorsements with the fire insurance contract is the addition of *other perils*. Discussed in the next sections of this chapter are the popular endorsements: "extended coverage," "dwelling building and contents—broad form," and "dwelling building and contents—special form." In recent years the Dwelling Property Forms of the Insurance Services Office, which include these coverages directly in the forms rather than as separate endorsements, have been widely used.[16]

The extended coverage endorsement

This packaged endorsement, known when it was first introduced in the 1930s as the "supplemental contract," provides in a single addition *extended coverage* protection against the perils of windstorm, explosion, hail, riot, smoke, and several other perils. The endorsement is not, in fact, an additional contract but is rather an extension of the protection of the fire insurance contract to cover other perils without at the same time increasing the face amount of the policy. The insured does not make a choice among the perils; all are automatically included when the premium for extended coverage is added in the declarations.

There are several varieties of the *extended coverage endorsement*, including one for coastal areas which includes loss by waves. One of the most common wordings is that found in the Dwelling Property *Basic*

---

[16] The analysis here centers on the wording in these forms, although some differences in coverage may be found in other forms and endorsements used in some jurisdictions.

Form (DP–1). The coverage is in force if a premium for extended coverage is indicated on the first page of the policy.

Seven perils are included in a policy extended in this manner: *(a) windstorm; (b) hail; (c) explosion; (d) riot* and civil commotion; *(e) aircraft* damage; *(f) vehicle* damage; and *(g) smoke* damage.

The coverage of the extended coverage endorsement is effected by a clause that substitutes the new perils to be covered for the word *fire* as it appears in the insuring clause of the statutory contract. All of the policy provisions are applied with respect to losses by the extended coverage perils exactly as they would be applied to a fire loss.

The $50 deductible clause of the dwelling property insurance form applies to losses caused by extended coverage perils, or sometimes only to losses caused by the wind and hail perils. In some jurisdictions full coverage is available for an additional premium, but the $50 deductible is the more usual. The deductible applies to each occurrence of loss and to each dwelling if more than one are insured in the same policy. In some jurisdictions the deductible applies to both a building and its contents.

Most of the wording of the extended coverage endorsement pertains to explanation of the perils, defining what is intended to be covered and what is not intended to be covered in the contract. For example, the *windstorm or hail* perils do not include coverage for rain, snow, sleet, sand, or dust unless wind or hail damages the building, causing an opening in the roof or walls. Also excluded is property when outside the building, such as awnings; signs; radio or television antennas, aerials, or towers; and rowboats or canoes. *Explosions* are defined so that steam explosions from boilers or pipes (owned, leased, or controlled by the insured) are not covered. Sonic booms are covered because they are not excluded. *Riot* coverage includes damage by striking employees and civil commotion, but it does not include indirect losses such as interruption of business. *Vehicle* coverage excludes damage by any vehicle owned or operated by the insured or a resident and damage by any vehicle to fences, driveways, and walks. *Aircraft* damage includes self-propelled missiles and spacecraft. *Smoke* coverage includes sudden and accidental damage from smoke but not smoke from fireplaces, agricultural smudging, or industrial operations. If a separate premium is shown in the declarations of DP Form 1, *vandalism and malicious mischief* is an added peril covered, excluding glass constituting a part of the building and theft. Damage caused by burglars is included. No coverage applies if the dwelling has been vacant for more than 30 days immediately before a loss.

An "apportionment clause" included in the extended coverage endorsement makes it important for the insured to have the extended coverage included in all fire policies covering the same property. If this is not done, the insurer pays proportionately: for example, if extended coverage is on two thirds of the property, only two thirds of the extended coverage loss would be paid.

The broad form endorsement

Another very common endorsement, the *dwelling building and contents—broad form,* is used to insure buildings (other than farm property) designed for occupancy by not more than four families or apartments and their contents.[17] The current use of all the dwelling forms has been limited by the popularity of homeowners' contracts (see Chapter 23), which include coverages similar to forms discussed here. The forms are also used where homeowners' policies are not applicable, such as rental properties, unoccupied new or for-sale homes, and homes of smaller value.

The broad form endorsement includes all of the perils just discussed in connection with the extended coverage endorsement. In addition, it broadens the coverage of 2 of those perils and adds 10 new perils to the scope of the fire insurance contract. The result is a very comprehensive coverage for the dwelling owner or tenant. Although it is a "named perils" type of endorsement, including only those perils specifically named or listed in the wording used, the broad form endorsement provides adequate protection for many insureds.

A $50 deductible for any one occurrence applies to property covered by the broad form endorsement in the form used by many states. The deductible can be waived for an additional premium, but it seldom is because of the higher cost. A special deductible applies for the perils of vandalism and malicious mischief: 2 percent of the insurance amount but not less than $100 nor more than $250.

The two extended coverage perils which are somewhat broadened are:

1. *Explosion.* This does cover explosion of *steam* boiler and pipes owned, leased, or controlled by the insured, because there are no specific exclusions.

2. *Damage by vehicles.* This includes damage to insured property done *by any vehicle owned or operated by the insured or by a resident of the premises,* except for damage to fences, driveways, or walks.

The 10 perils added by the broad form endorsement are:

1. *Sudden and accidental tearing apart, cracking, burning, or bulging* of a steam or hot water heating system, an air conditioning system, or an appliance for heating water.

2. *Freezing of plumbing, heating and air conditioning systems or household appliances.* Freezing is not covered when the building is va-

---

[17] See footnote 16. The analysis here is based upon the Dwelling Property *Broad* Form (DP–2).

cant, unoccupied, or under construction, unless reasonable care has been used to maintain heat in the building or the water has been drained and shut off.

3. *Vandalism and malicious mischief.* This covers willful or intentional damage or destruction of the property insured. It does not cover building glass breakage, which is separately covered (see item 9 below). Note the special deductible mentioned previously. This peril can also be included in the extended coverage endorsement as one added peril, if an additional premium charge is made.

4. *Burglars.* Damage done in breaking into the property for burglary is covered, but this is not intended to include the property taken by the burglars. A 30-day vacancy exclusion also applies for this peril.

5. *Falling objects.* This includes damage by falling trees. The windstorm peril would cover most of such losses, but occasionally trees do fall without any wind being involved. Damage to the contents or the building interior is covered when the roof or walls first sustain damage from the outside. Outdoor radio and television antennas and aerials, masts and towers, outdoor equipment, awnings, and fences are not covered.

6. *Weight of ice, snow, or sleet.* This includes physical injury to the building or contents due to the weight of such elements. As above, most outdoor property is excluded, and patios, pavements, swimming pools, walls, and docks are additional specific exceptions.

7. *Collapse.* The actual collapse of a building or any part of it is covered, but "settling, cracking, shrinkage, bulging, or expansion" is not covered. *Earth movement* (such as caused by earthquake and landslide) and water damage (from floods, backing up of sewers and drains, and seepage) are specifically excluded in all perils of the broad form endorsement. Unless the direct result of the building collapse, all the outdoor property mentioned above, and underground pipes, cesspools, septic tanks, and foundations are not covered.

8. *Accidental discharge or overflow of water or steam.* Such discharge or overflow from plumbing, heating, air conditioning, or household appliances is covered. Rain leaking through a roof is not included in this coverage. For example, a faucet unintentionally left running for a few hours can cause considerable damage to floors, walls, and contents. Water damage losses during vacancy of over 30 days or which occur off the described location are excluded. The damage to the system or appliance itself is not covered, but tearing out and replacing part of the building to effect repairs to the system is covered.

9. *Breakage of glass.* All glass which is part of the building, including storm doors and windows, is covered for loss by almost any cause except after 30 days' vacancy. The $50 deductible usually applied to all broad form perils is an important limitation.

10. *Electric current damage.* Sudden and accidental injury to property from artificially generated (thus not lightning) electric currents is covered. Tubes, transistors, and similar items are excluded.

Other features of the broad form endorsement are explained later as the homeowners' policy, which is often written to include the broad form perils, is discussed in the chapter on multiple-line insurance. For example, there is limited coverage against many perils (except windstorm) for *lawns, trees, shrubs,* and *plants.* The broad form also includes important *10 percent extensions* of coverage for contents off-premises (worldwide), other structures, improvements and alterations (if insured as a tenant), and rental value and additional living expense coverage. *Debris removal costs, reasonable repairs* to protect the property from further damage, and *removal* (up to 30 days) of property endangered by insured perils are covered.

The special form endorsement

The *dwelling buildings and contents—special form* is used to insure the same types of dwelling properties as those discussed for the broad form endorsement.[18]

One important distinction of this endorsement as compared with most others used with the fire insurance contract is that the special form is an "all-risks" coverage. It does not list or name the perils that are covered but merely states that "this policy is extended to insure against all risks of direct physical loss, except as hereinafter provided."

The result is among the broadest types of coverage available, even though some exclusions are necessary. The debate as to whether an "all-risks" coverage is much more comprehensive than a "named-perils" coverage is not important. An all-risks form with few exceptions may be broader than a named-perils form with few perils named or many exceptions noted. The reverse may also be true: an extensive listing in a named-perils form may provide better coverage than an all-risks form with many exceptions. In this case, the special form provides somewhat broader protection for most insureds. The difference is not too great, however, as can be surmised from the fact that in most territories the special form only costs a few cents more per $100 of insurance than the broad form.

Because an all-risks policy automatically *includes* all perils that it does *not* exclude, one advantage is that unusual losses and those that could not be reasonably anticipated are covered. A few illustrations for buildings insured under the special form are: spillage of a liquid stain on walls or floors; wind-driven rain that seeps in or comes through doors,

---

[18] The Dwelling Property *Special* Form (DP–3) has similar wording.

windows, or bad roofs, to damage interior paint or wallpaper; and squirrels or other animals that chew the front porch woodwork. Similar damage to contents would also be covered.

Most of the exclusions are similar to those discussed in connection with the broad form endorsement, such as earthquake, landslide, flood, freezing under certain conditions, vandalism during long-term vacancy, and some limitations on trees, plants, and other outside properties.[19]

An example of an additional type of exclusion particularly needed by all-risks coverage is the exclusion for *wear-and-tear* losses. Because the intention is to cover accidental and sudden losses rather than the gradual accumulation of losses that might normally be expected, the wear-and-tear exclusion includes: deterioration; rust; mold; smog or industrial smoke; damage by birds, vermin, or domestic animals; and the settling, cracking, bulging, or expansion of such properties as pavements, patios, or structural parts of the building.

A $50 deductible is almost always used in connection with the perils insured by the special form endorsement. The same type of all-risks coverage found in the special form is included in Forms 3 and 5 of the homeowner's policy, discussed in the later chapter on multiple-line insurance.

A REVIEW OF THE FIRE INSURANCE CONTRACT

Now that the forms, clauses, and endorsements to the basic fire insurance contract have been presented, it will be helpful to review these together with the preceding major parts of the contract around which this chapter has been organized. The entire typical contract (for dwelling building and contents), including its declarations, insuring agreement, conditions, and exclusions, is summarized from a different viewpoint in Figure 13–3. These parts of the whole contract are related to coverage in terms of *persons, property, perils and losses, premiums, locations, amounts, term, suspensions,* and *loss provisions.* Such an analysis is useful for any kind of insurance contract.

SPECIAL AND ALLIED FIRE LINES

As can be seen by the endorsements studied in the previous section, the field of fire insurance includes more than just the peril of fire. Windstorms, explosions, riots, water damage, smoke, and many other perils are often included in the fire insurance contract. A number of other

---

[19] The exclusions for flood and water are the same for broad form and special form endorsements: damage from flood, surface water, waves, below-ground-level water, and back-up of sewers and drains.

Figure 13–3. Analysis of the fire insurance contract

THE ENTIRE POLICY CONTRACT

Declarations	Insuring Agreement	Conditions and exclusions	Forms*	Clauses*	Endorsements*
Persons → Insurer, Agent, Insured (s), Mortgagee (s)	Legal representatives, Assignment	Mortgagee(s)	Insureds and family	Mortgage	Insureds and family
Property → Buildings, Contents, Etc.	Property described	Not uninsurable types	Outdoor equipment, All family personal property, Other structures, Improvements	Trees, plants, lawns, Etc. Not excluded property	Glass Not swimming pools, etc. Not seasonal
Perils and losses → Fire, Extended coverage, Other perils	Fire, Lightning, Removal, Direct, Not indirect	Added perils Not war, civil authority, neglect after loss, theft, explosion, riot, concealment, or fraud	Rental value, Additional living expense, Debris removal	Liberalization Not nuclear Not flood backup, seepage	Extended coverage and 10 other perils Not burglar damage Not earth movement

Premiums → Fire / Extended coverage / Other

In consideration of premium

Coverages A–E as specified

In consideration of added premium

Losses → Property described

Named locations
Removal (5 days)

Off-premises contents (worldwide)

Amounts → Insurance amount

Actual cash value
Insurable interests
Not increases from building codes
Not more than repair or replacement

Other insurance
Pro rata liability

Replacement cost

Coinsurance
Reinstatement

$50 deductible

Term of policy → Inception 1 or 3 years

Noon standard time† to expiration date

Cancellation to insured (5 days)

Cancellation to mortgagee (10 days)

Suspensions →

Increase in hazard
Vacancy (60 days)

Alterations and repairs permitted

Vacancy
Unoccupancy

Loss provisions →

Written notice
Protect property
Separate damaged
Inventory
Proof of loss
Exhibit books
Appraisal
Repair or replace
Subrogation
Not abandonment

Pro rata
Apportionment
Losses must begin during policy period

Loss
Loss payable
Loss of pair or set

Waiver of subrogation

* Assume that the contract includes the "dwelling building and contents—broad form" and the clauses and endorsements it contains. Where an item is found in one of these, it is not repeated in the lists for the others. The "dwelling property" broad form is similar.
† Now often changed by statute or policy to 12:01 A.M. at place of property insured.

miscellaneous perils are associated with fire insurance and included in the general term of *special and allied fire lines* of insurance. Some of these perils are written by endorsements on the fire contract; others are written predominantly by the fire insurance companies in separate contracts.

Appendix C, "Special and Allied Fire Lines," can be referred to for details of these many coverages. They are sometimes of importance to particular insureds, but their relatively infrequent use makes it unnecessary to include full discussion of their characteristics in this chapter. One of the most common is *sprinkler leakage insurance* for damage done by the accidental discharge of water from automatic sprinklers in a building. Legal liability for such sprinkler leakage damage is also an important type of coverage for those insureds who are responsible for sprinkler equipment. *Builder's risk insurance* is a special contract available for the changing values and ownership interest during construction. *Crop insurance* is written for specified types of crops for damage by weather, insects, and disease. *Flood insurance* is available in many areas with the federal government through private insurance agents (see Chapter 23). *Multiple-location contracts* are very important for larger businesses that need the flexible and automatic coverage of reporting forms. Other special and allied lines discussed in Appendix C are water damage liability and tenants' improvements and betterments.

CONCURRENCY

Policies designed to cover identical properties should be written as nearly alike as possible with the same terms and conditions. When there are discrepancies, the insurance is said to be "nonconcurrent," and this may have the effect of complicating the problem of loss adjustment or providing inadequate coverage. Very minor differences in details may not cause problems, but major ones often do so.

Nonconcurrency occurs most frequently in a combination of specific and blanket policies. The owner of several buildings forming part of one establishment may take out specific insurance on certain of the buildings and blanket insurance covering several or all of the buildings. Another form of nonconcurrency is to be found when several policies cover on a given risk, but some are written with coinsurance and others without it. A special "limit of liability" rule apportions the coverages among the several contracts in these cases.

There are many examples of nonconcurrent contracts in fire, inland marine, and casualty insurance. Most of the problems are solved by interinsurer cooperation under what is known as the 1963 *Agreement of Guiding Principles*. It is agreed in advance by almost all major insurers how any disputes in regard to overlapping coverages will be settled.

These rules of priority and apportionment specify which type of contract is to be primary coverage for stipulated losses and which is to be excess coverage. Generally, the policy that is more specific as to described property or location is the first to pay for a loss. For example, specific coverage on one building is paid before any other insurance, such as a "blanket" policy covering several buildings.

Also, coverage which is specific as to location applies before "floater"-type contracts which cover property wherever it is located, except where the floater policy is issued to a transportation carrier or bailee. In a loss of a fur coat insured under both the furrier's (bailee customers) insurance and under the off-premises coverage of homeowner's insurance, the bailee's policy would apply first and any excess of loss over that payment would be paid by the homeowner's policy. Thus the participation of several different insurance contracts in a loss is settled in an orderly and consistent manner, and the loss payment is made without unnecessary delay.

FOR REVIEW AND DISCUSSION

1. *Why and how* are insurance contracts standardized? Give examples from several different types of insurance contracts.

2. Compare the basic *purposes* of the three main sections in the standard fire contract.

3. What *significance* do the following terms have in fire insurance: *(a)* standard policy? *(b)* insurable interest? *(c)* proximate loss? *(d)* actual cash value? *(e)* friendly fire? and *(f)* pro rata liability clause?

4. Johnny can't read well, but he is sure that fire insurance is written to cover losses of more than just the property value of the owner. Illustrate why you believe Johnny to be correct.

5. What has the phrase *"direct* loss by *fire"* in the New York standard fire contract been interpreted to mean? Explain fully.

6. Is the *actual cash value* paid under a fire policy based upon: *(a)* assessed property valuation? *(b)* policyholder cost? *(c)* full replacement value? and *(d)* an amount for which the insured had offered it for sale?

7. Explain whether or not the fire insurer is liable in each of these cases:
   a. A roast cooking in the oven becomes badly burned, and smoke damages the dwelling and furniture.
   b. Some Kleenex on a mantelpiece accidentally catches fire. A person gathers up the tissue and throws it into a fireplace, not knowing that a diamond ring was in the burning Kleenex.
   c. Jewelry is thrown into a furnace with rubbish and destroyed.
   d. Mr. Gepeto negligently throws a match into a pile of shavings and destroys his woodworking plant.

8. The extended coverage endorsement is a widely used insurance endorsement. What is extended, and how is it accomplished?

9. How are the direct riot damage and the resulting fire loss covered by the usual fire insurance contract? Is this fair to insureds in rural areas?

10. What requirements does the insured have to meet after a fire loss? Is subrogation important in the fire insurance contract? Is your answer based on potential or actual benefits to the insurer or the insured?

11. Why may so many different forms and endorsements be added to what is supposed to be a *standard* fire contract?

12. Why would you agree that the dwelling building and contents forms add greatly to the coverage of the standard fire insurance contract?

13. Identify and contrast the purposes of the standard mortgage clause, the coinsurance clause, and the pro rata distribution clause.

14. Some clauses are restrictive, while others extend the coverage of the insurance contract. Give an example of each type, with explanation.

15. Why is the standard mortgage clause very favorable to the mortgagee?

16. Which of the following perils would probably be covered by a standard fire insurance contract with the broad form endorsement:
    a. Sonic boom damage?
    b. Steam boiler explosion?
    c. Vandalism not associated with a riot?
    d. Landslide or subsidence other than that caused by earthquake?
    e. Water leakage due to freezing of plumbing system?

17. Criticize the following statements about the fire coinsurance clause:
    a. "The insurance company merely pays 80 percent of the fire loss."
    b. "The purpose of the clause is to make more profit for the insurer."
    c. "The 80 percent coinsurance requirement is not important because in a large loss it does not matter."
    d. "Changing values for real estate or inventories do not affect the policyholder who insures with the coinsurance clause."

18. Barbara owns a building and carries insurance equal to 100 percent of its value, with an 80 percent coinsurance clause. Is she permitted to do this? What change would you make in her coverage?

19. Mr. I. M. Insecure has the following fire insurance on his business property, which is valued today at $200,000: $120,000 of insurance, with an 80 percent coinsurance clause included in the policy contract.
    a. Is his friend Mr. B. A. Success correct in telling him that he is not carrying enough insurance to meet serious losses and the coinsurance requirement? Explain.
    b. What would be paid in case of a $72,000 loss? Show your method.
    c. A $180,000 loss? Show your method.
    d. How would you explain to Mr. Insecure the reasons why he should carry more insurance in relation to his property values, and how the coinsurance clause does this in an equitable manner?

20. Would you, as an insured, prefer to have a "named-perils" or an "all-risks" contract? Explain. Can you relate your answer to fire "allied lines"?

21. Why do most insureds need either the broad form endorsement or the special form endorsement for protection of their dwellings?

22. Show how the entire fire insurance contract may be easily summarized as to its coverage of persons, property, perils, and amounts of insurance.

23. What is "nonconcurrency," and how are some of its problems solved?

Chapter 14

Outline of concepts

The general purposes of indirect loss insurance are to pay for "consequential losses" following direct property damages.

Classification divides the types into (1) *time element* and (2) *no time element* losses.

Time element losses include the most common type of indirect loss insurance, business interruption, as well as contingent business interruption, rents and rental value, extra-expense, and tuition fees insurance.

Business interruption insurance is discussed in terms of its:

Importance, because of severe losses, but very often overlooked.

Purpose, which is to pay for income loss, including future profits and expenses, from such perils as fire, wind, riot, and others.

Difference from profits insurance, which covers only the profit lost because of damage to inventories of manufacturers.

Insurance amount values, estimated from gross earnings.

Loss illustrations of calculating profits and continuing expenses.

Forms, which today are based upon the use of a *gross earnings form,* and for smaller businesses a *no coinsurance earnings* form.

Contingent business interruption insurance applies where direct damage to the *property of others* may cause income loss. *Off-premises power* and *selling agents' commissions* are also examples.

Rents and rental value insurance protects owners or tenants from loss of rental income or use of property following a loss such as fire.

Extra-expense insurance is significant for businesses where customer service must be continued at high additional costs after a direct loss.

Tuition fees insurance is a specialized need of colleges and schools.

No time element losses are those indirect losses in which the length of time required for restoration of property is not a determining factor:

Profits insurance on goods sold but not yet delivered.

Leasehold interest insurance to cover the loss of long-term favorable leases canceled after a serious fire or other direct damage.

Temperature damage insurance for loss to perishable property.

Matched set or parts insurance for jewelry or clothing.

Depreciation insurance for replacement costs over actual cash values.

Valuable papers insurance for expensive or important records.

Accounts receivable insurance for collection loss due to record damage, for "all risks."

Rain insurance for loss of profits due to unfavorable weather.

Indirect loss insurance

Few persons or organizations fail to insure their property against direct losses caused by the fire, windstorm, and other perils discussed in the previous chapter. However, many owners and tenants overlook the need for *indirect loss insurance,* which covers the *additional expenses* and *lost values* (such as *income* or *profits*) that occur as a result of direct physical damage or destruction. Chapter 14 explains the need for and the many kinds of indirect loss insurance, a much-neglected aspect of property insurance.

Too often, when policyholders run to check their insurance policies after a property loss, they find that indirect losses are not covered. The omission is a serious matter. For example, a business firm with a major building destroyed by fire may have ample coverage to replace it—but will the firm go bankrupt without any income during the six months or longer required to rebuild? Without business interruption insurance, many firms are unable to survive until normal operations are resumed.

GENERAL PURPOSES

Indirect loss coverages provide indemnity for losses that occur as a consequence of direct damage to property. Thus, such losses are sometimes called "consequential losses." For example, if an accidental fire destroys a store and its merchandise, the loss of the value of the building and its contents is a direct loss covered by the fire insurance contract. However, the owner of the store will also lose *income* because of the business interruption. This is an indirect loss of fixed expenses and *profits* over and above the actual physical damage to building and merchandise. Another example of an indirect loss is the loss of rental income due to fire causing property to be unusable. Indirect losses also have the purpose of protecting insureds against *extra expenses,* and several other special types of consequential property losses. Such losses may also include other perils such as windstorm, explosion, water, or riot. Indirect loss insurance is a form of after-the-loss insurance.

CLASSIFICATION OF TYPES OF INDIRECT LOSS INSURANCE

Indirect loss that is attributable to the time element required in order to restore damaged property to normal use is known as a *time element loss*. The coverages to provide insurance are known as time element coverages. Among the major time element losses are: (1) losses due to the *interruption of business* by damage to the insured's property; (2) *contingent* losses due to business interruptions; (3) loss of income from *rents,* or loss of *rental value,* caused by damage to the property; and (4) *extra expense* incurred to conduct business or maintain a home on a temporary basis following loss. Loss of *tuition fees* by educational institutions is an example of a special type of time element loss.

In contrast to indirect losses involving a time element, there are many indirect losses that have no relationship to the time required to restore property to normal use.[1] Among the major types are: (1) loss of *profits* on *manufactured goods* and (2) loss of *leasehold,* or excess rental value interest, due to the cancellation of a lease following damage to the property subject to the lease. Miscellaneous types include: loss of perishables due to *temperature change;* loss due to damage to *parts of matched sets;* losses that are the difference between actual value and *replacement cost* new (depreciation); loss or damage to *valuable papers;* loss due to damage to *accounts receivable* records; and loss of profits and expenses due to *rain.*

Most of the major types of indirect loss are written by adding a form to the standard fire contract. For each type of indirect loss insurance, a good understanding of the contract can be achieved by considering the following in analyzing the coverage: What *perils, losses, properties, locations, persons or interests,* and *amounts* are covered? Also, any conditions excluding or suspending coverage should be noted, and the insured's duties and insurer's options after a loss should be reviewed.

TIME ELEMENT LOSSES

Losses that are dependent upon the time necessary to restore the property to normal operations are among the best-known kinds of indirect losses. The amount of the loss is largely determined by the element of time after the loss which is required to repair, rebuild, or restore property to normal use. The losses include lost profits, lost income, lost use of property, contingent losses to other parties, and increased expenses. In effect, the topic is "business survival insurance."

---

[1] This chapter divides all indirect losses into "time element" and "no time element" losses. Another useful division could be between (1) losses which result in *decreases in income* and (2) losses which result in *increases in expenses.*

Business interruption insurance

Importance. Although more than 90 percent of owners carry insurance to protect the physical properties used for their businesses, probably not more than 30 percent of these owners carry *business interruption insurance* to protect the earnings of their businesses. In many cases this is like a sea captain watching out for icebergs on top of the water but forgetting that most of the danger lies underneath.

There is no fixed relationship between property damage loss or value and business interruption loss or value. The importance of business interruption insurance becomes apparent when it is recognized that a small property loss in a vital section of any business may cause a total suspension of operations with a resulting loss far in excess of the actual property damage loss. Consider, for example, the disastrous effects possible as the result of the destruction of an essential elevator or escalator in a department store. Damage of $5,000 to the elevator might result in the loss of $100,000 of earnings during a major sale. On the other hand, it is conceivable that very substantial property damage might occur without serious interruption of operations if the property could be quickly restored to provide normal business operations.

The great need for business interruption insurance is also apparent in the statement that "43 percent of all businesses suffering a serious fire loss never reopen—despite the fact that most carried insurance on building and contents."[2]

Purpose. *Business interruption insurance,* also known as *prospective earnings insurance* and *use and occupancy insurance,* protects against the *loss of income* because of the interruption of business *by fire or other perils.* Fundamentally, it is the *reduction* in gross earnings which is insured. Sizable business interruption losses are cuased not only by fires but also by *windstorms* and *explosions.*

The *riot* peril, too, is one which today should receive much greater attention in the insured's choice of perils to be included in the "BI" contract. New forms in recent years have clarified the interruption by a civil authority clause in these contracts. They cover loss of earnings due to a specific order denying access when there has been damage (such as by riot or civil commotion) adjacent to the insured's property. The damage must be within a few doors or city blocks at the most. Loss due to a general citywide curfew is not covered, however. In essence, the insured *peril* must damage *property,* thus interrupting for a *period* of time the *production* capacity to create *profits.*

The contract is one of indemnity for the net profits not realized, plus such fixed charges and expenses as necessarily continue during the inter-

---

[2] John D. Phelan, *Business Interruption Primer* (Indianapolis Rough Notes, 1970), p. 8. Later studies continue to verify this comment.

ruption, but only to the extent that such fixed charges and expenses would have been earned had no interruption due to an insured peril occurred. Business interruption insurance keeps the business in the position that it could have maintained for itself had there been no interruption. In a sense, its function for an employer is quite similar to the function of unemployment insurance for an employee. It has also been called "living insurance" or "disability insurance" for businesses.[3]

Distinguished from profits insurance. Business interruption insurance is to be distinguished from *profits insurance* in that profits insurance looks to the past whereas business interruption indemnity looks to the future. As will presently be noted, profits insurance protects the insured against the loss of potential net profits on finished stock in the hands of a manufacturer or held in storage. When this stock is damaged or destroyed, the direct loss insurance will cover only an amount necessary to repair or replace the damaged property, not potential profits. Hence, profits insurance is necessary for complete coverage. Time is not a crucial factor in determining the profits insurance loss. In the case of business interruption insurance, on the other hand, time is the essence of the contract. The contract looks to the future and protects the insured against the loss of future earnings during the time required to restore normal business operations after a physical damage loss.

The difference between the two forms of insurance is emphasized when it is realized that profits insurance on a mercantile stock will cover only the profit prevented on the stock on hand which is damaged or destroyed. For example, if a mercantile stock turns over 10 times each year, this would mean that an interruption of six months in the business would result in a loss of five turnovers of the stock. Business interruption insurance would cover this loss, but profits insurance would cover only the loss of profits on the inventory actually on hand and damaged at the time of the loss.

Business interruption insurance amount. The first step in determining the business interruption insurance needed by, for example, the owner of a mercantile store, is to estimate the total values exposed to loss. Usually, these are the *gross earnings* of the firm. In the case of an interruption of business, the store owner would not lose the entire gross sales income, for the net cost of the merchandise in the store would be covered by direct property insurance against fire and other perils. (Other items such as discounts and bad debts would not be lost, either, in an interruption.) Thus, the store owner first calculates gross sales *less* the net cost of merchandise and these other items in order to arrive at estimated gross earnings.

The estimate of the *insurance* amount necessary to cover a *business*

---

[3] Joseph R. Pierpont, "Business Interruption Insurance—What It Covers," *Risk Management,* December 1976, p. 34; and James R. Jorgensen, *Business Interruption Insurance— How It Works* (Mt. Prospect, Ill.: B. J. Publications, 1981), p. 1.

interruption value, or gross earnings, involves several other considerations. First, in a serious loss, would the store be able to get back in
business, at least partially (perhaps at a temporary location), sooner
than one year after the loss? Any factors such as the type of building
construction and the availability of facilities for reestablishing the business are important in determining the percentage of business interruption value to be covered. Second, would the earnings of the store be
subject to substantial fluctuation during the year, as for weddings in
June or Christmas in December? If so, the estimate of lost earnings
must consider the peak periods of the year rather than only the average
daily or monthly loss.

This suggests that the coinsurance requirements of the particular contract form to be used in writing the business interruption insurance
may vary considerably. The forms permit the choice of coinsurance to
be 50, 60, 70, or 80 percent of the gross earnings determined as the
insurable value. These coinsurance requirements give the insured a wide
latitude in the event of fluctuating earnings. For the average mercantile
business, 50 percent of the business interruption value is ordinarily adequate. Losses for minor peak periods are automatically covered so long
as adequate insurance to value is carried, but where the business is
heavily seasonal, larger amounts are indicated. Thus, perhaps 70 percent
of the estimated business interruption value might be chosen as the
insurance amount. Such a choice would be made on the assumption that
it would rarely take longer than about eight months to get back in business in full. If the loss occurred during peak seasonal sales periods, the
insured would have coverage for the larger losses that might result from
the ill-timed shorter period.

One of the contentions about estimating business interruption values
has been the supposed difficulty of predicting the amount of continuing
expenses, whether full or partial. Under the popular gross earnings form
(see later section), however, this is largely unnecessary, because almost
all expenses continue during the most likely interruption, one of short
duration.[4] In this case there are relatively few expenses which can be
deducted from gross earnings (see later example of a business interruption *loss*) in calculating the BI *value.* The major item by far is usually
ordinary payroll expense, which can be deducted when the insurance
contract is on an 80 percent or higher coinsurance form.[5] Aside from
this, probably only a small amount of power, heat, and refrigeration

---

[4] This reasonable observation is credited to correspondence from Richard B. (Ben) Mas-
ters, CPCU, retired, executive manager of the Insurance Educational Association, San
Francisco.

[5] Sometimes the payroll item is very large, and the insured wants coverage. A loss by
Warner-Lambert Co., for example, included a claim for explosion direct property damage
of $1 million, $2 million of lost profits, and $45 million of continuing payroll expenses,
as reported in the *Wall Street Journal,* November 22, 1977.

expenses not under contract could be deducted (an extra premium is charged for this coverage).

Thus, in the later illustration, the business interruption value could be quickly estimated by merely subtracting $250,000 of ordinary payroll from the estimated gross earnings (or "net sales," as this is sometimes called) of $495,000, and a BI value of $245,000 established. This could be larger in a more serious loss, but again it is mostly the discontinuable ordinary payroll item which would increase the deductions substantially, as unskilled workers are laid off. Much of this payroll would not be a discontinuable expense unless the interruption lasted for several months or longer.

The reasoning is similar to that in fire insurance, where in estimating values for the purpose of calculating the insurance amount needed in order to meet coinsurance requirements, some values are often excluded because they would not be damaged in a fire. (These deductions include the cost of excavation, the foundation, and underground piping.) In business interruption insurance, expenses are excluded that will not exist when there are no sales. These include such items as bad debts, discounts, sales tax, returns and allowances, prepaid outgoing freight, rent (when based on sales), commissions on sales, and a few other items deducted from gross income or sales in estimating gross earnings or net sales. The ordinary payroll realistically becomes deductible only in interruptions of longer duration. As the shutdown continues, more expenses begin to drop off, but the insurance amount stays in effect until it is used up in loss payments. Thus, insurance of 50 percent of the gross earnings for an insured with fairly regular earnings may often cover a loss for several months beyond six months, if some expenses discontinue but many remain.

In addition to providing indemnity to the insured for loss of profits and continuing expenses as a result of fire or other perils insured against, the policy agrees to pay *expenses incurred for reducing the loss* under the policy. This element is not computed in arriving at the business interruption insurable value, for it adds nothing to the risk. The operation of this clause is illustrated by the following example. Assume that a seasonal business suffers a fire just as it is about to fill a number of large orders. The loss of profits and continuing expenses is estimated to be $80,000, and work will probably be totally suspended for 90 days. As the business does not wish its customers to go to another concern, it rents a neighboring property, sets up machinery, and is operating at full capacity in 45 days. Although this involves working night and day shifts at increased labor costs of $20,000, the business considers it worthwhile since it is thereby able to maintain its contact with valuable customers. If by the expenditure of $20,000 the insured is able to reduce the loss to $40,000, for example, the insurance company is obligated to pay the $40,000 loss of profits and continuing expenses, plus the expediting expense item of $20,000. This makes the total loss payment $60,000 instead of the $80,000 that it would have been had the expediting expense not been incurred.

Business interruption loss. A business establishment is operated for its *earnings*. Every going business at any given time finds itself in one of three situations: it is being operated at a profit, at cost, or at a loss. While business interruption insurance aims primarily to indemnify the insured for loss of *profits* because of an enforced cessation or limitation of operations, it does not follow that an insured has no loss if the business is not making a profit. When a plant is shut down, certain fixed charges must go on if the business is to continue to function. The policy, therefore, not only covers the loss of net profits on business prevented from being carried on but also includes the payment of such *fixed expenses* as must continue during the business interruption. Fixed expenses are covered to the extent that they would have been earned had there been no loss. Finally, the coverage pays for *expenses for reducing loss,* to the extent that they do reduce loss.

The *duration* of the loss continues only until the insured property is restored to the condition it was in before the loss, not until production or sales are returned to the same level as before.

If a business is operating at a profit and a fire causes suspension, the loss includes both the profit item and the fixed-charge item, plus any costs incurred in order to minimize the loss. If the business is operating at cost and a fire occurs, the loss is the same, less the profit item. If the business is operating at a loss, it may still be earning part of its fixed charges, and these represent a loss if business is suspended.

Comprehensive work sheets have been prepared for business establishments in order to estimate their potential business interruption loss. As an example, the year's loss of a business may be illustrated as follows:

1.	Estimated *Gross Business Income* from sales or services for 12 months following		$1,000,000
2.	Discounts allowed	$ 2,000	
3.	Allowances for returns, etc.	$ 1,000	
4.	Charge-offs for bad accounts	$ 2,000	
5.	Net cost of merchandise or raw stock (whichever applies)*	$500,000	
6.	Total 2 through 5. Deduct from 1		$ 505,000
7.	*Estimated Gross Earnings*		$ 495,000
8.	Salaries, commissions, and wages that may not be paid if operations cease	$250,000	
9.	Delivery service, power, heat, refrigeration, telephone, insurance and tax rebates, and other operating expenses that may be discontinued	$100,000	
10.	Total of 8 and 9. Deduct from 7		$ 350,000
	Balance represents *Estimated Business Interruption Loss*		$ 145,000

* This includes anything, such as packaging, that goes out the door with the product and is used up and consumed in the manufacture of the product, or any services contracted outside, such as delivery service.

Business interruption *loss* is thus estimated by calculating *gross earnings* and subtracting *expenses* which would *not continue* after damage to the physical property has occurred. The remainder is an estimate of the future profits and continuing expenses which would be lost as a result of the interruption of business.

For the average small mercantile establishment, business interruption loss can be determined with the knowledge of *(a)* turnover and *(b)* markup. Averages for a large number of classes of business have been determined by and are available from Dun & Bradstreet and other such financial services. For example, a jewelry store has a low turnover with a high markup and seasonal peaks. On the other hand a meat market has a relatively low markup with a high turnover. In the case of a jewelry store with a stock valued at $80,000 with a 75 percent markup, the gross earnings on one turnover would be $60,000. If the turnover is twice each year, then the annual gross earnings would be approximately $120,000, or an average of $400 a day for 300 working days. The business interruption loss for a year would be $120,000, less the discontinuable expenses. On the assumption that these expenses were estimated at $20,000, for example, the business interruption loss would be $100,000 if the business was stopped completely for one year.

Business interruption forms. Business interruption contracts are usually created by adding a form to the basic part of the standard fire policy. There are only two basic forms: one for *mercantile* and nonmanufacturing risks and one for *manufacturing* risks. The forms make no daily or weekly limitation of payment but require coinsurance based upon the annual business interruption value of the business. These forms have an advantage over the older per diem and weekly forms in that they automatically adjust to fluctuating earnings.[6] The insurer is liable for any loss during the period of coverage, whatever the amount, provided that the face of the policy is equal to or exceeds the coinsurance percentage of the business interruption value.

Seasonal or daily fluctuations in earnings are automatically taken care of, and the actual loss sustained is paid. In the case of a department store, for example, this would mean a high amount of indemnity for Saturdays, with lower amounts for the less active days, as well as higher sums for the periods of greatest activity, such as during the Christmas shopping season, and lesser sums for the dull periods between seasons.

---

[6] Per diem valued forms of business interruption insurance are still written. Some tax and loss settlement advantages, such as for a new business where gross earnings are difficult to predict, offset in some cases the disadvantages of a per day limitation. No coinsurance is required, and the loss payments are usually not taxed as ordinary income as in the other forms. A disadvantage is that the rates are normally higher. Power plant coverages may still be written on a valued basis, and in this field the term *use and occupancy* still prevails.

Department stores, in order to keep their organization intact during short periods of suspension, usually continue most of their employees and for this reason should include in the coverage the item of ordinary payroll.[7] On the other hand, a manufacturing plant may exclude such payroll from its insurable value or may insure it for a limited period or for the entire policy period, whichever coverage best meets its needs.

The *gross earnings form* is most widely used today for most businesses. The business interruption loss is estimated as discussed previously, and a choice made as to the coinsurance percentage desired. The rate decreases as a higher coinsurance requirement is used. The insured's *ordinary payroll* is covered, though if payroll coverage is not desired it may be excluded by endorsement. Forms are written in some jurisdictions with an *agreed amount* instead of a percentage of coinsurance (if the insured files an annual statement of income and expenses), which has the advantage of eliminating the danger that the insured may become a coinsurer because of a deficiency in insurance.

A relatively new and promising solution to the difficulty of estimating coinsurance needs accurately is the *"no coinsurance" earnings forms* available in most states. Earnings forms are different from the *gross* earnings forms discussed previously. They are designed for small and medium-sized business and provide a simple method of determining the amount of insurance. The business estimates its need for income for one month after a loss, and the policy is written for four times that amount.[8] The policy pays for loss of earnings, defined as net profit plus payroll and other continuing expenses, less any noncontinuing operating expenses. Many smaller firms needing several thousand dollars of coverage per month find this form increasingly attractive because of its simplicity. Its disadvantages are that it is not permitted for manufacturers and that it may be higher in cost for larger firms than the gross earnings form.

The business interruption forms contain a number of special exclusions, and the nature of these depends upon whether or not the policy is designed for a mercantile or a manufacturing risk. The policy may provide that there shall be no liability for: *(a)* the destruction of any finished stock; *(b)* any increase of loss which may be occasioned by any ordinance or law regulating the construction or repair of buildings; *(c)*

---

[7] Mercantile establishments in particular have the need to retain the entire staff during a period of shutdown. However, in many other organizations competition for labor may create the necessity of retaining employees of all categories to be available when the business reopens rather than rely on the recruiting of a new staff.

[8] The four times one month's loss of earnings is the result of assuming a maximum restoration period of four months and of a common limitation in the contract of no more than 25 percent of the insurance being available during the first 30 days after loss. In many Western states the requirement is $33\frac{1}{3}$ percent, so the insurance amount is commonly set at three times the first month's estimated loss.

the suspension, lapse, or cancellation of any lease or license, contract, or order; *(d)* increase of loss due to interference with rebuilding by strikers; and *(e)* consequential or remote loss.

Contingent business interruption insurance

This type of indirect loss policy pays the insured for loss due to damage or destruction of property *not* owned or operated by the insured but upon which the business is dependent for continued operation. Major suppliers and major customers need this insurance coverage whenever they are heavily dependent on one or a few sales outlets or sources of supply.

General forms. There are two forms of contingent business interruption insurance: *(a) contributing properties* coverage and *(b) recipient properties* coverage. The first form provides indemnity if the insured business suffers an interruption loss due to the destruction of or damage to facilities of prime suppliers that provide materials, parts, or services to the insured. An example of the need for such insurance was a disastrous fire at Livonia, Michigan. A $50 million fire destroyed an essential transmission plant which supplied many General Motors automobile manufacturers. The vast business interruption suffered as a consequence by the automobile manufacturers was a contingent business interruption loss to them, resulting from the destruction of the properties of the prime supplier of transmission parts.

The second form, recipient properties coverage, insures against loss caused by damage to or destruction of facilities of prime customers of the insured. The subcontractor who supplies materials or parts to a prime contractor or customer might benefit from such coverage. If the business place of the prime customer (i.e., the "recipient property") is damaged or destroyed so that the prime customer cannot take the product of the insured, the subcontractor is covered for business interruption losses under recipient properties coverage. Such insurance is most important when a single large buyer purchases most of the total production and when the product has limited possibilities in other markets.

Another example of the second form of contingent BI coverage is the loss which a smaller store would suffer as a result of destruction or damage to a major department or food chain store in a shopping center. The loss of income caused by the decrease in customers of the smaller store could be insured as a contingent business interruption coverage.

Off-premises power plant insurance. Another type of contingent business interruption coverage becoming more popular as a result of energy shortages is a specialized contingent form covering the continued flow of utilities. Insurance is written to cover loss attributable to the interruption of the supply of electricity, heat, gas, water, or other energy from a public or a private utility. Since the coverage applies with respect to utilities received from plants *outside* the premises of the insured, the coverage is, in fact, a form of contributing properties business interruption insurance. It protects the insured against interruption of utilities due to fire, wind, explosion, or other perils causing damage at the source of supply. Interruption due to damage to transmission lines may be covered, as well as property damage at the generating plant.

Selling agents' commissions insurance. The selling agent who handles large quantities of the output of one or a few manufacturing establishments may suffer a severe loss of income if a continuous flow of the sales product is interrupted. The loss may be covered under a *selling agents' commission form* of contingent business interruption insurance, which is needed when a substantial volume of sales is derived from the output of a single plant. It also appeals to the agent or salesperson who spends the entire year taking orders for a future seasonable delivery. Orders for calendars and advertising novelties, for example, are taken the year around, but deliveries are made in early December. If the plant were destroyed before delivery of the goods, the agent might suffer a severe loss. The goods need not have been completed, since it is sufficient to support a claim if the selling concern is unable to make deliveries because of a peril covered by the policy. The rate charged is the rate for business interruption insurance at the location where the goods sold by the agent are manufactured.

Rents and rental value insurance

If a property is rendered untenantable by fire, there is, in addition to the direct loss or damage, a loss of rental income (if occupied by a tenant) or a loss of use (if occupied by the owner). Losses from this source are insurable under a rents or rental value form of business interruption insurance. *Rents* insurance indemnifies the owner of a property if the owner's rental *income* is cut off or interrupted by fire or other peril included in the coverage. Rents insurance is a particularly important coverage for estates or trusts if the beneficiaries depend largely upon income from real estate holdings. *Rental value* insurance covers the occupant and indemnifies the occupant for the *loss of use* of the premises. The occupant may be the owner, in which case the indemnity is based upon what it costs the owner to secure premises similar to those destroyed or damaged. If the occupant is a tenant under a lease drawn so that rent continues during the unusable period, the tenant can be paid on the same basis.

Rent insurance forms in common use are written with coinsurance requirements varying from 60 percent to 100 percent. The rate is less as the ratio of insurance to value required by the coinsurance clause increases. The amount of insurance necessary for full coverage is the amount of income received during the estimated period required to rebuild the property if it is totally destroyed. In seasonal risks, the policy is written to limit its liability for loss of rent only during the months of customary occupancy.

The period for which a loss may be collected begins with the happening of the fire, or other contingency insured against, and runs for the period required with the exercise of reasonable diligence to restore the property. The loss must originate during the term of the policy, though the liability may continute beyond its termination.

In order to compare rents and rental value insurance with extra-expense insurance (discussed next), Table 14–1 summarizes who needs these indirect loss coverages, the exposed values, the basis for the loss amount, and some restrictions on the loss payments.

The student should avoid confusion with leasehold interest (for tenants) and excess rental value (for owners) insurance, discussed in the later section of "no time element losses." These types of indirect loss insurance pertain only to *increased* rental costs or values based upon *long-term leases.*

Table 14–1. Comparison of rents, rental value, and extra-expense insurance

	Type of insurance		
	Rents	*Rental value*	*Extra-expense†*
Who needs coverage	Owners (including estates)	Owners or tenants occupying the premises	Owners or tenants
Exposed values*	Loss of *income* from tenants having to discontinue occupying the premises	Loss of *use value* due to having to discontinue occupying premises	Additional expenses in order to continue use of premises
Basis for loss amount	Loss of rents for the insured premises	Cost of renting similar other premises	Expenses beyond normal and expenses to reduce the loss
Restrictions on loss payments	Period required to restore property with reasonable diligence	Same as for rents insurance	Often sets limit on basis of insurance amount for one month (40%), two months (80%), or longer (100%)

* These losses must be caused by the perils insured against, such as fire, wind, explosion, and other allied fire perils.
† Called "additional living-expense" insurance for residents as opposed to business.

Extra-expense insurance

Business forms. Subject to the policy limits, *extra-expense insurance* covers all extra-expense or additional charges incurred by the insured *in order to continue* normal business following damage or destruction of buildings or contents by an insured peril. This may cover the cost of doing business at a location other than the usual premises of the insured. Business interruption insurance covers loss when the business is *discontinued.* Extra-expense insurance covers the additional cost of *continuing* a business following a loss. For example, if one location of a company with several production facilities were damaged, the company might incur additional expenses to put on an extra shift of employees at the undamaged locations.

The business interruption policy does cover some expenses incurred in order to continue part of a business or to get a business back into operation, limited to the extent that loss under the policy is reduced. Extra-expense insurance sets no such limitation and provides for any extraordinary outlay that is needed to keep a business in operation. It provides for the extra expense over and above normal operating costs that enables the insured to continue as nearly as practicable normal business operations immediately following damage or destruction to buildings or contents by the perils insured against. The policy does not cover loss of income in any respect.

The amount paid for extra expenses is limited by (1) the basic policy insurance amount and (2) a percentage of the total insurance amount which is set as the maximum that may be used each month following the beginning of indemnity. For example, a common requirement is a limitation of 40 percent during the first month of restoration, 80 percent during the first two months, and 100 percent for periods in excess of two months.[9] The period of indemnity continues during whatever time is necessary to restore the property to normal use.

Some types of businesses have a special need for protection against extra-expense losses. Such firms as banks, milk distributors, newspapers, laundries, and many others must provide at all costs *continuous service* to their customers. Otherwise, their clients are immediately lost to competitors. These businesses need somehow to continue daily service, and extra-expense insurance is an important means by which this can be accomplished. Extra help, services available at temporary locations, and airfreight costs to replace needed equipment are typical extra-expense costs.

---

[9] Coinsurance is not used in connection with extra-expense insurance, although the above monthly limitations serve a similar purpose in encouraging the insured to purchase an adequate amount of insurance.

Some businesses need *both* business interruption and extra-expense insurance. *Combined* BI–EE *insurance* is available in some rating territories. Although many retail stores may find business interruption insurance sufficient to repay them for the loss of fixed expenses and profits, other stores may decide that they could not be out of business very long before permanently losing a substantial number of customers to competitors. Only extra-expense insurance would help reduce these losses, by paying the additional costs of keeping the business in operation. Examples of the need include: unfortunate timing of a loss, perhaps when business is falling and a new store is opening up nearby; and a branch suburban store which needs to continue to operate in spite of a fire destroying the main downtown store.

The extra-expense coverage of this form is based upon 4 to 50 percent of the business interruption insurance amount, as selected by the insured. Separate percentage limits apply for shutdowns less than 30 days, 30 to 60 days, and more than 60 days. The protection is not an additional limit beyond that payable for a business interruption loss, but a part of it. The business interruption rate is increased from 20 to 100 percent, depending on the extra-expense limits chosen, for this type of combined BI–EE coverage.

Residential forms.   Extra-expense coverage known as *additional living-expense* is available for residents of dwellings and is written in connection with rental value insurance. This form bears the same relationship to rental value insurance that extra-expense insurance bears to business interruption insurance. Rental value coverage indemnifies the insured for the rental value of the home during the period that it is unfit for occupancy because of a loss caused by a peril covered by the insurance. The additional living-expense form reimburses the insured for excess expenses necessitated by living elsewhere during the period that the property is not habitable.[10] This coverage is included in the homeowners' contracts discussed in Chapter 23.

The additional living-expense contract covers reasonable and *necessary* living expenses. To establish a claim the expenses must be *incurred.* Thus, insureds may not create excessive charges to provide more luxurious quarters. Conversely, they may not move in with relatives or occupy less desirable quarters on a temporary basis and collect on the ground that they *could have* obligated the insurer for the better quarters under the terms of their policy.

Additional living-expense insurance is not written with a coinsurance

---

[10] Some cynical soul has coined the term *mother-in-law insurance* for extra living-expense cover, presumably because it obviates the need for going to live with in-laws while repairs to a dwelling are being made.

requirement, but the payment in any one month under the contract is limited to 25 percent of the face of the policy. This means that with excess costs of $250 monthly and an interruption of use of the premises of one month, $1,000 insurance would be required. The insurance should be at least four times the first monthly anticipated claim and should be in an amount sufficient to last for the time the family may be expected to occupy substitute quarters.

Additional living-expense insurance does not pay the full cost of substitute quarters but only the *excess* cost of the new quarters above the usual costs of living in the uninhabitable damaged property. Includable expenses in a typical claim for additional living expenses might be the *extra* costs of a hotel or motel for several weeks (perhaps followed by further rental of an apartment or house), eating meals out, laundry costs, extra travel expenses, and many other items.

Tuition fees insurance

Many educational institutions are dependent upon the income derived from tuition fees. A fire or other peril that destroys any substantial part of a school might require a temporary suspension of operations, with a consequent obligation to refund tuition collected or to cancel charges already made. After the work of reconstruction and repair is completed, some students formerly enrolled may not return.

Tuition fees insurance pays for loss occasioned by the necessity to return, or the failure to receive, tuition fees as the outgrowth of an insured peril. Recovery is not limited to the time required to restore the damaged property. If a school building is destroyed or damaged during a school term, the resulting transfers may not be determined until the opening of the next school year. If the reconstruction period runs to a date within 30 days of the opening of the next school year, the loss of tuition includes the loss from transfers that occurred because of the students' uncertainty regarding the completion date. The insured is expected to make use of other available property that will reduce the amount of the loss.

NO TIME ELEMENT LOSSES

Indirect losses in which the time required for the restoration of the physical property is *not* the determining factor in the payment of an insurance loss are of several types. Insurance of these losses is not as important as insurance of the time element losses previously discussed, but the consequences of not considering insurance protection for such losses can be serious in specialized situations.

Profits insurance

Profits insurance indemnifies the insured for loss of profits on finished goods. It is written by attaching a special form to the fire, windstorm, explosion, or other peril insurance contract. Under the fire or other direct loss contract, the measure of the damage to the insured is the cost to repair or replace. In the case of manufactured goods, this is limited to the manufacturing costs. If a warehouse is filled with completed goods not yet delivered, their destruction will result in a substantial loss of profits to the insured. Direct damage loss will be settled on the basis of the manufacturer's cost, rather than on the basis of the selling price for the goods.

In the case of seasonable goods, the profits of an entire year may be lost if fire occurs just before it is time to deliver the finished product. Christmas toys, for example, are ordinarily delivered during the month of October, but the manufacturing process takes place during the entire year. If the year's stock of toys of a manufacturing establishment is destroyed late in September, the loss of profits will be serious. Any business that has substantial amounts of finished stock in storage, regardless of their seasonable nature, can need profits insurance.

The distinction between profits insurance which covers profit loss on only one turnover of goods and business interruption insurance covering perhaps many business turnovers has already been made earlier in the chapter.

Two forms of profits insurance are written. One limits the liability of the insurer for loss of profits to the percentage of loss ascertained and adjusted under the direct property loss policies. A second form, known as the "unlimited form," adjusts the profits item without regard to the percentage of loss on the manufactured goods. The unlimited form is regarded as the most satisfactory protection.

Profits insurance is usually written only for a manufacturer. Loss of profits for a retailer is covered in business interruption insurance. It is expected that the retail merchant can replace at cost much of the damaged stock and would collect only the profits that were not earned during the restoration period. On the other hand, the manufacturer's finished goods cannot be replaced at cost for delivery according to the contract. The time needed for restoration is not a factor in the loss of the profit.

Contingent profits insurance is a special form used by insurance agencies whose commissions are contingent upon their loss experience. Many contracts between the agent and the insurer provide for an agreed commission, plus a contingent commission if the loss experience does not exceed a certain percentage of premiums. As the year's end approaches and the contingent commission is earned, there is the possibility that a serious loss might wipe out the contingent earnings of the agency. An insurance agency may purchase insurance against the loss of these anticipated contingent earnings.

Leasehold interest and excess rental value insurance

Leases often contain a cancellation clause which provides that either party to the lease may terminate it if a designated percentage of the property is destroyed. If a tenant possesses a particularly advantageous *long-term* lease, the lease will in all probability not be continued if the owner can terminate it. In that case, the tenant will lose a valuable interest in the lease. (Refer to Table 14–1 to help you understand how the types of insurance discussed in this section compare with rent, rental value, and extra-expense insurance.)

Leasehold value represents the increased rental value of premises to a tenant in excess of the actual rental agreement. Thus, it is quite possible that a property for which a 15-year lease calling for a $2,000 monthly rental was executed 10 years ago might bring $3,000 a month today. If this is so, the holder of the lease has a leasehold interest in the property valued at $1,000 a month for the remaining 60 months. The increased income value of the lease must be discounted at an assumed rate of normal interest, such as 6 percent or more, because it represents a value over a future time period. Leasehold insurance does not cover in the event of cancellation of the lease for any reason other than the happening of a loss due to one of the perils insured against.

In addition to the situation in which a tenant is paying less than the current market rental value of a property, there are other situations that create an insurable interest in a lease. Where good locations are scarce and are held under long-term leases, a prospective renter might find it profitable to pay a substantial lump-sum *bonus* to secure a present tenant's location. This sum would be lost entirely if the premises were destroyed and the tenant's lease canceled. The policy is written for a face amount equal to the bonus, with the amount of insurance decreasing monthly to reflect the amortization of the bonus. A tenant's *improvements and betterments* may be insured for direct physical loss or damage during the unexpired term of the tenant's lease. In some situations a property owner may agree to make certain renovations for a prospective tenant and require the payment of *advance rent* for a year or more. The cancellation of such a lease would cause the tenant to lose a proportional share of the advance rent for the unexpired term of the lease. Like the bonus and the improvements, this form of advance rent may be covered, with the amount of insurance decreasing over the term of the lease.

In a leasehold interest policy, the lease furnishes the key to the entire underwriting problem. Oftentimes a copy of the lease is attached to the policy. A satisfactory form will require that the property be over 50 percent destroyed by fire (or other specified perils) before the lease may be canceled. Statutes in the state where the property is located govern in case there is no cancellation clause in the lease itself.

Rates for leasehold interest insurance are governed by the building rate. Since a leasehold interest decreases in value from month to month as the term of the lease runs toward expiration, the form provides for a continued reduction in the amount payable. So that it may be equitable, the premium is based upon an average of the amount the insurer has at risk during the policy term. Leasehold interest policies may be written on an annual basis or for a term. If a change in the leasehold value takes place, the insurance may be adjusted to cover accordingly.

A converse of the leasehold interest contract is found in the *excess rental value policy,* which protects the *owner* of buildings who has an advantageous lease that if canceled could not be renewed on equally favorable terms.

Temperature damage insurance

If a temperature change follows a fire loss originating in the insured premises, any loss to merchandise caused by the change is generally held to be covered by the fire insurance contract. If the merchandise is located in a building that secures its heat or refrigeration from outside the insured property, the policy issued on cold storage warehouses, packing plants, greenhouses, and other such risks (where there is a liability for loss or damage by interruption of power or change of temperature) usually exempts the insurer from such indirect liability. Where temperature change may cause such liability, policies may be endorsed to provide *temperature damage insurance* for loss caused by failure of heat or refrigeration.

Matched set or parts insurance

Another source of indirect loss is the loss or damage of one part of a matched set. The risk is especially important in the clothing business, where different parts of a garment are often sent to several locations for processing. Indirect loss or damage by the insured perils due to the reduction in value of remaining parts of clothing or suits is covered by an endorsement, whether the loss or damage is caused at the insured's location or elsewhere. Jewelers also find a need for *matched set insurance* on such articles as earrings, bracelets, and necklaces where the value of the set may be more than proportionally lost by damage or loss of one part.

Depreciation insurance

The fire insurance contract covers the insured for loss or damage to the extent of the actual cash value of the insured property at the time of the loss. Actual cash value is often defined as replacement cost new, less depreciation. An insured building whose value is lessened by age and use, changing business conditions, neighborhood changes, and the like, may be covered under a fire insurance contract, and yet the insurance may be less than the amount necessary to replace the loss or the damaged property.

Depreciation insurance, sometimes called *replacement cost*[11] insurance, pays for full replacement cost new of the insured property without deduction for depreciation. It provides indemnity for the expenditures that the insured is obliged to make in order to restore the property to its full usefulness as before the loss or damage. Depreciation insurance substitutes a figure representing the cost of replacement new for the term *actual cash value.* Only seldom would the replacement cost figure cause a smaller loss payment, which could happen if underinsurance caused a coinsurance penalty to be applied.

Depreciation insurance through replacement cost endorsements or clauses has become increasingly important in the past decade. Homeowners' contracts for residential risks and business multiple-line package policies both often include such protection now. Depreciation insurance is ordinarily written to cover buildings only, including machinery and equipment incidental to building service. A few insurers have in recent years begun to offer such replacement cost insurance on *contents,* too. Coinsurance is usually required for 80 percent or more of the full replacement cost. Some insurers specify a time limit, such as 12 months, within which repair or replacement must be completed with due diligence. The possible increased moral hazard, because the contract pays on the basis of replacement cost (new for old), is carefully watched.

Valuable papers insurance

Many persons and businesses have a great need for *valuable papers insurance.* Lawyers, doctors, authors, architects, photographers, banks, insurance companies and agencies, and the like, suffer extensive losses when their records are damaged. Indeed, protection for the expenses of replacement (or irreplaceable values) is needed to some extent in almost every business.

The valuable papers and records forms provide insurance under two headings: *(a)* specified articles and *(b)* all others. Specified articles are

---

[11] Formerly the term *depreciation insurance* was applied to separate policies covering this risk, while *replacement* cost referred to endorsements to the fire policy. Note that in the former case only the difference between replacement cost and actual value is covered.

The next three types of insurance discussed (depreciation, valuable papers, and accounts receivable) are sometimes classified as types of direct loss insurance. However, they are included in this text as further examples of indirect loss insurance because of the peculiar characteristics of the contracts. They cover principally the additional indirect losses which occur as a consequence of direct loss to these special kinds of tangible property.

listed and valued, and the amount per article is the agreed value for the purposes of loss adjustment. All other papers and records are covered in a blanket amount, not separately valued. It is often required that the insured papers and records be maintained in a fireproof safe or receptacle, named and described in the policy, at all times except when they are in actual use. Good risk management may also be used to reduce valuable papers exposures, by having duplicate papers made and kept off the premises.

Accounts receivable insurance

Another type of insurance based upon losses resulting from damage to or destruction of records is *accounts receivable insurance*. This insurance may be writing on a reporting form or for a lump sum on a nonreporting form. For the reporting form monthly reports of values are submitted, providing greater flexibility where there is a considerable fluctuation in values. The nonreporting form appeals to smaller insureds who do not wish to be faced with the responsibilities entailed in monthly reports.

The policy covers as follows: *(a)* all sums due the insured from customers, including interest, provided that the insured is unable to collect credit payments as the direct result of loss of or damage to records or accounts receivable; *(b)* collection expense in excess of normal collection cost and made necessary because of such loss or damage; and *(c)* other expenses, when reasonably incurred by the insured in reestablishing records of accounts receivable following such loss or damage. A department store using many charge accounts for its sales is a good example of need for this policy. Were its records destroyed, many accounts would be uncollected. Even when duplicate records are maintained, they are seldom completely current and foolproof as an alternative method of treating this risk.

Notes are not covered by accounts receivable insurance. Losses due to electronic or magnetic injury, disturbance, or erasure of electronic recordings are not covered unless caused by lightning. Fidelity losses attributable to fraudulent or criminal acts of any insured are also excluded. The usual war damage and nuclear radiation or radioactive contamination exclusion apply, but the exclusions are few in comparison with the broad all-risks coverage of these policies.

Rain insurance

It would seem to be a far cry from covering direct loss or damage to property by fire to covering insurance for loss of profits due to rainfall. However, windstorm and earthquake losses became covered as extensions

of fire insurance, for both direct and indirect losses. A logical further
step was to provide indemnity for losses due to the interruption of a
business activity when weather is the cause of the loss. *Rain insurance*
pays for such loss incurred as a result of rain, hail, snow, or sleet, for
(1) loss of funds advanced for expenses and (2) loss of income.

Typical situations in which rain insurance can be helpful in providing
needed protection are graduation exercises, fairs, races, baseball and
other sports events, and many charity benefit performances.

An application for the policy must be made at least seven days before
the rain insurance policy attaches. Local agents are not authorized to
bind the insurance without authorization from the home office of the
insurer, and the business is not accepted until the premium has been
paid in advance. It is an unusual type of insurance in comparison with
more common insurance contracts, but nevertheless an indirect loss coverage of importance to some insureds. As someone has said, there's nothing dry about rain insurance!

Unlike other forms of insurance, rain insurance attaches for a very
brief period, usually for only a few hours in a single day. The policy
provides payment if rainfall occurs within certain specified hours. Two
types of coverage are available. One provides for the measurement of
the amount of precipitation, and the findings of an established weather
station are usually relied upon for these readings. The nonmeasurement
contract provides that payment shall be made under the policy if rain
in any amount falls during the specified hours.

There are three common forms of rain insurance coverage. All of them
are strict contracts of indemnity and pay only for the amount of loss
that the rain actually caused. This is determined in different ways for
different types of events. Some are based on income expectancy of previous years, some on fixed expenses incurred before the event, and some
on the necessary refund of advance ticket sales.

FOR REVIEW AND DISCUSSION

1. What basic types of insurance are there against indirect losses? Give two
   examples of each and mention for whom the insurance might be advisable.
2. Why is insurance for indirect losses an important form of insurance protection to the insurance consumer?
3. Barbara occupies loft space as a tenant in a two-story building which is
   destroyed by fire. What is the liability of the business interruption policy
   in the event that *(a)* the owner decides not to rebuild? *(b)* the owner decides
   to rebuild a four-story structure? *(c)* the owner will rebuild but takes several
   months to determine what to do?
4. Sarah claims that the gross earnings business interruption contract with
   50 percent coinsurance should be purchased only where a relatively short

period of business interruption appears likely, such as a total cessation of business for six months. Explain the error in this statement.

5. For the purposes of determining business interruption insurable *value*, distinguish between gross earnings for a mercantile risk and gross earnings for a manufacturing risk. What factor is the cause of the major difference?

6. Mr. Harnack says that since he is not the owner of his own business building he does not need indirect loss insurance. If a fire occurs, he claims that he would move to a new location. Advise him.

7. A store carries a "no-coinsurance earnings" insurance policy for $10,000. Assuming a loss of $5,000 monthly for three months, what will the insurer pay? Why may this policy be better than the gross earnings form?

8. Show the amount of insurance required under a gross earnings BI form with 50 percent coinsurance, based on the following data: *(a)* net sales $310,000; *(b)* merchandise at beginning of year, $40,000; *(c)* merchandise purchased during year, $150,000; and *(d)* merchandise at end of year, $20,000. Assume a 10 percent increase in business for the year ahead over the year to which the above data apply.

9. Is BI coverage limited to the fire peril, or may it include other perils?

10. The Solar Manufacturing Company is operating at a loss and cancels its BI policy on the ground that there will be no interruption of profits if the plant is shut down. Is the reasoning correct?

11. A retail store owner says that he cannot imagine why he might ever need both business interruption *and* extra-expense insurance. How would you advise him, and what contract would you recommend?

12. Extra-expense insurance is written for businesses as well as other risks. What *other risks*, and *how?*

13. Give several examples of the need for *(a) contingent* business interruption insurance, *(b) profits* insurance, and *(c) rent* insurance.

14. Describe a *unique* feature of the following "no time element" coverages for indirect losses: *(a) rain* insurance, *(b) accounts receivable* insurance, *(c) valuable papers* insurance, and *(d) depreciation* insurance.

Chapter 15

Outline of concepts

Major divisions of transportation insurance are *ocean marine* insurance and *inland marine* insurance.

Ocean marine insurance covers primarily sea perils of ships and cargoes, which can be protected from "warehouse to warehouse."

Development was as one of the earliest of all forms of insurance.

The basic contract and perils follow the old Lloyd's of London contract wording, and the contract is a 100 percent coinsurance, *valued* form covering perils of the sea, fire, enemies, jettisons, barratry, and "other like perils." (War and negligence of the crew are perils often added.)

The insurable interests include the *hull* (vessel), *cargo, freight,* and *liability* ("protection and indemnity"). Contracts can be written on *fleets* or *single* vessels, for *voyage* or *time,* and on *single-risk* or *open-cargo* forms.

Special ocean marine insurance concepts are important, some being the use of *implied warranties, average and loss clauses, coinsurance, sue and labor clause,* and *assignment.*

Marine insurance adjustments require special marine adjusters and involve unique terms such as *presumed lost, salvage,* and *abandonment.*

Rates are based on judgment of the ship's classification and many other factors; international competition is important.

Pleasure craft insurance has developed special contracts for yachts, cruisers, and outboard and inboard motorboats in recent years.

Inland marine insurance covers primarily the land or over the land (but sometimes water) transportation perils of property shipped by railroads, motortrucks, and other means of transport.

Needed is broad protection in many situations, in flexible contracts.

Development, based on changing needs of property owners, shippers, and the carriers, has been encouraged by the Nationwide Definition, which classifies the types of risks eligible for inland marine insurance.

Classes of inland marine insurance are basically four, with many varied contracts within each group:

Property in transit, in *trip transit, annual,* and *open* forms.

Bailee liability, for *legal liability* of the bailees, or for the customers.

Fixed transportation property, for bridges, tunnels, and others.

Floaters, which cover mobile types of property wherever it is located:

Personal floaters provide all-risks protection on a scheduled, or on a blanket basis, for many types of personal property or valuable personal articles such as furs, jewelry, cameras, fine arts, and collections.

Commercial floaters are needed for many diverse business properties, including physicians' equipment, salespersons' samples, radium, installations, conditional sales, agricultural machinery, and electronic data processing equipment. Special "block" policies for jewelers and other dealers provide unusually broad coverage.

Transportation insurance

The previous two chapters have discussed the basic fire and allied insurance contracts and insurance for indirect losses. Another important part of property insurance is the very broad field of *transportation insurance*, which is concerned with the perils of property in (or incidental to) transit as opposed to property perils at a generally fixed location. The term does not include normal automobile insurance and aviation insurance, which merit separate treatment in later chapters.

Why is a chapter on transportation insurance (or "marine" insurance, as it is often called) included in this text? You may think that you will never own a ship to insure, nor deal with international cargos that need insurance coverage. However, *ocean marine* insurance is important to you for other reasons. You may own a motorboat or sailboat. Also, ocean marine insurance is the source of many phrases and clauses in fire, liability, automobile, and homeowners' contracts which you will purchase. You are likely to use some of the many types of *inland marine* insurance analyzed here, too—for property in transit, movable equipment and personal property at various locations, or valuable personal articles.

If there were no transportation insurance, what corporation could, or would, own or finance a new $50 million "supertanker"? Or a shipment of $80 million of gold bullion from one location to another? Or an art collection worth $100 million on exhibition throughout the world? Or a new $30 million bridge handling thousands of cars and trucks every day? The probable answer—no one; and our mobile, intercoordinated society of today might come to a screeching halt. But *with* transportation insurance, all of this is possible and more, as communication satellites, robots, lasers, and computers expand insurance needs.[1]

Take one major ocean marine loss—the sinking of the *Amoco Cadiz*[2]

---

[1] William H. Rodda, "Inland Marine's Future," *Business Insurance*, September 13, 1982, p. 39.

[2] "Turbulent Wake of the Cadiz," *National Underwriter* (P. and C. ed.), April 7, 1978, p. 1; and William Kiechel, "The Admiralty Case of the Century," *Fortune*, April 23, 1979, p. 79.

—and what do we see? A concentration of values exposed to many perils in an ocean voyage, in which the one loss "which never could happen" did. The result was over $12 million in insurance paid for the ship and its machinery, more than that figure for the 220,000 tons of crude oil spilled from its mammoth tanks into the sea, and about $30 million of pollution liability damage. The problems of oil slick on nearly 120 miles of French tourist and fishing coastline involved the French and Liberian governments (under whose flag the ship was operating), an Italian crew, U.S. shipowners, Dutch cargo owners, the British charterer of the ship, and many others. Obviously, this loss was a challenge to the future ingenuity of insurers around the world.

MAJOR DIVISIONS

Transportation insurance, usually known in the insurance business as *marine* insurance, has two major divisions. The first of these, *ocean marine* insurance, is one of the oldest written forms of insurance and has to do primarily with the insurance of sea perils.[3] It makes credit for international trade possible.

The second division, of comparatively recent origin, is *inland marine* insurance, which is primarily for land perils such as railroad and motor-truck transportation and for inland waterway transportation risks. Inland marine insurance now includes a wide range of policy forms that embrace every conceivable method of transportation and communication outside of those risks that fall definitely within the ocean marine category.

OCEAN MARINE INSURANCE

Scope and development

Insurance historians tell us that the insurance of ocean marine perils preceded almost all other types of insurance. (See Chapter 3 for an account of the beginnings of such insurance several thousand years B.C.) The first ocean marine policies insured against the loss of the vessel or the cargo. Shippers found that even though they covered their goods while these were waterborne, damage such as total destruction by fire while the goods were on the docks at one end of the voyage or the other could be quite as disastrous as a total loss of the vessel at sea. The first extension of ocean marine coverages, then, was to provide insurance

---

[3] Those with a nautical bent will enjoy such insurance books as Thomas Chubb, *If There Were No Losses* (New York: John B. Watkins, 1957); and William Bronson, *Still Flying and Nailed to the Mast* (Garden City, N.Y.: Doubleday, 1963).

on the cargo while it was on docks or quays. From this, it was but a step to make the coverage effective at the warehouse of the shipper and to terminate the coverage at the warehouse of destination, by the so-called warehouse-to-warehouse clause. Thus was ocean marine insurance brought ashore to cover land and inland water transportation or other perils.[4]

The ocean marine business is highly specialized in its operation and is carried on primarily by large insurers. Most of the American marine risks are insured through the American Hull Insurance Syndicate, through which some 50 insurers cover several thousand ships for amounts up to $50 million or more per ship. Worldwide, Lloyd's of London is one of the famous insurers of ocean marine perils, and these perils account for about one third of its total insurance and reinsurance business. Ocean marine insurance provides protection for *(a)* ships or *hulls; (b)* goods or *cargoes; (c)* earnings such as *freight*, passage money, commissions, or profit; and *(d) liability* (known as *protection and indemnity*) incurred by the owner, or any party interested in or responsible for insurable property by reason of maritime perils.

The basic contract and perils covered

The modern ocean marine policies take their point of departure from the Lloyd's contract adopted in 1779. The perils clause in Lloyd's marine policy form as it is used today follows the original pattern and reads as follows:

> TOUCHING The adventures and Perils which we the assurers are contented to bear and do take upon us in this Voyage, they are, of the Seas, Men-of-War, Fire, Enemies, Pirates, Rovers, Thieves, Jettisons, Letters of Mart and Countermart, Surprisals, Takings at Sea, Arrests, Restraints and Detainments of all Kings, Princes and People, of what Nation, Condition, or Quality soever, Barratry of the Master and Mariners, and of all the other like Perils, Losses and Misfortunes that have or shall come to the Hurt, Detriment or Damage of the said Goods and Merchandises and Ship, etc., or any Part thereof.[5]

In the United States, the Lloyd's policy serves as the general core around which the various contracts offered by the insurance companies

---

[4] Including these land perils led to the establishment of that branch of marine insurance with the seemingly contradictory title of *inland marine* insurance.

[5] For history buffs who enjoy a sense of humor, a delightful booklet, *Shipping and Insurance Sketches, 1867*, was published in 1967 (Insurance Institute of London, 20 Aldermanbury, London EC 2, 92 pages). A picture of marine insurance is recreated, even to the careful observation that secretaries in miniskirts were not a part of the London office scene in 1867. (They wore trousers and beards!)

have been built. The value of the ancient phraseology and the reason for its retention lie in the fact that in the long period of its use, meanings have been definitely settled through the process of litigation.

Because of the international nature of marine insurance competition, coverages have considerable uniformity. In the United States the American Institute of Marine Underwriters standard clauses reflect the generally accepted practice in the American market. These clauses have met with considerable approval, but the fact remains that in the field of marine insurance there are no standard forms made mandatory by law.

Perils of the sea. Looking more closely at the perils listed in the Lloyd's marine policy, several are significant. *Perils of the seas* are mentioned first, and these include winds, waves, collisions, strandings, sinkings, and other such accidents. Not all perils *on* the seas are covered, however, for this would have a broader interpretation.

War. The older perils clause mentions *war*, but most policies used now do not list war in the basic policy. In order to include war, an endorsement is attached to the policy, including the *free-of-capture-and-seizure clause* (FC and S). The war perils covered are specified in a paragraph which more clearly identifies the actions considered as war, many of which are also listed in the original perils clause: actions of "capture, seizure, destruction or damage by men-of-war, piracy, takings at sea, arrests, restraints and detainments, and other warlike operations."[6] These include such actions before or after declaration of war, and also civil wars, rebellions, or revolutions. For more modern war perils, aerial bombardment, mines, torpedoes, and atomic or nuclear weapons are specifically included. A common alternative for insuring all of these war perils is to issue a separate policy covering them.

Fire. One of the important covered perils *on* the sea is *fire*, and it is therefore named as a separate covered peril in the perils clause of the basic policy. Both direct and consequential losses are insured, including damage done by water or other materials used to contain or extinguish fire.

Enemies. The listed peril of *enemies* is peculiar to marine insurance contracts, and this would generally include all types of taking the insured property by force, including pilferage. However, some contracts exclude pilferage by using the term *assailing thieves*. The pilferage peril is difficult to insure—pilferage is often the result of the shipper's negligence through improper packaging, and it leads to argument as to whether the carrier or the shipper had possession of the property at the time of loss. Thus, the pilferage peril is often excluded from the contract of the carrier, and if coverage is desired, it is insured by the shipper.

---

[6] For further interpretation, see Roland Rueger, "Understanding the 'Roll and Pitch' of the Adventure and Perils Clause," *Business Insurance,* September 13, 1982, p. 40.

Jettisons and barratry. Two unusual marine perils are *jettisons and barratry.* The *jettisons* covered are those that involve voluntarily throwing overboard parts of the ship or cargo in order to save the vessel from sinking or other damage. (See also later discussion under "general average" losses.) *Barratry* is also insured by the perils clause, and this generally means all kinds of fraud by the master or the crew with the intention of reaping gains at the expense of the owners. Examples include abandoning or setting fire to the ship, running the ship ashore or diverting it from its course, and embezzlement of the cargo.

All other like perils and losses. The final phrase in the perils clause covers *all other like perils, losses, and misfortunes,* which might seem to imply that the ocean marine policy is an all-risks contract. This is not the case. The coverage only applies to perils that are of the same nature as the perils previously enumerated and losses that are the outgrowth of those perils.

Negligence of the captain or crew. A decision having a lasting influence upon the policy of marine insurance was rendered in the case of the steamer *Inchmaree.* The crew's negligence caused a check valve to close with salt, with the result that a pump was damaged. The loss was held not to be covered under the "and all other perils, losses, and misfortunes" clause of the marine policy. The *Inchmaree clause* was introduced into hull policies in order to include *negligence of the master or crew* in the list of perils insured against. If, for example, insufficient fuel is placed aboard a ship and the master is obliged to burn furniture to bring it into port, this is not a fire loss. Negligence in providing the proper fuel is the proximate cause of the loss, and negligence of this nature is covered. Another example might involve an explosion caused by negligence of the captain or crew. Other explosions are usually included by adding an "explosion clause" to cover bursting boilers and other losses due to latent (undiscovered) defects in equipment.

The insurable interests

As with fire insurance, the insured must have a financial interest in the subject of insurance in order to have an enforceable contract. An *insurable interest* is present when the insured has a relationship to the property or interests protected, such that a real value is lost, if a loss occurs. The interest need not exist when the insurance is effected, but it is absolutely essential that it exist at the time of the loss.

Valued form and 100 percent coinsurance. In contrast to the situation in fire insurance, in ocean marine insurance the policy is usually written on a *valued* form, making the agreed valuation binding upon both parties at the time the insurance is placed. This is a measure of the *amount* of insurable interest or full value. Ocean ships often have values of many millions of dollars, with cargoes of equal or larger value.[7]

In the settlement of a loss under a marine policy, the liability of the insurer is similar to that of an insurer under a fire policy with the *100 percent coinsurance* clause. The principle is so thoroughly understood that it is recognized as established in law and need not be inserted in the policy in the form of a coinsurance clause. When rates are made, it is understood that the amount designated in the policy represents the full value of the risk. Failure to designate full value has no effect upon the insurance in case of total loss, and the full amount of the insurance is paid. In the event of partial loss, however, the insurer is obligated to pay only that portion of the partial loss that the amount of insurance bore to the value of the risk. To illustrate, if a cargo valued at $50,000 is insured for $25,000 and there is a loss of $10,000, even with $25,000 insurance the full amount of the loss cannot be collected. Since the amount of insurance to value is one half, the amount for which the insurer is liable is likewise one half.

Time and voyage policies.   Another method of describing the interests insured in ocean marine insurance is in relation to the *duration* of the coverage. The policy is either a *time policy,* providing coverage for a fixed period of time (usually one year), or a *voyage* policy, insuring the subject matter only for the specific voyage described in the contract.

Hulls, cargo, freight, and liability interests.   One of the most important classifications in ocean marine insurance divides contracts into four groups based upon the *type of interest* covered: (1) *hulls,* (2) *cargo,* (3) *freight,* and (4) *liability.* Each of these major types is next discussed in a separate section.

Hull.   Hull policies cover various types of vessels. These policies are adapted to ocean ships, sailing vessels, builder's risks, port risk policies, fleet policies, and the like. A hull policy may cover the liability risk by incorporating a collision or running-down clause into the form.

In the interest of a lower premium, hull policies are written that provide for either a deductible average or a minimum franchise form. When the *deductible average* form is used, any sum agreeable to the parties may be written into the contract. It may range from a few hundred dollars to hundreds of thousands, depending upon the risk and the amount of loss that the insured is willing to carry. Under deductible average, the deduction is made from any loss. Under the *minimum franchise* form, no claim is paid unless the loss reaches a certain limit, but if the loss reaches or exceeds the designated limit, it is paid in full. This is the most frequently used form of deductible. Ordinarily 3 percent is used, but the designated limit is sometimes as high as 10 percent.

---

[7] An example of one of the largest ocean marine losses in recent years was the German ship München, which was insured for $60 million with a cargo loss of $20 million.

The *builders' risk form* covers the perils peculiar to ship construction. The policy attaches from the laying of the keel, and it covers not only the hull itself but also tackle, engines, boilers, machinery, and all furniture and fixtures as well as all material used in construction. The policy covers against fire and other named perils, and risks of launching may be included. Excluded are claims originating from loss of life and personal injury, workers' compensation and employers' liability, strikes, riot, civil commotion, earthquake, and war risks.

With the development of large companies to operate fleets of vessels, it was found that insuring the *fleet* under a single coverage had certain advantages. The most important of these was the inclusion of the less desirable and older risks in the policy at an average rate. If the vessels in the fleet were insured individually, the poorer vessels might be rejected altogether by the underwriters or accepted only at a very high rate. Ships operated as fleets are today frequently separately owned as a matter of law through a corporation formed to own each ship in the fleet. Another corporation is formed to operate it. This legal device has the effect of limiting liability claims in cases of accident and calls for the *single vessel* coverage.

Even when navigation is *seasonal,* as in the case of the northern lakes, the vessel policies are written for a year, since fire and other perils are matters of concern whether or not the ship is in use. A winter-mooring clause requires satisfactory conditions. If the vessel is laid up in port, a return premium is allowed.

Cargo. Anyone shipping or receiving goods by sea may have need for *cargo* insurance. Cargo policies may be written under a *single-risk form* providing insurance for a particular ship, or they may be written under *floating or open forms* which provide coverage for goods of a certain class up to a certain limit, their values to be declared subsequently. Freight coverage may be included in such policies. Many shipments are usually covered under an open-cargo form, automatically covering all of the insured's shipments on and after an effective date.

Open-cargo forms are designed to accommodate exporters or importers who are shipping goods throughout the entire year. Goods consigned to them are often aboard and under way before notice is in the hands of the owner. Under the export form, the insured issues certificates of insurance without delay as evidence of the fact that insurance is in effect. The import policy is sufficiently broad to attach automatic coverage even before the insured or the insurer know that the cargo is shipped. All shipments are covered from the time the interest of the insured attaches.

Freight. Policies issued to cover freight interests are usually designed to cover hull or cargo interests as well. The freight interest is usually included in the valuation. If a ship undertakes a voyage and the freight to be earned is not payable until the cargo is delivered, the total loss of the ship will also involve the loss of the freight to be earned on the cargo. It is thus normal in insuring the hull to include the income expected from freight for the voyage. In the case of a cargo shipment, the shipping charges will represent part of the value at the port of destination, and it is customary to add shipping costs (freight) to the value at the port of embarkation. This form of insurance bears a close resemblance to the purposes of business interruption insurance discussed in Chapter 14.

Liability. Damage to an insured ship as a result of collision constitutes one of the perils covered under the marine policy. The policy without special provision does not cover the liability of the shipowner for damage caused to other ships. To cover this liability, the *collision* or *running-down clause* (RDC) is made a part of the hull policy. If the insured vessel is at fault in an accident, the RDC pays for the damages to the other ship. In case both vessels in a collision are found to be responsible, the liability of each vessel is fixed in proportion to the degree in which each vessel is at fault. The collision clause is limited to provide indemnity only in the case of liability for physical damage to another vessel and its freight and cargo, including loss of use of the damaged vessel. The clause does not assume liability for damage to cargo in the custody of the insured vessel, or damage to persons, or damage to docks, piers, and the like.

If collision insurance is provided for fleets under a common ownership, there would be no payment under the ordinary collision clause in the case of a collision of two ships in the same fleet.[8] The situation is covered by the so-called *sister-ship clause.* The insured would be paid under the policy as if the vessels were owned or managed separately.

The collision liability provided in the RDC is often broadened by *protection and indemnity* (P&I) *insurance* in a separate policy, though sometimes this is added by an endorsement. The coverage is a highly specialized form of marine legal liability insurance with respect to vessel operations. The policy "protects" and "indemnifies" the owner and operator of the insured vessel with respect to *(a)* crew members, *(b)* persons other than employees, *(c)* cargo, *(d)* fixed objects, and *(e)* miscellaneous claims, including liability for customs or other fines or penalties. Protection and indemnity insurance is much broader than the coverage provided in the *running-down clause,* which covers only damage to other *vessels* (and loss of use) and their freight or cargo interests.

Coverage for liability of the insured for personal injury to and death of *crew members* is the source of a large number of claims. Negligence

---

[8] One of the largest recent losses of this kind involved two mammoth supertankers, each nearly four football fields long, belonging to Bethlehem Steel Corporation. The collision occurred off the coast of South Africa, and damage claims of $35 million were estimated (*The Wall Street Journal,* January 16, 1978, p. 25).

is not necessarily a condition precedent for liability. A crew member who is injured or becomes ill while in the service of a vessel is entitled to wages to the end of the voyage, maintenance, return passage, and medical care. If negligence of the vessel is a factor, a liability suit may be filed against the shipowner. Liability of the vessel to *persons other than employees* for bodily injury and death is covered, including claims of passengers, stevedores, and any other persons who may be working on the vessel or be on board. Any responsibility of the vessel owner for damage to *cargo* carried by the vessel is covered. If damage is attributable to negligence, the cargo owner may proceed against the ship for losses resulting from improper stowage, contamination, the unseaworthiness of the vessel, and shortages. Damage to *fixed objects* such as piers, docks, bridges, marine cables, and aids to navigation may run to very sizable sums. Unlike the usual liability policy, the coverage will pay damages if property belonging to the insured, such as docks and wharves, is damaged. Also covered are liability for *customs, quarantine,* immigration, or other *fines,* or *penalties* for legal violations for which the owner, master, or agents of the vessel are liable. The P&I policy is written on a deductible basis, with deductibles ranging from $250 to as high as $15,000 or more a claim.

Under the terms of the Longshoremen's and Harbor Workers' Compensation Act (1927) and its amendments, every employer with one or more employees covered by the act is obliged to secure the payment of compensation either by insurance or by qualifying as a self-insurer. The coverage includes "disability or death, of an employee resulting from an injury occurring upon the navigable waters of the United States (including any dry dock), if recovery for the liability or death through Workers' Compensation proceedings may not be validly provided for by state law." This requirement does not extend to include the master or crew of any vessel. The insured's liability for compensation may be endorsed upon the marine policy that has been extended to cover P&I risks.

Special ocean marine insurance concepts

Ocean marine contracts are important for several concepts contained in additional clauses and features. The "implied warranties" of ocean marine contracts are unique in comparison with other insurance contracts. Other principles are found in many insurance contracts but were derived from the ocean marine field. These include the "average" and "memorandum" deductibles, coinsurance, the "sue and labor" clause, and assignment provisions.

Implied warranties. *Implied warranties* are seldom incorporated into the policy, for by law, they are made a part of the agreement without any expression on the part of the parties. Strict compliance is necessary since they form a condition precedent before an obligation exists on the part of the insurer. If the condition be broken at the inception of the risk, there is no contract whatever and the policy is void. In most other types of insurance, warranties (often interpreted as representations) can be breached without terminating coverage, although loss payment may then become voidable at the option of the insurer.

Among the more important of the implied warranties are those that have to do with *(a)* seaworthiness, *(b)* deviation, and *(c)* legality. The insurer has a right to expect that the vessel insured is *seaworthy*. Generally speaking, the ship must be tight; properly equipped with cargo properly stowed and not in excess of safe carrying capacity; with necessary food, fuel, water, and other stores; and with a competent master, officers, and crew and with a pilot when one is required by law or usage. The *deviation* warranty provides that the insured vessel must not deviate from the proper course of the voyage. (Exceptions are those deviations necessary for the safety or success of the voyage, such as to avoid an iceberg or a hurricane.) To comply with the warranty of *legality,* the venture must be lawful, and so far as it is within the control of the insured, it must be carried out in a lawful manner. Smuggling is an example of an illegal purpose.

Average and loss clauses. The term *average* appears frequently in connection with maritime insurance losses. The etymology of the term is not altogether certain, though the contention that it is derived from the French word *avarie* and means "loss" or "damage" is in line with its present-day use. For example, *general average losses* and *particular average losses* are discussed next.

General average losses. When the cargo, or a part thereof, is thrown overboard, or when a part of the vessel is sacrificed for the purpose of preventing the vessel from sinking or other damage, the property sacrificed is said to have been "jettisoned." Property jettisoned to save other property, by law, must be contributed for by all of the owners of the property saved. They each share proportionally, in relation to their values, in the loss. The contribution is termed a *general average loss*. There are three essentials, each of which must be present, in order to establish a claim for general average. The sacrifice must be (1) voluntary, (2) necessary, and (3) successful. If a mast is carried away in a storm, even though the ship rides more easily thereafter, there can be no claim for general average because of the act was not voluntary. The loss is covered, however, if the captain necessarily orders the mast cut away. If the property for which the sacrifice is made is not saved, obviously the owners derived no benefit from the sacrifice, and accordingly they are under no obligation to contribute to a general claim. The rules for settling general average losses vary in different countries.[9]

---

[9] Many nations follow the "York-Antwerp Rules" which cover disputable points such as the cost of repairing different ships, jettison of open deck cargo, and temporary repairs.

Particular average losses. A *particular average loss* differs from a general average loss in that it does not require contribution from other parties. It differs from a total loss in that the item of property insured is not destroyed or lost in its entirety. Thus, it is a partial loss to individual interests, such as that caused by a fire which damages the cargo of a particular person.

The rules for ascertaining the amount of a particular average loss differ with the interest involved. When a vessel's *hull* is damaged, the measure of indemnity is predicated upon the cost of repairs, less the customary depreciation deduction, depending upon the age, type, and condition of the vessel and the character of the repair. When certain items of a *cargo* are totally destroyed, the loss is determined by the proportion that the part lost bears to the value of the whole. Thus, if 5,000 barrels of potatoes are insured for full value at $100,000 and 1,000 barrels are totally destroyed, the loss is $20,000, or 20 percent of the insurance. If the goods are delivered at their destination in a damaged state, the difference between the sound and the damaged values at the port of arrival is determined. A partial loss of *freight* interest for the value of the shipping charges may be the result of a partial loss to either the ship or the cargo, or both. The measure of indemnity is determined by finding the proportion that the lost freight charges bears to the total freight charges.

Memorandum and FPA clauses. Under the broad coverage of the marine contract, insurers would be continually harassed by claims for trifling losses whenever shipments of certain susceptible types of merchandise were covered. To help solve the problem, a "memorandum clause" was added designating certain goods upon which the underwriter was relieved of all partial loss. On other goods less susceptible to damage, no loss was to be paid unless the damage amounted to a certain percentage of the value, known as the "average limitation." This was a "franchise" type of deductible, the claim being paid in full if the loss exceeded the deductible amount.

In modern cargo policies, the objectives of the memorandum clause are attained by the use of the *free of particular average (FPA) clauses.* A FPA clause may be issued with the intention that a loss shall usually be paid only if it is *total.* An example is the "free of particular average American conditions" (FPAAC) clause: "Free of particular average unless caused by the vessel being stranded, sunk, burned, or in collision but including jettison and/or washing overboard irrespective of percentage." This clause is used particularly for cargo shipped on deck, and partial losses are covered only for the specified perils. In the case of underdeck shipments, approved merchandise is ordinarily covered under the FPAEC (English conditions) clause: "Free of particular average under 3 percent unless the vessel be stranded, sunk, burned or in collision, each package separately insured." This clause relieves the insurer of paying petty claims, but if the loss to any package equals or exceeds 3 percent it is paid in full.

Sue and labor clause. A section of the perils clause provides that the insureds or their representatives are both permitted and obligated to take certain designated steps to prevent, limit, or reduce loss. This clause, known as the *sue and labor* clause, is a collateral agreement separate and apart from the provision to indemnify for loss or damage from the named perils. Payments made to an insured for expenses incurred under the sue and labor clause are not regarded as a partial loss and therefore are not subject to percentage restrictions that may apply to particular average claims. In the case of a total loss, compensation under the sue and labor clause might sometimes be payable over and above the face of the policy. The expenditure must be the act of the insureds or their agents and must definitely be made in order to save the ship or goods insured from damage by the perils insured against in the policy. Salvage charges are paid if the salvors act under contract with the insured.

Assignment clauses. Marine policies are usually assignable, but an insurable interest is required. The assignment may be invalid if the interests of the assignee materially change the character of the risk. After a loss covered by the policy, the policyholders may assign their rights of action to another. Cargo insurance policies have clauses to permit assignment before a loss and without the consent of the insurer by writing the insurance "on account of whom it may concern." In the case of hull policies, insurers, foreseeing the importance of moral hazard, incorporate in the policy a clause making the policy void if it is assigned without their consent.

Marine loss adjustments

The adjustment of marine losses involves a considerable degree of technical knowledge and, accordingly, is usually entrusted to experts. Marine adjusters represent all parties in the loss and, in effect, act as arbitrators in the settlement.

In order to establish a claim under the policy, it is necessary to present certain information which is obtainable from marine documents. As a source of proof that the loss was caused by one of the perils insured against, reference may be made to the *log* of the vessel and a document made by the master under oath termed the *master's protest.* In the case of a claim on a cargo, the *bill of lading* is presented to show that the goods on which the loss is claimed were actually aboard the ship in question. The *invoice* of the goods serves as a basis for arriving at the value of the shipment and for determining whether or not the insurance is adequate. The insurance policy or *certificate* is necessary in order to determine to whom the loss is payable.

An unusual circumstance prevails in ocean marine insurance if the ship has not been heard from after a reasonable time. It is then *presumed to have been lost,* and a claim for an actual total loss may be made. There is no time fixed by law after which a missing vessel should be presumed to be lost. In England, a notice of missing vessels is posted at Lloyd's, and 10 days thereafter claim may be made upon the insurers for total loss. In this country, 30 days may run before the payment for loss is due.

When used in connection with insurance and maritime law, the term *salvage* has two distinct meanings: (1) the property which is saved and (2) the compensation due to those who voluntarily assist in saving a ship or cargo in peril. Salvors have a legal interest in the property saved, and if they and the owners of the property are unable to agree upon an amount for a reward, the amount is fixed by an admiralty court. A vessel deserted by its crew without the intention of return is said to be a "derelict." In such cases an old rule awarded the salvors one half of the property saved, which is now held to be an upper limit for salvage. The actual amount depends upon the danger, risk, time expended, and skill necessary to save the threatened property. The work of salvors benefits the marine insurers, and the marine policy pays for the cost of salvage.

When the subject of insurance is wholly destroyed, irreparably damaged, or taken from the insured without hope of recovery, the loss is total and *actual.* Ships and cargoes, however, can suffer other types of losses. They may, for example, be stranded or sunk beyond recovery, or captured and taken from the insured's control. When the loss becomes total only because the subject matter of the insurance is abandoned, and the entire property is not actually destroyed, the loss is termed *constructive.* So far as the insured is concerned, the loss is total, though there may be some salvage to the insurer. In England, when the cost of repairing or recovering the ship or goods will exceed their value when restored, abandonment is permitted. In this country, claim for a total loss is permitted if the cost of repairs or expenditures will be in excess of 50 percent of the value of the property when restored. In these cases, there may be an *abandonment* (at the insured's option only) of the property. The insured gives up the property to the insurers, and the full insurance amount is paid. The insured must prove that a constructive total loss has occurred and make the decision to abandon promptly so that the insurers can salvage as much of the property as possible, if they choose to do so.

Rates

Ocean marine insurance has long been written on the basis of judgment rates quoted by underwriters after an appraisal of the entire risk. As in other fields, statistical data are accumulated. However, because the perils covered for each particular voyage tend to differ in so many respects, it is not easy to determine a rate that may be generally applied. Even in the case of ships that are nearly identical, differences in management and policies of operation could easily have the effect of requiring entirely different rates. Ships sailing over an identical course present risks in summer that are different from those in winter. In some areas hurricanes, icebergs, and fogs may create a seasonal hazard. Shoals, tides and currents, inadequate anchorages, and dangerous approaches affect navigation. In no other branch of the insurance business is judgment so important.

Marine insurance syndicates, such as the American Institute of Marine Underwriters, suggest advisory rates for certain types of cargo shipments made upon approved ships. Recent increased use of "containerization" (large sealed units and pallets) has decreased rates for theft and handling damages. In the case of a policy producing a sizable volume of business, the insurer would probably quote lower rates than those suggested. Conversely, a policy on susceptible merchandise might require rates higher than those quoted. The reputation of the shippers, their experience record, and the classification of the ship would modify the rates.

Vessel construction is an important factor in ocean marine rate making. Data bearing upon the construction and type of a vessel are assembled by *classification societies* and made available to insurance underwriters through periodic publications known as *registers*. The registers contain data on nationality; the number of decks; the condition of the rigging, engine, boiler, and equipment; and the date of the last survey.

The ocean marine insurance market tends to be international in its scope. The growth of world trade in recent decades has created new and challenging insurance problems, such as the giant "supertankers" whose future costs have been predicted as $100 million or more per ship. American insurers have been permitted exemptions from antitrust legislation that permit them to combine in order to develop rates and share risks. American businesses tend to insure with U.S. firms, but in some years approximately 50 percent of American marine business is insured abroad. The large size of each risk and the international market make ocean marine insurance a highly competitive field.

Pleasure craft insurance

Millions of motorboats and yachts are owned and used privately for pleasure purposes in the United States. Many of the smaller pleasure boats are provided limited insurance through the homeowner's contract, which automatically includes fire and theft coverage up to $500 on boats and equipment and liability protection for boats up to certain sizes (sailboats, 26 feet; outboards, 25 horsepower; inboards, 50 horsepower). Some larger boats can be added to the homeowner's contract by endorsement.

Special contracts have been designed to cover motorboats and outboard motors in use today. These *outboard policies* provide physical damage insurance for the motors, boats, trailers, and equipment. Although called "comprehensive" policies, they are usually named-perils coverage, typically including such perils as fire, theft, collision, wind, and loss of motor overboard. Bodily injury liability insurance is not provided in these contracts, but limited (usually to $500, or the hull value) coverage for property damage liability to other boats is included under the "collision or running-down clause." In order to secure more adequate liability protection, the owner should also purchase protection and indemnity coverage which covers liability for loss of life and personal injury and for property damage. Medical payments may be included, too.

Special *yacht policies* have been developed to meet the insurance needs of the owners of the larger boats, such as cabin cruisers, inboard motorboats, and sailing ships. Most such marine contracts are for a term of one year, covering the hull, sails, fittings, furniture, provisions, machinery, and equipment. If new, boats are valued at their purchase price; if secondhand, at cost plus improvements. The policy is valued, and full insurance to value is required.

The package policies usually include (1) the hull, (2) protection and indemnity, (3) federal compensation, and (4) medical payments insurance. The insured vessel is insured for perils of the sea and other waters described, fire, theft, barratry (employee fraud causing ship damage), general average and salvage charges, latent defects and negligence, jettison, and "other like perils." Exclusions often include wear and tear, pilferage, war risks, strikes, riots and civil commotions, and damage sustained while racing. Partial losses are covered in full if these are equal to the deductible franchise expressed in the policy, which ranges from $25 to $500 and is usually about 1 percent of the value of the ship.

Certain geographical limits are designated in the policy, and the coverage applies only within the territory of intended use specified in the contract. Leaving these limits without the consent of the insurer constitutes a deviation and suspends the policy until the insured vessel returns to the cruising limits undamaged. Liability during waterskiing is often excluded, or coverage amounts are restricted to basic limits. The rates vary considerably, and discounts are frequently given to accident-free boaters and boaters who have passed accredited Coast Guard safety courses.

INLAND MARINE INSURANCE

Inland marine insurance is much more recent in its origins than ocean marine contracts. The impetus for inland marine insurance coverages appeared in the railroad age, and it grew rapidly during the automobile and airplane eras. In our mobile society, many families and most businesses need to know about the different exposures to loss covered by the varied field of inland marine insurance. The related field of aviation insurance is discussed in Chapter 22.

The need

For many years shippers looked to the gigantic *railroads* for reimbursement in the event of loss or damage to the goods shipped. Much litigation and delay stemmed from the liability limitations that were incorporated into the bills of lading. A growing tendency to seek private transportation insurance was crystallized during World War I when the government took over the railroads. About the same time, *automobiles and trucks* were becoming an increasingly important factor in the transportation system. The shipper had little or no assurance of the ability of the trucking concern to meet large losses. If the shipper owned the trucks, the contents needed to be separately insured. The *airplane* also caused apprehension lest this method of transportation prove particularly hazardous.

Another important basis for inland marine insurance is the fact that the common carrier is *not* always liable for loss or damage to the goods owned by the shipper. The common-law liability of the carrier has been thus expressed: "The law charges this person thus entrusted to carry goods against all events, but Acts of God, and of the enemies of the King."[10] The early common law has been modified slightly to make a carrier not liable for a loss occasioned by an "act of God" (such as a tornado, lightning, or a flood), by an order of the public authority, by a public enemy, by faults of the shipper, or by the inherent vice or nature of the goods. The carrier is liable for fire, burglary, and other perils, and for its own negligence. However, developments in recent years have often limited the amount for which the carrier may be held under "released" bills of lading.

When goods in the hands of a common carrier have reached their destination and have been placed in reasonable safety, the status of the carrier automatically changes (usually in 48 hours) to that of a warehouser. The difference in status is that when the carrier becomes a warehouser, it is liable *only* for losses growing out of its negligence. Failure to provide adequate protection to meet such situations may entail a serious loss to the shipper.

The use of motortrucks as carriers led to a demand for insurance covering the legal liability of the carrier and other bailees who had temporary custody of goods for owners. Not all persons operating transportation facilities come within the legal classification of common carriers. Some

---

[10] *Coggs* v. *Bernard*, 2 Lord Raymond 909; 1 Smith's Leading Cases 369.

truckers who do not operate regularly established routes or who work primarily for one or two customers accept goods as bailees; in this instance, they are liable for negligence but are not virtual insurers of the goods, as are common carriers.

Development of inland marine insurance

Inland marine insurance does not refer only to the insurance of transportation risks on inland waterways. It developed out of the need for inland transportation insurance involving land risks or waterborne risks, or both. It was natural that appeal for the coverage should first be made to marine insurers that knew the problems of transportation risks and were authorized to write much broader coverages than could be obtained under the old fire or casualty contracts. The inland marine contracts were particularly desirable when there were concentrated values such as furs, jewelry, or art treasures. A single policy covering all risks had a tremendous appeal as compared with insuring the risks against burglary, fire, and other specific perils, particularly when the all-risks policy could be obtained for a lower cost. The fire insurance business had little flexibility with respect to policies, forms, and rates. Thus competition flared between the fire and marine insurers.

The fire insurers worked out a definition of marine insurance which in 1933 was approved by the National Association of Insurance Commissioners. This became known as the "Nation-Wide Definition and Interpretation of the Insuring Powers of Marine and Transportation Underwriters." In 1953, the definition was considerably broadened and modified by the NAIC. The title was shortened to *The Nationwide Definition,* and it is divided into two parts. The first part states the conditions under which marine and transportation policies may cover *(a)* imports; *(b)* exports; *(c)* domestic shipments; *(d)* bridges, tunnels and other instrumentalities of transportation and communication; and *(e)* personal property floater risks. The second part of the definition, known as the "restrictive section," specifies about six prohibited risks where the element of transportation is ordinarily lacking. A 1976 revision has now been adopted in most of the states, providing greater flexibility and dividing the floater risk category into two separate divisions—personal and commercial floaters. Electronic data processing policies are a significant commercial class that has become eligible under the definition of marine insurance.

Another step in putting an end to unregulated competition was the development of uniform rates and forms. The Inland Marine Insurance Bureau is now part of the Insurance Services Offices as a rating body, and IMIB rates and forms set the pattern for much of inland marine insurance. However, many of the contracts in the transportation field are still unregulated. Pipelines, radio and television towers, salespersons' samples, store and equipment floaters, installment risks, and fine arts policies are still in the unregulated areas.

Classes of inland marine insurance

Basically a risk must involve an element of transportation to be eligible for an inland marine contract. Either the property is actually in transit, is held by persons (bailees) who are not its owners, is at a fixed location which is an important instrument of transportation, or is a movable type of goods which is often at different locations. There are four divisions or classes of inland marine insurance: (1) property in transit, (2) bailee liability, (3) fixed transportation property, and (4) personal and commercial floaters.

Inland marine policies are written on an all-risks or a named-perils basis. When a policy is written on an *all-risks basis,* it provides broad automatic coverage of all risks without naming each peril in the contract. The only risks not included are those named in the listed exclusions of the policy. All-risks coverage does not necessarily include all losses, however, for some losses are certainties and do not involve risk. A loss must be attributable to some unpredictability that could not have been foreseen. Thus losses due to innate tendencies to deterioration or wear and tear are not covered. Policies written on a *named-perils basis* may provide a coverage limited to a few perils, or one that is virtually but not actually all risks.[11] The extent of the coverage will depend upon the number of perils which are specifically listed as being included in the policy coverage. Another name for such a contract is a "specified-perils" policy.

The wide variety of inland marine insurance contracts will be apparent as the classes of coverage are discussed. Appendix D offers a detailed list of the prospects for marine and all-risks contracts, indicating for a number of common businesses and situations the types of insurance property and the form of the policies recommended. For example, manufacturers are shown as prospects for the following inland marine contracts: trip transit; motortruck cargo; parcel post; and floater policies for neon signs, exhibitions, installations, installment sales, salespersons' samples, patterns, garment contractors, and many others.

Exclusions vary with the type of contract, with the addition of exclusions necessary to delineate properly the extent of the coverage. In a named-perils policy it is customary to exclude loss by leakage, breakage,

---

[11] For example, a policy written by one insurer on the George Washington Memorial Bridge spanning the Hudson River at New York covered against the perils of fire; explosion; collision; lightning, flood, floating ice, tornado, hurricane, windstorm, tidal wave, rainstorm, falling meteor, earthquake, or other acts of God; malicious mischief, banditry, sabotage, or other acts of violence; strikes, labor disturbances, riots, or other civil commotion; collapse or failure; and seizure or detention.

marring, scratching, and wet or dampness, and losses attributable to wear and tear or gradual deterioration. All policies exclude losses caused by the risks of war, nuclear or radioactive force, and confiscation of illegal goods by any government authority. Even in an all-risks contract, certain losses such as breakage of statuary, glassware, porcelains, and similar fragile articles are excluded. Losses caused by strikes, riots, or civil commotion may be excluded. Finally, it is customary to exclude loss or damage by any process while the property is actually being worked upon. Reference in every instance should be made to the particular contract to determine the exclusions which apply.

A valuable aid to the student of insurance is the understanding that all insurance contracts must have some exclusions. (See section in Chapter 13 for fire insurance excluded property perils.) In analyzing any policy, particularly in those of the inland marine all-risks type, it is most helpful to keep in mind the *general types of exclusions* which may normally be expected. These include losses that are: (1) *uninsurable* or *catastrophic;* (2) usually *separately insured* in other contracts; (3) *excessive or unusual,* thus requiring special information, endorsements, and premium charges; (4) *normally expected,* thus not really risks; and (5) *not accidental* in nature.

Property in transit.   The first major class of inland marine insurance is protection for property frequently exposed to loss while it is in transit from one location to another. Several different contracts are available for these risks, including the basic inland transit floater; the trip transit policy; the processing floater; the department store floater; and special forms which insure only one type of transportation, such as express, motortruck, parcel post, registered mail, first-class mail, or armored car and messenger shipments.

The insuring clause of the *basic inland transit policy* states briefly that the policy covers for an amount not exceeding the limit(s) of liability as stipulated in the attached form or endorsement(s). This is followed by a space on the face of the policy for the attachment of the proper form or endorsement so that it may be modified to fit the particular needs of the insured. There are standardized forms to cover goods and merchandise shipped by common carrier. Policies may be issued to cover a single shipment, or as in the case of the open-cargo form, merchants, manufacturers, or others who ship and receive goods continuously may cover all shipments. There are two forms of policy in use, differing only in the manner of computing the premium. An *annual form* requires a deposit premium based on an estimated valuation of shipments to be covered during the policy period. An annual audit is made of the total value of all the actual shipments, and an additional premium is charged or a return premium paid to the insured. The *open policy form* requires a monthly report, with premiums due and payable when the report is made. The form attached to the basic policy lists the perils covered as well as the exclusions. The more important clauses in the basic policy follow the pattern already noticed in connection with ocean marine insurance, including a sue and labor clause and an average clause. Territorial limits for the coverage are established. Certain other clauses parallel to a considerable degree clauses already noticed in connection with fire insurance contracts.

Trip transit policies are available for single shipments of merchandise, furniture, livestock, machinery, and other property while in transit by railroad, motortruck, and inland or coastwise steamers. The insurer is usually not liable for loss caused by theft, robbery, civil commotion, strikes, riots, war, and like perils, except by special endorsement. Exhibits, films, paintings, valuable stamp collections, and many strange and unusual risks involving transportation hazards have been covered. It would be difficult to draw a line beyond which marine insurers are unwilling to go in insuring special transportation risks.[12]

Inland marine insurance sometimes requires other special forms adapted both to the nature of the perils to be covered and to the means of shipment. Certain of these forms have, within limits, become reasonably standardized:

a. Express shipments policy, which covers all-risks of loss, including fire, windstorm, flood, earthquake, theft, transportation, and navigation;

b. Parcel post policy, which insures safe arrival of merchandise shipped by parcel post, first-class mail, or registered mail. This is an alternative to insurance available through the government postal system;

c. Registered mail policy, which covers shipments by registered mail and by express for business institutions having large values at risk, such as shipments of currency or securities;

d. Armored car and messenger policy, which provides insurance for shipments of money, securities, and other valuables;

e. Processing floater policy, for goods and merchandise sent from the premises of the owner to various locations for processing. This policy covers on a named-perils basis: *(a)* when the property is owned by the insured and is being processed by others and *(b)* while the property is in transit;

f. Department store floater policy, which is a special form of transit policy designed to meet the needs of department stores or other retail merchants that ship and receive merchandise. It covers all risks of loss

---

[12] Would you believe a barrel of monkeys? Well, an airplane full of them was insured from South America to a zoo in the United States. Other examples are numerous: a Gutenberg Bible that covered while the book was on display; an amount of $48,000 covering on a one-cent British Guiana stamp; and 4 million cryptolaemus bugs imported to kill the mealybug which was destroying citrus fruit.

or damage to the property insured subject to the usual inland marine exclusions.

Bailee liability.   To meet the needs of persons who have intentionally received temporary custody of the goods or property of others, the inland marine field has developed *bailee liability* coverages. The term *bailment* pertains to personal property which passes temporarily into the possession of a person or persons other than the owner. The "bailor" gives up possession of the property to the "bailee."

Common law classifies bailees into three categories based upon whether bailment is: (1) for the sole benefit of the *bailor,* with no compensation for the care of the property; (2) for the benefit of the *bailee,* such as in borrowing property without compensation; and (3) for the mutual benefit of the *bailor and the bailee,* such as in cases where the bailee is repairing, transporting, or storing property for some compensation.

The degree of care required differs in these situations. The bailee in the first category would be expected to exercise only *minimal* care of the property; in the second category, *exceptional* care; and in the third category, *ordinary* care, or that care reasonably taken by average persons caring for their own property.[13] In the absence of special agreements or statutes, most ordinary business transactions involving bailments fall into this last classification. The type of property in the bailment also affects the degree of care required. An innkeeper would be expected to handle money in quite a different manner from the way in which a trucker would be expected to handle a load of cement.

Various statutory liabilities apply to carriers, warehousers, and public garagekeepers, among others. Bailees are invariably liable for negligence or "failure to exercise the care that the circumstances justly demand."[14] The negligent performance of a required duty or failure to perform the duty will create a legal liability for damages on the part of the bailee. This is a liability imposed by law and not a liability which is the outgrowth of contract.

Insurance may be purchased to cover the bailee's *legal liability* for loss. In order to establish a loss, there must be (1) legal liability on the part of the bailee and (2) loss or damage due to a peril covered by the policy. Many losses involve no legal liability, yet the bailee because of the desire to maintain customer goodwill wishes to make good losses of property that occur while it is in the bailee's custody. Three forms of bailee policies are written: *(a)* for the sole benefit of the bailor, *(b)*

---

[13] *Levine* v. *Wolff,* 78 N.J.L. 306; 73 Atl., 73; *Mortimer* v. *Otto,* 206 N.Y. 89; 99 N.E. 189.

[14] A public carrier is not liable for loss or damage to goods due to an act of God. The negligence rule, however, makes such a carrier liable if through the negligence of the carrier the lost or damaged goods were brought within the operation of the destructive forces of the act of God (*Schwartz* v. *Adsit,* 91 Ill. App. 576).

for the sole benefit of the bailee, and *(c)* for the benefit of both. It is more usual today and more satisfactory to provide direct-damage insurance which pays for damage to the property in the hands of the bailee whether or not there is any element of legal liability.

Many forms of insurance are written that have a bailee interest. Fire insurance contracts include coverage, for example, on property held in trust or on commission but not sold. There are also three such major inland marine forms: (1) motortruck carriers, (2) bailees' customers, and (3) furriers' customers. Statutory laws compel licensed public truckers to purchase a prescribed minimum coverage for *truckers' legal liability* for their shipments.[15] Their legal liability as carriers may be written under a blanket form or under a gross receipts form on a named-perils basis. Under the blanket form, a list is made of the trucks operated by the insured, and a limit of liability is set for each truck. Under the gross receipts form, a rate is applied to the total receipts of the business. This form has an advantage in that a percentage of every charge goes for insurance and thus no insurance costs accrue when the trucks are idle or empty. *Bailees' customers policies* are written on a named-perils basis and cover direct damage without regard to legal liability to goods in the custody or control of the insured for services such as cleaning, repairing, laundering, and the like. While the policy may be adapted to the needs of any business institution, three forms have attained wide acceptance: laundries, dyers and cleaners, and rug and carpet cleaners. Furriers and department stores accepting furs for storage offer as part of their service *furriers' customers insurance* all-risks protection on the stored items. The policy is written on a special inland marine form, and the dealer is furnished insurance certificates to issue to customers. The policy provides not only legal liability coverage up to the valuation on the receipt issued to the owners of the furs but also direct loss or damage without regard to legal liability. The policy may be endorsed with the excess legal liability endorsement which covers any legal liability in excess of the receipt valuations.

Fixed transportation property. Bridges, tunnels, and other instrumentalities of transportation and communication are insurable under inland marine forms, although as a matter of fact they are fixed property. They are so insured because they are held to be an essential part of the transportation system.

Bridges are owned not only by various governmental units such as states and their political subdivisions but also by railroads and by companies that operate them for profit from the tolls. Enormous values are

---

[15] Additional insurance is required for liability for damages to *other* property and for injuries to persons. Trucks with gross vehicle weights of 10,000 pounds or more are subject to insurance requirements of $750,000 (up to $5 million for very hazardous materials) under the national Motor Carrier Act of 1980.

concentrated in a single structure, and oftentimes a bridge represents a major asset or substantial income. Policies must exclude buildings, their contents, and supplies held in storage. The bridge policy is written to cover either *(a)* direct damage or *(b)* indirect losses of use and occupancy.

Bridge insurance covers direct loss or damage to the bridge and its approaches "however caused" with a limited number of exceptions. Included are such losses as fire, flood, ice, collision, and explosion. The policy does not usually cover losses caused by or resulting from strikes, lockouts, labor disturbances, riots, civil commotions, sabotage, vandalism, or malicious mischief; from the violation of law; or from war risks. Losses occasioned by failure of the insured to maintain the structure properly are excluded. Examples of actual losses show that serious losses are possible and that insured amounts should be substantial.[16]

Next to bridges and tunnels in terms of insurable values come piers, wharves, and docks. The perils of fire, windstorm, and other perils ordinarily included in the fire contract may not be covered. Flood risks, collision, or collapse are insurable under the marine contract. Marine railways and dry docks, however, are insurable against all risks. Water pipelines are insurable, as are oil pipelines and power transmission lines. Radio towers are covered, and here the principal peril is collapse. Airway beacons and floodlights are insurable. Stop-and-go traffic signals often cost thousands of dollars. Dams may be insured, and the peril here is collapse or damage from ice or debris.

Floaters. In inland marine insurance, the term *floater* is used in the sense that insurance is provided to follow mobile insured property wherever it may be located, subject always to territorial limits of the contract. Floater policies are classified under the 1976 Nationwide Definition as *(a)* personal and *(b)* commercial. In the personal floater category are policies covering such items as jewelry, furs, silverware, and works of art. In the commercial floater category are policies covering contractors', physicians', and farm equipment; theatrical property; salespersons' samples; consignment, installation, and installment sales floaters; and many others.[17]

The basic contract for all floaters is the *scheduled property floater policy*.

---

[16] The collapse of the Narrows Bridge over Puget Sound, four months after its completion, resulted in an insured loss of $5 million under an all-risks inland marine form. Insurance on the Tappan Zee Bridge over the Hudson River was for $62 million direct damage and $6 million business interruption. Other examples of large U.S. losses were the "Silver Bridge" over the Ohio River, which failed with a tragic loss of almost 50 lives, and the collapse of a bridge over Tampa Bay in 1980 caused by a ship collision.

[17] The most complete text available for further reference on ocean marine insurance and the many inland marine floater policies is William H. Rodda, *Marine Insurance: Ocean and Inland*, 3d ed. (Englewood Cliffs, N.J.: Prentice-Hall, 1970).

It is a very simple policy that states on its face the usual insuring clause indicating that the policy covers "on property described below or in schedule attached." The property to be covered may be listed, and forms with additional clauses and stipulations attached. The standard clauses that appear in the basic property floater are in many cases repetitions of clauses that appear in policies already noticed.

Personal floaters. At some time or another everyone has personal property at a nonpermanent location. The baggage of a traveler is a pertinent example, as is clothing at a laundry, an overcoat in a checkroom, or equipment used for sports. A number of personal property floaters are available that provide broad protection or insure articles of higher value.

Several floater policies covering personal effects are prefixed by the term *personal*. The policies are so different and their names are so similar that it is important to distinguish the different forms. Those most likely to be confused are: *(a)* the personal property floater, *(b)* the personal effects floater, and *(c)* the personal articles floater. Closely akin to the foregoing is the tourist's baggage form.

The *personal property floater* provides all-risks coverage not only away from the insured's residence but in the residence as well. The policy covers "personal property owned, used or worn by the person in whose name this policy is issued and members of assured's family of the same household, while in all situations, except as hereinafter provided." The policy thus insures virtually every piece of personal property, with only a few exceptions such as boats, automobiles, and business property. Unforeseen and unexpected perils are automatically included in the all-risks protection, and only a few perils are excluded, such as the breakage of fragile articles, war, and wear and tear. The importance of this former classic example of all-risks insurance has decreased in recent years with the availability of similar broad coverage in the homeowners' policies (see Chapter 23).

The *personal effects floater* provides all-risks protection for the insured on personal property away from his or her residence. It does not specifically list the personal effects to be covered, but it includes all property usually carried by tourists and travelers.

The *personal articles floater* provides all-risks protection on furs, jewelry, cameras, silverware, fine arts, golfer's equipment, musical instruments, and stamp and coin collections. Formerly insured under separate contracts, these types of property may now all be combined in the personal articles floater policy, or added to homeowners' contracts.

Depending upon the nature of the risk, inland marine floaters utilize one of three forms. These are *(a)* blanket, *(b)* scheduled, and *(c)* blanket and scheduled. There are many classes of personal property that involve in the aggregate substantial values but include no single item or items sufficiently valuable or distinctive to require scheduling. Such properties are insured under the *blanket* form. For example, the golfer's equipment floater is an all-risks blanket policy.

Scheduled property floaters are used to cover properties involving a number of separate items, each of substantial value. Such policies may be written on a very broad all-risks basis with the few exclusions that are typical of all inland marine policies. Cameras and musical instruments are examples of property that is insured in this way. Snowmobiles are a new type of risk covered by a scheduled policy. To be covered under a scheduled policy, property must be carefully described to indicate clearly the item to be covered, and when more than one item is insured, each must be separately valued.

Furs and jewelry are often scheduled for coverage by individuals and their families. The policy covers worldwide against all risks. When new, the cost price is acceptable as a valuation; otherwise, an appraisal by a reliable furrier or jeweler is preferable. It is an underwriting practice not to insure furs for an amount greater than their cost. Insuring both furs and jewelry under a single policy is advantageous because as aggregate values exceed designated limits, the rate on the excess drops. A further reduction in the premium may be obtained if a $50-deductible clause is made a part of the policy.

There are certain types of personal property that lend themselves to a combination *blanket and scheduled* form of coverage. Items that have an unusual value may be scheduled, and other items may be covered on a blanket basis. The personal property floater, already noticed, is an example of a scheduled and blanket personal property form. Another example is the *fine arts floater*. The policy is used in insuring private or public collections of pictures, tapestries, valuable rugs, statuary, antique furniture, rare porcelains, books, and other valuable items. Special forms are available for museums, art galleries, dealers, or other commercial enterprises. A final example is the *wedding presents floater*. In order to protect wedding presents, wherever they may be and until they are permanently located, the wedding presents floater provides a worldwide coverage against all risks. The policy must be written to expire not over 90 days after the wedding.

Commercial floaters. Property that is frequently moved about in connection with a business or profession may be insured under a business or commercial floater. Some of the more widely used commercial forms will be described.

The *physicians' and surgeons' equipment floater* is designed to cover professional instruments and equipment used by the insured in the practice of medicine or dentistry. It is an all-risk policy covering instruments and equipment carried by the insured from place to place, and instruments not customarily carried are excluded from the protection. If there are any unusually valuable instruments they may be scheduled, though for most physicians or surgeons blanket insurance is adequate.

The *salespersons' floater* policies insure samples transported from place to place for display to prospective customers. There are as many classes of samples as there are types of business. Obviously, a case of shoe samples, with only one shoe of a kind, is less of an attraction to thieves than is a case of jewelry. Some samples are shipped by railroad or air, while others are transported in the automobile of the salesperson.

The radium floater policy protects one of the most peculiar types of property that has ever been made the subject of insurance. Radium is a rare substance, now widely used by the medical profession, particularly in the treatment of cancer. Infinitesimal amounts have a very high value. To indemnify the owner of radium in the event of its loss from any cause, war risks and gradual deterioration excepted, the all-risks radium floater is written by describing the individual items covered.

Installation floaters are written for a number of concerns whose business requires the complete installation of their product in working order in the premises of the customer before delivery is completed. For example, business firms specializing in store fixtures contract to remodel a given location, which may require anything from a new front to interior decoration. Machinery is often delivered installed, as are many other items. The business at any time will have goods partially installed in numerous locations and in transit. Such risks may be insured against fire and transportation perils, and against perils on the premises to which they have been consigned until installation is complete.

The *conditional sales approval floaters* may be written covering department stores and other businesses against the loss of goods sold on the installment plan, loaned, leased, or sent on approval. It is a usual practice to send out to prospective customers on approval or for trial such commodities as rugs, refrigerators, television sets, furniture, washers and dryers, and the like. Sales frequently involve installment payments. The floater covers goods in transit against many named perils and in buildings, excluding premises owned, rented, leased, or used by the insured.

There are several forms of *agricultural machinery equipment and farm animals floaters*. Some companies also write livestock mortality insurance on valuable farm animals, poultry, and dogs or other pets on a named-perils basis. The business floaters here noted serve only as examples of the many parts of inland marine insurance. Policies are also written on neon signs, theatrical equipment, rolling stock, contractor's equipment, and scientific instruments. An inland marine floater policy may be adapted to almost any conceivable type of risk involving property that is moving from place to place. Leased electronic data processing equipment is a modern example of risks newly eligible for floater coverage.

A final example of inland marine insurance adaptation in the business area is provided by the *inland marine block policies*. Originally written for jewelers and said to have originated with the underwriters at Lloyd's of London, block policies are written for jewelers, furriers, camera or musical instrument dealers, construction and agricultural equipment dealers, and others. The policies are written on an all-risks basis, with the list of exclusions tailored to meet the particular class of business to be covered. The property is covered without limitation as to time on the insured's own premises, in contrast to the usual marine contract. In addition, the block policy provides in a single package coverage for: *(a)* goods on the premises of others; *(b)* goods in transit, including salespersons' samples; and *(c)* goods of others in the custody of the insured. With the exception of the jewelers' block policy, whose form has been standardized, there are variations in the terms of the other forms just noted. Because the jewelers' form is the oldest and has become standardized, it will serve as an example of a block policy.

The *jewelers' block policy* is written to provide comprehensive coverage for pawnbrokers, silverware dealers, and diamond wholesalers. The policy provides an all-risk cover against loss or damage "arising from any cause whatsoever," subject to a few exclusions such as inherent vice or insufficient or defective packing. There are five specific limitations in the amount of coverage: (1) to property at the named premises; (2) to property shipped by first-class registered mail, railway express, or armored-car service; (3) to registered airmail or express shipments in a given day to one recipient at the same address; (4) to property handled by parcel transportation services; and (5) to property in the custody of insured's personnel away from the premises. In addition to property of the insured, the policy provides protection against loss of property owned by customers of the jewelers or by dealers who may entrust property to them. Policies generally cover "in or upon any place or premises whatsoever" in the United States and Canada and while being carried in transit. Particular emphasis is given to a number of conditions and warranties that appear. The insured is required to keep an accurate inventory so that the exact amount of loss can be determined. The insured also warrants that the protective devices and security guard service described in the proposal will be maintained. In all, the jewelers' block policy illustrates the specialized need of many businesses for the broad coverage of business floater contracts.

FOR REVIEW AND DISCUSSION

1. Explain *why* the need for transportation (marine) insurance has grown so rapidly in the past 50 years. In what parts of marine insurance has the development been most rapid?

2. Of what importance to a midwestern business is knowledge about ocean marine insurance? Is there any reason for an individual homeowner to understand ocean marine insurance, too?

3. Is the ocean marine policy a *standard* contract? Explain your answer.

4. Briefly explain the importance of the following principles in ocean marine insurance: *(a) warranties, (b) protection and indemnity insurance, (c) deductibles, (d) assignment,* and *(e) coinsurance.*

5. Any vessel used for pleasure purposes may be insured by yacht and motorboat insurance. What additional protection is afforded under the marine form that the fire policy cannot give?

6. Choose three terms of unique significance in ocean marine insurance losses and explain why each is important.

7. "Marine insurance rates are judgmental ones, and international in character." Explain why you agree, or disagree, with this statement.

8. Why did most states adopt *The Nationwide Definition,* and what were its important effects in the insurance business?

9. Identify the basic *classes* of inland marine insurance and give an example of each type.

10. What *general* types of exclusions should you expect to find in insurance contracts (even in "all-risks" inland marine policies)? Illustrate each general type with a specific exclusion found in some inland marine contract.

11. Why does a business need to know about bailments, and how does insurance relate to these situations? What difference does it make whether the bailee is a warehouser or a common carrier?

12. Mr. X, an employee of the Alpha Hotel, allowed a trunk being transported from the airport to become wet, destroying $500 worth of clothing. Is Alpha liable? If so, is the risk insurable?

13. Credit sales are very common. Many customers feel that they should not pay for something that is not fully theirs at the time the loss occurred. What form of coverage will provide adequate insurance, and what type of businesses need it most?

14. In a recently reported fire more than 200 clothing items at a dry cleaner were destroyed. Assuming that the cleaner was free of neglect, what form of inland marine insurance would cover such losses, and why is it needed?

15. Gilbert Stuart's portrait of George Washington has been appraised at $250,000. Would the fine arts floater policy cover loss to this picture occasioned by the malicious throwing of acids upon it? Explain.

16. What types of *personal* "floater" contracts might an individual or a family consider? Which are blanket coverage, and which are scheduled coverage?

17. What types of *commercial* "floater" contracts might be considered in the insurance program for a department store? for a jewelry store?

Chapter 16

Outline of concepts

The scope and magnitude of the liability risk involve every modern family or organization with increasing legal responsibility.

The legal basis for liability is *legal wrongs,* invading the rights of others. Legal wrongs may be *criminal* or *civil.* Criminal wrongs involve the public at large and are punishable by government action. Civil (or private) wrongs are based on (1) *contracts* or (2) *torts.*

    Liability under contract law occurs only as a result of the invasion of another's rights under a contract, by:

        Breach of contract, or not fulfilling promises in an agreement;

        Bailee liability, which has been discussed in Chapter 15; and

        Implied warranties, which often extend liability well beyond the specific written obligations of a contract.

    Liability under tort law involves all civil wrongs not based on contracts:

        Intentional acts or omissions, such as battery, assault, and trespass;

        Strict or absolute liability, which applies even if there is no fault present, is used increasingly in some circumstances; and

        Negligence liability, which requires:

            A legal duty to act or not act, under the circumstances;

            A voluntary unintentional wrong, determined by prudent conduct;

            A proximate relationship between the wrong, and

            An injury, a death, or property damage as the result.

    Modifications of the usual negligence liability rules sometimes occur by court cases or statutes:

        Comparative negligence, where each party causing losses pays in the proportion that he or she is held liable;

        Presumed negligence, which under certain circumstances may create a "prima facie" case of liability; and

        Imputed negligence, which may extend the liability of some persons or organizations to injuries or damages caused by *others.*

Specific kinds of liability situations illustrate many exposures, based on:

    Real property ownership (unsafe conditions causing injuries);

    Attractive nuisance hazards (injuries to children);

    Employees and agents (often hold employers or principals responsible);

    Animals (for injuries caused by dogs or other pets);

    Government units and charitable institutions (uncertain, decreasing immunity);

    Product liability (rapidly escalating claims);

    Nonownership liability (for employees' or rented automobiles); and

    Libel and other related types of liability.

The liability risk

"To sue or not to sue"—that is the question! The answer is increasingly in the affirmative—or at least the answer is a rhetorical "Why not!" Situations involving injuries or damages that a generation ago would invariably have been assumed by the injured person are now regularly the basis for lawsuits by one person against another person or an organization. The Tylenol tragedy illustrates vividly the unexpected nature and vast consequences of *the liability risk,* or exposure to claims and losses because of alleged or actual legal responsibilities.[1]

What has changed in our society to create such great uncertainty in this area? Many factors are involved, including changing personal or moral values and attitudes toward such institutions as the family, government, business, and the church.[2] The social environment, too, has changed with such trends as urbanization, geographic mobility, nondiscriminization, the "automobile economy," professionalism, and the affluent society. Our ideas of individual, corporate, and social responsibility have undergone many changes, and these changes have been reflected in a pronounced reliance upon law to determine the extent of the liability risk. One thoughtless act, defective product or package, hazardous property condition, or mistake (even unintentional) and the result can be a nightmare of legal battles for anyone.

What emerges is a world which places heavy emphasis on requirements and rights under the law. Whether one likes it or not, rarely can important decisions ever be made for family or business without considering

---

[1] "The Tylenol Tragedy," *Business Insurance,* October 11, 1982, p. 1. Seven Chicago deaths from cyanide in Tylenol capsules shocked the world—and resulted in losses estimated to be several hundred million dollars for the cost of destroying and recalling merchandise from the market, for lost future sales and profits, and for defending or paying more than $600 million of individual and class action lawsuits already filed against the manufacturers.

[2] In a provocative look at the future, Dr. John D. Long evaluates the "public moral hazard" as it is influenced by such trends in our society as (1) population, (2) inflation, and (3) relaxed theological pressures. Further ideas on achievement, property ownership, waste, apprehension, honesty, responsibility, and other "ethical pillars" of insurance are presented in his book, *Ethics, Morality, and Insurance* (Bloomington: Bureau of Business Research, Indiana University, 1971).

their legal implications. A birth, a death, a marriage, a divorce, the purchase of a home, a new job, a new car, a sales contract, or the formation of a business enterprise—all of these have significant legal consequences. The liability risks which accompany these and many other everyday events of our lifetime are the subject of this chapter.

SCOPE AND MAGNITUDE OF THE LIABILITY RISK

Sources

Because of the prevalence of claims, almost everyone is aware of the liability risk in operating an automobile. However, every form of personal, business, or professional activity is also to some degree exposed to loss because of liability claims based on negligence. If a negligent act or omission interferes with the rights of any individual, the party responsible for the negligence is liable for damages to the injured party. There is also always the danger of alleged negligence which may result in expensive litigation. There may also be the breach of liability assumed under a contract or the breach of an implied warranty, such as the implied warranty of a seller that goods are fit for the purpose for which they are sold. To meet the legal consequences of all these escalating exposures, liability insurance has become essential in our legalistic society. The insurance solutions are presented in Chapter 17.

Size of losses

The owner of a property knows that the limit of direct loss is the value of the property. Thus, if a building worth $80,000 is completely destroyed, it will result in a loss to the owner of $80,000. If an automobile worth $10,000 is stolen and never recovered, it represents a loss of no more than $10,000. In the case of liability claims, the limit may not be fixed with any reasonable certainty. This characteristic is in contrast to the situation in direct property insurance, where the direct maximum possible loss can be readily determined as the total property value.

Liability claims, therefore, may far exceed the capital invested in an enterprise. More than this, it requires a substantial sum of money to prove that there is no liability when a groundless claim is made. If there is liability and the injury is serious, such as one involving the permanent disability or disfigurement of an individual, in the absence of adequate insurance the verdict can bring financial ruin to an individual or business. The former limits for which liability policies were written are no longer regarded as adequate. Courts are taking judicial notice of dollar depreciation, and verdicts that would have been considered excessive in the past are no longer regarded as sufficient to compensate an injured person for loss sustained as the result of an injury.[3] The annual size of liability payments today in the United States has caused William E. Knepper, a past president of the International Association of Insurance Counsel, to refer to this multibillion-dollar cost as "the injury industry."

Liability verdicts today are not only high, and thus potentially ruinous to financial condition, but they are also extremely variable and unpredictable for an individual or business. Ten years ago losses were considered large if they exceeded $50,000 or $100,000. Today numerous examples of awards of more than $1 million for *one* person's injuries have appeared.[4] Contrary to popular notion, it is not only the urban states that have had large verdicts handed down by juries, for in many states the single-person awards have approached or exceeded $1 million. In 1978, $128 million, the largest judgment in U.S. history, was awarded to a 13-year-old boy against Ford Motor Company for burns resulting from a defective gas tank. This much-publicized award was later reduced to $6.3 million. For a single accident involving a number of persons, the claims and verdicts can skyrocket to many millions of dollars. High verdicts are by no means limited to those resulting from automobile accidents. Fires, explosions, building collapses, falls, poisonings, airplane crashes, and many other situations may create liability lawsuits.[5]

Although it is true that the majority of liability claims are settled or receive verdicts for far less than the original amounts asked in a court suit, this is poor consolation for the individual or business faced with a claim which may spell financial ruin after several years of uncertainty. The trend is significant, too, for the defendant may often be required to pay an award far beyond any expectation of maximum loss at the time insurance was purchased.

The large claims for liability are not always against big corporations, either. A California housewife was sued for over $800,000 of damages to residential homes on the basis that she was negligent in starting a backyard fire without a fire permit! The variability of liability claims,

---

[3] For example, in 1902 an award of $4,000 was held to be excessive for the loss of a right leg (*Chicago Railroad Company* v. *Jackson*, 55 Ill. 492; 8 Am. Rep. 661); and in 1911 a verdict of $10,000 was reduced to $5,000 in a case where both legs had been amputated (*St. Louis Railroad Company* v. *Hesterly*, 98 Ark. 240; 135 S.W. 874). Practically all settlements came within the usual $5,000 insurance limit, which today is sadly inadequate.

[4] About 400 such jury verdicts in the past two decades are noted by Jury Verdict Research, Inc. The increase in recent years has been rapid, with about 100 per year reported. *Insurance Facts* (New York: Insurance Information Institute, 1981–82), p. 42.

[5] Multi*billion* dollar claims resulted from a Kentucky nightclub fire (1977); a fire at the MGM Las Vegas hotel (1980); a skywalk collapse in a Hyatt Regency hotel in Kansas City (1981); and a Pan Am 727 jet crash in Chicago (1982).

even for similar accidents, is self-evident in the following recent contradictory headlines: "Failure to Yell 'Fore' Costs Golfer $25,140" and
"Golfer Must Accept Risk of Being Hit."[6]

Results of losses

Direct loss or damage to property destroys values already acquired,
but a liability claim may destroy more by obligating the party held responsible for the loss or injury to make payments for years in the *future*.
Legal obligations for serious negligence are not excused by bankruptcy.
Individuals who believed themselves to be judgment proof are sometimes
obliged to make weekly payments out of their incomes until judgments
are satisfied. A court judgment may reach out to take bank deposits,
securities, real estate, and a part of one's earnings for years to come.

Bankruptcy has sometimes been suggested as a way out for a person
without assets, and it is said to be judgment proof. This is not a simple
procedure, and the consequences in the way of injury to business reputation and credit standing amount to a lasting injury. In many states failure
to satisfy a judgment up to a given amount will result in the loss of a
car owner's right to drive and, in some jurisdictions, a jail sentence.
Travelers do not realize that they are subject to the laws of the place
where an accident occurs, and reciprocal agreements in another state
may cost motorists the right to drive.

Fraudulent claims

During recent years, great loss and annoyance have resulted from
fraudulent claims for alleged injuries. A number of individuals and gangs
have been apprehended, but the menace has grown to such proportions
that insurers have organized central index bureaus in different sections
of the country for the filing and tabulating of claims. This system brings
to light duplication of claims for the same alleged injury, and the frequency with which the names of doctors and lawyers appear in connection
with doubtful claims "spots" them for observation.[7]

Aside from the professional fakers of claims, there are the amateurs
who in any accident, however slight, go to bed immediately and experi-

---

[6] The first headline is from a Columbus, Ohio, newspaper; the second from Atlanta,
Georgia.

[7] Faked claims are sometimes made in such a manner as to prompt a quick adjustment
to avoid unfavorable publicity. One man, after eating part of a chicken pie in a restaurant,
would slip a dead mouse under the pastry and then "discover" the mouse presumably
cooked in it. Another man would swallow a tack and allege that it had been in the food.
Xray pictures would be presented and damages paid. His fraud was brought to light by
careful investigation of claims among several insurers.

ence all kinds of symptoms. Every claimant knows that it is expensive to contest a suit and that the defendant, disliking the attendant publicity, prefers a quick settlement. Insurers use their professional loss-adjustment services to minimize the harmful effects of fraudulent claims.

The above is not intended to accuse all injured persons of being dishonest. Most claimants are honest, but some are not, and these persons can cost insureds (and uninsureds) and insurers a considerable sum. The cost of property defense is high—for fraudulent as well as valid claims. The typical plaintiff's attorney receives from one fourth to one third of the settlement. Defense attorneys are paid on the basis of minimum or fixed fees, or on a time basis, instead of a percentage of the settlement. For many defense proceedings, several thousand dollars of expense for court costs and legal expenses are involved.

THE LEGAL BASIS FOR LIABILITY—LEGAL WRONGS

A claim based upon liability imposed by law develops as the result of the invasion of the rights of others. A legal right is more than a mere moral obligation of one person to another, for it has the backing of the law to enforce the right. Legal rights impose many specific responsibilities and obligations, such as not invading privacy or property, or not creating an unreasonable risk or actual harm to others.

The invasion of such legal rights is a *legal wrong*. The wrong may be: *(a)* criminal (public) or *(b)* civil (private). A *criminal wrong* is an injury involving the public at large and is punishable by the government. The action on the part of government to effect a conviction and impose fines or imprisonment is termed a "criminal action."

Civil wrongs are based upon: (1) torts and (2) contracts. *Torts* are wrongs independent of contract (for example, false imprisonment, assault, fraud, libel, slander, and negligence). *Contracts* may involve legal wrong when implied warranties are violated, bailee responsibilities are not fulfilled, or contract obligations are breached. Although the government takes action with respect to crimes, civil injuries are remedied by court action instituted by the injured party in a "civil action." The remedy is usually the award of monetary damages. The liability consequences of a crime are not usually insurable, but the liability for damages growing out of a civil wrong may, and often should be, insured.

Figure 16–1 illustrates the *legal basis for liability*. Although liabilities include criminal wrongs, for liability insurance the emphasis is on *civil wrongs* and particularly on the many legal wrongs based upon *torts*. Of greatest importance are torts resulting from *negligence* (unintentional acts or omissions), which are said to encompass more than 9 out of 10 claims for personal injury or property damage to others.

Figure 16–1. The legal basis for liability

Liability under contract law

Liability under contract law is based on the invasion of another's rights under a contract. It occurs only as a result of a *contract* between one party and another. In contrast, liability under tort law is based on the breach of one's duty to respect the rights of the general public. It may result from either common law or statute law.

In insurance terminology, the convenient but inaccurate term *legal liability* is sometimes used. All liability which is imposed by tort *and* contract law is "legal," since the rights of the injured party to damages are enforceable in courts of law.

Breach of contract. Not fulfilling promises made in an agreement, or *breach of contract,* is the most obvious type of civil wrong based on contracts. Contractual responsibilities often extend well beyond the specific written obligations of a contract, and insurance sometimes covers these civil wrongs based on contracts. Contract default in connection with surety bonds will be discussed in Chapter 21.

Bailee liability. *Bailee liability*, which results from bailment contracts, has been noted in Chapter 15. The responsibilities created in these special types of contracts are important enough to be listed as a separate category of liability under contract law, although the previous discussion is not repeated here.

Implied warranties. One of the most common extensions of liability under contract law concerns manufacturers and distributors of products. In connection with sales or a contract to sell, the law imposes certain obligations termed *implied warranties*. Where a buyer reasonably relies on the skill or judgment of the seller, there is an implied warranty that the goods are reasonably fit for the purpose for which they were sold.

A seller may also be held liable if products are supplied to a user without giving proper notice of their dangerous qualities. The dividing line between negligence and liability growing out of implied warranty is not always clear. The point to be emphasized is that the seller may be held liable for injuries which the product may cause after it leaves the seller. The Consumer Products Safety Act of 1972 increased the potential liability of many producers and sellers in this area. Products liability insurance is discussed in a separate section of Chapter 17.

Liability under tort law

Torts include all civil wrongs not based on contracts. As such, they are a broad residual classification of many private wrongs against another person or organization. They occur independently of contractual obligations and may result (1) from intentional acts or omissions, (2) from strict liability imposed by statute law, or (3) from negligence. The requirements for tort liability are enumerated in the later section on negligence liability, the most important type of tort liability.

Intentional acts or omissions. Lawsuits sometimes occur because of injuries or damage caused by intentional acts or omissions. One example is *battery*, which is the offensive or harmful touching of another without his or her express or implied consent. *Assault* is a second example, and this involves threatened battery. Other examples include *trespass* (entry on land of another without permission) and *false arrest or detention*, which results from the unprivileged restriction of another's freedom of movement. This may cause harm to another by damage to reputation or mental distress. *Fraud* involves intent to cause loss to another, too, and is such a broad category as to be separately treated in many discussions of this subject. *Libel* (written) and *slander* (oral) involve false statements made about someone else, which cause damage to character or invasion of privacy (see later section of this chapter). All of these acts are based upon planned or premeditated acts or omissions, although the harmful results may not have been anticipated.

Strict or absolute liability. The seriousness of the liability exposure is seen in a trend which in particular situations holds persons responsible for injuries or damages no matter how careful they may have been in trying to avoid losses to others. Under what is called *strict liability* or "absolute liability" certain persons are held liable for damages, regardless of whether or not fault or negligence can be proved against them. Although this doctrine is applied only in particular circumstances, the courts and statutes have been applying it with increasing frequency. Examples include: injury from blasting operations by contractors; injury caused by any type of wild animal kept in captivity (see also later section of this chapter about domesticated animals); and damage done by a release of pressure or weight of water, such as a weak dam bursting.

Other illustrations of this trend are the absolute liability, up to certain amounts, which airlines have for the safety of their passengers, and the broadest application of the "liability regardless of fault" idea, workers' compensation laws, which hold the employer liable for most employee work injuries and diseases.

In food cases, too, the doctrine is often applied when foreign objects cause injury to or sickness of the consumer. Automobile manufacturers are increasingly being sued for defects which cause automobile accidents. Different state laws may apply, but some are broadening to permit strict liability suits for serious car faults leading to damages. In such cases, the plaintiff would not have to prove that the manufacturer knew, or should have known, of the defect. A recent case held a merchant accountable under strict liability for sale of glue to a 13-year-old who died as a result of glue sniffing. In spite of a state law which made it illegal for anyone under age 19 to possess the glue, the court held that violation of the law barring such sale created strict liability on the seller's part.[8]

Negligence liability. *Negligence* is a tort, a civil wrong not based upon a contract. Most of the liability imposed by law stems from accidents attributable to negligence. If negligence can be shown to be the proximate cause of an injury to another, the negligent party is liable to the injured party for damages. Negligence is the *failure to exercise the proper degree of care* required by circumstances. It may consist of not doing what was required under the circumstances, or of doing something that ought not to have been done. Behavior in any circumstances that fails to measure up to that expected of a careful, *prudent* person in like circumstances

---

[8] "Sale of Glue to Minnesota Minor Imposes Strict Liability on Seller," *Weekly Underwriter,* November 24, 1973, p. 30 (*Zerby* v. *Warren,* 210 N.W. 2d 58). The strict liability doctrine had been accepted in most states, but it often applies only in limited cases with special circumstances present.

constitutes negligence. Faulty judgment may result in liability for negligence, even though the motive behind the act was the best.[9]

Requirements for negligence liability. Four *requirements* must exist before *negligence liability* is present: (1) a *legal duty*, (2) a *wrong*, (3) a *proximate relationship* between the wrong and an injury or damage, and (4) an *injury or damage*.

A *legal duty* to act, or not to act, depends on the circumstances and the persons involved. A bystander has no legal duty to try to prevent a mugging, but a police officer does. Lifeguards have a legal duty to attempt to save a drowning victim, but others usually do not. Whether or not a legal duty is owed to someone else is decided by the courts, and many factors may determine the degree of care required. Examples include the duty of one person to respect another's right to bodily safety, or his or her right to the use of another person's property.

Previous sections have indicated that negligence is one of the most common and important wrongs. A *wrong* is a breach of legal duty, based upon a standard of conduct that is determined by what a prudent person would have done or not done in similar circumstances. Criminal wrongs and the other kinds of civil wrongs (breach of contract or warranty) are not as pertinent as negligence is in this description of the word *liability*. To do a wrong, the act or omission must be *voluntary*. Thus, if a person in the course of avoiding great danger injures another person without intent, there is held to be no voluntary act and hence no liability. Negligence usually involves injury that is *unintentional*. On the other hand, it is no defense if the act which injures a party was done without intent to do an injury or if the motive behind the act was good and praiseworthy.

A third requisite for the fixing of liability is found in the rule that the voluntary act of the wrongdoer must have been the *proximate cause* of the injury. For the act to be held a proximate cause, there must have been a continuous succession of events from the act to the final event causing the injury. If there was an independent and intervening cause, the continuous succession of events was broken. Thus, a fire negligently ignited and spread by the winds is one continuous succession of events. If, however, a third party were deliberately pushed into the flames by someone else and injured, there would not have been a continuous sequence. No liability for the injury would attach to the party responsible for the fire.

The fourth requirement for negligence liability is that there be *injury* or *damage*. The guilty person must pay an amount that reasonably com-

---

[9] Even in these cases, the degree of care necessary to escape the charge of negligence varies. For example, a surgeon setting a fractured limb must exercise an entirely different degree of care from that exacted of a nonmedical person helping in an emergency.

pensates the injured party for *(a)* bodily and other personal injuries, *(b)* loss of income due to disability, *(c)* pain and suffering, *(d)* disfigurement, and *(e)* any other losses for which the negligence is the proximate cause.

Loss of income due to inability to work often comprises a large proportion of *bodily injury* liability cases. As an example of other losses, a husband may collect for the value of his wife's services as well as for "consortium," the term which the law applies to the companionship of the wife.[10] A parent may also collect for the loss of the services of an injured child and for the expenses attendant upon the injury. In the case of death, the heirs or next of kin may collect damages for the loss of the life. Some states fix a statutory limit for an instantaneous "wrongful" death; but if the party retains or regains consciousness after the injury and ultimately dies, the damage for conscious suffering is added to the damage for the death. Sometimes bodily injury is extended to include cases where no actual physical injury is suffered, but mental anxiety results from near accidents.

Compensation for *property damage* is measured by the difference in the value of the property before and after injury. Although the cost of repair and replacement may serve as a measure of damage, this does not always reflect the actual amount of the damage. If the cost to repair the damaged property is in excess of its value, then the measure of damage would be the value of the property immediately before the accident, less its salvage value immediately following the accident. Indirect losses resulting from the loss of use of the property may also be a part of property damage liability.

Modifications of the usual negligence liability rules. Several modifications, by court cases or statutes, sometimes change the usual rules pertaining to negligence liability. These include *comparative* negligence laws and the doctrines of *presumed* and *imputed* negligence.

Contributory and comparative negligence. Except where statutory enactments have modified the common-law rule, anyone who is so negligent as to contribute to his or her own injuries or damage cannot recover from another for these injuries. Such a person is said to be *contributorily negligent*.

The claimant frequently advances the plea that the alleged contributory negligence did not contribute to the injury, and that if the defendant had exercised reasonable care, the accident could have been avoided. There has developed a rule, known as the "doctrine of last clear chance," which holds that although the claimant is negligent, there is liability

---

[10] At common law the right to maintain a suit for loss of consortium was limited to the husband (*Koscialak* v. *Portland Railway, Light & Power Company,* 126 S.E. 307; 189 N.C. 120). However, many other decisions have held that the reverse is also true and authorized the wife to file suit.

if the defendant had a last clear chance to avoid the accident.[11] Today the rule is followed by statute in only a few states. It is, however, a concept often used in defense proceedings, sometimes successfully.

In its strict application, the old common-law doctrine of contributory negligence does not always produce equitable results. A very slight degree of negligence on the part of an injured person would bar recovery. Some 34 states have enacted statutes which provide that contributory negligence shall not bar recovery for damages. Such statutes apply the idea of *comparative negligence* and provide that damages shall be diminished in proportion to the amount of negligence attributable to the person injured or to the owner or person in control of the property damaged.

At first glance there seems to be substantial merit to having each person share the cost of an accident in proportion to their share of negligence. For example, 80 percent of the damages to others is paid if a person has been held 80 percent negligent. In a few states, however, under complete comparative negligence if both parties suffer losses, the person who was primarily responsible for the accident would also receive 20 percent of his or her damages. The critics of the comparative negligence law used in these states point out this drawback. *Partial* comparative negligence statutes are more common, under which in this example the plaintiff, if his or her negligence is less than the defendant's negligence (thus less than 50 percent), would receive 80 *less 20 percent*. The defendant would receive nothing, because the defendant's negligence exceeded 50 percent. Ohio's law, effective since mid-1980, is an example of this type. Legal authorities also stress other faults in both types of comparative negligence laws: the extreme difficulty or the impossibility of charging a jury to define liability with a precise percentage measuring stick and the tendency to increased litigation. For these reasons the contributory negligence rule as reasonably applied in many states remains an important rule of negligence. Slight negligence tends to be disregarded, and suit against the party primarily responsible is permitted. Settlements out of court also frequently ignore slight negligence or take it into consideration in making partial payments.

Presumed negligence. In order to establish a case, the claimant in ordinary circumstances must show a failure to exercise reasonable care. The burden of the proof, therefore, is on the claimant. In certain cases, however, *presumed negligence* may be assumed from the facts. The legal doctrine which applies—*res ipsa loquitur,* "the thing speaks

---

[11] The doctrine is said to derive from what attorneys refer to as the "Hobbled-Ass Case" (*Davies* v. *Mann,* 19 Eng. Rul. Cas. 189), decided in England in 1842. The defendant drove his carriage against a donkey tied in the street and pleaded that the owner of the donkey was contributorily negligent in leaving it so tied. The court held: "Although the ass may have been wrongfully there, still the defendant was bound to go along the road at such a pace as would be likely to prevent mischief."

for itself"—establishes a prima facie case of negligence. Negligence is presumed without the injured person having to prove it. The burden of proof is shifted to the defendant, an exception to the common-law rule that a plaintiff must prove the defendant's fault.

The doctrine operates when an accident causes an injury: *(a)* if the instrumentality would not normally cause injury without negligence, *(b)* if inspection and use of the instrumentality is within exclusive control of the party to be held liable, and *(c)* if the party to be held liable has superior knowledge of the cause of the accident and the injured party is unable to prove negligence.[12] There must be no contributory negligence, and the accident must be of such nature that injury would not ordinarily occur without negligence.[13] The inference of negligence is to be deduced from the attending circumstances and must be the only one that can reasonably be drawn. The rule does not apply if a definite cause for the injury can be established or if it can be shown that the injury probably resulted from an unavoidable cause, an act of a third person, or from causes due to other than a human agency.[14]

Modern situations to which this doctrine has been applied include automobile injuries (in cases where no witnesses are available), railroad or aviation injuries, medical malpractice claims (such as an operation on the wrong part of the body or the wrong person), and many damages caused by defective products.

Imputed negligence. Not only is a negligent person liable for *his* or *her* acts or omissions which cause injuries or damage to others, but sometimes the responsibility extends to negligence of *other* persons. Courts and statutes have extended the rules of negligence to apply to employers, landlords, parents, automobile owners, and many other parties.

If the negligent party acts in the capacity of employee or agent of another, the wrongdoer *and* the owner or operator of a property are sometimes liable. *Employers* are often personally liable for the torts of their employees. (See also later section in this chapter on liability for employees and agents.) Even in the case of employers hiring "independent contractors," whose actions are not in most cases directly under the

---

[12] *McCloskey* v. *Kopler et al.,* 329 Mo. 527; 46 S.W. (2d) 557.

[13] The doctrine arose in an old English case where all causes of an accident, other than that of negligence, were logically excluded by the facts themselves. A sailor sued and proved a broken axle as well as his injuries by being thrown from a stagecoach. The court held that a prima facie case was established and inquired: "What other evidence can the plaintiff give?" (*Christian* v. *Griggs,* 170 Eng. Rep. 1088). Speaking for the court, Chief Justice Mansfield stated: "When the breaking down or overturning of a coach is proved, negligence on the part of the owner is implied. He always has the means to rebut this presumption, if it be unfounded."

[14] *Francy* v. *Rutland Railroad Company,* 119 N.E. 86; 22 N.Y. 482; and *Corpus Juris Secundum,* Carriers, Sec. 764 (e); 10 *American Jurisprudence,* Carriers, Sec. 1625.

control of the employer, liability may be imputed to the employer if the employee is given faulty equipment or directions for the work. Imputed liability is also important in property rentals, where landlords may be held responsible for the actions of their tenants.

Parents, too, although generally not liable for negligent actions of their children, may be held liable by some state statutes. These usually impose limited liability up to several thousand dollars on the parents for damages caused by their children, but may extend further for specific types of dangerous instruments (guns, for example) used by minors. A child may also be legally liable for his or her own wrongful acts but is seldom able to pay substantial damages.

Under statutes called "vicarious liability" laws, liability in most states is imputed to *automobile owners* even though they are not driving or riding in their cars. Also, under the "family purpose doctrine" such liability applies particularly to the car owner whose family members negligently use the car, either under the idea of agency (when the car is used for family purposes) or on the basis of using a dangerous instrumentality.

Several dozen states have passed "dram shop" or liquor liability laws which make *taverns* or other businesses dispensing liquor liable for injuries that may be caused by their intoxicated patrons, such as in an automobile accident.

SPECIFIC KINDS OF LIABILITY SITUATIONS

Many kinds of special liability situations exist. The following discussion of some of these important aspects of liability is illustrative of the wide scope and variety of the liability risk. The solutions to these problems often involve various liability insurance contracts, but the significance of loss prevention should not be forgotten. (See beginning of section on liability risk management.) Many other examples will be found in the discussion of general liability insurance in Chapter 17 and in the important chapters on employers' liability and automobile insurance which follow.

Real property ownership

A dangerous or defective condition maintained on a property is termed in law a "nuisance." Owners of property are responsible for injuries attributable to dangerous conditions. Tenants are responsible for nuisances created by themselves or created by the landlords if the tenants do not effect corrections.

In the case of property owners, the prudence and diligence required differ with respect to the positions occupied by persons entering upon the property. The law divides such persons into two major classes: (1) trespassers and (2) invitees. One who goes without any right upon the lands of another is a *trespasser*. One who is expressly invited to enter primarily for the occupant's benefit is an *invitee*. Customers, letter carriers, and trash collectors fall into this class.[15]

It is held that trespassers take the risk of defects in the premises whether these defects be hidden or open, but that trespassers cannot be intentionally injured by a trap or other very dangerous situations.[16] The invitee, on the other hand, may hold the occupier of the premises liable for any loss or damage caused by a defect which though unknown to the occupier is of such a nature that a reasonable and prudent man would have discovered it by exercising reasonable diligence. The standard of care owed an invitee is to inspect, to correct, or to warn of dangerous conditions of all kinds which make the premises unsafe.

Snow and ice on public sidewalks may be the occasion of a liability claim, although not all jurisdictions have the same laws. The general rule holds that the owner of a property is not responsible for injury or damage caused by snow or ice that falls and forms naturally on sidewalks. A duty to correct the situation may arise if the sidewalks are used by the owner's customers or tenants. Municipal codes may require the removal of snow or ice within specified time periods after its accumulation. If some act of the owner or tenant creates a dangerous situation, liability for injury may follow. An overflow from a defective gutter or a drain will create liability, for example.

When private property is open to the public, the public by implication is invited to use all the facilities generally made available. The owner or tenant is obligated to exercise reasonable care to maintain the property so that it is reasonably safe and is expected to use reasonable foresight to anticipate any injury that might occur. If the design is such that it creates a dangerous condition, the owner or tenant may be held liable for injuries. With respect to stairways, entrances, ramps, and the like, there should be no dangerous conditions such as an unusual slippery condition or the absence of standard lighting and handrails. However, when persons have knowledge of the existence of any danger and deliberately expose themselves to it, they may not be able to collect damages for their injuries.

---

[15] A third category, a *licensee*, is sometimes noted in law as a person who has the owner's consent to be there, but is there for his or her own benefit. Usually, the duties of the owner to such a person are similar to the owner's duties to trespassers—that is, using reasonable care only to warn the licensee of concealed and dangerous conditions. Examples are solicitors or door-to-door salespersons.

[16] In a well-publicized case in Iowa, the state Supreme Court in 1971 awarded $30,000 to a *burglar* who was booby-trapped by a gun set up by the owners. The trap was held to be an unreasonable and malicious means of protecting their property in an unoccupied farmhouse.

Attractive nuisance hazards

An important exception to the usual liability for injuries to trespassers is in cases of injuries to children because of an *attractive* nuisance. A line of decisions known as "Turntable Cases" held that a boy injured by a railroad turntable was not in the position of a trespasser.[17] It was held that the turntable attracted young children so strongly that they were enticed to play upon it, and this fact being known to the railroad, it was bound to use ordinary care to protect them from harm, even if they were trespassing.

The laws of some states do not apply the doctrine at all, although juries may be sympathetic toward children anyway. Other states vary considerably as to how they apply the concept against owners or tenants of property, and as to the age of the children (often "under 10") to whom it pertains. Usually the nuisance is an artificial or uncommon object or condition which attracts children and is a threat to them because they do not realize the possible dangers.

The attractive nuisance doctrine is one of which both businesspersons and homeowners should be constantly aware in order to avoid or prevent such losses. Objects or situations that might become attractive nuisances are ladders, swimming or decorative pools, trampolines, bonfires, construction sites, gasoline, power lawn mowers, unlocked automobiles, motorbikes, elevators, machinery, and other properties of many kinds. All of these may give rise to liability claims on the attractive nuisance theory. This is an area in which loss prevention as a part of good risk management should be emphasized: building fences, using warning signs, hiring security guards, and not leaving keys in motor vehicles or machinery are examples of possible precautions.

Liability for employees and agents

Aside from the responsibility that attaches to the individual wrongdoer when acting in the capacity of agent or employee, responsibility may also attach to the principal or employer. The legal doctrine of *respondeat superior* holds a principal or employer liable to third parties for damage caused by the negligence of an agent or employee. Usually, the negligent act must be within the apparent scope of authority of the employee or agent. However, liability may extend to a wrongful act contrary to express instructions that is committed in the course of employment. For example, if a bank messenger uses a car contrary to orders and accidentally kills a person, the bank may be held liable for the tort of its em-

---

[17] *Keep* v. *Milwaukee and St. Paul Railroad Company,* 21 Minn. Rep. 207. This was an 1875 case. The turntable was a common railroad device at the end of the tracks upon which the railroad cars could be turned around.

ployee. The employer cannot escape responsibility by showing that the employee acted contrary to orders or by showing that the work being done was not the work that the employee had been instructed to do. The employer in such cases may have recourse against the employee for disobeying instructions (or the employee may be fired), but the employer still must pay the injured third party.

Liability for acts of animals

The keeping of a mischievous animal with knowledge of its propensities to injure or damage is a basis for absolute liability. In this group are to be found pets and other domestic animals, even sometimes animals ordinarily held to be harmless. Some states also have passed special statutes with respect to dogs, and in such states the owner is liable for injury notwithstanding a lack of knowledge of vicious propensities. To fix liability upon the owner of a domestic animal, the beast need be neither vicious[18] nor ordinarily classed as dangerous.[19] Wild animals are kept at the owner's peril; and the liability is absolute, regardless of diligence or absence of fault.

Liability of government and charitable institutions

Stemming from the feudal belief in the divine right of kings, the *doctrine of sovereign immunity* was borrowed in this country from England. In effect, this doctrine said that "the King can do no wrong" and thus could not be liable to anyone. Federal and state governments and political subdivisions of the states adopted this immunity from liability and could not be sued without their consent for the torts of their officers and agents.

Over the years, the courts developed a distinction between governmental and proprietary activities. Injury to an individual caused by a government officer engaged in a proprietary (profit-making) function was held not to be within the immunity that goes with governmental functions. Among the activities regarded as proprietary are the operation and maintenance of rental property, and utilities such as waterworks, sewer systems, electric plants, airports, and the like. The line of demarcation between governmental and proprietary functions is extremely nebulous. In the case of proprietary functions, the tendency is to hold the govern-

---

[18] In a Vermont case a young mastiff jumped up and put his paws on a visitor's shoulders. The visitor fell and broke his leg. Suit for damages was defended on the ground that the owner could not be liable unless the dog was vicious and the owner had knowledge of that fact. The court held that it was sufficient to fix liability if the owner knew that the dog was rough at play and might reasonably commit the injury.

[19] A California woman asked $25,000 damages from a neighbor for being kicked by a "giant" and "vicious" rabbit in her backyard.

mental unit to the same degree of liability as attaches to private enterprise.

There has also been a strong trend to curtail the scope of *governmental immunity*. For example, many states allow individuals to bring suit as the result of special legislation. In other instances states have set up administrative boards to investigate claims and, following the ordinary rules of liability, recommend legislative action. Other states have passed laws curtailing governmental immunity or eliminating it entirely.[20] The Federal Tort Claims Act makes the federal government liable for injuries to individuals in the same manner and to the same extent as a private individual. The tendency to hold more governmental units responsible for liability is clear, but the differences among various states and other units are numerous.

The question also presents itself as to the personal liability of individuals whose negligence gave rise to the loss or damage. Some courts have held that public policy should in any case prevent a diversion of public funds from public uses to settle private damages.[21] Such a holding does not preclude suit against a government officer, trustee, or employee individually. Generally speaking, the liability of public employees for private suit for negligence depends upon the positions and upon the nature of the act giving rise to the suit. Judges are held to have absolute immunity. For others, distinctions based on the nature of the wrong have been drawn.[22]

The theory that *charitable institutions* (such as churches and hospitals), like governmental units, are fully immune from liability for the negligence of employees or agents is far from safe. There is a wide diversity of state laws and legal opinion, and most courts tend to hold charitable organizations responsible for negligence.[23] The change from small

---

[20] For example, New York law provides: "The State hereby waives its immunity from liability and action and hereby assumes liability and consents to have the same determined in accordance with the rules of law as applied to actions in the Supreme Court against individuals or corporations, provided the claimant complies with the limitations of this Article" (113 N.Y. Laws 1929, ch. 467).

[21] *Devers* v. *Scranton*, 308 Pa. 13; 161 Atl. 540; *Taylor* v. *Westerfield*, 233 Ky. 619; 26 S.W. (2d) 557.

[22] For example, the personal liability of school board members with respect to *school bus* accidents is unsettled. Because of this uncertainty, automobile liability policies are endorsed to cover the legal liability of individual board members, bus owners, and bus drivers. Although a municipality cannot usually be sued for damages resulting from accidents caused by *fire apparatus*, some cases have held that the drivers must answer for damages when they are at fault.

[23] In *Fire Insurance Patrol* v. *Boyd* (120 Pa. 624; 15A, 553), the court stated: "This doctrine (that a public charity is bound to apply its funds in furtherance of the charity and not otherwise) is hoary with antiquity." In *McDonald* v. *Massachusetts Gen. Hosp.*, 120 Mass. 432 (1876), the first American decision to adopt the immunity doctrine, relied on an English case without realizing that the English decision had been overruled 10 years earlier. The early decision has long since ceased as a binding precedent in most jurisdictions.

charities to charitable institutions with large assets, income, and ability to meet damage claims has gradually set a trend from immunity to liability.[24] More recent decisions reject the immunity doctrine completely, so that it is extremely unwise for any charitable institution to assume that it is immune from liability for the negligence of its agents or employees. Rather than rely on uncertain immunity, many charitable organizations purchase liability insurance to cover these responsibilities.

Product liability

One of the most rapidly growing fields of liability risk is that of protection for *product liability exposures*. The expansion of the manufacturer's responsibility, as well as that of all dealers and handlers of goods, has been mentioned in connection with implied warranties. Few areas of insurance challenge the insight and the professional advising capacity of the insurance agent or risk manager more than this changing field.

The type, frequency, and severity of losses have skyrocketed in the past two decades.[25] About two thirds of the product liability claims payments are for bodily injury rather than for property damage claims. In terms of dollar amounts, less than 1 percent of the payments account for more than 50 percent of the payment dollars.[26] *Jury verdicts* often average nearly $400,000, and about one fourth of the liability verdicts exceeding 1 million dollars during the last 20 years have been product liability cases.[27] Large *claims* are more frequent than payments made and often more unusual, too. For example, a department store was sued by a woman for $2.8 million because they failed to correct a busted zipper on a pair of blue jeans. James Brady, injured in the assassination attempt on President Reagan, is seeking $100 million in damages from the manufacturer and distributor of the handgun used by John Hinckley![28]

Retailers, wholesalers, and manufacturers may be held liable for injury arising out of the use or consumption of merchandise *away from the*

---

[24] "Today they have become, in many instances, big business, handling large funds, managing and owning large properties. . . . It is idle to argue that donations from them will dry up if the charity is held to respond for its torts the same as other institutions" (*Foster* v. *Roman Catholic Dioceses of Vermont,* 17 C.C.H., Negligence Cases 858; see also *Administrator* v. *Hospital of St. Vincent de Paul,* 107 S.E. 785).

[25] Think, for example, of the heart pacemaker! See "Pacemaker Failure Presents Exotic Products Liability Case in New York," *Weekly Underwriter,* October 27, 1973 (*Friedman* v. *Metronic, Inc.,* 345 N.Y.S. 2d 637). The widening problems of products liability are well discussed in a special section of the *CPCU Annals* 27, no. 1 (March 1974), pp. 5–45.

[26] "Products Liability: The Facts and the Figures," *Journal of Insurance,* November–December 1977, p. 13. This article was based on a study by the Insurance Services Office of 25,000 claims in 1976–77.

[27] See footnote 4. Data is based upon studies through 1980.

[28] "Brady Sues Gun Manufacturer," *Business Insurance,* July 26, 1982, p. 2.

premises of the vendor. A well-known manufacturer, Bon Vivant, went bankrupt because of claims for contaminated soups. The liability for injury frequently arises with respect to food products, but almost every manufacturer or distributor has some product liability exposure.[29] In some cases, the risk is exceptionally high, as for example in the case of the manufacturer of an essential part of airplanes. An improperly constructed electronic system, or even a simple nut or bolt, could be held responsible for the loss of a jet aircraft worth millions of dollars. Sometimes a company has potential liability for injuries or diseases caused by products used many years after their sale, and even by successive purchasers of the product. A current example is the much-publicized dilemma of Manville Corporation, which is requesting bankruptcy as a result of more than 16,500 claims pending for asbestos lawsuits.[30]

Other cases illustrate the widespread nature of the product liability risk. One case involved a suit against a fire alarm company for $25,000 when the fire whistle stuck while a home burned! Smoke detectors, now sold by the millions, may cause similar claims if they are defective. Another case involved a lawsuit filed because a 375-pound body fell through the bottom of a casket at a funeral. Many liability cases have been against drug and chemical firms, such as the Salk polio vaccine personal injury losses and a Texas case of over $11 million damages which resulted when a wrong chemical was negligently put into cattle feed. The broadening of product liability risks is apparent in cases involving everything from a defective automobile to a football helmet, which was the cause of one $600,000 award. Soaps, deodorants, hair lotion, and cigarettes have been claimed to cause injuries and sicknesses ranging from allergies to fatal diseases such as cancer. The swine flu immunization program resulted in nearly 3,000 claims against the U.S. government, including one death claim for $1 billion!

Recent large product liability awards include $150,000 to a child injured by a defective power lawn mower; $250,000 because an injury resulted from a forklift designed without a safety device; $2 million because of improper stabilizers on the 720 jet; $500,000 because a drug was not properly tested before marketing; $140,000 to a boy whose T-shirt was held to be dangerously flammable; and $6.8 million to a man injured by a rifle when its safety catch malfunctioned.

Major increases in the product liability hazard have occurred for a number of reasons: (1) "privity" (direct contractual relationship) is no longer needed in most states, so that an injured person may sue the negligent manufacturer or other parties as well as the retailer who sells

---

[29] A 1982 settlement of $425,000 was paid because a woman's hair fell out after she bit into a beetle in a cup of yogurt.

[30] "Precedent-setter?" *Business Insurance,* September 6, 1982, p. 1.

the goods; (2) the doctrine of warranty has been extended, especially
the sales warranty under the Uniform Sales Act and the Uniform Commercial Code; (3) government commissions and private ombudsmen such
as Ralph Nader have displayed a renewed interest in the consumer;
and (4) the Consumer Product Safety Act of 1972, a federal law for testing,
researching, and investigating standards of products, has had far-reaching effects on potential consumer products liability hazards.

The seriousness of the product liability risk has been called a "crisis"
by many in recent years. Some 25 states have passed *tort reform acts*
which attempt to limit product liability, and many others have such
legislation under consideration. These statutes vary considerably, but
many (1) set a time limit during which lawsuits can be filed after the
manufacture or purchase of a product, or the discovery of a loss (2–12
years); (2) permit a "state of the art" defense based on new advances
in technical knowledge, or the defense that the producer has properly
warned the user about possible dangers; (3) restrict noneconomic damages
for intangibles such as pain and suffering; (4) allow defense on the basis
that a product met government specifications or standards; (5) eliminate
claims based upon alterations or changes in the product by the user;
or (6) reduce the application of strict liability rules in product liability
cases.[31]

A whole new area related to product liability has emerged with new
federal government regulations under the Environmental Protection
Agency. *Pollution liability* from sudden and gradual exposure to hazardous products is a tremendous potential exposure for many companies
that transport oil and other products, or those that generate or dispose
of hazardous waste. New standards of loss control and a billion-dollar
"Superfund" by the end of the 1980s are being set up to regulate these
industries under the Comprehensive Environmental Response, Compensation, and Liability Act of 1981.

The increasing trend toward major problems in product liability caused
the federal government to set up an interagency task force, which concluded that no widespread unavailability of insurance existed. However,
their proposals led to the Product Liability Risk-Retention Act of 1981.
This act facilitates the formation of "risk-retention groups" as insurers
in order to increase insurance availability and affordability in the product
liability market. Whether or not the desired effects of this act—or more
sources of competition through association captive insurers and less state
regulation of rates—will occur in the 1980s remains to be seen.[32]

[31] Jerry Geisel, "Product Liability Score Card," *Business Insurance*, September 20, 1982, p. 34.

[32] Eric A. Wiening, "The Risk Retention Act—A Solution to What Problem?" *CPCU Journal* 35, no. 3 (September 1982), p. 174.

Nonownership liability

Some perplexing questions of liability occur in connection with the ownership and operation of automobiles. Although many specific state statutes provide otherwise, it is the rule that when an automobile is borrowed (in good mechanical condition), the car owner is not usually called upon to pay for damages arising out of its operation. On the other hand, if the operator of a car doing damage occupies the position of employee or agent of the car owner, the owner may be held liable.

The liability is based upon the doctrine of *respondeat superior,* and it applies not only to chauffeurs driving cars owned by their employers but also to salespersons, agents, or other employees who in the course of their employment use *their own cars* in transacting business for their employers. Employers may always have liability when a car (or boat or plane) is *owned, leased,* or *hired* by them. In addition, other *nonowned vehicles* may impose responsibility on employers. For instance, an employee of a drugstore delivering a package on the way from work, an employee of a contractor going from one job to another, a salesperson or scores of others acting in their employer's interest and driving their own automobiles may involve their employers in huge accident claims. The danger is particularly acute in that the employee may have very few resources, while the employer is a logical target at which to aim heavy damage suits.

Libel and other related types of liability

A special liability risk, which is usually covered only by specific endorsement or in a separate contract, is faced by authors, publishers, and others. The exposure is that of libel and several other related perils.

Libel is something more than the liability due to negligence. A publisher or other person who holds someone up to scorn, contempt, or ridicule may be liable for heavy damages when an untrue and malicious statement is published. The law recognizes two classes of malice. When there is a deliberate desire to injure, there is malice in fact. A careless disregard for another's rights which results in errors constitutes malice in law. Absence of intent to libel does not constitute a defense. Publication of a retraction is not a complete defense and serves only to mitigate damages.

The exposure and losses are notable. For example, a much-publicized suit by a football coach at a Southern university resulted in a $3 million judgment against *The Saturday Evening Post,* for a libelous story which claimed that the coach had given a rival team its football plays. The case was settled before retrial for less than one sixth the original verdict. The biography of Howard Hughes was the basis for a large and complicated libel lawsuit. The late mayor of San Francisco was awarded $350,000, plus more than that in legal costs, for a malicious magazine article that linked him with the Mafia.[33]

Claims may be made for *slander* as well as libel. Libel is written defamation, and slander is spoken defamation of character. Radio and television stations may be sued, as may credit bureaus that make verbal reports to subscribers by telephone or otherwise. An insured may also become involved in claims for damages for *invasion of privacy.* The right of privacy concerns the peace of mind of the individual. Every person has some rights that private personal matters, such as insanity or adultery, should not be commented upon or ridiculed in public without his or her consent. (Public figures have fewer such rights.) Truth is not a defense to an action for the infringement of the right of privacy. Claims based upon *plagiarism* and *violation of copyright* against writers and publishers are further examples of the wide scope of these special cases of the liability risk in its many forms.

Other special situations

There are many special situations. The operator of a drugstore may incur professional liability claims that are an outgrowth of compounding prescriptions (a form of malpractice liability) or may incur products liability that may result from dispensing food. In fact, any person who sells foods may be subject to a liability claim based upon alleged injury from their use. *Professional and medical malpractice liability* situations are discussed separately in Chapter 17 because they involve specialized exposures and insurance coverages.

Property damage liability and personal injury may result from explosions, elevators, boats, and airplanes. Schools and colleges may be held responsible for injuries on their properties, particularly with reference to gymnasiums, swimming pools, grandstands, crowded auditoriums, and the like. In some instances the school itself may be liable for accident or injury, and in others liability may attach directly to a teacher or trustee.[34] Injury to others may grow out of participation in sports. In fact, a person may incur liability while simply walking along the street, as in the case of a man who is smoking and accidentally burns another

---

[33] "Alioto Is Awarded $350,000 plus Costs in *Look* Libel Case," *The Wall Street Journal,* May 4, 1977. The large legal costs of libel cases are also noted in a $2 million jury award in 1982 to the president of Mobil Oil, which was said only to cover the legal fees incurred by the plaintiff.

[34] Fortunately, for teachers and colleges the liability is not without some limit. The New Jersey Supreme Court ruled against a Columbia University student who had sued for $8,065 damages, claiming that the college had "failed to teach him wisdom." The judge sagely observed that "wisdom cannot be taught, if in fact it can be defined"!

person with a lighted cigar. In every instance the party concerned must exercise such care as a reasonably prudent person would use in the circumstances; and failure to do this, whether deliberate or unintentional, creates a liability for injury and damages if a person or property is injured as a result.

FOR REVIEW AND DISCUSSION

1. Describe the legal basis for liability and explain why this is important to insurance consumers.
2. Why are liability risks sometimes considered more important than property risks? Cite several examples.
3. What is an "attractive nuisance"? What effect does it have on a property owner's potential liability? How can the exposure to loss be reduced?
4. What is the relationship among "legal wrongs," "torts," "negligence," and liability insurance? (Include the requirements for "negligence.")
5. What is the difference between liability under *contract* law and liability under *tort* law? (Illustrate your answer with examples of each.)
6. "Torts are not always based on unintentional acts, nor on fault." Explain both parts of this statement.
7. "Presumed" and "imputed" negligence may each modify the usual negligence rules. Give an example of each of these rules, showing its results to the claimant.
8. Divide the class into two groups, asking one group to present the *advantages*, and the second group the *disadvantages* of *comparative negligence* statutes.
9. How does the concept of *strict or absolute liability* change the usual negligence situation? When does this concept apply?
10. Jerry is an employee of the federal government and drives a postal truck. May the federal government or this employee be sued?
11. Mrs. Swank, a Sunday school teacher, is injured when a piano leg collapses. Is the church liable in the event that suit is filed?
12. Explain how real estate property ownership may create liability risk to trespassers and invitees.
13. What legal liability rule may make a business responsible for actions of employees or agents who cause injuries to others or damages to the property of others? Illustrate your answer with several examples.
14. Discuss how persons or organizations can become liable for losses caused by property they do *not* own.
15. Explain how *libel* and other related types of liability may create liability risks.
16. "There are some situations where there is *immunity from liability*, but many changes in the extent to which this doctrine applies have occurred." Explain this statement.

Chapter 17

Outline of concepts

Liability risk management coordinates other methods with insurance.

Types of liability insurance are classified into major types as *bodily injury* and *property damage;* and *direct* and *contingent.*

The scope of major liability insurance contracts includes (1) *employers,* (2) *automobile,* and (3) *"general,"* which is further subdivided into: (1) *personal,* (2) *business,* (3) *professional contracts;* or (1) *primary* and (2) *excess contracts;* and *medical payments.*

The general liability insurance program is discussed:

    Nature of and rationale for the revisions.

    The basic policy format, with the three following parts:

    Declarations, including statements by the insured about the coverage,

    The policy jacket, with supplementary payments, definitions, and conditions applying to all general liability contracts of this type, and

    The coverage parts, which contain the insuring agreements and exclusions.

Personal liability insurance contracts, the *comprehensive personal liability* policy and farmers' CPL, cover individual and family interests.

Business liability insurance contracts are numerous. Most common are:

    Owners', landlords', and tenants' liability policy (OLT);

    Manufacturers' and contractors' liability policy (M&C);

    Comprehensive general liability policy (CGL);

    Other business liability coverages: *storekeepers', contractual, products and completed operations, protective,* and *automobile.*

Professional or malpractice liability insurance contracts differ greatly and are important to medical and many other professional persons.

Excess insurance is broad, additional high-limit coverage of catastrophe losses of individuals and businesses. This is contrasted with "primary" coverages which pay losses first (or are the only protection), before the excess contracts apply:

    Excess and surplus lines, often insuring risks difficult to place in normal markets, and adding unusual perils and broader coverage;

    The umbrella liability policy, a popular form for businesses and other organizations needing broader, higher limit insurance;

    Retroactive liability policies, which can be purchased to cover some losses that have already occurred; and

    Excess personal liabilities policies, for million-dollar or higher limit personal coverages, which can be easily added to many family homeowner's policies.

Medical payments coverage pays medical expenses, regardless of liability, and is often included in general liability contracts.

General liability insurance

The extensive size and variety of exposures to loss from "the liability risk" create almost unbelievable potential liability by every person and organization for injuries or damages to others. What can be done to reduce or prepare for liability losses? Applying the techniques of *risk management*, as discussed in Chapters 1 and 2, is the best answer. In this process, most individuals, businesses and other organizations will find *insurance* as one of the most essential methods of risk treatment.

General liability insurance, which covers all types of liability insurance other than employers' liability and automobile liability, thus becomes the emphasis of this chapter. The general liability insurance program is analyzed as the basis for many contracts. The declarations and policy jacket sections contain many standard terms. Then a "coverage part" is added that completes the contract. Thus, various personal, business, and professional liability policies are developed. Other excess insurance covers some unusual or catastrophic exposures.

LIABILITY RISK MANAGEMENT

The first two steps in *liability risk management*, identification and measurement of risk, are implicit throughout the prior chapter. First, by *identifying* the many types of text and contract liability and classifying the major categories as in Figure 16–1, the task of dealing with them is clarified. Then, the examples of the magnitude of these exposures show that the *measurement* of liability risk is extremely difficult because there are no maximum limits for liability losses as there are for property losses. Past claims and loss payments indicate to some extent the likely loss frequency and severity, but future costs remain essentially unlimited and very difficult to predict.

The third step in the risk-management process, the *choice of the methods* of risk treatment, suggests that several alternatives for liability exposures should be considered and evaluated. The best results are usually obtained by combining and coordinating the various techniques. Finally, risk *administration* can monitor and review the choices made in order to implement and change the methods as experience shows which techques are most effective.

For example, perhaps some liability situations can be *controlled*, through *avoidance* of exposure to loss, such as by not owning real estate or by leasing automobiles or other equipment instead of owning it. Other liabilities might be controlled by *combination* or *diversification* of similar loss exposures in larger entities in order to achieve greater predictability. In some cases, the opposite technique of *separation* of exposures may be used, as in creating separate corporations which have liability limited to the assets of each company. *Loss prevention and reduction,* as discussed in Chapters 1 and 2, have important applications in minimizing both frequency and severity of liability losses. Examples include maintaining property free of dangers which may cause injuries to the public; designing and testing products to reduce defects or hazards which could cause accidents; special protection for property held for others as a bailee; extra training of employees and agents to lessen the possibility of imputed negligence; and legal review of sales contracts to limit the implied or specific warranties extending liability.

Some potential liability losses can be *financed* through risk-*retention* methods such as by setting up savings, reserve, "self-insurance," or "captive insurer" plans. Perhaps some liability can be *transferred* to others, such as by "hold-harmless" agreements or other written contracts which make other persons responsible for part or all of liability losses.

However, several factors work against the exclusive reliance on many of these methods of risk treatment for liability situations. One is the complexity of the risk, based upon its legal nature, changing laws and interpretations, and the involvement of third parties (the claimant or injured person) in the legal liability process. Another is the large size of potential losses and the relative infrequency of loss as compared with most forms of property insurance. These characteristics make difficult the calculation of probabilities and variance of future losses. Many persons or firms are unable to use risk retention as a sole method of liability risk management, without the danger of serious financial trouble from the larger losses. Loss-prevention costs may be high and hard to justify. Risk transfer by contracts other than insurance are oftentimes cumbersome and ineffective.

Admittedly, some liability risks should be controlled by being avoided, or losses prevented, or risks transferred by special contracts—but by far the likeliest choice of individuals and businesses for financing most of the liability losses is to transfer the risk by purchasing *liability insurance.*

One thought for discussion is whether or not liability insurance may sometimes increase losses because of recklessness or carelessness. Although few studies document such an effect, it is possible that that such a tendency may exist when the financial losses caused by wrongdoers will be paid for by their insurers. Also, it may be argued that liability insurance has increased liability exposure because juries assume that defendants are adequately insured, and thus award larger verdicts when insurance-generated funds appear to be available.

TYPES OF LIABILITY INSURANCE

Liability insurance is *not accident insurance* or automatic payment for all accidents which cause damage. Rather, it defends the insureds when claims are made against them and settles with the claimants on reasonable terms *if* the insureds are legally liable for the loss or damage. The liability insurance policy makes such payments as the insureds would themselves have been obligated to pay because of the liability imposed by law. If there is no negligence on the part of the insureds and hence no legal liability, there is no obligation on the part of the insurer to make any payment to a claimant. The insurer, however, is obligated to defend the insureds against groundless claims, to bear the expenses thereof, and to make settlements subject to the limits of the policy in the event of unfavorable verdicts. In cases in which the question of liability is not clear, the insurer has the option to (and frequently does) make a settlement. By so doing, the insurer saves the expense of litigation, and the insureds are spared the inconvenience of a trial.

In the direct-damage insurance contract there are two parties to the agreement—the insurer and the insured; the insured receives payment from the insurer for a property loss. In the case of liability insurance, the third party who is injured or suffers a loss is not the insured. Because of this, liability insurance has sometimes been termed *third-party insurance*. The term is entirely in order, but in using it one should remember that the third party is not an insured and usually has no right of action against the insurer. (Louisiana is an exception, for direct suits against the insurer are permitted there.)

In writing liability coverage, insurers frequently separate the property damage from the bodily injury covers. Hence, the liability insurance field is divided into two major classifications: (1) *bodily injury liability insurance* and (2) *property damage liability insurance*. Bodily injury liability policies are sometimes written setting forth a limit applicable to *each person* and a limit applicable to *each occurrence*. Thus, for example, a liability contract may have limits of $50,000–100,000. This means that in any one occurrence not more than $50,000 will be paid for the claim of the given individual and not more than $100,000 as the aggregate of all claims for bodily injuries growing out of a single occurrence. In the case of property damage liability, a limit of liability is set that is applicable to any one occurrence. Exceptions to this practice are found, including some auto policies and the new general liability forms which specify only an occurrence limit of liability for bodily injury. In other contracts, an "aggregate limit" for the policy term is established. Thus, in the case of malpractice and product liability coverages, a limit per occurrence, with another aggregate limit for the entire policy term, is the practice.

Insureds frequently cause injuries to persons under circumstances in which negligence cannot be proven or imputed. In these circumstances, the liability insurance company is obligated to make no payment to the injured party. In connection with the ownership of an automobile, for example, the owner may feel morally obligated to make payments to injured passengers, in cases where there is actually no negligence. The insured, for such losses, can provide *medical payments coverage*. The protection is not technically liability insurance, but it is often an important part of the liability insurance contract. (See later section of this chapter.)

As in the property insurance field, liability insurance may also be divided into direct and indirect types. One type is written to cover the primary or *direct* liability of the insured, and a second type of contract is written on *contingent* liability. Contingent liability insurance (often called "protective" liability insurance) covers the insured in cases where the insured might still be held indirectly liable. For example, a subcontractor might be primarily liable for an accident, but the injured party might also sue the general contractor.

THE SCOPE OF MAJOR LIABILITY INSURANCE CONTRACTS

The types of liability insurance contracts for the many negligence and other liability situations are of great variety. As a consequence, no simple or logically inclusive classification is recognized. In this text, three major areas of liability insurance contracts are treated in separate chapters:

1. *Employers'* liability insurance contracts (and workers' compensation) in Chapter 18;
2. *Automobile* liability insurance contracts (and other types of automobile insurance) in Chapters 19 and 20; and
3. *General* liability insurance contracts in this chapter, including "excess" liability insurance policies.

The first two major areas deserve separate treatment based upon either their importance within other significant insurance contracts or on their special purpose of taking care of a particular kind of liability loss. The third area, *general liability insurance contracts*, includes all forms of liability insurance except for employers' and automobile liability insurance.

A simple division of *all* liability insurance contracts into "business" and "nonbusiness" categories is not a better classification. Although it is important to make this distinction within each of the indicated major areas, the distinction does not separate the usual liability insurance contracts meaningfully. For example, employers' liability insurance is almost always a business responsibility, yet some individuals need it for nonbusiness situations such as covering household or domestic employees. Automobile liability insurance is a major concern of individuals and families, but it may also be of great importance to business, nonprofit, or governmental organizations. Thus, *general liability insurance* is the best available term to describe the "all-other" area of liability insurance. Within the liability insurance business, the category is well known.

The field of general liability insurance may be divided into three distinct types of contracts according to the nature of the activity creating liability: those providing protection against (1) *personal* or individual liability perils, (2) *business* liability perils, and (3) *professional* or malpractice liability perils. According to the size of the loss to which the coverage applies, liability contracts may also be classified as those which provide protection against (1) *primary,* and (2) *excess* or catastrophe perils. These classifications are used in the following major sections of this chapter which discuss general liability insurance contracts. Since *medical payments* coverage is technically not insurance against liability but is often included in liability contracts, a separate section at the end of this chapter is devoted to this important type of insurance.

THE GENERAL LIABILITY INSURANCE PROGRAM

Nature of and rationale for the revisions

Extensive changes in liability contracts were set forth in 1973. Although not required by law, as in fire insurance, the standard provisions of the new general liability forms brought a commendable updating and uniformity to this field of insurance, both for members of the Insurance Services Office and for most independent insurers.

The general liability contract is now adaptable to many of the varied liability fields. Most important in these revisions was a reflection of the need for greater clarity and understanding in this very important segment of insurance. Changing liability exposures in our modern society, more liberal court interpretations, and changing needs of policyholders were all significant factors in making these revisions necessary.

In 1982, the Insurance Services Office released a proposed draft of a new general liability policy. After review by many insurance organizations, this form will probably begin to be used in many states. Some of the suggested changes are discussed in the following sections, where they may create important modifications in the coverage.

The basic policy format

The new contracts are based upon three parts: (1) a *declaration sheet;* (2) a *policy jacket* which contains all the supplementary payments, definitions, and conditions common to all general liability contracts; and (3) *coverage parts* which include the insuring agreements and exclusions. These three parts are put together to form a complete policy. The more common types of coverage parts added are comprehensive personal liability; owners', landlords', and tenants' liability; manufacturers' and contractors' liability; comprehensive general liability; and several types of medical malpractice liability contracts.

The policies contain the equivalent of the usual four sections of insurance contracts, that is, declarations, insuring agreements, conditions, and exclusions. However, standard definitions and conditions for all liability contracts are contained in the jacket of the policy, while the coverage part purposefully requires the insuring agreements to be immediately followed by the exclusions pertaining to that coverage. Clarity of intent and ease of understanding are the rewarding results of this format.

Declarations

The *declarations* include statements which identify both the insured and the insurer. Important data about the contract terms are typed in on the form to show who, what, where, and when the insurance covers. The declarations provide that by accepting the policy the named insured agrees with the representations made and that the policy is issued in reliance upon the truth of these statements.

The policy jacket

The provisions common to all general liability insurance contracts are contained in the standard policy jacket. Three sections are identified as "supplementary payments," "definitions," and "conditions." The reading and analysis are eased by centralizing these in the policy jacket, and the length of the various "coverage parts" added is correspondingly reduced.

Supplementary payments. The first section of the policy jacket, which is applicable to all of the coverage parts that may be used with it, mentions several extra costs which are payable by the insurer in addition to the policy liability limit. These include: (1) premiums on bonds to release attachments relating to lawsuits defended by the insurer; (2) bail bond cost up to $250 per bond required for traffic law violations arising out of vehicles to which the contract applies; (3) reimbursement to the insured for reasonable expenses incurred at the insurer's request in assisting the company in the investigation or defense of any claim or suit, including actual loss of earnings not to exceed $25 per day.

Definitions. More than the usual number of definitions appear in the policy jacket, but some are more important than others for particular types of general liability contracts.

Whenever the word *insured* is used in the contract without qualification, it is defined to include any director, executive officer, stockholder, or partner of the insured if the named insured is a corporation or partnership. The coverage to directors, executive officers, stockholders, or partners applies only while they are acting within the scope of their duties in connection with the furthering of the interests of the business. When the named insured is an individual, the spouse is also included.

Coverage is provided on the basis of *occurrence,* rather than on the basis of accident. Older policies covered liability imposed by law for injury or damage caused by "accident," which was defined as "a sudden and unforeseeable event." This required that the event happen at a definite time and place and that it be unexpected and unintended. The new wording covers injury or damage caused by an "occurrence" defined as "an accident, including continuous or repeated exposure to conditions, which results in bodily injury or property damage neither expected nor intended from the standpoint of the insured." It is not required that the event be a sudden one. The word *accident* is used in this definition in order to clarify the time of coverage as being from the time of injury rather than from the time of exposure. It also makes the policy limits applicable only once for each occurrence instead of having multiple limits apply on the basis of a series of events due to the same factor (for example, a contractor's equipment hitting four automobiles in a collision is considered one occurrence).

The proposed new ISO form may eliminate the word *accident,* by defining occurrence to include injuries only if they are *discovered* during the policy term. Alternative coverage would be purchasable, if desired, to cover only injuries for which *claims* are first made during the policy term. The change to "first discovery" or "claims made" coverage, as opposed to occurrence-based coverage, is being hotly debated.

Examples of the broadened coverage for liability losses based on an "occurrence" that would probably not be covered as an "accident" are:

1. Skin injury as a result of repeated use of a lotion.
2. Crops killed by fumes escaping continuously from a manufacturing plant.

3. Paint damage to homes by repeated exposure to dust and chemicals from trucks going to and from a construction site.
4. Sickness or disease caused by exposure to unsanitary conditions.
5. Injury resulting from assault and battery by an employee.

Another important definition helps clarify the difference between *product liability* and *completed operations coverages,* for some court decisions had held that these two kinds of liability were not separate. Contractors often had difficulty in determining whether or not installations in which defects later caused injuries were covered by product liability (usually) or completed operations. The policy jacket contains a detailed definition of "product liability" hazard as injury occurring after the relinquishment of possession and away from premises owned by or rented to the insured. "Completed operations" is defined as injury or damage (not the negligent act or accident) arising out of operations or out of reliance upon a representation or warranty occurring *after* the operations are completed. This time is at the earliest of the following: (1) when all of the operations by or on behalf of the insured are done, (2) when such operations at the site are done, or (3) when the portion of the work out of which the injury arises has been put to its intended use. The importance of such definition is that completed operations coverage must be purchased to cover many contracting situations which may cause losses after the events specified have occurred.

Bodily injury means "bodily injury, sickness or disease sustained by any person which occurs during the policy period, including death at any time resulting therefrom."[1] A coverage of increasing recent interest is the *personal injury hazard* which involves third-party claims for damages that are other than physical. The general liability program permits adding this coverage to the basic policies or writing it as a separate policy. Three groups of claims alleging the following offenses are covered by this liability insurance: (1) false arrest, detention, or imprisonment, and malicious prosecution; (2) libel or slander and invasion of privacy; and (3) wrongful entry or eviction. All businesses may have some exposure to these claims. The handling of shoplifting suspects by retail stores is an example of a serious and quite common exposure.

Property damage is defined to include "physical injury to or destruction of tangible property which occurs during the policy period, including

---

[1] Usually this requires physical harm, but some cases have involved mental or nonphysical injury. A Michigan truck driver received a $150,000 award for psychotic results of an accident in which no physical injury was involved. The case caused *Time* (February 16, 1964, p. 75) to define "emotional trauma" as "a state of mind precipitated by an accident, stimulated by an attorney, perpetrated by avarice, and cured by a verdict"! Recent cases have even involved lawsuits against physicians for emotional distress of parents and cost of care or loss of earnings of handicapped children born in unwanted pregnancies ("Suing for Being Born," *Newsweek,* March, 1982, p. 53).

loss of use thereof at any time resulting therefrom." This excludes such violations of intangible property rights as unfair competition or patent infringement. The new definition, separated into a second part of the 1973 revision, does not require physical injury before a loss is covered, which broadens the coverage to include loss of use in cases where no prior physical damage to property has occurred. For example, store owners might sue for loss of profits when contractor's equipment breaks down and blocks access to the stores.

The 1973 changes also eliminate the former per person limit of liability, with only per occurrence limits now applying (except for products and completed operations, where a per year aggregate limit applies). The policy has separate occurrence limits for bodily injury and for property damage liability. Basic limits are $25,000 and $10,000, but these should be increased in most cases. The changes also added an exclusion for pollution damage (which used to be commonly added by endorsement), except when the pollution is sudden and accidental.

Other definitions are included in the policy jacket, such as automobiles, mobile equipment (racing and snowmobiles are excluded), and policy territory. For the precise differences in wording and meaning, several charts comparing the older and newer policies are available.[2]

Conditions. The policy jacket also contains several important conditions upon which the obligations of the insurer and the insured are based.

The *insured's duties in the event of occurrence, claim, or suit* are a combination of three former requirements for notice of accident (in writing, as soon as practicable, explaining the circumstances), claim or suit (immediately), and assistance and cooperation of the insured (for settlement in hearings and trials, etc.). These are reasonable requirements that enable the insurer to provide proper defense and obtain a fair settlement or judgment for the claim. The insured may provide "first aid" at the scene of the accident, but should not jeopardize the insurer's position by trying to make payments or to arrange a settlement. Such actions may be held as a breach of this condition.

Clarification of the insurer's right to *inspect and audit* the insured's property and operations is an important change in the new general liability contracts. Some court decisions under the old wording had held this to be not only a right but also an obligation of the insurer, with possible negligence if the insurer did not do so. The new wording specifically states this as a right, without any warranty by the insurer "that such property or operations are safe or healthful, or are in compliance with any law, rule, or regulation."

---

[2] Such as those published by Underwriters Adjusting Company, General Adjustment Bureau, and others.

The *other insurance* condition determines what happens when there is more than one insurer. Instead of merely prorating or apportioning with other applicable insurance, this condition states that when the insurance is intended to be primary coverage, it shall pay before excess or contingent liability contracts contribute to the loss. If it happens that two or more contracts are both primary coverage on this basis (regardless of differences which may exist as to the policy limits), then each insurer shall pay on an "equal shares" basis. Each insurer would pay equal amounts of the loss up to the point at which the lower of the policy limits is exhausted, after which the higher limit policy would apply alone. For example, assume that for the same insured, insurer A has an applicable bodily injury limit of $250,000 and insurer B has a $500,000 limit. If a liability judgment for $700,000 is rendered against the insured, insurers A and B will each pay $250,000 and then insurer B will also pay the balance of the judgment, or $200,000 more.

Conditions of less importance are those pertaining to financial responsibility laws, premium bases, and assignment. Other conditions which have remained essentially the same are those permitting policy changes in writing, cancellation (by insured: anytime; by insurer: with 10 days' notice), the right of subrogration by the insurer, and action against the insurer by the insured only after the insured has complied with all policy provisions and the final judgment of settlement of the claim has been determined.

The coverage parts

Two basic parts of the general liability insurance program have been explained above—the declarations and the policy jacket. The addition of a *coverage part,* containing the *insuring agreement and exclusions* pertaining to the insurance, completes the contract. Many different coverage parts can be used to develop completed general liability insurance contracts known as:

1. *Personal liability:*
    a. Comprehensive personal liability policy.
    b. Farmers' comprehensive personal liability policy.
2. *Business liability:*
    a. Owners', landlords', and tenants' liability policy.
    b. Manufacturers' and contractors' liability policy.
    c. Comprehensive general liability policy.
3. *Professional liability:*
    a. Medical or malpractice liability policies.
    b. Other professional liability policies.

Other policies are more briefly mentioned. Some other policies permitted within this program include both general and automobile liability exposures, such as the comprehensive automobile liability policy, the comprehensive automobile and garage liability policy, and others. A total of more than 20 separate coverage parts may be used to create specific general liability insurance contracts.

The following discussion of specific contracts of the general liability insurance program is divided, as above, into three major groups: (1) *personal*, (2) *business*, and (3) *professional or malpractice* liability insurance contracts.

PERSONAL LIABILITY INSURANCE CONTRACTS

Two basic personal policies are the comprehensive personal liability policy and the farmers' comprehensive personal liability policy. The individual and the family need liability protection for numerous personal or individual situations. The ownership of residential property, participation in sports activities, the keeping of pets or animals, and many normal everyday activities all place a responsibility upon individuals not to cause injury or damage to other persons or their property.

Several other separate policies were used many years ago—a residence liability, a sports liability, and a dog liability policy—but now these coverages are almost always insured by the comprehensive personal forms instead.

Excess or catastrophe liability policies are discussed later in this chapter. Some of these provide coverages for individuals.

In the liability insuring clause, the comprehensive personal liability policies, unlike most liability policies, cover under a *single limit* the liability of the insured for damage on account of bodily injury to members of the public and to employees, and for damage to the property of others caused by an occurrence. The minimum single limit is $10,000, but as in the case of other liability coverages, policies are frequently written for larger limits, such as $50,000, $100,000, or more. The single limit represents the maximum liability of the insurer, regardless of the number of persons injured or the extent of property damage attributable to a single occurrence.

The comprehensive personal liability policy and the farmers' personal comprehensive liability policy are both designed to provide comprehensive liability protection for a named insured and the members of his or her household. However, certain perils in the farm risk are not found in the usual household, and the farmers' comprehensive form is adapted to them. Although based primarily upon the personal liability exposures, the farmers' form does include some business liability perils.

Today the CPL and the farmers' CPL are typically included, along with fire, theft, and other insurance, in the homeowners' or farmowners' multiple-line contracts explained in Chapter 23.

BUSINESS LIABILITY INSURANCE CONTRACTS

Many different business liability policies can be developed by adding a coverage part to the basic general liability insurance program. The three best known are: the owners', landlords', and tenants' policy (OLT); the manufacturers' and contractors' policy (M&C); and the comprehensive general liability policy (CGL). Many businesses now include protection similar to these contracts within the various business multiple-line contracts (see Chapter 23).

Several other coverage parts are either commonly added to, or at least should be considered with, the above policies, or they are designed to fit special liability needs of certain businesses. Storekeepers', contractual, completed operations and products, protective, and automobile liability coverage parts are briefly presented as "other" business liability.

For each of these coverage parts the basic addition to the declarations and policy jacket is the *insuring agreement*. The insurer promises to pay *on behalf of the insured* all sums which the insured shall become obligated to pay as damages because of (1) *bodily injury* or (2) *property damage*. The insurer agrees to defend any suit against the insured for these damages, even if the suit is groundless, false, or fraudulent. These costs may be considerable, and they are paid in addition to the policy limits. One exception is that the insurer is not obligated to defend any new suit after the applicable limit of the policy has been exhausted by payment of judgments or settlements.

Exclusions in the new policies are required to follow immediately after the insuring agreement. These exclusions are, in general, considerably more understandable because of this location. The specific exclusions vary according to the coverage part. In many coverage parts a separate section defines in further detail the persons insured, the limits of liability, and the policy period and territory.

Owners', landlords', and tenants' liability policy

The *owners', landlords', and tenants' (OLT) liability policy* covers loss or expense, or both, resulting from claims upon the insured on account of bodily injuries or property damage to any person or persons not employed by the insured. The occurrence must be alleged to have been caused by reason of the ownership, maintenance, or use of the premises occupied by the insured. The general types of *businesses* eligible for the OLT policy include retail stores, offices, and apartment building owners. (Residential tenants use personal liability forms such as the CPL or homeowner's tenants policy.) The OLT policy covers liability insurance for *premises, operations in progress,* and *elevators*. For coverage of the full scope of business liability, including products and completed operations, the CGL is recommended.

The coverage is twofold as to location. For many types of businesses the principal exposure is within the place of business, while in other businesses the outside peril constitutes a substantial part of the exposure. The *on-the-premises* hazards extend to elevators or sidewalks and passages adjacent. Examples of claims include injuries resulting from the collapse of a chair on which a customer was seated; falls on stairs, torn carpets, or slippery floors; toppling merchandise; and many others. The outside or *off-premises* hazards are important where accidents during the demonstration or installation of appliances in the customer's home may involve the employer of the salesperson in a claim for damages. New locations or activities are covered automatically if the insurer is notified within 30 days.

Two basic types of liability insurance are invariably included together in the OLT policy, although separate limits of liability apply to each: (1) *bodily injury* liability coverage and (2) *property damage* liability coverage. Under the *bodily injury* protection, the insurer agrees to pay all sums which the insured becomes legally obligated to pay because of bodily injury, sickness, or disease (including death) suffered by members of the public for operations carried on at and from the premises of the insured. *Property damage* liability covers injury to or destruction of property of others, including loss of use. Usually included now is water damage liability coverage, such as damage to buildings or contents from plumbing, heating, refrigerating, air conditioning, or automatic sprinkler systems.

The standard limits for the owners', landlords', and tenants' liability policy are $25,000 per occurrence, with a limit of $5,000 for property damage liability coverage. Limits can and should be increased for many businesses to $500,000 and $100,000 or more. The rate of such increased amounts of coverage decreases per thousand dollars of protection as the policy limits are raised.

Manufacturers' and contractors' liability policy

The *manufacturers' and contractors' M&C liability policy* provides protection for the manufacturer or contractor similar in nature to that afforded under the OLT policy. Coverage is adapted, however, to insure against claims from members of the public at all premises and for all operations of the insured, which for these types of businesses often include scattered and changing locations. Applicants for employment, visitors, salespersons, deliverypersons, employees of contractors, children, and trespassers—all form a part of the public.

Contractors engaged in construction are protected in the operation of the machinery and equipment used in their work, both while it is at the work location and while it is being taken to and from the work location. Coverage for elevator liability is included, and the use of hoists and elevators for handling materials is one of the serious hazards of many manufacturers and contractors. Inspections and recommendations for loss-prevention techniques can be a particularly valuable service of insurers for such exposures.

As with the OLT policy (the student should also review the previous section in order to understand the M&C policy), only incidental coverages for contractual (assumed) liability are included. These are: (1) leases of premises, (2) easements, (3) municipal ordinance indemnification agreements (for example, such as for signs), (4) railroad sidetrack agreements, and (5) elevator maintenance agreements. All other contractual liability requires the addition of a separate coverage part for this exposure, as is explained in a later section of this chapter.

Manufacturers or contractors also need to analyze carefully their products and completed operations liability exposure, for which coverage is oftentimes needed. Such coverage can be obtained through the use of the comprehensive general liability policy or as a separate coverage part if only those hazards are to be covered.

Comprehensive general liability policy

The most important of all business liability policies is the *comprehensive general liability (CGL) policy*. It is the best method by which most businesses (except small ones) can obtain the full scope of coverage for noncontractual general liability hazards. For some the OLT or M&C policy may be adequate, but for many the CGL policy is the best alternative.

Many of the comments in the two previous sections apply to the CGL coverage part. It includes the basic liability protection of the OLT and M&C policies for premises, operations, elevators, and incidental contractual exposures (such as for leases of premises and some easements). However, it is broader in that it automatically includes coverage for completed operations, products, escalators, and independent contractor (or protective) liability exposures. It is designed to include in a single contract insurance protection against all these liability perils.

The policy also provides full automatic coverage for claims arising because of the acquisition of some property subsequent to the writing of the policy and for the so-called unknown perils, about which the insured knows nothing, or which would usually not be covered by any named-perils policy.

The following exclusions also apply to the OLT and M&C policies: (1) assumed or contractual liability, except the named incidental types (see M&C policy section); (2) automobile or aircraft liability; (3) off-premises watercraft liability; (4) liability for war; (5) liability for injury or sickness of employees;[3] and (6) property damage to property owned by, occupied by, rented to, used by, or in the care, custody, or control of the insured. For specified types of insureds a few other exclusions apply, such as liquor liability and property damage liability for explosions, collapse, or underground damage.

In order to extend the CGL policy to many of the above excluded coverages, a *broad form CGL endorsement* (revised in 1981 by ISO) is quite popular. It has 12 sections, among which these are most important: blanket contractual liability (any oral or written agreement related to the insured's business); personal injury; premises medical payments; liquor liability (but not for those in the liquor business); fire legal liability (for real or personal property, but not for liability assumed by contract); broad form property damage; incidental malpractice; nonowned watercraft (under 26 feet in length, not carrying persons or property for a charge); limited worldwide liability (for product liability); additional insureds (officers, directors, employees); and extended bodily injury (for intentional acts to protect persons or property).[4]

Other business liability coverages

Several other coverages are or can be included in the three most common business liability policies just discussed.

Storekeepers' liability coverage. One coverage part, the *storekeepers' liability policy,* is an alternative to these three policies designed for small retail shops. A single insuring limit varying from a basic $25,000 to $100,000, is used for both bodily injury and property damage liability coverages. Coverage for limited contractual and products liability hazards is included.

Coverage for contractual liability. In many cases of liability assumed by contract, specific insurance is necessary if adequate protection is to be provided. It has been noted above that only limited and incidental contractual exposures are covered in the basic general liability policies. The addition to these policies of a separate coverage for *contractual liability* exposures is frequently needed. Occasionally a separate policy is written for just this purpose.

The insurer provides liability insurance for bodily injuries or property damage liability that the insured has agreed to assume under a *written* contract. The agreement under which liability is assumed is usually iden-

---

[3] Workers' compensation and employers' liability protection are not included in the basic policy or by endorsement. The peril regarding employees is covered *only* under the workers' compensation policy.

[4] *The John Liner Letter* (Wellesly, Mass.: Shelby Publishing, May 1982).

tified in the policy by reference, but in some instances a copy of the indemnity provisions of the contract is attached to the policy.

This policy finds frequent use in providing protection for contractors who are required to assume the responsibility for all liability of a municipality before they are issued a permit to store material on city streets, to bridge sidewalks, or to use public facilities in other ways. Other examples of the need for coverage of contractual liability hazards are written equipment leases, work or supply contracts, and hold-harmless agreements.[5] In hold-harmless agreements, which have increased in use in recent years, one party agrees to assume the liability of another party. Thus, the first party is "held harmless" (or not held liable) for some or all of the claims which may result. Leases and construction contracts often include such provisions.

Coverage for product and completed operations liability. The many examples of product liability exposures in the previous chapter emphasize the importance of product liability insurance.[6] For contractors the related coverage of claims for completed operations was noted as it appears in the policy jacket of the general liability insurance program.

Although product liability insurance became rather difficult and more expensive to purchase in the 1970s, especially for such exposures as drug and chemical manufacturers and distributors, no widespread unavailability of coverage was found by a federal task force. Every business should consider the need for product liability insurance and determine whether or not it has been insured properly. It can be separately insured or added in the OLT policy or other forms. It is automatically included in the CGL policy, but this coverage does not include (1) damage to the insured's product, (2) costs of withdrawing the product from the market,[7] or (3) loss of use claimed for failure of the product to perform as warranted.

The potential effect of the Risk Retention Act of 1981 in alleviating product liability market problems was mentioned in Chapter 16. The increasing problem of meeting pollution liability regulations and insurance requirements of the Environmental Protection Agency (EPA) by the mid-1980s was also noted. Although a specialized need of firms dealing with hazardous wastes, the need for loss control and insurance in this

---

[5] For a review of the purposes, legal principles, evaluation, and controls in this area, see *The Hold-Harmless Agreement* (Cincinnati: National Underwriter, 1978).

[6] One more example is literally mind-boggling. A few years ago Coors had a $2 million lawsuit for allegedly pickling a writer's brain with that popular beverage, beer. The writer was a novelist, not a textbook writer. No settlement on the claim has been announced.

[7] Insurance for this exposure is called "product recall" coverage. The need is apparent in the recent cases involving toxic shock syndrome from Rely tampons and death from cyanide-laced Tylenol capsules. Most of the millions of dollars of costs may occur from expenses of recall (and lost future business) rather than from actual injuries or deaths caused by these products.

area is strong evidence of the trend toward increasing product liability exposures for many businesses in the future.[8]

Product liability insurance pays claims for bodily injury or property damage caused by mistakes, imperfect ingredients, or foreign substances, as well as improper handling, labeling, packing, or delivering. The policy does not cover products consumed on the premises of the insured or any liability for injury to employees. Goods manufactured, sold, or distributed in violation of law are never covered. It is not necessary that the product actually be sold, since injury attributable to samples or souvenirs is covered.

The policy covers only for amounts for which the insured shall become legally obligated to pay as damages if the occurrence causing the loss occurs (a) away from the insured's premises and (b) after the insured has relinquished possession of the product to others. The policy is written with two limits: (a) a limit per occurrence and (b) an aggregate limit. The per occurrence limit fixes a total liability for claims from one common cause, such as from one prepared or acquired lot of goods. The aggregate limit is the total liability for all damages under the policy for one year. Basic limits are $25,000 and $50,000. Higher limits may be purchased, and limits of $1 million or more are often recommended.

Purchase order agreements are sometimes written with a "hold-harmless" clause under the terms of which the manufacturer agrees to hold the retailer harmless for liability claims. The hold-harmless agreement is an assumed liability that is excluded under the products liability policy but may be covered by endorsement.

Coverage for protective liability. Several types of *protective liability* insurance may be important to certain policyholders. (See previous section on types of liability insurance.) The *owners' and contractors'* protective liability policy is designed to provide owners of property with protection for the *contingent* liability that may develop as the result of an accident caused by the negligence of a contractor. Contractors purchase the coverage to provide themselves with the same protection for claims that develop as the result of the alleged negligence of subcontractors. Members of the public frequently file their suit for damages against the general contractor, or they file a joint suit.

The protective policy provides direct liability protection in those situations in which the law holds the owner or the principal contractor liable in spite of the negligence of an independent contractor. These situations develop in connection with (a) unlawful work, (b) responsibility that cannot be delegated, and (c) inherently dangerous work. An accident

---

[8] George Head, "The EPA's Balancing Act," *National Underwriter,* P. and C. ed., October 15, 1982, p. 19. See also Matthew Lenz, Jr., *Environmental Pollution: Liability and Insurance* (New York: Insurance Information Institute, 1982).

resulting from the violation of a municipal ordinance would fall into the first category. The principal contractor cannot delegate to others duty to the public, such as the maintenance of a safe sidewalk condition. Where an extremely hazardous operation, such as blasting, is a part of an operation, the principal contractor may not escape responsibility for injury to the public on the grounds that the dangerous work was let to a subcontractor.

Another form of contingent liability insurance that is occasionally needed is the *principal's* protective liability policy. Newspaper, milk, and baked goods distributors, for example, hire persons who may be called either employees or independent contractors. The policy provides protection under two insuring clauses: *(a)* liability *to* independent contractors and *(b)* liability *for* independent contractors. Thus, if the insured is held liable for injury or damages to a person described in the policy as an independent contractor, the insurance covers. On the other hand, if the insured is held liable for injuries by independent contractors to members of the public, protection also applies.

Coverage for automobile liability.   Many *automobile liability* coverages may now be combined in the new general liability program. Coverage parts for automobile physical damage, medical payments, garage, and comprehensive automobile liability are available. Single contracts can be developed for a comprehensive CGL and automobile policy, or an OLT and automobile policy, to provide packages of combined liability coverage.

PROFESSIONAL OR MALPRACTICE LIABILITY INSURANCE CONTRACTS

The treatment of a patient by a medical practitioner (such as a surgeon, physician, or dentist) with lack of care or professional skill and with injurious results, constitutes malpractice. Liability for personal injury in such instances is known as *professional* or *malpractice* liability.

Professional liability insurance was first written to indemnify medical professionals for loss or expense resulting from claims on account of *bodily injuries.* Any malpractice, error, or mistake committed, or alleged to have been committed, in performing medical services is covered.

Today, many other professional persons in addition to those in the medical fields find themselves defendants in heavy damage suits. Professional liability insurance has been extended into fields to cover losses where *monetary* damages (as opposed to bodily injury) are a consequence of the negligent professional services of the insured. Accountants, architects, advertisers, attorneys, insurance brokers or agents, real estate agents, stockholders, financial planners, consultants, data processors, and many others may all be held liable for their professional errors or mistakes. Failure to meet a standard of skill and care generally accepted for any of these professions or occupations, with resulting injury to the client, may obligate the responsible parties to defend themselves against claims for damages.

Professional malpractice liability for the medical fields

The medical forms are presented here first because of their many unusual liability features. The growing importance of professional liability insurance for many nonmedical professional groups is emphasized in succeeding sections.

Physicians', surgeons', and dentists' liability policy. This form (which can be attached to the general liability policy jacket) provides coverage for liability arising out of professional acts or omissions committed by the insured or by any person for whom the insured is legally responsible. Negligence is not required, as many medical acts are performed *intentionally,* and these are covered because the injury does not have to result from an accident.

The insuring clause providing indemnity to the insured for damages on account of malpractice or mistake is very broad. Any claim whatever arising from injuries either real or alleged comes within the scope of the policy. The policy covers such claims as errors in recommending treatment or in prescribing or dispensing drugs or medicines, and claims arising through the performance of surgery or autopsies. It also defends counterclaims in suits brought for the collection of fees. Physicians and other professional practitioners have frequently been victimized by claims based upon alleged moral turpitude while engaged in professional practice. Such claims are covered by this contract, as are claims based upon undue familiarity, assault, slander, libel, and malicious persecution. The policy covers claims for bodily injury, for property damage, for care and loss of services, and losses of an intangible nature, in one major insuring clause.

The policy does not cover the personal liability of the insured for claims that cannot be traced to the professional practice of the insured. The policy excludes claims arising by reason of the liability of the insured as proprietor, superintendent, or executive officer in any hospital, clinic, laboratory, or other business enterprise.

In the case of professional persons, defense is an important factor. While in other damage cases a settlement to avoid suit where liability is not clear or is even denied may be the most inexpensive and expedient way to handle a claim, professionals cannot afford to jeopardize their reputations in this manner. They therefore often need the right to refuse to allow payment for an alleged injury. A feature peculiar to this policy is the requirement that the insurer secure the written *consent of the insured* before settling any claim. When insureds feel that their professional reputations are at stake, they may require the company to resist the case to the court of last resort, even though the claimant offers to compromise on a basis satisfactory to the insurers. The insurer obligates itself to defend the insured's reputation and to pay, subject to the policy limits, such award as may be made against the insured. Some new forms are limiting this risk by prescribing arbitration for certain conditions or by deleting the requirement that the insured consent to claim payments.

Policies are written on an occurrence basis with a limit per claim and an aggregate limit of liability for the policy period. The per claim limit is in contrast to the per person limit to be found in certain of the other liability policies, and the aggregate limit has no reference to a single accident. Obviously, most insureds should purchase much higher limits than the basic ones.[9] In addition to the policy written for an individual, many policies are written through groups such as medical societies and partnerships.

The *distinguishing features* of the medical forms of professional liability insurance (most of which also apply to the nonmedical forms), as compared with other liability insurance, in summary include: (1) importance of *defense* factor for maintaining professional reputation, (2) *consent* of the insured *before settling claims,* (3) very broad coverage of *negligence and even intentional acts* on an occurrence basis, (4) *per claim* and *per occurrence limits,* (5) one insuring clause for all damage claims, and (6) *high-coverage limits needed,* but high cost and limited market for some professional specialties.

In many areas and in a number of medical specialties, such as surgery, radiology, and anesthesia, a crisis of market availability occurred in malpractice insurance beginning about the mid-1970s as claims and awards increased substantially. Several insurers dominant in the malpractice field restricted or eliminated the writing of these contracts. The result was a severe shortage of markets for buying malpractice coverages, even with annual premiums increasing more than ten-fold to about $1.3 billion a year in the past decade.

The solutions have been varied. In many states special legislation has been passed to permit the use of joint underwriting associations (JUAs), in which all insurers writing liability insurance are required to participate in providing malpractice coverage for hospitals and medical professionals. Risk-management techniques have been encouraged in several of these states. In Florida and Ohio, for example, substantial credits of 15 percent or more are granted for the implementation of written risk-management policies by hospitals, the hiring of risk managers, and the

---

[9] Indicative of the escalating needs of professionals to keep current in this area is a monthly publication now available, the *Professional Liability Reporter* (San Francisco).

formation of committees, including medical practitioners, to review losses and recommend loss-prevention practices. Other states have passed or are considering legislation which (1) requires that attorney's fees be on a declining sliding-scale basis for larger awards; (2) mandates arbitration panels; (3) reduces payments by the amount collected from collateral medical insurance contracts (hospital, surgical, and major medical coverage); (4) eliminates the "Ad Damnum" provision in liability suits, in which specific dollar amounts of claims are used in jury trials; or (5) shortens the statute of limitations on lawsuits, thus reducing the "long tail" or coverage from some claims that were delayed for many years, particularly in the case of minors filing suit after age 21.

Insurers have reacted by more restrictive underwriting requirements and by writing coverage on a "claims made" basis instead of the usual "occurrence" basis. Only claims made or reported during the current contract are covered, making pricing of the protection easier for the insurer by eliminating the need to estimate claims that may occur long after an alleged malpractice incident happened.[10] When policies or insurers are changed, it is important to have "discovery coverage" included for a period of one to three years beyond the expiration date. A number of medical societies have also formed their own insurers in order to provide malpractice insurance to their own medical practitioners.

The crisis of coverage availability is not over, but it has been alleviated by these legislative and market adjustments. The costs for malpractice insurance will undoubtedly remain high, and medical professionals will probably continue to pay increasing costs, sometimes many thousands of dollars a year, for adequate coverage of this current problem in the liability field.

Druggists' liability policy. This is a malpractice coverage which also extends to provide product liability insurance protection.

The contract provides insurance against claims for damages on account of bodily injury or death that results from actual or alleged error on the part of drugstores or their employees in preparing, dispensing, selling, or delivering drugs, medicine, or merchandise. Coverage is also provided for claims arising out of the consumption or use of beverages, food, or other products, including merchandise of every character. This extends to losses caused by errors in labeling or delivering. Hence, a claim originating because two correctly compounded prescriptions were accidentally exchanged in delivery is covered. Also covered are errors in reading or interpreting the physician's prescriptions.

---

[10] Robert C. Witt and George M. McCabe, "The Medical Malpractice Insurance Pricing Problem: An Economic View," *CPCU Annals* 30, no. 2 (June 1977), p. 140. For the controversial statutory limitation of malpractice claims to a specified dollar amount, see Richard B. Corbett, "The Medical Malpractice Problem: Are Limitations on the Amount of Recovery a Viable Solution?" in the same issue, p. 151.

An exclusion with respect to claims attributable to illegality assumes some significance in connection with this coverage. For example, the illegal employment of clerks, sales of prohibited drugs, or the compounding of a prescription by a person who is not legally qualified (except by an assistant present and under the pharmacist's direction) will void the coverage so far as these acts give rise to claims. Violation of the Medical Practice Act by prescribing treatment or violation of the Harrison Narcotic Act or of laws governing the sale of alcoholic liquors has the same effect. However, if the insured or the manager does not intentionally violate the law, the policy protects the drugstore from the illegal actions of employees who may knowingly commit an illegal act.

Hospital liability policy. Like the druggists' policy, this form is a combination coverage for malpractice and product liability. It is designed for use by hospitals, clinics, nursing homes, and mental-psychopathic and other health institutions.

Coverage is provided for liability arising out of malpractice, error, or mistake made in rendering or failing to render medical or nursing treatment, including the furnishing of food or beverages. Product liability insurance is included, both on and off the premises, for drugs or medical supplies or appliances furnished or dispensed by the insured.

The need of hospitals for such insurance protection has escalated with the malpractice problems of recent years. Some of the potential solutions have been discussed in the physicians', surgeons', and dentists liability section. Other solutions proposed include the elimination of multiple lawsuits (against both hospitals and medical practitioners) and "structured settlements," which substitute periodic payments for medical expenses in place of large lump-sum payments.[11] Large losses are illustrated by one settlement for a woman who had oxygen instead of anesthesia administered to her, resulting in a $2 million payment based on an estimate of more than $128,000 a year in future medical expenses.

Miscellaneous medical liability policy. This coverage is provided by endorsing one of the other professional liability policies. The policy to be used depends upon the professional classification of the applicant for insurance. The form is used to cover chiropodists, chiropractors, nurses, optometrists, opticians, veterinarians, dental hygienists, and other technicians.

Other professional liability insurance

Many *nonmedical* professions also have a great need for professional liability insurance contracts. Special contracts have been developed for

---

[11] William S. Gibson, "Medical Malpractice: A Recurring Crisis," *Journal of Insurance,* November–December 1981, p. 12.

attorneys, architects, and many other persons. The basic reason for these contracts is the expanding legal liability for the specialized professions—the law requiring a higher standard of care to be exercised by professionals in the performance of their duties. Few real professional persons should be without such insurance.

Errors and omissions insurance. Usually, professional liability insurance is called *errors and omissions insurance* when it applies to nonmedical professionals such as insurance agents.[12] These forms often use deductibles of $1,000 or more. They ordinarily do not require the consent of the insured to settle claims. A limit of liability per claim and in the aggregate for the policy period applies. Individual contracts are written, although many of these exposures are written in group policies offered to all the members of professional agent or adviser societies.

The growing responsibilities of financial planners and investment advisers deserve special attention, particularly with many persons (including insurance agents) and firms expanding to offer broad financial services. Potential legal problems and liability are serious, as written financial plans involving purchase or sale of securities require federal registration and compliance with many state licensing and regulatory acts. Loyalty to clients and disclosure of any conflicts of interest are essential in meeting requirements of the Investment Advisers Act, and in avoiding liability for damages under SEC regulations for any unsuitable recommendations.

Many other service businesses also have available to them special professional liability insurance policies. Examples include advertising agencies, television stations, management consultants, travel agents, real estate agents, and data processing companies. Symptomatic of the vulnerable position of many professionals today is the general public attitude of dissatisfaction toward them—even toward attorneys in our legalistic, "sue syndrome" society.[13]

One of the prime purposes of errors and omissions insurance is to provide the best possible defense for any claims which may damage the reputation of professional persons. In contrast to the medical professional liability contracts, these are not for bodily injury claims. It is *property damage liability* losses which are insured, and only a few exclusions apply: fraudulent or criminal acts, and libel or slander.

An interesting type of errors and omissions policy is one which protects *mortgagees*. Technically, it provides the insured mortgagee with property

---

[12] Ronald T. Anderson, *Agents' Legal Responsibility* (Cincinnati; National Underwriter, 1981).

[13] Such as was expressed in "The Troubled Professions," *Business Week*, August 16, 1976, p. 126; and in "Those #☆×¿!!! Lawyers," *Time*, April 10, 1978, p. 56. Even the clergy are not immune from professional liability lawsuits, as illustrated by claims for suicides and divorces alleged to have resulted from improper pastoral counseling.

insurance against indirect losses, rather than liability insurance against third-party claims. However, it is known as E and O insurance and is so similar that it is discussed here. Banks and other financial institutions that lend money with real estate as security are always faced with the possibility that through some neglect on the part of the property owner, insurance in force when the loan was made will not be renewed. Painstaking care in checking expirations still leaves a loophole—error on the part of the employees to whom this responsibility has been assigned. This insurance protects against losses arising out of failure to have in force proper insurance to protect the mortgaged property as a result of error or omissions. The policy protects only the mortgagee, not the mortgagor (owner), and it applies only when, through error and omission, specific insurance is invalid, insufficient, or has not been provided. Failure to record changes in ownership, insufficient insurance to meet coinsurance requirements, incorrect description, failure to report change of occupancy or increase of hazard when known, errors in ordering or renewing coverage, incorrect statements of ownership—these and scores of other errors are examples of the protection provided by this policy.

Directors' and officers' liability insurance.   As a specialized type of professional liability coverage, one of the most talked about examples of recent years has been *directors' and officers' liability insurance* paying on behalf of the executives (or also to reimburse their organization if the executives receive indemnification) for claims arising out of wrongful acts such as error, neglect, breach of duty, or misleading statements.[14] This insurance protects one of the most important assets of an organization—its management.[15]

Lloyd's of London and about a dozen U.S. insurers specialize in this market. Policy limits of $5 to $20 million or more are often purchased. Early forms of this important coverage were written only for the very large corporations, but today the market has expanded to include many smaller firms.[16] Increasing lawsuits by stockholders or even competitors (for antitrust or unfair competition, etc.) reinforce the need for D & O liability protection, in spite of yearly premium costs which often reach $10,000 or more. Deductibles of $5,000 to $20,000 are common, and a participation of 5 percent or more by the insured in loss payments is frequent. The intent is to cover negligence of innocent and loyal directors and officers and defense of such claims, but not active and deliberate fraud.

---

[14] See William E. Knepper, *Liability of Corporate Officers and Directors,* 3d ed. (Indianapolis: Allen Smith, 1978).

[15] James F. Donahue, "D & O Liability: Too Important to Overlook," *Risk Management,* April 1981, p. 46.

[16] Based on an annual survey by the Wyatt Company (Chicago) of 2,000 organizations, about three fourths had D & O contracts (averaging almost $10 million liability limits).

Many new liability exposures related to directors and officers are appearing. Alleged discrimination suits under the Equal Employment Acts or equivalent state or local laws are one example, and only a few insurers write this coverage. Another problem concerns "punitive damages," court awards in liability cases which go beyond ordinary compensatory payments to the injured party. The sizable nature of these increasing awards was brought dramatically to public attention with a $125 million award to a young burn victim (later reduced to less than $3 million) against an auto manufacturer for a faulty gas tank. Although this was in connection with a products liability claim, punitive damage awards could also involve corporate officers or directors. Whether or not punitive damages should be included in any liability insurance has been hotly debated.[17] The Insurance Services Office excluded but then decided to leave such protection in the standard CGL forms. Many D & O policies exclude this coverage unless it is specifically endorsed on the contract.

EXCESS INSURANCE

Liability contracts, in addition to being classified as covering personal, business, and professional liability exposures, may also be divided into (1) *primary* and (2) *excess* liability coverages. All of the contracts discussed on the previous pages are essentially primary, that is, they provide first (and often only) basic coverage for the perils insured. In contrast to primary coverages, *excess* insurance is designed as catastrophe protection to provide very large limits of coverage (millions of dollars) as *additional insurance amounts* for at least some unusual and larger exposures or perils which are not covered by any other insurance. Perils are covered first under primary contracts, and then the excess insurance applies as extra coverage, if needed—thus the term *excess insurance*. Some excess policies, such as the "umbrella" policy, also include *additional perils* not covered by any other insurance contracts.

If Rip Van Winkle were an insurance agent who woke up today after 20 years of sleep, he would have a difficult job in recognizing many of the titles used today in the business to describe insurance contracts. One of the most confusing areas would be the *excess insurance* field. Although some types of excess insurance have been available for more than 30 years, the popularity of these contracts has recently increased tremendously. The professional insurance man has a new vocabulary to learn, with "umbrella," "difference in conditions," "bumbershoot," "comprehensive ceiling," "surplus line," and many other terms important to agents and clients.

---

[17] John D. Long, "Should Punitive Damages Be Insured?" *Journal of Risk and Insurance* 44, no. 1 (March 1977), p. 1.

The *liability* area is very active in adapting the concept of excess insurance to its needs. It is here that most of the best-known excess contracts of recent years have evolved. Although the London and surplus lines insurers first developed these contracts, today there are dozens of U.S. insurers that write many of the types of excess liability insurance mentioned below. Sometimes they have "special risks" departments for this purpose. The coordination of excess coverages with primary coverages is an increasing problem.[18]

Some excess liability insurance is written for special situations requiring much higher limits of coverage than are normal for a particular single kind of liability insurance. Truck liability, products liability of manufacturers, and aircraft liability are examples of this type. The underlying prime contract determines the type of coverage, and the excess contract provides the same coverage and only adds an extra limit of insurance.

Excess and surplus lines

Excess insurance is taken here to mean insurance of high limits which is used to supplement basic policies or a substantial risk-retention program. Contracts of $1 million to $10 million or more, with a $1,000 to $10,000 deductible or more, would be typical. *Surplus line insurance* is often associated with excess insurance, for many such policies are designed for excess coverages. However, as it is defined in the state insurance codes, surplus line insurance usually refers to a difficulty in placement of the insurance in the normal markets. It is *not* extra in the sense of not being needed, as the term might imply. In addition to excess insurance, surplus lines are (1) substandard exposures, (2) unique or unusual perils, or (3) very broad coverages. Examples of each group are (1) tenements, bowling alleys, and supermarkets; (2) twin insurance, financial institution mortgage protection, and nonappearance of performers; and (3) "all risks" on buildings, valued use and occupancy, and builders' risk coverages. A current listing of all types of nonstandard and specialty contracts available would number more than 150.[19]

Although not technically examples of excess insurance (because they do not increase policy limits), some coverages sold in the surplus lines market supplement basic policies by extending the coverage to include many more perils. In the *physical damage* insurance area, *difference*

---

[18] Arthur E. Parry, "The Primary-Excess Insurance Policy Tangle," *Risk Management,* September 1977, p. 21; and Claude E. Stephenson, "Sorting Out the Layers of Umbrella and Excess Liability Placements," *Risk Management,* November 1981, p. 28.

[19] See *The Insurance Market Place* (Indianapolis: Rough Notes), and *Excess-Surplus Lines* (New York: *Weekly Underwriter*), both published annually. A loose-leaf manual is also available, *Excess and Surplus Lines Manual* (Santa Monica: Merritt).

in conditions (DIC) insurance has created strong interest in the merits of all-risks coverage. Essentially, this form converts named-perils insurance into all-risks insurance.[20] It covers perils such as flood, water damage, collapse, and earthquake, as well as unusual and unknown losses. It can be endorsed on other contracts. Because of the many differences in insurance contracts issued for large corporations doing business on a worldwide basis, this form is an important one for *international* businesses to consider. Its advantage is in providing similar coverage everywhere by insuring the differences which often exist in the usual contracts issued for properties insured in foreign countries.

DIC coverage is often written in large contracts covering property valued at $5 million to $10 million or more (separate limits may apply for the flood or earthquake perils). Deductibles of $5,000–$25,000 per loss or per claim usually apply. Lloyd's, Factory Mutuals, Industrial Risk Insurers, and several other major U.S. insurers provide a somewhat restricted but growing market for this unusually broad type of insurance.

Umbrella liability policy

One of the most popular forms of excess liability insurance for *business and organizations* during the past several decades is the *umbrella liability* contract. Many variations of this policy are nonstandard, and even those that follow a standard pattern have many important differences. The development has been from an extremely broad all-risks liability contract obtained through Lloyd's of London in the 1950s to a more restricted yet still very broad contract that is now available from perhaps 100 or more insurers.[21]

The umbrella liability contract is "excess" in two respects: (1) it provides *extra limits* with a combined blanket *single limit over other existing liability coverages,* usually the required basic auto policy (BAP) limits of $500,000 (as an example), a general liability contract for $100,000/$300,000/$100,000 limits, and employer's liability for $100,000; and (2) it is *extra (broader) coverage* for other liability exposures not covered by the underlying liability contracts, above a self-retention limit of about $25,000. The maximum limit is high—at least $1 million, and usually $5 million, $10 million, $50 million, or more. The retention deductible for smaller business firms is sometimes lowered from $25,000 to $10,000, or less.

---

[20] E. J. Leverett and David G. Oliver, "Comparing an 'Ideal' DIC Policy to What the Market Offers," *Risk Management,* September 1982, p. 40.

[21] A thorough analysis explaining the broad coverage but noting the many provisions to check carefully is found in *The John Liner Letter* (Wellesley, Mass.: Shelby Publishing), March 1982. Seventy umbrella forms are compared in *The Umbrella Book* (Newport Beach, Cal.: Warren, McVeigh, and Griffin, 1982).

The contract is an indemnity one, repaying the insured for a wide variety of liability losses. Although the contract forms vary, Figure 17–1 indicates the types of liability that are often included and the way in which the limits of coverages are applied. Note that the top of the "umbrella" (at the top of Figure 17–1) is uneven, providing $1 million limits *over* the basic amounts available and over the deductible amount. Some insurers also sell these contracts on an "up to $1 million," or other amount, basis.

The broad protection of the umbrella liability contract is shown by the addition of many coverages that the business does not usually have

Figure 17–1. Umbrella liability policy illustration ($1 million)*

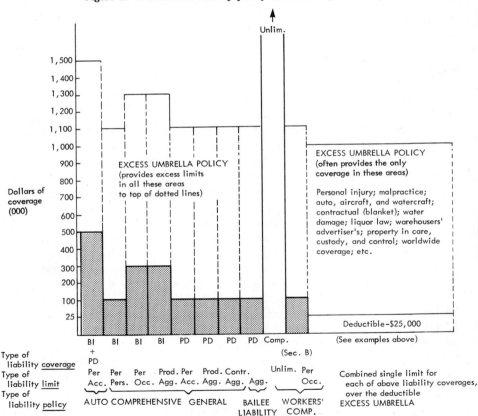

Abbreviations: BI (bodily injury); PD (property damage); Comp. (compensation); EL (employer's liability); Acc. (accident); Pers. (person); Occ. (occurrence); Prod. (product); Agg. (aggregate, per year); Unlim. (unlimited).
* Many umbrella liability policies would have higher limits, such as $5 million or $10 million or more. A $1 million limit policy is used in order to show more clearly the relationship to a deductible of $25,000 and primary coverages (darkened space) of $100,000 to $500,000.

in its underlying insurance, such as advertisers' legal liability, worldwide operations liability, personal injury liability, and many others. These are only insured above the insured's retention limit (or deductible) of $25,000. The result is that important catastrophe liability protection is achieved. The deductible does not apply to auto, general liability, and employers' liability losses, which are covered for the additional single limit of $1 million (or more, if the umbrella policy is larger) as soon as they exceed the basic underlying limits. Excess fidelity coverage is also included in some of these policies.

Examples of loss potential for the business insured are many: a salesperson leases an airplane, a company officer makes a business trip to Europe, an employee's automobile is driven to Mexico on business, or a security guard makes a false arrest. Large losses which indicate the need for catastrophe protection of the type that umbrella liability provides are: dams breaking and causing floods; thalidomide used that caused children to be malformed at birth; airplane crashes; rape and assault injuries to hotel or motel guests not provided with sufficient security; pollution damage by manufacturers; and many others.

The cost of the umbrella contract varies. Premiums, which must be partially based on judgment factors, decreased for several years but rose again with the increasing losses and appreciation of the loss potential of liability situations. Smaller insureds may pay less than $1,000 for their umbrella contract; larger firms may pay many thousands of dollars.

Retroactive liability policies

Can insurance be written to cover losses that have already occurred? Normally, no—because insurance covers uncertainties. Thus it may be a surprise to learn that there *are* circumstances in which retroactive insurance is both needed and insurable. The idea of such protection attracted worldwide attention following the 1980 multimillion dollar fire in the Las Vegas MGM Grand Hotel.

In a loss of such epic proportions, even after the loss happened there remained substantial uncertainty as to *who* would be held liable, *how much* would be payable, and *when* the courts would require payment. Therefore, it was reported that MGM purchased $170 million of *retroactive liability insurance* above the $30 million coverage existing at the time of the fire.[22] Three layers of excess liability insurance were written, shared by several dozen U.S. and British insurers. The first layer of $70 million was estimated to have cost about $27 million; the second layer of $25 million about $2.5 million; and the cost of the third layer

---

[22] "MGM Fire: Coping with the Loss," *Business Insurance,* September 1981, p. 1, 40–41.

of $75 million was not announced. The insurance contracts included a retroactive endorsement which back-dated the coverage to apply to claims and defense costs from the fire of the previous November. Some 600 lawsuits involving many millions of dollars have been filed. Other retroactive liability insurance for $40 million excess above existing $60 million coverage was purchased for the MGM fire loss by GK Technologies. This covers potential liability resulting from installation of electric wiring by one of their subsidiary companies, for which about 60 lawsuits are seeking a half billion dollars. The property insurance policy held by MGM on the hotel has been estimated as nearly sufficient to cover their losses, including about $60 million already paid for eight months of business interruption.[23]

In another catastrophic loss, the 1981 collapse of a skywalk in a Hyatt Regency Hotel in Kansas City, the purchase of retroactive insurance by the owner (Hallmark Cards) was considered but not done.

These two spectacular losses illustrate the use of retroactive liability insurance. Although unusual, retroactive coverage is far from completely new: (1) Lloyd's of London has written similar insurance for many years on ships that have been reported lost, but where the extent of the losses and possible salvage costs were uncertain; (2) product liability exposure has recently been written to protect against unreported but already incurred losses, when a change has been made from "claims made" to "occurrence" coverage; and (3) any liability policy written on a "claims made" basis without a limitation of a retroactive date is retroactive insurance.[24] As an example of insurer innovation in this area, one company began in 1982 to offer a "protection in retirement liability policy" which insures businessowners for past liability losses reported after they have retired and they have cancelled their regular liability coverage.[25]

Other excess business policies

A variation of the umbrella contract is used in the marine field, where it is called the *bumbershoot*. The purpose is to provide excess limits coverage above the primary marine protection and indemnity coverage. The problems of admiralty liability law and maritime workers' compensation are unique in this field, and careful coordination with or inclusion within the umbrella liability policy is necessary.

One of the innovations from Lloyd's of London is the combination of all-risks *property and* all-risks third-party *liability* in a single excess contract known as the *comprehensive ceiling coverage*. This contract is

---

[23] "MGM Grand Sues 2 Excess Insurers," *Business Insurance,* March 1, 1982, p. 1.

[24] Charles A. McAlear, "Retroactive Insurance: Turning the Clock Back for 300 Years," *Risk Management,* August 1982, p. 30.

[25] *The Bulletin,* Travelers Insurance Companies, June 21, 1982, p. 1.

very flexible and broad in its coverage. It serves as real catastrophe protection (usually $5 million or more) over the basic fire, business interruption, crime, and liability contracts of the insured. It may be excess over such basic contracts as the SMP policy, the 3-D policy, and the comprehensive general liability policy.

Excess personal liability policies

The *excess personal liability* area is one of substantial interest, concern, and sales potential. It is designed for *individuals,* in contrast to the excess contracts previously discussed for businesses and organizations. Based on the fact that professional or other persons with high income or assets are often the target for large liability claims, these contracts provide important defense and catastrophe liability coverage.

Many U.S. insurers have developed contracts of this type. Most are for limits of $1 million to $10 million above basic automobile liability coverage with $100,000/$300,000/$10,000 limits (or the combined single limit of $300,000 in the newer auto policies), and comprehensive personal liability coverage for $50,000. A deductible is chosen by the insured to apply to losses *other than* those covered by the basic coverages. Usually, this is about $1,000, but it may be as low as $250 or as high as $10,000.

These policies usually apply to the entire family and include residence, personal injury, automobile, employer's, aircraft, sports, snowmobile, and watercraft liability (over basic, if insured owns a larger than a 26-foot boat). Sometimes excess major medical coverage of $50,000 or more is included. The usual exclusions include business pursuits or professional malpractice liability (both of which may be added by endorsement), property damage to aircraft, and nuclear energy liability.

The cost for a $1 million personal excess liability contract with a $1,000 deductible is $50 or more a year. The cost is nominal in relation to the need for insuring the constantly changing large exposures to liability loss. The coverage can be written as a separate policy, but for many families it is easiest to have this protection added by an endorsement (HO–82) to the homeowner's policy. Excess personal liability insurance is a sound recommendation for great numbers of homeowners insurance buyers.[26]

MEDICAL PAYMENTS COVERAGE

A very important supplement to many general liability contracts is *medical payments* insurance. It is optional with most of the business liability policies but is automatically included in the comprehensive per-

---

[26] Roy C. McCormick, "The Case for Family and Individual Personal Injury Coverage," *Rough Notes,* June 1982, p. 18.

sonal liability policies. It is not written as a separate policy but as a part of liability and some other insurance contracts.

Medical payments insurance pays for all necessary and reasonable medical, surgical, ambulance, hospital, professional nursing, and funeral expenses for a person injured or killed in an accident arising out of the premises or operations of the insured, *regardless of negligence or liability*. In modern terms, it is a form of "no-fault" insurance (see Chapter 19).

The importance of medical payments coverage is that it avoids delay, difficulty, and costs involved in proving legal liability. It is most helpful for smaller losses, where a customer or a member of the public can be provided with rapid payment for such common injuries as sprains, cuts, bruises, or simple fractures. In many cases, the goodwill of a business can be enhanced greatly by medical payments coverage because the injured person does not have to prove liability or bring lawsuit against the business.

Medical payments coverage is often written in connection with the OLT policy and the CGL policy. It is rarely written with the M&C policy because the type of premises and the changing nature of locations is an exposure much different from that of the usual owner, tenant, or business firm dealing with customers from fixed locations used regularly by the public. Medical payments may not be written with coverage of the products liability hazard at all. The reasons include the possibility of many small claims from poisonings or faulty products, the potential cost of multiple injuries from one accident, and the probable encouragement of carelessness by the insured.

The usual limit for medical payments coverage is $500 per person. Quite frequently this limit is increased to $1,000 per person, and more is written with some policies. A second limit also applies, in the business liability contracts, per accident—usually $25,000 but occasionally more. The expenses paid for must be incurred within one year after the accident. Payments made under the medical payments coverage do not prevent the injured person from later deciding that further payment is warranted, by proving the legal liability of the insured.

There is no medical payments coverage for injury to the named insured, any partner of the insured, or any employee while engaged in the insured's employment. Thus it is *not* accident insurance for a whole family or other person residing regularly on the premises covered by the liability policy, or for an employee of the tenant or resident. In this respect, medical payments coverage under general liability policies differs from automobile medical payments coverage (see Chapter 20), where injuries to the insured and to the insured's family are among those covered by the insurance.

Some business establishments have a first-aid station with a nurse, often a physician, and with other first-aid assistance as part of their regular organizations. Where this is the case, a discount is allowed from the medical payments premium.

In summary, the medical payments coverage is an easy and worthwhile addition to many liability policies covering many small injuries for which the insured would normally feel obligated, morally or legally, to the injured person.

FOR REVIEW AND DISCUSSION

1. Risk management can be applied to some liability situations. Give three illustrations of this statement, other than insurance. Also explain why insurance is a commonly accepted technique for meeting liability risks.

2. What are the basic kinds of liability insurance losses, and how do these differ from accident insurance?

3. Illustrate three major types of general liability insurance contracts with an example of a specific policy of each type.

4. What changes have revisions brought to general liability insurance contracts? Include several examples of the benefits to (a) the insured and (b) the insurer.

5. Why is liability insurance coverage on an "occurrence" basis, as it is usually written now, generally considered broader than coverage for an "accident"?

6. The owners', landlords', and tenants' policy covers both *premises and off-premises* liability. It may also include protection for *protective, contractual,* and *products* liability. Explain the need for each of these types of liability insurance by a property owner.

7. Mr. Hubbard is the owner of a building leased in its entirety to a tenant who has assumed all liability in the event that anyone is injured on the premises. Is the owner relieved of all risks?

8. A general contractor repairing a bridge failed to provide either a barricade or lights, and an automobile accident injured the driver. Suit was filed and damages were awarded. How could the contractor have been insured? Would your answer change if subcontractors were hired by the general contractor?

9. X is covered by a comprehensive general liability policy. As a result of an error, he caused the arrest of B. B brought action against him for false arrest and alleged mental anguish. Does the policy cover?

10. Beth became ill in a restaurant as a result of eating spinach in which pieces of glass were later found. Is this risk insurable? Could a fake claim also be insured? Do other businesses (besides restaurants) have such liability? Explain.

11. "Malpractice liability contracts" insure physicians, hospitals, druggists, and other like practitioners. Discuss the extension of professional liability to include other professional persons, such as lawyers, and directors and officers.

12. What features of malpractice liability insurance for medical professionals distinguish it from other types of liability insurance?

13. Are the products and malpractice liability fields really in a "crisis" today? What statutory and other changes have been instituted in order to alleviate the problems of these fields?

14. *Why* does a business or organization need to consider *excess* insurance? Does the same situation exist for individuals?

15. Mr. Fischer says: "Why should I pay for adding medical payments coverage to my business liability policy? If I'm legally liable for someone's injuries, the policy will pay. If I'm not, I don't want to pay." *Explain* whether or not you agree with Mr. Fischer.

16. The idea of writing insurance to cover losses that have already occurred does not seem logical, but it is done in some circumstances. What is this type of unusual excess insurance called, and why might it be needed and useful?

Chapter 18

Outline of concepts

Employers' liability is a special part of liability law. The common-law employers' liability doctrines and statutes were largely replaced by:

Workers' compensation laws, making employers' "liability *without* fault for work injuries or diseases" usually the exclusive remedy of employees.

Constitutionality was tested in early court cases, but almost all states now have *compulsory* laws (a few are *elective*).

Scope and benefits of the laws include broad coverage of about 85 percent of employees. The basic benefits are (1) *medical expenses,* (2) *income,* (3) *death,* and (4) *rehabilitation* expenses. Occupational *injuries* and *diseases* are covered by benefits which vary widely by state.

Administration of the laws is usually by a state commission.

Financing of the benefits is by *employers,* through insurance plans.

Workers' compensation insurers: Alternatives include *private insurers, state funds* (in some states), or *self-insurance plans* (permitted in many states).

The standard workers' compensation and employers' liability policy is standardized not by law but by custom of the insurers, but it is nevertheless very uniformly accepted. Its basic parts include:

Declarations, providing basic underwriting data;

Insuring agreements, four in number, which identify workers' compensation and employers' liability coverages, definitions, and duration;

Exclusions, which are few; and

Conditions, which specify rights of insurer, insured, and employees.

Basic rating plans require approval of rates filed by rating bureaus, although a few states now have "open competition" laws.

Special rating plans are significant in workers' compensation because the basic or average rates are frequently modified for individual insureds by:

Experience rating plans, based on an individual employer's *past* loss experience, which is a direct incentive to the employer to reduce losses.

The premium discount plan, for decreasing *expenses* of larger insureds.

Retrospective rating plans, for *current* loss experience.

Second-injury funds encourage hiring partially disabled employees.

Workers' compensation losses differ from many other kinds of insurance because they are not based on fault and because the amounts and loss-settlement procedures are set forth in the state laws.

Other policy benefits are those which help *prevent* losses rather than pay for losses that have occurred. *Inspection services* are increasing.

Occupational Safety and Health Act (OSHA) and other federal laws are increasing federal involvement in workers' compensation.

Employers' liability and workers' compensation

When employers hire employees, they assume many responsibilities. Among the most costly, for many businesses and organizations, are the legal obligations under *workers' compensation* laws for occupational disability because of *work injury* or *disease*. The solution to the financial burden of disability because of employment is a dual one: many of the state government requirements are met by workers' compensation insurance contracts purchased from private insurers.

An unusual blend of social and private insurance results, which explains the inclusion of this type of insurance in Chapter 11 on government life and health insurance as well as in this chapter. Employers finance the social-private system of insurance, which costs about $16 billion dollars annually to provide the employee with compensation for work injuries and diseases.

The origin of workers' compensation laws is employers' liability law. Why and how employers' liability has been supplanted in the United States by the workers' compensation laws is evident in a brief review of the relationship between employer and employee in our changing industrial society. The development has been one progressing from *common-law liability*, to *employers' liability statutes*, and finally to the *workers' compensation laws* of the 20th century.

EMPLOYERS' LIABILITY

Common-law liability of employers

At common law an employer may be held liable to employees when the negligence of the employer is the cause of damages. However, the burden of proof rests squarely upon the employee to show that there was employer negligence and that this negligence was the cause of the employee's injury or sickness.

The employer has three strong *defenses* against employee claims under *common-law liability*. Under the *contributory negligence rule*, the employee must also show that he or she did not contribute to the negligence. Further, when an employee has knowledge of the ordinary risks involved, he or she is paid for assuming those risks and, therefore, cannot recover for injuries caused thereby. The doctrine has been extended to apply in cases in which the employee continues to work without complaint after the discovery of failure on the part of his or her employer to afford proper protection. The employer's defense against such claims is referred to as the *assumption-of-risk rule*. Finally, the common law relieved the employer of responsibility when the cause of the injury was the willful wrongdoing or negligence of a fellow servant (employee). This defense is known as the *fellow-servant* (or *common employment*) *rule*. When two employees are working together, for example, one employee might negligently drop a heavy tool, causing injury to the other employee.

Modifications of the common law

The difficulty of an employee in establishing a case of liability can readily be understood. Through statutory enactment and a tendency on the part of the courts to interpret the rules favorably to employees, the position of the worker was somewhat bettered. The class of fellow-servant employees was narrowed to exclude supervisors or managers. Other laws followed but were to a degree nullified by employers who required workers to sign contracts releasing them from liability.

A number of states adopted *employers' liability acts* about the turn of the century, modeled after employers' liability legislation in England, which held the employer responsible for accidents caused by defective machinery and the negligence of supervisors. Employers' liability acts were initially rejected by the courts. The federal Employers' Liability Act of 1906 was held unconstitutional, but later upheld by the U.S. Supreme Court. This law abrogated the fellow-servant rule and modified the operation of the contributory negligence and assumption-of-risk rules. Finally, the law provided that contracts intended to exempt the employer from liability created by the act should be void.

The employees' situation was improved, but negligence on the part of the employer still had to be proved. Many accidents occurred where negligence could not be shown. Great expense and delay were suffered by both employers and employees in litigation, and the award of a jury in any case was often unpredictable. The disadvantageous position of the employee was still severe, for the immediate result of filing a suit or making a claim against the employer was twofold: the employee lost his or her job, and expenses were incurred which the employee could usually ill afford.

WORKERS' COMPENSATION LAWS

Even though the liability acts were designed to improve the position of the employee, they were, nevertheless, far from satisfactory. Employers' liability acts in all jurisdictions in the United States have now been superseded by *workers' compensation laws.*

The theory behind workers' compensation legislation completely disregards the old idea of liability based upon negligence. Rather, the theory is based upon the idea that the cost of occupational disabilities is to be paid by the *employer, regardless of liability,* and then passed on to the consumer as a part of the cost of production.

Compensation laws make the employer responsible for indemnity to the disabled employee without regard to the matter of fault or negligence. The amount of indemnity to apply in particular cases is predetermined by the law, although it does not equal the full income received while employed. The laws relate payments to injuries or sicknesses; and if these are fatal, *death* benefits are provided for the employee's dependents. *Medical expenses, income,* and *rehabilitation benefits* are included.

Constitutionality

Just as employers resisted the trend toward liberalization under the employers' liability acts, so they questioned the constitutionality of the first attempts toward compensation laws. Courts held that the first statute that sought to impose a liability upon an employer "who has omitted no legal duty and has committed no wrong" was unconstitutional in New York. The states evolved a new plan to overcome the constitutional difficulties, giving employers a choice as to whether or not they would be governed by the workers' compensation act. Wisconsin had the first effective workers' compensation law in 1911, and many other states also passed such laws by the early 1920s. As an incentive to employers, the elective laws provide that if an employer fails to accept the compensation law, the employer loses the defenses of contributory negligence, negligence of a fellow employee, and assumption-of-risk by an employee. With the loss of the common-law defenses and the uncertainty as to jury awards, plus litigation costs, the compensation alternative was preferred by employers.

Scope of the laws

In the beginning, workers' compensation laws were enacted only to protect employees engaged in certain industries regarded as hazardous, such as coal mining, blasting operations, and explosive manufacturing. The tendency in compensation legislation has been to enlarge the application of the laws. No state at present brings all occupations within the operation of the law, but most occupations are covered, regardless of the extent of danger in the work. Most states cover all public employments and most private employments. The result is that about 85 percent of employees are now under workers' compensation laws. Agricultural, domestic, and casual labor are usually exempted, and about a dozen states exempt firms employing less than about three employees. In many states, some of these exempted employees are covered on a voluntary basis.

Compulsory and elective laws

Based upon the *employer's* rights, there are two types of workers' compensation laws: (1) compulsory and (2) elective. Almost all of the state laws are *compulsory,* which means that all employers to whom the laws apply are required to pay for work injuries or diseases as specified under the compensation statutes. Only three states still have the *elective* type of law (see above section on constitutionality) permitting the employer to accept or reject the workers' compensation act.[1] If the employer rejects it, the common-law defenses discussed earlier are lost to the employer. As a result, such a choice is very unusual.

Employees also usually come under workers' compensation laws on a compulsory basis. Some states still permit employees to reject the applicable compensation law in writing, but normally this must be done *before* a loss occurs. This is also rarely done, because the employer then retains the common-law defenses and a liability suit against the employer by the worker would be difficult to sustain. In some cases, the employee may elect not to come under workers' compensation after a loss has occurred, but this applies only in certain circumstances, such as when a minor has been illegally employed or when the employer has willfully injured the employee.

Perils covered in the laws

Compensation is provided for all *injuries* and *diseases arising out of and occurring in the course of employment.* No benefits under compensation acts are allowed when it is proved that the injury was occasioned by the willful intention of the employees or by their intoxication while on duty. An exception to the regulation covering intoxication is sometimes made if employers knew that the employees were intoxicated or that they were in the habit of being intoxicated while on duty.

---

[1] New Jersey, South Carolina, and Texas.

Occupational disability includes both *injury* and *disease*. Occupational diseases are defined as diseases peculiar to the occupation in which the employee is engaged and due to causes in excess of the ordinary hazards of employment. In recent years, suits claiming compensation for such diseases as those developing from exposure to chemical fumes and dust, radioactivity, prolonged industrial noise, and even "cumulative trauma" on the job have come increasingly to the attention of employers.

Liability for occupational disease is based upon the common-law doctrine requiring the employer to use all reasonable precautions to safeguard employees from injury and to warn them of the existence of any particular danger. By statute in one form or another, occupational diseases have been covered in all jurisdictions—in some by the workers' compensation laws, in others by separate occupational diseases acts. However, not all diseases contracted in the course of an occupation may be attributed to the work or its nature. In the case of an occupational disease there must be a cause-and-effect relationship between the occupation and the disease as well as a frequency and regularity of the occurrence of the disease in the particular occupation.[2] In some states, the exposure must be peculiar to the worker's occupation and extend over a specified minimum time period.

The problem created by the inclusion of occupational diseases within the scope of workers' compensation is a serious one both to insurers and to employers. Insurers and insureds alike have raised two questions: First, since occupational diseases in general are progressive and recurring, at what point of time does liability for compensation begin? And second, in the event that there are more than one employer, which employer is liable? The trend of court decisions indicates that employees are insured "in their then condition," and if their employment causes a disease to continue until they are incapacitated, the insurer at the time of the incapacity is liable.

Employees may be suffering over a long period from occupational diseases, such as silicosis or radiation, that are progressive in nature.[3] They may have changed their employment, yet the employers for whom they

---

[2] An occupational disease has been defined as "one which arises from causes incident to the profession or labor of the party's occupation or calling. It has its origin in the inherent nature or mode of work of the profession or industry, and is the usual result or concomitant" (*Victory Sparker & Spec. Co.* v. *Franks,* 147 Md. 368; 128 A. 635).

[3] One of the most famous occupational disease cases diagnosed cancer as attributable to radon gas latent for 33 years. Workers swallowed particles of radium when they wet with their lips the tips of brushes used in painting numerals on watch and clock dials. The lethal nature of the process was unknown until death occurred. Such delayed effects of new materials or processes cause considerable concern for insurers. Other cancer victims have also been held to be covered for compensation payments (see *Utter* v. *Austin Hill Mfg. Co.,* 309 A, 2d 583, reported in *Weekly Underwriter,* January 12, 1974, p. 58).

are working at the time their disease reaches a stage resulting in incapacity must bear the entire brunt of the compensation.[4]

Workers' compensation—an exclusive remedy?

Workers' compensation laws were instituted as a compromise between employers and employees as to their responsibilities for work disabilities. Employers accepted liability regardless of fault, and employees were generally held to have given up their rights to sue the employer for occupational hazards. However, recent developments indicate that workers' compensation benefits may not be the only right available to employees in some cases.[5]

The Ohio Supreme Court decided in 1982 (in *Blankenship* v. *Cincinnati Milacron*) that employees could sue for work-related disabilities if they were shown to be the result of an intentional act by the employer. The case involved work exposure to noxious fumes and chemicals which the employer knew were dangerous. Although workers' compensation benefits would ordinarily be the employees' sole remedy for the employer's *negligence,* the court said it would be against public policy to protect the employer from suit for an *intentional tort.*[6] The decision applied a "dual capacity" or "two-hat" theory. This doctrine added to Milacron's capacity as an employer a second potential capacity—that of a third-party tortfeasor (wrongdoer) for a common exposure from a product intended to be sold to the public. The case did not decide whether or not an employee could recover damages under both approaches from a single source, nor did it rule whether or not Milacron had committed an intentional tortious act.

Although unusual, the *Milacron* case was not the earliest to test workers' compensation as an exclusive remedy. The 1952 California case of *Duprey* v. *Shane* was among the first, and several other Ohio decisions have either upheld or denied application of the "dual capacity" concept. Related cases have been decided in Ohio, and in Minnesota, New York, and Massachusetts, where some WC provisions permit such actions.[7] An estimated 200 lawsuits have been filed, including one against Mon-

---

[4] An exception exists in those states with "second-injury funds" (see later section of this chapter).

[5] The following analysis is based upon articles by Donald S. Malecki in the April, July, and August, 1982 issues of *The Ohio Underwriter* (Cincinnati, Ohio), on p. 1, p. 9, and p. 1, respectively. See also "When Your Employee Takes You to Court," *Journal of American Insurance,* Winter 1981–82, p. 1.

[6] See Chapter 16 for the distinction among intentional and negligent (unintentional) torts and liability for breach of contract.

[7] *Mercer* v. *Uniroyal* (49 Ohio App. 2d 279, 1976); *Guy* v. *A. H. Thomas Co.* (55 Ohio St. 2d 183, 1978); *Delamotte* v. *Midland Ross* (64 Ohio App. 2d 159, 1978); and *Knous* v. *Ridge Machine Co.* (64 Ohio App. 2d 251, 1979).

santo for more than $2 billion. In addition to employers, developments in this complicated legal area will need to be watched carefully during the 1980s by insurance companies, self-insurers, and state funds insuring workers' compensation.

Types of benefits under the laws

The basic types of benefits include (1) *medical expenses,* (2) *income* benefits, (3) *death* benefits, and (4) *rehabilitation* benefits, which almost all of the states now provide.

Medical benefits. *Medical expenses* are a primary benefit, and all states provide for complete medical care without any waiting period. About one third of all workers' compensation benefits are for medical expenses.

Income benefits. Although the benefits for loss of *income* often differ by state, there are points of similarity in all the acts. *Definite schedules of benefits* are provided for different types of disability. While in certain cases lump-sum settlements may be made, it is usual to provide for the payment of benefits on a weekly basis. When used, the lump-sum benefits are in lieu of weekly benefits. For example, perhaps $25,000 might be paid for the loss of a leg or an arm, or $15,000 for an eye. The states vary greatly in terms of the size of the lump-sum settlement.

To discourage malingering, the weekly benefit is set at a fraction of the injured employee's weekly wage. Thus, a typical state might allow 66⅔ percent of the injured employee's weekly wage, which may be about 75 percent of take-home pay. A maximum of 100 percent of the state average wage and a minimum of $20–50 per week often applies. A maximum total payment in some states set in terms of amount, varying from about $40,000 to $120,000, or as a multiple of the weekly benefit, such as 200–600 weeks, or in terms of both. However, in most states the duration is life or the period of disability.

With rising workers' compensation costs in recent years, an interesting change in the Florida law is being watched. Since 1979, income benefits there have been payable only for periods during which an actual reduction or loss of earnings has occurred. With a few exceptions, *actual* wage loss is all that is paid.[8] Early results during 1980–81 have permitted employer premiums to be reduced by about 40 percent, but a 24 percent increase was requested in 1982. Other states are considering the wage loss system for limiting compensation benefits.

In order to eliminate the excessive expense of handling small losses

---

[8] More precisely, 95 percent of the difference between pre-injury and post-injury wage is paid. See "Florida's Bold Experiment in Cutting Worker Compensation Costs," *Journal of American Insurance,* Summer 1982, p. 21.

and to prevent malingering when the injury is of no serious consequence, some laws provide a period of from a few days to one week during which no compensation is paid. This interval is called a "waiting period," and it acts as a kind of deductible. This period is now decreasing in most states to about three days, and often full retroactive payment is provided for losses of more than two weeks.

An important feature of compensation legislation is fixing with as much detail as possible the exact benefit due in each specific type of injury. Substantial variations appear in the provisions of the acts of the various states, but the following injuries or disabilities are usually specifically provided for: *(a)* fatal injury, *(b)* temporary total disability, *(c)* permanent total disability, *(d)* temporary partial disability, and *(e)* permanent partial disability. Some laws provide benefits in the case of such disfigurements as might be a handicap in securing employment.

The trend in the level of income benefits has been upward. Maximum weekly benefits, for example, have gone up, and time and amount limits have also increased. The size of the increases has not been as rapid as the general wage level rises, but other factors are also present. One is the fact that the federal OASDHI program also provides benefits for serious disabilities (total and permanent). In some cases disabled workers can collect from both workers' compensation and OASDHI a total benefit of up to 80 percent of their wages before they were disabled. The limitation (since 1966) is appropriate because these disability income payments are tax-free, making them as much as or sometimes even more than net normal earnings.

Death benefits. Various categories of survivors (widows, widowers, children, and other dependents) are paid income as a *death* benefit. Benefits are usually the same amount as for the worker's permanent total disability, with an added amount in about nine states for children. Remarriage usually stops the parent's payments. Some of the states have an amount limit in their law, and this varies widely from about $20,000 to $250,000. Burial expenses are also paid, ranging from about $500 to $2,500.

Rehabilitation benefits. The value of *rehabilitation services* has been recognized by many insurers in recent years. The employee benefits by being rehabilitated or by being permitted to return to work at the earliest possible date. The cost of the claim to the insurer is reduced. The employer gets the worker back on the job sooner, and this ultimately reduces the cost of the insurance to the employer. In spinal cord injuries, for example, the average hospital stay can be reduced to four months at a rehabilitation center.[9] All of the state laws now provide for rehabilita-

---

[9] "Workers' Compensation: The Claims Dollar under Pressure," *Journal of American Insurance,* Summer 1977, p. 8.

tion benefits as a logical and important part of workers' compensation. Although some states only provide referral services to other rehabilitation programs, most states pay a retraining allowance.

Administration of the laws

While in some five[10] jurisdictions the administration of compensation law is left with the courts, the more usual method is to leave it with a special *state commission* (or administrator) appointed for the purpose. When the courts have jurisdiction, cases are heard by a judge or by a referee appointed by the judge.

In the interests of simplification and to expedite the settlement of disputed points, legislatures have preferred the appointment of a commission. These commissions have been invested with varying powers to make rules and regulations for the purpose of carrying out the provision of the compensation act. The state compensation administration is quasi-judicial but much more supervisory and administrative. Commissions are given authority to appoint investigators to hear the evidence and make decisions. Most states use an agreement method in which employer and employee agree on the benefit amounts, subject to approval by the state authority. In the absence of fraud, the decision of the commission upon all questions of fact is usually final, but questions of law may always be appealed to the courts.

Financing of the benefits under the laws

It is the employer who has the direct responsibility for paying benefits to qualified workers in accordance with the workers' compensation laws. Indirectly, the consumer may be paying these costs if the product is one of relatively inelastic demand (where price increases do not decrease sales).

To guarantee that the benefits will be paid to the worker, employers are required in all states to have some form of insurance. In many states they are given a choice among private insurers, state funds, and self-insurance. The next section of this chapter explains these alternatives available to the employer.

Regardless of the insurance method chosen, the cost of workers' compensation benefits are substantial. Nationally, the cost of workers' compensation is about $16 billion a year. The costs vary considerably by state, type of occupation, and individual business firm. The general level of benefits is determined by the state laws which set forth the income

---

[10] *Analysis of Workers' Compensation Laws* (Washington, D.C.: Chamber of Commerce of the United States, published annually) lists Alabama, Louisiana, New Mexico, Tennessee, and Wyoming.

percentage, the duration, and the minimum and maximum payments. Different classifications have extremely different costs, as the rates may vary from a few cents per $100 of payroll for such classes as office workers to over $50 per $100 for hazardous occupations such as sawmill operators and steeplejacks.

Workers' compensation is obviously a major cost factor for many businesses. Humanitarian objectives, too, are significant, for many occupational injuries or diseases may be prevented. The financial incentive which employers have under the workers' compensation laws which make them responsible and under the rating plans for insurance (see later section) has been the cause of industrial loss prevention with commendable results. Accident frequency and severity have been reduced by about one half during the past 50 years. Still, the overall costs of workers' compensation to business and industry are important, as these costs normally range from 1 to 2 percent of payroll from year to year.

WORKERS' COMPENSATION INSURERS

Employers are usually offered options as to how they shall guarantee the payment of workers' compensation claims. Insurance may be provided either through a *state fund* or by *private insurers* (stock, mutual, or reciprocal) authorized by the particular state to transact the business of workers' compensation. The exact requirements of the various states differ. Table 18–1 summarizes the number of states (1) in which the state fund has a monopoly[11] of the compensation business, (2) the state funds are in competition with private insurers, and (3) the business of compensation insurance is entrusted to private insurers. As an alternative in each of the three groups, in 47 states employers who can provide satisfactory proof of financial ability may carry their own risk; that is, they may *self-insure.*[12]

From time to time the question of whether or not a state shall establish or abolish a *state fund* becomes a political question. Advocates of the state fund contend (1) that since workers' compensation insurance is virtually compulsory, it should be the duty of the state to provide a means for buying the insurance; (2) that with respect to a compulsory coverage it is inappropriate that it be a source of profit to private insur-

---

[11] The "monopolistic state fund" means that the state is the *only* source of workers' compensation insurance and that private insurers may not write any workers' compensation insurance for risks in these states. The six states are: Ohio, West Virginia, Nevada, North Dakota, Wyoming, and Washington. The first and the last two named permit self-insurance as an alternative.

[12] Self-insurance is not permitted in Nevada, North Dakota, and Texas, although in Texas some risks are in effect self-insured by using a "fronting" policy. The 12 states that use "competitive state funds" include the large industrial states of New York, Pennsylvania, Michigan, and California.

Table 18–1. How insurance requirements of the state workers' compensation laws can be met in various states*

Type of insurer	Number of states
1. Private insurer	32
2. Competitive state fund	12
3. Monopolistic state fund	6

* In addition to the use of private insurers or state funds, 47 states permit larger employers to qualify as self-insurers if they meet certain requirements. Puerto Rico is not included above: it requires insurance in the state fund and does not permit self-insurance.

Source: *Analysis of Workers' Compensation Laws* (Washington, D.C.: Chamber of Commerce of the United States, published annually).

ance; and (3) that since the cost of workers' compensation insurance is a cost of production, to allow a profit reflects an unnecessary charge to the consumer. State funds currently pay about one fourth of all workers' compensation benefits.

In answer to this, those who favor private insurance (1) raise the question as to whether a state fund does, in fact, provide protection at the lowest possible cost, because in the absence of competition inefficiency in management may evidence itself; (2) point out that competition affords a superior service[13] (especially loss prevention) to policyholders, providing insurance on an interstate basis and that private insurers provide employers' liability protection, medical expense coverage, and other forms of protection not available through a state fund; (3) argue that under private insurance the cost is definitely established, whereas under a state fund an unseen cost may develop if the taxpayer is called upon to subsidize the fund to maintain its solvency; and finally (4) emphasize that in a system of private enterprise any activity that may be carried on to advantage by private business establishments should not be delegated to the government. Private insurers pay about 60 percent of all workers' compensation benefits paid each year.

The pros and cons of private insurers versus state funds are difficult to remove from political considerations. All of the six states with monopolistic funds have had the funds in existence for many years, and these states are very reluctant to give up or change a system that has been

---

[13] "State Funds for Workers' Compensation: A False Economy," *Journal of American Insurance,* Winter 1977–78, p. 28. An opposite conclusion is reached in "Comparing Comp Systems," *Business Insurance,* January 1982, p. 19.

in operation for so long a time. The only major change from a monopolistic to a competitive state fund occurred in Oregon in 1965. One investigation of that state fund, which compared it with private insurers in Massachusetts, concluded that the private insurers provided superior marketing and administrative services and higher benefits at a somewhat increased cost.[14] The factors are complex; and the influence of unions, employers (large versus small, sometimes), insurers, and other interest groups is crucial in assessing the chances for a change to a competitive system.[15]

The question of whether or not to *self-insure* the risk of workers' compensation is another important decision for most of the larger employers. The general arguments in favor of self-insurance are the alleged lower administrative costs, minimization of litigation and quicker delivery of benefits, encouragement of rehabilitation, improved cash flow in claims payments, increased managerial benefits of direct contact between employer and employee, and increased incentives for accident prevention.[16] The choice is not a simple one, for it involves careful consideration of the *particular* employer in a particular occupational group in a particular state or states at the present time. Critics of self-insurance point out the increased administrative and claims payment burden on a self-insured employer, the loss of a third-party guarantor of benefits and buffer between employer and employee, difficulties of obtaining excess insurance, and the decrease in valuable loss-prevention and loss-analysis services by the insurer.[17] A major disadvantage is that losses are usually only deductible as they are actually paid out for claims. (See Chapter 2 for further discussion of self-insurance.)

Self-insurance is quite common for large employers with sufficient assets and annual WC premiums of several hundred thousand dollars. With high loss frequency and sufficient spread of risk the workers' compensation peril becomes one of the best examples of the use of self-insurance plans.[18] Estimates of the total coverage of this type indicate that about 15 percent of workers' compensation losses are paid by self-insurers.

---

[14] Mark R. Greene, "Marketing Efficiency and Workmen's Compensation—A Case Study," *Journal of Insurance* 24, no. 4 (December 1962), pp. 467–502.

[15] T. L. Gerlacher, "Should Private Insurance Companies Be Permitted to Write Workmen's Compensation Insurance in Ohio?" (M.B.A. thesis, Ohio State University, 1967).

[16] Ralph R. Adams, "Advantages to Self-Insuring Workers' Compensation," *Risk Management*, December 1977, p. 10.

[17] C. Paul Kipp, "Evaluating the Feasibility of Self-Insuring Workers' Compensation," *Risk Management*, December 1977, p. 15. See also James S. Trieschmann and E. J. Leverett, Jr., "Self-Insurance of Workers' Compensation Losses," *Journal of Risk and Insurance* 44, no. 4 (December 1978), p. 635.

[18] For one method of analyzing this, see Larry D. Gaunt and Maurice E. McDonald, *Examining Employers' Financial Capacity to Self-Insure under Workers' Compensation* (Atlanta: Georgia State University, 1977).

THE STANDARD WORKERS' COMPENSATION AND EMPLOYERS' LIABILITY POLICY

There is no standard workers' compensation policy in the sense that a standard form is required by statutory enactment. Because of the diversity of the compensation laws as enacted in the various states, insurers developed a standard form sufficiently broad to meet the requirements of insureds and at the same time meet the legal demands in each jurisdiction. The form is known as the "standard workers' compensation and employers' liability policy."

That the policy has served well is evidenced by the fact that only one major revision, in 1954, has occurred since its introduction more than 50 years ago. The revision reduced to a minimum the number of endorsements necessary, and the majority of policies are issued to the average risk without endorsements. There are a few situations, due to statutory requirements, manual rules, or underwriting practices, in which endorsements are still required.[19]

The standard provisions for workers' compensation and employers' liability policies follow the pattern of liability policies with four main divisions: (1) declarations, (2) insuring agreements, (3) exclusions, and (4) conditions. Efforts have been made to follow the language of comparable provisions in liability policies. This rule makes for consistency and contributes to the understanding of both forms of insurance.

Declarations

The declarations consist of five items and cover such pertinent information as the name of the insured, the policy period, the states in which operations are carried on, and liability limits for employers' liability. The premium basis, rates, and classification of operations required by the insurer appear here. Basically the declarations provide the underwriting data relied upon by the insurer for the issuance of the policy.

Item 1 calls for the name of the insured, the address, the form of business organization, and all of the usual permanent workplaces of the insured.

Item 2 states the policy period. The policy runs from 12:01 A.M. standard time at the address of the insured. This reference is very important in the case of a risk that extends to a number of states and includes more than one time zone.

---

[19] See Albert J. Millus and Willard J. Gentile, *Workers' Compensation Law and Insurance* (New York: Roberts Publishing, 1976). The new form is approved for use in 43 states and the District of Columbia, but it does not apply in Arizona or the 6 states which have monopolistic state funds.

Item 3 is perhaps one of the most important of all the declarations. It states that coverage A of the policy applies to the workers' compensation law and any occupational disease law of the state or states listed. The policy covers all operations of the insured in the state or states listed. In the case of a concern operating on a nationwide basis, item 3 may list the states to be covered by inserting "all states except . . ." The excepted states are then listed. When this practice is followed, states with monopolistic state funds, states in which the insurer is not qualified to write compensation insurance, and states in which the insured is not within the provisions of the workers' compensation law must be listed as exceptions. Many insurers recommend an alternative method of obtaining wide geographic coverage—an *all-states endorsement* with monopolistic state fund states specifically included.

Item 4 classifies the operations of the insured. The estimated total annual remuneration of all employees is given as a premium basis. The rates per $100 of payroll are listed together with the minimum premium, the total estimated annual premium, and the deposit premium. If premium adjustments are to be made on a semiannual, quarterly, or monthly basis, this is indicated.

Item 5 supplies a single limit to apply to the employers' liability feature of the coverage. Sometimes provision is made for a different limit of liability for certain operations. This limit applies only to employers' liability coverage and not to workers' compensation benefits which are all fixed by the law.

Insuring agreements

There are four sections to the insuring agreements, designated by roman numerals. Insuring agreement I concerns coverage A for the insured's liability under the *workers' compensation* laws, and coverage B provides an *employers' liability* coverage with respect to injuries and sicknesses arising out of and in the course of employment. Insuring agreement II covers the matters of defense, settlement, and supplementary payments. Insuring agreement III provides for definitions. Insuring agreement IV is concerned with limiting liability to disease or injury that originates within the policy term.

Basic coverages. The standard workers' compensation and employers' liability policy basically affords the insured a two-fold coverage in *insuring agreement I:*

Coverage A—Workers' Compensation
To pay promptly when due all compensation and other benefits required of the insured by the workers' compensation law.
Coverage B—Employers' Liability

To pay on behalf of the insured all sums which the insured shall become legally obligated to pay as damages because of bodily injury by accident or disease, including death at any time resulting therefrom, sustained in the United States of America, its territories or possessions, or Canada[20] by any employee of the insured arising out of and in the course of employment by the insured either in operations in a state designated in Item 3 of the declaration or in operations necessary or incidental thereto.

Coverage A takes notice of the definition of "workers' compensation law." This is defined in insuring agreement III and applies with respect to the state or states indicated in the declarations.

Coverage B provides protection for the employer who is faced with a common-law or employers' liability claim. It is quite possible that such a claim be filed, particularly in those states providing employees with the option of coming within the operation of the compensation act. In most but not all states the workers' compensation acts have the effect of repealing employers' liability laws and terminating common-law liability. In addition to liability coverage for injury, a broad common-law disease coverage is afforded. It is to be noticed that the word *disease* appears in coverage B and not the words *occupational disease*. Thus, coverage is afforded with respect to a liability claim attributable to any disease to which the employment may be alleged as a contributing cause.

Coverage B has the effect of including liability claims for injuries not covered by the compensation laws. Even though groundless, these claims will be defended by the insurer. Coverage B affords protection only with respect to injuries "arising out of and in the course of employment." This means that a claim for coverage must be traceable to the operations of the insured in a state specified in the declarations. Other claims would be covered by one of the standard liability policies. To avoid duplication in coverage there is usually an exclusion in liability policies with respect to employers' liability.

Since compensation benefits are fixed by law, there is no limitation with respect to them in the policy. A policy limit for coverage B is established in the declarations. A widely used limitation is $100,000, although for many business institutions this limit is not considered adequate and the insured may elect higher limits of $500,000 or $1 million.

Defense and settlement. *Insuring agreement II* is similar in effect to like clauses in liability insurance coverages. The clause obligates the insurer to defend the insured and places the matter of negotiation and settlement with the insurer alone. There is the usual requirement to pay bond premiums and expenses in effecting a settlement and to reimburse the insured for reasonable expenses incurred at the insurer's request. Such expenses incurred are all in excess of the limit of liability

---

[20] Worldwide coverage is provided, if exposures are temporary.

with respect to liability coverages and in addition to the amounts required to be paid under a compensation law.

Definitions. *Insuring agreement III* concerns definitions, closely coordinated with the coverages provided under insuring agreement I, which uses such broad terms as *the workers' compensation laws, states,* and *bodily injury by accident or disease.*

Definition *(a)* ties the term *workers' compensation laws* as found in coverage A to the state or states indicated in item 3 of the declaration. If the state has a separate occupational disease law, coverage A provides occupational disease coverage unless it is specifically excluded from the policy endorsement. The definition of "workers' compensation law" does not include the U.S. Longshoremen's and Harbor Workers' Compensation Act.[21] Finally, the definition states that it "does not include those provisions of any such law which provide nonoccupational disability benefits."

Definition *(b)* makes the word *state* mean any state or territory of the United States and the District of Columbia, if listed in the declarations.

Definition *(c)* clarifies the meaning of "bodily injury by accident" and "bodily injury by disease" in such a way that it would be impossible for an injured employee to claim an accidental injury and then to hold the insurer liable for an occupational disease disability if a disease followed as a result of the injury. Under the terms of the definition, any given injury may be one or the other, but it cannot be both.

Definition *(d)* is usual to liability policies and provides that with respect to coverage B, assault and battery shall be deemed an accident unless committed by or at the direction of the insured.[22]

Time of losses. *Insuring agreement IV* has two parts. The first part of the agreement states that the policy applies only to an injury occurring during the policy period. The second part makes the insurer liable for an occupational disease that has developed over a long period of time. In the case of silicosis, for example, an employee may be exposed over a period of years during which the workers' lungs are gradually becoming affected. If the worker has been working in granite quarries and is now found to be disabled, even though several insurers provided coverage over the years, the one covering when the last injurious exposure developed assumes the liability.[23]

---

[21] Because of the wide difference in longshoremen's and maritime risks, they are only included in the definition by endorsement.

[22] To be compensable, an assault must be one "arising out of and in the course of employment" (*Heiz* v. *Ruppert,* 218 N.Y. 148). If the assault is not compensable, the assault is held to be an accident and the insurer will provide defense under coverage B.

[23] A few states require contributions from successive insurers of the same employee. In these states the policy is endorsed amending this agreement.

Exclusions

There are six exclusions. Other workers' compensation insurance, including coverage as a qualified self-insurer, is excluded in order to avoid duplicate coverage. Domestic or farm employment is excluded unless it is covered by the compensation law or described in the declarations. The remaining exclusions apply only under coverage B, the employers' liability coverage. The policy does not apply to assumed liability in a contract, to punitive damages for employees hired in violation of law or to any such employees hired in violation of law with the knowledge of the insured, to suits filed after 36 months after the end of the policy, or to obligations under unemployment or disability benefits laws of the states. The last exclusion also excludes employers' liability coverage for any obligations under workers' compensation or occupational disease laws of the states designated in the declarations section of the policy.

Conditions

The conditions follow closely those in policies making use of the national standard provisions program for liability policies. Most pertain either to calculation and payment of the premium, or to the settlement of losses.

Conditions relating to the premium. *Condition 1* of the policy deals with the manner of premium computation. Compensation premiums are computed as a percentage of the payroll of the insured. The premium that an employer must pay depends on *(a)* type of business, *(b)* number of employees, and *(c)* total amount of remuneration that is paid to them. This information is found in the declarations.

The first paragraph of condition 1 incorporates by reference "the manuals in use by the company." By virtue of this clause the preparation of the policy is enormously simplified. If an employer should carry on operations not mentioned in the declarations, the premium will be computed for those operations by the use of manual rates. The insured, moreover, agrees that any change in classifications, rates, or rating plans or any changes in benefits provided by the workers' compensation law all become a part of the policy by the issuance of an endorsement by the insurer.

The second paragraph describes what is meant by "remuneration" and that the remuneration of all employees engaged in operations covered by the policy, whether executive officers or not, shall be included. The payroll submitted for determining the compensation premium includes all other persons performing work "which may render the company liable under this policy for injury to or death of such persons." This means, for example, that if employers sublet work, they must include the payroll of subcontractors in their compensation premium unless those subcontractors already carry their own compensation insurance.

The third paragraph explains that since WC premiums are based on the actual payroll for the period covered, they cannot be computed until the end of the policy term. The policy is written with an estimated payroll. At the end of the policy term an audit is made; and if the estimated premium is in excess of the actual premium developed by the audit, the difference is returned to the insured. On the other hand, if the estimated premium is less than the premium developed by the audit, the insured is billed for the difference.

The fourth paragraph places an obligation on the insured to maintain all the necessary records for the purpose of computing the premium. The insurer may elect to ask the insured to forward those records for the purpose of computation of premium. However, except for small employers, it is the practice of the insurer to send an auditor to the office of the insured and there check payrolls and records. The right of the insurer is limited to "the information necessary for premium computation" and not to any other records or files.

Condition 2 concerns policies written for a period longer than one year. It makes all the provisions of the policy, including premiums and coverage amounts, apply separately to each consecutive 12-month period.

Conditions relating to loss settlement. Most of the remaining conditions in the standard workers' compensation and employers' liability policy have already been noticed in connection with previous insurance contracts. Several of the clauses specify rights of the *insurer* to (1) inspection and audit of the insured's books; (2) written notice of injuries, claims, or lawsuits, as soon as practicable; (3) assistance and cooperation of the insured in hearings, trials, obtaining witnesses, and the like; (4) proportional contribution from other insurance payable for covered losses; (5) subrogation for payments made under the contract; and (6) assignment of the contract only when the insurer consents to it in an endorsement.

Rights of the *insured* are also explained in several of the conditions. The insured who has complied with the policy terms has the right of action against the insurer if the employers' liability benefits are not paid as provided. Changes in the policy may be made by endorsement, and all terms in conflict with the compensation law are made to conform to it. The insured may cancel the contract at any time, and the insured also has the right to 10 days' notice in case the insurer cancels.

One condition (8) introduces a feature not usually found in liability coverages. In addition to protecting the named insured, the policy states that the provisions of the insuring clause relating to workers' compensation or employers' liability are the *direct obligation* of the insuring company *to any insured employee* (or, in the case of death, to dependents). Since the contract is made primarily for the benefit of employees and their dependents, they have a direct right of action against the insurer. Only recently have some auto and other liability contracts included such a right. The obligations of the insurer to the employee shall not be affected by the failure of the employer in any way to comply with the policy requirements, such as default in the payment of the premium after an accident, failure to give the insurer the proper notice, and death, insolvency, bankruptcy, or legal incapacity of the employer. A notice to the employer of an injury is presumed to be notice to the insurer.

BASIC RATING PLANS

Basic workers' compensation insurance rates are usually derived from total industry statistics, divided into industry groups such as "manufacturing," "contracting," and so on. These data are subdivided into rates for about 600 classifications of products and processes by rating bureaus that submit them in the various states for approval. In many states, deviations from the "manual" rates are permitted but only infrequently sought or approved. Competition by individual insurers occurs through dividend plans and the individual risk rating plans discussed in the next section.

Is there enough competition in setting the basic prices in workers' compensation insurance? The opinion is divided.[24] In 1980 the National Association of Insurance Commissioners suggested a model bill for "open competition" rating, requiring insurers to submit data on a uniform basis but prohibiting agreements to adhere to advisory rates. Each insurer would have to develop their own rates. About six states have passed such laws. Opponents claim such legislation will erode the data base for credible rating, such as that now provided by the National Council on Compensation Insurance in 31 states. Potential problems mentioned include the difficulty of regulating multiple manuals, loss of commitment to loss control by focusing on price, and the disadvantages of small insurers and insureds. The developments in these attempts to increase competition in the basic rating structure of workers' compensation insurance will be worth watching in the 1980s.

SPECIAL RATING PLANS

In addition to the basic classifications and rates, the *individual* insured may have several opportunities to benefit from *special risk rating plans* which include (1) *experience* rating plans, (2) *premium discount* plans, (3) *retrospective rating* plans.

---

[24] William O. Bailey, "Competitive Rating and Workers' Compensation," and Gary L. Countryman, "Open Competition Rating for Workers' Compensation," *Journal of Insurance Regulation* 1, no. 1 (September 1982), pp. 1 and 9.

Experience rating plans

Experience rating plans are based upon the *past loss experience* of the *particular risk* under consideration. All states permit experience rating. If the loss history shows a cost below normal for the class, a reduction in the rate is allowed, while an unfavorable experience result increases the manual rate. When the risk is very large, with a "credibility factor" of 1.00, the risk is said to be self-rated. To qualify for experience rating, the risk must produce a designated annual average premium figure at manual rates. In most states, the insured whose premium exceeds $750 per year must use the experience rating plan. For the purpose of determining experience, the plan requires a period of not less than one year and can usually include a maximum of three years.

The term *standard premium* is used to designate that premium determined by applying manual rates to the employer's payroll modified by experience rating. When the annual standard premium exceeds $1,000, two additional types of plans may further modify the premium charge. These include *(a)* the premium discount plan and *(b)* five retrospective rating plans.

The premium discount plan

Workers' compensation rating plans recognize that certain factors that enter into the premium charge do not increase proportionately as the premium increases. The principal factors considered are *(a)* losses, *(b)* claim expense, *(c)* engineering and accident prevention, *(d)* administration and payroll audit expenses, *(e)* acquisition costs, and *(f)* taxes. As the premium increases, it is the purpose of the plan to give credit for those expenses that do not increase proportionately. It is a mandatory device to reflect expense savings for larger risks. Premium in excess of $1,000 is grouped in brackets and larger discounts (up to 16 percent or more) are applied as the premium increases in amount. The theory upon which these premiums are computed is sometimes referred to as the "principle of graded expense."

Retrospective rating plans

Retrospective rating plans differ from the experience rating plans mentioned above. Modification for *current loss* experience is the distinguishing feature of the retrospective plans. These plans are not separate and apart from experience rating but are, in effect, supplementary to it. While experience rating looks definitely to the past to determine the rate for the future, retrospective rating bases the premium upon actual losses of the current policy year. It is an optional arrangement for eligible risks, typically larger firms with good loss records and loss-prevention programs. Minimum standard premiums of about $5,000 are required, but to be effective $50,000 or more is often needed.

At the inception date of the policy the actual anticipated experience can only be estimated. Under the retrospective plan, if the experience is particularly good, a credit is reflected in the premium charge. If the experience is unsatisfactory, the cost to the insured is reflected in an increased premium. In actual operation the plan provides for three premiums: (1) the minimum retrospective premium, (2) the maximum retrospective premium, and (3) the retrospective premium. The plan provides that the insured shall pay in any case the minimum retrospective premium. On the other hand, the insured can never be called upon to pay more than the maximum retrospective premium. The premium that the insured will actually pay will probably fall somewhere between the two; this is known as the "retrospective premium." It is determined by adding to the basic premium the losses incurred, modified to provide for taxes and claim adjustment expenses. Individual claims included in the loss experience are often limited beforehand to stipulated maximum amounts, such as $10,000. The term *cost plus* has sometimes been applied to this rating plan.

The retrospective rating plan gives the insured the same credit for decreasing administration and acquisition expenses as does the premium discount plan. In addition, however, the retrospective rating plan reflects current losses in the current premium charge. This is, in fact, a protected profit-sharing plan in which the insured shares the profits by receiving immediate credit for lower loss experience. Overall, one of the most important effects of the compensation rating plans is the direct incentive that they provide to all parties to use the best loss-prevention and loss-reduction techniques.

There are five forms of retrospective rating: plans A, B, C, and J, which apply to workers' compensation only, and plan D, which may also apply to liability, automobile, burglary, and glass insurance. These plans are alike in principle but vary in detail, principally with reference to the fixing of the maximum and minimum premiums. In addition, several states have adopted retrospective plans of their own.

As rating plans and electronic data processing capabilities have broadened in availability and application, the retrospective plans have increased in popularity. Techniques and costs have been refined so that the use of such plans is spreading to more types of insurance (with high loss frequencies) and more insureds.

SECOND-INJURY FUNDS

With the increasing use of experience and retrospective rating, attention has been focused on all of the factors that may increase or reduce loss experience and hence workers' compensation cost. Great emphasis has been placed upon accident-prevention service, and it has been natural to consider physical factors. This has directed attention to employees so incapacitated that a second injury would result in total disability.

The term *second injury* in compensation parlance refers to an injury that taken in connection with a previous injury will result in an incapacity greater than would have resulted had there been no previous injury.[25] For example, persons who have lost an eye or a hand could become totally incapacitated as a result of losing the remaining eye or hand. Unless the statutes provide specifically to the contrary, the cost of disability arising out of the second injury reflects upon the employer in whose employ the second injury is sustained. The result of this situation is to place an undue burden upon the employer who employs the already seriously injured person.

To counteract this situation and to encourage employers to hire workers already known to have a permanent physical disability, all but a few states have by statute limited the liability of the current employer to the disability resulting from the second injury. The statutes usually provide that after having paid benefits for 104 weeks, insurers or self-insured employers will be entitled to reimbursement for additional weekly benefits out of the *second-injury fund* administered by the state. It is usual to provide that the fund be financed by contributions from insurers and self-insured employers writing compensation insurance. Payments for the second-injury disabilities are made out of this fund. If the injury is total, special compensation is provided. It is also provided that if the injured worker is able to secure employment but not at the level of previous employment, the worker may receive compensation based upon the difference between present and past weekly earnings, before the second injury occurred.

Second-injury laws have not been as effective as expected in encouraging employment of the handicapped, largely due to the employer not being aware of their benefits and because of some limitations in applying the laws.

WORKERS' COMPENSATION INSURANCE LOSSES

About 2.5 million persons a year are hurt at work in the United States, according to the National Safety Council, which estimates the annual compensation payments and production losses at $30 billion, including 250 million workdays in time lost annually. No wonder employers are concerned about rising workers' compensation costs!

---

[25] Albert P. Rodriguez, "How 'Special Disability' Law Impacts Hiring Handicapped," *Risk Management,* September 1980, p. 50. The term *subsequent-injury* is sometimes used also.

Claims for injury or disease made by workers against employers are *(a)* compensation claims or *(b)* liability claims. The adjustment of *compensation* claims concerns itself with coverage and with the nature and extent of the injury without the necessity of determining negligence. The *liability* feature of the policy provides specified limits of liability protection in rare cases when the disability is not within the protection of the compensation act and negligence by the employer must be shown.

The provisions of a workers' compensation act or an occupational disease act determine the benefits with which the employer might be charged. All of these benefits are assumed by the insurer. Workers' compensation insurance is, in fact, group accident and sickness insurance limited to occupational disabilities. Not only do the acts relieve the injured workers of the necessity of proving negligence, but they also usually deny them the right to sue under the common law.

Compensation acts are "liability without fault" statutes and establish a uniform payment for the disabled employee that is measured by the nature and the extent of the injury. The standard of recovery varies from state to state but is in every instance fixed by the legislature. The amount of the award for any compensable injury is not a problem for the insurer, except that it must follow the employer-employee agreement procedure specified by the particular state. In establishing arbitrary awards for compensation claims, which are in many instances less than could be anticipated in negligence cases, the legislatures have based the amount of these awards on the assumption that prompt payment without delays, costs, and litigation is better for all parties than fuller compensation subject to such contingencies.[26]

Compensation laws require that an injured employee give *notice* of an injury within a specified period, usually 30 days. The time limit for diseases is longer. Upon receiving notice, the employer proceeds immediately to notify the insurer and the industrial commission.

In an *insurance investigation* the adjuster first determines that the injury or disease reported was one "arising out of and in the course of employment." The disabled person and witnesses are interviewed, and usually signed statements are taken. A death case may require an autopsy, and in such cases steps must be taken to secure the consent of relatives.

The adjuster incorporates all pertinent data in a *report* to the insured. The effect of the disability on the particular individual, a written report of the attending physician, any suggestions with respect to treatment, and any subrogation possibilities are included. A complete breakdown of income benefits due by weeks and amounts is determined. The report will also cover payments for medical benefits or any expected payments

---

[26] *Ruso* v. *Omaha & Council Bluffs Street Railway,* 98 Neb. 436; 153 N.W. 510.

that are anticipated. There is no limit on the amount or on the period of time for which the employer is obligated to provide medical care. This is considered good business from the point of view of the injured employee, the employer, and the insurer. The best medical care can reduce the disability period and the indemnity payments.

At the conclusion of the investigation, the adjuster undertakes to reach an *agreement* with the employee with respect to compensation under the provisions of the act. A memorandum concerning the details, signed by all parties, is filed in the office of the compensation commission. If, upon review, the commission finds the agreement to be in conformity with the provisions of the compensation act, it is approved. If the insurance adjuster and the employee fail to reach an agreement in regard to the compensation, appeal for an award must be made to the commission. After proper notice and hearings, a final decision is rendered by the commission.

OTHER POLICY BENEFITS

One of the most important benefits of workers' compensation insurance is the impetus to *loss-prevention* efforts that it provides to both insurer and insured. The individual risk rating plans have been shown to be of direct benefit to employers who lower their insurance costs by good loss experience. With rising costs, loss prevention and better employee motivation and understanding can be among the most effective controls of employers.

Loss prevention in industrial injuries and disease has also been achieved by considerable activities of the insurers, even though the workers' compensation contract does not legally oblige them to engage in such activities. The insurers inspect the workplaces covered and suggest to the insured such changes or improvements as may operate to reduce the number and severity of accidents. A high accident frequency may be attributable to poor management and indifference. Management sometimes overlooks hazards attributable to poor housekeeping, such as obstructions in aisles, slippery floors, lack of adequate handrails or guards, and the like. Improvements in housekeeping may be effected at modest cost. Safety meetings for the education of management and employees require some time and effort. If management is sincerely interested in reducing costs by improving its loss ratio and will cooperate with the inspection and engineering service of the insurer, improvement can frequently result.

Insureds realize that industrial injuries and diseases are a direct source of monetary loss. Work is interrupted; superintendents and others lose time from productive effort; machinery is broken and goods are spoiled because of the mental upset of witnesses to the accident. These and other factors tend to make the "hidden costs" of industrial accidents a serious drain, even though the employer's obligation to the injured worker is covered by insurance. These indirect costs, including such items as loss of time by other employees, the costs of replacement or rehiring, decreased productivity and morale, are estimated at four times the direct cost of workers' compensation insurance.[27]

Inspection service is becoming an increasingly important factor in the placing of compensation insurance. An unfavorable loss experience coupled with poor or indifferent management would place a business in the category of an undesirable risk from the insurer standpoint. On the other hand, hazardous occupations are insurable if management evidences an interest in loss-prevention activities. Some insurers and other firms have highly specialized engineering and research services for the purpose of investigating working conditions and of devising, if possible, safer methods and conditions. The knowledge of experienced loss-control and industrial hygiene experts proves of great assistance in discovering safe methods. If a favorable experience is reflected in the premium, the direct saving is often substantial. Services provided by insurers include the following: (1) engineering consultation service, (2) periodic inspection service, (3) employee and supervisor training programs, (4) distribution of informative materials, (5) claims services, (6) employee safety meetings, and (7) advisory committees to work with supervising officials.

OCCUPATIONAL SAFETY AND HEALTH ACT AND OTHER FEDERAL LAWS

Job safety for employees escalated to the top of the major workers' compensation issues with the passage of the *Occupational Safety and Health Act (OSHA) of 1970.* This federal law usurped from the state considerable control of work-safety regulations, and a state must put into effect rules at least as stringent as the federal standards if it wishes to maintain jurisdiction for work-safety conditions of employees within its borders. The penal (fines of $10,000 or more) and investigative rules of OSHA are extensive and far-reaching, with many employers feeling the effects of inspections across the nation by 1,200 federal compliance officers who are enforcing the safety regulations under the act. Although the long-range effects will be beneficial in creating a safer working environment and in preventing losses, employers must pay the costs, including the fines for OSHA violations. Some large fines have been levied,

---

[27] H. W. Heinrich, *Industrial Accident Prevention* (New York: McGraw-Hill, 1950), pp. 50–61. This book is a classic pioneering effort in the field of loss prevention. See also Daniel C. Peterson, *Techniques of Safety Management* (New York: McGraw-Hill, 1971); J. A. Grimaldi and R. H. Simons, *Safety Management* (Homewood, Ill.: Richard D. Irwin, 1975); and *Loss-Control Management* (Malvern, Pa.: Insurance Institute of America, 1981).

including $116,000 against grain elevators and $216,000 against steel companies. Insurers are facing potential increased liability if the laws are not met.

One pronounced effect of the Occupational Safety and Health Act of 1970 was the establishment of the National Commission on State Workers' Compensation Laws. Charged with the responsibility of "evaluating current state laws to determine if such laws provide an adequate, prompt, and equitable system of compensation," the commission published a comprehensive treatment of current state laws.[28] It specified 21 substantive minimum standards recommended to the state compensation systems, including unlimited medical care and rehabilitation benefits, higher income benefits, compulsory coverage of all employers and employees, and other changes. Most, but not all, of the states have improved their compensation laws to meet these standards.

The progress of OSHA has not been without difficulties and costs, but the benefits of a safer workplace appear worthwhile.[29] The Department of Labor, through the Occupational Safety and Health Administration, is responsible for setting the rules for legally permitted exposures to hazards in the workplace. Another organization, the National Institute for Occupational Safety and Health (NIOSH) conducts occupational health research and recommends standards for safe exposures to hazardous substances.

The scope of the immense task is illustrated by the fact that in 1977 the Labor Department rewrote the general industry standards in a 250-page document which *revoked* more than 1,100 regulations that were classified as outdated or "nitpicking" job safety rules. Complaints from employers, unions, and even employees themselves encouraged the revisions. OSHA has changed its regulatory focus from minor safety regulations to concentrate on routine inspections and reports from the 7,000 manufacturers whose operations cause about three fourths of the serious injuries.[30] A longer-range objective is to set health standards for some 2,000 chemicals suspected of causing cancer, which may cost industry and consumers as much as $100 billion.

One setback to OSHA authority occurred when U.S. Supreme Court ruled unconstitutional the unannounced inspections of workplaces. OSHA inspectors now may first have to obtain a search warrant from a judge, who may require proof that there is "probable cause" to believe

[28] National Commission on State Workmen's Compensation Laws, *Compendium on Workers' Compensation* (Washington, D.C.: U.S. Government Printing Office, 1973).

[29] Estimated costs of $2.5 billion annually during 1970–1980 are about 11 percent of the $23 billion cost of workplace accidents. John B. Ricker, Jr., "OSHA: the Balance Sheet," *Journal of Insurance,* November-December 1980, p. 2.

[30] "OSHA to Exempt 474,000 Employers from Some Filings," *The Wall Street Journal,* June 4, 1982, p. 10.

that safety hazards or violations are present in a workplace. In actual practice, few employers are requiring federal OSHA inspectors to obtain search warrants, in spite of the fact that employers can do so under the present law.[31]

There has been periodic pressure for *federalization* of the state workers' compensation acts to require minimum standards for workers' compensation laws in all the states. Such proposals have the desirable objectives of achieving greater uniformity among the states and of raising the coverage and benefit levels. However, the details and problems of applying workers' compensation standards on a national basis after about 70 years of state jurisdiction are considerable. State rights versus federal rights are involved in this issue; increased costs may result for many employers; and reaching agreement upon the exact standards would be difficult.

FOR REVIEW AND DISCUSSION

1. Is the peril of occupational disability taken care of by "social" or "private" insurance in the United States? Explain your answer.

2. State workers' compensation laws are almost all *compulsory* laws. They are also either *(a) monopolistic* or *(b) competitive.* What do these terms mean?

3. Why have workers' compensation laws been adopted in all of the states? Shouldn't injured employees be able to show negligence on the part of the employer before the employer is held liable?

4. What kinds of benefits are provided by the workers' compensation laws? How are the amounts determined?

5. The workers' compensation policy provides *(a) liability* and *(b) compensation* coverage. What is the extent of the compensation protection afforded? Is compensation always the exclusive remedy for the injured worker? Explain.

6. Do workers' compensation laws cover all, or just some, employees? Explain, including reference to changes that have occurred since the early laws.

7. Give an example of these types of disability: *(a)* temporary, *(b)* permanent partial, *(c)* permanent total, and *(d)* occupational disease.

8. There are a few monopolistic workers' compensation state funds, while some states offer state funds as an alternative to private insurance. Why, in your opinion, has the state monopoly idea not been more widely adopted?

9. Mrs. X works in a restaurant and contracts a skin infection caused by handling vegetables. Is this an occupational disease? Would this be covered by the standard workers' compensation policy? Illustrate why this peril is important.

10. Discuss the advantages and disadvantages which employers may have by

---

[31] "Job-Safety Inspectors Seldom Required to Get Warrants Despite Justices' Ruling," *The Wall Street Journal,* July 17, 1978, p. 10.

"self-insuring" their workers' compensation responsibilities, as is possible in most states for larger employers.

11. Physically handicapped employees sometimes find it difficult to secure employment because of increased costs under the experience-rated compensation plans. If you were a large employer, would you feel financially safe in employing persons already injured in industrial accidents or disabled veterans?

12. A.B. filed suit against his employer, claiming that he had contracted silicosis because the paint plant in which he worked was not properly ventilated. Suits from other employees followed. Why is the position of the employer better if the disease is covered by the compensation act?

13. What characteristics make the workers' compensation policy (a) simpler than other insurance contracts and (b) sometimes more difficult to write than other insurance contracts?

14. How are *basic rates* determined for workers' compensation insurance? What *special rating plans* for individual insureds may apply? Briefly explain their primary purposes.

15. Explain the importance of the following in workers' compensation insurance: (a) loss-prevention work, (b) "second-injury funds," (c) "self-insurance," and (d) rehabilitation.

16. What *types* of insurance do employers use to comply with the financial requirements of workers' compensation laws? Which of these types predominate?

17. How do workers' compensation contracts vary from other insurance contracts in their (a) loss provisions and (b) loss procedures for claims?

18. How is the *federal* government becoming more involved in (a) occupational disabilities and (b) workers' compensation plans?

19. One of the most significant laws concerning workers' compensation was the Occupational Safety and Health Act. Discuss its effects and difficulties.

Chapter 19

Outline of concepts

Automobile insurance is part of our "automobile economy" today, in which the car is both friend and foe. Problems for consideration include the needs for, the costs of, and the solutions provided by fault and no-fault insurance.

The need for automobile insurance is observed from three viewpoints: (1) society, (2) the motorists, and (3) the injured victims.

The cost of automobile insurance is a primary factor:

    Increasing costs are substantial, particularly rising *liability losses.*

    Rate regulation has aimed at maintaining—

        Price competition among rating bureaus and independent insurers.

        Nonprice competition, services by insurer and agent, also important.

        State regulation uses three approaches: *prior approval, file and use,* and *open competition* rating laws.

Solutions to the need for automobile insurance are evolving.

    Basic current and changing solutions have revised some tort liability systems, and various proposals of a social insurance nature have been adopted to meet the problems.

    Financial responsibility laws are the basic answer in 20 states to the need to encourage the purchase of automobile liability insurance.

    Compulsory liability insurance is used in about 30 states; evidence of insurance must be shown before license plates are issued.

    Automobile insurance (assigned risk) plans in about 40 states assure almost everyone that liability insurance can be purchased.

    Other "residual market" mechanisms include *reinsurance facilities, joint underwriting associations,* and, in one state, an automobile *state fund* insurer.

    Unsatisfied judgment funds in five states pay an innocent victim for losses caused by financially irresponsible motorists.

    Uninsured motorists coverage is available to insureds in all states, as one of the most successful methods devised for paying innocent victims.

    Automobile no-fault insurance plans of several types may help alleviate the liability system problems of automobiles. Sixteen states have "modified," and eight have "pseudo" no-fault laws. The pseudo types expand first-party "add-on" coverages but do not abolish tort liability suits.

    Another crucial solution is *automobile safety and loss prevention,* through the combined efforts of government, private insurance, and public demand.

Automobile insurance—fault and no-fault

Although insurance texts tell students that insurance is not gambling, insurance authors sometimes must be gamblers. Four years ago this writer gambled that the trend toward no-fault automobile insurance in some states would slow and that the chapter title above was the best possible. It remains so today for the 1980s.

Certainly no chapter that desires to have up-to-date relevance could be titled "tort" liability (fault) automobile insurance, yet it is not a reasonable prediction that the title should be only "no-fault" (not based on negligence). The title fault and no-fault implicitly says that the solutions for the future will contain both systems of automobile insurance. It is expected that the complex changes will adjust to a combination of both concepts.

For essential background, this chapter first discusses the *need* for automobile insurance today; then one of the basic factors, *cost;* and finally the current and changing *solutions,* including no-fault, which are being adopted by law and the insurance business to meet the needs of modern society.

THE NEED FOR AUTOMOBILE INSURANCE

One of the most obvious signs of affluence in the United States today is the number of automobiles—bulging over on the roads, the shopping centers, the parking lots, and even the eyesore auto graveyards. In suburbia a major problem is how to get two cars in a one-car garage, or three into a two-car garage!

Automobile—friend and foe

The "automobile economy" of the United States today is an amazing world of mobility, responsibility, and danger. It has provided many opportunities and advantages for work and recreation, yet at the same time it has created substantial risk and insurance problems. Could anyone really have imagined a generation or so ago that nearly 150 *million* motorists would be driving today over our highways? Or could the awesome effects of this era in terms of death, injuries, and monetary costs have been predicted?

The annual toll has reached alarming proportions: about 50,000 persons killed, 5 million persons injured in 28 million accidents, and $60 billion in lost wages, property damage, and legal medical, and insurance costs.[1] Almost 2 million American deaths have been due to highway accidents during the 20th century. Annual fatalities from automobiles are double the number caused by accidents in the home, 4 times the number caused by work accidents, 10 times the number resulting from fires, and 35 times the number resulting from aircraft accidents.[2]

Automobile liability insurance

With such obvious needs for insurance protection, it is little wonder that the automobile insurance field has grown to a gigantic size, exceeding $41 billion in annual premiums. More than 60 percent of the premiums are for *liability* and related insurance, with the remainder for physical damage coverage on the automobile of the insured. Thus, many of the ideas discussed in previous chapters about employers' and general liability insurance also apply to automobile insurance. Automobile liability insurance deserves separate treatment, however, and this chapter presents some of the major issues and proposed solutions to its current problems. The automobile coverages, especially the common "personal automobile policy" by which most private automobiles are insured today, will be discussed in the next chapter.

Viewpoints on the need

Three viewpoints are pertinent in appraising the need for automobile insurance, that of (1) the society, (2) the automobile motorist, and (3) the injured victims of automobile accidents. Automobile insurance must be looked at not only as an individual solution to an individual problem of risk but also in its *social* or public aspects. Among the responsible-thinking citizens in the United States, there is almost universal acceptance of the idea that everyone owning or using an automobile should purchase liability insurance. The uncertainty of financial disaster due to an automobile accident is so widespread a risk today that few persons are exempt from its possibility.

The losses are dramatic, and they are more often attributable to causes of human origin than most other losses. Nearly 9 out of 10 traffic accidents

---

[1] *Insurance Facts* (New York: Insurance Information Institute, 1982–83), p. 58.

[2] Ibid., pp. 46, 59, and 72.

involve *individual negligence*, such as failure to observe traffic laws, intoxication, or just plain poor driving habits. In many cases the multiple factors involved render it difficult to place responsibility for such accidents solely on one person. Some accidents are perhaps primarily the result of *social negligence*. For example, consider the effects of such underlying causes as the number of automobiles manufactured; the lack of adequate roads; improper engineering of highway grades, curves, and traffic signals; and weak driver-licensing laws and tests. The immediate cause of automobile accidents may *usually* be the "nut behind the wheel"—but perhaps the "freewheeling society" in which we live must shoulder its share of the blame, too.

The *individual* who owns or uses an automobile (or other motor vehicle) has some of the familiar risks which all property owners face. Part or all of the value of the automobile may be lost through a variety of perils, such as fire, theft, or collision. In addition, owners or drivers have an enormous risk in not knowing whether their automobiles will cause damage to the property of other persons, or injury to other persons, for which they may be held liable. Individuals or families may also suffer death or disability losses due to medical care expense and lost income as a result of an automobile accident. In summary, the individual risks require protection from all the important fields of insurance: (1) property, (2) liability, (3) life, and (4) health.

Another viewpoint from which automobile insurance should be considered is that of the victims. If they are *innocent unpaid automobile accident victims*, certain legal rights accrue to them against the parties responsible for their property damage or personal injury loss.[3] To obtain payment, they must usually prove the other party liable. Time and costs may be involved in carrying out the legal right, and even then the negligent parties may not be able to pay for the results of their irresponsibility. The result is that some innocent victims of automobile accidents remain uncompensated, and this is often an overlooked viewpoint. The presumption is that the victim is innocent, and that someone else, or everyone else, is responsible for the accident and/or for the lack of payment for the injuries and damages that the victim has suffered.

From *society's* viewpoint, the effects may be similar regardless of who was the cause of the accident. The victims and their families may become burdens of the government through various public welfare or social insurance programs. In addition, the results are costly for everyone: property is damaged, injuries are suffered, income is lost, and lives are wasted. Thus government also becomes involved in "the automobile problem,"

---

[3] Sometimes this problem is stated as that of the "uninsured motorist," but the result rather than the cause of the problem appears to be a better way of stating the difficulty today.

with studies and laws relating to accident causes, repair costs, auto safety features, and auto insurance costs and market inadequacies.

The need to consider all of the three viewpoints in reaching a conclusion about *how* and *how much* is to be paid, and *by whom* suggests that some governmental action encouraging or requiring insurance is necessary. Each of the solutions discussed later in this chapter shows that this is true, although the method and extent of the requirements differ greatly in the various types of state laws designed to cope with the problem.

The *automobile* is needed by many persons today, and it causes such great potential for *losses* that automobile *insurance* also becomes a necessity. Thus the *cost* of automobile insurance becomes so important that it is discussed separately in the next section. Remember, however, that the concern over cost is related to another major aspect of the problem— that of determining how the costs to the injured *victim* of automobile accidents can be met through insurer and government action. That is the major topic of this chapter—the section on current solutions.

THE COST OF AUTOMOBILE INSURANCE

"When a fellow says it hain't the money, but the principle o' the thing— it's th' money!"[4] So goes an old joke, but today in automobile insurance the joke is nothing to laugh at. With the annual cost of automobile accidents at about $60 *billion* in 1982, the money and the principles become undeniably significant. Some of the principles have been introduced in the preceding section. This section treats the cost aspects of the problem.

It is important for policyholders and students of insurance to know as much as possible about automobile insurance prices. They should at least be familiar with the reasons why the costs for automobile insurance are high and with how automobile insurance rates are regulated. What factors determine the cost for the many different classifications of insureds is also important to the individual consumer. That topic is discussed in Chapter 20.

Increasing costs

Automobile insurance is one of the important costs of operating an automobile. The costs are estimated as follows:[5]

---

[4] F. McKinney Hubbard, *Hoss Sense and Nonsense*, 1926.

[5] The analysis of such costs differs somewhat with the assumptions made. This is based on a Federal Highway Administration survey using a standard-size car driven 100,000 miles over 10 years in suburban Baltimore. Compact-size cars showed 3.3 cents insurance costs of a total cost of 21.4 cents, and subcompacts 3.1 cents of 18.9 cents. *Insurance Facts*, p. 42.

Depreciation	6.3 cents per mile
Maintenance	5.5
Garages, parking tolls	3.2
Gas and oil	5.6
Insurance	2.4
Taxes	1.6
Total	24.6 cents per mile

Some policyholders pay more for their automobile insurance than they do for gas or for maintenance. This comes as a shock. A greater shock comes to those automobile owners, especially young persons, who find that their annual cost for insurance may exceed the total value of their older-model car!

Automobile insurance costs have increased rapidly, approximately doubling in many areas during the last 10 years; yet in the past decade automobile insurers have lost several billion dollars writing the protection they provide for policyholders.[6] The reasons are many: the lag of rate increases behind the rising costs, changing marketing methods, the reluctance of state authorities to approve higher rates, the difficulty of predicting losses and expenses in a rapidly expanding field, and many other factors.

The fundamental reason for the increase in automobile insurance costs is traceable to the *loss* portion of the premium dollar paid for automobile insurance. During the last seven years the average costs for bodily injury and property damage liability claims each increased about 100 percent.[7] The expense portion of automobile insurance premiums has actually decreased (by about 10 percent during the last decade), in spite of the general tendency toward the higher cost of doing business today as compared with several years ago.

Thus, in analyzing the losses paid by automobile insurers, the reasons for much greater insurance costs are spotlighted. What, for example, would cause *bodily injury liability* payments and medical payments to increase? These factors emerge: (1) more cars, more drivers, more mileage driven, more accidents; (2) sharply rising hospital and medical costs for treating accidents; (3) more loss of income, based on rising wages, when injuries do occur; and (4) a sharp upward trend in the size and number of claims made, the settlements paid, and the verdicts granted by juries in personal injury cases.

What about *property damage liability, collision, and physical damage* insurance costs? Here other factors are pertinent: (1) higher property

---

[6] Losses and expenses have exceeded premiums received by all automobile insurers. Investment income, fortunately, has enabled the insurers to stay in business without destroying the financial strength of most companies. Some insurers have succeeded in making a profit; many others have suffered rather consistent underwriting losses.

[7] *Insurance Facts,* p. 59.

values, for cars as well as the property which automobiles damage; and (2) higher repair costs, especially for automobile repairs, based on increased labor and materials costs. With labor costs at an average $18 per hour or more, the cost of replacing the same selected parts went up from about $700 in a 1975 car to more than $1,600 in 1982.[8] A startling figure from industry studies shows that it would cost more than $27,000 to replace all the parts of a totally wrecked car with a factory price of $7,100.[9]

Inflation is an underlying factor in many of the reasons for rising automobile insurance costs. The prices of items important to insurance have increased sharply. Ironically, many of the reasons for cost increases are well beyond the control of the insurers themselves. Certainly it must be recognized, for example, that the insurance industry does *not* control hospital costs, repair bills, inflation, car design, highway construction, driver licensing, and many other parts of the problem. It may be true that some of the increased payments under automobile insurance contracts are due to fraud or exaggerated claims, but it can also be readily seen that many basic factors are responsible for the increases in the prices of all kinds of automobile insurance during recent years.

Rate regulation

The prices charged for automobile insurance contracts do vary, not just for different contracts and different territories but also for essentially identical policies in the same areas. This is contrary to the belief of most persons, consistently revealed by many consumer research surveys, that all insurers charge about the same price.

Price competition. How can the contradiction be explained? It is obviously based upon lack of information and understanding by the buying public. As to the reasons for that lack of information and understanding, two factors loom as most significant. First, the many pricing mechanisms for automobile insurance are not simple. They include many variations in both regulation and practice. The regulatory provisions of the 50 states differ greatly, both as to the objectives and wording of the laws and as to the extent to which the laws are applied. These differences appear in sharp focus when one analyzes the numerous automobile insurance markets and the actual practices of the competing insurers. Second, insurance consumers are after all, no more sophisticated in their approach to buying insurance than in their approach to buying most

---

[8] Ibid., p. 61. See also, on p. 62, the Insurance Institute for Highway Safety low-speed crash test results for 1981 cars. Federal requirements are shown as reducing costs substantially for five-mile-an-hour front and rear accidents, but these are only part of the total cost problem. Repair costs increase dramatically with 2.5 v. 5.0 mph bumpers.

[9] Based on an Alliance of American Insurers study for a 1982 Toyota subcompact.

other goods and services. Decisions are not always carefully calculated, and they are made with tremendous differences in education, ability, initiative, and interest. Indeed, like most other products, automobile insurance is probably purchased as often on the basis of emotional factors and partial information as on the basis of rational decision making with all the factors at hand.

Nonprice competition. Another point is most significant. Why shouldn't the prices for automobile insurance vary considerably? Contracts do differ in their terms, and even in identical contracts the product is largely a bundle of services, not limited merely to indemnification for loss. It also includes many hard-to-measure benefits. Just as important to most buyers of automobile insurance as its price (though price is certainly a dominant factor in many decisions, perhaps too many) are such needs as (1) the opportunity to learn about their requirements, and how insurance can provide the best solutions; (2) the advice and counsel of the insurer and agent in making the decision as to proper coverage; (3) the promptness, efficiency, and fairness of the loss payments; and (4) the careful protection of the insured's right to own and drive an automobile by meeting the various vehicle regulations of the states. Nonprice competition is very important to the automobile insurance buyer.

State regulation. The background for the main issue of state regulation of rates is set with the above observations. The problem is essentially one of the extent to which there should be price *competition* as opposed to price *cooperation* in automobile insurance, or put another way, the proper extent of public control of price competition in this field.[10]

A summary of the current methods of control is warranted. Three major legislative methods may be identified: (1) "prior approval," (2) "file and use," and (3) "open competition" laws. A few states use other methods, such as state-made rates (Texas, Massachusetts) or mandatory bureau rates (North Carolina), instead of rate filings by insurers.

Most of the states still use a *prior approval* law which permits rate changes only after the state has approved them. As a result of the McCarran Act (Public Law 15, 1945), these states adopted within a few years laws modeled after bills approved by the National Association of Insurance Commissioners. These are known as "all-industry laws," because many states adopted them, but this does not mean that all of the states did so. The laws apply to many forms of property-liability insurance in addition to automobile insurance. They permit insurers to choose among several alternatives: (1) filing their own rates, (2) adopting the rates filed by a rating organization, or (3) using deviated rates based upon their

---

[10] C. Arthur Williams, Jr., and Andrew F. Whitman, "Open Competition Rating Laws and Price Competition," *Journal of Risk and Insurance* 40, no. 4 (December 1973), p. 483. See also John D. Long and Robert I. Mehr, *The Illinois System of Insurance Pricing* (Bloomington, Ind.: Insurance Research Associates, 1981).

own experience. The rates must be filed with the state insurance department, and the insurance commissioner or superintendent must approve
them before they are used by the insurers. The laws basically permit
competition through independent, bureau, and deviated rates, and they
provide for regulated cooperation through the rating bureau approach
to rate making. The standards used by the states to evaluate compliance
with the objectives of these rate regulation laws vary considerably, as
does the application of those standards. Competition is encouraged but
somewhat controlled. The result in most states is that automobile insurance consumers find, if they look for it, a reasonable degree of price
competition.

About a dozen states use the *file and use* approach to automobile insurance rating. The law in these states does not mandate approval of the
rates by the insurance commissioner. Contracts and rates are filed but
can be used by the insurers immediately. The commissioner can disapprove the filings at a later time if such a decision is made. In some of
these states the bureau rates can be mandatory, but in most states they
are only advisory.

The *open competition* approach is based upon the idea that competition
is the best regulator of insurance prices. About 10 states follow this
practice, with laws which provide minimum regulation as long as the
general objective of maintaining competition in order to achieve rate
adequacy, reasonableness, and fair discrimination are met. Essentially
these are nonfiling systems, and the commissioner does not review forms
or rates. An NAIC model law in the early 1980s recommended an open
competition law for adoption in the states. Some empirical evidence during the past decade suggests that insurance costs are as low and stable
in open competition states as in other states.[11]

A review of the rationale and development of the various rating laws
shows the complexity of the current situation in regard to government
and consumer criticism of higher rates, cancellations, and underwriting
practices. The competitive-type laws have gained some support, but the
revision of the prior approval laws may take many years in some states.
The open competition approach is encouraged by (1) independent insurers
that desire more freedom in setting rates, (2) many stock and mutual
bureau insurers that want to achieve more adequate rate increases, and
(3) the desire of state regulators to squelch criticism from the federal
government of the inadequacy of state regulation in maintaining price
competition in automobile insurance. Conversely, increased auto insurance rates due to inflation and no-fault laws have caused support for

---

[11] Robert C. Witt and Harry Miller, "A Comparative Analysis of Relative Costs under
Competitive and Non-Competitive Rate Regulatory Laws," and "Rate Regulation, Competition, and Underwriting Risk in Automobile Insurance Markets," *CPCU Journal* 33, no.
4 (December 1980, p. 174), and vol. 34, no. 4 (December 1981, p. 202), respectively.

greater rate regulation in automobile insurance. The future changes remain unclear in many states.

SOLUTIONS TO THE NEED FOR AUTOMOBILE INSURANCE

The key to the family automobile(s?) is truly the sign of one of the highest standards of living that any nation has ever enjoyed. Yet, with the key goes a frightening responsibility for the control of the costs, both physical and financial, which are associated with it. To the individual, these costs create the need for automobile insurance.

The need, as shown in the various viewpoints on the problems and in regard to the costs of automobile insurance, have been discussed in preceding sections. The growth of competition and costs, financial losses of unparalleled proportions in some years, changing government regulations, and consumer mistrust combine to create continued expectation of change to achieve improvements in automobile insurance.

Basic current and changing solutions

The need is easily overdramatized in some of the types of "growing concern" noted in the early part of this chapter. However, the concern *is* there, and the public appeal *is* strong. News articles often sensationalize automobile accidents to obtain the reader's attention. Dramatic pictures of multivehicle crashes leave the public with the impression that automobile accidents are caused not by individuals but by a horrible series of unfortunate circumstances. For example, gasoline tankers explode, and smog or snow cause chain reaction accidents on crowded superhighways, involving many deaths, injuries, and property damage claims in seconds. The implication of these rather isolated cases is apparently (extrapolating the examples to *all* automobile accidents): "Who can possibly be blamed for automobile accidents?" Although the answer "no one" may be appropriate for some such accidents, the answer today may still be an identifiable "someone" for the more usual two-car and less-complex accidents.

The tort liability system is so basic a part of our society in the United States that its application to the automobile field will continue. Changes *will* occur, but they are likely to occur in an evolutionary manner rather than a revolutionary one. Some parts of the automobile liability risk may be determined as social in nature, requiring a social insurance plan as a solution. However, it is assumed here that for at least the span of this text edition, *individual* responsibility for many automobile accidents will continue to be the basis for much of the usual automobile insurance contract.

To try to predict the exact outcome of the many new state laws and experimental plans, however, would be impossible. Apparently some form of *no-fault* plan will be used in connection with *some* part of *some* of the automobile contracts for *some* insureds. Whether this no-fault trend will be for all on a compulsory basis or for some on an optional basis may take a decade or more to be decided.

This section aims first at understanding the *past* and *current* solutions to the need for automobile insurance. A later section will review briefly the newer no-fault programs, especially those that have appeared in recent years, which seem to characterize the changing and questioning attitudes of today's consumers, insurers, and regulators.

Aside from the practical need for protection against potentially severe losses, automobile insurance is *needed* because it is *required by government*. Thus, the current solutions are all fundamentally connected with *legislation* which requires some type of *insurance* plan.

In certain fields of business, the federal government and a number of states have enacted legislation making adequate vehicle coverage a condition which must be met before a license to operate is issued. Common carriers such as trucking concerns and taxicab or bus operators fall into this category. The Interstate Commerce Act requires all interstate common carriers to furnish evidence of liability insurance to the Interstate Commerce Commission. These requirements have been sharply increased by the Motor Carrier Act of 1980, with 1983 limits of $750,000 (and up to $5 million for vehicles hauling hazardous materials). Some states require that a certificate of insurance be on file in the case of private transit carriers. A few states also require insurance before issuing an automobile registration or license to certain individuals, such as minors under the age of 21 or 18.

The most important types of automobile insurance legislation and plans, however, apply to *all* or *nearly all* automobile owners or drivers. Table 19–1 summarizes the scope and general characteristics of these laws and plans. As to *purpose,* they can be divided into groups which attempt to (1) increase the universality of third-party liability insurance (nos. 1 and 2, *financial responsibility* and *compulsory liability laws*); (2) provide a pool or fund in which private insurers participate (nos. 3–5, *assigned risk, other residual market,* and *unsatisfied judgment* plans); (3) encourage the purchase of first-party coverage for the insureds own losses (nos. 6 and 7, *uninsured motorists* and *no-fault* plans); or (4) reduce losses (no. 8, *safety and loss-prevention* plans).

Each of these areas is discussed separately in the following sections of this chapter.

Financial responsibility laws

In connection with the operation of an automobile, about 20 states only *encourage* the purchase of liability insurance by means of financial

Table 19–1. Summary of automobile insurance legislation and plans

Type of legislation or plan	Purpose	Scope of use	General characteristics
1. Financial responsibility laws	To increase purchase of third-party liability insurance	About 20 states	Typical law requires security to pay for current accident, and purchase of liability insurance with 10/20/5 (or higher) limits, *after* being involved in an accident, for future liability claims
2. Compulsory liability laws	To increase purchase of third-party liability insurance	About 30 states	Require purchase of liability insurance *before* car license and plates are issued
3. Assigned risk (auto insurance) plans	To pool the higher-risk drivers	About 42 states	If motorists have been refused regular insurance, they may obtain coverage through such a plan, which apportions these insureds among all private insurers in the state
4. Other residual market mechanisms	To pool the higher-risk drivers	Nine states	Three types of laws pool loss experience of higher-risk drivers by a "reinsurance facility" (four states), a "joint underwriting association" (four states), or a "state fund" (one state)
5. Unsatisfied judgment funds	To pool payments to unpaid victims	Five states	Provide innocent victim with payment for losses caused by others who cannot be identified or by others who are unable to pay for judgments against them
6. Uninsured motorists coverage	To encourage insureds to purchase own coverage	All states	Adds coverage in insured's *own contract* for income and medical expense losses *caused* by uninsured motorists to any occupants of the insured's car
7. Automobile no-fault laws	To have insureds purchase *own coverage***	16–24 states	In 16 states the "modified" type abolishes tort liability suits except for serious injuries and has insureds collect losses from their *own* insurer (8 other states have "pseudo-type" laws)
8. Safety and loss-prevention plans	To reduce automobile accidents or losses	Many states; federal and industry plans	Promote traffic safety and laws, better driver-licensing laws, safer vehicle manufacture, and coordinated accident reporting and research

*Note that no-fault plans are *first-party* insurance contracts, for coverage with the insured's own insurance company, as opposed to the *third-party* coverage provided for *liability* of the insured to other persons in the other laws and plans of this table.

responsibility legislation but do not require everyone to buy it. These laws are designed to make it impossible for reckless and *financially irresponsible motorists* (those who have *become involved in an accident*) to secure a license to drive a car unless there is a guarantee that they are able to pay and will pay, within statutory limits, damages for which they become liable.

Early laws. The earliest financial responsibility laws required that once motorists were *found liable* for an accident, they must prove their financial responsibility or lose their license to drive. These were called "one-bite" laws because they required insurance for *future* accidents, but not for the first one.[12]

To strengthen the financial responsibility legislation other states passed laws under which motorists must immediately establish their ability to answer for damages if *involved in an accident*.[13] If motorists are not insured, they are required to furnish security that in the judgment of the state authorities will satisfy any judgment that may be recovered against them. In contrast to the earlier laws, these "security-type" laws require motorists involved in an accident to provide security immediately to cover any possible judgments for an accident that has already occurred, as well as insurance for future accidents.

Current laws. Most states today have the *security-type law*. All but a few statutes require at least minimum bodily injury of $10,000 per person and $20,000 per occurrence and property damage limits of $5,000. Many states require higher limits, such as 15/30/10 or 25/50/10.[14] There is no waiting until the motorist is convicted of a traffic violation or a judgment is awarded for damages. The motorist must be prepared to respond to damages immediately upon the happening of an accident. The law applies to the accident that has occurred as well as the accidents that may occur in the future. This type of law provides a powerful incentive to insure, since motorists understand that failure to satisfy the state authorities with respect to financial responsibility following an accident will result in the immediate suspension of license and registration. Financial responsibility must be evidenced at the time of any accident involving

---

[12] This type of plan generally fell short of the objective of financial responsibility legislation. One of the earliest such laws was passed in Connecticut in 1925. Financially irresponsible motorists continued to drive without insurance because many who met with injuries were unwilling to incur the cost of a suit if it appeared that the judgment would be uncollectible. In such circumstances, the negligent persons were not "found liable," and they suffered no penalty.

[13] This type of law appeared in New Hampshire in 1937. In many states the present legislation is based upon a model safety responsibility law that is applied not only after an accident but also in specified cases where the motorist has a number of serious motor vehicle violations, such as reckless driving or speeding.

[14] For a summary of the different statutory limits in each state, see *Insurance Facts*, p. 77. About 35 states have *bodily injury* limits higher than 10/20, and 25 have higher *property damage* limits than $5,000.

personal injuries, although many states do not apply the law to minor property damage accidents such as under $100 to $250.

The primary purpose of financial responsibility laws was to provide *encouragement for all* motorists to purchase liability insurance, *without compelling everyone* to do so. This goal the laws have reasonably achieved because most persons know that their driving privileges will be jeopardized if they have an accident while uninsured. The percentage of insured drivers has increased from 40 percent 40 years ago to over 85 percent in most of the states today. Many of the states with particularly effective financial responsibility law enforcement have increased the percentage to above 90 percent insured. Only a few states have less than 75 percent insured.

Compulsory liability insurance legislation

In contrast to the financial responsibility laws, about 30 states have *compulsory laws* which make the demonstration of financial responsibility a condition precedent to obtaining registration. All owners of automobiles are required to show proof of an insurance policy *before license and plates will be issued.*[15] In essence, this makes financial responsibility mandatory in order to own and use a car. It was not until 30 years after Massachusetts adopted a compulsory law in 1927 that a second state, New York, passed such a law. About 15 states adopted compulsory liability provisions in connection with no-fault laws instituted during the past dozen years.

Pros and cons.   Advocates of compulsory insurance point to the danger of a serious accident when an uninsured and financially irresponsible driver is liable for damages and unable to pay. As a guarantee of protection to the public against financial loss, compulsory insurance is held by its advocates to be superior to the typical financial responsibility law, under which approximately one out of eight registered vehicles remain uninsured in the United States.

Opponents of compulsory insurance object to the compulsion forced upon all car owners, whether or not they are bad drivers. They contend that this tends to increase recklessness, thereby causing more accidents. Insurers have little opportunity to select their risks, the loss suits tend to increase abnormally, and the rates increase faster in states with compulsory insurance laws.[16] There is also a belief that property damage

---

[15] Or in some states, sign a statement that insurance is in effect. As an alternative, the laws also permit the filing of cash, bond, or collateral in amounts equivalent to the required insurance contract limits of liability. Practically speaking, insurance is the only method used.

[16] "Compulsory Auto Insurance: How Well Does It Work?" *Journal of American Insurance,* Spring 1982, p. 21. Rates for 1976–80 of 6 states with compulsory laws were each compared with 3 other comparable states without such laws.

claims are fraudulently converted into bodily injury claims since only bodily injury coverage is required by many of the laws.

The compulsory law does *not* mean that all motorists are insured.[17] Of motorists licensed in the compulsory states, rarely less than 5 and often as many as 15 percent remain uninsured,[18] such as: (1) hit-and-run drivers, (2) drivers of stolen cars, (3) motorists insured when plates were issued but for whom the insurance has lapsed, and (4) fraudulently registered cars. Uninsured motorists may also include many (estimated at about 20 percent) out-of-state drivers. The cost of administering the compulsory law is high, involving millions of dollars annually in each state for record keeping and police to pick up license plates.

Another criticism is the tendency of the compulsory laws to provide less protection, as many persons expect the required minimums to meet their full needs. This may create an "underinsured" problem of inadequate policy limits. Policy coverage also tends to be restricted by political considerations, as promised lower rates are secured by limiting the policy coverage. In Massachusetts, for example, unless it is endorsed to do so, the policy does not cover (1) accidents occurring on private property, (2) accidents occurring out of state, or (3) guests in the car. A final objection raised is the possible threat to private enterprise that may result from a state insurance fund perhaps usurping a field of insurance which now accounts for 40 percent or more of the business of property-liability insurers.

The lack of complete data leaves many of the arguments for and against compulsory automobile liability insurance inconclusive. The idea and objectives are reasonable in many respects, but they are often misunderstood as automatically bringing a full solution to the problem.

Neither the compulsory laws nor the financial responsibility laws do much to increase the prevention of accidents, which is perhaps the fundamental and most-needed goal. Better enforcement of existing motor vehicle and safety laws is essential and tackles the problem at its root. The increasing and unnecessary losses on the highways should not be condoned under any of the current or proposed solutions to the problem of the automobile accident victim.

The compulsory law is apparently a growing but not popular choice. It has been defeated in many bills introduced regularly in many states, and support for it seems to have increased only when it has been adopted along with the new no-fault laws.

The current situation appears to cause less concern over compulsory

---

[17] Or that all auto accident injuries are covered. Those who are responsible for their own injuries, for example, as well as the victims injured by the several types of uninsured motorists mentioned in this paragraph, are not covered except under the no-fault laws.

[18] "Compulsory Auto Insurance"

automobile liability insurance among insurers and much more concern over changes which may usurp part or all of the tort liability system (see no-fault plans discussed later). Some of these plans are implicitly based upon compulsory features requiring insurance, so that compulsory insurance becomes less a separate decision and more a portion of a much greater and more complex change.

Automobile insurance (assigned risk) plans

As a corollary to either the basic financial responsibility law or the compulsory automobile liability insurance law, the *automobile insurance plans* (formerly called *assigned risk* plans) have been developed to meet the problem of rejected risks. Today, these plans assure almost all persons in about 42 states that insurance is available. Every state has felt the necessity of making insurance available to all who are entitled to it. Since private insurers have the right to select risks, an applicant may sometimes have difficulty in securing adequate insurance. Provision has been made under the automobile insurance plans for sharing this "residual market" of higher-risk drivers by equitably distributing individually rejected risks among all insurers.

The plans are not the same in all states, but they work similarly. Generally, if motorists have been refused insurance by one or more private insurers, they may apply to the manager of the assigned risk plan. If the applicant is found to be eligible for insurance according to the standards of the plan, the manager of the plan assigns the risk to an insurer. Assigned risks are rotated among the different insurers in proportion to the business that each insurer writes in the state. All insurers are obligated to accept risks as assigned with a few exceptions: applicants engaged in gambling, dealing in narcotics, or other illegal enterprises, and habitual violators of the law.[19] Insureds covered as assigned risks include not only persons with poor accident records, but also the hard-to-underwrite classes of drivers such as very old, inexperienced, or very young drivers in some areas.[20] Typically, only about 3 percent of all

---

[19] A decision of the U.S. Supreme Court held in 1951 that an insurer must assume its share of assigned risks. The constitutionality of the California law was questioned, and the decision was that the police power of the state "extends to all the great public needs," including the compensation of innocent victims of highway accidents (*California State Automobile Association Inter-Insurance Bureau, Appellant,* v. *John R. Maloney, Insurance Commissioner,* 340 U.S. 105; 71 Sup. Ct. 601, 95 Law Ed. 788).

[20] Only extreme cases of many law violations or accidents result in being refused insurance coverage in the assigned risk plans. Less than 1 or 2 percent of applicants are denied coverage. As classic examples of accident-proneness, a 39-year-old Ohio driver had 50 accidents in a nine-year period (in only two accidents was he found at fault), and two Wisconsin motorists collided with each other twice, at different intersections, within a half-hour period! (*Columbus Dispatch,* February 2, 1981, p. A–6.)

registered vehicles are insured in these plans, but the situation differs greatly by state and year, with several states having percentages of 5–20 percent in the plans.[21] Ninety-two percent of the shared market exposures were concentrated in 10 states.[22]

The policyholders who purchase their insurance protection through the automobile insurance plans usually pay a higher rate than other insureds. A surcharge of 10 percent to as high as 200 percent is often applied, depending on the policyholder's accident record, motor vehicle violations, and other factors. Many of the plans offer higher than basic liability limits and other automobile insurance coverages.

The latest figures available show that the higher charges do not offset the poorer loss experience for those classifications of automobile insureds. Underwriting losses have exceeded premiums by $4 billion during 1973–81 and exceeded $1 billion in 1981.[23] In order to operate successfully in the future, the automobile insurance plans must be helped by rate increases and by better driver-licensing procedures in all the states. Reexamination of all drivers every few years has been recommended by a National Traffic and Motor Vehicle Safety Act which has become effective in several states.

Other "residual market" mechanisms

In addition to the automobile insurance plans just discussed, several states have attempted to solve the "residual market" problem by using other methods to pool the loss experience of high-risk drivers. Nine states passed laws of three different types in the years 1973–81.

Four of the laws set up *reinsurance facilities*. Effective in Massachusetts, North and South Carolina, and New Hampshire, these mechanisms require insurers to accept all applicants for automobile insurance if they have valid driver's licenses. Then the insurer may decide to cede (reinsure) some of the highest risks to the reinsurance facility of its state, which operates a combined pool for all reinsured risks. Losses and expenses of the facility are shared among all insurers in proportion to the total automobile insurance they write in the state. Canada has used a reinsurance facility for more than 10 years.

Four states established *joint underwriting associations*, which differ from the reinsurance facilities in that they identify a small number (about 8–14) of insurers as "servicing carriers" which issue contracts,

---

[21] *Automobile Insurance Plans Service Office Insurance Facts* (New York: AIPSO, 1980).

[22] Jim Marks, "Auto Insurance—The Shared Market," *Journal of Insurance*, July/August 1982, p. 34.

[23] "Residual Market Losses Top Billion Mark," *Journal of American Insurance*, Fall 1981, p. 24.

collect premiums, and pay claims on behalf of the JUA. The JUA is proportionally owned and operated by all the insurers doing business in the state. Each agent or broker is assigned a servicing carrier in order to provide all agents and brokers with access to a market in which to place the higher risk. Florida, Missouri, Michigan and Hawaii each has a JUA which establishes rates and commission for high risks within the state. One difference is that Hawaii mandates that welfare recipients are entitled to free automobile insurance (up to the statutory minimum limits). New Jersey is also establishing a JUA plan this year.

One state, Maryland, chose to insure canceled or rejected drivers in an automobile insurance *state fund*. The state-run company guarantees the availability of 100/300/100 liability and physical damage limits and other coverages written through all the regular agents and brokers in the state. Claims are handled by the fund's own personnel. Deficits have been so large that now the private insurers are assessed proportionally, which in effect causes the voluntary market insureds to subsidize the annual residual market deficits.

Although the three different residual (involuntary) market mechanisms were intended as improvements on the automobile insurance plans (AIPs), research does not seem to show much progress, nor to permit definitive conclusions as to which system is more costly.[24] Thus many crucial questions remain unanswered. It would seem, however, that the alternative systems' lack of positive benefits (and the fact that only Michigan's 1981 plan was adopted during the past eight years) leaves most of the states with the AIPs as the major solution to the perplexing problems of the residual markets.[25]

Unsatisfied judgment funds

In addition to the residual market availability of insurance and other problems, another area of concern is the innocent unpaid victims of automobile accidents. How should they be paid for losses caused by others who cannot be identified, are uninsured, or are otherwise unable to pay for their mistakes?

Five states have adopted legislation which provides the innocent victim of an automobile accident with a source of payment for losses caused by a financially irresponsible motorist. A separate *unsatisfied judgment fund* (UJF) is established with the purpose of paying bodily injury losses,

---

[24] J. Finley Lee, *Servicing the Shared Automobile Insurance Market* (New York: National Industry Committee on Automobile Insurance Plans, August 1977).

[25] For two opposing views on the residual market plans, see Charles A. Barker, "Do Effective Involuntary Automobile Mechanisms Exist Today?" and Richard J. Decker, "Servicing the Shared Automobile Insurance Market," *CPCU Journal* 33, no. 2 (June 1980, p. 43) and vol. 33, no. 4 (December 1980, p. 131), respectively.

and in addition (in three states) property damage losses: (1) if the victim proves liability by obtaining a judgment against another party who was negligent in causing the accident and (2) if the victim shows that the judgment cannot be recovered, that is, remains unsatisfied.

The states which have established this type of fund are North Dakota (1947), New Jersey (1952), Maryland (1957), New York (1958), and Michigan (1965). Nine provinces in Canada have such plans, too, the earliest having been established in 1945. New York's plan set up a Motor Vehicle Accident Indemnification Corporation, which differs by using a nonprofit corporation (rather than a state fund) administered by the insurers to pay claims.

Maximum amounts of coverage apply: usually the basic limits of 10/ 20/5, with a deductible of $100–$200 for property damage.[26] Negligent motorists are not relieved of liability for the damages or injuries they have caused; their driving privileges are revoked until the UJF has been reimbursed for the amount paid to the innocent victim.

The basic financing of these funds is by a levy, usually assessed against the *uninsured* motorists of the state. However, two states also charge insured motorists a fee at the time of registration. Several states charge the *insurers* writing automobile business about one half of 1 percent of their net premiums. The fee charged the uninsured motorist has risen sharply in recent years. This fee is for the right *not* to purchase automobile liability insurance and it does not provide any liability protection for the uninsured motorist.

An evaluation of the merits and disadvantages of unsatisfied judgment funds refers to the following benefits: (1) providing some recourse to innocent victims; (2) keeping more irresponsible motorists off the road; (3) a small reimbursement of the funds, about 5 percent, by the uninsured motorists; and to the following faults: (1) the financial inequity of the costs being paid by insured motorists; (2) the fund deficits that have resulted from inadequate levies; and (3) the complicated, expensive, and cumbersome procedures used by the funds.[27]

With compulsory and no-fault automobile insurance plans, the need in many states for unsatisfied judgment funds has diminished. Some states have added a private insurer plan for pooling these risks, but most rely now on the widespread availability of uninsured motorists coverage, discussed next.

---

[26] G. Victor Hallman, *Unsatisfied Judgment Funds* (Homewood, Ill.: Richard D. Irwin, 1968), pp. 127–34.

[27] Sajjad A. Hashmi, "Unsatisfied Judgment Funds," *Journal of Risk and Insurance* 31, no. 1 (March 1964), p. 93. See also "The Problem of the Uninsured Motorist: A Proposed Solution," *Journal of Risk and Insurance* 24, no. 3 (September 1967), p. 363.

Uninsured motorists coverage

The typical method today of providing payment to victims of automobile accidents caused by financially irresponsible motorists is *uninsured motorists coverage* (UMC). For a small cost, usually about $10–$20 a year, insured motorists may include this coverage *in their own* automobile insurance contracts. It is basically protection for the entire *family* (and relatives in the household), as car occupants or pedestrians, against losses caused by uninsured motorists. Loss payments include medical payments and loss of income. Other persons riding in the insured auto are covered, and the coverage extends to other cars driven by an insured. UMC also covers hit-and-run cases, whose victims usually cannot collect their damages because they have no one to ask for payment.

The standard form of this coverage is treated in further detail in the later discussion of the personal auto policy in Chapter 20. Different contracts may have somewhat different wording, so the insured should read the endorsement to determine the extent of protection.

The state laws are also important, as all states now require that uninsured motorists coverage be offered in automobile insurance contracts. In many states the insured may refuse in writing to have the coverage included. Many states make the coverage mandatory, and it must be included in all policies written for automobiles in those states. Details of the coverage vary considerably in some states. Most states require 10/20 limits, and higher limits must be made available. Property damage coverage is included in only a few states. Newer contracts may also include *underinsured* motorist coverage.

Uninsured motorists coverage accomplishes the objective of payment to innocent victims without a separate system such as the UJF. It is not necessary that the victim secure a judgment against the wrongdoer; however, the victim must show that the negligent party had no liability insurance. Delays and administrative costs are reduced by having the insurer pay the insured for injuries for which the uninsured motorist is liable. In many states an arbitration process is used when this is necessary in order to arrive at a fair payment figure.

Evaluation of UMC shows that it is a valuable and relatively simple solution to many of the problems of unpaid automobile accident victims. Criticism of UMC points out that it would be more equitable to have the uninsured (rather than the insured) motorist pay the costs. It is also sometimes difficult for an insurer to decide that an uninsured motorist is liable in an accident, because then the insurer must pay the insured under the UMC coverage. The potential conflict of interest is troublesome.

An interesting expansion of UMC in most states includes within the definition of an "uninsured automobile" a motor vehicle for which liability insurance is in effect at the time of an accident but is uncollectible because of the *insolvency of the insurer*. Government investigations have stressed the number of automobile insurer insolvencies in recent years. Actually these have been relatively few in number, and they have usually involved high-risk, substandard specialty insurers. It is appropriate, however, for the consumer of automobile insurance to have this additional protection within the UMC coverage.

Automobile no-fault insurance plans

One of the major problems with a new word or phrase is that great misunderstandings result because so many meanings become attached to it during its formative stage. Thus, there are many different interpretations of no-fault *automobile insurance* at its current stage of development.

The meaning of no-fault. The "fundamental basis for a no-fault system is the *abolishment of tort liability* in automobile accidents, with drivers or owners accepting responsibility for *some or all* losses sustained by pedestrians and by occupants of their own vehicles in return for immunity from liability for those losses."[28] The need for establishing fault[29] before loss payments are made is largely eliminated by such plans, and the insured motorist at least in most cases, has the right to collect directly from his or her *own insurer*. Thus, *no-fault* insurance is primarily *first-party* (the insured), rather than third-party (other persons) coverage. Tort liability actions are either eliminated or, more usually, restricted to the more serious losses. (See Chapter 16 for discussion of torts and negligence.)

The distinction between "true" no-fault plans, "modified" no-fault plans, and "pseudo" no-fault plans is important. *True* no-fault plans abolish all liability claims. Sixteen states have no-fault plans of the *modified* type, with tort liability suits only permitted in cases of serious injuries. Eight states have adopted *pseudo* no-fault laws, which involve *no* restriction on liability lawsuits, even though they do expand medical expense and income loss payments to the first-party injured insureds. Sometimes these are called "add-on" plans, because they are additional coverages included in the insured's policy.

Public awareness of the no-fault concept has increased considerably in recent years, but much confusion still exists. Before any decision is made for or against no-fault, then, it is necessary to ask: *"What* no-

---

[28] Willis P. Rokes, *No-Fault Insurance* (Santa Monica: Merritt, 1972), p. 3.

[29] The term *liability-without-fault,* used with workers' compensation laws where compensation is the *exclusive* remedy, is not technically correct. Most auto no-fault plans are really *payment-without-fault* to the injured person, but other remedies may still be available. Thus the plans are more properly looked upon as *automobile accident insurance* rather than as a complete departure from the concepts of fault and liability.

fault plan or law?" Succeeding sections discuss the many proposals, experimental plans, and state laws which must be distinguished.

Legislative action needed. The place of legislation in the picture is prominent. In each of the previously discussed "solutions" to the problem of the unpaid auto accident victim, some legislative action by the states was required—a financial responsibility law, a compulsory automobile liability insurance law, an assigned risk plan setting up a placement facility for poorer risks or an unsatisfied judgment law. Even in the relatively successful uninsured motorists coverage the most rapid use has occurred in states that have legislated the coverage into existing contracts—either on a required or an optional basis.

Most of the no-fault plans also rely heavily upon legislative approval and changes. For this reason, fortunately, the revolutionary aspects of the suggested reforms have been slowed. However, when the reforms do obtain legislative sanction, the situation can undergo broad and rapid change.

The ultimate solution, however, is far from settled yet. About one third of the *states* have passed laws which deserve to be called no-fault according to the concepts discussed previously. However, these laws vary considerably in scope and detail. In addition, a *federal no-fault law* that would set minimum standards for the states has been debated. It is very difficult to predict whether a federal no-fault law will be passed, but there is little question that the possibility provides an impetus for state no-fault laws.

A brief review of early no-fault plans will provide a better perspective for discussion of the no-fault laws that have been adopted in the states.

No-fault plans before 1970. The basic concepts of no-fault automobile insurance plans have been recommended in plans dating back several decades or more. One of the first, the *Columbia plan,* advocated a "true" no-fault plan in 1932, in which no-fault compensation benefits would replace liability payments as the only payment to injured parties. Two other no-fault plans were recommended in the 1950s, one a "full-aid" voluntary plan of scheduled benefits and the other a compulsory plan that was based on actual individual economic loss (not including pain and suffering).[30] Since 1946 the *Saskatchewan plan* in Canada has required compulsory automobile accident insurance, in quite limited amounts, regardless of fault. Most medical expenses are covered by government health insurance and tort actions against negligent parties are permitted for larger claims, so only part of injury losses is covered by

---

[30] *Report by the Committee to Study Compensation for Automobile Accidents* (Columbia University: Council for Research in the Social Sciences, 1932; Albert A. Ehrenzweig, *"Full Aid" Insurance for the Traffic Victim* (Los Angeles: University of California Press, 1954); and Leon Green, *Traffic Victims: Tort Law and Insurance* (Chicago: Northwestern University Press, 1958).

the no-fault provisions. An experimental *family compensation plan* was introduced by the Nationwide Companies in the 1950s, in which their policyholders had the option of purchasing limited alternative compensation benefits for all injured persons in an automobile accident. The coverage was discontinued in 1967 after studies showed that it did not discourage many claimants from filing tort claims. A different proposed plan of this era was the *Conard plan,* which was not adopted by any state, but would have integrated social security disability income payments and Medicare-Medicaid medical expense payments by deducting such payments from tort liability claims.

A pronounced impetus for bringing no-fault plans to the attention of the states was provided in 1965. The *Keeton-O'Connell plan,* proposed by two law school professors, was a modified no-fault plan called "basic protection insurance."[31] The plan sought to do away with most automobile tort liability lawsuits by having insureds paid by *their own insurers* for most out-of-pocket medical expenses and income losses (up to $10,000 per person). It permitted regular tort claims only for pain-and-suffering losses exceeding $5,000. The advantages were alleged to include less fraud, more equitable distribution of losses, reduced court congestion and delays, faster loss payments, and reduced automobile insurance costs. In the late 1960s numerous critics evaluated these benefits as unlikely and claimed that the plan also possessed other disadvantages, such as encouraging indifference to safety, doubtful constitutionality, and rating problems (with better risks paying more and worse risks less).[32] Nevertheless, the industry and public discussion resulted in several additional steps toward other automobile no-fault insurance plans.

Competing insurer organizations advocated voluntary approaches during the late 1960s. An experimental *guaranteed benefits plan* put forward by the American Mutual Alliance was tried in several states. This plan offered automobile accident victims a choice of taking advance payments for some medical expenses and lost income, or suing under normal tort liability law. The American Insurance Association proposed a system in which the insured's own insurer provided *complete personal protection* for automobile accident injury payments. It abandoned the fault concept completely for economic (medical expenses and wage) losses.

Two plans were legislated outside the mainland United States in these

---

[31] Robert E. Keeton and Jeffrey O'Connell, *Basic Protection for the Traffic Victim—A Blueprint for Reforming Automobile Insurance* (Boston: Little, Brown, 1965). See also, by the same authors, *After Cars Crash—The Need for Legal and Insurance Reform* (Homewood, Ill.: Dow Jones-Irwin, 1967); and Jeffrey O'Connell, *The Injury Industry* (New York: Commerce Clearing House, 1971).

[32] An Illinois no-fault law was declared unconstitutional in 1972 on the basis that a medical expense threshold discriminated against low-income citizens. However, in many other states including Michigan in 1978 and Florida in 1982, the courts have upheld the constitutionality of no-fault laws.

crucial years of change. In Puerto Rico a *social protection plan* became effective in 1969. It pays unlimited medical benefits, death benefits up to $10,000, disability income of 50 percent of salary (for two years, with low weekly maximums), and other scheduled dismemberment and funeral benefits. The negligent party is relieved of liability up to about $10,000, with workers' compensation and other private insurance, other than life insurance, decreasing the benefit payments. The government administers the plan, which is financed by an annual tax on each motor vehicle. North of the border, most of the Canadian provinces adopted a *Canadian plan* in 1969. Private insurers pay injuries on an optional no-fault basis up to $5,000. Poorer risks are reinsured in a reinsurance facility that reduces the alleged social stigma of being placed in an assigned risk or automobile insurance plan, as in most states in the United States. Evaluation of this plan indicates that it has not been very successful, with continual problems of underwriting losses.[33]

State no-fault laws, 1970–1983. With this background of many different proposals and limited legislation for automobile no-fault insurance, the decade of the 1970s began an era of legislative action in which various U.S. states passed no-fault laws. Although the debate regarding the pros and cons continues in many state legislatures, (see next section), modified no-fault laws are here in 16, or one third, of the states.[34] These plans are "modified" rather than "true" no-fault laws because liability suits are still permitted if medical costs go above a certain level, or "threshold," usually $1,000 or less. Michigan's law is closest to a true no-fault plan for it does not use a threshold figure, and it severely restricts accident victims' lawsuits to those involving deaths or very serious injuries. Eight states add on medical expense and disability income no-fault coverage, without any restriction on tort liability claims, in a *pseudo* no-fault law.[35] These "add-on" laws require or provide optional no-fault benefits such as described in the next paragraph, but they do not limit liability suits for pain and suffering.

Massachusetts was the first state to enact a no-fault law in 1970, and by 1975 16 states had legislated no-fault benefits.[36] Since then, Nevada repealed its law in 1979, and the District of Columbia in 1982 adopted the only new no-fault law passed during the past seven years. The state laws vary considerably, and comparative analysis becomes quite complex.

---

[33] Lee, *Servicing the Shared Automobile Insurance Market,* p. 66.

[34] Including the District of Columbia.

[35] Arkansas, Delaware, Maryland, Oregon, South Carolina, South Dakota, Texas, and Virginia.

[36] Colorado, Connecticut, Florida, Georgia, Hawaii, Kansas, Massachusetts, Michigan, Minnesota, Nevada (since repealed), New Jersey, New York, North Dakota, Pennsylvania, Utah, and Kentucky. See *Analysis of Automobile No-Fault Statutes* (New York: General Adjustment Bureau, February 1977).

For example, the *no-fault benefits* for medical expenses are limited to a figure such as $2,000 to $25,000 in most of these states, while in three states such expenses are unlimited except by a requirement that the expenses be reasonable. Loss-of-income payment is restricted in many states by definite weekly, monthly, or total maximums, and often by duration maximums (one year, etc.) Some states combine medical and income losses and set one maximum for a combination of both, such as $5,000–$50,000. In many of the state laws other limits apply in various combinations for funeral expenses, substitute household service for the injured person, lost income with maximums in terms of weekly or monthly dollar amounts and/or percentages (60–85 percent), and death and survivors' benefits.

The important restrictions on *tort liability* lawsuits also vary considerably. The threshold of medical expenses above which tort claims are permitted is unreasonably low, such as $200 or $500, in about half of these states. This means that the number of liability claims is not substantially reduced. However, the trend in recent years has been toward a new method of setting the limits for tort action. More of the no-fault laws are restricting the circumstances under which plaintiffs can sue for pain and suffering, anguish, or other "general damages" to serious injuries or deaths. The law, for example, may verbally describe and specify permanent loss of body members or functions, or permanent scarring and disfigurement, or 60 days or more of disability, as the only permitted basis for lawsuits involving noneconomic losses. Thus far, these *verbal thresholds* seem to be an improvement, although it must be remembered the citizens of the states that use verbal definitions are giving up important liability rights to sue for such damages.

Vehicle damage liability does not come under the no-fault laws, so the tort system still applies. One exception is Michigan, where tort liability for damage over $400 to another person's vehicle is abolished. Research indicates that no-fault plans should not include property damage claims because the long delays and expensive attorney costs which characterize personal injury lawsuits are not present.[37]

Space does not permit an individual analysis of all the no-fault state laws. However, the relative success of the Michigan law suggests a more detailed description of this law to be advisable. In many ways this law is the broadest of the 16 no-fault laws. Every owner of a motor vehicle[38] must maintain 20/40/10 liability limits. Tort liability is abolished for

---

[37] Robert I. Mehr and Gary W. Eldred, "Should the No-Fault Concept Be Applied to Automobile Property Damage?" *Journal of Risk and Insurance* 42, no. 1 (March 1975), p. 17.

[38] Designed for public highway use, if it has more than two wheels. Under most of the state no-fault laws, private passenger cars are the only vehicles included, with commercial cars, all trucks, and motorcycles not subject to the laws.

(1) damages of more than $400 to covered motor vehicles except for intentional harm caused to persons or property; (2) noneconomic losses for pain and suffering, "unless the injuries result in death, serious impairment of body function, or permanent serious disfigurement"; and (3) damages for expenses, work loss, and survivors' loss in excess of the maximum limits of the law. No dollar amount threshold for medical expenses applies; instead the threshold is a "verbal" one as quoted above. Benefits for personal injuries, payable on a no-fault basis, include unlimited medical expenses (except hospital room charges must be equal to semi-private rates) and rehabilitation, funeral expenses up to $1,000, work loss of income (and substitute services of $20 per day) for three years up to $1,475 per month (plus annual cost-of-living increases). The benefits are reduced by the amounts payable under workers' compensation and social security. Property protection of up to $1 million damage to tangible property other than vehicles or their contents is included, with an optional $300 deductible. (Properly parked cars are covered as an exception to this property protection part of the law.) Subrogation rights by insurers for collision losses are eliminated. The law also requires insurers in Michigan to offer their policyholders the option of designating their health or accident insurance as primary coverage before the automobile coverage applies for medical expenses.[39]

Evaluation of the results of state no-fault laws.   No simple conclusion has yet emerged as to whether the state no-fault laws have been really successful. The effects of the laws on the total costs of automobile liability insurance have been studied in some states, with savings as compared with tort liability calculated as considerable in Massachusetts (about 50 percent) but as much smaller in Florida (about 25 percent).[40] Critics question these and other studies as being too limited, not current, and not including the increased costs of motor vehicle physical damage costs and other add-on costs of motor medical expense and disability income coverages. Other comparisons of how much rates have increased in the 16 no-fault states as compared with the other states indicate no significant total difference.[41] The savings on fewer liability claims and

---

[39] Pennsylvania does this, too. Considerable debate has arisen as to whether health insurance should be primary coverage, or whether costs are reduced more by having auto insurance as primary (as in New York and New Jersey). See also B. P. Russell, "The Issue of Primacy: Who Serves Best?" *Journal of Insurance,* January–February 1973, p. 2.

[40] Calvin H. Brainard, "Massachusetts: Loss Experience under No-Fault in 1971—Analysis and Implications"; and Calvin H. Brainard and John Fitzgerald, "First-Year Cost Results under No-Fault Automobile Insurance: A Comparison of the Florida and Massachusetts Experience," *Journal of Risk and Insurance* 40, no. 1 (March 1973), and vol. 41, no. 1 (March 1974), p. 95 and p. 29, respectively. See also Jerry D. Todd, "The Costing of Automobile No-Fault Insurance," *Journal of Risk and Insurance* 43, no. 3 (September 1976), p. 431.

[41] State Farm Insurance Company studies, in 1975 and 1981.

on reduced costs in settling directly with the insured for injuries often appear to be largely offset by payments to insureds who would not collect under tort liability.

Advocates of the no-fault laws emphasize other benefits besides costs. They claim that the purpose of no-fault laws is to pay more of the insurance premium dollar to automobile accident victims and to do so quicker and more equitably. Research shows (1) that less than half of claimants are able to recover benefits under the liability system (which excludes the negligent victims, one-car crashes, and combined or undetermined fault cases), (2) that serious injuries are compensated for only 30 percent of their losses while minor injuries are overpaid, and (3) that the average time to final settlement is 16 months after an accident.[42] Although the overall effectiveness of no-fault laws has not been established, some studies show that the portion of the premium dollar received by victims for economic losses has increased in certain no-fault states, such as Michigan and Florida.[43] It has also been found that the frequency of bodily injury liability claims has been cut substantially in some no-fault states.[44]

Opponents of no-fault legislation include some insurers, trial lawyers and their professional associations, and others. Such opponents vigorously deny that no-fault can reduce automobile costs and argue that legislation should not take away an individual's right to sue for pain and suffering. The effect of no-fault laws on personal responsibility for negligence, with possible increased carelessness as a result, is pointed out as a major defect. One of the greatest difficulties under no-fault is in changing rating systems which may inequitably allocate higher costs to persons involved in accidents who are in no way responsible for them. Injured persons may suffer serious losses, be only partially compensated under the no-fault system, and then have their rates increased. At the same time, the negligent parties may merely say "We're sorry" and have no losses or rate increases. Departing from the traditional legal concept that the person at fault in automobile cases should pay is repugnant to many persons, whether or not their livelihood depends on the tort liability system. Although there is legal precedent for such change in the U.S. workers' compensation system, treating automobile accidents as a social rather than an individual responsibility is not the same as holding employers liable without fault.

Interrelated issues. In summary, the jury is still out in deciding

---

[42] U.S. Department of Transportation, *Economic Consequences of Automobile Accident Injuries* (Washington, D.C.: U.S. Government Printing Office, 1970), vol. 1.

[43] *No-Fault Press Reference Manual* (Bloomington, Ill.: State Farm Insurance Companies, 1973 and continuously updated). This reference also refutes the idea that no-fault laws have caused heavy insurer losses in no-fault states, claiming that inflation and premium reductions have been the major causes of these losses. See also *Survey of 16 No-Fault States* (Washington, D.C.: U.S. Government Printing Office, 1977).

[44] Michigan and Colorado, in a 1978 actuarial study sponsored by the U.S. Senate Commerce Committee.

if no-fault laws are advisable. There is a shifting from the idea of having fault determine liability to the idea of no-fault compensation when someone is injured. However, all but one of the no-fault laws in the United States were passed before 1975, and progress in recent years has been minimal. *Whether or not the laws should* change in this way is not fully researched, documented, or supported by the public, the insurers, the legal profession, or other parties involved in the changes.[45] Just *how* the laws should change is also debatable in many respects.

The complexity of the issues is not limited to the no-fault concept, as many other related issues are involved. One author points out that the automobile reforms are really three clashes of principles between (1) *public* and *private* insurance, (2) *federal* and *state* regulation, and (3) *fault* and *no-fault* systems. He concludes that in the long range the key issue still in doubt is the first, whether government-operated or privately operated systems will prevail.[46]

It is more difficult to think of *un*related issues than it is to name problem areas which are related to the automobile and its insurance. (Pollution? Gas shortages? Discrimination? Safety? Product liability? Fraud?) *Cost inflation* in medical costs, jury awards, and automobile repair costs is also a major part of the problem in automobile insurance. When one considers that liability law has been applied to the automobile situation for 60 years or more, a few years' wait for a solution does not seem too long if better solutions can be formulated during that time. The problems are so serious, and so many alternatives have been considered, suggested, or partially adopted, that time appears to be one of the important ingredients required for the development of the successful answer.

The need for time is stressed by those who advocate *tort liability reform* in order to improve the existing liability systems. Reforms that will alleviate the undesirable aspects make good sense—*if* they can be achieved with reasonable rapidity by such things as better rating laws, fewer underwriting restrictions, advance claims payments, noncancellation guarantees, rehabilitation, more complete uninsured motorists coverage, and insurer insolvency protection. Many of these improvements will be needed regardless of state-by-state adoption of limited no-fault laws.

The relationship of automobile liability reforms to *all* areas of liability law is stressed in one recent report about the tort system.[47] This summary

[45] For research on no-fault systems in seven European countries (France, Great Britain, Germany, Italy, Netherlands, Sweden, and Switzerland), see Werner Pfennigstorf, *Compensation of Auto Accident Victims in Europe* (Chicago: American Mutual Insurance Alliance, 1972), which is also reported on by Everett T. Bartelbaugh, Jr., in the *CPCU Annals* 26, no. 2 (June 1973), p. 36, with the conclusion that the systems seem to be working well.

[46] Robert E. Keeton, "Beyond Current Reforms in Automobile Reparations," *Journal of Risk and Insurance* 40, no. 1 (March 1973), p. 31.

[47] "Righting the Liability Balance" (California Citizen's Commission on Tort Reform, Fall 1977), *Journal of Insurance,* January–February 1978.

is critical of the tendency in recent years to make most changes through the courts rather than through legislative action. Six recommendations are made that would affect the general applicability of the tort system to liability law: (1) the need for a conscious policy of statutory guidance; (2) the use of arbitration[48] for small cases, and on a compulsory basis for claims under $10,000; (3) the improvement of the legal process to eliminate unmeritorious cases and to hasten trials; (4) the tightning of key rules of law, such as by defining the "foreseeability" of injuries and by codifying comparative negligence laws; (5) the assurance of reasonable costs of legal counsel by limiting contingency fees to plaintiffs' attorneys, with smaller percentages for larger awards; and (6) the reformation of the court systems through careful study by state planning commissions. The report concludes that no-fault statutes must be prepared for, but adopted only if close monitoring of the experience of the best existing systems justifies their enactment. Recommendations for needed reforms in product, professional, and government liability and in workers' compensation systems are also included.

Another crucial solution: Automobile safety and loss prevention

One final solution to the automobile insurance problem(s) needs emphasis. *Traffic safety, or loss prevention* in regard to automobile accidents, should be a major objective of our society. Few of the insurance solutions discussed in this chapter include accident prevention among their goals. Nevertheless, these solutions must be evaluated in terms of their effect upon automobile accidents. For example, although insurance is blamed for rising automobile costs, how can it solve such a problem as the approximately 25,000 traffic deaths (about half of all traffic deaths) caused each year in the United States by the use of alcohol? Insurer support for tougher and mandatory penalties for driving while intoxicated (DWI) convictions, which one half of the states now have, is recommended.[49]

Efforts are being made to coordinate the safety work of insurers, government, and independent researchers, such as those in universities. The Insurance Institute for Highway Safety promotes research studies and traffic safety conferences. On the government level, the National Highway Traffic Safety Administration formulates safety regulations for states and automobile manufacturers, for crashworthy bumpers, seat belt systems, air bags, and other safety designs and equipment. The bureau also lists as the top-priority areas: (1) driver licensing, (2) traffic records, (3) alcohol, (4) emergency medical services, (5) motor vehicle

---

[48] Which is also strongly recommended by Warren E. Burger, "Litigation: Is It Out of Control?" *Journal of Insurance,* May–June 1982, p. 2.

[49] "The Anti-Drunk Driving Campaign: Can It Succeed?" State Farm Insurance Companies, July 30, 1982.

registration, (6) police traffic services, and (7) accident location and cause research.[50] The difficulties of applying safety standards are also noted: only 27 states now require periodic safety inspections of automobiles, after 8 states dropped such programs because of high costs and problems of enforcement; and NHTSA standards for crashes without damage were *lowered* in 1982 to 2.5 miles per hour.

It is also sad to note that cooperation by the public in auto accident prevention is woefully lacking. Although safety belts have been required for more than 10 years on all passenger vehicles manufactured in the United States, studies show that only 1 out of 10 drivers use them![51] Similar less-than-satisfactory results could be noted in the public's cooperation in complying with the national 55-miles-per-hour speed limit, which is also a proven means of saving lives on the highways of America.

To have the prettiest automobile rather than the safest one seems to be losing favor among automobile buyers, although beauty, style, and chrome are admittedly still much pleasanter to talk about than safety restraints, padded dashes, collapsible steering columns, double-lock doors, brake systems, and the hundreds of other features which determine the safety of an automobile. With more support from an educated and concerned public, progress in automobile and traffic safety should improve. One example is the research work being done to develop research safety vehicles (RSVs) that will produce safe, fuel-efficient, and reasonably priced automobiles for the future.[52]

One hopes that the solutions are less drastic than the bill passed by the California Senate (it did not become a law) to outlaw all gasoline-powered automobiles. Although this was proposed as an antipollution bill, it might also serve to shock some complacent persons into action leading to real solutions for automobile insurance! Another extreme example of how much further loss-prevention efforts can go is the recent sentencing of a Moscow drunken driver to execution by a firing squad.[53] This deterrent to bad driving habits illustrates how mild current U.S. punishments of traffic safety violators are.

The active role of insurers, as well as government and the public, in every field affecting automobile insurance will be needed in the future

---

[50] Examples of such research are: *Societal Costs of Motor Vehicle Accidents* (Washington, D.C.: U.S. Department of Transportation, National Highway Traffic Safety Administration, December 1976); and *Analysis and Summary of Accident Investigations, 1973–76* (Washington, D.C.: U.S. Department of Transportation, Federal Highway Administration, 1977).

[51] "Why Hardly Anybody Buckles Up," *Changing Times*, October 1982, p. 82. Automatic seat belts or air bags, required by late 1983, should help improve this situation.

[52] "The Socially Responsible Car," *Journal of American Insurance*, Summer 1977, p. 23.

[53] Reported in the *Columbus* (Ohio) *Citizens-Journal* on January 21, 1978, for truck driver Valentin Shimko, who killed seven and injured eight persons at a subway-trolley-bus stop.

in order to make progress in the crucial area of automobile loss prevention.

FOR REVIEW AND DISCUSSION

1. Why is automobile insurance needed? Whose viewpoints are pertinent, and how do those viewpoints differ?
2. Automobile liability insurance is unquestionably one of the great dilemmas of insurance today. It is a complex group of interrelated problems.
   a. What do you identify as *three* of the major problems?
   b. In your judgment, why has each of these problems arisen?
   c. What is being done about each of these problems by (1) the insurers and (2) the government?
   d. Show how the problems you have chosen are interrelated.
3. Is the increasing cost of automobile insurance due primarily to the *loss,* the *expense,* or the *profit* portion of insurance premiums? Explain why you did or did not choose each of these premium segments.
4. What factors have caused the rising costs of automobile bodily injury liability insurance? Automobile physical damage insurance?
5. How is state insurance regulation related to the problem of rising automobile insurance prices?
6. What approaches are used to regulate automobile insurance rates? Which approach is most widely used, and which is most effective?
7. Bob Beane says that automobile accident deaths are outrageous, and he doesn't "see why the bad drivers should be allowed to purchase automobile insurance." Rosa Beane disagrees, saying that "bad drivers are just the ones who most need the insurance and for the injured victims' sake should be required to have insurance." With whom do you agree and why?
8. Which of the "automobile insurance solutions" are based upon *government* action? Which on *voluntary* action by insurers or insureds? Explain.
9. What are automobile (assigned risk) insurance plans? Explain their *(a)* purpose, *(b)* method of operation, and *(c)* success, or lack of it. What other systems have some states adopted to solve the problems of the automobile "residual market"?
10. Discuss *(a)* the merits and *(b)* the faults of the following solutions to the "problem of the unpaid innocent automobile accident victim":
    a. Compulsory automobile liability legislation.
    b. Financial responsibility laws.
    c. Unsatisfied judgment funds.
    d. Uninsured motorists coverage.
    e. Automobile (assigned risk) insurance plans.
    f. No-fault automobile insurance plans.
11. Differentiate among the state laws what you consider to be the *three major* types of legislation that are designed to cope with the problem of the unpaid automobile accident victim.

12. What are the *(a)* advantages and *(b)* disadvantages of uninsured motorists coverage as a solution to the automobile accident victim problem?

13. Divide the class into groups and assign each group one of the automobile no-fault insurance solutions: *true* no-fault, *modified* no-fault, and *pseudo* no-fault laws. Have each group prepare a statement explaining why its solution is the best answer to the automobile dilemma today.

14. Relate automobile safety and loss prevention to the solution you choose as the best one for meeting the automobile insurance problem today.

15. Explain how the *modified* no-fault laws vary from others which have been called *pseudo* or "add-on" laws. How do the individual state laws differ?

16. How may the long-range problems of no-fault automobile insurance vary from the short-range ones?

17. Evaluate the trend and the success of state no-fault laws during the past decade. Explain how other legislation may be needed to change the situation.

Chapter 20

Outline of concepts

Basic coverages for automobile insurance usually include *liability, medical payments, uninsured motorists,* and *physical damages* protection.

Basic policy forms are partially standardized for insuring *personal* (emphasized in this chapter) and *business* auto exposures.

Underwriting is a major task of insurers trying to attain a profit by:

Selection of insureds—restricted today by the *"right to buy"* concept, limited rights to *cancel,* and broader *renewal* guarantees.

Rating, or pricing, for:

Automobile classifications, *private passenger, commercial, public.*

Private passenger auto liability premiums, which have classifications based on the age, sex, and marital status of the *operators;* the *use* of the auto; and *driver training, good student, multicar,* and *safe-driver* rules.

Physical damage premiums, based on *car's age and value,* and *deductibles.*

Basic parts of the personal policy (PAP), illustrating the *readable contract trend,* with *personalized and simplified format,* are:

Declarations, containing basic data about insureds, autos, and coverages, and the **insuring agreement and definitions.**

Part A—Liability is the most important coverage and includes:

Bodily injury and property damage in a *single limit of liability.*

Defense and supplementary payments for *defense, investigation, bonds.*

Covered persons insured are carefully defined.

Policy limits and **other insurance** are explained.

Part B—Medical payments is small in cost but pays *regardless of fault* for insured, family, and other occupants in the insured's car.

Part C—Uninsured motorists protection for the insured, family, and guests—for injuries caused by negligent uninsured motorists.

Part D—Damage to your auto is *physical damage* insurance for:

Collision coverage for damage by hitting other objects, even if the insured's own fault, usually on a $100 or more deductible basis.

Comprehensive (other than collision) coverage for "all risks."

Part E—Duties after an accident or loss—conditions insureds should fulfill so that the insurer will pay.

Part F—General provisions applies to the entire contract, explaining subrogation rights, assignment, and cancellation.

No-fault coverage in some states does away with at least some tort liability, and provides for payment by the insured's *own* insurance company.

The business auto policy (BAP) insures commercial vehicles and is also part of the readable, simplified contract trend.

Automobile insurance coverages

Did you ever wonder what would happen if all of the approximately 150 million motorists in the United States decided to "hit the road" at the same time? You've seen traffic jams—but imagine that one! With almost one car or truck for each motorist, the streets and highways would be filled, but no one could go anywhere. Each motor vehicle is an *individual* problem for its owner or driver, as well as a collective source of the problems of costs, losses, and need for insurance protection discussed in the previous chapter. This chapter explains how individual motorists solve many of their problems through the purchase of adequate *automobile insurance coverages*.

The good news is that, with very few exceptions, motorists can buy automobile insurance today in a form that represents one of the broadest of all insurance contracts, covering many different cars, drivers, and coverages (liability, property, and medical) in one convenient policy. In doing so, motorists transfer almost all of their risks to the insurers. The bad news is that some problems remain.

Several of the problems of automobile insurance were discussed in the previous chapter. The need was seen from the viewpoint of society, the motorists, and the injured victims. Insurers have difficulty because the rating laws in many states do not allow increaser in automobile insurance prices as rapidly as loss costs rise. The insurance solutions are compounded by the many different and changing state laws pertaining to financial responsibility, compulsory insurance, residual markets, and no-fault plans.

What remains for the insureds to criticize? The *cost* of the contract is probably the basis of most complaints, with generalized comments of "it's too high" or "it's gone up too much" appearing most frequently. *Coverage, availability,* and particularly the *services* that go with the contract are other major sources of grumbling by policyholders. The speed and amount of loss payment, the defense of claims, the advice on coverages and losses, and the cancellation of protection are among the other policyholder complaints related to automobile insurance coverages.

BASIC INSURANCE COVERAGES

Automobile insurance is the largest field of property-liability insurance, accounting for about 40 percent of total premiums. That makes it a $41 billion business today. There are two major divisions of the automobile insurance business. The first provides the *casualty* (mostly *liability*) coverages; and the second, the *physical damage* coverages. The casualty coverages are: *(a)* bodily injury liability, *(b)* property damage liability, *(c)* medical payments, *(d)* uninsured motorists, and, in some states, *(e)* no-fault coverage. In the physical damage category are those forms of automobile insurance that protect the insured from loss or damage to the car itself: *(a)* fire, *(b)* theft, *(c)* collision, and *(d)* a number of miscellaneous coverages such as windstorm, explosion, water damage, riot and civil commotion, and vandalism and malicious mischief. All of the perils mentioned in *(d)* are often combined with fire and theft coverage in what is called "comprehensive physical damage" coverage.

The portions of the total automobile insurance premiums for the major coverages are:[1]

Casualty (liability, medical payments, and uninsured motorists) coverage	60%
Physical damage coverage	40%
	100%

It is logical to discuss the two classes of business together. Although separate contracts were formerly written for liability and physical damages, today almost all of the contracts issued combine both major coverages in a single policy.

BASIC POLICY FORMS

Automobile insurance is not a field in which all contracts are alike. There are some similarities among the most common automobile contracts, and many provisions have been standardized by the voluntary action of insurers who use forms developed by associations of insurers or rating bureaus.[2] However, about 800 insurance companies sell automobile insurance, and the field is known both for price competition and for nonprice competition in the form of contract variations. Some contract differences are significant to the insurance buyer; others are sales "frills" and attention-getting features. Wise automobile owners read their automobile insurance contracts to determine exactly what has been purchased.

---

[1] *Insurance Facts* (New York: Insurance Information Institute, 1982–83), p. 22.

[2] The major ones are the Insurance Services Office and the National Association of Independent Insurers. Although some of the larger insurers have developed their own contracts, with minor differences from the bureau forms, this chapter analyzes the ISO contracts because of their wide use.

Different automobile contracts are used for different exposures to loss. The two general kinds of automobile exposures are those associated with *family* (personal) and *business* (commercial) use. As part of the trend toward more readable and understandable insurance contracts, the Insurance Services Office introduced new automobile insurance contracts in the late 1970s. The result is that most family automobile exposures are now insured under the *personal auto policy* (PAP),[3] and commercial automobiles are insured in a policy called the *business auto policy* (BAP). The analysis of the PAP contract is emphasized in this chapter, because of its widespread use for automobile insurance protection of individuals and families. The BAP contract coverage is summarized in the final section of this chapter.

UNDERWRITING

Basic parts and goals

Automobile insurance underwriting includes the functions of *selection* and *rating*. The purpose is to obtain a group of insureds who will in total provide the insurer with a reasonable profit and maintain its financial strength.

In automobile insurance during recent years this has been a considerable task. The job has been made more difficult in the past decade by factors such as were mentioned in Chapter 19:

1. The increasing costs of automobile accidents, for many underlying reasons such as rising medical and repair costs, income losses resulting from injuries, and jury verdicts.
2. The types of rate regulation applied by some states, which create a time lag between increasing costs and permitted rate increases.
3. Social considerations, in which insurance is required or encouraged by every state, cancellations are more restricted, and applications are harder to deny than ever before.

The underwriting *process* is usually performed through the combined efforts of the insurer, its agents, and some organizations outside the insurance business. Insurers have the main responsibility for the selection and rating of insureds because they are accepting the risk of loss. The initial responsibility, however, often falls on the agents. They are the ones who solicit the prospects for insurance or accept applications.

---

[3] Another new contract, used by many insurers that are members of the National Association of Independent Insurers (NAII), is the *Family Car Policy*. This has been approved in many states, and it has the same purposes of easy-to-read understandability as the PAP policy. Some individual insurers still use contracts designed only for use by their own insureds.

The application is ordinarily a signed *written statement* by the applicant, including basic information about the automobile, its location and use, its drivers, the amounts and types of insurance desired, and the insurance accident and traffic violation records. Oftentimes the agent may bind the coverage immediately, pending the writing of the actual contract at the insurer's home or branch office, or at the agency office. Agents strive to obtain a reasonable group of insureds for their insurers. If they do a poor job of selecting, with many insureds in the less desirable classifications or with high loss results, they may find that the insurer no longer wants them as representatives. Many agents are most interested in writing automobile insurance for persons or families that are (or are prospects for being) insured with their agencies for home, health, or other types of insurance as well as the automobile policy. Oftentimes, the underwriting decisions of the agent are supplemented by *credit investigations* (Equifax or others) and by motor vehicle department reports requested by the insurer. This is a common practice, especially for new applicants, younger drivers, and many other of the more difficult classifications. Insurers must use such information carefully to avoid lawsuits claiming inaccuracies under the Fair Credit Reporting Act.

The underwriting task requires a balancing of objectives. On the one hand, simplicity and economy of applying the rules, classifications, and rates are highly desired. On the other hand, a fair and equitable system, distinguishing by class and rate wherever a sizable difference can be determined accurately, is needed. The compromise is between the two extremes of (1) utmost simplicity (one rate to all) and (2) extreme but costly complexity (overrefinement into too many classifications). In essence, the goal is expressed but not precisely defined in the rating laws of many states as one which requires *fair* discrimination among insureds but prohibits rates that discriminate unfairly.

Selection

A growing public concept, summarized as the "right to buy insurance," has caused great concern to insurers in recent years. In automobile insurance, the idea manifests itself in an attitude that *everyone* ought to be able to buy insurance. Partially, this concept is derived from vague reference to inalienable rights under the Constitution, or rights to protect as well as own property. The growing social nature of automobile insurance (see Chapter 19), with the state requiring or highly encouraging its purchase, has probably been a major factor in the development of this attitude. The concept is contrary to one of the basic ideas of underwriting, that is, that the insurer should be able to *select* the insureds with whom it desires to do business.

How can these concepts be brought together? In practice, the theories must be applied on a less-than-absolute basis. The complete freedom of an insurer to select its insureds is impossible today, as all states have assigned risk plans through which almost all of the substandard, higher rated risks can obtain coverage. The complete right of an individual to buy insurance is tempered by several practical qualifications: except for a very small percentage of motorists (less than 1 percent is estimated, mostly alcohol or drug addicts and habitual traffic offenders), an individual can obtain insurance coverage. In effect, persons who are extremely bad risks may lose their right to have insurance. Other persons may be able to buy it, but will have to pay a premium much higher than the standard cost. They also may not be able to specify the insurer they want or to purchase the broader coverage and limits they desire.

The common practice by which insurers have voluntarily curtailed their *right to cancel* the automobile insurance contract further illustrates the growing restrictions on the selection of insureds. Starting two decades ago, many insurers guaranteed that the policy would not be canceled by the insurer after an investigation period of about 60 days, except for a few stated commonsense reasons. The exceptions included nonpayment of premiums, fraudulent misrepresentation, and/or loss of the driver's license by the insured, and several serious motor vehicle offenses, such as driving while intoxicated, leaving the scene of an accident without reporting, or three moving traffic violations within 18 months. The noncancellation agreement has been broadened by most insurers to permit cancellation only for (1) nonpayment of premiums or (2) suspension or revocation of the driver's license or motor vehicle registration of the insureds who customarily drive the automobile. Almost all state laws also similarly restrict the right of the insurer to cancel today. Reasons for cancellation are to be given the insured in the case of cancellation, and most states specify 10–30 days' notice before cancellation. On new business, most states permit cancellation (without the restrictions) during an underwriting period of about 60 days.[4]

The problem is broader than just noncancellation, however, which only guarantees the insured protection during the policy period (not over one year). Some insurers, including several large independent insurers, have extended the noncancellation provision to include a *five-year renewal* guarantee. A few additional exceptions beyond the two basic ones stated above are specified, such as convictions for a hit-and-run accident, driving while intoxicated or drugged, and motor vehicle homicide.

---

[4] The state laws are far from uniform, however, as many add other permissible reasons for cancellation, such as physical or mental conditions, endangering public safety, fraudulent claims, habitual use of drugs or alcohol, and others. See *Fire, Casualty, and Surety Bulletins* (Cincinnati: National Underwriter Company, Casualty-Surety Section Cra.) for comparisons of the individual states.

The criticism of insurers also extends to *refusal to write* certain classes of insureds, by age, occupation, or other such characteristics. Arbitrary refusal on such bases is now condemned by the major automobile insurance associations and by state laws which restrict the right of the insurer to refuse or to discontinue contracts indiscriminately.

Government needs to make real efforts to remove the irresponsible, unfit, and reckless drivers from the road. Then it is possible to apply the objective that everyone with a valid driver's license should be able to obtain automobile insurance. On behalf of the insurers it may be noted that (1) few, if any, drivers who really *deserve* to be driving are arbitrarily denied automobile insurance coverage; (2) cancellations and nonrenewals are a very small part of the total number of insureds; and (3) improvements in state laws, contract provisions, and insurer practices in automobile underwriting have been significant.

The dilemma of the insurer—and perhaps a reason why everyone should not have the "right to buy" automobile insurance—is shown in the following example from the State Farm Insurance Companies files. A 25-year-old applicant was turned down after admitting to two citations on his motor vehicle record in the past five years. He complained to the Department of Insurance and told it that he was getting a little disgusted with the way the so-called good agencies tried to take advantage of people. However, instead of two citations, he actually had 19, a total of 46 entries on his motor vehicle report, and he had been picked up 11 times for speeding. His car wasn't too hot either—six noisy muffler traffic tickets—and once he didn't even have any license plates for it.

Rating

If nearly all motorists are (or should be) insured, the practical emphasis of underwriting shifts from selection to *rating,* or pricing, of the automobile insurance contract.

Automobile classifications. Automobiles are classed as: (1) private passenger, (2) commercial, (3) public, (4) dealers', and (5) miscellaneous. These classifications are based to some degree upon the type of car and to a greater degree upon the use of the car. The class designations are for the purpose of differentiating among the various major types of automobile risks. The miscellaneous category includes a number of automobiles designed for special purposes, such as fire and police vehicles, ambulances, hearses, auto homes, motorcycles, snowmobiles, motor scooters, tractors (not of the truck type), and trailers or semitrailers. Automotive equipment not insurable under the automobile policy includes golf carts, lawn mowers, and power shovels. Risks of this type are normally insured under separate inland marine or other contracts.

Private passenger vehicles are the example chosen in this chapter for illustrating the classification and rating system of automobile insurance. (See the next several headings of this section.)

Commercial vehicles are classified by the size of the vehicle and the business use classification of the insured. In addition to factors of weight and use, some territories give consideration to a mileage-radius factor. Commercial trucks involving long-distance (more than 50 miles) operations are definitely more hazardous than those confined to a local territory. For rating purposes, *public* automobiles include private and public livery, taxicabs, and buses. Because public automobile rates are high and because there is no risk when the car is not in operation, a system of rating has been devised on an earnings basis per $100 of gross receipts or on a mileage basis. Garage, service station, and other automobile *dealers* are insured under special contracts. When there are five or more commercial or public cars under a single ownership, a "fleet" policy is issued, based upon discounts and the estimated average future exposure. The advance premium charged is adjusted at the end of the policy term by determining the actual number of vehicles and their use during the policy term.

Private passenger automobile liability premiums. As insured in the personal automobile policy, the rating procedure for private passenger automobiles illustrates the process of determining automobile insurance premiums. Different factors are important in calculating the price charged by the insurer for the various basic coverages, as discussed later in this chapter. However, the major portion of the price of automobile insurance applies to the liability and physical damage coverages. The medical payments coverage and the uninsured motorists coverage are relatively small parts of the total premium and therefore are not included in this description of the rating system.

The classification and rating system for private passenger automobile insurance in most states produces 161 classifications, not including differences in territory. This is the plan described in the following paragraphs. About four states use plans which result in 260 classes, and about a half dozen use nine classes.[5]

The *base premium* for bodily injury and property damage *liability* is determined by two factors: the *territory* and the *limits of liability* chosen for the contract. Tables showing the basic premiums for the minimum limits for bodily injury liability coverage and property damage liability coverage are developed for each territory. Higher limits are also available. The new personal auto policy uses tables with a single combined limit for all liability coverages (see later section).

---

[5] Some individual insurers also still use the nine-class system based upon the pre-1965 plan. Youthful male drivers under 25 are all put in one of two classes, married or unmarried, and no separate class for female drivers is used. Business use and driving to work are also factors.

The territorial designation is according to the state and territory in which the automobile is principally garaged and used. Some states have as many as 50 separate rating territories, while others have only a few. The differentiation is based upon both the usual rural-urban differences in exposure to loss and upon the loss experience in the territory for several years. Claims statistics in changing the rates are determined by accidents charged to the location where the car is principally garaged and used. Thus an accident caused by a person from a large city is not charged to a small city where the accident may have occurred. The rates vary considerably by territory. Even within the same state, the rate for the same coverage may be several times as high in one section as in another.

Primary rating factors.   Next, two sets of *classification factors,* primary and secondary, are determined, and the total is applied to the base premium. The *primary classification factors* are:

1.   *Age, sex,* and *marital status* of the automobile operators.
2.   The *use* of the automobile.
3.   *Driver training* and *good student* qualifications.

A growing controversy in recent years concerns the use of age and sex differentials in automobile insurance rating. About 10 states have passed laws which prohibit rate classifications based on age or sex, but several of these laws been repealed. Other states have maintained the system described here. Research indicates that these characteristics are reasonably good predictors of actual loss experience and therefore do not constitute unfair discrimination.[6]

Age of the drivers and owners is an important factor, for many research studies have shown that the younger age groups are the cause of many more accidents, particularly fatal and serious ones, than their proportion of the total number of drivers would indicate. For example, the National Safety Council reports that drivers under age 25 are 22 percent of all drivers but are involved in 37 percent of all accidents. The current system used in most states reflects statistics which show that the youngest drivers are the most likely to have accidents, but that the accident rate goes down gradually from age 18 to age 29.

Older operators are divided into three groups (no youthful drivers):

1.   Females, ages 30–64, only operator.
2.   Age 65 or over, one or more operators.
3.   All others.

---

[6] Ronald W. Spahr and Edmond L. Escolas, "1979 Automobile Accident Reports: Do Driver Characteristics Support Rate Discrimination?" *Journal of Risk and Insurance* 44, no. 1 (March 1982), p. 91.

The youthful operator classifications also reflect the fact that, in general, youthful *male* operators have more accidents[7] than youthful *female* operators and that youthful *unmarried* men have more accidents than youthful *married* men. The classes developed are in four groups, with further breakdowns for age 17 (or under), each age to 20, and combined age classes for ages 21–24 and 25–29. The number of classes developed total more than 100:

4. Females, unmarried, under age 25.
5. Males, married, under age 25.
6. Males, unmarried, under 25, and not owners or principal operators of the insured automobile.
7. Males, unmarried, under age 30, and owners or principal operators.

In approximate terms, the relationship among these groups is illustrated by the range of the factor applied, from less than 1.00 for the first group, 1.00 for the second and third, and a progressively large factor for groups 4–7, with group 7 males age 17 having a factor of more than 3.00 applied.

Operators affect the above classifications if they are residents of the same household as the insured or if they customarily operate the insured automobile. Unmarried females and males under age 25 who are absent from home while attending school over 100 miles away are rated as being married.

The above age-sex-marital factor is combined in tables with the *use* factor, based upon five classes.

1. Pleasure use.
2. Used to or from work less than 15 miles one way (10 miles, in some plans).
3. Used to or from work more than 15 miles one way (10 miles, in some plans).
4. Business use.
5. Farm use.

When the first group is rated as 1.00, the factor applied to groups 2–4 is higher and the factor applied to group 5 is lower.

Driver training is important for youthful drivers from age 17 through age 20. Generally, it saves lives, reduces accidents, *and* lowers insurance rates.[8] The standards for qualified courses are usually set by the state

---

[7] The age-old controversy over which sex drives better is not resolved by this fact alone. Where, when, and how much males and females drive may show otherwise. Let the argument continue, and *vive la différence!*

[8] Some research indicates that driver education courses, which in 28 states lower the minimum driving age, may actually *increase* auto accidents by teenagers. "Driver Education: Part of the Solution or Part of the Problem?" *Journal of American Insurance,* Fall 1981, p. 1.

education departments, often involving about 30 hours of classroom work and 6 hours of driving. Those with driver training receive a lower rating factor, about 5–10 percent less than that of drivers of the same age without driver training. This one factor can make a substantial dollar difference for many youthful drivers.

Good students also receive lower rates from some insurers by meeting certain qualifications (full-time students earning a B average, in the upper 20 percent of class, or on the honor roll or equivalent). The rates average about 20 percent less than those for other students. The theory is that the better students use automobiles less than other students.

Secondary rating factors. There are three types of *secondary classification factors*. The *multicar* exposure factor is based on the idea that if more than one private passenger car is owned by one person (or by relatives of the same household in joint names), the cars will not each be used as much as is the case where only one car is owned. This factor results in a combined premium that is at least 15 percent less than the total premium for single-car exposures would otherwise be.

For 1971 and later model cars, a secondary factor is applied to to classify autos by *type of vehicle* into standard, intermediate, and high performance cars and sports cars.

Another secondary factor is the *safe-driver rating plan* which is used by many insurers to distinguish among drivers on the basis of their accident record, traffic conviction record, and experience (for principal operator only). A "point system" is used to classify drivers into five groups. "Chargeable" accidents during the past three years count one point each whenever they involve bodily injury, or property of more than $200.[9] (The rates go up 30 percent for one accident, 70 percent for two, 120 percent for three, and higher!) Most plans vary somewhat, but 1–3 points are assigned against the insured for motor vehicle violations such as driving while intoxicated, hit-and-run accidents, and license suspension or revocation. Lack of experience (less than three years' license) by the principal operator of the insured automobile counts as one point against the insured. Although called a secondary factor (applied after the first factors), the importance of the safe-driver plan in increasing rates substantially is apparent in the indicated rate increases.

In review, the primary classification factors (age-sex-marital status, use, driver training, and good-student rules) and the secondary classification factors (multicar, type of vehicle, and safe-driver plans) are combined to be applied against the base premium for each car insured to determine the insurance premium.

---

[9] These do not include accidents in which the insured was not at fault, such as those in which (1) the insured is reimbursed by or has a judgment against someone else and (2) the car was legally parked.

Other rating factors. Other systems have been used in the past. During World War II, mileage (based on gas ration cards) was a simple system. Use and age factors were subsequently determined to be a more accurate basis for predicting losses. In the 1960s discounts were given for "compact" cars, but these, too, were determined to be unjustified by most insurers as better statistical experience was obtained. In fact, these cars have been determined to have personal injury risk 40 percent or more greater than that of full-size cars.[10] Undoubtedly, the future will bring other revisions in the system of rating, with some traditional factors being discarded and new ones accepted. One of the promising new systems in use by several insurers employs psychological tests as a method of classifying younger drivers.[11]

Private passenger automobile physical damage premiums. Automobile *physical damage* insurance premiums (for damage to the insured's *own* car) are also heavily dependent on the *territory* in which the motor vehicle is operated. The next elements for consideration are the *age and value of the car.* Four age groups are applicable to the comprehensive physical damage and collision coverages: for the current year model and for each preceding year up to three (or older). As the car becomes older, the premium decreases. Automobiles are grouped into different classes identified by the letters A–Z, according to their appropriate values. In anticipating collision and physical damage losses, it is recognized that a Cadillac owner should pay more than an owner of a lower priced car since damage and repair costs will be greater.

Collision insurance also uses premiums which vary by *use* of the car, and for the private passenger cars the classes are much the same as for liability insurance.

A final factor of importance is the use of *deductibles* in physical damage coverage. Most policyholders prefer to carry part of collision losses themselves, and the $100 deductible form is most often used. Deductibles of $200–$1,000 and higher are also now available. The insurance buyer should check on the difference between deductible coverages, for often a substantial saving is possible through the use of the higher deductibles. (See later section of this chapter on collision coverage.) For other physical damage losses, the "comprehensive" coverage used to be written without a deductible, but today many contracts have a $50 or a $100 deductible apply. Insureds should consider their ability to withstand smaller losses

---

[10] "The Small Car—A Mixed Blessing," *Journal of American Insurance,* Spring 1977, p. 1. The death rate in the smallest cars was about twice that in full-size cars in 1978–80. "Small Cars Aren't as Safe as Big Ones, Crash Data Indicate," *The Wall Street Journal,* January 1, 1982, p. 12.

[11] Grinnel Mutual Reinsurance Company has claimed good success with its system, adopted in the early 1960s, and broadened use is recommended. See William D. Wells, "Psychographics: A Critical Review," *Journal of Marketing Research,* May 1975, p. 196.

without strain on their financial budget. For many insureds, the use of a higher deductible with the premium saved going toward the purchase of higher liability limits or other coverages is a good risk-management decision.

THE PERSONAL AUTO POLICY (PAP)

One of the most serious obstacles to consumers understanding insurance has been the legal nature and form of its contracts. Since these contracts are written by legal and underwriting departments of insurers and often conform to state laws formulated by committees of legal experts, it is not surprising that most insurance contracts contain heavy doses of what critics call "legalese."

The readable contract trend

The encouraging trend toward simplicity in personal lines of coverage was led by the Homeowner's '76 contract, explained in Chapter 23, and the *personal auto policy,* [12] introduced in 1977.

Real progress in attaining more understandable language in insurance contracts will need cooperation among many insurers, their associations, and the legislatures. The trend has spread to commercial lines, where the *businessowner policy* (see Chapter 23) appeared in 1976, and the *basic auto policy* was introduced in 1978.

Contracts in plain English have also arrived in other fields. Sometimes this has happened because business firms have experimented with and voluntarily used new and more readable contracts. Banks have simplified consumer notes, mortgage loans, trust forms, and other documents. Widespread use, however, seems to require action by the lawmakers, such as the New York law which was the first one to require consumer contracts to be written in plain English.

The use of simpler language is not always advantageous to insurance consumers. From a legal standpoint, the changes may be a disadvantage sometimes (1) by reducing the value of legal precedents interpreting the language of older contracts and (2) by weakening the presumption that all ambiguities should be interpreted against the insurer.

Personalized and simplified format

One of the most noticeable changes in the readable contracts is the use of simplified language, particularly the references to "you" and "your" for the insureds, and "we" and "our" for the insurers writing

---

[12] Developed by the Insurance Services Offices (ISO) for use by its affiliated companies.

the coverages. In the personal auto policy the results are a reduction of one half, from 9,000 to 4,500 words. Larger printing, shorter sentences, emphasis of key words, a glossary of more technical terms, and fewer endorsements (reduced from 45 to about a dozen) also aid considerably in making the contract more understandable to the average policyholder. Definitions of terms are clarified to help simplify the contract coverage.

Declarations

In general appearance the PAP of different insurers may look quite different. The individual insurers following the Insurance Services Offices form may design their own cover and declarations page. The remaining parts are standardized, however, and these are discussed individually by sections in the following analysis.

Because sample policy kits[13] are available to most students, the entire automobile insurance contract is not reproduced here. Emphasis will be placed on evaluating the meaning of the major provisions of all the parts, but the student may occasionally benefit by referring to the actual contract wording in the policy itself as the PAP is explained.

The declarations page usually includes most of the basic information about the insurer, the insured, the policy period (usually one year, beginning at 12:01 A.M.), the automobile(s),[14] the premiums, and the limits of liability for each of the coverages. Several items give the insurer important data upon which the classification and premium for the insurance contract are based. These items include the description of the automobile or automobiles, their cost, their use, whether or not a mortgage or loan is in existence on them, the location at which they will be principally garaged, and whether or not within the past three years any insurer has canceled automobile insurance for the insured.

It is noted that the coverage parts listed in the declarations are identified as A through D. The contract is a "schedule" type of policy, as the policyholder chooses (by agreement with the insurer in the declarations) many of the coverages to be included by scheduling the limits of liability for each coverage and paying the appropriate premium charge. Part A (liability) and any of the coverages in Part D (damage to your auto) may be written alone or in conjunction with one another. Part B (medical payments) and Part C (uninsured motorists) can be written only with Part A. Medical payments coverage is optional, but uninsured motorists coverage is required by law in many states unless specifically excluded.

---

[13] Such as those published by the Insurance Information Institute, 110 William St., New York, N.Y. 10038, or the American Mutual Insurance Alliance, 20 North Wacker Drive, Chicago, Ill. 60606.

[14] Space is provided for two or more cars, since many families insure more than one car in the same policy, with a reduction in cost of 15 percent or more.

The usual contract will include all four of these coverages. In addition, the last two parts of the contract are included in all contracts, so the total six parts of the contract are:

Part A—Liability.

Part B—Medical payments.

Part C—Uninsured motorists.

Part D—Damage to your auto.

Part E—Duties after an accident or loss.

Part F—General provisions.

The valuation and territorial class, safe-driver plan points, and driver training and multicar rating factors are shown. The declarations page also refers by number to any endorsements which are attached to the later pages of the contract. On the bottom lines the contract is confirmed as a legal contract by signatures of authorized representatives of the insurer and states that the declarations, policy jacket, forms, and endorsements are all a part of the completed policy.

Automobiles eligible to be written under the PAP are those owned by an individual (or by a husband and wife residing together in the same household), not those owned by corporations. Vehicles with four-wheel drive, usually not including trucks, qualify for this coverage. Trucks which may be insured under this form include pickup, sedan delivery, or panel trucks not customarily used in the insured's business or occupation or used similarly by farmers, ranchers, or federal employees. The vehicles covered must be owned by the insured or leased from others under a contract of at least six months.

Insuring agreement and definitions

The front page of the policy includes a brief insuring agreement and a group of definitions applying to the entire contract.

The use of "you" and "your" is explained as referring to the named insured and spouse living in the same household. "We" and "us" and "our" mean the insurer.

"Covered auto" is any vehicle listed in the declarations, which includes any *owned* trailer of a type designed for use with a private passenger automobile. (Farm wagons or implements towed by such vehicles are also covered.) A *nonowned* auto or trailer used as a *temporary substitute* for an owned vehicle while it is being repaired is included. Full coverage also applies to *acquired vehicles in addition to* the ones described in the declarations if the insured asks that they be covered within 30 days after the acquisition. *Replacement vehicles* are also covered automatically except for physical damage coverage, and the insured may ask for Part D coverage within 30 days.

"Family members" are those persons related to the named insured or spouse by blood, marriage, or adoption, if they reside in the household of the named insured.

Part A—Liability

Bodily injury and property damage. The basic promise of the insurer in the liability portion of the PAP is to "pay for *bodily injury* or *property damage* for which any covered person becomes legally responsible because of an auto accident." Liability decisions aim at requiring those persons who are responsible for a loss to pay for it. Both injury to other persons, including death, and damage to the property of other persons are included. Gratuitous payments are not a part of liability coverage; a legal responsibility must exist before the insurer will pay the injured party under this provision of the contract.

Note that the PAP uses the word *accident,* not the word *occurrence* which was used in the earlier auto contracts and other general liability policies. Although this word is usually considered to be more limited in coverage, the continuous or repeated exposure included in the occurrence coverage of general liability insurance is not significant in auto risks. The intent of the change to the word *accident* in this contract is to make the coverage more understandable to the policyholder, not to limit the protection of the policy.

Single-limit coverage. One of the most significant features of the personal auto policy is the *single limit* of coverage for both bodily injury and property damage.[15] The single limit applies in any one auto accident, regardless of the number of covered persons, injured claimants, or property damage claims. For example, a $300,000 limit would provide coverage up to that amount for bodily injury to one person, or for several persons in total, or for property damage.

In the case of accident in another state which specifies higher financial responsibility limits than the single limit of the policy, the PAP will provide whatever coverage is required by the law. This also applies to compulsory insurance or no-fault laws in these other states.

Defense and supplementary payments. The insurer agrees to *settle or defend* any claim or suit asking for bodily injury or property damages because of an auto accident. This duty in the "defense clause" ends when the limit of liability has been exhausted. Settlement and defense costs include those of investigating claims, defense attorney fees, court costs, and other expenses of negotiation and defense.

In addition to the policy limit, there are several *supplementary pay-*

---

[15] If state laws require separate limits, the policy's single limit applies accordingly, but it will not increase the total limit of liability. For example, a $50,000 single limit policy in a state that requires 20/40/10 separate limits would provide $50,000 for bodily injury to one or more persons or for property damage, not $70,000.

ments provided for: (1) up to $250 for bail bonds when these are required after an auto accident resulting in covered damages (not for other traffic violations); (2) premiums on appeal and release of attachment bonds in suits defended by the insurer; (3) accrued interest on judgments that the insurer must pay, up to the time that payment is offered; and (4) reasonable expenses, and up to $50 a day for loss of earnings, of an insured attending hearings or trials at the request of the insurer.

Note that first-aid expenses after an accident are included for covered persons under medical payments coverage. In previous auto policies, these expenses were included for everyone injured in an auto accident by being specifically mentioned in the coverage.

Covered persons and autos. One of the broadest features of the personal auto policy is that it protects more than just the named insured. The insurance applies to ownership, maintenance, or use of any auto or trailer (as defined earlier) by a *covered person,* defined in the contract to include, with respect to *owned* automobiles:

1. The *named insured* and *spouse* and any *relative* (including wards or foster children) living in the same household. This includes persons temporarily away from the household, such as children boarding at college.
2. *Any other person* driving the named insured's auto, if the driver can demonstrate that a reasonable belief that permission to use the auto exists (in previous policies, permission for use had to be given by the insured).
3. *Any person or organization,* for liability arising out of any covered person's use of the covered auto on behalf of that person or organization (such as an employer).

With respect to *nonowned*[16] *automobiles* of the insured, the PAP provides liability coverage for:

4. *Any person or organization,* for the *named insured's* or *family members'* (see earlier definition) use of any auto or trailer, other than the covered auto or one owned by the person or organization. A common example is the borrowing or driving of someone else's car by the insured or members of the insurer's family (with reasonable belief of the right to use it.) This coverage is often called "drive-other-car coverage." It also provides protection to employers or organizations, for other cars which may be used on their behalf by a covered person.

---

[16] Don't let this word confuse you. Of course, all autos are owned by someone. As used in the auto contract and discussion here, a nonowned auto means one that is owned by *someone other than you,* the insured.

The extension of coverage under the automobile contract to these four categories of covered persons is seen as a very important part of the policy coverage. However, the coverage is limited by *exclusions*. Four exclusions pertain to the use of specific *types of vehicles:*

1. Vehicles used in the auto business (selling, servicing, parking, etc.).
2. Trucks used in any other business or occupation (except "covered autos," which may include pickup or panel trucks not customarily used in the insured's occupation, or such trucks used similarly by farmers, ranchers, or federal employees).
3. Vehicles with less than four wheels.
4. Any vehicles while they are used to haul property or persons for a fee (except in shared-expense car pools, which are covered).

Also excluded is bodily injury to *employees* of the insured (except domestic employees if workers' compensation is not required). Another exclusion is coverage for *property rented to, used by, or in the care of the insured* (*except* damage to a nonowned residence or garage, or damage to nonowned automobiles furnished or available for the regular use of the named insured or family members). The exception means that full *liability* coverage is restored for the insured and family members, including property damage liability for any nonowned autos in their care, custody, or control for regular use. A final exclusion refers to a certain kind of *wrongdoing* by any person, for *intentional* bodily injury or property damage.

Policy limits and other insurance. The importance of the single limit of liability under the PAP has been mentioned previously. Because all bodily injury and property damage claims come under the single limit, it is imperative for the policyholder to consider the purchase of as high a limit as is available and affordable. Although smaller standard limits (or those required by the state laws) are purchasable, few insureds should consider less than a $50,000 limit, and most should buy at least $100,000 or $300,000 liability limits. Most insurers will also quote the cost of even higher amounts, such as $500,000 or more, upon request.

The cost of the additional premium for higher limits is not as much as might be imagined. Most claims are small, so a premium increase of 20–40 percent over the $50,000 coverage will purchase the higher limits needed. The insurance contract can provide security and peace of mind to the insured only *if* proper limits are purchased. The insured who has a $50,000 policy but is sued for $250,000 (not an unlikely case today) has great uncertainty, perhaps for several years of uninsured worry during negotiations or trial. Thus the insurance will not do in this type of situation what it is intended to do—even if the actual payment eventually turns out to be much smaller than the amount originally claimed. Trying to save on the cost of automobile insurance by purchasing lower liability limits is generally unwise.

Illustrations of the potential need for high single-limit coverage under the PAP are plentiful and follow the examples of the large liability lawsuits and judgments mentioned in other liability situations (see Chapters 16, 17). In the auto field, multiple-car crashes are common, sometimes involving many persons. Property damages, too, can involve several $10,000 autos, $20,000–$40,000 buses, mobilehomes or trucks (plus valuable cargoes), and other property damage.

Motor vehicle accidents often involve more than one auto insurance contract. If a covered person is using someone else's car, the driver's PAP applies only as *excess* insurance over any other insurance covering the loss (such as the owner's insurance). In such cases the owner's insurance policy pays the loss up to the full limits of its liability, and only then does the driver's insurance policy pay up to its maximum liability for the remaining amount of the loss. Each time you loan your car to someone else, you should remember that your insurance will apply first. Suppose that Lisa borrows Tom's car, with a reasonable belief in her right to use it, and that she has an accident. Tom's insurance contract will provide the primary coverage for any liability claims, and Lisa's insurance contract will provide excess liability coverage only if needed.

Only in a few cases will the insured have *other insurance* on the automobile he or she owns, usually as the result of a mistake or a misunderstanding. If this does occur, then the PAP provides that it covers only "in the proportion that its limit of liability bears to the total of all applicable limits." Insurer A, for example, with a $50,000 limit, would pay only a one-third share of a liability loss if the insured also had a contract with a $100,000 limit on the same owned car through Insurer B. Insurer B would pay a proportional two thirds of the loss, up to its policy limit. The same prorating of duplicate coverage would apply if medical payments coverage in more than one contract were in existence on the same owned car.

Out-of-state coverage is automatically included in the PAP. If the other state requires higher limits than the policy, for meeting financial responsibility or compulsory insurance laws in that state or Canadian province (see Chapter 19), your covered auto is insured for the higher limits in an accident there.

Part B—Medical payments

The policyholder may include Part B—*medical payments* coverage in the personal automobile policy to cover the cost of *medical services* for the *named insured, relatives,* and *anyone else in the insured's car.* Part B does not apply to pedestrians, or to occupants of buildings or other vehicles into which an insured vehicle may crash. This is really automobile accident insurance for medical care costs, and the protection applies *without regard to whose fault* the accident was. In effect, this is one of the original no-fault coverages which has been available in auto insurance for many years.

The cost is small, usually varying from about $10 to $30 per year, depending on the basic charge in the policy for bodily injury liability and the limits of medical coverage chosen. Most policies have about a $2,000 limit *per person*, but that limit may be raised to $5,000 for only a few dollars more per year. The higher limits are recommended, and some insurers now offer $10,000 or more coverage. Increasing the protection amount by 10 times may only double the premium cost.

The advantage of having automobile medical payments coverage in addition to liability insurance is that payment is made promptly, without a wait for the determination of liability. This coverage also avoids many embarrassing or difficult liability claims or lawsuits by friends injured in your car, and it provides compensation for you and for members of your family who are often unable to sustain a liability claim against you. Also, under the "guest laws" in some states, the persons in your car must often prove "willful or wanton misconduct" by the owner or driver. This makes it unlikely that the liability portion of the contract will pay for the occupants of your car in these states. Medical payments coverage avoids these problems of establishing legal liability, and in addition it pays for many injuries which may be considered moral rather than legal responsibilities.

The coverage is quite broad, for *all necessary medical expenses* (including surgical, dental, ambulance, hospital, and nursing) are paid, as well as funeral expenses, up to the policy limit. Injuries occurring "in, upon, entering or alighting from" the automobile are covered. The high cost of medical services today makes the need for such protection obvious. With six persons injured in your car, per person policy limits of $2,000 could provide $12,000 of needed coverage for family and friends.

The PAP extends the coverage to medical expenses incurred within *three years* from the date of an accident. The coverage is primary for auto accidents, with benefits payable even though the injured persons may collect benefits from other hospitalization, accident, or disability insurance. However, payments are excluded under medical payments coverage if benefits are required or available under workers' compensation laws.

In the case of *nonowned* autos operated by the named insured or family members, the coverage applies only to the named insured or family members. (Other occupants are covered by the policy on the nonowned vehicle or by their own policies.) This coverage applies as excess over any other collectible auto insurance providing medical or funeral expenses.

The coverage applies to an insured struck as a pedestrian by any motor vehicle, including a motorcycle, but a specific exclusion applies while any person is occupying a motorized vehicle with less than four wheels. A few other exclusions prevent duplicate coverage, such as when persons are injured in public conveyances.

Part C—Uninsured (and underinsured) motorists coverage

The recognition of the need for insurance to pay the insured, family members, and their passengers for bodily injury caused by a negligent owner or operator of an uninsured motor vehicle has led to the inclusion in the personal auto policy of coverage C—*uninsured motorists* coverage. Increasingly popular during the past 20 years, this coverage is now mandatory in some states for every automobile insurance contract issued; and in most states it is included in the contract unless the insured specifically rejects it in writing.

Coverage is usually issued for a single limit of bodily injury liability as stated in the policy declarations.[17] A limit similar to that of the basic liability coverages normally applies. By definition, an *uninsured motor vehicle* is one which is not covered by a bodily injury[18] liability policy or bond at the time of an accident for at least the minimum statutory limits of the state where your auto is principally garaged. This would include a stolen car. The definition is extended to include a hit-and-run motor vehicle when the owner or operator cannot be identified.

Uninsured motorists coverage is relatively inexpensive. The premium is usually a flat amount for one automobile of about $10–25. An additional automobile is included for a lesser amount.

The named insured and family members are protected with insurance against accidents caused by uninsured motorists which occur when they occupy the owned automobile, operate bicycles, or are pedestrians. In any nonowned automobile operated by the named insured, only the named insured and family members are covered, and the coverage is excess over other collectible UM insurance.

The insurance business approaches this coverage with some reluctance since the adjustment of a loss involves two interests that are essentially diverse. The insured must show (although a lawyer is not necessary) that the uninsured person was negligent and that the negligence caused the injury. Suppose Mr. A is injured in an accident caused by Mr. B, who is uninsured. In the case of a disputed claim the insurer finds itself in the unhappy position of working against its own interest if it presses

---

[17] The reasons for this coverage and its relationship to the problem of the innocent unpaid automobile accident victim have been discussed in Chapter 19.

[18] *Property damage* (to the insured's car) is not included, except in a few states (with a $100 or more deductible).

the interest of Mr. A to the limit in an effort to establish liability on the part of Mr. B. If they fail to agree that Mr. A is legally entitled to recover damages against Mr. B, or if they fail to agree as to the amount thereof, the matter is settled by *arbitration* rules specified in the contract.

The purpose of the protection is to provide for the insured the amount that would have been collected from an uninsured driver. The negligent driver does not have to be insolvent; UM coverage applies if he or she is uninsured. It has been stated that the insured who carries liability insurance takes care of the "other person." In the case of uninsured motorists coverage, the insurance is comparable to the collision insurance on the insured's own car. Here, instead, it is bodily injury protection for the insured and others against negligent and uninsured motorists.

Underinsured motorists coverage is also available by an optional endorsement added to the PAP. It pays when the automobile bodily injury liability insurance carried by the negligent third party is exhausted. In such cases, your uninsured motorists coverage would not apply because the motorist responsible for your injuries *is* insured but with policy limits insufficient to pay your full loss. (Some insurers and court decisions in these *under*insured situations might interpret this as being *un*insured, but many have not.) Thus in many states today, insurers are required to offer underinsured motorists coverage. This covers you, your family members, and other occupants of your car for bodily injuries caused by other insured motorists who have inadequate limits of liability insurance. Because many motorists carry only the low statutory limits, it is recommended that you purchase underinsured motorists coverage. For example, if you buy $100,000 underinsured motorists limits, it would pay up to $80,000 when the other negligent insured motorist has a policy with only a $20,000 limit. In some states, you must accept or reject both uninsured and underinsured motorists coverage together, and they must both be for the same limits of coverage.

Part D—Damage to your own auto

Physical damage coverage for your own automobile is provided in the PAP under Part D, if the declarations page indicates a premium charge and policy limit for the protection. This coverage should not be confused with property damage liability, which is the damage to the property of other persons for which you are held liable.

Part D may include *all direct and accidental* losses to your auto, or *collision* losses may be excluded if the collision peril is not shown in the declarations as covered and a premium charge is not indicated. *Other than collision* losses (similar to the "comprehensive" coverage of the older forms) are covered by a separate premium amount. Towing and labor costs may be included in this part of the PAP, for emergency road service up to $25 per disablement, with an endorsement costing only a few dollars. The collision and comprehensive (other perils) coverage will be discussed separately, as each has its own insuring agreement.

The importance of physical damage insurance is related to the value of the automobile and to the need and ability of the owner to replace or repair the vehicle if it is damaged. Since most newer automobiles today are items of large value in relation to the assets of a family, most owners do need this insurance protection. However, as the value of an older car decreases, a time may be reached when physical damage insurance is not necessary to cover a possible maximum loss of a few thousand dollars. It is unwise to go without this coverage, however, if the value of the automobile is such that your income or assets could not readily replace the car as required for your work or family.

Sometimes you have little choice as to whether or not you purchase physical damage insurance. Most installment contracts for the purchase of automobiles require that sufficient physical damage insurance be purchased to protect the value of the car used as collateral. Two warnings are important in these cases: (1) the insurance which the bank or other creditor suggests or requires is usually limited to coverage on the car itself and should not be misunderstood as including the very important liability or other automobile coverages; and (2) if the insurance cost is included in the finance plan, be sure to ask what coverages are included and to know the cost involved.

Collision coverage. *Collision* insurance reimburses you for damage to your automobile sustained by reason of a collision with another car or with any other object, movable or fixed. The policy also specifically includes loss to the automobile caused by upset.

As with medical payments insurance, even if you did not carry collision insurance, you *might* be able to recover damages from another person who caused the accident. However, you would be wise to consider purchasing collision insurance since (1) you or the driver of your automobile may be responsible for the loss, whether or not another car is involved in the accident; *and* (2) if another party is responsible for the damage, you must prove negligence; *and* (3) there may be delay and uncertainty in collecting from a negligent person (who may not have sufficient assets or insurance to pay the damages). If you carry collision insurance, *regardless of whose fault* the loss is, you will be paid for the damages to your car.

Collision losses are one of the most common situations in which *subrogation* may apply. If you collect the damages from your insurer, the insurer may then take over your rights to sue the responsible party and recover the payment made to you. Whether or not the insurer will actually do so depends on many factors, including the accident facts, who was liable, the size of the loss, and whether or not proof of negligence is readily available and recovery of claims is likely from the other person.

Collision insurance is also a common illustration of the use of the *deductible*. It is the basic purpose of the deductible to avoid the high cost and administrative expense of frequent small collision losses. The normal collision deductible in the PAP, which also applies to the comprehensive (other than collision) perils, provides that there shall be no liability on the part of the insurer unless the loss exceeds a named amount. Then the amount of the loss payment is only so much of the loss as exceeds the deductible amount. For example, under a $100 deductible form, if the loss is $90, there is no payment by the insurer; if the loss is $300, the insurer pays the policyholder $200.

Although the $50 deductible is still used in auto insurance, deductibles of $100 or more are being used with increasing frequency. Some agents and insurers often advise a $250 deductible, and deductibles of up to $1,000 or more are available. The reduction in cost to you often justifies the decision to accept a larger portion of collision losses yourself. For example, if you can afford a $250 loss, and the reduction in premium for a $250 deductible as compared with a $100 deductible is $60, it may be unwise to have the smaller deductible. In effect, you may be paying a substantial premium for insurance you don't really need.

Some contracts used to waive the deductible (and some may still do so) if the loss was caused by a collision with another automobile insured by the same insurer. However, in the PAP there is no waiver of the deductible in such cases.

Ordinarily, you can expect to receive the deductible amount from the insurer if the insurer subrogates for the entire amount, including the deductible, and is successful in subrogation proceedings against another negligent party. The cost of the legal proceedings must be considered in a proportionate recovery. The insurer does not profit in subrogation cases and often recovers only a part of the payment it has made to you.

A most important fact is that the collision insurance applies not only while the named insured is operating the automobile but also while *other persons* are operating it with a reasonable belief that they have the right to do so.

One of the most significant changes in the PAP as compared with older contracts is that physical damage insurance applies only to *your* covered auto. *Nonowned or temporary substitute* cars which you or your family members use are *not* covered. However, under the new provisions of the liability section of the PAP, you are protected for *legal liability* for damages to such cars in your custody. Family members are similarly covered when they borrow or use other cars. A possible advantage of the new wording is that a deductible does not apply in those cases in which you or your relatives are liable for the physical damage to non-owned or temporary substitute cars.

The insurer's limit of liability is usually for indemnity based upon the *actual cash value* of the automobile,[19] although some contracts, especially for business vehicles, use a stated value form. The actual cash value wording protects the policyholder for losses on the basis of value as of the time of the loss, not exceeding the cost of repair or replacement. Other valid and collectible physical damage insurance of the insured on the automobile applies on a pro rata basis.

Escalating cost of new cars to the $10,000 or higher range makes automobiles the next most expensive purchase to their home for many families. However, cars depreciate much faster than homes. Thus some insurers in many states now offer *repair or replacement cost coverage* on new cars, for collision and other physical damage to your car, except fire or theft. The PAP endorsement pays the full cost of repairing or replacing your car (less the deductible if repairable), without any deduction for depreciation, whether or not the cost exceeds the car's market value. Suppose your new car costs $10,000, and three years later it is worth only $5,000. The policy would pay up to what it would cost you to buy a comparable new car. Although more expensive by about 15 percent, this new coverage may become popular in the future.

Comprehensive (other than collision) coverage. With the exception of collision losses, *comprehensive physical damage* is virtually an *all-risk* physical damage coverage. It is now written in the PAP instead of the limited coverages that were formerly used for fire, theft, and other named perils. Protection is afforded for any "direct and accidental loss to your covered auto including its equipment."

Although the broad wording of the contract would automatically include losses on an "everything but" basis, the clause does give specific examples of the types of perils that are *not* considered to be collision losses and are therefore covered. These perils are the following: fire; theft or larcency; windstorm; explosion or earthquake; hail, water, or flood; vandalism or malicious mischief; riot or civil commotion; missiles or falling objects, contact with birds or animals; and breakage of glass.

Many strange and unexpected losses have been included on this coverage. Mention may be made of cases involving damage to a fender kicked by a horse, damage to the finish of an automobile caused by arsenic tree spray or paint, damage by battery acid and Halloween vandals, and damage by running into a dog, deer, cow, or other animal.

---

[19] The principle is the same as that used in the fire insurance policy. No dollar amount for payment is stated in the contract except the maximum limit. The replacement cost less reasonable depreciation is a basis, and this is often determined by market value.

To be covered, the damage must be *accidental*. It is not accidental damage if you break a window so that you can get into the car with the keys locked inside. The breakage of glass due to a collision is included as a covered comprehensive physical damage loss, but in a policy provision that applies only to glass breakage in a collision, the insured may choose to have it considered a collision loss. This avoids having a double deductible apply to glass breakage as both a collision and a comprehensive loss.

Transportation expenses are provided in a clause which grants reimbursement for actual transportation expenses incurred following the theft of an automobile. This is a type of "loss of use" coverage that begins 48 hours after the theft and ends when the automobile has been returned to use or the loss has been paid. Coverage is limited to up to $10 per day to a maximum of $300. The amount paid is in addition to the loss payable for the damages caused by the theft.

Another change in the PAP is that personal effects in the auto are no longer covered. A very limited coverage had applied under previous policies.

Most of the other provisions of this section are applied to both comprehensive and collision coverages. Many are similar to the definitions, clauses, and exclusions already discussed in Part A of the personal automobile policy. The coverage applies to the owned automobile while it is being used either by the named insured or by anyone else using it with a reasonable belief of being entitled to do so. Nonowned automobiles are *not* covered. Newly acquired additional cars must be reported within 30 days of acquisition. A replacement automobile requires notification within 30 days after acquisition only if physical damage coverage is desired on the new vehicle. The insurance specifically states that it shall not directly or indirectly benefit any carrier or other bailee for hire.

Other exclusions are: (1) damage due to wear and tear, freezing, mechanical or electrical breakdown or failure, or road damage to tires[20] (except that caused by theft); (2) loss to custom furnishings or equipment on trucks or vans; (3) loss caused by war, radioactive contamination, or nuclear weapons; (4) camper bodies or trailers (unless specifically declared); (5) loss to CB radio, two-way radio, scanning receiver, or telephone equipment (unless endorsed on the policy); and (6) loss to equipment for the reproduction of sound (including tapes and records). The last two exclusions do not apply if the items are permanently installed in your covered auto.

The comprehensive coverage in the PAP is usually written for the amount of "actual cash value" or the amount necessary to repair or

---

[20] Note that ordinary flat tire losses are not included. To be covered by physical damage, the loss must be due to a collision or another identifiable covered peril.

replace the property. Several choices among deductibles are used, as for the collision coverage discussed previously. Similar advice applies with regard to using the largest deductible possible in order to lower the premium cost for the comprehensive coverages. Deductibles of $100–$200 are common.

Part E—Duties after an accident or loss

The simplified wording of this part of the PAP specifies what any person seeking coverage under the policy should do following an accident or loss. Many of the provisions are promises that you as the insured must fulfill before you can expect the insurer to make payments under the contract. Note that these are "conditions," although called "duties" in the contract, and that if you do not fulfill them, the insurer may not have to pay the loss. (Legally, a duty would permit the insurer to force you to meet the promises made.)

When an accident occurs, *prompt notice* should be given by you or on your behalf to the insurer or its agents. Oftentimes this would involve a phone call to the agent, followed up within a few days with a written signed report which the agent may help you prepare. The notice should contain reasonably obtainable information respecting how, when, and where the accident or loss happened, together with the names and addresses of any injured persons and witnesses. If a claim is made or a suit is brought, you should promptly *forward to the insurer copies of any notices or legal papers* that you have received. You must *cooperate with the insurer* in the investigation, settlement, or defense of any claim or suit.

With respect to the coverages you are not divested of all responsibility once you have turned the adjustment over to the insurer. In fact, you are required, if requested by the insurer, to *submit to physical exams* by physicians (selected and paid by the insurer), to *authorize them to obtain medical or other pertinent records,* and to *submit a proof of loss.*

Some additional duties pertain to uninsured motorists coverage: you must promptly notify the police if a hit-and-run driver is involved and promptly send the insurer copies of legal papers if a suit is brought. Also, under the coverage for damage to your auto, you must take reasonable steps after loss to protect your covered auto from further loss (the insurer pays reasonable expenses), promptly notify the police if your covered auto is stolen, and permit the insurer to inspect and appraise the damaged property before its repair or disposal.

In the event of an accident that may involve a claim for damages, printed forms indicating the nature of the *data desired by the insurer* are often used. Where there is a bodily injury, an estimate of the extent of the injury is needed. Significant items are whether or not the injured persons receive first aid or medical attention, the name of the attending physician, and the name and location of the hospital. If the driver of your car is someone other than you, the driver's name, address, and license number form an essential part of the report. The weather conditions and the condition of the highways should be noted, and a detailed sketch should be made showing the relative positions of the cars just before and after the collision. In complying with the *state requirements* for reporting accidents, you should make a duplicate copy of any written reports and forward a copy to the agent or insurer. If members of the police force were present at the accident scene, a notation should be made of their names or badge numbers.

You should *not* make any admission as to liability, and you should *not* make any efforts to negotiate a settlement of the claim. By virtue of the contract the insurer has exclusive control over the adjustment of the claim, and you should not make any attempt to effect a settlement without the consent of the insurance company. By doing so, you run a risk of forfeiting your right to indemnity under the policy.

To indicate in a legal action that you are covered by insurance may result in a mistrial or may reverse a judgment for the plaintiff. If the jury knows that an insurer and not the individual defendant is to pay the damages, there will be a temptation to be generous with the insurer's money. Reference to "insurance" directly or by inference may jeopardize the case, but this rule is not universally accepted in the light of the wide distribution of insurance and the use of some defense counsel that regularly represent insurers.[21] Where, however, the rule is in force, attorneys will be on the alert to turn it to their advantage whenever the opportunity presents itself.

Part F—General provisions

Some of the provisions are restrictions on the extent of liability of the insurer. Only automobile losses that occur in the *United States, Puerto Rico, and Canada* (including U.S. territories or possessions) or while you are being transported between ports of these countries are covered. Residents of the Southern border states and travelers who visit Mexico should note that separate protection must be purchased if they wish to be covered while driving in Mexico. Since Canada's required liability limits in some provinces exceed the financial responsibility laws of some states, care should be taken to check the insurance contract and laws before driving in Canada.

---

[21] *Carter* v. *Walker,* 165 S.W. 483. See also *Russell* v. *Bailey,* 290 S.W. 1108: "We would say that the custom of carrying casualty insurance is now so universal and so generally recognized that a mere individual reference to the fact that defendant was thus protected should not constitute error in absence of a showing of injury."

If the insurer makes payment under the policy, and the person to or for whom payment was made has a right to recover damages from another, the insurer is *subrogated* to (takes over) that right.[22] You or that person must do whatever else is necessary to enable the insurer to exercise their rights. It is also important that you or they do nothing after a loss to prejudice the subrogation rights of the insurer, either by relieving another of liability or by assuming responsibility. You may feel that you are to blame for an accident, but you may be mistaken, for example.

An *assignment* of the policy will not bind the insurer until it consents. To be valid, the assignment must be *in writing* and must be signed by an authorized officer of the insurer. Because of the nature of automobile coverages, the insurer wishes to underwrite its insureds carefully. In the event of the named insured's death, the policy shall then cover the named insured's spouse and legal representatives of the deceased person in performing their duties.

Cancellation provisions require the insurer to give the policyholder 10 days'[23] notice in writing, with a proportional return (or offer to return) of unearned premium to the end of the policy period. If the insured cancels, the return of premium is calculated on the customary short-rate basis. The personal automobile policy and many other automobile insurance contracts have recently limited the right of the insurer to cancel the liability portion of the coverage. (See discussion of underwriting selection of risks earlier in this chapter.)

No-fault coverage

The era of no-fault benefits also creates an expanding need for coverage that is adjusted to rapidly changing conditions. The PAP extends automatically (at no additional cost) coverages to pay no-fault benefits if covered persons drive into a state where they need no-fault protection. When applicable, the requirements of no-fault laws are available to the insureds.

If the insured lives in a state that has passed a no-fault law, it is necessary that the contracts be changed to include the no-fault provisions. For existing contracts this may be done by the law itself, while for new and renewal contracts the wording of the contracts are changed or endorsed to modify the contract coverage.

The endorsement provisions vary considerably by state. As an *example of "modified" no-fault insurance* (and in contrast to the more extensive Michigan no-fault insurance discussed in Chapter 19), *New Jersey* has

---

[22] The insurer's subrogation rights do *not* apply under Part D—Damage to Your Own Auto, against any person using *your covered auto* with a reasonable belief that that person is entitled to do so.

[23] This is the minimum for nonpayment of premium or if the notice is mailed during the first 60 days the policy is in effect. Otherwise, 20 days notice is required.

added a "basic personal injury protection endorsement" to accomplish this change. The endorsement is two pages long, and it specifies and defines the coverage to include automobile accident benefits payable, regardless of fault, for:

1. Medical expenses (all reasonable medical expenses, unlimited).
2. Income continuation (not exceeding $100 per week for one year, but optional coverage for 75 percent of income up to $35,000 annually is available for purchase).
3. Essential services (substitute cost of care and maintenance of insured and relatives, subject to daily limit of $12 with aggregate of $4,380 per person).
4. Survivors (above benefits become payable to dependent surviving spouse or children).
5. Funeral expenses (not exceeding $1,000).

The no-fault benefits are available in private passenger automobile accidents in New Jersey for bodily injury to the named insured; relatives who are residents of the household; "other persons" occupying the automobile or using it with the named insured's permission; and pedestrians. If the accident occurs outside New Jersey, "other persons" are covered only for medical expense. Excluded are persons committing a felony or high misdemeanor or attempting to avoid arrest by a police officer, and persons acting with intent to cause injury or damage. The insurance is compulsory for all owners who register or principally garage their car in New Jersey, and it also includes required liability limits of 15/30/5.

Injured persons can sue under tort liability *only* if the injury results in permanent disability, significant disfigurement, loss of a bodily function or bodily member, or death; or if medical expense exceeds $200, exclusive of hospital expenses. This is an extremely low "threshold," and many other states have been increasing their limit to $1,000 or more. The lower amounts do not reduce the number of tort liability claims and costs significantly. Any benefits collectible under workers' compensation or temporary disability laws, Medicare, or federal military programs are deducted from the no-fault payments.

The potential complexity and complications are apparent from this summary of the New Jersey no-fault endorsement. Automobile insurance consumers must be careful to understand their rights and obligations with these additions. (See earlier discussion of current no-fault laws in other states in Chapter 19).

THE BUSINESS AUTO POLICY

In addition to insurance for personal automobiles, the business student may sometimes need to know about how commercial vehicles (which account for about one fifth of all auto insurance) are insured. Since 1978 most motor vehicles used for business purposes have been insured in the *business auto policy* (BAP),[24] which covers autos, trucks, trailers, and semitrailers designed for public roads.

General nature

The business auto policy appeared as part of the trend toward contract simplification which was illustrated in the explanation of the personal auto policy. Many of the same objectives apply: reduction of the number of contracts and forms, personalized wording ("you," "we," etc.), single-limit liability coverage, and revised structure of the contracts and their provisions.

Designed as a self-contained contract, the *business auto policy (BAP)* will still provide an option for combination of coverage with the comprehensive general liability policy (CGL—see Chapter 17) by using a common declarations page. However, if this approach is used, both contracts should be insured with the same insurer to avoid any problems of overlapping or uninsured protection.

Following the declarations pages the BAP contract is divided into six parts, each of which will be separately discussed in the following sections. Liberalizations and limitations in this contract will be emphasized, rather than an item-by-item review of concepts already treated in the text for the personal auto policy. Particular attention in this brief summary will be given to provisions which are different for business as compared with personal auto exposures.

Declarations

The declarations pages are much more extensive than in the personal auto policy. The seven items pertain to (1) the named insured, (2) the schedule of coverages chosen, (3) the description of 10 covered auto "designation symbols," and schedules for (4) covered vehicles you own, (5) hired or borrowed vehicles, (6) employer's nonownership liability, and (7) gross receipts or mileage basis for public auto or leasing rental firms.

The major innovation is the use of the numbered designation symbols 1–10, which determine the choices made by you as to which vehicles are to be insured. Symbol 1 is the broadest designation, for *any* vehicle on a comprehensive basis. The others designate *owned* autos only (or are limited to private passenger autos, other than private passenger autos, or autos subject to no-fault or compulsory uninsured motorists laws); *specifically described* vehicles, *hired* vehicles, or *nonowned* vehicles

---

[24] Filed by the Insurance Services Office (ISO), the BAP or some version of it is used in all states except Texas. ISO filed a revised form in 1980.

only. To avoid any gaps in coverage, it is recommended that you purchase Symbol 1 coverage.

Item 2 in the declarations is very important, for this schedule of the coverages uses the designated symbols to indicate the liability, personal injury protection (no-fault), medical payments, uninsured motorists, and physical damage coverages which apply in the contract. Extreme care must be exercised by you and your agent to see that the appropriate designated symbol numbers are correctly inserted in this section of the declarations. Errors could mean lack of needed protection.

Six basic parts

Part I—Words and phrases with special meanings. This section contains a half page of definitions important to the contract. "You" are the person or organization insured, and "we" means the company providing the insurance. "Accident" is used rather than "occurrence," as in the PAP contract, but the definition includes continuous or repeated exposures resulting in bodily injury or property damage that you neither expected nor intended.

Of special significance to business auto risks is the fact that "auto" means a land motor vehicle, trailer, or semitrailer designed for travel on public roads, and that "mobile equipment" is separately defined to include such vehicles as bulldozers, graders, farm machinery, and those that are designed for use off public roads, for use solely on your premises, or are not required to be licensed.

Part II—Which autos are covered autos. The numerical designated symbols in the declarations determine which autos are considered covered autos for each of your chosen coverages. Vehicles acquired during the policy period are usually automatically covered, but if the coverage is only for specifically described autos (symbol 7) the newly acquired vehicle must be reported within 30 days. Temporary substitute vehicles are covered automatically for liability coverage only if coverage is carried for hired and nonowned autos. Physical damage coverage for these autos must be endorsed on the contract. Covered autos include trailers with a load capacity of 2,000 pounds or less and mobile equipment while it is being carried or towed by a covered auto.

Part III—Where and when this policy covers. Accidents or losses are covered in (or while being transported between) the United States, its territories or possessions, Puerto Rico, and Canada.

Part IV—Liability insurance. Most of the wording and interpretations for this section are similar to those of the personal auto policy already discussed. The single most important change is the *combined single limit* of liability for bodily injury and property damage. Insurers have conversion tables in order to advise policyholders of recommended amounts to assure adequate limits. For example, a policy formerly written for $100,000/$300,000/$50,000 limits should use a single limit of at least $350,000. Many businesses purchase a limit of $1 million or more.

An exclusion of special importance for business exposures is that "loading and unloading" excludes liability "resulting from the handling of property (1) before it is moved from the place where it is accepted by the insured for movement into or onto the covered auto, or (2) after it is moved from the covered auto to the place where it is finally delivered by the insured." A separate exclusion applies for "property moved by a mechanical device (other than a hand truck) not attached to the covered auto."[25] Because comprehensive general liability policies exclude loading and unloading, to avoid a gap in protection it is recommended that both your CGL and BAP policies be written by the same insurer.

Part V—Physical damage insurance. Two options for coverage apply in this section: "comprehensive" and "specified perils" (fire, theft, etc.). The specified perils coverage is written as a package, although fire, or fire and theft, perils can be written by special endorsements. The definitions correspond to previously discussed explanations of these coverages. Collision and towing charges may also be included in the physical damage insurance protection.

Part VI—Conditions. These conditions, which apply to the entire contract, are similar to the conditions of the personal auto policy. For businesses, the use of trailers is common and coverage for a trailer is clarified by stating that it applies only on an excess basis while it is used with a motor vehicle that you do not own.

FOR REVIEW AND DISCUSSION

1. *Who* is protected by the personal auto policy (PAP) and *what* automobiles?

2. Suppose your friend Barbara asks your advice on proper protection she should have for her new automobile. What explanations would you offer her for the most important coverages, and what approximate limits would you suggest that she include in the personal auto policy?

3. Are automobile insurance costs similar *(a)* for all insureds and *(b)* for similar protection for all insurers? *(c)* Should they be? Explain.

4. John Sure says: "Everyone has a *right to buy* automobile insurance because it's needed today by families as much as groceries or a house are needed." Suzy Dubious replies: "But automobile insurers must *underwrite* their business, or they will go broke." Divide the class into two groups to report on

---

[25] For examples, see *Fire, Casualty, and Surety Bulletins* (Cincinnati: National Underwriter), F. and C. Sections Auto (Casualty) B–7, and *The John Liner Letter* (Wellesly, Mass.: Shelby Publishing, March 1980).

(a) how these two ideas conflict; and *(b)* how these two ideas can, or are, brought together in the automobile insurance marketplace.

5. In determining the premium for automobile liability insurance, what factors are considered in addition to the territory in which the car is garaged?

6. Someone says to you: "Your private passenger automobile rate classification depends not upon *who* you are but upon *what* you do and have done, and upon your *car.*" Would you agree or disagree? Explain.

7. Mr. Riskee has just purchased a personal auto policy (PAP) with a $300,000 limit for bodily injury liability and property damage liability and a $5,000 limit for medical payments.
   a. What kind of property damage is covered? Give several examples.
   b. Does the medical payments coverage pay for losses even if Mr. Riskee is not liable for them? Explain. *Whose* injuries does it pay for?
   c. What additional coverages would you suggest that Mr. Riskee have on his *own* car? Explain each briefly.
   d. Would you recommend that the uninsured motorists coverage be included in this policy? Why or why not?

8. What are the "defense and supplementary payments" in the personal auto policy, and why may they be important to the policyholder?

9. Does a husband's personal auto policy cover his wife and children while they are driving the car of a friend? Explain. What difference does it make if the friend also has a similar policy?

10. A lends his automobile to B and rides with B. B negligently attempts to pass another car on a hill, and in a collision both A and B are seriously injured. Can A, the owner of the car and the named insured, sue B? If so, will A's policy protect B?

11. Mary, the daughter of X, is injured while riding to a Girl Scout meeting in a friend's car. Does the father's medical payments coverage on his personal automobile afford any relief in this situation?

12. X carries Part-D—damage to your own auto (comprehensive physical damage) coverage. Explain why you think the following losses would, or would not, be covered:
   a. Because of a delay in putting antifreeze into the automobile radiator, there is a freeze-up with serious damage.
   b. Would it be the same if there were damage resulting from the freezing of parts due to lack of lubrication?
   c. Vandals rip the car radio antenna off and dump red paint over the car.
   d. The car is stolen, and the thieves collide with an oncoming car in an attempt to escape from the police.
   e. X has both comprehensive physical damage and $100 deductible collision coverage. The car hits a telephone pole, causing $200 windshield damage.

13. Identify (by *letter*) the basic type of automobile insurance coverage from the list below which would provide protection for the following losses under the personal auto policy, and *explain briefly why:*

Coverage A—liability
Coverage B—medical payments
Coverage C—uninsured motorists
Coverage D—damage to your own car

Loss

a. Damage to your own car by colliding with a tree.
b. Medical expenses of a pedestrian because of your own negligence.
c. A broken finger by a passenger shutting the car door.
d. Damage to your own car by a tornado.
e. Damage to another person's car caused by negligent operation of your car.
f. Injury to your wife while she is riding in a friend's car, caused by another car driven by a person who has no insurance.
g. Loss of income of a person injured in another car caused by the negligent operation of your car.
h. Damage to a neighbor's front porch and lawn caused by the negligent operation of your car.
i. Cost to defend you against a lawsuit involving your car, even though nothing was paid.
j. Hospital expenses for you from an automobile accident in which you were negligent and ran off the road.

14. John has just had an accident. What recommendations would you give him as to *(a)* the *duties* he has under Part E of his PAP contract, and *(b)* what he should *not* do?

15. *Whose* injuries does the uninsured motorists coverage (C) of the personal auto policy cover? *When?*

16. What *additional* rights, and *reduced* rights, does an insured have under the no-fault laws in some states? How is the contract coverage of the insured *extended* to apply in other states in which the insured may be traveling, in regard to financial responsibility and no-fault laws?

17. How has the personal auto policy (PAP) made the contract more understandable to the average automobile insurance consumer? Explain fully.

18. "The business auto policy (BAP) is much like the personal auto policy (PAP), but important differences are found in the declarations and in some of the exclusions." Explain this statement.

Chapter 21

Outline of concepts

Crime insurance and suretyship both deal with the increasing peril of *dishonesty,* or *crimes against property.* Basic divisions are:

Burglary-theft insurance, which covers *nonemployee* dishonesty:

Perils are *burglary, robbery,* and *larcency* (*theft* includes all three).

Underwriting faces *moral hazard, adverse selection,* and *underinsurance.*

Basic contract parts are the declarations, insuring agreements, exclusions, and conditions.

Personal theft insurance is common today in homeowners' policies.

Business burglary-theft insurance (often in *special multiperil policies*) includes contracts for:

Mercantile open-stock burglary policy for merchandise.

Safe burglary policy for money, securities, and other property.

Mercantile robbery policy for inside or outside "holdup" coverage.

Paymaster robbery policy for large amounts of money coverage.

Forgery insurance, primarily for outgoing commercial paper.

Storekeepers'; and office, burglary, and robbery for $1,000 or less.

Money and securities policy (broad form) for *"all risks"* of loss.

Comprehensive 3-D policy for the broadest *dishonesty* insurance.

Blanket crime policy, with a single insurance amount.

Suretyship involves a *guarantee* that a person will perform an obligation.

Nature and development from personal to corporate sureties are traced.

Insurance and suretyship are compared and contrasted.

General divisions (*fidelity* and *surety* bonds) and basic features are noted.

Fidelity bonds insure the peril of *employee dishonesty* in:

Individual bonds, for a specific employee;

Schedule bonds, for named employees, or for a position;

Blanket bonds, for covering all employees, in either *blanket position* or in *commercial blanket* bonds; and

Public official bonds, often required by law.

Judicial bonds are of two types—*fiduciary* and *litigant* bonds.

Contract bonds are *construction, supply, maintenance,* and other types.

Crime insurance and suretyship

One of the characteristics of the total property-liability insurance field is the almost overwhelming variety of perils and coverages that it includes. Part IV has already introduced fire, indirect loss, transportation, liability, workers' compensation, and automobile insurance. The scope of the field does not stop there but also encompasses crime perils discussed in this chapter, including the closely related suretyship guarantees.

The relationship between the crime and surety fields may be seen by the size of their annual insurance premiums, as shown in Table-21–1.

Thus the total size of the crime and suretyship fields of insurance represents approximately $1.5 billion of annual premium—hardly insignificant, but relatively small in relation to fire and allied lines ($5 billion), transportation ($4 billion), liability ($7 billion), workers' compensation ($15 billion), and automobile ($41 billion) insurance.[1]

Separate treatment of these areas is warranted for several other reasons. The previous figures do not include crime insurance and bond premiums when these perils are included in the very popular multiple-line insurance coverages (see Chapter 23). Also, the insurance and risk-management concepts and principles for these fields are sometimes quite different from those for the types of property-liability insurance discussed previously. The specialized nature of these perils warrant a closer look at their problems and solutions, including the unusual features of the insurance coverages for them.

BASIC DIVISIONS OF CRIME INSURANCE, INCLUDING SURETYSHIP

Crime insurance, or as it is sometimes called, *dishonesty* insurance, pays owners for the loss of their property due to its being wrongfully taken by someone else. The related field of *suretyship* is partially based

---

[1] *Insurance Facts* (New York: Insurance Information Institute, 1982–83), p. 13.

Table 21–1. Crime insurance and suretyship coverage

Kind of insurance	Net premiums written	
Burglary-theft insurance		$ 135,000,000
Suretyship		
a. Surety bonds	$970,000,000	
b. Fidelity bonds	380,000,000	1,350,000,000
Total		$1,485,000,000

Source: *Insurance Facts* (New York: Insurance Information Institute, 1982–83), pp. 13 and 27. Premium figures are for 1981.

upon the dishonesty peril but also involves a broader guarantee of the satisfactory performance of duties by various persons.

Money is the type of property that is most commonly taken dishonestly. This area of crimes against property is likely to conjure up visions of "Bonnie and Clyde" bank holdups, but the field of crime insurance is much broader. First, the types of property insured include merchandise and many types of personal property other than money.[2] Second, the criminals taking property are either (1) members of the *public* (the most notorious being labeled "public enemies") or (2) *employees.*

The subject of the first major section of the chapter is *burglary-theft* insurance, which covers nonemployee dishonesty. Employee dishonesty, the basis of the *fidelity bond* business, is discussed in the second major section of this chapter as a part of *suretyship.* Suretyship also includes some bonds, such as judicial and contract bonds, which cover losses due to neglect as well as dishonesty.

Many of these types of bonds and insurance are for coverage of *business* exposures, which probably involves three fourths or more of the total premiums. Some of the burglary-theft insurance, particularly the important theft coverage that is now included in the homeowners' policies, and some of the surety bonds are for *personal* exposures.

BURGLARY-THEFT INSURANCE

Most crimes against property, except those committed by employees, are included in what the insurance business calls *burglary-theft* insurance. The direct effect of such losses is borne by individuals and organizations, and increasing insurance costs are a part of the burden. One innovative judge recently decided that burglars should pay their share, too, and sentenced a burglar to pay a restaurant's insurance costs for three years!

---

[2] Crime insurance as discussed in this chapter is mostly property insurance. The term also includes a few forms of liability insurance, however, such as innkeepers' and warehousers' legal liability, and safe deposit box insurance (see Appendix E).

Burglary-theft risk management

From a risk-management standpoint, crime coverages are important both because of the high concentration of certain types of property values exposed to loss and because of the frequency with which losses occur. Stolen property losses of about $6 *billion* occur each year, not including property losses due to auto theft or employee dishonesty, in 11.4 million robberies, burglaries, and larcenies.[3] The total annual cost of crimes against property includes many more billions of dollars of *uninsured* losses, and crime *prevention* efforts. *Risk identification* checklists and classifications of potential crimes are used to carry out the first step in the risk-management process.

The need to coordinate *risk control* (especially loss prevention) techniques with risk financing through insurance is increasingly recognized. Homeowners can use deadbolt locks, window alarms, better lighting, and security systems reporting to central stations or to the police. Businesses often add sophisticated alarm equipment, audit and inventory controls, watch dogs, security guards, and many other methods to reduce property thefts.[4]

Such private efforts also include collective plans as, for example, the Insurance Crime Prevention Institute supported by many insurers, and the National Crime Protection Institute to help train police officers in better crime protection techniques. The need to coordinate private and public efforts is also important. Increases in suburban crimes and in fire losses due to arson are examples of troublesome crime areas today where citizens can work to reduce crime rates.[5] Crime prevention efforts through the cooperation of industry and government authorities are an essential part of maintaining market availability for burglary-theft insurance.[6]

Partial *risk retention* can be used in burglary-theft insurance policies by having deductibles apply to the coverage, ranging from several hundred dollars to $1,000 or more.

Perils

Technically, the term *theft* is broad enough to include any act of stealing or taking another's property. This peril includes three parts: (1) bur-

---

[3] Ibid., p. 64. Burglaries totaled 3.8 million; larcenies, 7.1 million; and robberies, ½ million. (Definitions of these different crimes are noted in the next section of the text.)

[4] "The Face of Crime," *Journal of Insurance* 42, no. 2 (March–April 1981). This special issue has good advice on how to keep the burglar away from homes, how to cope with the corporate crook, and theft by computers.

[5] "Citizens Against Crime," *Journal of Insurance* 43, (May–June 1982), p. 9.

[6] An example of cooperative educational, statistical, and enforcement efforts is the National Crime Prevention Association. "Crime Prevention: a Common Cause," *Journal of Insurance* 38, no. 6 (September–October 1977), pp. 9–24.

glary, (2) robbery, and (3) larceny. Theft by business employees is discussed separately under fidelity bonds.

Burglary, robbery, and larceny are not always defined identically in the statutes of different jurisdictions. To eliminate any element of uncertainty, policies covering theft losses provide a definition of the peril to be covered. Briefly, *burglary* is the taking of the property of another by the forcible breaking and entering of the premises. *Robbery* consists of the carrying away of the personal property of others in their presence by violence or by putting them in fear. *Larceny* is any theft except burglary or robbery. Larceny losses would include thefts by sneak thieves, shoplifters, mechanics, or others having access to the premises of the insured.

Other losses related to the above perils are included in some burglary-theft contracts. *Damage to the property* of the insured by burglary, robbery, vandalism, and malicious mischief is often included. A few contracts, such as the "package" crime insurance coverages discussed later, include *destruction* by almost any cause, and some contracts include *disappearance,* where no proof that the property was taken is required.

Underwriting

Burglary-theft insurance is quite different from most of the types of insurance discussed so far in this text. One of the most unusual characteristics of burglary-theft insurance is the high degree of *moral hazard,* the increased possibility of loss because of fraud or dishonesty by the insureds themselves. The basic act of stealing is often difficult to prove, and deciding whether the insured or others are responsible is not an easy task in many crime coverages. The generally broad definitions used in many of the contracts (such as "theft," "mysterious disappearance," etc.) and the high concentration of value in many of the types of property covered (such as money, jewelry, etc.) also add to the moral hazard.

Normally, only those insureds with substantial exposure to loss insure against the burglary-theft perils. It was noted earlier that only $135 million in annual premiums insure these perils. The estimated $6 billion annual loss would indicate that only a very small proportion of such losses are insured. The tendency for the best insureds not to insure and for the worst ones (from the standpoint of potential loss) to insure is pronounced. Fortunately, some progress in reducing the effects of such *adverse selection* against the insurer is being made as more insureds purchase these types of insurance. For example, the homeowner's program, which automatically includes theft coverage, has helped spread burglary-theft coverage to most homes and families. The special multiperil (SMP) program for businesses, too, is making such coverage much more readily available to insureds as an optional choice in the contracts. (See Chapter 23.)

The basic tendency to *underinsure* the potential burglary-theft exposure is also a serious problem. For most other types of insurance, the insureds buy coverage at or close to the value of the property, either because they realize the possibility of serious or total loss (fire insurance) or because they are forced to do so (automobile collision and physical damage on financed cars). Most burglary-theft insureds purchase only a small amount of coverage, assuming that very large losses are unlikely. Two methods are used to encourage the insured to purchase insurance amounts in reasonable relationship to value. One method is the *coinsurance* clause, discussed later in connection with open-stock burglary insurance. This operates like the fire insurance coinsurance clause, but the percentage requirement is often permitted to be less than 80 percent of value, and a maximum loss-potential limit is usually established in order to reduce the required amount when certain types of property are insured. A second method is the *rating system,* which is based upon a graded or sliding scale that reduces the cost of burglary-theft insurance per $1,000 as more insurance is purchased. For example, the first $1,000 of personal theft insurance might cost the insured $80 per year; the second $1,000, only $50; and the third or more, $30.

Burglary-theft insurance is carefully underwritten by most insurers. Inspection reports are commonly used in order to determine such things as the condition of the premises, the neighborhood, and the protective features of the property. Loss-prevention advice by agents and insurers can be of substantial value to insureds, both in preventing losses and in reducing rates. Actual and potential burglary alarm or security guard systems, locking devices, safes, inventory and cash systems, and many other features should be carefully evaluated as the process of risk management is followed in developing recommendations for the prospective insured.[7] Increasing problems of availability of coverage in urban areas have also led the federal government to encourage loss prevention and the insuring of crime losses (see Chapter 24).

Basic contract parts

Policies in the burglary-theft category generally follow the pattern already noticed with respect to many other insurance contracts. There are four sections: (1) declarations, (2) insuring agreements, (3) exclusions, and (4) conditions. Most policies have about four pages. The printed policy is included in the first three pages, and the fourth is reserved for endorsements.

---

[7] A fast-growing industry has developed for home and business security systems, including American District Telegraph (ADT) and many others. Modern methods using electric eyes, perimeter systems, ultrasonic and microwave detectors, and other methods should be considered.

Declarations. The first page of the policy contains the declarations, which are basically all the essential statements and specifications required for the particular exposure. They contain the name, address, and business of the insured; the policy period and the coverage, together with the limits of insurance, the premium to be charged, and the premises to which the policy applies.

The declarations will state whether or not a burglar alarm or security guard system is maintained, or any other warranty with respect to special protective features that reflect in a reduction in premium. These protective measures are conditions which are usually interpreted as suspending the coverage while they are not maintained, or excluding the coverage of losses attributable to their absence. Finally, there is a statement with respect to a history of previous losses or cancellations during the past five years, and whether any such insurance has been declined by any insurer.

Insuring agreements. The insuring agreements are preceded by a short paragraph in which the insurer agrees to indemnify the insured named in the declarations for certain losses. The insurer does so in consideration of the payment of the premium and in reliance upon the statements in the declarations. The insuring agreements then describe the perils (see above section) against which the insurance is written and the property covered.

The insuring agreement may consist of one or more parts. While the insuring agreement establishes in a broad way the nature of the perils to be covered, the extent of the protection can be determined only in connection with the exclusions, definitions, and conditions contained in the contract.

Exclusions. The exclusions in theft coverages are designed primarily to save the insured from paying twice for the same coverage. For example, theft of an automobile is excluded since such vehicles are ordinarily specifically insured. Other exclusions deal with features that apply to the particular type of coverage. Most contracts exclude losses attributable to war.

Conditions. The conditions follow the types already noticed with respect to other insurance contracts. They provide for notice and proof of loss, subrogation, assignment, cancellation, other insurance, action against the insurer, changes, special statutes, and a clause covering payment, replacement, and recovery. These clauses are to be found in one form or another in all theft policies. The notice of cancellation when the insurer elects to cancel, is 15 days in most instances, but longer in some forms.

The conditions peculiar to an individual policy concern themselves primarily with *(a)* definitions and *(b)* ownership of the property covered. Because of the differences in statutory definitions of various forms of *theft,* the extent of the coverage is clarified by specific definitions of theft in the conditions. Other terms, such as *custodian, guard, messenger,* and *premises,* are carefully defined. Loss is defined to include damage. Other specific definitions appear where the coverage requires it. Following the definitions is a condition with respect to ownership of the property insured. Burglary policies usually provide coverage for both the property of the insureds and property for which they may be held liable.

Personal theft insurance

All theft insurance may be divided into (1) *personal* and (2) *business* types. The remainder of this section on burglary-theft insurance is separated in this manner.

Personal theft contracts are seldom written today as separate policies, but the coverage of the more common broad form is similar to that available to the insured in the popular homeowners' policies.

The *broad form personal theft policy* provides two major types of coverage: (1) theft from the premises or a depository and (2) theft away from the premises. The coverage is very broad in that the word *theft* includes burglary, robbery, and larceny. It may be attributable to burglars, occasional employees, or for that matter anyone except relatives permanently residing with the insured. The peril of *mysterious disappearance* is also named, but it is covered by interpretation rather than by being specifically defined in the contract. It applies to any insured property, except a precious or semiprecious stone removed from its setting in any watch or piece of jewelry. This means that if any piece of insured property is missing, with the exceptions noted, and there is no explanation for its disappearance, then the loss is covered by the policy. Suppose a watch worn by the insured disappears, but it is not known whether the watch was stolen, merely fell off, or was misplaced somewhere. Such loss would probably be covered as a mysterious disappearance.

Including the peril of "mysterious disappearance" affords an extremely liberal coverage. Frequently there is doubt as to whether the claims are actually the outgrowth of theft losses. The homeowners' program restricts its contracts to pay only for loss "from a known place under circumstances when a probability of theft exists."

Coverage includes the property of the insured, the insured's family, relatives, guests, residence employees, and other permanent members of the household. On-premises coverage applies automatically when the named insured moves to new premises. Off-premises coverage is worldwide and extends to provide coverage on property unattended in automobiles and property in charge of a carrier for hire. The policy also covers damage caused by burglars, robbers, and thieves to the insured property or to the premises occupied by the insured, and loss or damage caused by vandalism or malicious mischief.

For the purpose of insurance, property is classified into: *(a)* jewelry, sterling silver, and furs; *(b)* other property not specifically insured; and *(c)* specified articles described and insured for specific amounts. Specified limits of insurance are applied to the first two categories, and specified amounts are applied to each article in the third category. If a separate amount of insurance is set for the jewelry, silver, and furs group, and another for other property in the second category, this is called "divided coverage." It is not necessary, however, to separate jewelry, silver, and furs, although this is often done. Property not specifically insured is covered by "blanket coverage," the amount of insurance applying to any losses of general personal property, such as household furniture, clothing, rugs, musical instruments, cameras, money ($100 limit, usually), and securities. In addition, any particularly valuable items may be scheduled and insured for a separate amount, and this is called "specific coverage."

The insured may elect one or several combinations of divided, blanket, and specific coverage. The rates vary according to the choices of the insured, the occupancy of the premises, and the territorial classification.

Business burglary-theft insurance

Insurance against burglary-theft perils includes several basic types for most general businesses. Banks and other financial institutions have special forms (see Appendix E for some examples). Also very important today are the "package" crime coverages discussed at the end of this section. Many of these forms are now included in the SMP or other multiple-line insurance policies (see Chapter 23).

Mercantile open-stock burglary policy.   Basically, this policy provides *(a)* burglary insurance and *(b)* insurance coverage for property damage attributable to burglary. The burglary peril is defined in the policy, and by means of specific endorsements in connection with certain carefully underwritten risks, the policy may be extended to cover the perils of theft, larceny, and robbery.

Unlike insurance coverages for money and securities that are written on all-risks or broad forms, all-risks policies are never written to cover mercantile open stock. The policy is a specified-perils contract covering *(a)* burglary, *(b)* property damage, *(c)* robbery by threat or violence to a security guard, and *(d)* in some instances, theft.

The contract indemnifies the insured for loss of the insured property caused by *burglary* while the premises are not open for business. This includes breaking out (of someone hiding in the premises) as well as breaking in by actual force and violence as evidenced by visible marks made by tools, explosives, electricity, or chemicals. The policy covers all *merchandise* in the insured premises as well as furniture, fixtures, and equipment, but not money and securities.

The property insured must be on the "premises" described in the contract application, which means the interior of the building, excluding island showcases or outside show windows not opening directly into the interior of the premises. Specific types of property excluded are furs or fur articles taken from inside show windows by breaking glass from outside; any property over $100 taken from outside show windows that are inside the building line; jewelry in excess of $50 per article; manuscripts; and records. Several of these limitations can be removed by an endorsement for an additional premium. The property insured is basically merchandise, but it is also extended to include property that the insured holds as a bailee. Burglary losses caused or aided by the insured, an associate, or an employee are not covered.

As is usually the case in burglary insurance, *property damage* by a burglary or an attempted burglary is covered. This coverage includes merchandise, furniture, fixtures, and equipment in the premises, as well as damages to the premises if the insured is the owner or is liable for the damage.

Theft coverage is only rarely provided in this policy, and insurance is practically never the answer for retail stores, where shoplifting losses add an estimated 2 to 3 percent to the cost of merchandise. The importance of good risk-management practices to prevent employee theft is seen in the annual losses due to shoplifting: $4 billion in inventory shortages and 4 million shoplifters caught. The prevention of such losses through internal controls (audits, closed-circuit TV, sensormatic devices fixed to merchandise, security guards, and so on) is strongly advocated.[8]

All of the coverages apply only while the premises of the insured are closed to business. The contract is sometimes said to be a "nighttime, Saturdays, Sundays" policy. The other exclusions are: *(a)* loss in excess of actual cash value or cost to repair or replace, *(b)* losses contributed to by a change in the condition of the risk or occurring while a protective system for which a premium reduction is allowed is not maintained; *(c)* losses due to war, vandalism, malicious mischief, nuclear energy, and dishonesty of employees; *(d)* loss or damage that cannot be ascertained from the records of the insured; and *(e)* "mysterious disappearance" (unexplained) losses.

The mercantile open-stock burglary form introduces a feature peculiar to this type of policy. The rating manual provides for a classification

---

[8] Al Frantz, "Shoplifting—The $4 Billion 'Boost'," *Journal of Insurance* 39, no. 1 (January–February 1978), p. 24; "Shoplifting—Is Prevention the Only Insurance?" *Insurance Marketing,* June 1978, p. 30; and Peter Nulty, "Sensormatic Collars the Shoplifter," *Fortune,* February 25, 1980, p. 114.

of risks according to the type of business and establishes a limit known as the *coinsurance limit* for each classification. The coinsurance limit expressed for a class of business is in a dollar amount. It represents a maximum probable loss for the type of goods in the class. For example, the coinsurance limit might be set at $10,000 for heavy goods such as pianos, but at $20,000 for smaller, more stealable goods such as clothing. To determine the amount of insurance to be carried for a given risk, and therefore to avoid a coinsurance penalty, it is necessary to know *(a)* the value of the stock, *(b)* the coinsurance limit, and *(c)* the coinsurance percentage as determined by the rating territory.

There is also a *coinsurance clause* requirement expressed as a percentage of the value of the stock and based upon location. The country is divided into territories, and the requirement varies from 40 percent to 80 percent because of the larger or more frequent losses in urban areas.

To avoid penalty the insured must carry an amount of insurance which equals or exceeds the *smaller* of either the coinsurance limit *or* the amount determined by applying the coinsurance percentage to the value of merchandise at the time of loss. The operation of the coinsurance clause under the foregoing condition may be illustrated by the following example:

Value of inventory of a television store	$100,000
Coinsurance percentage for specified territory, 60 percent	60,000
Coinsurance limit for specified territory	40,000

To comply with the coinsurance clause, the insured must carry 60 percent of the value of the inventory; but since the coinsurance limit is less than 60 percent of the value of the inventory, the coinsurance requirement is fully satisfied if $40,000 of insurance is carried.

Safe burglary policy. The insurance agreement of this policy provides indemnity to the insured for loss of the insured property from within the vault or safe by safe burglary. The term *safe burglary* is defined to mean the felonious abstraction of insured property from the covered safe when all doors of the safe are duly closed and locked.

The property insured includes *(a)* money, *(b)* securities, and *(c)* other property. The coverage is not limited to strictly mercantile risks but may be issued to any person or organization owning a safe or vault. Money is defined as "currency, coins, bank notes, bullion and traveler's checks, registered checks, and money orders held for sale to the public." Securities include all negotiable and nonnegotiable instruments representing either money or other property, such as stamps, checks, drafts, bonds, and stock certificates or contracts. The policy also covers other property of any kind kept by the insured in the safe, except manuscripts, records, and accounts.

In order to establish a loss under a mercantile safe policy, it must be shown that a *burglary* actually occurred or was attempted. Entry to the safe or vault must have been effected by the use of tools, explosives, electricity, or gas or other chemicals upon the exterior of the safe, at a time when it was properly closed and locked by at least one combination or time lock. Evidence of the force used must appear on the exterior of the safe. An adequate set of books must be maintained from which the value of the lost or damaged items can be determined.

Under the safe burglary policy, the insurer is not liable for losses occurring while a combination or time lock, burglary alarm, vault, or private security guard service warranted in the policy declarations is not maintained. These protective measures are considered conditions of the contract, which if unmet will exclude coverage for losses. Losses effected by opening the door of the safe or vault by manipulation of the lock are regarded as theft losses not in the burglary category. If the manipulation is performed by an employee of the insured, the protection is available through a fidelity bond coverage.

The contract extends to cover *property damage* to the safe (or the insured's property inside) caused by burglary or attempted burglary of the insured's safe. It also covers property damage to furniture, equipment, and merchandise on the premises, if the insured is the owner or is liable for damages to the premises.

Rates for safe insurance are quoted per $1,000 of insurance and depend upon: (1) the type of safe, (2) the territory, (3) the class of business, and (4) the property covered. Safes are classified into groups of fire-resistive and burglar-resistive safes. Discounts are allowed for private security guards, safes equipped with an approved relocking system, or premises protected with tear-gas systems. Discounts are also allowed when there is more than one safe in a single location.

Mercantile robbery policy. Stores, offices, and other organizations are not immune from robbery during business hours; and messengers carrying money and valuables are held up and robbed. Messenger and robbery insurance coverages are: *(a)* inside holdup insurance, which covers robbery risks (and kidnapping, if included); and *(b)* outside holdup insurance, which covers the risk of messenger robbery. Either coverage is available separately in the *mercantile robbery policy.*

The *inside holdup* coverage covers loss or damage to the insured property through robbery or attempted robbery and loss or damage to furniture, fixtures, and other property. The coverage is effective on a 24-hour basis and furnishes protection only within the insured's premises. Loss or damage to merchandise stolen from a show window by a person who has broken the glass from the outside is covered while the premises are regularly open for business. *Kidnapping* is sometimes resorted to by robbers who hold an owner or an employee, usually off the premises, later forcing the person detained to open the premises or supply information, keys, or other means of admission.

The *outside holdup* feature of the contract covers the insured for robbery losses if the robbery or attempted robbery takes place outside the premises of the insured. It covers not only messenger robbery but also damage resulting from robbery or attempted robbery of money, securities, merchandise, or the messenger's container. The coverage provides 24-hour protection.

The premium for inside and outside robbery is dependent upon the territory in which the risk is located, the number of persons on duty within the insured's premises, the kind of business, the protective measures, and the kind of property. Credits on the rate under the messenger robbery form are allowed for the use of a private conveyance, a locked messenger chest or satchel attached by a chain or a wire strap to the custodian or vehicle conveying the funds, and a route limited to the interior of the building. Burglary (and robbery and theft, if desired) coverage in the home of the custodian may be endorsed to the policy.

Paymaster robbery policy. Many businesses and organizations need off-premises coverage only because they pay their employees in cash and transfer large sums of money from point to point. The *paymaster robbery policy* provides day and night protection for the insured from loss by robbery from a custodian *inside or outside* the insured's premises of money or checks held solely for *payroll* purposes. It also covers an amount not exceeding 10 percent of the amount of the insurance, for money and securities not intended solely for payroll purposes. Robbery losses attributable to kidnapping of a custodian are included. While on the premises of the employer, employees of the insured are protected against loss of money or checks which is the outgrowth of a robbery of the custodian or an attempt thereat. Payroll funds taken by a safe burglary do not come within the protection of the policy.

Paymaster robbery, or all-risks, coverage is also available by endorsement under the money and securities broad form policy (see later section).

Forgery insurance policy. The *depositor's forgery policy,* sometimes referred to as a "forgery bond," is issued to individuals, firms, or corporations. It is not issued to banks and savings and loan associations. The policy is divided into two sections: *(a)* covering outgoing items and *(b)* covering incoming items. The policy usually protects the insured only for outgoing items, against forgery losses on commercial paper (checks, drafts, notes, etc.) issued or presumed to have been issued by the insured or an authorized agent. The incoming coverage is seldom written today, as most of these losses should be guarded against by ordinary business credit procedures.

Storekeepers', and office, burglary, and robbery policies. A type of "package" crime insurance, including limited amounts of a number of types of burglary-theft insurance, is available to the small *storekeeper and merchant*. It provides at reasonable cost a convenient blanket burglary and robbery coverage.

The storekeepers' form in a single "all-or-none" policy covers the insured against loss of money, securities, and merchandise, together with damage to property. The coverage is provided under seven headings, with $250 insurance applying to each as follows: (1) inside robbery, (2) outside or messenger robbery, (3) kidnapping the custodian and forcing the custodian to open the premises, (4) safe burglary ($50 limit on money and securities), (5) theft from a bank depository or a custodian's home, (6) open-stock burglary, and (7) damage to the premises by burglary or robbery. The limit for each coverage may be increased in multiples of $250 to a usual maximum of $1,000. A broad form of this policy adds several other coverages, such as forgery, vandalism, and malicious mischief.

A policy similar to the storekeepers' policy is written to provide a burglary and robbery coverage for *offices*. It covers office equipment and other property but excludes merchandise. A $100 limit applies to money and securities. The class of risk for which the office form is designed includes accountants, architects, attorneys, insurance offices, brokers, contractors, dentists, doctors and the like. Policies similar to those for stores and offices are available to service stations and other businesses.

Money and securities policy (broad form). To provide a broader package of coverage, the *money and securities policy (broad form)* offers much more than burglary and robbery coverage. It insures *money and securities* for *all risks* of disappearance, wrongful abstraction, and destruction (including fire). Other property is covered only for safe burglary, robbery, or theft from a messenger's home. Damage to property caused by burglary or robbery is included.

The policy does not provide employee dishonesty coverage or open-stock burglary coverage. Available to many businesses, this policy has two optional insuring clauses: *(a)* inside protection and *(b)* outside protection. The policy may be written to cover either or both.

The policy may cover securities only. This form has a particular appeal to institutions and individuals that own large values in securities. Trustees or treasurers of endowed institutions, investment trusts, holding companies, and brokers frequently have in their possession securities of large values. Even with the protection afforded by the safe-deposit box, the possibility of loss growing out of mysterious disappearances, entry to the box by misrepresentation or fraud, as well as burglary or robbery, constitutes a real peril. In addition, fire, theft, tornado, riot, explosion, or other like perils might cause the destruction of the box and its contents. With the exception of certain bonds written for financial institutions, almost all other policies specifically exclude or limit losses growing out of the destruction of money and securities.

Comprehensive dishonesty, disappearance, and destruction policy. This contract, familiarly known as the 3-D *policy,* was designed to provide the broadest possible crime coverage for business firms.[9] Since it combines *fidelity and burglary* coverages, it is a convenient method of insuring all crime perils. It combines in a single document coverages that at one time were available only as separate policies.

The basic printed form, available in the 3-D policy or as an endorsement under the special multiple-peril policy (SMP), contains five separate and optional insuring clauses, with a separate limit of insurance for each:

1. Employee dishonesty coverage (in either the commercial blanket *or* blanket position bond forms discussed in the next section). Covered are loss of money, securities, or other property through any fraudulent or dishonest act or acts committed by any *employees,* acting alone or in collusion with others. Embezzlement is a common example.

2. Loss inside the premises coverage. The actual destruction, disappearance, or wrongful abstraction of *money or securities within* the insured's premises (or banking or safe-deposit premises) is included. The *broad form* perils of burglary, robbery, or theft are covered, and *other property* is covered for safe (or locked cash drawer) burglary or robbery.

3. Loss outside the premises coverage. Loss of money or securities is covered *off* the insured's premises, for destruction, disappearance, or wrongful abstraction while being conveyed by a messenger or an armored car vehicle or while within the living quarters of the home of a messenger. Loss of other property is covered for off-premises robbery in these same circumstances.

4. Money orders and counterfeit paper currency coverage. Loss is covered due to the acceptance in good faith of (1) any post office or express money order, if not paid on presentation, or (2) any counterfeit U.S. or Canadian paper currency. Such bogus items are sometimes called "incoming" risks.

5. Depositor's forgery coverage. Covered is loss for the insured, or any bank in which the insured has an account, through forgery or alteration of checks, drafts, promissory notes, or similar written promises to pay money. Examples of such "outgoing" risks include checks made or drawn in the name of the insured to fictitious payers, by anyone impersonating another, or payroll checks endorsed by someone without

---

[9] The student is referred to other sources for some policy details not included here. See Harold F. Gee, *Comprehensive 3-D Primer* (Indianapolis: Rough Notes, republished about every four years); and *Fire, Casualty,* and *Surety Bulletins* (Cincinnati: National Underwriter, loose-leaf).

proper authority. This coverage is not often purchased in the 3-D policy, because banks which cash such forgeries without proper identification of the payees would usually be responsible for such losses unless the insured's negligence contributed substantially to the forgery.

In addition to the five basic coverages, 13 other endorsements are available in order to include mercantile open-stock (burglary or theft), payroll, office equipment, credit card forgery, extortion, and other crime coverages.

Protection may be extended to virtually every conceivable type of crime loss. The insured elects those coverages desired in the policy. The policy does not have a uniform limit applying to each of the insuring clauses; an optional amount is chosen to apply to each of the various clauses. The broad protection of the 3-D policy and its advantage of convenience have made it one of the most popular methods for businesses to insure their crime and fidelity bond perils.

Blanket crime policy.   This contract is very similar to the 3-D policy. However, a major difference is that it includes the first five basic coverages as a package; all are included *automatically*. Another basic difference is that the *blanket crime policy* provides a *single insuring limit* rather than separate limits for each of the coverages. The minimum amount must be at least $1,000, but other minimums, such as $10,000 for fidelity coverage, may also apply. For example, a $100,000 policy would provide a total of that amount as needed for any of the fidelity, money and securities, or forgery coverages included in the contract. Office equipment theft, payroll, extortion, and other coverages are optional.

Some insureds prefer the automatic mandatory inclusion of the five basic perils under a single limit of coverage in the blanket crime policy; others, particularly those insureds with substantial fidelity exposures, prefer the flexibility of the 3-D policy.

SURETYSHIP

Nature and development

The contract of suretyship is a credit device that made its appearance with the earliest development of business obligations. Under the terms of a surety agreement, or *bond,* one party becomes answerable to a third party for the acts or neglect of a second party. The answerable party is the *surety,* and the one for whose debt or obligation the surety is responsible is the *principal debtor,* or more commonly referred to as the *principal* or *obligor.* The person protected by the agreement is called the *obligee.* For example, in a fidelity bond, the surety accepts the responsibility of the employee (the obligor) to the employer (the obligee) for faithful performance of the duties of employment. In a contract bond, the surety accepts responsibility of the contractor (the obligor) to the property owner (the obligee) for carrying out the construction or supply contract.

Before the writing of surety bonds became an established business, persons acting in a fiduciary capacity or occupying positions of trust requiring sureties were obliged to appeal to relatives or friends. More often than not, the *personal* surety signed a bond without remuneration and purely as a favor. This practice was the source of many difficulties, not to say loss and hard feelings. *Corporate* surety bonds were first offered in England to insure the honesty of servants, but it was not until the mid-1800s that the corporate fidelity business for insuring employees became established. Corporate suretyship, however, was slow in developing. As the idea of corporate sureties became better known, individuals became increasingly reluctant to assume obligations without remuneration. Also tending to stimulate the development of corporate suretyship were the permanence and stability of the surety corporations. These are subject to the regulations provided by the statutes; their chief function is to meet losses when they occur. Individual sureties are unable to supply a bond with the same safety and stability that a surety company can. For this reason, those requiring bonds today insist upon satisfactory corporate sureties.

Insurance and suretyship

Suretyship, especially fidelity bonding, is like insurance in some respects. The bonds look like insurance contracts, too, and they are often issued by agents who write both insurance contracts and surety bonds. The regulation of bonds usually falls under the state insurance departments. If the definition of insurance is limited to transfer of risk, bonds meet this criterion (although the pooling method and purpose do differ somewhat).

However, the surety bond differs from insurance in several ways. Bonds always have *three parties to the contract* (see previous section), whereas insurance contracts often have only two. *Individuals may* act as sureties, although they seldom do. In contrast to many insurance contracts, most surety bonds are *not cancellable by the surety.*

Also, a primary distinction is that in bonds there exists a *right of indemnity* between the surety and the principal debtor. If the surety is called upon to pay a loss under the bond, the surety may in turn proceed against the principal, who is primarily liable on the agreement. This is in contrast to the insurance contract, which obligates the insurer to pay losses in accordance with the policy terms without recourse to any other party to the contract. The liability of the principal is to be contrasted with the liability of third parties against whom an insurer may proceed under its rights of subrogation. In the case of subrogation, the third party is not a party to the contract.

Another basic difference is that most insurance contracts anticipate that there will be losses, the outgrowth of the happening of the contingency covered by the policy. In the surety contract, on the other hand, the promise of the surety is secondary, after the failure of the principal to perform a specific obligation. Failure may be occasioned by dishonesty, incompetence, or lack of resources. Surety bonds are usually written on the assumption that *losses* will be a *relatively small* part of the cost of the bond. They are written to strengthen the credit or provide a guarantee for the principal rather than with the primary purpose of paying losses. Fidelity bonds do anticipate losses and in this respect are more like insurance than are surety bonds.

In summary, the distinctions between suretyship and insurance are of some importance but do not always hold true if all types of insurance are compared with all types of bonds.

General divisions of suretyship

Bonding companies divide bonds into two classes: *(a) fidelity bonds* and *(b) surety bonds.* In general, all corporate bonds in which a surety agrees to answer for the nonperformance of a principal are surety bonds. However, a distinction is often made between a fidelity bond and a surety bond. In the case of a fidelity bond, the obligation of employees to be honest with their employers is implied rather than contractual. The bond reimburses an obligee (the employer) for loss of money or property growing out of dishonest acts of the principal (the employee). The surety bond, on the other hand, obligates the surety to be responsible for the performance of an expressed obligation of the principal. In the case of surety bonds, while a dishonest act may give rise to a loss, negligence and lack of ability on the part of the principal may also create a liability on the part of the surety. A default on the obligations, however caused, is covered.

The business of corporate suretyship has developed into three major divisions. These are: (1) fidelity bonds, (2) judicial bonds, and (3) contract bonds.[10] Some miscellaneous surety classes are of lesser importance (see Appendix E). A brief summary of each major class follows. Figure 21–1 shows the relationship among the classifications.

Under *fidelity bonds* the surety company reimburses employers for dishonesty losses of employees. The employer may be an individual, an

---

[10] Additional information is available in David Porter, *Fundamentals of Bonding* (Indianapolis: Rough Notes, 1978). Booklets on specific types of bonds are also published by the Surety Association of America (Metro Park, N.J.).

Figure 21–1. Types of fidelity and surety bonds

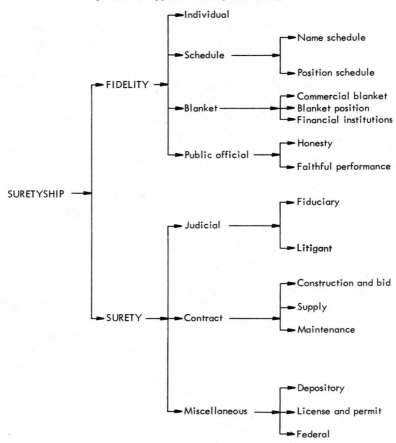

organization, or the public. Public official bonds are included as fidelity bonds because they basically concern dishonesty (and may be written for only that peril) and because the annual statement of insurers puts them in the fidelity classification.

Judicial bonds, sometimes referred to as "court bonds," are those required in court proceedings. There are two categories: *fiduciary* types are required of someone entrusted with property by the court; and *litigant* types are required of plaintiffs or defendants.

Contract bonds guarantee property owners who enter into contracts for construction that the work will be completed in accordance with the terms of the agreements. The surety company guarantees the performance of contracts and the credit of the person, such as contractors, who obligate themselves to build, supply or maintain some specific product or service.

Basic features of fidelity and surety bonds

There are certain features which are common to many fidelity and surety bonds. These characteristics will be discussed briefly before some of the more usual types of bonds are analyzed in reference to their specific provisions. Many of these features are concerned with identifying the limitations under which the surety promises to make payment for losses.

Underwriting. In order to issue bonds, the surety must have information about the principal and the function that is to be performed. Applications for bonds require an evaluation based on the three C's of suretyship—the applicant's *character, capacity,* and *capital.* The surety is only willing to make its guarantees or promises to pay on the basis of the obligors' reputation, general abilities and financial standing in carrying out their obligations.

Penalty of the bond. When a designated sum is written into the bond as a limit of the liability of the surety, the amount is called the *penalty* and the bond is a *fixed-penalty bond.* The penalty corresponds to the face or insurance amount of an insurance policy. Some bonds, known as *open-penalty bonds,* are written in which no amount of penalty is fixed. An example is a "lost instrument" bond which protects the issuer of a duplicate stock certificate or other legal paper that has been lost, stolen, or destroyed.

Obligation to bond. Persons who hold positions of trust should understand that negligent losses to property in their care can cause a *personal liability.* Failure by the directors to provide fidelity coverage upon employees of a bank is negligence, for example, and the directors may be held personally liable for dishonesty losses. Statutory requirements may be regarded as minimum requirements. What constitutes adequate bonding coverage must be decided by the circumstances surrounding each particular case.

Effect of fraud. If a surety has been induced by fraud of the principal to become a party to the bond, the *surety is still bound* to provide protection for an innocent obligee.

As to the obligation of the obligee to inform the surety of all the facts affecting the risk, it was originally held that the contract was *uberrimae fidei* (of utmost faith). The opinion now prevails that only when inquiry is made by the surety and disclosures by the obligee are incomplete, insufficient, misleading, or false, is the contract jeopardized.

Statute of frauds. Unlike other contracts of insurance, which are usually in writing (but are not required to be), surety contracts fall within the statute of frauds. Under these statutes, in most of our states, an agreement to answer for the debt, default, or miscarriages of any other person must be *in writing*. Thus, liability under fidelity and surety bonds is legally enforceable only if it is supported by written evidence of the agreement.

Assignment. Contracts of guarantee and suretyship are as a general rule assignable, even before a breach, unless by their terms assignment is limited or restricted. Fidelity bonds are not assignable before a loss without the consent of the surety because definite employees or positions are insured by the insurer, and others may not be substituted.

Subrogation. In contracts of suretyship, upon the payment by the surety of a debt of the principal, the surety is subrogated to all the rights of the creditor against the principal whose debt has been paid. This includes all securities, funds, liens, priorities, or equities held by the creditor as security.

Acts discharging surety. When a surety is liable for the honesty of an employee, upon the discovery of any dishonesty in connection with the duties for which the employee is bonded, the employer is obligated to dismiss the dishonest employee at once or to secure the consent of the surety for continued employment. Failure to follow this procedure will release the surety from any liability for loss occasioned by *further dishonest acts* of the employee.

Unless provided in the bond, no particular supervision over the bonded employee is required. It is usual, however, in the case of corporate fidelity bonds to require a warranty that periodic examinations or audits of the principal's accounts will be made. Failure to comply affords grounds for releasing the surety.

Contractor's bonds as a rule contain a clause permitting changes, alterations, or additions without the consent of the surety. However, if a change is such that the work becomes essentially different from that originally contemplated, the nonconsenting surety may be released.

Cosureties. Bonds issued in very large amounts are sometimes signed by more than one surety. Each company obligated on such a bond is known as a *cosurety*. When the individual limits of liability for the cosureties are set, it becomes necessary to do this through an agreement between the sureties that is known as a "side agreement."

Reinsurance. The laws of the various jurisdictions in this country fix a limit to the liability that is to be assumed by a surety company on a single risk. When attractive business is offered, but the limit of liability is in excess of that which the company may legally assume, or is willing to assume, it may write the bond and reinsure the excess liability with other surety companies, just as insurance companies reinsure their excess lines.

Indemnitors. An indemnity agreement is occasionally used when a contract bond is required by an applicant whose financial position or experience falls just short of meeting the surety's standards. The *indemnitors* are individuals who assume much the same responsibility as that assumed by an accommodation endorser of commercial paper. In the event of a default by the principal, the surety assumes the obligation but may in turn seek reimbursement from the indemnitors. Upon what grounds can a surety company justify asking for indemnitors if it is in the business of surety underwriting and is paid a premium for assuming the risk? The answer is the same as that which justifies a bank, which is in the business of lending money, in requiring endorsers before lending upon an unsecured note. The credit of the applicant is otherwise insufficient.

Legal capacity. To be bound on a contract of surety, the principal must have legal capacity to enter into the contract. For example, the agreement of an infant or an insane person is voidable. In the case of suretyship, the incapacity of the principal does not affect the liability of the surety. The surety is still liable even when the surety becomes a party to the agreement without knowledge of the incapacity of the principal, unless induced to do so through fraudulent concealment or misrepresentation.

Fidelity bonds

General classes. A fidelity bond pays an employer for loss growing out of *dishonest acts of employees*. Fidelity bonds are classified as to the extent of the protection they afford against (1) *larceny* and *embezzlement*, which are specific crimes for which conviction in the courts is necessary and (2) *dishonesty*. Most fidelity bonds today insure dishonesty, which includes all forms of theft, fraud, or misappropriation of an employer's property. For the purposes of underwriting, bonds are classified as: (1) bonds required by *private* employers to cover loss through dishonesty of employees and (2) bonds required of *public officers* for the faithful performance of their duties.

As to form, bonds are written as follows: (1) *individual* bonds, (2) *schedule* bonds, and (3) *blanket* bonds. Schedule bonds are written as *(a) name* schedule and *(b) position* schedule. Blanket bonds are subdivided into *(a) commercial blanket* and *(b) blanket position*. Since these classes represent some of the most important fidelity coverages, each will be discussed briefly in separate sections.

In addition to the foregoing, a large number of blanket bonds are written for banks and other financial institutions. The fidelity coverage often forms only a portion of the protection afforded. The specialized nature of these bonds causes them to be used less frequently by general business, so their discussion is reserved for more complete analysis in Appendix E.

Importance. Dramatic robberies with guns blazing and police sirens screaming are popular fare for television and movies, but it is the much less obvious "white-collar crime" that costs corporations and consumers an estimated $50 billion in *losses* every year. The notorious bank robber's haul only averages $10,000 according to FBI statistics, while the real growth industry for dishonesty is computer fraud, which exceeds $400,000 per loss. (See the Equity Funding scandal discussed in Chapter 28.)

A substantial part of the losses caused by criminals in gray flannel suits instead of stocking masks are caused by employees. The multibillion-dollar annual loss in the United States because of employee dishonesty is one example of the significance of fidelity bonds. Even more startling is the fact that only a very small part (probably less than 10 percent) of the total losses are recovered under fidelity bonds. Most financial institutions are bonded, but fewer than 25 percent of mercantile establishments protect themselves with fidelity bonds—and many of those are underinsured.[11]

Another reason for the importance of fidelity bonds is the use of these contracts in business *risk management*. Losses occur in fantastic amounts under the most unusual and unexpected circumstances. Many of the losses occur gradually over long periods of time, and only ultimate discovery shocks employers with the realization that thousands of dollars have been lost. Trusted bookkeepers steal money, but much more is lost through other employees who take tools, merchandise, raw materials, and other property. Purchasing agents, salespersons, clerks, supervisors, and executives all cause many losses, of the more obvious cash and financial assets as well as mundane by-product wastes that practically no one would expect to be stolen. For example, one employee in collusion with suppliers provided fraudulent samples of metal scrap to raise the price of purchased materials, and another sold broken glass to a competing bottle manufacturing plant.[12]

The only answer is for employers to exercise constant vigilance to reduce the probability and the extent of such losses *and* to purchase fidelity bond coverage. Many business firms have elaborate security systems involving many security guards, police dogs, and electronic devices. Others hire professional firms, such as Pinkerton's and the William J. Burns International Detective Agency, to design and maintain safeguarding systems, to perform the very important employee investigations, and to do other loss-prevention work. Because many businesses do not insure against employee dishonesty, the scope of the risk retained and the parallel need for loss prevention are increased. The techniques of embezzlement, for example, require close scrutiny of *every* employee because no

---

[11] *Insurance Facts*, p. 27.

[12] *Honesty Insurance*, booklet published by Insurance Company of North America.

clear-cut description of the typical embezzler is possible. The analysis of the causes of embezzlement, which include (1) need or desire, (2) rationalization, and (3) opportunity, furnishes the employer with many prospective methods by which management can control some employee dishonesty.[13]

Contract term and restoration clauses. Both individual and schedule fidelity bonds may be written on either a *term basis* or a *continuous basis*. If written for a term, the period is usually a year and the bond expires at the end of the term, as does an ordinary insurance policy, unless a continuation "certificate" is added. With the continuous form, which is the most common form for fidelity bonds, if premiums are paid when due, the bond remains in force until a party to the agreement cancels it.

Fidelity bonds may be canceled at any time by the employer or the bonding company. If the company wishes to cancel, notice is required and the conditions governing the notice are incorporated into the bond. In a bond for an individual employee, it also terminates on his or her death, resignation, or discharge.

Fidelity bonds provide coverage only if loss is sustained while the coverage is in effect or is discovered within a certain designated time. The cutoff period is usually one or two years. If a bond is terminated and a new one is purchased, the new surety usually agrees to pay for losses (up to the old limit) that occurred under the old bond but were not discovered until after the end of the discovery period of the old bond. This coverage formerly required special coverage called a "superseded suretyship rider."

There are two important types of *restoration clauses*. Under a simple restoration clause, a fidelity bond is automatically reinstated to its full amount after a loss. However, the amount reinstated is effective only for *future* losses. The most common and comprehensive restoration form is known as the "retroactive restoration clause," and it is used for most blanket bonds. The retroactive restoration clause automatically restores the full face of the bond as to *prior* losses following the discovery of a dishonest or fraudulent act. If a loss antedating the first loss is discovered later, that loss, as well as future losses, is covered in the full amount of the bond.

Individual bonds. The simplest bonds for private employers are *individual* bonds, which are written to guarantee against dishonest acts of a named individual. On the basis of an application from the employee, an investigation is made by the surety company. If the risk is acceptable, the surety company signs the bond, and this is delivered to the employer.

---

[13] A good survey of such controls, analyzed in flowcharts and with checklist questions to help evaluate present systems, is contained in *How to Reduce Embezzlement Losses* (New York: Royal Globe Insurance Companies).

Signature of the principal (employee) is the practice still followed, but it is not essential because the employee is liable for any dishonest act without regard to the bond itself. Separate individual fidelity bonds for each employee cause considerable confusion in keeping all employees covered and in renewing bonds as they expire.

Schedule fidelity bonds. To overcome this difficulty, the schedule bond is often used. The *name schedule bond* lists the names of all the employees to be covered and provides surety protection in a single document. The insuring clause indicates the acts of dishonesty to be covered. The name and a bond limit for each bonded employee is listed in the schedule. This permits flexibility in the amount of coverages. For example, the treasurer of a concern may be bonded on a name schedule bond for $100,000, while outside salespersons may be provided with satisfactory coverage in the amount of $25,000. As new employees are added to the staff, their names may be included in the coverage by endorsement; and if employees leave, they may be removed from the schedule. The persons named in the schedule are not required to sign the bond. Employees are required, however, to sign an application in which each agrees to indemnify the surety against any covered loss that he or she causes.

The principal difference between the name schedule bond and the *position schedule bond* is to be found in the method of preparing the schedule. In the name schedule bond, defaults of persons designated by name are covered. Instead of naming the persons to be covered, the position form contains a list of positions in the schedule, and the number of persons holding each of those positions. For example, a schedule might show one person in the position of treasurer and 20 persons as outside salespersons.

This bond appeals particularly to business concerns having a considerable turnover in personnel. In the schedule bond, each person within a listed position is bonded for the same amount. If two or more persons occupy the same position, the number in that position must be correctly listed. Otherwise, the employer will have to pay a share of any loss in proportion to the number of unlisted persons.

Under the position schedule bond, an automatic coverage for 60 days is provided which protects the employer in the event that additional persons are added to the same covered position. New positions of a class not already designated in the schedule may also be added automatically, but in this case it is usual to set a limit for the liability of the surety company. The automatic coverage is terminated at the end of 60 days unless a written request for continuation is filed by the employer and accepted by the surety.

Blanket fidelity bonds. Individual and schedule bonds involve considerable detail and care where there are frequent changes in personnel. In addition, losses frequently develop that are traceable to unbonded or inadequately bonded personnel. *Blanket fidelity bonds* cover *all employees.* There are two forms: *(a) commercial blanket bonds* and *(b) blanket position bonds.* Banks and other financial institutions have special blanket forms which are not available to general business firms (see Appendix E).

The commercial blanket bond is written for a stated limit *per loss,* with the aggregate lump sum applied collectively to all employees. The blanket position bond also covers all the employees of the insured. However, it differs in that the blanket position bond applies the loss limit to *each employee.* In the case of the blanket position bond, the company is theoretically liable for the penalty of the bond multiplied by the number of employees but only if the employees are in collusion. If a blanket position bond covers $20,000 per employee, for example, and five employees collaborate to each steal $15,000, a loss of $75,000 would be paid. (If one of the five stole $50,000 in such a case, however, then $30,000 would not be covered.)

The commercial blanket bond is the most popular type. It provides a catastrophe limit without requiring the choice of a separate limit of coverage for each employee. Also, the employer does not have to establish how much of a loss is caused by each employee in cases involving collusion by more than one employee.

The minimum limit sold is $2,500 per employee for the blanket position bond and $10,000 for the commercial blanket bond. The maximum limit is usually $100,000 for the blanket position bond, but no maximum limit is set, except by company practice, for the commercial blanket bond. Amounts such as $100,000 or more are quite common, and the cost of such a bond for a medium-sized retail store, for example, might be several hundred dollars per year. The rates vary with the number and type of the employees.

The Surety Association of America publishes an "exposure index" which suggests estimated bond limits on the basis of the sum of current assets (5 percent of goods and 20 percent of other current assets) and gross sales or income (10 percent). For example, a combined exposure index of about $100,000 might indicate a minimum bond of $50,000, or $5 million a bond of $500,000. The actual need would vary according to particular circumstances.

The definition of employees covered by the commercial blanket bond and the blanket position bond is identical. Both bonds cover all persons (except directors of the insured, if a corporation, who are not also officers of the corporation) who are in the regular service of the insured. They must be compensated by salary, wages, or commission, and they must be under the direction of the insured in the performance of their duties. The bonds do not cover agents or other like representatives. Territorial coverage includes all of the United States and Canada; and if desired, coverage may be extended to include approved employees in foreign countries. Executive officers of a corporation owning a majority of stock may be excluded from the coverage. Others excluded are canvassers, collectors, demonstrators, drivers, and outside salespersons of companies in certain designated lines of business. These employees are known as "Class A special employees," and they are sometimes excluded from the blanket bond and covered for a limited amount under a schedule bond at reduced cost.

The commercial blanket bond provides that the payment of a loss shall not reduce the amount payable for any other loss whether it is sustained before or after the shortage under consideration. This provision is unnecessary in the blanket position bond since the full penalty of the bond applies to each employee and a loss payable with respect to one employee in no way affects the coverage on the others.

There is also a difference in the discovery period after the termination of the entire bond. The commercial blanket bond allows 12 months, whereas the blanket position bond allows 24 months. Both forms provide group coverage in that fraudulence or dishonesty losses are paid if these are attributable to one or more employees even though the guilty party may not be designated.

Public official fidelity bonds.   The law requires that designated individual public officials be bonded, but losses frequently occur that are attributable to the acts of minor employees not covered by the statute. Thus, in order to cover all public employees, a *blanket bond* (with one limit per loss) or a *blanket position* (with a limit for each employee), is usually needed.

There are two forms written: *(a)* the *honesty* blanket bond and *(b)* the *faithful performance* blanket bond. Coverage under the faithful performance form provides protection against loss from the failure of employees to perform faithfully the duties of the office as required by law or to keep accurate accounts of all properties and monies in their control. In contrast, coverage under the honesty forms is limited to loss from dishonest or fraudulent acts committed by employees.

The blanket bond covers all officers and subordinates (except treasurers and tax collectors) who are not required by law to furnish an individual bond to qualify for office. All such employees may be covered on a single bond; or a separate bond may be executed for the different divisions or departments of any state, county, city, town, village, or other political subdivision.

Judicial bonds

All bonds filed in judicial proceedings are included within the category of judicial bonds. Judicial bonds also are sometimes referred to as "court bonds." The field is divided into two groups. *Fiduciary bonds* constitute the first group and include those bonds which guarantee the faithful performance of property administered under the supervision and jurisdiction of a court. The second group includes all those bonds required of *litigants* in a court action.

The coverage afforded by each subdivision is quite different. Fiduciary bonds, such as probate bonds, provide a guarantee that principals will discharge their trust honestly and in accordance with the law. The coverage is broader than one strictly against dishonesty since it also covers losses occasioned by negligence or lack of ability. In litigant bonds, which are used in connection with litigation, the obligation is the payment of money. Honesty, integrity, high standing, or ability have no effect in determining the obligation if the litigation is in the end decided against the principal. Examples include both those required of plaintiffs and defendants in various court actions.

Fiduciary bonds.   One of the most common types of fiduciary bonds is the *probate bond*. The guarantee of a probate bond is that fiduciaries will fulfill their trust in accordance with estate or other laws. It involves numerous specific obligations, such as the filing of inventories, taking prompt steps to conserve assets, properly investing funds, and properly making distributions where so directed. The surety company is interested not only in the honesty of the bonded persons but also in their knowledge of the fiduciary's responsibilities and their ability to fulfill the requirements of the trust. Among the more frequently used probate bonds are those required by law for administrators, executors, guardians, conservators, and testamentary trustees.

Because of the nature of the guarantee under a probate bond, surety companies are not always willing to assume the risk without retaining some control over the direction and management of the assets. In the writing of some bonds, a special *joint-control agreement* is executed at the time of application for the bond. When the principal and the surety agree to joint control, the principal is required to deposit all funds in a separate bank account. Checks may then be drawn on this account by the fiduciary, but they must be countersigned by a representative of the bonding company. Applicants frequently resent the request of surety companies for joint control, feeling that such a request reflects upon their honesty. However, the obligations placed by law upon fiduciaries are not always simple matters to those unacquainted with the duties of the position to which they have been appointed. Fiduciaries, by some improper act, though committed with the best intentions, or by the failure to act through carelessness or inadvertence, may cause huge losses. The fiduciary has nothing whatever to lose through permitting joint control and stands in a position to gain from the experience and knowledge of surety company representatives.

Fiduciary bonds *other than probate* are of several kinds. Into this classification fall fiduciaries appointed in many courts other than probate. Such fiduciaries are appointed to handle an estate or to manage property or a business when there are a number of conflicting interests; and when an impartial person is needed to safeguard and to distribute the assets equitably. In this group are to be found conservators, trustees, custodians, receivers, liquidators, assignees of creditors, and referees.

Litigant bonds. This category includes all bonds filed on behalf of litigants in connection with judicial proceedings in the courts. The *litigant bond* permits the principal to maintain an action when the court requires a surety to protect the other party from loss in the event that the action brought is unsuccessful. Liability under the bond, therefore, is not contingent upon the honesty or ability of the principal. The obligation assumed by the surety is the payment of money if the action comes to an unfavorable termination from the point of view of the principal.

Plaintiff's bonds are often required of those who bring legal actions against others. For example, a creditor who lives outside the state in which an action is brought against a debtor is required to file a bond guaranteeing the payment of the costs of the suit. If property of a defendant is held as a means for satisfying a claim if the action is successful, the plaintiff is required to file a bond guaranteeing the defendant against loss through having the property tied up. Also, if a plaintiff undertakes to compel a defendant to do or refrain from doing certain things, a bond is required to protect the defendant against loss if the plaintiff is unsuccessful.

Defendant's bonds are likewise often necessary or convenient. When property has been tied up pending the outcome of an attachment or injunction action, the defendant may release the property and secure its use by filing a bond. The use of some other defendant bonds is a matter of everyday routine in the courts. Bail bonds are one of the most common types.

Contract bonds

Contract bonds furnish a good example of the valuable services rendered by the surety bond business. Without such bonds, many contractors would not or could not perform their work. Contract bonds are basically credit guarantees. They encourage banks and suppliers to lend money or extend credit for needed working funds.

The three main *classes* of contract bonds are as follows: (1) construction, (2) supply, and (3) maintenance. There are other miscellaneous bonds for special purposes, such as a compensation bond of a self-insurer under a workers' compensation act.

Construction contract bonds. Contractors undertaking the construction of *public* works or public buildings are usually required by law to furnish a bond before bids or contracts are awarded. Examples include sports arenas, civic centers, highways, bridges, and tunnels. The advantages of the surety bond in guaranteeing the faithful performance of the contract have also proved attractive to *private* construction projects for apartment houses and business buildings.

The guarantee under a *construction contract* bond obligates the surety to indemnify the owner if the contractor fails to complete the project on schedule. Problems may be caused by weather delays, strikes, shortages, dishonesty, erroneous cost estimates, or many other uncertainties. To make the owner whole in the event of default by the contractor, the surety is faced with the choice of finishing the work or of reimbursing the owner for the cost in excess of the original contract price. In addition to the foregoing, most contract bonds guarantee that the contractor will pay all labor and material bills incurred. For losses occasioned by injury to employees or the public, the contractor purchases proper public liability and workers' compensation forms. Some element of maintenance may be incorporated into construction contracts as part of the bond, such as a guarantee to the owner for a year against incompetent work or the use of defective materials.

Bid bonds, sometimes termed "proposal bonds," are filed before the contract is awarded and usually accompany the bid. Their purpose is to guarantee that the bidding contractors, if awarded the contract, will sign the contract, supply such bond as is required, and carry on the work to a satisfactory conclusion. Bid bonds fall into three main types. Under the first type, if the contractor should fail to sign the contract and furnish a satisfactory *final bond,* the surety would be liable for an additional cost to the owner because of rebidding the contract. The second type is known as a *bid letter.* This is a communication addressed to the owner in which the surety company agrees to execute the final contract bond if the named bidder is awarded the contract. The third type is known as an *automatic bid bond.* It operates as the final bond if the bidder is successful and is awarded the contract. Frequently owners offer bidders the option of filing either a bid bond or a certified check. The amount of the bond or check is usually placed at about 5 to 10 percent of the contract price. In the case of automatic bonds the face will equal that required for final bonds.

By the terms of the *mortgagors' completion bond,* the surety guarantees the lender of money that the owner will complete the building described in a contract in accordance with its terms and deliver it free of liens. Bonds of this class are, strictly speaking, not contract bonds; however, they are used in connection with the financing of construction projects. The construction contract bond guarantees that if the owner makes payments to the contractor as they become due, the contractor will faithfully complete the work. A failure to make payments when due relieves the contractor of the obligation to finish, and there is no obligation on the part of the contractor's surety to proceed with the work since there has been no default by the contractor. In such circumstances, a bank or other lender might find a partially completed building, heavily encumbered with liens, on its hands. The completion bond is given by the owner, not the contractor, to the lender of money. It guarantees that no act or default of the owner will give grounds for failure by the contractor to complete the building.

A brief illustration will indicate the *relationship of bid, construction, and completion bonds* mentioned in a construction operation. Assume a group of persons with a valuable piece of land and a sum of money. They decide to erect a hotel but need $1 million more to use their land profitably. They bring their plans to a group of investment bankers, together with an estimated operating statement. The bankers wish to be assured that the building costs will remain within estimates and that a completed and unencumbered building will be available as security for the mortgage. When they advertise for bids, the promoters will require a bid bond of all bidders. This will guarantee that the successful bidders will undertake the work or indemnify the owners for any loss occasioned by their failure to do so. When the job is let, the contractor will furnish the owners with a construction bond, which guarantees that the contractor will fulfill the terms and conditions of the agreement. The bankers will require a completion bond from the owners of the property. This guarantees that the owners will make payments to the contractors so that the building will be completed unencumbered by liens.

Supply contract bonds. *Supply contract bonds* guarantee the faithful performance of contracts for furnishing supplies and material at an agreed price. A newspaper publisher might use such a bond to guarantee its newsprint supply. Supply contract bonds are often required by governmental units. The surety is liable for any loss sustained by the obligee through failure to secure the supplies in accordance with the conditions of the contract. This includes any additional expense in securing substitute supplies, and it may include loss or damage occasioned by delay.

Maintenance bonds. *Maintenance bonds* guarantee that the principal will maintain in good condition all or some part of a construction project. The bonds are also used in connection with supply contracts when the performance of the material sold is guaranteed by the seller. The maintenance bond finds frequent use in connection with highway construction work for various government jurisdictions. In connection with building contracts, the element of maintenance is most often found in the guarantee of a roof for a stated period of years. Maintenance guarantees against defective materials or work are sometimes also made in connection with materials such as waterproofing, insulation, and paint.

Miscellaneous surety bonds

A number of other *miscellaneous surety bonds* are briefly described in Appendix E. Included are those shown at the bottom of Figure 21–1, such as depository, license and permit, and federal bonds of various types. These bonds are used for specialized purposes and are further examples of the wide scope and variety of the field of suretyship.

FOR REVIEW AND DISCUSSION

1. Dishonesty is the major peril for the fields of crime insurance and suretyship. Explain why you agree or disagree with this statement.
2. Money stolen in a blaze of gunfire is the stereotyped crime insurance loss. What parts of crime insurance does such an example *not* include?
3. What makes burglary-theft insurance difficult for insurers to underwrite?
4. "A business has very wide choices in deciding how it should take care of the peril of nonemployee dishonesty." Discuss this statement in terms of *(a)* insurance and *(b)* risk management.
5. How has the multiple-line trend affected the personal and the business fields of burglary-theft insurance?
6. Classify the basic parts of the field of crime insurance in outline form. Why is it important to understand such classification?
7. Identify several of the "package" crime insurance contracts and explain their advantages to the insured.
8. What are the disadvantages of the storekeepers' burglary and robbery policy for a merchant's crime insurance needs, and what other contracts are available?
9. A fiction writer describes a masked man entering a store and taking cash at gunpoint. He remarks that the burglary policy had not been renewed, so the storekeeper was not paid for his loss. Why is this an incorrect inference?
10. A burglar's explosion of a safe damages a fine oil painting, but nothing is taken. Is the property damage loss covered under the burglary policy? Would destroyed paper money be covered?
11. What is the purpose of the fidelity bond? How does it differ from judicial and contract bonds?
12. In underwriting fidelity and surety bonds, what information does the surety company evaluate in regard to the principal or obligor?
13. A large manufacturer of color television sets reads about the tremendous losses resulting from employee dishonesty. What bond coverage should he purchase, and how else could he apply good risk management to this peril?
14. What are the similarities and the differences between "insurance" and "suretyship"?
15. A former bookkeeper and the treasurer of a corporation are suspected of collaborating in embezzling money, but the officers are unable to identify

what amounts each employee stole. What is the position of the corporation if each of the employees concerned is specifically bonded? What type of bond should this business probably have?

16. Contrast the protection of the blanket position bond with that of the commercial blanket bond. Which type is most popular and why?

17. "The 3-D policy is a type of blanket crime insurance but is not the same as the blanket crime insurance policy." Explain.

18. Probate bonds are required when a person is appointed by the court to safeguard the estate of an incompetent. What other situations may require fiduciary bonds? What other types of judicial bonds are there?

19. John Carter is investing in a large office building to be built by the Tucson Construction Company. What kinds of contract bonds might he need to know about? What guarantees will they provide? To whom?

Chapter 22

Outline of concepts

Miscellaneous property and liability insurance is a broad field:

    Aviation insurance has developed rapidly since the "jet age."

        Insurers include several large syndicates, or groups of insurers.

        Basic nature is like that of auto insurance, but with larger exposures.

        Aircraft classification: airline, private, industrial, commercial, special.

        Types of contracts include *hull, aircraft liability, admitted liability, medical payments,* and *comprehensive light plane.*

        Aviation rates are nonstandard, open market, and international.

    Boiler and machinery insurance combines property-liability insurance:

        Nature: *direct* and *indirect* losses to insured's property. Liability to others for their property or injury losses is included as direct loss.

        The basic contract is written separately, or with special multiperil policies.

        Direct losses are those by explosion, collapse, rupture, and other breakdowns of steam boilers, machinery, or electrical equipment.

        Indirect losses include *consequential, use and occupancy, outage,* and *power interruption.*

    Glass insurance is for expensive plate glass and other special types.

        Basic coverages are for "all risks" of breakage or damage by chemicals, with fast replacement of glass an important service.

    Credit insurance is catastrophe protection, for wholesalers primarily.

        Nature and development, a guarantee with insurance characteristics.

        Foreign or export credit insurance, helping to expand world trade.

        Underwriting the risk, based on credit ratings and coinsurance.

        The peril covered: insolvency of, or uncollectibility from, customers.

        Types of contract include general and extraordinary.

        Policy provisions define insolvency, normal loss, and other terms.

    Title insurance is important only in some geographic areas:

        The peril insured is undiscovered *past defects* in real estate title.

        The need arises from human errors in meeting legal requirements.

        The title insurer has extensive abstract research facilities.

        The basic policy is for indemnity to owners or mortgagees.

        Contract provisions include claim conditions and term (perpetual).

        Use of a group policy by mortgage companies is convenient.

Miscellaneous property and liability insurance

The property-liability insurance field offers a continual challenge for anyone choosing a career in it because of its almost unlimited variety of exposures and coverages. Persons employed in this segment of the insurance business must be familiar with dozens of contracts, many of which insure substantially different perils.

Property-liability agents are an example. Although much of their daily work may involve the automobile, fire, and liability insurance needs of their clients, the *usual* day will require their immediate attention to at least several other kinds of insurance exposures or losses. After writing a special "all-risks" policy for jewelry and furs, they may next consider a merchant's need for theft insurance or a bank's choice among several fidelity bonds. Before the day is finished, they will probably have at least one more unusual type of coverage or loss to analyze. Perhaps it will be a private yacht or airplane to insure, or a shopping center plate glass loss to settle.

All of these properties and perils are encompassed in the wide spectrum of property-liability insurance in Part Four of this text. Prior chapters have treated fire, indirect loss, transportation, liability, workers' compensation, automobile, and crime insurance. Chapter 22 takes up the remaining types of miscellaneous property and liability insurance, including *aviation, boiler and machinery, glass, credit,* and *title.* Each of these types of insurance has some unusual features which are not found in other insurance contracts.

The size of these miscellaneous markets is approximately $900 million of direct written premiums each year: aviation insurance, $160 million; boiler and machinery insurance, $380 million; glass insurance, $32 million; credit insurance, $80 million; and title insurance, about $250 million.[1]

---

[1] *NAII Greenbook* (Des Plaines, Ill.: National Association of Independent Insurers, 1982), pp. 12–13.

AVIATION INSURANCE

With changing modes of transportation come changes in risk. Aircraft accidents are not as frequent as the Caspar Milquetoasts think but when crashes occur, they are serious and they are well publicized in the newspaper headlines. Actually, the accident and fatality rates per million aircraft miles flown have decreased substantially in recent decades. Fatalities per 100 million passenger-miles decreased from 2.08 in the 1940s to .09 in the 1970s.[2] However, the rapid growth of the aircraft industry has caused many problems that have a direct effect on aviation accidents: larger planes (aircraft carrying 200–400 passengers), more planes (tripled in the last 10 years), crowded airport runways, pilot and traffic controller personnel requirements, and others.

The dramatic impact of airplanes on life in the United States is seen in the nearly 9 *billion* miles flown every year. The shrinking size of the globe is a real thing for many persons, either in terms of their own travel or in terms of the goods that come to them from throughout the world.

Are airplanes safe today? Compared with automobiles, where 28 million accidents cause 5 million injuries and 50,000 deaths annually in the United States, the 3,600 aircraft accidents that cause less than 1,400 deaths each year look small.[3] Almost 4 times as many persons die from poisons, 6 times as many from drownings, and 10 times as many from falls, as die from airplane crashes.[4] However, some observers say fewer aircraft accidents and less loss of life would occur if airport control systems were improved and airplanes were made safer by (1) better design and construction, fire suppression, and evacuation procedures, (2) rear-facing, anchored seats, and (3) reduced use of plastics in interiors.[5]

Development

The first aircraft insurance contracts that were issued made use of the fire or automobile forms. The early experience was far from successful, characterized by a considerable element of trial and error, high premiums, and large deductibles.

---

[2] George Will, "More People Flying the Friendly Skies," *Citizens Journal* (Columbus, Ohio), August 23, 1978, p. 13. Auto deaths by the same measure decreased from 2.74 to 1.56. For other data, see "Passenger Fatalities in Flying on Scheduled Airlines," *Statistical Bulletin*, Metropolitan Life Insurance, October–December 1981, p. 7.

[3] *Insurance Facts* (New York: Insurance Information Institute, 1982–83), pp. 58 and 72.

[4] *Newsweek*, September 13, 1982, p. 37.

[5] "Is Air Travel Becoming Too Dangerous?" *Changing Times*, June 1979, p. 25; and "Air Crashes: Can They Be Survivable?" *Journal of Insurance* 42, no. 6 (November–December 1981), p. 17.

The civilian aircraft industry is now a giant in the transportation field. Nearly 200,000 aircraft, including 2,000 commercial air carriers with 14,000 flights daily, are flying millions of passengers and billions of ton-miles of mail and freight. Many thousands of planes and helicopters are used by businesses. The increased use of aircraft is sufficient to label this the aerospace age. Examples of such uses include rental planes, crop spraying, advertising, cattle herding, pipeline patrols, fire fighting, hovercraft, and many others.

Insurers

Not all insurers write aircraft insurance, but several hundred U.S. insurers do. For many years almost all aircraft risks were written by insurers organized into underwriting groups (or syndicates). Two of the largest, the U.S. Aircraft Insurance Group and the Associated Aviation Underwriters, each has about 20 to 40 insurers or members. Such syndicates still account for a substantial part of the business, especially the protection for the large airline transportation and aircraft manufacturing companies. More than 20 syndicates at Lloyd's of London specialize in aviation insurance. International competition for aviation insurance is keen. Some of the larger individual insurers now cover many planes and helicopters that are privately owned or are owned or used by business firms.

With the passage of federal regulatory legislation, the Civil Aeronautics Board and the Federal Aviation Administration have made mandatory safety measures that might otherwise be disregarded. Control is exercised with respect to the certification of pilots, and regulations cover aircraft flights in the United States.

Adequate insurance facilities exist in this country for handling most aviation risks. However, many special aviation problems for insurers are appearing, and adequate market capacity for aviation insurance often requires many insurers and reinsurers throughout the world. Single aircraft values of $5 million to $50 million and desired liability limits of $10 million to $300 million illustrate the large and increasing exposures in aviation insurance today.[6] The supersonic "superbird" of the skies, the Concorde, is valued at more than $50 million, almost double the cost of the Boeing 747 aircraft.

Basic nature

Aircraft coverages basically parallel the automobile coverages. They are divided into two classifications: direct loss and liability coverages.

---

[6] Henry V. White-Smith, "Aviation Insurance—Past, Present, and Future," *Lloyd's Log,* November 1977, p. 18.

However, the perils in aircraft insurance differ so much from the perils in automobile insurance that aircraft coverages are unusual in many important features. Excluded from discussion here are the aviation accident insurance contracts issued to passengers, which are a type of health insurance treated in Chapter 9.

As compared with the automobile risk, aircraft insurance involves primarily a total loss business, and much larger sums. A modern 747 or DC-10 jet airliner equipped to carry more than 300 people costs $30 million or more. Direct loss insurance, depreciation, and obsolescence are factors of tremendous importance. Losses are in many instances much greater than and different from those attached to the automobile. One of the most important of the factors influencing aircraft losses is the physical condition, training, and experience of the pilot. Although it is true that inexperienced drivers of automobiles are responsible for many accidents, the incompetence of a pilot is disastrous. The adage has developed: "Good pilots die in bed." Automatic warning systems in modern aircraft aim to reduce pilot error of many kinds.[7]

The liability peril for U.S. domestic passengers stems from the same source as that of automobile liability and is also based upon the accepted common-law rules of negligence. However, several international agreements hold many foreign operators of aircraft absolutely liable, and sometimes apply a limit of liability of about $75,000 per person. In addition, the trend of legislation is in the direction of absolute liability. An example is the settlement of more than $62 million paid to 1,100 relatives of victims in the crash of the Turkish DC-10 near Paris, with payments ranging from $10,000 to $900,000.[8]

Because of the large amounts involved and the peculiar nature of the risk, the underwriting problems are usually handled by agents or managers who are specialists in aviation coverages. In total, the aircraft insurance business has become an unusual blend of features—combining aspects of automobile, fire, liability, and inland marine insurance in a specialized insurance area which also has close dependence on reinsurance availability around the world.

Classification of aircraft

Planes are classified by their use into five categories. The first classification applies to large scheduled and nonscheduled *air carriers*. The second

---

[7] For example, radar and "ground proximity warning systems." See "Topical Problems in Air Safety," *Sigma* (North American Reinsurance), September 1976.

[8] *Columbus* (Ohio) *Dispatch*, May 12, 1978. An excellent review of the complex rules of the 1929 Warsaw Convention, the 1955 Hague Protocol, and other agreements (not signed by the United States) appears in "Aviation Liabilities in the 1980s" (Swiss Reinsurance, 1981).

applies to individually owned aircraft used for *private business or pleasure*. *Industrial aid* corporate-owned aircraft are used to transport employees, executives, and guests. The *commercial* classification includes charter aircraft operated by a fixed-base operator. A number of risks involving unusual conditions, such as flying clubs, crop dusting, photography, law enforcement, and dealers are included in a *special-uses* group.

Types of contracts

The basic policy forms include: (1) *hull policies,* which cover the risks of loss or damage to the insured aircraft itself; (2) *aircraft liability coverages,* which are written to cover public and passenger liability and property damage liability; (3) *admitted aircraft liability coverage,* which provides for voluntary settlements to injured passengers; and (4) *medical payments coverage,* which provides medical expenses regardless of liability. These contracts and a *comprehensive light plane policy* which combines many of these coverages are each discussed separately in the following sections.

In addition, special forms are written for *(a) hangar keeper's liability,* which covers the bailee's liability with respect to aircraft stored for safekeeping or repair; *(b) airport and air meet liability,* which provide protection similar to the owners', landlords', and tenants' forms generally written for property owners; *(c) product liability,* which covers manufacturers and sales or repair organizations against liability claims attributable to defective products or work; *(d) aircraft workers' compensation and employers' liability; (e) aviation personal accident* insurance; and *(f) cargo liability,* covering legal liability for loss or damage to cargo or baggage.

Insurance against liability for damage to another's cargo is to be distinguished from property insurance covering the insured's own cargo. Cargo insurance is not classed as an aviation line but is written by inland marine departments. Cargo liability is written as a separate form and covers the aircraft owner for loss or damage to merchandise for which the airline may be legally liable. Passenger baggage liability covers aircraft owners' liability for loss or damage to passengers' baggage.

In aviation insurance, a distinction is made between *ground* coverages and *flying* coverages. Hangar fire, windstorm, and theft perils come within the scope of ground coverages, which cover while the aircraft is not in motion. Accidental damage or "crash insurance," public and passenger liability, and property damage are the more important flying coverages, during the aircraft's actual takeoff run and continuing until it has safely completed its landing run.

Only aircraft licensed by the U.S. Department of Commerce are regarded by insurers as risks eligible for insurance. Since the skill and experience of the pilot are said to constitute 90 percent of the insurer's risk, particular emphasis is centered on the qualifications and character of the pilots who will fly the insured planes.

Hull insurance. The hull policy provides insurance against direct loss or damage from the perils defined on the schedule of coverages attached to the policy. Policies are written on either a named-perils basis or an all-risks basis. When written on a *named-perils* basis, the policy may be arranged to include any or all of the following coverages: (1) fire, (2) crash insurance, (3) stationary land damage, (4) windstorm, and (5) theft. These perils are similar to coverages under other property insurance contracts, and "crash insurance" is merely a different name for the same type of protection afforded by automobile collision coverage.

When written on an *all-risks* basis, which is common today, the policy includes such perils as fire, crash damage, windstorm, earthquake, flood, and every other conceivable risk which may damage the plane.

The more usual all-risks hull coverages include: *(a)* all risks while the aircraft is not in motion, *(b)* all risks except while in flight (includes taxiing), and *(c)* all-risks ground coverage extended to include all risks while in flight. This last form is the most comprehensive obtainable. The usual exceptions are wear and tear, deterioration, conversion (taking without authority) by a person in possession of the aircraft, and loss due to mechanical breakage or structural failure.

Fire is essentially a ground hazard. The insured plane is covered against fire from any cause, as well as against explosion and lightning, while not in flight. The fire hazard in aviation is particularly great not only because of the plane itself but also because of the conditions usual to the hangars in which planes are stored. Causes of plane fires include backfiring engines, short circuits, and the development of static electricity. All airplane fire rates are "loaded" because of the conflagration hazard. A hangar fire, once started, burns furiously because of gasoline, and the chances of saving planes stored inside are negligible.

Windstorm is strictly a ground coverage and covers no loss whatsoever occasioned by flight, which is covered under crash insurance. The aircraft is covered while in the hangar or in the open for damage caused by hail, storm, rain, sleet, snow, earthquake, flood, or water. Windstorm insurance is an essential coverage for airplanes. Planes are carried into the air on strong winds and completely wrecked. An airplane safely housed in its hangar may also be seriously damaged by collapse of the hangar.

Crash insurance covers loss or damage that may occur to the insured aircraft by collision with the ground or another object during flight.

The policy provides that the insurer will pay the insured value of the plane, including its equipment, in the event of total loss. The rates for hull insurance are based on the assumption that the aircraft is insured for *100 percent of value.* No coinsurance clause actually appears in the contract, but the practice of requiring insurance 100 percent to value is similar to the inland marine business. Total loss payments are reduced by depreciation. In the case of partial loss, the liability of the insurer is limited to the cost of repairing the damaged property with material of like kind and quality.

Deductibles apply in a variety of ways and amounts. In the case of light planes, 5 percent of the insured value often applies as a deductible if the loss occurs while the aircraft is in motion. For other losses, a dollar amount, such as $100, usually applies. Larger aircraft often use 5 to 10 percent deductibles.

To provide participation of the insured in all losses and at the same time limit small claims, the *participation form* of policy is offered. Instead of reducing the loss by a flat amount deductible, the participation form requires the insured to bear a percentage of each claim, regardless of its size. The insured must determine whether it is more important to eliminate all partial losses up to a certain amount and to collect everything in excess of that, or to bear a percentage of all losses, which increases in dollar amount as the amount of the loss increases. With a $100,000 plane and a 10 percent deductible, in the case of a total loss the insured would collect $90,000. Insuring the same plane with a 25 percent participation would limit the amount of the claim to $75,000 in a total loss. The use of deductibles and participation forms has the effect of modifying the rate in favor of the insured. The higher the deductible or the rate of the participation, the lower will be the premium charged the insured.

Aircraft liability. With the exceptions to be noted, public and property damage liability afford essentially the same insurance protection as similar coverages in automobile insurance. Although the automobile policy generally covers the passenger bodily injury liability hazard automatically, in aviation policies the insured chooses separate coverage *(a)* for bodily injury liability excluding passengers and *(b)* for passenger bodily injury.

The bodily injury liability coverage excluding passengers does not cover: (1) liability imposed upon or assumed by the insured under any workers' compensation act or plan, or (2) liability for injuries sustained by employees or pupils of the insured. In the case of property damage liability coverage, the coverage excludes: (1) property belonging to, or in the custody of, the insured or the insured's employees or pupils; (2) property which is rented or leased and for which the insured is legally responsible; and (3) property carried in or upon the insured aircraft.

There is an "additional insured" clause similar to that found in the automobile liability policy, extending coverage to other persons while they are flying the plane of the insured. The policy also provides a fly-other-aircraft provision which protects the private owner insured while flying a borrowed plane. The policy excludes any liability in connection with racing, aerobatics, crop dusting, spraying, seeding, hunting, herding, or dropping objects from the aircraft.

Because of the values involved and the possibility of catastrophic accidents, basic limits for bodily injury other than passenger liability are $100/300,000. Property damage limits are often above $100,000. Passenger liability coverage is written with a standard limit of $5,000 per passenger seat (the pilot's seat is not counted). The CAB minimum requirements are $75,000 per seat for smaller, and $300,000 for major, commercial airlines. However, many policies are written for multimillion dollar limits. The terrific damage that a crashing airplane can do to both the human body and property emphasizes the need for even higher limits than those mentioned. Single death or disability cases have been settled for amounts well over $3 million. Multiple death claims from one aircraft accident have exceeded $150 million. In the case of property damage the need for high limits, sometimes overlooked, is likewise essential.

Admitted liability coverage. *Admitted liability* coverage is not common, but it is sometimes purchased by business aircraft owners. Added by endorsement, this is also called "voluntary settlement" coverage. In the event of bodily injury to a passenger, the insurer will offer a settlement on a definitely determined basis, regardless of whether the insured is legally liable. In consideration of the payment of these benefits, the claimant releases the insured from any further liability. If the injured passenger refuses to release the insured from further liability, the policy will pay any legal claims for damages that may be established up to the amount of the benefits indicated.

Medical payments. The similarity of medical payments to admitted liability coverage is found in the fact that medical payments are offered the injured passenger without the necessity of establishing liability. Under the admitted liability coverage, however, the policy limits are high enough to pay for more than just medical costs, and a release is required from the injured party. Medical payments cover not only passengers but the pilot as well. Coverage is written only in connection with passenger liability insurance. The limits for each passenger and the pilot are often $2,000 or more. As with automobile medical payments, payment is made for reasonable medical and funeral expenses.

Comprehensive light plane policy. A special hull policy has been provided for light planes—that is, planes weighing under 10,000 pounds fully loaded—to cover comprehensive risks, including crash. The perils are specifically named, but the policy covers a wide range of additional risks, such as earthquake, flood, denting, marring, and the like. Unlike the automobile comprehensive, this is usually not an all-risks cover. Moreover, the insured bears a portion of the crash loss in the form of participation and in return secures a considerably lower rate. A $100 deductible or more usually applies to all ground coverages except fire, theft, and transportation; and typically a deductible of $250 or more applies to in-motion coverages.

Aviation rates

In contrast to other property fields, aviation insurance provides no common rating schedule for insurers showing rates applicable to different classes of aviation risk. Rates, therefore, are not standard and are to a large degree based upon judgment. The final rate quotation is made only after the underwriter has been given an opportunity to appraise the physical condition, age, weight, flying characteristics, and value of the plane. If the plane is used in connection with a business operation, the operator with good equipment, a good reputation, and a good loss experience secures the most favorable rate consideration.

Rates are ordinarily quoted on an annual basis. Typical hull coverage rates may be 1 percent or more of the aircraft values. Dealers or business organizations that have an active turnover in the number of aircraft owned may secure a policy providing for periodic reporting of risks, with premiums computed from the reports of the number and nature of the planes at risk. In some instances crash insurance may be written based on the number of hours the insured plane is flown. Most of the coverages for scheduled airlines are written on a reporting basis.

BOILER AND MACHINERY INSURANCE

Nature

Insurance policies issued to many businesses upon boilers, turbines, electrical machinery, and similar objects provide coverage for two classes of loss: (1) direct loss and (2) indirect loss. A single policy may cover boilers or machinery, or both. Other names for boiler and machinery insurance are engineering, breakdown, and power plant insurance.

Examples of loss causes include explosions, the cracking of pressure vessels, electrical short circuits (without fire), lack of proper lubrication, bursting flywheels, and many others. The size of loss is large, often $100,000 or more, and sometimes many millions of dollars. The exposures continue to grow, with some exposures valued at more than $100 million each.

Direct loss provides indemnity in the following cases: *(a)* damage to the insured's property, whether to the insured object or to other property; *(b)* damage to the property of others for which the insured may be liable; *(c)* liability for loss of life and injury to employees when the coverage is not provided by the compensation laws of the jurisdiction; and *(d)* liability for loss of life and injury to persons who are members of the public—that is, not employees. Note that the use of the words *direct loss* here is different from its use in other types of property insurance, because it includes several kinds of *liability* losses (property damage liability; *b;* employer's liability, *c;* and bodily injury liability, *d*).

Indirect loss is covered as follows: *(a)* consequential loss to perishable materials when caused by accident to the boiler or other object insured; *(b)* business interruption under a use and occupancy form; *(c)* indemnity for indirect losses caused by an accident when there is no business interruption, under the outage form; and *(d)* power interruption due to loss of power from a source off the premises.

In addition to paying losses, boiler and machinery insurance is very important for the *loss-prevention and engineering* services of the insurer. About one third of the premium dollar is devoted to inspection costs, exposure analysis, repair suggestions, and other risk-management techniques.

The basic contract—types of direct loss perils insured

Boiler and machinery insurance is usually written in a separate contract. However, increasing use of the multiple-line contracts for businesses has rapidly expanded its inclusion (usually on an optional basis) in such contracts as the special multiperil policy, as discussed in Chapter 23.

The standard provisions of different insurers are not identical word for word. The basic policy is used for all power plant insurance, including the use and occupancy and the consequential loss forms as well as direct damage coverages.[9]

The basic policy is completed by attaching a number of schedules. Most of the newer contracts do not require the listing of separate objects, covering instead by "blanket" definitions groups of pressure equipment and machinery for the generation or use of power. A common definition for accident is used, applying to most objects insured.

The standard provisions allow for six forms of coverage in the *insuring agreements,* with *all but the bodily injury liability coverage* being *mandatory:*

1. The *property damage* section provides insurance for damage to the insured object, as well as damage to other property owned by the insured.

2. The *expediting charges* section reimburses the insured for reasona-

---

[9] A special form is used for residences with substantial premises or off-premises exposure to explosion of boilers, water heaters, and furnaces.

ble costs incurred in effecting the speediest possible replacement of the damaged property. These charges include expenses incurred for temporary repairs, for overtime work, or for rushing the transportation of material by an agency more expensive than would ordinarily be used. A limit for expediting charges, usually $1,000, applies.

3. The *property damage liability* section defends the insured against claims and makes payment for liability for damage to the property of others caused by an insured accident.

4. The *bodily injury liability* section is the *only optional coverage*, but if included, it covers the insured against bodily injury to persons injured by an insured accident. The usual defense and settlement provisions are included. Liability under any workers' compensation law is not covered, but there is no other exclusion with respect to liability to employees.

5. The *legal expenses* section covers the cost of defending liability claims, including interest on unpaid judgments, premiums on attachment and appeal bonds, and witness and attorney's fees. These costs do not reduce the amounts available for claim payments.

6. The *automatic coverage* section provides protection for newly acquired objects similar to those described in the schedules. The clause requires written notice to the insurer within 90 days after a newly acquired object is put in operation, and the premium is computed accordingly.

Boiler and machinery insurance is primarily a material damage coverage. The six coverages apply, *in sequence,* as needed. Bodily injury liability provided by the boiler and machinery policy is considered as excess and noncontributing insurance when there is other liability insurance. For example, suppose an insured has a $200,000 steam boiler contract, and a separate general liability contract with a $100,000 bodily injury limit per person. An explosion results in $50,000 damage to the boiler, $1,000 of expediting charges to repair the boiler, $25,000 of damages to the property of others, and a $130,000 bodily injury settlement with a member of the public. Payments would be made for each of these losses in the sequence mentioned. However, only $30,000 would apply to the bodily injury loss, because it applies only as excess coverage.

The policy defines the term *one accident* to include all resultant or concomitant accidents, regardless of the number of objects involved, as long as these accidents are the outgrowth of a single general occurrence. If two or more objects are involved, the highest limit applying to any one of the objects governs.

Large deductibles are commonly used, often $1,000 to $10,000. Separate deductibles may apply to direct and indirect losses, or a single one may be used for both coverages.

Direct losses—the types of property insured

Steam boilers and vessels. Coverage for steam boilers is written on the basic boiler and machinery contract and provides indemnity for loss or damage caused directly by the *explosion,*[10] *collapse,* or *rupture* of the insured boilers or vessels.[11] An identifying schedule listing the objects[12] covered, the pressure approved by the insurer for each, the kind of boiler, and other essential data is made a part of the policy. The boiler policy does not cover explosions in the firebox or tubes of the boiler unless such explosions are optionally included in the schedules or the contract is endorsed to cover furnace explosion.

The boiler coverage excludes loss or damage to property of the insured resulting from an explosion caused by the burning of the structure containing the boiler, or loss or damage to the insured's property by fire. Fire damage to the property of the insured is covered by the fire policy insuring the property. The liability coverage, however, includes the insured's legal liability for damage to the property of others resulting from an explosion caused by fire or from a fire caused by an accident covered by the policy. The policy excludes liability for loss or damage from the explosion of a boiler while any safety valve limiting the pressure in it is with the insured's knowledge and consent removed, inoperative, or set at a pressure in excess of that stated in the policy schedule.

Engines, electrical machinery, and turbines. Coverage may be written to insure breakdown of *engines* that derive their power from steam, oil, or gas. Pumps, compressors, and refrigerating machines are objects insurable under the form. The policy covers damage caused by sudden and accidental breaking, deforming, burning out, or rupturing of the insured machine or any of its parts. Lack of lubrication, loosened parts, or crystallization of moving parts by "fatigue" can result in such losses. Flywheel[13] insurance covers many types of revolving machinery, such as wheels, fans, blowers, dryers, and separators. Insurance for *electrical machinery* and *turbines* provides similar protection for breakdown

---

[10] The policy defines "explosion" as a sudden substantial tearing asunder of the boiler caused by the internal pressure of steam, air, gas, or liquid. Boiler insurance may provide *limited* coverage (against explosion caused by internal pressure) or *broad* coverage (losses caused by the accidental burning, bulging, cracking, or collapse of the boiler).

[11] The boiler policy is not confined to steam boilers but also often insures numerous other vessels which may explode from internal pressure, such as air tanks, kettles, refrigerating and air conditioning systems, steam pipelines, and water heaters.

[12] It is customary to apply the term *object* to the vessel covered, interpreted in the manual definitions. Thus, a boiler includes its parts, such as gauges, safety valves, superheaters, and pipes. Auxiliary piping for many objects should be specifically scheduled.

[13] A "flywheel explosion" can wreck property and cause injury and loss of life. Wheels weighing 10 tons have been thrown more than 1,000 feet!

losses.[14] Motors, generators, transformers, switchboards, and circuit breakers are examples of this coverage.

Indirect losses

There are four forms of boiler and machinery insurance covering indirect damage. These are *(a)* consequential loss, *(b)* use and occupancy, *(c)* outage, and *(d)* power interruption. The first three of these forms cover indirect loss caused by accident covered under the policy on the premises of the insured. Power interruption covers the insured for loss of power from a source off the premises.

Consequential loss. This form protects the insured against spoilage due to interruption of heat, burnout of motors, interruption of power, or failure of refrigeration caused by an accident to the insured object. In types of risk where there is danger of spoilage to perishable goods, the *consequential loss* may far exceed the direct damage caused by an accident.[15] Losses of this character are not covered unless an additional premium is paid and the consequential loss endorsement is attached to the policy.

Use and occupancy. *Use and occupancy* insurance covering any of the objects insured under power plant forms is also usually added to the direct damage policies by endorsement. In principle the coverage is the same as that of other business interruption forms (see Chapter 14), having as its purpose the payment of continuing fixed charges and indemnification for loss of profits due to shutdown as a result of accident. It may be written on either a stated (or "valued") basis or an actual loss (or "nonvalued") basis. Use and occupancy insurance for power sources is often overlooked. The violence that attends explosions sometimes leads to an undue emphasis upon direct damage and liability coverages and the neglect of the potential business interruption losses. The heart of an industrial plant is its power equipment. Apartments, hotels, public utilities, and other business establishments also are often dependent for income upon their heating and power plants. The cost may be thousands of dollars for each day that the plant or business cannot be operated.

---

[14] A turbine is a rotary engine with a delicately balanced rotor which turns upon the impact of the steam or water. The centrifugal force so generated is capable of terrific destruction. Large units, such as are used by public utility companies to generate power, each cost millions of dollars.

[15] A motor burning out in a dairy and causing even a few minutes' shutdown in pasteurizing might result in a large loss. A boiler out of commission in a greenhouse, or the refrigerating system in a cold-storage plant, may run a consequential loss to thousands of dollars while the direct damage loss is negligible.

Outage. Indirect loss for the period an insured object is out of use is called *outage*. Interruption of business is not a factor. Outage insurance differs from use and occupancy insurance, which provides only for loss caused by the interruption of business. Outage insurance provides for the payment of a stated hourly payment for each working hour that the insured object has been incapacitated because of an accident of the kind insured against for direct damage. The insurance is only written by attaching an outage endorsement to the direct damage policy.

Power interruption. An accident in a power plant off the insured's premises, which causes loss to a user of the power through the interruption of the service, is not covered by the electrical machinery policy. *Power interruption* insurance provides indemnity against loss arising from the total or partial deprivation of usable service furnished by a public utility. The policy is written separately from other boiler and machinery coverages and may include the service of electricity, steam, water, gas, or refrigeration. Two forms of coverage are available: *(a)* hourly indemnity for loss of use and *(b)* property loss due to spoilage, which is paid on the basis of the actual loss sustained. Business interruption is not a factor to the establishment of a claim under either form.

GLASS INSURANCE

The business uses of glass in buildings and interiors for light, display, and ornamentation are many. The growing use of large plates tends to concentrate substantial values. Glass is easily subject to breakage, especially when used in show windows. Riots, windstorms, explosions, strikes, runaway automobiles, and accidental or deliberate breakage by vandalism are some of the common hazards.

Basic coverages

The *comprehensive glass policy* provides a coverage that is an *all-risks* contract, with very few exceptions. Similar coverage is available in one of the special multiperil (SMP) forms (see Chapter 23). It pays the insured for all damages to glass, lettering, and ornamentation insured by the policy due to breakage of the glass or the accidental or malicious application of chemicals. Scratching of the glass is not included. The policy also provides three coverages for losses that may be incidental to glass damage: (1) damage to frames and bars, (2) installation of temporary plates, and (3) removal of obstructions. There are only three exclusions: *(a)* fire; *(b)* war, including invasion, civil war, insurrection, rebellion, or revolution; and *(c)* nuclear or radioactive energy.

The multiple-line package contracts now insure many glass exposures. Residence glass breakage is covered in the homeowners' policies, and either automatically or optionally, limited glass breakage is included (usually with limits of $50 per plate or $250 per occurrence) in the SMP policies for many businesses.

Broken glass. The policy provides that the insurer will replace broken glass described in the schedule and any lettering or ornamentation insured under the policy. Rapid and efficient *replacement service* is one of the prime benefits of glass insurance for many policyholders. Insurers can usually obtain service from glaziers more quickly, and at lower cost, than property owners can arrange for themselves.

Glass broken by windstorm, expansion cracks, flying substances, the settling of a building, earthquake, or other accident is covered by the policy. Protection is afforded for deliberate breaks, such as those by burglary, malice, or vandalism. As an alternative to replacing the glass, the insurer may pay for the replacement in cash. When a broken plate is replaced, the policy automatically covers the new plate and no additional premium is required.

Frames, temporary plates, and obstructions. The cost, not to exceed $75 each, is included for several incidental costs. Repairing or replacing window sashes contiguous to the insured glass with like material is covered if this is made necessary by damage to or breakage of the insured glass. Coverage is also provided for the cost of boarding up or installing temporary plates made necessary by unavoidable delay in replacing the damaged glass. Removing or replacing fixtures or any other obstruction in order to replace the damaged glass is covered by the policy, except for the cost of removing show window displays.

Other contract features

If needed, the type of indirect loss insurance provided by the above three $75 insuring agreements may be increased for the payment of an additional premium. Unless otherwise described in the schedule, each plate insured is covered as plain plate, flat glass set in frames. The policy payment is limited to the actual cost (up to the amount insured) of the glass, lettering, or ornamentation and its replacement, at the time of the breakage.

Glass insurance is not limited to ordinary window or plate glass. The comprehensive glass policy may also cover many special types of glass bricks and blocks, Thermopane, safety glass, and other building glass. Stained glass set in leaded sections may be covered under a form that also includes marring, scarring, and scratches. Neon and glass signs are also insurable under a comprehensive glass policy. Such signs are written on either a deductible basis or a full-cover basis. The deductible varies up to about $100 for each insured object, with a corresponding reduction in premium as the deductible increases.

In the event of loss, immediate written notice must be given either to the insurer at its home office or to its authorized agent. Such notice gives the insurer the opportunity to investigate the loss, and possibly to use its subrogation rights against persons responsible for the loss. The policyholder is further required to make all reasonable efforts to preserve the glass for salvage and to prevent further loss or damage.

CREDIT INSURANCE

Nature and development

Most businesses insure their physical property assets against catastrophes caused by perils such as fire and windstorm. Surprisingly, most firms do not insure their assets against uncollectible accounts and bad debts, in spite of rapidly increasing losses in recent years due to business failure.[16] Instead, they rely on selecting the customers to whom they extend credit and writing off normal bad debts as a part of operating expense. Some businesses, however, have a much greater exposure to larger credit losses.

Credit insurance[17] is a contract under which an insurer indemnifies the insured against *abnormal credit loss* occasioned by the insolvency of debtors. Most of the insureds purchasing this kind of insurance are *wholesalers,* but coverage is available for any manufacturer or distributor with annual sales of $500,000 or more.

The question was raised in the early days of credit insurance as to whether it was a contract of insurance or a surety guarantee. The courts have held that credit insurance agreements are, in fact, contracts of insurance for two reasons: (1) the credit risk is not based upon the individual standing of the primary debtor but rather upon the credit experience of a large group of debtors belonging to a certain class, and (2) in credit insurance, the policy may be obtained without any knowledge or consent on the part of the debtor, rather than as an accomodation to the debtor in securing credit.

Credit insurance is a small branch of the insurance business, though the demand for the coverage is increasing[18] and the coverage is appearing

---

[16] *Insurance Facts,* p. 73. The increase in 1981 was 45 percent, to about $6 *billion.*

[17] The distinction between the *commercial* credit insurance discussed here and *consumer* credit insurance such as credit life and health insurance is important. The term *credit insurance* has always been understood to mean the commercial type.

[18] A. A. Dilworth, "Commercial Credit Insurance: Safety Belt for the Business Roller Coaster," *Journal of Insurance* 34, no. 5 (September–October 1973), p. 26; and "Money Squeeze Prompts Another Look at Credit Insurance," *The John Liner Letter* (Wellesly, Mass.: Shelby Publishing, June 1980).

in new fields. For example, the area of *foreign* credit insurance has taken on increased significance.

Foreign or export credit insurance

Internationalism and the global concept have become bywords of the modern era. With improved transportation and communication, the exchange of goods and services throughout the world has increased to heights undreamed of, except perhaps by unusual men such as Wendell Willkie in his vision of "one world."

One of the world trade barriers which is gradually lessening is the availability of credit. Starting in the early 1960s, the United States began to encourage the expansion of exports with the first large-scale U.S. *foreign* or *export credit insurance plan*. The Foreign Credit Insurance Association, now including more than 60 U.S. insurers, was established.

The plan differs in some ways from the credit insurance discussed above. Foreign credit is designed as a credit guarantee plan for *exporters* and often includes coverage for losses from nonpayment due to "political" as well as "commercial" risks. *Insolvency* and *default* which result in the lack of payment for goods and services sold in foreign markets are the major perils insured against.

The FCIA is, in effect, a working partnership between the private insurance industry and the U.S. government-owned Export-Import Bank of Washington (Eximbank). Insurance companies bear the normal commercial credit risks of buyers' insolvency, while Eximbank covers such hazards as the inconvertibility to dollars of local currency, war, revolution, expropriation, and other political risks.

Short-term credit (up to six months) and medium-term credit (six months to five years) are insured up to 85 percent of losses due to commercial risks and up to 95 percent for political risks. The insurer wants the exporter to have a vested interest in potential losses. The exporter must furnish credit information to FICA on the purchasers. The normal approximate cost of the commercial risks is less than 1 percent of the value of the goods, depending on the (1) length of credit, (2) the type of risks insured, and (3) the country to which the goods are being sent. Political risks may be included for about three fourths of the cost of the commercial risks. The total cost thus varies from about 1 to 3 percent of the values insured.

The short-term credit policy is intended for exporters that ship consumer goods, but almost all products are eligible. The medium-term policy differs from the short-term policy by usually being available on a single-case basis rather than including all the shipments within a certain period. It also insures installment payments payable rather than accounts receivable, and it is used for larger transactions, such as shipments of heavy equipment and durable goods.

Two benefits to exporters that use these credit insurance policies are (1) the broader market they have because a major part of the risk is transferred to FCIA and (2) the greater ease with which financing can be obtained from banks when the exporters' foreign accounts are insured. The value of export credit insurance to a nation is also significant. Many other countries are more advanced in the use of credit insurance than the United States and insure a higher percentage of their exports.

The future of this type of insurance is bright, even though obstacles are present. The need for such insurance is based upon the difficulties of credit sales in foreign countries whose language and customs vary from those of the shipper's country. Increased foreign commerce, the fact that export credit insurance is now available for most foreign buyers, and the trend toward liberalized contract terms and rates are favorable factors in this expanding field of insurance.

Underwriting the risk

It is not the function of domestic commercial credit insurance to replace credit investigations with the contract of indemnity. Rather, the insurance is a form of indemnity for unforeseen abnormal losses where credit investigations are made. The function of credit insurance is to protect the working capital and to strengthen the financial statements of businesses. It is not intended for retailers, because the cost of credit investigations to determine potential insolvency of many small consumers would be prohibitive.

Insurers place upon the liability they will assume a limitation based upon the *credit rating* of the customers of their insureds. Credit ratings are usually determined by references to the services of established mercantile agencies such as Dun & Bradstreet.[19] The cost of credit insurance varies, but it is usually less than $1 per $1,000 of shipments.

Since control of the extension of credit rests with the insured, policies are written with a *coinsurance* stipulation that the insured bear an agreed percentage of each loss. The coinsurance features of the contracts vary. Percentages of 10 and 20 are usual. The higher percentages are used when the risk is greater or in the case of an inferior rating coverage with high limits. The condition is comparable to deductible coverage using a percentage of loss as the amount of the deductible. Unlike the user of coinsurance in the fire insurance contract, the insured never receives full recovery for a loss.

---

[19] Dun & Bradstreet is the agency widely used as a basis for underwriting, although the ratings of other agencies operating in a specialized field have been accepted.

The peril covered

Credit insurance covers the peril of loss by the insured arising out of the *insolvency of customers* to whom credit has been extended. The commercial credit insurance contract is most commonly issued to manufacturers and wholesalers, but it is now also available and used by service organizations such as advertising agencies. The insured assumes normal credit losses. The policy pays for any *abnormal or excess loss* resulting from the insolvency of debtors.

Careful credit analysis will not preclude the necessity for credit insurance. Although it is true that many credit losses result from business incompetence, it is equally true that a large proportion of credit losses are the outgrowth of fire, tornado, or other physical disasters. The accounts receivable of a business operating over a widespread area may be threatened by a catastrophe which extends credit losses throughout the country.

Types of contract

Only two companies write credit insurance in the United States: the American Credit Indemnity Company of New York, and the London Guarantee and Accident Company. One major difference in the contracts offered is that the "general coverage policy" is designed to cover all insurable accounts of the insured against credit losses in excess of normal, while "extraordinary coverage" provides insurance against credit losses on one or a few accounts. The rates vary substantially, but generally for the normal one-year contract they are less than one half of 1 percent of the covered sales volume. As to timing of the losses, credit contracts are written either to provide "back coverage" (for *insolvencies* during the policy period) or "forward coverage" (for *sales or shipments* made during the policy period).

Policy provisions

A debtor need not necessarily be adjudicated a bankrupt to be insolvent. Failure to meet obligations in the usual course of business is sufficient to hold the insurer liable for loss. Most contracts set forth at some length the conditions which will warrant a claim on the ground of *insolvency*. In addition to actual legal insolvency, the coverage extends to situations where collection might prove difficult because of assets impaired by the debtor's death or disappearance, or by the filing of receivership or bankruptcy proceedings against the debtor.

In every business, year in and year out, bad accounts are to be expected and are absorbed as an annual charge-off. The recurring amount of such *normal loss* can be calculated for any business within reasonably close limits, usually expressed as a percentage of gross sales. In the credit insurance policy it is termed the *primary loss*. It is not the function of credit insurance to provide indemnity for the primary loss. Every credit policy indicates a primary loss for the business insured determined by previous experience, and there is no liability by the insurer until the primary loss has been exceeded.

The policy sets forth the period within which the insured must file a *claim*. A usual period is 10 days after acquiring knowledge of the debtor's insolvency. In filing a claim, the whole account against the debtor is placed with the insurer for attention and collection. This notice constitutes authority for the insurer to effect an adjustment within a period not to exceed 60 days. The policyholder is obligated to assign to the insurer the claim allowed in adjustment and is required to warrant the legal validity of the indebtedness for the amount of the claim. Most credit insurance policies are now written with a provision affording the insured the right to file past-due accounts with the insurer for collection before these accounts shall have become more than 90 days past due under the original terms of sale. When a past-due account is filed with the insurer, it is treated as if the debtor were insolvent. After the collection charges and expenses are deducted, remittance is made to the insured.

Under general coverage policies there is no *cancellation* privilege. Under extraordinary coverage issued on individual debtors, the insurer or the insured is allowed the privilege of canceling coverage by written notice as to future shipments to any debtor.

TITLE INSURANCE

The peril insured

The peril covered by a title insurance contract is loss growing out of undiscovered defect in the title to an insured property.[20] The policy guarantees the title search to a purchaser, mortgagee, or other interested party, covering the insured against loss arising out of *undiscovered defects in existence* at the time the policy was issued.

In contrast to other forms of insurance, title insurance looks backward for the source of a claim rather than forward. The usual insurance con-

---

[20] An alternative to title insurance appears in some dozen states that have passed Torrens acts. Under the Torrens system, the property owner applies to a court which, after suitable hearing of any claims by other parties, registers absolute title in the name of the owner. These are voluntary systems that are used extensively only in a few large areas, including New York, Boston, and Chicago.

tract covers loss growing out of the happening of some unfavorable contingency subsequent to the issuance of the policy. Title defects which may arise following the issuance of a title policy are not within the scope of the coverage. To support a claim, the defect must have been in existence and undiscovered when the policy was issued.

The need for title insurance

The term *real property* refers to land and to rights issuing from the possession of land. Title to real property may be acquired in a number of ways, the more common being transfer with the consent of the owner, by will, and by descent regulated by statute. To secure title to the rightful owner, the law sets up certain formalities governing transfers which must be complied with in detail; otherwise, the transfers may be defective.

A transaction involving the sale of real estate usually involves substantial sums of money. The purchaser is interested in knowing that the seller has good title to the property being conveyed. A search is made at the record office covering all grants, conveyances, wills, liens, encumbrances, taxes, or other matters that might have the effect of clouding the title. A document called an "abstract" is prepared. It is referred to a lawyer who carefully examines it and gives an opinion as to the title. However, the most careful scrutiny of the records by a competent attorney will not in every case bring to light existing causes which may prove a title to be defective.[21]

The title insurance company

Title insurance companies are large corporations with resources that are ample to carry the risks assumed. Unlike other insurers, the need for investigating local legal records causes most of them to confine their activities to a limited territory. There are between 100 and 200 title insurers, with total annual premiums of several hundred million dollars. Loss ratios are very small (less than 5 percent of earned premiums), as about one half of the premium is devoted to the title search and the abstract. The costs of defense also take up a substantial portion of the premium.[22]

Since the abstract of title is the basis of the contract, title companies have built up and maintained up-to-date records for the real estate of

---

[21] *The Title Industry: White Papers, vol. 1: The Nature and Need for Title Insurance Services* (Washington, D.C.: American Land Title Association, 1976).

[22] Jerry D. Todd and Richard W. McEnally, "Profitability and Risk in the Title Insurance Industry—The Texas Experience," *Journal of Risk and Insurance* 41, no. 3 (September 1974), p. 415.

the territory in which their operations are conducted. These records are referred to as an "abstract plan," and this eliminates the necessity of making a complete search of title every time a transfer is made. The writing of a new policy upon a property formerly insured involves only a reference to the records covering changes since the issuance of the last previous policy.

In urban communities where values are high and real estate turnover is rapid, title companies render an important service. In communities where values are low and transfer is infrequent, the volume of business will not support a title insurance company. In such communities the purchaser of real estate or the mortgagee must be content with a title opinion without the guarantee of an insurance contract. The availability, types, and distribution methods used in title insurance vary greatly in different parts of the United States.[23]

The basic policy

Title insurance contracts are not at all uniform, but the usual forms issued to owners and mortgagees are alike in certain essentials. The insuring clause provides indemnity to the insured, heirs, and devisees, subject to an indicated limit: (1) by reason of any *defect of the title* of the insured to the estate or described interest; (2) by reason of the *unmarketability of the title* of the described insured; or (3) because of *liens or encumbrances* at the date of the policy except for those specifically excluded.

The schedule describing the subject matter of the insurance sets forth: (1) the estate or interest of the insured, (2) a description of the property whose title is insured, and (3) the deed or other instrument by which the title or interest is vested in the insured. A second schedule sets forth discovered defects that are, therefore, not within the scope of the protection.

Contract provisions

A final section of the policy contains the conditions and limitations of the contract between the insurer and the insured. *Assignment* of a title policy is not usually permitted unless the policy is held by the owner of a mortgage or other encumbrances, in which case the contract may be transferred to an assignee of the insured. Even when permitted,

---

[23] And special problems of tie-in sales with real estate producers exist in some areas, too. See Alfred E. Hofflander and David Shulman. "The Distribution of Title Insurance: The Unregulated Intermediary," *Journal of Risk and Insurance* 44, no. 3 (September 1977), p. 435.

the only safe method for obtaining adequate and full protection in the case of the transfer of equity is to secure a new policy or to have the current policy brought up to date.

Whenever a claim is settled by the insurer, the policy provides that the insurer shall be entitled to all *subrogation* rights and remedies which the insured would have had in respect to the claim. The insured is obligated to transfer these rights to the insurer and to permit the insurer to use the name of the insured in any necessary action in connection with recovery or defense. When payment does not cover in full the loss of the insured, the insurer's subrogation rights are limited to the proportion that the amount paid by the insurer bears to the entire loss.

The policy defends the insured against all actions or proceedings founded on a claim of title or an encumbrance prior to the policy date. The policy then sets forth in some detail the *conditions under which loss may arise,* such as actions of ejectment, dispossession, or eviction founded upon a claim of title, a lien, or an encumbrance. One common example would be the claim of a wife to her dower rights in real estate, which perhaps had not been properly satisfied and recorded by a prior purchaser.

In order to recover under a title contract, the insured must show that a loss has actually been sustained. When the insured is without title, the *measure of damages* under a title insurance contract usually would be the purchase price. When title actually passes but a lien is subsequently discovered, the measure of damage is the cost of discharging the lien. When the defect is in the form of an encumbrance, the measure of damage is the difference between the value of the property unencumbered and its value with the encumbrance. Arbitration is used to settle cases of disagreement as to damage amounts.

The title insurance policy is personal and does not follow the property. It is usually *perpetual,* though sometimes the coverage is limited to 25 years. When the insured property is transferred, the insurance terminates, and if the new owner desires coverage, a new policy is issued. Premiums are paid in a *single premium payment* at the time the policies are written, and no further payments are required during the term. The cost varies by location, type of policy, amount of insurance, and other factors.[24] A typical policy for the owner of a $70,000 home might cost several hundred dollars. Policies are sometimes written for a reduction in premium when they are reissued within five years from the date of the original insurance.

---

[24] Rating bureaus are used to set most rates, and studies indicate abolishing these bureaus to increase competition would not be beneficial. H. Lee Roussel and Moses K. Rosenberg, "The High Price of 'Reform': Title Insurance Rates and the Benefits of Rating Bureaus," *Journal of Risk and Insurance* 48, no. 4 (December 1981), p. 638.

Use of a group policy

A group title insurance policy is used for the convenience of large users of title policies. Life insurers and mortgage companies, for example, are issued a master policy with certificates indicating each risk to be covered. The group policy has particular appeal for the mortgagee who wants to know the type of coverage on every risk but who does not want to examine a number of different forms or policies.

FOR REVIEW AND DISCUSSION

1. What do the types of miscellaneous property-liability insurance in this chapter have in common? How are they unlike?
2. Discuss aviation insurance *(a)* from the viewpoint of loss severity and insurer capacity to provide coverage and *(b)* in regard to hull coverage and the use of "deductibles," "participations," and "coinsurance."
3. What forms of aviation insurance are written to protect against *(a)* damage to the owner's aircraft? and *(b)* liability for damages and injuries to other persons or their property?
4. What important differences from the automobile policy are found in the aviation policy with respect to claims for bodily injury?
5. "The inspection feature of a boiler and machinery (power plant) policy is of greater value than the insurance feature." Explain.
6. What changes have the multiple-line package policies brought to boiler and machinery insurance and to glass insurance?
7. What is the peril insured against by power interruption insurance? Does such insurance cover power interruption attributable to equipment owned or operated by the insured? Explain.
8. What insuring agreements provide coverage under the usual boiler and machinery insurance policy? How are indirect losses covered?
9. What is meant by the statement that "the bodily injury liability coverage of the boiler and machinery contract is *excess* insurance"?
10. When *should* a business firm purchase glass insurance? When should it *not* purchase such insurance?
11. The comprehensive glass policy is an "all-risks" contract. Explain why the following losses would or would not be covered:
    a. Fire in adjoining premises causes the glass to crack.
    b. The surface of the glass is scratched with a diamond ring.
    c. Several plates of glass are broken during a strike at the insured's property.
    d. Chemicals thrown on the glass ruin its surface.
12. How does *foreign* credit insurance differ from regular credit insurance?
13. Fire, flood, windstorm, drought, crop failure, or other local catastrophes may unfavorably affect the ability of a debtor to meet obligations. Will credit insurance prevent loss from these sources?

14. Credit insurance is said to be (a) "a guarantee of working capital" and (b) "an endorsement of the customer's promise to pay." Explain each of these statements.

15. For what, and to what extent, is the insurer liable under a title insurance policy? Would an assigned policy provide a new owner full protection?

16. In comparison with many other insurance contracts, what unusual features does a title insurance contract have? Explain three such features briefly.

Chapter 23

Outline of concepts

Multiple-line and all-lines insurance trends in the U.S. are very important.

  Product diversification trends "spread the risk" among types of insurance.

  Multiple-line insurance characteristics include its—

    Nature, a combination of traditional fire and casualty insurance.

    Development, which has been strong since the multiple-line laws.

    Significance, approximately $18 billion annual sales and many changes.

    Purposes, which are summarized in its policyholder advantages of *coverage, cost,* and *convenience;* and similar insurer advantages, plus greater *stability.*

    Disadvantages, restricting flexibility and causing misunderstanding.

  Multiple-line insurance contracts are different from multiple-line *insurers or groups;* or from *multiple-peril, package,* or *all-risks contracts.*

    Homeowners' multiple-line contracts have been very popular. The analysis centers on—*who* (persons), *what* (property and perils), *when* (policy duration), *where* (places), and *how* coverage applies (package, perils, premiums).

      Homeowners' plus contracts have been adopted in some states.

    Other personal multiple-line contracts include those for *mobile homes, farmers-ranchowners* and a few *miscellaneous* types.

    Business multiple-line insurance contracts have grown rapidly since the early *manufacturer's* and *block* policies, particularly with the popular:

      Special multiperil (SMP) policies now available to almost all commercial risks, combining broad coverage for property-liability perils.

      Businessowners' policies (BOP), in the new "readable" type package contract for smaller apartment, office, and retail store businesses.

  All-lines insurance is a separate and more recent trend.

    Nature and extent: writing *fire, casualty, life,* and *health* perils.

    Property-liability insurers have often become all-lines groups by forming or purchasing life insurer affiliates, or through holding companies.

    Life insurers are becoming all-lines groups, especially many of the largest.

    The future promises more all-lines *contracts* insuring home, auto, life, and health perils in one *combination personal-lines package policy.*

Expansion to financial services is the trend of the 1980s to watch.

  Growth and types of conglomerates are explained.

  Financial services conglomerates are the major trend today, by many financial institutions, including banks, brokers, and insurers.

  Financial supermarkets are aided by computers and telecommunications.

  The position of insurance is controversial, but insurers are expanding and salesforces are changing to professional financial advisers.

Multiple-line and all-lines insurance

A supermarket for insurance? That's what many insurance companies and agents are, because they offer an amazing variety of insurance products for sale to consumers of insurance. The insurance market not only offers the many "lines" of insurance in thousands of different individual contracts, as discussed in Parts Three and Four of this text, but also in various combination packages of *multiple-line* and *all-line* insurance. The trend toward combination packages began four decades ago, and it developed into an era of "one-contract buying" to meet the demands of the convenience-hungry consumer. The emerging *financial services* trend goes beyond insurance to include many related services, and is expanding "one-stop shopping" to new dimensions for the 1980s.

PRODUCT DIVERSIFICATION TRENDS

When one looks at the development of the total U.S. field of insurance and risk, it is amazing to find that the basic principle of *product diversification* went relatively unused until the second half of the 20th century. The marketing concept of selling many products and services so that good results in one kind of business will help offset bad results in another is an application of the adage "Don't put all your eggs in one basket." Insurers have long applied this idea of "spreading risk" in many of their underwriting rules, such as in fire and windstorm catastrophe limits for geographic areas, and in retention limits above which large exposures are transferred to reinsurers. However, they have been much slower in applying the concept by doing business in many "lines" of insurance. The reasons have been partially financial and managerial but also historical and regulatory.

The dynamic trend toward the combination of insurance coverages (and other related services) that have been treated for many years as separate and distinct businesses are illustrated by the three examples discussed in this chapter.

The first example, *multiple-line insurance,* which combines many of the kinds of *property and liability* insurance analyzed in Chapters 13–22, is an accomplished fact with numerous insurers and contracts today.

Chapter 23 includes a concise but reasonably complete description of its nature, significance, purposes, development, and contracts. Since multiple-line insurance is a merging of types of insurance already separately presented in Part Four of this text, unnecessary duplication of the coverage details is avoided. The important homeowners' contracts, however, are discussed carefully, and briefer examples of other personal and business multiple-line insurance are included.

All-lines insurance, the second example, is a newer and less complete part of the general trend. Because it involves the combination of *life and health* insurance (discussed in Part Two) with *property* and *liability* protection, a section near the end of this chapter concerns its progress and potential future development.

Financial services, the third example, is the most recent of the trends. Most of this development began to occur in the 1970s, and the expansion is continuing in the 1980s through mergers and holding companies. The broadening of insurers into related consumer services (and vice versa!), such as mutual and money market funds, credit, and investments of many types, has created financial conglomerates of increasing significance.

Figure 23–1 shows the relationship among product lines in insurance and risk and the development in related financial services.

MULTIPLE-LINE INSURANCE CHARACTERISTICS

Nature

Multiple-line insurance is the combination of the traditional "lines" or basic types of coverages known as *fire* and *casualty* insurance.[1] The most common illustration of multiple-line insurance combines fire perils with liability (and/or theft) protection. Individually these basic perils would be mono-line in character; in combination they become multiple-line insurance.

In discussing multiple-line insurance, it is necessary to recognize that the term includes many parts. For example, one might refer to or study separately such facets as multiple-line insurance *contracts* or multiple-

---

[1] One might be tempted here to replace the term *fire and casualty* with *property and liability.* Historically, under the legal definition by which the states have separated the fields of insurance, the term *fire and casualty* is necessary in describing the origin of multiple-line insurance. However, in theory, *property* insurance and *liability* insurance are properly contrasted as the two fundamental parts of multiple-line (nonlife) insurance. This is the more accepted use of the term today. *Casualty* insurance creates such difficulties of logical definition as almost to defy its use, but the term has long-standing legal and business acceptance as including the fields of liability, theft, workers' compensation, automobile, health, surety, and a wide variety of miscellaneous coverages. (See earlier discussion in Chapter 3.)

Figure 23–1. Product diversification trends

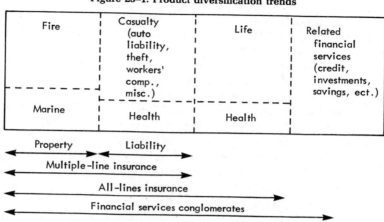

Note: Dotted lines represent past, or partial, barriers among product lines.

line *insurers*. Another subdivision of the topic of multiple-line insurance is multiple-line *groups*. A multiple-line group involves fire and casualty insurers combined by common ownership, management, or reinsurance arrangement. It may have a history, legal organization, and operations that are substantially different from those of a multiple-line insurer which involves only a single company or corporate identity writing both fire and casualty lines of insurance. Many insurance groups or "fleets" are operated, even today, as closely affiliated enterprises with the same officers for several of the individual insurers within the group. Other insurer groups are loosely related, and the separate insurers may have complete autonomy within their activities and substantially different personnel and practices. However, a multiple-line insurer must by definition be a single insurer.

Furthermore, basic functions of insurer activities may be separately defined and discussed under such terms as multiple-line *sales* (or *agents*), multiple-line *underwriting*, multiple-line *rating*, and multiple-line *claims adjustment*.

It is difficult to review in one chapter the entire field of insurance from a multiple-line viewpoint. It becomes necessary to emphasize only a portion of what is collectively known as the multiple-line insurance trend.

Development

The multiple-line trend has not been a rapid or a consistent change. Viewed the perspective of history, the trend appears as a long series of changes, including complete reversal of the trend at some points. Since the early 1940s, however, multiple-line insurance has been a relatively fast and continuous movement.[2]

The experience of foreign insurers with broad charters suggested that early American insurers might have adopted similar multiple-line operations. However, mono-line insurers were accepted almost from the beginning of American insurance, as almost all insurers through the 19th century did business within restricted lines of fire, marine, or other specialized areas. The voluntary acceptance of what became known as the "American system" of mono-line insurance was encouraged and required by insurance department regulations and laws of the states. One of the basic reasons for the compartmentization of insurance became, then, restrictive legislation. The states apparently concluded that it was easier and better to regulate insurance by licensing and limiting insurers to do business only in specific categories of insurance.

The first real adoption of the multiple-line principle began in the early 1900s with legislation in some states which permitted fire and marine insurers to combine, and later allowed fire insurers to have casualty subsidiaries and casualty insurers to own fire insurers. The success of the insurer group or "fleet" operations and the need for broader insurance coverages for automobiles, airplanes, and other valuable movable properties encouraged multiple-line operations. The trend slowed, however, with various restrictions on the expanding powers of marine insurance.

The modern multiple-line trend began with a resurgence of the insurer groups that wrote both fire and casualty protection in separate but closely related enterprises. The advantages of broader insurance powers were recognized in the Diemand Committee Report to the National Association of Insurance Commissioners in 1944. The states began to pass "partial multiple-line laws," permitting one insurer to write both property and liability protection for automobiles, aircraft, certain types of personal property, reinsurance, and insurance outside the United States. "Full multiple-line laws" followed, breaking the legal barriers which had existed between fire and casualty insurance for a century or more. As long as the insurer met the capital and surplus requirements for the various lines, it could be licensed to write all types of insurance protection except life insurance. The major landmark in this development was New York State's passage, in 1949, of such full multiple-line insurance legislation. By 1955 all of the states permitted, by specific legislation or departmental rulings, full multiple-line insurance operations.

The capital and surplus requirements for the formation of a multiple-line insurer vary among the states from $100,000 to about $5 million.[3]

---

[2] David L. Bickelhaupt, *Transition to Multiple-Line Insurance Companies* (Homewood, Ill.: Richard D. Irwin, 1961), p. 3.

[3] James E. Bachman, *Capitalization Requirements for Multiple-Line Property-Line Insurance Companies* (Philadelphia: S. S. Huebner Foundation for Insurance Education, 1978).

Insurance organizations doing business only within a single major line of insurance still exist. Almost all of the larger fire and casualty insurers today, however, operate as multiple-line organizations. They began as single-line insurers and broadened their licensing powers and insurance activities by charter amendments and mergers.

Significance

Multiple-line insurance extends the concept of product diversification to insurance. Just as manufacturers have discovered that it is often better to produce several related products rather than rely only on one, so insurers now sell protection against many perils.

One of the clearest indications of the place and growth of multiple-line insurance is its sales figures. Thus, Table 23–1 shows the amazing growth record of multiple-peril contracts. In 25 years the annual sales have increased from less than $200 million to almost $18 *billion*, or a 90-fold increase! Commercial multiple-line policies, which had a later start, have grown to become nearly 40 percent of the total multiple-line field.

Multiple-line insurer *groups* have grown steadily since the 1940s. About 270 stock and mutual insurer groups including about 1,000 separate insurers, were in business by 1982.[4] These groups wrote 90 percent of the total property-liability insurance premiums of $97 billion.

Table 23–1. Multiple-peril* contracts, selected years,
1956–1981
(in millions of dollars of premiums written)

Year	Homeowners' multiple-peril contracts	Commercial multiple-peril contracts	Total multiple-peril contracts
1956	$ 179	$ 18	$ 197
1960	764	56	820
1964	1,333	371	1,704
1968	2,077	993	3,070
1972	3,300	2,100	5,400
1976	5,420	4,030	9,450
1980	9,821	6,886	16,707
1981	10,780	6,870	17,650

* This term rather than *multiple line* is used in order to conform to the statistical source, The contracts noted here are also properly classified as multiple line. (See footnote 7.)

Source: *Insurance Facts* (New York: Insurance Information Institute 1982–83), p. 13 and previous years. Farmowners' multiple-peril contracts are reported separately in 1980 as $555 million, and in 1981 as $620 million.

---

[4] *Best's Aggregates and Averages* (Oldwick, N.J.: A. M. Best, 1982), pp. 10–36.

Insurers classified as multiple-line *insurers* (single corporate identities writing both fire and casualty insurance) wrote approximately $55 billion,[5] or 57 percent of the total premiums, by 1982.

Purposes

The amazing growth of multiple-line insurance is explained by the advantages of the multiple-line technique, which may vary considerably according to the viewpoint of the party involved.

Policyholder advantages. From the viewpoint of the *policyholders,* the advantages of multiple-line contracts may be summarized as improvements in (1) *coverage,* (2) *cost,* and (3) *convenience.* In effect, the results are better protection and service at lower costs, and a reduced number of contracts, companies, agents, and premiums for the insured. Cost economies are naturally uppermost in the minds of most policyholders, and these may be substantial. Oftentimes, the combination of coverages in a single multiple-line contract may bring savings of 20 to 40 percent as compared with the cost of protection in several separate property and liability contracts. The prime advantage of better coverage and service under a multiple-line contract should not be forgotten, however. The purchase of a multiple-line contract usually results in fewer gaps in protection than does the purchase of several individual policies covering separate perils. Also, overlapping coverages or overinsurance which may occur under separate policies are avoided through less confusion in regard to which policy covers which peril.

Insurer advantages. In many ways the objectives of insurers entering into multiple-line operations are also those of the policyholder, although further goals may be reasons for the insurers' interest. Fundamental to all of the insurer motives is the general impact which multiple-line operations should have in *stabilizing, or maximizing, underwriting profits* by diversifying the company's business.[6] The "spread of loss principle" which is basic to all insurance is applied in the acceptance of many kinds of perils. For example, the averaging of fire losses with liability and other losses over a period of time should result in greater stability of operating results, and thus financial strength, for an insurer. A bad year of fire losses may be offset by some profits from theft, liability, or other kinds of insurance.

In addition to achieving stability of earnings and profits, the multiple-line insurer may achieve increased *profits, power,* and *prestige.* If multiple-line contracts increase total sales and lower costs through increasing the average size of contracts, then a multiple-line insurer may obtain

---

[5] Ibid., pp. 57, 59, 5B, 7B. Stock and mutual insurers so classified numbered about 510.

[6] Howard F. Blasch, J. D. Hammond, and Ned Schilling, "Planning Insurance Company Line Mix for Profit Maximization," *Risk Management,* September 1977, p. 41.

greater influence, industry position, and prestige as an insurer. The benefits to policyholders mentioned above are also likely to bring success to
the insurer, for satisfied insureds are of great importance to the continuing growth of insurers.

Disadvantages

Possible disadvantages that may accompany the adoption of multiple-
line insurance should be mentioned. The policyholder usually does not
have quite the freedom of choice that exists when separate contracts
are selected. Certain minimum coverages must be included in most multiple-line contracts, and the insured may be paying for a few types of
unwanted protection. The same idea applies to the insurer—for example,
it may accept a good fire insurance policyholder at the expense of including some questionable burglary or liability business. Another basic problem is the general difficulty of readjusting to change, including the effort,
time, and costs that change requires. There is also the uncertainty that
arises from new contract wording, whose precise meaning often takes
a number of years of legal interpretation to determine. A final problem
is the unwarranted assumption that these broader multiple-line contracts
provide automatic and complete coverage for *all* losses. They do not
and cannot, and a false sense of security may be created from undue
reliance upon them to accomplish the impossible.

MULTIPLE-LINE INSURANCE CONTRACTS

The summary here of multiple-line insurance contracts can only include some of the major multiple-line coverages. For accuracy in detail
and timeliness the reader must supplement this chapter with reference
to the bureau and company forms, manuals, and rules applicable under
the laws of his or her own state.[7]

Terminology once again becomes significant in clarifying discussion
in this section on multiple-line insurance contracts. Caution must be
exercised in using terms which may be confused with the expression
"multiple line." For example, one might discuss *multiple-peril*[8] insurance

---

[7] For up-to-date specific information on multiple-line contracts, the reader should consult
such loose-leaf, continuing reference services as the *Fire, Casualty, and Surety Bulletins*
(Cincinnati: National Underwriter), the *General Insurance Guide* (Smithtown, N.Y.: Werbel
Publishing), or the *Policy, Form, and Manual Analysis Service* and other publications,
such as *Homeowners Guide, An Analysis of the SMP Policy* and *Businessowners Policy
Program* (Indianapolis: Rough Notes).

[8] Note that the preceding statistics on multiple-line growth are technically referred to
as multiple peril. The inconsistency is necessary because of the lack of other data. The
figures do not include "extended coverage" premiums when written only with the fire
insurance contract, but do include the premiums for this coverage when written in the
homeowners' and other "multiple-peril" contracts.

contracts, but multiple-peril contracts are not necessarily *multiple-line* insurance policies. The two perils combined may be all within one insurance line, such as fire. The extended coverage endorsement is multiple peril but not multiple line in nature because it includes only fire and allied lines of insurance. Similarly, the storekeepers' burglary and robbery policy combines several perils in one contract, but since all are casualty coverages, it is not a multiple-line policy.

A *package policy* is always a multiple-peril contract, because it includes a number of separate perils in one contract. One additional characteristic, however, makes package policies a distinctive part of the development of multiple-line insurance. In package contracts the policyholder must accept substantially all of the perils combined in the package; multiple-line contracts merely involve combining fire and casualty perils, which may be done either by "packaging" (*all-or-none* choice by the insured) or by "scheduling" (permitting choices as to the coverages included). Most modern package policy contracts are also multiple line in nature, but the differentiation is necessary for a proper understanding of how these closely related types of contracts have grown.

Similarly, the terms *all risks* and *comprehensive* may also cause confusion to insurance students and consumers if they are not properly used. Both of these terms include the attribute of broader coverage in insurance policy contracts, but each term may have precise meanings that are widely dissimilar. Many contracts are called *comprehensive* when they include only a few perils; other such contracts may include many perils. The term is not standardized in the insurance business, and it generally refers only to the fact that it is a combination form of comparatively liberal coverage. Examples include the comprehensive general-liability policy and the comprehensive automobile physical damage coverage.

All-risks contracts are distinguished by the type of insuring agreement used. If the policy lists each peril that it covers, it is a "named-perils" or "specified-perils" contract. If the contract says it covers, for example, "all-risks of physical loss except enumerated exclusions," then it is an all-risks type of contract. Note that "all-risks" should not be taken literally, for invariably a few exclusions are specifically identified. Examples of all-risks contracts are the personal property floater, the dwelling property special form, and the glass insurance[9] policy.

For further discussion, the multiple-line insurance contracts are separated into two basic groups, those that are essentially *personal* (individual, family, or nonbusiness) and those that are designed primarily for *business* situations.

---

[9] The title of the *comprehensive* glass insurance policy is an example of how the terms discussed above are used without making the distinctions explained.

Homeowners' multiple-line insurance contracts

The most popular and the best known of multiple-line insurance contracts today are the *homeowners' policies.* The use of these forms has been of the most significant and widely accepted of multiple-line techniques. Some other examples of personal multiple-line insurance contracts are briefly mentioned at the end of this section.

Development. During the past 30 years the homeowners' policies used by insurers and their bureau associations have had a half-dozen extensive revisions. Consumers in various states are not all using completely standardized forms. Some bureau policies, such as those of the Insurance Services Office (ISO), are widely used, but several large insurers (such as State Farm, Nationwide, Allstate, and St. Paul) have developed and use their own contracts.

Forty-five of the states have approved the use of the "Homeowners '76" program,[10] introduced by the ISO in 1976. The analysis in this chapter is thus based upon these popular homeowners' policies. A later section will summarize the "Homeowners/Plus" program, which has been adopted in some states during 1982–83.

Basically, the coverages in the Homeowners '76 program are both broadened and narrowed. The appearance and format have been extensively revised. The new personalized and simplified language (reduces the number of words by 40 percent, from 12,000 to 7,000) is the most obvious of the changes, with "you" referring to the named insured (and spouse) and "we" meaning the insurance company. The policies are in booklet form, and use 25 percent larger type than the former contracts. All of these changes aid readability, as explained in the Chapter 20 discussion of the personal auto policy.

The major parts of the contract are organized for understandability, and the traditional "165 lines" of the standard fire contract are eliminated. Their content is rewritten under five new section headings. "Definitions" (and boldface type for important words) precede the parts explaining "coverages," "perils insured against," "exclusions," and "conditions." Although contract analysis could follow these headings of the fundamental parts of the policies, the following evaluation is instead divided according to the contract's *purposes.* (This procedure was suggested to the reader as an alternative and meaningful method of contract analysis in Chapter 13 for the fire insurance contract.) Accordingly, the emphasis here is on *who* is covered, *what* is covered, *when* and *where* the protection applies, and *how* this protection is provided at a certain

---

[10] This program and the forms are copyrighted by the Insurance Services Office, with permission for their use granted to its members, subscribers, and service purchasers.

price. The old but effective outline of who, what, when, where, and how provides a convenient framework for analyzing homeowners' policies.[11]

Who is covered.   As to *who* is covered by the homeowners' policies, the primary purpose of these contracts is to provide multiple-line coverage to *owners* who occupy their private residences, and condominium unit-owners in form 6.[12] The eligibility rules also permit *tenants* to obtain the same combination of fire, theft, and liability perils, in a contents (tenant's) homeowner's policy form 4. Homeowners' policies are oftentimes insurance for the personal property and personal liability of the whole family. "Insured" means you as the named insured in the declarations (or insureds, if joint owners), as well as your relatives, or any other persons under the age of 21 who are in your care. Property of a student who is an insured is covered at a residence away from home, and theft coverage applies if the student has been there at any time during the 45 days immediately before a loss.

What is covered.   The homeowners' policies state *what is covered* by reference to the *property* and *perils* included in the coverage. The basic property covered includes the dwelling, related private structures, and personal property (except in a portion of the premises regularly rented to others). The homeowners' policies are basically combinations of the perils in the standard fire policy (and allied perils forms), the residence burglary and theft policy, and the comprehensive personal liability policy.

Six *additional coverages* are included for property. *Debris removal* occasioned by an insured loss is covered (up to 5 percent of the dwelling coverage, as an *additional* limit).[13] *Trees, shrubs, plants,* and *lawns* (up to 5 percent, or $500 each for the first three items mentioned) are covered for named perils only. These perils include fire, lightning, explosion, riot, aircraft, vehicles not owned or operated by a resident of the residence premises, vandalism, malicious mischief, and theft, but do not include windstorm or other unspecified perils. Other additional coverages are *reasonable repairs* to protect the property from further damage; *fire department charges,* up to $250; *property removed* from endangered premises, up to 30 days; and *credit card, forgery and counterfeit money,* up to $500.

The important *comprehensive personal liability* coverage was introduced earlier (in Chapter 17), but is reviewed briefly here as contained

---

[11] Detailed analysis is also available in current editions of the *Homeowners '76 Policy Program Guide* (Indianapolis: Rough Notes).

[12] The purpose is protection for essentially one- or two-family private and personal residential coverage, although some states permit insuring situations which include the owner-occupant of up to four-family houses and as many as two roomers or boarders.

[13] Form 8 includes debris removal coverage, but not as an additional limit. It also has a $250 limit instead of $500 for trees, shrubs, plants and lawns.

in Coverage E in Section II of the homeowners' policy forms. The premises liability protection applies to occurrences, defined as accidents including injurious exposures to conditions, which result in bodily injury or property damage on your premises. It includes your permanent residence, whether it is a dwelling owned by you or an apartment that you rent; a temporary residence of any insured, whether owned or rented; vacant land (except farmland); and even your cemetery lot. Secondary permanent residences may also be included in the declarations or added to the policy. The policy extends to provide protection for losses attributable to an insured's *(a)* pets, bicycles, and small boats (owned watercraft with outboard motors not over 25 horsepower, or other rented ones; and owned or rented inboards or inboard-outboards with not over 50 horsepower, or sailboats not over 26 feet long); *(b)* sports, such as golfing, hunting, or fishing; and *(c)* any type of occurrence away from home for which an insured is held responsible. The obligation of the insurer to defend any liability claims ends when the amount paid for an occurrence equals the stated limit of liability.

The contract covers your liability and that of the other insureds for loss or damage that is the outgrowth of personal activities, except in an automobile accident or in business or professional acts. Aircraft and motorized land vehicles designed for public road use and subject to motor vehicle registration are not covered. Neither are *owned* motorized snowmobiles and other such recreational motor vehicles off the insured locations, but coverage does apply on the residence premises or off the premises if such vehicles are rented or borrowed. Golf carts while used for golfing purposes are covered, whether owned or operated by any insured and whether on or off the premises.

The business pursuits of any insured are not covered in the basic policy, but the policy may be extended to include some business activities if an insured is not the principal owner or partner (examples: teachers or salespersons). Incidental business pursuits on the premises, such as a doctor's office, an art or music studio, and the like, may also be covered by an endorsement.

The standard limits of liability coverage are $25,000 per occurrence, but higher limits up to $500,000 are recommended, for small additional premiums. For example, the $300,000 limit is only about $14 more a year than the $25,000 limit (in Ohio—it may be more elsewhere).

The contract excludes assumed liability, except liability assumed under a written contract relating to the premises. The wording of the insuring clause taken together with the exclusion provides protection to you if certain liabilities are assumed in a "hold-harmless" clause under a lease. Employers' liability to full-time residence employees (not more than two in some states) is covered without charge if they are not entitled to benefits under any workers' compensation law. Fire legal liability coverage for damage to nonowned premises and furnishings is included. This protection appeals to tenants, particularly those who rent valuable seasonal properties. It protects you as a tenant from damage suits growing out of injury to or destruction of a home which you have rented or its contents, if the loss is caused by one of the perils noted.

Section II also covers three *additional coverages*. *Claims expenses* (up to the policy limit) in defending a suit against any insured are paid, including premiums on required bonds, reasonable expenses and loss of income incurred by you at the company's request (up to $50 per day), and interest accrued on any judgments against you. *First aid expenses* for others incurred by an insured are paid. Up to $250 per occurrence is paid for *damage to property of others* caused by an insured. For example, this last coverage would pay, *regardless of legal liability,* if your 15-year old son accidentally broke a neighbor's window, or if you damaged a lawnmower borrowed (not rented) from a friend. Intentional damage by any insured over 13 years old is not covered.

Medical payments (Coverage F of Section II—liability insurance) provides coverage of reasonable medical expense within three years for injuries to residence employees and to members of the public injured on or off the premises of the insured. It applies, regardless of legal liability, if the injuries are attributable to the activities of an insured or of your residence employees while they are engaged in your employment or of an animal owned by or in the care of any insured. The basic limit is $500 per person, but a few dollars increases this to $1,000, or $15 increases it to $5,000. Injuries to regular residents of your household (except residence employees) are *not* covered. This is liability insurance and not accident coverage for everyone. Nuclear or radiation contamination is excluded.

Theft coverage is defined in the homeowners' contracts as "attempted theft and loss of property from a known location when it is likely that the property has been stolen." Thus, "mysterious disappearances" are covered only from a known place when theft is the likely cause of loss. Theft from an unattended off-premises auto is not included unless there is forced entry. (Form 5 includes such losses, and the coverage for such unlocked-car losses can be added in other forms.) Any equipment for the recording or reproduction of sound (stereos, tape decks, CBs, etc.) is not covered for any perils, while in an automobile, except by endorsement.

Some important perils *excluded* in homeowners' contracts are: (1) *earth movement;* (2) *war;* (3) *water damage,* such as flood and backing up of sewers; and (4) *nuclear hazards.*

When coverage applies. The minimum duration of coverage is one or three years. Some insurers also issue continuous policies. Contracts can be paid for on an annual installment basis. The coverage begins at

12:01 A.M. at the location of the home. The insurance agent often has the power to bind coverage immediately for the insured while the policy is being prepared.

Where coverage applies. The protection is basically at a fixed location—the dwelling of the insured. However, coverages away from the dwelling are also significant. For example, personal property owned or used by any insured away from the dwelling is covered on a *worldwide* basis. Personal property is also covered while in transit to a new residence, and for 30 days after you begin to move the property there. A 10 percent limit off premises applies for property that is usually situated at another residence of an insured. The family liability and medical payments to other persons also apply both at home and away from the premises. Seasonal (secondary) dwellings in the same state may be added by endorsement.

How coverage applies. *How* the homeowners' policies provide the coverage discussed in the preceding paragraphs can be explained in several ways. The policies are *multiple line* in character, combining fire, theft, and liability protection in one contract. The policies are also *package* contracts in the sense that they must include certain coverages. The insured is given some leeway in choosing the amounts of coverage on the dwelling, personal property, liability, and medical payments. This characteristic of the insured having to accept basic perils, and to a certain extent amounts of insurance which are fixed by percentage formulas, makes the homeowners' policies essentially package rather than schedule type contracts. Coverages may be increased by endorsement, but the only decrease permitted is that personal property on premises may be reduced to 40 percent of the amount of coverage on the dwelling. The *all-risks* technique is also used in connection with homeowners' policies in forms 3 and 5, which cover "all risk of physical loss" to the insured property except for specified exclusions. Form 6 may be endorsed to provide all-risks coverage on alterations and additions by a condominium unit-owner.

Pricing, another part of how the homeowners' policies work, is accomplished by an *indivisible premium,* a combined charge for all basic property perils included in the contract. Premium charts are used to show the cost of the various forms based upon the amount of coverage for the dwelling. No separate charge is made for each of the individual perils included in the contract, contrary to fire insurance, in which the premium is calculated by adding together separate charges for fire and other perils. The homeowners' rate is a package premium for the minimum amounts of coverage in the package contract. Additional charges are calculated for the increases in insurance amounts permitted above the mandatory minimums. For example, the basic amount of insurance on the contents or personal property is automatically 50 percent of the dwelling insurance amount, but the coverage on the contents or personal property can be increased. The basic required liability limit of $25,000 can also be increased. (See later summary in Table 23–2.)

Deductibles are used in connection with each form. A $100 deductible usually applies to all property losses in Section I, except credit card losses and fire department service charges. You are covered only for that part of the loss over the deductible. Some of the state rules vary, but larger deductibles of $250 to $2,500 (at 4 to 30 percent credit) are available, or a $50 deductible at a 10 percent increased cost can be purchased. All forms except form 5 can eliminate the deductible. In form 8 a special theft deductible of $250 applies for losses from the residence premises. The "disappearing" deductible of the older forms, which pays in full for losses over $500, is still used in a few states.

One other important feature of the homeowners' policies is that *replacement cost coverage* is provided on the dwelling and the related private structures. This applies *if* the whole amount of the insurance on the buildings is *80 percent*[14] *or more* of the replacement cost, not including the value of the land and excavation. Thus depreciation will not be subtracted in calculating the claim payable, and the policyholder will receive full repair or replacement cost on these items. When the full replacement cost is more than $1,000 or more than 5 percent of the insurance amount, the property must be actually repaired or replaced before this provision applies. Note that this provision is *not* the same as a "coinsurance" requirement (see Chapter 13), which is seldom used in homeowners' contracts except in a few states such as New York. Payment on a replacement cost basis is an extra *benefit* to the insured in these contracts, rather than a penalty to be applied for underinsurance. For example, suppose the building values are $100,000, and a loss involving $50,000 of replacement cost occurs. If $80,000 or more insurance is carried, the full $50,000 loss would be paid. If there is only $60,000 insurance, the loss would be paid on the basis of actual cash value, which would be less than $50,000 because depreciation would be deducted.

Some insurers are also insuring replacement cost coverage on *personal property,* paying fully for losses of items even if they cost more now than when you bought them. This may be an advantage to you, especially for major furniture and appliance losses, but there is an increased premium cost of 15 percent (35 percent in forms 4 and 6). Insurers must be careful of the moral hazard, which could increase losses under this coverage. However, early reports indicate reasonable success with such increased coverage, which is becoming more widely available.

---

[14] A *special loss settlement* endorsement permits you to select 50, 60, or 70 percent, and retain this replacement cost feature of the contract. This may be advisable on older homes whose replacement value is high or difficult to determine.

An *inflation guard endorsement* is available at a small additional cost. The policy amount on all the insured properties is automatically increased 1 percent every three months (or 12 percent over a three-year policy), helping to meet rising construction and replacement costs. This is a convenient way of avoiding underinsurance caused by inflating property values. The quarterly percentage increase can be increased by one-half percent increments beyond the basic 1 percent.

Loss of use of the residence premises is provided for in Coverage D. *Additional living expenses* are paid when an insured peril causes the premises to be uninhabitable. The limit is 20 percent of the dwelling insurance amount (as additional insurance) under most forms, except form 1, which has a limit of 10 percent. Form 4 and form 6 apply the percentage limit to the contents amount (20 and 40 percent, respectively). This covers the extra costs of living elsewhere while repairs are being made. These expenses are often important in serious losses. *Fair rental value* of that part of the residence rented or held for rental to others is also paid, with the same percentage limits applying as added insurance.

An endorsement to the homeowners' policies of insurance for specifically listed *scheduled personal property* is often recommended. Very broad all-risks protection can be provided at low cost by scheduling valuable properties such as *jewelry, cameras, furs, musical instruments, silverware, golfer's equipment, fine arts, postage stamps,* and *coins.* Endorsements may also add protection for *theft* away from the premises from *unattended motor vehicles,* and for *earthquake* damage.

A few *special limits* apply to specific articles as to the amount of coverage. An attempt is made to provide reasonable coverage for valuable or hard-to-value articles such as money ($100 limit); watercraft and their trailers ($500 limit); other trailers ($500 limit); grave markers ($500 limit); and accounts, securities, and manuscripts ($500 limit). Specific theft limits apply to unscheduled jewelry, watches and furs ($500 per loss in the aggregate); to silverware, goldware, and pewter ($1,000 limit); and to guns ($1,000 limit). Several of these limits can be increased by endorsement; money to $1,000, jewelry and furs to $1,000, silverware to $10,000, and so on.

Comparison of coverages. A summary table may help to explain the homeowners' policy forms. Table 23–2 indicates the major property, perils, and amounts of coverage which the seven basic homeowners' forms provide. The most significant result of all these forms is to combine the fire and allied perils, theft, and liability insurance for owners who occupy their homes, and to achieve this same combination of coverages for tenants who use form 4 and condominium-unit owners who use form 6. The major differences among the seven forms are found in the scope of the *property perils* that are included in addition to the basic fire and lightning coverage: form 1 and form 8 add extended coverage perils;

Table 23–2. Homeowners' policies, summary of coverages

	Policy Section I (property coverage)				Policy Section II (liability coverage)
	Coverage A	Coverage B	Coverage C	Coverage D	Coverages E and F
	Dwelling	Related private structures	Personal property	Loss of use	Comprehensive personal liability and medical payments to others
AMOUNTS	This amount is chosen as the basic contract coverage Minimum $15,000 for forms 1, 2, 8; $20,000 for form 3; and $30,000 for form 5	10% of dwelling amount of insurance	50% of dwelling (worldwide, but only 10% of *contents* amount for property usually situated at secondary residences) Minimum for forms 4 and 6, $6,000	20% of dwelling, or 10% under form 1; and under form 4, 20% of the contents amount; and under form 6, 40% of the contents amount	Basic amounts are: $25,000 (liability) and $500 (medical payments); Coverage E—liability can be increased up to $500,000 and Coverage F—medical payments up to $5,000, for small added premiums

FORM		All forms include the above perils of (1) liability and (2) medical payments. (Additional coverage for "damage to property of others," up to $250, regardless of legal liability, is also a part of each form.)
Basic form (No. 1)	Fire and lightning Extended coverage perils (wind, explosion, smoke, and so on) Theft, vandalism	
Broad form (No. 2)	All basic form perils as above, plus miscellaneous perils such as falling objects, collapse, water damage, rupture of heating systems, and freezing (essentially these are the broad form fire endorsement perils)	
Special form (No. 3)	"All risks of physical loss" except those specifically excluded (such as flood, earthquake, landslide, war, backing up of sewers); broad form on contents	
Contents (tenants') broad form (No. 4)	Contents only covered—*not buildings* Covers same named perils as broad form 2 Can be used alone for tenants	
Comprehensive form (No. 5)	Covers same all-risks perils as special form 3 but includes both *dwelling and contents*	
Condominium unit-owners' form (No. 6)	Covers personal property same as contents broad form 4, but adds: basic limit of $1,000 for additions and alterations to the building, and loss of use up to 40 percent of the contents amount; endorsements permitted for theft when rented to others, and "loss assessments" by the condominium association	
Modified coverage form (No. 8)	Covers insureds who own *older homes* with market values much less than replacement values. All losses paid on basis of *actual cash value*, rather than have the replacement cost option apply. (This permits insureds to carry less than 80 percent to value.) The perils included are similar to *basic form 1*, but theft of personal property is limited to $1,000 from the residence premises only.	

forms 2, 4, and 6 add broad form perils; form 3 adds all-risks perils to building coverage; and form 5 covers all-risks on both buildings and contents. (See Chapter 13 for further explanation of the perils).

The special form (No. 3) is the most popular form for dwelling owners buying homeowners' policy contracts. Apartment renters need the contents form (No. 4). The market for the condominium-unit owners' form (No. 6) is increasing, and these insureds should consider increasing the $1,000 limit on additions and alterations which covers such improvements as fixtures, cabinets, and carpeting. More details on form 6, and form 8 for older homes, are included in Table 23–2. A few policyholders use the limited protection of the basic form (No. 1) or modified coverage form (No. 8), or the all-risks coverage of the comprehensive form (No. 5).[15] Special form (No. 3) provides all-risks coverage on the buildings similar to that of the dwelling buildings special form endorsement and the broad form named-perils coverage on the contents. The result is very adequate coverage, only excluding a few known perils such as spillage of liquids or animal damage to contents.

The amounts of coverage as to property and perils is illustrated by an example in Table 23–3 showing the insurance provided by the special form (No. 3).

Comparison of costs.   A comparison of approximate costs in Table 23–4 illustrates how the basic forms vary for a homeowner or tenant in a class 1–7 rating territory in the Midwest.[16] Thus, the small increase in premium for form 3 can be seen as compared with forms 1 or 2 ($10

Table 23–3. Example of coverage and amounts, homeowners' special form (No. 3)

Property and perils coverage	Amounts of coverage
Section I (property)	
a. Dwelling	$80,000
b. Separate garages or related private structures (total, not each)	8,000
c. Contents, or personal property worldwide ($4,000 limit if usually situated at another residence)	40,000
d. Loss of use (additional living expense, and fair rental value)	16,000
Section II (liability)	
e. Comprehensive personal liability	25,000
f. Medical payments (to others, regardless of fault)	500
g. Damage to property (of others, regardless of fault)	250

---

[15] In effect, form 5 provides all-risks coverage by combining the standard fire insurance policy (with the dwelling special form attached), the comprehensive liability policy, and the personal property floater policy. The higher cost relative to that of other forms discourages its use.

[16] Rates vary considerably by territory, class of fire protection, type of building, and urban-rural differences in exposure, as well as among various insurers.

Table 23–4. Homeowners' policies, summary of costs

Form	Basic coverage amount*	Approximate annual cost†
Basic (No. 1)	$80,000 dwelling	$193
Broad (No. 2)	80,000 dwelling	203
Special (No. 3)	80,000 dwelling	214
Contents (No. 4)	20,000 contents	97
Comprehensive (No. 5)	80,000 dwelling	289
Condominium unit-owners (No. 6)	20,000 unit	87
Modified coverage (No. 8)	80,000 dwelling	212

* For frame dwelling in forms 1, 2, 3, 5, 6, and for contents in fire-resistive building in forms 4, 6; the usual flat deductible of $100 per loss is applicable.

† Annual, although some contracts are written with premiums payable in installments. A few insurers write 3-year policies.

and $21 difference),[17] and the rather substantial increase for form 5 ($75). The reduced cost of the homeowners' policies over separate fire, theft, and liability contracts is estimated at about 25 percent. At the above rates, the homeowner under form 3 is insuring $128,000 of assets ($80,000 dwelling, $40,000 contents, and $8,000 for related private structures) plus the loss of use and basic liability coverages, for approximately one sixth of 1 percent a year of the values protected. In a serious loss, the homeowner could collect up to the above limits under each of the separate coverages.

A special word of advice is needed in regard to contents coverage. The best way to be sure that you have enough coverage is to take, and keep up to date, a household inventory. Agents and companies have forms that are helpful in doing this. Photographs of each room also help considerably.

Homeowners' plus policies. The first major revision of the ISO "homeowners '76" program was announced in 1982. Called *homeowners' plus,* the use of these policies began in California and were to be available in early 1983 in Colorado, Georgia, Massachusetts, Oregon, and Wisconsin. If successful, they will be introduced in other states during 1983.

Prior policy forms will continue to be identified as forms 1–4, 6, and 8, with form 5 provided by adding an endorsement to form 3 to expand coverage on unscheduled personal property to an all-risks basis.

The primary purpose of the changes is to upgrade coverage to higher average limits which reflect the increased needs caused by inflation. For

---

[17] Many agents recommend form 3 as the "best buy." See Saul Sokol, *Your Insurance Adviser* (New York, N.Y.: Harper & Row, 1977), p. 194.

example, in *Section II liability coverages* the basic liability limits for all forms are increased to $100,000, medical payments to $1,000, and voluntary payments for damage to property of others to $500. Liability for model airplanes has been specifically included.

In *Section I property coverages* the special limits for some personal property are increased: money to $200; securities, tickets, stamps, etc., to $1,000; watercraft to $1,000; and trailers (not used with watercraft) to $1,000. *Theft* coverage has also been increased: for jewelry and furs to $1,000; for guns to $2,000; and for silverware to $2,500. Theft of property from an unattended motor vehicle or watercraft (without visible sign of forced entry), which is a popular endorsement to the earlier forms, is now automatically included. Theft or unauthorized use of bank fund transfer cards is added. New *optional* coverages include business property up to $2,500, and landlord's furnishings up to $1,000.

Although most changes in the homeowners' plus policies increase coverage, the change of the base *deductible* for property losses to $250 is a decrease in coverage. The insured has the option of reducing this to the $100 deductible used in the other forms. Two changes in liability coverages also lessen coverage to some extent. Excluded are liability arising from (1) negligent entrustment of a motor vehicle, (2) written contracts, except those directly related to maintenance of an insured location, and (3) intrafamily suits and suits between persons covered by the same policy.

Other personal multiple-line contracts. The concept of combining coverages in homeowners' policies has been adopted in other personal lines policies for mobile homes and for farmers-ranchowners. A few miscellaneous multiple-line contracts even pre-date the development of homeowners' policies.

Mobilehome policy. The market for the *mobilehome policy* is expanding rapidly, as about one third of all the new single-family detached houses sold are mobilehomes. Almost 11 million Americans now live in mobile homes. A package policy approach is used, similar to that of the regular homeowners' policies. The policy combines fire, windstorm (very important), and allied lines coverage on the mobilehome; personal property; additions to the mobilehome (on an optional basis); loss of use expense; theft; and liability exposures. The eligible mobilehomes are those portable units that are built to be towed on their own chassis with frame and wheels and are designed for year-round living. The policy is not intended for small trailers. A minimum new-cost value of $4,000 is required (many mobilehomes cost $30,000 or more). Unscheduled personal property is insured for a minimum of $2,000, and additional living expense for $15 per day up to 45 days, but both of these limits may be increased. Many of the endorsements usual to homeowners' policies are available, such as deductibles higher than the usual $100 flat deductible, the earthquake peril, scheduled valuable personal property, and a secondary residence. A special endorsement for collision or upset coverage of the mobilehome is optional, with a $100 or $250 deductible.

Farmowner-ranchowner's policy. The *farmowner-ranchowner's policy* is an example of a multiple-line insurance contract which combines personal and business multiple-line insurance. The coverage is quite similar to that of the homeowners' forms. Fire, theft, and liability protection is provided on the dwelling ($12,000 minimum) and contents. Separate coverage amounts, in addition to those usually found in homeowners' policies, apply for other structures and for farm personal property. The coverage of property perils is either like that of the basic form (No. 1) or it includes more extensive named perils, as in the broad form (No. 2).

The liability insurance is the equivalent of the farmer's comprehensive personal liability policy now in use, covering liability, medical payments, and animal collision. The liability coverage includes the important product liability exposure. Liability for injuries to employees is not included in the farmers' CPL, except by endorsement. The animal-collision cover is optional; it provides a limited form of livestock mortality insurance for the insured. The policy pays the insured for loss by death of cattle, horses, sheep, hogs, and the like, if death is caused by collision between an insured animal and a motor vehicle not owned or operated by the insured or the insured's employees. The animal collision applies only to insured animals killed on a public highway while not being transported.

Miscellaneous multiple-line contracts. A number of other insurance contracts may be classified as multiple-line coverages. Each of these contracts combines fire and casualty insurance perils; in fact, the development and use of these contracts preceded by many years the homeowners' policies which today are the most popular multiple-line contracts. The *personal property floater,* the *personal articles floater,* the *outboard motorboat policy,* and the *valuable papers policy* are examples which have been discussed in previous chapters. They are better known as inland marine insurance contracts because they were developed prior to the real impetus and legal sanction for multiple-line contracts.

These forerunners of full multiple-line legislation in the states were a significant part of the multiple-line trend. Fire, allied, and theft perils were combined in the all-risks, worldwide protection of the personal property floater in the early 1930s. The personal articles floater also appeared then. It was designed for articles of high value which were scheduled in a specific list of items, such as jewelry, furs, collections, and historical and artistic objects. The valuable papers policy, which may also be used by businesses, provides coverage for hard-to-value properties such as blueprints, plans, and manuscripts. The outboard motorboat policy reveals a strong heritage from the ocean marine field of insurance and combines fire, theft, and even limited liability protection in one policy.

Business multiple-line insurance contracts

The tremendous growth of commercial multiple-peril contracts has been noted in Table 23–1. From less than $100 million in premiums, the field has grown in little more than two decades to about $7 *billion* in premiums a year!

General development. The development of multiple-line protection for business prior to 1970 was limited. Since then many new contracts have appeared, with rapid changes in this volatile area.[18] The special multiperil (SMP) and businessowners policy (BOP) programs of the Insurance Services Office (discussed in the next sections) have grown rapidly during the past decade. A brief review of the earlier business multiple-line contracts shows how these programs developed.

One of the early experiments in multiple-line insurance for business was the *manufacturer's output policy.* It covered all personal property of the manufacturer on an all-risks basis while the property was away from the premises of the insured. It was originally a specialized policy for the automobile industry only. Later it changed its title to the "manufacturer's policy" and became available to several hundred classes of manufacturers. Unlike most insurance contracts, the policy was continuous, remaining in effect until canceled. A minimum premium of $5,000 restricted the contract to large risks. A reporting form adjusted the premiums to the property values actually in existence during the year. Automobiles were covered at any location.

Block policy contracts were one of the first examples of business multiple-line coverage. The *jeweler's* block policy is still generally written. It is an inland marine policy covering the entire merchandise and contents of the jeweler's store on an all-risks basis both on and off the premises. Several similar policies include the *furrier's* block policy and a variety of *dealers'* block policies (equipment, appliances, cameras, instruments, and so on). They are multiple-line contracts, even though they are still written as part of the inland marine field.

All-risks *property* coverage was expanded in the 1960s to four other categories of business risks, by attaching forms to the fire insurance contract. Examples include (1) the *commercial property form* for merchants, (2) the *office contents form* for offices, (3) the *industrial property form* for smaller manufacturing businesses, and (4) the *public and institutional property* program for schools, churches, hospitals, and government

---

[18] Recommended for current and further details than are provided in this text are the form and manual loose-leaf services mentioned in footnote 7.

units. The special multiperil program, which provides property *and liability* protection in more complete multiple-line policies, rapidly replaced these forms.

Special multiperil (SMP) program. Package multiple-line coverages for business risks that have been adopted in some states have not been approved in others. Bureaus such as the Insurance Services Office have helped standardize many forms, but differences exist among the various states and also between bureau companies and independent insurers.

One of the early contracts that appeared as part of the special multiperil program was for mercantile properties, including retail and wholesale establishments. SMP contracts also became available for businesses whose primary function was to provide services rather than goods. The first of these to become available was a contract for *motel* (now *motel-hotel*) owners; then specialized policies emerged for *office* building owners, *apartment* building owners, and *processing or service risks,* such as cleaners, repair shops, barbershops, and many other classifications. After several years of experimentation with the development of these *separate* "programs," revised SMP rules were put into a single consolidated manual.

The outstanding characteristic of these policies is the provision of property *and liability* coverages in one policy. Usually, these coverages are mandatory, and include both real and personal property. The policies are a combination of the package and schedule approaches to insurance. The basic package includes some fire and liability insurance, but the insured optionally selects other coverages, such as theft, business interruption, boiler and machinery, glass, valuable papers, and other miscellaneous perils. The policies include either named property or all-risks perils. The basic liability form is not comprehensive, but the limitation of coverage to specified premises and only incidental operations can be changed to comprehensive general liability coverage. Combined single limits (without a separate per person limit) apply on a per occurrence basis and on an aggregate basis for bodily injury and property damage liability, which includes premises, protective, and products exposures (see Chapter 17).

As a hypothetical example of how the SMP benefits consumers, a small retail clothing store might have the lower costs and broader coverage of an SMP contract as illustrated by Table 23–5. In the example, for about 15 percent less cost the mercantile policy adds protection against business interruption, burglary and theft, and vandalism and malicious mischief, and increases the liability coverage to more adequate limits. Other examples might, of course, add similar or greater increases in coverage that would cause the total cost to exceed the original cost of individual policies.

Table 23–5. Cost and coverage comparison—individual policies
and special multiperil (SMP) policy

	Individual policies	Amounts of coverage	One-year cost* of Individual policies	One-year cost* of Mercantile package
1.	Standard fire policy with broad form coverage endorsement	$100,000 on building	$250	$170
2.	Standard fire policy with broad form coverage endorsement	$100,000 on contents	280	200
3.	Public liability	$100,000 bodily injury $25,000 property damage limits	120	80 (single lmt. of $300,000)
4.	Business interruption	$60,000 gross earnings	None carried	40
5.	Burglary and theft	$20,000 merchandise	None carried	70
	Total one-year cost		$650	$560

* Costs are illustrative and not exact. They would vary in actual practice by substantial amounts according to many factors such as sprinkler systems, store area, territory, and protective features. Insurance rates also differ between bureau and nonbureau members. If similar coverages are compared, the package discounts under SMP contracts may range between 5 and 35 percent for various business classes. Three-year policies are sometimes written, with annual installments.

Simplified SMP package. In 1977 a new *simplified SMP package* was adopted to eliminate the duplicate coverage of the many separate policies that had been developed to provide all-risks coverage of business personal property. The SMP now uses a policy "jacket" in booklet form of the declarations, insuring agreements, and general provisions common to all but a few policies. To this are added a form with basic conditions and definitions (MP-00-90) and a form to insure *buildings* (MP-00-10) and *personal property* (MP-00-12) on a *named peril* basis. Similar forms can be used to broaden the coverage to *all-risks* coverage for buildings (MP-00-13), and for contents (MP-00-14).

The SMP can now be used for *almost any type of commercial or institutional operation.* The only exceptions are farms, motor vehicle businesses, bowling alleys, rooming houses, apartment dwellings with fewer than three units, and very large business properties which may qualify for a special plan for "highly protected risks." The most important addition is the eligibility of the SMP for contracting risks.

A revised manual of rules is divided into *five parts:* general policy rules, and rules for the four specific coverage areas of property, casualty, crime, and boiler and machinery. Policy terms of one, two, or three years are permitted.

The *general conditions and definitions* in Form MP-00-90, together with the declarations page, replace the 165 lines of the old standard fire policy. The four parts are: (1) general conditions, stating the premium computation, time of inception (12:01 A.M.), cancellation, subrogation, and other items; (2) conditions applicable to Section I (property coverage), similar to much of the fire contract wording, but adding deductible (usually $100), coinsurance, and nuclear clauses; (3) conditions applicable to Section II (general liability), including an explanation of supplementary payments, the insured's duties after a loss, and other clauses; and (4) a page of definitions related to Section II.

Section I *(property coverage)* provides either named-perils or all-risks coverage on buildings and personal property. A flat deductible of $100 per occurrence for each building and for its contents applies (and $1,000 maximum per occurrence). Usually both the building and its contents must be insured, but a tenant may cover only the contents, or a landlord only the building. The named-perils forms include vandalism and malicious mischief. Reporting value coverage can be added by endorsement to provide for changing property values. Replacement cost coverage can also be purchased. Many optional forms are available for the addition of business interruption, extra expense, glass, water damage, earthquake, sprinkler leakage, and many other perils. These tailor the contract to meet the particular insured's needs. Automobiles are the major type of property not included in the SMP.

Section II *(general liability coverage)* provides standard liability coverage for a declared location and its incidental operations. *Combined single limits* (minimum of $25,000), on an occurrence and on an aggregate basis for *bodily injury* and *property damage* apply in the basic liability form (MP-200). If desired, dual limits are available. Products liability and completed operations liability are included, unless deleted. Separate optional medical payments coverage applies, with a minimum of $250 per person and per accident. Any of the standard general liability coverages that can be written in separate general liability contracts may now be provided in the SMP, including comprehensive general liability coverage (see Chapter 17). Automobile nonownership liability, and explosion, underground, and collapse (XCU) liability, can be added by endorsement. Workers' compensation is not included in the SMP.

Sections III and IV provide *crime* and *boiler and machinery coverage* on an optional basis. A wide range of choices permits the insured to choose among the types of perils discussed in Chapters 21–22—burglary, robbery, and theft (inside or outside the premises); blanket fidelity bonds (employee dishonesty); depositor's forgery; and boiler and machinery direct and indirect losses. The only significant related perils that cannot be included here are surety bonds, which must be written separately.

In all, the new simplified SMP package policy is a flexible multiple-line contract that enables many business risks to insure their total property and liability exposures, with the exceptions of workers' compensation, automobile, and surety bonds, as noted.

Another multiple-line policy, the businessowner's policy (BOP), has become increasingly popular for smaller businesses since the mid-1970s, and it deserves special attention.

Businessowner's policy program (BOP). An alternative to the SMP for many small and medium-sized businesses of the apartment, office, and retail store types is now also widely used. The *businessowner's policy (BOP)* which has been available since 1976, combines property and liability exposures.[19] It differs from the SMP by including: (1) more limited eligibility (specified types of businesses with a smaller building size and occupancy area); (2) a more fixed package of coverages, with somewhat less flexibility in choosing limits and coverages; (3) broader protection through the use of several automatic provisions for replacement cost coverage and the absence of coinsurance requirements; and (4) a more readable style of contract, replacing the 165 lines of the old standard fire contract with revised format and wording.

Eligible risks are described to include only buildings classified as *apartment* buildings (not more than six stories high and with no more than 60 dwelling units), *office* buildings (not higher than three stories or exceeding 100,000 square feet in area), and *mercantile* buildings (not over 7,500 square feet in area). Tenants may also purchase the BOP for offices of up to 10,000 square feet in one building, and for mercantile operations of up to 7,500 square feet. Many risks eligible for SMP contracts are specifically ineligible, such as condominiums, contractors, wholesalers, and banks. Retail stores are one of the largest eligible classes as a market for the BOP. Most of the BOP contracts have annual premiums of under $1,000.

The insured under the BOP contract makes *relatively few choices of coverage*. Two alternative forms are used for property coverages: a *standard* form (BU-0001) insuring named perils (fire, extended coverage, vandalism, and sprinkler leakage), and a *special* form (BU-0002) insuring all risks. The insured selects a full replacement value for insurance on the building and/or its contents, which, like the homeowners' policies, then automatically includes many additional coverages for a package of protection with an indivisible premium. Loss of income and rather high liability coverages are also built into the BOP. The insured may choose to add, for additional premium, optional coverages for employee dishonesty, boilers and machinery, glass, exterior signs, and earthquake exposures. Burglary and robbery are automatically included in the special (all-risks) form, and may be added to the standard (named-perils) form.

---

[19] The BOP contract discussed here was developed by the Insurance Services Office (ISO) after several independent insurers filed such contracts in the mid-1970s. For more detailed analysis, see the current editions of *Fire, Casualty, and Surety Bulletins* (Comm. Multiperil pages); and *Businessowner's Policy Program* (Indianapolis: Rough Notes).

The *premium rates* for the BOP package are based on an indivisible premium for the basic coverages. As compared with the costs of individual contracts for fire, theft, liability and other perils, these rates provide savings similar to those illustrated for the SMP in Table 23–5. The annual premiums are stated as provisional amounts, subject to audit at expiration time for all of the exposures covered. For example, if other premises are acquired during the policy term, there would be an additional charge for liability.

Analysis of the BOP *property coverages* indicates that they contain several additional unusual features as compared with those of the standard fire contract and the SMP program. The standard named-perils form (BU-0001), for example, includes an *automatic quarterly increase in the building coverage of 2 percent* (or higher, if so indicated in the declarations). Another automatic increase in the insurance amounts is a *25 percent increase in peak season fluctuations of business personal property*. It applies if the insured's average monthly values for the preceding 12 months are fully covered by declared insurance limits on this property. The SMP coverage for such fluctuations requires an endorsement. *Off-premises* property coverage is limited to $1,000 in the BOP, or to $10,000 for 30 days while the property is at newly acquired premises owned, leased, or operated by the insured. *No coinsurance* requirement applies in the BOP. Automatic coverage for *loss of income* with no stated limit is a part of the BOP contracts, to a maximum of 12 months of indemnity during the time that is required to resume normal operations. Other coverages included in the BOP, but not the SMP, are wind and hail protection for trees, shrubs, and plants (with limits of $250 per item, $1,000 per occurrence), and protection for collision and other damages to property in transit. The basic flat *deductible* is $100 per property loss in any one occurrence, applying separately to each building, its contents, and personal property in the open. The aggregate deductible applied in any one occurrence is $1,000.

The special form (BU-0002) property coverages are similar to those of the named-perils form, except that the perils included are on an *all-risks* basis. The special form property coverages include *theft* insurance for all business personal property, which is not covered in the named-perils form except by adding burglary and robbery coverage. Money and securities used in the insured's business are included in Coverage D automatically, but this is limited to $10,000 on premises and $2,000 off premises. A special deductible of $250 applies to theft and employee dishonesty losses.

The *liability coverages* in Section II of the BOP contracts, both the standard and special forms, are very extensive. The insured need only choose a *$300,000 or $1 million* liability limit. Medical payments coverage of $1,000 per person and $10,000 per accident is included, with no options.

The liability protection is comparable to that of comprehensive general liability coverage (see Chapter 17). It includes products and completed operations; fire legal liability to structures rented or occupied by the insured (special additional limit of $50,000); blanket contractual liability for written agreements; personal injury liability for false arrest, libel, slander, or invasion of privacy; nonowned automobile liability; and even host liquor liability at functions incidental to the insured's business. The "insured" is defined to include any employee of the named insured while acting within the scope of his or her duties, coverage which must be endorsed on most other general liability contracts. The liability coverage of the BOP illustrates vividly the broad coverage that this important multiple-line contract provides to businesses.

ALL-LINES INSURANCE

Nature and extent

All-lines insurance is a separate current trend, but one almost as apparent and significant as the multiple-line trend. The all-lines approach combines *property, liability, life, and health* insurance. Although this combination may be accomplished by a single contract or single insurer[20] only in a few examples and a few states, multiple-line insurers have created an all-lines trend for several decades by purchasing or forming separate life insurers. Eighty of the 100 largest property-liability insurer groups listed in *Best's Aggregates and Averages,* for example, have one or more life insurers in their group of insurers.[21] The groups now number more than several hundred, including life insurers that expanded by adding property-liability companies to their operations.[22] The result has been many all-lines insurer *groups,* although all-lines *contracts* and all-lines *insurers* are still rare except in limited cases.

Property-liability insurers have become all-lines groups

The most frequent action in the formation of all-lines groups has been taken by property-liability insurers. Either by purchasing a life insurer

---

[20] Emphasis is on the phrase "by a single contract or a single insurer." In contrast to the multiple-line trend, which started with (1) multiple-line *groups* and (2) extended to multiple-line *companies* and (3) then to the rapid growth of multiple-line *contracts,* the all-lines trend is still largely centered on the first phase, that is, all-lines insurance company *groups.*

[21] *Best's Aggregates and Averages* (Oldwick, N.J.: A. M. Best, 1982), pp. 8–9.

[22] Even prior to 1970, one source notes 253 groups of both life and nonlife companies with an average of more than four companies per group (Richard de R. Kip, "Insurance Company Groups," *CPCU Annals* 22, no. 3 [September 1969], pp. 197–202). This study does not differentiate between property-liability companies that added life companies or life companies that added property-liability insurers.

or by forming a new life affiliate, multiple-line insurers have often become all-lines groups.

Some of the early *reasons* why this trend emerged have been concisely reviewed: (1) basically, it caters to the buyer's convenience by providing one-stop shopping; (2) volatile loss ratios in property and liability insurance have caused property-liability insurers to look to life insurance as a stabilizer for their operations; (3) the property-liability insurers have a ready-made sales force for selling life insurance; and (4) many property and liability insurance agents deal with business firms, which makes for a natural entry into the group life insurance business of these firms.[23] The three C's—coverage, cost, and convenience—summarize many of the advantages.

Practically all of the larger property-liability insurers and many of the smaller ones now have life insurance affiliates. These groups emphasize the opportunities which property-liability insurers have in overcoming the most serious problem of life companies—finding life insurance prospects. Encouragement to the local agent to place more life insurance business along with the insureds' automobile, homeowner's, and other insurance has taken many forms. One of the most pointed methods was observed when one of the largest insurers offered agents higher commissions on property-liability business *if* certain quotas of life insurance production were met!

Exclusive agency companies have been very successful in building their life insurance operations to significant parts of their all-lines group operations. Examples are Allstate, Nationwide, and State Farm Life, which has become ranked as one of the top 10 life insurers.

Life insurers are becoming all-lines groups

Life insurers are expanding their operations by starting or purchasing property-liability insurers. In past years they have been held back by legal barriers that prevented a life insurer from owning substantial stock in other insurers. However, such prohibitions have been largely removed.[24] The entry of life insurers into all-lines operations will probably be a *gradual development* for a number of reasons: (1) licensing laws in most states prevent a single insurer from doing business in both the

---

[23] Benjamin N. Woodson, "All-Lines Underwriting: Five Years Later," *CLU Journal* 16, no. 3 (Summer 1962), pp. 239–42, reaches the interesting conclusion that the greatest change was the "applicability of life insurance methods to the underwriting and sale of personal-line and casualty coverages." Direct billing by the insurer, group insurance sales, and reduced commissions on renewals are examples.

[24] New York State's highest court reversed a former decision and stated that out-of-state life insurers might purchase fire and casualty companies. Although other legal barriers exist (such an antitrust and monopoly acts), this decision hastened the all-lines trend in the 1960s by permitting the purchase of Aetna Insurance Company by the Connecticut General Life Insurance Company.

life and property fields,[25] so the permitted insurer group technique of all-lines operations (which is sometimes more unwieldy) will have to be used; (2) about two thirds of life insurance is written by mutual insurers, and these are limited in expansion by the amount of their surplus; (3) profits in property-liability insurance in recent years have been volatile, especially in relation to those of the more stable life insurance field; and (4) the changes necessitated by all-lines operations are considerable, involving a major impact on management, product development losses and expenses, underwriting, marketing, education and training, regulation, and investments.[26] However, many observers feel that despite the problems in entering all-lines insurance, the movement will continue to grow. The reasons for expecting growth are competition, economy, and the growing recognition of the mass market and financial services concepts.

The legal problems have decreased with the advent of a related trend—that of "holding companies" which own several corporate enterprises. If state laws prevent a life insurer from owning a property-liability insurer directly, both the life insurer and the property-liability insurer can be owned by a holding company and operated as an all-lines group. Such reorganizations have been reinforced by the increased interest in broader financial services and by the general corporate merger trend.

Several large life companies acquired property-liability affiliates before 1970: Connecticut General Life—Aetna, Lincoln National Life—American States, State Mutual Life—Hanover, and others. During the last decade, the giants of the life insurance business moved into the property-liability field: Prudential, Metropolitan, Equitable, and John Hancock. Perhaps 100 other life insurers initiated or acquired property-liability operations in order to become all-lines insurers. A decreasing proportion of life insurers remain convinced that specialization in life insurance only is the best answer for the future. Management experts conclude that few life insurers by 1990 will be solely in life insurance.[27]

The Prudential and Metropolitan set up separate property-liability companies, causing shock and fear among the established property-liabil-

---

[25] Only 13 states permitted the early "inclusion of life, fire, and casualty writing powers in *single insurers.*" These were Alabama, Alaska, Connecticut, Delaware, Georgia, Maine, Mississippi, North Dakota, Oregon, Rhode Island, South Carolina, Tennessee, and Wisconsin. Any insurer doing business in New York cannot under the application of the Appleton Rule to out-of-state insurers use such broad powers. See Hugh D. Harbison, "Legal Environment for All Lines Insurance" in *All Lines Insurance* Dan M. McGill ed. (Homewood, Ill.: Richard D. Irwin, 1960), chap. 2, p. 23. More states have changed their laws, but many still do not allow one corporation to be an all-lines insurer.

[26] See chaps. 4–11 on each of these impacts of all-lines insurance. This was the first book to use the title *All Lines Insurance.*

[27] Philip H. Dutter, "The Coming Life Insurance Shake-up: Who Will Survive?", *CLU Journal,* 34, no. 4 (October 1981), p. 10.

ity insurers. The potential increased competition from their agents (Prudential has 25,000; Metropolitan has 19,000) was obvious. The *reasons* given by Prudential for becoming an all-line group include: (1) reaction to the competition from property-liability companies entering the life field, (2) the use of substantial life insurer surplus to increase the potential financial stability of total operations, (3) the opportunity to realize an investment return equal to or greater than investments in other ventures, and (4) the appeal of all-lines distribution to both the agent and the consumer.[28] Other reasons are the advantages of an integrated marketing and management system, better use of technical personnel, and the desire for a hedge against (1) loss of employee benefit markets to competition, (2) loss of health insurance markets to expanding social insurance plans, and (3) inflation factors, which increase premiums more for property-liability lines than for life insurance.

A strong *consumer interest in all-lines* agents was noted in Prudential's research a decade ago. State Farm and other property-liability insurers have been successful in selling on an all-lines basis. Even the life insurers' own research shows that three fourths of the public would prefer buying life insurance from an insurer that offers all types of insurance (or all types plus other financial services).[29]

The consumer is attracted to the concept. The ability of the life insurance agent to stay in regular personal (not just telephone) contact with his or her clients is indicated as a strong reason for the long-range success of life agents in property-liability insurance. The probable gradual nature of expansion is stressed because of the need for underwriting selectivity, the reluctance of clients to change insurers in a tightening market, and the need to retrain agents so that they can serve as all-lines family insurance counselors. The cost of retraining is a big factor: many insurers of all types are devoting much more time to expanding their agents' capabilities in new fields.[30]

Marketing results thus far have been reasonably successful for the life insurers, although the underwriting results for property-liability

---

[28] Leroy J. Simon, "Why the 'Rock' Moved into Property-Liability," *Journal of Insurance* 34, no. 4 (July–August 1973), p. 21.

[29] *MAP '76: Monitoring Attitudes of the Public* (Washington, D.C.: American Council of Life Insurance, 1976), p. 62. In 1982 these annual national surveys show that (1) banks generally have a more favorable public image than life insurers, (2) all but 3 percent of respondents feel that life insurance has become more expensive (in spite of widespread price reductions), and (3) the public feels extremely low levels of knowledgeability about life insurance, although they are convinced that they know more about financial affairs than in prior years.

[30] "Life and Casualty Insurers Meet Head-on," *Business Week*, August 29, 1977, p. 87. Nationwide devotes 30 percent of its training time to life insurance, for example, in contrast to only 10 percent a decade ago.

business have not always been good, as might be expected for high-cost initial operations in a new field.

The potential *benefits* of having life insurers sell in the property-liability areas cited are greater financial stability for the total insurance market, reaching difficult and broader markets, the introduction of new ideas, greater competition and thus less government intervention, increased total underwriting capacity, and a better long-range management viewpoint for insurance. Anticipated larger and steadier incomes for their agents are frequently mentioned by life insurers as expected benefits.

The future

Some executives predict that the division in the insurance industry will end in the next decade.[31] All-lines insurance has a long way to go before it earns its title fully, however. Perhaps in the future there will be many contracts that really deserve to be called *all-lines contracts*. At present only a few all-lines types of policies are written by a small number of insurers in a few states. An example is disability insurance and life insurance for a home mortgage, which is written along with a homeowner's contract (and automobile insurance, in some cases). Putting all of these coverages in one policy of total protection available to most insurance consumers is a prediction for the future.[32] If the trends noted here continue, it may happen sooner than many persons expect.

A *combination personal-lines package policy* is defined as a single policy with a specific premium computation plan with potential savings to the consumer over separate policies, offering at least one basic home and automobile coverage. A "true" personal-lines package policy is "one policy that encompasses all lines of insurance for a family and its possessions, meaning basic property, basic casualty, plus some form of life and health coverage."[33]

Early efforts at marketing these broad contracts were often limited and relatively unsuccessful. Burkhart notes the W. J. Perryman Co. (Alabama) in 1960 as the first insurer to include life coverage with home and auto, and the General America (Safeco) Companies in 1943 as the first insurer with a combined home-auto policy. The Founders Insurance Company was next, in 1951. The Cincinnati Insurance Company and the Midwestern Indemnity Company began writing a combination home-

---

[31] *Ibid.* Edward J. Noha, chairman of the CNA companies.

[32] Robert E. Bray, "The Insurance of the Future?", *Nevada Herald* (Missouri), May 10, 1981. (You don't have to be from Missouri to believe someone from there!)

[33] James S. Burkhart, "History, Development, and Future Potential of Combination Personal Lines Package Policies," *CPCU Annals* 26, no. 4 (December 1973), p. 129. Other specific references to companies in this section, unless otherwise noted, come from the same source.

automobile contract in 1957 and have "the distinction of being the only known early pioneers in this unique field to still actively market their home and auto combination policy."[34] More insurers, mostly small ones, adopted this practice in the 1960s.

Three big insurers broke into the field more recently. First, the Insurance Company of North America (1969), then, in 1973, the Continental Insurance Companies and the Travelers. INA's is almost a true personal-lines package, offering home and auto coverage, with optional "excess" personal liability (see Chapter 17) and accidental death and dismemberment. It uses a variable percentage savings discount and an indivisible premium. Continental's is a true all-lines "personal comprehensive protection" (PCP) policy, with combined home-auto property and liability, excess liability, hospital, and disability income and mortgage life insurance at unique premium modification rates. Extensive advertising in major magazine media featured the idea of covering "you, your home, and auto" all in one policy. A detailed 50-page comparison of the coverages with current homeowners' and auto contracts emphasizes the easier wording and broader coverage aspects of the comprehensive contract. The Travelers' "Com Pac" combines home and automobile insurance at a 10 percent discount, and recently added mortgage redemption life insurance.

The three major insurers mentioned above are sufficient evidence to suggest that the new era of true all-lines contracts for the personal field started before the 1980s. INA also merged with Connecticut General Life in 1981 to form an all-lines group known as CIGNA. Although it is much too early to predict lasting effects, these efforts by well-recognized insurers are too broad geographically to go unnoticed by consumers or competitors. It will take other large insurers to make this a real trend for the insurance business, but the convenience and cost savings features may well make these innovations grow more rapidly in the next decade.

Undoubtedly, increased competition in all-lines selling will be an important part of tomorrow's insurance market. The advantages of survey selling and such other features as automatic monthly check payment plans are obvious to many policyholders. Many agents or agencies have been operating as all-lines sales forces for years. Independent agents now write about one eighth of the new ordinary life insurance sold each year, and about 70 percent of this is written through the life insurance affiliate of one of the agency's property-liability insurers.[35] As a result of the rapid entry of property and liability insurers into all-lines opera-

---

[34] Ibid., p. 131. The Cincinnati Insurance Company also now can add homeowner's reducing term life insurance (in $25,000 or $50,000 amounts) to its combination contract.

[35] William B. Lusk and Douglas T. Hibbard, "The Independent Property-Casualty Agent Distribution System," *CLU Journal* 35, no. 1 (January 1981), p. 12–13.

tions by creating all-lines groups, and the need to protect their markets, life insurers have sound reasons for evaluating the prospects of all-lines insurance.

The insurance product of tomorrow may be a direct outgrowth of the trend to multiple-line and all-lines insurance. It may well be a market dominated by "package" contracts of property, liability, life, and health insurance. It must be consumer-oriented (see Chapter 29) if it is to be successful. The progressive insurer is reanalyzing its organization structure, its financing and training system for agents, and its total marketing and underwriting plans in order to provide better all-lines insurance for the modern buyer.

EXPANSION TO FINANCIAL SERVICES

Growth and types of conglomerates

One of the most pronounced characteristics of U.S. business for several decades has been the "urge to merge." Sometimes these *mergers* have involved only business firms that have competed directly in *one product or service.* The advantages of economies of larger scale and broader markets have been attractive in our increasingly mobile economy. Insurance has seen this type of growth in the multiple-line and all-lines insurance trends.

In many other cases, growth has taken place in a different sphere— that of combining businesses offering different but *related products or services.* Both vertical (production and distribution) and horizontal (on the same level) integration have occurred. Pooled capital, production, computer, and distribution facilities have helped combat rising material and labor costs. Product diversification has been desired for greater stability of operating results in a rapidly changing market. The "financial services conglomerate" is an example of this expansion.

The true "conglomerate" type of growth combining *unrelated businesses,* has appeared, too. Primarily during the past several years, this phenomenon has attracted much attention. It faces the restraints of some legislation and court action, particularly the antitrust provisions of the Sherman, Clayton, and other federal acts. However, many conglomerates have been successful in their operations, and some have involved insurance.[36] The Sears-Allstate Insurance combination was an early example, and the move by Kroger Food Stores in 1982 to set up financial centers in its grocery chain is an indication of what may increase in the future. Armco, Greyhound, Xerox, Montgomery Ward, and even Baldwin Piano have entered the insurance business.

---

[36] See Dan Cordtz, "What Does U.S.I. Do? Why, Almost Everything," *Fortune,* February 1973, p. 73, for what is called "the ultimate conglomerate."

Thus, the insurance business is a part of all three of the above tendencies toward combination of business firms and growth in their size. Mergers and expansion to multiple-line insurers increased rapidly during the 1960s. All-lines insurer groups, particularly property-liability insurers purchasing or forming life insurer affiliates, became numerous throughout the late 1960s and the 1970s.[37] Life insurers followed in their expansion to all-lines insurance throughout the past decade. During this same period the financial services conglomerate appeared, and that growing trend is the emphasis of the next section.

Financial services conglomerates

The *financial services conglomerate* is one of the most significant trends noted today. The "zaibatsu," which has long been a prominent form of business in Japan, uses the banking-financial base for its large-scale activities in many endeavors. Legislation by Congress and court interpretation may well determine the future of this method of business in the United States. The homogenization of financial services seems destined to continue, as the distinctions among the functions performed by financial institutions are disappearing.[38]

Banks rushed to transform themselves into holding companies during the last dozen years, and several thousand were operating mutual funds, finance companies, and other related activities by the early 1980s. They may be restricted from entering manufacturing and other industries, but their continued expansion beyond the traditional "banking" field to include other financial services is to be expected in a computer economy. Federal legislation in 1982 directly prohibits bank holding companies from providing insurance as principal, agent, or brokers. However, even with this restriction, the trend may slow but not stop their expansion into insurance. The law *exempts* (1) bank holding companies in towns of less than 5,000 population, (2) those with less than $50 million in assets, (3) many that already have insurance agency operations, and (4) sale of credit life and some credit property insurance.[39] One author concludes that "the movement to totally integrated financial services is irreversible and that all that is left is to clear some legislative hurdles."[40]

Savings and loan associations have also begun to market, in one payroll deduction, combinations of term life insurance, mutual fund shares, and

---

[37] Alan L. King, "Conglomeration within the Property and Liability Insurance Industry," *CPCU Annals* 27, no. 4 (December 1974), p. 314.

[38] Harold Skipper, Jr., "The Homogenization of the Financial Services Industry," *CLU Journal* 36, no. 1 (January 1982), p. 30.

[39] Title VI of the Depository Institutions Amendments of 1982 (H.R. 6267).

[40] Robert S. Cline, "Commercial Banks and the Distribution of Property and Liability Insurance," *CPCU Journal* 35, no. 2 (June 1982), p. 82.

savings programs. The first life insurer owned by a federally chartered savings and loan association appeared in 1982.[41] For the finally troubled savings and loan field, insurance may offer an enticing if not irresistible expansion in order to compete for consumers and financial-services profits in the future.

Stock brokerage firms are combining with insurance in many ways. E. F. Hutton began its own life insurer, which is in the forefront of the new universal life insurance market. Prudential purchased Bache, and Sears (which owns Allstate Insurance) added Dean Witter Reynolds (which owns Lincoln Benefit Life). American Express now owns both Fireman's Fund Insurance and the stock brokerage firm of Shearson Hayden Stone. Merrill-Lynch acquired Family Life Insurance Company.

Financial supermarkets?

The rush by banking institutions to provide customers, particularly large depositors, with broader financial services is well underway. Already, some offer new services in securities and mutual funds investments, travel arrangements, financial and tax planning, credit cards, and cash or asset management accounts.[42] Legislation in late 1982 even opened the door for their direct competition with the popular money market funds, by permitting banks to start money market funds that are federally insured.

If the financial supermarkets of the 1980s continue their growth, perhaps only the largest firms can take advantage of some of the forces behind the trend—deregulation and advances in technology. Computers and telecommunications permit fast and efficient cash and other transfers, but they require substantial capital investments. Some authorities suggest there will, however, continue to be plenty of room for smaller and more specialized financial firms, just as there has been a resurgence of convenience stores to compete with food chains and discount giants.[43]

The position of insurance

Where will insurance companies fit into the trend toward the "one-stop money shop"?[44] It appears that competition is escalating, and that bankers, brokers, and insurance agents will all be vying for each other's business. Many insurers are committed to broadening their financial

---

[41] "Illinois S&L Moves into Insurance Arena," *National Underwriter,* November 19, 1982, p. 48. Federated Assurance is owned by First Federal Savings and Loan Association of Chicago.

[42] Jane Bryant Quinn, "Banking for Fat Cats," *Newsweek,* July 12, 1982, p. 13D.

[43] Roger E. Birk, "Beyond the 'Supermarket'—a New Era in Financial Services," *Viewpoint* (Marsh-McClellan), Fall 1982, p. 5.

[44] Jane Bryant Quinn, "Your One-Stop Money Shop," *Newsweek,* July 19, 1982, p. 57.

services beyond insurance, as many have mutual funds, and some have stock market affiliates (Prudential-Bache), credit cards (Firemen's Fund-American Express), and money market funds (Hartford, Travelers). A few insurers have all of these services available to the consumer. Even insurance brokers have been purchased, as illustrated by the move by the Transamerica conglomerate back toward a financial services group in the acquisition of the fifth largest insurance broker, Fred S. James and Co.[45]

The salesforces are undergoing tremendous changes, too. Life insurance agents are retraining to become security brokers, and security brokers are obtaining insurance licenses. Both groups are competing for consumer recognition as financial advisers, through new professional designations such as Certified Financial Planner (CFP) and Chartered Financial Consultant (ChFC).[46]

The issue is still controversial. Many insurers have not yet expanded to all-lines insurance, and the leap to other related financial services is a difficult one. The potential advantages are increased income for their salesforces, cutting expenses, meeting competition, and improving services to insureds. However, the disadvantages may include the cost of retraining and reorganization, heavy start-up expenses, retaliation by businesses outside of insurance, and loss of identity as insurance experts. A majority may never take such steps, preferring instead to concentrate in insurance and its specialized services.

The search for profitability in the future may be an elusive target, even for the insurance giants. Success will be dependent upon increased productivity by companies and agents, and consumer acceptance of new ways of doing business. Although the financial services trend offers many new opportunities, it promises to be a challenge of unprecedented proportion to insurance in the years ahead. As one top insurance executive has said, the financial supermarket will be no panacea for solving all of the problems of insurance, and "success in the arena of financial services is going to come hard and slow."[47]

FOR REVIEW AND DISCUSSION

1. Product diversification is a trend that is seen in many types of businesses today. Compare and contrast product diversification in the past 20 years of insurance with that of other businesses.

---

[45] "Transamerica Builds on its Old Identity," *Business Week*, November 15, 1982, p. 39.

[46] These fast-growing national programs are administered by the College of Financial Planning (Denver, Colorado), and the American College (Bryn Mawr, Pa.), respectively.

[47] Dr. Joseph Melone, executive vice president of Prudential and chairman of the Life Insurance Marketing and Research Association (LIMRA), in "Pru Exec: Financial 'Supermarket' No Panacea," *National Underwriter*, March 19, 1982, p. 22.

2. Explain how the multiple-line and all-lines insurance trends are perhaps related to the risk-management concept (as discussed in Chapters 2 and 3).

3. If multiple-line insurance contracts provide greater coverage than comparable separate policies, how can the multiple-line contracts have a lower premium? Is this the only significant result of these contracts?

4. What is *multiple-line* insurance, and how does it compare with *all-lines* insurance? What separate parts can you identify in the multiple-line trend? Why are they significant?

5. Has the multiple-line trend been recent? Rapid? Continuous? Explain.

6. Are all insurers now multiple-line insurers? Why or why not?

7. What is the difference between multiple-line insurance and "package" policies? All-lines insurance? Multiple-peril contracts? All-risks policies?

8. What are the goals of multiple-line insurance for the insurers?

9. Mr. Riskee has just been married and has purchased a new suburban home. Why would you recommend a homeowner's policy to him? What form would you suggest, and why?

10. Give an illustration of four kinds of liability exposures covered in the comprehensive personal liability section of the homeowner's policy, indicating for each whether or not tenants as well as property owners might incur such losses.

11. Some of the homeowners' policies use the "named-perils" approach in providing protection, while some use the "all-risks" approach. (a) Differentiate these two approaches, indicating the basic perils included in one homeowner's form which uses each approach. (b) State your recommendations, with reasons, for the homeowner's form and the limits of coverage to be used by a family owning an $80,000 dwelling.

12. What is the primary purpose of the new "homeowners' plus" policy which has been adopted in some states? (Cite several examples to illustrate your answer.)

13. Why do you think the personal multiple-line contracts were developed on a large scale before the business contracts using the same technique?

14. What forms of business multiple-line policies were developed first? Did they include property or liability coverages, or both?

15. What features characterize the popular special multiperil (SMP) contracts, including the simplified SMP package policy, for businesses? How do these contracts compare with the businessowners' policies (BOP)?

16. Explain (a) several factors which may hasten and (b) several factors which may slow down the all-lines insurance trend. What part of the development of all-lines *groups* is most evident now? All-lines *contracts*?

17. Divide the class into two groups: one to discuss the benefits which a well-established life insurer may achieve as a leader in the life insurance business only, the other to show why the life insurer should expand to all-lines insurance or even noninsurance financial enterprises.

18. If you were the president of a property-liability insurer, what would you suggest to your executive committee as methods by which your agency force could be encouraged to sell life insurance for a proposed life insurer affiliate?

19. What *(a)* advantages and *(b)* disadvantages does a financial services conglomerate have to offer in relation to each of the major functions of an insurer, that is, product development, underwriting and rating, marketing, claims payment, and miscellaneous activities?

20. What future do you predict in the next decade for the financial services conglomerate? Carefully explain your reasoning and the factors involved, with emphasis on the position of insurers in this trend.

Chapter 24

Outline of concepts

Government property and liability insurance, although not a new field of study, is nevertheless one of *increasing* scope and *changing* complexity.

  General nature of the government's involvement is *more recent* and *less encompassing* than its involvement in the life and health insurance fields.

  A new era evolved after the Housing and Urban Development Act, with the federal government helping to *maintain insurance availability* for some *high-risk perils and areas.*

  Comparison with social insurance: plans are *optional,* not compulsory.

  An overview indicates the emphasis here on four programs.

FAIR plans in 28 states help urban property owners obtain insurance against *riot and related perils.*

  The problem is one of *serious civil disorders* of catastrophic proportions.

  The answer was *federal reinsurance of state* "fair access to insurance requirements" (FAIR) *plans* under the HUD department.

  How the FAIR plans operate as insurer pools in the states is explained, with agents of private insurers servicing the business.

Flood insurance is now available under a *federally insured* plan, using agents of private insurers to sell and service the contract.

  The problem was accentuated by many uninsured flood losses.

  National Flood Insurance Act of 1968 inaugurated the new plan.

  Coverage limits and community qualification rules are set by HUD.

  The results are much increased availability of limited flood coverage, and growth because of new rules for federal disaster relief.

  The change to direct federal flood insurance in 1978 had the government assume the flood insurance risk, and set higher available limits for covered properties (now more than 2 million policyholders for $100 billion coverage).

Crime insurance is another federally sponsored insurance program.

  The concept is like that of the FAIR plans, but involves the federal government directly as an *insurer* in urban areas at "affordable" rates.

  The contracts are for both residential and commercial properties.

  The results have been poor, and involve substantial problems.

The future of federal insurance and reinsurance plans may be decreasing in some areas, or could involve other alternatives such as the proposed National Catastrophe Insurance Act.

U.S. overseas political risks are insured in a unique government-private plan, encouraging direct U.S. private investments abroad.

Government-required liability insurance is a growing area, especially with *compulsory automobile insurance* under no-fault laws.

Government property and liability insurance

The first treatment of *government property and liability insurance* in a separate chapter of an insurance text appeared in the previous edition of this book. The rationale for the emphasis is that these government programs have unique features, and that they are substantial in size. Billions of dollars of U.S. property and liability exposures are now protected by government systems of insurance and reinsurance for floods, riots, crime, overseas private investment, and other property and liability perils. This chapter parallels Chapter 11, Government Life and Health Insurance, where the gigantic federal OASDHI program of social security, state workers' compensation,[1] and unemployment and nonoccupational disability income plans are discussed.

GENERAL NATURE

In property and liability insurance the emergence of government involvement in insurance has been more recent and less encompassing than in life and health insurance. Until the last decade only scattered examples of direct government insurance of property-liability perils are found. The emphasis was on selected losses, such as damage to property values by war, nuclear energy property and liability damages, credit losses on exports, crop insurance disasters, and savings account losses in bank and savings and loan association accounts. Most of the areas were those in which the risks were so large that unless government provided the insurance system, the private insurance business could not do so, or at least had not done so.

However, in the years following the Housing and Urban Development Act of 1968 there emerged a new era in which government became actively involved in providing *reinsurance* in order to maintain *existing* private insurance systems for high-risk urban properties against riot and other perils. In addition, the government decided that the neglected

---

[1] Work injury and sickness perils have been discussed in Chapter 18, Employers' Liability and Workers' Compensation, and are also so closely related to the health peril, that they are logically included in Part Two as part of government life and health insurance.

problem of floods and water damage in beach areas needed insurance not being provided by most private insurance plans. In some states, crime insurance was also difficult or very expensive. Thus government insurance systems were inaugurated in these areas during the 1970s.

Comparison with social insurance

The student of insurance and risk should note that many of the government property and liability insurance plans have some similarities to the concept of *social insurance,* as developed in Chapter 3, but also differ in some essentials. Basically, the purpose is similar—helping to provide economic security against some specific perils for the well-being of large groups of persons in our society. In contrast to the life-health social insurance plans, however, the insurance developed in the property area oftentimes is *not compulsory* for the properties exposed to loss. (Nuclear energy liability already is, and automobile liability is becoming, an exception to this statement.) Social plans in life and health insurance are largely based upon laws which *require* that all eligible persons be a part of the program (OASDHI), or that employers *must* provide certain benefits (workers' and unemployment compensation, for example). The federal or state government taxing power over employers and employees is used to enforce the compulsory feature of these laws.

Upon analysis, most other government property insurance plans will be found to lack the compulsory feature. Some plans may lack other characteristics which are important in describing social insurance, such as widespread application to meet universal problems of maintaining economic security in a society.

An overview

In describing the fields of insurance, Chapter 3 identified several insurance systems which were defined as "voluntary" government plans, where the government may provide the insurance but permits the coverage to be purchased on an optional basis. Included in this category are such programs as those of the Federal Crop Insurance Corporation, Federal Housing Administration insurance of mortgages, and title insurance under Torrens title laws in some states. The Federal Deposit Insurance Corporation and the Federal Savings and Loan Insurance Corporation, which insure deposits or shares up to $100,000 per account, are also sometimes[2] included in this classification of "voluntary" government insurance plans.

A few other plans might be included as government property-liability

---

[2] National and state banks which are required to carry this insurance are exceptions, and could be included in social insurance.

insurance. These include plans in some states and municipalities which have "self-insurance funds" for insuring government property against fire and other perils. Although some of these plans may qualify as true insurance systems, many lack some of the requirements for sound use of the insurance technique. In connection with workers' compensation, all but a few states have established a "second-injury fund" which encourages the hiring of handicapped workers. The employer is required to pay for a second disabling injury only to the extent that it separately causes loss of income and not for the combined results of both the first and second disability. The balance of payments comes from the state's second-injury fund.

Further details on all of these programs will not be included in this chapter. Several are mentioned elsewhere: foreign export credit insurance and state title insurance laws in Chapter 22, crop insurance in Appendix C, and nuclear energy property and liability insurance in Chapter 13. This chapter will concentrate on the *newer* federal *riot* and *crime* programs for urban properties, the *flood* insurance program of the Federal Insurance Administration, and on the *political risks* insurance program of the Overseas Private Investment Corporation (OPIC). A final section will look at the *future* potential for compulsory liability insurance (especially automobile) which could be classified as part of the government's increased interest in property-liability insurance.

FAIR PLANS

Fair Access to Insurance Requirements (FAIR) plans are now in operation in 28 states, the District of Columbia, and Puerto Rico, helping urban property owners to obtain riot and other insurance protection. In addition, property owners in high-risk areas along the Atlantic and Gulf Coasts in seven states have beach and windstorm plans available. Because the FAIR plans are so much larger, the following description concentrates on the FAIR plans for urban properties.

The problem

In response to the serious riots and civil disorders in many states during the 1960s, which caused restricted insurance availability in some urban areas, the federal government acted to bolster the private insurance business. The Urban Property Protection and Reinsurance Act of 1968 (Public Law 90-448) was the direct result of recommendations of the President's National Advisory Panel on Insurance in Riot-Affected Areas.[3]

---

[3] As part of the report of the National Advisory Commission on Civil Disorders, this commission's report was titled *Meeting the Insurance Crisis of Our Cities* (Washington, D.C.: U.S. Government Printing Office, 1968).

The problem was severe. Civil disorders had caused losses totaling more than $200 million during 1965–69 in Watts and California, Newark, Detroit, and in Washington, Baltimore, Chicago, and other locations following the assassination of Dr. Martin Luther King. Others continued to occur in scattered locations in the 1970s and 1980s, the largest in New York (1977) and Miami (1980). Many homeowners and businesspersons in the urban areas of primary concern had increasing difficulty in obtaining proper riot insurance coverage in connection with their fire and extended coverage contracts.

The answer

The federal government's answer was to make available a new riot reinsurance program through a National Insurance Development Fund under the Department of Housing and Urban Development (HUD). Although all insurers are not required to purchase this reinsurance, the many hundreds of insurers that do must also participate in HUD-approved and state-supervised FAIR plans or voluntary pools which make basic property insurance more readily available in the high-risk urban areas.

A model plan has been developed by leading insurance associations to meet the HUD requirements for approval. This is called the Model Uniform Basic Property Insurance Inspection and Placement Program. It requires inspection procedures for homes and businesses, a plan for placing the business with insurers, and a joint reinsurance plan within each state for the participating insurers. Other states may use individually developed plans, but these, too, must meet the fundamental federal requirements.

This was not the first time the U.S. government acted as a reinsurer. In World War II (1942–47) the federal War Damage Insurance Corporation provided catastrophic loss coverage for U.S. properties, with private insurers sharing profits and losses up to $20 million. Nuclear energy property and liability insurance has been available since 1956 through private insurers and pools which now provide approximately $300 million in property coverage and $160 million in liability coverage. Assessments against nuclear plants and the Atomic Energy Commission guarantee further indemnity up to $560 million. The HUD plan was a major impetus for the further expansion of private insurer-federal reinsurer plans for riot and related perils. The motive of government in these plans was not to serve as the primary insurer of the perils, but to initiate action by private insurers in these fields by serving as the reinsurer.

The FAIR reinsurance plan involves several layers of payments in this order: (1) out of the individual insurer's retention and participation (up to 2.5 percent of the premiums written in the state), (2) out of the reinsurance premium held in the National Insurance Development fund for each state (the percentage of losses payable to the insurers varies from 90–98 percent, depending on the size of the losses incurred), (3) out of potential assessments against all insurers that purchase riot reinsurance in the state (up to 2 percent of all property premiums collected), (4) out of state backup layers (up to 5 percent of all property premiums paid), and (5) from the borrowing authority of HUD (up to $250 million for catastrophic losses).[4] The last item is a loan which must be repaid from future reinsurance premiums charged the insurer. The premium rate charged to the insurer has varied from 1.25 percent on covered lines to 0.15 percent or less, following better-than-expected loss experience. The role of the federal government is clearly that of a backup for the private insurance system.

How the FAIR plans operate

Each state that has a FAIR plan has formed a pool or syndicate to make property insurance (principally riot, but also fire and allied lines[5] and theft insurance) available to property owners who cannot obtain coverage in the regular market. FAIR plan insurance is not intended to replace coverage normally available, but is for the purpose of providing "fair access to insurance" based on the physical characteristics of the property (rather than on rejection for its poor location). Agents of the insurers help the purchasers in making applications, obtaining the contracts, handling premiums, and filing claims as necessary. Insurers in each pool share in the losses and expenses of each plan in proportion to the property insurance premiums they write in the state. The insurers are required to reinsure losses for specified property insurance lines with the federal government plan.

The insured pays a standard rate unless the property insured fails to meet certain minimal requirements, as many properties do. The state plan sets the rates, and the states vary widely in the details of their rating plans. An application for coverage cannot be denied on the basis of location in a likely riot area or on the basis of other environmental hazards beyond the control of the property owner. When the property owner cannot obtain insurance in normal insurance markets, application is made through an agent for a free inspection of the property. If the property is acceptable under the usual underwriting requirements in regard to its structural condition (regardless of its location in an unaccept-

---

[4] John R. Lewis, "A Critical Review of the Federal Riot Reinsurance System," *Journal of Risk and Insurance* 38, no. 1 (March 1971), p. 32.

[5] Vandalism and malicious mischief must also be offered, except in states where the normal market is adequate.

able neighborhood), a contract is issued. If the property requires structural improvements of a serious nature, the insurance may be denied until the changes are made. In many cases, the deficiencies will be less serious and the property found insurable, with a surcharge. The excess charges often run from 50 to 100 percent of the standard rates, under either the FAIR plan or other "schedule excess" plans used in many states.[6] The owner can remove these surcharges by making the necessary improvements.

Individual insurers are not required to write coverage without limit, but they notify the plan of the limits that they will accept on each class of business. The minimum amount is $5,000, but the FAIR plan facility may submit an application to not more than five insurers, so that the property owner can obtain at least $25,000 of insurance. Maximums also apply, with $100,000 on habitational property and $500,000 on commercial property at any one location (including contiguous buildings).

The results

Twenty-eight states have the FAIR plans, which by 1982 were issuing about 940,000 contracts insuring property values of $36 *billion* for $190 million in premiums. These FAIR plans sustained annual losses of almost $73 million.[7] Only a few states have been able to make a profit on FAIR plan business to date. About one half of insured properties are commercial risks.

Special plans in operation in seven states offer *beach and windstorm coverage* along the Atlantic and Gulf Coast areas. The states are Alabama, Florida, Louisiana, Mississippi, North Carolina, and South Carolina, and Texas. Almost $6 billion of properties were insured, and underwriting losses were $14 million.[8]

Although the adequacy and equity of FAIR plan rates have been criticized, the initial crude rating system has been modified to include some improvements. Problems of "dumping" (by the insurers) of the poorest risks into the plans have occurred in some cases, but the lower commissions (usually 8–10 percent) allowable under the plans have encouraged agents to secure regular coverage in most cases where it is possible to do so. The use of FAIR plans by insureds varies greatly in the various states and cities in which these plans operate. Many states have less

[6] Andrew F. Whitman and C. Arthur Williams, Jr., "FAIR Plan and Excess Rate Plan Rates in Minnesota," *Journal of Risk and Insurance* 38, no. 1 (March 1971), pp. 44–51. See also Michael L. Smith and C. Arthur Williams, Jr., "FAIR Plan Insureds: Occupancy and Location Characteristics and Experience," *Journal of Risk and Insurance* 42, no. 1 (March 1975), p. 156.

[7] *Insurance Facts* (New York: Insurance Information Institute, 1982–83), p. 36.

[8] Ibid.

than 5 percent of the total fire and extended coverage premiums in the plans, while others may have more than 20 percent.

The federal riot reinsurance program has been compared with commercial excess reinsurance, which also provides stability and catastrophe protection on an aggregate excess-of-loss basis (see Chapter 26); while the noteworthy differences include the federal riot insurance program's application on a state-by-state basis, its highly arbitrary rating system, and its general inflexibility.[9] The same author summarizes its strengths (politically feasible and fiscally workable), and weaknesses (state-by-state application, the ultimate absorption by private insurers of a clearly social problem, the unwillingness of many states to expose general revenues to back up the FAIR plans, high costs, and vague definitions of the riots and losses covered).

Although the total program offered substantial relief and stability for the private insurers during a very critical period, the long-range effects of the government's action on the urban property insurance market and private insurance business remain largely to be seen. One possible undesirable effect, pointed out by the Government Accounting Office, is that these plans may be creating incentives for arson where the property owners are not required to verify building values. *HUD* reports claim that *FAIR* plans are not a cause of increasing arson-for-profit cases, and imply that lack of insurance is the villian behind the problems of property deterioration in the inner city. However, other studies dispute these conclusions. They blame inner city decay on the social and economic ills of unemployment, substandard housing, high taxes, rising crime rates, uncollected rents, and loan defaults. Lax underwriting criteria in the plans are also criticized, which leads this research to state that "the correlation between the *FAIR* plan and properties that are being torched is too obvious and recurrent to ignore."[10]

Who should pay for the high costs of insuring urban properties? Some of the costs are paid by the property owners—in *FAIR* plans, rates may be three or four times the regular market rates. However, the consistent losses of the plans, involving millions of dollars each year, are subsidized by the insurers and their other policyholders. The exposures are concentrated in certain states: for example, some $25 of $36 billion of the total insurance in force in *FAIR* plans is in only four plans—California, Michigan, New Jersey, and New York.[11] Fortunately, the trend toward high losses seems to be slowed, and insurers are writing more urban property

---

[9] Lewis, "A Critical Review," p. 34.

[10] "Urban Decay: A Real World Perspective," *Journal of American Insurance* 54, no. 1 (Spring, 1978), p. 1.

[11] *Insurance Facts,* pp. 36–37.

insurance without depending on the *FAIR* plans. (See later section on
the future of these plans.)

FLOOD INSURANCE

Another serious problem of insurance availability has been the flood
peril for fixed-location property, which was usually considered to be
"uninsurable" because of its catastrophic nature, high concentration or
risk, and economic unfeasibility. Standard homeowners' policies exclude
flood damage.

The problem

Sometimes associated with extensive hurricane losses, the many millions of uninsured losses by flood damages, such as those suffered in
Alaska (1964) and in Hurricane Betsy (1965) and Beulah (1967), prompted
action by the federal government in 1968. Fixed-property (real estate)
owners, in particular, were incapable of obtaining proper coverage except
in Lloyd's markets at high rates and under many limitations.

Private insurers emphasized the difficulties of adverse selection, with
the property owners in areas that were most likely to suffer sizable and
frequent losses being the only applicants for flood insurance. In addition,
the insurers stressed problems of equitable and marketable prices for
the cost of coverage in such areas, as compared with other areas that
had very infrequent but catastrophic losses. The result was that few
persons had insurance, and many hardships were created by this uninsured peril. Government declarations of "disaster areas" following flood
damage were primarily stopgap measures aimed at emergency aid and
restoring properties with low, long-term loans after the losses had occurred. The use of general tax revenues to do this for the specific unfortunate property owners was questioned.

The National Flood Insurance Act of 1968

To alleviate the problem, the National Flood Insurance Act was passed
to inaugurate a coordinated program of land-use and loss-prevention
measures, with an attempt to make flood insurance coverage more widely
available in the United States. Before-the-loss funding was chosen as a
much needed part of an insurance system to meet the flood peril.

Basically, the original act set up a reinsurance program of the federal
government in order to initiate action by private insurers at subsidized
rates. A pool of about 130 insurers, the National Flood Insurers Association (NFIA), was formed in order to underwrite the coverage in selected
areas which met the requirements of the Department of Housing and

Urban Development. The insurers, through their regular agents, wrote the protection at rates and commissions (15 percent) set by the government in communities that have satisfied the program standards. The federal government subsidized part of the cost of the insurance.

Coverage limits and community qualifications. The limitations of coverage were extensive. In addition to being restricted only to communities which agreed to meet (over a period of years) extensive land-use and control requirements set up by HUD, the eligible dwelling and smaller business properties could obtain insurance up to $17,500 per single-family dwellings, $5,000 on contents, and $30,000 on multiple-family dwellings, commercial, and nonprofit structures. A deductible of $200 or 2 percent of the insurance amount, if greater, applied. (See later section for current limits.)

HUD regulated the qualification procedure for communities that applied to participate in the program. The U.S. Corps of Engineers completed flood control and other studies of the area, and determined actuarial rates. (These requirements were mostly waived during an emergency period while the communities met qualification standards.)

Before flood insurance could be obtained in a community, the community must have applied to come under the program. Temporary approval was often obtained in a few weeks. The next step took the most time, as extensive delineation of flood-prone areas could take up to three years or more for large communities. The implementation of the survey, which might cost up to $2,000–$3,000 per mile of stream or river surveyed, took the flood insurance and flood control process out of the hands of the individual. Yet the individual could use the information that was available to determine whether a prospective property was exposed to the peril of flood and to see whether flood insurance was then advisable. Once the flood-prone areas were designated, the community had six months to change their zoning and building codes in these areas. Building was prohibited unless special flood proofing was used in the construction of new buildings. Other areas were identified for open-space use, such as for parks or golf courses.

Contributing to the peril of flood resulting from rain, rivers, tidal waves, hurricanes, melting snow, and rising sewers, are the hazards of urbanization. Where forests and grasslands once stood, square miles of rooftops, streets, and parking lots quickly divert precipitation to storm sewers that are not designed to handle these sudden surges of large volumes of waters.

Considerable incentive was given to the participating insurers to begin the flood insurance program: The NFIA's share of losses was limited by federal reinsurance, and HUD agreed to reimburse the insurers for 90 percent of their losses during the emergency period prior to acceptable actuarial rate studies. One insurer in each state was designated as the

servicing company for flood insurance contracts. All agents sent applications to the insurer, which issued a separate policy, not an endorsement
of existing fire and extended coverage policies. It covered flood and mudslide damage, including overflow of inland and tidal water or unusual
and rapid accumulation or runoff of surface water in normally dry land
areas. The backing up of sewers was not covered.

The coverage was not looked upon as a profit maker for either insurers
or agents. Insurers normally provided the coverage as a public service.
Agents tended to accept applications, but were criticized for lack of promotion in regard to the availability of the protection. Slowly, extensive
efforts were made to publicize the flood insurance program in the individual states.

The results.   For several years after the original act it was difficult
to characterize the flood insurance program as even reasonably successful. By mid-1970, only 158 areas had qualified, and only about 5,500
contracts had been issued.[12] Catastrophic and widely publicized flood
damage in South Dakota and much flood damage following Hurricane
Agnes on the Eastern seaboard in 1972 sharply increased interest in
the flood insurance program. Flood insurance became available in every
state under the program. Availability of coverage, even with federal
subsidization of up to 50 percent or more of actual estimated costs, was
only part of the problem. Because of the newness of the program and
the unfamiliarity of consumers with the substantial benefits, many property owners exposed to flood losses did not act to purchase the coverage.
An estimated 7,000 communities were in flood-prone areas, yet only a
third of these were eligible for the flood insurance program, and in Hurricane Agnes less than 1 percent of $3 billion in damages was covered
by the federally subsidized insurance program.[13]

The Flood Disaster Protection Act, effective in 1974, substantially increased the rather modest limits of coverage available under the flood
insurance program. Much discussion also occurred in regard to achieving
better "spread of risk" by including more disaster-type perils, such as
earthquake, landslide, and earth movement. (See later section on the
future.) The new statute also raised federal participation in the program
from a $4 billion limit to $10 billion, and forbade federally regulated
banks and savings and loan associations to make property loans in an
identified flood hazard area unless the property had minimum flood insurance.

Another impetus to the program occurred when new rules became
effective in regard to eligibility for federal disaster relief. In areas where

---

[12] Robert S. Felton, William K. Ghee, and John E. Stinton, "A Mid-1970 Report on
the National Flood Insurance Program," *Journal of Risk and Insurance* 38 no. 1 (March
1971), p. 4.

[13] "A New Effort to Control Flood Loss," *Journal of American Insurance,* Winter 1972,
p. 20.

federal flood insurance is available, unless property owners have purchased the insurance coverage within one year after its availability, their grants and loans under the disaster relief program may be reduced by the amount of flood insurance they could have purchased. These disaster relief benefits include long-term loans of 2 percent interest and "forgiveness" clauses of $2,000 or more.

The change to direct federal flood insurance

In 1978 HUD *discontinued the participation of private insurers in accepting flood insurance risks.*[14] The role of the insurers is now limited to serving as agents for the federal government, which assumes the full insured amounts under the program instead of sharing the risk, as it did under the former partnership. HUD has contracted with a private computer firm, EDS Federal Corporation, to act as the fiscal administrator under the Federal Insurance Administration.[15]

Coverage limits and rates. Under the new direct federal flood insurance program, the insurance limits, rates, and deductibles were increased in 1978. Some other coverage details were also changed in 1981–83.

When a community first qualifies for the flood insurance program, *emergency* status permits insuring up to $35,000 coverage on a single-family dwelling and contents coverage up to $10,000. Other residences, nonresidential risks, and small business (with assets not exceeding $5 million) are eligible for amounts of up to $100,000 on buildings, $10,000 on residential contents, and $100,000 on other contents. Current fixed rates, increased substantially in 1981, vary from $.40 to $.50 per $100 on buildings, and $.50 to $1.00 per $100 on contents.

Higher limits of coverage become available after HUD sets *regular* rates in an area: up to $185,000 on single-family dwellings, $250,000 on other residences and small businesses, and $200,000 on nonresidential structures. Contents limits increase to $60,000 on all residential risks, $300,000 on small businesses, and $200,000 on nonresidential risks. Actuarial rates (subsidized, but based on actual risk of flood damage) are charged for new or additional coverages purchased during the regular phase.

The commissions paid to agents on a one-year policy are 15 percent on the first $2,000 of premium, and 5 percent on all premiums in excess of $2,000 per policy. On three-year policies the commissions are 15 percent to $6,000 premium and 5 percent thereafter. Minimum premium

---

[14] For the developments to this date, see Samuel H. Weese and J. Wesley Ooms, "The National Flood Insurance Program—Did the Industry Drop Out?" *CPCU Journal* 31, no. 4 (December 1978), p. 186.

[15] For policy purchases, contact your local insurance agent. You can also call 800–638–6620, or write the National Flood Insurance Program, P.O. Box 34294, Bethesda, Md. 20817.

is $50, and minimum commission is $10 per policy. A waiting period of five days usually applies before the coverage is effective.

In 1982 the deductible was raised to $500, applying separately to both buildings and contents. Flood insurance on jewelry, precious metals, and art objects was reduced to $250. Replacement cost coverage is provided only for primary residences. Some properties are no longer eligible for flood insurance: new buildings constructed over water or seaward of mean high tide, unanchored mobile homes in special flood hazard areas, and mobile homes placed in new parks in coastal high hazard areas. As of October 1, 1983, new buildings built in certain undeveloped coastal barrier tracts along the Atlantic and Gulf coasts will not be insurable under the federal flood insurance program.

Overall evaluation. An analysis of the current status of federal flood insurance leads to two conclusions: (1) it is a very large and important program, second only to OASDHI of the federal insurance plans, and (2) it has some problems.

The program provides flood insurance in every state for property located in 17,000 of an estimated 20,000 communities considered to be flood-prone. There are about 2 million policyholders, one half of them in Florida, Texas, and Louisiana. The total written premiums are more than $200 million, covering about $100 billion of property.[16]

Although the intent and benefits of the program are good, the implementation is criticized for its red tape and errors. Agents, who tend to sell flood insurance primarily in areas where it is required by mortgage lenders, complain that (1) processing policies near renewal time is difficult, (2) telephone calls to the EDS servicing company are time-consuming and poorly handled, (3) the government is under no legal obligation to send any renewal notices, and (4) the hold-harmless agreement of the federal government with agents has not idemnified them in a few cases.[17]

Agents and agent associations appear reasonably optimistic for the growth of flood insurance, as improvements are being made to reduce rating problems and delays. Claims payments have generally been regarded as prompt and satisfactory. Suggestions as to why an agent should sell flood insurance, in spite of the problems, include the fact that if one agent does not another agent will do so. Also, flood insurance opens up contacts with various clients, avoids errors and omissions claims against agents, and is a most serious peril, since 90 percent of natural disasters are flood-related.[18]

---

[16] *Insurance Facts,* pp. 38–39.

[17] Noreen Lupo and Stuart V. d'Adolf, "The Leaky Flood Program," *Independent Agent,* October 1982, p. 39.

[18] Sajjad A. Hashmi, "Flood Insurance—1982," *CPCU Journal* 35, no. 1 (March 1982), p. 28.

Losses under the national flood insurance program have been heavy. In the past eight years, about $250 million more in claims have been paid out than the $1 billion paid in premiums. In 1980, a particularly bad year, the FIA paid out $3 for each $1 collected. To this extent, the program still depends upon subsidies which come from the U.S. taxpayer. More restricted coverage in the coastal areas and higher rates may help improve this situation.

CRIME INSURANCE

The *federal crime insurance program* started in 1971 under the Housing and Urban Development Act. Paralleling the problems of riot insurance availability in many urban areas was the increasing difficulty of property owners in obtaining crime insurance coverage.

The concept

The program is similar in concept to the FAIR plans, but the coverage is different in that it has always been written *directly* by the *federal* insurance administrator rather than indirectly through reinsurance. The FIA has the authority to write such insurance in any state in which there is a "critical" shortage of crime insurance coverage at "affordable" rates. These rates are determined by the Federal Bureau of Investigation (FBI) and census studies, in which an affordable rate is one that a reasonably prudent person should be willing to pay for coverage, on the basis of costs and benefits under the policy in his or her territory.

Crime insurance is thus made available for residences and businesses when regular theft insurance is not offered at affordable rates.

States are given the opportunity to establish pools or assigned-risk-type plans to provide the coverage, but if they fail to act within a certain time, then the federal government can offer the protection. The insurance is now written in about 27 states, using selected private insurers (Aetna Casualty, INA, and American Universal were early selections in some areas) as servicing agents. Coverage can be purchased through any licensed property insurance agent.[19]

The contracts

Both residential and commercial contracts are sold to eligible property owners. They must meet federal standards of loss-prevention efforts, in-

---

[19] Also, information can be obtained by phoning 800–638–8780, or writing to Federal Crime Insurance, Box 41033, Washington, D.C. 20014.

cluding such things as dead bolt locks on doors and locks on all windows. The requirements for commercial properties are more extensive, and may include alarm systems for certain high-risk classes of business. Free inspections are offered to determine protective device requirements for businesses.

The property owner has no choice but to accept or reject rather inflexible contracts offered by the FIA. The residential policy is a package of burglary and robbery coverage, with a maximum of $10,000 insurance. A deductible of $100 applies, or 5 percent of the gross amount of the loss, if greater. Annual premiums for the residential contract are $80 for $10,000 insurance. The commercial policy rates vary more, and deductibles range from $200 to $500, or 5 percent of the gross loss amount. Coverage can be purchased up to a maximum of $15,000, and the insured is permitted to buy burglary (merchandise, safe, etc.) and/or robbery (inside, outside, messenger, etc.) coverages. The cost varies according to annual gross receipts of the firm.

The results

Although early predictions for the rapid growth of the federal crime insurance program were made, the progress has been poor. By 1977, 33,000 policies were in force, 45 percent of them in New York City.[20] At the beginning of 1982, there were 70,000 policies, but this was a decrease of 15 percent from 1981, and the amount of coverage in force had decreased 51 percent to $576 million.[21]

Numerous problems in acceptability of the program and its contracts have been encountered. Some lack of enthusiasm on the part of agents in selling the coverage is connected with the federal standards for protective devices, which are somewhat stringent and often unclear. Commissions are looked upon as too low by many agents, especially for the smaller policies.

Federal crime insurance has clearly been the least successful of the three government property and liability insurance programs of the Federal Insurance Administration. With relatively few policyholders after 10 years of operations and losses of $32 million in 1981 (despite heavily subsidized rates), the program is summarized as one which never really sold, by Jeffrey S. Bragg, the Federal Insurance Administrator.[22]

---

[20] "HUD Crime-Insurance Program Is Slated to Be Renewed on Hill despite Little Use," *The Wall Street Journal*, March 15, 1977.

[21] *Insurance Facts*, p. 40. Fifty-eight percent of the policies, and 61 percent of the coverage, was in the state of New York.

[22] "Getting the Government out of Insurance," *Independent Agent*, June 1982, p. 22.

THE FUTURE OF FEDERAL PROPERTY INSURANCE AND REINSURANCE PLANS

Numerous questions are raised by such plans as the federal riot, flood, and crime insurance plans. Does availability in some areas, or for some types of property, discriminate against other areas and other types of property? Can inequities be avoided in the charges made to insureds, insurers, and taxpayers? What limits should be available per item of property (building or contents)? How far in total capacity can the private insurers, and the government, go? For what other perils should similar programs be considered? Does government participation as *reinsurer* of only very large FAIR plan losses contradict its other roles as *insurer* of crime and flood coverages and Medicare?

One example of an alternative future direction of federal property insurance and reinsurance is legislation in the form of a National Program of Catastrophe Insurance, first proposed in 1972. Under this bill, a *National Catastrophe Insurance Act* would set up a Catastrophe Insurance Corporation to hold reserves built up from a *mandatory* inclusion of catastrophe perils in all fire insurance contracts. The perils included would be flood, plus any other catastrophe peril as specified by the board of directors of the corporation after public hearings. It could include, but would not be limited to, such other perils as earthquake, wavewash, mudslide, war damage, subsidence, and nuclear accident. Claims would be payable only if the president of the United States declared losses as occurring in a major disaster area. Insurance amounts, deductibles, and eligibility requirements would be based upon recommendations of the corporation.

One author,[23] in reviewing this proposal, urges congressional action citing the advantages of an insurance program, rather than disaster relief,[24] as: (1) rates reflecting private equity, with social adequacy; (2) loss-prevention incentives; (3) discouraging high-risk construction in high-risk areas; (4) avoiding bureaucratic relief programs; (5) greater stability for federal and state budget planning; and (6) systematic and certain loss payments as a matter of right rather than charity.

A proposal by the National Association of Insurance Commissioners for similar catastrophe insurance (based on a tax-deductible reserve held by insurers instead of a federal corporation) is said to be inadequate,

---

[23] Andrew F. Whitman, "Proposed National Catastrophe Insurance Legislation," *CPCU Annals* 27, no. 3 (September 1973), p. 88.

[24] Which is itself called a disaster. See "It's A Disaster," *Fortune*, April 10, 1978. Cited are the inadequate definition of what constitutes a disaster, and complicated regulations of the Federal Disaster Assistance Administration to determine when "temporary" housing aid should stop.

as are other alternatives such as federal reinsurance, expansion of the state FAIR plans, and other voluntary approaches.

Another author stresses the difficulties of establishing a proper rating system for a broad catastrophe insurance system.[25] The outcome of these proposals remains very much in doubt in the 1980s. Although appealing to some observers, the practical problems and potential increased costs during a period of federal budget deficits make such a large new program unlikely.

In fact, the trend for future years appears headed in the direction of reducing federal government involvement in property insurance. The goal of the current Federal Insurance Administrator is to eliminate the crime and riot reinsurance programs during the next several years, and even the flood program at some later date.[26] He believes the private insurers are now capable of solving the problem of insurance availability in urban areas. As the relatively successful flood insurance program grows and stands on its own with less subsidy from the taxpayers, he sees private insurance as desiring to be more involved. Expansion by the FIA to provide other federal insurance programs is not favored. The developments in the 1980s will be important to watch.

U.S. OVERSEAS POLITICAL RISK INSURANCE

The *Overseas Private Investment Corporation* is an important and interesting combination of government and private insurance. Not to be confused with the oil cartel OPEC, this U.S. government firm protects assets of investors in specified developing countries. Political risk insurance has been called "one of hottest new products in the insurance industry."[27]

Purposes and growth

This program has the basic purpose of encouraging direct U.S. private investments abroad, primarily by making available investment guarantees against three types of political risks: *inconvertibility of foreign currency;* (2) *expropriation, nationalization, or confiscation* by a foreign government; and (3) *war, revolution, or insurrection.*

OPIC was created under the Foreign Assistance Act of 1961 and its 1969 amendments. Annual gross revenues were about $30 million by the beginning of 1983. OPIC's efforts to cover U.S. private investments are centered on insuring new investments in more than 90 eligible "less developed friendly countries and areas." OPIC also finances the investiga-

---

[25] Dan R. Anderson, "All Risks Rating within a Catastrophe Insurance System," *Journal of Risk and Insurance* 43, no. 4 (December 1976), p. 629.

[26] "Getting the Government out of Insurance," *Independent Agent,* June 1982, p. 22.

[27] "Insuring Against Risk Abroad," *Business Week,* September 14, 1981, p. 59.

tion and development of projects of U.S. investors in those countries and areas by coordinating the work of its Washington staff with that of U.S. embassy officers overseas.

Primary emphasis has been placed upon the needs of small and medium-sized U.S. companies and banks, and a special effort has been made to encourage mineral exploration in less developed countries. In recent years about 40 percent of insured projects were for projects of $500,000 or less and almost two thirds were for projects of $1 million or less.

Total OPIC insurance coverage of $1.5 billion written in the fiscal 1981 year to the end of September was approximately equally divided among inconvertibility, expropriation, and war risks. Hundreds of projects insured by OPIC have increased net foreign exchange and created new jobs in dozens of countries. Two thirds of the countries, primarily in Latin America and Asia, had less than $1,000 per capita gross national product.

Insurance and reinsurance pool

OPIC is required by statute to maintain its operations on a self-sustaining basis through insurance and reinsurance arrangements, with due regard to the principles of risk management.[28] It does this by combining private insurance and U.S. government guarantees through a unique pool called the Overseas Investment Reinsurance Group. U.S. and foreign private insurers participate in pool limits of $40 million per country and $80 million annual aggregate limits. Other pool limits apply to individual projects, such as $2 million for inconvertibility and $10 million for expropriation. The insured usually retains the risk of loss of at least 10 percent. A separate Lloyd's reinsurance agreement covers OPIC for maximum limits of nearly $25 million per country and a $75 million worldwide aggregate.

The OPIC program is guaranteed by the full faith and credit of the United States. Individual projects result from agreements with the approval of the host foreign government. The form of investment includes not only conventional equity and term loans, but also assets contributing to long-term projects, licensing and technical assistance agreements, production-sharing agreements, and joint ventures. Many of the insurance coverages run for long periods, and equity investments can be insured for up to 20 years.

The definitions of the three optional perils insured are generally quite broad. *Currency inconvertibility* includes measures taken by exchange authorities, denying access to foreign exchange, and the passive failure

---

[28] An example a risk management technique useful in this field is the hiring of inside or outside specialists to assess the risks in various countries. See Stephen J. Korbin "Assessing Political Risk Overseas," *The Wharton Magazine* 6, no. 2 (Winter 1981–82), p. 25.

of authorities to act on applications for foreign exchange within a specified period, such as 60 days. *Expropriation* is defined to include not only classic nationalization, but creeping expropriatory action lasting more than three months on institutional loans or more than a year on other losses. Expropriation of U.S. property in Chile, Cuba, Iran, and El Salvador is well-known, but the widespread dangers of more than 500 expropriations in nearly 80 countries during the past two decades are less recognized.[29] *War* risks are for war, revolution, or insurrection losses within the country in which the project is located, and a formal declaration of war is not necessary. Physical damage losses on covered property are insured, as is default on scheduled payments on debt contracts for periods of three to six months or longer.

Future development

Congressional renewals of OPIC's authority to operate the combined government-private insurance of these risks have sometimes been reluctant, but in 1981 the program was renewed through September 1985. The objection to OPIC stems from the allegation that domestic jobs are transferred overseas as a result of its activities, although OPIC denies this charge. The expansion of exports through OPIC-assisted projects, the improvement of U.S. access to mineral and energy resources, and the protection of competitive market positions abroad are held to improve the U.S. economy and employment position and to offset by far any such job losses in the United States. The growth of private insurance involvement is still a goal, but the need for OPIC in insuring expansion in developing countries is generally recognized. Private insurers, such as American International Group and INA during the 1970s, and Chubb, Continental and AFIA in the 1980s, entered the field of political risk insurance and are now writing more premium volume than OPIC. The growth of both the private and the government plans appears promising.

GOVERNMENT-REQUIRED LIABILITY INSURANCE

To achieve social objectives, some kinds of liability insurance are required by government. These requirements guarantee payment from a negligent person to an injured, innocent accident victim. The most widely discussed type of *compulsory liability* insurance is *automobile* liability insurance. The coverage is not universal yet in the U.S. Only 3 states (Massachusetts, New York, and North Carolina) adopted such legislation before the trend accelerated in the 1970s with the advent of no-fault automobile insurance laws in about 24 states, which typically have in-

---

[29] "Insuring Against Risk Abroad," p. 62.

cluded compulsory coverage as part of their plans.[30] About 20 states still prefer to encourage an automobile driver or owner to purchase such insurance as a result of "financial responsibility" laws, which do not make the insurance mandatory at the time a car is registered for a license.

The advantages and disadvantages of these alternative solutions to the problem of the unpaid automobile accident victim are discussed in Chapter 19. Separate evaluation in this chapter is not necessary, but the increasing importance of this trend should be carefully noted in connection with the expanding role of government in liability insurance.

In addition, some states require liability insurance for selected situations. The owners of public vehicles, such as buses and taxicabs, must often meet state requirements by purchasing automobile liability insurance with specified limits of coverage. Young drivers under 21 years of age or less are required to carry automobile liability insurance in some states. The Interstate Commerce Commission requires motor vehicle common carriers to purchase liability insurance with prescribed minimum limits. Milk distributors in some states are required to carry products liability coverage. Nuclear reactor operators must furnish millions of dollars of public liability insurance, and this has affected the development of nuclear power in our energy-short nation whenever such protection is unavailable.[31]

Many other examples may be found, even outside the liability insurance field. For example, bonds are often required in state statutes for such situations as public construction contracts and for certain state officials (such as treasurers). The federal government requires bonds for trustees of union funds and aliens. Court bonds are required by many courts in many legal procedures. All of these are illustrations of government-required insurance contracts, but the limited nature of their application to special situations tends to cause them not to be included in the discussion here of more broadly applicable government insurance plans for property and liability insurance.

Other proposals and laws for government insurance are increasingly frequent. In 1976, Congress passed a bill to insure foreign art exhibits in the United States for up to $50 million. Public interest has also encouraged the House to pass a bill (not yet law) to compensate crime victims

---

[30] Note that the compulsory feature under no-fault laws is automobile insurance *coverage* (on a no-fault basis), but that the compulsory provision applies to both the first-party (the insured) *and* his or her third-party liability to others, where applicable. Mention should also be made of another government insurance innovation, in Maryland, that started a state automobile insurance company for some insureds in that state in 1973.

[31] Dan R. Anderson, "The Price-Anderson Act: Its Importance in the Development of Nuclear Power," *Journal of Risk and Insurance* 30, no. 4 (December 1977), p. 253. See also William C. Wood, "Nuclear Liability After Three Mile Island," *Journal of Risk and Insurance,* vol. 48, no. 3 (Sept 1981), p. 450.

for their medical expenses. Twenty-four states already have limited plans for such losses.[32]

In all, this chapter, as the first in textbooks to separately discuss the increasing role of government in property and liability insurance, should warn the student of a major new viewpoint to consider in evaluating property-liability insurance as discussed in Chapters 13–24. It is possible that the government role in these fields of insurance will diminish. However, many indications are that the federal and state government positions will continue in sponsoring, initiating, requiring, insuring, and reinsuring property-liability insurance of the future.

FOR REVIEW AND DISCUSSION

1. Compare and contrast the area of government property-liability insurance with that of government life-health insurance.

2. What has happened in the past 15 years to escalate the involvement of the federal government in property and liability insurance?

3. How does the usual government involvement in property-liability insurance differ from the definition of "social insurance" developed earlier?

4. Describe the *problem* of "fair access to insurance requirements," and the *answer* which the FAIR plans help to provide property owners.

5. Can everyone obtain insurance coverage for his or her property exposures under the state FAIR plans? Explain why or why not.

6. Who assumes the major risk under the federal riot reinsurance plans? Explain.

7. How do you evaluate the success of the FAIR plans and the federal reinsurance program for urban properties?

8. Why were floods considered "uninsurable" for many years? How has this situation changed?

9. The federal flood insurance program is described as one that combines both loss prevention and insurance protection. Explain.

10. To what extent has flood insurance been a successful program for the government, insurers, and property owners? What is its likely future?

11. In what respects is the federal crime insurance program different from those for riot and flood insurance? What is predicted for its future?

12. What contradictions do you see in the four most recent and important areas of federal insurance involvement in the property-liability field?

13. How is government *liability* insurance involvement different from the major types of government property insurance?

14. Do you think a proposal such as the National Catastrophe Insurance Act, or a similar voluntary plan, is the solution to the hardships which disasters cause? Why or why not?

---

[32] "Measure to Compensate Victims of Crime Narrowly Clears House for the First Time," *The Wall Street Journal,* October 3, 1977.

15. What do the expanding automobile no-fault laws have to do with the role of government in liability insurance?

16. Explain *(a)* the purpose of the Overseas Private Investment Corporation and *(b)* the types of political risks insurance that are available through it.

17. Explain what private insurers are doing to slow the need for government (especially federal) plans for insuring property and liability risks. What should they do to help the current situation?

Part Four

THE STRUCTURE AND OPERATIONS
OF THE INSURANCE BUSINESS

The insurance business is analyzed in Part Four on the basis of the major **functions** performed by the insurer, and how these are regulated. Chapters 25–28 present the *insurer* viewpoint, in contrast to the consumer and risk-management viewpoints emphasized in previous chapters. Chapter 25 discusses how insurance and its accompanying services are *marketed* to the consumer through various insurers and agency systems. In Chapter 26, the unique task of *underwriting,* or the selection and pricing of insurance, is presented, together with several miscellaneous functions. The final function of major importance, *loss payment,* including types of insurance adjusters and procedures, is the subject of Chapter 27. The reasons and methods for the extensive *regulation* of the operations of the insurance business are the focus of Chapter 28. Regulation is closely tied together with so many of the major functions of carrying out insurer operations that it is beneficial to discuss the regulatory process as the concluding chapter of Part Four.

Chapter 25

Outline of concepts

Insurance marketing—the process of getting a "bundle of services" in connection with insurance contracts from the insurer to the insured—is a main part of the functional approach to the study of insurance. Although insurance agents are the best-known part of insurance, this chapter emphasizes the *who* and the *how* of the total process.

Comparisons of insurance and other marketing help in understanding *the insurance product and the insurance market*.

The legal types of insurer include *stock* and several types of *mutual* companies, as well as other relatively less important types such as *Lloyds, reciprocals, fraternals, savings bank life*, and *health associations*. Differences in purposes, ownership, pricing, financial security, assessment rights, price, incorporation, and policyholder services are distinguishing characteristics. A summary reviews these differences.

Criteria for choosing an insurer explain the factors which the insurance consumer should consider, including *financial strength, service*, and *cost*.

Types of insurer representatives are not limited to *agents* but also include *solicitors, brokers*, and *service representatives*. Their use and significance vary by type of insurance and territory.

The professional concept is growing in insurance, stressing the technical knowledge, educational requirements, advisory skills, integrity, and attitude of all insurance personnel in performing their marketing and other functions properly.

Criteria for choosing an agent or broker suggest that the insured should evaluate these factors: knowledge and ability, willingness, integrity and character, and representation.

Marketing methods in insurance include the alternatives among:

Agency versus direct-selling systems, with agency methods predominating in insurance because of the need for personal services to clients;

Life insurance agency systems using *general agents* and *branch managers;* with some changes occurring as a result of broader financial services;

Property insurance agency systems using:

Independent agents, who represent several or many insurers,

Exclusive agents, who are agents for only one insurer, and

Modifications or "mixed" agency systems that combine characteristics of both types of agents; and

Group insurance systems, well established in life-health insurance, with various *mass merchandising* plans growing in property-liability insurance.

Insurance marketing

Insurance agents are the most visible and the best-known part of insurance marketing. Of nearly 2 million persons employed in the insurance business, approximately one third are sales personnel and two thirds have nonsales jobs. About one half of the sales force derive 50 percent or more of their income, and the other half obtain less than 50 percent, from life insurance.[1] Selling insurance as a career is an important part of the insurance business, yet an understanding of the insurance marketing *process* includes much more than that. This chapter emphasizes the *total* insurance distribution system—its product, its insurers and their representatives, its marketing methods, and how its consumers make their choices within the different parts of the function of insurance marketing.

Why should insurance students care how the insurance business is organized to market its contracts and services? Several reasons may apply. First, some students may be considering career opportunities in insurance, and if so, there are many types of marketing jobs available. Second, as consumers of insurance, students may gain a better understanding about the many choices and decisions among insurers and agents which purchasers must make in buying insurance. Finally, the marketing process is a key function in insurance operations, and the methods used by insurers to sell and service insurance contracts are significant in determining their costs and usefulness.

Insurance personnel, and consumers too, are often quoted as emphasizing that insurance is different from other products common to our everyday life. But is insurance *really* a "unique" product? If so, is this primarily because insurance is complex and "intangible," or is it because insurance is a future, contingent, service, risk contract with substantial legal characteristics, as explained in Chapter 4?

---

[1] *Insurance Facts* (New York: Insurance Information Institute, 1982–83), p. 11; and *Life Insurance Fact Book* (Washington, D.C.: American Council of Life Insurance, 1982), p. 91.

COMPARISONS OF INSURANCE AND OTHER MARKETING

The similarities *and* the differences can be enlightening. How well the comparison is made will determine the depth of understanding that one has about insurance and its marketing process. This chapter differentiates among the various types of insurers, their marketing methods, and their representatives. It also explains the professional concept and the consumer viewpoint of insurance marketing. With this information, the most beneficial thinking can be that which asks: "Why is this so for insurance but not for other businesses (or vice versa?)"

Marketing the insurance product

Figure 4–1 of Chapter 4 should be reviewed by the reader, as it shows the relationship of marketing to the product design, underwriting, and loss payment functions as insurance is distributed from insurers to insureds.

Marketing, the directing of the flow of goods and services from the producer to the consumer or user, is a particularly important business activity for insurance. The insurance product is a written legal contract *plus* the "bundle of services" included with it. The educational, motivational, advisory, and other services prior to, at the time of, and after the issuance of the contract make the purchase of insurance at least in some ways dissimilar from buying automobiles, restaurant meals, or clothing. The nature and characteristics of different products help determine the best sales appeals, procedures, pricing methods, and techniques to be used in the distribution process.

Sales personnel in our society are sometimes unfairly stereotyped as being like Willy Loman in the famous play *Death of a Salesman*. However, the essential nature of the marketing activity cannot be forgotten. The insurance agent is the basis of marketing for the insurer. Unissued contracts in the agent's file cabinets are as worthless as overstocked buggy whips in the warehouse of a misguided manufacturer a few decades ago. The insurer must develop the marketing system that becomes the link between the insurer (producer) and insured (consumer or "policyholder"). Other businesses can have small yet profitable operations. Relatively, there is more need for an insurer than for other businesses to have a reasonably large and diversified market, because predictability of losses is usually increased by larger numbers and spread of risk. Thus, the marketing of insurance assumes a predominant place among functions performed by insurers.

The insurance market

In one sense, a *market* is a meeting of people who have as their purpose the transaction of business. The term can mean either the region in which a commodity is sold, or the group of persons who might be expected to purchase, or the place of purchase. As examples, there are, respectively, the central West Coast market, the young marrieds' market, and the local market.

In insurance terminology, *market* is used to indicate both the area of distribution and the available source of the different coverages. In the first instance, persons in the middle salary brackets might be referred to as a market for retirement annuities, or large industrial organizations as a market for group pension plans. The second use of the term applies it to the place or source for the purchase of different forms of coverage, such as the aviation, fire, or marine insurance markets. This concept of insurance marketing has already been discussed in Chapter 3, where the fields of insurance were classified into various lines of business. In addition to knowing *what* risks are the subject of insurance, one must know *who* distributes the insurance product and *how* the marketing is accomplished.

Insurance buyers or their agents have little difficulty in placing ordinary risks—that is, in "finding a market." As a risk tends to involve special features, the limitations of the market appear. Every company selects risks on the basis of underwriting judgment, and there are many classes that one company or another will not write at all. For example, some fire insurers will not insure restaurants. In the liability field, motorcycles or drag cars may not be insured. In life and health insurance, many insurers will not write insurance for scuba divers.

Local agents may limit their business to either life or property insurance, or they may embrace all forms of the insurance business. An all-lines agency represents companies that will afford facilities for all the classes of insurance that its customers require. Frequently, the limitations of local agents require that they seek outside facilities. In such instances, agents are said to "broker" the line, or as much of it as they are unable to handle. The transaction involves a division of commissions.

The risk manager for an organization selects agents and insurers, and must be familiar with the insurance market and its limitations. The usual coverages, such as fire and automobile insurance, are obtainable in every community through a local agency. For more hazardous lines that are not written in volume, the market is more limited. It is true that almost every measurable risk is insurable. It does not follow that every agent has the facilities for placing every insurable risk. Ability to place unusual lines is evidence that the agent or broker is well informed and provides broad professional services.

LEGAL TYPES OF PRIVATE INSURERS

The *insurer* that bears or carries the risk of insurance is sometimes referred to as a "risk bearer" or an "insurance carrier." The term *insurer* is more accurate than *insurance company* because some insurers are not incorporated.

Private insurers are divided broadly into three major groups by their *legal type* of organization, as follows: (1) *stock* companies, (2) *mutual* companies, and (3) other insurers. "Other" insurers include *(a)* reciprocal exchanges; *(b)* Lloyds associations; and *(c)* fraternal societies, mutual

Figure 25–1. Comparison of legal types of U.S. private insurers by number and sales, 1981 (figure above each type is number of insurers; figure below each type is billions of dollars of premiums)

* Excludes "voluntary government" types as explained in Chapter 3, whose premiums are about $3 billion.
† Most or all of these types write *property-liability* insurance. Totals are estimated.
Sources: *Life Insurance Fact Book, Insurance Facts, Best's Aggregates and Averages,* and *Source Book on Health Insurance Data,* 1982. Estimates included for some 1981 figures.

savings bank life systems, and health associations. These basic legal types also might be separated into those insurers that are *commercial* or proprietary in nature and those that are *cooperative* in nature. The first category has profit-seeking owners other than policyholders, such as in stock companies and Lloyds associations. Cooperatives are organized for the benefit of the policyholder-owners, such as in mutual companies, reciprocals, and fraternals.

Insurers may also be divided according to the *types of insurance* they write, as property, liability, life, and health insurers. Chapter 3 compared insurers in this way as it explained the fields of insurance.

According to *domicile*, U.S. insurers are considered *domestic* by the state in which they are organized, *foreign* by all other states, and *alien* if incorporated in another country.

Figure 25–1 summarizes the relationships among private insurers by legal type of organization. Observe that stock and mutual insurers are by far the most significant, both in terms of the number of insurers (about 85 percent of the total) and in terms of the sales volume (about 90 percent of the total). All "other" types of private insurers are relatively unimportant in regard to the total insurance business, but in particular types of insurance or geographic areas they may be more prominent. Examples are the fraternal life insurers in Wisconsin, the savings bank life insurers in Massachusetts, and the Blue Cross–Blue Shield plans in the hospital and surgical field.

Note that some insurers are excluded in the discussion of marketing in this chapter. *Government* insurers, although part of the total marketing aspects of insurance, operate on principles quite different from those of private insurers. *Self-insurers* are also excluded, since they are less a type of marketing for insurance than an alternative for treating risks (see Chapter 2).

Another meaningful way of classifying insurers, that of differentiating among the various insurance marketing *systems,* is emphasized in a later section of this chapter.

Stock companies

Stock insurance companies are incorporated business organizations organized as profit-making ventures and owned by stockholders. Sometimes they are termed "proprietary." Laws enacted by the various states govern their operation, and they must meet capital, reserve fund, asset, and investment requirements. The contracts they issue are usually written for a definitely stated consideration (premium). The insured receives no benefit (dividend) from the earnings of the company and pays no assessment or additional premium if losses exceed income. The insured's first cost is usually the final cost.

The capital subscribed by the *stockholders* serves as an extra amount in addition to premium payments out of which losses can be paid. Additions made to the surplus serve the same purpose. Stockholders are entitled to any of the *residual profits* after losses and expenses have been paid and proper reserves set up. Some of the larger stock companies are national or even worldwide in their scope. In the United States, stock companies generally write their contracts through local agents, paying them a commission on the business. Approximately one third of them write business in all or most of the states.

Stock insurance companies thus have the following basic legal characteristics: (1) they are incorporated and owned by stockholders who supply capital funds serving as part of the financial security for the firm's operations; (2) they issue contracts for a fixed cost (the contracts are non-assessable); and (3) they can pay residual profits to the stockholders.

Mutual companies

A *mutual insurance company* is a corporation owned by its *policyholders*. The policyholders also *participate* in the operations of the company, at least through voting rights, and share in the company's financial success and, sometimes, failure. The company is organized for the purpose of providing insurance for its policyholders at low cost. Every policyholder is a member of the company. There are no stockholders. The mutual policyholder-members elect the board of directors, and the board elects the executive officers who actually manage the company. The mutual corporation assumes the risks of its policyholder-members. When the premiums in a given period are more than adequate to meet losses and expenses, part or all of the excess is returned to the policyholder as a "dividend."

There are a number of different kinds of mutual insurers. These include (1) *advance-premium* mutuals, (2) *assessment* mutuals, and (3) *special-purpose* mutuals. They may differ greatly in some characteristics, but each is incorporated and is owned by policyholders who receive dividends if the company operations are successful.

Advance-premium mutuals. This type of company is best known and most important of mutual insurers, writing all but a few percent of total mutual insurance. Practically speaking, the operations of *advance-premium mutuals* may be very similar to those of the stock companies. Legally, the advance-premium mutuals are different because they are owned by the policyholders, have no stockholders, and usually pay policyholder dividends. However, they are like the stock companies that also operate on an advance-premium basis, collecting most or all of the cost of the insurance at the time the contract is written. They often do business in a wide variety of types of insurance and in a fairly large geographic area.

These advance-premium mutuals issue a nonassessable contract in which the maximum cost of the insurance is set when the policy is begun. Legal requirements for writing nonassessable policies require these mutuals to possess specified amounts of surplus to provide for the financial solvency of the company in case of temporary periods of heavier than normal losses or expenses. A few mutual companies in this category issue a partially assessable contract, but this is the exception.

Many of these advance-premium mutuals issue dividends to policyholders. The original price may be the same as the stock company rate. At the end of the policy period a return may be made as a dividend for any excess amount beyond the losses, expenses, and reasonable reserves and surplus of the company. The actual amount of the return is unknown to the policyholder until after the insurance contract expires, it being dependent upon the experience of the company for that policyholder classification. The actual net cost (original price less dividend) to the policyholder is thus uncertain until the dividend is paid.

In most states the advance-premium mutuals must comply with the same reserve, investment, policy form, and regulatory laws as apply to stock companies. Their organization requirements are somewhat different, as a minimum number of policyholders are required to start a company and the board of directors must be set up in the charter and bylaws as subject to the control of policyholders rather than stockholders.

In the life insurance field, practically all mutual companies operate on an advance-premium basis. They are often referred to as *legal reserve* companies and do not permit assessments against the policyholders.

Assessment mutuals. There are many *assessment mutuals* writing primarily fire and windstorm insurance for farm and small-town dwellings on an assessment basis. They probably number more than 1,000, but account for less than 2 percent of the total premium writings of all mutual insurers. In some rural communities, these township or county farmers' mutuals are well known, however, and they may write a majority of the farm property risks in some small local areas.

Assessment contracts are written in two ways, either with limited or unlimited rights of assessment against the insureds. Some require no advance premiums at all, relying entirely on assessments at the end of the policy period. A member who belongs to an insurer in which liability is unlimited is bound to pay a proportional share of all losses and legitimate expenses of the company. The unlimited liability for assessment has caused some concern to many who fear that a serious catastrophe might involve them in assessments greater than they could meet. On the other hand, because farm risks are so scattered, a farmers' mutual with a reasonable number of risks may be comparatively free from the catastrophe hazard, except for tornadoes or widespread windstorms. Most of the farm mutuals operate with the unlimited assessment plan, but others may state a definite dollar limitation on the assessment or limit it to a certain multiple of the policyholder's premium.

Special-purpose mutuals. Some mutual companies are considered *special-purpose mutuals* because they were organized with a special purpose in mind. Usually these organizations limit their insurance to a definite type of business, such as milling or grain, lumber, or drug manufacture. In the past these insurers were known as "class mutuals," and they wrote insurance only for the occupational class in which they had specialized knowledge. Many were started on this basis, with the objective of special low rates or forms of coverage, but now write business for many types of firms, even though they retain the old class name for the insurance company.

An important group of small *factory mutuals* in New England base their operations on the belief that prevention should be the first and basic aim in any effort to secure low-cost fire insurance. The Factory Mutual System developed in the 1800s to insure large manufacturing properties. A technical staff of trained engineers was organized, and a laboratory for research and testing was established. This group was largely responsible for the adoption of the automatic sprinkler system and many other fire safeguards. There are now about four companies organized together as the Associated Factory Mutual Insurance Companies, cooperating efficiently in engineering, inspection, research, and loss adjustment.

The Factory Mutuals require insureds to pay large deposit premiums, several times the yearly cost. At the end of the policy period, deductions are made for the substantial loss services, other expenses, and actual losses paid, and the balance is returned to the insured. The contracts are written using special representatives in the field but no agents. The purposes of the Factory Mutuals are to provide insurance for large and high-grade industrial and institutional properties and to emphasize loss prevention. Similar in regard to these purposes, about 100 stock insurance companies have organized an association known as the Industrial Risk Insurers, which operates through agents in writing these large exposures.

Other insurers

Although stock and mutual insurers write about 80 percent of the total private insurance business in the United States, there are other legal types that merit attention because (1) they represent the wide variety of insurers in the market, (2) they may be relatively significant in particular types of insurance, or (3) they help illustrate the principles of insurance in showing the student how insurance works, what problems it has, and what features the insurance consumers should be looking for in their choices of insurance contracts and services.

Lloyds. In contrast to stock and mutual insurers that accept risks as corporations are the *Lloyds insurers*, whose basic characteristic is that they are *individual* insurers. Although this type of insurance accounts for less than 1 percent of the total insurance sales in the United States, the concept of insurance written by individuals is important. Historically Lloyds organizations are significant, too, and in the world market they are very predominant in reinsurance and in insuring unusual and difficult risks. Two types of Lloyds should be distinguished: "Lloyd's of London," which is by far the most important, and the "American Lloyds," which are small and few in number.

Sometimes called the world's most fascinating marketplace, Lloyd's of London is one of the most famous institutions for the insurance of risks. It still bears the name of the coffeehouse in which it originated more than 300 years ago as a center of shipping news and financial information.[2] Lloyd's as a corporation neither subscribes to policies of insurance nor directly issues them. Insurance is written by individual "underwriting members" who sign "each for himself and not for another." The insurer, then, is not Lloyd's but the underwriters at Lloyd's. A policyholder insures *at* Lloyd's but not *with* Lloyd's.

Membership in Lloyd's has been compared with membership in the New York Exchange. The exchange sets up standards with which its members must comply, yet purchases of insurance are transactions between members and their customers. Members are elected to membership. Individually, they are insurers; collectively, they are Lloyd's. Regulatory measures add formal requirements of substantial initial net worth (about $200,000 for Americans) for the carefully selected members, an annual audit of their accounts, and restriction of commitments in relation to their capital. Also, a reserve fund requirement states that all current premiums must be segregated under a deed of trust as a fund out of which claims may be paid. Every penny of a member's assets stands squarely behind any risks assumed. Corporations are not admitted to

---

[2] There have been some intriguing books and even movies about Lloyd's of London. For two classic books on the subject, see C. E. Golding and D. King-Page, *Lloyd's* (New York: McGraw-Hill, 1952); and Ralph Straus, *Lloyd's: The Gentlemen at the Coffeehouse* (New York: Carrick & Evans, 1938). For those addicted to the late, late TV shows, watch for reruns of Tyrone Power in *Lloyd's of London*. An excellent color film of the same title is available through Lloyd's representatives, showing how the traditions are preserved: the famous Lutine Bell is rung once for bad news and twice for good news; red-coated messengers are called "waiters"; and major losses are entered in a book with a quill pen! Current review of Lloyd's operations is contained in a monthly publication, *Lloyd's Log* (London: Lloyd's).

membership. There is a further element of protection in a central guarantee fund, and a separate trust fund is held in the United States for American policyholders.

There are more than 20,000 *underwriting members* from around the world (also called "names") at Lloyd's, who supply capital but do not work at Lloyd's. These members are organized into approximately 400 *syndicates*, with a membership varying from a few to more than 1,000 in each.[3] A syndicate is operated by an agent or "underwriter," who commits the members of that syndicate to the risks insured. A policy is written through a "broker." There are about 260 firms of Lloyd's *brokers*. With an adequate description of the risk, the broker offers the insurance to the underwriters, and each underwriter who wishes signs a slip (underwrites his or her name to it, hence the term *underwriter*), indicating the amount of insurance accepted. When the broker has obtained enough signers so that the amounts they assume will total the required insurance, Lloyd's Policy Signing Office draws up the policy and affixes its official seal. This document, however, is not signed by the corporation but by individuals who must themselves pay their proportional share in the event of loss. The function of the corporation of Lloyd's is purely to supervise transactions and guard the reputation of the institution. The Lloyd's Act of 1982 gave disciplinary powers to a 27-member Council of Lloyd's, which has conducted investigations of recent malpractice and issued several suspensions.

The fame of Lloyd's of London is heightened by the unusual risks that have been insured there. Examples of this market's versatility include a prize of $2 million offered for the capture of the famous Loch Ness monster; Elizabeth Taylor's illness in the filming of *Cleopatra* (on which a $2 million loss was paid); Marlene Dietrich's legs and Jimmy Durante's nose against accidental injury; hole-in-one golf prizes of $50,000 or more; space missile launchings; and a wide variety of other unique risks.

Many of these spectacular risks obtain widespread publicity for Lloyd's of London. Although Lloyd's is not the biggest insurer in the world, its sales of insurance and reinsurance are nearly $3 billion a year, and it is probably the best known of all insurers. Today, marine risks make up one third of its total business, and nonmarine, motor, and aviation risks make up the bulk of its business. Some large life (term insurance) is written. Excess liability risks involving millions of dollars are quite commonplace. Practically any large loss in the world—whether it is a multimillion-dollar fire, a big ship or airplane crash, or a major hurri-

---

[3] H. A. L. Cockerell, *What Goes on in Insurance?* (Cambridge, Eng.: Woodhead-Faulkner, 1982), p. 56–57.

cane—involves Lloyd's of London as either an insurer or a reinsurer.

Lloyd's of London is licensed directly only in two states, Illinois and Kentucky, though Lloyd's brokers and agents operate throughout the United States and the rest of the world. Although the usual United States family would have little need for insuring at Lloyd's of London, businesses can insure at Lloyd's to obtain needed high-liability limits, special coverages such as worldwide package policies, or hard-to-obtain protection for large exposures or unusual perils.

In the United States there are a few "American Lloyds" associations. About 30, including several in Texas, write primarily auto-physical-damage insurance. In the American Lloyds each member is ordinarily liable for only a specified maximum, and the strict regulations of the London Lloyd's governing membership, deposits, and audits are not present. Each organization depends upon the financial strength of its individual members within their limited liability. Some insureds have not understood that the American Lloyds and the original London organization have no connection. The American Lloyds form of insurer plays a relatively insignificant role in United States insurance. However, the concept of having individuals rather than corporations write insurance is important. (See also Chapter 29 for information on a new development in the United States, the formation of "insurance exchanges.")

Reciprocals. In the property and liability insurance field another type of insurer combines some characteristics of a mutual insurer (owned by its policyholders) and a Lloyds association (individuals assume the risks).

The *reciprocal* exchange or interinsurance association is a type of cooperative insurance. Each policyholder under this form of insurance contract is insured by all of the others. Each insured is also an insurer, as contracts are exchanged on a reciprocal basis.

The reciprocal exchange is not in the legal sense a mutual insurer because the individual subscribers assume their liability as individuals, not as a responsibility of the group as a whole. Another basic difference from mutual insurers is that reciprocals are not incorporated as companies but are formed under separate laws as associations. Reciprocals are contrasted with Lloyds because Lloyds are: (1) proprietary or profit seeking and (2) the Lloyds insurer is not also an insured, as is always the case in a reciprocal.

The funds held by a reciprocal are the sum total of individual credits held for the account of individual subscribers. These subscribers are required to accumulate reserves representing a multiple ranging from two to five annual premiums before underwriting earnings, if any, are returned in cash. A separate account is maintained for each subscriber, and out of this is paid only a proportional share of each loss and expense. Beyond that, the reciprocal can usually levy an assessment of up to a multiple of premiums paid, such as 10 times, but the liability of each subscriber is definitely limited. Reciprocal insurance is quite distinctly an American development.

The policyholders, or subscribers, appoint a manager to whom is entrusted the responsibility of carrying on the business. The manager derives authority from a power of attorney and is known as an "attorney-in-fact." An advisory committee has ultimate control over the manager. Reciprocals are not incorporated, so no capital assets are available to prevent insolvency.

The major characteristics of reciprocals are (1) the dual nature of each insured as an insurer (with stated limits of liability), (2) the system of individual accounts, and (3) the use of an attorney-in-fact under the control of an advisory committee.

Reciprocals are relatively unimportant in the total business of insurance (only about 60 writing a few percent of all property-liability insurance), but in certain areas and for specific lines such as automobile insurance they have acquired some significance. Although usually small, a few reciprocal exchanges have grown to substantial size. Examples are the Farmers Insurance Exchange (Los Angeles), the Inter-Insurance Exchange of the Automobile Club of Southern California, and the United Services Automobile Association (San Antonio, Texas).

Fraternals, savings bank life, and health associations. Among other types of insurers are some specialized insurers that have unique characteristics as compared with all the preceding insurers that have been described.

In the field of life and health insurance there are several special types of insurers formed under provisions in the state laws separate from the laws applying to stock, mutual, reciprocal, and Lloyds associations. They are often essentially mutual in their operations and have the goal of low-cost insurance for members. They differ, however, by not being incorporated as insurance companies under the state insurance laws.

A *fraternal* society is a special type of insurer providing insurance benefits, particularly life insurance, for its members. The operations of the fraternal are closely related to and controlled by the bylaws of a lodge or a nonprofit social organization. Many fraternals are church oriented, such as the Lutheran Brotherhood and the Knights of Columbus fraternal benefit societies. The fraternal orders have tax exemptions. A possible undesirable feature is the fact that the fraternal order usually can assess the policyholder in case of financial difficulties. The popularity of the fraternal benefit societies declined in importance after the early 1900s, but several of the 200 operating today are quite large. Total fraternal life insurance in force of about $60 billion, however, is less than 2 percent of total life insurance in force in the United States.

Savings bank life insurance systems operate in three states. A centralized agency in each of these states administers a plan through which participating mutual savings banks may issue limited amounts of life insurance. The limits are $15,000 in Connecticut, $30,000 in New York, and $53,000 in Massachusetts. The policies are sold on an over-the-counter basis without the use of agents. The financial backing of the plans does not include the total assets of the banks, as only the insurance department assets of the bank and certain contingency funds of the state administrative agency are available to insureds. Although the life insurance in force is only about $14 billion, in these three states the amount represents approximately 3 percent of the total life insurance.

Health associations are important in the insurance of medical care expenses, especially in the prepayment of hospital and surgical expenses. More than 900 plans are in operation, but by far the largest and best known are the Blue Cross and Blue Shield associations. More than 100 of these plans write more than one half of the total U.S. hospital-surgical insurance. These are nonprofit, tax-exempt, unincorporated, voluntary organizations set up in most states under special enabling legislation. They are administered by trustees who represent the hospitals, the medical profession, and the communities involved in a particular geographic area, such as a part of or an entire state. A primary distinction from other insurers is that the objective of these associations is to provide health insurance for a very broad segment of the population. Impliedly, this aim includes such groups as the low-income classes and the aged and justifies the differences in taxation and regulation usually applied to Blue Cross–Blue Shield plans as compared with other insurers. Marketing distinctions also include the use of salaried representatives for enrollment in place of agents; contracts by the plans with hospitals and doctors to provide medical services rather than pay losses in dollars; and an emphasis on group enrollment through employers instead of individual contract sales, which enroll 10 percent of the subscribers.

Dental insurance has also adopted the service approach for prepayment plans, as dental service plans similar to those of Blue Shield have offered group dental insurance in many states since the mid-1960s. The Delta Dental Plans Association coordinates many of the nonprofit associations. More than 100 insurance companies, too, offer dental insurance as a part of regular group health insurance contracts. Dental insurance is said to be the fastest growing of all employee health insurance plans in the United States, with more than 80 million persons now covered (twice the number five years ago). About three of four major companies have dental insurance for their employees. Vision care insurance is also growing rapidly as an employee health insurance fringe benefit.

A wide variety of other health associations exist for the purpose of providing prepayment insurance plans for communities, unions, colleges, or clients of a group medical practice. Examples include the Health Insurance Plan of New York, the International Ladies' Garment Workers' Union plan, the Kaiser Foundation plans, and the Ross-Loop Medical

Group (Los Angeles). In the past decade much attention has been given to the formation of "health maintenance organizations," or HMOs, and some have been sponsored and financed by the larger life insurers (see Chapter 10).

Summary

The major differences among the primary legal types of insurers are presented in Table 25–1. Most consumers will purchase their insurance from stock and mutual insurers. However, in theory and for some insureds in some kinds of insurance, differences among the other types are also important to note.

The most significant reason for knowing these distinguishing characteristics is to understand *why* each may be important to the policyholder. Purpose and ownership of the insurer are determining factors in maintaining efficient control of the enterprise, and for possible conflicts of interest between owners and insureds. Financial strength is crucial to overall solvency and continuity of insurance. Prices may be fixed, or the net cost to policyholders may depend upon possible returns, based upon the future costs and expenses of the organization. Potential liability of the policyholder may also vary according to limited or unlimited assessment rights against the insureds. Wise consumers should know how these characteristics may affect the insurance purchased and its cost.

Table 25–1. Summary of differences among legal types of insurers

Distinguishing characteristic	Stock	Mutual	Lloyds	Reciprocals
Purpose	Profit to stockholders	Returns to policyholders (insurance at low cost)	Profit to individual members	Insurers are insureds
Ownership	Stockholders (incorporated)	Policyholders (incorporated)	Individual members	Individual subscribers (associations)
Financial strength	Based on capital and surplus	Based on surplus only (no capital)	Members' net worth and unlimited liability, reserves, trust funds	Individual accounts and reserves
Price	Fixed, known price	Net price not known	Fixed price	Possible returns on individual accounts
Assessment right	None	Some mutuals may assess policyholders, if needed	Entire personal assets of members	Limited assessment rights

CRITERIA FOR CHOOSING AN INSURER

How does the insurance consumer go about choosing an insurer that best meets his or her needs? With all the various legal types of insurers discussed in the previous sections, the selection is not easy. A good rationale must consider several major factors, plus some others which may overlap with the criteria for choosing an agent, discussed separately later.

Although Part Four of this text emphasizes the insurer viewpoint, it is necessary to keep the insured's (consumer) viewpoint always in mind. This is essentially the professional concept of insurance marketing, one of agents advising their clients as if the risk problems were their own. The agent's part in that concept is discussed in later sections of this chapter.

It might seem at first thought that the selection of the insurance company would be one of the first and most important decisions of the insurance buyer. Personal or business purchasers of insurance *may* select the insurer; however, often they do *not*, for most insurance is bought through agents. In *life and health* insurance, it is most common to have the agent represent only one insurer, so the selection process is a combination one. As the purchaser chooses the agent, the insurer is also automatically chosen. This may also be true in cases where the consumer selects the insurer (perhaps on the basis of the insurer's advertising or general reputation) and then looks for an agent who represents that insurer. The "exclusive," one-company representation, agency system in property and liability insurance, discussed later, is similar in its effects on the market selection process of the insurance buyer.

Although the purchaser is not always involved in choosing the insurer, the process of evaluating insurers may need to be understood. This is particularly important for the large business firm, with perhaps thousands or millions of dollars of coverage written by a few insurers, and in any of the (relatively) infrequent cases in which the purchaser does business directly with the insurer without the services of an agent.

Companies enjoying the best reputations ordinarily attract high-grade representatives. With state regulatory agencies scrutinizing the financial position of companies, the ability of companies to pay is rarely expected to become a problem. The attitude of companies with respect to claims may differ, however, and the insured is concerned with the company's attitude regarding technicalities and the reputation of the claim department for satisfactory dealings with insureds at a time of loss.

The insured is interested in knowing the scope of the contracts offered by an insurer and in whether or not the insurer is liberal with respect to underwriting. A company that is selective in choosing risks may prove unsatisfactory when a buyer has a more difficult type of risk to be insured.

The insurer's facilities for rate analysis and for loss-prevention recommendations that may reduce insurance costs are also important to the consumer.

The size of an insurer is not always a controlling factor in its selection; financial strength and size are not necessarily equivalents. Growth over a period of years is significant. The buyer who limits purchases to well-known and recognized companies and places business with an agent or broker of outstanding reputation will probably have accomplished much in choosing the best possible insurer. If statistical data about the insurer are needed for further analysis, several readily available sources are useful. The state insurance departments can provide some current information. Financial history, ratings, and analyses on individual insurers are published in annual volumes of *Best's Insurance Reports,* and other publications by A. M. Best Company.

Here are some of the criteria to be considered in choosing an insurer:

1. *Financial strength.*   Although surplus—or capital and surplus—is required by all states, the requirements vary considerably. The present net worth of the insurer is a starting point in the financial analysis of an insurer, but many other factors may need to be considered: the type of business written, the trends[4] observed over a number of years, the underwriting and investment activities analyzed separately, and the adequacy of reserves. The ratios of policyholders' surplus to liabilities (and to net premiums written) are particularly significant. More quantitative guidelines of financial strength are available in the NAIC, "early warning system" for insolvencies used in many states. Basic to all these factors is the general quality of the management, which over a period of time ultimately determines the financial strength of the company.

2. *Service.*   The ability of the insurer to provide proper protection for the insured is essential. Does the insurer specialize in a few lines of insurance contracts, or does it sell all coverages which the purchaser may need and want? Is the insurer experienced in offering all the contracts it will write? Will the insurer tailor-make contracts to meet individual needs of the insurance buyer? Does it have capacity and adequate reinsurance for the largest risks the buyer may require? Is it licensed in all states in which the buyer needs coverage? In addition to indemnification for losses, can the insurer provide the necessary engineering and loss-prevention services which the purchaser needs? What are the general attitude and reputation of the insurer with regard to prompt and fair settlement of all reasonable claims?

3. *Cost.*   Although often thought to be the most important criterion, cost should usually be considered and compared after the above two

---

[4] *Best's Insurance Trends* (Oldwick, N.J.: A. M. Best) is a new summary of this information.

criteria are analyzed. Costs do vary,[5] and a too low cost can be just as bad as a too high cost. Lower costs are an obvious direct benefit to the purchaser of insurance, but *too* low costs can result in an unduly strict attitude toward claims payment, inadequate reserves or other financial weaknesses, or perhaps undesirable decreases in the number or quality of agents and representatives who provide services to the insurance buyer.

Initial costs are only part of the necessary analysis, for final costs over a longer period of protection must be considered, including possible rate changes, dividends, assessments, or premium adjustments under audit or retrospective rating plans. In life insurance (see Chapters 6–8), *net* cost comparisons over a period such as 20 or more years, considering dividends, cash values, and interest factors, may be needed. For large businesses, the insurance costs should be analyzed with other risk-management costs, such as loss prevention.

TYPES OF INSURER REPRESENTATIVES

The insurance buyer is often most concerned, and rightly so, with the representative of the insurer with whom direct contact is made. The legal type of insurer or the marketing system used is often of secondary importance to the insured. The applicant for insurance makes contact with the insurer through one or more of the following: *(a)* agents, *(b)* solicitors, *(c)* brokers, and *(d)* service representatives.

Agents

The agent is a representative of the insurer, and the authority under which he or she operates is delegated through an agency contract. The agent is appointed by an insurance company to act for it, with authority to solicit, negotiate, and put contracts of insurance in effect.

The powers of the agent are governed by the "agency contract" with the insurer. The terms *general agent, local agent,* and *state agent,* among others, are frequently used in the insurance business. The local agent who makes contact with the applicant for insurance may be designated *general agent, regional agent,* or simply *agent.* All of these terms have a specialized significance within the business and may represent the nature of the agent's position with the company or the commission arrangement.

Legally, regardless of terminology, a property-liability agent is either

[5] See, for example, Joseph M. Belth, *Life Insurance: A Consumer's Handbook* (Bloomington: Indiana University Press, 1973); and *Life Insurance Rates and Data* (Cincinnati: National Underwriter Co., annual).

a *general agent* or a *limited agent*. A general agent (other than in life insurance) can bind a risk and thereby make insurance effective immediately and prior to the actual delivery of the policy. Many such agents do not have to wait for the contract to be written by the insurer, as the agent or the agency office writes the contract for such usual coverages as fire, auto, or homeowners' policies. If the agent's powers are limited or restricted, the scope of the delegated authority determines what may be done or not done. It has been noted in Chapter 4 that secret limitations may not apply, and the principal may be bound if the action is within the agent's implied or apparent authority.

Life. The life insurance business customarily limits the authority to issue or modify life insurance contracts to salaried company officers. Life insurance agents are *limited* agents. Generally speaking, life insurance agents are authorized to solicit, receive, and forward applications for the contracts written by their companies. Agents are authorized to receive the first premiums due on applications, but not subsequent premiums. An exception is the "industrial" life insurance agent, who does collect renewal premiums regularly at the home of the policyholder and forwards them to the company.

The authority of the life insurance agent is limited not only in the matter of collections but also in the ability to accept risks or bind the coverage. The life insurer issues the contract after receiving the written, signed application and also usually a medical examination report. The agent cannot "cover" the policyholder immediately, nor can contract modifications be made later without the approval of the insurer.

Property. Agents appointed to represent property and liability insurers are as a rule granted the powers of a *general* agent. The limitations to their authority are set forth in the agency agreement. Such agents may *bind* their companies by oral contract as well as waive policy provisions. Among other responsibilities they inspect risks and often also collect initial and renewal premiums.

Many such agents write contracts in their own offices for fire, auto, or homeowners' policies. Special contracts for business liability, steam boiler explosion, glass breakage, or other perils may have to be issued by the insurer in the home office or the branch office. Few agents have authority to bind or issue bonds.

Solicitors

A *solicitor* is an individual authorized by an insurance agent or broker to solicit contracts of insurance, acting only on behalf of the agent or broker. The solicitor does not have the authority to bind the insurer with respect to risk, but is authorized to collect premiums. The solicitor is an employee of the agent. The agent is responsible for acts or omissions within the scope of the solicitor's employment. In some urban areas, the larger insurance agencies may employ numerous solicitors.

Brokers

Brokers, who represent the *policyholder* rather than the insurer, may also be valuable in rendering service to the insurance purchaser. With widespread contacts and knowledge of many fields of insurance, many brokers offer significant advice and counsel to their clients.

The larger insurance brokerage firms are especially well equipped to handle the problems of insurance for a buyer with individual and specialized requirements. Examples include some firms with hundreds of employees, such as Alexander and Alexander, Johnson and Higgins, and Marsh and McLennan.

Unlike the agent, who legally represents the insurer, the broker *acts on behalf of the insured.* Thus, the broker is an independent contractor. The broker serves the insured by assisting the applicant for insurance in placing risks, yet is paid by the insurer. By informing themselves of rates, forms, and markets, brokers are useful and recognized intermediaries between the insurer, or the agent, and the insured.

Insureds are sometimes confused because they do not differentiate between an insurance broker and an agent. The insurance agent is acting under specific and delegated authority from the insurer and is often authorized to bind coverage within delegated limits. The broker, on the other hand, has no such authority. Because the broker is held to represent the policyholder, the insured is bound by the acts of the broker with respect to all the negotiations between insurer and insured. Any misrepresentation, mistake, breach of warranty, or fraud perpetrated by the broker on the insured's behalf makes the insured responsible as if the insured had committed the acts.

It is important to understand clearly that the broker cannot make insurance effective. The broker is not a party to the insurance contract as an insurer. However, many insurance agents may be licensed as both agents and brokers. The simplest illustration is to be found in the case of an agent who commits the insurer for a part of a line and acts as a broker in placing any excess coverage.

There are brokers called *excess line brokers* (or *surplus line brokers*).[6] These brokers write coverages for which there is no available market in the state, such as lines or exposures that have a high loss frequency or severity. Examples of business done by excess line brokers include

---

[6] The variety and complexity of these markets can be seen in the many markets discussed in publications such as the *Excess and Surplus Lines Manual* (Santa Monica, Calif.: Merritt); and *Agents and Buyers Guide* (Cincinnati: National Underwriter).

liability insurance for amusement parks and ski resorts, and many products liability exposures. Sometimes excess line brokers are obliged to seek a market such as that afforded by Lloyd's of London or other international insurers. Usually the business is placed with companies that have not been licensed to do business in a particular state and are known as "nonadmitted companies." Excess lines business should invite the careful scrutiny of the financial responsibility and reputation of the insurer by the prospective insured. The excess line broker may not always deal with the insured directly but may be sought out by the insured's broker. Many states require special licenses for excess line brokers.

While the major part of life insurance production is handled by company agents, there are a number of *life brokers* who place the business they produce with the company that they feel can best handle and service the line adequately. Group insurance has proved a fertile field for brokers. Since underwriting rules of companies differ so widely, the placing of a group risk may involve its submission to several companies. A significant volume of brokerage business also arises from life agents who fundamentally represent one life company but place business in another because clients want the particular plan or price it offers. Substandard and "jumbo risk" policies are often placed in this way. Estate planning and pension plans in which transactions are large and competition keen are other fields in which the life brokers are more and more making their influence felt. The dramatic change to increased brokerage in life insurance during the past 15 years brings with it some substantial training and financing problems as agents consider their allegiance to their primary insurers.[7]

Service representatives

Many companies and some large agencies employ specialists on a salaried basis to work with and assist agents in writing the more complex lines. Such employees are termed *service representatives,* and they may help an agent to sell or service insurance. Company officers, managers, or general agents of insurance companies employed on a salaried basis are not included in the category of service representatives. A license is not usually required by the state to act as a service representative.

Examples of service representatives are common in both the life and property insurance fields. In property insurance, "special agents" are used by many companies to initiate agency contracts, help the agent on special sales problems, and generally keep the agent informed of new contracts and services of the insurer. Engineering, appraisal, and

---

[7] Richard E. Johnson, "Life Insurance Brokerage and Its Impact upon the Exclusive Agency System," *CLU Journal* 36, no. 4 (October 1982), p. 60.

loss-prevention services are often provided by company specialists in conjunction with local agents. Company claims adjusters also work in cooperation with the agents on many of the losses involving large amounts or special problems.

In life insurance the service representatives include advanced under-writing specialists who aid the life agent in estate programming and pension or tax planning. Many salaried training specialists are used by general agents to recruit, supervise, and help the new life agent. Most companies writing group life and health coverages provide salaried company representatives who aid the life insurance agent in writing group contracts.

THE PROFESSIONAL CONCEPT OF INSURANCE MARKETING

The insurance business is placing increasing emphasis upon the value of education and training, based upon the premise that the insurance agent is no longer a mere canvasser for business. Instead, more agents are learning to diagnose and treat the broad risk and insurance needs of their clients. With the emphasis upon education and the focusing of insurance protection in such a manner that the needs of the applicant are cared for on the most economical basis possible, the *professional idea of personal service* was developed.

Emphasis on the professional status of the insurance agent does not carry any adverse reflection upon the term *business*. A business specialty can be just as much a *profession* as medicine, law, or other endeavors. The professional concept recognizes many forms of business negotiation in which representatives of differing interests meet on opposite sides of a bargaining table, and there is nothing unethical in such transactions.

Professional insurance agents bring technical knowledge and experi-ence to the service of their clients. In addition, they may call upon their company associates for assistance. These include highly trained special-ists. The professional concept makes the agent the representative of the policyholder in working out an insurance program that will best meet the insured's needs. The agent and the client are on the same side of the bargaining table. Agents can be successful only to the extent that they satisfy the needs of their clients. The fact that the agent legally represents the insurer does not prevent the agent from being fair and professional in serving the policyholder. The professional concept does, however, require the agent to exercise extra care in seeing that all advice and actions are in keeping with the highest possible ethics.[8]

The insurance business makes training and educational facilities at

---

[8] See Ronald C. Horn, *On Professions, Professionals and Professional Ethics* (Malvern, Pa.: American Institute, 1978).

all levels available. Correspondence courses and special home office training courses are offered. For those who wish to become specialized experts at the top of their profession, there are the vigorous educational programs and the examinations of the American College and the American Institute for Property and Liability Underwriters.[9] With the objective of establishing higher educational standards in life and health insurance, the American College awards to properly qualified persons the professional designation CLU (Chartered Life Underwriter) upon completion of a series of 10 national written examinations. A similar movement resulted in the formation of the American Institute for Property and Liability Underwriters. The term *underwriter* is used in a broad context, for not only do agents receive the professional designation of CPCU (Chartered Property Casualty Underwriter), but so do many home office or branch offices persons who perform other insurer functions. Ten written examinations are given, involving in addition to insurance knowledge the broad range of related business subjects such as risk management, accounting, finance, economics, law, and management. The usual procedure of a successful candidate is to participate in two-hour class study groups meeting weekly during a five-year continuing education program.

Almost 50,000 persons have now achieved the coveted CLU designation, and about 15,000 have the CPCU designation. In addition, tens of thousands of others have partial credit or are currently improving their capabilities through the CLU–CPCU programs. Also important are the certificate courses offered by the American College in about 10 advanced study areas; its Master of Science in Financial Services degree; its new Chartered Financial Consultant (ChFC) designation; and its continuing education program for practicing CLUs, operated jointly with the American Society of Chartered Life Underwriters.

The Insurance Institute of America (IIA), which is closely associated with the CPCU program, has a study program leading toward an IIA certificate in general insurance, and specialized associate designations in claims, management, risk and loss control management, underwriting, auditing, and planning and research. A sales training program in life and health insurance is offered by the Life Underwriter Training Council (LUTC), which each year enrolls more than 30,000 agents in its courses. The Life Office Management Association (LOMA) also has an extensive educational program of examinations for persons working in life insurance offices. Another growing professional designation, important in the emerging financial services trend, is that of Certified Financial Planner (CFP), administered by the College of Financial Planning.

---

[9] The student desiring further information about these programs can obtain bulletins and course study outlines by writing the American College at Bryn Mawr Avenue, Bryn Mawr, Pa. 19010, or the American Institute at Providence and Sugartown Roads, Malvern, Pa. 19355.

The professional concept assumes a client's reliance upon a person of particular skills or training. Professional ethics require conduct that will warrant implicit confidence on the part of a client. For example, the Society of CPCU has a Code of Ethics detailing 10 unethical practices, such as misrepresentation, which could lead to a CPCU's expulsion, suspension, reprimand, or censure. The insurance agent is sometimes compared to the pastor, the doctor, or the family lawyer. To the extent that insurance persons are experts bringing specialized knowledge concerning the principles and uses of insurance unselfishly to clients, the analogy is good. It is, therefore, proper to emphasize the professional status of the insurance agent, recognizing that a public attitude of respect must be earned.

It is also well to indicate that not all insurance agents or brokers are fully qualified to render a professional service. There are many agents who are needed in the insurance business without the skill and educational requirements necessary to plan a life estate satisfactorily or to serve the needs of a complex business establishment. More and more, however, the broadening use of insurance to meet a wide variety of family and business financial needs suggests that the insurance personnel of the future will often have to be of professional caliber. The wider viewpoints of "risk management" and "financial services" are good examples of the growing need and opportunities for professionalism in insurance.

CRITERIA FOR CHOOSING AN AGENT OR BROKER

Since most insurance is written through the agency system, the choice of a competent and reliable insurance agent is often the most important decision for the purchaser of insurance. If an "exclusive" agent who represents one insurer only is chosen, this selection also determines the insurer with which business is conducted. If an "independent" agent is chosen, the insurance buyer often leaves the selection of the insurer up to the agent, or at least relies heavily on the agent's recommendations.

A substantial part of the insurance premium, often between 5 and 25 percent, represents commission or salary to the agent. In the event that no service or inadequate service is rendered for this part of the premium, the insured is paying for something not received. The purchaser of insurance must determine whether or not the agent or broker is only an order taker. If so, the insured is getting something less than full value.

Some insureds place insurance with a number of agents. Frequently this distribution is made on a reciprocity basis to create goodwill or on a patronage basis to distribute a line among a number of friends. Sounder practice today suggests selecting one agent or broker (or as few as possible) to handle an entire insurance account. Skilled agents as well as the insurance buyer should prefer this practice. They would rather have fewer accounts for which they are fully responsible than a wide participation in risks where they contribute little in the way of service. Sometimes an account may be split so that the property and liability lines are handled by one agent, and the life, health, and pension business by another agent. It is usually not wise to have too many agents, however, for the more than one agent knows about your total insurance account, the better he or she may be able to analyze the risk and recommend protection for your total needs.

The insurance consumer who allows friendship to be the dominant factor governing the selection of an agent may suffer lack of adequate protection or pay an exorbitant amount for excessive or duplicating coverages. Placing insurance only on the basis of personal friendship is as foolish as selecting a doctor, a lawyer, or an architect on that basis. Because of the complex nature of various risks, insurance coverages, and rates, it is essential that the insurance and risk adviser be selected with the same care and discrimination that are used in choosing other professional assistance.

Here are some of the criteria that might be used to evaluate insurance agents and brokers:

1. *Knowledge and ability.* The agent or broker must do a two-fold job of education: (1) learn about your risk and insurance needs, and (2) help you understand the value of the services rendered to you as an insurance buyer. The agent must have the background and experience necessary to identify, analyze, and treat risk properly; and to learn and teach, ask and answer. One method of evaluating the agent's knowledge and ability is to ask questions such as these: "Are you a CLU or a CPCU? If not, are you working toward these or other educational program objectives on a regular basis? Are you a full-time agent?" Not all part-time agents, nor all agents who have not completed professional designations, are bad. However, agents who are fully committed to the insurance business are more likely to be able to do a really successful job for their clients by keeping abreast of rapidly changing knowledge requirements.

The insurance consumer needs a technically competent agent who performs the wide variety of services essential to proper insurance protection. These may include understanding needs, analyzing significant risks, finding markets, comparing alternative coverages and contracts, arranging for credit or installment payments, checking on the accuracy of classifications and the rates charged, providing loss-prevention or engineering services, making valuation appraisals, seeing that claims payments are made promptly, frequently reviewing changing needs, and many other important duties.

2. *Willingness.* If qualified, can and will the agent also take the time to *apply* his or her knowledge with an attitude of conscientiousness

that will result in the full appraisal of all your needs and alternatives? Unless this is done, you won't receive any benefit from all that knowledge and ability. The agent must be able and willing to take the time to see that services (including those of agency staff and companies) are performed in the most adequate way possible.

The agent should offer to recommend additional legal, accounting, or consulting services when these are needed. Loss-prevention suggestions and help with filing claims for losses are important parts of the service provided to the insurance buyer. The best-qualified agent who is "too busy" is no good for *you* unless the time and desire are present to perform these services regularly at the time you need them.

3. *Integrity and character.* Even willing and able agents or brokers lack an important requirement if they are unable to command the confidence and trust of the insured. An insurance purchaser who cannot believe and act on recommendations given is not receiving full value from the insurance dollar spent.

Since insurance advice is purchased in order to obtain certainty, agents or brokers must be able to give their clients both psychological and actual security. In other words, consumers need someone with whom they can identify closely in discussing their financial goals and needs. The values of agent and client, if similar, can aid them in establishing a good rapport with each other. The age of the agent in relation to that of the insured may be a factor in this regard, but differences in age are probably less important than differences in ideas and lifestyle. Confidential information from the purchaser is often required in order to provide good insurance counseling services; thus the agent or broker must respect the buyer's trust with as complete honesty as would a doctor, a lawyer, or an accountant.

4. *Representation.* Good agents do not represent poor insurers. They must represent or have contacts with one or many insurers that can provide the required protection and services for the insured. All the necessary coverages, including even special or unusual ones, must be available through the agents in a prompt and efficient manner at a reasonable cost. The insurer or insurers they represent should be capable of writing many different kinds of insurance, with a progressive attitude toward newer coverages and forms designed to meet the particular needs of individual buyers.

Whether to select an agent or broker as the intermediary in placing insurance in a given community will depend largely upon custom and the state law. In some large cities much of the insurance business is in the hands of brokers and very little contact with applicants for insurance is made directly by agents. In most areas opposite conditions prevail, and business is handled largely through agents representing the insurers.

Insurance agencies and brokerage firms vary from the individual agent to organizations having a large staff and offering a wide degree of specialization. Some are one-person agencies, others have a half-dozen agents and office personnel, while still others have as many as a hundred employees and operate much like a small insurance company. These organizations differ in the services they are able to offer, their methods of doing business, and the types and kinds of insurance they handle. In the multiple-line (property and liability) agency, life insurance today is often included to make it an all-lines agency. Frequently, the members of the agency who handle the life business limit their activities to this field. Also, in the large multiple-line agency certain persons become recognized experts in such lines as fire, liability, workers' compensation, or fidelity and surety coverages. In selecting the agent or broker with whom to deal, it is therefore important for the insurance consumer to determine whether or not the particular agent and agency office have the needed experience and service facilities.

The suggestion has been made that large business accounts be offered for competitive bids on an annual basis. This can sometimes achieve lower costs for insurance. However, some buyers have attempted to do this with not too satisfactory results. Agents who do not regard the insured as a permanent client may provide less service. Insureds have found the method detrimental because in a period of unfavorable losses a business firm may have no assurance of continued coverage, and competing insurers will be reluctant to participate. Thus, insurance buyers may seriously limit their market. This will not be the case if an insurer may expect over a period of years to recoup losses incurred in an unfavorable year. From the standpoint of the buyer as well as the agent, a long-term relationship on a professional basis seems to work out best in the long run.

Whatever choice of agent or broker is made by the applicant for insurance, the choice should be made carefully. For the businessperson or even for the family spending a substantial portion of income on insurance, this is not a selection to be made in a haphazard manner. Thoughtful evaluation of the representation offered by the agent or broker is required, including such factors as knowledge, ability, integrity, and attitude. Choosing an agent or broker is not an easy task, but for the insured it is an essential step toward a sound insurance and risk program.

MARKETING METHODS

Agency versus direct-selling systems

Insurance is distributed from insurers to policyholders in a variety of ways. The most important is the *agency system* of representatives who operate under the authority given them by insurers to make legal transactions with consumers of insurance. The complex nature of insurance and its usual significance to the insured make such personal contact through an intermediary essential to the sale of most insurance.

Insureds seldom come in contact with insurer officers. The contact between insured and insurer is usually made through an agent. The discussion of insurer representatives in this section assumes major importance when the widespread use of agency systems in marketing insurance is realized.

Direct-selling systems are the exception to the general rule that insurance is sold mainly through agents. Under these systems the insurer deals directly with the insured, without agents, through *employees* of the insurer. In specialized and limited lines in certain market segments of insurance, these systems may assume some importance. Airport vending machines for selling aviation accidental death protection are one example. Another common example is health insurers who operate by using direct-mail advertising. All correspondence is direct from the company to the prospect, and the insurance contract is written and serviced by mail or telephone without an agent. For another example, the Factory Mutuals deal directly with insureds in writing fire insurance for large businesses. A few automobile insurers, such as Government Employees Insurance Company (GEICO) and J. C. Penney Insurance Companies, have applied the direct-mail system successfully in writing automobile insurance. Some life insurance sales are also accomplished in this way. Direct-mail solicitation has been successful in recent years for books, records, clothing, and other products, and undoubtedly it will grow in insurance for qualified, carefully selected markets. Sales through credit cards are growing, too.

In life and health insurance the growth of *group insurance* (see Chapters 8 and 10) with sales through salaried employees in place of commissioned agents is evidence of a trend that might be called a compromise between direct and agency systems of marketing. The idea of selling through employers has also begun to be applied in the property-liability field, especially for automobile and homeowners insurance (see the last section of this chapter).

Life insurance agency systems

A distinction should be observed between the usual agency method of marketing life insurance as opposed to property insurance. In marketing life insurance, the insurers normally use agents who *represent only one insurer*. The agent sells life insurance for one company and therefore is restricted to the rules, rates and policy forms of that insurer. A *general agent* often provides field supervision of the sales in a given territory for the insurer and is in a position similar to that of a wholesaler of manufactured products who distributes goods for one major producer. The general agent works under the authority of the insurer, and hires, trains, and directs the activities of the life agents working for a given general agency office. The general agent is paid a commission for the business written, but the actual acceptance of the life insurance contracts is performed at the home office of the life insurer. Many insurers have a *branch manager* instead of a general agent. The branch manager usually operates more as an employee of the insurer than as an individual entrepreneur and is likely to be paid largely by salary. The distinctions are not always maintained.

Life and health insurance is sometimes highly specialized, and many representatives of life and health insurers devote themselves exclusively to these lines. Within the field are specialists who devote themselves to a particular line, such as business life insurance, group insurance, or pension plans.

A development of the last decade has some life insurance agents selling mutual funds or other investments as well as life insurance contracts. This may be regarded as an important change in life insurance agency systems, as different licensing, training, compensation, and organization may evolve from these broadening financial counseling services in the future.

Property insurance agency systems

In property insurance two major agency systems of marketing are used to distribute the fire, automobile, and other casualty insurance contracts: (1) *the independent agency system* and (2) the *exclusive agency system.*[10] The distribution system for property insurance is different from that for life insurance for many reasons. Among them might be the historical fact that in the property business the 10 largest companies have written a smaller share of the business; the need of property-liability agents to have several insurers in order to write large risks or varied types of insurance; and the short duration of the property-liability contract, which permits or requires property agents to change their clients' insurance from one insurer to another as needs and markets fluctuate.

The independent agency system. Traditionally the predominant method has been an agency system in which the agent *represents several* or *many insurers.* This is known as the *independent agency system.* The

---

[10] The primary terms used to describe insurance marketing systems have caused much confusion. The Committee on Property and Liability Insurance Terminology of the American Risk and Insurance Association agreed upon the basic terms used above: (1) direct-selling, (2) independent agency, and (3) exclusive agency systems. See also David L. Bickelhaupt, "Trends and Innovations in the Marketing of Insurance," *Journal of Marketing* 31, no. 3 (July 1967), pp. 17–22.

agent is independent in the sense that business is placed with any one of a number of insurers (perhaps as few as 3 or as many as 30) that the agent represents. The agent is not an employee of the insurers, and sells on a commission or fee basis as an independent contractor. The insurers recognize the *agent's* ownership, use, and control of policy and expiration records. The agent often has the authority to bind the insurer immediately for many of the kinds of insurance written for his or her policyholders. A branch office or general agency of each insurer may supervise the activities of the agent for a regional territory.

The exclusive agency system.   The *exclusive agency system* of marketing property insurance has risen in recent decades with the growth of automobile insurance and simplified insurance coverages (nonbusiness) for the individual. Here the agent normally represents only *one company,* as in the case of the typical life insurance agent. The agent's contract limits representation to one insurer or to a few which are under common management. It reserves to the *insurer* the ownership, use, and control of policy and expiration data. The agent may have binding authority. The larger exclusive agency insurers, such as State Farm Mutual, Allstate, and Nationwide Mutual, have made tremendous increases in their sales of automobile insurance in the last two decades, and more recently they have been showing substantial gains in fire, homeowners', and even life and health insurance.

Comparisons.   The advantages and disadvantages of these two marketing systems in property insurance are not easily seen by the policyholder. Certainly the terms are often misleading. Less desirable than the above contrast between independent and exclusive agency systems are the two terms *American Agency System* and *direct-writing system,*[11] which have been extensively used to describe, respectively, these two competing systems of marketing. Obviously, the direct-writing system can be just as "American" as the American Agency System, and the American Agency System just as "direct" as the direct-writing system! Even with the newer suggested terms, one should point out that independent agents are dependent to a certain extent on the insurers they represent and that exclusive agents may have some measure of independence from their insurer. Also, the exclusive agency system is not automatically better or of higher caliber, as its name may imply. In fact, its critics call it the "captive" agency system!

The marketing changes of recent years have resulted in considerable competition. Benefits to the consumer in the form of lower costs through

---

[11] A term unfortunately still in use. For summaries of the operations of these insurers, see George Nordhaus and Stephen Brown, *Marketing Property and Casualty Insurance* (Santa Monica, Calif.: Insurance Marketing Services, 1976), chap. 8. Note that some insurers, such as State Farm, use modifications of both systems: only established agents become, after about four years, "independent contractors," but only for that one insurer.

emphasis on reducing expenses and on increasing options for broader coverages have been a favorable result of the competitive era during the past several decades. Insureds must analyze their choices in terms of both *cost and service* from the individual agent, regardless of the name of the agency system. By some cost effectiveness measures, the use of exclusive agents appears to allow higher levels of sales at lower costs, but the quality of the service received by customers must also be compared. For example, duplication of activities by independent agents is greater, but it may help in the tailoring of service to their clients.[12]

The main advantage of the exclusive agents is lower cost, through reduced commissions or decreased expenses due to centralization of some functions, such as policy writing, record keeping, billing, training, advertising, and sales. The exclusive agent also has the potential advantage of receiving more education and training from an insurer that can design such programs specifically for the agent. The insurer has closer control over the education and the activities of the agent, and receives full and direct benefit from the success of the support it gives to the agent. Representing one insurer can simplify the agent's job but may narrow the help which the agent can give a client who, for example, needs to obtain a difficult type of coverage.

Independent agents have substantial advantages in representing more than one insurer and in their ownership of expirations. Since no one insurer is best in all lines and all territories, independent agents serve as experts in choosing the best companies to write insurance that will meet the individual needs of their clients. They thus have a wider choice and variety of coverages, prices, and services for their policyholders. Properly used, their position of "independence" can enable them to bring good benefits to clients by placing insurance with strong and reliable insurers at reasonable prices. This feature of being able to select from a wide variety of companies is emphasized in advertising by the agents who belong to Independent Insurance Agents of America (IIAA).

Trends. It is fair to predict that no one agency system will be destroyed by the other in the current era of changing distribution patterns of insurance. Each system has some merit, and each will retain and increase its share of the market to the extent that it meets the real services needed by the insurance consumer.[13] In striving to do this, both systems are increasing educational efforts for their agents, encouraging them to participate regularly in national and company professional pro-

---

[12] Michael Etgar, "Cost Effectiveness in Insurance Distribution," *Journal of Risk and Insurance* 42, no. 2 (June 1977), p. 211.

[13] These services are evaluated in J. David Cummins and Stephen N. Weisbart, *The Impact of Consumer Services on Independent Insurance Agency Performance* (Glenmont, N.Y.: I.M.A. Educational and Research Foundation, 1977).

grams of all kinds. Perhaps performance in this area will be the key to long-run changes.

The exclusive agency system has grown very rapidly, increasing their market share from about 25 to 50 percent in auto insurance during the period 1955–83, and by similar growth in homeowners' insurance from 1971 to 1983.[14] The new property-liability affiliates of major life insurers (Prudential, Metropolitan, and John Hancock, for example) have also used the exclusive, one-company representation, agency system successfully. The exclusive agency system has yet to show that it can adapt to the fields for business coverages, where the independent agency system still predominates.[15] However, certain exclusive agency companies have done well, particularly State Farm, in the smaller commercial policy market.

It seems that the two major agency systems, independent and exclusive, are becoming more mixed and similar each year. Several of the largest independent agency systems now issue exclusive agency contracts for their regular agents. These include: Insurance Company of North America, for all lines; and the Chubb Insurance Group and Royal-Globe Group, for personal (nonbusiness) lines. Other independent agency companies have one-company agreements, but only for special classes of agents, such as those just beginning in the business. The agent agrees in these contracts to place virtually all insurance with the one company. Many independent agency companies have also adopted techniques of premium payments similar to those of exclusive agency companies. The "direct-billing" system of having bills sent to the policyholder directly from the insurer, instead of from the agent, has gained in popularity consistently to become typical for many insurers today. Cost savings, especially with the use of computers, have hastened this trend. Under this method, the agent is relieved of the time-consuming and expensive task of extending credit to the consumer and then collecting the premiums.

Conversely, the exclusive agency insurers have adopted some of the successful methods of their competitors. For example, some of these companies have granted their larger and more successful agents certain rights that are similar to the ownership rights which independent agents have to renewals and records. Under these agreements, established exclusive agents are paid by the insurer for their book of business if they

---

[14] William B. Lusk and Douglas T. Hibbard, "The Independent Property-Casualty Agent Distribution System," *CLU Journal* 35, no. 1 (January 1981), p. 17. This article also notes that the number of independent agencies is estimated to have decreased by 10,000, or about 15 percent, in the seven years prior to 1980.

[15] The large independent agencies are particularly strong in business coverages, although larger size, by growth or merger, is not necessarily the road to cost economies. See J. David Cummins, "Economies of Scale in Independent Insurance Agencies," *Journal of Risk and Insurance* 44, no. 4 (December 1977), p. 539.

leave or retire from their exclusive agency company. The sums or renewal commissions to which the agents are entitled under these contract provisions with the insurer may be substantial. Also, more of the exclusive agency insurers are gradually permitting their agents to "broker" business with other insurers. This is particularly important in insurance for businesses, where large exposures sometimes require insurance with several insurers in order to place the total protection correctly. Increased brokerage by life insurers was also noted in a previous section as a major change for the 1980s.

Group insurance systems

One example of how the changes in insurance marketing have accelerated is *group* insurance. Marketing to consumers in this system is usually done on a group basis through the employer, with payroll deductions as the convenient method of premium payment. Labor unions, credit unions, finance companies, professional associations, and other groups may also be used to obtain the primary desired result, which is the lowering of insurance costs to the members of the groups.

Group life-health insurance. In *life* insurance the trend toward increased group insurance has been continuous since such plans began more than 50 years ago. Today one fourth of all life insurance premiums, and one half of the total life insurance in force, is group insurance. *Health* insurance, with the major growth occurring during the past 20 years, has used the group method of marketing even more extensively. More than three fourths of all health insurance premiums written by U.S. life insurance companies is group insurance, and for the other primary health insurer (Blue Cross–Blue Shield) the proportion is higher. *Annuities* or insured pensions, too, have used the system widely, with almost three fourths of the total premium income coming from group plans. The group insurance trend is shown in further detail in Chapter 8, where group annuities are discussed, and in Chapter 10, where group life and health insurance are treated.

Maxi-style business trends. The group phenomenon can be looked at as a part of the increased affinity for "big business," a move toward "maxi-style"[16] systems of marketing. Perhaps it is a reaction to the gargantuan billion-dollar business enterprises that there is also this increased tendency toward "big purchasers." Contracts of purchase of a whole new specialized type are appearing in many fields of business: automobile manufacturers sell in thousand-car lots to governmental

---

[16] Portions of the following section are adapted from David L. Bickelhaupt, "Insurance Marketing: Maxi-Style for the 1970s," *Bulletin of Business Research* (Ohio State University) 46, no. 3 (March 1971), p. 1.

agencies and international automobile leasing companies; institutional buyers of securities negotiate with special brokerage firms for millions of shares of stocks; discount department stores buy entire product lines of some producers; and realtors sell whole communities of housing developments. The power of the group buyer is matched to that of the group seller.

Group property-liability insurance.   What does mass buying and selling have to do with *property-liability* insurance? *Mass merchandising* is quite apparent in property-liability insurance today, as well as in the life-health fields. It is important to know *why* this trend has occurred. Most explanations center on the prospective efficiency of group coverage. However, the consumers emphasis on lower prices also helps explain why insurance mass merchandising exists.

Mass merchandising plans in property-liability insurance *are* different from group life-health insurance in some respects, particularly in that most such plans have individual selection, rating, and contracts instead of group underwriting. However, employer participation is involved in the arrangements for the plans, premiums are collected through payroll deduction, and the causes and objectives of the plans are similar to those of group life-health insurance. Although not technically group insurance, mass merchandising is a part of the trend. The terminology is neither well developed nor consistent. The term *mass merchandising* boils down to selling and servicing personal lines of insurance to large groups, usually with a common employer, through a payroll deduction plan. Other terms closely allied to mass merchandising are *mass marketing* (a broader term, denoting sales to much larger groups without any common ties such as employment), *group insurance* (a legal term, usually requiring group underwriting techniques and special legislation), *franchise merchandising* (payroll deduction), and *collective merchandising* (including some of all the preceding attributes).[17]

Mass merchandising plans for groups of several hundred or many thousands of persons naturally vary considerably in detail. Automobile insurance has been the primary coverage, but many also offer homeowners', personal excess liability, and, recently, even life and health insurance. Several plans incorporating the characteristics of group insurance (group selection and rating, guaranteed coverage, and employer payment of at least part of the premium) have appeared. A listing of the major efforts by insurers thus far encompasses many of the larger property-liability insurance company groups. Although none have yet had great success, the Travelers Companies recently announced major plans for a new mass merchandising plan. Group plans aimed at trade associations

---

[17] Bernard Webb, *Mass Merchandising of Automobile Insurance* (Santa Monica, Calif.: Insurors' Press, 1969).

instead of employers may be emphasized by these insurers in the decade ahead.

Future mass merchandising plans are likely to grow in the personal lines. Almost all households have need for auto and home property and liability insurance. An insurance teacher[18] has pointed out that this is primarily because of the agency system, which has built the path to mass merchandising by convincing the public that insurance is a social necessity!

How far, how fast is the crucial question. Probably less than 10 percent of property-liability insurance premiums is collected today under mass merchandising plans. Some persons predict that 25 to 50 percent will be sold in these systems by the 1990s.[19] The speed with which the plans grow will depend on many other developments, such as:

1. *Liability system changes.* The combination of no-fault auto insurance and mass merchandising trends might merge, for both systems emphasize cost savings as their most salable point.

2. *Union attitudes.* The United Auto Workers unions and others consider this an important new "fringe benefit" and a major area of negotiation.

3. *Costs—inflation trend.* This pushes insurance costs up (faster than rate changes) and causes clamor for change.

4. *Regulation changes.* With existing laws, public interest, and other factors, the prevailing attitude seems to be one of a "holding action" only. Many states permit such plans, while many others do not. It is increasingly apparent, however, that legislation is more and more geared to the consumer, and the trend is toward state laws that approve these plans. Another factor is possible tax law changes: Could these new plans become a tax-deductible, nonincome employee fringe benefit? If so, the impetus would be rapid.

5. *Employer attitude.* Probably the most significant factor is what the *employer* decides about all this. That is the key. What reaction will the employer get from the employee, if take-out pay exceeds take-home pay? Will the employer be blamed for poor claims adjustment or rate increases or cancellations? Worse yet, will the employer have any legal liability if errors are made or coverage is not adequate? The payroll deduction plan sounds good, but what about the cost? How far should the employer go? Should banking, credit, gasoline purchases, and even auto purchases also be provided on a payroll deduction group plan? How does the employer make the vital choice as to who should do the employee counseling—agent or insurer (company) employee? Many agents feel that

---

[18] Robert Mehr, University of Illinois.

[19] "Commercial Mass Marketing," *Independent Agent*, November 1982, p. 105.

the employee may lose substantial benefits of individual personal service in the mass merchandising plans.

The estimates of savings are one of the problems of any such new type of distribution system. Some insurers have said that the costs will be lowered as much as 15 percent; others say that the costs will be lowered only 5 percent. Administrative savings may not be as much as expected, and perhaps will only be passed on to the employer in various hidden costs, such as the payroll deduction costs or the labor costs of having employees discuss insurance on "company time," either in formal counseling appointments or in informal discussions with other workers.

Coverage may be less than under individual plans, but will the employee recognize this and purchase an additional policy, or will the tendency be to accept the group coverage? Discrimination is also raised as a potential problem, especially from a regulatory viewpoint. It seems difficult to try to appraise this aspect of the problem without knowing the details of a specific plan. Who is a plan being unfair to—the worker who doesn't own a car, or the better driver, perhaps? Is it a mandatory plan or a voluntary plan that the worker can accept or reject? How is the rate calculated?

There could be some benefits.[20] If mass merchandising is efficient for the insurer as a means for achieving volume and profit, then it may be for the agents, too (at least some of them). Safety and loss prevention are important potential benefits. About 2 percent of costs in most plans are allocated for such things as driver clinics and safety contests. Most deaths under age 40 are from automobile accidents, and savings in rehiring and retraining could be large. Other risk management techniques such as loss analysis and control might also be effective in mass-merchandised personal insurance.

Some of the goals of mass merchandising, if achieved in an orderly, meaningful way from the insurance consumer's standpoint, may help solve some other insurer problems, such as auto insurance costs and increasing government intervention. Pertinent is the observation that the United States is the only country in the world with group insurance as a major part of the private insurance business (about one fourth of life, three fourths or more of annuities and health insurance). Yet the United States is also the country with the largest private insurance business and the least social insurance encroachment into the private sector. Group insurance systems may have helped in preserving the private insurance business from the expansion of social insurance systems

---

[20] John R. Lewis reviews eight of these in "Observations on Mass Merchandising of Property and Liability Insurance," *CPCU Annals* 24, no. 2 (June 1971), p. 174, as he critiques Spencer Kimball and Herbert S. Denenberg, *Mass Marketing of Property Insurance* (Washington, D.C.: U.S. Government Printing Office, June 1970), p. 6. See also "Why Group Marketing?", *Independent Agent*, September 1982, p. 53.

into life-health insurance. Perhaps it will also have a similar impact in property-liability insurance for the future.

FOR REVIEW AND DISCUSSION

1. John says: "Insurance marketing means insurance *agents.*" Marcia says: "Partially, yes, but the insurance marketing *process* means much more." Explain these statements.

2. "Insurance marketing is really quite different from the marketing of other products." Explain *(a)* whether or not you agree with this and *(b)* what difference it makes to the insurer.

3. Match the characteristic in column 2 with the type of insurer in column 1. Use each number only *once* for the *most closely* related item.

Column 1		*Column 2*	
a.	Reciprocals	1.	Emphasize loss prevention
b.	Lloyds associations	2.	Are often assessable
c.	Stock companies	3.	Mostly write life insurance
d.	Mutual companies	4.	Insure lumber, drug, etc., exposures
e.	Health association	5.	Interinsurance exchanges
f.	Savings bank insurers	6.	Have capital and surplus
g.	Fraternals	7.	Individual insurers
h.	Farm mutuals	8.	Blue Cross–Blue Shield
i.	Factory mutuals	9.	Life insurance, in 3 states
j.	Class mutuals	10.	Policyholder dividends

4. What are the basic characteristics of advance-premium, assessment, and special-purpose mutuals? Why is each type important in the insurance market?

5. Discuss points of similarity and differences among London Lloyd's and *(a)* the American Lloyds *(b)* mutual insurers, and *(c)* reciprocals.

6. Insurers may be differentiated on the basis of their ownership and their stated objectives. How do stock companies, mutuals, Factory Mutuals, fraternals, and health associations differ as to ownership and objectives?

7. How do stock companies, advance-premium mutuals, assessment mutuals, reciprocals, and Lloyds differ in their use of surpluses and their sources for deficits?

8. By what type of insurer is the major volume of each type of insurance business written? Can you explain some of the differences noted?

9. Divide the class into two groups, one defending and the other criticizing the proposition that "direct-selling systems in insurance are likely to increase."

10. Why do the agency systems in life and property insurance differ? Does the power of the typical agent in these fields differ, too?

11. Who owns the agent's records, and therefore the expirations, under the "independent agent system"? Would your answer be different for an "exclusive agent"?

12. Distinguish between an agent and a broker. May the same individual be both? What is an "excess line broker"? How are brokers becoming more important?

13. Mr. I. M. Goodfellow operates a retail store and feels that for business purposes he should divide his insurance business among his customers. Can you see any dangers in this practice? What is the solution you recommend?

14. What does the "professional concept" of insurance marketing include? Does this explanation offer any reasons as to why agency systems are more important than direct-selling systems in marketing insurance?

15. Explain three criteria which a business executive should follow in choosing an insurer and three other factors of importance in selecting an insurance agent or broker. Would you answer this question differently if the insured were an individual or a family rather than a business?

16. Which is more important to the ordinary insured, the choice of an insurer or the choice of an insurance agent? Why?

17. Explain what "mass merchandising" is, and two potential benefits and two problems for the (a) insurer, (b) insured, and (c) agent.

18. Who is the key to the future expansion of "mass merchandising" group insurance plans? Explain why you think so. Identify and explain why one other development may also be important in this growth.

Chapter 26

Outline of concepts

Underwriting, which is closely **related to other insurance functions,** includes the *selection, pricing,* and *reinsurance* of insurance contracts.

Purposes of underwriting are a reasonable and *profitable* group of risks in spite of the tendency toward *adverse selection.*

Selection of risks is ultimately done by the *insurer,* but the *agent* and other sources of *underwriting information* are crucial in many lines.

Rating, or *pricing,* of insurance contracts is the field of *actuarial science.*

  Fire insurance rates are used as a basic example to show how insurance prices are determined.

    Rating bureaus help insurers analyze the various *factors* affecting loss and set *class* rates for groups of like properties and *specific,* or *schedule,* rates for *larger* individual business properties.

    The insured can lower insurance costs by decreasing the poor features and increasing the good features of the property insured.

  Automobile insurance has rating factors different from those for fire insurance and uses both class rates and individual rate modifications.

Special problems of underwriting are noted:

  Deductibles, for reducing costs and loss payment problems, include *straight* (most common), *franchise, aggregate,* and other types.

  Minimum premiums, to recoup expenses, prevent adverse selection.

  Annual and term policies, to set fair prices for various durations.

  Installment plans, to permit convenient regular payments.

Reinsurance is the transfer of insurance from one insurer to another.

  Its purposes are to spread risks, especially large ones, to permit growth of insurers, and to provide technical advisory services.

  Reinsurance organizations are of several types: *professional reinsurers* writing only reinsurance, *reinsurance departments* of insurers, and *reinsurance pools.*

  Reinsurance agreements include *treaty,* or automatic, and *facultative,* or specific, types.

  Reinsurance contracts are of the *share-of-risk* and the *excess-of-loss* types, which distribute the insurance or losses between insurer and reinsurer.

  Retrocessions occur when reinsurers insure with other reinsurers.

  International aspects are important in reinsurance competition.

Other functions of insurers, often overlooked but vital to success of the underwriting and other major functions of insurers, include "auxiliary" services such as legal, educational, actuarial, research, public relations, and administrative.

Insurance underwriting and related functions

Insurance is a "business affected with a public interest" and a business which provides a wide variety of coverages to almost everyone. However, the insurer is not usually required to write an insurance contract for each person who applies for one.[1] At first glance, there appears to be something wrong with a business that can refuse to do business with persons most likely to have losses (who perhaps need the product most), while continually striving to accept as clients those persons who are least likely to have losses. A few second thoughts are pertinent: in addition to the "public needs," doesn't the insurer also have a primary obligation to all its insureds and its owners to do business so that it remains financially solvent and obtains reasonable profits? The dilemma is real, accentuated today by the growing importance of many social problems and by the recognition of insurance as a frequent and useful solution to the financial consequences of these problems.

UNDERWRITING RELATED TO OTHER INSURANCE FUNCTIONS

Part Four of this text approaches the study of insurance on a functional basis. The previous chapter discussed the marketing of insurance. The next major part of the process of insurance is *underwriting,* the selection and rating of the risks that are insured. *Reinsurance* is so important to underwriting that it merits a separate section in this chapter. Several other auxiliary functions are also mentioned briefly at the end of this chapter examining insurance from the viewpoint of the insurer.

The functions of an insurer are necessarily closely related to one another. No one activity exists alone, and each activity has many direct effects on the others. The student is advised to look again at Figure 4–1 to see these relationships. For example, the types of contracts offered

---

[1] A few exceptions apply. For example, some states may require insurers to accept all applications, as in automobile insurance for licensed drivers in a state with compulsory liability insurance laws. The contract, however, may be a limited one, assigned proportionally to all insurers in a special plan.

by an insurer may determine how the contracts are distributed through an agency system to the policyholders. Agents are often important in helping to redesign insurance contracts to meet specific needs of the insurance market.

The interrelationship of the major insurance activities is nowhere more apparent than in the underwriting process. An insurer that has organized a good system of distributing a wide range of insurance contracts still cannot operate successfully without proper attention to the selection and pricing of its product. The *underwriters*[2] of a company are those who have the task of accepting, rejecting, or revising insurance contracts which the marketing system brings to the insurer. Whether or not the underwriting function is properly carried out, of course, has an important effect on the frequency and size of insurance losses. Unless contracts are properly priced and reinsured, the acceptance of risks can cause the financial insolvency of insurers.

PURPOSES OF UNDERWRITING

A general description of *underwriting* is simple: it is the selection and rating of risks which are offered to an insurer. The process is based on *selection,* so this part of the definition of underwriting is discussed first. *Rating* and *reinsurance* (the purchase of insurance by insurers) are so significant a part of the total process as to be explained in separate sections of this chapter.

Selection implies that there are some acceptances and some rejections, or that not all risks will be accepted for insurance. An understanding of why some risks must be selected by an insurer and some rejected will make clear that insurance underwriting is one of the major functions of an insurer. It is also an activity that is not found in most other businesses. A somewhat comparable activity exists in banks and savings and loan institutions, where the credit selection process assumes a similar major role.

Suppose an insurer were willing to write an insurance contract for every person or business its agents had sold on completing an application for insurance. Would it be sound business practice for an insurer to operate in this manner? The student may answer: "Of course. The company needs large numbers of risks and a diversification or spread among

---

[2] In everyday insurance language the term *underwriter* is also used to refer to the agent or salesperson. The professional designations CLU (Chartered Life Underwriter) and CPCU (Chartered Property Casualty Underwriter) mean anyone who writes or does business in insurance. Sometimes the underwriters are the actual insurers, as when one refers to the underwriters at Lloyd's of London. The term originated there, with the practice of underwriters signing their acceptance of part of the risk under the broker's description of the desired insurance.

various kinds of risks, geographic locations, and so on. Why shouldn't an insurer accept all the separate risks it can get?" After further consideration the student might add: "Naturally, the insurer won't want the bad risks, or those which seem to offer a high probability of loss, for it will lose money in writing such poor risks."

A more complete answer might then suggest itself. The insurer does not want bad risks, it is true; but even bad risks could be accepted if the price charged for the contract were high enough to pay for all losses and expenses and still permit the insurer a profit on the business. Here is the crux of the problem—the insurer must accept only policyholders who will in total be *profitable* risks. The purpose of underwriting is thus found to be the acquisition by the insurer of selected insureds who at least in the long run will return a profit to stockholders (or policyholders of a mutual-type insurer).

An important corollary to understanding the underwriting function is the fact that most insurance prices are based upon an *average* rate for an entire class or group. Some insureds within each class will be better than average and some worse than average. Which type of policyholders will an insurer that does no selection of risks tend to have? A moment's thought will give the answer. Those persons who are better than average are most likely not to want or need the insurance, and conversely, those persons who know they are worse than average will be most likely to desire the insurance contract. This result is natural, for in everyday language the bad risks at the average rate are obtaining a bargain.

An example of how class rates are useful in achieving equity among similar exposures within each class is shown in Figure 26–1. All exposures with an indicated loss rate of between $1.00 and $2.20 are combined in one class (A) for an average rate of $1.60 per $100 of insurance. How-

Figure 26–1. An illustration of class or average rates

ever, if the individual insureds are separable on the basis of underwriting information (potential loss characteristics, or past losses), it is fairer to establish two classes (B and C) with rates of $1.30 and $1.90, respectively. If the classes are large enough to retain predictability, a third choice is to establish four classes of average rates (D, E, F, and G), with respective rates of $1.15, $1.45, $1.75, and $2.05. More equity is thus achieved, for the differences between exposures at the low end and the high end of each class are reduced. Within each class, no matter how large it is, remains the problem of the poorer risks being most likely to apply for insurance, but inequity in the rates is lessened as the classifications are refined by having more classes.

The tendency for insurance contract applications to include a preponderance of "poorer than average for the class" risks is found throughout the field of insurance. Whenever the applications result from free choice on the part of the individuals who wish to transfer their risks to an insurer, the choice will be *against the insurer*. The worst risks will be most apt to apply for insurance, and the better risks most likely not to apply. This tendency is called *adverse selection*, and every insurer must be aware of its existence and results. The results of adverse selection can be financial disaster, as the insurer ends up with poor risks but obtains only an average price for the protection it provides. The result will be the opposite of the stated purpose of insurance underwriting—a large, safely diversified, profitable group of risks.

Two illustrations of adverse selection show why an insurer usually cannot just accept all insurance applications. In life insurance, the most likely persons to apply if no medical examinations or statements were required before the writing of the contract would be persons in poor health. In theft insurance, the typical application would tend to come from applicants who have had many thefts or from situations in which valuable properties lack proper burglary or robbery protection.

The major need for insurance underwriting thus stems from the tendency toward adverse selection which without underwriting would be ruinous to insurers. Even with selection by the insurer of the risks it will accept, some adverse selection always exists whenever a class or group rate is used. Profitable risks can only be achieved by careful selection of risks which reasonably offsets the adverse selection factors involved in insurance applications. The insurer also needs to have information about the policyholders it accepts, for only then can fair classifications and sufficient prices be determined.[3]

The process of underwriting is the means by which the insurer evalu-

---

[3] Underwriting techniques vary by type of insurance. The Associate in Underwriting Program is providing new publications for study by underwriters, such as G. William Glendenning and Robert B. Holtom, *Personal Lines Underwriting,* and others in this series published by the Insurance Institute of America (Malvern, Pa.).

ates the potential risks it has been asked to accept. A compromise is often necessary between two objectives: (1) to obtain a *large number* of individual risks within each classification, so that reasonable predictability of losses is possible, and (2) to obtain *homogeneity* of risks within each classification, so that reasonable equity between the better and poorer individual risks is achieved. The care with which an insurer combines these objectives is vital to its underwriting success and thus the whole operations of the insurer.

Consequently, underwriters may be looked upon as the backbone of the insurance business. Their job is essential. They must say no many times, but their function is also oftentimes to say yes by helping the consumer become insurable.[4] Proper rate classes and prices, with good loss-prevention practices, can help make insurance available to all persons who need it.

SELECTION OF RISKS

The selection of risks and the pricing of the contracts which are to be issued are closely related. If an adequate price for a class of risks has been established, the insurer must underwrite to secure at least an average group of policyholders. Otherwise, losses paid will exceed the premium income for paying losses. If the pricing for an insurance contract is inadequate, then even normal underwriting methods will fail to produce a profitable group of insureds. The alternative in such a case is to increase prices or to practice severe risk selection, only accepting the best risks of each class. Despite the necessary interrelationship between pricing and selection in the underwriting process, pricing is separately treated here with a number of examples.

The agent and insurer as underwriters

For most insurers the choice of policyholders begins with the underwriting done by the agent. Except for the relatively few applications which are initiated by the insured, there is substantial selection of risks by the agent in most lines of insurance. Each time an agent prepares a prospect list or, for example, telephones Mr. White instead of Mr. Green to sell insurance, the first step in underwriting is performed. If an insurer appoints well-qualified agents, they will usually try to choose clients with average or better loss exposure characteristics.

Even though the agent does some underwriting for the insurer, much

---

[4] The social and consumer responsibilities of the underwriting function are well emphasized in J. J. Launie, J. Finley Lee, and Norman A. Baglini, *Principles of Property and Liability Underwriting,* 2d ed. (Malvern, Pa.: Insurance Institute of America, 1977).

of the underwriting is performed by salaried employees in the home offices and branch offices. That is why underwriting must ultimately be considered an insurer function. This is true for a combination of reasons. Agents, though they should have their companies' interests in mind as they sell insurance, cannot perform all the needed underwriting services. Their position is not completely unbiased, either, for they are paid on a commission basis, regardless of the quality of the contracts they sell. Sometimes they may not be qualified to make the selection, as in life insurance, or may not have all the necessary information as in automobile insurance, where only preliminary underwriting information is secured by the agent. The insurer is in a much better position to check with the state motor vehicle department for the applicant's past accident record and with credit investigation companies for financial and moral faults. Agents' lack of data and their technical inability in specialized fields such as medicine or engineering place the prime responsibility for underwriting with the insurer. This is logical, for it is the insurer that is accepting the risks and the insurer that is obligated to pay the losses if they occur.

The general technique of the insurer is to provide underwriting rules to be carried out by its agents and company personnel in the underwriting departments. Agents receive instructions on what risks not to write as well as encouragement in the form of directives and sales contests which specify what types of contracts and what kinds of policyholders are particularly desired. In fire and liability insurance, *underwriting guides* are common. One insurer may specify bars and bowling alleys, for example, as generally unacceptable. Another insurer may prohibit insurance on lumberyards, seasonal hotels, and plastics factories.

Other types of applicants are often specified as insurable only after the insurer has detailed information and an opportunity to have a company representative investigate or inspect the applicant's property. Examples of situations where the agent may not have authority to bind the coverage immediately, are steam boiler explosion risks and comprehensive liability risks for businesses. Automobile insurers may request referral of taxi firms, youthful or elderly drivers, long-haul truckdrivers, motorcycle risks, and others.

The *binding* authority which many agents possess for putting the contract into effect immediately is a good example of the fact that agents do perform important underwriting services for their insurers. Many property insurance contracts go into effect by the agent issuing the contract immediately. Sometimes a "binder," or temporary contract, is issued for a period of about 20 days until the actual contract is written. The insurer may then decide not to write the contract, or may cancel the contract written by the agent, but this would be an unusual case. Even in somewhat doubtful cases, the insurer is more likely to continue the protection and perhaps ask for additional information prior to renewal of the contract. Underwriting by the insurer and the agent takes place not only at the time of the original application but also at each expiration and renewal of the insurance contract. Loss experience and other new information are significant in renewal underwriting.

Sources of underwriting information

Underwriting is not just the technique of saying no to all difficult or doubtful risks. Both the agent and the insurer must frequently explain how an applicant can become acceptable with loss prevention or other methods. Good judgment and good information are needed in this process. The sources of underwriting information upon which insurers rely include: (1) the applicant, (2) the agent, (3) the insurer's own inspection or claim department, (4) insurer bureaus and associations, and (5) outside agencies. Note that some of the sources are internal to the insurer, while several involve external information from others.

The *applicant* for an insurance contract often makes both written and oral statements. Signed written statements are normal procedure in life and health insurance, and the applications become a part of the contract. Automobile and business risk applicants also frequently prepare written statements as a means of giving the company basic underwriting details. *Agents* for many kinds of insurance provide their companies with reports, opinions, and recommendations which are valuable aids to the insurers in selecting their policyholders. Many *insurers* maintain separate *inspection departments* to provide the underwriters with physical inspection and engineering reports on the properties of applicants. The insurer's claim department, too, may be a source of important underwriting data for renewal decisions.

Insurers also combine efforts to maintain *bureau or association* lists of undesirable insurance applicants. The Medical Information Bureau (MIB) for life insurance and the Index Bureau of the American Insurance Association for automobile and other insurance offer a centralized index service of applicants who have been refused insurance, had frequent losses, or had suspicious or fraudulent claims. Used by most of the major insurers, their files are an effective means of spotting claims repeaters and fraud attempts. Other bureaus representing many insurers are maintained for regular inspection and rating services such as are discussed in regard to fire insurance in the next section of this chapter.

Many kinds of insurance use *outside agencies* to supplement the information gathered from the applicants, agents, and insurer representatives. Physicians supply life insurance companies with medical reports after physical examination of the applicants. Standard financial rating services such as Dun & Bradstreet are used for many insurance applications from business. Life insurers have used credit investigations by outside firms for many years. Automobile insurers have increasingly used such investigations to check motor vehicle reports and court records of new applicants, especially younger drivers. These are not just financial investigations for credit purposes but are also valuable in determining poor habits or moral problems of the prospect from such sources as employers, neighbors, or associates. The judgment of *moral hazard* is crucial, yet difficult, for many kinds of insurance. The mental attitudes which cause increased losses were discussed in Chapter 1. The aim of these investigations is not only to obtain negative information but to obtain positive character reports that will permit insurance to be written. The importance of independent investigative companies to insurers is apparent from the size of the largest firm, Equifax, Inc., which employs about 10,000 persons. Hooper-Holmes and other firms are also important in the field of providing underwriting information to insurers. They now have the increased challenge of performing their important tasks in compliance with the Fair Credit Reporting Act of 1970 and the Privacy Act of 1974. Insurers must also meet these requirements, as well as other state laws such as the N.A.I.C. Privacy Protection Model Act (1980), which has been passed in about ten states.

RATING (OR PRICING)

General

The pricing of insurance contracts is a specialized part of underwriting which requires the services of experts. Basically, insurance rates are calculated by *actuaries* who apply sound principles of mathematics to the particular pricing problems of insurance. The manuals, rate charts, and formulas which actuaries develop for insurers and company bureaus are used by agents as they quote the contract price of insurance to policyholders. Underwriters, too, perform substantial parts of the rate-making process, including classification of risks and applying rates.

The fundamental basis for most insurance rates is the estimate of future losses. The task of making this estimate is complicated in some kinds of insurance by the lack of data in regard to past loss experience. In life insurance, the job of setting correct prices is aided by a wealth of past experience but hampered by the need to make predictions that extend many years into the future. The scope of life insurance mortality data is amazing, and the techniques of analyzing and graduating the recorded data are part of the field of study known as *actuarial science*.

Fire insurance as an example

As an example of property insurance rating methods, the field of fire insurance offers a valuable insight into the many different factors that must be considered in setting the price to be charged for insurance. The problems involved are numerous, and it is through the cooperation of insurers in rating bureaus that many of the solutions are reached.

Rating bureaus. The work of fire insurance rating is placed in the hands of specialized *rating bureaus*. Some operate only within one state, others combine several states, and some are national in scope. One of the most widely used is the Insurance Services Office (ISO).

Fire insurance rates are usually regulated by the state, although some states do not regulate them. Most states make provision for (1) rating organizations, (2) advisory organizations, and (3) individual insurers to file rates. In these states, insurers are obliged to file with state authorities all rates, plans, and rules that they propose to use, except inland marine risks, which are exempt. An insurer may satisfy its obligation to make such filings by becoming a member of or a subscriber to a licensed rating organization which makes such filings on its behalf. The license issued authorizes the *rating organization* to promulgate rates, examine policies, and make reasonable rules for such procedures as the correction of any error or omission found by the rating organization. In contrast to a rating organization, the bill defines an *advisory organization* as an organization which assists insurers by collecting and furnishing loss or expense statistics or by submitting recommendations, but which does not make rate filings. In effect, these rating and advisory organizations are monopolies, permitted under state statutes in order to allow cooperation and limited price fixing for fire insurance, subject to regulation of their activities by the states. Reasonable uniformity and competition are also achieved by permitting *individual insurers* to file separate rates.

It is the function of the rating bureau to apply the rating schedule in use in the territory to each property that is the subject of insurance. The task requires a staff of inspectors, engineers, and other experts. Rate manuals and prices are published, and corrections are furnished from time to time to insurers and their representatives. Application for a new rate or for rerating a building already rated may be filed with the rating organization either by the owner of the property, an insurance agency, or an insurer.

Rate analysis. Insureds who handle their affairs in a businesslike manner will not be content to be told that the rate on their buildings is 2 percent of value per year when they know that across the street a property owner pays one half of 1 percent. First, they will want the discrepancies justified, and second, they will want to know to what extent a downward revision of their own rates is within their control. All of this information is obtainable through an analysis of the makeup of the rate.

The effort to eliminate as far as possible the element of judgment in evaluating hazards makes the problem of rate determination for a sizable structure a complicated and technical procedure. The average insurance agent does not make a rate analysis. This work is done by the rating bureaus. The agent and the insured, however, may take the makeup of the rate and determine where it will be profitable to eliminate hazards for which charges are made in the rate.

The *perils* included in a fire insurance contract often include more than just fire damage. Although the rate analysis example here refers only to fire as a cause of loss, separate prices are developed by the fire rating bureaus for such perils as "extended coverage" (for windstorm, smoke, explosion, riot, and other perils); business interruption loss of income, rents, and extra expenses; water damage and sprinkler leakage; and earthquake.

The price of fire insurance also varies with the location or *territory* of the property, the structure or *construction* of the building, the use or *occupancy* of the property, the loss-prevention or *protection* facilities, and the proximity or *exposure* to other risks. For example, the factor of structure or construction class changes the price significantly. Standards for the classes are carefully defined by the rating bureaus, and a "frame" building pays a higher rate than a "brick" or a "fire-resistive" building.

Two types of fire insurance rates are set by the bureau: (1) *class* rates, or "tariff" rates, for groups of average properties; and (2) *specific* rates, or "schedule" rates, for individual properties. The idea of having some rates for groups of risks with similar characteristics and other, individual rates for risks that differ widely in their specific characteristics is common to many types of insurance. A further look at these two types of rates follows.

Class rates.   Class rates are group rates, an average price applying to each similar category or classification. The outstanding example of class rating is to be found in separate *dwellings* or *residential* homes. Class-rated dwellings are subdivided into groups in accordance with construction, with a rate assigned to such classes as frame or brick and to combustible or noncombustible roof. The rate also varies as to the fire protection classification of the city or town and the number of families occupying the property. In addition, many jurisdictions apply class rates to buildings where the elements of construction and occupancy are similar enough to permit a ready grouping into rate classes. Insurance Services Office filings expand class rating to most smaller buildings in "general" classes (mercantile, churches, schools, warehouses, offices) and to "habitational" classes (apartments, motels, boardinghouses). Class rates must be used for properties to which such rates apply.

The purposes of class rates are economy and simplicity, yet reasonable equity, so that the individual buildings within a given class do not vary too much with regard to potential loss-causing characteristics. Thus, for example, all one-family brick dwellings in a midwestern town of 200,000 population and with fire hydrants might have a one-year fire rate of $0.30 per $100 of insurance.

Specific or schedule rates.   When class rates do not apply, the rate is said to be "specific." *Specific rates* are set by the rating bureaus for larger mercantile and manufacturing properties, educational institutions, public buildings, and many types of *business* establishments. Specific rates are determined by the application to the particular risk of a schedule designed to measure the relative quantity of fire hazard with respect to the particular risk. The system is known as *schedule rating*. Most larger buildings use specific rates developed after a physical inspection of the individual property. These include sprinklered, manufacturing, hotel, restaurant, and other risks.

Schedule rating is a plan by which differences in hazards with respect to different properties are measured. It takes into consideration the various items that contribute to the peril of fire, including the construction of the building, its occupancy or use, its protection, and its exposure to nearby buildings. Credits and charges representing departures from standard conditions as to each of these items are incorporated into the schedules. Thus, a schedule rate is the sum of all charges less the sum of credits.

Schedule rating has not by any means solved the fire insurance rating problems. A schedule, of itself, is partially an arbitrary standard. However, among insureds using the same schedule, equity and uniformity may be obtained.

Municipal grading schedule (Insurance Services Office).   In both class and schedule rating of properties, another factor to consider is the municipality in which the properties are located. ISO has helped in this process by evaluating cities of over 10,000 population. An engineering survey is done, grading many *physical conditions of the city* and *fire defenses*. For example, in cold climates there is a heating hazard as well as a hazard growing out of difficulty in getting fire apparatus to respond quickly and operate efficiently in cold weather. In hot, dry climates there is increased combustibility, and fires may be spread rapidly by high winds. Likewise, earthquakes, tornadoes, hurricanes, floods, forest fires, and other unusual conditions contribute to the conflagration hazard. The *municipal grading schedule* considers these factors, as well as water supplies, the adequacy and capability of police and fire department equipment and personnel, fire prevention programs, building laws, and other items. Deficiency points are assigned on the basis of regular inspections which grade areas into 10 classes of protection from 1 (the best) to 10 (the worst). Cities can obtain a higher classification and thus a lower basic insurance rate by making recommended improvements and having a new inspection survey performed. To the extent that individuals can influence the city government to update fire department equipment or training programs, or to reduce or eliminate fire hazards, a lower community rate may be obtained. (Recently, a new system of grading cities of more than 500,000 population considers only the *loss* experience of those cities.)

What the insured can do to lower rates. The details of schedule rating are many, and they make the problem of rating seem complicated. The insured is primarily interested in knowing that it is possible to reduce the insurance premium through the elimination of chargeable construction defects or the installation of protective devices. The following examples show the wide range of what can be done by insureds to lower their costs of insurance.

One of the first points that the insured should consider is charges for features of *construction* classed as "other than standard." Frequently, by means of some inexpensive modification, the standard requirements may be met and a substantial saving effected. In the case of such things as stairs, heating, lighting, and electrical wiring, slight alterations to correct defects may result in savings far in excess of the cost. Another factor to consider is the *exposure* from adjoining buildings. If a building of superior construction is exposed on any side by a high-rated risk, such as a small frame addition at the rear of a brick building, the exposure charge can be eliminated by removing the unneeded addition. A rate may also be materially lessened by entirely closing unprotected openings with standard fire doors, fire shutters, or wire-glass windows set in steel sash and frames. It frequently happens that a hazardous *occupancy* or use of the property is eliminated, and through neglect or oversight no application is made for rerating. Whenever there have been any changes in occupancy in either the insured property or an adjacent property, an investigation to ascertain their effect upon the rate is in order. Charges for hazards growing out of *faults of management* are usually the outgrowth of carelessness or indifference. Since such hazards are readily corrected, a charge is made which aims to make their elimination profitable to the insured. Charges are made for such hazards as broken plaster or windows, heating pipes improperly placed near combustible material, improper receptacles for oily or other waste, the accumulation of rubbish, and other indications of slack housekeeping. The insured will find it inexpensive as well as common sense to correct such faults.

Perhaps no single improvement to a property will have a greater effect on a rate reduction than the installation of an *automatic sprinkler system*. In buildings where the temperature is below the freezing point of water, a dry system is available. Instead of being filled with water, the pipes contain air under pressure up to the sprinkler head. When a sprinkler head is opened, the compressed air is released and water then flows through the system and through the opened valve to drench the fire. The cost of sprinkler installation is unreasonably high for risks involving small values. However, when large values are involved, over a term of years the savings on the insurance premium will pay for the sprinkler system. In addition, many fire losses can be avoided or substantially reduced by sprinkler systems, and both lives and property saved.

Credits on the rate are also allowed for *other protective features* designed to minimize the risks of fire. Among these are approved fire extinguishers, automatic smoke and fire alarms, and security guard service. When the installation of such equipment is contemplated, care should be exercised to see that it meets the standard of rating requirements.

When *new building construction plans* are being considered, their submission to the fire insurance rating bureau will frequently bring forth suggestions to increase the safety of the property and lessen the insurance cost. A slight addition to the thickness of a floor or wall; a change in roof specifications; changes in floor openings, elevators, vents—all may become profitable investments by saving on insurance premiums. The planning stage is the best time to catch and eliminate chargeable hazards at little or no cost. Improvements can be made that would be too expensive to consider in a completed building. Through submission of the plans and specifications to the rating bureau, a complete rate analysis may be obtained for study before final acceptance and approval of the plans.

The lower fire insurance rates that can be achieved by eliminating hazards are perhaps the least important of a number of benefits that policyholders should consider. Indirect losses, some probably not insured, could be substantial. The desire for the safety of human lives may also be an overwhelming factor in deciding to do all that is possible to prevent fire losses.

Automobile insurance as another example

Rating plans usually must try to establish insurance rates so that insurers can pay total claims and expenses, while at the same time providing reasonable equity among the prices charged the various insureds. In pricing automobile insurance *class* rates are the usual rating method. The location and use of the property are the basic loss-causing characteristics classified. Because of higher loss frequency than in fire insurance, it is also common to develop *individual* rate modifications for insureds on the basis of their accident record experience.

Territorial differences in price are important in automobile insurance. Each rating territory, which may be as large as a whole state or as small as a part of an urban area, pays a rate based on the losses attributable to automobiles garaged in that territory. Thus, a New York automobile or driver causing a loss in Florida would affect New York liability rates, not those of Florida. Generally, rural areas pay lower prices for automobile insurance than do urban areas, but the actual losses of the area are also important. One city may have a much higher rate than another city of the same size because of poor loss experience. The loss-producing characteristics may be largely uncontrollable, such as snow, ice, fogs, and hills, or they may be partially controllable, such as poor roads, lenient juries, and lax police enforcement.

The *use* factor in automobile insurance rates is primarily related to classification of drivers. The principal and secondary drivers are grouped in hundreds of classifications based on age, sex, and marital status. Generally, married persons have lower rates than unmarried persons; persons over age 30 lower rates than persons under 30; and females lower rates than males. Separate classifications also apply to private passenger automobiles used primarily in a business, as opposed to those used mostly for pleasure and those used for transportation to and from work regularly more than a stated number of miles. Commercial vehicles, such as large trucks, have separate rating plans.

Experience of the drivers is also a significant factor in pricing. Many rating plans require higher rates if the driver (or family members using the automobile) have had recent automobile accident *losses*. The driving record thus influences the charges considerably. For example, being responsible for one accident within the past three years might increase the price of insurance by 20 percent, while two accidents could cause a 50 percent or more increase. These "demerit" plans of rating bureaus and independent insurers vary in the percentage additions to cost. Price discounts of about 15 percent are granted for driver education courses completed by drivers under age 21, and to owners of two or more automobiles if they insure them in the same policy. The system of individual rate modifications based upon loss experience is somewhat like the "schedule" rates for fire insurance on individual business properties. In place of estimating the prospective effect of good and bad features of the property through a physical inspection, the individual rates are developed by increasing the class rate by percentages on the basis of actual automobile insurance losses of the individual insured. Some insurers also vary collision and physical damage rates according to loss experience by classes of specific car models. A Pontiac Firebird may pay higher rates, for example, than a Buick Skylark.

A few states have passed legislation banning the use of age and sex as rating factors in automobile insurance. Claiming unfair discrimination, Massachusetts, North Carolina, and Hawaii are requiring the use of other rating factors such as driving experience and mileage use, but these types of laws are being challenged by many insurers. (See also Chapter 20.)

Special problems

Deductible clauses. A deductible clause made its early appearance in marine insurance contracts because in the case of goods particularly susceptible to damage there would otherwise be many claims for insignificant losses, or for losses that could reasonably be anticipated. Thus, marine contracts on cargo shipments usually provide that the insurer is relieved of all partial losses on certain types of goods. In other classifications of goods the loss must exceed a designated percentage of value, or a specified dollar amount, in order to be collectible.

This type of deductible is known as a *franchise deductible*. The percentage of value or specified amount which is not paid is called the "franchise." No loss is payable unless the loss equals or exceeds the franchise percentage or amount. If the loss reaches this figure it is paid in full. For example, if a policy has a 3 percent franchise deductible on property valued at $100,000, no payment is made for a loss of under $3,000. If the loss is $3,000 or more, the payment is for the full amount of the loss.

Much more common in most other forms of insurance is the second major type of deductible, called the *straight deductible*. Such a deductible provides that a named percentage of the loss or a stated dollar amount is *always* deducted from the claim and the amount above this deductible is paid the insured. Usually, the deductible is a specific dollar amount, often relatively small, such as $50 or $100, but it may be much larger.

The straight deductible is very important in property insurance. In automobile insurance, for example, owners of automobiles might be perfectly satisfied to have small damages repaired themselves. If the insurer is liable for the repair of minor losses, the cost of handling the claims is entirely out of proportion to the damage sustained. For this reason, automobile insurance for the car of the insured is frequently written with a straight deductible clause providing that the company is not liable unless the loss exceeds an amount named in the clause, such as $50 or $100 or $250, and then the insurer pays only the amount by which the loss exceeds the specified deductible.

Small deductibles written in connection with property insurance are sound in theory. They effectively eliminate most of the small "nuisance" claims, and in the long run they make possible a lower insurance premium. The insured receives a reduced premium where a deductible is used. Adjustment expense in settling a small nuisance loss is often more than the amount of the loss. A $50 loss payment may often involve $100 or more in agents' and adjusters' time and completion of necessary forms. The loss records show that the adjustment and payment in full of such claims do increase insurance costs considerably because for many types of insurance the greatest number of losses are small ones. With rising loss costs, deductibles as a means of reducing insurance premiums are often increasingly advantageous to consumers in holding insurance costs down. (See Chapter 2 for other discussion on the reasons for using deductibles.) One additional factor for insureds to consider is the federal income tax deduction for *uninsured* casualty losses. With the 1982 Economic Tax Equity Act, only such losses that are more than 10 percent of gross adjusted income are deductible (previously losses over $100 were deductible).

It has not proved feasible in connection with most property insurance to provide a franchise type of deductible for payment in full if the loss exceeds the amount of the deductible. In the case of a $100 deductible there is a grave temptation to stretch an $80 or $90 loss to the point where it exceeds the deductible, if by so doing the full amount of the claim is to be paid. A combination of the straight and franchise deductibles is the so-called variable, diminishing, or *modified* deductible.[5] For example, in the case of a $100 loss or less, the full amount of the deductible applies. The amount payable for loss between $100 and $500 may be 125 percent of the amount in excess of $100. When the loss is $500 or more, the franchise loss deductible disappears. This is illustrated as follows:

Amount of loss	Deductible amount	Loss less deductible	Amount collectible	Franchise amount
$100	$100	0	0	$100.00
200	100	$100 × 125%	$125.00	75.00
400	100	300 × 125%	375.00	25.00
500	100	400 × 125%	500.00	0

The modified type of deductible has the advantage of not encouraging exaggerated claims by the insured in order to receive loss payment. In keeping with the theory that a deductible's purpose is to eliminate small losses but *not* to reduce a loss payment when the loss is *large,* it is an equitable method. Its disadvantage is greater complexity and possible lack of understanding by the insured. In fact, the major disadvantage of all deductibles is the practical problem of educating insureds to understand that the reduced cost and other benefits of deductibles more than offset the slightly lower loss payments they receive.

Sizeable deductibles have been introduced in fire insurance for large business and other properties. Forms are offered that allow deductibles at the insured's option ranging from $5,000 to $250,000 or more. A sched-

---

[5] Widely used for homeowners' policies during the 1970s, the modified deductible is used for these contracts in only a few states today. Most homeowners' policies have a straight deductible of about $100 per loss.

ule of rate credits is applicable according to the percentage of value represented by the deductible amount which the insured selects. The higher the percentage which the deductible bears to the basis of insurance, the greater is the credit allowed. Experience shows that the less the amount of the loss, the more frequent the occurrence. If insureds can handle losses up to a given point and eliminate such losses from their insurance coverage, the loss experience will be reflected in much lower rates. Consumers should not cling to traditional deductibles, and should periodically review their choices of deductible amounts.[6] The choice of the optimal size of deductible can be a complex decision, based on what the insured can afford, the insured's degree of risk aversion, the loss frequency and severity, and the premium savings.[7]

Newer types of deductibles are becoming more common, too. In addition to the straight, franchise and modified deductibles just discussed, the *aggregate deductible* is increasing in popularity. This is applied to *total losses in a year* rather than to each loss. Its use is appearing frequently in liability (particularly for product claims) and some forms of health insurance.

Minimum premiums. There are certain *fixed costs* involved in issuing an insurance policy. Neither insurers nor agents can afford to write contracts with very small premiums. For example, a certain amount of expense is involved in the office labor required in preparing the policy. That cost alone often exceeds $25 per contract written. For this reason it is customary to require a *minimum premium*, sometimes referred to as a "policy fee."

In some fields of insurance a large expense is caused by *inspections* or other such services. If the amount of insurance ordered does not bring the premium up to a specified minimum, the underwriting requirements indicate a charge that must be met regardless of the rate. Finally, there are *short-term exposures* in which there is a tendency of applicants for insurance to apply for coverages for a period of a few months when circumstances tend to increase the risk. Examples would include auto insurance only during winter driving months, or fire insurance only while the heating system is turned on. If such insurance were written at the proportional part of the annual rate, there would be a tendency to create a situation of adverse selection against the insurer. The minimum premium has to be set at an amount sufficiently large to reimburse the insurer for the increased risk.

---

[6] But choose the large deductibles carefully. A recent $1 million loss at First National Bank of Chicago involved the good news that the bank had insurance coverage but the bad news that its insurance contract had a deductible—for $1 million (*Newsweek,* October 24, 1977).

[7] Harris Schlesinger, "The Optimal Level of Deductibility in Insurance Contracts," *Journal of Risk and Insurance* 48, no. 3 (September 1981), p. 465.

Annual and term policies. The time specified in the policy during which the coverage is effective is its *term.* A property insurance policy written for one year is called an *annual policy;* if written for a longer period, it is called a *term policy.* Certain types of risks are accepted on an annual basis only; others are written for a longer term, sometimes with a rate reduction; still others are written for less than one year at an increased short-term rate.

When policies are written on the term basis with a prepaid premium for the entire term, most contracts are for one year, although some are written for three years. A discount used to be given for prepaid contracts of more than a year, but today most insurers follow Insurance Services Office rules which charge the *full* annual rate for each year. The advantage of such policies is that they do not have to be rewritten each year, and the rate is guaranteed for the policy term against rate increases.

Policies written for a period of less than a year are ordinarily written for a special purpose, such as to bring about an expiration date at a particular time or to add to insurance during the period of a temporary inventory increase. Policies written for less than a year are charged on what is termed the *short-rate basis.* Tables are prepared to show short-rate premium calculations, as if a regular contract were written and then canceled. For example, a 180-day contract would cost 60 percent of the annual premium. (ISO now applies a new method, charging 90 percent of the full unearned premium.)

In the early days of fire insurance *perpetual* policies were offered, and a few insurers continue the practice today. Perpetual policies are written under a continuous contract for a single premium. While the insurance is in force, the investment return on premium deposits is used to pay claims and operating expenses.

Installment plans. Term rates for longer than a year with annual *installment payments* are allowed in some types of insurance. For example, in the casualty field 2.5 times the annual premium plus 5 percent is the charge for a three-year term policy if paid in installments of 50, 30, and 20 percent for the first, second, and third years, respectively. To permit taking advantage of term discounts with equal annual installment payments, the deferred premium plan (DPP) provides for an annual DPP rate which is 105 percent of the one-year regular rate.

A wide variety of premium payment plans have recently appeared in insurance. With automobile insurance costs rising, six-month policies or premiums are quite common. Policyholders are often faced with the need to spread their insurance premiums over a number of payments. Some insurers have set up separate finance plans to permit the insured to do this on a quarterly, semiannual, or monthly basis. Larger agencies have also designed such finance plans to aid their clients. The trend appears to be toward monthly payments, which are especially suitable for the all-lines insurer groups that can offer the insured a plan with one convenient monthly premium for all types of insurance.

REINSURANCE

The underwriting process is closely related to reinsurance, and the underwriter must know how his or her ability to accept risks is both broadened and limited by reinsurance available to the insurer. *Reinsurance* is the transfer of insurance from one insurer to another insurer. It is insurance purchased by insurers.

Purposes

How can an insurer accept large risks that today sometimes exceed $50 million in a single building, a ship, or an airplane? How can liability contracts for business firms be written that have policy limits of $100 million or more? How can a person now have in excess of $10 million of life insurance? Few, if any, insurers could absorb such loss payments without endangering their financial solvency. In exposures affecting many insureds at one time, such as hurricanes, how can insurers avoid the concentration of loss that occurs? Gigantic losses do not occur frequently, but when they do they illustrate the "real why" of insurance—protection against losses which perhaps could only be met by the insurance system.

In recent years the examples of insured losses in catastrophes illustrate the size and variety of such unfortunate events: *in 1979,* Hurricane Frederic ($750 million), loss of RCA "Satcom" satellite ($70 million), DC–10 airplane crash in Chicago ($122 million), and collision of tankers in the Caribbean ($42 million); *in 1980,* settlement because of faulty construction of three liquefied gas freighters ($300 million), fire in U.K. aircraft spare parts warehouse ($176 million), capsizing of North Sea and Alaskan oil rigs ($68 and $36 million), race riots in Miami ($65 million), and tornados in three states ($62 million); *in 1981,* Texas hail damage ($152 million), Scandanavian North Sea storms ($102 million); and *in 1982,* Mississippi floods and a Hawaiian storm each causing more than $100 million of insurance claims. Worldwide during the past 12 years the causes of major losses have been about 30 percent natural catastrophes, 30 percent road, rail, and waterborne traffic, 18 percent each aviation and fires, and 4 percent miscellaneous.[8]

The fact that catastrophes do occur explains the most important purpose of reinsurance, the spread or *diversification of exposures and losses.* One insurer can write large amounts of insurance on a single property

---

[8] *Sigma* (New York: North American Reinsurance Corporation), October 1982, p. 14.

or in a concentrated area; then reinsurance shifts part of the risk to many others. Large losses are thus shared, and excessive losses in one occurrence do not cause financial instability of individual insurers. Without reinsurance, each insurer would be limited to its own financial ability to pay losses. With reinsurance, financial strength is enhanced by the spreading of losses throughout the entire insurance business.

Reinsurance also has other purposes. Reserve requirements for insurers as they write insurance contracts cause a drain on surplus and restrict growth, particularly for newer or smaller companies. More rapid *growth* can be achieved by having a reinsurer take over from the insurer part of the requirements for maintaining reserves, which permits the insurer to increase their writing of more business. Reinsurers also offer many *technical advisory services* to new insurers or those expanding to new types of insurance or territories. From the standpoint of the reinsurer, the normal purpose or motivation for reinsurance is *profits*.

Reinsurance organizations

Reinsurers are of two basic types: (1) *professional reinsurers* that do a reinsurance business only, and (2) *reinsurance departments* of insurers that write mostly insurance but also write some reinsurance. About three fourths of the market for reinsurance in the United States is written by the full-time professional reinsurers. There are about 35 professional reinsurers in the United States and approximately 200 more worldwide.[9] However, in the past two decades the number of U.S. insurers that have organized reinsurance departments has almost tripled to about 100.

A special type of reinsurer is the *reinsurance pool,* which is an association for the exchange of reinsurance among two or more insurers according to an automatic agreement. Each reinsurer receives a certain amount or proportion of the risks or losses of the other reinsurer or reinsurers, and each cedes or gives to all the others a predetermined part of its risks or losses. These pools are also used for spreading infrequent catastrophic types of risks among insurers of a company group or fleet. Examples of such reinsurance pools, sometimes called syndicates, are those found for such risks as nuclear fission, insurance in foreign countries, marine insurance, large industrial risks, and aviation insurance. Well known in these fields are the American Nuclear Insurers, the American Foreign Insurance Association, the American Hull Insurance Syndicate, the Factory Insurance Association, and the United States Aviation Underwriters.

---

[9] *Sigma,* July–August 1981, p. 5.

Reinsurance agreements

There are two principal forms of reinsurance agreements in regard to the method by which the reinsurance goes into effect: (1) specific, or facultative, reinsurance; and (2) treaty, or automatic, reinsurance.

Specific, or facultative. *Specific* reinsurance, also termed *facultative* reinsurance, is *optional* to both the insurer and reinsurer. Each contract under specific reinsurance is written on its own merit and is a matter of individual bargaining between the original insurer and the reinsurer. This form is termed facultative because the reinsurer is under no obligation through previous agreement of reciprocal arrangement to accept the risk. Also, the insurer may or may not offer the risk to the reinsurer. Each party thus retains the faculty or privilege of accepting or rejecting the reinsurance agreement. Facultative reinsurance is still widely used because some risks will always fall outside the scope of the automatic arrangements discussed next.

Treaty, or automatic. *Treaty*, or *automatic*, reinsurance exists when the insurer agrees in advance to "cede" or offer some types of risks and the reinsurer agrees to accept those risks. The individual risks may be undetermined at the time of the agreement. The reinsurer agrees to insure an amount or a proportionate part of a designated class of past or future business written by the insurer. Treaties controlling the major part of the business today are *obligatory*, the reinsurer agreeing to accept a specific part (the ceded or reinsured amount) of each risk assumed by the original insurer, and the original insurer on its part agreeing to cede a like portion of the risk. The liability of the reinsurer attaches as soon as the original insurer assumes the risk. Automatic[10] protection is thus assured for the original insurer, as the reinsurer has agreed beforehand to accept all risks within the terms of the treaty.

Reinsurance contracts

Facultative and treaty reinsurance agreements may use either of two basic ideas in distributing the insurance risk between the original insurer and the reinsurer. The reinsurer agrees to accept either (1) *a share* of the *amounts of risk* which the insurer writes or (2) an *excess* of the *losses* beyond certain established limits.

A special type of contract which is not regularly used by an insurer is called "portfolio reinsurance." This occurs when the reinsurer takes

---

[10] Sometimes the insurer retains the option of determining what it will reinsure, and the treaty is termed an "open treaty" or a "facultative treaty." Here the automatic part of the arrangements for reinsurance is limited to the general type of reinsurance contract and its provisions, but the actual risks and amounts to be ceded to the reinsurer are subject to negotiation.

over all the risks of certain lines of insurance from the original insurer, oftentimes when the insurer is discontinuing such business.

Share-of-risk contracts. Reinsurance contracts that share risks may involve two fundamental ways[11] of distributing the business written by the insurer. In one type, known as *quota or pro rata share*, the insurer cedes a proportional share of every insurance contract of a given kind. For example, in fire insurance the insurer might keep only one third of each risk and the reinsurer accept two thirds. In that case the reinsurer would receive two thirds of the premium (less commissions paid by the insurer to agents) and pay two thirds of any losses. This form of reinsurance contract enables the original insurer to write much larger amounts of insurance than it otherwise could, and it is particularly useful to smaller insurers that want to expand rapidly.

Another common type is the *surplus share*, in which the reinsurer does not participate in every risk of the original insurer but accepts only that part of the risk which goes over certain limits. Usually the limit is established in relation to the "line" retained by the original insurer, and the reinsurer may, for example, agree to take three lines above the retention. The reinsurer does not participate unless the insurance exceeds the net retention. Surplus treaties are one of the most common types of reinsurance arrangement in fire insurance. Often a second or third surplus treaty is used, involving several different reinsurers on the same risk for amounts up to 5 or 10 times the amount of risk kept by the original insurer.

Excess-of-loss contracts. The second basic type of reinsurance contract, *excess-of-loss*,[12] is designed to afford protection against large *losses* only. *Individual* coverage is used when protection is desired on a single, large exposure. *Catastrophe* coverage applies to classes of exposures, irrespective of the number of risks involved, or against an accumulation of losses in excess of a stipulated limit. The coverage may be limited to a certain area, such as a designated city, or it may be nationwide in scope. A special form of catastrophe coverage may be limited to a definite class where an insurer desires to protect underwriting profits by having the reinsurer pay all losses when the loss ratio exceeds an agreed percentage of the earned premiums. This is called "excess-of-loss ratio" reinsurance. There are many other variations.

---

[11] Reference here is primarily to property-liability reinsurance contracts. In the life insurance field two basic types are also used: the "coinsurance" type and the "yearly renewable term" type. Since life risks involve total losses only rather than total or partial losses, reinsurance contracts in the life and property fields are not completely analogous. Basically, however, the "coinsurance" type is closest to the share-of-risk contract and the "yearly renewable term" is most like an excess-of-loss contract.

[12] Excess-of-loss reinsurance is sometimes confused with "catastrophe covers," which have similar goals of protecting against large losses only but are written as direct insurance between policyholder and insurer.

Unlike the quota share cover, in the case of loss under excess-of-loss reinsurance there is no obligation on the part of the reinsurer until the gross claim is shown to be in excess of the amount payable by the ceding company. The reinsurer shares *only* a portion of *losses* in excess of the retention; it does not receive a full proportional share of the premium. Thus, this type is sometimes called "nonproportional" reinsurance. Sometimes, in order to hold the ceding company interested in the gross amount of the loss settlement, the agreement is written so that the ceding company continues to participate in the excess loss in an agreed percentage.

Excess-of-loss contracts are the type of coverage by which many insurers, especially in automobile, liability, and other types of casualty insurance, cover the catastrophe risk. Fire and allied lines such as windstorm insurance have also used this type of reinsurance with increasing frequency. American and alien companies accepting reinsurance write the coverage, and Lloyd's of London writes many of these increasingly popular reinsurance contracts.

A summary of the types and characteristics of reinsurance organizations, reinsurance agreements, and reinsurance contracts is presented for review in Table 26–1.

Retrocessions

Reinsurance enjoys no immunity from the operation of the principles governing sound practice for insurers. The reinsurer must also avoid a concentration in "conflagration" areas or catastrophe situations and must maintain a wide distribution of its risks. Since the reinsurer may have lines ceded from a number of different sources, it might find itself with an unwarranted accumulation of risk in a single policyholder or a given locality or class. To avoid too large an exposure to loss, the reinsurer would itself have to resort to reinsurance. The act of reinsuring any part of a reinsurance contract is termed a *retrocession*. In compensation, liability, and life risks, the reinsurer sometimes finds the amount of reinsurance far greater than it is willing to carry. In such cases, it can accept the entire excess and in turn seek reinsurance through retrocession, retaining only as much of the risk as it deems prudent.

An example of reinsurance

The entire area of reinsurance is an example of the essential need to spread risk among many risk bearers. Much of the process goes on without policyholders being aware of its existence, since they are not a party to the reinsuring arrangements. Yet it is an important part of the security behind many insurance contracts. Without reinsurance, most

Table 26–1. Summary of types of reinsurers and reinsurance

Types	Characteristics
1. *Reinsurance organizations*	
a. Professional reinsurers	Write reinsurance only
b. Reinsurance departments	Write reinsurance, but are primarily insurers
c. Reinsurance pools	Associations of insurers writing or sharing reinsurance jointly
2. *Reinsurance agreements*	
a. Specific, or facultative*	Optional choice allowing ceding insurer to offer, and reinsurer to accept, individual insurance risks; neither party obligated in advance to do so
b. Treaty,* or automatic	Binding agreement in advance to have ceding insurer offer, and reinsurer accept, some proportion or amount of designated types of insurance
3. *Reinsurance contracts*†	
a. Share-of-risk	Reinsurer shares *risks* (premiums and losses) with insurer
a. Quota or pro rata share	Reinsurer and original insurer share part (or a percentage) of the entire premiums and claims on the risks insured
b. Surplus share	Reinsurer shares risk only above a net retention by insurer
b. Excess-of-loss	Reinsurer shares only *losses* proportionally with insurer
a. Individual contracts	Reinsurer agrees to pay losses on a single exposure above the retention amount paid by insurer
b. Catastrophe	Reinsurer agrees to pay catastrophic losses on classes of exposures above the amount, or a specified loss ratio, retained by insurer (generally liability insurance)

* A variation may combine these two types in a "facultative treaty," in which the agreement in advance is limited to the general terms that will apply for the reinsurance. The insurer is not required to reinsure nor the reinsurer to accept business, but if they do so, the terms of the reinsurance agreement automatically apply.

† Life insurance uses two other types not described here: "yearly renewable term" and "coinsurance" plans.

insurers could accept only a limited amount of insurance on any one risk, perhaps only a few thousand dollars. With reinsurance, many insurers can accept millions of dollars of insurance from an insured and through reinsurance distribute a large share of the risk to many others.

Consider the hypothetical illustration[13] of an agent who sells $9 million of fire insurance on a manufacturer's plant. Three insurers may each

---

[13] Recommended for further explanations and examples of reinsurance are two books by Robert W. Strain: *Reinsurance* and *Reinsurance Practices* (New York: College of Insurance, 1980 and 1982, respectively).

Figure 26–2. An example illustrating the use of reinsurance contracts

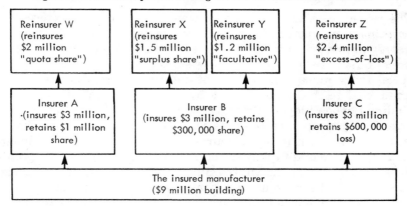

take $3 million of coverage in separate policies. Perhaps Insurer A has a quota share treaty reinsurance agreement with Reinsurer W that takes two thirds of this $3 million policy. Insurer B may have a surplus share treaty with Reinsurer X to take five "lines" above a $300,000 retention by Insurer B, or $1.5 million. This would leave $1.2 million to be arranged by Insurer B in a facultative reinsurance agreement with Reinsurer Y in a second surplus agreement. The third $3 million policy may be spread to Reinsurer Z in an excess-of-loss contract, in which Insurer C agrees to take care of all losses up to $600,000 and Reinsurer Z will pay any loss exceeding that amount up to $3 million. Any of the reinsurers, or all of them, may decide that their total risk is too great and through retrocession transfer some of their risk to other reinsurers. See Figure 26–2 for illustration of this example of the use of reinsurance contracts.

The example illustrates how one policyholder's risk may result in several insurance contracts and many reinsurance and retrocession agreements. The relatively large dollar figures in the example should not be taken to mean that reinsurance is used only for large business risks. It is in everyday use by practically all insurers for many risks. Fire insurance on homes and automobile liability insurance of more than $50,000, as well as many other common types and sizes of insurance contracts, have reinsurance regularly involved. The "retention" by the original insurer, of course, may be smaller, or it may be larger where the insurer is large enough to absorb such losses.

Other reinsurance illustrations could involve millions of dollars. The 1980 MGM Grand Hotel fire in Las Vegas and the 1981 Hyatt Regency Hotel skywalk collapse in Kansas City each involved reinsurance amounts in excess of $100 million and dozens of reinsurers.

International aspects

The reinsurance area is noted for several unusual characteristics: its *international* character, its extreme *flexibility* and freedom from insurance regulation as to forms and rates, and its high level of business *conduct* on a basis of good faith between the contracting parties. A substantial reinsurance business, about one third of all U.S. reinsurance, is conducted in the United States by reinsurers from other countries, including London Lloyd's. Branch companies of alien reinsurers are also active. These companies compete with the full-time professional U.S. reinsurers[14] and with the reinsurance departments of U.S. insurers, which have increased rapidly in recent years. The reinsurance premium that is exported from the United States is an item of some importance in the balance of payments, involving several billion dollars each year.

The widespread market for reinsurance—a world spread that is needed by all countries—is partially responsible for the great flexibility which reinsurers have in designing new and special contracts for the individual needs of insurers. The large and sometimes complex nature of reinsurance arrangements and the necessarily high caliber of reinsurance personnel for such contracts make reinsurance a unique part of the insurance business. It is only on an international basis that giant risks can be spread throughout the world, even to the USSR in its "Ingosstrakh"[15] reinsurance company, by the process of reinsurance. Risks of $10–$100 million may be placed in the competitive reinsurance market in only a few days. Increasing losses and increasing needs for multimillion-dollar reinsurance coverages for fire, windstorm, riot, liability, aircraft, shipping, and many other types of damages promise to make reinsurance of growing importance in the international marketplace.

OTHER FUNCTIONS OF INSURERS

Many of the following functions facilitate the underwriting function. This brief treatment of the "auxiliary" departments of insurers should not be taken to mean that these functions are unimportant. In fact, the success of many insurers can be traced to the excellent support given by these departments to the primary operating departments of marketing, underwriting, and claims. The *investment* department has become

---

[14] Examples of the largest reinsurers are: U.S. professional—General Reinsurance, Employers' Reinsurance, and American Re-Insurance; alien professional reinsurers—Swiss Reinsurance, Munich Reinsurance, and Gerling.

[15] Surprisingly, the USSR does have a reinsurer that writes insurance outside the Communist Bloc. It also has a government insurer (Gosstrakh), and citizens own and insure buildings and other property, but not liability exposures there. See Paul P. Rogers, "Property Insurance in the Soviet," *CPCU Journal* 35, no. 2 (September 1982), p. 145.

so crucial to all insurers today that it is separately treated in the final chapter.

The *legal* department, for example, often works closely with the underwriting and claims departments of property and liability insurers. It is generally also responsible for meeting general incorporation, licensing, rating, and taxation laws of the many states in which insurers do business. Oftentimes it helps design insurance contracts, drafts agency agreements, and provides general legal counsel for the insurer. In life insurance it offers substantial aid to the sales and underwriting departments by reviewing tax problems.

The *actuarial* department is most closely related to the rating or underwriting department of insurers. Life insurance companies, in particular, need a separate actuarial staff to diagnose mortality trends, determine costs for the various contracts, and provide research for many phases of their activities. Close cooperation is needed with the accounting, statistical, and computer areas in order to coordinate expense, loss cost, and other studies.

Separate *research* departments are not common for most insurers, but increasingly the need for economic and social research is being realized. Some companies now have substantial staffs to analyze economic trends, policyholder opinion surveys, market potentials, investment opportunities, and other factors important to insurer operations. An organization including many of the research directors, the Society of Insurance Research, was formed about a decade ago. It has national and regional meetings to discuss research activities, and publishes the *Research Review*. A new Insurance Research Institute was also started by insurer-sponsored organizations five years ago.

A *public relations* department is maintained by some insurers. News releases, claim dissatisfactions, and general service to the community and public are part of its activities. Coordination with the claims, education, and advertising departments may be essential in many of its projects. Several major trade associations for public relations are supported by many insurers.

Education is another growing area of insurance organizations. Several hundred directors of educational activities for insurers are joined together nationally in a professional effort to improve insurance education through the Insurance Company Education Directors' Society. Many insurers today provide extensive programs of education for management development and the training of claimspersons and underwriters, as well as regular separate schools for agents and employees. They also support many professional educational organizations (see Chapter 25).

Many general *administrative* services are necessary for the efficient operation of an insurer. There are numerous jobs for personnel managers, purchasing experts, computer programmers, secretaries, and many other types of administrative personnel. A successful insurer must be well organized in the administrative areas to provide efficient results. Automation offers substantial help today for many problems in handling administrative services, but it is unlikely that the current ratio of two nonsales jobs for each sales job in insurance will change rapidly. The wide scope of employment in the insurance business is seen in this chapter to include personnel from practically all the fields of marketing, finance, management, and the information sciences.

FOR REVIEW AND DISCUSSION

1. After your study of the underwriting function, do you feel that insurers must write insurance for all applicants? Explain your position.
2. Why do rating and reinsurance topics pertain to underwriting? How is underwriting related to the other major functions of an insurer?
3. Why can't an insurer just accept all applicants for insurance when a "class" rate is used for the price of the contract?
4. What limitations does the insurer set in relying upon the agent to perform the selection of proper risks?
5. What sources of underwriting information are commonly used in various kinds of insurance?
6. What is "adverse selection," and how does the insurer overcome this problem? Give examples from life, health, fire, and automobile insurance.
7. What is a class fire rate, and how is it found? How does a specific fire rate differ from the class rate, and how is it determined? Give an example of each.
8. The Medical Office Building has just been completed, and application for a fire rate filed. A substantial charge is included in the rate because the building has wooden interior walls. Wherein did the owners fail concerning this rate? What other features of this risk would heavily influence the insurance rate that the building owners will have to pay?
9. Can a public interest campaign be used to make the classification of a city for its fire insurance rate a community affair and perhaps reduce the rate?
10. What is the purpose of a "schedule" fire insurance rate? How does this compare with the purpose of "merit" rates for automobile insurance?
11. How can individual business property owners lower fire insurance costs?
12. Substantial deductibles may encourage self-insurance. Why do deductibles of $10,000 or upward have a place in the insurance business?
13. What are the purposes of deductibles? term policies? installment plans?
14. *Straight* deductibles are most common, but *franchise* deductibles are sometimes used in insurance. Explain the difference.
15. Mr. Foster finds an unusual "modified" deductible in his homeowner's contract. How is it modified? Is its purpose sound in theory and practice?

16. Explain the principal reasons for reinsurance and distinguish between: *(a)* facultative and treaty reinsurance; *(b)* reinsurance and retrocession; and *(c)* share-of-risk and excess-of-loss reinsurance.

17. To what extent is reinsurance an international activity? Why?

18. Briefly explain how three "auxiliary" departments of insurers may help in their performance of the underwriting function.

Chapter 27

Outline of concepts

Insurance loss payment is the primary reason for, and result of, many insurance contracts. Uncertainty about losses creates the need for insurance.

The significance of this function is widespread. The spectacular losses, such as multimillion-dollar fires, explosions, and windstorms, are the ones that get the headlines. However, the thousands of everyday smaller claims paid by insurers are those that benefit most policyholders.

The purposes of "loss adjusting" are *fair* and *prompt* payment of justified claims. The *reputation* of the insurer is greatly influenced by the manner in which loss payments are made.

Insurance adjusters are of *five types*. Which type is used for a particular loss depends on many factors, such as the kind of insurance, the volume of business written by the insurer, the frequency and difficulty of the claims, the ability of the agent, and the insured.

Agents often settle smaller losses and help in many other losses, depending on the type of insurance.

Staff adjusters are full-time, salaried employees of one insurer and are active in such fields as automobile losses.

Independent adjusters represent various insurers on some losses.

Adjustment bureaus regularly represent many insurers and are especially useful in fire, windstorm, and other property damage losses.

Public adjusters are hired by the insured in some difficult claims.

Claims procedures vary among the different kinds of insurance.

Fire insurance losses are based upon proper *notice* and *proof* of loss by the insured, and usually the insurer's payment of *actual cash value* follows certain *rights and conditions* stated in the contract. Some special problems in valuing buildings, merchandise, and other types of property are noted.

Liability insurance losses are more difficult to settle because a third-party claimant is involved. Also, the responsibility for injury, its extent, and its future results must be determined. Bodily injuries are more difficult to evaluate than property damages.

Life insurance losses are usually paid directly by the insurer through the agent to the beneficiaries. The payment is usually a *fixed-dollar* amount, with some *settlement option* choices available and relatively few legal problems except for the incontestable clause, suicide, and accidental death claims.

Insurance loss payment

Did you ever hear of a moose stomping a compact car?[1] A bull wrecking a swimming pool? A can of hair spray that exploded, after having been put in a toilet, blowing the user from the toilet seat into the bathtub? A patient who billed the insurance company for a seashore vacation because the doctor had prescribed salt water for an injured toe—and later sued the doctor for malpractice because the toe became infected? Well, insurance adjusters have had all of these claims—but most losses are *not* so funny.

The payment of losses is certainly the most obvious of the important functions of insurance. Without claims culminating in loss payments there would be no insurance business. To Joan and John Q. Public, insurance *is* losses—dollars of payment for unfortunate happenings. Not all "happenings" in the language of today's generation are losses, and not all losses are paid for by insurance—but many are.

Before you read this chapter, it is recommended that you first look back at Figure 4–1 to review the relationship of loss payment to all the other major functions of insurers. It is the purpose of this chapter to provide a broad picture of insurance in action, explaining *who* pays insurance losses and *how* they do so. Specific illustrations from three major fields of insurance show the scope of insurance losses and how *claims procedures* vary in fire, liability, and life insurance losses.

SIGNIFICANCE

The basic function of loss payment is commonly referred to as *insurance adjusting*. The term is not very satisfactory, but it has become well fixed in the business of insurance. It is hoped that some better term may be adopted in the future, for "adjustment" connotes something that

---

[1] Into a subcompact car, no doubt. The losses mentioned in the first paragraph of this page are among those noted in "Humor Found in Insurance Claims," *Columbus* (Ohio) *Dispatch*, April 8, 1977. To make things worse, or funnier at least, that person who landed in the bathtub told his story to the ambulance attendant, causing him to laugh so hard that he dropped the stretcher and broke both of the patient's wrists.

requires a compromise or change before settlement is reached. Since this is not always true, a better phrase might be *claims payment,* with the persons who do this work referred to as *claimspersons.* However, since the more common reference today is to adjusting and adjusters, these terms will be used frequently in this chapter. Insurance adjusting does have the same objective as the perhaps more accurate terms *loss payment* and *claims payment.* A loss, a claim, and an adjustment may logically be three different amounts, though here the term *adjustment* is used to mean the final insurance payment by the insurer.

Loss payments are a daily part of the routine of the insurance business. Thousands of loss checks are delivered to insureds every day—for automobile accidents, hospital expenses, burglaries, explosions, deaths, and occupational injuries. Sometimes the routine becomes the spectacular, and losses such as Hurricane Frederic in 1979 can affect hundreds of thousands of persons. That loss was the largest national disaster for insurance ever to occur in the United States. Its almost 1 million claims and $750 million of insured losses were seven times the damage done by the San Francisco earthquake in the early 1900s. Single-building fires can sometimes be amazingly large, too, as was shown in the more than $100 million losses for the MGM Grand Hotel in Las Vegas in 1980. Tornados,[2] floods, explosions, and other natural catastrophes also destroy property values and cause deaths or injuries. Many large losses attributable to human failures may result in multi-million-dollar liability lawsuits, too.

The repayment for the values which have been lost is often the point at which policyholders have the strongest possible realization of why they purchased insurance contracts. Up to that time they may have had a feeling that there were a number of vague reasons why they purchased the protection. When they actually receive a loss check which makes it possible for them to rebuild their homes or replace their automobiles, they have specific and tangible knowledge of why they needed the insurance. They may often wonder what they would have done if they lacked the proper insurance coverage. Other times, they may merely wish that they had the foresight to have bought insurance before losses occurred.

PURPOSES

Insureds who have honestly suffered loss or damage need approach the insurance company in no apologetic frame of mind. The claim settlement which they ask for is theirs by right of purchase. It should be

---

[2] For a detailed study of "Insurance Copes with Catastrophe: The Xenia Tornado," by the Columbus chapter of CPCU, see the *CPCU Annals* (now *Journal*) 29, no. 20 (June 1976).

the objective of both insurers and insureds to arrive at a fair and equitable measure of the loss. There will frequently be areas of disagreement. With both parties resolved to reach an equitable adjustment, disagreements are usually readily reconciled.[3]

Insurance adjusters today are an important contact between the insurer and the policyholder. It is incumbent upon them to deliver the goods which the agent has sold. The insurance business recognizes that years of insurance programming and planning will come to nothing if the insured is faced with difficulty following a loss. New adjusters are taught that it is their function to settle claims equitably and not, as is sometimes believed, for the least sum to which they can get insureds to agree. Adjusters are further instructed, when insureds do not know what is due them under their contracts, to take steps to explain what amounts should be included in their claims. By the same token, in the interest of equity in the business, adjusters are trained to recognize sharp practices and to resist padded claims or fraudulent demands. Fairness to the uninformed *and* resistance to wrongful claims are for the benefit of both the insurance business and the insureds, who in the long run must pay rates based upon loss experience.

From the point of view of the insurer, claims adjustments afford an attractive area of competition, especially in types of insurance where premium rates are relatively similar and price competition is a minor factor. Although only a minority of all insureds have a loss in a given year, the reputation of the insurer rests not only on how satisfied the claimants are but also on how many other persons the claimants tell about their losses and payments. Ironically, dissatisfied policyholders will tell *everyone* why they believe they were unfairly treated, whereas satisfied claimants will take their payment as a matter of course. If the insurer fails in effecting a prompt and equitable adjustment following loss, it will have failed in the most crucial of all competitive areas.

This is not to say that there should be competition among insurers by overpayment of claims, which only results in higher insurance costs for all. There is no one who recognizes prompt services and sound practices with respect to the settlement of claims more readily than does the agent or broker. If independent agents become dissatisfied with the adjustment practices of a company, they will direct their business to other insurers. Exclusive agents cannot change their business to another insurer, but because of the sizable business they write they can effectively criticize their insurer if it is being unfair or too reluctant in paying just claims. Likewise, experienced insurance buyers soon learn the reputation of insurers with regard to claim service.

---

[3] See Willis Rokes, *Human Relations in Handling Insurance Claims* (Homewood, Ill.: Richard D. Irwin, 1981).

Loss adjustments are set in motion when insureds file notices of loss with their insurers. The adjustment is the means for accomplishing the ultimate aim of insurance. Claims are filed under only comparatively few of the many thousands of insurance policies written. It is the purpose of the adjustment to determine the question of liability for a given loss and to reach an agreement with respect to the loss or damage payable under the insurance contract. In paying losses, adjusters have been advised to follow the "4–F rules"—be *fair, frank, friendly,* and *firm.*

INSURANCE ADJUSTERS: TYPES AND ORGANIZATION

Since insurance policies are contracts, the terms and conditions are carefully stated so that in the event of losses insureds have their contracts to follow in effecting an adjustment. As a matter of practice, a company representative approaches the insured, and if investigation shows the loss to be legitimate, a settlement is attempted, sparing the insured as much technical detail as possible. All such persons who aid in the loss payment are termed *claimspersons,* or in more common language, *adjusters.* It has been said that "insurance adjusters are not well liked because they *hold* all the money." Perhaps, however, they *should* be popular precisely because they *pass out* all the money! Adjusters fall into five categories: (1) agents as adjusters, (2) staff adjusters, (3) independent adjusters, (4) adjustment bureaus, and (5) public adjusters. The relationship of these five types of adjusters is illustrated in Figure 27–1.

Figure 27–1. Insurance adjusters*

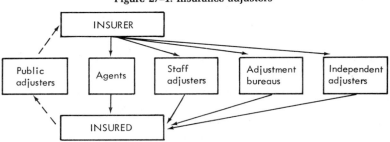

* A special type of adjuster is also noted for marine insurance, in Chapter 15.

Agents as adjusters

It is common sense on the part of the insurer to allow the agent whenever possible to pay the smaller losses to the policyholder. After all, the agent is usually closest to the client, is familiar with the insurance contracts which the insured has, and normally has the earliest facts on the occurrence of the loss. The agent has, too, a prime interest in seeing that the consumer receives prompt and fair treatment in the loss payment. Satisfaction of the policyholder is important to the agent in terms of goodwill and continued business with the insured and his or her friends.

In *property* insurance many agents have the authority of their companies to settle a claim with the policyholder immediately. For smaller and uncomplicated losses this is the most expedient and efficient way to pay claims. For example, local agents may be given permission by their companies to settle all losses of certain kinds up to a stated dollar amount. For a new agent or a small agent this authority may only extend up to $100. For larger and more seasoned agents the authority may extend to $500 or more, and in addition agents may be given responsibility for actually issuing checks in the name of their companies. The custody of such a checkbook, of course, must be carefully controlled by the company. An abnormal number of losses would occasion a review by the insurer to be sure that the agent was not being overly liberal in paying claims. For agents it is a valuable right which enables them to render prompt service to their policyholders with a minimum of paperwork. Some of the kinds of losses where this practice is common are fire, windstorm, medical payments under home and automobile contracts, and automobile collision and miscellaneous damage (to the insured's car).

In larger losses or losses which involve more complex adjusting methods, such as in *liability* insurance, it is necessary to provide specialized help to the agent and the insured. One of the four other types of adjusters will be used in such cases. This is reasonable because it is the duty of the insurer to see that losses are equitably paid. An agent with little legal background should not be permitted to attempt to settle liability claims, nor should one with little experience in adjusting an infrequent business interruption loss be given sole authority to determine the company's liability and amount of loss payment. The funds for loss payment are the prime responsibility of the insurer. A wrongful claim payment would be improper for the insurer, for the agent, for the policyholder, and for other policyholders whose rates may be raised in the future by careless or exaggerated claims payment.

In *life* insurance the agent is often directly involved in loss payment. The claims procedure for smaller contracts is a simple one—notice to the company and a death certificate are often all that is required before the policy amount can be paid. The life agent usually forwards the death notice and certificate to the insurer, and the check is issued by the company for delivery to the policyholder's beneficiary by the agent. Life insurers do not have the problem of determining the extent of loss payment that is common in property insurance losses, for the contract itself states the amount to be paid upon loss. An exception would be the extra payments for accidental death, which require legal investigation and definition in some cases. For the larger policies, various installment payment options in place of a lump-sum cash payment may need to be explained by the agent. In health insurance loss payments, agents may often use special personnel from the claims departments of their insurers.

One of the most rewarding feelings for an agent is the personal satisfaction received as a result of actually seeing "insurance in action." It may be the disabled husband thanking the agent for having included disability income protection in health insurance which provides the family with steady income during a long period in which he cannot work. Or perhaps it's a dream home that can be built again on the ashes of a fire that otherwise would have caused the loss of a lifetime of savings. Many life insurance agents can point with quiet pride to families whose sons and daughters have grown up to attend college without financial hardship in spite of the unexpected early death of family breadwinners. Because agents see firsthand the value of insurance in such circumstances, the almost missionary zeal of some agents can be understood—and appreciated. This aspect of an agent's work—being able to see the results of a job well done—can make it one of the most satisfying of all careers.

Staff adjusters

The contact between local agents of property-liability insurers and the home office is maintained through special agents or state agents who sometimes may, as part of their duties, help with loss adjustments. Other insurer representatives who make adjustments are known as company or *staff adjusters*. In the casualty field in particular, they are usually employees who devote their entire time to loss settlements. Automobile claims lend themselves to the services of staff adjusters since in most instances only one insurer is concerned with such claims. Also, the volume of claims is such that companies have found it to their advantage to maintain claims offices staffed by specialists in the various lines they write. Some automobile insurers in larger cities maintain "drive-in" claims locations where immediate estimates and payments for damages are made.

The use of staff adjusters depends on the volume and kinds of business written in the territory in which the loss occurs. To support a full-time staff adjuster in a given area the insurer must have enough claims to be adjusted. Some companies use staff adjusters almost exclusively, while others are more apt to use the services of the other types of adjusters available.

Independent adjusters

Independent adjusters are experts who have made loss adjusting a business. Some have specialized in particular fields. Others possess a general knowledge and undersanding of adjustment procedure and handle losses whenever it is impossible or inconvenient for the staff or other types of adjusters to do so. Some independent adjusters operate as individuals within a limited area; others have built up sizable organizations and extend their operations on a regional or national basis. For example, Crawford and Company (Atlanta) has more than 3,000 employees and 500 branch offices. Several thousand independent adjusters are members of the National Association of Indpendent Insurance Adjusters. Its members are encouraged to participate in the educational program of the Insurance Institute of America leading toward professional examinations for the Associate in Claims (AIC) designation.

Independent adjusters work for the insurers who request their services. A typical use would be in automobile insurance where the insurer has only a small volume of business in a given area or where the policyholder has an accident while traveling there. It would be expensive and inefficient to send a staff adjuster from the home or branch office to settle the occasional claim which occurs in such areas. Instead, the insurer hires an independent adjuster to do the job. The independent adjuster often builds up a continuing working relationship with particular insurers, in addition to accepting infrequent adjusting assignments from a larger number of insurers. The tremendous variety of claims and the goal of reaching loss payments equitable to both insurer and insured make the career of an independent adjuster a challenging one.

Adjustment bureaus

Very important in all fields of claim adjustment except life insurance are the *adjustment bureaus*. These are separate corporations, not insurers, whose sole business is claim adjustment. Bureau adjusters are highly trained and experienced employees who devote their entire time to adjusting losses. Insurers look with favor upon the trend toward bureau adjustment, feeling that it tends toward an equitable treatment of all insureds and is particularly efficient when several insurers are involved in the same loss. Bureau adjusters aim to effect prompt and satisfactory adjustments with a minimum of controversy or litigation; on the other hand, they are equipped to cope with fraud or false claims.

One of the largest and best-known adjustment bureaus is the GAB Business Services, Inc., which is very active in settling fire and windstorm losses, automobile physical damage, and other types of claims and services. The organization has a national headquarters in New York City and regional offices in New York, Atlanta, Dallas, Chicago, and San Francisco. Annually over 1 million losses are adjusted with less than 1 in 100,000 going to court. GAB Business Services has 650 branch offices with about 3,500 employees. One other large organization, the Underwriters Adjustment Company, has headquarters in Chicago and provides adjustment facilities for 13 states in the Midwest. Such large-scale adjustment bureaus are especially important in coordinating loss adjusters for the tremendous burden of thousands of claims within a few days after a major disaster. With the increasing frequency of southeastern windstorms in the early autumn, GAB sometimes has even sent hundreds of adjusters to the Southeast in advance of the actual storms.

Public adjusters

As the name implies, *public adjusters* represent the public, in contrast to the adjusters who represent insurers. The public adjuster is retained *by the insured* to negotiate the loss settlement. (Note the direction of the arrows in Figure 27–1.) Public adjusters offer their services, usually on a fee basis, using their expert insurance knowledge in estimating damages and effecting loss settlements. It is sometimes assumed that a staff adjuster is biased and will make borderline decisions to the advantage of the insurer. Such situations are the exception, for most insurers strive toward fair loss payments. Insureds who feel inadequate to approach such a problem of adjustment without assistance in representing their interests can turn the loss over to a public adjuster. Sometimes attorneys will be retained by the insured to perform a similar function.

In some states public adjusters are required to obtain a license from the insurance department of the state. An examination may be required, and the state licensing authority exercises control to ascertain that the practices of the adjusters are on an ethical basis. One reason why this is important is that public adjusters acts as agents for the insureds within the scope of their employment. If the public adjuster perpetrates a fraud in an attempt to get a generous adjustment then the policy is voided quite as much as if the fraud were perpetrated by the insured. To permit any other holding regarding the operations of a public adjuster would open wide the door to fraud. All that would be necessary to perpetrate a fraud upon the insurer would be the insured's complete delegation of the responsibility for adjusting a loss to a public adjuster whose acts might be later disavowed.

CLAIMS PROCEDURES

A general insurance text cannot give consideration to all the aspects of claims and adjustment procedures for all types of insurance. The following major types of claims will be discussed here: (1) fire, (2) liability, and (3) life. The examples are selected because of the significant differences of one class from the others and because of the importance of these three types of insurance to the average insurer purchaser. The student will also find other claims procedures discussed in sections of earlier chapters. For example, the chapters on transportation insurance, workers' compensation, automobile insurance, and health insurance will provide additional contrasts for the study of claims methods.

Fire insurance losses

Rights and conditions. The fire insurance contract imposes definite conditions upon the insured immediately upon the occurrence of a loss. (See Chapter 13 for specific contract wording on "loss provisions.") All of the post-loss provisions are conditions on the insured, rather than duties or obligations. However, the insurer may deny loss payment if these conditions are not met.

The purpose of *notice of loss* to the insurer is so that the insurer may take whatever steps it deems necessary to investigate the loss. The policy specifies "immediate" written notice, but usually companies waive this provision and proceed with the adjustment after the insured notifies the agent in any manner. What constitutes immediate notice is dependent upon the circumstances surrounding each case. The insured should exercise due diligence and forward the notice without unnecessary delay, usually the day the loss occurs, or at least the following day. In one case, the policy was in a safe in the building that was burned and could not be obtained until 53 days after the fire; yet the notice was held sufficient. In another case, a notice given 14 days after a fire, unaccompanied by any circumstance excusing the delay, was held not to be immediate notice, and payment was denied. The penalty to the insured for lack of proper notice is severe, for the insurer can treat the contract as voidable on the ground that the insured has failed to meet an important condition of the policy.

The submission by the insured of a *proof of loss* is the second condition for loss payment. This document is a signed statement in regard to the *property*, the *loss*, and the *insurance*. It includes information as to the knowledge and belief of the insured as to the time and origin of the fire, title to the property, the cash value of each item and the amount of loss, loans outstanding, other insurance, and the like. The proof of loss, unless waived, should be furnished to the insurer or its agent within 60 days after the termination of the fire. Blank forms designed to meet the requirements of the insurer are often used. *Values* are a point of the utmost importance to all parties to the contract. Proving the loss rests upon the insured, and this requires the ability to demonstrate the values of the property and the loss. The insurer is usually obligated to indemnify the insured to the extent of the *actual cash value* of the property destroyed or damaged, with deductions for depreciation. However, some policies may pay full *replacement cost* including depreciation.

A limit is fixed by the cost of repairing or replacing the destroyed or damaged property within a reasonable time with material of like kind and quality.

A misconception of some insureds is that after a fire the damaged property should not be touched until it is examined by the adjusters. Insureds are under no obligation to leave the property undisturbed; on the contrary, they should do everything reasonable to *prevent further damage.* Insureds who fail to protect their property adequately from further loss after a fire cannot collect for the additional loss thus occasioned. For example, they may need to dry machinery to prevent rusting, board up windows, or provide temporary roof repairs to avoid further damage to the contents of a building.

The insured should make a complete *inventory* stating the quantity and cost of each article and the amount claimed as a loss. If the goods destroyed have an established open-market value, the quotations on the day of the fire (considering freight charges and discounts) form the basis of the valuation for adjustment purposes. In the case of a manufacturer, the production or acquisition cost serves as a basis. It is the insured's job to prepare the inventory, although the agent or adjuster often gives advice or helps in other ways to see that the inventory is complete.

In the event that an agreement on values lost cannot be reached, provision is made in the policy for an *appraisal procedure* which either party may demand. Many adjusters who have spent a lifetime in adjusting have never had a loss go to appraisal, but the procedure is still of potential value where an honest difference of opinion exists. The insurer and the insured each select an appraiser, and these two appraisers select a third appraiser. Awards signed by two or three of the appraisers determine the amount of the loss. Neither party can appeal from that decision, except on the ground of fraud, mistake, or willful misconduct on the part of the appraisers.

Besides appraisal, when insureds have complied with all the conditions of their policies and still fail to effect a settlement, they may have recourse to *lawsuit* in the courts. In order that questions of liability may not accumulate against insurers indefinitely, the usual policy provides that "no suit or action on this policy, for the recovery of any claim, shall be sustainable in any court of law or equity unless commenced within twelve months next after the fire."

The fire insurance contract provides for two *options of settlement by the company:* (1) replacing or restoring the subject matter of the insurance to its former condition, or (2) taking all or any part of the property at the agreed or appraised value. If a company feels that it may rebuild the damaged property with like kind and quality at less cost than would be required to make a payment for damages, it may elect to do so. The option to repair or replace involves the insurer in the business of repairs or construction, and when at all possible, insurers prefer to settle losses by a cash payment. Under the second option the insurer may sometimes settle a loss by taking all or part of the property and paying its agreed or appraised value to the insured. This method is fairly common for damaged merchandise property, which the insurer turns over to a professional *salvage* company to be sold. The amount realized is credited to the insurers, who, in turn, pay the insured a total loss. However, the insured has no right to ask the insurer to take the property and salvage it. The policy specifically says that there can be no abandonment of the property by the insured to the insurer. Several salvage companies have repair facilities for drying, airing, sorting, and auctioning goods damaged by fire, smoke, or water. An example is the Underwriters Salvage Company of New York, with offices in more than 20 major cities.

Special problems. In the event of a *total loss of merchandise in a business*, a physical inventory is, of course, impossible. The value of the destroyed property must be determined by the books and accounts of the insured. If the books are properly kept and inventories are accurately taken at stated periods, it is comparatively simple to compute the value of goods on hand at the time of the fire. To accomplish this, one must take an inventory as a starting point, add to this purchases made, and deduct sales. Since purchases are recorded on the basis of cost and sales income is recorded on the basis of selling price, it is essential to reduce the item of income from sales to a figure that will represent the cost of the items sold. In the following example, sales of $900,000 are divided by 1.50 (assuming a mark-up of 50 percent in order to calculate the $600,000 cost of goods sold.

Inventory calculation for statement of loss

Inventory of stock on hand at beginning of year (cost)		$1,000,000
Adjustment for depreciation		40,000
Actual value of stock at beginning of year		$ 960,000
Subsequent purchases		500,000
Total goods to be accounted for		$1,460,000
Sales	$900,000	
Less profit at 50% mark-up	$300,000	
Cost of goods sold (sales ÷ 1.50) $600,000 Deduct		$ 600,000
Value of stock on hand at time of fire		$ 860,000

The problem of determining value and loss or damage is more difficult for *buildings* or *machinery*. Because such fixed assets are designed for use over a long period of years, the problems of depreciation and obsolescence become factors of major importance. In relation to a fixed asset, *depreciation* has been defined as the inevitable decrease in value resulting from wear, tear, and the lapse of time. When the decrease in value is the outgrowth of market changes in the demand for or usefulness of the property, the loss is due to *obsolescence.* Arbitrary accounting chargeoffs on the straight-line basis often are not or do not attempt to be an accurate measure of the value. A property built during a period of low construction costs might actually be growing *more* valuable each year as building costs advance; yet a straight-line depreciation of some arbitrary percentage, say 5 percent, would furnish a book value of less than cost. The actual value would be greater than cost in this case.

In recent years, the availability and use of *replacement value coverage,* particularly for buildings, has grown rapidly. For buildings not more than 20 or 30 years old, insurers will today often write insurance that will pay full replacement cost without any deduction for depreciation. This avoids any problems of estimating depreciation to be subtracted in the loss payment. Insurance consumers should consider this coverage when it is available. Many insurers are also beginning to offer such coverage for insurance on contents and personal property.

Because of the difficulties involved in fixing a building value, a satisfactory and competent *appraisal* (an expert estimate of valuation—not the loss appraisal procedure mentioned earlier) may be needed. For any building of substantial value, an appraisal made by a reputable appraisal firm is a cost which the insured should be willing to accept in return for its importance in the event of a serious loss. The American Appraisal Company is an example of a company providing specialized appraisal services. For smaller buildings, the agent or insurer may help the insured without separate cost to appraise the value of the property. Values may be brought up to date with a table of price indexes for various types of construction, such as brick, frame, or steel.[4]

When an adequate appraisal of buildings has been made by competent appraisers and has subsequently been kept up to date, the problem of valuation is not a difficult one. Even when there is a *total loss* and no appraisal has been made, blueprints, photographs, or building permits will generally help to fix the date of construction, the estimated depreciation, and the replacement cost. Several methods are used for fixing value when neither appraisal nor plans are available as a guide: the "discount method," based upon computing future earnings of the building on the basis of past experience, and the "square-foot method," based upon the estimated cost of other buildings of like construction. In the event of *partial loss* to a building, the customary procedure is to obtain from a reliable contractor or builder an estimate of the cost to repair and replace the damaged property. Frequently, a builder representing the insured and another representing the insurer work together in making the estimate of loss.

---

[4] A useful compilation describing various price indexes and their sources is *Catalog of Indices* (Bethesda, Md.: All-Industry Research Advisory Council, March 1982).

Several other special problems of fire insurance losses are discussed in Chapter 13.[5] Special limitations on the insurer's liability are treated there, including the important problems of *contribution and apportionment* (where several contracts insure the same property), *coinsurance* requirements (to encourage insurance amounts reasonably close to total values of the property), and *nonconcurrence* (which involves conflicting provisions in different policies).

Liability insurance losses

Differences from other losses. The adjustment of liability claims differs from the adjustment of property insurance claims in that the *claimant is not the insured.* In representing the insurer, the adjuster is usually dealing with a "third party," not a customer of the insurer.

A liability claim carries with it a basic element of conflict with respect to the claim because one person has caused someone else either (1) property damages or (2) personal injuries. Mental attitudes frequently intensify the degree of conflict. Different individuals have different approaches and attitudes toward a given situation. The owner of a new Cadillac might want a scratch on a fender to be removed at considerable expense. To another individual such a scratch is incidental, and that person would neither spend a substantial sum to repair the scratch nor expect an insurer to do so. Finally, a difference in the attitude of a claimant from that of a defendant regarding the extent of a personal injury is natural. Persons injured in accidents tend to exaggerate the nature and extent of the injury, while it is natural for the defendant to discount or minimize its importance.

Property damages. The extent of a claim for *damage to property* is measured by the amount of the loss occasioned the property owner. The measure of loss is the difference in value between the property undamaged and the property in its damaged condition. While the *cost of repair* may serve as a measure of damage, there is no obligation to restore a property to its original condition if the cost for repair exceeds the value of the property before the damage. For example, an old automobile virtually demolished is worth a claim only for the value of the car before the accident, less its salvage value.(A few new policies that provide full repair or replacement costs are exceptions to this statement.)

Property damage liability claims must be differentiated from direct-loss insurance claims. A fire claim, for example, usually includes only

---

[5] Further details of property loss adjustments can be studied in Paul I. Thomas, *How to Estimate Building Losses and Construction Costs* (Englewood Cliffs, N.J.: Prentice-Hall, 1976); and Paul I. Thomas and Prentiss B. Reed, *Adjustment of Property Losses* (New York: McGraw-Hill, 1977).

payment for the direct damage to the property unless additional coverage is purchased to provide for the indirect results of the loss of use of the property, such as loss of profits or rents. In property damage liability claims, however, the *loss of use* may be included. The rental cost of a similar automobile, for instance, would be included in a liability claim against the person causing damage serious enough to prevent the use of an automobile for some time.

Personal injuries. Determining an adequate amount of compensation for a *personal injury* is not a simple process.[6] This statement is supported by the number of verdicts in widely different amounts for seemingly identical injuries. In no other area of loss adjustment will the measure of damages be influenced to such a large degree by the fallibilities and prejudices that are characteristic of human nature. The difficulties increase when a jury or a judge attempts to assign a monetary value to a severe personal injury. A disabling injury is a more severe financial loss to a wage earner than to a housewife. Who can measure the loss of the housewife's love and care of small children? Who will differentiate with respect to the amount of pain suffered? What impact will social position, financial circumstances, and reputation of the claimant have upon the amount of the settlement? Finally, what will be the effect of the ability, resourcefulness, forensic talents, and persuasiveness of the claimant's attorney if the case goes to trial? All of these factors must be weighed by the adjuster in an attempt to reach a settlement that can be conscientiously recommended to the insurer.

Some liability contracts use the words *bodily injury* instead of *personal injury*. These terms are not identical in the coverage they may provide. The broader coverage is personal injury, which may also include other types of harm, such as psychic trauma without any actual physical injury. Personal injuries were also seen in Chapter 17 to encompass claims for libel, slander, wrongful detention, invasion of privacy, and other actions.

Minor injuries that involve primarily a loss of time are not too difficult to handle. The same is true with respect to medical bills and hospital expenses, if any. The area of uncertainty in such cases involves suffering and inconvenience. These cases are settled on the basis of consideration given to income lost or expected to be lost because of the injury, the age of the injured person, the number of dependents, the amount of medical care expense, the nature of the injury, and the extent of pain suffered. For a person suffering from a broken leg, for example, medical expenses and income lost, plus a settlement for suffering, are the usual measures of damages.

---

[6] Many legal references would indicate this difficulty, and authors have written many pages on the subject. For example, see James H. Donaldson, *Casualty Claim Practice* (Homewood, Ill.: Richard D. Irwin, 1976).

The situation is quite different with more serious injuries. In the case of fatality some states limit recovery by statute. Where there is a statutory limitation for death, the law may specify "instantaneous death." If the injured party is not killed instantaneously, claim may be made for an additional amount for medical expenses, for loss of wages before death, and for "conscious suffering," depending upon the magnitude of the injury and the length of time. When the injured party lives and suffers permanent injury, the problem of damages becomes increasingly complex. In some low-verdict areas the judgments vary substantially from those of high-verdict areas.

In recent years, many insurers have adopted procedures to reduce the time and cost of settling personal injury cases. One such method is to make an "advance payment" to the claimant in situations where liability is quite evident. The amount is deducted from the final settlement. This method has the advantage of lessening financial hardship to the injured claimant and his or her family and of permitting the best medical and rehabilitation treatment immediately. It also enables better relations to be maintained between the claimant and the insurer during the sometimes long period of several years before final settlement,

Steps in the claim process. Following an occurrence that may involve a liability claim, *notice* should be given the insurance company "as soon as practicable," whether insureds feel themselves to be liable or not. Insurers have printed forms indicating the nature of the data the insured will be expected to acquire. Whether or not injured persons received first aid or medical attention and the name of the attending physician and hospital should appear in the report. The name and address of the car owners, drivers, and witnesses are required. It is important to note the exact location of the accident and weather conditions. A detailed sketch should show the relative positions of the cars just before and after the collision. In complying with the state requirements for reporting accidents, insureds should make duplicate copies of any written forms or reports and hold them for the insurance adjuster.

Liability policies vest much control of claims and litigation arising out of them with the insurer. The insurer is entitled to the prompt notice previously noted "so that it can *control* a claim: attempt an early settlement . . . contact witnesses . . . take statements, etc."[7] In very clear language it is provided that the insured shall not admit or voluntarily assume any liability, offer to settle any claim, or incur any expense without the written consent of the insurer. Although insureds may believe themselves to be liable, the interpretation of the law may be different than they think. An admission of liability by insureds can jeopardize

---

[7] "Reporting Requirements: For Losses . . . Claims . . . Occurrences," *John Liner Letter* 19, no. 12 (November 1982), p. 1.

both insurers' right of "subrogation" against others and protection under the policy for the insureds. Basic control of settlement should remain with the party that has the most effective legal resources and that is to pay the indemnity—namely, the insurer.

When the report of an accident involving a claim reaches the insurer and coverage is verified, company representatives will conduct an *investigation* to determine whether there was, in fact, negligence and whether the negligence was the proximate cause of the damage. A police report, if available, will be obtained. All pertinent facts are secured promptly from the insured, and then contact with claimants is made immediately. Witnesses are interviewed, and oftentimes written or taped statements are taken. A factual statement in simple, straightforward terms is the goal.[8]

The *summary report* prepared by the adjuster will contain all pertinent information and reach a conclusion as to liability. It will then appraise the nature of the injuries or property damage. In the case of personal injuries a settlement value is assigned in an amount which in the adjuster's opinion would be a proper settlement from the point of view of the insurer and the insured. Such an evaluation establishes a reasonable figure that would enable payment without suit. Any points that will help to bring the case to a conclusion, such as the attitude of the claimants or their attorneys, are mentioned.

Although the insurer controls an adjustment in any offer of compromise, the insurer is obligated to defend any suit against the insured with respect to the perils covered, even if such suit is groundless, false, or fraudulent. The insurer may elect to effect a settlement within the policy limits; otherwise it must assume the defense of the insured. A serious question occasionally develops when the insurer receives an *offer to settle within the policy limits* from the claimant. The position of the insurer becomes a precarious one when it refuses such an offer of settlement and elects to go to trial. If a judgment is then awarded against the insured in an amount in excess of the policy limits, the insured may claim that the insurer should pay the full amount of the trial award. If the conduct of the insurer is such that the insured suffers (1) because of *negligence* or (2) *bad faith,* then the insurer may be held liable for the full verdict without regard to policy limits. The insurer cannot abandon or neglect a defense or deliberately settle a claim in its own interest at the expense of the insured except at its own peril. On the other hand,

---

[8] Here are a few classic examples of policyholder statements that fell short of this objective: "To avoid a collision, I ran into the other car"; "I collided with a stationary bus coming the other way"; "I consider that neither vehicle was to blame, but if either was to blame, it was the other one"; and "I bumped into a lamppost which was obscured by a pedestrian."

the insurer should, and can, resist any settlement that it feels is excessive or fraudulent.

Following an accident that results in a claim for damages, the responsibility of the insureds does not cease when they turn the adjustment over to the insurer. The *cooperation clause* obligates the insured to render full assistance in the settlement or adjustment of a suit. The clause is held to be a material condition, and if the insured fails to comply with its requirements, the contract may be voidable. Insureds may feel sorry for the claimant. However, any willful obstruction on the part of insureds to the defense of the insurer violates the cooperation clause. Insureds must give full and truthful accounts of all the circumstances, and they must attend court and testify to these facts as witnesses if requested to do so.

When liability has been established and a value placed on a claim, insurers prefer to make a prompt *settlement*. Although an adjuster may refuse a claim that is unreasonable, litigation is avoided if possible. Nothing is to be gained by bringing a case to trial that can be settled reasonably in any other way, and the nearer a case comes to litigation, the more expensive it becomes. In many cases the fees of the plaintiff's attorney are a percentage of the settlement. Thirty percent or more is very common. Court costs, assessed by the court on either or both parties, may be in addition to this figure. Most cases, therefore, are settled as a result of negotiations between the claimant and the insurance adjuster. For an increasing number of claims, *arbitration* may be used to settle losses under a few thousand dollars.

Where there is definite liability and the amount of the claim does not seem to be too excessive, the insurer may elect to pay rather than assume the uncertainties of litigation and additional costs. There are other situations in which liability is doubtful and the insurer may be able to defeat the claimant's suit against the insured. If a case of this kind can be settled for a reasonable sum, the insurer may prefer to close the case with such a settlement. Finally, there are cases that on the basis of the insurer's investigation would indicate no liability. However, because of the limitations of witnesses, the possibility of an unsympathetic jury or a persuasive opposing attorney, and the trend of verdicts in the jurisdiction, a reasonable settlement is to be preferred to the risk of an excessive trial verdict.

It is apparent that a loss may be settled at any one of several stages. The claims adjuster may settle following the investigation. Failure to settle may result in suit. After a suit is filed, the case may be settled before trial, sometimes "on the courthouse steps." If the case goes to trial, which only a few percent of all claims do, settlement will be based upon the verdict except where an appeal is entered. Every effort should be made, and usually is, to effect a satisfactory adjustment at the earliest possible stage of the claim.

Life insurance losses

The settlement of life claims is usually taken care of by the life insurance agent. Unlike other fields of insurance, for life insurance there is no specialized claims adjuster. The definiteness of the death peril and the amount of insurance payable make it possible for the agent to arrange for the payment from the insurer. In the unusual situation where a claim is questioned, the law and claims departments of the insurer will provide the necessary legal advice.

Life insurance in its simplest form pays a lump sum (called a "face value") upon the death of the insured. Technically, the life insurance policy does not provide for payment upon death but rather for payment upon submission of *proof of death* to the insurer. This notice may be given by a beneficiary or the legal representative of the insured. Many claims are paid within a few days or weeks.

Life insurance contracts provide that the policy shall be *incontestable* by the insurer after a certain designated period during the lifetime of the insured, usually two years. The clause gives the company time to investigate any factors bearing on the application, and at the same time it results in greater certainty to insured and beneficiary after the two-year period. In most cases the insurer is prevented from raising defenses later that would be hard for policyholders or their beneficiaries to disprove, such as those based upon misrepresentation or fraud. Misstatements of age are treated in a separate clause; the contract is not voidable in such cases, but is corrected to provide benefits for the true age of the insured.

In determining the liability of the insurer for a death claim under a life insurance policy, the question of whether or not the insured committed *suicide* may upon occasion become important. The policy provides for a return of premiums paid in the event of self-destruction within a period of a year or in some instances within two years. If suicide is suspected but cannot be proved, there is a presumption against it. This means that if the life insurance company contests the payment of a policy on the basis of suicide, it must establish the fact by a preponderance of evidence so that no other reasonable inference may be drawn from the circumstances.

In cases where policies provide that if the insured dies as a result of *accidental death,* double (or sometimes more) the face of the policy is to be paid the beneficiaries, proof must be submitted that the death was accidental. The question of accidental death is often surrounded by uncertainty, arising out of court decisions and the different wording of the various insurance contracts themselves.[9] Death by accidental means must usually be "independent of all other causes," with no liability if death is due directly or indirectly to disease or bodily or mental infirmities. The final resort for determination is a jury.

It is a simple matter if the policy provides for a distribution under lump-sum payment or one of the *settlement options*. If, however, the insured has not chosen a settlement option, then the beneficiary may choose the settlement option. The settlement of the claim will utilize the policy proceeds for cash, interest, installments, or life income payments, subject to the approval of the insurance company. Not only may options be combined, but the agreement may include the power to change from one option to another, the privilege of increasing or decreasing installment payments, and withdrawal privileges. In making these choices in a planned settlment option to minimize taxes and meet various needs, the life insurance agent can be of substantial service to the purchasers and beneficiaries of life insurance.

FOR REVIEW AND DISCUSSION

1. How would you describe the purposes which policyholder and insurer should have in effecting a loss payment under an insurance contract?

2. "Losses are the reason for insurance," says Percy Pessimist. "Perhaps true," says Oliver Optimist, "but that's not why I buy my insurance." With which of these persons would you side in an argument over the purposes of insurance, and why?

3. Who adjusts insurance losses? Why are different types of adjusters used in the various fields of insurance? Include reference to the major advantages of an insurer using different types of adjusters.

4. The agent's authority to settle losses directly with the insured varies greatly. What factors are involved in this disparity?

5. Mr. Rogers owns a warehouse in which musical instruments are stored. A fire occurs, burning a hole in the roof. He advises his employees to touch nothing until the adjusters arrive. Is this good advice? Explain.

6. In adjusting a fire insurance loss, it is usually necessary to determine "the actual cash value of the property at the time of loss." How is this done?

7. Compare the special problems of loss payment in fire, liability, and life insurance. Rank these three types of insurance in terms of the difficulty of loss adjustment, and explain your order of ranking.

8. Under the fire insurance contract, what should the insured do after a loss has occurred? Are the policy provisions "duties" or "conditions"?

---

[9] In *Landress* v. *Phoenix Mutual Life Insurance Company* (291 U.S. 491), Mr. Justice Cardozo referred to accident insurance law as the "Serbonium bog." The reference from Milton's *Paradise Lost* (book 2, line 592) reads, "A gulf profound as that Serbonium bog. Betwixt Domiata and Mount Casius old, Where armies whole have sunk."

9. Are valuation problems in a fire insurance loss different for buildings, merchandise, and other types of property? Explain how the insured can reduce these problems.

10. What options does an insurer have in settling a fire insurance loss? Explain any preferences that the insurer will usually have.

11. Why are loss payments under liability insurance contracts usually under the control of the insurer rather than the insured? Does this mean that the policyholder has nothing to do in regard to a liability claim?

12. X brought action against Y, an insured, for bodily injuries. X offered to settle for a sum that was within the policy limits of $50,000. The insurer refused the offer, allowed the case to go to trial, and the claimant obtained a verdict of $125,000. Why might the insurer be liable for the amount in excess of the policy limits?

13. Why are liability insurance losses, as opposed to property insurance losses, more difficult to settle? As opposed to life insurance losses?

14. Assume that your friend Carl has had an automobile accident. He believes he was responsible, but he does not want to tell his insurer about it because he has a good driving record. The accident only involved a dented fender and a few minor bumps to the occupants of the other car. (a) What advice and procedure do you recommend? (b) If Carl was injured but not at fault for the accident, what advice do you offer him?

15. The loss payment function of insurers is carried out by many different persons. Discuss the various career opportunities that adjusting losses may provide for college students.

Chapter 28

Outline of concepts

Insurance regulation, particularly regulation by the states, is more extensive than regulation for many other businesses.

Why insurance regulation is needed can be seen from its purpose of protecting the public and insureds in what is basically a *long-term, complex, future, financial promise* contract.

Methods of insurance regulation are *two:*

Self-regulation of insurance is considerable but sometimes ineffective.

Government regulation of insurance involves *three* types:

Government legislation, primarily *state laws,* is based upon Public Law 15 which followed the famous SEUA decision in 1944.

Administrative action is very important, with the *insurance commissioner* in each state exercising broad enforcement powers of licensing and examination of companies and agents in an *insurance department.*

Court action helps interpret the insurance laws or *codes.*

Kinds of insurance regulation by the states include the birth, life, and death of an insurer.

Formation and licensing of insurers require *incorporation,* meeting minimum *financial requirements,* and other standards.

Insurer operations are supervised as to—

Contracts and forms, with *basic wording* approval for some (but not all) kinds of insurance required by the state insurance department.

Rates are controlled to some extent in *fire* and *auto* insurance with much current discussion centering on some states changing from "prior approval" to "open competition" types of rate regulation.

Expense limitations are placed upon *life* insurance in some states.

Reserves are required: *legal* reserves for life insurance, and *unearned premium* and *loss* reserves for property-liability insurance.

Asset and surplus values are watched closely.

Investments are limited to the safest securities for most assets of life insurers; more lenient rules apply to property-liability insurers.

Agents' licensing and trade practices aim at qualified, honest, and fair treatment of policyholders.

Taxation of insurance is an important (about $4 billion) revenue producer for the states through a special *premium tax.*

Rehabilitation and liquidation of insurers are supervised carefully.

Some current regulatory issues include: *insurer guaranty funds, federal versus state regulation,* and *other issues.*

Insurance regulation

Regulation or deregulation: that is the question. To paraphrase Shakespeare, is it nobler to suffer the slings and arrows of outrageous controls, or to take action against a sea of troubles and by opposing end them? Insurers and regulators might well ponder the words in *Hamlet* in relation to the trend of the early 1980s toward less regulation in their heavily supervised business.

All forms of private enterprise have some regulation of their activities, either by self-imposed rules and customs or by specific regulations of government. Sometimes the government provides extensive controls, including almost every phase of the operations from creation to liquidation. At other times there is minimum government regulation, perhaps only for the purposes of providing necessary tax information. The purpose of this chapter is to explain *why* and *how* the business of insurance is regulated.

WHY INSURANCE REGULATION IS NEEDED

The general purpose of insurance regulation is to protect the public against insolvency or unfair treatment by insurers. From the state's viewpoint, regulation is also important as a revenue producer through state taxes on insurance premiums.

The insurance business is among the types of private enterprise subject to much government regulation. It is generally classed as a business which is "affected with a *public interest.*" This characteristic is the reason why many forms of government supervision[1] of insurance are deemed necessary. Although competition is an effective regulator for some businesses, in insurance *uncontrolled* competition would work a hardship upon the buyers of insurance, most of whom do not understand insurance contracts. Much of the insurance written is to protect third parties who have not participated in making the contracts. The value of the contracts depends upon the ability of the insurers to fulfill their promises to the

---

[1] Used here as a synonym for regulation, which is sometimes thought to have a stronger connotation of active direction.

public, sometimes many years after the issuance of a policy. Ability to carry out the provisions of contracts depends upon many factors, including the efficient operation of the insurer, the selection of satisfactory risks, the determination of proper premium rates, and the wise investment of adequate reserves. Consequently, the needed integrity and *long-range financial stability* of insurers place insurance in an area which has traditionally been considered appropriate for government regulation.

The question of how much regulation is necessary is a more difficult one. Insurance does not belong in the same class as banks and public utilities, which are examples of the most complete public regulation requirements. Many banks are subject to federal charters, whereas insurers are not.[2] Unlike insurance companies,[3] public utilities have close government control of their organization (under "certificates of necessity"), their complete rate schedules, and their maximum profit return in relation to invested capital. The extent of regulation of insurance is reviewed in succeeding sections of this chapter by descriptions of the major methods and kinds of insurance regulation.

METHODS OF INSURANCE REGULATION

The *state* government is undoubtedly most important in the regulation of insurance. Before considering this and other phases of government insurance regulation, however, it is logical to summarize the self-regulation of insurance.

Self-regulation of insurance

To the extent that a business provides adequate self-regulation, government regulation is often unnecessary, or at least diminished in some degree. In insurance it is not realistic to think that the entire job of regulation can be done by internal, as opposed to external, methods of supervision. However, cooperation by insurers to regulate themselves is permitted by law and is extensive.

There are many insurer and trade association groups that exercise considerable control or provide advice in regard to each of the major functions of insurance. For example, forms and rates for many fire, automobile, liability, and other types of insurance are filed by the Insurance

---

[2] Though such charters have been advocated for parts of the business, such as interstate life insurer charters on a voluntary basis and mandatory federal charters for auto insurance.

[3] All insurers are not technically "companies" or corporations, but the use here refers to all private insurers. *Social* insurance systems such as are discussed in Chapters 11 and 24 are closer to the concept of a public utility, and their regulation and administration are correspondingly more complete.

Services Office on behalf of individual member companies for approval
by the state insurance departments. This saves much duplication and
reduces costs. In claims administration, the adjustment bureaus handle
losses for insurers, so that several insurers involved in the same losses
do not need to provide separate loss investigation and payment services.
Many insurers cooperate with one another in coordinating loss prevention; examples include the Insurance Institute for Highway Safety, the
National Auto Theft Bureau, and the Insurance Crime Prevention Institute. Marketing activities are regulated by rules applying to members
of numerous organizations of insurance agents and brokers. Research
is enhanced by insurers' joint efforts in the Life Insurance Marketing
and Research Association and the Society of Insurance Research. Better
public relations and legislation are promoted by the American Council
of Life Insurance, the Insurance Information Institute, and the Risk
and Insurance Management Society.[4] In improving insurance education
and setting standards for professional courses and designations the following organizations are important: the American Academy of Actuaries,
the American College, the American Institute (and the related Insurance
Institute of America), the Life Office Management Association, and the
Life Underwriter Training Council. Teachers of insurance and other industry personnel exchange much valuable information through meetings
and publications of the American Risk and Insurance Association and
the Insurance Company Education Directors Society.

Many insurers and these types of organizations supply representatives
directly to industry committees that work in conjunction with government regulatory bodies to draft legislation, coordinate programs, and
improve both self-regulation and public regulation of insurance. For example, the National Association of Life Underwriters (NALU) has sponsored much legislation for implementation in state legislative bodies.
Extremely different methods and results may be found in particular
lines or classes of insurance, or in the various states. Self-regulation is
no panacea; it works extremely well in some parts of insurance, while
in others it is disappointingly ineffective. Difficult areas for self-regulation
include many aspects of insurance which are closely related to competition, such as regulation of production costs, commissions, advertising,
and rates.

In some foreign countries, such as England and the Netherlands, self-
regulation has worked well. So little government regulation exists in
England that this general comment has been heard: "In England, insurers may do anything, the only requirement being that they publicize

---

[4] Some organizations function in several types of self-regulation activities. RIMS, for
example, is active in education, research, public relations, and the promotion of legislation
on behalf of its members.

Figure 28–1. Methods of insurance regulation

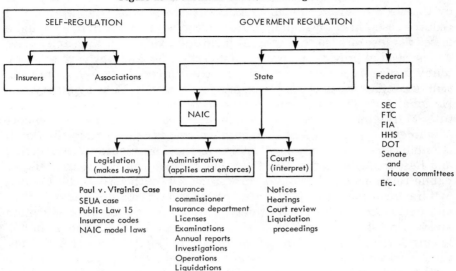

what they are doing!" Still, cooperative action of the insurers has succeeded in achieving high standards of financial solvency and fair treatment to policyholders. The reasons attributed to the excellent success
of self-regulation in England include the philosophy, attitudes, and traditions of English insurers, as well as their smaller number and size. Even
the Swiss, the epitome of democracy and freedom, have a proverb which
says: "Anything that is not prohibited ought at least to be regulated!"
Other countries, such as West Germany and the Scandinavian nations,
follow the strictest patterns of governmental regulation of insurance,
including approval procedures for most forms, commissions, and rates.
The United States seems to fall between the extremes. Self-regulation
is relied upon much more in the United States than in West Germany,
but much less than in England.

As a review of this section on self-regulation and as an introduction
to the next section on governmental regulation, see Figure 28–1, which
summarizes the methods of insurance regulation.

Government regulation of insurance

Three basic methods of providing insurance regulation are available
to government: (1) legislation, (2) administrative action, and (3) court
action. Corresponding to the three main branches of the government,
each of these methods is significant in the supervision of insurance. Legis-

lation is the foundation of insurance regulations, for it creates the insurance laws. The insurance laws of each state are often combined in what is known as an *insurance code*,[5] and these codes are of primary importance. Administrative action is also very important, as the application and enforcement of insurance laws are left in the hands of the insurance *superintendent or commissioner* in each state. Court action has great value in regulation because of its effect in providing detailed interpretations of troublesome parts of the law.

Government legislation. The regulation of the insurance business *by the states* was well established by the late 1800s and continues today as the predominant form of regulation. The practice is based upon a series of court decisions, and it has been continued in the face of some contention that because of the number of jurisdictions, insurance might better be regulated by the federal government. The classic case is *Paul* v. *Virginia*, in which the United States Supreme Court decided in 1868 that insurance "is *not* a transaction of commerce" and thus can be neither interstate commerce nor subject to federal regulation.[6] Until 1944, a period of 75 years, the Paul decision was upheld by the Supreme Court.

In 1941, complaints were made to the Department of Justice that certain insurance company practices were in violation of the Sherman Antitrust Act. As a result a momentous four-to-three decision was handed down in 1944 by the U.S. Supreme Court before one of its largest audiences in history. This case, *United States* v. *South-Eastern Underwriters Association et al.*,[7] now known to the legal profession and to the insurance business as the SEUA *case*, held that insurance *is* commerce. Thus, because of its interstate nature it would often be subject to federal regulation. As a matter of practice, because of delegation of authority by Congress, the regulation of the business of insurance remains a state function.

The specific delegation to the states of the power to regulate insurance occurred with the passage of *Public Law 15* in 1945.[8] Congress made the Sherman Act, the Clayton Act, and the Federal Trade Commission Act applicable to the business of insurance after January 1, 1948, "to

---

[5] The insurance code for an individual state may be bound in a volume which today often exceeds several hundred pages.

[6] Today it is difficult to rationalize such a decision, but in 1868 the now-famous decision stated: "Issuing a policy of insurance is not a transaction of commerce. They are not commodities to be shipped or forwarded from one state to another and then put up for sale. . . . Such contracts are not interstate transactions, though the parties may be domiciled in different states. They are, then, local transactions and are governed by local law" (*Paul* v. *Virginia*, 231 U.S. 495).

[7] 64 U.S. 1162.

[8] Also known as the McCarran-Ferguson Law, C 20, 79th Cong., 1st sess. For those students wishing to have an excuse for a birthday party in its honor, the law was passed on March 4, 1945. Members of the Ohio State University Alpha chapter of Gamma Iota Sigma (national insurance fraternity) did so in 1977.

the extent that such business is not regulated by state law." In other words, jurisdiction for regulating interstate insurance was left with the individual states as it had been for many years, but the important proviso was added that would permit the federal government to take over insurance regulation whenever the state regulation became inadequate.

Most cases indicate that federal jurisdiction will not usurp the states' powers as long as legislative action to provide insurance supervision has been taken.[9] Most states increased their insurance regulation heavily in laws passed as a result of the SEUA decision and Public Law 15, and they have continued their efforts to retain the power to supervise insurance. Investigations totaling thousands of pages of testimony have been carried out by the Senate Antitrust and Monopoly Subcommittee. Alleged inadequacies in state insurance laws have been pointed out, but federal legislation has not taken over any significant part of state regulation of insurance. Targets for Senate and House investigations have been automobile insurance (particularly substandard or high-risk insurers), the credit life insurance field, and insurance activities of bank holding companies, insurer solvency funds, product liability, and automobile no-fault plans.

Thus, the development of insurance regulation by the states has had a colorful history. Interesting details on some of its other landmarks, such as the Armstrong Investigation of 1905, the Merritt Committee Investigation of 1911, the Temporary National Economic Committee studies in 1939–41, and investigations of health insurance practices in 1910 and 1951–58, are contained in other volumes.[10]

In summary, the regulation of insurance by governmental legislation has been found to be almost completely a matter of insurance laws passed by the individual states. The state insurance codes have the distinct disadvantage of lacking uniformity. The critics of state regulation emphasize the duplication, complexity, and inefficiency that may result from nonuniformity. With increasing mobility, more uniformity of state laws is needed. The taxes and fees (see later section on taxation) paid by insurers to the states in the annual amount of nearly $4 *billion* in 1982 are stark evidence of the stakes involved. Legal precedent to date has firmly established for the individual states the regulatory responsibility for insurance and its benefits in tax revenue. (See later section of this chapter on regulatory issues.)

---

[9] *FTC* v. *National Casualty Company* (1958) and *FTC* v. *Travelers Health Association* (1959). The first serious effort in many years to advocate a repeal of the McCarran-Ferguson Law occurred in 1977, with hearings conducted by the House Judiciary Committee.

[10] Including appendix I of the classic reference: Edwin W. Patterson, *The Insurance Commissioner in the United States* (Cambridge, Mass.: Harvard University Press, 1927).

Administrative action. The broad powers which the *insurance commissioner*[11] of each state possesses are the key to the enforcement of insurance laws by the states. The administrative powers of the commissioners are derived from statutes which create the office. Usually these statutes are not very detailed in defining the authority and responsibility of the commissioner. The thousands of bills and laws that today concern insurance matters and the general increased reliance on administrative law have made the position of commissioner increasingly important in state government. The commissioner's wide authority extends from the licensing of insurers and agents to requiring annual reports from the insurers to approving forms and rates (in some but not all lines of insurance) and investigating complaints of many kinds.

In most states the insurance commissioner is *appointed* by the governor and is a member of the governor's cabinet. The logic of this method of choosing the head insurance regulatory official is that the governor is ultimately responsible for the business success of his or her term of office and therefore should be able to appoint a person to carry out this responsibility. The prime disadvantage of this method is that political influence may be asserted on the commissioner's decisions. The short tenure of appointed commissioners, averaging two to three years, is also bad. In about 10 states where the job of insurance commissioner is an *elective* office, the disadvantageous situation of a short term in authority is also complicated by the vagaries of voter appeal. One wonders whether the electorate could choose a person of the necessary high caliber and integrity with any better measure of success than appointments by the governors have produced. The dilemma of obtaining better commissioners and longer terms of office seems unavoidably tied to the political party system of our government.

The insurance *department* with which most insurance commissioners carry out their duties may vary from a few persons in some of the smaller states to about 950 employees in such a state as New York. Approximately 20 states each have more than 100 employees, including company examiners. Many departments have existed for a century or more. Some states have relied upon New York as a guide for their insurance legislation and administrative action. Also of importance is the fact that New York laws usually apply to *all* insurers licensed there, including those domiciled in other states. This is important in creating uniformity in regulations among many states, and it has become known as the *Appleton Rule*.

---

[11] Most of the states use this title or "commissioner of insurance"; about nine "director of insurance"; and four "superintendent of insurance." *Insurance Facts* (New York: Insurance Information Institute, 1982–83), pp. 79–81.

The major powers of the insurance commissioner have been mentioned as licensing, examination, and investigation. After following the required incorporation procedure if it is a domestic organization, each insurer in the state must be *licensed* for the lines of business it plans to write. The commissioner has broad interpretative powers in deciding whether or not an insurer is qualified, financially and otherwise, to operate in the state. After issuance, licenses are usually renewable on an annual basis. The insurance commissioner has considerable power to refuse to issue a renewal license as well as the power of suspension or revocation. Examinations are also conducted which determine licensing of insurance agents or brokers.

The *examination of insurers* once they have been licensed is also an important task of the commissioner. The continued solvency of insurers is the major objective of such detailed examinations, which are conducted according to law at intervals of from three to five years. The checking of assets, liabilities, and reserves is part of this procedure, as is the review of underwriting, investment, and claim practices of the insurer. A zone system is used in cooperation with the National Association of Insurance Commissioners (NAIC) to avoid unnecessary duplicate examination by many states. In this way the examination of insurers licensed in many states is standardized and simplified, and the results of the regular zone examination are accepted by all states in which the insurer does business. In the intervening years between complete examinations of insurers, every state requires the filing of an *annual statement* with the insurance commissioner. This is a report of current financial conditions and of changes which have occurred during the year. A standard NAIC form is used which, for most details, provides uniformity of the information requested in the statement. These annual statements are available to the public in the state insurance department offices.

The National Association of Insurance Commissioners is a voluntary association of the top insurance administrator from each state. It is important not only for the zone examination procedures but also for its influence through the commissioners on uniformity of insurance laws in the various states. Recommendations and *model laws* are studied by its committees and discussed at semiannual meetings. The position of the commissioners has aided to some extent in the adoption of such suggestions by the states. However, major criticism has been aimed at the NAIC for its inability to bring about greater uniformity in state insurance legislation. A revitalized NAIC and interest in increased cooperative action among the states has been observed.[12] Many model laws have been recommended for such areas as holding companies, variable

---

[12] See Jon C. Hanson, "The NAIC: Its Nature and Scope," *CPCU Annuals* 26, no. 1 (March 1973), p. 10. The addition of a research unit was an improvement.

contracts, guaranty funds, life insurance replacement,[13] and unfair advertising. Major research projects have been completed, covering automobile
insurance, premium taxation, competitive rating, credit life and health
insurance, and mass marketing. Statistical reporting systems both for
testing company solidity ("early warning tests") and for measuring profitability have been operational for more than a decade.

In most states a wide variety of *investigation* powers of the insurance
commissioner determines whether or not insurers or their representatives are meeting the requirements of the statutes. Free access to records
and books of insurers and hearings on such matters as rate violations
or unfair trade practices are examples of this authority. As a result of
such procedures, which are often informal, the commissioner may issue
administrative rulings or advisory opinions in regard to the business
conduct of insurers or their agents. In extreme cases the commissioner
may declare the insolvency of an insurer in liquidation or rehabilitation
proceedings. All such powers have as their major goal the protection
of insurance policyholders and claimants. These parties should not treat
the functions of an insurance commissioner as a guarantee against any
and all possible loss, but the commissioner's insurance regulatory powers
provide important means of preventing or reducing such losses and ·
abuses.

Figure 28–2 shows the relationships of the company examination and
audit, agent licensing, rating and forms approval, and policyholder service functions. Substantial statistical record keeping is a part of the
insurance department's work. The warden aids in enforcing the laws
passed by the legislature and interpreted by the courts, and in carrying
out the administrative rulings of the department. The magnitude of the
task is considerable. For example, in a recent year in Ohio there were
more than 1,200 companies licensed; 50,000 agencies with 190,000 licenses for individual agents issued; 30,000 rate filings submitted; and
in excess of 10,000 agents' license examinations administered. The spirit
of consumerism has increased attention by insurance department personnel to their responsibilities for taking care of policyholder complaints.
Some departments have installed consumer "hot lines" to accept toll-
free telephone calls. Many calls are not complaints (which center on
auto, health, and direct-mail insurance), but merely requests for information.

Court action.   The extremely broad authority of insurance commissioners is subject to some measures of review and interpretation by the
courts. The *notice* and *hearing* procedures which are conducted by commissioners in order to arrive at official rulings may be reviewed by the

---

[13] James W. Newman, Jr. and Harold Skipper, Jr., "Regulating Life Insurance Replacement Activity," *Journal of Insurance Regulation* 1, no. 1 (September 1982), p. 93.

Figure 28–2. The organization of a typical state insurance department

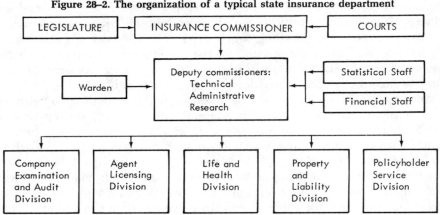

courts to determine whether the commissioner's duties have been in conformity with the statutes.

Examples are actions to compel the commissioner to issue a license to an insurer or to prevent its cancellation, and court review of decisions to permit rate increases or of refusals to do so. Not only may the courts be used in private actions (or by the attorney general of the state) against an insurance commissioner, but the reverse may also be true. The commissioner may, for example, petition the courts to enforce compliance with laws or rulings.

KINDS OF INSURANCE REGULATION BY THE STATES

The specific state laws which regulate insurance cannot be discussed in detail in this chapter. The insurance codes, as well as the general business laws, of each of the 50 jurisdictions vary too much to permit a complete treatment of the subject. For specific insurance laws, administrative practices, and court decisions, the lawyer and the student of insurance must refer to the regulatory activities in a particular state. However, a general picture of the kinds of insurance regulation in the states is also necessary. This section of the chapter summarizes the regulation usually found in the more important insurance jurisdictions, such as New York State. Care must be taken to compare the specific state laws and rulings with the general review presented here.

Insurance regulation by the states is largely aimed at the insurers that conduct an insurance business within their jurisdiction. Some regulation is also provided for agents, brokers, and other persons who are part of the marketing of insurance contracts and services provided to insurance policyholders. The regulation of insurers falls into the following categories: (1) formation and licensing requirements, (2) supervision of operations, and (3) liquidation procedures. The second category includes a wide variety of regulatory controls, some extensive and some slight, over such activities as contract forms, rates, reserves, assets, and trade practices. Truly, the birth, life, and death of an insurer are in the hands of the state regulators.

Formation and licensing of insurers

Insurance companies are required to meet specific standards of organization, often higher ones than are set for general business organizations. The rationale for such higher standards has been discussed in the first section of the chapter. Basically, the need is for methods which have the objective of assuring the solvency, competence, and integrity of the insuring organization. The first step is *incorporation,*[14] an introductory process in which the state recognizes and approves the existence of a new legal identity. Today all but one state use this method of formation for insurance companies.[15] The New York Insurance Law, for example, outlines in detail the procedure to be followed under the incorporation statute, including written proposal to the superintendent of insurance, name to be used, territories and kinds of business in which operations are planned, and public notice in newspapers of intention to incorporate.[16]

The next step, *licensing,* is a check on the insurer's financial condition to ascertain that it has the required capital and surplus for the kinds of insurance permitted in the license. The statutory requirements for licensing must be met by *domestic* (domiciled or having their home office in the state), *foreign* (out of state), and *alien* (out of the United States) insurers. The requirements sometimes vary among these three types of insurers, but the laws usually specify at least as high standards for foreign and alien insurers as for domestic insurers. Standards also vary by legal type of insurer, with requirements for mutual insurers being somewhat different from those for stock insurers. For example, the financial requirements for mutual companies are stated in terms of surplus rather than capital plus surplus, and additional requirements are set for the minimum number of policyholders with which to start a mutual company.

The financial standards that insurers must meet in order to obtain and retain a license vary tremendously in the different states. In some states as little as $25,000 of capital or surplus is required to write a

---

[14] Reciprocals, Lloyds associations, fraternals, and some health insurance associations do not legally become incorporated by this process. They do, however, file similar statements of their present status and proposed activities as stated in their charter and bylaws.

[15] Rhode Island, where insurers must petition the General Assembly.

[16] *New York Insurance Law,* secs. 48–49.

specific kind of insurance, such as fire insurance. Each additional kind of insurance for which the company is to be licensed requires an additional amount of capital or surplus. For multiple-line insurance, including all kinds except life insurance, the states also exhibit wide variation: the most lenient state requires only $100,000, while the strictest state requires almost $4 million. About 20 states set $1 million or more as the minimum standard for a new domestic multiple-line company.[17]

The licensing procedure is not dependent on financial requirements alone. Many states give the insurance commissioner leeway to apply considerable judgment in acting, or refusing to act, upon a license application. The objective of licensing is to assure a preliminary method of lessening the chance of the insurer's financial insolvency, particularly during the more difficult formative years. A license may be denied for many other reasons, including the bad faith or reputation of the proposed incorporators or management of an insurer. General managerial ability is undoubtedly as important as capital and surplus requirements in achieving sustained financial stability for an insurer. For that reason, the insurer's license is no more a guarantee against failure than an automobile driver's license is a guarantee against accident.

Insurer operations

As a protection against insolvency and unfair treatment of policyholders, insurance regulation continues after the formation and licensing of an insurer. The states exercise some control over many phases of the operations of insurers. The basic idea of continual regulation is that most obligations of insurers extend years into the future and that the state should provide supervision to see that the promises in the contracts are fulfilled. The ways in which insurer operations are supervised are strikingly different among the states and among the various kinds of insurance. Most states do provide some regulation of the following types: contracts and forms, rates, expense limitations, reserves, asset and surplus values, investments, agents' licensing and trade practices, and taxation.

Contracts and forms. The strictest regulation of contracts is applied to fire insurance, where the states stipulate the exact wording for the standard fire insurance contract. All states require a standard fire insurance contract, and almost all states use the New York form (see Chapter 13). Many differences in the wording of other contracts are found, how-

---

[17] David L. Bickelhaupt, *Transition to Multiple-Line Insurance Companies* (Homewood, Ill.: Richard D. Irwin, 1961), p. 65. The requirements have only increased by relatively minor amounts during the past two decades. See James E. Bachman, *Capitalization Requirements for Multiple-Line Property-Liability Insurance Companies* (Philadelphia: S. S. Huebner Foundation for Insurance Education, 1978).

ever, and independent insurers and the various rating bureaus may have individualized contracts which vary in some important particulars. Life insurance contracts are not standard contracts in the sense that similar forms or benefits are required. Most states do, however, provide some uniformity by requiring a number of "standard provisions" in life contracts pertaining to such items as the grace period, loan and surrender values, and the like. Examples of little regulation over contracts and forms are found in the marine and health fields. Except for a few required provisions, these contracts are the most nonuniform of insurance contracts and should be carefully studied by policyholders in order to determine what benefits, conditions, and exclusions they contain.

Rates. The price of insurance contracts is also controlled to a varying degree in the different lines of insurance. In some kinds of insurance, such as aviation and marine insurance, practically no regulation exists in the states. In life insurance regulation involves maintaining minimum reserves rather than setting the prices which must be charged. Most other major kinds of insurance are subject to some direct-rate regulation. Every state has statutory standards set forth in an insurance rating law.

Objectives of rate regulation. Basic standards recognized by rating laws usually require (1) that rates be *reasonable* and *adequate* for the class of risks to which they apply; (2) that no rate *discriminate unfairly* between risks involving essentially the same hazards and expense elements; (3) that consideration be given to the past and prospective loss *experience* and a reasonable underwriting profit. Rates are considered reasonable (not too high) and adequate (not too low) when they produce sufficient revenue to pay all losses and expenses of doing business, and in addition produce a reasonable profit.[18]

Early development of rating laws. The early attempts to establish rate making on a sound basis through various regional organizations generated opposition on the basis that cooperative action was monopolistic and contrary to the public interest. Various state legislators undertook to prohibit cooperative rate making by the enactment of bills (known as "anticompact laws") which prohibited combinations between insurers for the joint fixing of rates. It became apparent, however, that unlimited competition could also be injurious. Prices for insurance could be inadequate unless they were based upon estimated minimum costs of losses, expenses, and services. Insurance commissioners realized the importance of safeguarding the solvency of insurers. They determined that the disastrous consequences of unrestricted competition could be avoided through rating bureaus using statistical information combining the loss experi-

---

[18] Frederick G. Crane, "Insurance Rate Regulation: The Reasons Why," *Journal of Risk and Insurance* 39, no. 4 (December 1972), p. 511.

ence of many insurers. Laws were then enacted authorizing the association of insurers for the purpose of making rates.

NAIC model rating law. Many of the states passed rating laws some 35 years ago that followed a model bill set forth in the National Association of Insurance Commissioners "All-Industry Bill." (The bill's name does *not* mean that all states adopted it, merely that many insurers supported its provisions.) In these states, the laws provide specifically that there is no intent to prohibit or discourage reasonable competition, nor do they prohibit or discourage uniformity. The state insurance department passes upon the reasonableness of the rules and regulations of rating organizations. A rating bureau may not exclude or withhold its facilities from any insurers, each of which has the statutory right to become a bureau subscriber by paying reasonable fees. The laws permit, but do not require, concerted rate making.

When rates have been promulgated (set), allowing any return of the insurance premium to an insured, except dividends to a class, is regarded as discrimination. A concession in rates is contrary to the law, whether it is made in the form of a direct payment or a credit on premium or by means of any subterfuge. The statutes do not prohibit the payment by one broker or agent of a part of his or her commission or other compensation to other licensed agents or brokers.

The proposed rates are made by the rating bureaus or by individual insurers if their size and experience justify separate rates. The bureau method is used in fire insurance, workers' compensation, surety bonds, automobile insurance (by some but not all insurers), and other lines. Individual insurer rate making has increased in the past decade and has become an important factor in automobile insurance and the new forms of multiple-line homeowners' and commercial policy contracts.[19]

Approval of the proposed bureau or individual rates for these lines of insurance is required by the insurance commissioner *before the rates may be used by the insurers.* Thus, these types of laws that followed the NAIC model bill became known as "prior approval laws." About one half of the states still use this system of rate regulation for most property-liability insurance.

Current types of rating laws. Today, one of three types of rating laws prevail for most states: (1) *prior approval* laws, (2) *file-and-use* laws, and (3) *open competition* laws. A fourth type, in which the state makes the rates, is less important because only a few states use it.[20]

The *prior approval laws* have just been discussed. With the desire

---

[19] One of the conclusions reached by the U.S. Department of Justice Task Force on Antitrust Immunities in *The Pricing and Marketing of Insurance* (Washington, D.C., U.S. Government Printing Office, January 1977) is that too rigid rate regulation reduces competition.

[20] Texas and Massachusetts, for example. Similar is the North Carolina law which makes the bureau rates mandatory.

for increased competition, potentially lower rates, and deregulation of insurance, the prior approval law has come under strong fire during the past 15 years. Although some states have adopted other types, the strict regulation of prior approval laws remains predominant.

Many subissues are involved in the controversy, such as: (1) The present *extent of competition* in the major fields of property-liability insurance (particularly automobile insurance); (2) The proper *measurement of underwriting profits* for insurers on an "adjusted" or "statutory" basis, whether or not investment profits should be included, and the appropriate asset or sales basis for calculating rates of return; (3) The relative *effectiveness* of the present prior approval rate regulatory laws of most states (rate bureau membership permitted, and rate filing and approval required) versus the other types of rating laws; and (4) The relationship of the rate regulatory problem to the *state versus federal regulation* arguments discussed later in this chapter (if present state rate regulation proves inadequate, a new strong argument for federal regulation of insurance emerges).

About 10 states employ the *file-and-use law,* which permits the immediate use of filed rates, without affirmative approval by the insurance commissioner. The commissioner, however, may disapprove the rates within a certain time limit, such as 30 or 60 days. Some states, such as Ohio, use this method for one type of insurance (automobile) while retaining the prior approval rule for fire and other kinds of insurance.

The *open competition law,* which was pioneered in California, has also been adopted in about 19 other states. It relies upon competition to set the price for property-liability insurance. Open competition between rating bureaus (membership not required) and independent insurers is permitted and encouraged by the lack of requirements for filing or obtaining approval of rates. These laws require the insurance commissioner to monitor competition and to disapprove rates, if competition in the marketplace is substantially threatened on the basis of "share of market" and "workable competition" standards. The need for good definitions and for enforcement of antitrust laws in these states is stressed.[21] The goal is rate adequacy but not rate excessiveness, with sufficient markets for the needed coverages of insurance. New York has experimented with open competition since 1970. According to some studies, the experience of several states has been favorable in reducing rates.[22] Other research

---

[21] "Monitoring Competition: A Means of Regulating the Property and Liability Insurance Business" (Milwaukee: NAIC, 1974).

[22] For Illinois, see John D. Long and Robert I. Mehr, "The Illinois System of Insurance Pricing—Practices and Attitudes of Selected Insurers," (Bloomington, Ind.: Insurance Research Associates, 1981). For a more complete comparison of many states in automobile insurance, see Robert C. Witt and Harry Miller, "Rate Regulation, Competition, and Underwriting Risk in Automobile Insurance Markets," *Journal of Risk and Insurance* 34, no. 4 (December 1981), p. 202.

indicates no significant difference in rates of return earned by nonlife insurers under open competition as compared with other methods.[23]

The danger that open competition, no-filing laws will become synonymous with *no* regulation is a factor of considerable importance. This could have the undesirable result of encouraging federal legislation to fill the possible gap in state regulation. The potential effects on overall competition, agency systems, rating bureau services, small and large insurers, and many other parts of the insurance business must also be considered. A national opinion study gives some clues as to the possible future direction of insurance rate regulation. The open competition concept was favored by 51 percent, and prior approval by 33 percent (16 percent had no opinion). The reasons given centered on keeping prices down, free enterprise, and that government can still control excessive prices.[24]

Expense limitations.   Other than direct regulation of insurance prices by required rate approval, some state laws supervise the cost of *life* insurance by limiting the expense portion of the premium. The New York law is most influential in this regard because all insurers doing business in that state must conform to its limitations for all insurance contracts that they write anywhere. Maximum commissions and allowances of 55 percent during the first year are set for business written by life insurers in New York State.

Reserves.   The states require insurers to set up as a liability a reserve considered adequate to meet policy obligations as they mature. The only insurers excepted are certain types of mutual insurers operating on an intrastate basis and usually confining their operations within a small local area. In the case of these local mutuals, the reserve requirement may vary, depending upon the assessment liability provided in the policy.

In life insurance the *legal reserve* is an amount which augmented by premium payments under outstanding contracts and interest earnings will enable the life insurer to meet its policy obligations. These include death benefits and nonforfeiture benefits, such as policy loans and surrender values.

In the field of property insurance the *unearned premium reserve* must at all times be adequate to pay a full proportionate return premium to policyholders in the event of the cancellation of a policy before it expires. The reserve should be adequate to reinsure the business, if necessary. The basic purpose of the reserve is to meet all liabilities under the contract and to pay expenses of claim services *in the future*. At the same

---

[23] Robert A. Hershbarger, "An Analysis of Rates of Return Earned by Non-Life Insurance Companies by Type of Rate Regulation: A Case Study," *Journal of Insurance Issues and Practices,* June 1981, p. 60.

[24] *Public Appraisal of Pricing, Profits, and Regulation—A Public Appraisal of Auto Insurance* (New York: Insurance Information Institute, January 1980).

time, it accounts for income received but not yet earned and for repayment if the contract is discontinued.

A second type of reserve required of property insurers is the *loss reserve*. Since many contracts of this type do not involve immediate payment of all losses *that have occurred,* a reserve must be set up to assure their payment. For example, a workers' compensation claim may be made against the insurer today. In many cases the loss payments may be made gradually according to law during a long future period of disability. In automobile liability cases it may be several years after a loss before a court decides who is liable and for how much. In such cases, an estimate of the reserve that will be needed to pay the insurer's obligation is made and carried on its books as a loss reserve. In this way, losses and loss expense for claims that are known but not yet paid are provided for by the insurer under the loss reserve laws of the states.

Assets and surplus values. The value of assets appearing in the balance sheets of insurers must be correct in order that liabilities, reserves, and residual surplus items have true meaning. Nearly 50,000 individual securities held by insurers are valued according to practices adopted by a committee of the National Association of Insurance Commissioners. Stocks are usually given year-end market values, while bonds are carried at amortized values (a few are given estimated or "Convention" values). The valuations are advisory only to the states, but the result is a good example of voluntary and state regulation working together. For some insurers, such as mutual insurers, both surplus accumulation and distribution are subject to regulation aimed at providing equitable treatment for all policyholders.

Investments. To protect the solvency of insurers, most states have laws governing the types of securities that may be purchased for investment. The strictest regulations apply to life insurers since they hold many billions of dollars of assets for many years for their policyholders.

Life insurers are subject to vigorous supervision of their investment portfolios.[25] Each annual statement filed with the insurance department lists every individual investment with detailed information about its acquisition, costs, values, and earnings. The insurance laws require a high standard of investment quality. Mortgages and bonds are the prime investments in the portfolio of life insurers, involving a large majority of total assets. Most states grant some limited permission for other investments. Stocks may be limited, for example, to about 10 percent of assets or to 100 percent of surplus. Real estate holdings, especially commercial properties and housing projects, are also limited to a maximum of between 5 and 20 percent in various states. The legality of all holdings

---

[25] J. David Cummins, ed. *Investment Activities of Life Insurance Companies* (Homewood, Ill.: Richard D. Irwin, 1977).

of the insurer is checked carefully in periodic audits of the securities.

The investment of assets by *property and liability insurers* is also supervised, although the laws are more lenient and vary greatly among the states. The laws of each state must be consulted in order to determine the investment restrictions. The general practice aims at requiring the safest types of investments for all assets held as reserves (unearned premium and loss reserves) and other liabilities. Cash, bonds of high grade and specified experience, and perhaps preferred stocks of proven equality may be permitted for such assets. The remainder of assets (representing capital and surplus) may be invested in a wider range of securities, including common stocks meeting certain standards. Limitations on real estate holdings, on the size of single investments in relation to total assets or surplus, and on investments in out-of-state companies, as well as many other restrictions, are also common.

Many states prohibit insurers from financing debt by issuing their own bonds. Most other financial institutions are similarly restricted by state laws. This is an important difference that must be borne in mind when the investment portfolios and practices of insurers and other commercial enterprises are being compared.

Agents' licensing and trade practices. An important control on insurer operations is maintained through laws in all states which require insurance agents and brokers to be licensed. The insurance departments usually administer these laws, with the objective of permitting only competent and trustworthy representatives to be used by insurers. The standards vary tremendously, from mere payment of a license fee to a comprehensive written *examination* following required attendance in insurance courses approved by the department. New York's written examinations require 90 classroom hours of study. They have influenced some other states, such as Florida, to raise their licensing requirements for insurance agents. The examinations are often divided into separate tests for life insurance, health insurance, and multiple-line insurance. In states that license brokers, the examinations for insurance brokers are usually more difficult and extensive than those given to agents. Some adjusters and consultants are licensed, also, in a few states.

Special laws in many states, called *countersignature laws,* require that all property insurance contracts written in a state must be signed by an agent who is a resident of that state. Such laws are often criticized because they may add to the cost of insurance without providing any real services to the consumer. Agents must also represent only insurers that are authorized and licensed in the state. An exception is made under some *surplus line laws* which in some states permit a special licensed agent to represent unauthorized insurers in cases where the risks cannot be fully protected by licensed insurers within the state.

Unfair trade practices in insurance are made illegal in all states under laws similar to the Federal Trade Commission Act. These laws aim at retaining jurisdiction for the states (under the provisions of Public Law 15) in preventing fraudulent and unethical acts of agents and brokers. They provide fines and, more important, suspension or revocation of licenses as penalties for violations. Examples of such unfair practices in insurance include (1) *rebating,* the returning of any part of the premium (except in dividends) to the policyholder by insurer or agent as a price-cutting sales inducement; (2) *twisting,* a special form of misrepresentation in which an agent may induce the policyholder to cancel disadvantageously the contract of another insurer in order to take out a new contract; (3) *misappropriation,* in which the agent unlawfully keeps funds belonging to others; (4) *commingling,* which some states prevent by requiring a separate bank account for the agent's premium funds; and (5) *misleading advertising,* which is restrained by many regulations for full and fair information in advertisements by insurers and agents. The insurance commissioner has broad powers to prevent the above unfair practices and exercises this authority by investigating complaints as well as initiating investigations of any questionable acts of insurers or their representatives.

Taxation. Revenue for the states has become an important reason for insurance regulation. The insurers pay what amounts to a sales tax on gross premiums received from all their policyholders. This *premium tax* is usually about 2 percent, although some states charge up to 4 percent of premiums. The tax is paid by insurers; its cost, of course, is included in the price of insurance contracts and thus is paid indirectly by the policyholders. Premium taxes, and other license and miscellaneous fees, were about $4 billion in 1982.

That the taxes are primarily for revenue purposes rather than to pay for the cost of insurance regulation is obvious from the statistics compiled annually by the Insurance Industry Committee (Columbus, Ohio). The state premium tax goes into the general revenue fund of the state, with insurance department expenses being based on separate appropriations from that fund. Only about 5 percent of the above total tax revenue and fees is used for operation of the state insurance departments. Approximately one half of the states even use less than the amount of the separate license and miscellaneous fees (not the much larger premium tax) collected from insurers, in order to pay the costs of insurance department regulation. The range is quite diverse, from less than 50 percent of these fees, to more than 400 percent. If public regulation of insurance is lacking in any respect, the state legislatures should first look to see whether the insurance departments are provided with adequate funds and personnel to carry out the necessary supervision of insurance in a consistent and equitable manner.

Federal *income* taxes also apply to insurers. *Property-liability insurers*

pay regular corporate income taxes on statutory underwriting profits
and on net investment income. Some of the smaller mutual insurers
and reciprocals are exempted from these taxes (if their income is less
than $150,000 a year), but only 2 or 3 percent of the total business is
written by these insurers. For *life insurers,* taxable investment income
is first calculated by deducting from net investment income an amount
of interest (estimated by a formula) required to maintain policy reserves.
Then, if the gain from operations, after dividends and some special deductions, is greater than taxable investment income, one half of the excess
is added to the tax base.[26] There is debate as to whether stock or mutual
life insurers pay more income taxes in relation to the insurance business
they do. No definitive answer appears possible on the basis of the available
data, for the comparisons are often incomplete. There is evidence that
life insurers experience a tax burden much greater than other general
corporations and financial institutions.[27] In addition, changes in the tax
laws under the Tax Equity and Fiscal Responsibility Act of 1982 (TEFRA)
increase taxes for many life insurers, because policyholder dividends
are no longer deductible against investment income. Prior to this, modified coinsurance plans of reinsurance were often used in order to permit
the deduction of dividends.

Rehabilitation and liquidation of insurers

The insurance commissioner of a state not only officiates at the birth
and growth of an insurer but also at its demise if necessary. An insurer
may be *liquidated* for a number of reasons, including financial insolvency. Some liquidations may be made voluntarily in order to effect a
corporate reorganization or merger. Reinsurance of all outstanding liabilities and contracts may be achieved, so that no loss results to policyholders. For example, for the past 75 years no life insurance policyholder
of a New York–licensed insurer has suffered loss through an insurer
failure. Such losses have been prevented in other states for periods of
30 or more years.

The insurance commissioner acts under the insurance laws as the official in charge of supervising rehabilitation (if the insurer can be restored
to financial stability through reorganization) or liquidation if the insurer
is dissolved. The purpose of both actions is to conserve as much of the
insurer's assets as possible and to provide fair treatment for claimants,
policyholders, and investors. A good example of how the collapse of an

---

[26] Louis Garfin, "Current Issues in the Federal Taxation of Life Insurance Companies,"
Journal of Insurance Issues and Practices, June 1982, p. 1.

[27] A. E. Hofflander and C. L. Zollinger, "California Taxation of Life Insurance Companies," *Journal of Insurance Regulation* 1, no. 1 (September 1982), p. 23.

insurer can be averted short of liquidation proceedings, and of how an insurer can be rejuvenated (by restricting its expansion and imposing underwriting and expense limitations) occurred in the mid-1970s for the Government Employees Insurance Company (GEICO). This was one of the largest insurers ever to undergo such rehabilitation proceedings.

Sometimes the license of an insurer is *suspended* temporarily, for not meeting financial solvency standards or for other noncompliance with department rulings on rates, advertising, and so on. This may be a prelude to liquidation proceedings or only a temporary situation to enforce changes in the insurer's operations. Nevertheless, it is a powerful tool of enforcement.

SOME CURRENT REGULATORY ISSUES

The age of "consumerism" has created the environment for greater inquiry into insurance than has ever been made before.[28] The increase in consumer-oriented regulation seems to have peaked in the past decade, with the general trend toward deregulation perhaps being an offsetting factor—at least for the early 1980s. Several regulatory issues continue, however, to attract state and federal attention.

Insurer guaranty funds

The need. One of the most shocking financial news items of the 1970s was the exposure of the Equity Funding Corporation of America fraud in California. Allegedly involving life insurance contract amounts of more than $2 billion, the scheme was perpetrated through the use of false computer records. Bogus policies were recorded for an affiliate, Equity Funding Life Insurance Company (an Illinois company), and re-sold to reinsurance companies. Twenty-two persons were indicted for taking part in the fraud, which saw Equity Funding Corporation stock soar from $7.50 to more than $80 in a few years. This was primarily a stock swindle in which 60,000 life insurance policy sales on nonexistent persons were recorded as the basis for showing false corporate growth. Most of the real 20,000 life insurance policyholders did not lose their investments. In contrast, most investors recovered only 15 to 20 percent of their dollars in a reorganization into a new company, Orion Capital Corporation, in 1977. National Investors (of Arkansas) assumed 1,000 policies that it had formerly coinsured; some contracts were reinsured; and others were protected by the real assets of Equity Funding Life.

---

[28] The escalating popularity of insurance regulation topics can be seen in many journals and trade publications in the insurance field during the past decade. A new separate *Journal of Insurance Regulation* published its first issue in 1982.

This case illustrates that life insurance solvency regulation by the states is needed. It also shows that insurance regulatory laws could be helpful to the consumer even in a most complicated ruse involving the Securities and Exchange Commission and many stockbrokers. The ability to perpetrate the fraud is not an indictment of state regulation of insurance, considering the freak nature of the occurrence. Life insurance reserve requirements created real assets for bona fide policyholders, and only the phony policies were backed by phantom assets.[29]

Some insurers do suffer liquidation because of financial difficulty. In some states the number of liquidations is a cause for concern, particularly in some kinds of insurance, such as automobile insurance (and mostly for high-risk, substandard, newer insurers). The result has been some support for a federal guaranty fund for insurers that would operate somewhat as the FDIC does for banks. State deposit laws and several special state workers' compensation security funds are already in use which are similar in principle to this idea. The need for a federal plan for all kinds of insurance has not yet been proved conclusively.

The solution. In recent years, all 50 states have adopted *insurance guaranty fund plans* to protect consumers against the insolvency of *property-liability insurers*. Model legislation proposed by the NAIC encouraged states to adopt such laws, which do not include life insurance. The plans are administered on a state-by-state basis, but basically they assess solvent insurers in order to pay the unpaid claims of an insolvent company and to return unearned premiums to its policyholders. Insurers each pay a proportional share of the losses, based on their premium volume in the state.

During 1969–81 the funds paid out approximately $330 million to cover 67 company insolvencies, including five in 1981.[30] The guaranty funds appear to be doing a good job of protecting the consumer, with several improvements being adopted in some states. These concern (1) giving the funds immediate access to assets of the insolvent insurer (rather than waiting until liquidation proceedings are completed), (2) giving the funds priority before general creditors to obtain assets of the insolvent insurer, and (3) permitting a tax offset against premium taxes to solvent insurers for money paid into the guaranty funds.[31]

---

[29] "Equity Funding Ruse a Freak—State Regulation Not Indicted," *National Underwriter* (Property and Casualty Edition), September 14, 1973, p. 1. See also Lee J. Seidler, Frederick Andrews, and Marc J. Epstein, *The Equity Funding Papers* (New York: John Wiley & Sons, 1977).

[30] *Insurance Facts* (New York: Insurance Information Institute, 1982–83), p. 33. Not included are payments made under a pre-assessment fund in New York which has a $200 million ceiling. The largest assessments have been in California, Florida, Illinois, and Pennsylvania.

[31] "Insolvency Laws: Better Protection for the Insurance Consumer," *Journal of American Insurance,* Winter 1976–77, p. 1.

Part of the solution to protecting the buyers of insurance against insurer insolvencies may become increasingly significant for the future. Rather than merely a system to pay for insolvencies, a logical supplement is an attempt to detect troubled insurers in advance of insolvency proceedings. The National Association of Insurance Commissioners began in the 1970s an "early warning system" based upon 11 financial ratio tests. Primarily involving loss ratios and reserves, several new methods of predicting insolvencies by including other tests for asset changes and potential management mistakes and dishonesty have also been recently proposed.[32]

Federal versus state regulation

This chapter emphasizes regulation of insurance by the *states* because most government legislation, administrative action, and court decisions pertaining to insurance have been at the state level. The legal foundation for state regulation was decided with the passage of the McCarran–Ferguson Act (Public Law 15) in 1945. This law reaffirmed the predominant role in insurance regulation by the states, which still continues, because the law exempts insurance from major federal statutes such as the Sherman, Clayton, Robinson–Patman and other acts. Only to the extent that state legislation is inadequate does federal regulation apply.

The *federal* government has increased its regulation of insurance in some specific and limited areas of insurances. For example, federal agencies have regulated some aspects of interstate advertising and mergers through the Federal Trade Commission (FTC), variable life insurance and annuities through the Securities and Exchange Commission (SEC), occupational safety (OSHA), and pensions under the Employee Retirement Income Security Act (ERISA) under the Department of Labor and the Department of Health and Human Services.

With the exception of ERISA, the federal government involvement in insurance during the last several years has slowed. Federal budget restraints on many of the federal agencies have decreased controls in the present era of "deregulation," and legislative studies and proposals have lessened. Also, the growth of federal government insurance programs in the property-liability insurance fields has been noted in Chapter 24 as a declining goal of the federal insurance administrator.

Why should regulation of insurance be performed by the states? Advocates of *state regulation* have pointed out such reasons as: (1) the local

---

[32] James R. Eck, "Detecting Financially Troubled Property-Liability Insurers," *Journal of Business Research* 10, no. 4 (December 1982), p. 445; and Ran Bar–Niv, Financial Insolvency in the Property-Liability Insurance Industry," Ph.D. dissertation, Ohio State University, 1983.

nature of many insurance transactions, for which any difficulties can best be solved on a state basis; (2) the reasonable success of state regulation for many years during which insurance has become an important and sound business; (3) the value of regulation on a state-by-state basis, which permits changes and innovations in regulation without applying to the entire country all at once; and (4) the help of the National Association of Insurance Commissioners (NAIC) in recommending model legislation to the states in order to achieve some uniformity in insurance regulation. While recognizing that state regulation is not perfect, it is claimed that federal regulation would be much worse: cumbersome, expensive, less effective, and fragmented among dozens of agencies.[33]

The proponents of *federal regulation* of insurance have criticized state regulation on many points, emphasizing (1) inconsistencies and lack of uniformity in regulation of insurer licensing and insolvency, agent licensing, and many other insurance operations; (2) inadequate funding for the important tasks of the insurance commissioners, and the short term and political disadvantages of their term of office; (3) greater standardization needed in insurance contracts to cover many interstate exposures; and (4) increased competition as desired in order to assure availability and lower and fairer prices for insurance.[34] Implicit in these criticisms of the present state of insurance regulation is the idea that federal regulation would be better.

The controversy will undoubtedly continue. Although unlikely that the federal government will assume the major role in insurance regulation, the threat of federal regulation wherever the states fail to perform adequately has the benefit of being a constant impetus to improving state insurance regulation.

Other regulatory issues

The sample of current regulatory issues discussed in this chapter is merely indicative of the wide range and significance of regulation in insurance. It is hoped that these examples pique the interest of the reader and will spur further inquiry into regulation, which has and will continue to be crucial to the development of insurance.

Almost any listing of current insurance topics has a regulatory dimension. Regulation of special problems in regard to specific types of insurance is frequently mentioned in previous chapters. In *risk management,* for example, the growth of "captive" insurance companies is seen to

---

[33] *Regulation of Insurance* (Chicago: Alliance of American Insurers, 1977), p. 5.

[34] For example, the Insurance Competition Improvement Act proposed in 1980, which seeks to eliminate antitrust immunity and increase competition in automobile and property insurance rates.

result in new licensing and taxation problems. In *life insurance,* the trends toward increased price disclosure, new "universal" life insurance policies, and replacement of older contracts are changing the rules under which insurers operate. The tremendous impact of ERISA and related laws on *annuities and pensions* is significant. In *property* insurance, product liability and no-fault automobile insurance is noted as changing traditional tort laws. In the trend toward *broader financial services,* many problems of reorganization for regulation are apparent: mergers of insurers, licensing of financial advisors, and increased competition from interests outside of the insurance field.

In the final chapter on consumer, business, and social issues, some additional selected regulatory aspects in regard to insurance will also be treated.

FOR REVIEW AND DISCUSSION

1. For each of the following statements that is *false,* explain *why* it is not true:
   a. Self-regulation of insurance by cooperative voluntary efforts of insurers is considerable, but it does not work for some insurance activities.
   b. Most insurance regulation is performed by the federal government.
   c. The insurance commissioner in the states is more of a figurehead than a powerful administrator.
   d. Competition is always beneficial to the buyers of insurance.

2. Is self-regulation an effective means by which the insurance business can be regulated? Cite several examples and contrast it with administrative action.

3. *Explain* the relationship among the three basic methods by which government regulates insurance, that is: (1) legislation, (2) administrative action, and (3) court action.

4. Does the federal government or do the state governments provide most of the regulation for insurance? Explain the importance of (1) the *Paul* v. *Virginia* Case, (2) the South-Eastern Underwriters (SEUA) Case, and (3) Public Law 15 in the development of insurance regulation.

5. The insurance commissioner (or superintendent) in each state has powerful regulatory duties. Discuss several of the major *functions* of this official. What are some of the principal *problems* in connection with proper insurance supervision by the commissioner?

6. Evaluate the need for state regulation of insurance in each of the areas of *(a)* incorporation and licensing, *(b)* operations, and *(c)* liquidation.

7. Briefly discuss the extent of state regulation of insurance as to *(a)* contracts and forms, *(b)* rates, *(c)* reserves, and *(d)* investments. Include examples of how state regulation differs for some of the major fields of insurance.

8. In addition to income taxes and other taxes which may apply to many business enterprises, are insurers subject to any special forms of taxation? If so, explain the kind and extent of such taxation.

9. "Open competition" rate laws have been adopted by several states that have had "prior approval" laws for many years. Explain the difference, if any, in *(a)* the purposes and *(b)* the methods of these laws. Are there any alternatives?

10. "It is better for state insurance regulation to concentrate on maintaining insurer *solvency* and *not* trying to regulate the *price* which insurers charge for their contracts." Do you agree or disagree, and why?

11. In your opinion, has insurance regulation improved or decreased in effectiveness during the past 20 years? Explain your rationale.

12. What lessons might be learned in regard to the Equity Funding Corporation fraud case by *(a)* insurers, *(b)* regulators, and *(c)* consumers?

13. Explain how insurer guaranty funds solve a need in insurance regulation and what limitations these solutions have.

14. Air bag restraint systems may soon be required in automobiles. Discuss, on the basis of this chapter's reading, *(a)* what kind of government regulation this is, *(b)* whether it should be based on federal or state regulation, and *(c)* how such regulation might affect the insurance business.

15. Why is insurance regulation by the *states* advantageous to consumers and to the states? What arguments in favor of *federal* regulation are advanced by its proponents?

16. Two opposing trends are occurring in insurance regulation of the 1980s: (1) increased regulation and (2) "deregulation." Cite two examples of each trend.

Part Five

THE FUTURE OF INSURANCE

A wise author has said that "we should all be concerned about the future because we will have to spend the rest of our lives there."* This simplistic yet profound thought summarizes why the *future* is the topic for this final chapter, which almost a decade ago was the first such separate emphasis in an insurance text.

No business will have much future unless it looks frequently and carefully ahead. One of the most common characteristics of successful private enterprises is their ability to predict the future. Innovation and research to anticipate rather than merely react to inevitable changes are hallmarks of strong growth industries. Insurance should be no exception—in fact, insurance is inherently based on uncertainties in regard to *future* economic losses.

Thus, understanding insurance must include more than looking at the past and present. IBM's motto "Think!" could be paraphrased as "Think *ahead!*" to emphasize the need for long-range planning for future years. Studying today's trends and issues in order to prepare for tomorrow's solutions is the goal.

Chapter 29 discusses issues—divided into (1) consumer, (2) business, and (3) social viewpoints—that are likely to be major developments in the 1980s and beyond. It is intended to serve as an opportunity to take another look at some fields that have been studied, and to relate *selected* topics to the future changes that seem to be indicated. The topics have been chosen on the basis of (1) their *significance* and timeliness of the subject, (2) their potential *interest* to the student of insurance, and (3) their *expected value* in reviewing some concepts and introducing several other valuable ones. In essence, they are topics which the student of tomorrow is likely to see emphasized in *change*—which will always be essential to the success of any dynamic field.

---

* Charles Francis Kettering, *Seed for Thought,* 1949.

Chapter 29

Outline of concepts

Consumer, business, and social issues cover areas of interest and importance to insurance *students of the future.*

Consumer issues emphasize consumer needs and viewpoints on insurance:

> **Consumerist** trends show the significance and *increased role* of better educated and more vocal purchasers.

> **Potential effects** on insurance are *widespread,* as the "marketing concept" in an affluent society pays more attention to consumer behavior.

> **Current examples** include *hot lines* to insurers or state departments, *consumer guides,* more *readable contracts,* and better *cost comparisons.*

Business issues are many; only a few of major importance are selected.

> **Internationalism** represents a crucial issue for insurance management.

>> **Growth of world business** is seen *everywhere* in its global aspects.

>> **Rationale for world insurance** involves *spread-of-risk principles and the motivating factors of policyholders, profits, power, prestige.*

>> **Dimensions of international insurance** show the *predominance of U.S. and European* marketing, and *great disparity in development.*

>> **U.S. insurers in the world market** have progressed from *reinsurance* and *associations* of insurers to direct insurance sales abroad.

> **Marketing methods in insurance** are changing traditional "exclusive" and "independent" agency systems, with many modifications and new types.

> **Arson problems** are a major and growing dilemma for property insurance.

> **Insurer investments** are large and of increased importance.

> **Insurance exchanges** are new markets in New York, Illinois, and Florida.

> **New types of insurance** include *kidnap-ransom* and *legal-expense.*

Social issues are influencing the insurance environment greatly.

> **The ethical pillars of insurance** are vital to the future, with adaptation to "social responsibility" and changing personal and social attitudes.

> **Government regulation** crosses many areas of discussion, including:

>> **No-fault automobile laws,** in development in about 20 states.

>> **Environmental control laws,** increasing many federal standards.

>> **Consumer Products Safety Act,** bringing increasing difficulties.

>> **Pension reform legislation** on "vesting" and funding under the Pension Reform Act has increased federal regulation of private pensions.

>> **Group property-liability insurance** legislation is being formulated by the states in a competitive battle among different types of insurers.

>> **Property-liability insurance rating and profitability** is a complex area.

Other social issues include crucial questions for all to ask.

Consumer, business, and social issues

Today's insurance controversies or issues are likely to become tomorrow's areas of change.[1] A good teacher seeking to have students analyze an issue always suggests that the topic under discussion be scrutinized from several viewpoints.

THREE MAJOR VIEWPOINTS

The changes occurring, and those possible or likely to take place, include at least three major viewpoints: the *consumer,* the *insurance business,* and *social (government).* Each of these groups may be subdivided into more specific viewpoints, such as personal or business consumers, insurers or agents as part of the business, and federal or state governments.

In effect, this technique is used as a framework for this entire text; for Part One emphasizes the consumer and risk-management viewpoints in regard to risk and insurance; Chapters 11, 24, and 28 concentrate on the viewpoint of government insurance regulation and systems; Parts Two and Three adopt a "line" approach to the study of specific types of insurance, partially including the perspective of all three viewpoints; and Part Four looks at insurance from the business viewpoint of the insurer.

These three viewpoints are used in this chapter in order to classify the topics discussed. However, it is important to recognize that few, if any, of the subjects are issues which affect only one viewpoint. The *primary* effect may be characterized as most important from one viewpoint, but invariably each of the issues—no matter how classified—may also be considerably influenced by (and have great effect on) the other viewpoints. It is the *combined* result of thinking through each of these issues from all sides that will help most in a proper understanding of the selected topics.

The issues are chosen from among hundreds of others that might have

---

[1] For one survey based on this concept, see Lawrence G. Brandon, *Tomorrow Begins Today—A Study of the Future* (Malvern, Pa.: American Institute, 1982).

been singled out for discussion.[2] They are representative of the many issues which often cut across all lines of insurance and encompass all viewpoints. Some of these topics are mounting "problems," the answers to which are unclear, and may remain unclear for many years. All are issues, however, which are projected as significant for the future of insurance.

Predictions are dangerous, but they *do* have value. They become warnings to planners and guidelines for decision makers. Even at their worst, they serve in retrospect as amusing and useful examples of cloudy crystal-ball gazing. Another valuable purpose is that looking to the future forces human thinking away from the channels of everyday concern to encompass broader perspectives than would ever be achieved otherwise. The present is rarely satisfying by itself; it is in the future that improvements and ideals reside. Thus insurance *should* look to the future, despite the perils of prediction, in order to find the best potential for development.

CONSUMER ISSUES

The consumer viewpoint on insurance and risk, which in many respects has been underemphasized in the past, has been popularized as part of the general trend toward "consumerism." The needs and position of the consumer are receiving much greater attention than ever before.

Significance of insurance to consumers

For example, observers of the insurance business frequently and justifiably applaud the significance of insurance as an essential part of our democratic society. The logic of this point has been shown in Chapter 3, with statistics on the multi-billion dollars of sales, assets, and investments by insurance, which serves as the cornerstone of an expanding free world. Forgotten sometimes is the fact that these dollars come from families and businesses that want a foundation of security in a rapidly changing, and often insecure, environment.

The importance of insurance to our society *and* its citizens is emphasized by the Ohio Insurance Institute with statistics that summarize what would happen if insurance ceased to be available for just one day in the state.[3] The results are illustrated with figures on lost taxes; increased unemployment; unstarted buildings and business firms; reim-

---

[2] Dr. Walter Diehl, general manager of Swiss Reinsurance Company, has said that "anyone attempting to comment on the future of insurance finds . . . an embarrassing situation on account of the many possible aspects to the topic," *Sigma* (North American Reinsurance Corp., July 1978, p. 1). This author agrees, but embarrassment is more desirable than neglecting to attempt to choose and discuss pertinent factors in the future of insurance.

[3] *Ohio Insurance Guide* (Columbus, Ohio: Ohio Insurance Institute, 1982–83), p. 66.

bursed losses to homes, automobiles, and other property; foreclosed mortgages; unmade bank loans; financial hardship for families whose breadwinners died or were disabled; and various other cutbacks in what are today taken for granted as normal business activities.

The message is clear—insurance *is* significant, influencing almost every facet of our society. An important corollary is that, more so than ever before, insurance has become a business *profoundly* affected with a *public* interest. Its position and influence are such that, like it or not, this new dimension demands increasing attention from all those persons and organizations that are concerned with insurance in the era of consumerism. Consumers have achieved an unparalleled status in the decision making of the marketplace and in governmental activities.

For a decade or more, the uncomfortable dissatisfaction of the consumer who is rightfully looking for new values and who voices new-muscled complaints has been stressed.[4] One controversial example is the publication of *The Invisible Bankers* by Andrew Tobias in 1982.[5] It has been long since any book about insurance has received such publicity—or created such a stir in the popular press. Although it makes a somewhat unfair comparison of banking and insurance (they *are* different!), it is provocative, which is what any investigative reporter desires. Occasionally appreciative of the values of insurance, the author's attack on insurance is not scholarly, but it is readable with humor in its many anecdotes. It is more flippant than specific in advice to policyholders. Insurers are criticized as inefficient, agents as evasive, and consumers as larcenous. Reportedly successful in sales, in spite of vehement negative reaction from insurance circles for its misleading generalities, this book at least shows how much insurance needs to increase public understanding of its business.

Anyone who believes that the consumer-protection trend will fade away should appraise the account of its origins, causes, and probable future.[6] It is probably less true to call consumerism "a new wave" than to recognize it as an old idea with a new name. Basically it means honesty, information, and fair play for the buyer; but it *is* here to stay—and with it the need for business to adjust to the new relationships created by the more powerful consumer. These observations apply in spite of some consumer-protection rules which appear to be losing strength in the early 1980s, such as diminishing power of the Federal Trade Commission in controlling deceptive advertising.

---

[4] *A Sentry Study,* a national opinion poll conducted for Sentry Insurance Companies by McBain Research, 1980.

[5] Andrew Tobias, *The Invisible Bankers* (New York: Linden Press/Simon & Schuster, 1982).

[6] Frederick D. Sturdivant, *The Future of Consumerism in Retailing* (College of Administrative Science, Ohio State University, Reprint Series, March, 1978), p. 99.

Potential effects on insurance

Closely related to consumerism is a relatively new approach to solving some of the problems of marketing. Called the *marketing concept* in the textbooks, the idea is based upon the income revolution which has happened in most family budgets. The rise of all incomes, and particularly the incomes of persons in the middle-income group, permits many more expenditures for *discretionary* items than ever before. Instead of food, shelter, and clothing, consumers contemplate choices among automobiles, household appliances, travel and vacations, sports equipment, personal computers, and many new luxuries of today's society.

The result is a tremendous strengthening of the role of the consumer, providing a new focus for marketing effort. In general the transition has been one from an emphasis on selling what a company had, to *producing* the goods and services that are needed and wanted by the consumer. This new era of consumer-oriented marketing is the sphere within which changes in the insurance business are occurring today.

Take a careful look at insurance consumers today. That's fundamentally what all the new "surveys of buying habits" and "consumer behavior studies" are trying to do. Lifestyles are changing, and with the new emerging attitudes toward instant gratification, the family, religion, leisure, sex, work, and other values, the consumer must be studied in adapting marketing strategies to a new era.[7] Consumers today are more highly educated, have the advantage of "instant communication" via television and other media, and have access to many more markets than ever before. They have more assets and more income with which to purchase protection for those assets. Even so, they are apt to be more cost conscious than in years past, because they *know* they now have a wider choice of insurers, agents, contracts, services, and costs. They understand the need for insurance better than ever before, but would still like to find the best way to keep costs down in our society of rising inflation and taxes. The "best" way also involves, in their thinking, the simplest and most convenient way to obtain the most adequate insurance coverage. The advantages they are searching for in their role of making choices as consumers are: (1) the lowest *cost,* (2) the broadest *coverage,* and (3) the most *convenient* method.

Insurers are caught up in the consumer revolt in a number of ways. One example is the increasing emphasis on the cost of insurance, repeatedly seen in the growing reluctance of regulators to grant price increases for certain types of insurance coverages. The power of the press and the increased interest of unions in such rate increases are also readily

---

[7] Roger Blackwell and Wayne Talarzyk, "Changing Lifestyles: Input for Adaptive Strategies," *Bulletin of Business Research* (Ohio State University) 53, no. 1 (January 1978), p. 1.

apparent. More complete and explicable answers must be found to satisfy legislators and the public on the true profits in the property-liability insurance field. (See later section on this as a "social issue.") Insurers must strive to develop and explain pricing systems for all forms of insurance to consumers.

Another effect of consumerism on insurance is an accelerated adoption of the risk-management concept—a maxi-viewpoint of insurance *and* loss prevention *and* other alternatives for handling risk.[8] Inherent in the consumerist society is the need for much broader insurance education and research.

Current examples of the consumer trend

Typical of the desire for more information, and of the willingness of business and government to provide it, are the *consumer hot lines* installed by many insurers and state insurance departments. An example is the opening of an "Office of Consumer Information" by the Travelers Insurance Companies in the 1970s. Most of the more than *1 million* inquiries during the first decade of operation came through toll-free telephone calls. The answers were given, often following immediate checks with department heads, by volunteer and retired employees rehired to staff the new effort at consumer contact. Surprisingly, almost two thirds of the calls were from noncustomers of the insurer. More than 60 percent of the calls were made in order to get information, facts, and explanations. Less than 20 percent were made to complain, urge action, or berate the insurer. The mood of the caller was characterized as "friendly" in more than 40 percent of the calls; 17 percent of the callers were "frustrated"; and less than one fourth were "hostile" or "had been offended." In follow-up research, more than 80 percent of the callers were found to be very satisfied with the first contact made in response to their inquiries. The questions that were most frequently asked centered on automobile rates, no-fault plans, and cancellations; readability of contracts; how to cut insurance costs; homeowner's contract value increases with inflation; rapidity of claims payment; differences among basic life insurance contracts; and health insurance and Medicare.[9]

Ohio, Kansas, Michigan,[10] and other states have had similar experience with hot lines installed in their state insurance department offices. Inqui-

---

[8] George L. Head, "Continuing Evolution of the Risk-Management Function and Education in the United States," *Education Exchange,* December 1982.

[9] From correspondence with the Office of Consumer Information, Travelers Insurance Companies; and *Answers to Questions People Have Been Asking Us about Insurance* (Hartford, Conn.: Travelers Insurance Companies).

[10] "Call the Michigan Consumer Hotline A Success," *National Underwriter,* July 23, 1982, p. 10.

ries have been encouraged by publicity in regard to this service. The highest percentage of calls (about 40 percent) concern auto insurance, and life and health each prompt about 20 percent of the calls.

Another example of worthwhile attempts by the state insurance departments to improve understanding is the publication of pamphlets concerning topics of interest and importance to the insurance consumer. Topics of *shopper's guides* include hospital and surgery charges, comparative life and auto insurance costs, checklists on how to pick a good agent and insurer, and contract coverages. The NAIC also approved a buyer's guide and policy *cost* summary for life insurance which has been adopted by many insurers and is now required in about one half of the states. Although criticized as incomplete and unfair by some insurers, the information given to the public is generally commendable for having improved consumer education about insurance.

Also important to mention as examples of how insurers have responded to consumerism are the FAIR plans (see Chapter 24), urban investment programs in blighted areas of large cities by life insurers,[11] and the new "readable" homeowners' and auto insurance contracts discussed in previous chapters. In Chapter 6 the topic of price disclosure in life insurance was explored, showing how policyholders have more "interest-adjusted" cost comparisons available than ever before.

Government has also responded with many consumer affairs bureaus and commission and study groups on both federal and state levels. Legislation of considerable importance to the consumer has been passed: the Occupational Safety and Health Act; the Consumer Products Safety Act; the riot, crime, and flood insurance initiated by the Housing and Urban Development acts; pension plan rules under ERISA; and pollution controls by the Environmental Protection Agency. These actions have had and will continue to have far-reaching effects on consumers and on the insurance business.

BUSINESS ISSUES

The issues presented in this section are merely samples of the problem (and opportunity!) areas of insurance which directly affect the conduct of the insurance business. The international trend is emphasized because it will probably increase greatly in the future and therefore should be of particular interest to any student of insurance. Marketing philosophies, arson problems, insurer investments, insurance exchanges, and unusual new types of insurance are also mentioned.

---

[11] Life insurers now publish a regular report on their social investments, community projects, equal employment opportunities, company contributions, environmental concerns, and other activities. See *Response* (Washington, D.C.: Clearinghouse on Corporate Social Responsibility), and their annual report titled *Social Report*.

Internationalism

Forty years ago one of the most courageous and bestselling books of the modern era proclaimed that "our thinking in the future must be world-wide."[12] Few indeed are the topics or issues today which can be discussed merely on a national scale; the ramifications beyond national boundaries are too frequent and too important to omit. The broader aspects of international activities are crucial to today's work market-place. Increased and faster travel and communication continue this trend toward interdependence every year.

Growth of world business. Everywhere one sees evidence of interest and activity in the global aspects of business—in new products for import and export, in new international organizations, firms, and departments. The revival of some foreign languages, the vast increases in foreign travel and contacts, and the new curricula developed in the colleges for international business studies are further examples of forces combining to make the "foreign" world not as foreign as it used to be.

International business (and particularly insurance) has a potential which can reasonably be compared to the 1400s when Columbus piqued the imagination of Queen Isabella and opened the doors of the New World, or the 1800s when U.S. envoy Townsend Harris negotiated the opening of doors for trade with Japan. With world trade at record levels, and U.S. investments abroad and foreign investment in the United States increasing rapidly, the interrelationships of world business are readily apparent. The insurance program of the Overseas Private Investment Corporation (OPIC), discussed in Chapter 24, is an example. The reopening of trade with Communist China in 1979 is another.

The Parker Pen Company 55 years ago advertised that its pen "wrote in every language." Now look at any issue of *Time, Business Week, Fortune,* or similar publications, and count the companies which feature their international marketing prowess! In the current generation the pace of international business has quickened until it permeates almost every aspect of modern life. Gen Hirose, president of the Nippon Life Insurance Company, has claimed that the *economic* basis of world friendship is making more progress than the political basis and international insurance may well be one of the leaders in this trend.[13]

Rationale for world insurance. "Thinking big," in a geographic sense, is as valuable in insurance as in general business. The advantages

---

[12] Wendell L. Willkie, *One World* (New York: Simon & Schuster, 1943), p. 2. See also Edward Bates, "Impacts of Current Socio-Economic Forces," *International Insurance Seminars: Reports and Studies,* August 1977.

[13] At the International Insurance Seminars, Tokyo, Japan, 1970. The concept has been repeatedly expressed at similar seminars held during the past decade in Mexico, Spain, Norway, the Philippines, Brazil, and Canada.

of surveying the world insurance scene are many.[14] The principle of free trade advocated long ago by Adam Smith and other economists has an important application in insurance, which involves a basic need for diversification and spread of risk. What else motivates insurance companies to operate outside their home country? The incentives[15] to international insurance are:

1. *Policyholders.* The objective is more clients, retention of existing business relationships, and better-satisfied customers. Protecting or expanding markets is the description of this process. U.S. businesses, for example, need protection for their overseas operations.
2. *Profits.* This goal is a logical one for any private enterprise economy. It may take the form of *higher* immediate profits (short-run), higher long-run profits, or—separately or in combination with these goals— the desire for greater *stability* of profits through diversification and spread of risk among different countries. Developing nations have considerable insurance profit potential.
3. *Power.* The objectives of growth, in terms of policyholders, contracts, or assets, may sometimes be for its own sake, rather than a method by which to achieve profits. International business involves competition among large firms.
4. *Prestige.* This term may be used to describe the desire to improve a public image for the company or its executives. It can also be a legitimate and valuable tool by which the previous goals can be reached.

The four "p's"—policyholders, profits, power, and prestige—are an artificial but quite complete method of reviewing the goals and advantages of foreign market operations. Even though only hundreds of the 10,000 insurers in the world now operate on a truly international scale, the stake is big and growing bigger.

Dimensions of international insurance. To appreciate the dimensions of international insurance, one should first look at how insurance looks in the whole world.

The free world insurance market, not including the social insurance systems, totaled $435 billion in premiums during 1980,[16] up from $212

---

[14] In fact, one might argue that insurance, with the insuring of U.S. astronauts in their trip to the moon, has already gone "out of this world." Losses have, too, as the largest claim ever ($77 million) for a space test satellite explosion was paid in 1979.

[15] Mention should also be made of at least one deterrent to a truly international community—nationalism, which sometimes needlessly restricts business with foreign companies. See Edwin W. McCrae, "The International Business Environment," (Ohio State University) *Bulletin of Business Research* 52, no. 4 (April 1977), p. 1.

[16] *Insurance Facts* (New York: Insurance Information Institute, 1982–83), p. 12, for figures in this paragraph.

Table 29–1. The world's leading insurance countries in 1980
(Premiums rounded to billions of U.S. dollars)*

Position	Country	Nonlife premiums	Life premiums	Total premiums	% of total world premiums
1	United States	$125	$ 65	$190	44
2	Japan	19	40	59	14
3	West Germany	23	17	40	9
4	Great Britain	15	16	31	7
5	France	17	6	23	5
6	Canada	7	5	12	3
7	Netherlands	5	3	8	2
8	Italy	6	1	7	2
9	Australia	5	2	7	2
10	Switzerland	3	3	6	1
	Totals	225	158	383	89

* Excludes the Eastern-bloc countries and social insurance taxes.
Source: North American Reinsurance Corporation, as reported in *Insurance Facts* (New York: Insurance Information Institute, 1982–83), p. 12.

billion in 1975 and $70 billion in 1965. The U.S. part of this total was $190 billion, or approximately 44 percent, representing 7 percent of the nation's gross national product. More than a dozen other countries have a ratio of private insurance premiums to gross national product of 5 percent or higher. Such progress is not universal, however, as is shown in the per capita insurance premium figures, which are about $960 in Switzerland, $830 in the United States, and $650 in West Germany,[17] but are less than $20 in such countries as Brazil, Mexico, and India. Table 29–1 shows the world's leading insurance countries in terms of premium volume. Headed by the United States, Japan, West Germany, Great Britain, and France, the top 10 countries write almost 90 percent of the global insurance. Another contrast shows the United States with $4 trillion of life insurance values in force, but only a few countries, such as Canada, the United States, New Zealand, Sweden, Japan, Australia, and the Netherlands with life insurance greater than one year's national income. The conclusions are: (1) insurance is a big world business; (2) the United States is particularly important, and (3) there is great disparity in the development of insurance among individual areas and nations of the world.

The basic tenet of insurance—spread or diversification of risk—underscores the ideas that world business is dependent upon insurance and that insurance is dependent upon the existence of an international market. Of particular significance is the mechanism of reinsurance, by which

---

[17] *Life Insurance Fact Book* (Washington, D.C.: American Council of Life Insurance, 1982), p. 102.

insurers spread their risks throughout the world. For many concentrated, high-value properties, such as ships, airplanes, refineries, and dams, and for certain perils with catastrophic potential, such as hurricane, flood, earthquake, and aviation crashes, the majority of insurance contracts just could not be written without the world reinsurance market capacity. Would any insurance company want to take on, alone, a $300 million exposure for the damage and injury one 747 airplane could cause? Or a $200 million dam or utility exposure? Or a $100 million building?

In summary, much of the insurance written in the world is dependent upon the ability of insurers to write insurance or reinsurance outside their own country. For example, U.S. insurers write about $1 billion of reinsurance premiums for coverage in foreign countries and pay out $2 billion in reinsurance premiums to foreign reinsurers.[18]

U.S. insurers in the world market. Insurers are meeting the challenge of international insurance needs in several ways. One method is by the established *reinsurance* market, which has for many years solved the bulk of problems in making insurance a global product. Some 100 U.S. insurers have entered the reinsurance market in the past two decades, many on an international basis. Another way is through the use of *associations* in insurers, such as the American Foreign Insurance Association (AFIA)[19] and the American International Group (AIG), which have been active for 45 years. A third method, popular with U.S. insurers since the 1960s (an exception is the Insurance Company of North America, which earlier established direct branches of its company) is the *direct purchase or start of a foreign subsidiary insurer,* or *an international joint venture*[20] or *cooperative agreement* between foreign and U.S. insurers. Among these are: Aetna Life and Casualty (Assicurazioni Generali), Travelers (Guardian and Riunione Adriatica), Lincoln National Life (Union), Continental of New York (Phoenix), Occidental (Heiwa Life), Continental (Winterthur), and Nationwide (Neckura). Also operating overseas are the Atlantic Companies, Combined Group, Hartford Companies, Kemper Group, and many others.

International insurance, in addition to its consumer and social effects in various countries, also has a direct economic effect on the balance of payments. For example, U.S. insurers have traditionally purchased much more reinsurance abroad than they have sold in the foreign reinsurance markets, while other countries (notably the United Kingdom

---

[18] "More Reinsurance Flows Out of United States Than In," *Business Insurance,* October 1982, p. 30.

[19] Sylvia McGriff, "The Old AFIA Brings New Thrust to International Insurance," *Hartford Agent,* June 1982, p. 14.

[20] John D. Hogan, "Innovations in Insurance Marketing: The International Joint-Venture" (paper presented at the American Risk and Insurance Association annual meeting, Miami, Florida, August 1973).

and Switzerland) have sold more than they have bought.[21] Losses paid under such contracts also affect the net inflow or outflow of capital.

Marketing methods in insurance

Insurance buyers are the focal point of dramatic changes occurring in the marketplace. Probably at no point in recent history have insurance purchasers been in more of a "buyers' market" than during the early 1980s. They have the enviable position of an era which combines low prices and increased competition from many new marketing methods.

Life insurance. The general level of prices for life insurance has dropped perhaps 20 percent or more in the past decade to the lowest level ever experienced for individual coverages. Individual annuities are available with tax-deferred benefits through Individual Retirement Accounts (IRAs). The new "universal life" contract provides protection with savings accumulated at current market rate earnings. Better price disclosure rules provide more information to consumers in order to compare prices. The growth of group life insurance at favorable rates continues. Added to all these developments is emerging competition for insurers from the "financial supermarkets,"[22] with dozens of new companies jumping into insurance from other fields such as investments. Reorganizing for complete financial services are large firms both from within the insurance business and from other businesses, including Shearson/American Express; Prudential; Sears, Roebuck; Merrill Lynch; J. C. Penney; Continental Can; Travelers; and many others.

Property and liability insurance. Change seems everywhere in property and liability insurance. In the *personal lines,* the competition begun 40 years ago continues between *"exclusive" and "independent" agency systems.* As discussed in Chapter 25, the exclusive agency companies (led by State Farm, Allstate, and Nationwide) have increased their market share in a little less than three decades from one fourth to about one half of the automobile and homeowners' insurance markets. Direct billing to policyholders, revised rating classifications, brokerage agreements with competing insurers, and many other changes have been adopted by both types of agency systems. There appear to be as many "mixed" agency systems of marketing as there are examples of the traditional types.

In addition, the marketing phenomenon of *franchising* has spread to insurance agencies. Franchises are contracts to sell products or services in a specified territory. The advantages claimed are national identifica-

---

[21] See footnote 18.

[22] "How They Manage the New Financial Supermarkets," *Business Week,* December 20, 1982, p. 50.

tion of the franchises with the franchiser's name and advertising. The franchiser sets quality control standards for the marketing process and provides help such as customer referral services, education, market information, and other services to the franchisee. About four insurance franchise operations are already active: Insurance Systems Unlimited (ISU–Cal.), Insurance Consortium of America (ICA–Conn.), Marketforce International (MI–Mo.), and Insurance World Corporation (IWC–Cal.).[23] At least six other franchisers have been proposed or are in formative stages. Continental Insurance Companies has also entered into a joint venture to sell homeowners' insurance policies through franchised real estate agents of Century 21.[24] The developments will be important to watch in the 1980s.

Group property-liability insurance marketing of automobile and homeowners' insurance has been noted in Chapter 25. Although not yet widespread, some insurers are active in writing these coverages through employers and associations in states where legislation permits them to do so (see later section of this chapter on these legislative restrictions).

In the *commercial lines* the current market is more competitive than ever before. Insurers and agents are marketing business *multiple-line contracts* (see Chapter 23) with aggressive and cost-cutting techniques that result in prices that have dropped to dangerous levels. Examples of renewals at 50 percent or less than previous contracts are criticized as causing more switching of coverages for clients than most agents can ever remember in their careers. Agents writing the business are elated, but those losing customers wonder when the intense competition will lessen. Insurers that have reduced rates to increase premium volume and "cash flow" will undoubtedly suffer higher loss ratios, which will eventually lead to another cyclical round of price increases.

Two other trends are occurring simultaneously. The increased importance of *corporate risk managers* was observed in Chapters 1 and 2, bringing new challenges for insurers and agents to provide much more comprehensive insurance and loss-control services. The big *national insurance brokers* are improving their risk-management expertise and also are setting up networks of service offices. The six largest brokers have multistate offices (some acquired by purchasing large insurance agencies) in about 200 cities, providing headquarters in all the top sources of insurance business.[25] These include Marsh & McLennan, Alexander & Alexander, Corroon & Black, Fred S. James, Frank B. Hall, and Rollins Burdick Hunter.

---

[23] Richard J. Kasyjanski, "Insurance Agency Franchising," *Independent Agent,* December 1981, p. 39.

[24] "Continental's Experiment in Personal Lines Sales," *Independent Agent,* February 1982, p. 26.

[25] "The Rise of the Brokers," *Independent Agent,* February 1982, p. 53.

Arson problems

One of the perplexing problems of property insurance during the last decade has been the rise of *arson*, the deliberate setting of fires for fraudulent purposes such as collecting insurance, which seems to have reached almost epidemic proportions. The National Fire Protection Association estimated in 1981 that arson caused 820 civilian (nonfirefighter) deaths and property losses of $1.7 billion, or 28 percent of all building fire dollar losses.[26] A recent study by the All-Industry Research and Advisory Council (AIRAC) found that between 11 and 40 percent of all fires studied involved arson.[27]

Although the immediate effect of arson falls on the insurers that suffer increased losses, there are also many indirect effects—displaced tenants, uninsured losses, increased claims expenses, lost lives and injuries, business insolvencies and increased unemployment, the straining of fire department facilities and risks to fire-fighting personnel, and many others. The results have been depicted in television reports, books,[28] and articles as disastrous for many of the persons involved. The total annual cost may exceed $10 billion.

Thus far the battle against arson has been relatively ineffective, and major new efforts and changes seem needed. In spite of high costs, possible liability suits for alleged arson, and the difficulty of legally proving arson, insurers must intensify their investigations and their resistance to paying suspected arson losses. Research indicates that insurers should (1) pay more attention to the financial position of the insured in the underwriting process, (2) use more scientific investigative techniques, and (3) support legislation to reclassify the seriousness of arson as a crime.[29] Rewards for arson information leading to conviction have been offered by some insurers, but it remains difficult to prove intent in arson cases. Failure to heed the advice of researchers in implementing all available means to combat arson will be foolish indeed.

The need is for *combined* efforts by government officials in combating the crime of arson, insurer cooperation in the investigations, and even consumer help through vigilante organizations. Some cities, such as Boston and Cleveland, have mobilized various interests in attempts to reduce widespread arson, but in many areas little is being done. The Anti-Arson

---

[26] "The Arson Epidemic," *Insurance Backgrounder* (State Farm Insurance Companies, October 1982), p. 1.

[27] The *Arson Incidence Claims Study*, as reported in "Arson: What it Costs, Who's to Blame," *Journal of American Insurance*, Summer 1982, p. 13.

[28] John Barracato and Peter Michelmore, *Arson!* (New York: W. W. Norton, 1976). Also, by the first author is a booklet "Fire—Is It Arson?" (Aetna Casualty and Surety, 1979).

[29] Robert A. Hershbarger and Ronald K. Miller, "The Impact of Economic Conditions on the Incidence of Arson," *Journal of Risk and Insurance* 45, no. 2 (June 1978), p. 275.

Act of 1982 makes arson a federal crime if it involves property affected by interstate commerce and makes arson a major crime requiring reports to the FBI. Other national efforts have included a model arson penal code proposed by insurer groups for adoption in the states and the levying of severe penalties for many arson cases which cause or threaten death or injury to firefighters or other persons. A number of states[30] have also already passed model reporting-immunity laws, protecting insurers against any potential liability arising from giving information on suspected arson to authorities. Legal aspects of arson have been prominent in more than a dozen articles published during the last several years by the American Bar Association.

Insurance exchanges

The *insurance exchange* is an innovative concept that permits an underwriting syndicate marketplace in the United States. Similar to Lloyd's of London or a stock exchange in some respects, the U.S. exchange underwriting members are not, however, individuals with unlimited liability. Instead, they are usually corporations organized as "syndicates" to insure or reinsure risks as members of an exchange. The syndicates are the insurers, not the exchanges.

Three states have passed legislation permitting insurance exchanges. The New York Insurance Exchange commenced operations in 1980 with 14 underwriting syndicates and now has 25; the Illinois Insurance Exchange started in 1981 with 3 syndicates; and the Florida Insurance Exchange (also called the Insurance Exchange of the Americas) is scheduled to open in late 1982 with a reported membership of about 30 syndicates.[31]

The classes of insurance written on the exchanges varies. New York and Florida provide for reinsurance of all kinds and for direct insurance of non-U.S. risks. Illinois does not restrict the sites of risks insured but prohibits life insurance and direct insurance below a minimum premium of $50,000. New York also has a "free trade zone" for specially licensed insurers to write high-premium ($100,000 or more) or unusual high-risk types of insurance without prior regulatory approval of rates and forms. The syndicates in New York may only write direct insurance when it has been rejected by the free trade zone insurers.

---

[30] Connecticut, Georgia, Illinois, New York, North Carolina, Ohio, and Texas. "Arson Lab Fights Fire With Facts," *Journal of American Insurance* 54, no. 1 (Spring 1978), p. 9.

[31] Thomas L. Stevens, *Legal Structure of Insurance Exchanges* (American Bar Association, 1982), p. 887. Reprinted from *The Forum* 17, no. 4 (Spring 1982), this source is used for the additional data in this section unless otherwise noted.

Admission requirements set minimum capital and surplus for the syndicates or underwriting members. To write all kinds of property, casualty, and life insurance, the requirements vary in the three states from about $2 to $6.5 million, although limited lines set lower amounts. Numerous other regulations are imposed by the exchanges on syndicates and brokers.

The need for insurance exchanges and their operations are still controversial. Early predictions for reducing the flow of insurance to foreign markets and for rapid growth have not been achieved. However, in New York the annual premium volume has grown to about $100 million. A Canadian exchange is planned for 1983. One problem that may restrict the growth of the exchanges is the tax status of individual investors in the syndicates. A tax bill expected to be passed in late 1982 may discourage capital growth of the exchanges from investments by individuals, yet projections for the long-range potential for growth of the exchanges are optimistic.[32]

Insurer investments

Few topics in the 1980s are likely to be more prominent in insurance discussions than the effect of high (or low?) investment returns in insurance company operations. The investment earnings of insurers, in today's high interest rate economy, have become a major source of income and of great importance in (1) providing financial strength for the insurers and (2) reducing the overall costs of insurance by making effective use of the sizable assets that many insurers have. The prepaid nature of many insurance payments by policyholders, especially in life insurance, creates funds which the insurer must invest productively and wisely.

The prospective earnings of *life insurers* on total assets, which at the start of 1982 were $526 *billion,* are a primary factor in the pricing process of life insurance. About 25 percent of the total income of life insurers comes from investments. The approximate holdings of life insurers by types of assets are summarized in Table 29–2.

Although 81 percent of these assets represent the "legal reserves" of the contracts for policyholders and must be invested largely in long-term secure investments such as bonds and mortgages, life insurers also have major choices to make among many other investment alternatives for the remainder of their assets. Millions of dollars are invested every day by life insurers in such varied areas as the aviation industry (which is said to be supported by insurers to the extent of more than 40 percent

---

[32] Bill Densmore, "The Tax Bill Could Hinder Growth of Exchanges," *Business Insurance,* October 25, 1982, p. 27; and Jim Synder, "The Florida Exchange: A Face to the Future," *Journal of Insurance* 43 (January–February 1982), p. 10.

Table 29–2. Investments of U.S. life insurance companies, 1982 (beginning)

Type of asset	Billions of $		Percent of total assets
1. Mortgages		138	26
2. Government securities		39	8
3. Corporate securities			
Bonds	194		37
Stocks	48		9
Total corporate bonds and stocks		242	46
4. Real estate		18	3
5. Policy loans		49	9
6. Cash and miscellaneous		40	8
Total all assets		526	100

Source: *Life Insurance Fact Book* (Washington, D.C.: American Council of Life Insurance, 1982), p. 68.

of its outstanding bonds), home mortgages, urban redevelopment housing projects, shopping centers, office buildings, and space exploration.

The impact of these assets is significant. Life insurers provide financial capital to the economy. Bonds and mortgages are the primary type of investments, totaling almost two thirds of all assets. Stocks have been increasing in the overall portfolio and now are valued at $48 billion. They total only about 9 percent of assets, but a changing philosophy, a lessening of legal restrictions, and the growth of insured annuity funds are creating increased interest in stock market activity by life insurers.

In recent years the importance of investment income to *property-liability insurers* has become strikingly apparent. Although traditionally the insurers in these fields have stressed *underwriting* profits from insurance operations, for most insurers underwriting losses (in 5 of the past 10 years) have been supported by *investment* profits. Investments have served (1) to provide the primary source of stockholder dividends and (2) to strengthen the surplus to protect policyholders. Investment income has not been a direct consideration in the pricing of property and liability insurance.[33] Today, however, it has taken on increased significance in the total activities of property-liability insurers. During 1972–81 the property-liability insurers suffered an *underwriting loss* of $16 billion, whereas during the same period they had an *investment profit* of about $65 billion.[34] With this importance, the proper use of assets for invest-

---

[33] This attitude is in sharp contrast to the life insurance situation. For example, note that the booklet *Insurance Facts,* 1982–83 (New York: Insurance Information Institute), contains only two pages on the investment use of assets of the property-liability business. The *Life Insurance Fact Book, 1982,* pp. 67–87, has 20 pages of detailed information on investments! The volatility of property-liability investment profits or losses and the difficulty of determining the source of such income as due to policyholder or other assets have been advanced as the reasons for this contrast.

[34] *Insurance Facts,* pp. 16–17.

ments attains a new perspective and the investment function has assumed a much greater role in this field of insurance.[35] The current picture is summarized in Table 29–3.

Almost 60 percent of the total assets of $228 billion of property-liability insurers is invested in bonds, while stocks account for one fourth of total assets. Less than 1 percent of assets is in mortgages, in contrast to 26 percent of the assets of life insurers. The short-run nature of the obligations of property-liability insurers and the greater need for liquidity to meet catastrophe losses explain some of the differences between life and property-liability investment holdings. Note the higher percentage of bonds held by property-liability insurers (58 percent, as opposed to 37 percent). The stock portfolio of 25 percent, in contrast to the life insurers' 9 percent, is partially the result of fewer legislative restrictions on investments by property-liability insurers. It is also caused by the need for investments which increase in value along with inflation, in order to meet the growing loss payments of property-liability contracts.

The table also shows distinct differences between stock and mutual company investments. Relatively more bonds and less stock holdings are found in mutual companies. Tradition, the types of insurance contracts written, and the size of the insurers are major factors in these differences.

What do these figures in Tables 29–2 and 29–3 mean in regard to the investment function of insurers? The contrasts between life insurers and property-liability insurers have been pointed out. More important for all types of insurers are the facts that insurer assets are tremendous, totaling more than $750 *billion* in 1982, and that these assets need proper management. The assets are *not* automatically invested in certain types of holdings according to precise state laws but are, within regulatory limits, the result of the decisions made by many financial committees and experts of the insurers. The opportunities are bright for investment and financial management personnel in insurance companies. The size of their responsibility and the relative importance to the insurer of their activities promise to make their task of increasing significance in the future.

Investments of insurer assets will continue to be a top priority issue for the 1980s. For the life insurers, investment earnings on their sizable portfolios will determine how well they can compete with other businesses in offering policyholders current returns in new life insurance and annuity contracts. For the property-liability insurers, the current underwriting losses make maximum investment earnings crucial. Some observers predict that these losses may continue for several years longer

---

[35] For further information on insurer investments, see Robert W. Cooper, *Investment Return and Property-Liability Insurance Ratemaking* (Homewood, Ill.: Richard D. Irwin, 1974); and J. David Cummins, ed., *Investment Activities of Life Insurance Companies* (Homewood, Ill.: Richard D. Irwin, 1977).

Table 29-3. Investments of property-liability insurers, 1982 (beginning)

Type of asset	Billions of $			Percent of total assets		
	Stock	Mutual	Total	Stock	Mutual	Total
1. Bonds						
Government	13.3	6.7	20.0	8.0	13.5	9.3
Other	79.3	24.3	103.6	47.5	49.2	47.9
Total bonds	92.6	31.0	123.6	55.5	62.7	57.2
2. Stocks						
Preferred	7.1	1.1	8.2	4.3	2.3	3.8
Common	34.8	9.7	44.5	20.9	19.6	20.6
Total stocks	41.9	10.8	52.7	25.2	21.9	24.4
3. Mortgages	1.2	.1	1.3	.7	.2	.6
4. Real estate	1.4	1.0	2.4	.8	2.1	1.1
5. Premium balances	13.8	3.5	17.3	8.3	7.1	8.0
6. Cash and miscellaneous	15.8	3.0	18.8	9.5	6.0	8.7
Total all assets	166.7	49.4	216.1	100.0	100.0	100.0

Source: *Best's Fire and Casualty Aggregates and Averages* (Oldwick, N.J.: A. M. Best, 1982), pp. 54, 2B. Data include 1204 stock companies and 319 mutual companies, representing more than 95 percent of the total business written. Reciprocals and Lloyd's associations are omitted in these figures.

than is usual for the typical underwriting cycle, or perhaps even indefinitely.[36] Thus, investments by insurers will be increasingly significant to success—and survival.

New types of insurance

Did you ever hear of "antimonster insurance"? Believe it or not, that's one of the recent kinds of insurance developed for any attack against swimmers who compete in races in Scotland's Loch Ness. Such specialized innovations continue to appear every year in the insurance field, but of greater importance are newer insurance coverages that are developed for much broader use in many directions. The new and different ideas in insurance are limited only by the insurer's imagination, some legal regulations, and consumer acceptance.

Many new coverages for changing risk exposures have become available in the past decade. One example is *skyjacking* insurance, paying airline travelers as much as $100 a day for delays caused by airplane hijackers. This insurance was popularized by the numerous skyjackings a decade ago, but the need for it has been substantially lessened by government requirements for baggage inspections and increased security at airports.

Problems of insolvency in the investment field created the need for a government-industry insurance plan to protect clients against the *failure of securities brokers.* The securities industry cooperated with the federal government to bolster public confidence by forming the Securities Investor Protection Corporation (SIPC), insuring customers up to $40,000 in cash or $100,000 in securities for losses caused by the insolvency of securities broker-dealers. SIPC does not protect customers against losses due to fluctuating security prices.[37]

High interest rates and increased mortgage defaults in the 1980s have created the need to offer an insurance plan for homeowners who help finance sales, especially on second mortgages. Several insurers will insure *seller-financed mortgages,* working through the banks or other lending institutions, to protect against the buyer's default.[38]

With restrictions by auto manufacturers on new-car warranties, which decreased typical warranties from five years or 50,000 miles to one year or 12,000 miles, new insurance contracts are now available for *mechani-*

---

[36] Barry D. Smith, "The Property and Liability Underwriting Cycle," *CPCU Journal* 35, no. 3 (September 1982), p. 138.

[37] Harold C. Krogh, "The Securities Investor Protection Corporation: Financial Stringency in Securities Forms," *CPCU Annals* 30, no. 1 (March 1977), p. 78. The limits of coverage were doubled in 1977 amendments.

[38] Jane Bryant Quinn, "A New Security Blanket," *Newsweek,* August 2, 1982, p. 54.

cal breakdown. These contracts extend the warranty for parts and labor costs by three to five years at prices of $175 to $225 for new cars; such contracts are also available in most states on some used cars.[39] Related to this type of insurance is another insurance contract called the "lemon-aid policy," sold to automobile dealers in some states. The policy pays 85 percent of the dealer's loss when a state law permits a new car buyer to demand a full refund for cars that have persistent defects or major breakdowns.

Two other new types of insurance, not discussed previously in this text, are next presented as current examples of how insurers must adapt to the changing needs of insurance consumers.

Kidnap and ransom insurance. Large businesses have become an increasing target for kidnappings of company executives or members of their families. After the widely publicized Lindbergh case in the 1930s, Lloyd's of London wrote some *kidnap-ransom insurance* contracts for relatively modest amounts up to $100,000 (it reportedly paid $50,000 for the Lindbergh's baby). However, it was not until the 1970s that numerous kidnappings in South America began to escalate interest in such protection, and the largest single ransom payment was more than $14 million.[40] Italy has become infamous for crimes involving corporate or political hostages, crimes that culminated with the world-shocking murder in 1978 of the former premier Aldo Moro.[41] The 1976 Venezuela kidnapping of William Niehous, vice president of Owens-Illinois Corporation, brought the potential exposure to U.S. firms sharply into focus. He was rescued by police after being held captive for more than three years.

Kidnappings are of two types: criminal (for profit) and terrorist (for political purposes). The 1974 abduction of Patricia Hearst is an example of the second type, with her father being forced to give away several million dollars of food to the poor. Another political type was the 1979 Iranian case involving 62 American hostages held for 14 months in order to try to force the return of the exiled Shah. Ransom demands are sometimes staggering, and two recent payments were for $11 million (by Lloyd's Bank) and $60 million (by Bunge Born, Argentina's largest private firm).[42]

It is no wonder that kidnap-ransom insurance is one of the fastest growing types of coverage today. A Conference Board report from New

---

[39] "Insuring Cars against Breakdown," *Money,* July 1978, p. 50.

[40] "The Growing Spectre of Executive Kidnapping," *TWA Ambassador,* August 1976, p. 22. In 1970–73, 250 kidnapped executives were reported freed by ransom payments totaling millions of dollars.

[41] "Striking at Italy's Heart," *Newsweek,* March 27, 1978. Some 50–75 kidnappings were reported there in each of the previous three years.

[42] Roger M. Williams, "Executive Kidnapping: The Rise of a Grim New Business," *Saturday Review,* January 1, 1980, p. 13. Rolf Schild, a British businessman, also is said to have paid $26 million after being kidnapped in Sardinia.

York in 1979 estimates several thousand incidents of political terrorism each year, that three fourths of the largest 200 multinational corporations have insurance for kidnappings, and that 25 percent of the incidents are directed against American businesses.

Kidnap-ransom insurance is written primarily by only a few insurers in the United States[43] and by Lloyd's of London. Some persons criticize writing it at all as against public policy (for encouraging such crimes), but generally it is recognized as a legitimate need. The contracts[44] normally written have several unusual features: (1) insureds first have to pay ransom from their own resources (to avoid being in a position to pay larger or quicker ransom demands); (2) notification to and cooperation with the police is required; (3) a policy condition requires secrecy about the existence of the insurance; and (4) a survey of security systems and guards is made, with appropriate discounts in insurance costs allowed. The policy is usually issued for worldwide coverage, although certain countries can be excluded. The name, size, type of industry, and number and geographic distribution of covered employees for a company are important in determining the premium cost, which varies from a few thousand dollars for $500,000 coverage to $30,000 or more for $5 million limits. Threats to kill or injure an insured (extortion) as well as actual kidnapping and ransom demands are covered in some contracts. In all, this coverage is an unusual example of the response of insurers to the changing needs of business for catastrophic protection against a real exposure in a society that seems to be increasingly lawless.

Legal-expense insurance. A new and large market for prepaid legal services in group insurance plans for employees is emerging for development in the 1980s. An outgrowth of group life and health insurance as a fringe benefit through your place of employment, *group legal insurance* is becoming a popular coverage for middle-income Americans. Although group legal insurance was somewhat reluctantly supported by bar associations and insurers in the formative years of the early 1970s, its development has been spurred by two legal changes. The Taft-Hartley amendments of 1973 allowed legal services to be a part of union negotiations, and the Tax Reform Act of 1976 stated that neither employer contributions nor the value of group legal services were taxable income to employees.

Thus far most of the group insurance coverage for "legal health" services has resulted from collective bargaining agreements, with several thousand contracts now in existence covering a total of several million workers. Large groups adding such benefits are plans covering 150,000

---

[43] Such as American Home, Chubb and Son, Nation Union Fire, First State, and Stewart-Smith.

[44] Anthony A. Cassidy, "Lloyd's Kidnap-Ransom Insurance," *Risk Management,* September 1976, p. 6. Loss-prevention techniques are emphasized in Marsh and McLellan's *Kidnap or Hostage Situations* (1978).

Chrysler Corporation employees and 85,000 New York State public employees. However, the potential market is estimated at 70 million persons and annual premiums of $3 billion.[45] This large market is beginning to attract insurers, and many new plans are being approved by the insurance departments of various states. Credit unions, bar associations, and even Blue Cross associations[46] are sponsoring legal-expense insurance plans. College students are covered by about 200 plans, too. Although growth of the plans has been slow, the changing attitude of bar associations and the need for such plans to help in budgeting and paying for rising legal costs are seen as creating mounting pressure for more widespread availability.[47]

The legal-expense insurance plans vary considerably in several respects. Some are "closed panel" types, with the insured choosing among a panel of attorneys employed to provide specified legal services to a group. Others are "open panel" plans, permitting individuals to choose their own attorneys. In regard to the scope of the legal services covered, some plans are very limited and others are comprehensive in nature, including preventive or consultative legal advice (wills, uncontested divorces, bankruptcies, etc.), defense in civil and criminal actions, and plaintiff actions in nontort situations not covered by other sources. The limits of coverage range from $500 to $5,000 a year, and the premiums range from $5 per month per insured to two or three times that amount.

One of the unanswered questions is whether these group insurance plans will lower legal costs, as is one of their prime objectives, or whether the existence of such insurance may create rising costs from the legal profession. The broader marketing possibilities, now that the Supreme Court has ruled that soliciting and advertising professional services is not prohibited by any bar association code of ethics, will be an important factor in determining the longer range costs of prepaid legal-expense insurance. The developments will be an interesting part of the insurance scene to watch in the decade ahead.

SOCIAL ISSUES

The close relationship of insurance to the environment within which it operates is being examined more now than ever before. Although some experts warn that the social insurance area is growing too fast in competi-

---

[45] John S. Clayton, "Legal Insurance for the Middle Class," *Insurance Marketing,* October 1977, p. 10.

[46] "Insurance to Cover the Lawyer's Bill," *Business Week,* April 18, 1977, p. 46. Blue Cross of Western Pennsylvania has three plans, ranging from $60 to $140 per family cost for a year's coverage of $450 to $5,000 of various legal services.

[47] Claude C. Lilly, *Legal Services for the Middle Market* (Cincinnati: National Underwriter, 1974).

tion with the voluntary insurance system, most agree that the application of insurance techniques to individual, social, *and* combined individual-social problems will all be important in the future.

The ethical pillars of insurance

One of the most revealing looks to the future has been taken by Dr. John Long of Indiana University.[48] In questioning the flexibility of insurance to meet expected changes in the environment, he analyzes the projected environment to the year 2000 to wonder whether or not insurance can thrive, or even exist, given the anticipated changes. Will the basic attitude toward achievement and acquisitiveness, for example, change so that the motivations to work will drastically affect the desire to earn and possess wealth (and insurance to protect such assets)? Will the desire for more leisure affect insurance positively or adversely? The basic attitude toward the preservation of values and the distaste for waste are examined in their relationship to insurance. Also, personal attitudes are rapidly changing; and with any decreases in apprehension for the future, in honesty, in obedience to laws, and in the desire to preserve stabilizing traditions of personal responsibility and charity, come fundamental changes in attitudes toward insurance.

The institution of insurance is seen as surrounded by these "pillars of strength," any one of which could drastically change the desire, need, and significance of future insurance systems. The ramifications of thoughtful consideration of such topics are sobering, if not frightening. The adaptability of insurance to meet whatever environmental changes occur should be one of the most important objectives of forward-thinking insurance management. Rarely and only partially can insurance change the environmental conditions under which it works. Most progress must occur by the insurance business adjusting in a responsive way, both before and as personal and social values change. Only in this manner can the industry remain healthy in our society of the future.

The era of increasing "social responsibility" is already upon the American business scene. Insurance companies will have to reshape their priorities in order to accommodate many of the areas of social concern. For example, the tremendous life insurance investment departments will have to balance the obligations for profit and stability which they hold to policyholders and stockholders against increased responsibility to our society as a whole. This will be a challenging task and one which, if done poorly, could easily cause an adverse attitude of consumers toward the product of insurance.

---

[48] John D. Long, *Ethics, Morality, and Insurance: A Long-Range Outlook* (Bloomington: Bureau of Business Research, Indiana University, 1971). See also "The Ethical Pillars of Insurance," *CLU Journal* 26, no. 1 (January 1972), p. 61.

Many predictions, both general in nature and specific to insurance, are available to students of insurance who have a concern for the future.[49] Although the data and conclusions can always be questioned, all are valuable in encouraging thoughts forward in time in order to anticipate probable or possible changes. Insurance will of necessity be forced to deal with these changes, and looking ahead is an important step in preparing for future success.

Government regulation

Another area of great concern for insurance is the legislative framework within which it operates. The following are some examples of the kinds of issues at hand in both federal and state legislation related to insurance.

No-fault automobile laws. Chapter 19 shows no-fault insurance in about 20 states' no-fault plans by 1982. The trend in adopting these laws has slowed since the mid-1970s, with the District of Columbia's law the only new one during the past seven years. Although the issue has been treated by state laws thus far, the impending threat of a federal no-fault law is by no means merely idle conjecture. Congressional committees have only narrowly defeated federal proposals for minimum no-fault standards, and these proposals could obtain the necessary increase in support at any time. There is confusion of insurers, agents, and regulators on the many and varied no-fault plans. Consumers are understandably confused, also, but in general the idea has gained acceptance among them, even if that acceptance is based upon sketchy knowledge of the real effects of the laws on their tort liability rights and their potential cost savings. The situation could perhaps best be stated by saying that "the issue is yet in doubt," but there is no doubt that no-fault plans will continue to be a prominent topic during the 1980s.

One important, unresolved issue is the extent to which, if the no-fault concept is more universally applied in the automobile insurance area, the idea might be useful in other areas. No-fault divorce laws are already operable in some states, but what about extension of the concept to medical malpractice lawsuits and the even larger area of products liability claims?

Environmental control laws. A seeming myriad of federal laws are extending controls to many parts of manufacturing and business activities that were previously regulated only by the states. Examples

---

[49] As examples, see Alvin Toffler, *The Third Wave* (New York: Bantam Books, 1980); and J. Finley Lee, "Insurance in the 21st Century," *Journal of Insurance* 41, no. 6 (November–December 1980), p. 4, which summarizes a major research study sponsored by the Florida Association of Insurance Agents. Another study, called "Future I," was in progress by insurers and the Independent Insurance Agents of America in 1982.

in the 1970s include the Clean Air Act, the Water Pollution Act, the Pesticide Control Act, the Occupational Safety and Health Act (see Chapter 18), and the Noise Act. In 1976 the first federal hazardous waste statute, the Resource Conservation and Recovery Act, focused attention on environmental pollution. The 1980 Comprehensive Environmental Response, Compensation, and Liability Act (called "Superfund" for its $1.6 billion now being used to clean up waste sites) added specific mandatory liability requirements of $14–$50 million for vessel owners, oil rigs, and port operators. To take effect in the late 1980s, these new rules will have important effects on future insurers, insureds, and consumers.[50]

The Consumer Products Safety Act. In a field burgeoning with problems of increasing multimillion-dollar lawsuits, products liability costs are now becoming a major factor in the pricing policies of many businesses. Insurers have difficulty in setting realistic insurance rates to cover the rapidly expanding products liability claims. Although availability of insurance seems adequate in the early 1980s, the longer-range problems have not been solved. Even the Product Liability Risk Retention Act of 1981, a federal law aimed at relieving problems in this area by permitting group purchases of liability insurance, hardly seems to have begun to answer the real needs.[51]

The Consumer Products Safety Commission, which is a powerful new federal regulatory agency, requires notification by manufacturers, distributors, and retailers of any substantial product hazard of which they are aware. Failure to comply may result in civil penalties of up to $500,000 and one year in jail. The burden seems to have shifted from the consumer to the vendor; and this trend will have much effect on future liability lawsuits and insurance to cover the increasing liability caused by failures to meet the detailed requirements of the commission for design, management, record keeping, and other provisions (see also Chapter 17).

Pension reform legislation. For a decade there has been increasing concern about the major changes necessary in the control of pension plans. The classic case of a Studebaker plant in Indiana which closed with 4,000 workers receiving only about 15 percent of "vested" benefits was frequently cited as reason for the need for federal minimum standards. Vesting, which concerns the right of the employee to obtain contributions which the employer has made under pension plans, is a major issue. The Pension Reform Act of 1974 (ERISA), discussed in Chapter 8, requires private pension plans to guarantee gradual nonforfeitable rights accumulating during the first 10 to 15 years of work to full rights

---

[50] Leslie Cheek, "Pollution: The Peril Around Us," *Journal of Insurance* 42, no. 6 (November–December 1981), p. 2.

[51] Eric A. Wiening, "The Risk Retention Act: A Solution to What Problem?" CPCU *Journal* 35, no. 3 (September 1982), p. 174.

to these proceeds (regardless of whether the pension plan stops or employees leave their jobs before retirement). The act also includes mandatory
insurance to guarantee these benefits, strong fiduciary rules, and special
tax incentives to those workers who are not in private pension plans,
so that they can set up their own individual retirement programs. The
combined efforts of consumers, employers, and government in regard
to these extensive and expensive controls are readily seen as a continuing
priority issue for the future. The goals of ERISA are commendable, but
the myriad of detailed rules make this legislation one of the most costly
laws ever to be administered by federal agencies.

Group property-liability insurance legislation. Many of the states
already permit some forms of mass merchandising plans through employers and employees (see Chapter 25). Few, however, permit automobile,
homeowners', and other personal insurance contracts on a "true group"
basis, with full group rating and underwriting, as in life and health
insurance. In order to permit this, the state insurance laws in regard
to discrimination and marketing practices must be changed. The issue
of what the benefits and problems of such plans really are to consumers,
insurers, employers, and agents is still largely unresolved. Regulators
are uncertain as to what additional legal controls are necessary, although
pressure for permitting these plans has increased. About half of the
states have laws or regulations prohibiting "ficticious" groups organized
solely for the purchase of insurance, and 11 have rules for collective
merchandising plans.[52]

Some large insurers are actively marketing such plans already, while
others have not done so for their commercial clients. It appears that
two key factors, in addition to employer and union interest, will be important in the future: the possibility of extending tax deductions for employer
contributions to the cost of personal insurance in these plans, and the
battle between automobile insurers and Blue Cross–Blue Shield associations as to whether auto insurance or health insurance will be the primary coverage for medical costs of automobile accidents under the new
no-fault laws. The outcome of these issues may determine the future
of mass merchandising in the property-liability lines.

Property-liability insurance rating and profitability. Another
area of special interest to consumers, but directly affecting insurers and
government as well, is the question of how rates are set, and how profitable (or unprofitable) the property-liability business has been in recent
years. The issue was raised to prominence by a study[53] which indicated
that there have not been excessive rates in this sector of the business,

---

[52] Ibid., p. 189.

[53] *Studies on the Profitability, Industrial Structure, Finance, and Solvency of the Property
and Liability Insurance Industry* (Boston: Little, Brown, 1970).

but the complexities of choosing the proper rate base and formulas have created much discussion and criticism.[54] The NAIC has developed a form of measuring profits which may become an authoritative standard that regulators can use in approving the rates of insurers, but wide acceptance has not yet been attained.

A broader area of discussion also promises to provide continued debate within the industry, and with regulators, during the years ahead. This is the analysis of competition in property-liability insurance, particularly in regard to the tremendous task which the insurance department has of administering rate regulation (laws for automobile and homeowners' lines, especially) in many of the states. The issue is not limited only to this phase of the business, as life insurance, too, comes in for its share of the problem of maintaining reasonable competition in a business that also requires cooperative efforts to bring the consumer the best possible products at prices that are high enough (but not too high) and fair to different purchasers.[55]

The traditional methods of rating automobile insurance have been one of the hottest topics for debate during the early 1980s. Geographic territories, age, sex, and marital status as major pricing factors have been challenged in many states. Age and sex differences are now prohibited in about eight states, including Hawaii, North Carolina, and Massachusetts. These restrictions mostly benefit young male drivers, who in most plans now pay the highest automobile insurance premiums, by increasing rates for other groups, particularly older drivers. Even though accident statistics also clearly vary for urban and rural areas, basing premiums on geographic boundaries within a state has been claimed as unfair and social undesirable. (It may be unfair not to do so, too, as the opponents of this view point out.) Some states are trying to restrict the ways in which insurers classify risks by territory, by requiring the combination of urban and suburban (or rural) territories. The political appeal of lowering high auto insurance costs in urban areas by this method is a powerful factor in the clamor for challenging existing rating classifications, in spite of the years of accident data which indicate large differences in accident rates and costs in smaller territorial classes.

Surcharges on the rates charged inexperienced (mostly young) drivers are being tried in several states as an important new rating factor. Also,

---

[54] George L. Head, "Synopsis of Measurement of Profitability and Treatment of Investment Income in Property-Liability Insurance," *CPCU Annals* 24, no. 4 (December 1971), p. 379; and Stephen W. Forbes, "Profitability in the Nonlife Insurance Industry, 1955–74," *CPCU Annals* 30, no. 2 (June 1977), p. 126.

[55] Mark S. Dorfman, "Workable Product Competition in Life Insurance Markets," *Journal of Risk and Insurance* 34, no. 4 (December 1972), p. 613; and Peter Praetz, "Returns to Scale in the U.S. Life Insurance Industry," *Journal of Risk and Insurance* 47, no. 3 (September 1980), p. 525.

greater reliance on individual accident records seems indicated in the newer rating plans. The validity of such merit rating systems, with low rates for accident-free drivers and drivers with no traffic violations, is questioned, however, because of the unreliability of motor vehicle records in many states. The perfect rating system is probably unattainable, but there is no doubt that in the years ahead government, insurers, and consumers will be increasingly involved with many changes which treat auto insurance costs as a major social issue.

Other social issues

This chapter could easily continue for many pages more to point out issues for discussion from a social viewpoint. Many of the other issues have been mentioned in preceding chapters. The student is encouraged to review some of the earlier chapters to locate further problems which will undoubtedly also be major issues for the future.

Consumers will always be significant in social issues. A review[56] of the current public view lists many concerns related to insurance: (1) government regulation (nearly half of respondents think there is too much business regulation); (2) government responsibilities (most believe taxes too high and are evenly divided as to whether cutbacks are needed to reduce inflation); (3) financial planning, advising, and services centers (much interest, but individuals admit they have done or used little); and (4) retirement and Social Security (great interest, but many doubts).

Can you think of other social issues that will be increasing in importance during the rest of the 1980s? How about skyrocketing health care costs, nuclear energy exposures, or unemployment due to the computer age? Or the effects of the world population explosion with a 50 percent increase by the year 2000?[57] The need for greater productivity at work, but a desire for more leisure? Career women and families?

These issues and all those discussed in the chapter will affect *you and insurance* in the future. Continuing to use the Socratic method of teaching by asking questions, in regard these issues, this text ends by raising one more: *"How?"*

FOR REVIEW AND DISCUSSION

1. Give an example of how the *consumer, business,* and *government* viewpoints are related to each other in discussing one major issue in insurance today.

2. How and why has *consumerism* occurred in the United States? Is it really a new idea? How is the recent increased role of the consumer different from the consumer's earlier role?

---

[56] *Current Social Issues* (Washington, D.C.: American Council of Life Insurance, Summer 1982).

[57] Peter Neckermann, "Societal Changes in the Eighties," *Research Review,* July 1982.

3. What examples of the *response* to consumerism can you cite from the fields of insurance? What changes do you see in the next five years?

4. *Other than* the examples mentioned in this chapter, what are insurers doing to adapt to the era of consumerism?

5. Why is internationalism of special significance to the insurance business?

6. What rationale can an insurer develop for becoming international in scope?

7. Explain two important factors about the dimensions of international insurance today.

8. *How,* primarily, have insurers been international in the past? What new changes are appearing in the expansion to global insurance markets?

9. Does insurance help a nation's international balance-of-payments situation? Explain.

10. Marketing systems are changing in the property-liability field. How and why?

11. What can be done about the "arson epidemic" of recent years, and whose responsibility is it to provide the solution?

12. New "insurance exchanges" have been established in New York, Illinois, and Florida. What may be their potential benefits and problems?

13. Discuss the need for and the potential problems of *(a) kidnap-ransom* and *(b) legal-expense* insurance as recently developing new types of insurance. What other new types of insurance have you read about lately?

14. If you were the manager of investments, how might your job vary if you worked for a life insurer instead of a property-liability insurer?

15. Contrast the investments of different insurers, indicating the possible reasons for the differences in the portfolios of the insurers you discuss.

16. Has the relative importance of the investment and underwriting operations of insurers changed in the past decade? If so, what might this mean for finance majors in a college of business?

17. What new marketing methods are changing the distribution of insurance? What benefits in these changes are there for consumers?

18. Explain how the traditional methods of auto insurance rating are being criticized today, and how this is becoming a major issue effecting consumers, insurers, and legislators.

19. Discuss some of the "ethical pillars" upon which the future of insurance will be based. Which ones may cause problems for insurance, and which may enhance its position?

20. What evidence can you give of the increasing "social responsibility" of insurance? What examples of the *lack* of it?

21. Which of the social issues in regard to government regulation of insurance are being solved primarily on (1) the state level, (2) the federal level, and (3) on both the state and federal levels?

22. Safety has grown in the past decade as an area for increased government regulation. Explain two such changes.

23. What other social issues not featured in this chapter would you choose as being of considerable importance to the future of insurance?

Appendixes

Appendix A: Compound interest and present value tables

	Column 1 Amount of 1 at *compound interest* for selected interest rates, or $(1 + i)^n$			Column 2 Present value of 1 at compound interest for selected interest rates, or $v^n = (1 + i)^{-n}$			
n	2½%	3½%	5%	2½%	3½%	5%	*n*
1	1.02500	1.03500	1.05000	.97561	.96618	.95238	1
2	1.05062	1.07122	1.10250	.95181	.93351	.90703	2
3	1.07689	1.10872	1.15762	.92860	.90194	.86384	3
4	1.10381	1.14752	1.21551	.90595	.87144	.82270	4
5	1 13141	1.18769	1.27628	.88385	.84197	.78353	5
6	1.15969	1.22926	1.34010	.86230	.81350	.74622	6
7	1.18869	1.27228	1.40710	.84127	.78599	.71068	7
8	1.21840	1.31681	1.47746	.82075	.75941	.67684	8
9	1.24886	1.36290	1.55133	.80073	.73373	.64461	9
10	1.28008	1.41060	1.62889	.78120	.70892	.61291	10
11	1.31209	1.45997	1.71034	.76214	.68495	.58468	11
12	1.34489	1.51107	1.79586	.74356	.66178	.55684	12
13	1.37851	1.56396	1.88565	.72542	.63940	.53032	13
14	1.41297	1.61869	1.97993	.70773	.61778	.50507	14
15	1.44830	1.67535	2.07893	.69047	.59689	.48102	15
16	1.48451	1.73397	2.18287	.67362	.57671	.45811	16
17	1.52162	1.79468	2.29202	.65720	.55720	.43630	17
18	1.55966	1.85749	2.40662	.64117	.53836	.41552	18
19	1.59865	1.92250	2.52695	.62553	.52016	.39573	19
20	1.63862	1.98979	2.65330	.61027	.50257	.37689	20
21	1.67958	2.05943	2.78596	.59539	.48557	.35894	21
22	1.72157	2.13151	2.92526	.58086	.46915	.34185	22
23	1.76461	2.20611	3.07152	.56670	.45329	.32557	23
24	1.80873	2.28333	3.22510	.55288	.43796	.31007	24
25	1.85394	2.36324	3.38635	.53939	.42315	.29530	25
26	1.90029	2.44596	3.55567	.52623	.40884	.28124	26
27	1.94780	2.53157	3.73346	.51340	.39501	.26785	27
28	1.99650	2.62017	3.92013	.50088	.38165	.25509	28
29	2.04641	2.71188	4.11614	.48866	.36875	.24295	29
30	2.09757	2.80679	4.32194	.47674	.35628	.23138	30
40	2.68506	3.95926	7.03999	.37243	.25257	.14205	40
50	3.43711	5.58493	11.46740	.29094	.17905	.08720	50
60	4.39979	7.87809	18.67919	.22728	.12693	.05354	60
70	5.63210	11.11283	30.42643	.17755	.08999	.03287	70

n = number of years; v = value; i = interest rate.
Column 1 shows growth of $1 left at compound interest.
Column 2 shows what $1 due in future years is worth now.

Appendix B:
Life insurance premium calculations

The net single premium

The "net natural premium" represents the amount that each insured must pay into the insurance fund at the beginning of a year so that the beneficiary of each insured who dies during that year may receive the amount of the insurance. This premium has sometimes been defined as "the cost to each individual of the death claims of the group." The net natural premium is computed by applying an interest credit to the natural premium computed from the mortality table. The natural premium on the age of 35 was noted in Chapter 5 as $2.51. Applying credit for interest on the basis of 2.5 percent, the net natural premium becomes $2.44.

A lump sum that will pay in advance and in full the annual premiums on any type of insurance policy is computed by finding the sum which if paid when the policy is issued and augmented by interest earnings during the term will pay the benefit as it comes due. This sum is known as the *net single premium* (NSP).

For a five-year term policy. The computation may be simply illustrated for the five-year term policy. Assume entrants at the age of 35, each insured for $1,000. The mortality table indicates that during the first year there will be 23,528 deaths, and, accordingly, during that year $23,528,000 will be paid as death claims. To compute a five-year term premium, the process is repeated for each of the succeeding years through the five-year term. The rate computation is based upon the assumption that the death benefits are paid at the end of the year in which the deaths occur. To arrive at the basic equation expressing equality between the premiums and the benefits, it is necessary to reduce the benefits to the present value at the beginning of the policy term. The payments due at the end of the first year, therefore, are discounted for one year; those due at the end of the second year, for two years; and so on throughout the term. (See Appendix A for the discount factors.) The sum of the discounted benefits is then found and divided by the total number of entrants at the beginning of the term, and the result is the net single premium for the term.

This is illustrated for the five-year term policy at 35 years for $1,000 as follows:

1st year 23,528 claims = $23,528,000 due end of year
2d " 24,685 " = 24,685,000 " " " "
3d " 26,112 " = 26,112,000 " " " "
4th . " 27,991 " = 27,991,000 " " " "
5th " 30,132 " = 30,132,000 " " " "

Applying the discount factor,

$23,528,000 × 0.975610 = $ 22,954,152.08
24,685,000 × 0.951814 =   23,495,528.59
26,112,000 × 0.928599 =   24,247,577.09
27,991,000 × 0.905951 =   25,358,474.44
30,132,000 × 0.883854 =   26,632,288.73
                          $122,688,020.93

$122,688,020.93 ÷ 9,373,807 = $13.09

The sum of $122,688,020.93 represents the present value of all esti-
mated death claims during the five-year term. To find the net single
premium for each insured, this sum is divided by 9,373,807 (the number
of entrants), and the premium thereby determined is $13.09. Thus, if
at the beginning of the term each entrant pays $13.09, the insurer will
have sufficient funds to pay $1,000 to the beneficiary of each insured
who dies during the term.

For a whole life policy. The net single premium of a whole life
policy is computed exactly like that for the term policy except that instead
of finding the mortality costs for a definite number of years, the computation runs through the entire mortality table from the year of entrance.
The result is the net single premium for a whole life policy at the age
of 35. This works out as follows:

Year	Age	Number living	Deaths each year	Death claims payable	Discount factor	Present value of future death claims
1	35	9,373,807	23,528	$23,528,000 × 0.975610 = $		22,954,152.08
2	36	9,350,279	24,685	24,685,000 × 0.951814 =		23,495,528.59
3	37	9,325,594	26,112	26,112,000 × 0.928599 =		24,247,577.09

[This process is continued throughout the table. In the interest of
brevity, only the first three and the last calculations are shown.]

| 65 | 99 | 6,415 | 6,415 | $ 6,415,000 × 0.200886 = | | 1,288,683.69 |

$3,938,192,458.72

$3,938,192,458.72 ÷ 9,373,807 = $420.13

The present value of the total payment of 9,373,807 entrants at the
age of 35 from the above calculations is $3,938,192,458.72. This sum
divided by the number of entrants gives the amount of $420.13, which
is the net single premium for a whole life policy for $1,000 at the age
of 35.

The term policy and whole life forms here noted illustrate the method
of computing the net single premium. The method is the same for other
policy forms.

Most insureds are reluctant to pay a lump sum for insurance coverage. In the case of an early death, the cost of the insurance would be very high under the single-premium plan as compared with the annual-premium basis. There is also the practical fact that most persons are not able to pay for life insurance on a single-premium basis.

The net level premium

The net single premium represents a full cash-in-advance payment for a life insurance contract. To provide an installment premium plan that is mathematically equivalent to the net single premium, a premium may be charged that remains the same from year to year throughout the premium-paying period. This is known as the *net level premium plan* (NLP). To the insurer, each premium paid is a periodic payment of income, or an annuity.

Utilizing the annuity principle. Under the level premium plan, the time of death definitely determines the aggregate amount of premium paid by each insured. The annual premium is identical for each member of the group; but even though the member dies during the first policy year after the payment of a comparatively small first annual premium, the beneficiary will still receive the face of the policy with no obligation for further premium payments. The insured who pays premiums for many years receives identical treatment.

Since the level premium plan calls for the annual payment of premiums during the premium payment period by living policyholders, it is necessary to examine the anticipated mortality experience to determine (a) the number of premiums that may be expected and (b) the year in which it may be expected that each premium will be paid.

Annuity plans are based on the payment of installment benefit amounts to all the members of the group that survive from year to year in return for a large annuity premium deposit made previously. The lump sum or cost of the annuity is the equivalent of all of the annual payments discounted and divided by the number of entrants. The problem of converting a net single premium to a net level annual premium is the reverse of determining the cost of an annuity. For the annuity, the payments are known and the cost is found by discounting the payments. To determine the level premium from the known single premium, the net single premium is converted to the equivalent annuity due.

Ordinarily, an annuity contract calls for the first annuity payment to be made at the end of one year and annually thereafter. If the annuity is payable at the first of each year, beginning with the first year, it is called an *annuity due*. In the case of an annuity due, all the entrants receive an annuity payment the first year, but each year thereafter a payment is made only to the survivors. Since every insured in a group pays a premium when the policy is issued, it is the annuity due that is comparable to the annual premiums paid on a level premium basis for a life insurance contract. To convert a net single premium to a net level premium, it becomes necessary to find the annuity due that is its mathematical equivalent.

Converting the NSP to an NLP. A net single premium is converted to the equivalent of an annuity due through the use of simple proportion. If an annuity due of $1 yearly may be purchased for $20, then to purchase the same annuity due in the amount of $5 will take $100. The amount is determined by dividing the cost of the annuity due of $1 into the amount available. To convert a net single premium into a net level premium, which amounts to the same thing as converting it to an annuity due, the amount of the net single premium is divided by the value of an annuity due of $1 for the premium-paying term of the policy.

The whole life annuity due. To determine the value of an annuity, the mortality table is used to determine the number of entrants at the required age. Contrary to life insurance, annuity payments are concerned with the number of survivors. For a life annuity due for $1 a year at age 35, since there are 9,373,807 entrants, there will be due immediately $9,373,807. At the end of the second year, since there are 9,350,279 survivors, there will be due $9,350,279; but to reduce this amount to its present value the one-year discount factor must be applied. This process is continued, applying the appropriate discount factor throughout the annuity term. The sum of all annuity payments discounted is found and divided by the number of entrants, and the result is the net cost of the annuity due in question. A temporary annuity due of a year for five years at age 35 is illustrated as follows:

Age		Number living	Present value of $1 @ 2½ %	Present value of annual payments
35	$1 due now	9,373,807	$1.00	$ 9,373,807.00
36	$1 due one year from now	9,350,279	0.975610	9,122,225.70
37	$1 due two years from now	9,325,594	0.951814	8,876,230.93
38	$1 due three years from now	9,299,482	0.928599	8,635,489.69
39	$1 due four years from now	9,271,491	0.905951	8,399,516.54
				$44,407,269.86

The present value of all annuity payments is $44,407,269.86. This sum divided by the number of entrants equals $4.74, the individual share of the present value of all annuity payments. This is the net cost for an annuity payment of $1 a year beginning immediately at the age of 35 and continuing for five years.

The five-year term is here used as a simple explanation of the principle. To determine the premium of an annuity due to continue for the whole life, the same procedure is followed to the end of the mortality table. Thus:

Age		Number living	Present value of $1 @ 2½ %	Present value of annual payments
35	$1 due now	9,373,807	$1.00	$ 9,373,807.00
36	$1 due one year from now	9,350,279	0.975610	9,122,225.70
37	$1 due two years from now	9,325,594	0.951814	8,876,230.93

[As for the whole life policy, this procedure is carried out until there are no survivors. As before, only the first three and the last calculations are given.]

99	$1 due 64 years from now	6,415	0.205908	1,320.90
				$222,860,196.46

Individual share equals $222,860,196.46 ÷ 9,373,807 = $23.775 = $23.78

Summary of the NLP computation. To consolidate what has thus far been stated, the computation of a net level premium involves four steps: *(a)* find the present value of the benefits; *(b)* divide by the number of entrants in the group to determine the net single premium; *(c)* find the present value of an annuity for $1 for the term premium payments are to be paid; and *(d)* divide the net single premium by the present value of the annuity due.

Let:

B = Discounted benefits
E = Entrants in a given group
A = Present value of annuity due of $1 for premium-paying period
NSP = Net single premium
NLP = Net level premium

We then have:

$$B \div E = \text{NSP}$$
$$\text{NSP} \div A = \text{NLP}$$

The value of an annuity due of $1 a year for a five-year term at age 35 has just been computed to be $4.74. The net single premium for a five-year policy of $1,000 at age 35 has also been found to be $13.09. The problem is to determine from these two figures the five-year net level annual premium. If $1 a year for five years has a present value at the age of 35 of $4.74, then it follows that the payment for five years that is equivalent to $13.09 is $13.09 divided by $4.74, or $2.76. This figure represents the net annual level premium of a five-year term policy at age 35. The solution is a matter of simple proportion: $4.74 : $13.09 = $1 : x. The product of the means equals the product of the extremes. Hence, $4.74x = $13.09, and x = $2.76.

Appendix C:
Special and allied fire lines

Nature of special and allied fire coverages

There are a number of perils and losses that are so closely associated with the fire business that inclusion of the lines in the general field of fire insurance was logical. For example, the writing of sprinkler leakage insurance is a natural accompaniment of fire insurance.

Sprinkler leakage insurance

The automatic sprinkler system is a device designed to make fire, itself, a security guard. A building protected with a sprinkler system is piped throughout, and at given intervals, "heads" are set. These heads open if the temperature rises to a predetermined point. Some systems are *wet* (with water in the pipes up to the sprinkler head); others, where freezing may occur, are *dry* (with compressed air in the pipes, which when released at the sprinkler head, permits water to flow). Thus, when a fire occurs in the vicinity of a sprinkler head, the head is opened and water released on the fire. Water damage caused by the opening of sprinkler heads to extinguish an accidental and unfriendly fire is covered under the fire policy.

It occasionally happens, however, that water is discharged from the sprinkler system when no fire is involved. The fire policies do not cover the damage. The *sprinkler leakage contract* provides indemnity against direct property loss or damage caused by the discharge or leakage of water or other substances from within an automatic sprinkler system, including valves, pumps, pipes, and tanks. The sprinkler policy may be written to cover buildings or their contents, or both. Damage caused by the collapse or fall of tanks which form a part of the sprinkler system is a very important coverage, since water tanks located on the roof of a building can cause terrific loss when the supports collapse. Damage to the sprinkler system itself is covered in some forms.

Not only may sprinkler leakage insurance be written to cover direct damage, but it may also cover all of the indirect losses for which fire insurance is written. (See Chapter 14.)

Sprinkler leakage policies usually require at least 25 percent coinsurance. The rates are reduced so sharply as the percentage in the coin-surance clause is increased that the insured will do well to consider carefully the advisability of a high amount of insurance with a high coinsurance clause.

A sprinkler system in a building may result in serious loss or damage to the property of others, and if any element of negligence can be shown, the owner may be held legally liable. One of the most frequent causes of *sprinkler leakage liability* loss is freezing. Other causes which may introduce the element of liability include not maintaining the system properly, faulty parts, and unsafe construction. In all sprinkler leakage policies covering contents items there is a limited legal liability protection for loss to property similar to the insured's and held in trust or storage or on commission. For claims of a tenant attributable to sprinkler leak-age, a policy is needed that covers liability imposed by law. If there is any assumed liability, there is a special form by which that extra risk is included.

Water damage insurance

The sprinkler leakage policy excludes liability for water damage losses except for water leaking from inside the sprinkler system. To provide complete water damage insurance, the *water damage policy* is essential. The policy covers direct loss or damage caused by the accidental dis-charge, leakage, or overflow of water or steam from plumbing systems, tanks, standpipes for fire hose, appliances, and heating, refrigerating, and air conditioning systems. The policy also covers loss or damage caused by rain or snow admitted directly to the interior of the building through defective roofs or downspouts, or by open or defective windows, ventila-tors, or skylights.

The coverage does not usually include seepage, leakage, or influx of water through building walls, foundations, or lowest basement floors. Losses attributable to aircraft, fire, lightning, windstorm, earthquake, and explosions are not covered. Such losses are expected to be covered by the policies written to cover loss against these perils. Direct damage caused by the water leakage is covered, but there is no coverage for damage to the system, tank, or other source of the water damage loss.

As with sprinkler leakage, there are three forms of *water damage liability* protection: *(a)* limited protection under the property damage form, *(b)* liability imposed by law, and *(c)* assumed liability.

Tenant's improvements and betterments

It is customary for a business tenant to lease real estate in a condition requiring repairs or renovation involving substantial expenditure of money. To have an insurable interest in *improvements or betterments,* it is not necessary that the tenant have a written lease nor is it necessary that the improvements be installed during the term of the lease. It is required, however, that they be installed at the expense of the tenant who is the insured and that after installation the tenant have no legal right to remove them.

Insurable tenant's improvements, therefore, are of a nature that makes them a part of the building. They cease to be the property of the lessee and instead are the property of the owner of the building. Nevertheless, they are available for the tenant's use so long as the rental agreement remains effective. It is this loss-of-use interest in the improvements that the policy covers.

Insurance is written frequently as an endorsement to the fire insurance contract to include improvements and betterments in the contents item of the fire insurance coverage. This permits recovery by the tenant entirely independently of and apart from recovery by the owner of the real estate. In the event that improvements and betterments are damaged or destroyed during the policy term by the perils insured against, there is coverage for two situations: *(a)* where the owner refuses to restore but the lease is not canceled and *(b)* where the lease is canceled.

If the owner pays for restoring the improvements, it is apparent that the tenant has suffered no loss. The owner secures title to the improvements once they become part of the real estate, and their value should be considered for valuation and coinsurance purposes. On the other hand, *if the owner refuses to replace* the betterments, *but the lease is not canceled,* and the tenant pays for them, then the tenant's insurance covers. Settlement is made on the basis of the actual cash value of the damaged improvements or betterments.

The improvements and betterments may be destroyed, or they may be partly damaged. If the premises, however, are sufficiently (often 50 percent is stated) damaged to warrant cancellation of the lease, then from the standpoint of the tenant the betterments are a total loss. *If the lease is canceled,* settlement is made by paying the insured pro rata for the unexpired term of the lease based on the original cost of the improvements. No consideration is given to either depreciation or increased costs.

Builder's risk

A building in the process of construction presents a situation in which values are constantly changing. If insurance is placed at infrequent intervals, there will be periods of overinsurance and periods in which the insurance is inadequate. To eliminate such a situation and at the same time provide an equitable insurance plan, three *builder's risk forms* have been devised. The first provides no automatic coverage as values increase and is usually undesirable because of the frequent endorsements needed.

To provide automatic coverage and at the same time eliminate the necessity of monthly reports, a *completed value form* provides for placing insurance at the commencement of construction for the full projected value of the building when it will be completed. The rate charged is usually about 50 percent of the 100 percent coinsurance builder's risk rate, to allow for any overinsurance of values during construction.

All of the forms usually cover not only the building under construction but also fences, tool houses, builder's machinery, implements, supplies, and materials of every description used in connection with the construction if these are located on the insured or adjacent premises. The completed value form is the most popular method of insuring builder's risk exposures because (assuming proper values) the insured is fully protected throughout the construction period and no further reports of values are required.

Another method of covering increasing values automatically is the *reporting form*. A policy is written as soon as there is any insurable property on the premises for a beginning provisional amount. The total limit of liability for the completed value of the building is also stated. The insured is required to furnish the insurer with a monthly statement of values. Upon receipt of the statement, an endorsement is attached to the policy showing the increase in the insurable value and premium. The policy protects the insured automatically as the value at risk increases, pending the attachment of the monthly endorsements. To illustrate its operation: If at the time of the last report the values were $100,000 and just before the time for the next report they had increased to $120,000 and a fire occurs, the policy covers for the full value of $120,000, even though this amount is not endorsed on the policy. The "full reporting" clause (like 100 percent coinsurance) is mandatory. The interest of the contractor[1] or owner, or both, may be covered under the policy, and the usual fire, extended coverage, and vandalism and malicious mischief perils may be included. All-risks coverage is also available by a special endorsement.

In some states a contractors' form automatically provides a binder to cover for 30 days any new projects started. A newer special builders' form is also available in some jurisdictions, insuring builders similarly for automatic coverage at new project locations without the need to issue separate new policies.

Flood insurance

Insurance against rising water is to be distinguished from insurance against leakage or rain. The term *flood insurance* is applied to forms

---

[1] Also recommended is including all *subcontractors*. See "Name All Subcontractors Under Builders' Risk Policy?" *John Liner Letter* (Wellesley, Mass.: Shelby Publishing, July 1982), p. 1.

covering against direct loss by flood, such as the overflow of a river or a tidal wave. Marine policies covering the perils of transportation include loss or damage from the rising of navigable waters, and flood losses are covered under the all-risks transportation floater. Policies covering bridges may include flood loss. Automobiles are covered by comprehensive physical damage coverage in personal and business auto contracts, and in auto dealers' forms.

Insurance against flood loss to buildings and contents is now frequently written in many areas, through a federal flood insurance program (see Chapter 24) which now covers about $100 billion of property in nearly 2 million policies.[2]

Crop insurance

Among the numerous perils that threaten the destruction of crops are unfavorable weather conditions, hail, floods, insects, and disease. The distress resulting from widespread crop failure has focused the attention of agricultural interests upon the necessity for *crop insurance*. Private insurers write about $500 hundred million dollars in crop insurance premiums annually for this specialized risk.

The application ordinarily provides that the coverage will be effective provisionally 24 hours after the application has been received by the insurer, during which time the insurer has an opportunity to decline the business if it wishes to do so. The insurance coverage is reduced pro rata as harvesting progresses.

No liability is assumed for loss or damage resulting in injury to trees, vines, leaves, bushes, plants, blooms, or blossoms, when such products as fruits, beans, grapes, or strawberries are insured. There is liability only to the extent that the product itself has been affected. It is usual to provide a limit of liability per acre, and policies may include a clause that there shall be no liability on the part of the insurer unless the crop is damaged more than a certain designed percentage—5 percent is a figure frequently used. If the crop can be reset or reseeded, the insurer pays only the actual cost of these operations.

Underwriting insurance on growing crops presents numerous difficulties. At the planting season it is impossible to know what the market will be at the time of harvest. The insurer usually pays losses[3] on the basis of the decreased yield. This plan provides indemnity to the insured for a partial loss, even though much of the crop may be salvaged and a profit shown for the year's operation.

Frost and freeze coverages are written for owners of orchards or growing citrus fruits or other crops that are particularly susceptible to frost

---

[2] *Insurance Facts* (New York: Insurance Information Institute, 1982–83), p. 38.

[3] Ibid., p. 28.

damage. One of the major difficulties is the effect that serious frost losses have upon the market price of the balance of the crop. If the frost losses throughout a wide territory are severe enough to reduce the entire crop seriously, then part of the loss is regained by the increased value in the part of the crop that is marketable. This increased value is, of course, of no assistance to the orchard owner whose entire crop is destroyed. If, however, part of the crop is salvaged, the scarcity is beneficial. Providing for only a partial settlement at the time the damage occurs and a final settlement based upon income received when the salable crop has been marketed, is a normal procedure.

Crop-hail insurance is a popular form of crop coverage and usually provides indemnity for the percentage of physical damage resulting from hail or from wind accompanied by hail. To establish a loss it must be shown that the actual hail damage equaled or exceeded 5 percent of the loss. Crops are usually insured on a "specific amount per acre" basis, which varies considerably by the type of product.

Crop insurance is written by some private insurers on an *all-risks* basis to cover such perils as blight, insect pests, and drought. All-risks crop insurance differs from other forms of crop insurance in that it is virtually a crop guarantee. Instead of determining the amount of loss or damage attributable to an insured peril, the insurer is obligated to pay the insured any difference between the coverage and the amount of the crop actually produced. Efforts have been made to eliminate the moral hazard by reducing the amount of insurance to a part of the average yield, such as three fourths.

The insurance of crops has also been provided for many years by the *Federal Crop Insurance Corporation,* an agency of the U.S. Department of Agriculture. Federal crop insurance is not available in all counties, nor on all crops. This is a type of voluntary government insurance, as defined in Chapters 3 and 24. The Agricultural Consumer Protection Act of 1973 extended federal crop insurance on an all-risks basis for serious damage (of more than one third of the potential crop).

Growing competition of the FCIC with private insurers led to the 1980 Federal Crop Insurance Act which set up a new partnership between government and the insurance business.[4] Crop insurance is sold by the FCIC through licensed private insurance agents. Private insurers are reimbursed for operating and administrative costs, through reinsurance by the federal government. In addition, the act provided for multiple-peril coverages to be developed with federal reinsurance and permitted fire and hail losses to be excluded by the FCIC policies in order that private insurers could compete effectively. Effective in 1983, the govern-

---

[4] "Crop Insurance: A New Partnership," *National Underwriter,* April 10, 1981, p. 25.

ment policies must be sold by licensed agents of private insurers.[5] Private insurers, through their Crop Insurance Research Bureau and other associations, have recommended numerous improvements for the programs.[6]

Multiple-location contracts

The trend of big business frequently results in the distribution of property values among many locations. To provide complete and adequate protection for insureds having contents at a number of locations and with fluctuating values over the year, the *multiple-location forms* have been prepared. All locations may be covered by a single policy, with automatic coverage for new locations. Property suitable for coverage under the multiple-location forms includes contents only. Among the insurable items are merchandise, machinery, supplies, furniture, fixtures, and the insured's interest in betterments.

Reporting forms eliminate the necessity of canceling and rewriting or endorsing policies where the values at various locations fluctuate. Savings are reported in commissions and administration, as it is less expensive to write one policy for 100 or more locations than it would be to write a separate policy for each location. Comparable economies are achieved in accounting, collection expense, credit reports, and underwriting. Multiple-location rate adjustments apply only to that portion of the basic annual premium which is in excess of $1,000. Both the reduced costs and the convenience of having a single contract cover all locations appeal to the insured.

The insurance is written under two general types of coverage: (1) reporting and (2) coinsurance. The forms differ with respect to the number of locations required, whether or not they are reporting forms, the rating plans, and the requirements for minimum premiums.

It is the intent of reporting forms to follow fluctuating values so that whenever a loss occurs full insurance to value will be provided. The insurer obligates itself in this respect, but to make the contract effective the insured must meet certain obligations.

The *value-reporting requirement* obligates the insured to report in writing to the insurer not later than 30 days after the last day of each calendar month: (1) the exact location of all property covered, (2) the total actual cash value of insured property as each location, and (3) the specific insurance in force.

Failure on the part of the insured to make the required report causes *penalties for noncompliance*. The obligation of the insurer is limited to

---

[5] "IIA Wins Victory in Crop Insurance Fight," *Independent Agent,* July 1982, p. 114.

[6] "Associations Unite to Aid Crop Insurance," Mutual *Insurance Bulletin,* August 1982, p. 12.

no more than the amounts included in the last report filed prior to a loss, less specific insurance. The form also contains an "honesty clause" which provides that if the last reported value prior to a loss is less than the actual cash value at the time the report is made, then the insurer is liable only in the proportion that the value reported bears to the actual value. If an insured reports a $50,000 value where there is $100,000 actual value and sustains a $10,000 loss, the insurer is liable only for $5,000, or 50 percent of the loss.

Since the full amount of insurance coverage that the policy will provide cannot be known at the outset, the forms are written with a *provisional amount of insurance.* A deposit premium is collected, and the premium is adjusted at the end of the policy term on the basis of actual values reported.

Reporting forms also provide a *maximum limit of liability* for the insurer which is to be distinguished from the provisional amount of insurance. Where two or more locations are involved, a separate limit is established for each location. If reports are made showing values in excess of liability limits, premiums are collected for the full values reported, but if the values exceed the liability limits established, the liability limits apply. If values are ever determined to be in excess of liability limits, steps should be taken immediately to have the limits increased.

Where *specific insurance* is written and is considered in the computation of the final premium, the insured is obligated either to continue the specific insurance in force or to increase the limit of liability immediately under the reporting form if the specific insurance expires. Multiple-location coverages are usually excess over specific insurance payments. Limits of liability for multiple-location coverages are always determined by subtracting the specific insurance from peak values.

In effecting the final *premium adjustment,* an average of the total monthly values reported for the term of the policy is determined, and if the premium on this average at the applicable rate exceeds the provisional premium, the insured is required to pay for the excess. If the premium is less than the provisional premium, the insurer is obligated to return any excess paid, above any minimum premium that may apply.

Appendix D:
Partial prospect list for marine, inland marine, and "all-risk" lines*

Insurable property	Form of policy
Art collectors, dealers, and galleries	
Paintings, works of art, antiques, and objects of art or historical value	Fine arts
Banks	
Customers' furs for storage	Furriers' customers
Electric signs	Neon sign
Financed installment accounts	Installment floater
Fine arts	Fine arts
Securities, currency	Armored car and messenger
	Registered mail
Floor plan accounts	Floor plan
Bridge owners and mortgagees	
Bridges	Bridge property damage
	Bridge use and occupancy
Broadcasting stations	
Radio towers	Individually drawn
Churches and chapels	
Paintings, works of art, and stained-glass windows	Fine arts
Projection machines	
Religious articles and vestments	Camera
	Special floater
Clubs	
Guns	Special floater
Horses and saddlery	Livestock floater
Paintings, works of art, and stained-glass windows	Fine arts
Paraphernalia	Special floater
Power lawn mowers	Special floater
Projection machines	Camera

Insurable property	Form of policy
Property on exhibition	Exhibition floater
Theatrical scenery, costumes, and "props"	Theatrical floater
Colleges and schools	
Athletic equipment	Special floater
Bandplayers' uniforms	Special floater
Guns	Special floater
Horses and saddlery	Livestock floater
Musical instruments	Musical instrument floater
Paintings, works of art, rare books, manuscripts, and art glass windows	Fine arts
Paraphernalia	Special floater
Projection machines	Camera
Property on exhibition	Exhibition floater
Scientific instruments	Special floater
Theatrical scenery, costumes, and "props"	Theatrical floater
Tickets (for athletic events sent by mail)	Individually drawn
Trophies (possessing quality of fine arts)	Fine arts
Contractors	
Equipment	Contractors' equipment floater
Machinery, tanks, etc.	Installation floater
Department stores	
Customers' furs for storage	Furriers' customers
Electric signs	Neon sign
Fur stock	Furriers' block

* Reprinted by permission of the Royal Liverpool Insurance Corp. A similar list is published as a supplement to *Visiguide* (Hartford Insurance, 1981).

Insurable property	Form of policy	Insurable property	Form of policy
Jewelry stock	Jewelers' block	Tunnels (vehicular and rail)	Property damage
Paintings, pictures, etc.	Fine arts		Use and occupancy
Merchandise	Department store floater	Voting machines	Voting machine
	Exhibition floater	Works of art	Fine arts
	Installation floater	**Individuals**	
	Installment floater	Cameras, furs, jewelry, and silverware	Personal articles floater
	Motortruck merchandise floater		
	Marine cargo policy	Coin collection	Coin collection
	Parcel post	Golfers' equipment	Golfers' equipment
	Transportation	Guns	Special floater
Doctors		Model railroads	Special floater
Medical lamps	Physicians' and surgeons' floater	Musical instruments	Musical instrument floater
Radium	Radium floater	Outboard motorboats and motors	Outboard motorboat
Surgical and scientific instruments and apparatus	Physicians' and surgeons' floater	Paintings, other objects of art, and antiques	Fine arts floater
Dyers and cleaners		Personal effects	Personal effects floater
Customers' furs for storage	Furriers' customers	Personal property	Personal property floater form
Customers' goods	Dyers and cleaners		Trip transit
Exhibitors		Power lawn mowers	Special floater
Property on exhibition	Exhibition floater	Riding horses and equipment	Livestock floater
Works of art	Fine arts	Stamp collections	Stamp collection floater
Exporters or importers		Trophies (with qualities of fine arts)	Fine arts
General merchandise	Marine cargo policy Transportation— location	Wedding presents	Wedding presents
Farmers		Yachts and motorboats	Yacht
Livestock	Livestock floater	**Jewelers**	
Mobile agricultural machinery and equipment	Mobile agricultural machinery and equipment floater	Electric signs	Neon sign
		Jewelers' stock	Jewelers' block
Horses and wagons	Livestock floater	Parcel post shipments	Parcel post
Governments (town, city, county, and state)		Street clocks	Neon sign
Bridges	Bridge property damage	**Libraries**	
	Bridge use and occupancy	Books (while loaned, leased, or rented)	Transportation— location
Musical instruments	Musical instrument floater	Paintings, works of art	Fine arts
Power lawn mowers	Special floater	Property on exhibition	Exhibition floater
Road machinery and equipment	Contractors' equipment	Rare books and manuscripts	Fine arts
Securities, etc.	Registered mail	Stained-glass windows	Fine arts
Surveyors' instruments	Special floater		

Insurable property	*Form of policy*
Manufacturers, distributors, wholesalers, and retailers	
Electric signs	Neon sign
Exhibitions	Exhibition floater
General merchandise	See policies listed for department stores
Ladies' and men's wear	Garment contractors' floater
Patterns	Transportation—location
Privately owned rolling stock and locomotives	Individually drawn
Musicians, bands, and orchestras	
Musical instruments and orchestrations	Musical instrument floater
Bandplayer's uniforms	Special floater

Insurable property	*Form of policy*
Photographers	
Cameras and equipment	Camera
Photographic supplies	Parcel post
Property of others	Bailees' customers
Publishers and printers	
Books, magazines, etc.	Parcel post (transportation—location)
Property out for processing	
Truckers	
General merchandise	Motortruck merchandise floater
Warehousers	
Customers' furs for storage	Furriers' customers
Household goods and general merchandise	Motortruck merchandise floater
	Transportation floater

Appendix E:
Special crime insurance and bonds

CRIME INSURANCE AND BONDS
FOR FINANCIAL INSTITUTIONS

Bank burglary and robbery insurance

Since the greatest concentration of money and securities is in banks and other financial institutions, these institutions are targets for burglary and holdup. The individual burglary and robbery policy is still used *(a)* for institutions that do not require or want the broad protection furnished by a blanket bond (which includes burglary and robbery losses), and *(b)* as excess cover for large institutions that require more burglary and robbery insurance than the blanket bond provides.

The standard bank burglary and robbery policy provides four distinct coverages: (1) burglary, (2) robbery, (3) property damage caused by either burglary or robbery, and (4) property damage caused by vandalism or malicious mischief. The form was developed in cooperation with the American Bankers Association. A separate limit of liability and a separate premium are designated in the policy for each peril. The property damage feature provides indemnity for loss sustained as the result of damage to money and securities or to the premises, furniture, fixtures, vaults, and safes, when caused by burglary or robbery or any attempt thereat. Providing protection for vandalism losses eliminates the possibility of a dispute as to whether the damage in a particular case is actually an attempted burglary. Fire damage to money and securities is covered, but fire losses to premises and other contents are never insured in this policy, regardless of how the fire is caused. There is no loss under a burglary policy if the vault is left unlocked or if it is opened through a manipulation of the combination. Bank burglary and robbery rates apply special discounts for approved alarm systems, locks, security guards, and other features.

Safe-deposit boxes insurance

In the absence of negligence there is usually no liability on the part of a bank for loss to the contents of rented safe-deposit boxes. However,

937

the question of liability is sometimes uncertain, and the owners of valuables in rented boxes are also interested in insurance against loss of the contents.

Bank forms. The *bank safe depository policy* covers against the risks of loss of property in customers' safe-deposit boxes through burglary or robbery, damage or destruction caused by the hazards or attempts thereat and vandalism or malicious mischief. All property is covered, including money. Damage to the premises, safes, vaults, and other furnishings of the bank is covered. The measure of loss is the pecuniary loss, not sentimental value. Damage to the premises, equipment, or furnishings of the bank is paid for first, and the balance of the insurance is prorated among the boxes. The interest of box renters is covered regardless of the liability of the bank, but the protection afforded may be limited to legal liability by endorsement. There are no restrictions as to how the loss or damage must occur, nor is there any limitation as to the amount applicable to each box.

Lessee form. The *lessee policy* insures the renters of safe-deposit boxes for loss or damage to their own property or to property for which they are liable. The burglary coverage is effective while such property is contained in boxes in a designated vault. The robbery feature provides coverage inside the premises of the bank while at least one officer or employee of the bank is on the premises. The most popular form is an all-risks securities safe-deposit form providing insurance against any form of theft or larceny, unexplainable disappearance, or misplacement of securities.

Blanket bonds for financial institutions

There are many blanket bonds designed to meet the fidelity and other theft protection needs of financial institutions such as banks, savings and loan associations, stockbrokers, credit unions, and insurance companies.

The blanket bond idea was the outgrowth of a demand for comprehensive protection designed to cover not only the fidelity risks but also all other theft perils in a single contract. The broadest and most widely used is the *bankers' blanket bond* (Form 24). It consists of three major divisions: *(a)* the insuring clauses which indicate the risks covered; *(b)* the exclusions indicating the risks not insured or to what degree the coverages are modified; and *(c)* the discovery period, which covers such features as the notice requirements in event of loss, the reinstatement provisions, and the like. It is the intent of the bond to provide as complete coverage as possible for property of the insured, or property of others held by the insured. It is insured against such acts as embezzlement, burglary, robbery, theft, larceny, and forgery. The bond is not in actual fact an all-risks cover in that it has not been found feasible to cover losses due to clerical errors, carelessness, and incompetence. In addition to the perils noted, the bond covers indemnity for loss of property through damage, destruction, misplacement, and mysterious disappearance.

A special *insurance company blanket bond* is written, similar to the blanket bond protection available for banks. The form for life insurance companies is extended to indemnify the insured against the dishonest acts of general agents, soliciting agents, and servicing agents. The bond contains six insuring clauses: *(a)* dishonesty of employees, *(b)* on-premises hazards, *(c)* in-transit hazards, *(d)* forgery or alteration, *(e)* securities coverage, and *(f)* counterfeit currency. Endorsements may delete the forgery and securities protection or may extend the policy to cover loss of property while the property is within the premises of agents.

Liability insurance for crime losses

Policies covering the *liability* of the insured imposed by law upon custodians are included in the crime insurance category because burglary and robbery are among the principal sources of loss. Two specialized forms are: *(a)* innkeepers' liability and *(b)* warehousers' liability.

The *innkeepers' liability form* protects the innkeeper in the event of liability for the injury to, destruction of, or loss of property of guests. The policy provides no protection directly for the guests. The liability of an innkeeper is considerably greater than that of a bailee. Originally, innkeepers were held liable for almost all losses, unless the loss was occasioned by negligence or misconduct of the guest or by an act of God or the public enemy.[1] The common-law liability has been limited by statute in all the states, but to provide protection against the various liabilities that may arise, the hotel and innkeeper's policy is needed. Contractual liability is excluded, with the exception that written agreements made with a guest before a loss do not fall within this exclusion. Losses caused by loss of or damage to automobiles or property in automobiles, as well as property in the insured's custody for cleaning, or merchandise for exhibition, sale, or delivery by guests, are not covered, except by endorsement.

The *warehousers' liability form* covers warehousers and other like bailees for their liability for loss of property in their custody. Burglary and robbery losses from any cause, subject to limited exclusions, are covered. The policy is usually written with a deductible applying to each occurrence, which may be as little as $50 or as much as $10,000 or more. The exclusions include war risks, money, securities, and perishable goods. Because of legal requirements, in some states fire and sprinkler

---

[1] *Wilkins* v. *Earle*, 42 N.Y. 172.

leakage losses are not covered, and these risks are in such circumstances insured separately.

OTHER SURETY BONDS

Surety bonds other than contract

A number of miscellaneous surety bonds that involve financial guarantees are not included in the judicial or contract bond classification (see Figure 21–1): (1) depository and miscellaneous, (2) license and permit, and (3) federal. Many of these forms comply with statutory requirements.

Depository and miscellaneous bonds. *Depository* bonds guarantee that a bank in which funds (usually public) are deposited will pay the funds so deposited on demand. With the advent of the government Federal Deposit Insurance Corporation, such bonds are rarely required today.

In the miscellaneous category are to be found public *warehouse* and *grain elevator* bonds guaranteeing that merchandise shall be delivered on presentation of the storage receipt. *Auctioneer* bonds guarantee to the owner of property entrusted to an auctioneer for sale that the auctioneer will faithfully account for the proceeds. *Lost securities* bonds guarantee that when a valuable instrument is lost, the person to whom a duplicate is issued will reimburse the issuing party for any loss or expense suffered should a claim subsequently be made under the original instrument. *Insurance companies* are required to make a deposit of securities or to file a bond in a sum prescribed by the statutes which guarantee the payment of any liability incurred under their policies. States frequently require *investment or securities companies,* or their agents or representatives, to file a bond guaranteeing compliance with statutory requirements.

State and municipal license and permit bonds. *License and permit* bonds are required by various political subdivisions to guarantee to the public authority that the licensee or permittee will comply with the terms of the license or permit. In some instances bonds are required to indemnify third parties who may be injured. Examples include: blasting operators, collection agencies, contractors, detectives, electricians, employment agencies, funeral directors, taxi drivers, loan companies, pawnbrokers, plumbers, public accountants, and travel bureau operators.

Federal bonds. The federal government requires the filing of bonds in a number of situations. Before a permit is granted to manufacture and distribute certain articles (such as liquors or tobacco products) subject to an *internal revenue tax,* a bond is filed with guarantees that the principal shall comply with the regulations and pay all taxes in the manner required. Some articles destined for *export* may be shipped free of tax, but with the export permit the government requires a bond guaranteeing the amount of the tax and providing for a penalty if the goods are not actually exported or if after export they fraudulently reenter the country. Under the federal immigration laws, *aliens* not otherwise eligible for admission may be temporarily admitted for medical care or as students, tourists, or visitors. When so admitted, they assume an obligation to leave the country within an agreed period and file a bond guaranteeing departure or guaranteeing that the alien shall not become a public charge. *Customhouse* bonds are required when permits are obtained for the temporary importation of dutiable items. These bonds are used particularly in connection with exhibits, works of art, models, and samples.

Author and case index

943

Cheit, Earl F., 320 n
Chicago Railroad Company v. *Jackson,* 487 n
Chicago, St. Louis and New Orleans Railroad Company v. *Pullman Southern Car Company,* 104 n–5 n
Christian v. *Griggs,* 496 n
Chubb, Thomas C., 74 n, 456 n
Churchill, Winston, 70 n
City National Bank v. *Lewis,* 198 n
Clayton, John S., 906 n
Cline, Robert S., 737 n
Cockerell, Hugh A. L., 70 n, 75 n, 776 n
Coggs v. *Bernard,* 470 n
Cole, Mitchell J., 55 n
Conant, Roger R., 230 n
Cook, Thomas J., 345 n
Cooper, Robert W., 901 n
Corbett, Richard B., 529 n
Cordtz, Dan, 736 n
Corpus Juris Secundum, 496
Countryman, Gary L., 563 n
Crane, Frederick G., 869 n
Cummins, J. David, 52 n, 796 n, 797 n, 873 n, 901 n

D

D'Adolf, Stuart V., 754 n
Daenzer, Bernard, 46 n
Daniel, Hawthorne, 74 n
Dann, Donald R., 200 n
Davies v. *Mann,* 495 n
Davis, Herbert J., 200 n
Dawson, Christopher M., 48 n
Decker, Richard J., 591 n
Delamotte v. *Midland Ross,* 550 n
Demmas, Con G., 179 n
Denenberg, Herbert S., 801 n
Densmore, Bill, 899 n
Devers v. *Scranton,* 501 n
Dickerson, O. D., 254 n
Diehl, Walter, 886 n
Dilworth, A. A., 692
Dinney, G. R., 183
Donahue, James F., 532 n
Doñaldson, James H., 848 n
Dorfman, Mark S., 248 n, 911 n
Drake, Russell A., Jr., 21 n
Draper v. *Delaware State Grange Mutual Fire Insurance Company,* 105 n
Drucker, Peter F., 233 n
Duprey v. Shane, 550
Durant, Ariel, 71, 317

Durant, Will, 71, 317
Dutter, Philip H., 732 n

E

Eck, James R., 879 n
Ehrenzweig, Albert A., 595 n
Eilers, Robert D., 347 n
Eldred, Gary W., 598 n
Epstein, Marc J., 878 n
Escolas, Edmond L., 614 n
Etgar, Michael, 796 n

F

Fayol, Henri, 18 n
Felton, Robert S., 752 n
Fire Insurance Patrol v. *Boyd,* 501 n
Fitzgerald John, 599 n
Forbes, Stephen W., 911 n
Foster v. *Roman Catholic Dioceses of Vermont,* 502 n
Francy v. *Rutland Railroad Company,* 496 n
Frantz, Al, 651 n
Freeman, Douglas K., 373 n
Friedman v. *Metronic,* Inc., 502 n
Freifelder, Leonard R., 52 n
FTC v. *National Casualty Company,* 862 n

G

Gantt, Michael D., 52 n
Garfin, Louis, 876 n
Gatza, James, 52 n
Gee, Harold F., 656 n
Geisel, Jerry, 504 n
Gentile, Willard J., 557 n
Gentry, Ralph E., 39 n
George v. *Jesson,* 148 n
Gerlacher, T. L., 556 n
Ghee, William K., 752 n
Gibson, William S., 530 n
Glendenning, G. William, 9 n, 56 n, 808 n
Golding, C. E., 775 n
Gordon, Nahum L., 373 n
Goshay, Robert C., 36
Grace v. *Adams,* 103 n
Grant, Larry D., 556 n
Green, Leon, 595 n
Greene, Mark R., 40 n, 52 n, 59 n, 556 n
Greenebaum, Mary, 181 n
Greenough, William C., 229 n, 248 n
Gregg, Davis W., 129 n, 254 n, 279 n, 287 n, 370 n
Greider, Janice E., 106 n, 146 n, 191 n, 204 n

Subject index

This book has been set CAP, in 10 and 9 point Century Schoolbook, leaded 2 points. Part and chapter numbers are 28 point Melior Bold. Part titles are 14 point Melior Bold and chapter titles are 18 point Melior Bold. The size of the type page is 28 by 46 picas.